Andy Lackow
Illustrator
Page 40

Michael Fleishman
Illustrator
Page 266

Claire Scafa
Art Publisher
Page 168

1989 Artist's Market

Acknowledgements

The editor wishes to thank contributing editor Robin Gee and editorial assistants Mary Tonnies and Karen Karr for their assistance in planning and preparing the 1989 edition of Artist's Market.

Distributed in Canada by Prentice Hall of Canada Ltd., 1870 Birchmount Road, Scarborough, Ontario M1P 2J7.
Also distributed in Australia by Ruth Walls Books Pty. Ltd., P.O. Box 282, Paddington, N.S.W. 2021.

Managing Editor, Market Books Department: Constance J. Achabal

International Standard Serial Number 0161-0546
International Standard Book Number 0-89879-332-7

Cover illustration by Garry Nichols

1989 Artist's Market

Where & How to Sell Your Art Work

Edited by
Susan Conner

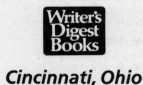

Cincinnati, Ohio

The Markets

Contents

From the Editor

Our work on the fifteenth edition of *Artist's Market* began by listening to you. We conducted a survey to find out what features in the book are most helpful to artists, and, most importantly, how we could better serve artists' needs. Using your suggestions, we included these new features in the 1989 edition:

- A new gallery section to meet the needs of illustrators who also sell their paintings, and of fine artists who crossover into the illustration market.
- To highlight the business aspect of art (which so many of you expressed interest in), the article at the front of the book, "Getting Serious About Gag Cartooning," zeros in on the fundamentals of selling cartoons, with tips on how to approach markets and recordkeeping. Practical advice on collecting payment is the focus of "Getting Your Due." The essentials of handling initial presentations, portfolios, contracts, taxes, recordkeeping and mailing procedures are covered in "The Business of Art."
- A special feature titled "How to Work with Small Businesses" presents tips on how to establish yourself locally, one of your prime concerns.

The *1989 Artist's Market* introduces over 800 new markets, each marked with an asterisk (*) (except in the gallery section, where all the listings are new) so you can locate them easily. In addition, we have updated the markets which ran last year. In these returning listings, there have been 49 company name changes, 154 address/phone changes, 194 contact person changes, 205 listings whose needs have changed and 171 changes in pay rates.

The 2,500 market listings provide more than just a company name and address. Here you can find the names of contact persons, art needs, payment terms, submission requirements and even inside tips from the markets you plan to approach. Over 50 illustrations *show* you what buyers are seeking while the detailed captions explain what made each piece successful.

The fourteen Close-up interviews spotlight artists, art directors, and gallery owners who share their secrets and insights into the freelance world. Such prominent artists and art directors as children's book illustrator Uri Shulevitz, designer Mike Quon and Richard Newcombe of Creators Syndicate provide valuable hints on making initial presentations, negotiating payment terms and establishing contacts.

The introduction to each market section provides helpful tips on the art requirements, trends and payment terms unique to each market. Don't forget to refer to the Glossary to find the definition of a term you may not know. You will also find in the introductions the names of additional publications that supply names and addresses of galleries and art buyers (but no marketing information). These publications usually can be found in reference or business libraries; otherwise, they can be ordered from the publisher or a bookstore. The addresses of these publications are found in the Artist's Resource List at the back of the book.

There's one more chapter to the *Artist's Market*, but it's not written yet. That's the story of how this book helps you as an artist. Each success story has to begin somewhere. We want to hear how yours began. We want to hear the whole story about the market you contacted and why, what samples you sent, and what was your first assignment—even how much you were paid, if you want to share that information. We will feature some of these "first-time" stories in the next edition. I look forward to receiving your stories and letters.

Susan Conner

Please Note

The Artist's Market welcomes new listings. If you are a user of freelance design and illustration or if you are a gallery director seeking new artists to represent and would like to be considered for a listing in the next edition, contact the editor by March 1, 1989.

The *Artist's Market* also welcomes you to submit artwork for possible inclusion in the next edition. The policy for submission is as follows:
(1)artwork must be submitted by a freelance artist or a market who uses freelance work;
(2)the artwork must have been published by one of the markets listed in the book.
If you have material to submit which fits these guidelines, send it to: Editor, Artist's Market, 1507 Dana Ave., Cincinnati, OH 45207.

Using Your Artist's Market

Markets in this book are organized according to their professional category, such as book publishers or magazines. However, you've probably found that your talents apply to many categories. For example, if you're a painter who also illustrates, you will find opportunities (for your fine art) not only in the gallery and art publisher sections, but also (for your illustration) in the magazine, book publishing and greeting card sections. Cartoonists look to advertising agencies, businesses, associations, greeting card companies, magazines, newspapers and syndicates. Because the companies' needs are so diverse, you will be able to find opportunities for your work in almost every section, no matter what your specialty is.

Interpreting the market listings

Listings include information on whom to contact, what type of work is needed, how artists are used, payment method and amount. Note the features illustrated by this sample listing:

contact information (2) **description (4)** **type of work (6)**	**(1) ADI ADVERTISING/PUBLIC RELATIONS**, Box 2299, Ft Smith AR 72902. **(2)** President: Asa Douglas. **(3) (4)** Ad agency/PR. Clients: retail, personal service, small manufacturing, political. **Needs: (5)** Assigns 150-200 freelance jobs/year. Regional artists only, within two-days' mail time. **(6)** Works on assignment only. Uses artists for consumer and trade magazines, billboards, brochures, catalogs, newspapers, stationery, signage and posters.
how to contact (7) **reporting time (9)** **portfolio information (11)** **payment (12)**	**First Contact & Terms: (7)** Send brochure showing art style. **(8)** Samples are filed. Samples not filed are returned by SASE. **(9)** Reports back only if interested. **(10)** Write to schedule an appointment to show a portfolio, **(11)** which should include roughs, original/final art, final reproduction/product and photographs. **(12)** Pays for design by the hour, $10-100. Pays for illustration by the hour, $25-300. **(13)** Considers complexity of project, client's budget, skill and experience of artists when establishing payment.
rights purchased (14) **advice from art buyer (15)**	**(14)** Buys all rights. **Tips: (15)** "Creative needs are satisfied with unusual, often unknown, ideas. Show complete scope of your ability to work from production through design."

(1) If this were a new listing, an asterisk (*) would precede the listing. This is not a new listing.
(2) Names of contact persons are given in most listings. If not, address your work to the art director or person most appropriate for that field.
(3) Dates indicating when the market was established are given in this area of the listings only if they are 1986, 1987, 1988. This indicates the firm or publication is new and possibly more open to freelance artists. The risk is sometimes greater when dealing with new companies. So far as we know, all are reputable but some are unable to compete with larger, older companies. Many do survive, however, and become very successful.
(4) Company descriptions and/or client lists appear to help you slant your work toward that specific business.

(5) The number or percentage of jobs assigned to freelance artists or the number of artists a market uses gives you an idea of the size of the market.
(6) Many firms work on assignment only. Do not expect them to buy the art you send as samples. When your style fills a current need, they will contact you. This section also tells you what type of artwork the company needs.
(7) Submit materials specified by the listing. If a market instructs you to query, please query. Do not send samples unless that is what they want you to do.
(8) Many art directors keep samples on file for future reference. If you want your samples returned, include a self-addressed, stamped envelope (SASE) in your mailing package. Include an International Reply Coupon (IRC) if you are mailing to a foreign market.
(9) Reporting times vary, and some—such as this listing—will only contact you if interested in your work.
(10) Markets want you to either mail portfolio materials or present them in person. Note whether to call or write for an appointment to show your portfolio.
(11) The type of samples you include in your portfolio reflect your understanding of the market; inappropriate samples signify a lack of market research.
(12) Payment terms.
(13) Markets often negotiate payment terms. Therefore, they do not specify the amount of payment but list the factors they consider when establishing payment.
(14) Note what rights the market purchases. If several types of rights are listed, it usually means the firm will negotiate. But not always. Be certain you and the art buyer understand exactly what rights you are selling. This advertising agency buys all rights.
(15) Read the tips added to many of the listings. They give you personalized advice or a view of general market information.

Getting Serious About Gag Cartooning

by Stan Barker

People think you're funny—and to you, that's a compliment. You dream up clever gags, and your drawings put them across. You *know* your work is as good as anything you've seen in print, and you're pretty sure you could be the next Gary Larson. Can your talents bring you fame and fortune as a gag cartoonist?

Probably. But first there's some not-so-funny business you'll have to attend to. Gag cartooning is a highly competitive field, thousands of freelancers vying with each other for limited magazine space available. It's a race that goes to the fittest, and your fitness will be measured not by your work alone but by how well you market it.

"Every cartoonist wears a number of hats," says Eric Decetis, whose work appears regularly in *Hustler*, *Penthouse*, *Campus Life*, and *National Lampoon*. "You've got your humorist's hat, and your artist's hat, but just as importantly, there's your *salesman's* hat. A lot of people starting out don't realize that, but a cartoonist is like any other entrepreneur with a product—making the sale is the name of the game."

There's no guarantee you'll make every sale—even established gag cartoonists have material rejected now and then—but there are ways to increase your chances. Here are tips from the pros on the right way to market your work.

Breaking in

The first step, of course, is knowing *where* to market your work. Studying magazines on the newsstand is a good way to familiarize yourself with the type of cartoons different publications use. Unfortunately, it won't tell you if a particular magazine is buying freelance work. For that reason, many cartoonists start with the market listings in *Artist's Market*. "It narrows it down for me," Decetis says. "If a listing mentions that artists' guidelines are available, it's a good idea to send for them, too." The guidelines, which are usually free for a self-addressed stamped envelope will give you further information about what type of cartoons a magazine is looking for, formats and pay rates.

Harley Schwadron, a cartoonist who's sold to over 100 markets, including the *Wall Street Journal*, *Saturday Evening Post*, *Omni*, *Good Housekeeping*, and *Psychology Today*, also recommends *Artist's Market*, as well as *The Gag Recap* and *Trade Journal Recap* (available from Al Gottlieb, Box 86, East Meadow, NY 11554). Each publication lists the major markets among general and trade publications, and the cartoons they've printed each month, along with the name of the person to contact, address and kinds of cartoons being bought.

Should you start at the top, sending your cartoons to major markets like *The New Yorker* and *Playboy*, or should you try breaking in by way of lower-paying markets—trade magazines, newsletters, local newspapers? Should you, when starting out, ever work for free, just to see your cartoons in print?

It depends on the individual. "Seeing your work in print for the first time can be a tremendous psychological boost," says Decetis. "Sometimes it might be worth more than money."

Stan Barker *is a Contributing Editor for* The Artist's Magazine *who takes the cartoon genre very seriously, indeed.*

He sold his first cartoon to *Deltiology*, a magazine for antique postcard collectors. "I must have put eight hours work into it, and probably got about five bucks. But it spurred me to go on." Starting gradually with low- or non-paying markets can pay off, he adds, by providing the beginning cartoonists with tear sheets of their work, and credits they can mention in cover letters to larger magazines.

"A lot of cartoonists focus on the major markets," says Schwadron. He's sold to more than his share of these, "but I never forget about the smaller circulation magazines and newsletters. For instance, my type of humor seems to go over well with doctors and lawyers, and I sell a lot to their professional journals—some of which pay very well." One of the keys to the business, he says, is: "Don't give up on a cartoon if it hasn't sold for top dollars. Try to keep your cartoons in the mail. Progress may seem to come slowly that way, but it *will* come, by gradually building your clientele."

Schwadron recognizes that it may be worth a beginner's time to do a freebie or two, but cautions against giving cartoons to national magazines. "They're big enough to pay for your work."

Submitting your work

Once you've found a market that seems right for you, the next step is to submit your cartoons. In the "good old days" when most major magazines—and most cartoonists—were located in New York City, Wednesday was "look day," when freelancers trekked to each editorial office to present their work. Today, with magazines and cartoonists spread across the country, mail is the route for submissions.

Don't phone ahead—most cartoon editors and art directors are too busy to field phone calls from contributors they don't know; besides, there's no way they can see your work over the phone. "The best thing is to send a nice batch of cartoons, maybe 8 to 12 really good ones, in a slick package," says Decetis. "I put mine in an acetate cover, with cardboard backing, and always include a self-addressed, stamped manila envelope for returns."

Schwadron includes a flyer he's had printed with samples of other work. "It's a way of showing other things you've done. An art director might see something there that leads to an assignment."

Both Decetis and Schwadron send original art, keeping good photocopies on file against possible loss. However, Jonathan Schneider, former president of the Cartoonist's Guild and now an artist's representative, feels it should be the other way around. "Most major markets

Artist: Eric Decetis

This cartoon is from Eric Decetis's regular feature in Chic magazine. He says, "Use your head when submitting ideas. Put thought and feeling into what you're doing so that your work will be more marketable. Work up a variety of thumbnails on one gag and choose the best. Do this for 10 to 12 samples if you're not published."

"Jump ball! Bring out the players' attorney for the offence and the players' attorney for the defence."

Artist: Schwadron

Cartoonist Harley Schwadron sold this cartoon to World of Sport. A former newspaperman, the Ann Arbor, Michigan cartoonist focuses on timely topics for his gags. "I think current cartoons deal more with social trends than they used to." He keeps detailed records of sales and submissions so that he can devote more time to cartooning. "It's best to submit cartoons through the mail, because editors like to see your work. Cartoonists work in a visual medium, and cartoons can't be seen over the phone. After all, it's the gag and the artwork that sells cartoons, not your name."

accept photocopies today," he says. The best bet is to send whichever format is requested in the market listing or artists' guidelines.

Always address your sample package to the name and title specified in the listings or guidelines. If none is given, send to "Art Director." (Few publications other than men's magazines have "Cartoon Editors.") And always include a cover letter, introducing yourself. Eric Decetis recommends keeping it short, but adds: "Saying you're a fan of the magazine, and enjoy the cartoons they print is a nice touch." In other words, remember to wear your salesman's hat.

Following up

Once you've sent your first batch of cartoons to a magazine, keep submitting to that magazine on a regular basis. The art director there needs to know you're the kind of cartoonist they can depend on for a steady stream of material. Here, being a *pro* means being a *pro*lific *pro*ducer. "Start with the majors and submit a minimum of eight cartoons every month," Jonathan Schneider advises. "If you're not that prolific, this may not be the business for you."

Clockwork submissions will get your name known at a magazine, even if your early material is rejected. "Rejections are all part of the game," says Schwadron. "A magazine might not be buying because it has a lot of cartoons on stock, but it will start buying when its inventory starts getting low. I've sent material to a magazine for six months straight, without one take. Then, all of a sudden, I've sold the same magazine six cartoons in a single month." Of course, he adds, you should only keep submitting if the magazine returns your rejected art. "If you don't hear back from them, don't send to them again."

What else can you do if your artwork is not returned? Unfortunately, says Schneider, the cartoonist has little recourse but to "keep sending letters" to the recalcitrant art director. However, Decetis says this has never been a problem for him. "The listings or guidelines will tell you how long you should wait to hear from a publisher, and generally you will hear from them in that time. If you haven't, write them again, explaining when you sent your cartoons, and asking if they got your package." And despite all the bad things you hear about the postal service, it is rare for a package to be lost in the mail. One safeguard against this would be to send your cartoons by certified mail, with a return receipt requested. Use your own judgment if the small added expense is worth it to you.

What you do when your work is returned is a much simpler matter: Send it off to another magazine. Again, don't take rejections personally. "The more magazines you send to," says Schneider, "the more you'll sell." The trick here—as well as the key to tracking down missing artwork—is to keep a good record of *what* you've sent *where* and *when*.

Keeping track

With the advent of personal computing, some cartoonists have begun keeping records of their submissions on floppy disks, but most still follow the old-fashioned formula of numbering each cartoon and logging it in a simple loose-leaf notebook. Decetis numbers his according to the date when he completed the drawing—for instance, a cartoon done on June 8, 1988 is numbered as 688. He records this number and the cutline (caption) of the cartoon, along with the name of the magazine it was submitted to and the date on which it was sent. Later, if the cartoon was accepted, Decetis will add a notation of how much he was paid; if it's bounced back, he notes the date on which it was rejected.

Schwadron's system differs in that he has a code number for each magazine he sends to. He keeps a list for each cartoon, on which he checks off the number of each magazine, noting dates and results. He has done thousands of cartoons but only sends to a hundred or so magazines. Numbering the publications "helps keep the administrative work down. This part of cartooning isn't much fun," he adds, "but it's absolutely necessary."

Schneider suggests a time saver: using a changeable four-digit rubber stamp to number the back of your cartoons. Since you should always put your name, address, and phone number on the flipside of your work, he recommends having a stamp made with this numbering system on it.

Always keep good Photostats or photocopies of your original work on file—you never know when you may need them.

Under present law, your work is automatically protected by copyright from the moment you finish it. In selling a work, you are assigning a portion of your rights to a magazine so they can print your work. Though it's true that most magazines copyright their contents, you can make sure your work is protected by putting the © symbol, followed by your usual signature, on your cartoon. If, by chance, your cartoon is being printed in a magazine whose contents are *not* copyrighted, you must include the © symbol on your work in order to safeguard it.

Pay rates should be set forth in a magazine's market listing or artist's guidelines. As a rule, they are not negotiable. (The usual exception to this is when an established cartoonist is put under exclusive contract to a particular magazine.) The listings/guidelines should also clearly state what rights to your work the magazine is buying. Some top markets such as *Penthouse* buy all rights; but in dealing with others—certainly all smaller markets—*always* try to sell first North American serial rights. This means that the magazine buys only the right to print your work for the *first time* in the United States and Canada; after that first appearance, all rights to the cartoon revert back to you. In submitting your work, always make clear what

CARTOON LOG Pg. 2 (continued)	Kiwanis -James Patterson -6/17/87	Inside Detective -Sonia Malave -6/30/87	Prevention -Wendy Ronga -10/16/87
Ironing Board Lady 23			
Movie Line 24			
Kite Finish Line 25			
How's Water 26		√	
Mind Taking Picture 27	√		√
Mouse Shadow 28			
Subway Rider 29			√
Not Santa 30			

Cartoonist Jim Meadows of New York City keeps detailed records of his cartoon submissions. For each submission, he records the name of the business or publication, the contact person and the submission date at the top of a log sheet, as shown above. On the left side he lists cartoons ready for submission. "With each chart," he says, "I can easily log submissions by putting check marks next to the magazine I'm submitting a certain cartoon to."

rights you are selling. Schneider adds, "If you do a freebie, don't go crazy and also give away all rights."

If you have sold first North American rights, you are free to resell your cartoon for reprints, especially among smaller-circulation magazines, and marketing reprints can be a very lucrative way of increasing your sales. Always inform the publication when and where your cartoon was previously published. Often you may submit a photocopy of the published work.

Resales/reprints are the only instance where it's acceptable to submit a cartoon to more than one magazine simultaneously. Never send multiple submissions of fresh, unpublished work. Magazines are highly competitive, and, says Schneider, multiple cartoon submissions are "considered highly unethical." Decetis agrees. "It's one way to create a lot of bad will for yourself."

Other options

If you're not selling a lot at first, you may want to use your talents in other areas. Decetis regularly cartoons for public information brochures put out by the California Air Resources Board. Other freelancers ply their skills for advertising agencies and graphics firms, or submit ideas to greeting card companies.

Humorous illustrator Ned Shaw of Bloomington, Indiana won the Silver Funnybone Award at the Society of Illustrators Humor Show. Shaw says many cartoonists call themselves "humorous illustrators" because the label opens many markets, including advertising and book illustration. "I did line work for so long, but it is low paying. I find many more jobs with humorous illustration."

Schneider advises his clients to call themselves *humorous illustrators*. "It's very hard to make a living as a gag cartoonist." Being a humorous illustrator opens the door to assignments illustrating magazine articles and covers, even books." It's not for everyone, he stresses. One of the attractions of gag cartooning is its creative freedom; humorous illustrators must follow the guidelines set down for an assignment by an art director.

Ned Shaw is a good example of a cartoonist who found his niche as a humorous illustrator. For him, cartooning was too low-paying. "I know some cartoonists make up to $100,000 a year," he says, "but I wasn't one of them. I've found many, many more jobs as a humorous illustrator . . . it's much more marketable now than cartooning." It's proved to be more rewarding aesthetically as well—Shaw's work has received the "Silver Funnybone" Award for Humorous Illustration from the Society of Illustrators.

Making it

So you still think you're cut out to be a gag cartoonist? Good. Here are some final tips and words of encouragement.

If you can't brainstorm enough gags on your own, do what other cartoonists do—find a gag writer. Cartoon trade publications and *Writer's Digest* magazine have sections in which you can advertise for writers. *Writer's Market*, published annually, will also include your listing, and at no charge. You may wind up with more gags than you can handle. The standard agreement is to pay the writer 25 percent of what the magazine has paid you for the collaborative cartoon.

Or you can try Decetis' method for getting new ideas. "I keep stacks and stacks of old magazines on hand, and when I'm dry, I look through them at other people's work. Not to steal ideas, but to get my own flowing. I might see something and say, 'Hey, I haven't done a housewife-in-kitchen-with-mad-husband situation lately!' Or I might think, 'Now what if that gag had been done this other way.' Pretty soon, I've got a new cartoon."

Another Decetis tip: Ask your mailman to leave all oversize packages on your doorstep. "You don't want to see what returned cartoons look like after they've been crammed into a mailbox!"

Ned Shaw's advice: "Always do your best, because editors aren't interested in what you would have done if you'd had more time, a bigger budget, a more creative assignment. All you are is your work. And keep hustling—whether it's a friend's business card or a magazine assignment."

Schwadron's advice: "Look through magazines to determine what kinds of cartoons they're buying. Slanting your gags saves both you and the art director time and effort. But always play to your strengths. Find your own particular style and type of humor. What you enjoy doing is usually what you'll do best."

Decetis agrees: "Don't waste your time on areas you're not good at. Learn to narrow down your markets."

And Schwadron, once more:

"Cartooning is a field where you have to learn by doing. If you stick to it, anyone with drawing talent and the ability to see things humorously will make it.

"Persistence pays off."

Getting Your Due

by Susan Conner

Has this happened to you one too many times? The art director of a local magazine asks you to illustrate a feature story. Even though the deadline is short and the job entails a tight, realistic rendering, you accept the assignment. Despite some complications, you work hard and are able to deliver the artwork a day ahead of schedule. Basking in the glow of the art director's praise, you hand him your invoice. "Great," he beams, "the check will be in the mail tomorrow."

You wait a few days, and no check. Fine, it takes a few days for the accounting system to issue the check. A few weeks later, still no check. In fact, you never get paid. You're angry, hurt and a few dollars short. You know what you'd like to do, but you don't know what you can really do. Your assignment was verbal; it's your word against the art director's.

There is no foolproof way to always collect what's owed to you, but you can take certain precautions against not being paid. If the precautions don't produce results, there are certain legal actions you can take to collect payment.

Preventive medicine

First, you must protect yourself by using a written agreement for all assignments. The mere thought of signing a contract is threatening to many people. Signing on the dotted line con-

Joseph Shoopak of San Diego, California was asked to illustrate an article about collecting delinquent payments for Legal Economics Magazine. *Shoopak says, "A close watch must be kept on overdue accounts to insure that they are eventually received."*

jures up visions of giving your life away because of what you don't read in the fine print. *On the contrary, a contract is a business tool that protects you and your business.*

A written contract or agreement clarifies exactly what's expected of both you and the client. It clears up misunderstandings before they happen. Often, it means the difference between staying in business and going under. It merely takes some understanding of what a contract is to waylay those irrational fears.

A contract is simply an exchange of promises between two or more people which, ideally, is enforceable by law. When you order pancakes at your local diner, you form a contract that says, "I will pay $3.50 for a stack of pancakes that are delivered to my table within a reasonable amount of time." You do the same thing at the gas station or at the grocery store. During your business hours, you must send out invoices or bills of sale, which are agreements or contracts that a buyer will pay for your services a set amount within a certain time frame.

To be enforceable, a contract must contain certain terms. It must contain an offer, such as "*Art Magazine* will pay me $75 for an illustration." Consideration is tendered in the promise to deliver the goods: "I will pay if you deliver on time." Both parties must agree to the terms of the contract, which is the acceptance, and they must be of reasonably sound mind to be considered competent.

The simplest contract

A contract does not have to be a long-winded affair. It can be as simple as a letter. "Letters are an invaluable, nonthreatening way to have the terms of your agreement reduced to writing," says attorney Jean S. Perwin, who specializes in entertainment law. She suggests using a simple, four-sentence letter for most situations you encounter as a freelance artist in the beginning of your career.

> Dear (Art Director's Name):
>
> It was a pleasure to speak with you on (date) about (the nature of your assignment). It is my understanding that I will supply you with (specific materials), for which I will give you (whatever rights apply), and that you will pay me (amount agreed upon), payable half now and half on final delivery of (the specific materials). All reproduction rights are reserved to me except those granted to you in this letter.
>
> I look forward to working with you.
>
> Sincerely,
> (Signature)
> (Printed or typed name)

In presenting the letter, you can explain this is your standard business procedure and is used to record your assignments. This is a nonthreatening way of getting your agreement in writing. Samuel Goldwyn once said that an oral contract is not worth the paper it's written on, and he's right. While an oral agreement is legally binding, it is difficult to enforce. A written contract eliminates potential problems in advance by clarifying exactly what the assignment entails before you are surprised by extra work, which might not be billable, or the client is dismayed when he receives your roughs rather than the finished art he expected.

Discuss all the issues involved in the assignment, resolve them, and write them down. Better to negotiate now, than lose a valued client later.

Whether you sell your work directly, by consignment, or through an agent, make sure there is a contract between the seller and the buyer. Direct sales account for the majority of transactions for many artists selling through fairs, shows and studios. In many cases, the only documentation for a direct sale is a receipt showing the piece, date and sales tax (if needed).

Formal contracts

Contracts are essential when you are entering a long-term business relationship. If your work is going to be published and reproduced in multiple copies, you are involved in a relationship that will exist over a long period of time. "Circumstances change," says Perwin. "When they do, problems arise, and a contract can prevent little problems from becoming big, expensive ones."

If you are involved in a complex situation, such as licensing or syndication, it's a good idea to see a lawyer. Keep in mind that any contract drafted by a large organization is designed to protect the organization, not you. An attorney can advise you about the contract terms and help you negotiate more favorable ones. Ask friends for recommendations or ask your local bar association if there is a nearby Volunteer Lawyers for the Arts. Try to find an attorney who is familiar with the arts.

By inserting certain terms into your agreement, you can increase your chances for getting your due. Your agreement—no matter if it's a letter or a full-blown contract—should contain the following points:

- ***Terms of payment***. Specify how, when and how much you are to be paid. For example, illustrator Mary Artist specifies that she will be paid the agreed upon flat fee of $120 ten days after final delivery, while designer Paul Proposal states that one-third of this fee will be paid after the concept stage; one-third due after the presentation of the dummy; and the third, plus expenses, is due upon completion of the project. Many artists insert a kill fee in case the artwork is not accepted.
- ***Due date***. Make sure your contract states that the account is due within a certain period. Standard business procedure is to make all accounts payable in 30 days. This means that, on day 31, payment is late. Have your due date marked clearly on your agreement or bill.
- ***Rights***. By specifying that no rights are transferred until full payment is received, you can prevent use of your artwork through a court-ordered injunction. If your artwork is reproduced by the client without paying you, the reproduction will be solid evidence in a copyright infringement case.
- ***Penalties***. Many established artists warn clients they will face a penalty for late payment. This usually takes the form of interest on the amount due. The threat of extra charges encourages timeliness. Also, many artists feel that charging the client attorney fees for collection efforts is an even better incentive.

Past due

There are many clients who maintain poor records of their accounts and simply forget to pay their bills on time. What they need is a friendly reminder. Send another copy of your bill and mark it "Past Due." A ready-made stamp speeds up your monthly collection efforts. Ask for late payment within at least 15 days.

If the "past due" reminder doesn't produce results, follow up with a letter demanding payment, and send it by certified mail with a return receipt requested. Use increasing firmness of tone as the past due period lengthens. The first letter should be a friendly nudge, followed by an appeal, then a push. Here are two letters that take in consideration the increasing seriousness of the situation. Along with the letter, send another copy of the original bill stamped "Past Due."

> Dear Client:
>
> Apparently you have overlooked your bill for $150 for the illustration I completed October 23. In the past, you have paid your bills promptly. That's why I am surprised to find your account is approximately 15 days overdue. Please check my bill for $150 dated October 23 and forward payment. If you have a special reason for withholding payment, please let me know.
>
> Many thanks for your prompt attention.

> Dear Client:
> I again call your attention to your past-due account of $150. A detailed statement of the account has been mailed to you several times already. I would appreciate payment in settlement of this amount by return mail.

If you don't receive payment after sending several letters, send a note outlining the steps you have taken to collect the money. The note will be valuable evidence later if you take your case to court.

If the client is short of cash, work out either a payment schedule or settle for a lesser amount than the balance owed. Remember that if the client declares bankruptcy, chances of collecting money are slim.

If you're not paid after 90 days, you must decide how long you're willing to play games. If the client hasn't paid by now, he's probably not going to pay at all. This is the time to evaluate what your next step is. If the amount due is less than $100, you might consider chalking it up to "experience." It's not worth the legal fees to collect it. If the amount and the principle are worth it to you, then you have other options.

When push comes to shove

In situations where the amount due is around $1,000, you may want to represent yourself in Small Claims Court. Check in your phone book under "Local Government" to find the number of the Clerk of Small Claims Court. The clerk will tell you the court's procedures. Each jurisdiction puts a different ceiling on claims. For example, New York City's ceiling is $1,500.

Court procedure is simple. Generally, each party presents his or her case without the help of an attorney, and cases are heard by either a judge or an arbitrator, not a jury. The presentation of the case usually takes a few minutes, but you may or may not know of the outcome immediately. Many decisions are mailed to you, while others are rendered in your presence.

Before you bring your case to court, you (now called the claimant) must take certain actions to file your claim. First, you must pay a nominal fee, usually $5 to $10, to file the claim. Next, you must file a statement explaining your claim; the statement names the creditor (you) and the debtor (the client), the amount of the debt and other pertinent details. Then you must summon the client, explaining that you will bring a civil suit against him unless payment is made immediately. If you don't get paid, it's time for your day in court.

It helps to prepare for your appearance. Bring along your contract, ledger sheets, invoices or letters you have written requesting payment. If your agreement with the client is oral, you will need the testimony of a witness.

If you are granted the decision, the next step is to collect the money. Collecting is up to you, not the court. Sending a letter asking for prompt payment and attaching a copy of the judgment may produce results. You can enlist the help of the local sheriff or city marshal through a court order to collect the money from the debtor's wages or bank account. You are given a certain amount of time to collect. If you collect the sum, you usually must file a "satisfaction of judgment" form with the court. This certifies that your case is closed.

If you do not want to deal directly with your client, and your claim is rather significant, you might consider hiring a collection agency. An agency generally exerts pressure in an aggressive and impersonal way by making calls and writing letters. They charge either a flat fee or a percentage of the amount collected, usually from 20 to 40 percent. The Yellow Pages will list your local agencies.

If the agency does not collect the money, it usually suggests starting a lawsuit and recommends an attorney. Since collection agencies levy claims only against corporations, it might be wise to go directly to an attorney if you feel the amount due can offset attorney's fees and court costs. Even attorneys won't accept collection jobs unless they involve substantial sums of money. Their payment is usually based on an hourly rate or a percentage of the amount collected. To contact an attorney, ask for referrals from your friends, call the local bar association referral service or the local Volunteer Lawyers for the Arts. Many times a strongly-worded letter from an attorney produces results without commencing a lawsuit.

Getting yours

Hopefully you will not have to resort to such heavy-handed methods as court action. By sharpening your own recordkeeping and collection methods, you can avoid many hassles. You must maintain an accurate and efficient billing system in order to document your sales. Not many of us are skilled accountants, but your recordkeeping needs can be eased by the computer, whose software makes daily bookkeeping a simple matter.

Even though you are in a creative business, you are still in business. Always be professional but firm in all your dealings with clients. Establish a good working relationship by getting everything in writing. If someone owes you money, remember that it's *your* money. You are entitled to it by law after you agree to take an assignment or sell a painting. It's time you get your due.

The Business of Art

Whether you're a painter, illustrator, graphic designer or cartoonist, you constantly deal with the business of art. If you're just starting your career, the thought of selling your work seems intimidating. The creative side is difficult enough, you say, without having to face self-promotion, taxes and recordkeeping. In reality, good business practices enable you to fulfill your creative potential. They pave the way for those long-awaited sales and shows.

This section provides general guidelines to building and securing your business through self-promotion, submitting your work and professional business practices.

Self-promotion

No matter what your specialty is, the secret to success is building your own reputation. You must let everyone know who you are, what you do and how well you do it. You're not going to be "discovered" without making contacts with the right people at the right time.

At first, the best place to be "discovered" is right in your own backyard. Your friends, relatives and neighbors all have contacts, many of whom might own a business, run a gallery or organize a show. The more people who know you are available, the better your chances are of getting an assignment or a show.

Local contacts are mainly established through word of mouth and referrals, which take time to build. Volunteer your services to paint portraits for the community center's annual bash or illustrate posters for local fundraising events. Even if you're not getting paid for volunteer duties, request a credit line, which gives you extra publicity and credibility, plus another piece in your portfolio. Always do your best job, because it could lead to other possibilities. Read the special feature by Michael Fleishman in the Business section to get more pointers on how to establish local connections.

The sample package

After you complete a few assignments or show your work at fairs, shops or galleries locally, the next step in establishing yourself as a professional artist is to develop a sample package. Reading the listings in the *Artist's Market* will help you to determine where you want to sell your work and compile a mailing list of names, addresses, phone numbers and contact people of your best prospects. Note if the company wants to be contacted through the mail, by phone or through an agent and also what materials the art director likes to review. Now you're ready to make contact.

You'll either make contact through the mail or by phone. If you're calling, be pleasant and succinct. State your name and why you're calling. Keep in mind that the person at the other end of the phone is a stranger, too, and you are trying to find out as much about him as he is about you. You should follow up your call by mailing a sample.

Your initial contact through the mail will be your sample package. The main purpose of this package is to provide a concise overview of your talents. Since you know your budget, you know how ambitious you can be with your package. No matter what the size, make it visually exciting. A small coordinated brochure and résumé present a much better image than a sizable yet unimaginative package.

The contents of your promotional package can vary, but the basic components include: a cover letter, business card, samples and a self-addressed, stamped envelope (SASE). Gallery directors like to see brochures and resumes illustrated with examples of your work (especially if the other samples are to be returned). Optional materials are a self-addresssed, stamped reply card (with check-off responses to prompt action) and a client list (especially if past experience increases assignment possibilities).

The cover letter personalizes your presentation; you're talking directly to someone about your best qualifications. It should be typed on your letterhead, never longer than one page, and concisely state who you are, what you do, what services you can provide and what follow-up (if any) you plan to make. Indicate whether samples are to be returned or filed; if they are to be returned, be sure your SASE contains sufficient postage. If they are to be filed and you have not included a reply card, your SASE may be a #10 legal-size envelope for a letter response.

A résumé lists your arts-related experience, education and achievements. It spotlights your best features and your most outstanding qualifications. A résumé is one of the most important tools in a fine artist's sample package, because it contains in a nutshell what a gallery director is looking for when reviewing work.

Résumés come in all shapes and sizes. Some are one-page listings of art shows or assignments, while others are elaborate full-color pamphlets. When designing your own, keep in mind that a résumé is a list of items that pertain only to your career as an artist; it is not a lengthy autobiography.

Your résumé should contain the following points:

- *Your professional name and address*. Graphic artists should list a phone number, while fine artists should attach a business card listing the number to select clients.
- *Education and scholarships*. List only post-high school degrees if they're art-related and also non-degree studies such as art seminars, workshops and lectures.
- *Exhibitions*. Exhibitions pertain more to a painter, but an illustrator can list them as evidence of stature and appeal. List every place that has handled your work, the year of the exhibition, the name of the gallery and its location. Also list whether it is a one-person or group show. If you have several shows, it is wise to separate exhibitions under subheadings such as "Solo Shows" and "Group Shows." Also include invitational and juried shows. List these in reverse chronological order, listing the most recent and working backwards.
- *Competitions and awards*. You will need three or more awards and competitions to warrant a special category. Otherwise, list them under exhibitions.

You can also list commissions, special projects, professional affiliations, collections, notices and reviews (note the publication, date and page number).

If you have just graduated from art school, emphasize the quality of your education (a note about prominent professors helps) over the lack of professional experience. Established artists emphasize prestigious accounts and awards, with their educational background as a last note. In other words, state your strongest evidence in the beginning, then back it up with additional strengths.

A brochure can be a multi-purpose folder, a one-page flyer or a multi-purpose booklet. Used in your promotional package, it should provide a brief synopsis of your talents, plus a few striking examples of your work. It should never be larger than 8½x11" so it can fit easily into an art director's files. If it is to be your only mailing piece, it must be comprehensive in scope; it must supply all the necessary information about your skills and successes.

A business card can be a calling card, an addendum to your package or a leave-behind after an interview. It should list your name, phone number and address plus a mention of your specialty. Use simple, clear type and standard dimensions (2x3½").

Samples are your visual candy; they are visual statements that best convey your style and technique. Select only the most appropriate and only the best. Many art directors claim they judge you by the worst piece they see. Gear your samples to the specific needs of the market you're approaching.

Types of samples

Art directors most commonly request to see transparencies, photographs, Photostats, photocopies and tear sheets. Black-and-white work lends itself to photocopies and Photostats (produced by a photographic process utilizing paper negatives). Color work is best depicted by either photographs or transparencies (a transparency is a positive image on a translucent film base; a slide is a 35mm transparency in a mount). Transparencies reproduce a greater range of tones than any other method of printing and can be made in varying sizes (2¼x2¼", 4x5" and 8x10"). Tear sheets, which are examples of published work, bolster your professional image and give an art director a notion of how your work appears in print. Tear sheets should be laminated to prevent tearing and folding.

Label everything. With photographs, Photostats and photocopies, use the back to stamp your name, address and phone number (a pre-printed label hurries this process); arrows indicating which way is up; the size of the original; and, if submitting several, mark each "1 of 5 photographs" or "2 of 5 Photostats". These numbers may also refer to a separate information sheet which gives details of how the illustration or design was used. If you send one, add "See info sheet" under the number.

Slides are labeled in similar fashion. On the "front" (image is correct when held up to a light), list your name, size of original work, medium, number and arrows indicating the top. If your slides are accompanied by an info sheet, indicate reference to it on the slides. Your full name, address and phone number may be printed on the reverse side.

Portfolio

You've been able to get your foot into the door with your first submission of self-promotional materials and samples. You've called to request an appointment to show your portfolio to the art director, either through the mail or in person, and he has agreed. Now is the chance to display to him the creative and professional artist you really are.

The overall appearance of the portfolio affects your professional presentation. A neat, organized three-ring binder is going to create a better impression than a bulky, time-worn leather case. The most popular portfolios are simulated leather with puncture-proof sides that allow the use of loose samples. The size of the portfolio should be dictated by the size of your work. Avoid the large "student" variety because they are too bulky to spread across an art director's desk. The most popular sizes are between 11x14" and 18x24".

No matter what format you choose for the case, you must follow a few basic principles in presenting its contents. Choose only your best work. Quality is better than quantity. Your portfolio should show a broad range of application—black-and-white and color work, different methods of print production, humorous and serious subjects, people and objects. Show a variety of jobs but not of styles. Your portfolio is your personal advertisement, and it must communicate directly and swiftly.

Since the drop-off policy is prevalent, have at least two or three portfolios at hand. One can be left when necessary, another can be used on personal calls, while the third can be sent to out-of-town prospects. Mini-portfolios are handy for simultaneous submissions. Let it be known that you will retrieve your portfolio either the next morning or the following evening. Most businesses are honorable; you don't have to worry about your case being stolen. But things do get lost, so, just in case, make sure you've included only duplicates, which can be insured at a reasonable cost.

When you're showing work to a gallery director, it's likely that you will be showing a few pieces of original work. If you work in several media, show one of each, then back them up with slides of further works. Choose work that is appropriate to the gallery. Don't drag along everything you've ever done, because you will not only confuse and bore the director, you'll also have to transport all that work to the gallery.

Packaging

Your primary goal in packaging is to have your samples, portfolio or assigned work arrive undamaged. Before packaging original work, make sure you have a copy (Photostat, photocopy, photograph, slide or transparency) in your file at home. If changes are necessary on an assigned job, you can then see on your copy what the art director is discussing over the phone. Most importantly, if your work is lost, you can make a duplicate.

Flat work can be packaged between heavy cardboard or Styrofoam. Cut the material slightly larger than the piece of flatwork and tape it closed. It is wise to include your business card or a piece of paper with your name and address on it on the outside of this packaging material in case the outer wrapper becomes separated from the inner packing. The work at least can then be returned to you.

The outer wrapping, depending on package size and quality of inner wrapping, may be a manila envelope, a foam-padded envelope, a "bubble" package (one with plastic "bubbles" lining the inside), or brown wrapping paper. Use reinforced tape for closures. Make sure one side is clearly addressed.

Check the various types of envelopes and packaging materials available at your local art supply, photography or stationery stores. If you're going to be doing a lot of mailing, buy in bulk quantities. The price is always lower.

Packing original works such as paintings takes several layers of protective coverings. The outer layer protects the work from physical damage, while the inner layer provides a cushion. The outer package must be sturdy, yet easy to open and repack. If you are mailing a flat work that is unframed, consider rolling it into a cardboard tube that can be found at appliance and furniture stores. A cardboard container is adequate for small pieces, but larger works should be protected with a strong outer surface, such as laminated cardboard, masonite or light plywood. Mounted, matted or framed pieces are irregularly shaped and require extra cushioning material such as Styrofoam. When packaging a framed work, wrap it in polyfoam or heavy cloth, cushion the outer container with spacers (any cushioning material that prevents a work from moving), then pack the artwork carefully inside so that it will not move when shipped.

Mailing

The U.S. Postal Service mail classifications with which you will be most concerned are First Class and Fourth Class, more commonly called parcel post. First Class mail is the type used every day for letters, etc. If the piece you are mailing is not the usual letter size, make sure to mark it First Class. Fourth Class is used for packages weighing 1 to 70 pounds and not more than 108 inches in length and girth combined.

The greatest disadvantage to using these classes of mail is that you cannot be guaranteed when the package/letter will arrive. If time is of the essence, consider the special services offered by the post office such as Priority Mail, Express Mail Next Day Service, and Special Delivery.

Today there is a growing number of airfreight services which make overnight delivery common. Check to see which ones are available in your area, but some of the more familiar names are Emery, Purolator and Federal Express. These firms offer varying rates according to weight of the package and urgency.

Certified mail includes a mailing receipt and provides a record of delivery at the addressee's post office. This type of mail is handled like ordinary mail, but you can request a return receipt on certain types of mail as your proof of delivery.

Cost is determined by weight, size and destination of the package and automatically includes insurance up to $100. You can purchase additional insurance.

UPS does have wrapping restrictions. Packages must be in heavy corrugated cardboard, with no string or paper on the outside, and be sealed with reinforced tape. UPS cannot guarantee how long it will take a package to arrive at its destination, but will track lost packages. It also offers Two-Day Blue Label Air Service to any destination in the U.S., and Next Day Service in specific zip code zones.

Greyhound Bus Lines and some commercial airlines also offer same-day or overnight package delivery. Check locally for rates and restrictions.

Pricing

Negotiation is the art of reaching a mutual agreement so that both parties feel satisfied with the outcome. When a client describes a project to you, you are hearing the client's needs and wants. He will never know *your* needs unless you speak up.

Each job will present you with a new and different pricing situation. Experience is often the best teacher, but even in the beginning, there are a few rules to follow. First, convey a positive attitude and listen carefully. Try to put yourself in your client's place so you can "hear" what he is really saying. When you speak, do it slowly and distinctly so the art buyer will slow down and listen to you.

So that you will be in a position to quote a price that is fair to both you and the client, you need to develop an hourly rate. This is especially important if you are a newcomer who can only estimate what your time is worth. After you establish an hourly rate and have completed many jobs, you will be able to quote a fee by knowing how long it usually takes to complete a similar assignment.

To arrive at an hourly rate, you need to know the annual salary of a person on staff who is doing similar work, such as a graphic designer on staff at an advertising agency. Take the annual salary, divide it by 52 (the number of weeks in a year) to get the weekly rate of pay. Then, divide the result by 40 (the number of hours in a work week) to arrive at the hourly rate for this type of job. Finally, add the extra expenses incurred in your overhead (rent, electricity, heat, supplies, etc.) by multiplying the result by 2.5. Check with other freelance artists to see if this figure is competitive and realistic.

Keep detailed records of your paintings in order to determine a fair price for them. Record when you started and completed a piece, plus the number of hours you worked on it. Also note the materials you used (both the amount and the cost). Then factor in your labor costs and overhead.

Remember that your prices should cover all costs and provide some profit. Also take into consideration the fact that you probably won't sell all the work you produce in a year. If you have sold your work for several years, you probably know how much you can demand for a work to make a profit. For example, if you complete 30 oils in a year and regularly sell only 15, you might have to double the amount you charge for each work. If the total costs involved in producing the work came to $175, you will have to ask at least $350 for each piece just to recover your costs for all the paintings you have completed during the year.

Contracts

In simplest terms, a contract is an agreement between two or more persons containing an offer, acceptance and consideration. Contracts may be written, oral or tacit, but to protect yourself from misunderstandings and faulty memories, make it a practice to have a written contract signed and dated by you and the party you are dealing with.

The items you want specified in your contract will vary according to the assignment and the complexity of the project; but some basic points are: your fee (the basic fee, possibly a kill fee, payment schedule, advances, expense compensation, etc.); what service you are providing for the fee; deadlines; how changes will be handled; and return of original art.

Read carefully any contract or purchase order you are asked to sign. If the terms are complex, or if you do not understand them, seek professional advice before signing. If it is a preprinted or "standard" contract, look for terms which may not be agreeable to you, such as "work-for-hire."

Further information on contracts is available in *The Artist's Friendly Legal Guide*, Tad Crawford's *Legal Guide for the Visual Artist*, and *Contracts for Artists* by William Gignilliat.

Copyright

According to a report published in *Graphic Artist's Guild Newsletter*, there are approximately 250,000 artists working in the visual arts. Yet, in 1986, only 51,258 works of visual art were registered for a copyright at the U.S. Copyright Office. Since most visual artists create at least one work a year, this means that only about 20% of the works created in a year are registered for copyright.

These figures point to a sad lack of knowledge about the copyright law. This section will touch upon the basics of copyright law so that you will be able to enjoy your creative rights.

The copyright law protects the creator of a work when the idea for a work is fixed in tangible form. Copyright protects the *expression* of an idea, not the idea itself. A copyright gives its owner the exclusive rights to reproduce, sell, distribute, display and publish artwork and to make reproductions from it. "Copyright is an exclusive right," says Roger Gilcrest, a patent attorney based in Cincinnati, Ohio. "It excludes other people from copying your work without your permission."

What can you copyright? A wide range of artwork is protected under the 1976 Act. It defines "pictorial, graphic, and sculptural work" that can be copyrighted as "original works of authorship fixed in any tangible medium of expression." This means that the work must spring from your own creative efforts and that it must be "fixed" on paper or any other tangible medium such as canvas or even in computer memory. Reproductions are copyrightable under the category of compilations and derivative works.

What can't be copyrighted? Ideas are not copyrightable. To protect an idea, you must use non-disclosure agreements or apply for a patent. Copyright protects the form but not the mechanical aspects of utilitarian objects. While you can copyright the form of your "Wally the Whale" lamp, you can't stop other people from making lamps. You can also copyright the illustration of Wally painted on the lamp.

How do you get copyright protection? Your work is automatically protected from the date of completion until the date of publication. When your work is published, you should protect your work by placing a copyright notice on it.

What is a copyright notice? A copyright notice consists of the word "Copyright" or its symbol ©, the year of first publication and the full name of the copyright owner. It must be placed where it can easily be seen, preferably on the front of your work. You can place it on the back of a painting as long as it won't be covered by a backing or a frame. Always place your copyright notice on slides or photographs sent to potential clients or galleries. Affix it on the mounts of slides and on the backs of photographs (preferably on a label).

If you omit the notice, you can still copyright the work if you have registered the work before publication and you make a reasonable effort to add the notice to all copies. If you've omitted the notice from a work that will be published, you can ask in your contract that the notice be placed on all copies.

When is a work "published"? Publication occurs when a work is displayed publicly or made available to public view. Your work is "published" when it is exhibited in a gallery, reproduced in a magazine, on a poster or on your promotional pieces.

How long does copyright protection last? If the work is created after January 1, 1976, protection begins the moment a work is completed and lasts for the life of the artist plus 50 years. For works created by two or more people, protection lasts for the life of the last survivor plus 50 years. For works created anonymously or under a pseudonym, protection lasts for 100 years after the work is completed or 75 years after publication, whichever is shorter.

How do I register a work? Write to the Copyright Office (Register of Copyrights, Library of Congress, Washington DC 20559) for Class VA forms for visual arts. After you receive the form, you can call the Copyright Office information number (202/479-0700) if you need any help. You can also write to the Copyright Office (address your letter to Information and Publications, Section LM-455) for information, forms, and circulars. After you fill out the form, return it to the Copyright Office with a check or money order for $10, a deposit copy or copies of the work and a cover letter explaining your request. For almost all artistic works, deposits consist of photographs, either transparencies (35mm or 2¼x2¼) or prints (preferably 8x10). For unpublished works, send one copy; send two copies for published works. You will need a certificate of registration which offers you more in-depth protection than the copyright notice can.

Do I have to register my work? You can register either before or after publication. The only time you must register your work is when you are planning to sue for infringement. However, it is always better to be protected from the start. You will not be entitled to attorney's fees or statutory damages if the infringement occurs before the date of registration (unless, in the case of a published work, registration is made within three months after publication).

What is a transfer of copyright? Ownership of all or some of your exclusive rights can be transferred by selling, donating or trading them and signing a document as evidence that the transfer has taken place. When you sign an agreement with a magazine for one-time use of an illustration, you are transferring part of your copyright to the magazine. The transfer is called a license. An exclusive license is a transfer that's usually limited by time, place or form of reproduction, such as first North American serial rights. A nonexclusive license gives several people the right to reproduce your work for specific purposes for a limited amount of time. For example, you can grant a nonexclusive license for your teddy bear design originally reproduced on a greeting card to a manufacturer of plush toys, to an art publisher for posters of the teddy bear, or to a manufacturer of novelty items for a teddy bear eraser.

What constitutes an infringement? Anyone who copies a protected work owned by someone else or exercises an exclusive right without authorization is liable for infringement. In an infringement case, you can sue for an injunction, which means you can stop the infringer from reproducing your work; for damages (you must prove how much money you've lost); and to prevent distribution of the infringing material.

For further information on copyright, refer to *The Artist's Friendly Legal Guide* and *How to Protect Your Creative Work* by David A. Weinstein.

Recordkeeping

If you haven't kept good business records, all your talent and art skills will mean nothing when it comes time to give an account of your business profitability to the IRS. Recordkeeping is usually considered a drudgery by artists, yet it is an essential part of your business. A freelancer is an independent businessperson, and, like any other entrepreneur, must be accountable for financial statements.

You don't have to be an accountant to understand basic recordkeeping principles. Two accounting terms that you'll need to know are the accounting period and the accounting method. Your accounting period determines the time frame you'll use to report income and claim deductions. Most likely you'll elect a calendar year accounting period, beginning January 1 and ending December 31. An accounting period other than a calendar year is known as a fiscal year.

Once you've selected your accounting period, you'll need to determine which accounting method best suits your business. Your accounting method will determine what income and expenses will be reported during a particular accounting period.

There are two basic accounting methods, the cash method and the accrual method. The cash method, which is used by most individuals, records income when it is received, or when a gallery or agent receives it for you. Similarly, expenses are recorded when you pay them. Expenses paid in advance can only be deducted in the year in which they occur. This method typically uses cash receipts and disbursement journals, which record payment when received and monthly paid expenses.

The accrual method is a little more involved. In this method, you report income at the time you earn it instead of when you receive it. Also, you deduct expenses at the time you incur them rather than when you pay them. If you use this method, you will probably keep accounts receivable and accounts payable journals, which list projects as they are invoiced or expenses as they are incurred. The accrual method is best for artists with huge inventories.

You are free to choose any accounting method you wish. However, once you've made that decision, you may only change your accounting method with the approval of the IRS. In order to request a change of accounting method, you must file Form 3115, Application for Change in Accounting Method, with the Commissioner of the Internal Revenue Service in Washington, D.C. not more than six months after the beginning of the year in which you wish to make a change.

The next step to good recordkeeping is to decide which records to keep. A good rule is to keep any receipt related to your business. It's important to hold on to cancelled checks, sales slips, invoices, cash receipts, cash register tapes, bank statements, bills and receipts for goods and services you have bought. Ask for a receipt with every purchase. If you're entertaining a client at a business dinner, ask the waiter or cashier for a receipt. Keep a record of the date, place, cost, business relationship and the purpose of the meeting. Don't forget to record driving expenses. Keep your business and personal records separate. Also, if you're a painter and an illustrator, keep separate records for each pursuit.

Here are a few tips for setting up an effective recordkeeping system. The first thing you should do is to divide your income and expense records into separate headings. Then you should divide each into various subheadings. A handy method is to label your records with the same categories listed on Schedule C of the 1040 tax form. That way you'll be able to transfer figures from your books to the tax form without much hassle. Always make an effort to keep your files in chronological order.

There are various bookkeeping systems at your disposal. A single-entry bookkeeping system records expenses as they are incurred; you add them up at the end of the year. This can be recorded in a journal or diary. A double-entry system is more complicated, involving ledgers and journals in which every item is entered twice—once as a debit and once as a credit so the books are always in balance.

Taxes

Knowing what income you must report and what deductions you can claim are the two most important factors in computing your taxes. To know these factors, you must first determine whether you are a professional or a hobbyist. You must prove you are a professional in order to claim business-related deductions which reduce the amount of taxable income you have to report.

Some of the factors which set you apart as a professional are: conducting your activity in a business-like manner (such as keeping accurate records, keeping a business checking account); your expertise and training; the time you devote to your work and if you have no other substantial source of income; and your history of income or losses. In the past a professional had to show two out of three years of profit. Now, under the Tax Reform Act of 1986, you must show a profit for three years out of five to attain a professional status.

As a professional who is the owner of an unincorporated business, you must report business expenses and income on Schedule C of Form 1040, Profit (or Loss) from Business or Profession. Remember that only 80 percent of your business meals, entertainment, tips, cover charges, parking and related expenses is deductible. Home office expenses are now deductible to the extent of net income from self-employment. The IRS's *Publication 553* (Highlights) covers the details (such as what items are 80% deductible) entailed in the Reform Act.

Under the Tax Reform Act of 1986, expenses incurred in creating artwork must be deducted through capitalization rules rather than be deducted when they occur. The new Uniform Capitalization Rule states that expenses such as art materials are investments in your business and should therefore be captialized rather than deducted. Capital expenditures, as art materials are now considered, must be *amortized* over three years. Amortization lets you recover these expenditures in a way similar to straight line depreciation. Amortization requires equal deductions taken in the years allowed. (This book is printed before the U.S. legislature votes on the exemption of artists from the Uniform Capitalization Rule. Check with the I.R.S. on how to report art-related expenses.)

Estimated tax is the method you use to pay tax on income which is not subject to withholding. You will generally make estimated tax payments if you expect to owe more than $500 at year's end and if the total amount of income tax that will be withheld during the year will be less than 90% of the tax shown on the previous year's return. In order to calculate your estimated tax, you must estimate your adjusted gross income, taxable income, taxes and credits for the year. Form 1040ES provides a worksheet which will help you estimate how much you will have to pay. Estimated tax payments are made in four equal installments due on April 15, June 15, September 15 and January 15. For more information, refer to IRS Publication 505, Tax Withholding and Estimated Tax.

The self-employment tax is a Social Security tax for individuals who are self-employed and therefore cannot have Social Security tax withheld from their paychecks. In order to be liable for self-employment tax, you must have a net self-employment income of $400 or more. Your net income is the difference between your self-employment income and your allowable business deductions. You will compute the amount of self-employment tax you owe on Schedule SE, Computation of Social Security Self-Employment Tax.

Depending on the complexity of your business and tax expertise, you may want to have a professional tax adviser to consult with or to complete your tax form. Most IRS offices have walk-in centers open year-round and offer over 90 free IRS publications containing tax information to help in preparation of your return. The booklet that comes with your tax return forms contains names and addresses of Forms Distribution Centers by region where you can write for further information. The U.S. Small Business Administration offers seminars on taxes, and arts organizations hold many workshops covering business management, often including detailed tax information. Inquire at your arts council, local arts organization or a nearby college/university to see if a workshop is scheduled.

You will be asked to provide your Social Security number or your Employer Identification number (if you are a business) to the person/firm for whom you are doing a freelance project. This information is now necessary in order to make payments.

Home office deduction

A home office deduction allows you to claim a business portion of the expenses incurred for the upkeep and running of your entire home. You may deduct business expenses that apply to a part of your home only if that part is used exclusively on a regular basis as your principal place of business at which you meet or deal with clients, or a separate structure used in your trade or business that is not attached to your residence. Your office must be a space devoted only to your artwork and its business activity.

You may have another business which generates more income than you derive from the sale of your art. For instance, you may have a fulltime job where you have an office at another location. You can still take your home office deduction as long as it's your principal place of business for your secondary source of income.

When a studio is part of the principal residence, deductions are possible on an appropriate portion of mortgage interest, property taxes, rent, repair and utility bills, and depreciation.

There are two ways to determine what percentage of your home is used for business purposes. If the rooms in the house are approximately the same size, divide the number of rooms used as your office into the total number of rooms in your house. If your rooms differ in size, divide the square footage of your business area into the total square footage of your house.

Your total office deduction for the business use of your home cannot exceed the gross income that you derive from its business use. In other words, you cannot take a net business loss resulting from a home office deduction.

Because the IRS keeps close tabs on the home office deduction, you should keep a log of business activities taking place in your home office. Record the dates and times the office was in use, what business was discussed, and all sales and business transacted.

Consult a tax adviser to be certain you meet all of the requirements before attempting to take this deduction since its requirements and interpretations frequently change.

Sales tax

Check regarding your state's regulations on sales tax. Some states claim that "creativity" is a service rendered and cannot be taxed, while others view it as a product you are selling and therefore taxable. Be certain you understand the sales tax laws to avoid being held liable for uncollected money at tax time. Write to your state auditor for sales tax information.

If you work on consignment with a shop or gallery, you are not responsible for collecting sales tax since it is the shop or gallery which is making the sale to the consumer. If you sell wholesale, you need not collect sales tax for the same reason. However, you must exchange resale numbers so both parties can show the numbers on their invoices.

In most states, if you are selling to a customer outside of your sales tax area, you do not have to collect sales tax. However, check to see if this holds true for your state.

Important note on the markets

- *Listings are based on editorial questionnaires and interviews. They are not advertisements (markets do not pay for their listings) nor are listings endorsed by the* Artist's Market *editor.*
- *Listings are verified prior to the publication of this book. If a listing has not changed from last year, then the editor has told us that his needs have not changed—and the previous information still accurately reflects what he buys.*
- *Remember, information in the listings is as current as possible, but art directors come and go; companies and publications move; and art needs fluctuate between the publication of this directory and when you use it.*
- *When looking for a specific market, check the index. A market might not be listed for one of these reasons: 1) It doesn't solicit freelance material, 2) It has gone out of business, 3) It requests not to be listed, 4) It did not respond to our questionnaire, 5) It doesn't pay for art (we have, however, included some nonpaying listings because we feel the final printed artwork could be valuable to the artist's portfolio), 6) We have received complaints about it and it hasn't answered our inquiries satisfactorily.*
- Artist's Market *reserves the right to exclude any listing that does not meet its requirements.*

The Markets

Advertising, Audiovisual & Public Relations Firms

We see advertising every day in the morning newspaper, in magazines and on television. We know what it does—it tells about a product in the hopes of selling it, but it's hard to define what it is. The distinctions between advertising and publicity have blurred; advertising has become any type of activity that promotes ideas, goods or services. For example, sponsorships of an athletic event or support of a political cause has become a form of advertisement.

Most advertising agencies create print ads for newspapers and magazines and ads for broadcasting media such as radio and television. Types of agencies range from full-service houses to specialized ones, classified by the products they advertise—food, beverage, fashion, cosmetics, and so on. Agencies can be as large as megacorporations with international offices or as small as a one-person office.

No matter what size an agency is, all rely on artists to create a certain look that sets their ads apart from the competition. Generally, art directors look to freelancers for an outsider's fresh approach or a unique look. Because of the agency's variety of clients and products, styles range from humorous illustration to detailed renderings, from realistic to abstract. Cartoons are often used to lighten a message or deliver a humorous tone.

Illustration is mostly used for print advertisements, brochures, direct mail packages, posters and catalogs. It is also used for making presentations to clients in the form of comprehensives or storyboards.

Since the Crash of 1988, advertising agencies have reduced their inhouse staffs and are seeking more creative help from freelancers. Faced with tight deadlines, artists are expected to "produce," that is, create artwork to specifications and do it on time. In order to show that you can produce, include in your portfolio your best work accompanied by a brief description of the project's instructions. Make sure you gear your portfolio to the agency's needs or types of clients; if the agency handles food companies, include renderings of food. Mention other advertising campaigns you have participated in, noting your exact involvement, the client, the art director and your price range. Read the agency's listing in this section or call the art director and ask what samples should be included; some wish to see your conceptual work (roughs and comprehensives) while others prefer to see only finished pieces. Always include a leave-behind such as a tear sheet or brochure—not just a business card—for the art director's files. The art director will contact you when an assignment arises that he feels fits your style.

Read the Close-up in this section to see how illustrator Andy Lackow handles payment and contract negotiations with agencies. They frequently ask for buyouts because their clients may want to use the artwork again. If you feel a buyout is called for, make sure you are compensated for it, but hold on to the ownership of the piece. Also, try to have the originals returned to you.

Agencies pay by the hour or by the project. Factors determining your fee depend on where the ad appears (in a major daily or in a local paper); if it's black-and-white or color; if the client is national or local; or if the ad is full-page or a spot. Other variables include turnaround time and the scope of the client's budget.

Public relations firms

Public relations firms are hired to convey a message or to maintain a favorable image for a company. The firm generally researches the market, then develops a plan to change or maintain a company's image. They call upon freelance artists for a variety of jobs, from designing a corporate logo to illustrating brochures.

Audiovisual firms

Audiovisual firms produce slide shows, filmstrips and motion pictures that are used for educational purposes, public relations, or for employee training. They rely upon artists to illustrate or design images that can be transferred to slides or films. Since their images are often incorporated into a project, artists who work with audiovisual companies must understand how their work will be used in order to avoid complications later. For example, the color scheme you use for your slides may clash with the rest of the presentation. Also keep in mind the correct format so that the image you create will fit with any copy that is superimposed.

While audiovisual firms are open to working long distance with artists, most advertising and public relations firms prefer working closely with local artists because of short deadlines and last-minute revisions. Freelance artists are used on a regular basis only when the workload is too heavy for inhouse staff.

Additional names and addresses (but no marketing information) can be found in the *Standard Directory of Advertising Agencies*, the *Audio Video Market Place, O'Dwyer's Directory of Public Relations Firms*, and the *Madison Avenue Handbook*. Read the weeklies *Advertising Age* and *Adweek* to keep current on the changes in the advertising field.

Alabama

J.H. LEWIS ADVERTISING AGENCY INC., Box 6829, Mobile AL 36660. (205)476-2507. Senior Vice President/Creative Director: Larry D. Norris. Ad agency. Clients: retail, manufacturers, health care and direct mail. Buys 15 illustrations/year.

Needs: Works with illustrators and designers. Uses artists for mechanicals and layout for ads, annual reports, billboards, catalogs, letterheads, packaging, P-O-P displays, posters, TV and trademarks.

First Contact & Terms: Prefers southern artists. Query. SASE. Reports in 5 days. No originals returned to artist at job's completion. Pays for design by the hour, $30-60. Pays for illustration by the project, $750-1,500. Pays promised fee for unused assigned work.

SPOTTSWOOD VIDEO/FILM STUDIO, 2520 Old Shell Rd., Mobile AL 36607. (205)478-9387. Contact: Manning W. Spottswood. AV/film/TV producer. Clients: industry, education, government and

advertising. Produces mainly public relations and industrial films and tapes.
Needs: Assigns 5-15 jobs/year. Artists "must live close by and have experience." Uses approximately 1 illustrator/month. Works on assignment only. Uses artists for illustrations, maps, charts, decorations, set design, etc.
First Contact & Terms: Send resume or arrange interview by mail. Reports only if interested. Pays for design by the hour, $25 minimum; by the project, $150 minimum. Considers complexity of project, client's budget, skill and experience of artist, geographic scope of finished project, turnaround time, rights purchased and quality of work when establishing payment.
Tips: "We are very small and go from project to project—most of them very small."

Arizona

***EVANS/PHOENIX**, Suite 400, 2122 E. Highland, Phoenix AZ 85016. (602)957-6636. Art Director: Michael Smith. Ad agency. Clients: retail, restaurants, state lottery, financial, homebuilders and industrial firms.
Needs: Works with 4-5 illustrators/month. Uses freelance artists for billboards, consumer and trade magazines, brochures, posters and newspapers.
First Contact & Terms: Send resume or promotional piece by mail; follow up with phone call for interview. Works on assignment basis only. Payment is by the project; negotiates according to client's budget.

FARNAM COMPANIES, INC., Box 34820, Phoenix AZ 85067-4820. (602)285-1660. Creative Director: Trish Spencer. Inhouse advertising agency—Charles Duff Agency—for animal health products firm. Client sells through distributors to feed stores, tack shops, co-ops, pet stores, horse and cattle industry.
Needs: Works with 3-10 freelance artists/year. Works on assignment only. Uses artists for illustrations for brochures, labels and ads. Especially looks for realism, skill in drawing animals and quick turnaround.
First Contact & Terms: Send query letter with resume and tear sheets to be kept on file. Prefers any type of samples "which clearly show quality and detail of work." Samples not filed are returned only if requested. Reports back only if interested. To show a portfolio, mail original/final art, final reproduction/product and tear sheets. Pays for illustrations by the project, $100 minimum. Considers client's budget, skill and experience of artist, and geographic scope for the finished product when establishing payment. Rights purchased vary according to project.
Tips: "Mail us samples of work. They should be of animals (horses, dogs, cats, cattle and small animals) with rates and time estimates if possible."

FILMS FOR CHRIST ASSOCIATION, 2628 W. Birchwood Circle, Mesa AZ 85202. Contact: Paul S. Taylor. Motion picture producer and book publisher. Audience: educational, religious. Produces motion pictures, videos, and books.
Needs: Works with 1-5 illustrators/year. Works on assignment only. Uses artists for books, catalogs, and motion pictures. Also uses artists for animation, slide illustrations and ads. Prefers tight, realistic style, plus some technical illustrations; prefers airbrush, watercolor, acrylics and markers.
First Contact & Terms: Query with resume and samples (photocopies, slides, tear sheets or snapshots). Prefers slides as samples. Samples returned by SASE. Reports in 1 month. Provide brochure/flyer, resume and tear sheets to be kept on file for future assignments. No originals returned to artist at job's completion. Considers complexity of project, and skill and experience of artist when establishing payment.

GILBERT ADVERTISING, LTD., Suite 107, 77 E. Weldon Ave., Box 7450-A, Phoenix AZ 85011-7450. Creative Director: T.R. Gilbert. Specializes in corporate identity; newspaper and magazine ads; brochures, catalogs and catalog sheets; and direct mail programs. Clients: primarily small firms in manufacturing and commercial services.

The asterisk before a listing indicates that the listing is new in this edition. New markets are often the most receptive to freelance submissions.

Needs: Works with 10-20 freelance artists/year. Artists "must be willing to sell all rights to reproduction of artwork for established or agreed-upon fee. We do not deal through artist's agents." Works on assignment only. Uses artists for advertising, brochures, catalogs, mechanicals, retouching, direct mail packages, charts/graphs, AV presentations, lettering and logos.
First Contact & Terms: Send query letter with brochure, resume, business card, slides, Photostats, photocopies, photographic prints, and/or tear sheets to be kept on file. Do *not* send original work. Samples not kept on file are returned by SASE. Reports only if interested. Pays for design by the project, $100-1,000 average; for b&w illustration by the project, $50-400 average; for color illustration by the project, $500-2,500 average. Considers complexity of project and client's budget when establishing payment.

PAUL S. KARR PRODUCTIONS, 2949 W. Indian School Rd., Box 11711, Phoenix AZ 85017. (602)266-4198. Contact: Paul Karr. Utah Division: 1024 N. 250 East, Box 1254, Orem UT 84057. (801)226-8209. Contact: Michael Karr. Film and video producer. Clients: industrial, business, educational, TV and cable.
Needs: Occasionally works with freelance filmmakers in motion picture and video projects. Works on assignment only.
First Contact & Terms: Advise of experience and abilities.
Tips: "If you know about motion pictures and video or are serious about breaking into the field, there are three avenues: 1) have relatives in the business; 2) be at the right place at the right time; or, 3) take upon yourself the marketing of your idea, or develop a film or video idea for a sponsor who will finance the project. Go to a film or video production company, such as ours, and tell them you have a client and the money. They will be delighted to work with you on making the production. Work, and approve the various phases as it is being made. Have your name listed as the producer on the credits. With the knowledge and track record you have gained you will be able to present yourself and your abilities to others in the film and video business and to sponsors."

PHILLIPS-RAMSEY, 829 N. 1st Ave., Phoenix AZ 85003. (602)252-2565. Senior Art Director: David Robb. Ad agency. Clients: savings and loan, racetrack, hotel, restaurant, high-tech, public utility, consumer goods, medical, home builders. Client list provided for SASE.
Needs: Works on assignment only. Uses artists for illustration, photography and production.
First Contact & Terms: Send brochure to be kept on file. Reports only if interested. Pays by the project. Considers complexity of the project, client's budget, geographic scope for the finished product, turnaround time and rights purchased when establishing payment. Buys all rights; "Our agency only works on a buy-out basis."

Arkansas

ADI ADVERTISING/PUBLIC RELATIONS, Box 2299, Ft. Smith AR 72902. President: Asa Douglas. Ad agency/PR. Clients: retail, personal service, small manufacturing, political.
Needs: Assigns 150-200 freelance jobs/year. Regional artists only, within two-days mail time. Works on assignment only. Works with 2-3 freelance illustrators and 5-10 freelance designers/month. Uses artists for consumer and trade magazines, billboards, brochures, catalogs, newspapers, stationery, signage and posters.
First Contact & Terms: Send brochure showing art style. Samples not kept on file are returned by SASE. Reports only if interested. Write to schedule an appointment to show portfolio, which should include roughs, original/final art, final reproduction/product and photographs. Pays for design by the hour, $10-100; pays for illustration by the hour, $25-300. Considers complexity of project, client's budget, skill and experience of artist and rights purchased when establishing payment. Buys all rights.
Tips: "Creative needs are satisfied with unusual, often unknown, ideas. There is a need for creative thinking on paper that can be added to a complete campaign. Show complete scope of your ability to work from production through design."

MANGAN RAINS GINNAVEN HOLCOMB, 911 Savers Federal Bldg., Little Rock AR 72201. Contact: Steve Mangan. Ad agency. Clients: recreation, financial, consumer, industrial, real estate.
Needs: Works with 5 designers and 5 illustrators/month. Assigns 50 jobs and buys 50 illustrations/year. Uses artists for consumer magazines, stationery design, direct mail, brochures/flyers, trade magazines and newspapers. Also uses artists for illustrations for print materials.
First Contact & Terms: Query with brochure, flyer and business card to be kept on file. SASE. Reports in 2 weeks. Call or write to schedule an appointment to show a portfolio, which should include final reproduction/product. Pays for design by the hour, $42 minimum; all fees negotiated.

California

***ANKLAM FEITZ GROUP**, 146 N. Golden Mall, Burbank CA 91502. (818)842-5163. Art Director: Russell Holmes. President: Barry Anklam. Full-service advertising and design agency providing ads, brochures, P-O-P displays, posters, and menus. Clients: high-tech, electronic, restaurants, photographic accessories.
Needs: Works with 8 freelance artists/year. Assigns 15-20 jobs/year. Uses artists for brochure illustration, newspaper and magazine ad illustration, mechanicals, retouching, direct mail packages, lettering and charts/graphs.
First Contact & Terms: Contact through artist's agent or send query letter with brochure showing art style. Samples are filed. Reports back only if interested. To show a portfolio, mail tear sheets, photographs, color and b&w. Pays for design and illustration by the project. Considers complexity of project, client's budget and turnaround time when establishing payment. Rights purchased vary according to project.

VICTORIA BASLER & ASSOCIATES, 1 S. Fair Oaks Ave., Pasadena CA 91105. (818)793-3015. Art Director: Julia King. Ad agency. "We are a full-service advertising agency providing collateral, brochures, print, radio and television production and media. We also have public relations and marketing departments." Clients: car rental, fashion, banks, computers, medical, nonprofit organizations. Client list provided upon request.
Needs: Works with 10-20 freelance artists/year. Assigns 10 jobs/year. Prefers local artists. Works on assignment only. Uses artists for design, illustration, brochures, catalogs, newspapers, consumer and trade magazines, mechanicals, retouching, billboards, posters, lettering and advertisements.
First Contact & Terms: Send query letter with resume. Samples are filed, "or if artist wishes," returned by SASE. Reports back within 2 weeks. Write to schedule an appointment to show a portfolio. Pays for design by the hour, $10-20. Pays for illustration by the project, $50 minimum. Considers complexity of project, client's budget, turnaround time and skill and experience of artist when establishing payment. Rights purchased vary according to project.
Tips: "Save time by not calling first, but simply writing a letter and/or resume to agency. When freelance artists call, we have our receptionist request a letter/resume."

BEAR ADVERTISING, 1424 N. Highland, Hollywood CA 90028. (213)466-6464. President: Richard Bear. Clients: fast food enterprises, sporting goods firms and industrial. Assigns 50-100 jobs/year.
Needs: Works with 1-2 illustrators and 2 designers/month. Local artists only. Uses artists for illustrations for annual reports, design of direct mail brochures, mechanicals and sign design.
First Contact & Terms: Call for interview. No originals returned. Negotiates pay.

ALEON BENNETT & ASSOC., Suite 212, 13455 Ventura Blvd., Van Nuys CA 91423. President: Aleon Bennett. Public relations firm.
Needs: Works with 2 freelance artists/year. Works on assignment only. Uses freelance artists for press releases and advertisements.
First Contact & Terms: Send query letter. Samples are not filed. Samples not filed are not returned. Does not report back.

RALPH BING ADVERTISING CO., 16109 Selva Dr., San Diego CA 92128. (619)487-7444. President: Ralph S. Bing. Ad agency. Clients: industrial (metals, steel warehousing, mechanical devices, glass, packaging, stamping tags and labels), political, automotive, food and entertainment.
Needs: Local artists only. Works on assignment only. Uses artists for consumer and trade magazines, brochures, layouts, keylines, illustrations and finished art for newspapers, magazines, direct mail and TV. Prefers pen & ink.
First Contact & Terms: "Call first; arrange an appointment if there is an existing need; bring easy-to-present portfolio. Provide portfolio of photocopies and tear sheets, and client reference as evidence of quality and/or versatility." Reports only if interested. No original work returned to artist at job's completion. Pays by the hour, $5-50 average; by the project, $10 minimum. Considers complexity of project and client's budget when establishing payment.
Tips: "Prefer to see samples of finished work; do not want to see classroom work."

COAKLEY HEAGERTY, 122 Saratoga, Santa Clara CA 95051. (408)249-6242. Creative Directors: Susann Rivera and J. D. Keser. Art Director: Bob Peterson. Full-service ad agency. Clients: consumer, high-tech, banking/financial, insurance, automotive, real estate, public service. Client list provided upon request.
Needs: Works with 100 freelance artists/year. Assigns 500 jobs/year. Works on assignment only. Uses

freelance artists for illustration, retouching, animation, lettering, logos and charts/graphs.
First Contact & Terms: Send query letter with brochure showing art style or resume, slides and photographs. Samples are filed. Samples not filed are returned by SASE. Does not report back. Call to schedule an appointment to show a portfolio. Pays for illustration by the project, $600-5,000. Considers complexity of project, client's budget, skill and experience of artist and rights purchased when establishing payment. Rights purchased vary according to project.

***GEORGE CARSON AND ASSOCIATES, INC.**, Suite B, 3555 Harbor Gateway S., Costa Mesa CA 92626. (714)549-1421. President: George Carson. A full-service advertising agency, providing collateral, sales materials, video films, TV commercials, radio spots, complete campaigns and publicity. Clients: automotive, sporting goods, financial, consumer goods, business-to-business.
Needs: Works with 6 artists/year. Assigns 100 jobs/year. Prefers local artists within 40 miles with at least 3 years of experience who have own studio or will work at agency. Works on assignment only. Uses artists for brochure design and illustration, catalog design and illustration, newspaper and magazine ad design and illustration, P-O-P displays, mechanicals, retouching, billboards, posters, films and logos.
First Contact & Terms: Send query letter with resume and photocopies. Samples are filed. Reports back only if interested. Write to schedule an appointment to show a portfolio or mail Photostats and tear sheets (if possible). Pays for design by the project, $150-8,000. Pays for illustration by the project, $30-1,650. Considers complexity of project, client's budget and turnaround time when establishing payment. Negotiates rights purchased.
Tips: "In a portfolio, include photos (transparencies are fine) and photocopies of work. Do not send originals, nor an assignment that the artist was not involved with less than 70%."

COPY GROUP ADVERTISING, Box 315, Encino CA 91316. Contact: Len Miller. Clients: resorts, travel spots, vacation areas and direct mail.
Needs: Uses artists for cartoons, illustrations, spot drawings and humorous sketches. "Artists with experience in book publishing, advertising and greeting cards would probably have the skills we're looking for. Prefers pen & ink."
First Contact & Terms: Send a small sampling of material for review. Prefers photocopies as samples; do *not send original work*. Reports within 10 days. Pays by the project, $25-150.

DIMON CREATIVE COMMUNICATION SERVICES, Box 6489, Burbank CA 91510. (818)845-3748. Art Director: Bobbie Polizzi. Ad agency/printing firm. Serves clients in industry, finance, computers, electronics, health care and pharmaceuticals.
First Contact & Terms: Send query letter with tear sheets, original art and photocopies. SASE. Provide brochure, flyer, business card, resume and tear sheets to be kept on file for future assignments. Portfolio should include comps; does not want to see newspaper ads. Pays for design by the hour, $20-50. Pays for illustration by the project, $75 minimum. Considers complexity of project, turnaround time, client's budget, and skill and experience of artist when establishing payment.

DJC & ASSOCIATES, 6117 Florin Rd., Sacramento CA 95823. (916)421-6310. Owner: Donna Cicogni. Ad agency. Assigns 120 jobs/year.
Needs: Works with 1 illustrator/month. Local artists only. Works on assignment only. Uses artists for consumer and trade magazines, stationery design, direct mail, TV, brochures/flyers and newspapers.
First Contact & Terms: Call to schedule an appointment to show a portfolio which should include original/final art, final reproduction/product, etc. No originals returned to artist at job's completion. Negotiates pay.

***DUDKOWSKI-LYNCH ASSOCIATES, INC.**, 150 Shoreline Highway, Mill Valley CA 94941. (415)332-5825. Vice President: Marijane Lynch. "We are a video facility providing Quantel Paintbox images to agencies, producers, corporations and institutions."
Needs: Works with 5 artists/year. "We need airbrush talent, motion graphics, cartoon, and general painting (any medium)." Prefers artist with strong art background and skill, and experience in video or film; best if artist has Quantel Paintbox experience. Uses artists for P-O-P displays, animation, films, video, logos and charts/graphs.
First Contact & Terms: Send resume. Samples are filed. Samples not filed are returned only if requested by artist. Reports back within 1 month. Call to schedule an appointment to show a portfolio, which should include final reproduction/product, photographs, color, b&w, and video tape. Pays for design by the hour, $15-30 or by the project. Pays for illustration by the hour, $20-30 or by the project. Considers complexity of project, client's budget, turnaround time and skill and experience of artist when establishing payment. Rights purchased vary according to project.
Tips: "Send resume, follow up call in two weeks. Have samples of work."

EXPANDING IMAGES, Suite 126, 18 Technology, Irvine CA 92718. (714)272-3203. President: Robert Denison. Audiovisual firm. Clients: mixed.
Needs: Works with 6 freelance artists/year. Uses artists for graphics, photography, illustration and design.
First Contact & Terms: Works on assignment only. Send samples to be kept on file. Prefers tear sheets as samples. Samples not filed are returned by SASE only if requested. Reports only if interested. Pays by the project. Considers client's budget and skill and experience of artist when establishing payment. Buys all rights.

HANNA-BARBERA PRODUCTIONS INC., 3400 Cahuenga Blvd., Hollywood CA 90068. (213)851-5000. Producer: Harry Love. TV/motion picture producer. Clients: TV networks. Produces animation and motion pictures.
Needs: Uses artists for animation and related artwork as needed. Uses mostly local artists.
First Contact & Terms: Provide resume to be kept on file for future assignments.

HUBBERT ADVERTISING AND PUBLIC RELATIONS CO., INC, 3198-M Airport Loop, Costa Mesa CA 92626. Senior Art Director: Chris Klopp. Ad agency. Clients: real estate and miscellaneous (all product, service).
Needs: Works with 5-10 freelance artists/year. Local artists only (southern California). Uses artists for line art/paste-up, advertising collateral illustration, b&w and 4-color; and layout comps. Especially seeks professionalism (marker skills); efficiency (clean); and deadline awareness (fast turnaround).
First Contact & Terms: Send query letter with resume and samples to be kept on file. Accepts any kind of copy that is readable as samples. Samples not filed are returned by SASE. Reports back only if interested. Write for appointment to show portfolio. Pays by the hour, $10-35 average. Pays in 60 days. Considers complexity of the project, client's budget and turnaround time when establishing payment. Rights purchased vary according to project.

***INNERQUEST COMMUNICATIONS CORPORATION**, 6383 Rose Lane, Carpinteria CA 93013. (805)684-9977. Producer: Don L. Higley. Estab. 1986. Audiovisual and public relations firm specializing in television mini-series and weekly series.
Needs: Uses artists for animation.
First Contact & Terms: Send query letter with brochure showing art style. Samples are filed. Reports back within 2 weeks only if interested. Pays by the project, $25-1,000. Considers client's budget when establishing payment. Buys all rights.

***LONGENDYKE/LOREQUE INC.**, Suite 10, 3100 W. Warner St., Santa Ana CA 92704. (714)641-9209. Lead Artist: Karen Kerfoot. "We are a slide graphic firm specializing in multi-image and videographic animation and special effects." Clients: audiovisual producers, ad agencies.
Needs: Works with 4-5 artists/year. Prefers local artists with knowledge of camera-ready art for AV. Uses artists for animation, logos, charts/graphs and camera-ready art for multi-image.
First Contact & Terms: Send resume and slides. Samples are filed. Samples not filed are returned only if requested by artist. Reports back only if interested. Write to schedule an appointment to show a portfolio, which should include original/final art and slides. Pays for design by the hour, $10-20. Considers complexity of project, turnaround time and skill and experience of artist when establishing payment.
Tips: "Artist must have knowledge of typesetting, multi-image screen formats and extensive use of Amberlith, and understand AV animation."

WARREN MILLER ENTERPRISES, 505 Pier Ave., Hermosa Beach CA 90254. (213)376-2494. Owner: Warren Miller. Produces sports documentaries, commercials, television format films and video cassettes for home use.
Needs: Works with 1 ad illustrator and 1 advertising designer/year. Works on assignment only. Uses artists for direct mail brochures, magazine ads and posters.
First Contact & Terms: Send query letter with samples (original sports illustration—skiing, sailing, windsurfing, etc.) or write for interview. Reports within 2 weeks. Buys nonexclusive rights. Samples returned by SASE. Provide resume to be kept on file for future assignments. "We pay by the project and since they range from brochures to full color film posters, it is impossible to give a fair range. Some of these are complicated; some already laid out and need only finished art." Considers complexity of project and skill and experience of artist when establishing payment.
Tips: There is "less 'standard' work and a trend toward contemporary, avant-garde art in our area of business. We prefer to work with artists who have done sports illustrations and recreation-oriented art, but we respond to great talent. Please send some kinds of samples and background information on assignments."

MOOSE COMMUNICATIONS, Box 5096, Bear Valley CA 95223. (209)753-6210. Producer: Doreen Nagle. Audiovisual firm. "We are a full-service media firm specializing in film and video production for training aids, promotional features, TV, sales aids, marketing, home distribution. We are also experienced in print and radio media. We serve all types of clients who need our services."
Needs: Works with 5 freelance artists/year. Assigns 12 jobs/year. Uses artists for design, illustration, brochures, consumer and trade magazines, P-O-P displays, retouching, animation, direct mail packages, press releases, motion pictures, lettering, logos, charts/graphs and advertisements. Perfers computer illustration, then pen & ink, airbrush, colored pencil, watercolor, collage, markers and calligraphy.
First Contact & Terms: Send query letter with resume, tear sheets, Photostats, photocopies, slides and photographs. Samples are filed. Samples not filed are returned by SASE. Reports back within 2 weeks only if interested. Write to schedule an appointment to show a portfolio or mail "any samples." Pays for design and illustration by the hour, $50 minimum; by the project, $150 minimum; by the day, $300 minimum. Considers complexity of project, client's budget, skill and experience of artist, how work will be used and rights purchased when establishing payment. Rights purchased vary according to project.
Tips: "We don't want to see a resume. We do want to see a client list and 3-5 samples of work."

ON-Q PRODUCTIONS, INC., 618 E. Gutierrez St., Santa Barbara CA 93103. President: Vincent Quaranta. Audiovisual firm. "We are producers of multi-projector slide presentations. We produce computer-generated slides for business presentations." Clients: banks, ad agencies, R&D firms and hospitals.
Needs: Works with 10 freelance artists/year. Assigns 50 jobs/year. Uses artists for illustration, retouching, animation and lettering.
First Contact & Terms: Send query letter with brochure or resume, and slides. Samples are filed. Samples not filed are returned by SASE. Reports back only if interested. Write to schedule an appointment to show a portfolio, which should include original/final art and slides. Pays for design by the hour, $20 minimum, or by the project, $100 minimum. Pays for illustration by the hour, $20 minimum or by the project, $100 minimum. Considers complexity of project, client's budget, turnaround time and skill and experience of artist when establishing payment.
Tips: "Artist must be *experienced* in computer graphics and on the board. The most common mistake freelancers make are "poor presentation of a portfolio (small pieces fall out, scratches on cover acetate) and they do not know how to price out a job."

ORLIE, HILL & CUNDALL, INC., (formerly Cundall/Whitehead Advertising Inc.), 20 Liberty Ship Way, Sausalito CA 94965. (415)332-3625. Contact: Alan Cundall. Ad agency.
Needs: Works with 6 designers/month. Uses artists for consumer magazines, stationery design, direct mail, slide shows, brochures/flyers, trade magazines and newspapers. Also uses artists for layout, paste-up and type spec.
First Contact & Terms: Send query letter and resume to be kept on file for future assignments. No originals returned to artist at job's completion. Pays for design by the hour, $35 minimum. Considers budget and complexity of project when establishing payment.
Tips: "We're an ad agency with expertise in direct marketing. What I want to see is brilliant selling ideas, magnificently interpreted into ads and other forms of communication."

PALKO ADVERTISING, INC., Suite 207, 2075 Palos Verdes Dr. N., Lomita CA 90717. (213)530-6800. Account Services: Judy Kolosvary. Ad agency. Clients: business-to-business, retail and high-tech.
Needs: Uses artists for layout, illustration, paste-up, mechanicals, copywriting and P-O-P displays. Produces ads, brochures and collateral material.
First Contact & Terms: Prefers local artists. Send query letter with brochure, resume, business card and samples to be kept on file. Write for appointment to show portfolio. Accepts tear sheets, photographs, photocopies, printed material or slides as samples. Samples not filed returned only if requested. Reports back only if interested. Pays for design by the hour, $15-30. Pays for illustration by the hour, $15-30, or by the project, $50-1,500. Negotiates rights purchased.

RICHARD SIEDLECKI DIRECT MARKETING, Suite C-170, 2674 E. Main St., Ventura CA 93003-2899. (805)658-7000. Direct Marketing Consultant: Richard Siedlecki. Consulting agency. Clients: industrial, publishers, associations, air freight, consumer mail order firms, and financial. Client list provided for SASE.
Needs: Assigns 15 freelance jobs/year. Works with 2 freelance designers/month. Works on assignment only. Uses artists for consumer and trade magazines, direct mail packages, brochures, catalogs and newspapers.
First Contact & Terms: Artists should be "experienced in direct response marketing." Send query let-

ter with brochure, resume and business card to be kept on file. Reports only if interested. Pays by the hour, $25 minimum; by the project, $250 minimum. Considers complexity of project and client's budget when establishing payment. "All work automatically becomes the property of our client."
Tips: Artists "must understand (and be able to apply) direct mail/direct response marketing methods to all projects: space ads, direct mail, brochures, catalogs."

DANA WHITE PRODUCTIONS, INC., 2623 29th St., Santa Monica CA 90405. (213)450-9101. Owner/Producer: Dana C. White. Audiovisual firm. "We are a full-service audiovisual production company, providing multi-image and slide-tape, video and audio presentations for training, marketing, awards, historical, and public relations uses. We have complete inhouse production resources, including slide-making, soundtrack production, photography, and A/V multi-image programming." Clients: "We serve major industry, such as GTE, Occidental Petroleum; medical, such as Oral Health Services, Whittier Hospital, Florida Hospital; schools, such as University of Southern California, Pepperdine University, and Clairbourne School; and public service efforts, such as fund-raising."
Needs: Works with 4-6 freelance artists/year. Assigns 12-20 jobs/year. Prefers artists local to greater LA, "with timely turnaround, ability to keep elements in accurate registration, neatness, design quality, imagination and price." Uses artists for design, illustration, retouching, animation, lettering and charts/graphs.
First Contact & Terms: Send query letter with brochure or tear sheets, Photostats, photocopies, slides and photographs. Samples are filed. Samples not filed are returned only if requested. Reports back within 14 days only if interested. Call or write to schedule an appointment to show a portfolio. Payment negotiable by job.

GLORIA ZIGNER & ASSOCIATES INC., Suite C-1, 245 Fischer, Costa Mesa CA 92626. (714)545-1990. President: Gloria Zigner. Advertising/PR firm. Clients: hotels, insurance companies, hospitals, restaurants, financial institutions, manufacturers, electronic companies, corporate identities, builders and developers. Buys 12-24 illustrations/year.
Needs: Works with 2-3 illustrators and 2-3 designers/month. Uses artists for billboards, P-O-P displays, consumer magazines, stationery design, multimedia kits, direct mail, brochures/flyers, trade magazines and newspapers. Also uses artists for design, color separations, layout, lettering, paste-up and type spec.
First Contact & Terms: Local artists only. Write for interview. Reports only if interested. Provide brochure, flyer, business card, resume and tear sheets to be kept on file for future assignments. No originals returned at job's completion. Pays promised fee for unused assigned work.

Los Angeles

N.W. AYER, INC.,888 S. Figueroa, Los Angeles CA 90017. (213)486-7400. Chairman/CEO: John Littlewood. Creative Directors: Bill Stenton, Jerry Murff. Art Directors: Gaye Burrows, Jacqueline Christie and Bianca Juarez. Ad agency. List of clients provided upon request.
Needs: Uses 1-2 illustrators/month. Uses artists for billboards, P-O-P displays, consumer magazines, direct mail, television, slide sets, brochures/flyers, trade magazines, and newspapers.
First Contact & Terms: "People interested should research what type of clients N.W. Ayer has in such references as *Advertising Agency Register* and in the Red Book." Provide tear sheets, original art or photocopies to be kept on file for future assignments. Pays for design by the project, $200-2,000. Pays for illustration by the project, $250-3,500. Negotiates payment based on client's budget and amount of creativity required from artist. No originals returned at job's completion.

BANNING CO., Suite 210, 11818 Wilshire Blvd., Los Angeles CA 90025. (213)477-8517. Art Director: Ismael Anda. Ad agency. Serves a variety of clients.
Needs: Works with 2 comp artists and 2-3 designers per month. Works on assignment only. Uses designers for P-O-P displays, consumer and trade magazines, stationery design, direct mail, brochures/flyers and newspapers.
First Contact & Terms: Call for interview. Prefers slides as samples. Samples returned by SASE. Reports within 2-3 weeks. Provide business card and brochure to be kept on file for future assignments. No originals returned at job's completion. All pay is based on job. Considers complexity of project, client's budget, turnaround time and rights purchased when establishing payment.
Tips: "This is a business first; art folks need some business skills—not just artistic ones. Have patience and confidence."

***BIG TIME PICTURE CO., INC.**, 12210½ Nebraska Ave., Los Angeles CA 90025. (213)207-0921. Operations Manager: Craig Saavedra. Audiovisual firm providing motion picture post-production services and facilities. Clients: major and independent film studios.
Needs: Uses freelance artists for animation.

BOSUSTOW VIDEO, 3030 Pennsylvania Av., Santa Monica CA 90404. (213)453-7973. Contact: Tee Bosustow. Video production firm. Clients: broadcast series, feature films, corporate, media promotion and home video.
Needs: Works with varying number of freelance artists depending on projects. Works on assignment only. Uses artists for titles, maps, graphs and other information illustrations.
First Contact & Terms: Hires per job; no staff artists. Send brochure showing art style and resume only to be kept on file. Do not send samples; required only for interview. Samples not filed are returned by SASE. Reports only if interested. Pays by the project, $50-500. Considers complexity of project, skill and experience of artist, client's budget and turnaround time when establishing payment. Usually buys all rights; varies according to project.

BROYLES GARAMELLA FITZGERALD & CZYSZ, 8226 Sunset Blvd., Los Angeles CA 90046. (213)650-9888. Senior Art Director: John Brogna. Ad agency specializing in entertainment, marketing, advertising, design, lifestyle/leisure products.
Needs: Works with 15 freelance artists/year. Assigns 50 jobs/year. Works on assignment only. Uses freelance artists for design, illustration, brochures, catalogs, consumer and trade magazines, P-O-P displays, mechanicals, animation, billboards, posters, direct mail packages, motion pictures, lettering, logos and advertisements.
First Contact & Terms: Send query letter with tear sheets, or "telephone." Samples are filed. Reports back only if interested and project requires specific artist style." Call to schedule an appointment to show a portfolio, which should include thumbnails, roughs, Photostats and tear sheets. Pays for design by the hour, $15 minimum. Pays for illustration by the project, $800 minimum. Payment is negotiable. Considers complexity of project and turnaround time when establishing payment. Buys all rights.

DYER/KAHN, INC., 8360 Melrose Ave., Los Angeles CA 90069. (213)655-1800. Creative Director: Bill Murphy. Ad agency and audiovisual firm. "We are a multi-media design studio providing advertising, sales materials, P-O-P displays and corporate identity for a variety of clients, including film and record companies, real estate developers, fashion and restaurants."
Needs: Works with 10-15 freelance artists/year. Prefers local artists. Uses artists for design, illustration, brochures, catalogs, books, newspapers, consumer and trade magazines, P-O-P displays, mechanicals, retouching, animation, billboards, posters, direct mail packages, press releases, motion pictures, lettering, logos, charts/graphs and advertisements.
First Contact & Terms: Send a resume. Samples are filed. Reports back only if interested. Drop-off policy (Thursday 9-9:30 a.m.). Payment "varies project by project." Considers complexity of project, client's budget and turnaround time when establishing payment.
Tips: "Use drop-off policy. If an AD is available he/she will see you. If not, work will be looked at by noon and ready for pick-up."

THE HALSTED ORGANIZATION, 3519 West Sixth St., Los Angeles CA 90020. (213)386-8356. Art Director: Damon G. Shay. Ad agency, public relations and marketing firm. Clients: manufacturers, medical/dental, sporting goods and general consumer. Client list provided upon request.
Needs: Works with 15-20 freelance artists/year. Prefers local artists with own studio. Uses artists for design, illustrations, brochures, mechanicals, retouching, posters, direct mail packages, press releases, lettering and logos. Looks for "clean work, type spec ability is rewarded, photo retouch is great,"
First Contact & Terms: Send query letter with brochure showing art style or resume and tear sheets, Photostats, photocopies, slides and photographs. Samples not filed are returned only if requested. Reports back within 10 days. Call to schedule an appointment to show a portfolio, which should include roughs, original/final art, tear sheets and b&w. Pays for design by the hour, $12.50 up; by the project, $120-no limit; by the day, $100-no limit. Pays for illustration by the hour, $15-40; by the project, $100-no limit; by the day, $90-no limit. Considers complexity of project, turnaround time, client's budget, and rights purchased when establishing payment. Buys one-time rights or reprint rights; rights vary according to project.
Tips: "In your portfolio, I do not want to see stationery, greeting cards, forms, fine art or school design projects."

NATIONAL ADVERTISING AND MARKETING ENTERPRISES, (N.A.M.E.), 7323 N. Figueroa, Los Angeles CA 90041. Contact: J. A. Gatlin.
Needs: Works on assignment only. Uses artists for graphic design, letterheads and direct mail brochures.

First Contact & Terms: Send query letter with tear sheet, Photostats and photographs. Samples not returned. Sometimes buys previously published work. Reports in 4 weeks. To show a portfolio, mail appropriate materials. Pays by the hour, $15-40.
Tips: "Submit repros of art, not originals."

San Francisco

ARNOLD & ASSOCIATES PRODUCTIONS, 2159 Powell St., San Francisco CA 94133. (415)989-3490. President: John Arnold. Audiovisual and video firm. Clients: general.
Needs: Works with 30 freelance artists/year. Prefers local artists (in San Francisco and Los Angeles), award-winning and experienced. "We're an established, national firm." Works on assignment only. Uses artists for multimedia, slide show and staging production.
First Contact & Terms: Send query letter with brochure, tear sheets, slides and photographs to be kept on file. Call to schedule an appointment to show a portfolio, which should include final reproduction/product, color and photographs. Pays for design by the hour, $15-50; by the project $500-3,500. Pays for illustration by the project, $500-4,000. Considers complexity of the project, client's budget and skill and experience of artist when establishing payment.

***BASS/FRANCIS PRODUCTIONS**, 737 Beach St., San Francisco CA 94109. (415)441-4555. Production Manager: Martha Edwards. "A multi-media, full-service organization providing corporate communications to a wide range of clients."
Needs: Works with 10 artists/year. Assigns 35 jobs/year. Prefers solid experience in multi-image production. Works on assignment only. Uses freelance artists for mechanicals, lettering, logos, charts/graphs and multi-image designs. Prefers loose or impressionistic style.
First Contact & Terms: Send resume and slides. Samples are filed. Samples not filed are not returned. Reports back within 1 month only if interested. To show a portfolio, mail slides. Pays for design by the project, $100-1,000; by the day, $200-350. Pays for the illustration by the hour, $18-25; by the project, $100-250. Considers turnaround time, skill and experience of artist and how work will be used when establishing payment. Rights purchased vary according to project.
Tips: "Send resume, slides, rates. Highlight multi-media experience. Show slide graphics also."

CHARTMASTERS, 201 Filbert St., San Francisco CA 94133. (415)421-6591. Art Manager: Michael Viapiana. Audiovisual firm.
Needs: Works with 5-6 freelance artists/year. Artists must sign W-2 form and work on premises as temporary employee." Uses artists for designs, illustrations, mechanicals, animation and charts/graphs. Experience in 35mm slide production, presentation and multi-image shows essential.
First Contact & Terms: Send resume and slides. Samples not filed are returned. Reports back only if interested. Call or write to schedule an appointment to show a portfolio. Pays for design by the hour. Considers complexity of project and skill and experience of artist when establishing payment. Rights purchased vary according to project.

HEAPING TEASPOON ANIMATION, 4002 19th St., San Francisco CA 94114. (415)626-1893. Owner: Chuck Eyler. Audiovisual firm. Clients: ad agencies, other production firms and local businesses.
Needs: Works with 5 freelance artists/year. Uses artists for design, mechanicals, animation and motion pictures. "Artists should have good pencil line quality and inbetweening experience."
First Contact & Terms: Send query letter with brochure showing art style or resume, tear sheets, photocopies and renderings/designs. Samples not filed are returned by a SASE. Reports back within 3 months with SASE and only if interested. Call or write to schedule an appointment to show a portfolio, which should include thumbnails, roughs, original/final art and video reels. Pays for design by the project, $100-800; for illustration by the hour, $8-25. Considers complexity of project, client's budget and skill and experience of artist when establishing payment. Rights purchased vary according to project.

KETCHUM COMMUNICATIONS, 55 Union St., San Francisco CA 94111. (415)781-9480. Executive Creative Director: Millie Olson. Ad agency. Serves clients in food, athletic footwear, farm products, air express, toys.
Needs: Uses freelancers for consumer and trade magazines, newspapers, print ads and TV.
First Contact & Terms: Call for appointment to show portfolio. Selection based on portfolio review, mailers from freelancers, referrals from colleagues and contacts by reps. Negotiates payment based on client's budget, amount of creativity required from artist and where work will appear.
Tips: Wants to see in portfolio whatever best illustrates freelancer's style. Include past work used by other ad agencies and tear sheets of published art.

***LORD & BENTLEY PERSUASIVE MARKETING**, 646 Ashbury, San Francisco CA 94117. (415)564-8384. Creative Director: Allan Barsky. Ad and marketing agency.
Needs: Works with 20 freelance artists/year. Prefers experienced artists only. Works on assignment only. Uses artists for design, illustrations, brochures, catalogs, magazines, newspapers, P-O-P displays, mechanicals, retouching, billboards, posters, direct mail packages, logos and advertisements. Artists must "understand reproduction process; the job is to enhance copy strategy."
First Contact & Terms: Send 6 photocopies of published/printed work. Samples not filed are not returned. Does not report back. To show a portfolio, mail appropriate materials, only photocopies of final reproduction/product. Pays for design by the project or hour, $20-75. Pays for illustration by the hour, $20-100. Considers skill and experience of artist when establishing payment. Buys all rights.

LOWE MARSCHALK, 574 Pacific, San Francisco CA 94133. (415)981-2250. Creative Director: John McDaniels. Ad agency. Clients: primarily travel, wine and food.
Needs: Works with 3-4 freelance illustrators and 2 freelance designers/month. Uses freelancers for billboards, consumer and trade magazines, direct mail, brochures/flyers, newspapers, P-O-P displays, stationery design and TV.
First Contact & Terms: Call for appointment to show portfolio. Selection based on past association and review of portfolios. Negotiates payment based on usage and where work will appear.
Tips: Wants to see features that demonstrate freelancer's originality and competency.

HAL RINEY & PARTNERS, INC., 735 Battery, San Francisco CA 94111. (415)981-0950. Contact: Jerry Andelin. Ad agency. Serves clients in beverages, brewery, computers, confections, insurance, restaurants, winery and assorted packaged goods accounts.
Needs: Works with 5-6 freelance illustrators/month. Uses freelancers in all media.
First Contact & Terms: Call one of the art directors for appointment to show portfolio. Selection based on portfolio review. Negotiates payment based on client's budget, amount of creativity required from artist and where work will appear.
Tips: Wants to see a comprehensive rundown in portfolio on what a person does best—"what he's selling"—and enough variety to illustrate freelancer's individual style(s).

EDGAR S. SPIZEL ADVERTISING INC., 1782 Pacific Ave., San Francisco CA 94109. (415)474-5735. President: Edgar S. Spizel. AV producer. Clients: "Consumer-oriented from department stores to symphony orchestras, supermarkets, financial institutions, radio, TV stations, political organizations, hotels, real estate firms, developers and mass transit, such as BART." Works a great deal with major sports stars and TV personalities.
Needs: Uses artists for posters, ad illustrations, brochures and mechanicals.
First Contact & Terms: Send query letter with tear sheets. Provide material to be kept on file for future assignments. No originals returned at job's completion. Negotiates pay.

UNDERCOVER GRAPHICS, Suite 1-C, 20 San Antonio Pl., San Francisco CA 94133. (415)788-6589. Creative Director: Helen Schaefer. AV producer. Clients: musical groups, producers, record companies and book publishers.
Needs: Works with 2-3 illustrators and 2-3 designers/month. Uses artists for billboards, P-O-P displays, corporate identity, multimedia kits, direct mail, TV, brochures/flyers, album covers and books.
First Contact & Terms: Send query letter with brochure or resume, tear sheets, slides, photographs and/or photocopies. Samples returned by SASE. Provide brochures, tear sheets, slides, business card and/or resume to be kept on file for future assignments. Reports in 4 weeks only if interested. To show a portfolio, mail roughs, original/final art, tear sheets and photographs. Originals returned to artist at job's completion. Pays $250-5,000, comprehensive layout and production; $10-25/hour, creative services; $25-500, illustrations. Considers complexity of project, client's budget, skill and experience of artist and rights purchased when establishing payment. Pays original fee as agreed for unused assigned illustrations.
Tips: Artists interested in working with us should "be creative and persistent. Be different. Set yourself apart from other artists by work that's noticeably outstanding. Don't be content with mediocrity or just 'getting by' or even the 'standards of the profession.' *Be avant-garde.*"

> ***"There is much more use of computer graphics for industrial video/film productions."***
>
> ***—Doreen Nagle, Moose Communications***
> ***Bear Valley, California***

Colorado

BROYLES ALLEBAUGH & DAVIS, INC., 31 Denver Technological Center, 8231 E. Prentice Ave., Englewood CO 80111. (303)770-2000. Executive Art Director: Kent Eggleston. Ad agency. Clients: industrial, high-tech, financial, travel and consumer clients; client list provided upon request.
Needs: Works with 12 illustrators/year; occasionally uses freelance designers. Works on assignment only. Uses freelance artists for consumer and trade magazines, direct mail, P-O-P displays, brochures, catalogs, posters, newspapers, TV and AV presentations.
First Contact & Terms: Send business card, brochure/flyer, samples and tear sheets to be kept on file. Samples returned by SASE if requested. Reports only if interested. Arrange interview to show portfolio or contact through artist's agent. Prefers slides or printed pieces as samples. Negotiates payment according to project. Considers complexity of project, client's budget, skill and experience of artist, geographic scope of finished project, turnaround time and rights purchased when establishing payment.

***CINE DESIGN FILMS**, 255 Washington St., Denver CO 80203. (303)777-4222. Producer/Director: Jon Husband. Audiovisual firm. Clients: automotive firms, banks, restaurants, etc.
Needs: Works with 3-7 freelance artists/year. Uses artists for layout, titles, animation and still photography. Clear concept ideas that relate to the client in question are important.
First Contact & Terms: Works on assignment only. Send query letter to be kept on file. Reports only if interested. Write for appointment to show portfolio. Pays by the hour, $20-50 average; by the project, $300-1,000 average; by the day, $75-100 average. Considers complexity of the project, client's budget and rights purchased when establishing payment. Rights purchased vary according to project.

COLLE & MCVOY ADVERTISING AGENCY, INC., 6900 East Belleview Ave., Englewood CO 80111. (303)771-7700. Creative Director: Celia Sheneman. Ad agency. Clients: Health, retail, banks, resorts, various high-tech, hospital and amusement park.
Needs: Works with 10-12 freelance artists/year. Prefers creative Colorado artists. Uses artists for design, illustrations, brochures, catalog, magazines, newspapers, P-O-P displays, mechanicals, retouching, animation, billboards, posters, direct mail packages, logos, charts/graphs, advertisements and radio.
First Contact & Terms: Send query letter with brochure showing art style or resume and tear sheets, Photostats, slides, photographs, etc. Samples not filed are returned only if requested. Call or write to schedule an appointment to show a portfolio, which should include thumbnails, roughs, original/final art, final reproduction/product, color, tear sheets, photographs, b&w, etc. Pays for design and illustration by the project, $150 minimum. Rights purchased vary according to project.
Tips: "We are interested in style and conceptual flexibility. We call on artists to extend and enhance a concept."

STARWEST PRODUCTIONS, 1391 N. Speer Blvd., Denver CO 80204. (303)623-0636. Creative Director: Steve Pettit. Ad agency/audiovisual firm. Clients list provided upon request with SASE.
Needs: Works with 2-4 freelance artists/year. Local artists only, experienced in audiovisual, print, storyboard. Works on assignment only. Uses artists for full concept to paste-up. Especially seeks paste-up skills.
First Contact & Terms: Send resume and slides, tear sheets, Photostats to be kept on file. Samples not filed are returned. Reports within 30 days. Write for appointment to show portfolio. Pays by the project, $1,000. Considers client's budget, and skill and experience of artist when establishing payment. Negotiates rights purchased.
Tips: "Always looking for someone with 'new' ideas."

STRADE INDUSTRIES, 12600 W. Colfax, Lakewood CO 80222. (303)232-8282. Production Manager: Sharon Adams. Audiovisual firm. "We are a communications firm specializing in print and slide presentation and computer graphics." Clients: banks, telecommunication companies, oil companies, aerospace companies, design firms, newspapers and real estate.
Needs: Works with 3 freelance artists/year. Assigns 20 jobs/year. Prefers local, experienced artists. Works on assignment only. Uses freelance artists for animation, charts/graphs, computer graphics and slide production.
First Contact & Terms: Send query letter with brochure or resume and slides. Samples are filed. Samples not filed are returned only if requested by artist. Reports back within months only if interested. Write to schedule an appointment to show a portfolio, which should include original/final art, final reproduction/product, slides and video disks. Pays for design and illustration by the hour, $8-15. Considers complexity of project, client's budget, turnaround time and skill and experience of artist when establishing payment. Buys all rights.

Close-up

Andy Lackow

Illustrator
New York City

While many artists prefer the artistic freedom of editorial illustration, Andy Lackow prefers the fast world of advertising, where he is given specific instructions and a quick turnaround time.

"Advertising provides less complicated jobs and better pay," Lackow says. Lackow works primarily on advertising campaigns with projects ranging from advertisements for pharmaceutical firms to movie posters to animation for Coca-Cola ads. The airbrush artist finds that magazines offer lower budgets and more complex assignments than do advertising agencies.

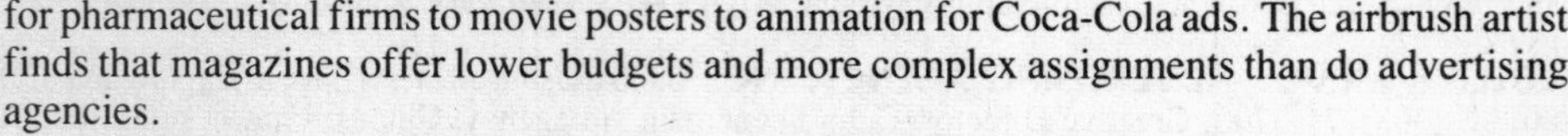

"I would knock myself out producing a full-page illustration, when I could have completed many other assignments for twice the price. I'm a perfectionist, but I don't like to spend a lot of time on a job when I could be making more money." Also, Lackow likes the security of knowing a substantial check will be in the mail as promised. "If you're working for a big company, you know you're going to get paid."

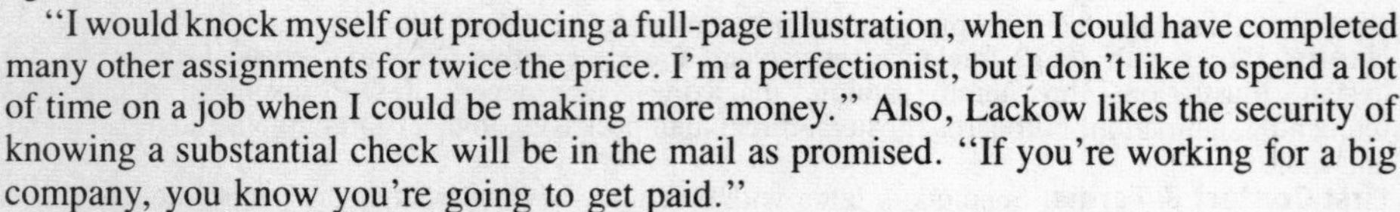

Working on advertising campaigns has its drawbacks, however. Deadlines, which are notoriously short, are occasionally moved up. This means that deadlines for other jobs might overlap. Then, after the deadline, the art director might ask for changes in the color scheme or the composition. "Hopefully, I've got my answering machine on when he calls so I can have some time to think about what to say." Lackow has established a policy of doing revisions but charging extra for those that are not specified during the original agreement.

Lackow is at that enviable point in his career when clients seek his services. He has developed a good reputation for creative work with a touch of humor, all done on time. Most of his assignments now come from his ads in talent directories such as *The Creative Black Book*; others come from referrals from clients and friends.

He does his own market research by calling other artists who advertise in the talent directories, asking what works for them in terms of self-promotion. He's found that what works for one artist might not work for another. "It's up to the artist to make his ad or self-promotional piece personable, to make it a memorable image."

Lackow carefully plans each self-promotional ad, often taking time off from assignments to design the right logo and the appropriate image. His ads display his versatility and his distinctive style, which are important qualities in working with advertising agencies.

His life as a freelancer hasn't always been so easy. Just out of school (he attended the Rhode Island School of Design and the School of Visual Arts), Lackow faced the same problems as other newcomers. "I had the innate talent but my work wasn't that sophisticated at that point." He was also an airbrush artist when the technique was in its infancy. He found a staff job silkscreening T-shirts and then textile goods. Working on staff made him realize that freelancing was the route for him.

Determined to make it on his own, he made a list of art directors by going to newsstands, reading magazine mastheads, and writing down names and phone numbers. He would call to make an appointment to show his portfolio, which consisted of pen-and-ink and airbrush work. "It's horrible to make cold calls, but most art directors try to be kind. You've got to get your feet wet." His first assignment came from *Crawdaddy* for a spot illustration for $50.

Because he is personable and forthright, plus an accomplished illustrator, Lackow now has no trouble negotiating his own terms with clients. He has set certain guidelines for himself. With the initial phone call, he collects as much information as possible about the client and the job. "You'll know right away if the terms or the client is unattractive. There shouldn't be any maybe's." After accepting the job, he first establishes exactly what the job entails, what the deadline is and how much money is budgeted. "An agency is given a price list by the company. If the agency says it doesn't know the budget, it's lying, because they assume illustrators will undersell themselves." In this situation, Lackow advises artists to say that you need to know the budget because you're busy and must know if the job fits into a price range you'd feel comfortable working with. Give the client a grace period to check his figures and ask to call back. If the agency still refuses to reveal the budget, Lackow asks who the client is. "If the client is Budweiser, and they want me to do a billboard, I have a certain pay schedule in mind." In general, the more complicated the job, the more Lackow expects in payment.

Being a successful freelance artist takes talent and perserverance. "You'd have to love what you do to put up with everything," says Lackow. "I can stay up til 5 A.M., eyelids drooping, trying to do everything to keep awake to finish a job. But through all this I feel like I really love what I'm doing. I feel like I'm creating magic on call."

—Susan Conner

This is Lackow's 1988 ad in the* Creative Black Book. *Because he receives so many calls from potential clients who have seen his annual ads, he sets aside time each year to create a striking piece. His ads show his versatility with an airbrush at various subjects. He sends the tearsheets received from the ad as mailers, reminders and drop-off pieces.

Tips: "Do not just drop in. Contact by letter or phone. Please keep in mind that schedules can be very hectic for managers and be patient (never rude). A delay in answer does not always mean 'no.' "

Connecticut

AV DESIGN, 1823 Silas Deane Hwy., Rocky Hill CT 06067. (203)529-2581. President: J.J. Wall. Audiovisual firm specializing in multi-media, multi-projection slide shows, meeting planning, computer graphics, typography, art and photo lab for corporations and ad agencies.
Needs: Works with 3 artists/year. Prefers local artists with paste-up experience (no job entry). Uses freelance artists for mechanicals, animation, logos, charts/graphs, slides, multi-image and E-6 lab work.
First Contact & Terms: Send resume. Samples are filed. Samples not filed are returned only if requested by artist. Reports back within weeks only if interested.

BRADFORD ADVERTISING, INC., 1 Cheney St., Ivoryton CT 06442. (203)767-0173. Art Directors: Gabrielle Kahane and Carole Mattia. Ad agency. Clients: automotive, industrial, bank, modular home manufacturer and sporting goods.
Needs: Works with approximately 10 freelance artists/year. Prefers local artists. Works on assignment only. Uses freelance artists for design, illustration, brochures, catalogs, P-O-P displays, mechanicals, billboards, posters, direct mail packages, press releases, logos and advertisements.
First Contact & Terms: Send brochure. Samples are filed. Samples not filed are returned only if requested. Does not report back. Call to schedule an appointment to show a portfolio, which should include thumbnails, roughs, original/final art, tear sheets and slides. Pays for design by the hour, $25-100; by the project, $250-1,500; by the day, $250-500. Pays for illustration by the hour, $50-300; by the project, $100-1,000; by the day, $250-1,500. Considers complexity of project, client's budget, turnaround time, skill and experience of artist, how work will be used and rights purchased. Negotiates rights purchased; rights purchased vary according to project.
Tips: "When contacting our firm, please send samples of work."

ERIC HOLCH/ADVERTISING, 49 Gerrish Lane, New Canaan CT 06840. President: Eric Holch. Clients: companies who advertise in trade magazines.
Needs: Works with 10 freelance artists/year. Works on assignment only. Prefers food, candy, packages, and seascapes as themes for advertising illustrations for brochures, ads, etc. Pays $100-3,000 average.
First Contact & Terms: Send query letter with brochure showing art style or samples to be kept on file. Write to schedule an appointment to show a portfolio, which should include roughs, photocopies and original/final art. Pays for design by the hour, $25-50. Pays for illustration by the project, $100-3,000. Buys one-time rights, all rights or negotiates rights purchased depending on project. Considers skill and experience of artist and client's preferences when establishing payment.

JACOBY/STORM PRODUCTIONS INC., 22 Crescent Rd., Westport CT 06880. (203)227-2220. President: Doris Storm. AV/TV/film producer. Clients: schools, corporations and publishers. Produces filmstrips, motion pictures, slide sets, sound-slide sets and videotapes.
Needs: Assigns 6-8 jobs/year. Uses artists for lettering, illustrations for filmstrips and to design slide show graphics.
First Contact & Terms: Prefers local artists with filmstrip and graphics experience. Query with resume and arrange interview. SASE. Reports in 2 weeks. Usually buys all rights. Pays $20-30/frame, lettering; $50-100/frame, illustrations. Pays on acceptance.

LISTENING LIBRARY, INC., 1 Park Ave., Old Greenwich CT 06870. (203)637-3616. Catalog Editors: Nancy Keller and Jill Rich. Produces educational AV productions.
Needs: Requires illustrators for front covers for 8-10 catalogs/year. Uses artists for catalog and advertising design; advertising illustration; catalog and advertising layout, and direct mail packages.
First Contact & Terms: Local (New York City, Westchester County, Fairfield County, etc.) artists only. Works on assignment only. Send resume and nonreturnable samples to be kept on file for possible future assignments. Samples not returned. Original work not returned to artist after job's completion. "Payment is determined by the size of the job, and skill and experience of artist." Buys all rights.

THE McMANUS COMPANY, Box 446, Greens Farms CT 06436. (203)255-3301. President: John F. McManus. National advertising/marketing/PR agency. Serves clients in data processing, corporate, consumer, industrial, social agencies, automotives and other industries.

Needs: Works with 4 illustrators/month. Works on assignment only. Uses artists for art direction (TV commercials), graphic design (print ads and collateral pieces), illustration, publications, filmstrips, multimedia kits, storyboards and packaging.
First Contact & Terms: Send resume (to be kept on file for future assignments). Samples returned by SASE; reports back on future assignment possibilities. Write for interview to show portfolio. "Payment is determined on use of creative work, whether it will appear in national or regional media."

***PELICAN SOFTWARE INC.**, 768 Farmington Ave., Farmington CT 06032. (203)677-6288. Vice President, Design: Susan Swanson. "We produce software (K-6) and books."
Needs: Works with 7-15 artists/year. Assigns 10-25 jobs/year. Uses freelance artists for catalog illustration, book design, magazine ad illustration and animation. Needs computer artists and illustrated stories.
First Contact & Terms: Send query letter with brochure showing art style. Samples are filed. Samples not filed are returned by SASE. Reports within 3 weeks. Call or write to schedule an appointment to show a portfolio. Pays for design by the project, $300-5,000. Pays for the illustration by the project, $100-1,000. Considers complexity of project when establishing payment. Buys all rights or reprint rights.
Tips: Looks for artists with "talent and imagination."

SMITH, DORIAN & BURMAN, INC., 1100 New Britain Ave., Hartford CT 06110. Production Manager: Richard A. Mikush. Industrial clients.
Needs: Uses artists for layout, illustration and retouching for trade magazines, collateral, direct mail and P-O-P display.
First Contact & Terms: Call for interview; local artists only. Prefers photographs and Photostats as samples. Samples returned *only* if requested. Reports in 2 weeks. Works on assignment only. Provide business card and tear sheets to be kept on file for possible future assignments. Payment by the project varies.

THE WESTPORT COMMUNICATIONS GROUP INC., 155 Post Rd. E., Westport CT 06880. (203)226-3525. Art Director: H. Lindsay. AV producer. Clients: educational and corporate. Produces filmstrips, multimedia kits, slide sets, sound-slide sets and booklets.
Needs: Works with 10-15 illustrators/year. Uses artists for filmstrip, slide, booklet and brochure illustrations.
First Contact & Terms: Send query letter and tear sheets to be kept on file. Reports within 1 month. Arrange interview to show portfolio. Pays $35/educational filmstrip frame; negotiates pay on other assignments.

Delaware

CUSTOM CRAFT STUDIO, 310 Edgewood St., Bridgeville DE 19933. AV producer.
Needs: Works with 1 illustrator and 1 designer/month. Works with freelance artists on an assignment basis only. Uses artists for filmstrips, slide sets, trade magazine and newspapers. Also uses artists for print finishing, color negative retouching and airbrush work. Prefers pen & ink, airbrush, watercolor and calligraphy.
First Contact & Terms: Send query letter with slides or photographs, brochure/flyer, resume, samples and tear sheets to be kept on file. Samples returned by SASE. Reports in 2 weeks. No originals returned to artist at job's completion. Pays for design and illustration by the project, $25-100.

SHIPLEY ASSOCIATES INC., 1300 Pennsylvania Ave., Wilmington DE 19806. (302)652-3051. Creative Director: Jack Parry. Ad/PR firm. Serves clients in harness racing, industrial and corporate accounts, insurance, real estate and entertainment.
Needs: Works with 2 illustrators and 1 designer/month. Assigns 9 jobs/year. Works with freelance artists on assignment only. Uses artists for annual report illustrations, mechanicals, brochure and sign design.
First Contact & Terms: Query with previously published work. Prefers layouts (magazine & newspaper), mechanicals, line drawings and finished pieces as samples. Samples not returned. Reports within 2 weeks. Provide resume, samples and tear sheets to be kept on file for possible future assignments. No originals returned at job's completion. Pays for design by the hour, $8 minimum. Negotiates payment.
Tips: Looks for "versatility and technique, individual style, good production skills."

District of Columbia

***DE LA CROIX PRODUCTIONS INTERNATIONAL INC.**, P.O. Box 9751 NW, Washington DC 20016. (301)-990-1426. Executive Producer: Maximilien De Lafayette. Produces shows, plays, music, and various artistic projects; recruits, trains, promotes and manages artists, actors, actresses, choreographers, designers, dancers, singers and stage directors as well as freelance painters and illustrators.
Needs: Works with 110 freelance artists/year. Uses artists for advertising, brochure, catalog, and magazine/newspaper design, illustration and layout; AV presentations; exhibits; displays; signage; posters and design for plays and artistic productions.
First Contact & Terms: Send resume, at least 2 letters of reference and samples to be kept on file; write for appointment to show portfolio. Prefers Photostats as samples. Reports within 2 weeks. Works on assignment only. Pays by the project. Considers skill and experience of artist when establishing payment.
Tips: Looks for "originality, new style, creativity, ability to meet work schedule, precision and flexibility when considering freelance artists."

JAFFE ASSOCIATES, Suite 200, 1730 Rhode Island Ave., Washington DC 20036. (202)331-9700. Office Manager: Laura Atkins. PR and marketing firm. Clients: commercial real estate, banks, national associations, architectural and engineering, health care, law firms and accounting. Places advertising only to limited extent.
Needs: Works with several designers. Uses artists for stationery design, multimedia kits, direct mail, television, slide sets and brochures/flyers. Prefers pen & ink, calligraphy, and computer illustration.
First Contact & Terms: Send resume and portfolio for review. "Freelancers are employed on basis of past experience, personal knowledge or special expertise." Provide brochures, flyers, business cards, resumes and tear sheets to be kept on file for future assignments. Originals returned only if prearranged. Pays for design by the project, $100 minimum. Negotiates payment based on client's budget, amount of creativity required from artist and artist's previous experience/reputation.
Tips: "Interested in samples of produced work and details regarding availability and ability to produce work on short time schedules. *Do not* deluge account executives with calls."

MANNING, SELVAGE & LEE, INC., Suite 300, 1250 Eye St. NW, Washington DC 20005. (202)682-1660. Contact: Creative Director. PR firm. Clients: pharmaceutical firms, nonprofit associations, real estate developers, corporations and high-tech firms.
Needs: Uses artists for illustration, paste-up and design.
First Contact & Terms: Send tear sheets, Photostats, photocopies, slides and photographs. Call or write to schedule an appointment to show a portfolio, which should include best work. Pays for design by the hour, $15-65; by the project, $150-5,000.

O'KEEFE COMMUNICATIONS, INC., 2135 Wisconsin Ave. N.W., Washington DC 20007. (202)333-7832. Art Director: Jane P. Anderson. "We produce multimedia audiovisual presentations, films and video as well as some printed media. We have a fully equipped photo lab, art department, video and editing department. We also produce set designs and convention displays with multi-image back-up." Clients: large trade associations and corporations.
Needs: Works with 15 freelance artists/year. Prefers local artists with previous AV knowledge. Will consider outside illustrators. "Good production skills are a must." Uses artists for design, illustration, brochures, mechanicals, animation, posters and lettering. Prefers pen & ink, airbrush, colored pencil, watercolor, markers and rubylith.
First Contact & Terms: Send query letter with resume, tear sheets, photocopies and slides. "Personal interviews are great if we have the time." Samples are filed. Samples not filed are returned only if requested by artist. Reports back only if interested. Call or write to schedule an appointment to show a portfolio, which should include roughs, original/final art, final reproduction/product and slides. Pays for mechanicals production and paste-up by the hour, $7.50-12. Pays for design by the hour, $10-14. Pays for illustration by the hour, $12-100. Considers complexity of project, client's budget and skill and experience of artist when establishing payment. Buys all rights. Rights purchased vary according to project.
Tips: "Our busy seasons are spring and early fall. All resumes and samples received throughout the year will be filed and reviewed at those times. The more samples of your work you include, the better your chances are of being called in during the crunch. Gear your samples to those you feel would translate well into AV communication and stress any AV experience you have in a cover letter."

Florida

JOSEPH ANTHONY ADVERTISING AGENCY, INC., 8300 Congress Ave., Boca Raton FL 33499. (305)994-2660. Art Director: Dennis Mastando. In-house direct mail firm. Clients: American consumer homes.
Needs: Works with 3-4 artists/year. Artist must have direct mail experience. Works on assignment only. Uses artists for advertising design and catalog layout; brochure design.
First Contact & Terms: Send query letter with resume, copies or print. Samples not filed are returned only if requested. Reports back within 3 months. Write to schedule an appointment to show a portfolio, which should include thumbnails, roughs, original/final art and final reproduction/product. Pays for design by the hour, $8-15. Pays for mechanical paste-up/keyline by the hour, $7-10. Considers complexity of project, client's budget, how work will be used, turnaround time and rights purchased when establishing payment.

COVALT ADVERTISING AGENCY, 12907 N.E. 7th Ave., North Miami FL 33161. (305)891-1543. Creative Director: Fernando Vasquez. Ad agency. Clients: automotive, cosmetics, industrial banks, restaurants, financial, consumer products.
Needs: Prefers local artists; very seldom uses out-of-town artists. Artists must have minimum of 5 years of experience; accepts less experience only if artist is extremely talented. Works on assignment only. Uses artists for illustration (all kinds and styles), photography, mechanicals, copywriting, retouching (important), rendering and lettering.
First Contact & Terms: Send query letter with brochure, resume, business card, tear sheets, Photostats, and photocopies to be kept on file. Samples not filed not returned. Reports only if interested. Call for appointment to show portfolio, which should include Photostats, photographs, slides, original/final art or tear sheets. Pays for design by the hour, $35 minimum; by the project, $150 minimum. Pays for illustrations by the project, $200 minimum. Considers complexity of project, client's budget, skill and experience of artist, and turnaround time when establishing payment. Buys all rights or reprint rights.
Tips: "If at first you don't succeed, keep in touch. Eventually something will come up due to our diversity of accounts. If I have the person, I might design something with his particular skill in mind."

CREATIVE RESOURCES INC., 2000 S. Dixie Hwy., Miami FL 33133. (305)856-3474. Chairman and CEO: Mac Seligman. Ad agency/PR firm. Clients: travel, hotels, airlines and resorts.
Needs: Works with 6 illustrators/designers/year. Local artists only. Uses artists for layout, type spec and design for brochures, ads, posters and renderings.
First Contact & Terms: Send query letter with resume and samples. No file kept on artists. Original work returned after completion of job. Call or write to schedule an appointment to show a portfolio, which should include thumbnails. Pays for design by the hour, $20-40 or negotiates pay by job or day. Pays for illustration by the hour, $40; amount varies by the project and day. Considers complexity of project, client's budget, and skill and experience of artist when establishing payment.

IMAGEWORKS® INC., Box 8628, Naples FL 33941. (813)598-3040. President: J. Paul Jodoin. Audiovisual firm. "We provide speaker-support slides, slide/tape programs, etc. for conventions, seminars, inhouse training, marketing, general information transfer." Clients: real estate developers, bankers, physicians, engineers, photographers, entertainers, attorneys, TV news personnel, PR and advertising agency representatives.
Needs: Works with 6 freelance artists/year. Assigns 20 jobs/year. Prefers local artists. Works on assignment only. Uses artists for P-O-P displays, mechanicals, retouching, animation, lettering, logos, charts/graphs and advertisements.
First Contact & Terms: Send query letter with resume and slides. Samples are filed. Samples not filed are not returned. Reports back only if interested. To show a portfolio, mail slides. Pays for design and illustration by the hour, $10-25. Considers complexity of project, client's budget, turnaround time, skill and experience of artist and how work will be used when establishing payment. Rights purchased vary according to project.

MEDIA DESIGN GROUP, 4862 SW 72nd Ave., Miami FL 33155. (305)663-3327. Production Coordinator: Tab Licea. AV producer. Clients: industry (80%) and advertising (20%). Produces "sales and marketing primarily, with some financial reporting and a little training."
Needs: Assigns approximately 100 jobs/year. Works with 2-3 illustrators and 1-2 designers/month. Works on assignment only. Uses artists for overall show design, cartoon work, paste up and board work.
First Contact & Terms: "We prefer AV experience and demand a high energy level." Send resume, then arrange interview by phone. Provide resume and business card to be kept on file for possible future assignments. No originals returned after publication. Buys all rights.

***MULTIVISION PRODUCTIONS**, 7000 SW 59th Place, S. Miami FL 33143. (305)662-6011. President: Robert Berkowitz. AV/film producer. Serves clients in industry and advertising. Produces multi-image sound-slide materials.

Needs: Assigns 50 jobs/year. Prefers "in-camera slide art specialists." Works with 2 animators and 3 designers/month. Uses artists for multi-image, AV/film projects.

First Contact & Terms: Send samples (prefers slides) and arrange interview by mail. Samples not kept on file returned. Reports within 1 week. Portfolio should include resume, samples and business card to be kept on file. Pays by the project. Method of payment is negotiated with the individual artist. No originals returned following publication. Buys all rights.

Tips: "Forox and animation specialists are needed for slides."

PRUITT HUMPHRESS POWERS & MUNROE ADVERTISING AGENCY, INC., 516 N. Adams St., Tallahassee FL 32301. (904)222-1212. Ad agency. Clients: business-to-business, consumer. Media used includes billboards, consumer and trade magazines, direct mail, newspapers, P-O-P displays, radio and TV.

Needs: Uses artists for direct mail, brochures/flyers, trade magazines and newspapers. "Freelancers used in every aspect of business and given as much freedom as their skill warrants."

First Contact & Terms: Send resume. Provide materials to be kept on file for future assignments. Negotiates payment based on client's budget and amount of creativity required from artist. Pays set fee/job.

Tips: In portfolio, "submit examples of past agency work in clean, orderly, businesslike fashion including written explanations of each work. Ten illustrations or less."

Georgia

ATLANTA AUDIO-VISUALS, 66 12th St., Atlanta GA 30303. Telex: 6501072756 MCI. Director: Robert Foah. AV producer. Serves clients in corporations. Produces multi-image materials.

Needs: Works with 3 illustrators/month.

First Contact & Terms: Send resume. Provide business card to be kept on file for possible future assignments only. Works on assignment only. Reports within 3 months. Pays by the project. Amount of payment is negotiated with the individual artist and varies with each client's budget. No originals returned after publication. Negotiates rights purchased.

***BURST VIDEO/FILM INC.**, Box 5354, Atlanta GA 30307. President: Fran Burst. Video production firm. Clients: major corporations, religious organizations, nonprofit groups. Client list provided on request with SASE.

Needs: Works with 5 freelance artists/year. Artists in Atlanta area only; minimum 2 years of experience. Uses artists for design and layout of graphics for 16mm film, slides and printed material, and some conceptual design for slide art. Artists should have a "good handle on graphic design and layout."

First Contact & Terms: Works on assignment only. Send query letter with resume to be kept on file. Reports only if interested. Pays by the hour or by the project. Considers client's budget, skill and experience of artist, turnaround time and rights purchased when establishing payment. Rights purchased vary according to project.

CAMP COMMUNICATIONS, 1718 Peachtree St. NW, Atlanta GA 30309. (404)874-3989. Creative Director: Lisa Cannon. Ad agency for the business-to-business, industrial segment. Clients: electronics, chemical, manufacturing, mining.

Needs: Works with 6 freelance artists/year. Assigns 20-30 jobs/year. Works on assignment only. Uses artists for design, illustration, brochures, trade magazines, retouching, lettering, logos and charts/graphs.

First Contact & Terms: Send query letter with brochure. Samples are filed. Does not report back. Call to schedule an appointment to show a portfolio. Pays for design by the hour, $25-50; by the project, $100-5,000. Pays for illustration by the project, $100-13,000. Considers complexity of project, client's budget, turnaround time and skill and experience of artist when establishing payment. Buys all rights; ("will *not* negotiate.")

Tips: "Set appointment; keep presentation short, show materials that relate to *our* clients. Follow up once a month."

CHANNEL ONE INC., 1727 Clifton Rd., Atlanta GA 30329. President: W. Horlock. AV producer. Clients: educational, nonprofit, religious.

Needs: Works with 3-4 illustrators/month. Uses artists for album covers, motion pictures and graphic and set design.
First Contact & Terms: Prefers slides, photographs, Photostats and b&w line drawings as samples. Samples returned by SASE. Reports in 2 months. Works on assignment only. Provide business card, brochure/flyer, resume and samples to be kept on file for possible future assignments. Originals returned to artist at job's completion if part of job contract. Payment depends on project.

WILLIAM COOK ADVERTISING/ATLANTA, 368 Ponce De Leon, Atlanta GA 30308. (404)892-3716. Senior Art Director: Darryl Elliott. Ad agency. Clients: hotels, industry and food.
Needs: Works with very few freelance artists. Works on assignment only. Uses artists for illustrations, mechanicals and layouts. Artist should have "good layout skills, visualization, speed, accuracy."
First Contact & Terms: Send query letter with resume and samples. Samples not filed are returned by SASE. Reports only if interested. Write to schedule an appointment to show a portfolio, which should include roughs, final reproduction/product and tear sheets. Pays for design by the hour, $14-50. Pays for illustration by the project, $100-2,000. Considers complexity of project, client's budget, how work will be used and turnaround time when establishing payment. Buys all rights.

FILMAMERICA, INC., Suite 209, 3177 Peachtree Rd. NE, Atlanta GA 30305. (404)261-3718. President: Avrum M. Fine. Audiovisual firm. Clients: corporate producer, advertising agencies.
Needs: Works with 2 freelance artists/year. Works on assignment only. Uses artists for film campaigns. Especially important are illustration and layout skills.
First Contact & Terms: Send query letter with resume and photographs or tear sheets to be kept on file. Samples not filed are returned only if requested. Reports back only if interested. Write for appointment to show portfolio. Pays for design by the project, $1,000-2,000. Pays for illustration by the project, $1,500-2,500. Considers complexity of the project and rights purchased when establishing payment. Rights purchased vary according to project.
Tips: "Be very patient!"

PAUL FRENCH AND PARTNERS, INC., 503 Gabbettville Rd., LaGrange GA 30240. (404)882-5581. Contact: Ms. Gene Ballard. Audiovisual firm. Client list provided upon request.
Needs: Works with 3 freelance artists/year. Works on assignment only. Uses artists for illustration.
First Contact & Terms: Send query letter with resume and slides to be kept on file. Samples not filed are returned by SASE. Reports back only if interested. To show a portfolio, mail appropriate materials. Pays for design and illustration by the hour, $25-100 average. Considers client's budget when establishing payment. Buys all rights.
Tips: "Be organized."

GARRETT COMMUNICATIONS, Box 53, Atlanta GA 30301. (404)755-2513. President: Ruby Grant Garrett. Production and placement firm for print media. Clients: banks, organizations, products-service consumer. Client list provided for SASE.
Needs: Assigns 24 freelance jobs/year. Works with 1 freelance illustrator and 1 freelance designer/month. Experienced, talented artists only. Works on assignment only. Uses artists for billboards, brochures, signage and posters. Prefers loose or realistic style and technical illustration occasionally.
First Contact & Terms: Send query letter with resume and samples to be kept on file. Samples returned by SASE if not kept on file. Reports within 10 days. Write to schedule an appointment to show a portfolio which should include roughs and tear sheets. Pays for design by the hour, $35-50; by the project, $100 minimum; by the day, $150 minimum. Pays for illustration by the hour, $35 minimum, by the project, $100 minimum; by the day, $100 minimum. Considers client's budget, skill and experience of artist and turnaround time when establishing payment. Negotiates rights purchased.
Tips: Send "6-12 items that show scope of skills."

THE GORDON GROUP, INC., Suite 106, 3305 Breckinridge Blvd., Duluth GA 30136. (404)381-6662. President: M.J. Gordon. Ad agency/AV and PR firm; "full-service marketing communication programs." Clients: business-to-business, industry, service, non-retail, non-foods.
Needs: Assigns 20-30 freelance jobs/year. Uses artists for trade magazines, direct mail packages, brochures, catalogs, filmstrips, stationery, signage, P-O-P displays, AV presentations and posters. Artists should make contact "any way they can." Works on assignment only. Pays by the hour, $20 minimum. Pay "depends on the job and the budget. We pay hourly or on a project basis." Considers complexity of project, client's budget, skill and experience of artist, turnaround time and rights purchased when establishing payment. Buys all rights, material not copyrighted.
Tips: "Don't spend a lot of money on materials. Turn us on with a creative letter instead."

***JONES-KELLEY & KILGORE, INC.**, Suite 300, 550 Pharr Rd. NE, Atlanta GA 30305. (404)261-7000. Creative Director: Michael Jones-Kelley. Ad agency. Clients: industrial and consumer.
Needs: Works with 3 freelance illustrators/month. Uses freelancers for billboards, consumer and trade magazines, direct mail, brochures/flyers, newspapers, P-O-P displays, stationery design and TV.
First Contact & Terms: Send samples. Prefers work "that has been produced—rather than daydreams." Samples are filed and not returned. Negotiates payment based on individual needs of job.

LEWIS BROADCASTING CORP., Box 13646, Savannah GA 31406. Public Relations Director: C.A. Barbieri. TV producer.
Needs: Uses artists for direct mail brochures, billboards, posters, public service TV spots and motion picture work. Perfers pen & ink, charcoal/pencil, colored pencil, watercolor, acrylics, oils, pastels, markers, calligraphy and computer illustration. Works on assignment only.
First Contact & Terms: Send query letter with resume and printed photocopied samples. Reports in 2 weeks. Provide business card and resume to be kept on file. Originals returned to artist at job's completion. Pay "depends on job."
Tips: "Be willing to flesh out others' ideas."

PRINGLE DIXON PRINGLE, Suite 1500, Marquis One Tower, 245 Peachtree Center Ave., Atlanta GA 30303. (404)688-6720. Creative Director: Perry Mitchell. Ad agency. Clients: fashion, financial, fast food and industrial firms; client list provided upon request.
Needs: Works with 2 illustrators/month. Local artists only. Works on assignment basis only. Uses freelance artists for billboards, consumer and trade magazines, direct mail, P-O-P displays, brochures, catalogs, posters, signage, newspapers and AV presentations.
First Contact & Terms: Arrange interview to show portfolio. Payment varies according to job and freelancer.

J. WALTER THOMPSON COMPANY, One Atlanta Plaza, 950 East Paces Ferry Rd., Atlanta GA 30326. (404)365-7300. Executive Art Director: Bill Tomassi. Executive Creative Director: Mike Lollis. Ad agency. Clients: mainly financial, industrial and consumer. This office does creative work for Atlanta and the southeastern U.S.
Needs: Works with freelance illustrators. Works on assignment only. Uses artists for billboards, consumer magazines, trade magazines and newspapers.
First Contact & Terms: Send slides, original work, stats. Samples returned by SASE. Reports only if interested. No originals returned at job's completion. Call for appointment to show portfolio. Pays by the hour, $20-65 average; by the project, $100-6,000 average; by the day, $150-3,500 average. Considers complexity of project, client's budget, skill and experience of artist and rights purchased when establishing payment.
Tips: Wants to see samples of work done for different clients. Likes to see work done in different mediums. Likes variety and versatility. Artists interested in working here should "be *professional* and do top grade work." Deals with artists reps only.

***TUCKER WAYNE & CO.**, Suite 2700, 230 Peachtree St. NW, Atlanta GA 30043. (404)521-7600. Creative Department Business Manager: Rita Morris. Ad agency. Serves a variety of clients including packaged products, food, utilities, transportation and agriculture/pesticide manufacturing.
Needs: A total of 8 art directors occasionally work with freelance illustrators. Uses freelancers for consumer and trade magazines, newspapers and TV.
First Contact & Terms: Call creative secretary for appointment. Selection based on portfolio review. Negotiates payment based on budget, where work will appear, travel expenses, etc.
Tips: Each art director has individual preference.

Idaho

I/D/E/A INC., One I/D/E/A Way, Caldwell ID 83605. (208)459-6357. Creative Director: Ben Shuey. Ad agency. Clients: direct mail.
Needs: Assigns 12-15 freelance jobs/year. Uses artists for direct mail packages, brochures, airbrush and photographs.
First Contact & Terms: Call before sending query letter with brochure, resume and samples to be kept on file. Write for artists' guidelines. Prefers the "most convenient samples for the artist." Samples not kept on file returned only if requested. Reports only if interested. Works on assignment only. Pays by the project, amount varies. Considers complexity of project, client's budget, and skill and experience of artist when establishing payment. Rights purchased vary with project.
Tips: "Most work goes into catalogs or brochures."

Illinois

THE BEST COMPANY, 109 N. Main St., Rockford IL 61101. (815)965-3800. Vice President: Richard (Ric) Blencoe. Ad agency producing radio/TV commercials, brochures, newspaper and magazine ads, logo and corporate identity programs. Clients: mainly consumer accounts. Client list provided upon request.
Needs: Works with 10-20 freelance artists/year. Uses artists for design, illustration, brochures, consumer magazines, retouching, billboards, lettering and logos.
First Contact & Terms: Send query letter with brochure or resume, tear sheets, Photostats and slides. Samples are filed. Samples not filed are returned only if requested. Reports back within 2 weeks only if requested. Call or write to schedule an appointment to show a portfolio or mail roughs, original/final art and tear sheets. Pays for design by the hour, $20-45; by the project, $50 minimum. Pays for illustration by the hour, $50 minimum; by the project, $300 minimum. Considers complexity of project, client's budget and skill and experience of artist when establishing payment. Buys all rights; negotiates rights purchased.
Tips: "Do some research on agency and our needs to present portfolio in accordance. Will not see walk-ins."

***BRACKER COMMUNICATIONS**, 330 W. Frontage Rd., Northfield IL 60093. (312)441-5534. President: Richard W. Bracker. Ad agency/public relations/publishing firm. Clients: construction, financial, acoustical, contractors, equipment manufacturers, trade associations, household fixtures, pest control products.
Needs: Works with 4-6 freelance artists/year. "Use only artists based in the Chicago area for the most part. We look for ability and have used recent graduates." Works on assignment only. Uses artists for graphic design/key line. Especially important are type specing, design/layout and photo handling.
First Contact & Terms: Phone or send resume to be kept on file. Reviews any type of sample. Reports within 2 weeks. Write for appointment to show portfolio. Negotiates and/or accepts quotations on specific projects. Considers complexity of project, skill and experience of artist, and turnaround time when establishing payment. Buys all rights.
Tips: "Don't make assumptions about anything."

BRAGAW PUBLIC RELATIONS SERVICES, 800 E. Northwest Hwy., Palatine IL 60067. (312)934-5580. Principal: Richard S. Bragaw. PR firm. Clients: professional service firms, associations, industry.
Needs: Assigns 12 freelance jobs/year. Local artists only. Works on assignment only. Works with 1 freelance illustrator and 1 freelance designer/month. Uses artists for direct mail packages, brochures, signage, AV presentations and press releases.
First Contact & Terms: Send query letter with brochure to be kept on file. Reports only if interested. Write to schedule an appointment. Pays by the hour, $25-75 average. Considers complexity of project, skill and experience of artist and turnaround time when establishing payment. Buys all rights.
Tips: "We do not spend much time with portfolios."

CAIN AND COMPANY (ROCKFORD), 2222 E. State St., Rockford IL 61108. (815)399-2482. Senior Art Director: Randall E. Klein. Ad agency/PR firm. Clients: financial, industrial, retail and service.
Needs: Assigns 6 freelance jobs/year. Uses artists for consumer and trade magazines, billboards, direct mail packages, brochures, catalogs, newspapers, filmstrips, movies, stationery, signage, P-O-P displays, AV presentations, posters and press releases "to some degree."
First Contact & Terms: Send query letter with brochure, resume, business card, samples and tear sheets to be kept on file. Call or write for appointment to show portfolio. Send samples that show best one medium in which work is produced. Samples not kept on file are not returned. Reports only if interested. Works on assignment only. "Rates depend on talent and speed; could be anywhere from $5 to $30 an hour." Considers skill and experience of artist and turnaround time when establishing payment. Buys all rights.
Tips: "Have a good presentation, not just graphics."

***CORONET/MTI FILM & VIDEO**, 108 Wilmot Rd., Deerfield IL 60015. Art Director: Tina Primer. Assistant Art Director: Judith Orr. Distributor of educational and training market film and videos. "We are an in-house advertising/marketing agency." Clients: in-house agency promotes company's products through catalog work, also single sheets, brochures and promotional flyers.
Needs: Works with approximately 8 freelance artists/year. Assigns jobs as needed. Prefers local artists, work in-house or in your home. Works on assignment only. Uses artists for advertising design and

layout, brochure and catalog design, illustration and layout, display fixture design and posters. Prefers realistic or technical style.
First Contact & Terms: Send query letter, resume and samples. Samples are not filed and returned only if requested by artist. Reports back only if interested. Pays for design and illustration by the hour, $6 minimum; by the project, $6 minimum and by the day, $48 minimum. Considers complexity of project, skill and experience of artist and turnaround time when establishing payment.
Tips: "Include samples of design and illustration capabilities showing neatness and accuracy."

JOHN CROWE ADVERTISING AGENCY, 1104 S. 2nd St., Springfield IL 62704. (217)528-1076. Owner: Bryan J. Crowe. Ad/art agency. Clients: industries, manufacturers, retailers, banks, publishers, insurance firms, packaging firms, state agencies, aviation and law enforcement agencies.
Needs: Buys 3,000 illustrations/year. Works with 4 illustrators and 3 designers/month. Works on assignment only. Uses artists for color separations, animation, lettering, paste-up and type spec for work with consumer magazines, stationery design, direct mail, slide sets, brochures/flyers, trade magazines and newspapers. Especially needs layout, camera-ready art and photo retouching. Prefers pen & ink, airbrush, watercolor and markers.
First Contact & Terms: "Send a letter to us regarding available work at agency. Tell us about yourself. We will reply if work is needed and request samples of work." Prefers tear sheets, original art, photocopies, brochure, business card and resume to be kept on file. Samples not filed returned by SASE. Reports in 2 weeks. Pays for design by the project, $5-50; pays for illustration by the project, $10-100. No originals returned to artist at job's completion. No payment for unused assigned illustrations.
Tips: "Current works are best. Show your strengths and do away with poor pieces that aren't your stonghold. A portfolio should not be messy and cluttered."

DYNAMIC GRAPHICS, 6000 N. Forest Park Dr., Peoria IL 61614. Art Director: Frank Antal. Graphics firm for general graphic art user.
Needs: Works with 50 freelance artists/year. Works on assignment only. Uses artists for illustrations. Needs artists with "originality, creativity, professionalism."
First Contact & Terms: Send query letter with portfolio showing art style or tear sheets and photocopies. Samples not filed are returned. Reports back within 1 month. To show a portfolio, mail appropriate materials, which should include final reproduction/product or Photostats. Pays by the project; "we pay highly competitive rates but prefer not to specify." Considers complexity of project, skill and experience of artist and rights purchased when establishing payment. Buys all rights.
Tips: "Submit styles that are the illustrator's strongest and can be used successfully, consistently."

FILLMAN ADVERTISING INC., 304 W. Hill St., Champaign IL 61820. (217)352-0002. Art/Creative Director: Mary Auth. Ad agency. Serves clients in industry. Assigns 60 jobs and buys 10 illustrations/year.
Needs: Works with 1-2 illustrators and 2-3 designers/month. Uses mostly local artists. Works on assignment only. Uses artists for posters, direct mail, brochures/flyers, trade magazines. Prefers realistic and technical style.
First Contact & Terms: Send query letter with originals, photographs, b&w line drawings, photocopies of inputs or finished printed pieces. Samples returned by SASE. Reports in 2 weeks. Send business card and resume to be kept on file for possible future assignments. No originals returned to artist at job's completion. Pays for design by the hour, $15-40. Pays for illustration by the project, $50-400. Pays promised fee for unused assigned illustrations. Considers skill and experience of artist when establishing payment
Tips: Does not want to see oversize samples of portfolios.

IMPERIAL INTERNATIONAL LEARNING CORP., Box 548, Kankakee IL 60901. (815)933-7735. President: Spencer Barnard. AV producer. Serves clients in education. Produces filmstrips, illustrated workbooks, microcomputer software, video tapes.
Needs: Assigns multiple jobs/year. Works with variety of designers/year. Works on assignment only. Uses artists for original line art, color illustrations and graphic design, computer graphics.
First Contact & Terms: Send query letter and tear sheets to be kept on file, Samples returned only if requested. Reports back only if interested. Method and amount of payment are negotiated with the individual artist. No originals returned to artist following publication. Considers skill and experience of artist when establishing payment. Buys all rights.

ELVING JOHNSON ADVERTISING INC., 7804 W. College Dr., Palos Heights IL 60463. (312)361-2850. Art/Creative Director: Michael McNicholas. Ad agency. Serves clients in industrial machinery, construction materials, material handling, finance, etc.

Needs: Works with 2 illustrators/month. Local artists only. Uses artists for direct mail, brochures/flyers, trade magazines and newspapers. Also uses artists for layout, illustration, technical art, paste-up and retouching. "We need technical illustration." Prefers pen & ink, airbrush, watercolor and markers.
First Contact & Terms: Call for interview. Pays for design and illustration by the project, $100 minimum.
Tips: "We find most artists through references and portfolio reviews."

***LAUREN INTERNATIONAL LTD.**, 7336B Route 34, Oswego IL 60543. Contact: Lauren Grey. Produces industrial films, filmstrips, print pieces and multimedia presentations.
Needs: Works with writers, illustrators, graphic designers, bottom lit slide artwork artists and photographers. Works on assignment only.
First Contact & Terms: Prefers slides or photos or whatever's applicable as samples. Reports back whether to expect possible future assignments. Pay depends entirely on person and job. Provide brochures/flyers and resume to be kept on file for future assignments. No originals returned to artist at job's completion.
Tips: "Professionals only, please."

LERNER SCOTT CORP., 1000 Skokie Blvd., Wilmette IL 60091. (312)251-2447. Vice President/Managing Art Director: Mark Bryzinski. Direct marketing/ad agency. Clients: insurance and communications companies, wholesale distributors, entertainment and consumer products.
Needs: Works with 8 freelance artists/year. Chicago area artists only. Works on assignment only. Uses artists for advertising design, illustration and layout; P-O-P displays, and signage. Prefers pen & ink, airbrush, watercolor, acrylics and markers.
First Contact & Terms: Send query letter with business card, photocopies or tear sheets to be kept on file. Samples not filed returned only if requested. Reports only if interested. Call for appointment to show portfolio. Pays for design by the hour, $20-80; by the project, $120 minimum. Pays for illustration by the project, $60 minimum. Considers complexity of project when establishing payment.
Tips: "I look for versatility—someone who can do a variety of styles and subjects. Also, I look for quality and seasoning. I don't have time for hand-holding or re-dos."

MARTINDALE & ASSOCIATES, #102, 350 West Kensington, Mount Prospect IL 60056. (312)437-6400. President: R. Martindale. Financial consultants. Clients: banks and savings and loans. Media used include billboards, consumer and trade magazines, direct mail, newspapers, radio and TV.
Needs: "Work load varies; usually our extra assignments (beyond what our regular staff can service efficiently) bunch up in active months such as January, May, September and October. Those extra assignments might be 5 or 6 newspaper ad layouts, 2 or 3 brochures, and perhaps a special design assignment." Works on assignment only. Uses artists for work in direct mail, brochures/flyers and newspapers.
First Contact & Terms: Write and request personal interview to show portfolio. Provide resume to be kept on file for future assignments. Reports within 10 days. Pays by the hour or by the project. Considers complexity of project, client's budget, skill and experience of artist, and turnaround time when establishing payment.
Tips: "We prefer to let the individual decide what he or she wants to show. If they can't show a strong portfolio, we can't expect them to be strong enough for our purposes." Artist should "stay within the *guidelines* of the assigned project."

ARTHUR MERIWETHER, INC., 1529 Brook Dr., Downers Grove IL 60515. (312)495-0600. Production Coordinator: Lori Ouska. Audiovisual firm, design studio and communications services. Clients: industrial corporations (electronics, chemical, etc.) plus consumer clients.
Needs: Works with 10-20 freelance artists/year. Artists should have minimum 2 years of experience. Prefers local artists, will occasionally work with out-of-state illustrators. Uses artists for keyline/paste-up, illustration and design. Especially important are knowledge of audiovisual and print production techniques.
First Contact & Terms: Send query letter with resume, business card, slides and tear sheets. Samples returned by SASE. Reports only if interested. Payment varies per project and artist's experience. Also considers client's budget, skill of artist and turnaround time when establishing payment. Rights purchased vary according to project; usually buys all rights.

MOTIVATION MEDIA INC., 1245 Milwaukee Ave., Glenview IL 60025. (312)297-4740. Contact: Creative Graphics Manager. Clients: consumer and industrial. Producers of multi-image programs, speaker support and sound-slide programs, filmstrips, motion picture and videotape productions.
Needs: Works with 10 production artists and 5 designers/month. Assigns approx. 675 jobs/year. Works on assignment only. Prefers pen & ink and markers.
First Contact & Terms: Query with resume and nonreturnable samples (photocopies, duplicates,

etc.). SASE. Replies in 2 weeks if interested. Provide resume to be kept on file for future assignments. Pays $12-25/hour, multi-image, charts/graphs art direction; $10-30/hour, illustrations; also pays by the job. Considers complexity of project, client's budget, skill and experience of artist and turnaround time when establishing payment. Pays 30 days after receipt of invoice.
Tips: "Send resume and copies of work. Our schedule does not allow us extensive time for interviewing. Though I need people who know slide production, I'm interested in people who know all areas of art production. Be able to see a project through from input to completion. In your resumes, be brief and to the point; list experience. In your portfolio, specify AV or slide experience."

TELEMATION PRODUCTIONS, INC., 3210 W. Westlake, Glenview IL 60025. (312)729-5215. Art Director: Mitch Levin. Video production house. Clients: automotive firms, corporate clients, advertising agencies and private producers.
Needs: Works with 3-5 freelance artists/year. Computer graphics experience and art background required. Works on assignment only. Uses artists for design, illustrations, animation, logos, charts/graphs and advertisements. Artists should have "good illustration skill, a strong sense of design and be visually oriented."
First Contact & Terms: Send query letter with resume and samples. Samples not filed are not returned. Reports only if interested. Pays for design by the hour, $10-15. Considers skill and experience of artist when establishing payment. Buys all rights.
Tips: Artists should "be enthusiastic toward learning a new computer graphic system." Looks for "use of color, 3-D, texture."

Chicago

AUDITIONS BY SOUNDMASTERS, Box 8135, Chicago IL 60680. (312)224-5612. Executive Vice President: R.C. Hillsman. Produces radio/TV programs, commercials, jingles and records.
Needs: Buys 125-300 designs/year. Uses artists for animation, catalog covers/illustrations, layout, paste-up, multimedia kits and record album design.
First Contact & Terms: Mail 8x10 art. SASE. Reports in 3 weeks. Pays $500 minimum, animation; $100-350, record jackets; $50-225, layout; $35-165, paste-up. Material copyrighted.

N.W. AYER, INC., One Illinois Center, 111 E. Wacker Dr., Chicago IL 60601. (312)645-8800. Contact: Iris Rogers. Ad agency. "We cover a very wide range of clients."
First Contact & Terms: Call for personal appointment to show portfolio. Negotiates payment based on client's budget and the amount of creativity required from artist.
Tips: Portfolio should consist of past work used by ad agencies and commercial art.

E. H. BROWN ADVERTISING AGENCY, INC., 20 N. Wacker, Chicago IL 60606. (312)372-9494. Art Director: Arnold G. Pirsoul. Ad agency. Clients: insurance, schools, banks, corporations, electronics, high-tech, etc.
Needs: Works on assignment only. Uses artists for design, illustration, newspapers, retouching, lettering, charts/graphs and advertisements.
First Contact & Terms: Send Photostats, photocopies and photographs. Samples are filed. Samples not filed are not returned. Reports back only if interested. Call or write to schedule an appointment to show a portfolio, which should include roughs, tear sheets, color and b&w. Pays for design by the hour, $35-50. Pays for illustration by the project, $400-1,200. Considers complexity of project, client's budget, turnaround time, skill and experience of artist, how work will be used and rights purchased. Negotiates rights purchased; rights purchased vary according to project.
Tips: "Be precise and efficient about the job to be done. Avoid delays and be on time when the job is contracted. Stick with the estimate."

FRANK J. CORBETT, INC., 211 E. Chicago Ave., Chicago IL 60611. (312)664-5310. Creative Director: Dick Jacobs. Ad agency. Serves clients in pharmaceuticals.
Needs: Works with 12-14 freelance illustrators/month. Uses freelancers "for almost everything."
First Contact & Terms: Call for appointment to show portfolio or make contact through artist's agent. Selection based on portfolio review. Negotiates payment based on client's budget.
Tips: Wants to see the best of artist's work including that used by ad agencies, and tear sheets of published art. Especially interested in good medical illustration, but also uses a wide variety of photography and illustration.

DARBY MEDIA GROUP, 4015 N. Rockwell St., Chicago IL 60618. Creative Director: Tony Christian. Production Manager: Dennis Cyrier. Audiovisual/offset printing firm. Clients: corporate, ad agencies, educational.

Needs: Works with 10-20 freelance artists and designers/year. Uses artists for production and illustration. Especially important for artists to have knowledge of audiovisual production.
First Contact & Terms: Local artists only (Chicago metropolitan area). Send query letter with resume and samples (if possible) to be kept on file. Write for appointment to show portfolio. Prefers slides as samples. Samples not filed are returned. Reports back only if interested. Pays by the hour, $10-25 average; by the project or by the day. Considers complexity of the project, client's budget, skill and experience of artist and turnaround time when establishing payment. Rights purchased vary according to project.
Tips: "Be design-oriented. Be knowledgeable on all aspects of AV and print production. Supply your own working tools."

***JOHN DOREMUS, INC./MUSIC IN THE AIR**, Suite 1801, 875 N. Michigan Ave., Chicago IL 60611. (312)664-8944. Vice President: Katherine Danielson. Director Global Marketing: Alexis Sarkisian. "We are a company which has as its specialty audio tape production. This is any and all forms of production, including music production along with documentary production. We also have on staff an emmy award winning video producer, and can provide this service as well." Clients: airlines, government agencies, and any company that needs music or audio programming.
Needs: Works with 50 artists/year. Assigns 100 jobs/year. Prefers AFTRA audio talent.
First Contact & Terms: Send query letter with resume. Samples are filed. Reports back within 1 month. Write to schedule an appointment to show a portfolio. Considers complexity of project when establishing payment.

FINANCIAL SHARES CORPORATION, 62 W. Huron, Chicago IL 60610. (312)943-8116. Vice President: Jennifer Dinehart. Training and public relations firm. Helps financial institutions achieve profitable results through high-quality customized consulting services. Our services include: market research, strategic marketing planning, product design and pricing, public and investor relations, sales training. We also develop and implement sales incentive and measurement programs. Clients: all financial institutions.
Needs: Works with 6 freelance artists/year. Assigns 50 jobs/year. Prefers local artists only. Uses artists for design, brochures, newspapers, logos, charts/graphs and advertisements.
First Contact & Terms: Send query letter with brochure. Reports back in 2 weeks. Write to schedule an appointment to show a portfolio, which should include original/final art, Photostats and final reproduction/product. Pays for design by the project. Considers client's budget, turnaround time and skill and experience of artist when establishing payment. Rights purchased vary according to project.
Tips: "We need artists who know about the finance/banking field."

GARFIELD-LINN & COMPANY, 142 E. Ontario,, Chicago IL 60611. (312)943-1900. Contact: Art Directors or Creative Director. Ad agency. Clients: "wide variety" of accounts; client list provided upon request.
Needs: Number of freelance artists used varies. Uses freelance artists for billboards, consumer and trade magazines, direct mail, brochures, catalogs and posters.
First Contact & Terms: Query with samples; arrange interview to show portfolio. Works on assignment basis only. Payment is by the project; negotiates according to client's budget.

IMAGINE THAT!, Suite 4908, 405 N. Wabash Ave., Chicago IL 60611. (312)670-0234. President: John Beele. Ad agency. Clients: broadcast, insurance firm, University of Illinois sports program, pharmaceuticals, retail furniture stores, real estate and professional rodeo.
Needs: Assigns 25-50 jobs and buys 15 illustrations/year. Uses artists for layout, illustration, mechanicals and photography.
First Contact & Terms: Arrange interview to show portfolio with Sheila Dunbar. Pay is negotiable.

***KOCH/MARSCHALL PRODUCTIONS, INC.**, 4310 N. Mozart St., Chicago IL 60618. President: Phillip Koch. Audiovisual firm.
Needs: Works with approximately 1 freelance artist/year. Assigns 1 job/year. Works on assignment only. Uses artists for films.
First Contact & Terms: Send query letter with brochure or resume. Samples are filed. Samples not filed are returned by SASE. Does not report back. Pays for design and illustration by the project, $200-1,000. Considers complexity of project, client's budget and how work will be used when establishing payment. Rights purchased vary according to project.

McCANN HEALTHCARE ADVERTISING, (formerly Sieber & McIntyre), 625 N. Michigan Ave., Chicago IL 60611. (312)266-9200. Contact: Creative Services Manager. Ad agency. Clients: pharmaceutical and health care fields.

Needs: Work load varies. Works on assignment only. Uses freelancers for medical trade magazines, journal ads, brochures/flyers and direct mail to physicians. Especially needs sources for tight marker renderings and comp layouts.
First Contact & Terms: Send query letter with resume and samples. Call for appointment to show portfolio, which should include roughs, original/final art, final reproduction/product, color, Photostats and photographs. Reports within 2 weeks. Pays by the hour, $10-50. Negotiates payment based on client's budget, where work will appear, complexity of project, skill and experience of artist and turnaround time.
Tips: "Rendering with markers very important." Prefers to see original work rather than reproductions, but will review past work used by other ad agencies. Needs good medical illustrators but is looking for the best person—one who can accomplish executions other than anatomical. Artists should send resume or letter for files.

MARKETING SUPPORT INC., 303 E. Wacker Dr., Chicago IL 60601. (312)565-0044. Executive Art Director: Robert Becker. Clients: plumbing, heating/cooling equipment, chemicals, hardware, ski equipment, home appliances, crafts and window covering.
Needs: Assigns 300 jobs/year. Works with 2-3 illustrators/month. Local artists only. Works on assignment only. Uses artists for filmstrips, slide sets, brochures/flyers and trade magazines. Also uses artists for layout, illustration, lettering, type spec, paste-up and retouching for trade magazines and direct mail.
First Contact & Terms: Arrange interview to show portfolio. Samples returned by SASE. Reports back only if interested. Provide business card to be kept on file for future assignments. No originals returned to artist at job's completion. Pays $15/hour and up. Considers complexity of project, client's budget, and skill and experience of artist when establishing payment.

O.M.A.R. INC., 5525 N. Broadway, Chicago IL 60640. (312)271-2720. Creative Director: Paul Sierra. Spanish language ad agency. Clients: consumer food, telephone communication, TV station and public utilities.
Needs: Number of freelance artists used varies. Local artists only. Works on assignment only. Uses artists for consumer magazines, posters, newspapers and TV graphics.
First Contact & Terms: Send query letter with resume of credits, slides or originals (color) and Photostats (b&w); follow with phone call. Samples returned by SASE. Reports within 3 weeks. Payment is by the project; negotiates according to client's budget. Buys all rights.
Tips: Artists interested in working here "must have sensitivity to the Hispanic culture. An artist should never sacrifice pride in his/her work for the sake of a deadline, yet must nevertheless meet the specified time of completion. Show only your best work during an interview, and don't take too much time."

POLYCOM TELEPRODUCTIONS, 142 E. Ontario, Chicago IL 60611. (312)337-6000. Executive Producer/Director: Mr. Carmen V. Trombetta. Producer: Debbie Heagy. Videotape teleproducer. Clients: 60% are major Chicago advertising and PR firms and educational/industrial enterprises and 40% are corporate enterprises. Produces filmstrips, motion pictures, multimedia kits, overhead transparencies, slide sets, sound-slide sets, videotapes and films.
Needs: Works with 2-3 illustrators/month. Works on assignment only. Assigns 150-200 jobs/year. Uses artists for motion pictures, videotape teleproduction, television copy art, storyboard animation and computer animation.
First Contact & Terms: Query with resume, business card and slides which may be kept on file. Samples not kept on file are returned by SASE. Reports in 2-3 weeks. Original art returned to artist at job's completion. Negotiates pay by project.
Tips: "Artists must be familiar with film and videotape. We need more videotape and computer graphics artists."

Indiana

ASHER AGENCY, 511 W. Wayne, Fort Wayne IN 46802. (219)424-3373. Creative Director: Renee Wright. Ad agency and public relations firm. Clients: automotive firms, hospitals, convention centers, apartment development, area economic development agencies.
Needs: Works with 10 freelance artists/year. Assigns 50 jobs/year. Prefers area artists. Works on assignment only. Uses freelance artists for design, illustration, brochures, catalogs, consumer and trade magazines, retouching, billboards, posters, direct mail packages, logos and advertisements.
First Contact & Terms: Send query letter with brochure showing art style or tear sheets and photocopies. Samples are filed. Samples not filed are returned by SASE. Reports back only if interested. Write to schedule an appointment to show a portfolio, which should include roughs, original/final art, tear sheets and final reproduction/product. Pays for design by the hour, $20 minimum.

Pays for illustration by the hour. Considers complexity of project, client's budget, turnaround time and skill and experience of artist when establishing payments. Buys all rights.
Tips: In portfolios, "we'd like to see rough or comp layouts as well as finished, printed work."

***BLOOMHORST STORY O'HARA INC.**, 200 S. Meridian, Indianapolis IN 46225. (317)639-4436. Art Directors: Curt Chuvalas, Ken Bloomhorst. Full-service advertising agency. Clients: retail.
Needs: Works with 30 artists/year. Uses freelance artists for brochure, catalog, newspaper and magazine ad illustration; P-O-P displays; mechanicals; retouching; animation; films; lettering and charts/graphs.
First Contact & Terms: Send query letter with brochure showing art style or tear sheets, photocopies and slides. Samples are filed. Samples not filed are returned only if requested by artist. Does not report back. Call to schedule an appointment to show a portfolio, which should include roughs, Photostats, tear sheets, photographs, color, b&w, and slides. Pays for illustration by the project, $100-10,000 + Considers complexity of project, client's budget, turnaround time, how work will be used and rights purchased. Rights purchased vary according to project.
Tips: "Please do not leave your phone number asking us to call you back to set up an interview."

C.R.E. INC., 400 Victoria Centre, 22 E. Washington St., Indianapolis IN 46204. Senior Art Director: Mark Grouse. Ad agency. Clients: industrial, banks, agriculture and consumer.
Needs: Works with 15 freelance artists/year. Works on assignment only. Uses artists for line art, color illustrations and airbrushing.
First Contact & Terms: Send query letter with resume, and photocopies to be kept on file. Samples not filed are returned. Reports back only if interested. Call or write to schedule an appointment to show a portfolio, or mail original/final art, final reproduction/product and tear sheets. Pays by the project, $100 minimum. Considers complexity of the project, client's budget, skill and experience of artist and rights purchased when establishing payment. Buys all rights.
Tips: "Show samples of good creative talent."

CALDWELL VAN RIPER, INC. ADVERTISING-PUBLIC RELATIONS, 1314 N. Meridian St., Indianapolis IN 46202. (317)632-6501. Creative Coordinator: Kathy Hendry. Ad agency/PR firm. Clients are "a good mix of consumer (banks, furniture, food, etc.) and industrial (chemicals, real estate, insurance, heavy industry)."
Needs: Assigns 100-200 freelance jobs/year. Works with 10-15 freelance illustrators/month. Works on assignment only. Uses artists for consumer and magazine ads, billboards, direct mail packages, brochures, catalogs, newspaper ads, P-O-P displays, storyboards, AV presentations and posters.
First Contact & Terms: Send query letter with brochure, samples and tear sheets to be kept on file. Call for appointment to show portfolio. Accepts any available samples. Samples not filed are returned by SASE only if requested. Reports only if interested. Pay is negotiated. Considers complexity of project, client's budget, skill and experience of artist and rights purchased when establishing payment. Buys all rights.
Tips: "Send 5 samples of best work (copies acceptable) followed by a phone call."

Kansas

LANE MARKETING GROUP, INC., (formerly Lane & Leslie Advertising Agency, Inc.), Riverview Bldg., Box 578, Wichita KS 67201. President: David W. Lane. Ad agency. Clients: banks, savings and loans, consumer products.
Needs: Works with 1 illustrator and 6 designers/month. Uses artists for storyboards, billboards, P-O-P displays, filmstrips, multimedia kits, direct mail, slide sets, brochures/flyers, trade magazines and newspapers. Also uses artists for photography and retouching.
First Contact & Terms: Send query letter with resume, tear sheets, Photostats, photocopies, slides and photographs. Call or write to schedule an appointment to show a portfolio, which should include original final art, final reproduction/product, tear sheets, Photostats and photographs. No originals returned to artist at job's completion. Pays by the hour and by the project; payment based on project. "We prefer to buy all rights."

MARKETAIDE, INC., Box 500, Salina KS 67402-0500. (913)825-7161. Production Manager: Eric Lamer. Full-service advertising/marketing/direct mail firm. Clients: financial, agricultural machinery, industrial, some educational, and fast food.
Needs: Prefers artists within one-state distance and possessing professional expertise. Works on assignment only. Uses freelance artists for illustrations, retouching, signage.
First Contact & Terms: Send query letter with resume, business card and samples to be kept on file.

Accepts any kind of accurate representation as samples, depending upon medium. Samples not kept on file are returned only if requested. Reports only if interested. Write for appointment to show portfolio. Pays by the hour, $15-75 average; "since projects vary in size we are forced to estimate according to each job's parameters." Considers complexity of project, skill and experience of artist, how work will be used, turnaround time and rights purchased when establishing payment.
Tips: Artists interested in working here "should be highly-polished in technical ability, have a good eye for design and be able to meet all deadline commitments."

MARSHFILM ENTERPRISES, INC., Box 8082, Shawnee Mission KS 66208. (816)523-1059. President: Joan K. Marsh. Audiovisual firm. Clients: schools.
Needs: Works with 1-2 freelance artists/year. Works on assignment only. Uses artists for illustrating filmstrips. Artists must have experience and imagination.
First Contact & Terms: Send query letter, resume and slides or actual illustrations to be kept on file "if it is potentially the type of art we would use." Samples not filed are returned. Reports within 1 month. Write for appointment to show portfolio. Considers client's budget when establishing payment. Buys all rights.

TRAVIS-WALZ AND ASSOCIATES, INC., 8417 Santa Fe Dr., Overland Park KS 66212-2749. Vice President/Creative Director: Gary Otteson. Ad agency. Serves clients in food, finance, broadcasting, utilities, pets, gardening and real estate.
Needs: Works with 2-4 illustrators/month. "We generally work with in-town talent because of tight deadlines." Commissioned work only. Uses illustrators for billboards, P-O-P displays, consumer magazines, direct mail, brochures/flyers, trade magazines and newspapers. Prefers pen & ink, airbrush, and charcoal/pencil. Also uses artists for retouching. Does not buy design or layout. Agency has its own design staff.
First Contact & Terms: Send query letter with brochure showing art style or tear sheets, Photostats and photocopies. Samples returned by SASE. Reports only if interested. Call to schedule an appointment to show portfolio, which should include final reproduction/product and tear sheets. No originals returned to artist at job's completion. Pays for illustration by the project, $120 minimum. Considers complexity of project, client's budget and turnaround time when establishing payment.
Tips: "We must see your work to buy. The best way to sell yourself is by your samples shown in person or brochure mailed to us. We prefer printed samples, photoprints or original work. Don't want to see slides-useless to judge work. We see 4 to 5 freelancers a week. More and more illustrators are entering the market. Our market is flooded so the competition is very stiff. Try to find a specialty that no one else is doing."

Kentucky

***SHEEHY & KNOPF INC. ADVERTISING**, 10400 Linn Station Rd., Louisville KY 40223. Creative Director: Tom Korkaw. Ad agency. Clients: investment companies, entertainment, health care, interior design and industrial.
Needs: Works with 10 freelance artists/year. Works on assignment only. Uses artists for illustrations, mechanicals, retouching, animation and lettering.
First Contact & Terms: Send query letter with brochure showing art style or resume and samples. Samples not filed are returned only if requested. Reports only if interested. Call or write to schedule an appointment to show a portfolio, which should include original/final art, final reproduction/product, color, tear sheets, Photostats and photographs. Pays for design by the hour, $35-60. Pays for illustration by the project, $50 minimum. Considers complexity of project, client's budget, skill and experience of artist, how work will be used, turnaround time and rights purchased when establishing payment. Rights purchased vary according to project. "We like to hear from students."
Tips: "Be concise. Make appointments before calling on anyone. Leave samples for reference of style and information on where to be reached including phone number. Call occasionally with updates."

Louisiana

CARTER ADVERTISING INC., 800 American Tower, Shreveport LA 71101. (318)227-1920. President: Bill Bailey Carter. Ad agency. Clients: banks, real estate, airline, toy manufacturing, fast food and hospital. Assigns 150 jobs and buys 50 illustrations/year.
Needs: Works with 2-3 illustrators and 2-3 designers/month. Prefers local artists. "Must have heavy production experience." Uses artists for billboards, P-O-P displays, filmstrips, consumer magazines,

stationery design, multimedia kits, direct mail, television, slide sets, brochures/flyers, trade magazines, album covers, newspapers, books and mechanicals.
First Contact & Terms: Query with resume or arrange interview to show portfolio. SASE. Reports within 2 weeks. Provide brochure, flyer, business card, resume, tear sheets, etc., to be kept on file for future assignments. No originals returned at job's completion unless otherwise agreed upon. Pay negotiated by project. Considers complexity of project, client's budget, skill and experience of artist, geographic scope of finished project, turnaround time and rights purchased when establishing payment.

CUNNINGHAM, SLY WADSACK INC.,Box 4503, Shreveport LA 71134-0503. Creative Director: Harold J. Sly. Ad agency. Clients: industrial/financial.
Needs: Works with 6-10 freelance artists/year. Works on assignment only. Uses artists for layout/design, illustrations, photo retouching, mechanical art and airbrushing. Especially looks for mechanical skills.
First Contact & Terms: Send query letter with brochure, resume, business card and samples to be kept on file. Samples not filed are returned only by request. Reports back only if interested. Pays by the hour, $20-50 average. Considers complexity of the project, client's budget and turnaround time when establishing payment. Rights purchased vary according to project.

DUKE UNLIMITED, INC., Suite 1709, 1 Galleria Blvd., Metairie LA 70002. (504)836-5150. President: Lana Duke. Ad agency. Clients: industrial, investment, medical, restaurants, entertainment, fashion and tourism.
Needs: Assigns 50 freelance jobs/year. Works with 2 freelance illustrators and 1 freelance designer/month. Works on assignment. Uses artists for consumer and trade magazines, billboards, direct mail packages, brochures, catalogs, newspapers, filmstrips, movies, stationery, signage, P-O-P displays, AV presentations, posters and press releases.
First Contact & Terms: Send query letter with brochure, business card, Photostats and tear sheets to be kept on file. Samples returned only if requested. Reports only if interested. Pays by the project, $150-1,000 average. The artist must provide a firm quotation in writing. Considers complexity of project, client's budget, skill and experience of artist, turnaround time and rights purchased when establishing payment. Buys all rights.

Maryland

SAMUEL R. BLATE ASSOCIATES, 10331 Watkins Mill Dr., Gaithersburg MD 20879-2935. (301)840-2248. President: Samuel R. Blate. Audiovisual and editorial services firm. Clients: business/professional, U.S. government, some private.
Needs: Works with 5 freelance artists/year. Only works with artists in the Washington-Baltimore-Richmond metro area. Works on assignment only. Uses artists for cartoons (especially for certain types of audiovisual presentations), illustrations (graphs, etc.) for 35mm slides, pamphlet and book design. Especially important are "technical and aesthetic excellence and ability to meet deadlines."
First Contact & Terms: Send query letter with resume and tear sheets, Photostats, photocopies, slides and photographs to be kept on file. "No original art, please. SASE for return." Call or write for appointment to show portfolio, which should include final reproduction/product, color, photographs and b&w. Samples are returned by SASE. Reports only if interested. Pays by the hour, $20-40. "Payment varies as a function of experience, skills needed, size of project, and anticipated competition, if any." Also considers complexity of the project, client's budget, turnaround time and rights purchased when establishing payment. Rights purchased vary according to project, "but we prefer to purchase first rights only. This is sometimes not possible due to client demand, in which case we attempt to negotiate a financial adjustment for the artist."
Tips: "The demand for technically-oriented artwork has increased. At the same time, some clients who used artists have been satisfied with computer-generated art."

IMAGE DYNAMICS, INC., Suite 1400, 1101 N. Calvert St., Baltimore MD 21202. (301)539-7730. Art Director: Erin Ries. Ad agency/PR firm. Clients: wide mix, specializing in restaurants and hotels, associations, colleges, hospitals and land developers.
Needs: Local artists only. Uses artists for illustration, design and paste-up; frequently buys humorous and cartoon-style illustrations. Prefers various styles in b&w and full-color.
First Contact & Terms: Call to arrange interview to show portfolio; "please do not drop in. Bring lots of b&w and color samples; have printed or produced work to show." Samples are returned. Reports only if interested. Provide business card and samples to be kept on file for possible future assignments. Pays

by the project, $100-1,500, depending on project and budget. Considers complexity of project, client's budget, skill and experience of artist and turnaround time when establishing payment.
Tips: "We are able to use freelance illustrators more towards a more creative product."

SHECTER & LEVIN ADVERTISING/PUBLIC RELATIONS, 2205 N. Charles St., Baltimore MD 21218. (301)889-4464. Production Executive: Virginia Lindler. Ad agency/PR firm. Serves clients in real estate, finance, professional associations, social agencies, retailing, apartments and manufacturing.
Needs: Works with 3-4 illustrators/month. Uses designers for billboards, consumer magazines, stationery design, direct mail, television, brochures/flyers, trade magazines and newspapers. Also uses artists for layouts and mechanicals for brochures, newspaper and magazine ads.
First Contact & Terms: Write for an interview to show portfolio. No originals returned to artist at job's completion. Negotiates pay.

MARC SMITH CO., Box A, Severna Park MD 21146. (301)647-2606. Art/Creative Director: Marc Smith. Advertising agency. Clients: consumer and industrial products, sales services and public relations firms.
Needs: Works with 6 illustrators/month. Local artists only. Uses artists for layout, illustration, lettering, technical art, type spec, paste-up and retouching. Uses illustrators and designers for direct mail, slide sets, brochures/flyers, trade magazines and newspapers; designers for billboards, P-O-P displays, film strips, consumer magazines, stationery, multimedia kits and TV. Occasionally buys humorous and cartoon-style illustrations.
First Contact & Terms: Send query letter with brochure showing art style or tear sheets, Photostats, photocopies, slides or photographs. Keeps file on artists; does not return original artwork to artist after completion of assignment. Call or write to schedule an appointment to show a portfolio, which should include thumbnails, roughs, original/final art, final reproduction/product, color and tear sheets. Pays by the hour, $25-150.
Tips: "More sophisticated techniques and equipment are being used in art and design. Our use of freelance material has intensified. Project honesty, clarity and patience."

VAN SANT, DUGDALE & COMPANY, INC., The World Trade Center, Baltimore MD 21202. (301)539-5400. Executive Creative Director: Stan Paulus. Creative Director: Glen Bentley. Ad agency. Clients: consumer, corporate, associations, financial, and industrial.
Needs: Number of freelance artists used varies. Works on assignment basis only. Uses freelance artists for consumer and trade magazines, brochures, catalogs, newspapers and AV presentations.
First Contact & Terms: Negotiates payment according to client's budget, amount of creativity required, where work will appear and freelancer's previous experience.

Massachusetts

ALLIED ADVERTISING AGENCY INC., 800 Statler Office Bldg., Boston MA 02116. (617)482-4100. Creative Director: Paul Beatrice. Ad agency and public relations firm. "We are a full-service ad agency providing advertising and collateral material for clients in the print, video and audio media." Clients: electronic, consumer products, film industry, food.
Needs: Works with 10-15 freelance artists/year. Assigns 20-30 jobs/year. Prefers local artists but will go farther for specific talents." Uses artists for illustration, retouching, animation, motion pictures, logos and advertisements.
First Contact & Terms: Send query letter with brochure, or resume, tear sheets, Photostats, photocopies, slides and photographs. Samples are sometimes filed. Samples not filed are returned by SASE. Reports back only if interested. Call or write to schedule an appointment to show a portfolio. Pays for design by the hour, $15-100. Pays for illustration by the project, $50 minimum. Considers complexity of project, skill and experience of artist and rights purchased when establishing payment. Buys all rights or reprint rights; negotiates rights purchased. Rights purchased vary according to project.

COSMOPULOS, CROWLEY & DALY, INC., 250 Boylston St., Boston MA 02116. (617)266-5500. Chairman of the Board/Creative Director: Stavros Cosmopulos. Associate Creative Director: Rich Kerstein. Advertising and marketing agency. Clients: banking, restaurants, industrial, package goods, food and electronics.
Needs: Works with 6 illustrators and 1 animator/month. Works on assignment only. Uses artists for billboards, P-O-P displays, filmstrips, consumer magazines, stationery design, multimedia kits, direct mail, television, slide sets, brochures/flyers, trade magazines and newspapers.
First Contact & Terms: Send business card, Photostats or slides. Samples not filed are returned by

SASE. Reports only if interested. Make an appointment to show portfolio. No originals returned to artist at job's completion. Pays for design by the project, $250 minimum. Pays for illustration by the project, $100 minimum. Considers complexity of project, client's budget, geographic scope of finished project, turnaround time and rights purchased when establishing payment.
Tips: "Give a simple presentation of the range of work you can do including printed samples of actual jobs—but not a lot of samples. I look for specific techniques that an artist may have to individualize the art."

***FLAGLER ADVERTISING/GRAPHIC DESIGN**, Box 1317, Brookline MA 02146. (617)566-6971. President/Creative Director: Sheri Flagler. Specializes in corporate identity, brochure designs, fashion and technical illustration. Clients: cable television, finance, real estate, fashion and direct mail agencies.
Needs: Works with 10-20 freelance artists/year. Works on assignment only. Uses artists for illustration, mechanicals, retouching, airbrushing, charts/graphs and lettering.
First Contact & Terms: Send resume, business card, brochures, photocopies or tear sheets to be kept on file. Call or write for appointment to show portfolio. Samples not filed are not returned. Reports back only if interested. Pays for design by the project, $100-1,500 average; for illustration by the project, $150-1,200 average. Considers complexity of project, client's budget and turnaround time when establishing payment.
Tips: "Send a range and variety of style showing clean, crisp and professional work."

SIMMONS PRODUCTIONS, 660 Main St., Woburn MA 01801. President: Peter Simmons. AV/video producer. Clients: corporations. Main uses: sales and marketing.
Needs: Works with 2 designers/art directors/month. Uses designers for multi-image slide shows and video graphics. Some storyboarding and illustration.
First Contact & Terms: Write for interview to show portfolio, or send resume, business card or brochure/flyer to be kept on file for future assignments. SASE. Works on assignment only. Pays going rates. Negotiates pay based on amount of creativity required and artist's previous experience/reputation.

TR PRODUCTIONS, 1031 Commonwealth Ave., Boston MA 02215. (617)783-0200. Production Manager: Tom Cramer. Audiovisual firm. Clients: industrial and high-tech.
Needs: Works with 5-10 freelance artists/year. Assigns 20-50 jobs/year. Prefers local artists. Works on assignment generally. Uses artists for slide graphics, layout, mechanical, computer graphics, charts/graphs, advertisements, and 2-color and 4-color collateral design. Especially important is clean, accurate board work.
First Contact & Terms: For slide work, artist must have experience in design and mechanicals for slides/multi-image. Send query letter with brochure showing art style, resume and slides to be kept on file. Samples not filed are not returned. Reports only if interested. Call to schedule an appointment to show a portfolio. Pays by the hour, $10-25 average. Considers complexity of project, client's budget, skill and experience of artist and turnaround time when establishing payment. Buys all audiovisual rights.

Michigan

BLAVIN, HARTZ & MOLNER, INC., Suite 153, 23077 Greenfield Rd., Southfield, Michigan 48075. (313)557-8011. President: Monroe "Bob" Molner. Clients: Variety of industries.
Needs: Buys 100-150 illustrations/year. Local artists only. Works on assignment only. Uses artists for print ads, TV storyboards, layouts, and fashion and furniture illustrations.
First Contact & Terms: Query. SASE. Reports in 1 week. Pays $10-50, fashion or furniture illustration; $20-30/hour, layout. Pays original fee as agreed for unused assigned illustrations. No originals returned to artist at job's completion.

LEO J. BRENNAN ADVERTISING, 2359 Livernois, Troy MI 48083-1692. (313)362-3131. Financial and Administrative Manager: Virginia Janusis. Ad agency and public relations firm. Clients: mainly industrial, automotive, banks and C.P.A.s.
Needs: Works with 10 freelance artists/year. Artist must be well experienced. Uses artists for design, illustrations, brochures, catalog, retouching, lettering, keylining and typesetting.
First Contact & Terms: Send query letter with resume and samples. Samples not filed are returned only if requested. Reports only if interested. Call or write to schedule an appointment to show a portfolio, which should include thumbnails, roughs, original/final art, final reproduction/product, color, tear sheets, Photostats, photographs and b&w. Considers complexity of project, client's budget, skill and experience of artist, and turnaround time when establishing payment. Buys all rights.

BROGAN KABOT ADVERTISING CONSULTANCY, INC., #475, 3000 Town Center, Southfield MI 48075. (313)353-9160. Creative Director: Anna Kabot. "We are a multimedia firm specializing in TV, print and radio." Clients: retail, medical, automotive and political.
Needs: "Doesn't use much freelance work but interested in increasing usage." Prefers local artists "but not exclusively." Works on assignment only. Uses artists for design, illustration, brochures, catalogs, P-O-P displays, mechanicals, direct mail packages, lettering, logos, layouts and storyboards.
First Contact & Terms: Send query letter with brochure or resume, tear sheets, Photostats, photocopies, slides and photographs; "anything that shows style and ability." Samples are filed. Samples not filed are returned only if requested. Reports back within 30 days. Call to schedule an appointment to show a portfolio or mail thumbnails, roughs, Photostats, tear sheets and slides. Pays for design by the project, $100-1,000. Pays for illustration by the project, $100-1,500. Considers complexity of project, client's budget and skill and experience of artist when establishing payment. Rights purchased vary according to project.
Tips: "Be prepared, be brief and be flexible."

COMMON SENSE COMMUNICATIONS, INC., 602 S. Michigan Ave., Saginaw MI 48602. (517)790-7404. Art Director: Robert Lauka. Serves clients in machinery, automobiles, insurance, building supplies and banking.
Needs: Buys 25 full-color illustrations/year. Works on assignment only. Uses artists for illustrations, color separations, layout, lettering, paste-up, retouching and type spec for ads, annual reports, billboards, catalogs, letterheads, packaging, P-O-P displays, posters, TV and trademarks.
First Contact & Terms: Send slides, printed samples, business card, brochure/flyer, resume, tear sheets or "all the information an artist has available for analyzing assignments" to be kept on file for possible future assignments. SASE. Reports within 4 weeks. Agency pays for unused completed work ("assignments usually approved or disapproved at tissue stage").
Tips: "Have a complete portfolio of work showing how you developed a project right through the finished product."

CREATIVE HOUSE ADVERTISING INC., Suite 301, 30777 Northwestern Hwy., Farmington Hills MI 48018. (313)737-7077. Executive Vice President/Creative Director: Robert G. Washburn. Advertising/graphics/display/art firm. Clients: residential and commercial construction, land development, consumer, retail, finance and manufacturing. Assigns 20-30 jobs and buys 10-20 illustrations/year.
Needs: Works with 3 illustrators and 2 designers/month. Local artists generally. Uses artists for filmstrips, consumer magazines, multimedia kits, direct mail, television, slide sets, brochures/flyers, trade magazines and newspapers. Also uses artists for illustration, design and comp layouts of ads, brochures, catalogs, annual reports and displays.
First Contact & Terms: Query with resume, business card and brochure/flyer to be kept on file. Samples returned by SASE. Reports in 2 weeks. No originals returned to artist at job's completion. Arrange interview to show portfolio, which should include originals, reproduced and published pieces. Pays for design by the project, $200-2,000. Pays for illustration by the project, $150-8,000. Considers complexity of project, client's budget and rights purchased when establishing payment. Reproduction rights are purchased as a buy-out.
Tips: "There is more development in computer graphics. The computer is becoming a major influence in illustration and design as a tool, like airbrush, markers or technical pens." In a portfolio, "show flexibility, but make dominant the category you are most proficient in."

***D'ARCY MASIUS BENTON & BOWLES, (DMB&B),** 1725 N. Woodward, Box 811, Bloomfield Hills MI 48303. (313)258-8300. Contact: Art Director or Art Coordinator (send for list of art directors). Ad agency.
Needs: Uses freelancers for consumer and trade magazines, brochures/flyers and newspapers.
First Contact & Terms: Call art coordinator or art director for appointment to show portfolio.
Tips: Each art director has individual specifications.

***DUBOIS/RUDDY AUDIOVISUAL PRODUCTION SERVICE, INC.**, 2145 Crooks, Troy MI 48084. (313)643-0320. President: Jim DuBois. Full-service art studio, audiovisual production service and corporate communications service.
Needs: Works with 10 artists/year. Local artists only. Uses freelance artists for brochure design and illustration, catalog design and illustration, book design, newspaper ad design and illustration, direct mail packages, magazine ad design and illustration, P-O-P displays, mechanicals, retouching, animation, billboards, posters, direct mail packages, films, lettering, logos, charts/graphs and keyline illustration.
First Contact & Terms: Send query letter with brochure showing art style or resume, tear sheets,

Photostats, photocopies, slides, photographs or any type of sample. Samples are filed. Samples not filed are not returned. Does not report back. Call to schedule an appointment to show a portfolio. Pays for design and illustration by the hour, $10. Considers skill and experience of artist when establishing payment. Buys all rights.

LAMPE COMMUNICATIONS, INC., Box 5339, West Bloomfield MI 48033. (313)332-3711. Production Manager: A.M. Lampe. PR firm. Clients: industry.
Needs: Assigns 100 freelance jobs/year. Works with 1 freelance illustrator and 2 freelance designers/month. Works on assignment only. Uses artists for trade magazine ads, brochures, stationery, signage and press releases.
First Contact & Terms: Send query letter with business card to be kept on file. Samples not kept on file are returned by SASE. Reports only if interested. Considers complexity of project, client's budget, and skill and experience of artist when establishing payment. Buys all rights.

THE MESSAGE MAKERS, 1217 Turner, Lansing MI 48906. Contact: Terry Terry. Audiovisual firm. Clients: industrial, commercial, government. Client list provided for SASE.
Needs: Works with 10-20 freelance artists/year. Works on assignment only. Uses artists for voice and camera talent, photography and graphics. Especially looks for communication skills and professional attitude.
First Contact & Terms: Send query letter with brochure showing art style or resume and tear sheets, Photostats, photocopies, slides and photographs. Reports back only if interested. Write to schedule an appointment to show a portfolio, which should include thumbnails, roughs, original/final art, final reproduction/product, tear sheets, Photostats and photographs. Pays for design and illustration by the hour, $8 minimum. Considers complexity of the project, client's budget, and skill and experience of artist when establishing payment. Rights purchased vary according to project.

PHOTO COMMUNICATION SERVICES, INC., 6410 Knapp NE, Ada MI 49301. (616)676-2429. President: Michael Jackson. Audiovisual firm. Clients: commercial and industrial; "local to international, large variety."
Needs: Works with 10 freelance artists/year. Works on assignment only. Uses artists for multi-image slide presentations, film and video. Prefers pen & ink, airbrush, calligraphy and computer illustration. Especially important is knowledge of animation and pin registration.
First Contact & Terms: Send query letter with brochure, resume, business card, photographs or slides to be kept on file. Samples not filed are returned by SASE only if requested. Reports back only if interested. Call or write for appointment to show portfolio. Negotiates payment by project. Considers complexity of the project, client's budget, skill and experience of artist, geographic scope for the finished product, turnaround time and rights purchased when establishing payment. Negotiates rights purchased.
Tips: Wants samples that are "a good cross reference that will fit in a file folder. Too big or too small gets lost."

THOMPSON ADVERTISING PRODUCTIONS, INC., 31690 W. 12 Mile Rd., Farmington Hills MI 48018. (313)553-4566. Vice President: Clay Thompson. Ad agency. Clients: automotive, marine and industrial.
Needs: Works with 20 freelance artists/year. Works on assignment only. Uses artists for design, illustrations, layout, retouching, and creative concept. Artist should have a "strong sense of design communication."
First Contact & Terms: Send resume and samples. Samples not filed are returned only if requested. Call or write to schedule an appointment to show a portfolio, which should include thumbnails, roughs and original/final art. Pays for design and illustration by the hour, $10-25. Considers complexity of project, client's budget, and skill and experience of artist. Rights purchased vary according to project.
Tips: Artist should "be prepared to show samples of layout work and demonstrated skills and be prepared to quote a price. Portfolio should include original layouts and artwork. Do not show examples without a concept support."

J. WALTER THOMPSON COMPANY, 600 Renaissance Center, Detroit MI 48243. (313)568-3800. Assistant Art Administrator: Maryann Inson. Ad agency. Clients: automotive, consumer, industrial, media and retail-related accounts.
Needs: Usually does not use freelancers; deals primarily with established artists' representatives and art/design studios.
First Contact & Terms: Contact only through artist's agent. Assignments awarded on lowest bid. Call to schedule an appointment to show a portfolio, which should include thumbnails, roughs, original/final

art, final reproduction/product, color, tear sheets, Photostats and photographs. Pays for design and illustration by the project.
Tips: Agency deals with proven illustrators from an "approved vendor's list." New vendors are considered for list periodically. "Portfolio should be comprehensive but not too large. Organization of the portfolio is as important as the sample. Mainly, consult professional rep."

Minnesota

BADIYAN PRODUCTIONS INC., 720 W. 94 St., Minneapolis MN 55420. (612)888-5507. President: Fred Badiyan. Audiovisual firm. Client list provided upon request.
Needs: Works with 50 freelance artists/year. Works on assignment only. Uses freelance artists for design, brochures, mechanicals, press releases and motion pictures.
First Contact & Terms: Send query letter with brochure or resume, tear sheets, photocopies and slides. Samples are filed. Samples not filed are returned. Write to schedule an appointment to show a portfolio or mail appropriate materials. Pays for design and illustration by the hour or by the project.
Tips: "Send a letter and sample of work."

BUTWIN & ASSOCIATES ADVERTISING, INC., Suite 128, 3601 Park Center Blvd., Minneapolis MN 55416. (612)929-8525. President: Ron Butwin. Ad agency. "We are a full-line ad agency working with both consumer and industrial accounts on advertising, marketing, public relations and meeting planning." Clients: banks, restaurants, clothing stores, food brokerage firms, corporations, full range of retail and service organizations, etc.
Needs: Works with 12-15 freelance artists/year. Prefers local artists when possible. Uses artists for design, illustration, brochures, catalogs, newspapers, consumer and trade magazines, P-O-P displays, retouching, animation, direct mail packages, motion pictures and lettering. Prefers pen & ink, airbrush, watercolor, markers, calligraphy and computer illustration.
First Contact & Terms: Send brochure or resume, tear sheets, Photostats, photocopies, slides and photographs. Samples are filed. Samples not filed are returned only if SASE is enclosed. Reports back only if interested. Call to schedule an appointment to show a portfolio. Pays for design and illustration by the project. Considers client's budget, skill and experience of artist and how work will be used when establishing payment. Buys all rights.

FABER SHERVEY ADVERTISING, 160 W. 79th St., Minneapolis MN 55420. (612)881-5111. Creative Director: Paul D. Shervey. Ad agency. Clients: business-to-business, industrial and farm.
Needs: Works with 25 freelance artists/year. Prefers local artists. Uses artists for retouching, line art, keyline, illustration.
First Contact & Terms: Send brochure and business card. Do *not* send samples. Does not report back. Call or write for appointment to show portfolio. Pays by the hour, $20-80 average. Considers complexity of project when establishing payment. Buys all rights.

LINHOFF COLOR PHOTO LABORATORY, Box 24005, 4400 France Ave. S, Minneapolis MN 55424. (612)927-7333. Art Director: Lynn Koskiniemi. Audiovisual firm. Clients: banks, computer companies and financial services companies.
Needs: Works with 2-6 freelance artists/year. Local artists only; must work inhouse. Works on assignment only, or as vacation replacement. Uses artists for keylining, artwork, computer graphics and typesetting. Especially important are ruling; an eye for layout; good word skills for proofreading; copy camera capabilities; graphic arts computer; typesetting knowledge a plus (Comp-Edit 5810). Experience with audio-visual preparation preferred.
First Contact & Terms: Send query letter with resume and photocopies to be kept on file. Samples not filed are returned by SASE. Reports within 2 weeks. Call to schedule an appointment to show a portfolio, which should include color and original/final art, AV projects (slides, viewgraphs). Pays by the hour, $8 minimum. Considers skill and experience of artist when establishing payment. Buys all rights.
Tips: "Much of our art preparation is predesigned and often 'mechanical' or repetitive. This is not a forum for an artist with flamboyant design skills. Instead, we want people that can envision the final AV product and can create clean yet exciting visuals."

EDWIN NEUGER & ASSOCIATES, 1221 Nicollet Mall, Minneapolis MN 55403. (612)333-6621. President: Ed Neuger. "We are a full-service public relations firm which specializes in financial relations for companies of all sizes." Clients: general. Client list provided upon request.
Needs: Works with 10 freelance artists/year. Assigns 25 jobs/year. Prefers local artists because "most

assignments are not extremely large or time is a factor." Uses artists for design, illustration, brochures, catalogs and annual reports.
First Contact & Terms: Samples are filed. Samples not filed are not returned. Does not report back. Call or write to schedule an appointment to show a portfolio. Pays by the project, such as on annual reports. Considers complexity of project, client's budget and skill and experience of artist. Buys all rights.

Missouri

BRYAN/DONALD, INC. ADVERTISING, Suite 2712, 2345 Grand, Kansas City MO 64108. (816)471-4866. President: Don Funk. Ad agency. Clients: food, fashion, pharmaceutical, real estate.
Needs: Works on assignment only. Uses artists for design, illustration, brochures, catalogs, books, newspapers, consumer and trade magazines, P-O-P displays, mechanicals, retouching, animation, billboards, posters, direct mail packages, lettering, logos, charts/graphs and advertisements.
First Contact & Terms: Samples are filed. Reports back only if interested. Call to schedule an appointment to show a portfolio.

BRYANT, LAHEY & BARNES, INC., Suite 210, 4200 Pennsylvania, Kansas City MO 64111. (816)561-9629. Art Director: Terry Pritchett. Ad agency. Clients: agricultural and veterinary.
Needs: Local artists only. Uses artists for illustration and production, including keyline and paste-up, consumer and trade magazines and brochures/flyers.
First Contact & Terms: Query by phone. Send business card and resume to be kept on file for future assignments. Negotiates pay. No originals returned to artist at job's completion.

PREMIER FILM VIDEO & RECORDING, 3033 Locust St., St. Louis MO 63103. (314)531-3555. Secretary/Treasurer: Grace Dalzell. AV/film/animation/TV producer. Serves clients in business, religion, education and advertising. Produces videotape, motion 35mm, 16mm and Super 8mm, strip films, cassette dupes, 8-tracks, TV and radio spots.
Needs: Assigns 50-60 jobs/year. Works with 8-10 illustrators, "a few" designers/month. Works on assignment only. Uses artists for strip film and slide presentations, TV commercials and motion picture productions.
First Contact & Terms: Send resume to be kept on file. "We do not accept samples; we review them during interviews only." Reporting time varies with available work. Pays by the project; method and amount of payment are negotiated with the individual artist. Pay varies with each client's budget. No originals returned to artist following publication; "copies supplied when possible." Buys all rights, but sometimes negotiates.
Tips: "In developing a brochure, begin by simply stating work capability and area of work most capable of producing, i.e., animation, cartoons, production, direction or editing—whatever you want to do for a living. Be specific."

***ROSENFIELD-LANE, INC.**, 29th Floor, 106 W. 14th, Kansas City MO 64105. (816)221-4443. Vice President, Senior Art Director: Bob Coldwell. Estab. 1987 (split from firm estab. 1965). Full-service agency providing advertising, marketing, public relations to retail, consumer clients. Clients: hats, liquor, autoglass, pizza, hospital, auto, fast food.
Needs: Works with 30-50 artists/year. Assigns 100 jobs/year. Prefer local/regional talent for price and turnaround time. Uses freelance artists for brochure and catalog design and illustration, newspaper ad illustration, direct mail packages, magazine ad design and illustration, P-O-P displays, retouching, animation, billboards, posters, films, lettering, logos, charts/graphs, comps and photography.
First Contact & Terms: Send query letter with resume, tear sheets, Photostats, photocopies, slides or photographs. Samples are filed. Samples not filed are returned only if requested by artist. Reports back only if interested. To show a portfolio, mail Photostats, tear sheets, final reproduction/product, photographs, color, b&w, slides, or video disks. Pays for design by the project, $100-1,000. Pays for the illustration by the project, $100-2,500. Considers complexity of project, client's budget, turnaround time, skill and experience of artist, how work will be used and rights purchased when establishing payment. Rights purchased vary according to project.

STOLZ ADVERTISING CO., Suite 500, 7701 Forsyth Blvd., St. Louis MO 63105. (314)863-0005. Art Director/Creative Supervisor: Paul MacFarlane. Ad agency. Clients: consumer firms.
Needs: Works with 2-4 illustrators/month; occasionally uses freelance designers. Works on assignment only. Uses freelance artists for billboards, consumer and trade magazines, direct mail, P-O-P displays, brochures, posters, newspapers and AV presentations.

First Contact & Terms: Arrange interview to show portfolio or query with samples. Pays for design by the hour, $25-50. Pays for illustration by the project, $100 minimum.
Tips: "I give more work to less-experienced people who have real vision—outstanding or potentially outstanding, yet 'unknown' work. I respond to professional, buttoned-down books." The most common mistakes freelancers make in presenting samples or portfolios are "too much work shown and showing unrelated or poorly presented work."

Nebraska

MILLER FRIENDT LUDEMANN INC., 300 Corporate Center, 1235 K St., Lincoln NE 68508. Art Director: Dave Christiansen. Ad agency/PR firm. Clients: bank, industry, restaurants, tourism and retail.
Needs: Works on assignment only. Uses artists for consumer and trade magazines, billboards, direct mail packages, brochures, newspapers, stationery, signage, P-O-P displays, AV presentations, posters, press releases, trade show displays and TV graphics. "Freelancing is based on heavy workloads. Most freelancing is paste-up but secondary is illustrator for designed element."
First Contact & Terms: Send query letter with resume and slides to be kept on file. Samples not kept on file are returned by SASE. Reports within 10 days. Write for appointment to show portfolio, "if regional/national; call if local." Portfolio should include thumbnails, roughs, original/final art, final reproduction/product, color, tear sheets and Photostats. Pays by the project, $100-1,500 average. Considers complexity of project, client's budget, skill and experience of artist, turnaround time and rights purchased when establishing payment. Buys all rights.
Tips: "Be prompt, have work done on time and be able to price your project work accurately. Make quality first."

J. GREG SMITH, Suite 102, Burlington Place, 1004 Farnam St., Omaha NE 68102. (402)444-1600. Art Director: Shelly Mitchell. Ad agency. Clients: financial, banking institutions, associations, agricultural, travel and tourism.
Needs: Works with 3 illustrators/year. Works on assignment only. Uses freelance artists for consumer and trade magazines, brochures, catalogs and AV presentations.
First Contact & Terms: Send query letter with brochure showing art style or photocopies. Reports only if interested. To show a portfolio, mail original/final art, final reproduction/product, color and b&w. Pays for design by the project, $700-2,000. Pays for illustration by the project, $200-5,000. Buys first, reprint or all rights.
Tips: Current trends include a certain "flexibility." Agencies are now able "to use any style or method that best fits the job."

Nevada

STUDIOS KAMINSKI PHOTOGRAPHY LTD., 1040 Matley Lane, Reno NV 89502. (702)786-2615. President: T.J. Kaminski. AV/TV/film producer. Clients: educational, industrial and corporate. Produces filmstrips, motion pictures, multimedia kits, overhead transparencies, slide sets, sound-slide sets and videotapes.
Needs: Works with about 3 illustrators/year. Has need of illustrators to paint portraits from photos once in a while. Uses artists for slide illustration and retouching, catalog design and ad illustration.
First Contact & Terms: Arrange interview to show portfolio. Samples returned by SASE. Reports within 1 week. Works on assignment only. Provide brochure/flyer, resume or tear sheet to be kept on file for possible future assignments. Pays $20-50/hour; $150-400/day.
Tips: Have good samples and be qualified.

New Hampshire

***ENTELEK**, Box 1303, Portsmouth NH 03801. Audiovisual and public relations firm. A client list is provided upon request with a SASE.
Needs: Works with 3 artists/year. Assigns 6 jobs/year. Uses freelance artists for brochure design and illustration, book design, direct mail packages and mechanicals.
First Contact & Terms: Send query letter with brochure showing art style. Samples not filed are not returned. Reports back only if interested. Considers client's budget and skill and experience of artist when establishing payment.

New Jersey

ADLER, SCHWARTZ INC., Suite 406, 2 University Plaza, Hackensack NJ 07601-6202. (201)461-8450. Art Director: Fred Witzig. Specializes in brand identity, corporate identity, displays and direct mail. Clients: corporate.
Needs: Works with 100 freelance artists/year. Uses artists for design, illustrations, mechanicals and retouching. Prefers airbrush, the pen & ink, watercolor, acrylics, pastels and markers. Uses computer illustration for charts, graphs, retouching and newsletter design.
First Contact & Terms: Send query letter with brochure showing art style or resume and samples. Samples not filed are returned only if requested. Reports only if interested. Call to schedule an appointment to show a portfolio, which should include roughs, marker comps, original/final art, final reproduction/product, tear sheets and photographs. "No spec work."Pays for design by the hour, $25-60. Pays for illustration by the project, $100-3,500. Considers complexity of project, client's budget, skill and experience of artist, how work will be used, turnaround time and rights purchased when establishing payment.

DAVID H. BLOCK ADVERTISING, INC., 33 S. Fullerton Ave., Montclair NJ 07042 (201)744-6900. Executive Art Director and Vice President: Karen Deluca. Clients: finance, industrial, consumer, real estate, bio-medical. Buys 100-200 illustrations/year.
Needs: Prefers to work with "artists with at least 3-5 years experience in paste-up and 'on premises' work for mechanicals and design." Uses artists for illustrations, layout, lettering, type spec, mechanicals and retouching for ads, annual reports, billboards, catalogs, letterheads, brochures and trademarks.
First Contact & Terms: Arrange interview. SASE. Reports in 2 weeks. Pays for design by the hour, $15-50.
Tips: "Please send some kind of sample of work. If mechanical artist; line art printed sample. If layout artist; composition of some type and photographs or illustrations."

CABSCOTT BROADCAST PRODUCTIONS, INC., #1 Broadcast Center, Blackwood NJ 08012. (609)228-3600. Creative Director: Anne Foster. Audiovisual firm, production company. Clients: retail broadcasters (radio and TV), ad agencies and industrial users.
Needs: Works with 10 freelance artists/year. Assigns 25 jobs/year. Prefers local artists experienced in television storyboarding. Works on assignment only. Uses artist for art, layout and storyboard creation. Especially important are freehand skills.
First Contact & Terms: Send query letter with brochure showing art style, resume and slides to be kept on file. Prefers any type sample that gives an idea of artist's style. Samples are returned by SASE if requested. Reports only if interested. To show a portfolio, mail appropriate materials, which should include tear sheets, Photostats and photographs. Negotiates payment by the project. Considers complexity of project, client's budget, skill and experience of artist and turnaround time when establishing payment. Negotiates rights purchased.

CHAMPION ADVERTISING AGENCY, 86 Davison Place, Englewood NJ 07631. Art/Creative Director: Jerry Hahn. Clients: jewelers, manufacturing and retail.
Needs: Assigns 100-150 jobs/year. Need for freelance illustrators varies and uses 2 design studios for needed work. Works on assignment or on speculation basis if okay. Uses freelancers for fine line art, scratchboard or pen & ink of jewelry products for newspaper reproductions. Uses artists for catalog design, illustrators for packaging and display concepts.
First Contact & Terms: Query in person or via direct mail with proofs, Photostats or repros of line art, tear sheets or previously published work. Do not send original art or slides unless specifically requested. Samples returned only if requested. Reports in 1 week. Provide business card, brochure/flyer, resume, sample proofs and tear sheets to be kept on file for possible future assignments. Pays $25-65 depending on product, scratchboard or pen & ink. Considers complexity of project and client's budget when establishing payment.
Tips: "My agency is a prospect for photographers, retouchers and scratchboard or line artists with jewelry or cosmetic experience, but hourly rates vary and are confidential. I look for graphic honesty . . . true product renderings in pen & ink for newspaper reproduction."

COOPER COMMUNICATIONS & PRODUCTIONS, INC., 2115 Millburn Ave., Maplewood NJ 07040. President: Dan Cooper. Vice Presidents: Ron Cooperman and Robin Vitullo. Production Manager: Peggy Augustine. Full-service ad agency with print, video and multi-image capabilities. Clients: all except retail—specialize in technology communications. Client list provided upon request.
Needs: Works with 4-5 freelance artists/year. Assigns 25 jobs/year. Prefers local artists. Works on

assignment only. Uses artists for design, illustration, brochures, catalogs, newspapers, P-O-P displays, mechanicals, animation, posters, direct mail packages, press releases, logos, charts/graphs and advertisements.
First Contact & Terms: Send query letter with brochure or resume. Samples are filed. Samples not filed are returned only if requested by artists. Reports back only if interested. Call or write to schedule an appointment to show a portfolio. Likes to see work samples and price list. Pays for design and illustration by the hour, $15-20 minimum. Considers complexity of project and turnaround time when establishing payment. Rights purchased vary according to project.

DAVIS, HAYS & COMPANY, 426 Hudson St., Hackensack NJ 07601. (201)641-4910. Contact: Art Director. Public relations and promotional consulting firm. Clients: service industries, business-to-business, marketing research, health and beauty.
Needs: Works with 3-5 freelance artists/year. Artist must have experience working with agencies. Uses artists for design, layout, mechanicals, illustration and production. "Professionalism and deadline and budget restrictions awareness are important."
First Contact & Terms: Send query letter with Photostats to be kept on file. Samples not filed are returned only if requested. Reports within 1 month. Call or write to schedule an appointment to show a portfolio, which should include roughs and original/final art. Pays for design by the hour, $20-50. Pays for illustration by the project, $200 minimum. Considers complexity of the project, client's budget and turnaround time when establishing payment. Buys all rights.
Tips: "We are looking for positive thinkers: those who say 'we'll find a way to do it' even when there are no easy answers. Also looking for artists with knowledge of MacIntosh graphics."

DIEGNAN & ASSOCIATES, Box 298, Oldwick NJ 08858. (201)832-7951. President: Norman Diegnan. PR firm. Clients: commercial.
Needs: Assigns 25 freelance jobs/year. Works on assignment only. Uses artists for catalogs and AV presentations.
First Contact & Terms: Send brochure and resume to be kept on file. Write for appointment to show portfolio; may also send portfolio. Reports only if interested. Pays artist's rate. Considers client's budget when establishing payment. Buys all rights.

***GERO & BIERSTEIN, INC.**, 692 Sunderland Rd., Teaneck NJ 07666. Art Director: Boris S. Bierstein. Advertising agency. "Multi-media, full-service agency providing comsumer and trade print campaigns, and collateral materials to long-term clients." Clients: manufacturers, real estate and financial.
Needs: Works with approximately 6 freelance artists/year; assigns 10 jobs/year. Prefers New York/New Jersey metro area artists. Works on assignment only. Uses artists for brochure, catalog, newspaper and magazine ad illustration, P-O-P displays and films.
First Contact & Terms: Send query letter with brochure. Samples are filed. Reports back only if interested. Pays for illustration by the project. Considers complexity of project and skill and experience of artist when establishing payment. Buys all rights.
Tips: "Contact us by mail with samples, if possible. If we are interested, we'll call."

***GILBERT, WHITNEY & JOHNS, INC.**, 110 S. Jefferson Rd., Whippany NJ 07981. (201)386-1776. Art Director: Eileen Tobin. Full-service agency providing print and broadcast advertising, trade and consumer, plus full range of collateral. Clients: national advertisers.
Needs: Works with 10-12 artists/year. Assigns 20 jobs/year. Works on assignment only. Uses freelance artists for brochure illustration, magazine ad illustration, mechanicals, retouching and films.
First Contact & Terms: Send query letter with brochure showing art style. Samples are filed. Samples not filed are not returned. Reports back only if interested. Call or write to schedule an appointment to show a portfolio. Pays for design and illustration by the hour, $50. Considers complexity of project, client's budget and how work will be used when establishing payment. Negotiates rights purchased.

INSIGHT ASSOCIATES, Bldg. E, 373 Rt. 46 W., Fairfield NJ 07006. (201)575-5521. Audiovisual firm. "Full-service business communicators; multimedia, videotape, print materials, sales meetings . . . all of the above from concept to completion." Clients: organizations in need of any audiovisual, audio and/or print." Client list provided upon request.
Needs: Works with 50-100 freelance artists/year. Assigns 50 jobs/year. Works on assignment only. Uses artists for design, illustration, brochures, catalogs, P-O-P displays, mechanicals, retouching, animation, direct mail packages, press releases, lettering, logos, charts/graphs and advertisements.
First Contact & Terms: Send query letter with brochure or resume. Samples are filed. Samples not filed are returned by SASE. Reports back within 3 weeks only if interested. Write to schedule an appointment to show a portfolio or mail brochure or resume. Payment varies. Considers complexity of

project, client's budget, turnaround time and how work will be used when establishing payment. Rights vary according to project.
Tips: Artists need "experience with audiovisual productions, i.e., multi-image, video, etc."

JANUARY PRODUCTIONS, 249 Goffle Rd., Hawthorne NJ 07507. (201)423-4666. Art Director: Karen Neulinger. AV producer. Serves clients in education. Produces videos, sound filmstrips and read-along books and cassettes.
Needs: Assigns 5-10 jobs/year. Works with 5 illustrators/year. "While not a requirement, an artist living in the same geographic area is a plus." Works on assignment only, "although if someone had a project already put together, we would consider it." Uses artists for artwork for filmstrips, sketches for books and layout work.
First Contact & Terms: Send query letter with resume, tear sheets, photocopies and photographs. To show a portfolio, call to schedule an appointment. Portfolio should include original/final art, color and tear sheets. Pays for illustration by the project. No originals returned following publication. Buys all rights.

J. M. KESSLINGER & ASSOCIATES, 37 Saybrook Place, Newark NJ 07102. (201)623-0007. Art Director: J. Dietz. Advertising agency. Serves business-to-business clients.
Needs: Uses 1-2 illustrators/month for illustrations, mechanicals, direct mail, brochures, flyers, trade magazines and newspapers. Prefers local artists. Works on assignment only.
First Contact & Terms: Phone for appointment. Prefers Photostats, tear sheets, slides as samples. Samples returned by SASE only if requested. Reports only if interested. Does not return original artwork to artist unless contracted otherwise. Negotiates pay. Pays by the hour, $15-50 average. Pay range depends on the type of freelance work, i.e. mechanicals vs. creative. Considers complexity of project, client's budget, skill and experience of artist, and rights purchased when establishing payment.

***KEYES, MARTIN GABY LINETT**, 841 Mountain Ave., Springfield NJ 07081. (201)376-7300. Ad agency. Art Director: Marvin Slatkin. Clients: manufacturing, retailing, banking, social agencies, communications and insurance. Media used include: billboards, consumer and trade magazines, direct mail, newspapers, P-O-P displays, radio, and TV.
First Contact & Terms: Send resume and portfolio for review. Negotiates payment based on client's budget and artist's rate.

***OPTASONICS PRODUCTIONS**, 186 8th St., Creskill NJ 07626. (201)871-4192. President: Jim Brown. Specializes in multi-image, audio for AV, displays, exhibits, print media and graphics. Clients: industry, theatre.
Needs: Works with varied number of freelance artists/year. Prefers local artists. Works on assignment only. Uses artists for advertising, brochure and catalog design and illustration; and graphics for multi-image slide shows.
First Contact & Terms: Send query letter with brochure/flyer, business card or resume which may be kept on file. Negotiates payment.

STARBUCK CREATIVE SERVICES, 26 Steven Tr., West Orange NJ 07052. Senior Vice President: B. Siegel. Ad agency. Clients: health care. Client list provided for SASE.
Needs: Works with 2-5 freelance artists/year. Uses artists for special projects and back-up.
First Contact & Terms: Send query letter with brochure, resume, business card and Photostats, photographs, slides or tear sheets to be kept on file. Samples not filed are returned by SASE only if requested. Reports within 3 weeks. Write for appointment to show portfolio. Payment open. Considers complexity of the project, client's budget, skill and experience of artist, geographic scope for the finished product, turnaround time and rights purchased when establishing payment. Rights purchased vary according to project.

***TPS VIDEO SERVICES**, Box 1233, Edison NJ 08818. (201)287-3626. Contact: R.G. Burks. Audiovisual firm. Clients: industrial, broadcast.
Needs: Work with 50 artists/year. Assigns 200 jobs/year. Works on assignment only. Uses freelance artists for brochure design, P-O-P displays, mechanicals, retouching, animation, posters, lettering, logos and charts/graphs.
First Contact & Terms: Send query letter with resume and any type of sample. "Must have SASE included for return." Samples are filed. Reports back within 1 week only if interested. Write to schedule an appointment to show a portfolio.

TROLL ASSOCIATES, 100 Corporate Dr., Mahwah NJ 07430. Vice President, Production: Marian Schecter. AV producer/book publisher. Audience: children. Produces books, records, filmstrips and multimedia.

Needs: Buys approximately 200 designs/year. Uses artists for catalog covers/illustrations, direct mail brochures, multimedia kits, record album designs and book illustrations.
First Contact & Terms: Local artists only. Query with resume and samples (slides preferred). SASE. Reports in 4 weeks. Provide resume, samples, brochure/flyer or business card to be kept on file for future assignments. No originals returned to artist at job's completion. Pays by the project. Buys all rights.

WREN MARKETING COMMUNICATIONS CO.,5 Independence Way, Princeton NJ 08540. (609)520-8500. Director of Creative Services: Debbie Goodkin. Communications consulting firm. Clients: industrial, Fortune 500 (automotive, pharmaceutical, financial, etc.).
Needs: Works with 5-10 freelance artists/year. Artists should have minimum of 1-2 years of experience. Uses artists for mechanical preparation, photography, storyboard and design, video crew, typesetting, project management. Especially important are design, mechanical preparation skills, rendering and storyboarding. Prefers pen & ink, airbrush, charcoal/pencil, colored pencil, markers and calligraphy.
First Contact & Terms: Send query letter with resume and samples. Letter and resume are filed; samples are returned if postage is paid by the artist. Reports back only if interested. Call for appointment to show portfolio. Pays by the hour, $8-35; by the project, $100 minimum; by the day, $100-350. Design rates vary according to skill level and project; photography rates vary according to project. Considers client's budget, and skill and experience of artist when establishing payment. Rights purchased vary according to project.
Tips: "Wren Marketing Communications is very interested in attracting experienced designers and producers. We are most interested in seeing samples of completed projects which demonstrate strong conceptual skills. Freelance artists who are interested in our firm but do not fulfill this experience level should be able to show their level of expertise in the production of slides, print and/or video."

ZM SQUARED, 903 Edgewood Lane, Box C-30, Cinnaminson NJ 08077. (609)786-0612. Executive Director: Mr. Pete Zakroff. AV producer. Clients: industry, business, education and unions. Produces slides, filmstrips, overhead transparencies and handbooks.
Needs: Assigns 8 jobs/year. Works with 2 illustrators/month. Prefers artists with previous work experience who specialize. Works on assignment only. Uses artists for cartoons, illustrations and technical art.
First Contact & Terms: Send resume and samples (slides preferred). Samples returned by SASE. Provide samples and brochure/flyer to be kept on file for possible future assignments. Reports in 3 weeks. Pays by the project, $100-2,500. Payment varies with each client's budget. No originals returned to artist following publication. Buys all rights.
Tips: "We look for simplicity in style, facial expressions in cartoons."

New York

ACKERMAN ADVERTISING COMMUNICATIONS INC., 31 Glen Head Rd., Glen Head NY 11545. (516)759-3000. Creative Director: Skip Ackerman. Art Director: Maxine Brenner. Serves clients in food, finance and tourism.
Needs: Works with 4 illustrators and 2 designers/month. Local artists only. Uses artists for layout, paste-up, illustration and retouching for newspapers, TV, magazines, transit signage, billboards, collateral, direct mail and P-O-P displays.
First Contact & Terms: Arrange interview. No originals returned.

***AD METHODS ADVERTISING, INC.**, 317 E. Main St., Smithtown NY 11787. (516)724-9075. President: Hesso Bellem. Advertising agency and public relations firm. A full-service, business-to-business firm serving industrial clients.
Needs: Works with approximately 5-10 freelance artists/year; assigns 25-30 jobs/year. Prefers local artists with experience and good design skills. Uses artists for brochure and catalog design and illustration, direct mail packages, magazine ad design and illustration, P-O-P displays, mechanicals, retouching and posters.
First Contact & Terms: Send query letter with brochure, photocopies, slides or photographs. Samples are filed. Samples not filed are not returned. Reports back only if interested. Write to schedule an appointment to show a portfolio, which should include thumbnails, roughs, Photostats, tear sheets, photographs, color, b&w and slides. Pays for design by the hour, $12-18; by the project; or by the day $100-150. Pays for illustration by the project. Considers complexity of project, client's budget, skill and experience of artist when establishing payment. Buys all rights.
Tips: "Send samples of comps and illustrations."

ASSOCIATED INDUSTRIAL DESIGNERS, INC., 32 Court St., Brooklyn Heights NY 11201. (718)624-0034. President: Robert I. Goldberg. Ad agency. Clients: manufacturers.
Needs: Works with 6 freelance artists/year. Uses artists for design, illustration, mechanicals, retouching, lettering and logos.
First Contact & Terms: Send query letter with samples showing art style. Samples are filed. Pays for design by the hour, $18 minimum. Pays for illustration by the hour, $15 minimum. Considers complexity of project and client's budget when establishing payment. Buys all rights.

CAMPUS GROUP COMPANIES, 24 Depot Sq., Tuckaho NY 10707. (914)961-1900. Contact: Melanie Suskin. Audiovisual firm.
Needs: Works with 25 freelance artists/year. Works on assignment only. Uses artists for design, illustrations, brochures, catalogs, books, mechanicals, animation, posters, direct mail packages, press releases, motion pictures, logos, charts/graphs and advertisements. "Artists must have computer art skills, good design and board skills."
First Contact & Terms: Send query letter with resume and samples. Samples not filed are returned only if requested by artist. Reports within 12 weeks. Write to schedule an appointment to show a portfolio, which should include as much as is relative. Pays for design and illustration by the hour, $10-30. Considers complexity of project, skill and experience of artist and turnaround time when establishing payment. Purchases all rights.
Tips: "Our company does not train artists; we have only skilled experienced artists."

***CMS DIRECT**, 2000 Winton Rd. S., Rochester NY 14618. (716)272-2500. Contact: Creative Director. Full-service direct marketing and advertising firm serving consumer and business-to-business clients.
Needs: Works with 50 freelance artists/year. Assigns 150-250 jobs/year. Prefers "world-class" artists. Uses artists for brochure, catalog and newspaper ad design and illustration, direct mail packages, magazine ad design and illustration, P-O-P displays, mechanicals, retouching, animation, posters, films, lettering, logos and charts/graphs.
First Contact & Terms: Send brochure or tear sheets and Photostats. Samples are not filed and are not returned. Reports back only if interested. Call to schedule an appointment to show a portfolio, which should include roughs, original/final art, Photostats, tear sheets, final reproduction/product, photographs, color, b&w and slides. Pays for design by the project, $100-5,000. Pays for illustration by the project, $100-3,000. Considers complexity of project, client's budget, turnaround time, skill and experience of artist, how work will be used and rights purchased when establishing payment.

COMMAND COMMUNICATIONS , 62 Bowman Ave., Rye Brook NY 10573. (914)937-7000. Contact: Studio Manager. Clients: industrial and corporate. Produces video animation, multimedia, slide presentations, videotapes and print materials.
Needs: Assigns 25 jobs/year. Uses artists for layout of brochures, design catalogs, corporate brochures, annual reports, slide shows, layouts, mechanicals, computer graphics and desk-top publishing.
First Contact & Terms: Local artists only (New York City, Manhattan and Westchester). "Send note on availability and previous work." SASE. Reports in 2 weeks. Provide materials to be kept on file for future assignments. No originals returned at job's completion. Pays $15-25/hour.

ALAN G. EISEN CO. INC., R.D. 2, Box 310, Narrowsburg NY 12764. President: Alan G. Eisen. PR firm. Clients: consumer and individual product manufacturers, service organizations and financial firms.
Needs: Works with 6-8 freelance artists/year. Assigns 2-3 jobs/year. Works on assignment only. Uses illustrators for jobs dealing with direct mail, brochures/flyers, trade magazines, annual reports and newspapers.
First Contact & Terms: Send query letter with resume and photographs. Samples not returned. Reports within weeks. To show a portfolio, mail Photostats upon request only. Pays for design by the project, $200 minimum. Pays for illustration by the project, $100 minimum. Considers complexity of project, how work will be used and rights purchased when establishing payment. Total rights purchased.

TONI FICALORA PRODUCTIONS, 11 Janet Terrace, Irvington NY 10533. (914)591-7344. Film/TV commercial producer. Serves clients in advertising.
Needs: Assigns 50 jobs/year. Prefers artists who specialize. Works on assignment only. Uses artists for "elaborate sets requiring freelance stylist and prop persons."
First Contact & Terms: Send query letter with resume, no samples. Call to schedule an appointment to show a portfolio, which should include color and photographs. Reports within weeks. Pays by the project. Amount of payment is negotiated with the individual artist and varies with each client's budget. No originals returned to artist after publication. Buys all rights.

FORDHAM EQUIPMENT & PUBLISHING CO., 3308 Edson Ave., Bronx NY 10469. (212)379-7300. President: Al Robbins. AV producer. Clients: schools. Produces filmstrips, multimedia kits, overhead transparencies and children's books.
Needs: Uses artists for filmstrip animation and children's book illustrations.
First Contact & Terms: Arrange interview to show portfolio. Prefers b&w line drawings as samples. Samples returned. Provide brochure/flyer to be kept on file for future assignments. Reports in 2 weeks. Works on assignment only. Pays by job.

***HERB GROSS & COMPANY**, 84 Edgerton St., Rochester NY 14607. (716)244-3711. Production Coordinator: Jim Hughes. Advertising agency. "We are an ad agency/production company specializing in consumer and retail advertising. We are highly experienced in film, TV, radio and music production." Clients: retail chains, sporting goods, optical, automotive of any kind, office supplies, and bedding.
Needs: Works with approximately 6 freelance artists/year; assigns 35 jobs/year. Prefers experienced, flexible artists. Uses artists for brochure, catalog, newspaper and magazine ad illustration, mechanicals, billboards, direct mail packages, and lettering.
First Contact & Terms: Send query letter with resume and tear sheets. Samples are filed. Samples not filed are not returned. Reports back only if interested. To show a portfolio, mail final reproduction/product, Photostats, tear sheets, photographs, color and b&w. Pays for design and illustration by the hour, $25 minimum; or by the project. Considers complexity of project, client's budget, turnaround time, skill and experience of artist and rights purchased when establishing payment. Buys all rights.

LLOYD S. HOWARD ASSOCIATES INC., Box N, Millwood NY 10546. Art/Creative Director: L. Howard. Ad agency. Serves clients in interior furnishings, lighting, swimming pools, recreation and publishing.
Needs: Works with 2 illustrators and up to 5 designers/month. Uses artists for consumer magazines, direct mail, brochures/flyers, trade magazines and newspapers. Also uses artists for mechanicals and finished art for newspapers, magazines, catalogs and direct mail. Especially needs layout/comp artists.
First Contact & Terms: Local or New York City artists only. Works on assignment only. Call for interview between 9 a.m.-noon. Prefers layouts, dupes, finished samples or Photostats as samples. Samples not returned. Reports in 2 weeks. Provide business card and tear sheets to be kept on file for possible future assignments. No originals returned to artist at job's completion. Pays by the project; pay "depends on assignment."
Tips: "Show actual comps or roughs."

HUMAN RELATIONS MEDIA, 175 Tompkins Ave., Pleasantville NY 10570. (914)769-7496. Editor-in-Chief: Michael Hardy. Audiovisual firm. Clients: junior and senior high schools, colleges, hospitals, personnel departments of business organizations.
Needs: Works with 5 freelance artists/year. Prefers local artists. Uses artists for illustrations for videotape. "It is helpful if artists have skills pertaining to science-related topics." Computer graphics preferred.
First Contact & Terms: Send query letter with resume and samples to be kept on file. Samples not filed are returned by SASE. Reports back only if interested. Call for appointment to show portfolio, which should include videotape, slides or tear sheets. Pays for illustration by the project, $65-1,500. Considers complexity of the project, number of illustrations in project, client's budget, skill and experience of artist and turnaround time when establishing payment. Rights purchased vary according to project.
Tips: "It is important that samples are seen before face-to-face interviews. We look for a strong, simple graphic style since the image may be on screen only 10 seconds. We require the ability to research and illustrate scientific subjects accurately."

KOPF & ISAACSON, 35 Pinelawn Rd., Melville NY 11747. Art Directors: Art Zimmermann or Evelyn Rysdyk. Ad agency. Clients: technical, i.e. telephones, computer firms etc.; some consumer, i.e. clothing manufacturing, travel agencies.
Needs: Works on assignment only. Uses some illustrations and some layout/comp. Prefers pen & ink, airbrush, acrylics, oils and computer illustration.
First Contact & Terms: Send query letter with resume and slides or tear sheets to be kept on file. No phone queries. Samples are not returned. Write for appointment to show portfolio. Pays for design by the project, $100-1,000. Pays for illustration by the project, $200-6,800. Considers complexity of the project, client's budget, skill and experience of artist, and geographic scope for the finished product when establishing payment. Rights purchased vary according to project.

McANDREW ADVERTISING, 2125 St. Raymond Ave., Bronx NY 10462. (212)892-8660. Art/Creative Director: Robert McAndrew. Ad agency. Clients: industrial and technical firms. Assigns 200 jobs

and buys 120 illustrations/year.
Needs: Works with 2 illustrators and 4 designers/month. Uses mostly local artists. Uses artists for stationery design, direct mail, brochures/flyers and trade magazines. Prefers realistic, precise style. Prefers pen & ink, airbrush and markers.
First Contact & Terms: Query with photocopies, business card and brochure/flyer to be kept on file. Samples not returned. Reports in 1 month. No originals returned to artist at job's completion. Call or write to schedule an appointment to show a portfolio, which should include roughs and final reproduction/product. Pays $20-40/hour and $100 minimum by the project for annual reports, catalogs, trade magazines, letterheads, trademarks, layout and paste-up. Considers complexity of project, client's budget, and skill and experience of artist when establishing payment.
Tips: Artist needs an "understanding of a product and the importance of selling it."

McCUE ADVERTISING & PUBLIC RELATIONS INC., 91 Riverside Dr., Binghamton NY 13905. Contact: Donna McCue. Ad/PR firm. Clients: retailers, nonprofit and industrial.
Needs: Artists with at least 2 professional assignments only. Uses artists for direct mail, television, brochures or flyers, trade magazines, newspapers, mechanicals and logo design.
First Contact & Terms: Send a query letter with resume, brochure, flyer, business card and tear sheets to be kept on file. No originals returned at job's completion. Negotiates payment.

***NATIONAL TEACHING AIDS INC.**, 1845 Highland Ave., New Hyde Park NY 11040. (516)326-2555. Contact: Aaron Becker. Publisher. Produces educational silent filmstrips, models and slides.
Needs: Uses artists for books and catalogs. Also uses artists for technical illustration.
First Contact & Terms: Local artists only. Arrange interview. Provide brochures/flyers to be kept on file for future assignments. No originals returned at job's completion. Negotiates pay.

THE NOTEWORTHY CO., 100 Church St., Amsterdam NY 12010. (518)842-2660. Contact: Tom Constantino. Advertising specialty manufacturer. Clients: advertising specialty jobbers with clients in real estate, banks, chain stores, state parks and community service groups. Buys 150 illustrations/year.
Needs: Uses artists for catalogs, packaging and litterbags, coloring books and pamphlets.
First Contact & Terms: Query with samples. SASE. Reports in 2 weeks. Provide resume and brochures to be kept on file for future assignments. No originals returned to artist at job's completion. Pays $200 minimum, litterbag design.

RICHARD-LEWIS CORP., Box 598, Scarsdale NY 10583. President: R. Byer. Clients: machinery, tool, publishers, office supplies, chemical, detergent, film and printing supplies.
Needs: Local artists only. Uses artists for illustrations, retouching and some ad layout and mechanicals. Prefers airbrush and markers.
First Contact & Terms: Query with resume or arrange interview to show portfolio. SASE. Reports in 2-3 weeks. Pays by the hour; negotiates pay.

RONAN, HOWARD, ASSOCIATES, INC., 11 Buena Vista Ave., Spring Valley NY 10977-3040. (914)356-6668. President: Muriel Brown. Ad/PR firm. Clients: video production products; lighting products; electronic components.
Needs: Works with 2-3 freelance artists/year. Uses artists for mechanicals, retouching, charts/graphs and AV presentations.
First Contact & Terms: Send query letter. "Samples and/or other material will not be returned. Please do not send unordered material with a demand for return. It is an unwarranted burden on our shipping department." SASE. Reports immediately. Pays $25 minimum for illustrations, layout, lettering, paste-up, retouching and mechanicals for newspapers, magazines, catalogs and P-O-P displays. Pays promised fee for unused assigned illustrations.

RIK SHAFER ASSOC. INC., 260 Main St., Northport NY 11768. (516)754-1750. President: Rik Shafer. Full-service agency.
Needs: Works with 12 freelance artists/year. Prefers artists in the Northeast region. Works on assignment only. Uses artists and graphic designers for advertising and brochure design and layout, brochure illustration, and posters.
First Contact & Terms: Send query letter, brochure, resume and Photostats to be kept on file. Samples not kept on file are returned. Reports back to artist. Pays by the project. Considers complexity of project, skill and experience of artist, and how work will be used when establishing payment.

***SPITZ ADVERTISING AGENCY**, 530 Oak St., Syracuse NY 13203. Contact: William Spitz, Nick Bibko or Chris Slater. Serves clients in plastic products, hotels, finance and electronics.
Needs: Uses artists for illustration, design, animated cartoons, technical art layout and retouching for

catalogs, direct mail, graphics, trademarks, letterheads, newspapers, trade magazines, radio, TV and billboards.
First Contact & Terms: Mail samples. Payment varies with job.

WALLACK & WALLACK ADVERTISING, INC., 33 Great Neck Rd., Great Neck NY 11021. Art Director: John Napolitano. Ad agency. Clients: fashion eyewear, entertainment, health and fitness and industrial.
Needs: Works with 10-15 artists/year. Uses artists for mechanicals, layout and design, illustration, photography and retouching. Mechanical and print production skills are important.
First Contact & Terms: Send query letter with brochure showing art style or resume, business card and photocopies to be kept on file. Samples returned only if requested. Reports only if interested. To show a portfolio, mail roughs and final reproduction/product. Considers complexity of the project, client's budget, skill and experience of artist, turnaround time, geographic scope for the finished product, and rights purchased when establishing payment. Rights purchased vary according to project.
Tips: "Present the work you like best and are good at. Specialists are remembered for future assignments. Generalists are better as staff. If a piece in your portfolio didn't come out exactly the way you intended, do it over. A perfect comp of an idea is better than a printed piece that misses the mark."

WINTERKORN LILLIS INC., Hiram Sibley Bldg., 311 Alexander at East Ave., Rochester NY 14604. (716)454-1010. Creative Director: Wendy Nelson. Ad agency. Clients: medical/health care and industrial firms; national level only—few regional accounts.
Needs: Works with 8-10 new illustrators/year; 6-10 new designers/year. Works on assignment only. Uses freelance artists for trade and consumer magazines, direct mail, P-O-P displays, brochures, posters, AV presentations and literature, and coverage for sales promotions and sales meetings.
First Contact & Terms: Query with samples to be kept on file. Prefers slide carousel or laminated tear sheets as samples. Samples returned only if requested. Reports only if interested. Pays by the project, $700-8,000 average. Considers complexity of project, client's budget, skill and experience of artist, turnaround time and rights purchased when establishing payment.
Tips: "Present only top professional work, 18 pieces maximum, in a very organized manner."

WOLF MANSFIELD BOLLING ADVERTISING, INC., 506 Delaware Ave., Buffalo NY 14202. (716)854-2762. Executive Art Director: Tod Martin. Ad/PR firm, marketing communications. Serves clients in a variety of industries.
Needs: Assigns a minimum of 3 jobs and buys 25 illustrations/year. Uses artists for illustrations, mechanicals, layout and retouching.
First Contact & Terms: Local artists primarily. Works on assignment only. Query with resume and arrange interview to show portfolio. Especially looks for "neatness and creativity of presentation." SASE. Reports in 3 weeks. Provide business card, brochure/flyer or resume to be kept on file for possible future assignments. Pays $12-50/hour.

New York City

***A.V. MEDIA CRAFTSMAN, INC.**, Room 600, 110 E. 23rd St., New York NY 10010. (212)228-6644. President: Carolyn Clark. AV firm. Clients: public relations firms, publishers, banks, security firm, ad agencies, educational publishers and internal corporate communications departments. Produces filmstrips, multiscreen slide shows, multimedia kits, overhead transparencies, cassettes, sound-slide sets and videotapes. Assigns approximately 20 jobs/year.
Needs: Works with audiovisual designers only and mechanical artists on a project basis. "Artists must have total knowledge of graphic slide production and kodalith pin registration techniques. Others please do not apply." Local, experienced audiovisual artists only.
First Contact & Terms: Provide resume and tear sheets or a photocopy of art to be kept on file. Samples not filed are not returned. Reports only if interested. "You may be called to bid on projects. Jobs on *freelance* basis only. Educational and training budgeting on the lower side, generally."

***ADELANTE ADVERTISING INC.**, 386 Park Ave. S, New York NY 10016. (212)696-0855. Executive Vice President, Creative Director: David Krieger. Ad agency. Clients: national consumer. Client list available.
Needs: Works with a varying number of freelance artists. Seeks experienced professionals. Sometimes works on assignment only. Uses artists for a variety of jobs.
First Contact & Terms: Send query letter, brochure, resume and samples to be kept on file. Prefers photographs, slides or tear sheets as samples. Samples not filed are not returned. Reports only if interested. Call for appointment to show portfolio. Pays by the hour, $15 minimum. Considers

complexity of the project, client's budget, skill and experience of artist, geographic scope for the finished product and turnaround time when establishing payment. Rights purchased vary according to project.

ANITA HELEN BROOKS ASSOCIATES, PUBLIC RELATIONS, 155 E. 55th St., New York NY 10022. (212)755-4498. President: Anita Helen Brooks. PR firm. Clients: fashion, "society," travel, restaurants, politics and diplomats, books. Special events; health and health campaigns.
Needs: Number of freelance jobs assigned/year varies. Works on assignment only. Uses artists for consumer magazines, newspapers and press releases. "We're currently using more abstract designs."
First Contact & Terms: Call for appointment to show portfolio. Reports only if interested. Payment determined by client's needs. Considers client's budget and skill and experience of artist when establishing payment.
Tips: Artists interested in working with us must provide "rate schedule, partial list of clients and media outlets. We look for graphic appeal when reviewing samples."

LAWRENCE BUTNER ADVERTISING, INC., 228 E. 45th St., New York NY 10017. (212)682-3200. Vice President: Nevil Cross. Ad agency specializing in direct response, consumer and trade advertising. Clients: publishers, discount brokerage and insurance companies.
Needs: Prefers local artists only. Uses freelance artists for design, brochures, newspapers, consumer and trade magazines, P-O-P displays, mechanicals, retouching, posters and direct mail packages.
First Contact & Terms: Send query letter with brochure or resume and tear sheets. Samples are filed. Samples not filed are returned only if requested. "We pay by experience."

CANAAN COMMUNICATIONS INC., 310 E. 44th St., New York NY 10017. (212)682-4030. President: Lee Canaan. PR firm. Clients: restaurants, hotels, celebrities, authors, corporate accounts, advertising agencies, political, art museums and galleries. Client list provided for SASE.
Needs: Assigns 12 freelance jobs/year. Works on assignment only. Uses artists for consumer and trade magazines, brochures, catalogs, newspapers, filmstrips and stationery.
First Contact & Terms: Send query letter with brochure, resume, business card, samples and tear sheets to be kept on file.

***CDBIII-KRISTY**, Suite 18D, 400 West 43rd St., New York NY 10036. (212)244-6187. Artistic Director: Charles David Brooks III. Ad agency and audiovisual firm. Clients: merchants. Client list provided for SASE.
Needs: Works on assignment only. Uses artists for design, illustrations, brochures, newspapers, posters, direct mail packages, press releases and advertisements.
First Contact & Terms: Send query letter with brochure showing art style or resume and tear sheets. Samples not filed are not returned. Reports only if interested. To show a portfolio, mail tear sheets. Considers complexity of project, client's budget, and skill and experience of artist.

***THE CHRISTOPHERS**, 12 E. 48th St., New York, NY 10017. (212)759-4050. Editor: Joseph R. Thomas. Multimedia public service organization engaging in various publishing and TV ventures.
Needs: Works with 3 artists/year. Prefers local artists with experience in nonprofit field. Works on assignment only. Uses freelance artists for brochure design and illustration, book design and direct mail packages.
First Contact & Terms: Send query letter with brochure showing art style. Samples are filed. Samples not filed are returned by SASE. Reports back within 1 week. Write to schedule an appointment to show a portfolio. Pays for design and illustration by the project, $150 minimum. Buys all rights.

DA SILVA ASSOCIATES, 137 E. 38th St., New York NY 10016. (212)696-1657. Creative Director: Raul da Silva. TV/film/animation/AV producer and limited publishing firm. Clients: entertainment.
Needs: Works with 3-4 illustrators and 1 designer/month. Also seeking designers, plus illustrators capable of rendering sci-fi/fantasy art in the *Heavy Metal* style—see the magazine for the years '77-'79." Works on assignment only. Uses artists for motion pictures, storyboards and titles.
First Contact & Terms: Send resume including references with phone numbers and addresses, and electrostatic copies which will *not* be returned. Samples returned by SASE only if requested; samples "always kept on file if they merit space. Do not send any original work without obtaining our request for it." Returns only solicited work. Reports within 2 weeks only if interested. Payment for illustrations and layout "depends completely on end use." Storyboards, $15-50/frame; continuity design, $300 and up/program. Considers complexity of project, client's budget, skill and experience of artist, turnaround time and rights purchased when establishing payment.
Tips: "We are a small, highly professional studio using only committed, *skilled* professionals who enjoy having their good work appreciated and rewarded. Hobbyists, dabblers usually do not make the grade for us."

DITTMAN INCENTIVE MARKETING, 22 W. 23rd St., New York NY 10010. (212)741-8040. Direct all inquiries to: Wendy Whetsel Design, 5 Mill St., Putnam Valley NY 10579. AV producer/print sales promotion agency. Serves clients in corporations.
Needs: Uses mechanical artists, photographers, illustrators and hand letterers.
First Contact & Terms: Provide resume and slides, original publications to be kept on file for possible future assignments. Reports within weeks. Pays by the project or by the hour, "depending on task." Considers complexity of project, client's budget, turnaround time and sometimes skill and experience of artist and rights purchased when establishing payment. No originals returned to artist following publication. Negotiates rights purchased.
Tips: "We maintain extremely high standards, and only those artists who feel that their work is extraordinary in creation and execution should contact us. We work only with artists who have a high level of imagination and intense pride in the finished product—supported, of course, by samples that prove it."

JODY DONOHUE ASSOC., INC., 32 E. 57th St., New York NY 10022. (212)688-8653. Contact: Interview, Review Portfolios Department. PR firm. Clients: fashion and beauty. Media used includes direct mail and P-O-P displays.
Needs: Works with 1-5 illustrators and 1-5 designers/month. Uses artists for P-O-P displays, stationery design, multimedia kits, direct mail, slide sets and brochures/flyers.
First Contact & Terms: Send brochure to be kept on file. Call for personal appointment to show portfolio. No originals returned to artist at job's completion. Negotiates payment based on client's budget, amount of creativity required from artist, and where work will appear.
Tips: Wants to see recent work that has been used (printed piece, etc.) and strength in an area (i.e., still life, children, etc.).

ERICKSEN/BASLOE ADVERTISING, LTD., 12 W. 37th St., New York NY 10018. Production Manager: Catherine M. Reiss. Full-service advertising agency providing all promotional materials and commercial services for clients. Clients: entertainment, home video, television, television syndication, movies, etc.
Needs: Works with 50 freelance artists/year. Assigns 50 jobs/year. Works on assignment only. Uses artists for illustration, advertising, video packaging, brochures, catalogs, trade magazines, P-O-P displays, mechanicals, posters, lettering and logos. "Must be able to render celebrity likenesses." Prefers oils and colored pencil.
First Contact & Terms: Contact through artist's agent or send query letter with brochure or tear sheets and slides. Samples are filed. Samples not filed are not returned unless requested; unsolicited samples are not returned. Reports back within 1 week only if interested. Does not report back to all unsolicited samples. Call or write to schedule an appointment to show a portfolio; "only on request should a portfolio be sent." Pays for illustration by the project, $500-5,000. Considers complexity of project, client's budget, turnaround time, skill and experience of artist, how work will be used and rights purchased when establishing payment. Buys all rights and retains ownership of original.
Tips: "I need to see accurate likenesses in your portfolio."

RICHARD FALK ASSOC., 1472 Broadway, New York NY 10036. (212)221-0043. PR firm. Clients: industry, entertainment and Broadway shows.
Needs: Uses 5 artists/year. Uses artists for consumer magazines, brochures/flyers and newspapers; occasionally buys cartoon-style illustrations. Prefers pen & ink and collage.
First Contact & Terms: Send resume. Provide flyer and business card to be kept on file for future assignments. No originals returned to artist at job's completion. Pays for illustration and design by the project, $100-1,000.
Tips: "Don't get too complex—make it really simple."

FLAX ADVERTISING, 1500 Broadway, New York NY 10036 (212)944-9797. Art Director: Debra Israel. Clients: women's fashions, men's wear and fabrics. Assigns 100 jobs and buys around 20 illustrations/year.
Needs: Uses artists for mechanicals, illustrations, technical art, retouching and lettering for newspapers, magazines, fashion illustration, P-O-P displays, some cartooning and direct mail.
First Contact & Terms: Local artists only. Arrange interview to show portfolio. Reports in 1 week. Pay varies.

***THE FOOD GROUP INC.**, 292 Madison Ave., New York NY 10017. Vice President/Creative Director: Phil Pearlman. Advertising agency. Full-service agency, specializing in food service advertising. Clients: major food manufacturers.
Needs: Works with approximately 6 freelance artists/year. Prefers local artists. Uses artists for

brochure and catalog design and illustration, direct mail packages, mechanicals, retouching, posters, lettering, logos and charts/graphs.
First Contact & Terms: Send query letter. Samples are filed. Reports back only if interested. Call to schedule an appointment to show a portfolio, which should include roughs, original/final art and tear sheets. Pays for design by the hour, $25-40 or by the day, $150-350. Pays for illustration by the project, $500-5,000. Considers complexity of project, client's budget, turnaround time and skill and experience of artist when establishing payment. Buys all rights.
Tips: "Have some food experience."

ALBERT FRANK-GUENTHER LAW, 61 Broadway, New York NY 10006. (212)248-5200. Senior Art Director: Dom Algieri. Multi-media, full-service ad agency. Clients: brokerage firms, hotels, banks and corporations.
Needs: Works with 5-20 freelance artists/year. Assigns 25-50 jobs/year. Works on assignment only. Uses artists for brochure, newspaper and magazine ad illustration and retouching.
First Contact & Terms: "Send any copy that shows work quality." Samples are filed. Samples not filed are not returned. Reports back within 2 months only if interested. Call to schedule an appointment to show portfolio, or mail Photostats, tear sheets and final reproduction/product. Pays for illustration by the project, $500-5,000. Considers client's budget, skill and experience of artist, how work will be used and rights purchased when establishing payment. Rights purchased vary according to project.
Tips: "Show your very best only."

PAUL FROEHLICH, PRODUCER, #8E, 910 West End Ave., New York NY 10025. (212)865-8630. Producer: Paul Froehlich. Audiovisual firm. "I produce multimedia presentations, audiovisual presentations, video shows for industrial and broadcast application." Clients: corporate communication departments, high-tech firms and a variety of associations.
Needs: Works with 4 freelance artists/year. Assigns 10-15 jobs/year. Uses artists for brochures, press releases, charts/graphs, storyboards, slide show design, set design and costuming for video.
First Contact & Terms: Send query letter with brochure. Samples are filed. Samples not filed are returned only if requested. Call to schedule an appointment to show a portfolio. Pays for design by the hour, $15-30; or by the project. Pays for illustrations by the project. Considers complexity of project, how work will be used and rights purchased when establishing payment. Rights purchased vary according to project.

GETO & DE MILLY, INC., 130 E. 40th St., New York NY 10016. (212)686-4551. Senior Account Executive: Stuart Fischer. Public relations firm specializing in public relations, governmental affairs, political consulting. Clients: real estate developers and builders, nonprofit organizations and public officials.
Needs: Works with 15 freelance artists/year. Assigns 15 jobs/year. Prefers local artists. Uses freelance artists for design, illustration, brochures, mechanicals, direct mail packages, lettering, charts/graphs and advertisements.
First Contact & Terms: Send query letter. Samples are not filed. Samples not filed are returned by SASE if requested. Reports back only if interested. Write to schedule an appointment to show a portfolio. Pays for design and illustration by the project, $250 minimum. Considers complexity of project, client's budget, turnaround time, skill and experience of artist, how work will be used and rights purchased. Rights purchased vary according to project.

MARC GLAZER AND COMPANY, INC., Suite 405, 249 W. 34th St., New York NY 10001. (212)244-3010. Contact: Marc Glazer. "We are a party planning and special events coordinator." Clients: banks, ad agencies, PR firms and other corporate accounts. Client list provided upon request.
Needs: Works with 15-20 freelance artists/year. Works on assignment only. Uses freelance artists for design, brochures, posters, direct mail packages, press releases, lettering, logos and advertisements.
First Contact & Terms: Send query letter with brochure or resume. Samples are filed. Reports back only if interested. Call to schedule an appointment to show a portfolio. Pays for design by the project, $100 minimum. Pays for illustration by the project, $200 minimum. Considers client's budget and skill and experience of artist when establishing payment. Rights purchased vary according to project.

THE GRAPHIC EXPERIENCE INC., 341 Madison Ave., New York NY 10022. (212)867-0806. Contact: Production Manager. Ad agency/direct marketing firm. Clients: national corporations and financial institutions. Assigns 800 jobs/year.
Needs: Uses 3-4 illustrators and 6-10 designers/month. Uses artists for consumer magazines, direct mail and brochures/flyers. Also uses artists for annual reports, catalogs, direct mail brochures, packaging, P-O-P displays and print media advertising.
First Contact & Terms: Query with nonreturnable samples or arrange interview. No work returned.

Provide brochures/flyers and business card to be kept on file for possible future assignments. Originals returned to artist at job's completion "only if a prior agreement has been made. If not, all art becomes property of agency." Pays $15-20/hour, mechanicals. Negotiates payment by job for color separations, design, illustrations, layout, paste-up, retouching, lettering and type spec.

GRAPHIC WORKSHOP INC., 230 Lexington Ave., New York NY 10016. (212)689-0303. Creative Director: Al Nudelman. Sales promotion agency. Clients: AV, computer accounts, industrial tools, men's wear, ladies' wear.
Needs: Works with 10-15 freelance artists/year. Prefers local artists with a minimum of 3-5 years of experience; "retail layout and some design background helpful." Works on assignment only. Uses artists for illustration, paste-up and mechanical, design comps. Especially looks for knowledge of type and good design sense.
First Contact & Terms: Send query letter with business card and slides or "whatever shows work off the best". Samples not filed are returned only if requested. Reports back only if interested. Pays by the hour, $10-15 average; by the day, $75-100 average. Considers client's budget, complexity of the project, and skill and experience of artist when establishing payment. Buys all rights.

GREY ADVERTISING INC., 777 3rd Ave., New York NY 10017. Print Business Manager: Gerda Henge. Needs ad illustrations.
Needs: Works on assignment only.
First Contact & Terms: Call for an appointment to show a portfolio, which should include/original final art. Pays by the project. Considers client's budget and rights purchased when establishing payment.
Tips: "Most of our advertising is done with photography. We use illustrations on a very limited basis."

GREYFALCON HOUSE, Suite 443, 496-A Hudson St., New York NY 10014. Art Director: Ann Grifalconi. Audiovisual and design firm. Clients: public service and corporate.
Needs: Occasionally uses outside artists for paste-up and lettering. Especially important are animation and layout, medical, storyboard, etc. Prefers airbrush, watercolor, collage and computer illustration.
First Contact & Terms: Local artists only, minimum 3 years of experience. Works on assignment only. Call and outline special skills and background; send simple resume and 1 sample only to be kept on file for 1 year. Prefers Photostat or tear sheet as sample. Sample not filed is not returned. Reports only if interested. Pays by the hour, $15-30 average; by the project, $250-1,000 average; by the day, $50-200 average. Considers complexity of the project, budget, skill and experience of artist, geographic scope for the finished product, turnaround time and rights purchased when establishing payment. Negotiates rights purchased according to project.
Tips: "I need work that is useful for film/audiovisual work."

CHARLES HANS FILM PRODUCTIONS INC., 25 W. 38th St., New York NY 10018. (212)382-1280. Art Director: Evelyn Simon. AV producer. Clients: industrial and corporate. Produces filmstrips, motion pictures, multimedia kits, overhead transparencies, slide sets, sound-slide sets, slide-a-motion and videotapes.
Needs: Works with 10-15 illustrators/year. Works on assignment only. Uses artists for "all phases of artwork," including chart work, paste-ups, mechanicals and some illustration and design as in animation or spot illustrations. The majority of the work is for slides.
First Contact & Terms: Send query letter with slides to be kept on file. SASE. Reports within 2 weeks. Call to schedule an appointment to show a portfolio, which should include original/final art. Pays for design by the hour, $15-20; payment for illustration varies.

HERMAN & ASSOCIATES INC., 488 Madison Ave., New York NY 10022. President: Paula Herman. Serves clients in insurance, electronics/computers, travel and tourism.
Needs: Prefers local artists who have worked on at least 2-3 professional assignments previously. Works on assignment only. Uses artists for mechanicals, illustrations and retouching for newspapers and magazines.
First Contact & Terms: Send brochure showing art style and whatever best represents artist's work as samples. Samples returned by SASE. Reporting time "depends on clients." Reports back whether to expect possible future assignments. Write to schedule an appointment to show a portfolio. Pays by the project.
Tips: "There is a trend toward more illustration. Artists interested in working with us should be persistent—keep following up. The illustrator should be an 'idea' contributor as well. Add to the concept or see another possiblity. Freelancers need to provide 'leave behinds,' reminders of their work."

***HOMER & DURHAM ADVERTISING, LTD.**, 115 Fifth Ave., New York NY 10003. (212)477-5400. Studio Manager: Jody Jobe. Full-service advertising agency. Clients: banks, high-tech companies, ho-

tels, travel, insurance, wine importers, men's fashion, steamship lines, etc.
Needs: Works with approximately 10 freelance artists/year. Prefers all work done in-house. Uses artists for brochure design and illustration, direct mail packages, magazine ad illustration, P-O-P displays, mechanicals, lettering and charts/graphs.
First Contact & Terms: Send query letter, resume and tear sheets. Samples are filed. Samples not filed are not returned.. Reports back only if interested. To show a portfolio, mail original/final art, tear sheets, final reproduction/product and photographs. Pays for design by the day, $150-400. Pays for illustration by the project, $250-5,000. Considers complexity of project, client's budget, turnaround time, skill and experience of artist, how work will be used and rights purchased when establishing payment. Rights purchased vary according to project.

JOCOM INTERNATIONAL, Suite 701, 250 W. 57th St., New York NY 10019. (212)586-5544. Vice President, Marketing: Patricia Crane. TV producer. Serves clients in industry, education and government. Produces films, videotape, teleconferences and multi-city closed-circuit satellite telecasts.
Needs: Assigns 6-12 jobs/year. Works with 2 illustrators and 2 designers/month. Uses artists for film and videotape.
First Contact & Terms: Send query letter. Works on assignment only. Provide samples, business card and tear sheets to be kept on file for possible future assignments. Reports in 2 weeks. Method and amount of payment are negotiated with the individual artist. No originals returned to artist following publication. Negotiates rights purchased.

KENWOOD CREATIVE, (formerly The Creative Establishment), 115 W. 31st St., New York NY 10001. (212)563-3337. Producer: Diana Davis. AV/film/multi-image producer. Serves clients in industry. Produces materials for business meetings, product introductions, corporate image and P-O-P.
Needs: Assigns 20 jobs/year. New York metropolitan area artists only. "Artists must have at least 1 year of experience in work applied for." Works with 5 board artists, 1 animator and 2 designers/month. Uses artists for most projects. Prefers airbrush and computer illustration.
First Contact & Terms: Send resume. Reporting time depends on current needs. Call or write to schedule an appointment to show a portfolio, which should include storyboards/final slides. Pays for design by the day, $400 maximum; pays for illustration by the project, $50-650 maximum. No originals returned to artist after publication. Negotiates rights purchased.
Tips: "With more use of computer art, freelancers now need a more technical background."

CHRISTOPHER LARDAS ADVERTISING, Box 1440, Radio City Station, New York NY 10101. (212)688-5199. President: Christopher Lardas. Ad agency. Clients: paper products, safety equipment, chocolate-confectionery, real estate, writing instruments/art materials.
Needs: Works with 6 freelance artists/year. Local artists only; must have heavy experience. Works on assignment only. Uses artists for illustration, layout, mechanicals.
First Contact & Terms: Send query letter with brochure showing art style or photocopies to be kept on file. Looks for "realistic product illustrations." Samples not filed are returned only if requested. Reports back only if interested. Write for appointment to show portfolio, which should include roughs, original/final art, color, b&w or tear sheets. Pays by the hour. Considers client's budget when establishing payment. Buys all rights.
Tips: "Artists generally don't follow-up via mail! After artists make initial phone contact, we request a mail follow-up: e.g. photocopies of samples and business card for future reference. Few comply."

WILLIAM V. LEVINE ASSOCIATES, 31 E. 28th St., New York NY 10016. (212)683-7177. Vice President: Steve Graniere. AV producer. Serves clients in industry and consumer products. Produces sales meeting modules, slides for speaker support and printed literature.
Needs: Assigns 10 jobs/year. Works with 1-2 artists/month. Works on assignment only. Uses artists primarily for cartoons or design of booklet, brochures.
First Contact & Terms: Send resume. Reports in 2 weeks. Pays by the project. No originals returned to artist after publication. Negotiates rights purchased.

LIGHTSCAPE PRODUCTIONS, 420 W. 45th St., New York NY 10036. Associate Producer: Mari Geraci. "We are a video and film production company, producing commercials, news releases and industrials. Clients: advertising agencies and industrial institutions.
Needs: Works with 10 freelance artists/year. Assigns 10 jobs/year. Uses artists for mechanicals, animation and lettering.
First Contact & Terms: Send query letter with brochure. Samples are filed. Samples not filed are returned only if requested by artist. Reports back only if interested. Write to schedule an appointment to show a portfolio. Considers complexity of project, client's budget and skill and experience of artist when establishing payment. Buys all rights.

LINTAS, NEW YORK, (formerly SSC&B Inc.), 1 Dag Hammarskjold Plaza, New York NY 10017. (212)605-8000. Senior Art Buyer: Patti Harris. Ad agency. Clients: home products, cosmetics, and food.
Needs: Works with 150 freelance artists/year. Works on assignment only. Uses photographers and illustrators for magazines, newspapers, and billboard advertisements. Artist should have "good design sense, color quality and reproduction knowledge."
First Contact & Terms: Send letter with tear sheets. Samples filed are not returned. Does not report back. Call to schedule an appointment to show a portfolio, which should include tear sheets, photographs and b&w. Negotiates payment. Considers complexity of project, client's budget, how work will be used, turnaround time and rights purchased when establishing payment. Rights purchased vary according to project.
Tips: Artist should contact art buyers "only if work is applicable to agency's accounts."

MANHATTAN VIDEO PRODUCTIONS, INC., 12 West 27th St., New York NY 10001. (212)683-6565. Production Coordinator: Benay Forrest. Video production firm serving banks, Fortune 500 companies.
Needs: Works with 3-5 freelance artists/year. Works on assignment only. Uses artists for brochures, mechanicals, logos and ads. Currently needs graphic artists.
First Contact & Terms: Send query letter with brochure showing art style. Samples not filed are returned by SASE. Reports only if interested. To show a portfolio, mail appropriate materials. Pays for design by the hour, $10 minimum. Pays for illustration by the hour, $10 minimum. Considers client's budget, skill and experience of artist and turnaround time when establishing payment. Rights vary according to project.
Tips: "No phone calls."

MARTIN/ARNOLD COLOR SYSTEMS, 150 5th Ave., New York NY 10011. (212)675-7270. President: Martin Block. Vice President Marketing: A.D. Gewirtz. AV producer. Clients: industry, education, government and advertising. Produces slides, filmstrips and Vu Graphs, large blow-ups in color and b&w.
Needs: Assigns 20 jobs/year. Works with 2 illustrators and 2 designers/month. Works on assignment only.
First Contact & Terms: Send query letter with resume to be kept on file. Call or write to schedule an appointment to show a portfolio, which should include original/final art and photographs. Pays for design by the hour, $15 minimum; pays for illustration by the hour, $25 minimum. Original artwork returned to artist after publication. Negotiates rights purchased.

MULLER, JORDAN, WEISS, INC., 666 5th Ave., New York NY 10103. (212)399-2700. Creative Director: Dale Calvert. Ad agency. Clients: fashion, agricultural, plastics, food firms, financial, corporate—"wide variety of accounts."
Needs: Works with 25 illustrators/year. Uses freelance artists for consumer and trade magazines, direct mail, P-O-P displays, brochures, posters, newspapers and AV presentations.
First Contact & Terms: Phone for appointment. Works on assignment basis only. Pays for design by the project, $300-3,000. Pays for illustration by the project, $200-3,000.

NEWMARK'S ADVERTISING AGENCY INC., 253 W. 26th St., New York NY 10001. Art/Creative Director: Al Wasserman. Art/ad agency. Clients: manufacturing, industrial, banking, leisure activities, consumer, real estate, and construction firms.
Needs: Works with 1 designer/every 2 months. Uses artists for billboards, P-O-P displays, consumer magazines, slide sets, brochures/flyers and trade magazines. Also uses artists for figure illustration, cartoons, technical art, paste-up, retouching and 3-D model building.
First Contact & Terms: Provide stat samples to be kept on file for future assignments. No originals returned to artist at job's completion. Pays $8-15/hour, paste-up and $75-3,000 or more/job.

OVATION FILMS INC., 15 W. 26th St., New York NY 10010. (212)686-4540. Contact: Art Petricone.
Needs: Works on assignment only. Uses artists for design and animation.
First Contact & Terms: Arrange interview. Prefers "original art where possible" as samples. Samples returned by SASE. Provide samples and tear sheets to be kept on file for possible future assignments.

PHOENIX FILMS INC., 468 Park Ave. S., New York NY 10016. (212)684-5910. President: Heinz Gelles. Vice President: Barbara Bryant. Director of Advertising/Promotion: Ren Patterson. Clients: libraries, museums, religious institutions, U.S. government, schools, universities, film societies and businesses. Produces and distributes motion pictures and educational films. Assigns 20-30 jobs/year.
Needs: Local artists only. Uses artists for motion picture catalog sheets, direct mail brochures, posters

©Blair Entertainment

Illustrator Mangal of New York City sold all rights for one-year use of this illustration to advertising agency Muller Jordan Weiss in New York City. Creative director Dale Calvert gave the illustrator one weekend to complete a tight layout and the final rendering, done in gouache and oils. "The experience of doing a rush job successfully is always satisfying," says Mangal, who is also a portrait painter, "as is having to use mixed media to achieve the effect of neon type and figures on one board."

and study guides.
First Contact & Terms: Query with samples (tear sheets and photocopies). SASE. Reports in 3 weeks. Buys all rights. Keeps all original art "but will loan to artist for use as a sample." Pays for design by the hour, $12-20. Pays for illustration by the hour, $12-20; by the project, $200-2,000. Free catalog.

RICHARD H. ROFFMAN ASSOCIATES, Suite 6A, 697 West End Ave., New York NY 10025. (212)749-3647. President: Richard R. Roffman. PR firm. Clients: restaurants, art galleries, boutiques, hotels and cabarets, nonprofit organizations, publishers and all professional and business fields.
Needs: Assigns 24 freelance jobs/year. Works with 2 freelance illustrators and 2 freelance designers/month. Uses artists for consumer and trade magazines, brochures, newspapers, stationery, posters and press releases.
First Contact & Terms: Send query letter, SASE (for response) and resume to be kept on file; call or write for appointment to show portfolio. Do not mail samples. Prefers photographs and Photostats as samples. Reports only if interested. Pays by the hour, $10-25 average; by the project, $75-250 average; by the day, $150-250 average. Considers complexity of project, client's budget, and skill and experience of artist when establishing payment. Buys first rights or one-time rights. Returns material only if SASE enclosed.
Tips: "Realize that affirmative answers cannot always be immediate—do have patience."

PETER ROTHHOLZ ASSOCIATES INC., 380 Lexington Ave., New York NY 10017. (212)687-6565. President: Peter Rothholz. PR firm. Clients: government (tourism and industrial development), publishing, pharmaceuticals (health and beauty products), business services.
Needs: Works with 2 illustrators, 2 designers/month. Works on assignment only.
First Contact & Terms: Call for appointment to show portfolio, which should include resume or brochure/flyer to be kept on file. Samples returned by SASE. Reports in 2 weeks. Assignments made based on freelancer's experience, cost, style and whether he/she is local. No originals returned to artist at job's completion. Negotiates payment based on client's budget.

PHOEBE T. SNOW PRODUCTIONS, INC., 37 W. 26th St., 7th Fl., New York NY 10010. (212)679-8756. Vice President: Lisbeth Bagnold. AV production company. Serves clients in industry. Produces slides, film and video materials.
Needs: Assigns 50 jobs/year. Works on assignment only. Uses artists, designers and illustrators for slides, film and video materials.
First Contact & Terms: Send resume to the attention of Barbara Bagnold, Producer; arrange interview by phone. Reports within 1 week. Pays by the project or by the hour. No originals returned following publication. Buys all rights.

TALCO PRODUCTIONS, 279 E. 44th St., New York NY 10017. (212)697-4015. President: Alan Lawrence. TV/film producer. Clients: nonprofit organizations, industry, associations and public relations firms. Produces motion pictures, videotapes and some filmstrips and sound-slide sets.
Needs: Assigns 4-10 jobs/year. Works with an average of 1 illustrator/month for filmstrips, motion pictures, animation and charts/graphs. Prefers local artists with professional experience.
First Contact & Terms: Send query letter with resume. SASE. Reports only if interested. Portfolio should include roughs, final reproduction/product, color, Photostats and photographs. Pay varies according to assignment; on production. On some jobs, originals returned to artist after completion. Buys all rights. Considers complexity of project, client's budget and rights purchased when establishing payment.
Tips: "Do not send anything but a resume!"

TOTAL VISUALS, 145 W. 45 St., New York NY 10036. (212)944-8788. Vice President: Joanne Breiter. Audiovisual firm providing slide presentations. Clients: investment firms, ad agencies, banks and PR firms.
Needs: Prefers artists from New York City and boroughs; "mainly need chartists, mechanical artists." Works on assignment only. Uses freelance artists for illustration, mechanicals, lettering and charts/graphs.
First Contact & Terms: Send resume, photocopies and slides; "call." Samples are filed. Reports back within weeks. Call to schedule an appointment to show a portfolio, which should include original/final art, Photostats, final reproduction/product and slides. Pays for mechanical art by the hour, $15-20. Pays for illustration by the project. Considers complexity of project, client's budget, turnaround time and skill and experience of artist when establishing payment.
Tips: Artists "must produce neat work under pressure!"

VAN VECHTEN & ASSOCIATES PUBLIC RELATIONS, 48 E. 64th St., New York NY 10021. (212)644-8880. President: Jay Van Vechten. PR firm. Clients: medical, consumer products, industry. Client list provided for SASE.
Needs: Assigns 20+ freelance jobs/year. Works with 2 freelance illustrators and 2 freelance designers/month. Works on assignment only. Uses artists for consumer and trade magazines, brochures, newspapers, stationery, signage, AV presentations and press releases.
First Contact & Terms: Send query letter with brochure, resume, business card, photographs or Photostats. Samples not kept on file are returned by SASE. Reports only if interested. Write for appointment to show portfolio. Pays by the hour, $10-25 average. Considers client's budget when establishing payment. Buys all rights.

North Carolina

CAROLINA BIOLOGICAL SUPPLY, 2700 York Rd., Burlington NC 27215. (919)584-0381. Art Director: Dr. Kenneth Perkins. AV producer. Serves clients in education. Produces filmstrips, charts and booklets, educational games.
Needs: Assigns 20 jobs/year. Works with 2 illustrators/month. Prefers artists located in the southeast who do good line work and use watercolor, acrylic or airbrush. Works on assignment only. Uses artists for illustration work, both biological and medical. "We buy some cartoons for our pamphlets, filmstrips and advertising and some cartoon-style illustrations."
First Contact & Terms: Send query letter with resume and samples (prefers Photostats or slides) to be kept on file. Samples not filed returned by SASE. Reports within 1 month. Call or write to schedule an appointment to show a portfolio, which should include roughs, original/final art, final reproduction/product and tear sheets. Amount of payment is negotiated with the individual artist; by the hour, $12 minimum. Considers complexity of project, skill and experience of artist and rights purchased when establishing payment. No originals returned to artist following publication. Buys all rights.

CLASSROOM WORLD MEDIA PRODUCTIONS, 14 Glenwood Ave., Raleigh NC 27603. Contact: E.E. Carter. AV producer. Clients: educational, industrial, governmental and religious. Produces filmstrips, multimedia kits, sound-slide sets and video programs.
Needs: Works with 1 designer/month. Uses artists for filmstrip animation, slide illustrations and catalog design.
First Contact & Terms: Query with resume and samples. Reports in 1-4 weeks. Provide brochures, flyers, resume and samples to be kept on file for future assignments. Negotiates pay; sometimes pays royalties.

HEGE, MIDDLETON & NEAL, INC., Box 9437, Greensboro NC 27408. President: J.A. Middleton, Jr. Ad agency.
Needs: Assigns 200 freelance jobs/year. Works with 5 freelance illustrators and 5 freelance designers/month. Works on assignment only. Uses artists for consumer and trade magazines, billboards, direct mail packages, brochures, catalogs, newspapers, stationery, signage, P-O-P displays and posters.
First Contact & Terms: Send query letter with brochure, resume, business card, photographs and tear sheets to be kept on file. Samples returned by SASE if requested. Reports only if interested. Write for appointment to show portfolio. Pays by the project, $20-6,000. Considers complexity of project, client's budget, skill and experience of artist, geographic scope of finished project, turnaround time and rights purchased when establishing payment. Buys all rights.

LEWIS ADVERTISING, INC., 1050 Country Club Ln., Rocky Mount NC 27804. (919)443-5131. Senior Art Director: Scott Brandt. Ad agency. Clients: fast food, communications, convenience stores, financials. Client list provided upon request with SASE.
Needs: Works with 20-25 freelance artists/year. Works on assignment only. Uses artists for illustration and part-time paste-up. Especially looks for "consistently excellent results, on time and on budget."
First Contact & Terms: Send query letter with resume, business card and samples to be kept on file. Call for appointment to show portfolio. Artists should show examples of previous work, price range requirements and previous employers." Samples not filed returned by SASE only if requested. Reports only if interested. Pays by project. Considers complexity of the project, client's budget, turnaround time and ability of artist when establishing payment. Buys all rights.

MORPHIS & FRIENDS, INC., Drawer 5096, 230 Oakwood Dr., Winston-Salem NC 27103. (919)723-2901. Art Director: Rick Langford. Ad agency. Clients: banks, restaurants, clothing, cable, industry and furniture.
Needs: Assigns 20-30 freelance jobs/year. Works on assignment only. Works with approximately 2 freelance illustrators/month. Uses artists for consumer and trade magazines, billboards, direct mail packages, brochures and newspapers.
First Contact & Terms: Send query letter with photocopies to be kept on file. Samples not filed are returned only if requested. Reports only if interested. Call to schedule an appointment to show a portfolio, which should include roughs and final reproduction/product. Pays by the hour, $20 minimum. "Negotiate on job basis." Considers complexity of project, client's budget, skill and experience of artist, geographic scope of finished project, turnaround time and rights purchased when establishing payment. Buys all rights.
Tips: "Send a letter of introduction with a few samples to be followed up by phone call."

MORRIS INTERNATIONAL, 301 E. Boulevard, Charlotte NC 28203. (704)376-0736. Creative Director: Sid Morris. Ad agency. Clients: consumer, sports, construction, nonprofit organizations, retail, food, communications, manufacturing.
Needs: Assigns 5-15 freelance jobs/year. Uses artists for consumer and trade magazines, billboards, direct mail packages, brochures, catalogs, newspapers, stationery, signage, P-O-P displays, AV presentations and posters.
First Contact & Terms: Send query letter with samples. Call for appointment to show portfolio. Prefers originals, reproduced, as samples. Samples returned by SASE if not kept on file. Reports only if interested. Works on assignment only. Pays by the hour, $10-60 average; by the project, $25-1,500 average. Considers complexity of project, client's budget, and skill and experience of artist when establishing payment. Buys all rights.
Tips: There is a "trend toward more illustration using airbrush techniques. An artist's portfolio should include a wide variety of subjects/projects—emphasis on detail—with ability for marketing."

THOMPSON AGENCY, Suite 200, 1 South Eastern Center, 112 S. Tyron St., Charlotte NC 28284. (704)333-8821. Art Director: Jennifer Owens. Ad agency. Clients: banks, soft drink, resort, utility and insurance agency.
Needs: Assigns approximately 50 freelance jobs/year. Works with 3 freelance illustrators/month.

Works on assignment only. Uses artists for consumer and trade magazines, billboards, direct mail packages, brochures, newspapers, signage, P-O-P displays and posters.

First Contact & Terms: Send query letter with brochure showing art style or photocopies to be kept on file. Samples returned by SASE if requested. To show portfolio, mail appropriate materials or write to schedule an appointment; portfolio should include final reproduction/product. Reports only if interested. Pays for design by the project, $500-7,500; pays for illustration by the project, $350-3,000. Considers complexity of project, client's budget, skill and experience of artist, turnaround time and rights purchased when establishing payment. Buys all rights.

Tips: "In general, we see a bolder use of ideas and techniques. We try to screen all work before appointment. Work must be professional and very creative."

Ohio

***BUTLER LEARNING SYSTEMS**, 1325 W. Dorothy Ln., Dayton OH 45409. (513)298-7462. President: Don Butler. Produces training programs.

Needs: Works with 2 freelance artists/year. Local artists only. Uses artists for design, illustrations, catalog and books.

First Contact & Terms: Contact by phone. Samples not filed are returned only if requested. Reports back within 7 days. Call to schedule an appointment to show portfolio, which should include thumbnails, roughs and original/final art. Payment varies. Considers complexity of project and client's budget when establishing payment. Buys all rights.

FAHLGREN & SWINK ADVERTISING INC., 120 E. 4th St., Cincinnati OH 45202. (513)241-9200. Ad agency. Senior Art Director: Curt Tweddell. Serves clients in household products, utilities, industrial equipment manufacturers.

Needs: Works with 1-2 illustrators/month. Uses artists for billboards, consumer and trade magazines, direct mail, newspapers, P-O-P displays and brochures/flyers.

First Contact & Terms: Call for appointment to show portfolio (illustrations, designs and photography). Works on assignment only. Provide sample folders, brochures, etc. small enough to be kept on file for future assignments. Negotiates pay based on client's budget and amount of creativity required from artist/photographer.

FAHLGREN & SWINK, INC., Suite 901, 1 Seagate, Toledo OH 43604. (419)247-5200. Creative Director: Steve Drongowski. Ad agency. Serves clients in healthcare and finance.

Needs: Works with 5-6 freelance illustrators/month. Uses freelancers for consumer and trade magazines, A/V direct mail, brochures/flyers, newspapers and P-O-P displays.

First Contact & Terms: Call for appointment to show portfolio or make contact through artist's rep. Selection is usually based on reviewing portfolios through reps but will see individual freelancers. Negotiates payment based on client's budget, amount of creativity required from artist and where work will appear.

Tips: Pieces that are produced are best in portfolio. "Printed pieces have a lot more credibility."

THE FILM HOUSE INC., 6058 Montgomery Rd., Cincinnati OH 45213. (513)891-0035. President: Ken Williamson. TV/film producer. Clients: industrial and corporate. Produces filmstrips, motion pictures, sound-slide sets and videotapes.

Needs: Assigns 30 jobs/year. Uses artists for filmstrip animation and ad illustrations. Works on assignment only.

First Contact & Terms: Send a query letter with resume and business card to be kept on file. Samples returned by SASE. Reports in 1 week. Negotiates pay; pays by the project.

Tips: "Maintain contact every 45 days."

***FREEDMAN ADV. INC.**, 814 Plum, Cincinnati OH 45202. Senior Art Director: Edward Fong. Advertising agency. "We are a multi-media, full-service agency." Clients: retail, business-to-business, restaurant and industrial.

Needs: Works with approximately 25 freelance artists/year; assigns 50 jobs/year. Prefers artists with three years experience and up. Works on assignment only. Uses artists for brochure and newspaper ad illustration, P-O-P displays, mechanicals, retouching, animation, logos and charts/graphs.

First Contact & Terms: Contact only through artist's agent, who should send resume and photographs. Samples are filed. Samples not filed are returned only if requested by artist. Reports back only if interested. Call to schedule an appointment to show a portfolio, which should include roughs,

original/final art, tear sheets and final reproduction/product. Pays for illustration by the project; "we usually bid job out first."
Tips: "Work should be at least on a national level. We use artists all over the U.S."

GERBIG, SNELL, WEISHEIMER & ASSOC., Suite 600, 425 Metro Pl. N., Dublin OH 43017. (614)848-4848. Vice President, Creative Director: Christopher J. Snell. Senior Art Director: Diane Hay. Ad agency. Clients: business-to-business, financial and medical.
Needs: Works with 30 freelance artists/year. Works on assignment only. Uses artists for illustration, design, keyline and photography.
First Contact & Terms: Send query letter with brochure, resume, business card and Photostats, photographs, slides or tear sheets to be kept on file. Samples not filed returned only if requested. Reports only if interested. Write for appointment to show portfolio. Pays for design by the hour, $25-60 and by the project, $25-1,000. Considers complexity of the project, client's budget, skill and experience of artist, geographic scope for the finished product and turnaround time when establishing payment. Rights purchased vary according to project.
Tips: Looks for "work which we can use at a reasonable fee and the ability to turn around quickly with a minimum of direction."

***HAMEROFF/MILENTHAL, INC.**, Suite 450, 1 Capital South, 175 S. 3rd St., Columbus OH 43215. (614)221-7667. Vice President/Creative Services: Bill Gallagher. Ad Agency. Clients: "wide variety" of accounts; client list provided upon request.
Needs: Number of freelance artists used varies. Uses freelance artists for billboards, consumer and trade magazines, direct mail, P-O-P displays, brochures, catalogs, posters, signage, newspapers and AV presentations.
First Contact & Terms: Make initial contact by letter with resume. Works on assignment only. Payment varies according to job. Considers complexity of project, client's budget, turnaround time and rights purchased when establishing payment.

HAYES PUBLISHING CO. INC., 6304 Hamilton Ave., Cincinnati OH 45224. (513)681-7559. Office Manager: Marge Lammers. AV producer/book publisher. Produces educational books, brochures and audiovisuals on human sexuality and abortion. Free catalog.
First Contact & Terms: Send slides and photographs. Samples returned by SASE. Reports in 2 weeks. Provide business card to be kept on file for possible future assignments. Pays by job.

IMAGEMATRIX, 2 Garfield Pl., Cincinnati OH 45202. (513)381-1380. President: Peter Schwartz. Total communications for business.
Needs: Works with 25 freelance artists/year. Local artists only; must have portfolio of work. Uses artists for paste-up, mechanicals, airbrushing, storyboards, photography, lab work, illustration for AV; buys cartoons 4-5 times/year. Especially important is AV knowledge, computer graphics for video and slides and animation understanding.
First Contact & Terms: Works on assignment only. Artwork buy-out. Send business card and slides to be kept on file. Samples not filed are returned by SASE. Reports within 2 months. Write for appointment to show portfolio. Pays for design by the hour, $8-35; by the project, $90 minimum. Pays for illustration by the hour, $8-15; by the project, $150 minimum. Considers complexity of the project, client's budget, skill and experience of artist and turnaround time when establishing payment. Buys all rights.
Tips: "Specialize your portfolio; show an understanding of working for a 35mm final product. We are using more design for video graphics and computer graphics."

GEORGE C. INNES & ASSOCIATES, Box 1343, 110 Middle Ave., Elyria OH 44036. (216)323-4526. President: George C. Innes. Ad/art agency. Clients: industrial and consumer. Assigns 25-50 jobs/year.
Needs: Works with 3-4 illustrators/month. Works on assignment only. Uses illustrators for filmstrips, stationery design, technical illustrations, airbrush, multimedia kits, direct mail, slide sets, brochures/flyers, trade magazines, newspapers and books. Also uses artists for layout and design for reports, catalogs, print ads, direct mail/publicity, brochures, displays, employee handbooks, exhibits, products, technical charts/illustrations, trademarks, logos and company publications. Prefers pen & ink, airbrush, watercolor, acrylics, oils, collage, markers and computer illustration.
First Contact & Terms: Send query letter with brochure showing art style or tear sheets, Photostats, photocopies, slides and photographs. Samples not filed are not returned. Reports in 2 weeks. To show a portfolio, a freelance artist should mail appropriate materials. No originals returned to artist at job's completion. Pays for design and illustration by the hour, $5-30.

MERVIN N. LEVEY CO., 3338 Kingsgate Blvd., Toledo OH 43606. (419)536-8186. President: M.N. Levey. Advertising agency and marketing consultant to manufacturers of consumer products in the U.S., Canada, Europe and the Far East. Clients: manufacturers, distributors, land developers, real estate, insurance, machinery, home furnishings, major appliances, floor coverings, foods, automotive, pet foods, health and beauty aids, department stores, supermarket and drug store chains.
Needs: Original art, layout and paste-up for newspapers, magazines, TV, direct mail and P-O-P.
First Contact & Terms: Area artists only. Prefers Photostats as samples. Samples returned. Reports within 4 weeks. Pays by the hour, $12-20 average. Considers client's budget, and skill and experience of artist when establishing payment.
Tips: "We'd like to have a group located in nearby cities to do keyline and lettering (full page newspaper ads) once monthly."

LIGGETT-STASHOWER, 1010 Euclid Ave., Cleveland OH 44115. (216)771-0300. Executive Art Director: Larry Pillot. Full-service ad agency. Clients: consumer firms.
Needs: Works with 8 illustrators/year. Local artists primarily. Works on assignment only. Uses freelance artists for billboards, consumer and trade magazines, direct mail, P-O-P displays, brochures, catalogs, posters, signage, newspapers and AV presentations.
First Contact & Terms: Query with resume of credits and samples. Payment is by the project; negotiates according to client's budget, amount of creativity required, where work will appear and freelancer's previous experience. Pays for design and illustration by the hour, $10 minimum.

LOHRE & ASSOCIATES, 1420 E. McMillan St., Cincinnati OH 45206. (513)961-1174. Art Director: Charles R. Lohre. Ad agency. Clients: industrial firms.
Needs: Works with 2 illustrators/month. Local artists only. Works on assignment only. Uses freelance artists for trade magazines, direct mail, P-O-P displays, brochures and catalogs.
First Contact & Terms: Send query letter with resume and samples. Call or write to schedule an appointment to show portfolio, which should include final reproduction/product. Especially looks for "excellent line control and realistic people or products." Pays for design by the hour, $12 minimum; pays for illustration by the hour, $6 minimum.
Tips: Looks for artists who can draw well and have experience in working with metal fabrication.

CHARLES MAYER STUDIOS INC., 168 E. Market St., Akron OH 44308. (216)535-6121. President: C.W. Mayer, Jr. AV producer since 1934. Clients: mostly industrial. Produces film and manufactures visual aids for trade show exhibits.
Needs: Works with 1-2 illustrators/month. Uses illustrators for catalogs, filmstrips, brochures and slides. Also uses artists for brochures/layout, photo retouching and cartooning for charts/visuals. In addition, has a large gallery and accepts paintings, watercolors, etc. on a consignment basis, 33%-40% commissions.
First Contact & Terms: Send slides, photographs, Photostats or b&w line drawings or arrange interview to show portfolio. Samples not kept on file are returned. Reports in 1 week. Provide resume and a sample or tear sheet to be kept on file for future assignments. Originals returned to artist at job's completion. Negotiates pay.

ART MERIMS COMMUNICATIONS, 750 Prospect Ave., Cleveland OH 44115. (216)664-1113. President: Arthur M. Merims. PR/advertising firm. Clients: industry.
Needs: Assigns 10 freelance jobs/year. Prefers local artists. Works on assignment only. Works with 1-2 freelance illustrators and 1-2 freelance designers/month. Uses artists for trade magazines, brochures, catalogs, signage and AV presentations.
First Contact & Terms: Send query letter with samples to be kept on file. Call or write for appointment to show portfolio, which should include "copies of any kind" as samples. Pays by the hour, $20-50 or by the project. Considers complexity of project, client's budget, and skill and experience of artist when establishing payment.
Tips: When reviewing samples, looks for "creativity and reasonableness of cost."

TRIAD, (Terry Robie Industrial Advertising, Inc.), 124 N. Ontario St., Toledo OH 43624. (419)241-5110. Vice President/Creative Director: Janice Robie. Ad agency/graphics/promotions. Clients: industrial, consumer, medical.
Needs: Assigns 30 freelance jobs/year. Works with 1-2 freelance illustrators/month and 2-3 freelance designers/month. Works on assignment only. Uses artists for consumer and trade magazines, brochures, catalogs, newspapers, filmstrips, stationery, signage, P-O-P displays, AV presentations, posters and illustrations (technical and/or creative).
First Contact & Terms: Send query letter with resume and slides, photographs, Photostats or printed samples to be kept on file. Samples returned by SASE if not kept on file. Reports only if interested. To

show a portfolio, mail appropriate materials or write to schedule an appointment; portfolio should include roughs, original/final art, final reproduction/product and tear sheets. Pays by the hour, $10-60; by the project, $25-2,500. Considers client's budget, and skill and experience of artist when establishing payment. Negotiates rights purchased.
Tips: "We are interested in knowing your specialty."

Oklahoma

***ADVERTISING INCORPORATED**, Box 707626, Tulsa OK 74170. (918)747-8871. Director of Illustration: David Butterfield. Ad agency. Clients: industrial, financial, retail.
Needs: Works with 12+ freelance artists/year. Uses artists primarily for finished illustration; also design and layout. Especially important are the ability to take direction, quick turnaround and prompt delivery, and tight, clean illustration.
First Contact & Terms: Works on assignment only. Send query letter with brochure and samples to be kept on file; call or write for appointment to show portfolio. Prefers Photostats, photographs or slides as samples. Samples not filed are returned by SASE. Reports back only if interested. Pays by the project, $100 minimum. Considers complexity of the project, client's budget, skill and experience of artist, turnaround time and rights purchased when establishing payment. Buys all rights.
Tips: "We expect quick turnaround time."

Oregon

***ADFILIATION ADVERTISING & DESIGN**, 323 W. 13th Ave., Eugene OR 97401. President/Creative Director: Gary Schubert. Advertising agency. "We provide full-service advertising to a wide variety of regional and national accounts. Our specialty is print media, serving a predominantly industrial and business-to-business advertisers." Clients: forest products, heavy equipment, software and sporting equipment.
Needs: Works with approximately 4 freelance artists/year. Assigns 20-24 jobs/year. Works on assignment only. Uses artists for brochure and magazine ad illustration, retouching, animation, films and lettering.
First Contact & Terms: Send query letter, brochure, resume, slides and photographs. Samples are filed. Samples not filed are returned by SASE only if requested. Reports back only if interested. Write to schedule an appointment to show a portfolio. Pays for design by the hour, $25-40. Pays for illustrations by the hour, $25-40; by the project, $400-800. Considers complexity of project, client's budget, turnaround time and skill and experience of artist when establishing payment. Buys first rights, one-time rights, or all rights; rights purchased vary according to project.
Tips: "We're busy. So follow up with reminders of your specialty, utilizing current samples of your work and convenience of dealing with you."

BOAZ-GREEN ADVERTISING, 1176 W. 7th St., Box 2565, Eugene OR 97402. (503)343-2548. Art Director: Robert E. Smith. Full-service ad agency with marketing and PR services.
Needs: Assigns 10-20 jobs/year. Uses artists for illustration, layout, mechanicals, occasional design work. Prefers experienced local artists. Works on assignment only. "We use freelancers primarily for overflow work and for special projects. Out-of-area artists are considered only if their specialized skills are better suited to a particular job than those of our inhouse staff."
First Contact & Terms: Send query letter with resume and samples to be kept on file. "Photocopies will do if they adequately show artist's work." Samples not filed are returned by SASE. Reports only if interested. Pays by the hour for inhouse production work, by the project for outside services. Considers nature of project, client's budget, and artist's skill when establishing payment. No originals returned unless agreed to in advance. Negotiates rights purchased.
Tips: "Our needs are as varied as our clients, so present a wide range of samples. Strong production skills a must."

CREATIVE COMPANY, INC., 345 Court St. NE, Salem OR 97301. (503)363-4433. President/Owner: Jennifer Larsen. Specializes in corporate identity and packaging. Clients: local consumer-oriented clients, professionals and trade accounts on a regional and national level, all in the Salem/Valley area.
Needs: Works with 3-4 freelance artists/year. Prefers local artists. Works on assignment only. Uses artists for design, illustration, retouching, airbrushing, posters and lettering. "Clean, fresh designs!"
First Contact & Terms: Send query letter with brochure, resume, business card, photocopies and tear sheets to be kept on file. Samples returned only if requested. Reports only if interested. Call for

appointment to show portfolio. "We require a portfolio review. Years of experience not important if portfolio is good. We prefer one-on-one review to discuss individual projects/time/approach. Pays for design and illustration by the hour, $20-50 average. Considers complexity of project and skill and experience of artist when establishing payment.
Tips: Common mistakes freelancers make in presenting samples or portfolios are: "1) poor presentation, samples not mounted or organized, 2) not knowing how long it took them to do a job to provide a budget figure, 3) not demonstrating an understanding of the printing process and how their work will translate into a printed copy, 4) just dropping in without an appointment, 5) not following up periodically to update information or a resume that might be on file."

Pennsylvania

ANIMATION ARTS ASSOCIATES INC., Lee Park, Suite 301, 1100 E. Hector St., Conshohocken PA 19428. (215)825-8530. Executive Producer/Art Director: Harry E. Ziegler. AV/motion picture/TV producer. Clients: government, industry, education and TV. Audience: engineers, doctors, military, general public. Produces 35/16mm films, sound/slide programs and filmstrips.
Needs: Works with designers and illustrators. Uses artists for filmstrips, motion pictures and animation.
First Contact & Terms: Call for interview. Provide resume to be kept on file for possible future assignments. No work returned at job's completion. Pays $5-10/hour, cartoon and technical animation.

TED BARKUS CO. INC., 1512 Spruce St., Philadelphia PA 19102. President/Creative Director: Allen E. Barkus. Ad agency/PR firm. Serves clients in finance, retailing, industrial products, consumer products, appliance manufacturers, fashion, food, publishing, travel destinations, and interior design.
Needs: Works with 2 illustrators and 1 designer/month. Local and New York artists with experience working with similar firms only. Works on assignment only. Uses designers for billboards, P-O-P displays, consumer and trade magazines, stationery design, multimedia kits, direct mail, TV, slide sets and newspapers. Uses illustrators for brochures/flyers.
First Contact & Terms: Send business card, slides, photographs and b&w line drawings to be kept on file. Samples returned by SASE. Reports in 2 weeks. No original work returned after job completed. Pays by the project or by the hour, $10-25 average. Considers complexity of project and skill and experience of artist when establishing payment.

***EDUCATIONAL COMMUNICATIONS INC.**, 761 Fifth Ave., King of Prussia PA 19406. Contact: Art Director. Audiovisual firm. Clients: automotive, pharmaceutical.
Needs: Works with 2-3 freelance artists/year. Works on assignment only. Especially important are cartoon or technical illustration skills.
First Contact & Terms: Send query letter with resume, tear sheets, Photostats, photocopies, slides and photographs to be kept on file. Samples are not returned. Does not report back. Write to schedule an appointment to show a portfolio, which should include original/final art, final reproduction/product, color, tear sheets, b&w and slides. Pays by the hour, $15 minimum. Considers complexity of the project, and skill and experience of artist when establishing payment. Buys all rights.
Tips: "Work submitted must be clean, professional, and corporate in nature. Speed, ability to follow directions, and ability to think creatively are important. Ability to meet deadlines essential."

HARDMAN EASTMAN STUDIOS, INC., 1400 E. Carson St., Pittsburgh PA 15203. (412)481-4450. General Manager: Barbara Jost. Audiovisual firm. Clients: audiovisual and industrial.
Needs: Works with 1-2 freelance artists/year. Local artists only. Works on assignment only. Uses artists for design, illustration, mechanicals and charts/graphs. Artists should have the "experience to design art for 35mm slide and TV crop format, also the ability to communicate with clients and translate input into what is required for end use."
First Contact & Terms: Send query letter with resume. Samples not filed are not returned. Reports only if interested. Write to schedule an appointment to show a portfolio, which should include roughs, original/final art, color and photographs. Payment varies. Considers complexity of project, client's budget, skill and experience of artist, and turnaround time when establishing payment. Buys all rights.
Tips: "Do not call. Send letter and resume!"

JERRYEND COMMUNICATIONS, INC., Rt. #2, Box 356H, Birdsboro PA 19508. (215)689-9118. Vice President: Gerard E. End, Jr. Advertising/PR firm. Clients: industry, banks, technical services, professional societies and automotive aftermarket.
Needs: Assigns 3-5 freelance jobs/year. Works "primarily with local artists for time, convenience and accessibility." Works on assignment only. Uses 1-2 freelance illustrators/month. Uses artists for trade

magazines, brochures, signage, AV presentations, posters and press releases.
First Contact & Terms: Send query letter with brochure showing art style to be kept on file. Samples not filed returned by SASE. Reports within 2 weeks. Call to schedule an appointment to show a portfolio, which should include roughs, final reproduction/product and tear sheets. Pays for design by the hour, $25-50 average. Considers complexity of project, client's budget, turnaround time and rights purchased when establishing payment. Buys all rights.
Tips: Have a "realistic approach to art; clients are conservative and not inclined to impressionistic or surrealistic techniques."

KRUSE CORPORATE IMAGE , (formerly Tom Weigand, Inc.), Morgantown Rd RD1, Box 61-B, Reading PA 19601. Owner/President: Dan Kruse. Art Director/Producer: Joe Reighn. Audiovisual firm. "We provide multi-image/video production for corporate image, product introduction and sales meetings." Clients: manufacturers, financial, medical, chemical, service.
Needs: Works with 3-5 freelance artists/year. Assigns 10-15 jobs/year. Prefers local or regional artists. Works on assignment only. Uses artists for design, animation and AV programming. Prefers calligraphy, then pen & ink, watercolor and markers.
First Contact & Terms: Send query letter with resume. Samples are filed. Samples not filed are returned if requested. Reports back only if interested. Write to schedule an appointment to show a portfolio, which should include tear sheets and slides. Pays for design by the hour, $6-25. Pays for illustration by the hour, $10-30, or by the project. Considers complexity of project, client's budget and turnaround time when establishing payment. Rights purchased vary according to project.
Tips: "I look to see what style(s) artists handle best and how creative their solutions have been while still matching the requirements of the project. They sometimes fail to present materials as solutions to certain communication objectives—as all our projects are."

NEW YORK COMMUNICATIONS, INC., 207 S. State Rd., Upper Darby PA 19082. Creative Director: Paul Greeley. Motion picture/TV/marketing consulting firm. Clients: radio & TV stations.
Needs: Uses artists for motion pictures and storyboards. Works with 2 illustrators and 1 designer/month.
First Contact & Terms: Query with resume. Reports within 1 week. Works on assignment only. Provide resume, sample storyboards, business card, brochure/flyer to be kept on file for future assignments. Samples not kept on file returned by SASE. No originals returned to artist at job's completion. Pays for design by the project, $300-1,200. Considers skill and experience of artist and turnaround time when establishing payment.
Tips: Looks for "the ability to capture people's faces, detail and perspective."

THE REICH GROUP, INC., 230 S. Broad St., Philadelphia PA 19102. (215)546-1636. Art Director: Ken Mehler. Ad agency. Specializes in print media and direct mail/collateral material. Clients: banks, insurance companies, business to business services, associations, religious groups.
Needs: Works with 15-20 freelance artists/year. Uses artists for advertising and brochure design and illustration, design of direct mail kits and illustrations for association magazines. Rarely uses unusual techniques; prefers primarily realistic styles. No cartoons.
First Contact & Terms: Send query letter with photocopies or nonreturnable samples to be kept on file. Reports only if interested. Works on assignment only. Write for appointment to show portfolio. Pays by the hour, $12-25 average; by the project, $125-400 average. Considers skill and experience of artist, turnaround time and rights purchased when establishing payment.
Tips: "Show commercial work that has been used in print. No school samples or experimentals."

THE SLIDEING BOARD, INC., 322 Blvd. of the Allies, Pittsburgh PA 15222. (412)261-6006. Production Manager: Cindy Len. "Audiovisual and multi-image firm for sales, marketing, training and capabilities presentations." Clients: consumer, industrial, financial, business-to-business.
Needs: Works with 20-30 artists/year. Assigns 75-100 jobs/year. Prefers local artists only. Uses artists for design, mechanicals, lettering and charts/graphs.
First Contact & Terms: Send query letter with resume and slides. Samples are filed. Samples not filed are returned. Reports back within 10 days only if interested. Call to schedule an appointment to show a portfolio. Pays for design and illustration by the hour, $5-20. Considers complexity of project, client's budget, turnaround time and skill and experience of artist when establishing payment. Buys all rights.
Tips: Artists must "have produced art for multi-image presentations before."

E.J. STEWART, INC., 525 Mildred Ave., Primos PA 19018. (215)626-6500. Production Coordinator: Karen Brooks. TV producer. Serves clients in industry, education, government, interactive video and advertising. Produces videotape programs and commercials.
Needs: Assigns 50+ jobs/year. Works with 2 illustrators and 2 designers/month. Philadelphia area

artists only. Works on assignment only. Uses artists for set design and storyboards.
First Contact & Terms: Send resume, brochure/flyer and business card to be kept on file. Reports in 3 weeks. Method and amount of payment are negotiated with the individual artist. No originals returned to artists following publication. Buys all rights.
Tips: "There is more interest in computer generated animation in our field. 10% of work is cartoon-style illustrations."

***THOMAS R. SUNDHEIM INC.**, The Benson East, Jenkintown PA 19046. Vice President/Creative Director: John F. Tucker, Jr. Serves clients in industrial and scientific products and services.
Needs: Works with 3 illustrators, 3 designers/year. Prefers local artists. Works on assignment only. Uses artists for illustration, technical art, retouching, trade magazines, direct mail and collateral; also work on P-O-P displays, stationery design and newspapers.
First Contact & Terms: Provide business card, brochure/flyer and samples to be kept on file. Prefers roughs through final as samples. Samples returned by SASE. No originals returned to artist at job's completion. Call to schedule an appointment to show a portfolio.
Tips: "Imitation is all I'm finding—and imitation of pretty bad stuff." Looks for the artist's *style* in samples or a portfolio.

South Carolina

***BRADHAM-HAMILTON ADVERTISING, INC.**, Box 729, Charleston SC 29402. (803)884-6445. Art Director: Mike Schumpert. Ad agency. Clients: financial institutions, fashion, hotel, resort, mall, dairy, restaurants, fast food, contractor, manufacturer.
Needs: Assigns 100 freelance jobs/year. Works with a total of 2-3 freelance illustrators and 2-3 freelance designers. Uses artists for consumer and trade magazines, billboards, direct mail packages, brochures, newspapers, filmstrips, P-O-P displays, AV presentations and posters. Needs pen & ink, pencil, wash, acrylic and airbrush.
First Contact & Terms: Send query letter with brochure and samples to be kept on file. Call for appointment to show portfolio. Prefers Photostats or tear sheets as samples. Samples not kept on file returned by SASE. Reports within 2 weeks. Works on assignment only. Pays $50-500 average. Considers complexity of project, client's budget, skill and experience of artist and turnaround time when establishing payment. All rights purchased.
Tips: "Approach us in a business-like, professional way: write a letter and follow-up with a phone call. Submit samples of specific type of work requested."

THE BROOM AGENCY INC., (formerly Broom & Bussell, Inc.), 2927 Devine St., Box 50710, Columbia SC 29250. (803)256-3337. Creative Director: Ralph Broom. Full-service advertising agency. Clients: real estate, banks, health care, department stores, radio station, government agencies, child care centers, car dealers.
Needs: Works with 20 freelance artists/year. Assigns 400 jobs/year. Works on assignment only. Uses artists for design, illustration, mechanicals, retouching, animation, posters, direct mail packages, lettering, logos and charts/graphs.
First Contact & Terms: Send query letter with brochure or tear sheets, Photostats, photocopies, slides and photographs. Samples are filed. Samples not filed are returned only if requested. To show a portfolio, mail thumbnails, roughs, Photostats, tear sheets, photographs and color. Pays for design and illustration by the project, $50 minimum. Considers complexity of project, client's budget and turnaround time when establishing payment.
Tips: "Send photocopied samples with cost charged on each."

***SHOREY & ASSOCIATES**, 450 E. Park Ave., Greenville SC 29607. (803)242-5407. Senior Art Director: Chris Harrison. Full-service ad agency specializing in industrial clients.
Needs: Uses illustrators.
First Contact & Terms: Query with samples. Provide materials to be kept on file for future assignments. Samples not returned. Does not report back. Works on assignment only. No originals returned at job's completion. Pays by the project. Considers complexity of project, client's budget, and skill and experience of artist when establishing payment.

SYNERGY PRODUCTIONS, INC., 614 Meeting St., West Columbia SC 29169. (803)796-0173. Art Director: Carol Harward. Audiovisual firm. "We are an audiovisual communications company specializing in multi-image slide presentations. We are also involved in the production of computer-generated slides." Clients: corporations, banks, industrial plants. Client list provided upon request.

Needs: Works with 3 freelance artists/year. Assigns a few jobs/year. Prefers local artists. Works on assignment only. Uses artists for design, illustration and mechanicals. Prefers pen & ink technical illustration or computer illustration.
First Contact & Terms: Send query letter with brochure or slides and photographs. Samples are filed. Reports back within 2 weeks only if interested. To show a portfolio, mail Photostats, tear sheets, photographs and slides. Pays for design and illustration by the project, $65 minimum. Considers complexity of project, client's budget and turnaround time when establishing payment. Rights purchased vary according to project.
Tips: "Need to see photography, illustrations, technical graphics and mechanicals; no paintings."

Tennessee

JANUARY & ASSOCIATES, 5560 Franklin Pike Circle, Brentwood TN 37027. (615)377-9111. Owner/CEO: John January; Creative Director: Tim Liddle. Ad agency. Clients: banks, fast food restaurants, industry, hospitals, music, entertainment and retail stores.
Needs: Assigns 26 freelance jobs/year. Works with 2 freelance illustrators and 2-5 freelance designers/month. Local artists only. Works on assignment only. Uses artists for trade magazines, billboards, brochures, catalogs, newspapers and filmstrips.
First Contact & Terms: Send resume to be kept on file. Write or call for appointment to show portfolio. Prefers slides, photographs or Photostats as samples. Pays by the hour or by the project. Considers complexity of project and client's budget when establishing payment. Negotiates rights purchased.

***LETTER GRAPHICS**, 180 Racine, Memphis TN 38111. (901)458-4584. Creative Director: Michael Somers. Creative support services for clients and agencies: art, design, logos, type, printing, illustration.
Needs: Works with 20 artists/year. Prefers experienced professionals. Works on assignment only. Uses freelance artists for brochure, catalog, newspaper and magazine ad design and illustration, direct mail packages, P-O-P displays, mechanicals, retouching, animation, billboards, posters, films, lettering and logos.
First Contact & Terms: Send query letter with photocopies, slides or photographs. Samples are filed. Samples not filed are not returned. Reports back only if interested. Call or write to schedule an appointment to show a portfolio, which should include photocopies or photos of color. "Quotes based on work required." Considers client's budget, skill and experience of artist and rights purchased when establishing payment. Rights purchased vary according to project.
Tips: "Show me what you can do—I'll call when I have something that fits your talent."

Texas

ALAMO AD CENTER, INC., 217 Arden Grove, San Antonio TX 78215. (512)225-6294. Art Director: Mike Villanueva. Ad agency/PR firm. Serves clients in medical supplies, animal breeding, food, retailing (especially jewelry), real estate and manufacturing.
Needs: Works with 6 illustrators and 4 designers/month. Local artists only. Works on assignment only. Uses artists for work in consumer magazines, brochures/flyers, trade magazines, album covers, architectural renderings and "overflow work."
First Contact & Terms: Send brochure, flyer, business card, resume and tear sheets to be kept on file. SASE. Reports within 4 weeks if interested. Arrange interview to show portfolio, which should include tear sheets. No originals returned at job's completion. Pay is negotiable. Considers skill and experience of artist when establishing payment.

BERNETA COMMUNICATIONS, INC., 701 Park Pl., Amarillo TX 79101. (806)376-7237. Vice President: Gladys Pinkerton. Ad agency and audiovisual firm. "We are a full-service communications and production firm." Clients: banks, automotive firms, museums, various businesses, hotels, motels, jewelry stores and politicians. Client list provided upon request.
Needs: Works with 12 freelance artists/year. Assigns 1,000 jobs/year. Works on assignment only. Uses freelance artists for design, illustration, brochures, catalogs, animation, posters, direct mail packages, lettering, logos, charts/graphs and advertisements.
First Contact & Terms: Send query letter with brochure. Samples are filed. Samples not filed are returned only if requested. Reports back only if interested. To show a portfolio, mail thumbnails, roughs, original/final art, Photostats, tear sheets, final reproduction/product, photographs, color, b&w,

slides and video disks. Pays for design by the project, $100-1,500. Pays for illustration by the project, $100-1,900. Considers complexity of project, client's budget, turnaround time, skill and experience of artist, how work will be used and rights purchased when establishing payment. Rights purchased vary according to project.
Tips: "Be organized. Be able to present yourself in a professional manner."

BOZELL JACOBS KENYON & ECKHARDT, Box 619200, Dallas-Ft. Worth Airport TX 75261-9200. (214)556-1100. Creative Directors: Ron Spataro, Neil Scanlan, Artie McGibbens. Ad agency. Clients: all types.
Needs: Works with 4-5 freelance illustrators/month. Works on assignment only. Uses freelancers for billboards, newspapers, P-O-P displays, TV and trade magazines.
First Contact & Terms: Call for appointment to show portfolio. Reports within 3 weeks. Provide business card, brochure/flyer, resume and samples to be kept on file for possible future assignments. Samples not kept on file are returned. Payment is negotiated.
Tips: Wants to see a wide variety including past work used by ad agencies and tear sheets of published art.

CLAYPOOLE, BURK & HUMMEL, Suite 501, 8585 N. Stemmons Freeway, Dallas TX 75247-3805. Vice President: Bailey Burk. Ad agency. Clients: petroleum, financial, insurance, retail, plastics and high-tech electronics firms.
Needs: Works with 2-3 illustrators/month. Uses freelance artists for billboards, brochures, AV presentations, print and collateral pieces.
First Contact & Terms: Send query letter with brochure showing art style or tear sheets, Photostats and photocopies. Write to schedule an appointment to show a portfolio, which should include original/final art and final reproduction/product. Pays for design by the hour, $30-50 or by the project. Pays for illustration by the project, $200-1,500. Considers client's budget or where work will appear when establishing payment.
Tips: "In the field, there are more promotions to complement advertising campaigns. Also, computer graphics should be a strong medium for the last part of the twentieth century. As for approaching our firm, set reasonable prices on the total layout of artwork. Don't show consumer applications to a business-to-business shop."

DYKEMAN ASSOCIATES INC., 4115 Rawlins, Dallas TX 75219. (214)528-2991. Contact: Alice Dykeman or Laurie Christopher. PR/marketing firm. Clients: business, industry, sports, environmental, energy, health. Assigns 150 jobs/year.
Needs: Works with 5 illustrators/designers per month. "We prefer artists who can both design and illustrate." Local artists only. Uses artists for design of brochures, exhibits, corporate identification, signs, posters, ads, title slides, slide artwork and all design and finished artwork for graphics and printed materials. Prefers tight, realistic style. Prefers pen & ink, charcoal/pencil, colored pencil and computer illustration.
First Contact & Terms: Arrange interview to show portfolio. Provide business card and brochures. No originals returned to artist at job's completion. Pays by the project, $250-3,000 average; "artist makes an estimate; we approve or negotiate." Considers complexity of project, creative compatibility, client's budget, skill and experience of artist and turnaround time when establishing payment.
Tips: "Be enthusiastic. Present an organized portfolio with a variety of work. Portfolio should reflect all that an artist can do. Don't include examples when you did a small part of the creative work. Have a price structure but be willing to negotiate per project." Finds most artists through portfolio reviews.

***EDUCATIONAL FILMSTRIPS & VIDEO**, 1401 19th St., Huntsville TX 77340. (409)295-5767. Contact: K.L. Russell. Editor: Julee Miller. Producer of audiovisual materials for school use (junior high, high school, college).
Needs: Works with 10 artists/year. Assigns 6 jobs/year. Uses freelance artists for animation, films, lettering and charts/graphs.
First Contact & Terms: Send query letter with brochure showing art style. Samples are not filed. Samples not filed are returned. Reports back within 1 month. To show a portfolio, mail original/final art, final reproduction/product, photographs, color, b&w and slides. Pays for design and illustration by the project, $10-6,000 or royalty. Considers complexity of project, client's budget, turnaround time, skill and experience of artist and rights purchased when establishing payment. Negotiates rights purchased; rights purchased vary according to project.

***EMERY ADVERTISING**, 1519 Montana, El Paso TX 79902. (915)532-3636. Art Director: Henry Martinez. Ad agency. Clients: automotive firms, banks, restaurants.
Needs: Works with 5-6 freelance artists/year. Uses artists for design, illustration, production.

First Contact & Terms: Works on assignment only. Send query letter with resume and samples to be kept on file; call for appointment to show portfolio. Prefers tear sheets as samples. Samples not filed returned by SASE. Reports back. Considers complexity of project, client's budget and turnaround time when establishing payment. Rights purchased vary according to project.
Tips: Especially looks for "consistency and dependability."

EVANS WYATT ADVERTISING, Gibralter Savings Bldg., 5151 Flynn Pkwy., Corpus Christi TX 78411. (512)854-1661. Contact: Mr. E. Wyatt. Advertising/exhibit/display/director.
Needs: Assigns 400 freelance illustrations/year; uses some cartoons and humorous and cartoon-style illustrations. Works on assignment only.
First Contact & Terms: Send a query letter with resume, brochure/flyer, tear sheets and photocopies to be kept on file. "No originals, please." Samples not filed are returned. Reports in two weeks. Arrange an interview to show portfolio, which should include scrapbook, slides or stats. Pays by the project, by the day, or by the hour, $75-150, with a $500 maximum. Considers client's budget and skill and experience of artist when establishing payment. "We pay flat for all rights."
Tips: More "by the project" assignments at negotiated charge. "Send 6-12 copies of general scope of work plus best specialty and price expected."

GOODMAN & ASSOCIATES, 601 Penn St., Fort Worth TX 76102. (817)332-2261. Production Manager: Susan Whittenberger. Ad agency. Clients: financial, fashion, industrial, manufacturing and straight PR accounts.
Needs: Works with 3-6 illustrators/month. Uses freelance artists for billboards, consumer and trade magazines, direct mail, P-O-P displays, brochures, catalogs, posters, signage and AV presentations.
First Contact & Terms: Local artists only. Arrange interview to show portfolio. Works on assignment basis only. Payment is by the project, by the hour or by the day; negotiates according to client's budget.

HEPWORTH ADVERTISING COMPANY, 3403 McKinney Ave., Dallas TX 75204. (214)526-7785. Manager: S.W. Hepworth. Full-service advertising agency. Clients: financial, consumer and industrial.
Needs: Works with 3-4 freelance artists/year. Uses artists for brochure and newspaper ad design, direct mail packages, magazine ad illustration, mechanicals, billboards, and logos.
First Contact & Terms: Send a query letter with tear sheets. Samples are not filed and are returned only if requested by artist. Does not report back. Portfolio should include roughs. Pays for design and illustration by the project. Considers client's budget when establishing payment. Buys all rights.
Tips: Looks for variety in samples or portfolio.

***IMAGEMATRIX DALLAS**, 6305 N. O'Connor Rd., Irving TX 75039. Creative Director, Design Group: Sam Johnson. "The design group specializes in design/production of print communications in general." Clients: real estate developers, food manufacturers/distributors, travel industry, hotels, industrials. A client list is provided upon request with a SASE.
Needs: Works with 12 artists/year. Assigns 20 jobs/year. Local artists only (Dallas/Fort Worth area). Works on assignment only. Uses freelance artists for brochure, newspaper and magazine ad design and illustration, direct mail packages, P-O-P displays, mechanicals, retouching, animation, billboards, posters, lettering and logos.
First Contact & Terms: Send query letter with brochure showing art style or tear sheets, Photostats, photocopies, slides and photographs. Samples are filed. Samples not filed are not returned. Reports back within 1 month only if interested. Write to schedule an appointment to show a portfolio, which should include thumbnails, roughs, original/final art, tear sheets, final reproduction/product, photographs, color, b&w and slides. Pays for design by the hour, $25-35. Illustration is bid out. Considers complexity of project, client's budget, turnaround time, skill and experience of artist, how work will be used and rights purchased when establishing payment. Buys all rights.
Tips: "Be patient and persistent. We're busy people!"

KNOX PUBLIC RELATIONS, Suite A, Guthrie Creek Park, 708 Glencrest, Longview TX 75601. (214)758-6439. President: Donna Mayo Knox. PR firm. Clients: civic, social organizations, private schools and businesses.
Needs: Works on assignment only. Uses artists for billboards, stationery design, multimedia kits, direct mail and brochures/flyers.
First Contact & Terms: Send query letter with brochure showing art style or resume and samples. Samples returned by SASE. Reports in 3 weeks. Call or write to schedule an appointment to show a portfolio. Originals returned to artist at job's completion. Pays for illustration by the hour.
Tips: "Please query first."

LEVEL FOUR COMMUNICATIONS, Three Dallas Communications Complex LB134, Irving TX 75039-3510. (214)869-7620. President: Doris Seitz. Ad agency. Clients: corporate and banking.
Needs: Works with 5-6 freelance artists/year. Uses local artists with a minimum of three years of experience. Works on assignment only. Uses artists for design, illustrations, brochures, catalog, books, magazines, newspapers, P-O-P displays, mechanicals, retouching, billboards, posters, direct mail packages, press releases, motion pictures, lettering, logos, charts/graphs and advertisements. Looks for "first-quality, high-level corporate design capability; a clean, sophisticated style."
First Contact & Terms: Contact through artist's agent or send query letter with resume and samples. Samples not filed are not returned. Reports only if interested. To show a portfolio, mail original/final art, final reproduction/product, color, tear sheets and photographs. On a typical brochure, pays for design by the project, $200 minimum. Pays for illustrations by the project, $200 minimum. Considers client's budget, skill and experience of artist, turnaround time and rights purchased when establishing payment. Purchases all rights but can negotiate; rights purchased vary according to project.

McCANN-ERICKSON WORLDWIDE, Suite 1900, 1360 Post Oak Blvd., Houston TX 77056. (713)965-0303. Senior Vice President/Creative Director: Jesse Caesar. Ad agency. Clients: all types including consumer, industrial, gasoline, transportation/air, entertainment, computers and high-tech.
Needs: Works with about 20 freelance illustrators/month. Uses freelancers in all media.
First Contact & Terms: Call for appointment to show portfolio. Selection based on portfolio review. Negotiates payment based on client's budget and where work will appear.
Tips: Wants to see full range of work including past work used by other ad agencies and tear sheets of published art in portfolio.

McNEE PHOTO COMMUNICATIONS INC., 9261 Kirby, Houston TX 77006. (713)796-2633. President: Jim McNee. AV/film producer. Serves clients in industry and advertising. Produces slide presentations, videotapes, brochures and films. Also a brokerage for stock photographs.
Needs: Assigns 20 jobs/year. Works with 4 illustrators/month. Prefers local artists with previous work experience. Uses artists for brochures, annual reports and artwork for slides, film and tape.
First Contact & Terms: "Will review samples by appointment only." Provide resume, brochure/flyer and business card to be kept on file for possible future assignments. Works on assignment only. Reports within 1 month. Method of payment is negotiated with the individual artist. Pays by the hour, $30-60 average. Considers client's budget when establishing payment. No originals returned after publication. Buys all rights, but will negotiate.

ROMINGER ADVERTISING AGENCY, 3600 Commerce, Dallas TX 75226. Art Director: G. Nelson Greenfield. Ad agency. Clients: hotels, real estate, corporate and industrial.
Needs: Works with 2-3 illustrators/year. Local artists only. Works on assignment basis only. Uses freelance artists for billboards, consumer and trade magazines, direct mail, P-O-P displays, brochures, catalogs, posters, signage, newspapers, and AV presentations and production.
First Contact & Terms: Query with resume of credits and samples. Payment is by the day or by project.

***VISIONS**, 14546 Broadgreen, Houston TX 77079. (713)589-1612. President: Jim Scott. Full-service ad agency specializing in package goods, new product introductions and promotions, corporate service/product market. Clients: package goods, high-tech, industrial, financial.
Needs: Works with 10-15 artists/year. Works on assignment only. Uses freelance artists for brochure, newspaper ad and magazine ad design and illustration; P-O-P displays, posters, direct mail packages, lettering and logos. Prefers pen & ink, airbrush, charcoal/pencil, watercolor, acrylics, pastels, markers, calligraphy and computer illustration.
First Contact & Terms: Send query letter with resume, tear sheets, Photostats, photocopies, slides and photographs. Samples are filed. Samples not filed are returned only if requested by artist. Reports back within 10 days. Call to schedule an appointment to show a portfolio, which should include original art and finished printed product. Pays for design by the hour, $20-50; pays for illustration by the project, $100-2,500. Considers client's budget when establishing payment terms. Negotiates rights purchased; rights purchased vary according to project.
Tips: "Call to set appointment or find out what material to present if not local." Finds most artists through references, then portfolio reviews.

ZACHRY ASSOCIATES, INC., Box 1739, 709 N. 2nd, Abilene TX 79604. (915)677-1342. General Manager: Marvin Kirkham. Ad agency, audiovisual and printing firm. Clients: industrial, institutional and religious service. Client list provided for SASE.
Needs: Works with 6 freelance artists/year. Works on assignment only. Uses artists for illustration, calligraphy and mechanical preparation.

First Contact & Terms: Send query letter with samples, if available, to be kept on file. Samples not filed are returned by SASE. Call or write to schedule an appointment to show portfolio, which should include roughs, final reproduction/product or anything pertinent to talent offered. Pays for design by the hour, $10 minimum. Pays for illustration by the project, $35 minimum. Considers complexity of the project, client's budget and turnaround time when establishing payment. Rights purchased vary according to project.

Vermont

***KELLIHER/SAMETS**, (formerly Image), 130 S. Willard St., Burlington VT 05401. (802)862-8261. President: Linda Kelliher. Ad agency. Clients: restaurants, automotive, ski resorts, banks, universities. Client list provided upon request.
Needs: Works with 3 freelance artists/year. Works on assignment only. Uses artists for illustrations and mechanical preparation when busy.
First Contact & Terms: Send query letter with resume and samples to be kept on file. Samples not filed returned only if requested. Reports within 2-3 weeks. Write for appointment to show portfolio, which should include Photostats, photographs, slides or tear sheets. Considers complexity of project, client's budget, skill and experience of artist, geographic scope for the finished product, turnaround time and rights purchased when establishing payment. Rights purchased vary according to project.

Virginia

***DEADY ADVERTISING**, 17 E. Cary St., Richmond VA 23219. (804)643-4011. President: Jim Deady. Specializes in industrial and financial, displays and publications. Clients: tobacco, zinc die castings and savings and loans.
Needs: Works with 10-12 freelance artists/year. Local or regional artists only with minimum of 2 years of experience with an agency. Works on assignment only. Uses artists for design, illustration, mechanicals, retouching and airbrushing; brochures, magazine and newspaper advertisements, radio and television commercials.
First Contact & Terms: Send query letter with resume to be kept on file; also send samples. Other samples are returned. Reports back only if interested. Call or write for appointment to show portfolio, which should include Photostats. Pays for design by the hour, $35-75 average, or by the project, $250-2,500 average; for illustration by the project, $275-1,500 average. Considers client's budget, skill and experience of artist and turnaround time when establishing payment.
Tips: "Be on time with all projects."

GOLDMAN & ASSOCIATES, 408 W. Bute St., Norfolk VA 23510. (804)625-2518. Creative Director: Oliver Raoust. Ad/PR firm.
Needs: Uses artists for work in building and mechanical renderings, airbrushing, animation, TV animation, TV/film production, P-O-P displays, filmstrips, consumer magazines, multimedia kits, slide sets, brochures/flyers and finished work. Negotiates pay.
First Contact & Terms: Query with samples of previously published work. SASE. Provide brochures, flyers, resume, tear sheets, samples and 3/4" video tape when possible to be kept on file for future assignments. Originals returned at completion on some jobs.

PAYNE ROSS & ASSOCIATES ADVERTISING, INC., 206 E. Jefferson St., Charlottesville VA 22901. (804)977-7607. Creative Director: Lisa Ross. Ad agency. Clients: resorts, service industries, manufacturing, banks.
Needs: Works with 12-20 freelance artists/year. Uses artists for photography, illustration and copy-writing; occasionally for paste-up.
First Contact & Terms: Send query letter with brochure showing art style or resume and tear sheets, Photostats, slides, photographs and other printed pieces. Reports back only if interested. To show portfolio, mail appropriate materials, which should include original/final art, final reproduction/product, Photostats and photographs. Pays for design by the hour, $15-40; pays for illustration by the project, $200-1,500. Pay varies according to "experience, type of work, etc." Considers skill and experience of artist and turnaround time when establishing payment. Rights purchased vary according to project.
Tips: "There is increasing popularity in use of illustration for brochure and print advertising. Also there is more acceptance of this by client, particularly photography and illustration together. We find more integration between copy and design in conceptual stage. Therefore designer, illustrator, photographer must be flexible."

SIDDALL, MATUS AND COUGHTER, Fidelity Bldg., 9th & Main Sts., Richmond VA 23219. Art Directors: Jessica Welton, Bob Shira, Suzanne Dashiell. Ad agency/PR firm. Clients: computer, travel, land development, bank, chemical, retail.

Needs: Assigns 50 freelance jobs/year. Works on assignment only. Works with 4 freelance illustrators/month. Uses artists for consumer and trade magazines, billboards, direct mail packages, brochures, newspapers and posters.

First Contact & Terms: Send query letter with samples and tear sheets to be kept on file. Call or write for appointment to show portfolio, which should include printed samples to be kept on file. Samples returned only if requested. Reports only if interested. Pays for design by the hour, $30-60. Pays for illustration by the project, up to $15,000. Considers complexity of project, client's budget, skill and experience of artist, geographic scope of finished project, turnaround time and rights purchased when establishing payment. Buys all rights.

Washington

MAGICMATION INC., Suite 1560, 1100 Olive Way, Seattle WA 98101. (206)682-8235. Vice President: Robert T. O'Dell. "Magicmation is a computer graphics service center using state-of-the-art technology, talented artists and sales staff to create, produce, and image high-resolution business graphics, pictures, paintings, photographs, etc. Clients: advertising, corporations, printers, photographers, software companies, research and development.

Needs: Works with 2 freelance artists/year. "Artists must have basic knowledge of computer graphics machines." Uses artists for design, illustration, mechanicals, retouching and charts/graphs.

First Contact & Terms: Send query letter with brochure or resume and slides. Samples not filed are returned only if requested. Reports back only if interested. Write to schedule an appointment to show a portfolio, which should include roughs, photographs, color and slides. Pays for design and illustration by the hour, $12-25. Considers skill and experience of artist when establishing payment. Buys all rights.

Tips: "Color, design, speed and *knowledge* of our equipment are very important."

***WATTS-SILVERSTEIN**, 1921 2nd Ave., Seattle WA 98101. (206)443-4200. Contact: R. Lindberg. AV producer. Serves clients in industry and advertising. Produces multi-image slide shows and print collateral.

Needs: Assigns 5 jobs/year. Works with 1 illustrator and 1 animator/month. Works on assignment only. Uses artists for "all our slide shows."

First Contact & Terms: Send resume and samples (slides preferred). Samples returned with SASE. Provide resume, samples and business card to be kept on file for possible future assignments. Reports within 2 weeks. Method and amount of payment are negotiated with the individual artist. Original art returned after publication. Negotiates rights purchased.

West Virginia

GUTMAN ADVERTISING AGENCY, 600 Board of Trade Bldg., Wheeling WV 26003. (304)233-4700. President: D. Milton Gutman. Ad agency. Clients: finance, glass, resort, media, industrial supplies (tools, pipes) and furniture.

Needs: Works with 3-4 illustrators/month. Local artists only except for infrequent and special needs. Uses artists for billboards, stationery design, television, brochures/flyers, trade magazines and newspapers. Also uses artists for retouching work.

First Contact & Terms: Send materials to be kept on file for possible future assignments. Call for an appointment to show a portfolio. No originals returned at job's completion. Negotiates payment.

Wisconsin

BARKIN, HERMAN, SOLOCHECK & PAULSEN, INC., 606 E. Wisconsin Ave., Milwaukee WI 53202. (414)271-7434. Administrator: John Ericsen. Wisconsin's oldest PR firm. Clients: educational organizations, financial, manufacturing, health care, insurance, brewery, leisure time and real estate development.

Needs: Works with freelance illustrators and designers according to client needs. Uses artists for all communications media. Prefers technical illustration; pen & ink, airbrush, calligraphy and computer illustration.

First Contact & Terms: Call administrator for appointment to show portfolio. Negotiates payment depending on job requirements.

BRIEN LEE & COMPANY, 1845 N. Farwell Ave, Milwaukee WI 53202. (414)277-7600. President/Creative Director: Brien Lee. Audiovisual firm. Video tape producer and agency specializing in wide range of sales and marketing presentations both on a per project and speculative basis. Clients: business, industry, the arts.
Needs: Works with 10 freelance artists/year. Assigns 20 jobs/year. Works on assignment only. Uses artists for design, illustration, P-O-P displays, mechanicals, computer graphics, animation, motion pictures and storyboards.
First Contact & Terms: Send query letter with resume, tear sheets, Photostats, photocopies and slides. Samples are filed. Samples not filed are returned. Reports back within 10 days. Write to schedule an appointment to show a portfolio, or mail Photostats, tear sheets, slides and videotape. Pays for design by the hour, $25-80. Pays for illustration by the hour, $40-100. Considers complexity of project, client's budget and turnaround time when establishing payment. Negotiates rights purchased.
Tips: Artists need "an understanding of videotape and motion/animation design."

SORGEL-STUDIOS, INC., 205 W. Highland Ave., Milwaukee WI 53203. (414)224-9600. Contact: Art Director. AV producer. Clients: business, corporate, multi-image and videotapes. Assigns 100 jobs/year.
Needs: Works with 10 illustrators/year. Uses artists for stylized illustrations, human figures and animation. Works with production artists familar with producing film work, cutting rubylith, etc. for Marron Carrel special effects camera.
First Contact & Terms: Query with resume and samples (slides). SASE. Reports in 3 weeks. Provide resume and brochures/flyers to be kept on file for possible future assignments. No originals returned to artist at job's completion. Pays for design by the hour, $7.50-20.50. Pays for illustration by the hour, $7.50-30.50.
Tips: "Most of our artwork is now computer generated and that limits our use of freelancers." Looking for "work that relates directly to multi-image, logo design , hand lettering and computer graphics experience. We do not want to see mangy, poorly organized portfolios."

VISUALS PLUS INC., 810 N. Plankinton Ave., Milwaukee WI 53203. Vice President/Creative Director: John D. Peterman. Audiovisual firm. "We are a multimedia firm specializing in computer-generated business graphics. We also have a complete art department and inhouse b&w/color photographic labs." Clients: private amateur/professional photographers. Produce graphics, art and multi-images for corporate and commercial businesses.
Needs: Works with 5 freelance artists/year. Assigns 40-50 jobs/year. Prefers local metro-Milwaukee artists. Works on assignment only. Uses artists for design, illustration, brochures, catalogs, books, newspapers, trade magazines, mechanicals, animation, direct mail packages, press releases, lettering, logos, charts/graphs and advertisements.
First Contact & Terms: Send query letter with brochure or resume and slides. Samples are filed. Reports back within 10 days "if applicable." Write to schedule an appointment to show a portfolio or mail roughs, tear sheets, final reproduction/product and slides. Pays for design by the hour, $4-10; by the project, $30-350. Pays for illustration by the hour, $8-20; by the project, $60-700. Considers turnaround time and skill and experience of artist when establishing payment. Buys all rights.
Tips: "Provide an honest response by mail with representative samples depicting experience and specific skills in area requested."

Canada

CRAWLEYS ANIMATION INC., 19 Fairmont Ave., Ottawa, Ontario K1Y 1X4 Canada. (613)728-3513. Recruitment Consultant: Pierre-Paul Lafreniere. Animation production house. Produces animated motion pictures—cartoon and technical, series, features. Clients: corporate interests, government, small business and broadcasters.
Needs: Works with many freelance artists. Local artists perferred. Works on assignment only. Uses artists for animation, background and layout art. Artists must have "a graduate diploma from a classical animation program or a minimum of 3 years of experience in an animation studio and a demo reel of sample materials."
First Contact & Terms: Send query letter with resume and slides, photographs and demo reels. Samples not filed are returned only by request. Reports only if interested. Call or write to schedule an appointment to show a portfolio, which should include thumbnails, roughs, original/final art, photographs and demo reels.

DYNACOM COMMUNICATIONS, Box 702, Snowdon Station, Montreal, Quebec H3X 3X8 Canada. Director: David P. Leonard. Audiovisual/TV/film producer. Clients: large industries,

government, education and health institutions.
Needs: Produces motion pictures, multimedia kits, overhead transparencies, slide sets, sound-slide sets, color videotapes and multiscreen mixed media "for training, motivation, sales, orientation and entertainment." Uses artists for album covers.
First Contact & Terms: Query with resume. Reports "only if we have a requirement." Buys all rights. Negotiates time of payment. Pays $20-40/frame, animated cartoons; $15-60, charts/graphs and technical art. Payment by hour: $5-15, advertising and illustrations; $5-10, lettering and mechanicals.

McCANN-ERICKSON ADVERTISING OF CANADA, Britannica House, 151 Bloor W, Toronto, Ontario MS5 1S8 Canada. (416)925-3231. Contact: Art Directors. Ad agency. Clients: consumer food, beverage and service industry accounts.
Needs: Local artists only. Works on assignment only. Uses freelance artists and photographers on all accounts.
First Contact & Terms: Especially looks for a "unique style" in a portfolio—also "enthusiasm and dedication." Call to schedule an appointment to show portfolio with individual art directors. Payment is by the project; negotiates according to client's budget and freelancer's previous experience.
Tips: "Artists should be more selective in the work they show. One poor piece of work lets down the whole portfolio."

***PULLIN PRODUCTIONS, LTD.**, 822 Fifth Ave. SW, Calgary, Alberta T2P 0N3 Canada. Creative Director: Art Feinstough. Audiovisual firm.
Needs: Works with 4 freelance artists/year. Works on assignment only. Uses artists for design, illustrations, brochures, P-O-P displays, animation, motion pictures, lettering and charts/graphs.
First Contact & Terms: Send query letter with resume and samples. Samples not filed are not returned. Reports only if interested. To show a portfolio, mail appropriate materials. Pays for design by the hour, $10-50. Considers complexity of project, client's budget, skill and experience of artist, how work will be used and turnaround time when establishing payment. Buys all rights.

WARNE MARKETING & COMMUNICATIONS, Suite 810, 111 Avenue Rd., Toronto, Ontario M5R 3M1 Canada. (416)927-0881. President: Keith Warne.
Needs: Works with 8 freelance artists/year. Works on assignment only. Uses artists for design, illustrations, brochures, catalogs, P-O-P displays, mechanicals, retouching, billboards, posters, direct mail packages, logos, charts/graphs and advertisements. Artists should have "creative concept thinking." Prefers charcoal/pencil, colored pencil and markers.
First Contact & Terms: Send query letter with resume and photocopies. Samples not filed are not returned. Reports only if interested. Write to schedule an appointment to show a portfolio, which should include roughs and final reproduction/product. Pays for design by the project, $85 minimum. Pays for illustration by the project, $150 minimum. Considers complexity of project, client's budget, and skill and experience of artist when establishing payment. Buys all rights.
Tips: Artist should "send samples (photocopies) and wait for assignment. There is an increasing need for technical illustration in the field."

Ireland

***ARKS LIMITED ADVERTISING AND MARKETING** , Harcourt Centre, 50/53 Harcourt St., Dublin 2, Ireland. Phone: 757981. Creative Director: Eamonn O'Flaherty. Ad agency. Clients: beer, cars, cosmetics, farm produce, computers. A client list is provided upon request.
Needs: Works with 20 artists/year. Assigns 2000 jobs/year. Uses freelance artists for catalog design and illustration, newspaper ad design and illustration, posters, lettering and TV storyboards.
First Contact & Terms: Send query letter with brochure showing art style or tear sheets and photographs. Samples are filed. Samples not filed are returned only if requested by artist. Reports back within 1 week. Call or write to schedule an appointment to show a portfolio, which should include roughs, photographs, slides and video disks. Pays "market value." Considers complexity of project, client's budget, turnaround time, skill and experience of artist and how work will be used when establishing payment.
Tips: Don't "waste my time."

Art/Design Studios

Art/design studios offer artists a wide range of freelance opportunities. There are studios which specialize in a particular area of design, but many accept any type of assignment from a client—corporate identity, product/brand identity, publication design, the design or illustration of direct marketing materials, catalogs, annual reports, brochures, exhibits, direct mail pieces and so on.

Because many companies do not have their own design departments, they often call upon design studios, either directly or through the company's advertising agency, to develop total programs that include not only a visual image but also a marketing strategy that unifies the message with the artwork.

The designer will coordinate disparate elements such as typography, illustration, color and space into a pleasing unity. Designers might take an entire project from conception to print, or they may only carry out the direction of the client's or agency's art director for the design.

Art studios are called upon mainly for illustration, while design studios specialize in design. Both may offer a range of services from design, illustration and layout to mechanicals, paste-up and retouching.

Depending on their size, studios either employ artists to handle duties in-house or hire freelance help. The one-person studio generally turns to freelance help when the workload becomes too heavy, while the large operation may turn to outside help for either a fresh approach or for basic mechanical skills such as paste-up.

The key to getting assignments from studios is to show a portfolio that contains only your best work and presents it in a neat, organized fashion. Focus on the needs of the studio and select samples that show your ability to fill those needs. If you're showing your work to a studio that specializes in corporate identity, include logos and letterheads instead of airbrush illustrations of food. Make sure you note what your involvement is in each project, such as designing the logo or lettering the piece. Art directors like to see how you conceptualize a project, so include thumbnails, roughs and comprehensives as well as the final illustration. It's also a good idea to have more than one portfolio to cover the prevalent drop-off policy in major metropolitan areas and also one for submissions through the mail.

Follow the lead of studios themselves and mail reminders and updates of your work to keep on file. Then when the need arises, you'll be in the running if your work is at hand.

Payment is usually based on the hour or the project. The amount of payment depends upon the complexity of the project, turnaround time, rights purchased and your reputation. Include in your estimate time spent in consultation with the client and any extra services you provide.

Design studios keep a high profile in order to be visible for potential clients. The most comprehensive directory of design firms (names and addresses are noted, but no marketing information is provided) is the *Design Directory*. Other sources are *Adweek's Portfolio of Graphic Design* and the *Creative Black Book*. Consider joining a professional design organization, because it puts you in touch with a network of designers both in your area and nationally. The American Institute of Graphic Arts (AIGA), for example, sponsors exhibitions and competitions and publishes a monthly journal plus a membership directory.

A.T. ASSOCIATES, 63 Old Rutherford Ave., Charlestown MA 02129. (617)242-6004. Partner: Daniel N. Kovacovic. Specializes in industrial design, model making, corporate identity, signage, displays and packaging. Clients: design firms, corporate clients, small business and ad agencies.
Needs: Works with 10-25 freelance artists/year. Prefers local artists, some experience necessary. Uses artists for model making, mechanicals, logos, brochures, P-O-P displays, charts/graphs and design.
First Contact & Terms: Send resume and nonreturnable samples. Samples are filed. Reports back within 30 days only if interested. Call or write to schedule an appointment to show a portfolio, which should include thumbnails, roughs, original/final art, final reproduction/product, tear sheets, Photostats, photographs, b&w and color. Pays for design and illustration by the hour, $10-25; by the day, $48-200. Considers complexity of project, client's budget, skill and experience of artist, turnaround time and rights purchased when establishing payment. Rights purchased vary according to project.

AARON, SAUTER, GAINES & ASSOCIATES/DIRECT MARKETING, Suite 230, 320 E. McDowell Rd., Phoenix AZ 85004. (602)265-1933. President: Cameron G. Sauter. Specializes in brand identity, direct marketing, direct response ads, catalogs and P-O-P displays for retail stores, banks, industrial, mail order and service companies.
Needs: Works with 5-10 freelance artists/year. Uses artists for advertising, brochure and catalog design and illustration, mechanicals, retouching and direct mail packages.
First Contact & Terms: Seeks artists with professionalism, speed and experience only. Works on assignment basis. Send query letter with brochure, resume and business card to be kept on file. Prefers original work, photos or slides as samples. Samples returned by SASE if not kept on file. Reports only if interested. Pays for design by the hour, $15-50 average; by the project, $100-1,000 average; by the day, $50-100 average. Pays for illustration by the hour, $25-75 average; by the project, $100-2,000 average; by the day, $100-150 average. Considers complexity of project, client's budget, skill and experience of artist and turnaround time when establishing payment. "All art is purchased with full rights and no limitations."

AD SYSTEMS INC., 723 S. Wells St., Chicago IL 60607. (312)427-4025. Creative Director: Patricia Kestler. Art agency. Specializes in print advertising and promotions relating to it. Clients: manufacturers and retailers.
Needs: Uses artists for P-O-P displays, direct mail, signage, brochures/flyers and slide sets. Prefers markers, then pen & ink, airbrush, colored pencil and watercolor.
First Contact & Terms: Local artists only. Arrange interview to show portfolio. SASE. Prefers Photostats, b&w line drawings, layout, roughs, comps, marker rendering, and previously published work as samples. Provide material to be kept on file for future assignments. No originals returned. Pays for design by the hour, $20-30. Pays for illustration by the hour, $25-30.
Tips: "Always show roughs and comps, then the finished printed piece. Show knowledge of paste-up or production."

***ADVANCE DESIGN CENTER**, Suite 200, 2501 Oak Lawn Ave., Dallas TX 75219. (214)526-1420. President: Jaime Sendra. Specializes in brand identity and package design for food products.
Needs: Works with 10-15 freelance artists/year. Prefers local talent. Prefers realistic, three-dimensional art; hard-edge, crisp style. Uses freelance artists for P-O-P displays, mechanicals, retouching, airbrushing, logos and food package illustration.
First Contact & Terms: Send query letter with brochure showing art style or tear sheets, photocopies, slides and photographs. Call to schedule an appointment to show a portfolio which should include original/final art, final reproduction/product, photographs, b&w, color or slides. Payment is based on project.
Tips: "Bring finished art with printed samples."

***ALLISON AND BAUM DESIGN**, 10 W. Hinsdale Ave., Hinsdale IL 60521. (312)654-2272. Principal: Barbara Allison. Specializes in direct mail and publications. Clients: corporate, trade associations.
Needs: Works with 10 freelance artists/year. Works on assignment only. Uses freelance artists for bro-

The asterisk before a listing indicates that the listing is new in this edition. New markets are often the most receptive to freelance submissions.

chure design and illustration, catalog illustration, book design, mechanicals, retouching, airbrushing, direct mail packages, charts/graphs, lettering, logos and design of advertisements.
First Contact & Terms: Send query letter with photocopies. Samples are filed. Reports back only if interested. Write to schedule an appointment to show a portfolio, which should include original/final art and final reproduction/product. Pays for design by the hour, $15-20. Pays for illustration by the project, $100-5,000. Considers complexity of project, client's budget, skill and experience of artist, how work will be used and turnaround time when establishing payment. Buys all rights.
Tips: "Be reliable and communicative."

ANCO/BOSTON, 48 Eliot St., South Natick MA 01760. (617)650-1148. Graphic Director: Fran Jarvis. Art agency. Clients: educational publishers, commercial and industrial.
Needs: Works with 10 illustrators. Local artists only. Uses artists for books, charts, graphs, technical art and paste-up. Most of the artwork required is one-color line art.
First Contact & Terms: Send query letter with resume and photocopies. All art becomes the property of Anco/Boston. To show portfolio, mail appropriate materials or call to schedule an appointment; send examples of work with resume. Pays for design by the project, $25 minimum; pays for illustration by the project, $10 minimum.
Tips: "We are interested only in b&w line art. Our work is for educational materials and is frequently of a technical nature."

***ANCONA 2 DESIGNERS INC.**, Suite 1001, 19 West 21st St., New York NY 10010. Vice President: Jane Ancona. Specializes in displays, interior design, packaging, product design and exhibits. Clients: large and small manufacturing companies.
Needs: Uses freelance artists for brochure and catalog design, P-O-P displays, mechanicals, retouching, logos, package design and comps. Especially needs "competent and versatile packaging, product and graphic designers."
First Contact & Terms: Send query letter with resume and photocopies of work. Reports back only if interested. To show a portfolio, mail thumbnails, roughs, original/final art, final reproduction/product, tear sheets, Photostats, photographs, b&w or color. Pays for design by the hour, $15 minimum. Considers complexity of project, client's budget, skill and experience of artist, how work will be used and turnaround time when establishing payment. Rights purchased vary according to project.

ANDREN & ASSOCIATES INC., 6400 N. Keating Ave., Lincolnwood IL 60646. (312)267-8500. Contact: Kenneth E. Andren. Clients: beauty products and tool manufacturers, clothing retailers, laboratories, banks, cameras and paper products.
Needs: Assigns 6-7 jobs/month. Local artists only. Uses artists for catalogs, direct mail brochures, flyers, packages, P-O-P displays and print media advertising.
First Contact & Terms: Query with samples or arrange interview. SASE. Reports in 1-2 weeks. Pays $15 minimum/hour for animation, design, illustrations, layout, lettering, mechanicals, paste-up, retouching and type spec.

ANTISDEL IMAGE GROUP, INC., 3242 De La Cruz Blvd., Santa Clara CA 95054. (408)988-1010. President: G.C. Antisdel. Specializes in annual reports, corporate identity, displays, interior design, packaging, publications, signage and photo illustration. Clients: high technology 80%, energy 10%, and banking 10%.
Needs: Works on assignment only. Uses artists for illustration, mechanicals, retouching, airbrushing, direct mail packages, model making, charts/graphs, AV materials and lettering.
First Contact & Terms: Send query letter with resume, business card and tear sheets to be kept on file. Reports back only if interested. Call or write to schedule an appointment to show a portfolio, which should include color, tear sheets, photographs and b&w. Pays for design by the hour, $10-40 or by the project $40-18,000. Pays for illustration by the project, $40-10,000. Considers complexity of project, client's budget, skill and experience of artist, how work will be used, turnaround time and rights purchased when establishing payment.
Tips: "Our top grade clients are not subject to 'trendy' fads."

THE ART WORKS, 4409 Maple Ave., Dallas TX 75219. (214)521-2121. Creative Director: Fred Henley. Specializes in annual reports, brand identity, corporate identity, packaging, publications, signage, illustration and photography.
Needs: Works with 15-20 freelance artists/year. Uses artists for advertising, brochure, catalog and book design and illustration; advertising, brochure and catalog layout; P-O-P displays, mechanicals, retouching, posters, direct mail packages, lettering and logos.
First Contact & Terms: Send brochure, business card slides, original work to be kept on file. Samples returned by SASE only if requested by artist. Reports within 7 days. Call or write for appointment to

show portfolio. Pays for design and illustration by the project. Considers complexity of project, client's budget, skill and experience of artist and turnaround time when establishing payment.

***AXION DESIGN**, Box 629, San Anselmo CA 94960. Contact: Recruiting Principal. Specializes in brand identity and consumer packaging design for Fortune 500 Companies.
Needs: Works with 15 freelance artists/year. Prefers artists in San Francisco Bay area. Uses artists for mechanicals, lettering, package design and illustration (especially of food). Especially needs international quality graphic designers with packaging design experience.
First Contact & Terms: Send resume and samples. Samples are filed. Samples not filed are returned if accompanied by SASE. Reports back only if interested. Write to schedule an appointment to show a portfolio, which should include original/final art, final reproduction/product, tear sheets, Photostats and photographs. Pays for design by the hour, $10-35. Pays for illustrations by the hour, $20 minimum; by the project "prices negotiable." Considers complexity of project, client's budget, skill and experience of artist, how work will be used when establishing payment. Buys all rights.

BAKER STREET PRODUCTIONS LTD.,216 Belgrade Ave., Mankato MN 56001. (507)625-2482. Contact: Mark Ahlstrom. Specializes in publications. Clients: publishers.
Needs: Works with 2 freelance artists/year. Prefers colorful juvenile-style art. Uses artists for illustrations, catalogs and books.
First Contact & Terms: Send query letter with resume and tear sheets. Samples not filed are returned by SASE only if requested. Reports within 3 months. Write to schedule an appointment to show a portfolio, which should include roughs, tear sheets and photographs. Pays for design and illustration by the project. Considers complexity of project, client's budget and skill and experience of artist when establishing payment.

BARNSTORM DESIGN/CREATIVE, Suite 301, 2502½ W. Colorado Ave., Colorado Springs CO 80904. (303)630-7200. Owner: Douglas D. Blough. Specializes in corporate identity, brochure design, multi-image slide presentations and publications. Clients: ad agencies, high-technology corporations, restaurants.
Needs: Works with 2-4 freelance artists/year. Works with local, experienced (clean, fast and accurate) artists on assignment. Uses artists for design, illustration, brochures, mechanicals, retouching, AV materials and lettering.
First Contact & Terms: Send query letter with resume and samples to be kept on file. Prefers "good originals or reproductions, professionally presented in any form" as samples. Samples not filed are returned by SASE. Reports only if interested. Call or write for appointment to show portfolio. Pays for design by the project, $100 minimum. Pays for illustration by the project, $50 minimum, b&w; $100, color. Considers client's budget, skill and experience of artist, and turnaround time when establishing payment.
Tips: "Portfolios should reflect an awareness of these trends. We try to handle as much inhouse as we can, but we recognize our own limitations (particularly in illustration)."

BASIC/BEDELL ADVERTISING SELLING IMPROVEMENT CORP., Suite 103, 2040 Alameda Padre Serra, Santa Barbara CA 93103. President: C. Barrie Bedell. Specializes in publications, advertisements and direct mail. Clients: national and international newspapers, publishers, direct response marketers, retail stores, hard lines manufacturers and trade associations plus extensive self-promotion.
Needs: Uses artists for publication design, book covers and dust jackets, direct mail layout and pasteup. Especially wants to hear from publishing and "direct response" pros. Negotiates payment by the project. Considers client's budget, and skill and experience of artist when establishing payment.
Tips: "Substantial increase in use of freelance talent and increasing need for true professionals with exceptional skills and responsible performance (delivery as promised and 'on target'). It is very difficult to locate freelance talent with expertise in design of advertising and direct mail with heavy use of type. If work is truly professional and freelancer is business-like, contact with personal letter and photocopy of one or more samples of work that needn't be returned."

LAWRENCE BENDER & ASSOCIATES, 512 Hamilton Ave., Palo Alto CA 94301. (415)327-3821. President: Lawrence Bender. Specializes in annual reports. Clients: electronic manufacturers.
Needs: Uses artists for design, illustration, mechanicals, retouching and airbrushing.
First Contact & Terms: Send query letter with resume, business card and samples to be kept on file. Samples not kept on file returned only if requested. Reports only if interested. Call or write for appointment to show portfolio. Pays for design by the hour, project or day. Pays for illustration by the project. Considers complexity of project, client's budget, skill and experience of artist and rights purchased when establishing payment.

MAY BENDER DESIGN ASSOCIATES, INC., 7 Deer Park Dr., Princeton Corp. Plaza, Monmouth NJ 08856. (201)329-8388. President: May Bender. Specializes in corporate identity, displays, packaging, product design and signage. Clients: manufacturers of consumer products, i.e. R-J Reynolds, Bausch and Lomb.
Needs: Works with variable freelance artists/year. Uses artists for illustrations, mechanicals, retouching, design, comprehensives, airbrushing and lettering.
First Contact & Terms: Send brochure. Samples are filed. Samples not filed are returned only if requested. Call or write to schedule an appointment to show a portfolio, which should include original/final art. Pays for design by the hour, $15-25, or by the project, $10-20. Considers complexity of project, client's budget and turnaround time when establishing payment. Rights purchased vary according to project.
Tips: "I like to see a few 'how they got theres', finished art and repros if possible."

SUZANNE BENNETT AND ASSOCIATES, 875 Avenue of the Americas, New York NY 10001. (212)564-8050. Contact: Suzanne Bennett. Specializes in direct mail, publications and book design. Clients: PR firms, magazines, book publishers and nonprofit organizations.
Needs: Works with 15 freelance artists/year. Uses artists for mechanicals, retouching, airbrushing and charts/graphs.
First Contact & Terms: Samples not filed are not returned. Does not report back. Write to schedule an appointment to show a portfolio. Considers client's budget, skill and experience of artist, how work will be used and turnaround time when establishing payment. Rights purchased vary according to project.

BARRY DAVID BERGER & ASSOCIATES, INC., 9 East 19th St., New York NY 10003. (212)477-4100. Contact: Monya Steele. Specializes in brand and corporate identity, P-O-P displays, product and interior design, exhibits and shows, corporate capability brochures, advertising graphics, packaging, publications and signage. Clients: product manufacturers and marketing organizations.
Needs: Works with 10 freelance artists/year. Uses artists for advertising illustration, mechanicals, retouching, direct mail package design, model making, charts/graphs, photography, AV presentations and lettering.
First Contact & Terms: Send query letter, then call for appointment. Works on assignment only. Prefers "whatever is necessary to demonstrate competence" as samples. Samples returned if not kept on file. Reports immediately. Provide brochure/flyer, resume, business card, tear sheets and samples to be kept on file for possible future assignments. Pays by the project for design and illustration.

J.H. BERMAN AND ASSOCIATES, Suite 621, 2025 I St. NW, Washington DC 20006. (202)775-0892. Senior Vice President: Jackie Deitch. Specializes in annual reports, corporate identity, publications and signage. Clients: real estate developers, architects, high-technology corporations and financial-oriented firms (banks, investment firms, etc.).
Needs: Works with 10-15 (6 consistently) freelance artists/year. Uses artists for design, illustration, brochures, magazines, books, P-O-P displays, mechanicals, retouching, airbrushing, posters, model making, AV materials, lettering and advertisements. Especially needs designers, illustrators, technical illustrators, architectural renderers and mechanical/production artists.
First Contact & Terms: "Artists should be highly professional, with at least 5 years of experience. Highest quality work required. Restricted to local artists for mechanicals only." Send query letter with brochure, resume, business card and samples to be kept on file. Call or write for appointment to show portfolio or contact through agent. "Samples should be as compact as possible; slides not suggested." Samples not kept on file returned by SASE. Reports only if interested. Pays for design by the hour, $12-50 average. Pays for illustration by the project, $200 minimum. Considers complexity of project, skill and experience of artist, how work will be used, turnaround time and rights purchased when establishing payment.
Tips: Artists should have a "totally professional approach."

THE BERNSTEIN DESIGN GROUP, INC., Suite 918, 500 N. Dearborn, Chicago IL 60610. (312)644-2474. President: Daniel Bernstein. Specializes in annual reports, corporate identity and direct mail. Clients: direct clients and PR firms.
Needs: Works with 3 freelance artists/year. Prefers local artists only. Works on assignment only. Uses artists for illustrations and retouching. Prefers pen & ink, colored pencil, watercolor, pastels and markers.
First Contact & Terms: Send query letter with brochure. Samples are filed. Samples not filed are not returned. Reports back within months only if interested. To show a portfolio, mail limited print promotional material. Pays for design by the hour, $30-60. Pays for illustration by the project, $50-1,000. Considers complexity of project, client's budget and time involved when establishing payment. Buys all rights.

Tips: "I do not have time for personal contact until the need arises. I want printed material only, not originals. They will be kept on file until needed. My freelancer needs are minimal."

THE BLANK COMPANY, 1048 Lincoln Ave., San Jose CA 95125. (408)289-9095. Art Director: Jerry Blank. Specializes in annual reports, corporate identity, direct mail, packaging and all collateral material. Clients: hi-tech firms, variety and food service.
Needs: Works with 3 freelance artist/year. Prefers artists with "experience that is reflected in a strong portfolio presentation; local artists only." Works on assignment only. Prefers sophisticated, contemporary and creative artists. Uses artists for design, illustrations, brochures, catalogs, P-O-P displays, mechanicals, posters, lettering, logos and advertisements.
First Contact & Terms: Send query letter with resume, tear sheets, Photostats, photocopies and photographs. Samples are filed. Samples not filed are returned by SASE only if requested. Reports back only if interested. Call or write to schedule an appointment to show a portfolio.

BOB BOEBERITZ DESIGN, 247 Charlotte St., Asheville NC 28801. (704)258-0316. Owner: Bob Boeberitz. Graphic design studio. Clients: galleries, retail outlets, restaurants, textile manufacturers, land developers, computer software, record companies and publishers.
Needs: Works with freelance artists on occasion. Uses artists primarily for illustration. Prefers pen & ink, airbrush and acrylics.
First Contact & Terms: Send query letter with brochure, resume, Photostats, photocopies, photographs, business card, slides and tear sheets to be kept on file. "Anything too large to fit in file" is discarded. Reports only if interested. To show a portfolio, mail appropriate materials or write to schedule an appointment; portfolio should include original/final art, final reproduction/product, color and b&w. Pays for illustration by the project, $50 minimum. Considers complexity of project, client's budget, skill and experience of artist and turnaround time when establishing payment. Buys all rights.
Tips: "Show sketches. Sketches help indicate how the person thinks. In illustration, show both the art and how it was used." Likes to see "ideas, concepts, actual mechanicals (not just reproduction samples)."

THE BOOKMAKERS, INCORPORATED, 298 E. South St., Wilkes-Barre PA 18702. (717)823-9183. President: John Beck. Specializes in publications and technical illustrations. Clients: mostly book publishers.
Needs: Works with 10-20 freelance artists/year. Uses artists for illustrations, brochures, catalogs, retouching, airbrushing, posters and charts/graphs.
First Contact & Terms: Send query letter with resume, tear sheets, Photostats, photocopies, slides and photographs. Samples not filed are returned by SASE. Reports only if interested. Write to schedule an appointment to show a portfolio, which should include thumbnails, roughs, original/final art, final reproduction/product, tear sheets, Photostats and b&w. Pays for illustration by the project, $20-2,400. Considers complexity of project, client's budget, skill and experience of artist, how work will be used and turnaround time when establishing payment. Buys all rights.
Tips: "We are especially interested in versatility."

BOWYER ASSOCIATES, INC., 160 Broadway Ave., Toronto, Ontario M4P 1V9 Canada. (416)484-8848. President: Robert Bowyer. Studio. Clients: retail, industrial and commercial.
Needs: Assigns approximately 200 jobs/year to freelance artists. Works with 2 freelance illustrators/month. Sometimes works on assignment. Uses artists for illustrations and finished artwork.
First Contact & Terms: Send resume to be kept on file if interested. Reports only if interested. Pays for design by the project, $50-1,000. Pays for illustration by the project, $50-1,500. Considers complexity of project, client's budget, and skill and experience of artist when establishing payment. Buys all rights.
Tips: Looks for "good, clean, commercial artwork." Artists should "show only top quality work, anything artist thinks is good, in a range from brochures to advertisements. Do not show artwork that you did in school."

BROOKS STEVENS DESIGN ASSOC., 1415 W. Donges Bay Rd., Mequon WI 53092. (414)241-3800. President: Kipp Stevens. Specializes in corporate identity, packaging and industrial design. Clients: manufacturing companies.
Needs: Works with 5 freelance artists/year. Uses artists for illustrations, P-O-P displays, retouching, model making and logos.
First Contact & Terms: Send query letter with resume. Samples not filed are returned only if requested. Reports only if interested. Call or write to schedule an appointment to show a portfolio, which should include roughs, original/final art, final reproduction/product and color. Pays for design by the hour, $11 minimum; by the project, $100 minimum. Pays for illustrations by the hour, $11 minimum; by the project, $100 minimum. Considers complexity of project, client's budget, skill and experience of artist, and turnaround time when establishing payment.

BUTLER KOSH BROOKS, 940 N. Highland Ave., Los Angeles CA 90038. (213)469-8128. Estab. 1987. Specializes in corporate identity, displays, direct mail, fashion, packaging and publications. Clients: film companies, fashion, medical and home video distributors.
Needs: Works with 12 freelance artists/year. Works on assignment only. Uses artists for design, brochures, catalogs, books, P-O-P displays, mechanicals, retouching, posters, model making, direct mail packages, lettering and logos.
First Contact & Terms: Send query letter with brochure or resume. Samples are filed. Samples not filed are returned by SASE. Reports back within 1 week only if interested. To show a portfolio, mail appropriate materials. Pays for design and illustration by the hour, $15. Considers complexity of project, client's budget, skill and experience of artist, how work will be used, turnaround time and rights purchased when establishing payment. Rights purchased vary according to project.

CANYON DESIGN, # 102, 20945 Devonshire St., Chatsworth CA 91311. (818)700-1173. Art Director/Owner: David O'Connell. Specializes in brand identity, corporate identity, displays and packaging. Clients: manufacturers, distributors and others.
Needs: Works with 28 freelance artists/year. Uses artists for design, illustrations, P-O-P displays, retouching, and lettering. "We are looking for an office manager/production manager and junior designer."
First Contact & Terms: Send query letter with brochure showing art style. Samples not filed are returned by SASE. Reports only if interested. Call to schedule an appointment to show a portfolio, which should include roughs, original/final art, final reproduction/product, color and tear sheets. Pays for design by the project, $500-4,500. Pays for illustration by the project, $500-1,500. Considers complexity of project, client's budget, skill and experience of artist, how work will be used, turnaround time and rights purchased when establishing payment.
Tips: "Check the going rates in the area before asking for Madison Ave. fees. Location of an agency or studio has a lot to do with determining the prices charged to a client. Don't include pieces in your portfolio that you have to make excuses for. More emphasis on creativity and less on production. The L.A. market has a strong color palette—atomic and neon colors." Looks for "innovations in materials and techniques. Airbrushed photorealism is dead. Photo illustration is very exciting. We like the concept of modifying reality by work over a real photograph with paint and other media."

THE CHESTNUT HOUSE GROUP INC., 540 N. Lakeshore Dr., Chicago IL 60611. (312)222-9090. Creative Directors: Norman Baugher and Miles Zimmerman. Clients: major educational publishers. Arrange interview.
Needs: Illustration, layout and assembly. Pays by job.

WOODY COLEMAN PRESENTS, INC., 490 Rockside Rd., Cleveland OH 44131. (216)661-4222. President: Woody Coleman. Artist's agent. Clients: ad agencies, PR firms and direct corporations.
Needs: Works with 25 freelance artists/year. Artists must have three years of experience. Especially needs photorealistic with figure and product. Uses artists for illustrations.
First Contact & Terms: Send query letter with brochure showing art style or tear sheets, slides and 4x5 transparencies. Samples not filed are returned by SASE. Reports only if interested. To show a portfolio, mail color and 4x5 transparencies. Pays for illustration by the project, $400-10,000. Considers complexity of project, client's budget, skill and experience of artist, how work will be used, turnaround time and rights purchased when establishing payment.
Tips: Artist should send "8 of their 10 best samples within their area of expertise."

COLLS DESIGN, INC., 716 Yarmouth Rd., Palos Verdes Estates CA 90274. (213)541-8433. President: William J. Colls. Specializes in annual reports, corporate identity, displays and exhibits. Clients: industry, governmental agencies and educational or health related organizations.
Needs: Works with 3 freelance artists/year. Uses artists for advertising, brochure and catalog design, illustration and layout; P-O-P displays, exhibits, mechanicals, retouching and logo design.
First Contact & Terms: Prefers artists in or near the South Bay area of Los Angeles. Works on assignment only. Send query letter with resume. Prefers Photostats and printed work as samples. Write for appointment to show portfolio. Provide resume, business card and sample copies to be kept on file for possible future assignments. Pays $50-500 average/project for design; $50-300 average/project for illustration. Pays for design by the hour, $10-30 average. Pays for illustration by the hour, $10-25 average; also negotiates. Considers client's budget, and skill and experience of artist when establishing payment.
Tips: "A successful freelance artist is usually talented, business-like, professional, dependable and knowledgeable about his or her specialty."

COMMERCIAL ARTS, LTD./MARKET DIRECT, 5929 Rockhill Rd., Kansas City MO 64110-3155. (816)523-0482. President: Lanie Bethka. Specializes in corporate identity, direct mail and publications.

Clients: real estate companies, banks, software houses, light manufacturers, engineering firms, colleges, insurance groups and medical groups.
Needs: Works with 1-5 freelance artists/year. Prefers local artists. Works on assignment only. Uses artists for illustrations, retouching, airbrushing, charts/graphs, AV materials and lettering. Prefers tight, realistic style or technical illustration; pen & ink, airbrush, acrylics, markers, computer illustration and mixed media.
First Contact & Terms: Send query letter with brochure or resume, tear sheets, Photostats, photocopies, slides and photographs. Samples are filed. Samples not filed are returned only if requested. Write to schedule an appointment to show a portfolio, which should include thumbnails, roughs, original/final art, final reproduction/product, tear sheets, Photostats, photographs, b&w and color. Pays for design by the project, $50-5,000 or more. Pays for illustration by the project, $35-1,000. Considers complexity of project, client's budget, skill and experience of artist, how work will be used and turnaround time when establishing payment. Buys all rights.
Tips: Finds most artists through portfolio reviews and samples.

***THE CONSULTANTS**, 333 Sandy Springs Circle, Atlanta GA 30328. (404)256-5839. President: Annette Joseph. "We design small specialty stores; we are a turnkey operation for design and visual merchandising. We do all construction drawings and supervisions."
Needs: Works with 3-4 freelance artists/year. Prefers local artists, must have drafting experience, do not need experience in visual merchandising. Works on assignment only. Uses freelance artists for advertising design, illustration and layout, interior design and renderings, architectural renderings, design consulting and visual merchandising.
First Contact & Terms: Send query letter with brochure showing art style or resume and sample of work for job interested in. Samples are filed. Samples not filed are returned only if requested by artist. Reports back within 2 weeks. Call or write to schedule an appointment to show a portfolio, which should include thumbnails, roughs, original/final art, final reproduction, color, renderings and drafting plans. Pays for design by the hour, $20-30. Pays for drawings by the hour, $20. Considers complexity of project, turnaround time and client's budget when establishing payment.

***CORPORATE GRAPHICS INC.**, Floor 17, 655 Third Ave., New York NY 10017. (212)599-1820. Chairman/Art Director: Bennett Robinson. Specializes in annual reports, corporate identity and publications. Clients: insurance, food products, banking, communications.
Needs: Works with many freelance artists/year. Works on assignment only. Uses artists for brochure illustration, mechanicals, charts/graphs. Portraiture and annual reports illustration is also needed for products, maps, situations, etc.
First Contact & Terms: Send resume and tear sheets. Samples are filed. Samples not filed are returned only if requested by artist. Reports back only if interested. Call to show a portfolio or to schedule an appointment. Mail tear sheets, Photostats, photographs, b&w and color. Pays mechanical artists by the hour, $15-20. Considers complexity of project, client's budget, skill and experience of artist, how work will be used and turnaround time when establishing payment.
Tips: "We want top-notch quality and sophistication of style. Mechanical artists need to know stat camera and color-key skills."

COUSINS DESIGN, 599 Broadway, New York NY 10012. (212)431-8222. Vice President: Morison Cousins. Specializes in packaging and product design. Clients: manufacturing companies.
Needs: Works with 10-12 freelance artists/year. Prefers local artists. Works on assignment only. Uses artists for design, illustrations, mechanicals, retouching, airbrushing, model making, lettering and logos. Prefers airbrush, colored pencil and markers as media.
First Contact & Terms: Send query letter with brochure or resume, tear sheets and photocopies. Samples are filed or not filed. Samples not filed are returned only if requested. Reports back within 2 weeks only if interested. Write to schedule an appointment to show a portfolio, which should include roughs, final reproduction/product and Photostats. Pays for design by the hour, $20-40. Pays for illustration by the hour, $20 minimum or a fee. Considers skill and experience of artist when establishing payment. Buys all rights.

CREATIVE COMPANY, INC., 345 Court St. NE, Salem OR 97301. (503)363-4433. President/Owner: Jennifer Morrow. Specializes in corporate identity and packaging. Clients: local consumer-oriented clients, professionals, and trade accounts on a regional and national level, all in the Salem/Valley area.
Needs: Works with 3-4 freelance artists/year. Uses artists for design, illustration, retouching, airbrushing, posters and lettering. "We are always looking for illustrators and cartoonists."
First Contact & Terms: Prefers local artists. "We also require a portfolio review. Years of experience not important if portfolio is good." Works on assignment only. Send query letter with brochure, resume, business card and samples to be kept on file. Accepts photocopies or tear sheets as samples. "We prefer

one-on-one review of portfolio to discuss individual projects/time/approach." Samples returned only if requested. Reports only if interested. Call for appointment to show portfolio. Pays for design by the hour, $20-40 average. Pays for illustration by the hour $25-40 average. Considers complexity of project, and skill and experience of artist when establishing payment.
Tips: "Don't drop in, always call and make an appointment. Have a clean and well-organized portfolio, and a resume or something to keep on file."

***CREATIVE FREELANCERS, INC.**, 62 West 45th St., New York, NY 10036. (212)398-9540. Artist representatives specializing in mechanicals and illustration.
Needs: Local artists only, except for realistic illustrators. Minimum 3 years of professional experience. Especially needs fast, accurate mechanical artists with good inking skills. Must be available days for on-premises work in New York City.
First Contact & Terms: Portfolio drop-off policy on Mondays or send resume and samples. Samples are not filed but returned if accompanied by SASE or picked up. To show a portfolio, mail appropriate materials or drop off book. "Anyone good enough will know what belongs in their book." Considers client's budget when establishing payment.

***CREATIVE IMAGES IN INC.**, 1501 Broadway, New York NY 10036. Creative Director: Marvin Berk. Specializes in corporate identity, direct mail, packaging and publications.
Needs: Works with 10-20 freelance artists/year. Prefers three years of experience. Uses freelance artists for brochure and catalog illustration, mechanicals, retouching, airbrushing, AV materials and lettering. Prefers airbrush, pen & ink and colored pencil as media.
First Contact & Terms: Send query letter with brochure showing art style or resume and samples. Samples are filed. Samples not filed are returned only if requested by artist. Reports back only if interested. To show a portfolio, mail roughs, final reproduction/product, tear sheets, b&w or color. Pays for design by the hour, $20 minimum or by the project, open. Pays for illustration by the project, $100 minimum or by the day, $200-500. Considers complexity of project, client's budget, skill and experience of artist, how work will be used and rights purchased. Rights purchased vary according to project.

CREATIVE WORKS, Suite A, 8295 N. Military Trail, Palm Beach Gardens FL 33458. (305)627-3388. Interior Designer (Drafting): Suzi Addessa. Art Director (Mechanicals): David Wright. Director of Product Design: Douglas Medema. Specializes in corporate identity, displays, interior design, packaging, signage, product and sales offices. Clients: ad agencies, public relations firms, real estate developers, manufacturers and promoters.
Needs: Works with 50 freelance artists/year. Uses local (work inhouse), experienced artists. Uses artists for design, illustration, mechanicals, airbrushing, model making and drafting. Especially needs drafting/mechanical people.
First Contact & Terms: Send query letter with resume to be kept on file. Samples not kept on file are returned by SASE only if requested. Reports within 1 week. Write to schedule an appointment to show a portfolio, which should include original/final art and photographs. Pays by the project for drafting and mechanicals. Considers complexity of project, client's budget, skill and experience of artist and turnaround time when establishing payment.
Tips: "Send resume for interest and follow by appointment."

CREEL MORRELL INC., Suite 1000, 301 Congress Ave., Austin TX 78701. (512)476-0000. Graphic Designer: Mary Conrade. Specializes in annual reports, corporate identity, displays, landscape design, interior design, technical illustrations, publications and signage.
Needs: Uses artists for illustrations, mechanicals, retouching, airbrushing, model making, copywriting and AV materials.
First Contact & Terms: Send query letter with brochure, resume, business card and whatever samples available to be kept on file. Samples not filed are returned only if requested. Reports only if interested. To show a portfolio, mail appropriate materials or call to schedule an appointment; portfolio should include final reproduction/product, color, tear sheets, Photostats, photographs or slides of work. Payment depends on each situation. Considers client's budget, skill and experience of artist, how work will be used and rights purchased when establishing payment.

CSOKA/BENATO/FLEURANT INC., 134 W. 26th St., New York NY 10001. (212)242-6777. President: Robert Fleurant. Clients: insurance, national retail chains and communications.
Needs: Uses artists for record jacket covers and sales promotion projects.
First Contact & Terms: Assigns 10-20 jobs/year. Arrange interview. Pays $15-25/hour, layout; $8-15/hour, paste-up and mechanicals; $500 maximum/job, record jacket covers. Negotiates payment by job for annual reports, catalogs, packaging, posters and P-O-P displays.
Tips: Professional presentation of work is a *must*.

***CWI INC.**, 255 Glenville Rd., Greenwich CT 06831. (203)531-0300. Contact: Geoffrey Chaite. Design studio. Specializes in packaging, annual reports, brand identity, corporate identity, point of purchase and collateral material, displays, exhibits and shows. Clients: packaged goods, foods, tools, publishing, drugs, tobacco, banks and sports.
Needs: Works with up to 10 illustrators and 2-3 designers/month. Minimum 8-10 years of experience. Uses artists for P-O-P displays, stationery design, multimedia kits, direct mail, slide sets, brochures/flyers, trade magazines, newspapers, layout, technical art, type spec, paste-up, retouching and lettering. Especially needs photography, illustration and paste-up.
First Contact & Terms: Send flyers, business card, tear sheets, b&w line drawings, roughs, previously published work, comps and mechanicals to be kept on file for future assignments. May return originals to artist at job's completion. Payment is negotiated.

***D.F.I. INC.**, 341 Linwood Ave., Buffalo NY 14209. (716)883-2095. Design Director: Jack Snyder. Specializes in displays, interior design, direct mail, packaging, publications, trade promotions and sales meetings for corporations.
Needs: Works with 10-15 freelance artists/year. Uses freelance artists for brochure design and illustration, P-O-P displays, retouching, airbrushing, AV materials, illustrations and renderings.
First Contact & Terms: Send query letter with brochure showing art style or resume and samples. Samples are filed. Reports back only if interested. Write to schedule an appointment to show a portfolio or mail thumbnails, roughs, original/final art and final reproduction/product. Pays for design by the hour, $25 minimum; by the project, $500 minimum. Pays for illustration by the hour, $25; by the project, $500. Considers complexity of project, client's budget, skill and experience of artist, turnaround time, rights purchased and quality when establishing payment. Rights purchased vary according to project.

DANMARK & MICHAELS, INC., Suite 308, 5728 Major Blvd., Orlando FL 32819. (305)351-6311. Art Directors: Mark de Stefano or Michael de Stefano. Specializes in technical illustrations. Clients: publishers of textbooks.
Needs: Works with several freeelance artists/year. Artist should have some experience in technical illustrations. Uses artists for illustrations, airbrushing, charts/graphs and maps. "We are always looking for good illustrators."
First Contact & Terms: Send query letter with resume and photocopies. Samples not filed are returned only if requested. Reports only if interested. Call or write to schedule an appointment to show a portfolio, which should include original/final art. Payment varies. Considers complexity of project, skill and experience of artist, and turnaround time when establishing payment.
Tips: "Artist must meet the deadlines required and have the ability to do the job."

***DELANY DESIGN GROUP, INC.**, 68 S. Main St., Providence RI 02903. (401)521-0096. President: George Delany. Specializes in annual reports, corporate identity, displays, fashion, packaging, publications, signage and fine art printings on canvas. Clients: furniture, human services, electronics, jewelry, real estate, health and fashion.
Needs: Works with 2-3 freelance artists/year. Prefers local artists. Works on assignment only. Prefers artists with production skills. Uses freelance artists for mechanicals, charts/graphs and AV materials. Occasionally uses freelance artists for brochure design and illustration, catalog design and illustration and book design.
First Contact & Terms: Send query letter with resume. Pays for design by the hour, $5-10. Considers complexity of project, client's budget, skill and experience of artist and turnaround time when establishing payment. Rights purchased vary according to project.
Tips: "We don't use many freelance artists. We like to keep control over quality and budget by working under our own roof."

***JOSEPH B. DEL VALLE**, Suite 1011, 41 Union Square West, New York NY 10003. Director: Joseph B. Del Valle. Specializes in annual reports, publications, book design and illustration. Clients: major publishers and museums.
Needs: Works with approximately 6 freelance artists/year. Artists must have experience and be able to work on a job to job basis. Uses artists for design, and mechanicals.
First Contact & Terms: Send query letter with resume. Reports only if interested. Call or write to schedule an appointment to show a portfolio, which should include final reproduction/product. Pays for design by the hour, $15-25. Considers client's budget and turnaround time when establishing payment.

DEMARTIN*MARONA*CRANSTOWN*DOWNES, 911 Washington St., Wilmington DE 19801. (302)654-5277. Vice President: Richard Downes. Specializes in annual reports, corporate identity, direct mail, packaging and publications. Clients: banks, radio stations and chemical companies.

Needs: Works with 3 freelance artists/year. Prefers 4-7 years of experience. Prefers mechanical artists. Uses artists for mechanicals and retouching.
First Contact & Terms: Send query letter. Samples are filed. Samples not filed are not returned. Reports back only if interested. Call to schedule an appointment to show a portfolio, which should include photographs. Pays for design by the hour and by the day. Pays for illustration by the project, amount varies. Considers skill and experience of artist when establishing payment. Buys all rights.

***DE NADOR & ASSOCIATES**, 14 Yellow Ferry Harbor, Sausalito CA 94965. (415)332-4098. Principal: Dudley De Nador. Specializes in annual reports, brand identity, corporate identity, displays, direct mail and packaging.
Needs: Works with 10 freelance artists/year. Prefers local artists (San Francisco & Marin County). Uses freelance artists for catalog illustration, P-O-P displays, mechanicals, retouching, airbrushing, direct mail packages and AV materials. Especially needs freelance artists to do paste-up and mechanicals.
First Contact & Terms: Send query letter with brochure showing art style or resume and tear sheets. Samples are filed. Samples not filed are returned only if requested by artist. Reports back only if interested. To show a portfolio, mail thumbnails, roughs, original/final art, final reproduction/product, tear sheets, b&w and color. Pays for design and illustration by the hour, $15-30. Considers complexity of project, client's budget, skill and experience of artist, how work will be used and turnaround time when establishing payment.
Tips: "Be concerned with excellence and have a positive mental attitude."

DESIGN & PRODUCTION INCORPORATED, 7110 Rainwater Pl., Lorton VA 22079. (703)550-8640. Senior Vice President: Jay F. Barnwell, Jr. Specializes in displays, interior design, signage and exhibition design. Clients: ad agencies, PR firms, architectural firms, institutions and major corporations.
Needs: Works with 10-20 freelance artists/year. Uses artists for design, illustration, brochures, catalogs, mechanicals, model making and exhibit design.
First Contact & Terms: Prefers local artists who are established professionals. Works on assignment only. Send query letter with brochure, resume and samples to be kept on file; call for appointment to show portfolio. Prefers slides or tear sheets as samples. Samples not filed are returned by SASE. Reports within 2 weeks. Pays for design by the hour, $50-200 average; by the project, $1,000-15,000 average. Pays for illustration by the hour, $25-50 average; by the project, $1,000-3,000 average. Considers complexity of project, client's budget, and skill and experience of artist when establishing payment.
Tips: "Only experienced freelancers need apply. Develop a style, a definite, recognizable trait that can be associated to you exclusively."

***DESIGN ASSOCIATES**, 10503 Nile Ct., Tampa FL 33615. (813)855-6129. President; Thom Hammond. Specializes in corporate identification, architectural delineation and product design and illustration.
Needs: Works with 5 freelance artists/year. Artists must have 3-5 years of experience in a specific area. Uses artists for the design, illustrations and layout of advertising and brochures plus product design, P-O-P displays.
First Contact & Terms: Send query letter with brochure showing art style or tear sheets, Photostats, photocopies, slides and photographs. Samples not filed are returned if accompanied by SASE. Reports back within 10-30 days. Call to schedule an appointment to show a portfolio, which should include thumbnails, roughs, original/final art, final reproduction/product, color, tear sheets, Photostats and photographs. Pays for design by the hour, $25-50. Pays for illustration by the project. Considers complexity of project, skill and experience of artist, how work will be used and turnaround time when establishing payment.
Tips: "The presentation or packaging of art has to be professional. A highly stylized artist is probably at a disadvantage because often times we need someone who can imitate a style our client is already accustomed to. The more flexible the artist the more work we can provide them."

DESIGN HORIZONS INTERNATIONAL, 520 W. Erie St., Chicago IL 60610. (312)664-0006. Creative Director: Carl Miller. Specializes in annual reports, corporate identity and publications. Clients: ad agencies, PR firms, builders/developers and travel firms.
Needs: Works with 6 freelance artists/year. Prefers artists with minimum 5 years of experience. Uses artists for illustrations, mechanicals, retouching, airbrushing and charts/graphs.
First Contact & Terms: Send query letter with brochure or resume, tear sheets, Photostats and photocopies. Samples are filed. Reports back only if interested. To show a portfolio, mail roughs, final reproduction/product, tear sheets and Photostats. Pays for design by the hour, $15-50. Considers complexity of project, client's budget and skill and experience of artist when establishing payment. Buys all rights; negotiates rights purchased.

***DESIGNMARKS CORPORATION**, 1462 W. Irving Park Rd., Chicago IL 60613-1997. (312)327-3670. President: Nathaniel Ascher Marks. Specializes in annual reports, brand identity, corporate identity, displays, direct mail, packaging, publications and signage. Clients: corporations, associations and government agencies.
Needs: Works with various freelance artists/year. Uses artists for illustrations and mechanicals.
First Contact & Terms: Send query letter with resume only. No samples. Reports only if interested. Write to schedule an appointment to show a portfolio, which should include thumbnails, roughs, original/final art, final reproduction/product, color and tear sheets. Considers complexity of project, client's budget, skill and experience of artist, how work will be used, turnaround time and rights purchased when establishing payment.

THE DESIGN OFFICE OF STEVE NEUMANN & FRIENDS, Suite 103, 3000 Richmond Ave., Houston TX 77098. (713)629-7501. Contact: Cynthia J. Whitney. Specializes in corporate identity and signage. Clients: architects, interior designers, developers, hospitals, universities, etc.
Needs: Works with 2-4 freelance artists/year. Artists must be local with "good background." Uses artists for design, illustration, retouching, model making, drafting and signage. Prefers pen & ink, colored pencil and calligraphy. Especially needs full-time and/or part-time production person.
First Contact & Terms: Send query letter with brochure, resume, references, business card and slides to be kept on file. Call for follow up after 15 days—ask for Cynthia Whitney. Pays for design by the hour, $8-12, based on job contract. Considers complexity of project, client's budget, skill and experience of artist, and how work will be used when establishing payment.

THE DESIGN QUARTER INC., 2900 4th Ave., San Diego CA 92103. (619)297-7900. Executive Vice President/Design: Brian Lovell. Specializes in annual reports, corporate identity, direct mail and publications. Clients: corporations and publishers.
Needs: Works with 6 freelance artists/year. Uses artists for catalogs, books, mechanicals, retouching, airbrushing, model making and charts/graphs. Prefers charcoal/pencil, colored pencil, watercolor, oils, pastels and computer illustration.
First Contact & Terms: Send business card to be kept on file. Prefers Photostats, photocopies and tear sheets as samples. Samples not kept on file are returned only if requested by SASE. Reports back only if interested. Call for appointment to show portfolio. Pays for design by the hour, $15-40 average; by the project. Pays for illustration by the hour, $25-50 average; by the project, $100-5,000 average. Considers complexity of project, client's budget, and skill and experience of artist when establishing payment.
Tips: "Show not only final work but also how you got to that final piece. Show tissues, comps and thumbnails."

DESIGNS FOR MEDICINE, INC., 301 Cherry St., Philadelphia PA 19106. (215)925-7100. President: Peter W. Bressler. Specializes in annual reports, corporate identity, packaging, technical illustrations, product design and graphic design. Clients: ad agencies, manufacturers and inventors.
Needs: Works with 8 freelance artists/year. "Local artists only to work in our office primarily; experience required varies." Works on assignment only. Uses artists for design, illustration, brochures, mechanicals, airbrushing, model making, lettering, logos and advertisements.
First Contact & Terms: Send query letter with brochure, resume, business card and samples to be kept on file, except for slides which will be returned to sender. Prefers slides and tear sheets as samples. Samples not filed returned. Reports within 3 weeks. Write for appointment to show portfolio. Pays for design by the hour, $5-20 average (quotation basis). Considers complexity of project, client's budget, and skill and experience of artist when establishing payment.
Tips: "Be aggressive, very talented and creative."

DESIGN TRANSLATIONS, 1 Tracy Ln., Milford OH 45150. (513)248-0629. Contact: Richard Riggs. Specializes in graphic design. Clients: technical firms, medical firms, and miscellaneous businesses.
Needs: Works with 1-2 freelance artists/year. Uses artists for mechanicals.
First Contact & Terms: "Artist must have superb craft and meticulous attention to detail; must be able to understand directions." Send query letter with resume and stats and/or slides to be kept on file. Samples not kept on file are returned by SASE only if requested. Reports back only if interested. Pays on a per job basis. Considers complexity of project, client's budget, skill and experience of artist, and turnaround time when establishing payment.

***DESIGN VECTORS, INC.**, #2, 408 Columbus Ave., San Francisco CA 94133. Contact: Tony Williams or Jim Tetzlaff. Specializes in brand identity, corporate identity, displays, direct mail, packaging, magazine design, publications and signage. Clients: public relation firms, banks, ad agencies and other corporations.
Needs: Works with 12 freelance artists/year. Local artists only. Uses artists for design, illustration, bro-

chures, magazines, mechanicals, airbrushing, charts/graphs and advertisements.
First Contact & Terms: Send query letter with brochure showing art style or resume and samples to be kept on file. "Send only resume or samples that we can keep." Reports back only if interested. Pays for design and illustration by the hour, $10 minimum. Considers complexity of project, client's budget, skill and experience of artist and turnaround time when establishing payment.

DESIGNWORKS, INC., Davis Square, 48 Grove St., Somerville, MA 02144. (617)628-8600. Design Director: Jennie R. Bush. Provides design for publishing industry. Specializes in educational publications. Clients: book publishers.
Needs: Works with 10 freelance artists/year. Prefers artists with three years of experience; local for design or paste-up. Works on assignment only. Uses artists for book illustration, charts/graphs, brochure and book design and mechanicals. Prefers styles "appropriate for educational materials." Prefers pen & ink, airbrush and colored pencil.
First Contact & Terms: Send query letter with brochure showing art style or resume tear sheets or photocopies. Samples are filed or returned by SASE if requested. Reports back only if interested. To show a portfolio, mail thumbnails, roughs, original/final art, tear sheets, Photostats or b&w or call to schedule an appointment. Pays for design by the hour, $18-25. Pays for illustration by the project, $300-5,000. Considers complexity of project, client's budget when establishing payment.

DESKEY ASSOCIATES, INC., 45 W. 36th St., New York NY 10018. Vice President Graphics Operations: Emmitt B. Sears. Specializes in brand and/or corporate identity, computer-generated art, displays, packaging, illustration and mechanical art. Clients: corporations.
Needs: Works with freelance artists for design, illustration, P-O-P displays, mechanicals, retouching, airbrushing, model making, lettering and logos.
First Contact & Terms: "Artists should present their resume, hourly wages and make a written request to present their work." Send query letter and resume to be kept on file. Prefers to see "best final samples of areas in which the artist may be of help and show some conceptual sketches or thumbnails." Samples are not returned. Write to schedule an appointment to show a portfolio. Pays for design by the hour, $10 minimum or by contract. Pays for illustration by the project, $250 minimum. Considers complexity of project, client's budget, skill and experience of artist, and turnaround time when establishing payment.
Tips: "Too often artists present work that is a finished product—one wonders what efforts or contributions were made to develop the final product."

GABRIEL DI FIORE ASSOC., 625 Stanwix St., Pittsburgh PA 15222. (412)471-0608. Owner: Gabe Di Fiore. Specializes in annual reports, corporate identity, direct mail and publication. Clients: ad agencies, PR firms and corporations.
Needs: Works with 20 freelance artists/year. Uses artists for illustrations, mechanicals, retouching, charts/graphs and lettering. Especially needs mechanicals and illustrations.
First Contact & Terms: Send query letter with brochure showing art style or resume, tear sheets and slides. Samples not filed are returned by SASE. Reports only if interested. Call or write to schedule an appointment to show a portfolio, which should include thumbnails, roughs, original/final art and tear sheets. Pays for design by the hour, $10 minimum; pays for illustration by the hour, $10 minimum. Considers complexity of project, client's budget and how work will be used when establishing payment.

DI FRANZA-WILLIAMSON INC. (a unit of Ketchum Communications, Inc.), 16 W. 22nd St., New York NY 10010. (212)463-8302. Contact: Martin Blass. Clients: businesses and advertising agencies.
Needs: Assigns 450 jobs/year; local artists with 5 years minimum of experience only. Uses artists for layout, comps, illustration, lettering and retouching for catalogs, direct mail brochures, flyers, packaging, P-O-P displays and slides.
First Contact & Terms: Send query letter with resume and request interview. No work returned. Payment for design, layout and illustration by the job; $15-20, mechanicals and paste-up; $15-22, type spec. Considers complexity of project, client's budget, skill and experience of artist, and how work will be used when establishing payment.
Tips: There is a "need for designers who can draw and put down their ideas in a presentable fashion. Show me roughs and layouts, not just finished pieces."

ANTHONY DI MARCO, DESIGN AGENCY, 2948 Grand Route St. John, New Orleans LA 70119. (504)948-3128. Creative Director: Anthony Di Marco. Specializes in brand identity, packaging, publications, and technical illustration. Clients: individuals and major corporations.
Needs: Works with 5-10 freelance artists/year. Seeks "local artists with ambition. Artists should have substantial portfolios and an understanding of business requirements." Uses artists for design, illustration, mechanicals, retouching, airbrushing, posters, model making, charts/graphs. Prefers highly pol-

ished, finished art; pen & ink, airbrush, charcoal/pencil, colored pencil, watercolor, acrylics, oils, pastels, collage and markers. Computer-generated graphics are a current interest.
First Contact & Terms: Send query letter with resume, business card and slides and tear sheets to be kept on file. Samples not kept on file are returned by SASE. Reports back within 1 week if interested. Call or write for appointment to show portfolio. Pays for design and illustration by the project, $50-500 average. Considers complexity of project, skill and experience of artist, turnaround time and rights purchased when establishing payment.
Tips: "Keep professionalism in mind at all times. Artists should put forth their best effort. Apologizing for imperfect work is a common mistake freelancers make when presenting a portfolio."

DIAMOND ART STUDIO LTD., 11 E. 36th St., New York NY 10016. (212)685-6622. Creative Directors: Gary and Douglas Diamond. Vice Presidents: John Taylor, Mary Nittolo, Phil Rowley. Art studio. Clients: advertising agencies, corporations, manufacturers and publishers. Assigns 800 jobs/year.
Needs: Employs 10 illustrators/month. Uses artists for comprehensive illustrations, cartoons, charts, graphs, illustrations, layout, lettering, logo design, paste-up, retouching, technical art and type spec. Prefers pen & ink, aribrush, colored pencil, watercolor, acrylics, pastels and markers.
First Contact & Terms: Send resume and tear sheets to be kept on file. SASE. Write for interview to show a portfolio. Pays for design by the hour. Pays for illustration by the hour and by project. Considers complexity of project, client's budget, skill and experience of artist, and turnaround time when establishing payment.
Tips: "Leave behind something memorable and well thought out."

DONATO & BERKLEY INC., 386 Park Ave. S, New York NY 10016. (212)532-3884. Contact: Sy Berkley or Steve Sherman. Advertising art studio. Specializes in direct mail response advertising, annual reports, brand identity, corporate identity and publications. Clients: ad agencies, public relations firms, direct response advertisers and publishers.
Needs: Works with 1-2 illustrators and 1-2 designers/month. Local experienced artists only. Uses artists for consumer magazines, direct mail, brochures/flyers, newspapers, layout, technical art, type spec, paste-up, lettering and retouching. Especially needs illustrations, retouching and mechanical paste-up. Prefers pen & ink, airbrush, watercolor and oils as media.
First Contact & Terms: Call for interview. Send brochure showing art style, flyers, business card, resume and tear sheet to be kept on file. No originals returned to artist at job's completion. Call to schedule an appointment to show a portfolio, which should include thumbnails, roughs, original/final art and final reproduction/product. Pays for design by the hour,$25-50. Pays for illustration by the project, $75-1,500. Considers complexity of project and client's budget when establishing payment.
Tips: "We foresee a need for direct response art directors and the mushrooming of computer graphics. Clients are much more careful as to price and quality of work."

***JAMES D. DOOLEY, DESIGN (ILLUSTRATION)**, 595 May St., N. Attleboro MA 02760. Specializes in technical illustrations and publications for industrial clients.
Needs: Works with 1 or 2 freelance artists/year. Prefers local artists with 3 plus years of experience. Works on assignment only. Uses freelance artists for mechanicals, retouching, airbrushing and inking constructions sketches. Prefers pen & ink, airbrush, colored pencil, watercolor, pastels, collage and markers.
First Contact & Terms: Send query letter with brochure showing art style or resume and Photostats and photocopies. Samples are filed. Reports back only if interested. Call to schedule an appointment to show a portfolio, which should include original/final art, final reproduction/product, b&w and color. Pays by the project. Rights purchased vary according to project.

***MARSHA DREBELBIS STUDIO**, Suite 208 S., 8150 Brookriver Dr., Dallas TX 75247. President: Marsha Drebelbis. Specializes in annual reports, corporate identity, displays and publications for corporations.
Needs: Works with 3 freelance artist/year. Works on assignment only. Local artists only with three years of experience. Uses freelance artists for mechanicals, retouching, airbrushing, model making and lettering.
First Contact & Terms: Send query letter with brochure showing art style. Samples are filed. Samples not filed are not returned. Reports back only if interested. Write to schedule an appointment to show a portfolio, which should include original/final art, tear sheets and Photostats. Pays for design and illustration by the project, $100 minimum. Considers complexity of project, client's budget, skill and experience of artist, how work will be used, turnaround time and rights purchased when establishing payment.

EDITING, DESIGN & PRODUCTION, INC., 4th Floor, 400 Market St., Philadelphia PA 19106. (215)592-1133. Production Manager: Jacqui Brownstein. Specializes in publications. Clients: publishers.
Needs: Works with approximately 18 freelance artists/year. Uses artists for design, illustrations, books and mechanicals. Especially needs designers of college textbook interior and/or covers. Prefers pen & ink and computer illustration.
First Contact & Terms: Send query letter with brochure showing art style or resume, tear sheets and photocopies. Samples not filed are returned only if requested. Reports within 2 weeks. Call to schedule an appointment to show a portfolio, which should include roughs, final reproduction/product, tear sheets and Photostats. Pays for design by the project, $250-600. Pays for illustration by the project, $10-30/piece. Considers complexity of project and client's budget when establishing payment.
Tips: "Our textbooks can be very complex and we require typed specifications and tissue layouts for every element in the book. We find we need a larger number of designers because we need the diversity to please various publishers. Some designers use the same elements in their design all the time and the publishers want each book to look different and unique." In presenting samples or portfolios, include art/designs that pertain to books (medical, computer, college textbooks). "I do not want to see paintings, landscapes, portraits, brochures, logos, and in general things you'd never see in connection with textbooks."

EHN GRAPHICS, INC., 244 E. 46th St., New York NY 10017. (212)661-5947. President: Jack Ehn. Specializes in annual reports, book design, corporate identity, direct mail, publications and signage.
Needs: Works with 10-12 freelance artists/year. Uses artists for illustrations, books, mechanicals, retouching and direct mail packages.
First Contact & Terms: Send query letter with samples. Samples not filed are returned only if requested. Reports only if interested. Call or write to schedule an appointment to show a portfolio, which should include original/final art and final reproduction/product. Considers complexity of project, client's budget, and skill and experience of artist when establishing payment.

DAVE ELLIES INDUSTRIAL DESIGN, INC., 2015 W. Fifth Ave., Columbus OH 43212. (614)488-7995. Project Director: John Ayotte. Specializes in corporate identity, displays, interior design, packaging and signage.
Needs: Works with 10 freelance artists/year. Prefers regional freelance artists with 3-5 years of experience. Works on assignment only. Uses artists for design, illustration, mechanicals, model making, AV materials and logos.
First Contact & Terms: Send query letter with resume, business card and slides to be kept on file. Samples not kept on file returned by SASE. Reports within 2 weeks. Call or write for appointment to show portfolio. Considers complexity of project, client's budget, skill and experience of artist and turnaround time when establishing payment.
Tips: Especially looks for "quality not quantity, professionalism, variety and effective problem solving" in samples.

***EMERSON, WAJDOWICZ STUDIOS, INC.**, 1123 Broadway, New York NY 10010. (212)807-8144. Creative Director: Jurek Wajdowicz. Specializes in annual reports, corporate identity and publications for corporations and publishing companies.
Needs: Works with 10-15 freelance artists/year. Works on assignment only. Uses freelance artists for mechanicals, airbrushing and AV materials.
First Contact & Terms: Send query letter with brochure showing art style or resume and samples. Samples are filed. Samples not filed are not returned. To show a portfolio, mail original/final art, final reproduction/product and tear sheets. Considers complexity of project, client's budget, skill and experience of artist, how work will be used, turnaround time and rights purchased when establishing payment.

***RAY ENGLE & ASSOCIATES**, 626 S. Kenmore, Los Angeles CA 90005. (213)381-5001. President: Ray Engle. Specializes in annual reports, corporate identity, displays, interior design, direct mail, packaging, publications and signage. Clients: ad agencies, PR firms and direct clients.
Needs: Works with 6 freelance artists/year. Prefers local artists; top quality only. Uses freelance artists for brochure and catalog design and illustration, book and magazine design, P-O-P displays, mechanicals, retouching, airbrushing, posters, model making, charts/graphs, lettering and logos. Prefers pen & ink, airbrush, colored pencil, markers and calligraphy.
First Contact & Terms: Send query letter with brochure showing art style or resume and tear sheets, Photostats, photocopies, slides or photographs. Samples are filed. Samples not filed are return if accompanied by a SASE. Reports back only if interested. Call to schedule an appointment to show a portfolio. Mail thumbnails, roughs, original/final art, final reproduction/product, tear sheets, Photostats, photographs, b&w and color. Pays for design by the hour, $25-50; by the project, $100 minimum; by the

day, $200-400. Pays for illustration by the project, $75 minimum. Considers complexity of project, client's budget, how work will be used, turnaround time and rights purchased when establishing payment. Rights purchased vary according to project.
Tips: "Think of how you can be of service to us—not how we can be of service to you."

MEL ERIKSON/ART SERVICES, 31 Meadow Rd., Kings Park NY 11754-3812. (516)544-9191. Art Director: Toniann Dillon. Specializes in publications and technical illustration. Clients: book publishers.
Needs: Works with 8-10 freelance artists/year. Local artists only. Uses artists for advertising illustration, book design and illustration, mechanicals, retouching and charts/graphs.
First Contact & Terms: Send query letter with resume and photocopies to be kept on file. Samples not kept on file are not returned. Does not report back. Call to schedule an appointment to show a portfolio, which should include final reproduction/product. Pays for design by the hour, $4.50-20; by the project, $50-1,000; by the day, $40-100. Pays for illustration by the hour, $4.50-$9; by the project, $25-$100; by the day, $40-80. Considers complexity of project and client's budget when establishing payment.
Tips: "Call first—show only work relative to my needs."

ETC GRAPHICS, INC., (formerly ETC Communications Group), Box 7046, New York NY 10128. (212)645-6800. President: King F. Lai. Specializes in marketing-oriented corporate communications materials. Clients: Fortune 500 corporations, ad agencies, PR firms, magazine publishers, small- and medium-size companies.
Needs: Works with 17 freelance artists/year. Minimum 2-3 years of experience. Works on assignment only. Uses artists for design, illustration, mechanicals, retouching, airbrushing and comp rendering.
First Contact & Terms: Send query letter with resume, brochure, business card and tear sheets or photocopies to be kept on file. Write for appointment to show portfolio. Pays for design by the hour, $10-30; for illustration by the hour, $10-30, or by the project. Considers complexity of project, client's budget, skill and experience of artist, how work will be used, turnaround time and rights purchased when establishing payment.

FINN STUDIO LIMITED, 154 E. 64th St., New York NY 10021. (212)838-1212. Creative Director: Finn. Clients: theatres, boutiques, magazines, fashion and ad agencies.
Needs: Uses artists for T-shirt designs, illustrations, calligraphy; creative concepts in art for fashion and promotional T-shirts.
First Contact & Terms: Mail slides. SASE. Reports within 4 weeks. Pays $50-500; sometimes also offers royalty.

***FITZPATRICK DESIGN GROUP**, 1111 Lexington Ave., New York NY 10021. (212)535-9707. Vice President: Robert Herbert. Retail planning and design firm.
Needs: Works with 10 freelance artists/year. Prefers experienced freelancers with references. Works on assignment only. Uses freeelance artists for interior design and renderings and design consulting.
First Contact & Terms: Send query letter with brochure showing art style or resume. Samples are filed. Samples not filed are returned by a SASE only if requested. "We usually ask the artist to call after we have had time to review the material." Write to schedule an appointment to show a portfolio, which should include photographs and whatever materials the artist thinks is pertinent. Negotiates payment. Considers complexity of project, skill and experience of artist, turnaround time and client's budget when establishing payment.
Tips: "Never call 'out of the blue'. Never show up without an appointment."

5 PENGUINS DESIGN, INC., 1648 W. Glenoaks Blvd., Glendale CA 91201. (818)502-1556. President: Dauri Pallas. Specializes in corporate identity and packaging. Clients: advertising for the motion picture industry, television and home video.
Needs: Works with varying number of freelance artists/year. Uses artists for design, mechanicals and production.
First Contact & Terms: Artists should be "very experienced and professional." Send query letter with resume, business card, tear sheets, photocopies, etc. to be kept on file. Samples not kept on file are not returned. Reports back only if interested. Pays for design by the hour at varying rates. Considers skill and experience of artist when establishing payment.

HANS FLINK DESIGN INC., 7-11 S. Broadway, White Plains NY 10601. (914)328-0888. President: Hans D. Flink. Specializes in brand identity, corporate identity, packaging and signage. Clients: corporate, packaged products.
Needs: Works with 10-20 freelance artists/year. Uses artists for design, illustration, P-0-P displays, mechanicals, retouching, airbrushing, model making, lettering, logos and package-related services.

First Contact & Terms: Send query letter with brochure and resume to be kept on file. Reports back only if interested. Call or write for appointment to show portfolio. Pays for design by the hour, $10-35 average; by the project, $500-3,000 average; by the day, $100-250 average. Pays for illustration by the project, $250-2,000 average. Considers complexity of project, client's budget, skill and experience of artist, how work will be used when establishing payment.

FREE LANCE EXCHANGE, INC., 111 E. 85th St., New York NY 10028. (212)722-5816. Multi-service company.
Needs: Uses artists for cartoons, charts, graphs, illustrations, layout, lettering, logo design and mechanicals.
First Contact & Terms: Mail resume and photocopied samples that need not be returned. "Say you saw the listing in *Artist's Market*." Provide materials to be kept on file for future assignments. No originals returned to artist at job's completion.

***HELENA FROST ASSOCIATES, LTD.**, 117 E. 24th St., New York NY 10010. (212)475-6642. President: Helena R. Frost. Estab. 1986. Specializes in packaging, publications and textbooks "at all levels in all disciplines." Clients: publishers.
Needs: Works with over 100 freelance artists/year. Works on assignment only. Prefers realistic style. Uses artists for book design, mechanicals and charts/graphs.
First Contact & Terms: Send query letter with brochure. Samples are filed. Samples not filed are returned only if requested by artist. Does not report back. Write to schedule an appointment to show a portfolio, which should include roughs, final reproduction/product and tear sheets. Pays for design and illustration by the project. Considers client's budget, turnaround time and rights purchased when establishing payment. Buys one-time rights.

STEPHANIE FURNISS DESIGN, 1327 Via Sessi, San Rafael CA 94901. (415)459-4730. Contact: Stephanie Furniss. Specializes in corporate identity, architectural and environmental graphics, supergraphics, interior design, packaging, sculpture and signage.
Needs: Works with 5 freelance artists/year. Uses artists for lettering and production work. Prefers pen & ink.
First Contact & Terms: Send query letter with resume and business card. Call or write to schedule an appointment to show a portfolio. Pays for illustration by the hour, $8-25. Considers complexity of project, skill and experience of artist, and turnaround time when establishing payment.

GAILEN ASSOCIATES, INC., Suite 105, 800 Oak St., Winnetka IL 60093. (312)446-5003. President: Bob Gailen. Specializes in annual reports, brand identity, corporate identity, packaging, publications and signage. Clients: corporations, ad agencies, marketing firms.
Needs: Works with 5 freelance artists/year. Works on assignment basis. Uses artists for illustration, photography, airbrushing and model making.
First Contact & Terms: Send query letter with resume and samples to be kept on file. Does not report back. Pays for design by the hour, $25 minimum; for illustration, per illustrator's quote. Considers complexity of project, client's budget, and skill and experience of artist when establishing payment.

***STEVE GALIT ASSOCIATES, INC.**, 5105 Monroe Rd., Charlotte NC 28205. (704)537-4071. President: Stephen L. Galit. Specializes in annual reports, corporate identity, direct mail, publications, and technical illustrations. Clients: ad agencies and corporate.
Needs: Works with 15 freelance artists/year. Looks for "expertise, talent and capability." Uses freelance artists for brochure and catalog illustration, retouching, airbrushing, model making, charts/graphs and lettering.
First Contact & Terms: Send query letter with brochure showing art style or tear sheets, Photostats, photocopies, slides or photographs. Samples are filed. Samples not filed are returned if accompanied by a SASE. Reports back only if interested. Call or write to schedule an appointment to show a portfolio. Negotiates payment. Considers client's budget, skill and experience of artist and how work will be used. Rights purchased vary according to project.

GEMINI II ADVERTISING AND GRAPHICS, INC., 8580 Production Ave., San Diego CA 92121. (619)695-6955. Vice President: Barbara A. Brewer. Specializes in high-tech and business-to-business advertising. Clients: business and high-tech.
Needs: Works with 4 freelance artists/year. Prefers illustrators, designers and layout artists. Works on assignment only. Uses artists for design, illustrations, brochures, catalogs, magazines, P-O-P displays, mechanicals, retouching, airbrushing, direct mail packages and advertisements.
First Contact & Terms: Send query letter with resume and photocopies. Samples are filed. Reports back only if interested. "We will call to schedule an appointment to show a portfolio." Pays for design

and illustration by the project, $200-5,000. Considers complexity of project, turnaround time and rights purchased when establishing payment. Buys all rights.
Tips: Artists "must have experience with agency work. No freelancer considered without having three years or more agency experience inhouse."

***GIOVANNI DESIGN ASSOCIATES**, 137 E. 36th St., New York NY 10016. (212)725-8536. Contact: John E. Frontino. Specializes in packaging. Clients: industry and fragrance/cosmetic firms.
Needs: Works on assignment only. Uses artists for advertising, brochure and catalog design, illustration and layout; P-O-P displays, mechanicals; poster, book and direct mail package design and illustration; AV presentations, lettering and logo design "as needed."
First Contact & Terms: Send brochure/flyer, slides, resume, business card and tear sheets to be kept on file. Samples not kept on file are returned by SASE. Reports "as soon as possible." Submit portfolio for review. Negotiates payment method and payment.

ERIC GLUCKMAN COMMUNICATIONS, INC., 60 E. 42nd St., New York NY 10165. (212)697-3670. President: Eric Gluckman. Specializes in corporate identity, direct mail, publications, industrial advertising and promotion, corporate capability brochures and sales promotion (trade). "We usually deal directly with client."
Needs: Works with 20 freelance artists/year. Artists should have 3 years of experience minimum. "All rights to art and photography revert to client." Works on assignment only. Uses artists for design, illustration, brochures, mechanicals, retouching, airbrushing, direct mail packages, posters, charts/graphs, lettering, computer generated art, logos and advertisements. Prefers pen & ink and acrylics.
First Contact & Terms: Send query letter with resume and samples to be kept on file. No slides as samples. Samples not kept on file returned by SASE. Reports only if interested. Call or write for appointment to show portfolio. Pays for design by the hour, $20-50; by the project, $250-5,000. Pays for illustration by the project, $50-3,500. Considers complexity of project, client's budget, skill and experience of artist, and turnaround time when establishing payment. Buys all rights.
Tips: "Be professional, make deadlines."

GOLDSMITH YAMASAKI SPECHT INC, Suite 510, 900 N. Franklin, Chicago IL 60610. (312)266-8404. Industrial design consultancy. President: Paul B. Specht. Specializes in corporate identity, packaging, product design and graphics. Clients: industrial firms, institutions, service organizations, ad agencies, government agencies, etc.
Needs: Works with 6-10 freelance artists/year. "We generally use local artists, simply for convenience." Works on assignment only. Uses artists for design (especially graphics), illustration, retouching, model making, lettering and production art. Prefers collage and marks.
First Contact & Terms: Send query letter with resume and samples to be kept on file. Samples not kept on file are returned only if requested. Reports only if interested. Call or write to schedule an appointment to show a portfolio, which should include roughs and final reproduction/product. Pays for design by the hour, $20 minimum. Pays for illustration by the project, payment depends on project. Considers complexity of project, client's budget, skill and experience of artist, how work will be used, turnaround time and rights purchased when establishing payment.
Tips: "If we receive many inquiries, obviously our time commitment may necessarily be short. Please understand. We use very little outside help, but it is increasing (mostly graphic design and production art)."

ALAN GORELICK DESIGN, INC., Marketing Communications, One High St., Morristown NJ 07960-6807. President/Creative Director: Alan Gorelick. Specializes in corporate identity, displays, direct mail, signage, technical illustration and company and product literature. Clients: health care and pharmaceutical corporations, industrial, manufacturing.
Needs: Works with 6-10 freelance artists/year. Works with "seasoned professional or extremely talented entry-level" artists only. Uses artists for design, illustration, brochures, mechanicals, retouching, airbrushing, posters, direct mail packages, charts/graphs, logos and advertisements.
First Contact & Terms: Send query letter with brochure, resume, business card, Photostats, slides, photocopies and tear sheets to be kept on file. Samples not filed are returned by SASE only if requested. Reports only if interested. Write for appointment to show portfolio, which should include thumbnails, roughs, original/final art, final reproduction/product, color, tear sheets, Photostats, photographs and b&w. Pays for design by the hour, $20-50. Pays for illustration by the hour, $15-50; by the project, $250-5,000. Considers complexity of project, client's budget, and skill and experience of artist when establishing payment.
Tips: Requires "straight talk, professional work ethic and commitment to assignment."

GRAPHIC DESIGN INC., 23844 Sherwood, Center Line MI 48015. (313)758-0480. General Manager: Norah Heppard.
Needs: Works on assignment only. Uses artists for brochure design, catalog design, illustration and layout, direct mail packages, advertising design and illustration and posters.
First Contact & Terms: Send query letter with resume and photocopies. Samples are filed. Samples not filed are returned only if requested. Reports back within 1 week. Write to schedule an appointment to show a portfolio or mail thumbnails, roughs, original/final art, final reproduction/product, color, b&w, tear sheets, Photostats and photographs. Pays by the project, $50-2,000. Considers complexity of project, available budget, turnaround time and rights purchased when establishing payment. Buys all rights.
Tips: Artists must have the "ability to make deadlines and keep promises."

GRAPHIC GROUP, 203 Mamaroneck Ave., White Plains NY 10601. (914)948-3151. Studio Manager: Leslie Matteson. Specializes in annual reports and corporate identity. Clients: Fortune 500.
Needs: Works with 10 freelance artists/year. Uses artists for design, illustrations, brochures, catalogs, books, magazines, newspapers, P-O-P displays, mechanicals, posters, direct mail packages, charts/graphs, AV materials and logos.
First Contact & Terms: Send query letter with resume and slides. Samples are filed. Reports back only if interested. Write to schedule an appointment to show a portfolio, which should include roughs, Photostats and b&w. Pays for design and illustration by the hour, $15-20. Considers client's budget and turnaround time when establishing payment. Buys first rights.

***THE GRAPHIC SUITE**, 235 Shady Ave., Pittsburgh PA 15206. (412)661-6699. Creative Director: Ronnie Savion. Specializes in annual reports, corporate identity, direct mail, fashion and publications. Clients: corporate, healthcare, retail, industry.
Needs: Works with 20 freelance artists/year. Works on assignment only. Uses freelance artists for brochure and catalog illustration, mechanicals, retouching, airbrushing, posters and lettering. Prefers pen & ink, airbrush, colored pencil and watercolor.
First Contact & Terms: Send query letter with brochure showing art style. Samples are filed. Samples not filed are returned if accompanied by a SASE. Reports back within 3 weeks. Call to schedule an appointment to show a portfolio which should include original/final art, final reproduction/product, b&w and color. Pays for illustration by the hour, $30. Considers complexity of project, client's budget and how work will be used when establishing payment. Buys all rights or rights purchased vary according to project.

***GRAPHICUS ART STUDIO**, 2025 Maryland Ave., Baltimore MD 21218. (301)727-5553. Art Director: Charles Piccirilli. Specializes in annual reports, advertising campaigns, brand and corporate identity, displays, packaging, publications and signage. Clients: recreational sport industries, fleet leasing companies, technical product manufacturers, commercial packaging corporations, direct mail advertising firms, realty companies and software companies.
Needs: Works on assignment only. Uses artist for advertising, brochure, catalog and poster illustration, retouching and AV presentations. Especially needs high quality illustration.
First Contact & Terms: Send query letter with resume, photocopies and photographs; prefers originals as samples. Samples returned by SASE. Reports on whether to expect possible future assignments. To show a portfolio, mail appropriate material or call to schedule an appointment; portfolio should include original/final art. Pays by the project.
Tips: Artists should have "versatility."

GRIMALDI DESIGN INC., Box 864, Murray Hill Station, New York NY 10016. (212)532-3773. Assistants to Director: James Moksette, Andrew Thornley. President: Joseph Grimaldi. Specializes in displays, interior design, packaging and signage.
Needs: Works with 6-8 freelance artists/year. Uses artists for illustration, mechanicals and model making.
First Contact & Terms: Prefers 3 years of experience. Works on assignment only. Send resume and samples to be kept on file. Prefers slides as samples. Samples not kept on file returned. Reports within 2 weeks. Write for appointment to show portfolio. Pays for design by the hour, $10 maximum. Illustration rates on request. Considers complexity of project and client's budget when establishing payment.

GROUP FOUR DESIGN, 147 Simsbury Rd., Avon CT 06001-0717. (203)678-1570. Production Manager: Stephen Licare. Specializes in corporate communications, product design and packaging design. Clients: corporations dealing in consumer products and office products.
Needs: Works with 5-10 freelance artists/year. Artists must have at least two years of experience. Uses artists for illustrations, mechanicals, airbrushing and model making.
First Contact & Terms: Send query letter with resume and slides. Samples not filed are returned. Re-

ports only if interested. To show a portfolio, mail roughs and original/final art. Pays for design by the hour, $12-20. Considers client's budget, and skill and experience of artist when establishing payment.
Tips: "We look for creativity in all artists seeking employment and expect to see that in their resume and portfolio."

HALL DESIGN, 707 California St., Mountain View CA 94041. (415)969-4255. President: Jack Hall. Specializes in brand identity, corporate identity, displays, interior design and packaging. Clients: corporations such as Motorola, Fujitsu and Scott Paper.
Needs: Works with 4 freelance artists/year. Prefers artists with 5 or more years of experience, local only. Works on assignment only. Prefers abstract graphic design, typography-based designs. Uses artists for design, P-O-P displays, mechanicals, model making, direct mail packages, AV materials and logos.
First Contact & Terms: Send resume and slides. Samples are filed. Samples not filed are returned. Reports back only if interested. To show a portfolio, mail original/final art and color. Pays for design by the project, $200-5,000. Considers complexity of project, client's budget, skill and experience of artist, how work will be used, turnaround time and rights purchased when establishing payment. Buys all rights.
Tips: "Be patient. The right job may not come along right away."

PAIGE HARDY & ASSOCIATES, 1731 Kettner Blvd., San Diego CA 92101. (619)233-7238. Contact: Paige Hardy or Lorie Kennedy. Specializes in corporate identity, publications, technical illustration and advertising art. Clients: retail firms and publications.
Needs: Works with 25 freelance artists/year. Usually works on assignment only. Uses artists for advertising, brochure and catalog design, illustration and layout; mechanicals, retouching and logo design. Especially needs production artist/paste-up with heavy experience.
First Contact & Terms: Send query letter with resume. Samples not returned. Reports in 1 week. Call or write for appointment to submit portfolio for review. Pays by the hour and project; negotiates payment.

HARPER & ASSOCIATES, INC., 2285 116th Ave. NE, Bellevue WA 98004. (206)462-0405. Creative Director: Randi Harper. Office Manager: Kelley Wood. Specializes in brand and corporate identity. Clients: high-tech, manufacturers, professional services, (i.e., architects, doctors, attorneys, yacht brokers, stockbrokers, etc.), food, fashion, etc.
Needs: Works with 10-12 freelance artists/year. Works on assignment only. Uses artists for illustration and airbrush.
First Contact & Terms: Send resume and slides. Samples returned by SASE. Reports only if interested. Pays for design by the hour, $8-20; for illustration by the hour, $10-30, or by the project. Considers complexity of project, client's budget, skill and experience of artist, how work will be used, turnaround time and rights purchased when establishing payment.
Tips: "Be honest about your abilities and do not be afraid to turn down an assignment if it is not appropriate for you."

***HARRINGTON-JACKSON, INC.**, 10 Newbury St., Boston MA 02116. (617)536-6164. Specializes in collateral materials—brochures, flyers, posters and other sales/promotional pieces. Clients: manufacturers and trade (industrial).
Needs: Works with 3-4 freelance artists/year. Local artists only with 2-3 years of experience. Works on assignment only. Uses artists for illustration, brochures, mechancials, retouching and airbrushing. "We especially need experienced (2-3 years) mechanical artists who can work in our studio."
First Contact & Terms: Send query letter with resume to be kept on file for 6 months. Reports only if interested. Call for appointment to show portfolio. Pays for illustration by the hour, $6-10; for mechanical art, $6-10. Considers skill and experience of artist when establishing payment.
Tips: "Call 2-3 hours in advance to make sure someone is available to review portfolio."

HILLMAN ADVANCED DESIGN STUDIO, 1021 Pearl, Boulder CO 80302. (303)443-6099. President: Jack L. Hillman. Specializes in corporate identity, displays, industrial design and packaging. Clients: manufacturers.

> ***"In a sample package, I must see some photocopies. A query letter alone with no indication of style is useless."***
>
> ***—Yvette Cohen, Plum Graphics***
> ***New York City***

Needs: Works with 12 freelance artists/year. Prefers local and experienced artists. Works on assignment only. Uses artists for design, brochures, mechanicals, posters, model making, charts/graphs, AV materials, lettering and logos. Especially needs "an experienced, well-rounded industrial designer."
First Contact & Terms: Send query letter with brochure, resume, business card and samples to be kept on file. Samples "originally should be any medium appropriate to the subject. In person I like to see originals or the finished piece." Samples not filed are returned by SASE only if requested. Reports within 1 week. Pay varies. Considers client's budget and skill and experience of artist when establishing payment.
Tips: "Only the best are considered: ability to meet schedules, professionalism, neatness; organization."

DAVID HIRSCH DESIGN GROUP, INC., Suite 622, 205 W. Wacker Dr., Chicago IL 60606. (312)329-1500. President: David Hirsch. Specializes in annual reports, corporate identity, publications and promotional literature. Clients: PR, real estate, financial and industrial firms.
Needs: Works with over 30 freelance artists/year. Uses artists for design, illustrations, brochures, retouching, airbrushing, AV materials, lettering, logos and photography.
First Contact & Terms: Send query letter with promotional materials showing art style or samples. Samples not filed are returned by SASE. Reports only if interested. Call to schedule an appointment to show a portfolio, which should include roughs, final reproduction/product, tear sheets and photographs. Considers complexity of project, client's budget and how work will be used when establishing payment.
Tips: "We're always looking for talent at fair prices."

GRANT HOEKSTRA GRAPHICS, INC., 333 N. Michigan Ave., Chicago IL 60601. (312)641-6940. President: Grant Hoekstra. Specializes in publications. Clients: publishers, ad agencies and corporations.
Needs: Works with 15 freelance artists/year. Local artists with experience only. Works on assignment only. Uses artists for design, illustration, brochures, retouching and lettering. Especially needs "illustrator who understands 'fundamental Christian' market."
First Contact & Terms: Send samples and prices to be kept on file. Call for appointment to show portfolio. Prefers photocopies as samples. Pays for design by the hour, $35-75. Pays for illustration by the project, $25-1,000. Considers complexity of project, client's budget and how work will be used when establishing payment.

THE HOLM GROUP, 3rd Floor, 405 Sansome, San Francisco CA 94111. (415)397-7272. Specializes in corporate identity and collateral. Clients: corporations.
Needs: Works with 5-10 freelance artists/year. Uses artists for illustration, mechanicals, retouching, airbrushing, lettering and logos.
First Contact & Terms: "Artist must send 'leave behind' first; then, we may call at a later date to see portfolio." Send query letter with leave behind and/or resume to be kept on file (except for bulky items or items requested returned). "Photocopies of samples are fine if they demonstrate the quality of work." Samples not kept on file are returned by SASE. Reports only if interested for a specific project (may be much later). Pays for illustration by the project, $350-1,000 average. Pays $15-20 in production. Considers complexity of project, client's budget and turnaround time when establishing payment.
Tips: "Put together an eye-catching resume to leave behind."

***MEL HOLZSAGER/ASSOCIATES, INC.**, 275 Seventh Ave., New York NY 10001. (212)741-7373. President/Art Director: Mel Holzsager. Specializes in corporate identity, packaging and general graphic design. Clients: publishers and manufacturers.
Needs: Works with occasional freelance artists according to the work load. Prefers local artists. Uses artists for advertising and brochure illustration, mechanicals and retouching.
First Contact & Terms: Send brochure showing art style to be kept on file. Samples returned if requested. Call or write to schedule an appointment to show a portfolio, which should include thumbnails, roughs and original/final art. Negotiates payment.
Tips: A mistake artists make is "trying to be too versatile. Specialization would be an advantage."

FRANK HOSICK DESIGN, Box H, Vashon Island WA 98070. (206)463-5454. Contact: Frank Hosick. Specializes in brand identity, corporate identity, packaging, product design and model building. Clients: manufacturers.
Needs: Works on assignment only. Uses artists for illustration, mechanicals, retouching, airbrushing and model making.
First Contact & Terms: Send query letter with brochure, resume, business card and samples to be kept on file. Samples not kept on file are returned only if requested. Reports only if interested. Call for appointment to show portfolio. Pays for design by the hour, $15-50 average; by the project, $100 mini-

mum; or by the day, $75-350 average. Pays for illustration by the hour, $15-50 average; by the project, $100-1,500 average; or by the day, $75-350 average. Considers complexity of project, client's budget, skill and experience of artist, and how work will be used when establishing payment.
Tips: Especially looks for "creativity, craftsmanship and quality of presentation" when reviewing a portfolio. Changes in the field include "big influence by computers, both in concept work and execution. Computer knowledge is helpful."

THE HOYT GROUP, INC., Box 686, Franklin Lakes NJ 07417-0688. (201)337-9002. President: Earl Hoyt. Specializes in corporate identity and packaging, and develops package structures. Clients: Fortune 500 firms.
Needs: Works with 10-15 freelance artists/year. Seeks experienced professionals. Works on assignment only. Uses artists for design, mechanicals, airbrushing, model making, lettering and logos.
First Contact & Terms: Send brochure to be kept on file. Send reproductions only as samples—no original art. Reports only if interested. Write for appointment to show portfolio. Pays for design by the project, $350-2,000. Pays for illustration by the project, $200-1,500. Considers client's budget, and skill and experience of artist when establishing payment.
Tips: Looks for "artistic flair." The most common mistake freelancers make in presenting samples or portfolios is "showing old, old work, plus everything they have ever done."

HUSTON AND BECK DESIGNERS, INC., 102 Lake St., Burlington VT 05402-1034. (802)864-5928. Principal: B. Huston. Specializes in displays, interior design, packaging, publications and signage. Clients: manufacturers, communication departments, museums and corporations.
Needs: Works with 24-50 freelance artists/year. Works on assignment only. Uses artists for design, illustrations, books, P-O-P displays, mechanicals, model making, charts/graphs and AV materials.
First Contact & Terms: Send query letter with resume. Samples not filed are returned only if requested. Reports only if interested. Call to show a portfolio, which should include thumbnails, roughs and photographs. Pays for design by the hour, $9-15. Pays for illustration by the hour, $25-75. Considers complexity of project, client's budget, skill and experience of artist, and turnaround time when establishing payment.

IDENTITA INCORPORATED, Suite 515, 1000 N. Ashley Dr., Tampa FL 33602. (813)221-3326. Interior and graphic design firm providing consultative services to health care facilities. Clients: institutional, hospitals, courthouses and parking garages.
Needs: Works with 3 freelance artists/year. Works on assignment only. Uses artists for architectural renderings, interior and graphic design and signage.
First Contact & Terms: Send query letter. Samples returned. Reports within 2 weeks. Payment varies according to job.

IDENTITY CENTER, Suite Q, 1340 Remington Rd, Schaumburg IL 60173. President: Wayne Kosterman. Specializes in brand identity, corporate identity, print communications and signage. Clients: corporations, hospitals and banks.
Needs: Works with 6-10 freelance artists/year. Prefers 3-5 years of experience minimum. Uses artists for illustration, mechanicals, retouching and lettering.
First Contact & Terms: Send resume and photocopies. Samples are filed. Samples not filed are returned. Reports back within 1 week. To show a portfolio, mail original/final art, Photostats and photographs. Pays for design by the hour, $15-20. Pays for illustration by the hour, $10-25. Considers client's budget, skill and experience of artist and how work will be used when establishing payment. Buys one-time rights; rights purchased vary according to project.
Tips: "Not interested in amateurs or 'part-timers'."

***IMAGE INK STUDIO, INC.**, 12708 Northup Way, Bellevue WA 98005. (206)885-7696. Creative Director: Dennis Richter. Specializes in annual reports, corporate identity and packaging for manufacturers.
Needs: Works with 2 freelance artists/year. Uses freelance artists for brochure and catalog illustration, mechanicals, retouching and airbrushing. Prefers pen & ink and airbrush.
First Contact & Terms: Send query letter with brochure showing art style or tear sheets. Samples are filed. Reports back only if interested. Call or write to schedule an appointment to show a portfolio, which should include tear sheets. Pays for illustration by the project, $50 minimum. Considers complexity of project, client's budget, skill and experience of artist and how work will be used when establishing payment. Buys one-time rights or all rights.

IMAGES, 1835 Hampden Ct., Louisville KY 40205. (502)459-0804. Creative Director: Julius Friedman. Specializes in annual reports, corporate identity, poster design and publications. Clients: corporate.

Needs: Works with approximately 100 freelance artists/year. Prefers experienced artists only. Uses artists for advertising illustration and layout, brochure and catalog design and illustration, brochure layout, mechanicals, retouching, poster design, book design and illustration, charts/graphs, lettering and logo design.
First Contact & Terms: Send brochure/flyer or resume and business card as samples to be kept on file. Samples not filed returned by SASE. Works on assignment only; reports whether to expect possible future assignments. Pays by the project for design and illustration.

INDIANA DESIGN CONSORTIUM, INC., Box 180, 300 River City Market Bldg., Lafayette IN 47902. (317)423-5469. Senior Art Director: Bryce Culverhouse. Specializes in corporate identity, displays, direct mail, publications, signage, technical illustrations, advertising and marketing communications. Clients: industrial, agricultural and medical.
Needs: Works with 10-20 freelance artists/year. Prefers very experienced illustrators. Uses artists for illustrations, mechanicals, retouching, airbrushing, model making and lettering.
First Contact & Terms: Send brochure. Samples are filed. Samples not filed are returned by SASE. Reports back only if interested. Call or write to schedule an appointment to show a portfolio, which should include roughs, original/final art, final reproduction/product, photographs, b&w and color. Pays for design and illustration by the project. Considers complexity of project, client's budget, skill and experience of artist and turnaround time when establishing payment. Negotiates rights purchased.

INNOVATIVE DESIGN & GRAPHICS, Suite 214, 1234 Sherman Ave., Evanston IL 60202-1343. (312)475-7772. Contact: Tim Sonder and Maret Thorpe. Specializes in publications. Clients: magazine publishers, corporate communication departments, associations.
Needs: Works with 3-15 freelance artists/year. Local artists only. Uses artists for illustration and airbrushing.
First Contact & Terms: Send query letter with brochure showing art style or resume, tear sheets, Photostats, slides and photographs. Reports only if interested. Write to schedule an appointment to show a portfolio, which should include original/final art, final reproduction/product, tear sheets and Photostats. Pays for illustration by the project, $100-700 average. Considers complexity of project, client's budget and turnaround time when establishing payment.
Tips: "Interested in meeting new illustrators, but have a tight schedule. Looking for people who can grasp complex ideas and turn them into high-quality illustrations. Ability to draw people well is a must."

JMH CORPORATION, 921 E. 66th St., Indianapolis IN 46220. (317)255-3400. President: Michael Hayes. Specializes in corporate identity, packaging and publications. Clients: publishing, consumer products, corporate and institutional.
Needs: Works with 10 freelance artists/year. Prefers experienced, talented and responsible artists only. Works on assignment only. Uses artists for advertising, brochure, catalog design, illustration and design, P-O-P displays, mechanicals, retouching, charts/graphs and lettering.
First Contact & Terms: Send query letter with brochure/flyer, resume and slides. Samples returned by SASE, "but we prefer to keep them." Reporting time "depends entirely on our needs." Write for appointment. Pay is by the project for design and illustration. Pays $100-1,000/project average; also negotiates. Considers complexity of project, client's budget, skill and experience of artist, how work will be used, turnaround time and rights purchased when establishing payment.
Tips: "Prepare an outstanding mailing piece and 'leave-behind' that allows work to remain on file."

JOHNSON DESIGN GROUP, INC., 3426 N. Washington Blvd., Arlington VA 22201. (703)525-0808. Art Director: Leonard A. Johnson. Specializes in publications. Clients: corporations, associations and public relations firms.
Needs: Works with 12 freelance artists/year. Works on assignment only. Uses artists for brochure and book illustration, mechanicals, retouching and lettering. Especially needs line illustration and a realistic handling of human figure in real life situations.
First Contact & Terms: Send query letter with brochure/flyer and samples (photocopies OK) to be kept on file. Samples are not returned. Negotiates payment by the project.

JONES MEDINGER KINDSCHI INC., Fields Ln., RFD 2, North Salem NY 10560. Contact: Wynn Medinger. Specializes in annual reports, corporate identity and publications. Clients: corporations.
Needs: Works with 30 freelance artists/year. Works on assignment only. Uses artists for illustration.
First Contact & Terms: "*No* phone calls!" Send query letter with tear sheets, slides, Photostats or photocopies to be kept on file. Samples not kept on file are returned by SASE only. Reports only if interested. Pays for illustration by the project $500-5,000 average. Considers client's budget, skill and experience of artist and how work will be used when establishing payment.
Tips: "We mainly use editorial-style illustration for corporate house organs."

JONSON PIRDLE PEDERSEN ALCORN METZDORS & HESS, 35 E. 20th St., New York NY 10003. Clients: corporations and publishers.
Needs: Prefers local artists. Uses artists and photographers for annual reports, publications, catalogs, etc. Pays $15-20, mechanicals and paste-up. Negotiates pay for color separations, illustrations, lettering, retouching and technical art.
First Contact & Terms: Query. SASE.

DAVID KAGEYAMA DESIGNER, 2119 Smith Tower, Seattle WA 98104. Contact: David Kageyama. Specializes in annual reports, corporate identity, displays, packaging, publications and signage. Clients: public service agencies, corporations, banking and insurance.
Needs: Works with 12 freelance artists/year. Works on assignment only. Uses artists for advertising, brochure, posters, direct mail packages, book and catalog illustration; retouching, AV presentations and calligraphy. Especially needs good, quick line/wash and/or humorous illustrator. Also specialists, such as, technical, airbrush, calligraphers. Perfers pen & ink, airbrush, colored pencil, watercolor, collage, calligraphy and computer illustration.
First Contact & Terms: Send brochure/flyer or resume, business card and nonreturnable samples to be kept on file for possible future assignments. Prefers photos (prints), actual illustrations and printed pieces as samples. Call for appointment. Pays $100-300 average/project for quick line illustrations.
Tips: "We are much more apt to respond to the artist with a specific style or who specializes in a particular topic rather than the generalist. Keep in touch with your latest work. I like to see rough sketches as well as finished work. My firm buys all illustration used for our clients. Commerical art degree or full-time artists, please!"

***AL KAHN GROUP**, 221 W. 82nd St., New York NY 10024. (212)580-3517. Contact: Al Kahn. Specializes in annual reports, corporate identity, packaging and publications. Clients: industrial, high tech, entertainment, fashion and beauty.
Needs: Works with 36 freelance artists/year. Works on assignment only. Uses artists for advertising design and layout, brochure and catalog design, illustration and layout; poster design and illustration, model making, charts/graphs, lettering and logo design. Prefers 3-dimensional construction style.
First Contact & Terms: Send brochure/flyer or resume, slides, b&w photos and color washes. Samples returned by SASE. Reports in 1 week. To show a portfolio, mail roughs, original/final art, final reproduction/product, tear sheets and photographs or call to schedule an appointment. Pays for design by the hour, $15 minimum; by the project, $250 minimum. Pays for illustration by the hour, $20 minimum; by the project, $250 minimum.
Tips: "We specialize in 'emotional response' advertising and image building."

KELLY & CO., GRAPHIC DESIGN, INC., 5530 First Ave. N., St. Petersburg FL 33710. (813)341-1009. Art Director: Ken Kelly. Specializes in annual reports, brand identity, corporate identity, displays, direct mail, packaging, publications, signage and technical illustrations. Clients: industrial, banking, auto, boating, real estate, accountants, furniture, travel and ad agencies.
Needs: Works with 6 freelance artists/year. Prefers artists with a minimum of 5 years of experience. "Local artists preferred, in my office. Non-smokers. Must be skilled in all areas. Must operate stat camera. Must have a good working attitude. Must be balanced in all styles." Uses artists for design, illustrations, brochures, catalogs, magazines, newspapers, P-O-P displays, mechanicals, retouching, airbrushing, posters, model making, direct mail packages, charts/graphs, lettering and logos. Prefers pen & ink, airbrush, colored pencil, watercolor, acrylics and markers.
First Contact & Terms: Send query letter with resume, tear sheets and photocopies, or "copies of work showing versatility." Samples are filed. Reports back only if interested. Write to schedule an appointment to show a portfolio, which should include roughs, tear sheets and b&w photocopies. Pays for design by the hour, $8.50-15; by the day, $60-70. Pays for illustration by the hour, $10-18; by the day, $90-110. Considers complexity of project, client's budget, skill and experience of artist and turnaround time when establishing payment. Buys all rights.
Tips: "Don't smoke! Be highly talented in all areas with reasonable rates. Must be honest with a high degree of integrity and appreciation."

LARRY KERBS STUDIOS INC., 419 Park Ave. S., New York NY 10016. (212)686-9420. Contact: Larry Kerbs or Jim Lincoln. Specializes in sales promotion design, some ad work and placement, annual reports, corporate identity, publications and technical illustration. Clients: industrial, chemical, insurance and public relations.
Needs: Works with 3 illustrators and 1 designer/month. New York, New Jersey and Connecticut artists only. Uses artists for direct mail, layout, illustration, slide sets, technical art, paste-up and retouching for annual reports, trade magazines, product brochures and direct mail. Especially needs freelance comps through mechanicals; type specification.

First Contact & Terms: Mail samples or call for interview. Prefers b&w line drawings, roughs, previously published work as samples. Provide brochures, business card and resume to be kept on file for future assignments. No originals returned to artist at job's completion. Pays $14-18/hour, paste-up; $18-20/hour, comprehensive layout; $18-22/hour average, design; negotiates payment by the project for illustration.
Tips: "Improve hand lettering for comps; strengthen typographic knowledge and application."

ANDRÉ RICHARDSON KING—ARCHITECTURAL GRAPHICS DESIGNERS, Suite 2200, 220 S. State St., Chicago IL 60604. (312)922-7757. Owner: André R. King. Specializes in corporate identity, displays, publications, signing and technical illustrations. Clients: developers, architects, landscape architects, planners, manufacturers and municipalities, etc.
Needs: Works on contract only. Uses artist for design, brochures, catalogs, charts/graphs, logos and advertisements.
First Contact & Terms: Send resume and tear sheets. Samples are filed. Samples not filed are returned only if requested by artist.

KMH, INC., 161 S. Twelve Mile Rd., Ceresco MI 49033. (616)979-1221. President: Douglas F. Wolff. Specializes in brand identity, corporate identity, packaging and signage. Clients: manufacturers.
Needs: Prefers product designers and prototype makers. Uses artists for design, brochures, mechanicals, retouching, airbrushing, model making, AV materials and logos.
First Contact & Terms: Send query letter with resume, Photostats, photocopies and slides. Samples are filed. Samples not filed are returned. Reports back within 5 days. To show a portfolio, mail roughs and original/final art. Pays for design by the hour, $15 minimum. Pays for illustration by the project, $250 minimum. Considers complexity of project, client's budget, skill and experience of artist and turnaround time when establishing payment. Buys all rights.

KNT PLUSMARK INC., Suite A, 1200 Main St., Irvine CA 92714. (714)261-1161. Senior Designer: John Hamlin. Specializes in brand identity, corporate identity, packaging and advertising. Clients: Fortune 500 companies.
Needs: Works with 15-25 freelance artists/year. Uses artists for design, illustrations, mechanicals, retouching, airbrushing, model making, lettering, logos and marker comps.
First Contact & Terms: Send query letter with resume. Samples not filed are returned by SASE. Reports only if interested. Call to schedule an appointment to show a portfolio, which should include roughs, original/final art, final reproduction/product, color, photographs and b&w. Pays for design by the hour, $15-20 and by the project. Pays for illustration by the project. Considers client's budget, skill and experience of artist and turnaround time when establishing payment.

***KRAMES COMMUNICATIONS**, 312 90 St., Daly City CA 94015. Senior Designer: Stephanie Zuras. Specializes in health and wellness and medical publications.
Needs: Works with 10-12 freelance artists/year. Works on assignment only. Prefers cartoon, realistic, medical styles. Uses artists for 8-16 page brochure illustration.
First Contact & Terms: Send query letter with tear sheets, Photostats and slides. All samples are reviewed and filed. Samples are returned only if requested by artist. Reports back only if interested. To show a portfolio, mail appropriate materials. Pays for illustration by the project, $5,000-8,000. Considers complexity of project, skill and experience of artist and turnaround time when establishing payment. Buys all rights, and retains original artwork.

KRUDO DESIGN ATELIER, LTD.,, Suite 220, 540 N. Lakeshore Dr., Chicago IL 60611. (312)644-0737. Contact: Shlomo Krudo. Specializes in annual reports, corporate identity, displays, direct mail, fashion, publications, signage and environment design. Clients: banks, law firms, financial service firms, cultural and educational institutions.
Needs: Works with about 6 freelance artists/year. Works on assignment only. Uses artists for illustration, mechanicals, keyline and paste-up.
First Contact & Terms: Send query letter with resume and samples. Samples are filed. Samples not filed are returned only if requested by artist. Reports back only if interested. Call or write to schedule an appointment to show a portfolio, which should include "whatever is appropriate to the individual's experience." Payment varies. Considers complexity of project, client's budget, skill and experience of artist, how work will be used, and turnaround time when establishing payment. Negotiates rights purchased; rights purchased vary according to project.

F. PATRICK LA SALLE DESIGN/GRAPHICS, 225 Sheridan St., Rockford IL 61103. (815)963-2089. Contact: F. Patrick La Salle. Specializes in corporate identity, displays, direct mail, packaging, publications and signage. Clients: small corporations, ad agencies, book publishers and hospitals.

Needs: Works with 10-15 freelance artists/year. Experienced artists only. Uses artists for design, illustration, brochures, catalogs, books, magazines, newspapers, P-O-P displays, mechanicals, photography (studio and on-location), retouching, airbrushing, posters, direct mail packages, model making and AV materials.
First Contact & Terms: Send query letter with brochure and samples to be kept on file. Call for appointment to show portfolio. "Photocopies as samples okay if technique is clear." Samples not kept on file are not returned. Reports back only if interested. Pays for design by the hour, $10-25 average. Pays for illustration by the hour, $20-35 average. Considers complexity of project, client's budget and turnaround time when establishing payment. "Artist will be paid after client has paid invoice."
Tips: "Most freelancers work here at the studio with provided supplies. Payment schedules set up with client *before* work is begun. Frequently, there is a 45-60 day wait for payment after billing has been completed. Recently, our clients have depended a great deal on our co-ordination and consultation with small to elaborate audiovisual presentations. Some have included live actors with slide support for demonstrations. Many artists, in the form of freelance support and production companies, have been involved."

***LORNA LACCONE DESIGN**, Suite 6E, 123 E. 54th St., New York NY 10022. (212)688-4583. President: Lorna Laccone. Specializes in corporate identity, publications and general graphic design for communications firms and major retailers.
Needs: Works with 10 freelance artists/year. Prefers reliable local freelancers to work on premises or off. Uses freelance artists for brochure design, mechanicals and airbrushing. Especially needs neat, clean fast mechanicals, comps/layouts.
First Contact & Terms: Send query letter with samples. Samples are not filed but returned if accompanied by a SASE. Reports back within 7-10 days. To show a portfolio, mail roughts, original/final art and tear sheets. "Published pieces are always nice to see, plus crisp comps." Pays for design by the hour, $25 minimum; by the project, $100 minimum. Pays for illustration by the hour, $25. minimum; by the project, $50 minimum. Considers complexity of project and turnaround time when establishing payment.

JIM LANGE DESIGN, 213 W. Institute Pl., Chicago IL 60610. (312)943-2589. Contact: Jim Lange. Specializes in lettering, logo design and corporate communications. Clients: agencies, PR firms.
Needs: Works with 12 freelance artists/year. Prefers expert craftsmanship. Uses artists for illustration and retouching.
First Contact & Terms: Send samples. Samples are filed. Pays for illustration by the project, $75-800. Considers complexity of project, client's budget, skill and experience of artist, how work will be used, turnaround time and rights purchased when establishing payment. Buys all rights.

***LEBOWITZ/GOULD/DESIGN, INC.**, 3 W. 18th St., New York NY 10011. (212)645-0550. Associate: Cyndy Travis. Specializes in corporate identity, packaging and signage. Clients: corporations, developers, architects, city and state agencies.
Needs: Works with 6 freelance artists/year. Works on assignment only. Uses freelance artists for mechanicals and drafting for architectural graphics.
First Contact & Terms: Send query letter with resume and slides. Samples are filed. Samples not filed are returned only if requested by artist. Call or write to schedule an appointment to show a portfolio, which should include roughs, final reproduction/product, Photostats, photographs and reduced working drawings (where appropriate). Pays for mechanicals and drafting by the hour, $12 minimum. Considers client's budget and turnaround time when establishing payment. Buys all rights.

LEE GRAPHICS DESIGN, 395 19th St. NE, Salem OR 97301. (503)364-0907. Owner/Art Director: Lee Ericksen. Specializes in advertising, promotions, capabilites folders, brand identity, corporate identity, displays, direct mail, packaging, publications, signage and illustrations. "We are a full-service graphics studio." Clients: individuals, ad agencies and PR firms.
Needs: Works with approximately 3-5 freelance artists/year. Artist must have talent, creativity and basic design ability. Uses artist for design, illustrations, brochures, catalogs, books, magazines, newspapers, P-O-P displays, mechanicals, airbrushing, posters, direct mail packages, charts/graphs, AV materials, lettering, logos, advertisements and anything that appears in print form. Prefers pen & ink, charcoal/pencil, colored pencil, collage and markers.
First Contact & Terms: Send query letter with resume. Reports only if interested. Call to schedule an appointment to show a portfolio, which should include thumbnails, roughs, original/final art, final reproduction/product, color, tear sheets, Photostats, photographs and b&w. Pays for design by the hour, $10-25; by the project, $10-25. Pays for illustrations by the hour, $10-25; by the project, $10-25. "Usually get estimate by artist." Considers complexity of project, client's budget, skill and experience of artist, how work will be used, turnaround time and rights purchased when establishing payment.
Tips: "Always show respect for your artwork with presentation; follow directions. Be versatile in all areas of graphics."

LEGAL ARTS, 711 Twelfth Ave., San Diego CA 92101. (619)231-1551. Contact: James Gripp. Specializes in displays; technical illustration; and forensic exhibits including: medical illustration, scale diagrams and models; and charts and graphs. Clients: law firms.
Needs: Works with 3-5 freelance artists/year. Prefers "degreed artists (AA or BA); local to San Diego County." Works on assignment only. Uses artists for illustration, airbrushing, model making, charts/graphs and AV materials. Especially needs medical illustrator and model maker.
First Contact & Terms: Send query letter with resume and samples to be kept on file. Write for appointment to show portfolio. "Samples may be shown by appointment in lieu of portfolio. Artist must send at least 5 photocopy samples with query letter." Reports back within 5 days. Pays for design and illustration by the hour, $7.50 minimum. Considers skill and experience of artist, and turnaround time when establishing payment. "Always 'work for hire' due to legal application of original art."
Tips: Especially looks for "diversity of media, specific applications towards my needs and superior craftsmanship" in samples for portfolio. "If you are a 'generalist', good! We do work that will be used as evidence in court—it must be accurate *every* time. In the legal field, the background of the artist (i.e. degrees), is of great importance to the courts. One must qualify as being educationally capable rather than just physically capable of preparing exhibits for trial use. Hence, the freelancer must have some documented background that a non-artist (judge or juror), will deem as being necessary before the artist can truthfully, accurately and honestly portray whatever is in the exhibit."

LEO ART STUDIO, Suite 610, 320 Fifth Ave., New York NY 10001. (212)736-8785. Art Director/Owner: Mr. Leopold Schein. Specializes in textile design for home furnishings. Clients: wallpaper manufacturers/stylists, glassware companies, furniture & upholstery manufacturing.
Needs: Works with 12-15 freelance artists/year. Prefers artists trained in textile field, not fine arts. Must have a portfolio of original art designs. Should be able to be in NYC on a fairly regular basis. Works both on assignment and speculation. Prefers contemporary and/or traditional styles. Uses artists for design, airbrushing, coloring and repeats. "We are always looking to add full-time artists to our inhouse staff (currently at 9). We will also look at any freelance portfolio to add to our variety of hands."
First Contact & Terms: Send query letter with resume and slides. "We prefer to see portfolio in person. Contact via a phone is OK—we can set up appointments within a day or two notice." Samples are not filed. Samples not filed are returned. Reports back within 5 days. Call or write to schedule an appointment to show a portfolio, which should include original/final art. Pays for design by the project, $200-500. "Payment is generally two-thirds of what design sells for—slightly less if reference material, art material, or studio space is requested." Considers complexity of project, skill and experience of artist and how work will be used when establishing payment. Buys all rights.
Tips: "Do not call if you are not a textile artist. Artists must be able to put design in repeat, do color combinations and be able to draw well on large variety of subjects—florals, Americana, graphics, etc. We will look at student work and advise if is correct field. We do not do fashion or clothing design."

LEONE DESIGN GROUP INC., 7 Woodland Ave., Larchmont NY 10538. President: Lucian J. Leone. Specializes in corporate identity, publications, signage and exhibition design. Clients: museums, corporations, government agencies.
Needs: Works with 10-15 freelance artists/year. Uses artists for exhibition design, brochures, catalogs, mechanicals, model making, charts/graphs, AV materials and logos.
First Contact & Terms: Send query letter with resume, samples, photocopies and photographs. Samples are filed unless otherwise stated. Samples not filed are returned only if requested. Reports back within 2 weeks. Write to schedule an appointment to show a portfolio, which should include thumbnails, original/final art, final reproduction/product, photographs, b&w and color. Pays for design by the hour or project. Considers client's budget and skill and experience of artist when establishing payment.

WES LERDON ASSOCIATES, INDUSTRIAL DESIGN, Box 21204, 3070 Riverside Dr., Columbus OH 43221-0204. (614)486-8188. Owner: W.E. Lerdon. Specializes in corporate identity and technical illustrations. Clients: manufacturers.
Needs: Works with 4 freelance artists/year. Prefers Ohio area designers with skill. Uses artists for design, illustrations, brochures, mechanicals, model making and logos. Prefers pen & ink, charcoal/pencil, colored pencil and markers.
First Contact & Terms: Send query letter with resume. Samples not filed are returned only if requested. Reports only if interested. Call or write to schedule an appointment to show a portfolio, which should include thumbnails, roughs, original/final art and photographs. Pays for design and illustration by the hour, $10-30. Considers complexity of project, client's budget, skill and experience of artist, and turnaround time when establishing payment.
Tips: "In presenting samples or portfolios, freelancers need to put them in time-ordered sequence of old work first and newest work last. . .to show improvement. Too often they are a jumble of old and recent work that confuses the impression of the artist's skill. Do not want to see slides; only original work."

LESLEY-HILLE, INC., 32 E. 21st St., New York NY 10010. (212)677-7570. President: Valrie Lesley. Specializes in annual reports, corporate identity, publications, advertising and sales promotion. Clients: financial, fashion, nonprofit organizations, hotels, restaurants, investment firms, oil and real estate firms.
Needs: Works with "many" freelance artists/year. "Experienced and competent" artists only. Uses artists for illustration, mechanicals, airbrushing, model making, charts/graphs, AV materials and lettering.
First Contact & Terms: Send query letter with resume, business card and samples to be kept on file. Accepts "whatever best shows work capability" as samples. Samples not filed are returned by SASE. Reports only if interested. Call or write for appointment to show portfolio. Pay varies according to project. Considers complexity of project, client's budget, skill and experience of artist, and turnaround time when establishing payment.
Tips: Designers and artists must "be *able to do* what they say they can and agree to do . . . professionally and on time!"

LIBBY-PERSZYK-KATHMAN-L.P.K., 225 E. 6th St., Cincinnati OH 45202. (513)241-6330. Design Director: James Gabel. Specializes in corporate identity and packaging. Clients: industrial firms.
Needs: Works with 12-20 freelance artists/year. Uses artists for illustration, mechanicals, retouching, airbrushing, model making and lettering. Especially needs illustration.
First Contact & Terms: Works on assignment only. Send query letter with brochure and samples/slides to be kept on file. Prefers slides, printed material or printed sheet as samples. Samples not kept on file are returned only if requested. Reports back only if interested. Write for appointment to show portfolio. Pays for illustration by the project, $50-3,000 average. Considers complexity of project, client's budget, skill and experience of artist, and turnaround time when establishing payment.

JAN LORENC DESIGN, INC., #460, 3475 Lenox Rd., Atlanta GA 30326. (404)266-2711. President: Mr. Jan Lorenc. Specializes in corporate identity, displays, packaging, publications, architectural signage design and industrial design. Clients: developers, product manufacturers, architects and institutions.
Needs: Works with 10 freelance artists/year. Local artists only—senior designers. Uses artists for design, illustration, brochures, catalogs, books, P-O-P displays, mechanicals, retouching, airbrushing, posters, direct mail packages, model making, charts/graphs, AV materials, lettering and logos. Especially needs architectural signage designers.
First Contact & Terms: Send brochure, resume and samples to be kept on file. Prefers slides as samples. Samples not kept on file are returned. Call or write for appointment to show portfolio, which should include thumbnails, roughs, original/final art, final reproduction/product, color, Photostats and photographs. Pays for design by the hour, $10-25; by the project, $100-3,000. Considers complexity of project, client's budget, and skill and experience of artist when establishing payment.

LUBELL BRODSKY INC., 270 Madison Ave., New York NY 10016. (212)684-2600. Art Director: Ed Brodsky and Ruth Lubell. Specializes in corporate identity, direct mail, promotion and packaging. Clients: ad agencies and corporations.
Needs: Works with 10 freelance artists/year. Works on assignment only. Uses artists for illustration, mechanicals, retouching, airbrushing, charts/graphs, AV materials and lettering.
First Contact & Terms: Send business card and tear sheets to be kept on file. Reports back only if interested. Considers complexity of project, client's budget, skill and experience of artist and turnaround time when establishing payment.

JODI LUBY & COMPANY, INC., 808 Broadway, New York NY 10003. (212)473-1922. Contact: Jodi Luby. Specializes in corporate identity, direct mail, publications and signage. Clients: corporate, publishing, manufacturing.
Needs: Works with various number of freelance artists/year. Works on assignment only. Uses artists for illustrations, mechanicals, retouching, airbrushing and lettering.
First Contact & Terms: Send query letter with brochure or resume, tear sheets, Photostats and photocopies. Samples are filed. Samples not filed are not returned. Reports back only if interested. Call to schedule an appointment to show a portfolio. Pays for design by the hour, $12-30. Considers complexity of project, client's budget, how work will be used and rights purchased when establishing payment.

***TED MADER & ASSOCIATES**, Suite 416, 911 Western, Seattle WA 98104. Creative Head: Tom Drapper. Specializes in annual reports, brand identity, corporate identity, displays, direct mail, fashion, packaging, publications and signage. Uses freelance artists for mechanicals, retouching, airbrushing, model making, charts/graphs, AV materials and lettering.

First Contact & Terms: Send resume and samples. Samples are filed. Write to schedule an appointment to show a portfolio. Considers skill and experience of artist when establishing payment. Rights purchased vary according to project.

***AARON MARCUS AND ASSOCIATES**, 1196 Euclid Ave., Berkeley CA 94708-1640. (415)527-6224. Principal: Aaron Marcus. A consulting, training, and product development firm that researches, plans and develops the visual design of user interfaces, and electronic publishing documents, including information displays for computer graphics systems. Clients: corporations, manufacturers, government, utilities.
Needs: Works with 5-10 freelance artists/year. Prefers Macintosh experience; usually local designers with 3 years information-oriented graphic design experience. Uses artists for brochure and catalog design and illustration; book, magazine and newspaper design; P-O-P displays (especially on computer screens); mechanicals; charts/graphs/diagrams; AV materials; logos and screen design. Especially needs info-oriented graphic designers with Macintosh experience, symbol designers and chart, diagram designers.
First Contact & Terms: Send query letter with resume and photocopies. Samples are filed. Samples not filed are not returned. Reports back within 1 month. Call or write to schedule an appointment to show a portfolio, or mail original/final art, final reproduction/product, tear sheets, Photostats, photographs, b&w, color or photocopies. Pays for design and illustration by the hour, $5-25. Considers complexity of project, client's budget, skill and experience of artist, how work will be used, turnaround time and rights purchased when establishing payment.
Tips: "We don't need general graphic artists. We're a specialized studio doing pioneering work in computer graphics design and need people who have serious motivation and/or experience in our project areas."

MCGRAPHICS DESIGN, Suite 320, 5607 N. Figuero St., Los Angeles CA 90047. (818)223-7522. Owner: Kathleen McGuinness. Specializes in brand identity, corporate identity, direct mail and packaging. Clients: corporations (manufacturers and distributors), some public relation firms and printers.
Needs: Works with 10 freelance artists/year. "Local artists only, personable and presentable in the corporate environment." Works on assignment only. Uses artists for illustration, catalogs, mechanicals, retouching, airbrushing and newsletters. Especially needs b&w line illustration.
First Contact & Terms: Send brochure, business card and samples to be kept on file. Call or write for appointment to show portfolio. Prefers brochures with some information about artist and samples of work. Samples not kept on file are not returned. Reports back "only if the artist calls and follows up." Pays for design by the hour, $10-20 average. Pays for illustration line products by the project, $100-250 average. Considers complexity of project, client's budget, and skill and experience of artist when establishing payment.
Tips: "Send samples first then make an appointment. Show up on time and *follow up* if we say we are interested."

MCGUIRE WILLIS & ASSOCIATES, 249 E. Cooke Rd., Columbus OH 43214. (614)262-8124. Partner: Sue Willis. Specializes in annual reports, audiovisual and publications. Clients: schools, training departments of companies, sales and banking.
Needs: Works with 20 freelance artists/year. Works on assignment only. Uses artists for advertising, brochure, catalog, poster, direct mail, packaging, book design, illustration, and mechanicals.
First Contact & Terms: Send query letter with Photostats, slides, brochure/flyer and samples to be kept on file. Samples returned by SASE if not kept on file. Reports in 2 weeks. Reports back on whether to expect possible future assignments. Negotiates payment.

ROB MacINTOSH COMMUNICATIONS, INC., 93 Massachusetts Ave., Boston MA 02115. President: Rob MacIntosh. Specializes in annual reports, advertising design and collateral. Clients: manufacturers, graphic arts industry, nonprofit/public service agencies.
Needs: Works with 12 freelance artists/year. Portfolio and work experience required. Uses artists for advertising and brochure design, illustration and layout, mechanicals, retouching and charts/graphs. Occasionally uses humorous and cartoon-style illustrations.
First Contact & Terms: Send samples to be kept on file. Irregular sizes or abundant material will not be filed. "Never send original work unless it's a printed sample. A simple, compact presentation is best. Often Photostats are adequate." Reports only if interested and "generally only when we require more information and/or services." Pays for design by the day, $100 minimum. Pays for illustration by the project, $100 minimum. Considers complexity of project, client's budget, skill and experience of artist and turnaround time when establishing payment.

MCS, 194-198 Rt. 46, East Fairfield NJ 07006. (201)882-7705. Director: Sharon Dowd. Specializes in brand identity, corporate identity, displays and packaging. Clients: consumer product companies.
Needs: Works with 10 freelance artists/year. Prefers local artists. Works on assignment only. Uses artists for illustration, retouching, airbrushing and AV materials.
First Contact & Terms: Call or write for appointment to show portfolio. Prefers slides and printed material as samples. Samples not kept on file returned by SASE. Reports only if interested. Pays for design and illustration by the hour. Considers complexity of project, client's budget and turnaround time when establishing payment.
Tips: "The cool fine artist approach is a turn-off. Professionalism, clean work, originality and a cooperative attitude is a plus. If excessive verbal explanation of work is necessary then obviously the visual doesn't communicate on its own."

***DONYA MELANSON ASSOCIATES**, 437 Main St., Boston MA 02129. Contact: Donya Melanson. Art agency. Clients: industries, associations, publishers, financial and government.
Needs: Most work is handled by staff, but may occasionally use illustrators and designers. Local artists only. Uses artists for stationery design, direct mail, brochures/flyers, annual reports, charts/graphs and book illustrations.
First Contact & Terms: Query with brochure, resume, Photostats and photocopies. Reports in 1-2 months. Provide materials (no originals) to be kept on file for future assignments. Originals returned to artist after use only when specified in advance. To show a portfolio, call or write to schedule an appointment or mail thumbnails, roughs, original/final art, final reproduction/product, color, tear sheets, Photostats, photographs and b&w. Pays $10-25/hour, cartoons, design, illustrations, lettering, retouching, technical art and logo design. Pays $10-20/hour, mechanicals. Considers complexity of project, client's budget, skill and experience of artist and how work will be used when establishing payment.
Tips: "Be sure your work reflects concept development."

***MENON ASSOCIATES**, Suite 406, 100 N. Travis, Sherman TX 75090. (214)893-8989. Owner: Das Menon. Specializes in brand identity, corporate identity, displays, direct mail, packaging, publications, signage and technical illustrations for local firms (north Texas area).
Needs: Works with 3-4 freelance artists/year. Works on assignment only. Uses freelance artists for brochure illustration, P-O-P displays, airbrushing, model making, AV materials, logos and industrial design.
First Contact & Terms: Send query letter with samples. Samples are filed. Samples not filed are returned only if requested by artist. Reports back within 1-2 weeks. Write to schedule an appointment to show a portfolio, which should include thumbnails, final reproduction/product. Pays for design by the project, $25-100. Pays for illustration by the project, $200-600. Considers client's budget, skill and experience of artist and turnaround time when establishing payment. Rights purchased vary according to project.
Tips: "Client satisfaction is the prime objective. Be creative only to that extent."

MG DESIGN ASSOCIATES INC., 824 W. Superior, Chicago IL 60622. (312)243-3661. Contact: Michael Grivas or design director. Specializes in trade show exhibits, museum exhibits, expositions and commercial interiors. Clients: industrial manufacturers, consumer-oriented product manufacturers, pharmaceutical firms, state and federal government, automotive parts manufacturers, etc.
Needs: Works with 4-6 freelance artists/year. Artists must be local exhibit designers with minimum of five years of experience. Works on assignment only. Uses artists for design, illustration, detail drawings and model making.
First Contact & Terms: Send resume, slides and photocopies to be evaluated. Samples not kept on file are returned only if requested. Write for appointment to show portfolio. Considers complexity of project, client's budget, and skill and experience of artist when establishing payment.

MILLER + SCHWARTZ, 3359 Coy Dr., Sherman Oaks CA 91423. (818)907-1493. Creative Director: David Schwartz. Specializes in real estate collateral. Clients: commercial real estate.
Needs: Works with 20 freelance artists/year. Works on assignment only. Uses artists for illustrations, mechanicals, retouching, airbrushing and lettering.
First Contact & Terms: Send resume. Samples are filed. Samples not filed are not returned. Reports back only if interested. Call to schedule an appointment to show a portfolio, which should include roughs and printed pieces. Pays for mechanicals by the hour, $15-20. Pays for illustration by the project. Considers complexity of project, client's budget, how work will be used, turnaround time and rights purchased when establishing payment. Rights purchased vary according to project.

***MIRANDA DESIGNS INC.**, 745 President St., Brooklyn NY 11215. (718)857-9839. President: Mike Miranda. Specializes in annual reports, corporate identity, direct mail, fashion, packaging, publications

and signage. Clients: agencies, PR firms, corporate and retail.
Needs: Works with 20 freelance artists/year. Works with all levels from juniors to seniors in all areas of specialization. Works on assignment only. Uses freelance artists for brochure design and catalog design and illustration, magazine and newspaper design, mechanicals, model making, direct mail packages, charts/graphs and design of advertisements.
First Contact & Terms: Send query letter with resume and photocopies. Samples are filed. Samples not filed are not returned. Does not report back. Call to schedule an appointment to show a portfolio, which should include thumbnails, roughs, original/final art and final reproduction/product. Pays for design by the hour, $10 "for juniors to whatever the market demands and budget permits." Considers complexity of project, client's budget and skill and experience of artist when establishing payment. Rights purchased vary according to project.
Tips: "Be professional, but not stand offish."

MIRENBURG & COMPANY, 43 W. 33rd St., New York NY 10001. (212)573-9200. Creative Director: Barry L. Mirenburg. Specializes in annual reports, brand identity, corporate identity, packaging, publications, signage and technical illustrations. Clients: Fortune 500, PR firms, etc.
Needs: Uses artists for design, illustrations, brochures, catalogs, books, magazines, newspapers, P-O-P displays, mechanicals, retouching, airbrushing, posters, model making, direct mail packages, charts/graphs, AV materials, lettering, logos and advertisements.
First Contact & Terms: Send resume and tear sheets, Photostats, photocopies, slides and photographs. Samples are filed. Samples not filed are not returned. Reports back only if interested.

***E.M. MITCHELL, INC.**, 820 2nd Ave., New York NY 10017. (212)986-5595. Vice President: Steven E. Mitchell. Specializes in brand identity, corporate identity, displays, direct mail and packaging. Clients: major corporations.
Needs: Works with 20-25 freelance artists/year. "Most work is done in our studio." Uses artists for design, illustration, mechanicals, retouching, airbrushing, model making, lettering and logos.
First Contact & Terms: Send query letter with brochure, resume, business card, Photostats, photographs and slides to be kept on file. Reports only if interested. Call or write for appointment to show portfolio, which should include roughs, original/final art, final reproduction/product, color, Photostats and photographs. Pays for design by the hour, $20 minimum; by the project, $150 minimum. Pays for illustration by the project, $250 minimum. Considers complexity of project, client's budget, skill and experience of artist, how work will be used, turnaround time and rights purchased when establishing payment.
Tips: "Call first."

MIZEREK ADVERTISING, 48 E. 43rd St., New York NY 10017. (212)986-5702. President: Leonard Mizerek. Specializes in catalogs, jewelry fashion and technical illustration. Clients: corporations—various product and service-oriented clientele.
Needs: Works with 25-30 freelance artists/year. Experienced artists only. Works on assignment only. Uses artists for design, illustration, brochures, retouching, airbrushing and logos.
First Contact & Terms: Send query letter with tear sheets and Photostats. Reports only if interested. Call to schedule drop off or an appointment to show a portfolio, which should include original/final art and tear sheets. Pays by the project, $500-2,500. Considers client's budget and turnaround time when establishing payment.
Tips: "Contact by mail; don't press for interview. Let the work speak for itself. Show commercial product work not only magazine editorial."

MOBIUM CORPORATION FOR DESIGN & COMMUNICATION, (formerly Kovach Associates Inc.), 414 N. Orleans St., Chicago IL 60610. (312)527-0500. Vice President: Ronald Kovach. Specializes in annual reports, corporate identity, packaging, publications and signage. Clients: real estate, industrial manufacturers, public relations and retail manufacturers.
Needs: Uses artists for advertising, brochure, poster and direct mail package illustration. Prefers a classic look for annual reports and packaging; "probably includes illustration for logotype or company mark when appropriate."
First Contact & Terms: Send query letter with brochure/flyer or resume. Prefers finished art or finished products as samples. Samples returned by SASE. Reports within 2 weeks. Provide resume, business card and brochure/flyer to be kept on file for possible future assignments. Call or write for appointment. Pays $100-3,000 average/project for design or illustration; also negotiates.
Tips: "Most good work relationships center on the personal relationship between parties. Although direct mail solicitation is effective, if you see a company you like, visit with them personally as often as possible."

***MODERN ARTS PACKAGING**, 38 West 39th St., New York NY 10018. Art Director: Mindy Waters. Specializes in the design of shopping bags.
Needs: Works with 4-5 freelance artists/year. Works on assignment only. Uses freelance artists for mechanicals and logos.
First Contact & Terms: Send query letter with resume. Reports back within 1 month only if interested. Call to schedule an appointment to show a portfolio, which should include photographs. Pays for design by the hour, $10 minimum; by the project, $75 minimum; by the day, $50 minimum. Considers complexity of project, client's budget and skill and experience of artist when establishing payment. Buys reprint rights.

BARBARA MOSES DESIGN, 225 W. Ohio, Chicago IL 60610. (312)644-2882. Contact: Barbara Moses. Clients: Direct response advertising.
Needs: Works with about 10 freelance artists/year. Prefers artists. Uses artists for finished art.

MARTIN MOSKOF & ASSOCIATES, INC., 154 W. 57th St., New York NY 10019. (212)333-2015. President: Martin Moskof. Specializes in annual reports, corporate identity, magazine and book design, exhibits, and signage. Clients: corporations and institutions, colleges (e.g., IBM, Carnegie Hall).
Needs: Works with 30-40 freelance artists/year. Local artists only, 2-3 years of experience. Works on assignment only. Uses artists for brochure and catalog design, illustration and layout; book design and illustration; mechanicals, retouching, direct mail packages, charts/graphs, AV presentations and logos.
First Contact & Terms: Send query letter with tear sheets, photocopies, slides and photographs to be kept on file. Reports only if interested. Call or write for appointment to show portfolio, which should include roughs, final reproduction/product, color and tear sheets. Pays for design by the hour, $15-25; by the day, $90-200. Pays for illustration by the project, $150-5,000. Considers complexity of project, client's budget and skill and experience of artist when establishing payment.

MOSSMAN DESIGN ASSOCIATES, 364 E. Palmetto Pk. Rd., Boca Raton FL 33342. Account Supervisor: Stanley Mossman. Specializes in corporate identity, direct mail, publications, health care institution brochures, book jacket and book design. Clients: publishers, manufacturers, hospitals, agencies, nonprofit institutions, etc.
Needs: Works with 3-5 freelance artists/year. Interested in "local artists with strong portfolio, a few years of experience, neat work and understanding of mechanicals." Uses artists for design, mechanicals, charts/graphs and photography.
First Contact & Terms: Send query letter with resume, business card and samples to be kept on file. Prefers copies, tear sheets and mock-ups as samples. Reports back within 5 days. Call or write for appointment to show portfolio. Pays for design and illustration by the hour, $5-20 average. Considers complexity of project, and skill and experience of artist when establishing payment.
Tips: Especially looks for creative samples or portfolio, clean and organized. A mistake artists make is "not knowing their own limitations, not being honest about their skills."

MULLER & COMPANY, 112 W. Ninth St., Kansas City MO 64105. (816)474-1983. Associate Creative Director: John Muller. Specializes in annual reports, corporate identity, displays, interior design, direct mail, fashion, packaging, publications and signage.
Needs: Works with 50-60 freelance artists/year. Works on assignment only. Uses artists for illustrations, brochures, catalogs, books, airbrushing, posters, charts/graphs, AV materials, lettering, advertisements and comp artists.
First Contact & Terms: Send resume, tear sheets, slides and photographs. Samples are filed. Reports back only if interested. To show a portfolio, mail thumbnails, roughs, original/final art, final reproduction/product and tear sheets. Considers complexity of project, client's budget, how work will be used and rights purchased when establishing payment.

MURAMATSU INCORPORATED, 10716 Reagan St., Los Alamitos CA 90865. Contact: Art Director: Amy Tamura. Specializes in trade show exhibits, product design, and interior design. Clients: various manufacturers.
Needs: Works with 10-15 freelance artists/year. Local artists preferred. Works on assignment. Uses artists for graphic production and interior design support services.
First Contact & Terms: Send query letter with resume. Reports only if interested. To show a portfolio, call or write to schedule an appointment. Pays by the hour, $10-35. Considers complexity of project, client's budget, skill and experience of artist, turnaround time when establishing payment.
Tips: "Contemporary design philosophy."

CAROL NAUGHTON & ASSOCIATES, INC., 213 W. Institute Place, Chicago IL 60610. (312)951-5353. President: Carol Naughton. Specializes in corporate identity, displays, interior design and

signage. Clients: real estate developers, manufacturers corporations and hospitals.
Needs: Works on assignment only. Uses artists for illustrations, model making, lettering, renderings and maps.
First Contact & Terms: Send query letter with resume, tear sheets and photocopies. Samples are filed. Samples not filed are returned. Reports back only if interested. Call to schedule an appointment to show a portfolio, or mail original/final art, tear sheets, photographs, b&w and color. Pays for design and illustration by the hour, $10-50. Considers complexity of project, client's budget and skill and experience of artist when establishing payment.

SID NAVRATILART, 1305 Clark Bldg., Pittsburgh PA 15222. (412)471-4322. Contact: Sid Navratil. Specializes in annual reports, corporate identity, desk-top publishing, direct mail, publication, signage, technical illustration and 3-dimensional designs. Clients: ad agencies and corporations.
Needs: Works with 5 freelance artists/year. Experienced artists only with a minimum of 5 years of experience; "I prefer artist to work on my premises at least during revision work, if that is possible." Works on assignment only. Uses artists for design, illustration, brochures, mechanicals, retouching, airbrushing, charts/graphs, lettering, logos and advertisements.
First Contact & Terms: Send resume, photocopies and business card to be kept on file. Material not filed is returned only if requested. Reports within 10 days. Write for appointment to show portfolio. Pays for design and illustration by the hour, $20-30 average. Considers complexity of project, client's budget, and skill and experience of artist when establishing payment.
Tips: "In illustration, we prefer the daring, innovative approach. The subject is usually industrial in nature, done for corporations such as PPG, USS, Alcoa, Rockwell. Do not send expensive photos and brochures. A brief resume with few xerox copies of work is sufficient."

LOUIS NELSON ASSOCIATES INC., 80 University Pl., New York NY 10003. (212)620-9191. Contact: Louis Nelson. Specializes in brand identity, corporate identity, displays, interior design, packaging, publications, signage, product design, exhibitions and marketing. Clients: corporations, associations and governments.
Needs: Works with 8 + freelance artists/year. Works on assignment only. Uses artists for design, illustration, mechanicals, model making and charts/graphs.
First Contact & Terms: Considers "quality, point-of-view for project and flexibility." Send query letter with brochure showing art style or tear sheets, slides and photographs. Samples are returned only if requested. Reports within 2 weeks. Write to schedule an appointment to show a portfolio, which should include roughs, final reproduction/product, color and photographs. Pays for design by the hour, $8-35 average; by the project, $60-5,000 average. Pays for illustration by the project, $100-500 average. Considers complexity of project, client's budget, skill and experience of artist and rights purchased when establishing payment.
Tips: "I want to see how the person responded to the specific design problem and to see documentation of the process—the stages of development. The artist must be versatile and able to communicate a wide range of ideas. Mostly, I want to see the artist's integrity reflected in his/her work."

NICHOLAS ASSOCIATES, 232 N. Ridgeland Ave., Oak Park IL 60302. (312)383-8506. Design Director: Nicholas Sinadinos. Specializes in annual reports, brand identity, corporate identity, packaging, signage and name development. Clients: ad agencies, PR firms, marketing firms, developers and direct accounts.
Needs: Works with 10 freelance artists/year. Prefers competent artists. Works on assignment only. Uses artists for design, illustrations, mechanicals, retouching, model making, AV materials and lettering.
First Contact & Terms: Send query letter. Samples are filed. Samples not filed are returned by SASE. Does not report back. Call to schedule an appointment to show a portfolio, which should include final reproduction/product and tear sheets. Pays for design by the hour, $20-50. Pays for illustration by the project, $50-10,000. Considers complexity of project and client's budget when establishing payment. Rights purchased vary according to project.
Tips: "Follow up."

***NICHOLS GRAPHIC DESIGN**, 80 8th Ave., New York NY 10011. President: Mary Ann Nichols. Specializes in corporate identity, direct mail and publications. Clients: ad agencies, PR firms, publisher, children's fashion manufacturer, industrial manufacturer, mailing house.
Needs: Works with 20 freelance artists/year. Prefers local artists. Works on assignment only. Uses freelance artists for brochure and catalog illustration, mechanicals, retouching, airbrushing, direct mail packages, charts/graphs and lettering. Prefers pen & ink, airbrush, watercolor and acrylics. "I am exploring the use of computers to aid in design. Freelancers with a computer/design background would be essential."

First Contact & Terms: Send query letter, resume and "samples you can spare." Samples are filed. Samples not filed are not returned. Reports back only if interested. Portfolio should include thumbnails, roughs, original/final art (if available) and final reproduction/product. Pays for design by the hour, $15-18. Pays for illustration by the project, $250-700. Considers complexity of project, client's budget, skill and experience of artist and how work will be used when establishing payment. Rights purchased vary according to project.
Tips: "I do not want to see disorganization" when presenting a portfolio.

NIIMI DESIGN ASSOCIATES INC., 451 N. Racine, Chicago IL 60622. (312)666-8383. Contact: B. Hoolehan. Clients: hardware consumer products.
Needs: Assigns 20-100 jobs/year. Uses mostly local artists. Uses artists for design, illustrations, layout, lettering, paste-up, retouching and technical art for packaging, P-O-P displays, catalogs, charts/graphs, exhibits and print media advertising.
First Contact & Terms: Query with samples or arrange interview. SASE. Pay determined by job.

***NORWOOD OLIVER DESIGN ASSOCIATION**, 501 American Legionway, Point Pleasant Beach NJ 08816. (201)295-1200. Vice President: Madan P. Vazirani A.I.A. Interior design firm. Design for department stores, malls, restaurants, hotels, and other commercial and retail clients.
Needs: Works with varied number of freelance renderers/year. Prefers renderers that have 5-10 years experience and within driving distance. Works on assignment only. Uses renderers for interior design and renderings, architectural renderings, design consulting, model making and wall hangings. Especially needs perspective renderings of interiors.
First Contact & Terms: Send resume and photocopies. Samples are filed. Samples not filed are not returned. Write to schedule an appointment to show a portfolio, which should include Photostats, photographs and color. Pays per rendering, $300-500. Considers client's budget, skill and experience of artist, and "whether piece is b&w, color or airbrush" when establishing payment. Buys first rights.

NOSTRADAMUS ADVERTISING, #1128A, 250 W. 57, New York NY 10107. (212)581-1362. Creative Director: Barry N. Sher. Specializes in publications. Clients: ad agencies, PR firms, nonprofit organizations, political candidates.
Needs: Works with 7 freelance artists/year. Uses artists for design, illustrations, mechanicals, logos and advertisements.
First Contact & Terms: Send resume and samples. Samples are filed. Samples not filed are not returned. Does not report back. Pays for design by the hour, $15 minimum. Pays for illustration by the project, $25 minimum. Considers complexity of project, client's budget and skill and experience of artist when establishing payment. Buys all rights.

NOTOVITZ & PERRAULT DESIGN, INC., 47 E. 19 St., New York NY 10003. (212)677-9700. President: Joseph Notovitz. Specializes in corporate design (annual reports, literature, publications), corporate identity and signage. Clients: finance and industry.
Needs: Works with 10 freelance artists/year. Uses artists for brochure, poster, direct mail and booklet illustration, mechanicals, charts/graphs and logo design.
First Contact & Terms: Send resume, slides, printed pieces and tear sheets to be kept on file. Samples not filed are returned by SASE. Reports in 1 week. Call for appointment to show portfolio, which should include roughs, original/final art and final reproduction/product. Pays for design by the hour, $15-50; by the project, $200-1,500. Pays for illustration by the project, $100-5,000; also negotiates.
Tips: "Send pieces which reflect our firm's style and needs. They should do a bit of research in the firm they are contacting. If we never produce book covers, book cover art does not interest us."

ANNA OHALLA GRAPHIC DESIGN, 317 Market St., Rockford IL 61104. (815)968-1533. Art Director: Anna Ohalla. Specializes in annual reports, brand and corporate identity, direct mail, packaging, publications and signage for corporations.
Needs: Works with 5 freelance artists/year. Prefers artists with 5 years plus of experience. Works on assignment only. Uses artists for illustrations, retouching and airbrushing.
First Contact & Terms: Contact through artist's agent or send query letter with samples. Samples are filed. Samples not filed are returned only if requested. Reports back only if interested. To show a portfolio, mail thumbnails, roughs, original/final art, final reproduction/product, tear sheets or photographs. Pays for design and illustration by the hour, $30-60. Considers client's budget, skill and experience of artist, turnaround time and rights purchased when establishing payment. Buys all rights.

OVERLOCK HOWE CONSULTING GROUP, 4484 W. Pine Blvd., St. Louis MO 63108. (314)533-4484. Vice President, Creative Director: Richard Deardorff. Specializes in brand identity, corporate identity, displays, packaging and signage. Clients: regional, national and international companies.

Needs: Works with 20-30 freelance artists/year. Prefers local artists with three years of experience, and national illustrators. Works on assignment only. Uses artists for illustrations, P-O-P displays, mechanicals, retouching, airbrushing, model making, direct mail packages, charts/graphs, AV materials, lettering and advertisements.
First Contact & Terms: Send query letter with resume and tear sheets, Photostats, photocopies, slides and photographs. Samples are filed. Reports back only if interested. Write to schedule an appointment to show a portfolio or mail original/final art, final reproduction/product, tear sheets, Photostats, photographs, b&w and color. Pays for illustration by the project, $200 minimum. Considers complexity of project, client's budget, skill and experience of artist, how work will be used, turnaround time and rights purchased when establishing payment. Rights purchased vary according to project.
Tips: Artist should be "well-organized, show full capabilities and be very professional."

PERSECHINI & COMPANY, #303, 1575 Westward Blvd., Los Angeles CA 90024. (213)478-5522. Contact: Shannon Heiman. Specializes in annual reports, corporate identity, displays, packaging, publications and signage. Clients: health care, real estate, hospitality, institutional ad agencies, public relations firms, and internal communications departments.
Needs: Works on assignment basis only. Uses artists for design, illustration, mechanicals, retouching, airbrushing and lettering. Occasionally uses humorous and cartoon-style illustrations.
First Contact & Terms: Send query letter with brochure, business card and Photostats and photocopies to be kept on file. Samples not kept on file are returned by SASE. Reports back only if interested. Pays for design by the hour, $10-20 average. Pays for illustration by the project, $100-2,500 average. Considers complexity of project, client's budget, skill and experience of artist, how work will be used, turnaround time and rights purchased when establishing payment.
Tips: "Our clients seem to want a very sophisticated look for their ads, brochures, etc. Occasionally we have a call for humor."

PGD INC., Box 98, Syracuse NY 13201-0098. General Manager: Mr. James. Specializes in corporate identity, publications and technical illustrations. Clients: educational, institutional, industrial and commercial.
Needs: Works with 10-15 freelance artists/year. Prefers local, versatile, fast designers and technical illustrators. Works on assignment only. Uses artists for design, illustrations, brochures, catalogs, books, magazines, mechanicals, retouching, airbrushing, posters, charts/graphs, logos and advertisements.
First Contact & Terms: Send query letter with resume, Photostats and photographs. Samples are filed. Samples not filed are returned. Reports back within 4 weeks. Write to schedule an appointment to show a portfolio or mail thumbnails, roughs and final reproduction/product. Pays for design by the hour, $25 minimum. Pays for illustration by the hour, $20-40 minimum. Considers complexity of project, turnaround time and rights purchased when establishing payment. Buys all rights.

PHARES ASSOCIATES INC., Consultant Designers-Industrial Design, 37704 Hills Tech Dr., Farmington Hills MI 48018. (313)553-2232. Administrative Assistant: Penelope Phares. Specializes in interior design and product design. Clients: manufacturing and architectural firms and advertising agencies.
Needs: "At least 2 years of experience, speed and accuracy a must." Works on assignment only. Uses artists for design, illustration and model making. Special needs include architectural rendering, product design and drafting.
First Contact & Terms: Send query letter with brochure, resume, business card, slides, tear sheets or photographs to be kept on file. Samples not filed are returned by SASE. Reports within 2 weeks. Call or write for appointment to show portfolio. Pays for design by the hour, $8-20 average. Pays for illustration by the hour, $8-15 average. "Speed and quality are the determining factors regarding pay." Considers complexity of project, and skill and experience of artist when establishing payment.
Tips: "Our firm likes to use the work of artists who can take direction and meet short deadlines with quality work."

HERBERT PINZKE DESIGN INC., 1935 N. Kenmore, Chicago IL 60614. (312)528-2277. President: Herbert Pinzke. Specializes in annual reports, corporate identity and publications. Clients: corporations.
Needs: Works with 4 freelance artists/year. Works on assignment only. Uses artists for illustrations, brochures, catalogs, books, magazines, mechanicals and model making.
First Contact & Terms: Send query letter with brochure or resume and samples. Samples are filed. Samples not filed are returned by SASE. Reports back only if interested. Call or write to schedule an appointment to show a portfolio, which should include thumbnails, roughs, original/final art and final reproduction/product. Pays for illustration by the hour, $15-50. Considers complexity of project, client's budget, skill and experience of artist, how work will be used, turnaround time and rights purchased when establishing payment. Rights purchased vary according to project.

***PORRAS & LAWLOR ASSOCIATES**, 15 Lucille Ave., Salem NH 03079. (603)893-3626. Art Director: Victoria Porras. Specializes in corporate identity, direct mail and publications. Clients: banks, high-tech industry and colleges.
Needs: Works with 10 freelance artists/year. Prefers artists living in New England with one year of experience. Uses freelance artists for brochure illustration, mechanicals, airbrushing, AV materials and lettering.
First Contact & Terms: Send query letter with brochure showing art style or samples. Samples are filed. Reports back only if interested. Call or write to schedule an appointment to show a portfolio, which should include thumbnails, original/final art, final reproduction/product or photographs (whatever is applicable to artist). Pays for illustration by the project, $50.-4000. Considers complexity of project, client's budget, skill and experience of artist, turnaround time and rights purchased when establishing payment. Negotiates rights purchased; rights purchased vary according to project.

***PRECISION GRAPHICS**, 119 W. Washington St., Champaign IL 61820. (217)359-6655. Owner: Jeff Mellander. Specializes in technical illustration for book publishers.
Needs: Works with 5-10 freelance artists/year. Uses artists for catalog and textbook illustration, primarily charts, graphs and medical illustration.
First Contact & Terms: Seeks artists experienced in drawing with technical pens and with highly developed skills in the area of technical illustration. Send query letter with resume, business card and samples to be kept on file. Write for appointment to show portfolio. Prefers Photostats as samples, but will accept good-quality photocopies. Samples not filed are returned by SASE only if requested. Reports only if interested. Pays according to accepted job bid of artist. Considers complexity of project, skill and experience of the artist, and turnaround time when establishing payment.
Tips: Looks for "quality—not quantity—and consistency" when reviewing work. "Beginning artists just out of school tend to show too much; try to hit on too many areas. Show what you *like* to do and what you do best."

PRODUCT SYSTEMS INTERNATIONAL, (formerly Herbst, Lazar, Rogers & Bell, Inc.), 40 N. Cherry St., Lancaster PA 17602. (717)291-9042. Office Manager: Sarah Campbell. Specializes in brand identity, corporate identity, displays, interior design, packaging, publications, signage, technical illustration, human factors, market research, product design and engineering, and cost reduction. Clients: manufacturers and retailers.
Needs: Works with 20 freelance artists/year. Artists should be within driving distance; "prefer freelancers to work inhouse." Works on assignment only. Uses artists for illustration, brochures, catalogs, mechanicals, model making, charts/graphs, lettering, logos advertisements and market research. Prefers airbrush, charcoal/pencil and markers.
First Contact & Terms: Send query letter with brochure, resume and business card to be kept on file; slides to be returned. Samples not kept on file are returned. Reports within 30 days. To show a portfolio, mail appropriate materials and write to schedule an appointment; portfolio should include thumbnails, roughs, final reproduction/product and photographs. Pays for design by the hour, $7-30; pays for illustration by the hour, $10-$30. Considers complexity of project, and skill and experience of artist when establishing payment.

***PRODUCTION INK**, 2826 Northeast 19th Dr., Gainesville FL 32609. (904)377-8973. Art Director: Nancy Blackmon. Specializes in publications.
Needs: Works with 6-10 freelance artists/year. Works on assignment only. Uses artists for brochure illustration, airbrushing and lettering.
First Contact & Terms: Send resume, samples, tear sheets, Photostats, photocopies, slides and photography. Samples are filed. Samples not filed are returned if accompanied by a SASE. Reports back only if interested. Call or write to schedule an appointment to show a portfolio, which should include original/final art. Pays for illustration by the project, $100 minimum. Considers complexity of project, client's budget, skill and experience of artist, how work will be used, turnaround time, and rights purchased when establishing payment. Buys reprint rights; rights purchased vary according to project.

PULSE, INC. COMMUNICATIONS, 7518 W. Madison St., Forest Park IL 60130. (312)366-1770. Creative Director: Frank G. Konrath. Specializes in annual reports, corporate identity, displays, landscape design, interior design, packaging, publications, signage and technical illustration. Clients include corporations.
Needs: Works with 5-15 freelance artists/year. "Local artists preferred. I will always consider talent over experience." Works on assignment only. Uses artists for projects involving many different specialities.
First Contact & Terms: "Pulse Inc. is an artist cooperative, so we work exclusively with freelancers. Our "staff" consists of artists who have taken office space at our studio complex. Send query letter with

business card to be kept on file. Pays by project. Staff listing available with SASE."
Tips: "Because we work directly with freelance artists within a cooperative format, an abilty to work with other artists and a background in art direction are imparitive ."

THE PUSHPIN GROUP, 215 Park Ave. S., New York NY 10003. (212)674-8080. Senior Vice President: Phyllis Rich Flood. Specializes in annual reports, brand identity, corporate identity, packaging, publications and signage. Clients: individuals, ad agencies, corporations, PR firms, etc.
Needs: Works with 5-6 freelance artists/year. Generally prefers designers to illustrators. Uses artists for design, illustrations, brochures, books, magazines, mechanicals, retouching, airbrushing, charts/graphs and lettering.
First Contact & Terms: Send query letter with resume, tear sheets, Photostats and photocopies. Samples not filed are returned only if requested. Reports only if interested. Call or write to schedule an appointment to show a portfolio, which should include roughs, original/final art, final reproduction/product, color, tear sheets, Photostats, photographs and b&w. Pays for design by the hour, $15-20. Considers complexity of project, client's budget, skill and experience of artist, and turnaround time when establishing payment.

QUALLY & COMPANY INC., #2502, 30 E. Huron, Chicago IL 60611. (312)944-0237. Creative Director: Robert Qually. Specializes in advertising, graphic design and new product development. Clients: major corporations.
Needs: Works with 20-25 freelance artists/year. "Artists must be good and have the right attitude." Works on assignment only. Uses artists for design, illustration, mechanicals, retouching and lettering.
First Contact & Terms: Send query letter with brochure, resume, business card and samples to be kept on file. Samples not kept on file are returned by SASE. Reports back within several days. Call or write for appointment to show portfolio. Considers complexity of project, client's budget, skill and experience of artist, how work will be used, turnaround time and rights purchased when establishing payment.
Tips: Looks for talent, point of view, style, craftsmanship, depth and innovation in portfolio or samples. Sees "too many look-alikes. Very little innovation. Few people who understand how to create an image, who know how to conceptualize, who can think." Artists often "don't know how to sell or what's involved in selling."

THE QUARASAN GROUP, INC., Suite 300, 630 Dundee Rd., Northfield IL 60062. (312)291-0700. President: Randi S. Brill. Technical Resource Manager: Joy Christensen. Specializes in books. Clients: book publishers.
Needs: Works with 100-300 freelance artists/year. Artists with publishing experience only. Uses artists for illustration, books, mechanicals, charts/graphs, lettering and production.
First Contact & Terms: Send query letter with brochure or resume and samples to production manager to be kept on file. Prefers "anything that we can retain for our files; Photostats, photocopies, tear sheets or dupe slides that do not have to be returned" as samples. Reports only if interested. Pays for production by the hour, $8-15 average; for illustration by the project, $75-3,500 average. Considers complexity of project, client's budget, how work will be used and turnaround time when establishing payment. "For illustration, size and complexity are the key factors."
Tips: "More publishers are finding that solid publishing service groups, with strength in art procurement, are an asset. They want us to work with the artists. This is good for artists, too. By working with us their work and talents can be displayed to all of our clients. It works well!"

MIKE QUON DESIGN OFFICE, INC., 568 Broadway, New York NY 10012. (212)226-6024. President: Mike Quon. Specializes in corporate identity, displays, direct mail, packaging, publications and technical illustrations. Clients: corporations and ad agencies (e.g. American Express, Chemical Bank, PaineWebber, Clairol and Shearson Lehman Hutton).
Needs: Works with 10-15 freelance artists/year. Prefers good/great people "local doesn't matter." Works on assignment only. Prefers graphic style. Uses artists for design, brochures, P-O-P displays, mechanicals, model making, charts/graphs and lettering. Prefers pen & ink. Especially needs precision inking people.
First Contact & Terms: Send query letter with resume, tear sheets and photocopies. Samples are filed. Samples not filed are returned if accompanied by a SASE. Reports back only if interested. Write to schedule an appointment to show a portfolio or mail thumbnails, roughs and tear sheets. Pays for design by the hour, $12-20. Pays for illustration by the project, $50-500 and up. Considers complexity of project, client's budget, skill and experience of artist, turnaround time and rights purchased when establishing payment. Buys one-time rights; rights purchased vary according to project.

R.H.GRAPHICS, INC.251 Park Ave. S., New York NY 10010. (212)246-0040. President: Roy Horton. Vice President: Irving J. Wittleman. Specialized in brand identity, corporate identity, displays, direct mail and packaging.

Close-up

Mike Quon

Designer

New York City

Mike Quon leads a staff of seven in turning out bold, colorful graphics for such clients as AT & T, American Express, Shearson Lehman Hutton, Coca-Cola, ITT and Paine Webber. The team of Mike Quon Design Office must produce a product that captures the essence of the client's purpose and also the graphic identity of Mike Quon. As an employer, Quon either hires associates to work inhouse or commissions freelancers to work for him.

Many of the major corporations Quon works with ask him to shape an entire identity program for them. This includes creating a logo and incorporating that with a certain "look" that appears on display stands, signage, point-of-purchase displays and posters as well as in brochures and catalogs. Quon's strong visual work gives him the leading edge in this type of project, because it delivers a clear message that carries across all mediums. He encourages other designers to develop a "personality" to their work so that it makes a mark in the minds of clients.

Quon has learned that a designer must be a good listener. "A designer must understand the client, what he stands for, what image or message he wants to get across. The designer should make every effort to learn as much as possible about the client." He feels that many artists make the mistake of listening carefully to a point, then letting their imaginations wander off with their own ideas about the project, instead of comprehending the whole picture. Quon keeps his focus on the client by asking a series of questions about the client, his outlook and the specifics of the job. Careful listening at this point enables him to avoid costly changes during the later stages.

Because he takes the proverbial extra step in understanding his client's needs, Quon has established a good reputation; clients trust him. "When you have the trust of your clients, you have the freedom to perform at your fullest. Your clients will also allow you to take a project one step further and spend the money for creative ideas—that's not easy." This position also allows him to experiment and thus establish a unique look that sets both him and the client apart from the competition. "I don't like to go for a safe solution. I like to be daring. That keeps the work interesting for me, too."

Before setting up his studio in 1972, Quon laid the foundation for his own business by working as a freelancer on many types of projects. As a graduate of UCLA and the Art Center in Los Angeles, he first created window displays for a department store. As art director for a number of advertising agencies, such as J. Walter Thompson in Los Angeles and Young & Rubican in New York, he established invaluable contacts throughout the industry. He also learned to always keep his eyes open for situations that needed a "design fix." With camera in hand, he still walks down streets and snaps photos of signage that could be improved. Then he makes some sketches and proposes his improvements to the company. As a result of his street photography, he has recently been sprucing up the signage of national fast food chains.

Unlike many design firms, Quon does not have a sales representative that pitches ideas to potential clients. Most clients seek Quon out, but, if he wants to attract a new client, he prepares his own pitch. He studies what the company has done in the past and then applies his own ideas to a new project, drawing accurate mock-ups. He feels that his strong portfolio of past clients and his carefully prepared proposals close many deals.

Just as freelancers do, Quon works with clients directly and through advertising agencies or public relations firms. He prefers to deal directly with the corporate representative instead of through a go-between because he can present his own ideas more clearly this way. "Through an agency you never get to talk to a client. The agency isn't as committed to my design as I am. I am my own best salesman."

He applies his design sense to his own self-promotional efforts. His logo—a big Q with a pencil as its tail—ties together his direct mail pieces, stationery, envelopes, business card and flyers. He constantly updates this package with images from new campaigns.

His self-promotional efforts don't stop there. He has assembled a slide show, which he presents at various art-related functions. You find him listed in all the talent sourcebooks. He also sends out press releases whenever he picks up a new client or finishes a noteworthy campaign, such as the logo for the 1988 Presidential debates. He keeps himself in print.

This master of self-promotion advises newcomers to keep their eyes constantly open for possible contacts. "Make contacts with people out in the world, too. You can meet people in elevators, at parties—potential clients are everywhere. Sometimes, just calling up a favorite store or company at the right time could have positive results."

What's the secret of Quon's success? "If you'd really like to know, it's done with mirrors," he jokes. "But seriously, it's a combination of persistence, hard work, talent, salesmanship, a love for what I do, a big ego and more hard work."

—Susan Conner

Citibank asked Quon through its advertising agency to illustrate and design this promotional piece. Done in pen & ink and flat plastic adhesive colors, the piece advertised a special promotion the bank sponsored. Quon was asked to illustrate the dining treats certain American cities feature. Quon says, "I liked doing the piece because it was not a detailed map but an illustrative one."

Needs: Works with 5-8 freelance artists/year. Artists must have ten years of experience. Especially needs mechanicals and ruling. Uses artists for P-O-P displays, mechanicals, retouching, airbrushing and lettering.
First Contract & Terms: Send query letter with brochure showing art style or resume and tear sheets. Reports only if interested. Write to show a portfolio, which should include roughs and original/final art. Pays for design by the hour, $18-25. Pays for illustration by the project, $50-250. Considers client's budget, and skill and experience of artist when establishing payment.

JOHN RACILA ASSOCIATES, 340 W. Butterfield Rd., Elmhurst IL 60126. (312)279-0614. Creative Director: John Neher. Specializes in brand identity, corporate identity, displays, interior design, packaging, publications and signage. Clients: manufacturers of consumer goods.
Needs: Prefers local artists to work on premises, minimum three years of experience or consumer product experience. Works on assignment only. Uses artists for design, illustrations, mechanicals, retouching, airbrushing, model making, AV materials, lettering and advertisements.
First Contact & Terms: Send query letter with brochure. Samples are filed. Samples not filed are returned only if requested. Reports back only if interested. Call to schedule an appointment to show a portfolio, which should include roughs, original/final art, final reproduction/product, tear sheets and color. Pays for design by the hour, $8 minimum. Pays for illustration by the project, $50 minimum. Considers complexity of project, client's budget, skill and experience of artist and turnaround time when establishing payment. Buys all rights.

COCO RAYNES GRAPHICS, INC., 35 Newbury St., Boston MA 02116. (617)536-1499. President: Coco Raynes. Specializes in brand identity, corporate identity, displays, direct mail, packaging, publications and signage. Clients: corporations, institutions (private and public) and architects.
First Contact & Terms: Send query letter with resume, tear sheets, and photocopies to be kept on file. Reports only if interested. Write to schedule an appointment to show a portfolio, which should include original/final art, photographs and b&w. Payment varies. Considers client's budget, and skill and experience of artist when establishing payment.
Tips: "Be on time, present yourself well. Show only your best pieces; smile, laugh."

RENAISSANCE COMMUNICATIONS, INC., 7835 Eastern Ave., Silver Spring MD 20910. (301)587-1505. Art Director: Joseph Giacalone. Specializes in corporate identity, publications, brochures, general illustrations and audiovisual presentations. Clients: government design and high-tech firms.
Needs: Works with 30-40 freelance artists/year. Uses artists for design, illustration, mechanicals, retouching, airbrushing, charts/graphs, AV materials and lettering. Prefers pen & ink.
First Contact & Terms: Send query letter with resume to be kept on file. Reports back only if interested. Pays for design by the hour, $10-20 average; for illustration by the hour, $15-25: for art production by the hour, $6-15 average. Considers complexity of project, skill and experience of artist and turnaround time when establishing payment.

RENQUIST/ASSOCIATES,INC., 2300 Washington Ave., Racine WI 53405. (414)634-2351. Vice President/Design: Dick Huennekens. Specializes in annual reports, brand identity, corporate identity, displays, landscape design, interior design, direct mail, fashion, packaging, publications, signage and technical illustrations. Clients: consumer and industrial.
Needs: Works with 10-12 freelance artists/year. Uses artists for illustrations, retouching, airbrushing, AV materials and lettering.
First Contact & Terms: Send query letter with brochure showing art style or resume, slides and photographs. Samples not filed are returned only if requested. Reports within 2 weeks. Call or write to schedule an appointment to show a portfolio, which should include thumbnails, roughs, original/final art, final reproduction/product, color and tear sheets. Pays for design by the hour, $15-50. Pays for illustration by the hour, $15-50. Considers complexity of project, client's budget and turnaround time when establishing payment.

***RESTAURANT PROMOTION & MARKETING INC.**, 251 Arden Rd., Gulph Mills PA 19428. (215)525-5768. President: Neale West. Specializes in packaging, publications and P-O-P color printing. Clients: food service industry.
Needs: Prefers local artists. Works on assignment only. Uses artists for brochure design and illustration, P-O-P displays, lettering, logos and design of advertisements.
First Contact & Terms: Send photocopies. Samples are filed. Samples not filed are returned if requested by artist. Reports back only if interested. Pays for design by the hour, $45-100. Pays for illustration by the hour, $45-125. Considers client's budget when establishing payment. Buys all rights.
Tips: "Most subjects deal with food and food art/photography."

"My assignment was to re-create Blanche Fischer Wright's original illustration for the 1916* Real Mother Goose,*" says freelance illustrator Janice Fried. Valerie Ritter, art director of Ritter & Ritter, Inc., in New York City, commissioned Fried, who presented her portfolio to Ritter. Deadline for the illustration, rendered in pen and ink and watercolor, was one week. The illustration was used in Macmillan's catalog and promotional materials.

***WILLIAM REYNOLDS DEPICTION & DESIGN INC.**, 314 W. Reno Ave., Bismarck ND 58501. (701)258-1864. President: William Reynolds. Specializes in corporate identity, displays, landscape design, interior design, signage and technical illustrations. Clients: sign companies, outdoor advertisers, architects and miscellaneous businesses.
Needs: Works with 2 freelance artists/year. Uses artists for mechanicals and lettering.

***ROY RITOLA, INC.**, 714 Sansome, San Francisco CA 94111. (415)788-7010. President: Roy Ritola. Specializes in brand identity, corporate identity, displays, direct mail, packaging and signage. Clients: manufacturers.
Needs: Works with 6-10 freelance artists/year. Uses artists for design, illustrations, airbrushing, model making, lettering and logos.
First Contact & Terms: Send query letter with brochure showing art style or resume, tear sheets, slides and photographs. Samples not filed are returned only if requested. Reports only if interested. To show a portfolio, mail final reproduction/product. Pays for design by the hour, $15-50. Considers complexity of project, client's budget, skill and experience of artist, turnaround time and rights purchased when establishing payment.

***RITTER & RITTER, INC.**, (formerly Arthur Ritter, Inc.), 45 W. 10th St., New York NY 10011. (212)505-0241. Art Director: Valerie Ritter. Specializes in annual reports, corporate identity, brochures, catalogs and promotion for publishers, corporations, nonprofit organizations and hospitals.
Needs: Works with 5 freelance artists/year according to firm's needs. Does not always work on assign-

ment only; "sometimes we need a freelance on a day-to-day basis." Uses artists for advertising design and illustration, brochure design, mechanicals, charts and graphs. Prefers "elegant, understated, sensitive design without self-conscious trendiness."
First Contact & Terms: Prefers experienced artists, although "talented 'self-starters' with design expertise/education are also considered." Send query letter with brochure, resume, and samples to be kept on file. "Follow up within a week of the query letter about the possibility of arranging an appointment for a portfolio review." Prefers printed pieces as samples. Samples not filed are returned by SASE. Pays for mechanicals by the hour, $14-20. Pays for design by the project, $100-500 average; or by the day, $90-150 average. Pays for illustration by the project, $50-500 average. Considers complexity of the project, client's budget, skill and experience of the artist and turnaround time when establishing payment.
Tips: "Variety is important, only if the portfolio is well-edited. Often, excellent work can be obscured if it is presented in the context of a cluttered portfolio which includes weaker work. Although it is never clear which pieces a potential client will respond to, it is essential that a portfolio have a consistent level of quality as well as versatility."

PHILLIP ROSS ASSOCIATES LTD., 310 W. Chicago Ave., Chicago IL 60610. Creative Director: Phillip Ross. Specializes in brand identity, corporate identity, displays, posters, direct mail, fashion, packaging, publications and signage. Clients: ad agencies, public relations firms, corporations and poster publishers.
Needs: Works with 10 freelance artists/year. Prefers artists with three years of experience. Uses artists for design, illustration, brochures, catalogs, P-O-P displays, mechanicals, retouching, airbrushing, posters, direct mail packages, lettering, logos and advertisements. Especially needs experienced artists for graphic design and art production.
First Contact & Terms: Send query letter with resume, Photostats and slides to be kept on file. Reports within 30 days. Call for appointment to show portfolio. Pays for design by the hour, $10-20 and by the project. Considers complexity of project and client's budget when establishing payment.
Tips: Especially looks for "visual impact, simplicity, sensitivity to typography and color, and clean line when reviewing work."

JOHN RYAN & COMPANY, 12400 Whitewater Dr., Minnetonka MN 55343. (612)936-9900. Senior Designer: Jim Henke. Specializes in brand identity, corporate identity, displays, interior design, fashion, packaging and signage. Clients: major national retail chains, book publishers and retailers, food, clothing and high-tech manufacturers and retailers. "50% of our business is in retail banking."
Needs: Works with 30-50 freelance artists/year. "Local and regional artists are preferred, but I will work with talented people anywhere. Professionalism is more important than experience; quality must be of the highest. Artists must be fast and priced within normal market rates." Uses artists for illustration, brochures, books, P-O-P displays, mechanicals, retouching, airbrushing, posters, direct mail packages, AV materials, lettering, logos and advertisements. Especially looking for "fresh new talent in black-and-white, graphic, airbrush and classic painterly styles, plus people working in new media such as 3.0 and paper sculpture."
First Contact & Terms: Send query letter with brochure, resume, business card and samples to be kept on file. Accepts color stats, slides, photocopies, Photostats or printed samples, "preferably in 8½x11 format so they can be filed." Samples not filed are returned by SASE only if requested. Reports within 1 month. Call for appointment to show portfolio. Pays for design by the hour, $30-75 average; by the project, $50-300 average. Pays for illustration by the project, $200-3,000 average. Considers complexity of project, client's budget, skill and experience of artist, turnaround time and rights purchased when establishing payment.
Tips: "Artist's work should be fresh in approach, superlative in execution, turned around in reasonable deadline, priced along normal rate guidelines. Creative problem solving and dazzling execution are premiums here."

SCHAFER ASSOCIATES VISUAL COMMUNICATIONS GROUP, 2001 Spring Rd., Oak Brook IL 60521; 32A Mills Pl., Pasadena CA 91105. (312)572-1890; (818)304-0346. Senior Vice President: Nicholas Sinadinos. Specializes in annual reports, brand identity, corporate identity, interior design, packaging, signage and name development. Clients: direct, agencies, PR firms, marketing firms and developers.
Needs: Works with 10-25 freelance artists/year. Prefers competent artists. Works on assignment only. Uses artists for design, illustrations, mechanicals, retouching, model making, AV materials, lettering and writing.
First Contact & Terms: Send query letter. Samples are filed. Samples not filed are returned by SASE. Does not report back. Call to schedule an appointment to show a portfolio, which should include final reproduction/product and tear sheets. Pays for design by the hour, $20 minimum; by the project, $100

minimum. Pays for illustration by the project, $100 minimum. Considers complexity of project and client's budget when establishing payment. Rights purchased vary according to project.
Tips: "Send materials and/or call. Follow up consistently."

JACK SCHECTERSON ASSOCIATES INC., Suite 204, 274 Madison Ave., New York NY 10016. (212)889-3950. Contact: Jack Schecterson. Art/ad agency. Specializes in packaging, product design, annual reports, brand identity, corporate identity, displays, exhibits and shows, publications and signage. Clients: manufacturers of consumer/industrial products.
Needs: Uses local artists. Works on assignment only. Uses artists for annual reports, catalogs, direct mail brochures, exhibits, flyers, packaging, industrial design, slide sets, album covers, corporate design, graphics, trademark, logotype design, sales promotion, audiovisuals, P-O-P displays and print media advertising. Especially needs package and product designers.
First Contact & Terms: Send query letter with brochure showing art style or resume and tear sheets, or write for appointment. Samples returned by SASE. Reports "as soon as possible." Pays by the project for design and illustration; negotiates payment. Reproduction rights purchased.

SCHROEDER BURCHETT DESIGN CONCEPTS, 40 Park Ave., New York NY 10016. Designor & owner: Carla Schroeder Burchett. Specializes in packaging drafting, marketing. Clients: manufacturers.
Needs: Works on assignment only. Uses artists for design, mechanicals, lettering and logos.
First Contact & Terms: Send resume, "if interested, will contact artist or craftsperson and will negotiate." Write for appointment to show portfolio, which should include thumbnails, final reproduction/product and photographs. Negotiates payment for design. Considers skill and experience of artist when establishing payment.
Tips: "Creativity depends on each individual. "Artists should have a sense of purpose & dependability."

SERIGRAPHICS ETC., Box 7200, Dallas TX 75209. Contact: Michael Truly. Specializes in packaging, publications and technical illustration, displays and signs. Clients: electronic companies, direct mail catalog industry—wholesale and retail, household appliance manufacturers, architectural firms, decorators and restaurants.
Needs: Works with 2-3 freelance artists/year. Works on assignment. Uses artists for advertising and catalog design, illustration and layout; P-O-P displays, mechanicals, retouching, posters, signs, charts/graphs, logos and architectural models.
First Contact & Terms: Artists must be careful and accurate, and able to interpret rough layouts. Send query letter with brochure, resume and business card to be kept on file. Write for appointment to show portfolio, which should include photographs or Photostats. Samples returned only if requested. Reports only if interested. Pays for design and mechanical production work by the hour, $6-7 average. Considers complexity of project, client's budget, skill and experience of artist, how work will be used and turnaround time when establishing payment.
Tips: "Show neat, accurate samples, if possible, that have been used in publication."

DEBORAH SHAPIRO DESIGNS, 150 Bentley Ave., Jersey City NJ 07304. (201)432-5198. Owner: Deborah Shapiro. Specializes in annual reports, brand identity, corporate identity, direct mail, packaging and publications. Clients: corporations and manufacturers.
Needs: Works with 10 freelance artists/year. Works on assignment only. Uses artists for illustrations, retouching and airbrushing and photography.
First Contact & Terms: Send query letter with brochure or resume, tear sheets, Photostats and photocopies. Samples are filed. Samples not filed are not returned. Reports back only if interested. To show a portfolio, mail original/final art, final reproduction/product, tear sheets and photographs. Pays for illustration by the project, $200-2,000. Considers complexity of project, client's budget, skill and experience of artist, how work will be used, turnaround time and rights purchased when establishing payment. Buys one-time rights.

SHERIN & MATEJKA, INC.404 Park Ave. S, New York NY 10016. (212)686-8410. President: Jack Sherin. Specializes in corporate communications, publications and sales promotion. Clients: banks, consumer magazines and insurance companies.
Needs: Works with 25 freelance artists/year. Prefers artists located nearby with solid professional experience. Works on assignment only. Uses artists for advertising and brochure design and illustration, mechanicals, retouching, model making, charts/graphs and lettering.
First Contact & Terms: Send query letter with brochure showing art style to be kept on file. Samples returned by SASE. Reports in 1 week. Call to schedule an appointment to show a portfolio, which should include original/final art and tear sheets. Pays $15-40/hour for design; negotiates illustration

payment method. Considers complexity of project, client's budget, skill and experience of artist, and how work will be used when establishing payment.
Tips: "We buy many humorous illustrations for use in corporate publications."

***ROGER SHERMAN ASSOCIATES, R.S. INTERIORS**, Suite 300, 13530 Michigan Ave., Dearborn MI 48126. (313)582-8844. Contact: Jan Sellars. Interior design and contract purchasing firms providing architectural and interior design for commercial restaurants, stores, hotels and shopping centers and complete furnishing purchasing. Clients: commercial.
Needs: Artists with past work experience only, able to provide photos of work and references. Works on assignment only. Uses artists for architectural renderings, furnishings, landscape and graphic design, model making and signage; also for special decor items as focal points for commercial installations, such as paintings, wood carvings, etc.
First Contact & Terms: Send query letter with brochure/flyer or resume and samples to be kept on file. Prefers slides and examples of original work as samples. Samples not returned. Reporting time depends on scope of project. Call or write for appointment. Negotiates payment; varies according to client's budget.

SMITH & DRESS, 432 W. Main St., Huntington NY 11743. (516)427-9333. Contact: A. Dress. Specializes in annual reports, corporate identity, displays, direct mail, packaging, publications and signage. Clients: corporations.
Needs: Works with 3-4 freelance artists/year. Local artists only. Works on assignment only. Uses artists for illustration, retouching, airbrushing and lettering.
First Contact & Terms: Send query letter with brochure showing art style or tear sheets to be kept on file (except for works larger than 8½x11). Pays for illustration by the project. Considers client's budget and turnaround time when establishing payment.

***JAMES C. SMITH, ART DIRECTION & DESIGN**, Box 558, Glen Ridge NJ 07028. (201)429-2177. Freelance Artist: Lucille Simonetti, 14 Edgemere Rd., Livingston NJ 07039. Clients: food processors, cosmetics firms, various industries, corporations, life insurance, office consultant.
Needs: Works with 10-20 freelance artists/year. Requires quality and dependability. Uses freelance artists for advertising and brochure design, illustration and layout; interior and landscape design and renderings; architectural renderings; design consulting; furnishings; charts and maps.
First Contact & Terms: Send query letter with brochure showing art style or resume and tear sheets and Photostats. Samples are filed. Samples not filed are returned only if requested by artist. Reports back within 1 week. Call to schedule an appointment to show a portfolio, which should include roughs, original/final art, final reproduction and color. Pays for design by the hour, $15-30. Pays for illustration by the hour, $25 minimum. Considers complexity of project and client's budget when establishing payment. Buys all rights. Also buys rights for use of existing non-commissioned art.
Tips: "Know what you're doing & do it well!"

HARRY SPRUYT DESIGN, Box 6500, New York NY 10128. Principal: Harry Spruyt. Specializes in structural packaging, product design and invention. Clients: product manufacturers, design firms, consultants and ad agencies.
Needs: Works with various freelance artists/year. Works on assignment only. Uses artists for illustrations, model making and accurate perspective drawings of products.
First Contact & Terms: Portfolio should include thumbnails, roughs, original/final art, final reproduction/product, photographs of models and color. Pays for design and illustration by the hour, $10-25. Considers "usable work, competence in doing job and rate of accomplishment with assignments" when establishing payment.
Tips: "Be succinct in conversation. Give a high value to our time together."

GORDON STROMBERG DESIGN, 5423 N. Artesian, Chicago IL 60625. (312)275-9449. President: Gordon Stromberg. Specializes in corporate identity, publications, interior design, direct mail and signage. Clients: professional offices, book publishing, small businesses, manufacturers, public relations firms, nonprofit organizations, Christian groups/charities and magazine publishers.
Needs: Works with small number of artists/year. Uses illustrators for, brochures, retouching and charts/graphs. "Open to seeing samples of your computer generated charts, illustrations and technical illustration."
First Contact & Terms: Looks for "quality, price and appropriateness in artists' work." Works on assignment only. Send query letter with brochure, resume and samples—"anything that will give me insight into your ability"—to be kept on file. "A phone call will only delay the process until you send brochure or samples or photocopies of samples." Prefers slides; accepts photocopies. Samples are returned

by SASE only if requested. Write for appointment to show portfolio. Considers complexity of project, client's budget, skill and experience of artist, how work will be used, and turnaround time when establishing payment.

SYNTHEGRAPHICS CORPORATION, 940 Pleasant Ave., Highland Park IL 60035. (312)432-7699. President: Richard Young. Specializes in publications. Clients: PR agencies, ad agencies and book publishers.
Needs: Works with 4-5 freelance artists/year. "Prefer local artists, particularly ones good at juvenile, multi-ethnic illustrations." Works on assignment only. Uses artists for advertising and brochure design, illustration and layout; book design and illustration; mechanicals and charts/graphs.
First Contact & Terms: Send resume and photocopies to be kept on file. Reports only if interested. Call for appointment to show portfolio, which should include thumbnails, roughs, original/final art, color, tear sheets and Photostats. Pays for design by the hour, $15-25 average. Pays for illustration by the hour, $10-15 average. Considers complexity of project, client's budget, and skill and experience of artist when establishing payment.

TESA DESIGN INC., 6122 Nancy Ridge Dr., San Diego CA 92121. (619)453-2490. President: Thomas E. Stephenson. Specializes in brand identity, corporate identity, packaging, signage and technical illustration. Clients: original equipment manufacturers.
Needs: Works with 4 freelance artists/year. Works on assignment only. Uses artists for design, illustration, brochures, catalogs, P-O-P displays, mechanicals, airbrushing, model making and logos.
First Contact & Terms: Send brochure and resume to be kept on file. Samples not kept on file are returned by SASE. Reports only if interested. Call for appointment to show portfolio. Pays for design and illustration by the project. Considers complexity of project, skill and experience of artist, and how work will be used when establishing payment.
Tips: "Portfolio should include industrial or mechanical subject matter."

TESSING DESIGN, INC., 3822 N. Seeley Ave., Chicago IL 60618. (312)525-7704. Principals: Arvid V. Tessing and Louise S. Tessing. Specializes in corporate identity and publications. Clients: publishers, educational institutions and nonprofit groups.
Needs: Works with 8-12 freelance artists/year. Works on assignment only. Uses artists for design, illustrations, books, magazines, mechanicals, retouching, airbrushing, charts/graphs and lettering.
First Contact & Terms: Send query letter with brochure. Samples are filed. Samples not filed are not returned. Reports back only if interested. Call to schedule an appointment to show a portfolio, which should include original/final art, final reproduction/product and photographs. Pays for design and illustration by the project. Considers complexity of project, client's budget, skill and experience of artist, how work will be used, turnaround time and rights purchased when establishing payment. Rights purchased vary according to project.

THARP DID IT, Suite 21, Fifty University Ave., Los Gatos CA 95030. (408)354-6726. Design Administrator: Sidney French. Specializes in brand identity, corporate identity, displays, packaging and signage. Clients: direct.
Needs: Works with 10-15 freelance artists/year. Prefers local artists/designers with experience. Works on assignment only. Uses artists for illustrations, P-O-P displays and retouching.
First Contact & Terms: Send query letter with brochure, resume or printed promotional material. Samples are filed. Samples not filed are returned by SASE. Reports back within 2 years only if interested. To show a portfolio, mail appropriate materials. Pays for illustration by the project, $50-5,000. Considers client's budget and how work will be used when establishing payment. Rights purchased vary according to project.
Tips: "Hang in there. If you're good we'll keep you on file. We may call this month, but if a project suited to you does not arise, you may not hear from us for a year or two."

THOMAS & MEANS ASSOCIATES, INC., 1428 Duke St., Alexandria VA 22314. (703)684-2215. Associate Director: Linda Kahn. Specializes in annual reports, corporate identity, publication, audio visual presentation and programs and communication consultation. Clients: corporations, government agencies, architects and developers, and associations.
Needs: Works with 12 freelance artists/year. Prefers local artists. Works on assignment only. Uses artists for design, illustration, brochures, magazines, mechanicals, retouching, airbrushing, charts/graphs, AV materials and logos.
First Contact & Terms: Send query letter with resume, tear sheets and photocopies to be kept on file. Samples not kept on file returned by SASE only if requested. Reports only if interested. Call for appointment to show portfolio. Pays for design by the hour, $15-35 average. Pays for illustration by the project, $300-2,500 average. Considers complexity of project, client's budget, skill and experience of artist,

how work will be used, turnaround time and rights purchased when establishing payment.
Tips: "Be persistent and show enthusiasm. Budgets are getting smaller again and clients are looking for the lowest bidder."

***TOKYO DESIGN CENTER**, Suite 928, 548 S. Spring St., Los Angeles CA 90013. (213)680-1294. Creative Art Director: Mac Watanabe. Specializes in corporate identity, advertising and packaging. Clients: fashion, cosmetic, architectural and industrial firms.
Needs: Works with 4 freelance artists/year. Uses artists for design, illustration, brochures, catalogs, books, P-O-P displays, mechanicals, airbrushing, charts/graphs and advertisements.
First Contact & Terms: Send samples to be kept on file. Samples not kept on filed not returned. Reports only if interested. Pays for design and illustration by the project. Considers client's budget when establishing payment.

TOKYO DESIGN CENTER, Suite 252, 703 Market St., San Francisco CA 94103. Contact: Curtis Tsukano. Specializes in annual reports, brand identity, corporate identity, packaging and publications. Clients: consumer products, travel agencies and retailers.
Needs: Uses artists for design and illustration.
First Contact & Terms: Send business card, slides, tear sheets and printed material to be kept on file. Samples not kept on file are returned by SASE only if requested. Reports only if interested. Pays for design by the project, $50-1,000 average. Pays for illustration by the project, $100-1,500 average. Considers client's budget, skill and experience of artist, turnaround time and rights purchased when establishing payment.

***TOTAL DESIGNERS**, Box 888, Huffman TX 77336. (713)688-7766. President: Ed Lorts. Specializes in corporate identity, displays, interior design, signage, technical illustrations and exhibit design.
Needs: Works with 2-3 freelance artists/year. Works on assignment only. Uses artists for brochure and catalog illustration, P-O-P displays, mechanicals and logos. Especially needs entry-level artist.
First Contact & Terms: Send query letter with brochure, resume and samples. Samples are filed. Samples not filed are returned. Reports back only if interested. Call or write to schedule an appointment to show portfolio, which should include thumbnails, roughs and original/final art. Pays for design by the project, $100 minimum. Pays for illustration by the project, $250. Considers complexity of project, skill and experience of artist, turnaround time and rights purchased when establishing payment. Buys all rights; rights purchased vary aocording to project.
Tips: "Bring turnkey,projects, thumbnails and roughs through to finished."

TRAVER AND ASSOCIATES, INC., 195 E. Columbia Ave., Battle Creek MI 49015. (616)963-7010. Vice President Operations: Chris Kreps. Specializes in brand identity, corporate identity, direct mail, packaging, publications and technical illustrations. Clients: food, auto, industry, health care, editorial design.
Needs: Works with 5 freelance artists/year. Prefers 2 years of experience. Works on assignment only. Uses artists for design, illustration, magazines, mechanicals, retouching, airbrushing, model making and AV material. Prefers airbrush, markers and computer illustration as media.
First Contact & Terms: Send query letter with brochure showing art style, resume, tear sheets, Photostats or photocopies. Samples are filed. Samples not filed are returned only if requested. Reports back within 1 month. Write to schedule an appointment to show a portfolio which should include final reproduction/product, tear sheets, photographs and color. Pays for design and illustration, $20-50. Considers complexity of project and skill and experience of artist when establishing payment. Rights purchased vary according to project.
Tips: Freelancers should "demonstrate an enthusiasm for their chosen field and willingness to take creative chances. Think beyond what is asked of them when appropriate. Have an awareness and interest in current trends and leaders in the industry."

TRIBOTTI DESIGNS,15234 Morrison St., Sherman Oaks CA 91403. (818)784-6101. Contact: Robert Tribotti. Specializes in annual reports, corporate identity, packaging, publications and signage. Clients: PR firms, ad agencies, corporations.
Needs: Works with 2-3 freelance artists/year. Prefers local artists only. Works on assignment only. Uses artists for illustrations, brochures, catalogs, mechanicals, retouching, airbrushing, charts/graphs, lettering and advertisements. Prefers markers, pen & ink, airbrush, pencil, colored pencil and computer illustration.
First Contact & Terms: Send query letter with brochure. Reports back only if interested. Call to schedule an appointment to show a portfolio, which should include thumbnails, roughs, original/final art, final reproduction/product, tear sheets, Photostats, photographs, b&w and color. Pays for illustration by the project, $75-1,000. Considers complexity of project, client's budget, skill and experience of

artist, how work will be used and rights purchased when establishing payment. Buys one-time rights; negotiates rights purchased. Rights purchased vary according to project.
Tips: "We will consider experienced artists only. Must be able to meet deadline."

THE T-SHIRT GALLERY LTD., 154 E. 64 St., New York NY 10021. (212)838-1212. Vice President: Flora Azaria. Specializes in t-shirts.
Needs: Works with 10 freelance artists/year. Uses artists for design and illustrations.
First Contact & Terms: Send query letter with resume and samples. Samples not filed are returned only if requested. Reports within weeks. To show a portfolio, mail appropriate materials. Pays for design by the project, $50-500. Pays for illustrations by the project, $50-500. Considers how work will be used when establishing payment.

UNICOM, 4100 W. River Lane, Milwaukee WI 53209. (414)354-5440. Senior Partner: Jay Filter. Specializes in annual reports, brand identity, corporate identity, packaging, publications and signage. Clients: retailers, industrial firms, fashion and professionals.
Needs: Works with 3-4 freelance artists/year. Works on assignment only. Uses artists for brochure and catalog design and illustration, P-O-P displays, charts/graphs, AV materials, lettering and logos.
First Contact & Terms: Send query letter with resume and slides.Samples not kept on file returned by SASE. Reports only if interested. To show a portfolio, mail thumbnails and roughs. Considers complexity of project, client's budget, skill and experience of artist, how work will be used and turnaround time when establishing payment. Rights purchased vary according to project.

UNIT 1, INC., 1556 Williams St., Denver CO 80218. (303)320-1116. President: Chuck Danford. Specializes in annual reports, brand identity, corporate identity, direct mail, packaging, publications and signage.
Needs: Uses artists for design, brochures, catalogs, P-O-P displays, mechanicals, posters, direct mail packages, charts/graphs, logos and advertisements. Prefers airbrush, markers and calligraphy.
First Contact & Terms: Send resume and samples to be kept on file. Samples not kept on file are returned. Reports only if interested. Call or write for appointment to show portfolio. Pays for design by the hour, $10 minimum or by the project, $100 minimum. Considers skill and experience of artist when establishing payment.

UNIVERSAL EXHIBITS, 9517 E. Rush St., South El Monte CA 91733. (213)686-0562. President: M.A. Bell.Specializes in displays and interior design. Clients: ad agencies and companies.
Needs: Works with 5 freelance artists/year. Prefers local artists, up to 40 miles, with excellent sketching abilities. Works on assignment only. Uses artists for design and model making.
First Contact & Terms: Send resume and samples to be kept on file. Prefers slides as samples; reviews original art. Samples not kept on file are returned only if requested. Reports back within 5 days. Call for appointment to show portfolio. Pays for design by the hour, $10-25 average. Considers client's budget and turnaround time when establishing payment.

WALTER VAN ENCK DESIGN LTD., 3830 N. Marshfield, Chicago IL 60613. (312)935-9438. President: Walter Van Enck. Specializes in annual reports, brand identity, corporate identity, displays, direct mail, packaging, publications and signage. Clients: book publishers, financial associations, health care institutions, investment advisory corporations and medium-sized corporations.
Needs: Works with 2-3 freelance artists/year. Prefers local artists. Works on assignment only. Uses artists for design, illustration, mechanicals, retouching, model making and lettering.
First Contact & Terms: Send query letter with business card and "slides or Photostats that do justice to line art" to be kept on file. Samples not kept on file are returned only if requested. Reports within 1 week. Call or write for appointment to show portfolio. Pays for illustration by the project, $500-2,500 average.

VIE DESIGN STUDIOS, INC., 830 Xenia Ave., Yellow Springs OH 45387. (513)767-7293. President: Read Viemeister. Specializes in corporate identity, packaging, publications and signage.
Needs: Works with 2 freelance illustrators/photographers per year. Artists must be local, or have a "very special style." Works on assignment only. Uses keyliners for mechanicals and charts/graphs. Prefers pen & ink.
First Contact & Terms: Send query letter with resume to be kept on file. Prefers to review Photostats and prints. Samples not kept on file are returned by SASE. Reports only if interested. Write for appointment to show portfolio. Pays for design by the hour, $20-30. Pays for illustration by the project, $100-300. Considers turnaround time when establishing payment.
Tips: "Smaller budgets require that design solutions be designed around existing resources, thus freelancer must be a known quantity."

***WARHAFTIG ASSOCIATES, INC.**, 48 West 25th, New York NY 10010. Production Coordinator: Chik Fung. Specializes in collateral, advertising, sales promotion for Fortune 500 companies.
Needs: Works with 20-30 freelance artists/year. Prefers very experienced artists. Uses freelance artists for brochure design and illustration, magazine design, mechanicals, retouching, charts/graphs, AV materials, lettering, logos and design of advertisements.
First Contact & Terms: Send query letter with resume and tear sheets. Samples not filed are returned if accompanied by a SASE. Does not report back. Write to schedule an appointment to show a portfolio, which should provide an adequate representation of style, concepts, work. Pays for design by the hour, $20-30. Pays for illustration by the project. Considers complexity of project, client's budget, skill and experience of artist, how work will be used, turnaround time and rights purchased when establishing payment. Rights purchased vary according to project.

BRUCE WASSERMAN & ASSOCIATES, Suite 1107, 568 Broadway, New York NY 10012. (212)226-4500. President: Bruce Wasserman. Specializes in annual reports, corporate identity, displays, packaging and signage. Clients: manufacturers and ad agencies.
Needs: Works with 10-20 freelance artists/year. Prefers local/mechanical people and illustrators. Works on assignment only. Uses artists for illustrations, mechanicals, retouching, airbrushing and lettering.
First Contact & Terms: Send query letter with tear sheets. Samples are filed. Samples not filed are returned only if requested. Reports back only if interested. Call or write to schedule an appointment to show a portfolio, which should include thumbnails, original/final art, final reproduction/product, tear sheets and photographs. Pays by the project. Considers complexity of project and client's budget when establishing payment. Buys all rights.

WHITEFLEET DESIGN INC., INE WIJTVLIET, 440 E. 56th St., New York NY 10022. (212)319-4444. Contact: Design Production. Specializes in annual reports, brand and corporate identity, displays, exhibits and shows, packaging, publications, signage and slide shows. Clients: large corporation in computers and engineering, retail stores, hospitals, banks, architects and industry.
Needs: Works with 8 freelance artists/year. Uses artists for brochure and catalog layout, mechanicals, retouching, model making, charts/graphs, AV presentations, lettering and logo design. Especially needs good artists for mechanicals for brochures and other print. Prefers Swiss graphic style.
First Contact & Terms: Send brochure/flyer and resume; submit portfolio for review. Prefers actual printed samples or color slides. Samples returned by SASE. Reports within 1 week. Provide brochure/flyer, resume and tear sheets to be kept on file for possible future assignments. Pays $10-15 average/hour for mechanicals; pays by the project for illustration.
Tips: Artists should "not start so high if unknown; give a break on the first 2 days to work in."

WISNER ASSOCIATES, Advertising, Marketing & Design, 2349 N.W. Flanders, Portland OR 97210. (503)228-6234. Creative Director: Linda Wisner. Specializes in brand identity, corporate identity, direct mail, packaging and publications. Clients: small businesses, manufacturers, restaurants, service businesses and book publishers.
Needs: Works with 7-10 freelance artists/year. Prefers experienced artists and "fast clean work." Works on assignment only. Uses artists for illustration, books, mechanicals, airbrushing and lettering.
First Contact & Terms: Send query letter with resume, Photostats, photocopies, slides and photographs to be kept on file. Prefers "examples of completed pieces, which show the abilities of the artist to his/her fullest." Samples not kept on file are returned by SASE only if requested. Reports only if interested. To show a portfolio, call to schedule an appointment or mail thumbnails, roughs, original/final art and final reproduction/product. Pays for illustration by the hour, $10-20 average. Pays for paste-up/production by the hour, $8.50-10. Considers complexity of project, client's budget, skill and experience of artist, how work will be used and turnaround time when establishing payment.
Tips: "Bring a complete portfolio with up-to-date pieces."

BENEDICT NORBERT WONG MARKETING DESIGN, 55 Osgood Pl., San Francisco CA 94133. (415)781-7590. President/Creative Director: Ben Wong. Specializes in direct mail and marketing design. Clients: financial services companies (banks, savings and loans, insurance companies, stock brokerage houses) and direct mail marketing firms (ad agencies, major corporations).
Needs: Works with 15 freelance artists/year. Uses artists for design, illustration, brochures, catalogs, mechanicals, retouching, posters, direct mail packages, charts/graphs, lettering, logos and advertisements. Especially needs "experienced designers in area of direct mail."
First Contact & Terms: Send query letter with resume, business card and samples to be kept on file. Prefers tear sheets as samples. Reports back only if interested. Call for appointment to show portfolio. "Payment depends on experience and portfolio." Considers complexity of project, client's budget, skill and experience of artist, how work will be used, turnaround time and rights purchased when establishing

payment.
Tips: "Please show imaginative problem-solving skills which can be applied to clients in direct marketing."

***WORDGRAPHICS, INC.**, Suite 208, 1372 Peachtree St. NE, Atlanta GA 30309. Art Director: Marilyn Shira. Specializes in typesetting, mechanical art, corporate identity, publications, slides, maps, ads and all graphics. Clients: printers, ad agencies, sales organizations, PR firms, publishers and manufacturers.
Needs: Works with varied number of freelance artists/year. Works on assignment only. Uses artists for mechanical preparation, layout, design and illustration and typesetting.
First Contact & Terms: Send query letter with resume to be kept on file. Call for appointment to show portfolio, which should include thumbnails, roughs, original/final art and final reproduction/product. Pays for design by the hour, $15-30; pays for illustration, $10-15.

WW3/PAPAGALOS, 313 E. Thomas, Phoenix AZ 85012. (602)279-2933. Creative Director: Nicholas Papagalos. Specializes in annual reports, corporate identity, displays, packaging, publications and signage. Clients: business to business.
Needs: Works with 10 freelance artists/year. Works on assignment only. Uses artists for illustrations, retouching, airbrushing, model making, charts/graphs, AV materials and lettering.
First Contact & Terms: Send query letter with brochure or resume and samples. Samples are filed. Samples not filed are returned only if requested. Reports back within 5 days. Call or write to schedule an appointment to show a portfolio, which should include thumbnails, roughs, final reproduction/product, Photostats and photographs. Pays for design and illustration by the project, $100 minimum. Considers complexity of project, client's budget, skill and experience of artist, how work will be used, turnaround time and rights purchased when establishing payment. Rights purchased vary according to project.
Tips: In presenting samples or portfolios, "two or three samples of the same type/style are enough."

"Artists need to learn to write a cover letter. A cover letter tells me if you can express yourself, and artists need to communicate well to be able to give presentations to a client. I would sooner give up some creativity to know how you're able to impact the needs of a client."

—M.J. Gordon, The Gordon Group
Duluth, Georgia

Art Publishers and Distributors

Art publishers reproduce and sell prints and reproductions. There *is* a difference between a print and a reproduction. Prints are original works of art created solely for the print medium. Lithographs, etchings, mezzotints, woodcuts and linocuts are original works of art, because the printmaking methods used to make them produce unique effects that only those methods can produce. Reproductions, on the other hand, are copies of original work. When a reproduction is made, a painting is usually photographed and reproduced.

Artists can sell an original painting only once, whereas they can enjoy repeat income from reproductions of the same painting. Prints are generally more affordable than paintings and are thus more accessible to art buyers. Both prints and reproductions offer illustrators and fine artists creative freedom, repeat income and widespread exposure.

Prints are usually produced as limited editions, which involve a specific number of prints, say 250 or 500, and therefore command a high retail price. Reproductions fall into three categories: limited editions, unlimited editions and posters. There is a limit to the number of unlimited edition prints run in each edition, but there is no limit to the number of editions that can be run if it is popular. Usually printed in large runs by photomechanical means (much like illustrations in a magazine), posters have evolved from an advertisement of an event or product into an affordable and collectible art form decorating homes and offices.

Art publishers issue printed works—either prints or reproductions—for sale. This means that an artist, a dealer, gallery, printer or businessperson who commissions or buys a work can be a publisher. There are artists who handle the whole process themselves—creating the image, printing and selling it. Others rely on the skills of professional printers and publishers, while some turn to dealers, who sell directly through their own galleries and possibly wholesale to other galleries. Most of the art publishers listed in this section are wholesale publishers who sell to galleries, frame shops and manufacturers, and other retail stores. Read the Close-up of Claire Scafa in this section for more details on how a wholesale publisher works.

Many publishers also handle the distribution of prints. Distribution entails marketing and selling works that have already been printed; either the artist has available editions or he is willing to have prints made at his own expense. The publisher/printer handles only the reproduction of works, leaving the actual distribution to the artist.

Publishers/distributors seek quality, saleable work with widespread appeal. An image must have good composition, reproduce well (have quality of line and good contrast) and appeal to a wide audience. Wholesale publishers must follow trends, since their decorative images must fit in with current decor. Certain subjects always sell better than others, such as children, florals and landscapes, but current trends favor animals such as cats, cows and large animals. Favorite color schemes also fluctuate every year, this year's being Southwest colors such as copper and bronze, and also flaming red, taupe and pastels.

When contacting an art publisher, remember that you're a potential investment to him. Send a résumé listing galleries representing you plus other professional art credits. A proven record of accomplishment helps. Your sample package should include slides or transparencies of your previously published or exhibited work. Label samples with information on size, medium and orientation (top, left, etc.). Be sure to include a self-addressed, stamped envelope that is large enough to return your samples.

Publishers generally offer either a flat fee or a royalty arrangement. The flat fee is based on an estimate of your sales potential and costs of printing and distribution. This arrangement is best if you are new to the field, unless you are confident that your edition will sell out. Royalties are based on a percentage of the retail price; they will be higher for established names and for smaller editions. Royalties for unlimited editions run 2.5 to 5% of wholesale price. This means that, for an edition of 5,000 reproductions sold wholesale for $15 a piece, you would earn $1,875 with a 2.5% royalty (5,000 × $15 = $75,000; $75,000 ÷ .025 = $1,875); this assumes, of course, that all 5,000 reproductions are sold.

Know what services the company is furnishing and what is expected of you before you sign a contract. You should retain the right to reproduce the image in other media, while selling to the publisher the right to reproduce the image as a certain type of print for a limited amount of time. Always retain ownership of the original work. The contract/agreement should also include the names and addresses of both parties, a description of the work, the size of the edition, payment and insurance terms, guarantee of a credit line and copyright notice plus the extent of promotion.

Keep current with the field by reading *Decor, Art Business News, Architectural Digest* and *Interior Design*. The Pantone Color Institute publishes the monthly *Color News*, and each year the Color Marketing Group publishes a list of colors that are popular for the year. Attend trade shows such as the Art Expo and the Art Buyers Caravan to meet people in the trade, plus trade shows in the decorative market such as the New York Gift Show and the National Housewares Show to see what subjects and themes are currently popular.

AARON ASHLEY INC., Suite 1905, 230 5th Ave., New York NY 10001. (212)532-9227. Contact: Philip D. Ginsburg. Produces unlimited edition fine quality 4-color offset and hand-colored reproductions for distributors, manufacturers, jobbers, museums, schools and galleries. Publishes 10 new artists/year. Pays royalties or fee. Offers advance. Negotiates rights purchased. Exclusive representation for unlimited editions. Written contract. Query, arrange interview or submit slides or photos. SASE. "Do not send originals." Reports immediately.
Acceptable Work: Considers oil paintings, watercolor and tempera. Prefers photo realistic wroks; unframed series.

ALJON INTERNATIONAL, 1481 SW 32 Ave., Pompano Beach FL 33069. (305)971-0070. President: Ronald Dvoretz. Art distributor of watercolors, acrylic and oil paintings, enamels on copper and collages. Clients: galleries, furniture stores, home show people, interior designers and other wholesalers and jobbers. Distributes work for 18 domestic artists/year. Pays flat fee. Negotiates payment method; very often pays on weekly basis. Negotiates rights purchased. Requires exclusive representation. Provides insurance while work is at distributor, promotion and shipping to and from distributor. Send query letter with brochure, slides or photos of originals. Samples returned only if requested. Reports only if interested. Call or write for appointment to show portfolio.
Acceptable Work: Considers oil and acrylic paintings, watercolors, mixed media and enamels on copper. Especially likes large (4'x5' or larger) acrylic abstracts—can be college work.
Tips: "Disregard retail pricing and come equipped with adequate samples. We must know colors. Subject matter is not of utmost importance."

***ALL SALES CO., INC.**, 3219 N. Cherry St., Hammond LA 70401. (504)542-8530. President: Tim Curry. Art publisher, distributor and agent handling limited editions, unlimited editions, handpulled originals and posters for galleries, department stores, etc. Pays royalties of 8% or payment method is negotiated. Offers an advance when appropriate. Buys all rights, reprint rights or negotiates rights purchased. Requires exclusive representation of the artist. Provides insurance while work is at firm. Send query letter with tear sheets, slides and transparencies. Samples not filed are returned by SASE only if requested. Reports back only if interested. Call or write to schedule an appointment to show a portfolio, or mail color.
Acceptable Work: Considers oil paintings, acrylic paintings, pastels, watercolor and mixed media. Prefers individual works of art and unframed series.
Tips: "Don't be your own critic. Work with a publisher, it's your name and his company's money."

AMERICAN ARTS & GRAPHICS, INC., (formerly AA Graphics, Inc.), 1200 N. 96th St., Seattle WA 98103. Licensing Coordinator: Shelley Pedersen.Publishes posters for a teenage market, minimum 5,000 run for department, record and poster stores, also discount drug stores. Artist's guidelines availa-

ble. Send query letter with tear sheets, Photostats, photocopies, slides and photographs; then submit sketch or photo of art. SASE. Reports in 2 weeks. Usually pays royalties of 10¢ per poster sold and an advance of $500 against future royalties.
Acceptable Work: Prefers 7x11" sketches; full-size posters are 23x35". Prefers airbrush, then acrylics and oils.
Tips: "Become familiar with popular posters by looking at designs in poster racks in stores. We do not want to see abstracts or geometrics."

***AMERICAN QUILTING ART**, Box S-3283, Carmel CA 93921. (408)659-0608. Sales Manager: Erica Summerfield. Art publisher of offset reproductions, unlimited editions and handpulled originals. Publishes/distributes the work of 3 artists/year. Payment method is negotiated. Offers an advance when appropriate. Buys all rights. Prefers exclusive representation of the artist. Provides in-transit insurance, insurance while work is at firm and shipping from firm. Send query letter with brochure showing art style or "any available material." Samples are filed. Samples not filed are returned by SASE. Reports back within 2 weeks. Write to schedule an appointment to show a portfolio.
Acceptable Work: Considers watercolor, pen & ink line drawings, oil paintings, acrylic paintings, pastels, tempera and mixed media. Prefers framed series.

***ANNEX ART STUDIO**, 2431 E. Las Olas Blvd., Ft. Lauderdale FL 33301. (305)524-8184. Owner: Laurence Crooks. Art publisher and distributor of limited editions and serigraphs to galleries. Publishes/distributes the work of 3 artists/year. Pays flat fee; $1,000-5,000, or payment method is negotiated. Offers an advance. Buys all rights. Requires exclusive representation of the artist. Provides shipping to and from firm. Send resume, tear sheets, Photostats, photographs and transparencies. Samples not filed are returned. Reports back within 10 days only if interested. Call to schedule an appointment to show a portfolio, or mail one print.
Acceptable Work: Prefers contemporary, photorealistic, impressionism. Prefers individual works of art and pairs, 20x28 maximum.
Tips: "We have a screen printing studio available in Florida for any artist wishing to pull his or her own prints. All necessary equipment, ink & paper will be provided free as part of the negotiated rights."

HERBERT ARNOT, INC., 250 W. 57th St., New York NY 10107. (212)245-8287. Vice President: Peter Arnot. Art distributor of original oil paintings. Clients: galleries. Distributes work for 250 artists/year. Pays flat fee, $100-1,000 average. Provides promotion and shipping to and from distributor. Send query letter with brochure, resume, business card, slides, photographs or original work to be kept on file. Samples not filed are returned. Reports within 1 month. Call or write for appointment to show portfolio.
Acceptable Work: Considers oil and acrylic paintings. Has wide range of themes and styles—"mostly traditional/impressionistic, not modern."
Tips: "Professional quality, please."

ART BEATS, INC., 2435 S. Highland Dr., Salt Lake City UT 84106. (801)487-1588. President: Robert Gerrard. Vice President: Jill Gerrard. Art publisher and distributor of limited and unlimited editions and offset reproductions. Clients: gift shops, frame stores, department stores and galleries. Publishes 20 freelance artists/year. Distributes work for 50 artists/year. Pays royalty of 10%; negotiates payment method. Sometimes offers an advance. Prefers to buy all rights or first rights. Requires exclusive representation. Provides promotion, shipping from firm and written contract. Send query letter with brochure showing art style or tear sheets, slides and photographs to be kept on file. Include SASE, address and telephone number and information on artist's background. Samples not filed returned only if requested. Reports within 1 month. To show a portfolio, mail tear sheets, Photostats and photographs.
Acceptable Work: Considers oil paintings, watercolors and mixed media; no b&w. Especially likes children's, country and floral themes, "but always interested in new things."

***ART EXCHANGE LTD**, Box 526, 20A Roundhill Mall, Zephyr Cove NV 89448. (702)588-7353. Marketing Director: Peggy Cain. Art publisher, distributor and secondary market for limited editions, handpulled originals and sculptures. Clients: galleries. Pays flat fee; $200-1,500; on consignment basis, firm receives 50% commission; payment method is negotiated. Offers an advance when appropriate.

The asterisk before a listing indicates that the listing is new in this edition. New markets are often the most receptive to freelance submissions.

Negotiates rights purchased. Provides insurance while work is at firm and a written contract. Send query letter with brochure and resume. Samples not filed are returned. Reports back within 20 days. Call or write to schedule an appointment to show a portfolio.
Acceptable Work: Considers oil paintings, acrylic paintings and sculptures.
Tips: "We are a very active business. Please have patience in returns of inquiries."

ART IMAGE INC., 1577 Barry Ave., Los Angeles CA 90025. (213)826-9000. President: Allan Fierstein. Publishes and produces unlimited editions and limited editions that are pencil signed and numbered by the artist. Also distributes etchings, serigraphs, lithographs and watercolor paintings. "Other work we publish and distribute includes handmade paper, cast paper, paper weavings and paper construction." All work sold to galleries, frame shops, framed picture manufacturers, interior decorators and auctioneers. Publishes 12-16 artists per year; distributes the work of 24 artists. Negotiates payment. Requires exclusive representation. Provides shipping and a written contract. Send query letter with brochure showing art style, tear sheets, slides and photographs. SASE. Reports within 1 week. To show a portfolio, mail appropriate materials or write to schedule an appointment; portfolio should include photographs.
Acceptable Work: "All subject matter and all media in pairs or series of companion pieces."
Tips: "We are publishing and distributing more and more subject matter from offset limited editions to etchings, serigraphs, lithographs and original watercolor paintings."

*ART RESOURCES INTERNATIONAL, LTD.**, 98 Commerce St., Stamford CT 06902-4506. (203)967-4545, (800)228-2989. Fax: (203)967-4545. Telex: 3712965. Vice President: Robin E. Bonnist. Art publisher. Publishes unlimited edition offset lithographs. Clients: galleries, department stores, distributors, framers throughout the world. Publishes 100 freelance artists/year. Distributes work of 200 artists/year. Also uses artists for advertising layout and brochure illustration. Pays by royalty (5-10%), or flat fee of $250-1,000. Offers advance in some cases. Requires exclusive representation of the artist for prints/posters during period of contract. Provides in-transit insurance, insurance while work is at publisher, shipping to and from firm, promotion and a written contract. Artist owns original work. Send query letter with brochure, tear sheets, slides and photographs to be kept on file or returned if requested; prefers to see slides or transparencies initially as samples, then reviews originals. Samples not kept on file returned by SASE. Reports within 1 month. Call or write for appointment to show portfolio, or mail appropriate materials, which should include transparencies, slides and photographs.
Acceptable Work: Considers oil and acrylic paintings, pastels, watercolors and mixed media. Prefers pairs or series, triptychs, diptychs.
Tips: "Please submit any and all ideas. We prefer to work with artists who are creative, professional and open to art direction."

***ART SOURCE**, Unit 2, 210 Cochrane Dr., Markham, Toronto, Ontario L3R 8E6 Canada. (416)475-8181. Art publisher and distributor. Produces posters, offset reproductions, art cards, handpulled originals, and prints using offset, lithograph, screen and etching for galleries and department stores. Publishes 20-30 freelance artists/year; distributes the works of 20-30 artists/year. Negotiates payment method. Negotiates rights purchased. Provides insurance while work is at publisher, promotion and a written contract. Negotiates ownership of original art. Send query letter with brochure, resume, and tear sheets, slides and photographs to be kept on file. To show a portfolio, mail thumbnails, tear sheets, Photostats and photographs. Samples not kept on file returned by SASE if requested. Reports within 14 days.
Acceptable Work: Considers oil and acrylic paintings, pastels, airbrush, acrylics, oils, gouache, tempara, watercolors, mixed media and photographs. Themes and styles open. Prefers pairs and series; unframed.
Tips: "Show us your work in its best possible way. We see you through what you show us." One of today's most popular mediums is the poster—"we publish many of them." Portfolio should include transparencies and a complete range of work. "No rude or violent work."

ART SPECTRUM, division of Mitch Morse Gallery, Inc., 334 E. 59th St., New York NY 10022. (212)593-1812. President: Mitch Morse. Art publisher and distributor. Produces limited editions (maximum of 250 prints) and handpulled originals—all 'multi-original' editions of lithographs, etchings, collographs, serigraphs. Serves galleries, frame shops, hotels, interior designers, architects and corporate art specifiers. Publishes 8-10 freelance artists/year; distributes the works of 15-20 artists/year. Negotiates payment method. Offers advance. Negotiates rights purchased. Provides promotion and shipping. Artist owns original art. Send query letter with resume, slides and photographs to be kept on file. Call or write for appointment to show portfolio, which should include original/final art and photographs. Samples not kept on file are returned. Reports within 1 week.
Acceptable Work: Considers original fine art prints only. Offers "subjects primarily suitable for cor-

porate offices. Not too literal; not too avant-garde." Prefers series; unframed (framed unacceptable); 30x40"maximum.
Tips: "Do not stop by without appointment. Do not come to an appointment with slides only—examples of actual work must be seen. No interest in reproductive (photo-mechanical) prints—originals only. Submit work that is "an improved version of an existing 'look' or something completely innovative." Actively seeking additional artists who do original paintings on paper. Trends show that the "current demand for contemporary has not yet peaked in many parts of the country. The leading indicators in the New York City design market point to a strong resurgence of Old English."

***ART WORLD INDUSTRIES/COLLIER PUBLISHING**, 5966 Bowcroft, Los Angeles CA 90016. Director of Operations: DeAnne Davenport. Estab. 1986. Art publisher and distributor of limited editions to galleries, department stores, decorators and auctions. Publishes/distributes the work of 2-4 artists/year. Pays flat fee; $1,000 minimum - $10,000, or payment method is negotiated. Offers an advance when appropriate. Negotiates rights purchased. Provides insurance while work is at firm, shipping to and from firm to clients only and a written contract. Send query letter with resume, slides and transparencies. Samples are not filed, but returned by SASE. Reports back within 2 weeks only if interested. To show a portfolio, mail slides and transparencies.
Acceptable Work: Considers oil paintings, acrylic paintings, pastels, watercolor, gouache, collage, tempera and mixed media. Prefers individual works of art.
Tips: "Show slides only. I do not want to see published work."

***ARTHUR'S INTERNATIONAL**, Box 10599, Honolulu HI 96816. President: Marvin C. Arthur. Art distributor handling original oil paintings primarily. Distributes limited and unlimited edition prints. Clients: galleries, collectors, etc. "We pay a flat fee to purchase the original. Payment made within 5 days. We pay 30% of our net profit made on reproductions. The reproduction royalty is paid after we are paid." Artists may be handled on an exclusive or non-exclusive basis. Send brochure, slides or photographs to be kept on file if interested. No originals unless requested. Artist biographies appreciated. Samples not filed returned by SASE. Reports back normally within 1 week.
Acceptable Work: Considers all types of original art works. Purchases have been made in pen & ink, charcoal, pencil, tempera, watercolor, acrylics, oils, gouache and pastels. "All paintings should be photographic in texture or have an eye appeal of the subject matter that is not a modern art puzzle."
Tips: "We desire fine quality work. It may be realism, impressionism or an eighteenth or nineteenth century styling, as long as the artist has given proper attention to detail. Having a track record is nice, but it is not a requirement. Being known or unknown is not the important thing, being talented and being able to show it to our taste is what is important."

ARTHURIAN ART GALLERY, 5836 Lincoln Ave., Chicago IL 60053. Owner: Art Sahagian. Estab. 1985. Art distributor/gallery handling limited editions, handpulled originals, bronzes, watercolors, oil paintings and pastels. Works with 40-50 artists/year. Pays flat fee, $50-1,000 average. Rights purchased vary with work. Provides insurance while work is at firm, promotion and a written contract. Send query letter with brochure showing art style or resume, photocopies, slides and prices. Samples not filed returned by SASE. Reports within 30 days. To show a portfolio, mail appropriate materials or write to schedule an appointment. Portfolio should include original/final art, color, final reproduction/product and photographs. Considers complexity of project, client's budget, and skill and experience of artist when establishing payment.

***ARTISTS' MARKETING SERVICE**, Box 984, Bowie MD 20715. President: Jim Chidester. Estab. 1987. Distributor of limited and unlimited editions, offset reproductions and posters. Clients: galleries, frame shops and designers. Distributes the work of 75-100 freelance artists/year. Pays on consignment basis (50% commission). Offers an advance when appropriate. Purchases one-time rights. Does not require exclusive representation of artist. Provides insurance while work is at firm and shipping to and from firm. Send query letter with brochure, tear sheets and photographs. Samples are filed. Samples not filed are returned by SASE only if requested by artist. Reports back within weeks. Write to schedule an appointment to show a portfolio, or mail tear sheets and slides.
Acceptable Work: Prefers traditional themes, landscapes, seascapes, nautical, wildlife, Americana, impressionistic, and country themes. Prefers individual works of art.
Tips: "We are only interested in seeing work from self-published artists who are interested in distribution of their prints. We are presently *not* reviewing originals for publication."

ARTISTWORKS WHOLESALE INC., 32 S. Lansdowne Ave., Lansdowne PA 19050. (215)626-7770. Contact: Michael Markowicz. Art publisher and art distributor of offset reproductions and handpulled originals. Clients: distributors, galleries, decorators and other retailers. Works with 2-4 freelance artists/year. Negotiates payment method. Advance depends on payment method. Negotiates rights purchased.

Requires exclusive representation. Provides in-transit insurance, insurance while work is at firm, promotion, shipping to and from firm and written contract. Send query letter with resume, slides and photographs to be kept on file. To show a portfolio, mail appropriate materials, which should include original/final art, final reproduction/product and photographs. "We only review original work after first seeing slides." Samples not filed returned by SASE.
Acceptable Work: Considers oil and acrylic paintings, pastels and watercolors; serigraphs. Especially likes still life/landscapes.
Tips: "We are looking for very well-executed still lifes and landscapes. We are not looking for traditional pieces but would rather work with a contemporary look. We have also received many more submissions than we can possibly publish. Artists should realize that we can only publish a few of the best works submitted. Submit only if you are producing high-quality, contemporary art."

ATLANTIC GALLERY, 1055 Thomas Jefferson St. NW, Washington DC 20007. (202)337-2299. Director: Virginia Smith. Art publisher/distributor. Publishes signed prints using offset lithography and hand-colored, handpulled restrike engravings. Also publishes architectural prints. Clients: retail galleries, department stores, decorators, large commercial accounts, and manufacturers. Publishes 3 freelance artists/year. Pays flat fee, $250-1,000 average. Offers advance. Buys one-time rights. Provides in-transit insurance, insurance while work is at publisher, promotion, shipping to and from publisher and a written contract. Negotiates ownership of original art. Send query letter with brochure, resume, slides, photographs and tear sheets to be kept on file. Samples not kept on file returned by SASE. Reports within 3 weeks. Call or write for appointment to show portfolio.
Acceptable Work: Considers oil and acrylic paintings, pastels and watercolors. Prefers traditional art and landscapes.

BECOME A POSTER, (division of Photo Environments), 2021 Vista del Man Ave., Los Angeles CA 90068. (213)465-9947. President: Joan Yarfitz. Works on assignment only. Uses freelance artists for marketing and advertising, posters, brochures and collateral materials. Send query letter with brochure showing art style or samples. Samples not filed are returned by SASE if requested. Call or write to schedule an appointment to show a portfolio. Negotiates payment. Considers clients' preferences when establishing payment. Negotiates rights purchased.
Acceptable Work: Considers illustration, b&w, color and photography.

BERNARD PICTURE CO. INC., Springdale Graphics, Box 4744, Stamford CT 06907. (203)357-7600. Art Director: Michele Beckhardt. Art publisher. Produces high quality reproductions using offset lithography for galleries, picture framers, distributors, and manufacturers worldwide. Publishes over 50 freelance artists/year. Pays royalties to artist of 10%. Offers advance against royalties. Buys all rights. "Sometimes" requires exclusive representation of the artist. Provides in-transit insurance and insurance while work is at publisher, promotion, shipping from firm and a written contract. Send query letter with brochure showing art style or slides and transparancies. Samples returned only if requested. Reports within 2 weeks. Call or write for appointment to show portfolio.
Acceptable Work: Considers oil paintings, acrylic paintings, pastels, watercolor and tempera. Prefers individual works, series and sets; unframed.

***BUCKHORN FINE ART PUBLISHING**,Box 10, Buckhorn, Ontario K0L 1J0 Canada. (705)657-1107. Sales Manager: Penny Beliveau. Art publisher, distributor, gallery, framing shop and promotions firm handling limited editions, offset reproductions, unlimited editions and greeting cards, calendars, reproductions on canvas. Clients: galleries, department stores, promotion companies, distributors in United States, Britain, Japan and Germany. Publishes the work of 10 freelance artists/year and distributes the work of 15 freelance artists/year. Payment method is negotiated, "depends on size of editions, size of prints, popularity of artist, promotion, etc." Occasionally offers an advance. Negotiates rights purchased. Sometimes requires exclusive representation of the artist. Provides insurance while work is at firm; negotiates other services. Send query letter with brochure showing art style or resume, tear sheets, photographs and any promotional information. Samples are filed. Samples not filed are returned. Reports back within 10 days. To show a portfolio, mail original/final art and final reproduction/product.
Acceptable Work: Considers pen & ink line drawings, oil paintings, acrylic paintings, pastels, watercolor, tempera and mixed media. "We prefer wildlife, landscapes, floral, seascapes, but are open to anything." Prefers individual works of art, pairs and unframed series.
Tips: "Be sure to show a good variety and sampling of work."

C.R. FINE ARTS LTD., 249 A St., Boston MA 02210. (617)236-4225. President: Carol Robinson. Art publisher/distributor/gallery handling limited editions, sculptures and fine art posters. Clients: galleries, poster stores, department stores, decorators, art consultants. Publishes 5-6 artists/year; distributes work of 30 artists/year. Pays royalty (15-30%) or works on consignment (40% commission);pays a flat

fee of $500; payment method is negotiated. Offers advance. Negotiates rights purchased. Provides in-transit insurance, insurance while work is at firm, promotion, shipping to and from firm and a written contract. Send query letter with resume and slides to be kept on file. Samples not filed returned by SASE only if requested. Reports within 3 weeks. Write for appointment to show portfolio.
Acceptable Work: Considers pastels, watercolors and mixed media; serigraphs, and stone or plate lithographs. Especially likes landscapes, seascapes, contemporary themes, beach scenes, animals, music themes, abstracts.
Tips: "We look for landscape artists who have a perspective and a depth of composition. Colors are important and a textural quality."

CANADIAN ART PRINTS INC., 736 Richards St., Vancouver, British Columbia V6B 3A4 Canada. (604)681-3485. President: Jasar Nassrin. Publishes limited edition handpulled originals and offset reproductions for galleries, card and gift shops, department stores, framers and museum shops. Publishes 40-50 artists/year. Send slides or photos. Reports within 5 weeks. Provides promotion, shipping from publisher and written contract. Pays royalties.
Acceptable Work: Considers paintings, pastels, watercolors, intaglio, stone lithographs and serigraphs.

CARIBBEAN ARTS, INC., 985 Westchester Pl., Los Angeles CA 90019. (213)732-4601. Director: Bernard Hoyes. Art publisher/distributor of limited and unlimited editons, offset reproductions and handpulled originals. Clients: galleries, stores, bookstores, corporations, art dealers and collectors. Works with 2-3 artists/year. Pays $50-1,200 flat fee; 15% royalties or on consigment. Payment method is negotiated. Offers an advance. Purchases first rights or negotiates rights purchased. Provides in-transit insurance, insurance while work is at firm, promotion, shipping from firm and a written contract. Send query letter with brochure or resume and slides. Samples are filed. Samples not filed are returned only if requested. Reports back within 10 days. Call or write to schedule an appointment to show a portfolio, which should include original/final art.
Acceptable Work: Considers oil paintings, pastels and watercolor. Prefers original themes and primitivism. Prefers individual works of art. Maximum size 30x40"
Tips: "Do a lot of original work."

***CAVU RANCH, INC.**, 41295 Hwy 184, Mancos CO 81328. (303)533-7277. Creative Director: Barbara Lockard. Art publisher and manufacturer of unlimited editions and screened fabric. Clients: giftware industry, department stores, galleries and direct mail catalogs. Publishes the work of 15 freelance artists/year. Pays flat fee, $50-200; payment is negotiated. Buys all rights. Provides insurance while work is at firm, shipping from firm and a written contract. Send query letter. Samples are not filed and returned only if requested. Reports back only if interested. Write to schedule an appointment to show a portfolio, or mail roughs and tear sheets.
Acceptable Work: Considers pen & ink line drawings and hand-cut screens. Prefers Southwest images and wildlife. Prefers individual works of art, 24x36 maximum.
Tips: "Must have working knowledge of silk screen printing."

THE CHASEN PORTFOLIO, 6 Sloan St., South Orange NJ 07079. (201)761-1966. President: Andrew Chasen. Art publisher/distributor of limited editions and handpulled originals for galleries, decorators, designers, art consultants and corporate art buyers. Publishes work of 3 artists/year and distributes the work of 10-15 artists/year. Payment method is negotiated. Negotiates rights purchased. Requires exclusive representation. Provides in-transit insurance, insurance while work is at firm, promotion, shipping to and from firm and a written contract. Send query letter with brochure or tear sheets, photographs and slides. Samples are filed. Samples not filed are returned by SASE only if requested. Reports back only if interested. Call or write to schedule an appointment to show a portfolio, which should include original/final art, final reproduction/product and color. Payment method is negotiated.
Acceptable Work: Considers oil paintings, acrylic paintings, pastels, watercolor, monoprints, lithographs, serigraphs, etchings and mixed media. Prefers architecture, figurative, still life, landscapes and impressionism. Prefers individual works of art, pairs and unframed series.

CIRRUS EDITIONS, 542 S. Alameda St., Los Angeles CA 90013. President: Jean R. Milant. Produces limited edition handpulled originals for museums, galleries and private collectors. Publishes 3-4 artists/year. Send slides of work. Prefers slides as samples. Samples returned by SASE.
Acceptable Work: Contemporary paintings and sculpture.

CLASS PUBLICATIONS, INC., 237 Hamilton St., Hartford CT 06106. (203)951-9200. Vice President: Leo Smith. Art publisher of offset reproductions. Publishes work of 2-3 artists/year. Pays $500-1,500 flat fee. Offers an advance. Buy all rights. Provides promotion, shipping from firm and a written con-

tract. Send query letter with brochure or slides and transparencies. Samples are not filed. Samples not filed are returned only if requested. Reports back only if interested. To show a portfolio, mail slides.
Acceptable Work: Considers oil paintings, acrylic paintings and airbrush. "Our posters are published on 100 lb. text, retailing for $4.50, for the college market. Artwork should be creative using strong colors with good detail. Common areas of humor are very much sought after. Examples of those areas include money, sex, married life, medicare." Prefers individual works of art.
Tips: "Take a look at the artwork. Does it have a broad market appeal? We look for artwork that will have the qualities of sophistication and mass appeal combined."

***COLONIA ART PUBLICATIONS**, 654 Santa Cruz Ave., Menlo Park CA 94025. (415)329-0740. President: David Newton. Art publisher of limited editions and posters for galleries and interior decorators. Publishes/distributes the work of 4 artists/year. Pays royalties; payment is negotiated. Negotiates rights purchased. Provides in-transit insurance and promotion. Send query letter with photographs and slides. Samples are not filed and are returned only if requested. Reports back within 10 days. Call to schedule an appointment to show a portfolio, or mail appropriate materials.
Acceptable Work: Considers acrylic paintings and watercolor. Prefers unframed series.
Tips: "Particularly, we are looking for a style which is original—the pieces should be capable of being developed as a series. A key requirement is a large amount of detail in the execution—this can be developed for pieces for publication."

GREG COPELAND INC., 10-14 Courtland St., Paterson NJ 07503. (201)279-6166. President: Greg Copeland. Art publisher and distributor of limited editions, handpulled originals, editions of sculpture, cast paper, paintings and dimensional sculpture. Clients: designers, architects, galleries, commercial designers, department stores, galleries and designer showrooms. Publishes 10-15 freelance artists/year. Works with 25-40 artists/year. Pays in royalties of 5% or negotiates payment method. Negotiates rights purchased. Provides shipping to firm. Send query letter with samples; or call or write for appointment to show portfolio. Prefers original work as samples. Samples are returned. Reports within 10 days.
Acceptable Work: Considers pen & ink line drawings, acrylic paintings, pastels, watercolors, mixed media, dimensional sculpture and sculpture; serigraphs. Looks for "beauty-excitement." Especially likes still lifes; modern style.

***COOPERATIVE ARTISTS PUBLISHING SERVICES**, 1414 S. Third St., Box 746, Minneapolis MN 55458-0746. (612)333-5498. Artists Coordinator: Cheri Anderson. Services Coordinator: Scott Owens. Primarily a distributor for artists, will assist in publishing. Handles a range of work from handpulled originals to mass market reproductions. Clients: high-end and mass-market retail, design professionals, end viewer, and alternative means of distribution including volume purchasers and other distributors. Distributes many artists each year. Payment method is negotiated consignment (maximum 90% to artist). Requires exclusive right to distribute accepted works for a specific period of time. Shares in promotion, provides insurance on premises, and written contract. Send query letter with brochure, resume, tear sheets, photographs, slides or transparencies. Reports within five days. Samples not filed are returned by SASE.
Acceptable Work: All works considered. "Cooperative Artists Publishing Services believes that, to the maximum extent possible, the public should 'jury' submissions. At the same time, the accomplishments of previously published artists must be respected." New artists will be presented in separate forums.
Tips: "Cooperative Artists Publishing Services is not a conventional distributor/publisher. It offers both higher reward and higher risk for the confident artist who desires a service bureau to make his or her product available in the marketplace."

***CROSS GALLERY, INC.**, 180 N. Center, Suite 1, Box 4181, Jackson WY 83001. (307)733-2200. Director: Mary Schmidt. Art publisher/distributor/gallery. Publishes/distributes, limited editions, offset reproductions and handpulled originals; also sells original works. Clients: galleries, retail customers, and corporate businesses. "We are just getting started and are developing galleries in other areas of the US for distributing work." Payment method is negotiated. Offers an advance when appropriate. Requires exclusive area representation of the artist. Provides insurance while work is at firm and shipping from firm. Send query letter with resume, tear sheets, Photostats, photographs, slides and transparencies. Samples are filed. Samples not filed are returned by SASE. Reports back within "a reasonable amount of time." Call to schedule an appointment to show a portfolio and mail Photostats, tear sheets, slides, transparencies, color.
Acceptable Work: Considers pen & ink line drawings, oil and acrylic paintings, pastels, watercolor, tempera, and mixed media. Prefers Western Americana with an emphasis on realism as well as contemporary art.
Tips: "We look for originality."

***CUPPS OF CHICAGO, INC.**, 221 Stanley, Elk Grove IL 60007. (312)593-5655. President: Dolores Cupp. Art publisher and distributor of limited editions, offset reproductions and original oil paintings for galleries, frame shops, designers and home shows. Publishes the work of 10 freelance artists/year and distributes the work of 200 freelance artists/year. Pays flat fee; and royalties of 10%. Offers an advance when appropriate. Negotiates rights purchased. Provides promotion and a written contract. Send query letter with brochure showing art style or resume and photographs. Samples are filed. Samples not filed are returned only if requested. Reports back only if interested. Call or write to schedule an appointment to show a portfolio, which should include original/final art.
Acceptable Work: Considers pen & ink drawings, oil paintings and acrylic paintings. Considers "almost any style—only criterion is that it must be well done." Prefers individual works of art.
Tips: "Work must look professional."

DANMAR PRODUCTIONS, INC., 7387 Ashcroft, Houston TX 77081. (713)774-3343. Vice President: Marlene Caress. Estab. 1985. Art publisher of limited and unlimited editions, offset reproductions and handpulled originals for galleries, designers and contract framers. Publishes work of 10-15 artists/year. Pays 10% royalties. Payment method is negotiated. Offers an advance. Negotiates rights purchased. Requires exclusive representation. Provides insurance while work is at firm, promotion, shipping from firm and a written contract. Send query letter with brochure or tear sheets, photographs, slides and transparencies. Samples not filed are returned by SASE. Reports back within 10 days. To show a portfolio, mail original/final art, tear sheets, slides, final reproduction/product and color.
Acceptable Work: Considers oil paintings, acrylic paintings, pastels, watercolor and mixed media.
Tips: "We are looking to work with talented people who maintain a professional attitude. Originality is important and color is critical in our industry. We welcome all new talent and offer a quick, honest appraisal."

***DEL BELLO GALLERY**, 363 Queen St. W., Toronto M5V 2A4 Canada. (416)593-0884. Owner: Egidio Del Bello. Art publisher and gallery handling handpulled originals for private buyers, department stores and galleries. Publishes the work of 10 freelance artists/year. Payment method is negotiated. Offers an advance when appropriate. Negotiates rights purchased. Provides promotion. Send query letter with resume, photographs and slides. Samples are filed. Samples not filed are returned by SASE within 2 weeks. Call to schedule an appointment to show a portfolio, which should include original/final art and slides.
Acceptable Work: Considers material suitable for lithography. "Interested in all styles." Prefers individual works of art.

DESIGNART, 2700 S. La Cienega Blvd., Los Angeles CA 90034. (213)870-0021. President: Carole Franklin. Art distributor of limited editions, offset reproductions and handpulled originals for designers, architects, art consultants and galleries. Distributes work of 200 artists/year. Payment method is negotiated. Buys one-time rights. Provides insurance while work is at firm and shipping from firm. Send query letter with brochure or resume, tear sheets, photographs and slides. Samples are filed. Samples not filed are returned only if requested. Reports back within 2 weeks. Call or write to schedule an appointment to show a portfolio, which should include original/final art.
Acceptable Work: Prefers contemporary, sculptural, 3-D, traditional and original themes and impressionism. Uses airbrush, watercolor, acrylics, oils, gouache, collage, mixed media, pastels and 3-D paper sculpture. Prefers individual works of art, pairs and unframed series.

***DODO GRAPHICS, INC.**, Box 585, 119 Cornelia St., Plattsburgh NY 12901. (518)561-7294. Manager: Frank How. Art publisher of offset reproductions, posters and etchings for galleries and frame shops. Publishes the work of 5 freelance artists/year. Payment method is negotiated. Offers an advance when appropriate. Buys all rights. Requires exclusive representation of the artist. Provides a written contract. Send query letter with brochure showing art style or photographs and slides. Samples are filed. Samples not filed are returned by SASE. Reports back within 3 months. Write to schedule an appointment to show a portfolio, which should include original/final art and slides.
Acceptable Work: Considers pastels, watercolor, tempera, mixed media and airbrush. Prefers contemporary themes and styles. Prefers individual works of art, 16x20 maximum.
Tips: "Do not send any originals unless agreed upon by publisher."

DONALD ART CO. INC., and division Impress-Graphics, 30 Commerce Rd., Stamford CT 06904-2102. (203)348-9494. Art Coordinator: Barbara Nieder. Produces unlimited edition offset reproductions for wholesale picture frame manufacturers, and manufacturers using art in their end products, for premiums and promotions. Send query letter with resume and duplicate photos or slides. Exclusive area representation required. Provides in-transit insurance, insurance while work is at publisher, shipping, promotion and written contract. Samples returned by SASE. Negotiates rights purchased.

Acceptable Work: Publishes 150 artists/year. Considers all types of paintings: oil, acrylic, watercolor, pastels, mixed media. Also needs work suitable for gallery posters.
Tips: "We have developed our division, Impress Graphics, for the publication and distribution of gallery posters. We will also be entering into the limited edition field, with some limited edition subjects already available. Look at the market to see what type of artwork is selling."

EDELMAN FINE ARTS, LTD., Suite 1503, 1140 Broadway, New York NY 10001. (212)683-4266. Vice President: H. Heather Edelman. Art distributor of original oil paintings. "We now handle watercolors, lithographs, serigraphs and "work on paper" as well as original oil paintings." Clients: galleries, interior designers and furniture stores. Distributes work for 150 artists/year. Pays $50-1,000 flat fee or works on consignment basis (20% commission). Buys all rights. Provides in-transit insurance, insurance while work is at firm, promotion, shipping from firm and written contract. Send query letter with brochure, resume, tear sheets, photographs and "a sample of work on paper or canvas" to be kept on file. Call or write for appointment to show portfolio or mail original/final art and photographs. Reports as soon as possible.
Acceptable Work: Considers oil and acrylic paintings, watercolors and mixed media. Especially likes Old World and Impressionist themes or styles.
Tips: Portfolio should include originals and only best work.

***EDITIONS, INC.**, 433 E. Broadway, Salt Lake City UT 84111. (801)531-0146. President: Ruby Reece. Art publisher/printer for limited and unlimited editions, offset reproductions, posters and advertising materials. Clients: artists, distributors, galleries, publishers and representatives. Provides insurance while work is at firm. Send photographs, slides, transparencies (size 4x5—8x10) and/or originals. "Contact offices for specific pricing information." Samples are filed. Samples not filed are returned by SASE. Reports back within 1 week. Call or write to schedule an appointment to show a portfolio or mail original/final art, slides and transparencies.
Acceptable Work: Considers pen & ink line drawings, oil and acrylic paintings, pastels, watercolor, tempera and mixed media. Accepts all styles.

ATELIER ETTINGER INCORPORATED, 155 Avenue of the Americas, New York NY 10013. (212)807-7607. President: Eleanor Ettinger. Flatbed Limited Edition Lithographic Studio. "All plates are hand drawn, and proofing is completed on our Charles Brand hand presses." The edition run is printed on one of our 12-ton, Voirin presses, classic flatbed lithographic presses hand built in France over 100 years ago. Atelier Ettinger is available for contract printing for individual artists, galleries and publishers. Provides insurance while work is on premises. Printed editions for established artists such as Agam, Warhol, Bearden, Neel, as well as emerging artists such as Johnson, Van Epps and Stavrinos and Odom. For printing estimate, send good slides or transparencies, finished paper size, and edition size required.

ELEANOR ETTINGER INCORPORATED, 155 Avenue of the Americas, New York NY 10013. (212)807-7607. President: Eleanor Ettinger. Established art publisher of limited edition lithographs, limited edition sculpture, unique works (oils, watercolors, drawings, etc.). Currently distributes the work of 21 artists. All lithographs are printed on one of our Voirin presses, flat bed lithographic presses hand built in France over 100 years ago." Send query letter with visuals (slides, photographs, etc.). Reports within 7 days. Call for appointment to show portfolio.
Acceptable Work: Oils, watercolors, acrylic, pastels, mixed media, and pen & ink.
Tips: "Our focus for publication is towards the School of American Realism."

FINE ART DISTRIBUTORS, 5954 Coca Cola Blvd., Columbus GA 31909. (404)563-9130. President: Wayne Bonner. Art publisher/distributor of limited and unlimited editions, offset reproductions and originals for art galleries, frame shops, gift shops, furniture stores, and interior designers/decorators. Publishes work of 4-5 artists/year and distributes the work of 35 artists/year. Pays 15% royalties and on consignment (50% commission of retail). Payment method is negotiated. Buys first rights. Negotiates rights purchased. Requires exclusive representation of the artist "we publish." Provides in-transit insurance, insurance while work is at firm, promotion, shipping from firm and a written contract. Send query letter with brochure or resume, tear sheets, Photostats, photographs, photocopies, slides or transparencies. Samples are not filed. Samples not filed are not returned. Reports back within 1 month only if interested. Call or write to schedule an appointment to show a portfolio, which should include final reproduction/product and color.
Acceptable Work: Considers acrylic paintings, pastels, watercolor, tempera and mixed media. Prefers contemporary, original themes and photorealistic works. Prefers individual works of art, pairs and unframed series. Maximum size 24x30".

FINE ART RESOURCES, INC., 335 Babcock, Palatine IL 60067. President: Gerard V. Perez. Art publisher. Publishes limited editions of handpulled original prints for galleries. *Does not* publish reproductions. Publishes 80 artists/year. Pays flat fee, $500-5,000 average. Offers advance. Negotiates rights purchased. Requires exclusive representation of the artist. Provides insurance while work is at publisher, promotion and a written contract. Plates or screens destroyed after printing. Send query letter with slides, photographs or tear sheets. Samples kept for future reference. Reports within 10 days if interested.
Acceptable Work: Any representational style.

RUSSELL A. FINK GALLERY, Box 250, 9843 Gunston Rd., Lorton VA 22079. (703)550-9699. Contact: Russell A. Fink. Art publisher/dealer. Publishes offset reproductions using five-color offset lithography for galleries, individuals, framers. Publishes 3 freelance artists/year. Pays 10% royalties to artist or negotiates payment method. Negotiates rights purchased. Provides insurance while work is at publisher, promotion and shipping from publisher. Negotiates ownership of original art. Send query letter with slides or photographs to be kept on file. Call or write for appointment to show portfolio. Samples returned if not kept on file.
Acceptable Work: Considers oil and acrylic paintings and watercolors. Prefers wildlife and sporting themes. Prefers individual works of art; unframed. "Submit photos or slides of at least near-professional quality. Include size, price, media and other pertinent data regarding the artwork. Also send personal resume and be courteous enough to include SASE for return of any material sent to me."
Tips: "Looks for composition, style and technique in samples. Also how the artist views his own art. Mistakes artists make are arrogance, overpricing, explaining their art and underrating the dealer."

***THE 5 G COLLECTION ART PLUS & COLLECTORS ART PLUS**, 1000 Clint Moore Rd., Boca Raton FL 33434. (305)994-3300. Director: Renee Goldsmith. Art publisher/distributor of limited editions and gallery. Clients: galleries, decorators and the public. Publishes/distributes the work of 5 artists/year. Pays flat fee; $2,500-5,000; payment method is negotiated. Offers an advance. Purchases first rights or one-time rights. Requires exclusive representation of the artist. Provides promotion and shipping to firm. Send query letter with brochure, resume, tear sheets and slides. Samples are filed. Samples not filed are returned only if requested by artist. Reports back within 10 days. Write to schedule an appointment to show a portfolio, or mail original/final art, tear sheets and slides.
Acceptable Work: Considers pen & ink line drawings, oil paintings, acrylic paintings, pastels, watercolor, tempera and mixed media. Prefers contemporary and original themes. Prefers individual works of art, "the bigger the better."

FOXFIRE DIV., TOB, INC., 2730 N. Graham St., Charlotte NC 28206. Art Director: Larry O'Boyle. Series 500-750 outlets. "We sell lithographs, limited editions to frame shops, galleries and the like." Send query letter with resume and slides. Samples not filed are returned by SASE. Reports back within 10 days. To show a portfolio, mail appropriate materials, which should include slides. Artist receives flat fee; on acceptance. Considers saleability of artwork and rights purchased when establishing payment. Negotiates rights purchased.
Acceptable Work: Prefers watercolors/oils, with wildlife themes.

FOXMAN'S OIL PAINTINGS LTD., 3350 Church, Skokie IL 60203. (312)679-3804. Secretary/Treasurer: Harold Lederman. Art distributor of limited and unlimited editions, oil paintings and watercolors for galleries, party plans and national chains. Publishes work of 4 artists/year and distributes work of 115 artists/year. Payment method is negotiated. Negotiates rights purchased. Requires exclusive representation. Provides promotion, shipping from firm and a written contract. Send query letter with resume, tear sheets, photographs and slides. Samples are not filed. Samples not filed are returned. Reports back within 2 weeks. Call to schedule an appointment to show a portfolio, which should include original/final art.
Acceptable Work: Considers oil paintings, pastels, airbrush, watercolor, acrylics and collage. Prefers simple themes, children, barns, countrysides and black art. Prefers individual works of art. Maximum size 48x60, contemporary, modern.

***G.R. FINE ART**, Suite 4, 1322 18th St., Santa Monica CA 90404. (213)828-2714. President: Gillie Richards. Art publisher of limited and unlimited editions and offset reproductions. Clients: major distributors in U.S.A. and Europe and galleries. Publishes the work of 10 freelance artists/year. Distributes the work of 20 freelance artists/year. Pays royalties of 20%; payment method is negotiated. Offers an advance when appropriate. Buys first rights or reprint rights. Requires exclusive representation of the artist. Provides promotion, shipping from firm and a written contract. Send query letter with photographs and slides. Samples are filed. Samples not filed are returned by SASE. Reports back within 1 month. To show a portfolio, mail appropriate materials.

Acceptable Work: Considers oil paintings, acrylic paintings, pastels, watercolor, tempera and mixed media. Prefers realism or impressionism. Prefers individual works of art. Maximum size: 36x48"

GALAXY OF GRAPHICS, LTD., 460 W. 34th St., New York NY 10001. (212)947-8989. President: Reid A. Fader. Art publisher of unlimited editions and offset reproductions. Clients: galleries, distributors and picture frame manufacturers. Publishes 25-50 freelance artists/year. Works with several hundred artists/year. Pays royalty of 10%. Offers advance. Buys all rights for prints or posters. Exclusive representation. Provides insurance while work is at firm, promotion, shipping from firm and written contract. Send photos or color slides or mail original/final art, final reproduction/product, color and photographs. Call or write for appointment to show portfolio. Samples are returned. Reports within a few days.
Acceptable Work: Any media. "Any currently popular and generally accepted theme welcomed."
Tips: "Traditional imagery is becoming very strong."

***GALLERY IN A VINEYARD**, Benmarl Vineyards, Marlboro NY 12542. (914)236-4265. Owner: Mark Miller. Art publisher, gallery and studio handling limited editions, offset reproductions, unlimited editions, handpulled originals, posters, and original paintings and sculpture. Clients: galleries and department stores. Publishes/distributes the work of 1-2 artists/year. Pays on consignment basis: firm receives 50% commission; payment method is negotiated. Negotiates rights purchased. Provides a written contract. Send "whatever artist prefers." Samples are not filed and returned only if requested. Reports back within 3 weeks only if interested. To show a portfolio, mail "whatever artist prefers."
Acceptable Work: Considers any media. Prefers contemporary, original themes. Prefers individual works of art.
Tips: "Subjects related to wine are currently especially interesting."

***GALLERY PUBLISHERS**, 137 Orange Ave., Coronado CA 92118. (619)435-3336. President: Jim Ebbert. Estab. 1986. Art publisher of limited editions and handpulled originals. Clients: galleries and retail customers. Payment is negotiated. Offers an advance when appropriate. Negotiates rights purchased. Provides promotion and a written contract. Send query letter. Samples are filed. Samples not filed are returned. Reports back within 30 days. To show a portfolio, mail tear sheets, slides and transparencies.
Acceptable Work: Considers oil and acrylic paintings and pastels. Prefers individual works of art.

***GALLERY REVEL**, 96 Spring St., New York NY 10012. (212)925-0600. Assistant Director: Shelley O'Connor. Gallery handling oil and a few watercolor originals. Distributes the work of 15 artists/year. Pays flat fee of $200 average or consigns work; payment is negotiated. Send query letter with brochure showing art style or resume and slides. Samples not filed are returned. Reports back within 15 days. Call to schedule an appointment to show a portfolio, which should include original/final art and slides.
Acceptable Work: Considers oil and acrylic paintings, all on canvas. Prefers impressionistic landscapes, realism and bronze sculpture.
Tips: "I am not interested in figurative and depressive work."

GEME ART INC., 209 W. 6th St., Vancouver WA 98660. (206)693-7772. Art Director: Gene Will. Publishes fine art prints and reproductions in unlimited editions. Clients: galleries, department stores—the general art market. Works with 40-80 artists/year. Publishes the works of 15-20 artists; distributes 23-40. Payment is negotiated on a royalty basis. Normally purchases all rights. Provides promotion, shipping from publisher and a contract. Query with color slides or photos. SASE. Reports only if interested. Call or write for appointment to show portfolio. Simultaneous submissions OK.
Acceptable Work: Considers oils, acrylics, pastels, watercolor and mixed media. Themework is open.

***GENRE LTD. INC.—ART PUBLISHERS**, 620 S. Glenoaks Blvd., Burbank CA 91502. (818)843-7200. President: Mrs. Akiko Morrison. Art publisher of limited editions, offset reproductions, unlimited editions and posters. Clients: catalog/direct mail, corporate, department stores, galleries, chains, high-end. Publishes the work of 8 freelance artists/year. Pays flat fee, $250-2,000; royalties of 10% for posters; consignment basis: firm receives 1/3 commission. Payment method is negotiated. Offers an advance when appropriate. Buys reprint rights; negotiates rights purchased. Provides insurance while work is at firm, promotion, shipping to firm and a written contract. Send query letter with brochure showing art style or slides. Samples are filed. Samples not filed are returned only if requested. Reports back within 2 weeks. Call to schedule an appointment to show a portfolio, or mail slides.
Acceptable Work: Considers pen & ink line drawings, oil paintings, acrylic paintings and mixed media. Prefers "black & white photographic dramatic style. We can create titles." Prefers unframed series.

GESTATION PERIOD, 1946 N. Fourth St., Columbus OH 43201. (614)294-4659. Operations Manager: Bob Richman. Art distributor of offset reproductions. "We do not publish." Clients: galleries, framers, college stores, gift stores, poster shops. Distributes 5-10 new artists/year "depending on what's available for our market." Payment method is negotiated. Generally offers an advance. Negotiates rights purchased. Generally does not require exclusive representation. Provides promotion packaging and shipping from firm. Send query letter with brochure and/or published samples to be kept on file. Samples not filed returned only if requested. Reports within 1 month.
Acceptable Work: Considers any medium including photography. Especially likes fine art/exhibition posters and humor.

GRAPHIC ORIGINALS INC., 153 W. 27th St., New York NY 10001. (212)807-6180. President: Martin Levine. Art publisher and distributor of graphics and paper art. Produces limited editions of etchings and silkscreens for galleries. Negotiates payment and rights purchased. Call for appointment to show a portfolio. Send resume, photos or originals. Samples returned by SASE. Reports within 3 weeks.
Acceptable Work: Considers contemporary and realistic themes. Prefers unframed works.

GRAPHICS INTERNATIONAL, Box 13292, Oakland CA 94661. (415)339-9310. Vice President: Rob R. Kral. Art publisher/distributor of limited and unlimited edition handpulled original etchings. Clients: galleries, frame shops, distributors and department stores. Number of artists worked with per year varies. Negotiates payment method. Buys all rights. Requires exclusive representation. Provides shipping from firm and a written contract. Send query letter with brochure, resume and samples to be kept on file. Accepts slides, photographs or original work as samples. Reports only if interested.
Acceptable Work: Considers pen & ink line drawings, watercolors and color etchings. Especially likes traditional style.

GREAT CANADIAN PRINT COMPANY LTD, 404-63 Albert St., Winnipeg, Manitoba R3B 1G4 Canada. (204)942-7961. Officers: Gary Nerman and Allan Kiesler. Art publisher and distributor. Produces limited edition silkscreens for galleries, native craft stores. Publishes 15 artists/year. "We publish and distribute only native (Indian) art with preference towards Canadian or Woodland. We will not look at queries from other sources and recommend that non-native artists not submit to us." Pays by royalty. Buys all rights. Requires exclusive representation of the artist. Provides a written contract. Send query letter with resume to be kept on file. If samples are requested, prefers to see original works, slides or photographs. Samples not kept on file returned only if requested. Reports within 4 weeks.
Acceptable Work: Prefers works on paper, any medium. Looks for "a unique style that still conforms to the parameters that make up native (Indian) art."

GUILDHALL, INC., 2535 Weisenberger, Fort Worth TX 76107. (817)332-6733; 1-800-356-6733. President: John M. Thompson III. Art publisher/distributor of limited and unlimited editions, offset reproductions and handpulled originals for galleries, decorators, offices and department stores. Also provides direct mail sales to retail customers. Publishes work of 6 artists/year and distributes work of 10 artists/year. Pays $250-2,500 flat fee; 10-20% royalties; 33% commission on consignment. Payment method is negotiated. Negotiates rights purchased. Requires exclusive representation for contract artists. Provides insurance while work is at firm, promotion, shipping from firm and a written contract. Send query letter with resume, tear sheets, photographs, slides and 4x5 transparencies. Samples are not filed. Samples are returned only if requested. Reports back within 2 weeks. Call or write to schedule an appointment to show a portfolio, or mail thumbnails, tear sheets, slides, 4x5 transparencies, color and b&w.
Acceptable Work: Considers pen & ink drawings, oil paintings, acrylic paintings, watercolor and bronze and stone sculptures. Prefers historical themes, Native American, westerns, abstract, equine and religious. Prefers individual works of art.

HADDAD'S FINE ARTS INC., Box 3016 C, Anaheim CA 92803. President: James Haddad. Produces limited and unlimited edition originals and offset reproductions for galleries, art stores, schools and libraries. Publishes 40-70 artists/year. Buys reproduction rights. Pays royalties. Provides insurance while work is at publisher, shipping from publisher and written contract. Submit slides or photos, representative of work for publication consideration. SASE. Reports within 60 days.
Acceptable Work: Unframed individual works and pairs; all media.

ICART VENDOR GRAPHICS, 8568 Pico Blvd., Los Angeles CA 90035. (213)653-3190. Director: Sandy Verin. Art publisher/distributor/gallery. Produces limited and unlimited editions of offset reproductions and handpulled original prints for galleries, decorators, corporations, collectors. Publishes 3-5 artists/year. Distributes 30-40 artists/year. Pays flat fee, $250-1,000; royalties (5-10%) or negotiates payment method. "We also distribute." Offers advance. Buys all rights. Usually requires exclusive rep-

resentation of the artist. Provides insurance while work is at publisher. Negotiates ownership of original art. Send brochure, photographs, not slides. Samples returned by SASE. Reports within 1 month.
Acceptable Work: Considers oils, acrylics, watercolors and mixed media, also serigraphy and lithography. Likes airbrush. Prefers Art Deco period styles." Prefers individual works of art, pairs, series; 30x40" maximum.
Tips: "Be original with your own ideas. Present clean, neat presentations in original or photographic form (no slides). Prefers Art Deco style or good contemporary. However, other work is certainly considered. No abstracts please."

***IMAGE CONSCIOUS**, 45 Sheridan, San Francisco CA 94103. (415)626-1555. Creative Director: Joan Folkmann. Art publisher/distributor of offset reproductions and posters. Clients: poster galleries, frame shops, department stores, design consultants, interior designers and gift stores. Payment method is negotiated. Negotiates rights purchased. Provides promotion, shipping from firm and a written contract. Send query letter with brochure, resume, tear sheets, photographs, slides and transparencies. Samples are filed. Samples not filed are returned by SASE. Reports back within 1 month. To show a portfolio, mail tear sheets, slides, transparencies, final reproduction/product and photographs.
Acceptable Work: Considers oil paintings, acrylic paintings, pastels, watercolor, tempera, mixed media and photography. Prefers contemporary, landscapes and still lifes. "Looking at a wide variety of work." Prefers individual works of art, pairs or unframed series.Tips: "Be aware of current trends in the market."

***INTERNATIONAL EDITIONS, INC.**, 1642 Westwood Blvd., Los Angeles CA 90024. (213)475-1233. Marketing Director: Sam Kasoff. Art publisher and distributor of limited editions and handpulled originals. Clients: galleries. Works with 3-4 artists/year. Negotiates payment method. Buys all rights. Provides insurance while work is at firm, promotion and a written contract. Send query letter with brochure, resume and business card. Prefers photographs as samples. Samples are returned. Reports within 1 month.
Acceptable Work: Considers oil and acrylic paintings, pastels, watercolors and mixed media; serigraphs and stone lithographs.

ARTHUR A. KAPLAN CO. INC.,, 460 W. 34th St., New York NY 10001. (212)947-8989. National Sales Manager: Reid Fader. Art publisher of unlimited editions, offset reproduction, prints and posters. Clients: galleries, department stores and picture frame manufacturers. Publishes approximately 40 freelance artists/year. Works with 300 + artists/year. Pays a royalty of 5-10%. Offers advance. Buys all rights. Requires exclusive representation. Provides insurance while work is at firm, promotion, shipping from firm and a written contract. Send resume, tear sheets, slides, photographs and original art to be kept on file. Material not filed is returned. Reports within 2-3 weeks. To show a portfolio, mail appropriate materials or call to schedule an appointment. Portfolio should include original/final art, final reproduction/product, color, tear sheets and photographs.
Acceptable Work: Considers oils, acrylics, pastels, watercolors, mixed media, photography.
Tips: "We cater to a mass market and require fine quality art with decorative and appealing subject matter. Don't be afraid to submit work—we'll consider anything and everything."

KEY WEST GRAPHICS, INC., 232 S.E. 10th Terrace, Fort Lauderdale FL 33301. (305)463-1150. President: Jennifer Roberts. Estab. 1985. Clients: galleries, interior design firms and private art dealers. Uses artists for illustrations and color. Send query letter with brochure showing art style or resume, tear sheets, slides and photographs. Samples not filed returned by SASE. Reports within 5 weeks. To show a portfolio, mail appropriate materials or write to schedule an appointment. Portfolio should include original/final art, color and tear sheets.
Acceptable Work: Considers saleability of artwork and rights purchased when establishing payment. Negotiates rights purchased. Considers pen & ink with washes and paintings and pastels. Prefers landscapes and figurative work as themes. Prefers oils and acrylics.

***KINGFISHER PRINTS LTD.**, 230 E. Boulevard, Charlotte NC 28203. Art Director: John Stephenson. Publishes unlimited editions of offset lithographs for distribution to trade picture manufacturers such as department stores and wholesalers. Publishes approximately 150 originals/year. Publishes 10 freelance artists/year. Send query letter with resume, slides or photographs with SASE. Samples are returned. Reports within 2 weeks. Buys all rights. Provides in-transit insurance while work is at firm, shipping from firm and a written contract. Send query letter with resume, slides and photographs. Write to schedule an appointment to show a portfolio, which should include original/final art, final reproduction/product, photographs and good color copies. Pays outright fee of $400-600; buys reproduction rights. Original art returned on completion of publication.
Acceptable Work: Considers all subjects suitable for sale to department stores, etc. Especially needs

landscapes with a traditional approach and contemporary work on most subjects.
Tips: "Within the contemporary market we see a move towards softer pastels such as peach/grey and black and white photographic imagery (illustration). Themes: Nostalgia, 50's, American imagery. We react to changes in fashion or trends in parallel fields, whether or not it be fashion design/color, or architective/decoration, and we select our artwork and artists accordingly. Artists would now be working in conjunction with inhouse designers and illustrators for a more professional approach to achieving the desired results. If the artist has a portfolio to show, and he/she thinks it is suitable for our market, then he/she should not hesitate to call, as we are always on the look out for new artists."

***LAKAR PUBLISHING**, Box 1163, Oakbrook IL 60521. (312)655-4554. President: Mr. Karth. Art publisher and distributor of limited editions, offset reproductions, unlimited editions and handpulled originals. Clients: galleries, frame shops, corporate art consultants and interior designers. Publishes/distributes the work of 4 artists/year. Payment method is negotiated. Offers an advance. Buys all rights. Requires exclusive representation of the artist. Provides in-transit insurance, insurance while work is at firm, promotion, shipping to and from firm and a written contract. Send brochure showing art style. Samples are not filed but returned. Reports back only if interested. Call to schedule an appointment to show a portfolio, which should include original/final art, tear sheets, slides and color.
Acceptable Work: Considers oil paintings, acrylic paintings, watercolor and tempera. Prefers American realism. Prefers individual works of art.

***LAUGHTER GRAPHICS** ™, 8133 High Dr., Leawood KS 66206. (913)648-6690. President: John Francis Borra. Estab. 1987. Art publisher of offset reproductions and posters for gift shops, department stores, frame shops, galleries, novelty shops, book stores, specialty shops/distributors. Payment method is negotiated. Offers an advance when appropriate. Negotiates rights purchased. Provides marketing. Send query letter with brochure showing art style and roughs or photocopies. Samples are filed. Samples not filed are returned by SASE. Reports back only if interested. Write to schedule an appointment to show a portfolio. "Never send portfolio unless requested!"
Acceptable Work: Considers pen & ink line drawings. Currently only interested in humorous themes. Prefers individual works of art, 16x20".
Tips: "Our company was established to produce and market cartoons as a legitimate art form; we consider everything we promote as high-quality art prints. We are open to any ideas that artists and writers feel is appropriate. Currently, our art prints are single-panel cartoons with and without gag lines. We are a young company, so our marketing strategies are still in formulation. We believe that themes, topics or characters with broad market appeal are best; however, a cartoon that has a very strong appeal to a rather narrow market may be just as promising. Don't edit yourself; if you have an idea you think is funny and believe others will find it funny, send it! Keep it reasonably clean, but you needn't be prudish."

DAVID LAWRENCE EDITIONS, Suite 153, 19528 Ventrua Blvd., Tarzana CA 91356. (818)996-3509. President: David Lawrence. Art publisher/distributor handling limited and unlimited editions of offset reproductions. Clients: galleries and frame shops. Publishes 5-10 freelance artists and distributes work for 25 artists/year. Negotiates payment method and rights purchased. Requires exclusive representation. Provides promotion, shipping from firm and a written contract. Send a resume and "anything that gives a good representation of work" to be kept on file. Reports back only if interested. Call or write for appointment to show portfolio.
Acceptable Work: Considers all media for publication and distribution.

LESLI ART, INC., 3715 Benedict Cyn. Ln., Sherman Oaks CA 91423. (818)986-6056. President: Stan Shevrin. Art publisher and artist agent handling paintings for art galleries and the trade. Works with 20 artists/year. Payment method is negotiated. Offers an advance. Requires exclusive representation. Send query letter with photographs and slides. Samples not filed are returned by SASE. Reports back within 1 month. To show a portfolio, mail slides and color photographs.
Acceptable Work: Considers oil paintings, acrylic paintings, pastels, watercolor, tempera and mixed media. Prefers realism and impressionism—figures costumed, narrative content. Prefers individual works of art. Maximum size 36x48".

LESLIE LEVY PUBLISHING, Suite D, 7342 E. Thomas, Scottsdale AZ 85251. (602)945-8491. Assistant Director: Carol Nance. Materials to be sent to: Leslie Levy Gallery, 7141 E. Main St., Scottsdale AZ 85251. (602)947-0937. Art publisher and distributor of limited editions, offset reproductions, unlimited editions, posters and miniature prints. Publishes/distributes the work of 9 artists/year. Pays flat fee; $.50-.75 each for posters. Insists on reprint rights. Requires exclusive publishing of the artist. Send query letter with resume, tear sheets, photographs, slides or transparencies—"highest quality of any of the above items." Slides, etc. are returned by SASE. "Portfolio will not be seen unless interest is generated by the materials sent in advance."

Acceptable Work: Considers oil paintings, acrylic paintings, pastels, watercolor, tempera, mixed media and photographs.
Tips: "First, don't call us before sending materials. We will contact you if we are interested. We are known in the industry for our high quality prints and excellent skilled artists. Please do not waste your time or ours if you are not a skilled artist."

LITHOS' Publishers and Distributors of Collector Prints, 6301 B Delmar, St. Louis MO 63130. (314)862-0674. Publisher: Linda Thomas. Handles limited edition prints (maximum 1,000/edition). Clients: framers, galleries, interior designers and art collectors. Pays negotiable royalty. Negotiates rights purchased. Provides insurance while work is at firm, promotion, shipping from firm and a written contract. Send query letter with resume, business card, slides and photographs.
Acceptable Work: Oil paintings, acrylic paintings, pastels and watercolors. Especially likes contemporary themes or styles.
Tips: "We are interested in never-before published images of black American subjects only. Artist should be prepared to give Lithos' exclusive publication rights for at least sixty months. Broad name recognition is not a prerequisite; good work is!"

LITTLE CREATURES INC.,7385 N. Seneca Rd., Milwaukee WI 53217. President: Dianne Spector. Publishes open editions, offset reproductions for gift shops, department stores and country shops. "National sales distribution established." Buys from or publishes 10 artists/year. Pays a flat fee of $150-350; royalties of 5%; payment method is negotiated. Send query letter with brochure showing art style, slides or photographs. Samples are returned by SASE. Reports back within 1 month.
Acceptable Work: Considers oil and acrylic paintings, markers, watercolor and mixed media. "Items with mass appeal; the folk art market for the upscale customer."
Tips: "Our customers are women aged 25-50, decorating their homes or purchasing affordable gifts. We publish the art, frame it and distribute it. Subjects should be warm and friendly but of high quality and with uniqueness of ideas. Don't let our name confuse you. Our business is selling art as framed pictures to furniture stores, gift shops, bath shops, miniature stores etc. We began our company with cute gift-type art and are looking for more of that style. We are also known for pioneering ideas of innovative American folk art and other subjects with mass appeal. If we like your style, we'll have you create a series for us. A new, separate division of our company purchases open edition art prints you have already published."

***LOLA LTD./LT'EE**, 325 N. Main, High Point NC 27260. (919)275-8005. Owner: Lola Jackson. Art publisher and distributor of limited editions, offset reproductions, unlimited editions and handpulled originals. Clients: art galleries, architects, picture frame shops, interior designers, major furniture and department stores and industry. Distributes the work of 87 freelance artists/year. Payment method is negotiated. "Our standard commission is 50% less 30-50% off retail." Offers an advance when appropriate. Provides insurance while work is at firm, shipping to firm and a written contract. Send query letter with brochure showing art style or resume, tear sheets, Photostats, photographs, photocopies or transparencies. "Actual sample is best." Samples are filed. Samples not filed are returned only if requested. Reports back within 2 weeks. To show a portfolio, mail original/final art or final reproduction/product.
Acceptable Work: "Handpulled graphics are our main area"; also considers oil paintings, acrylic paintings, pastels, watercolor, tempera, or mixed media. Prefers unframed series, 30x40" maximum.
Tips: "We need samples to work from to take orders on. We do not pay for samples. We have sales reps throughout U.S. to sell for you."

LONDON CONTEMPORARY ART, INC., 20526 N. Milwaukee, Deerfield IL 60015. (312)520-7779. President: Gerard Perez. Art publisher of handpulled original limited edition prints for art galleries. Publishes work of 60 artists/year. Pays 5% royalties. Buys all rights. Requires exclusive representation. Provides insurance while work is at firm. Send query letter with photographs. Samples are not filed and are not returned. Reports back only if interested. To show a portfolio, mail color photos.
Acceptable Work: Any and all media. Prefers pointilism, impressionism and landscapes.

***LUBLIN GRAPHICS, INC.**, 95 E. Putnam Ave., Greenwich CT 06830. (203)622-8777. Sales Manager: Paul LaBell. Art publisher/distributor/gallery. Publishes and distributes limited editions, offset reproductions, posters and art books. Clients: galleries, frame shops, books stores and corporations. Publishes/distributes the work of 15 artists/year. Payment method is negotiated. Provides promotion and a written contract. Send query letter with resume, slides and photographs. Samples not filed are returned by SASE. Reports back within 2 weeks. To show a portfolio, mail appropriate materials.
Acceptable Work: Considers graphics. Prefers individual works of art.

***LYNNS PRINTS**, 101 Wooster St., Lodi OH 44254. Owners: Diane and Ted Graebner. Art publisher, gallery and graphic arts printer of limited and unlimited editions and offset reproductions. Clients: galleries, department stores, and "country" stores. Currently publishes/distributes the work of 1 artist. "Looking for more to publish." Payment method is negotiated. Buys all rights; negotiates rights purchased. Provides a written contract. Send query letter with brochure, tear sheets, photographs or transparencies. Samples not filed are returned by SASE. Reports back within 2 weeks. To show a portfolio, mail thumbnails, tear sheets and/or slides.
Acceptable Work: Considers all 2-dimensional works in any media. Prefers acrylics and watercolor. Prefers contemporary, primitive and country images. Prefers individual works of art and pairs.
Tips: "Works must have good, strong design with a theme involved."

MARCO DISTRIBUTORS, 1412 S. Laredo, Aurora CO 80017. (303)752-4819. President: Mark Woodmansee. Art publisher and distributor of limited editions, handpulled originals, oil washes and oil on canvas. Clients: corporations, galleries and interior designers. Publishes 2 freelance artists/year. Distributes work for 10 artists/year. Pays flat fee or royalty of 20%; or negotiates payment method. Buys all rights or reprint rights or negotiates rights purchased. Requires exclusive representation. Provides promotion, shipping to and from firm and written contract. Send brochure and samples to be kept on file. Prefers photographs, tear sheets or original work as samples. Samples not filed are not returned. Reports back to artist. Call or write for appointment to show portfolio; or contact through artist's agent.
Acceptable work: Considers oil and acrylic paintings, pastels, watercolors and mixed media; serigraphs, stone lithographs, plate lithographs and woodcuts. Especially likes landscapes, some unique figures and impressionist style.
Tips: "Send photos of your work; follow with a call."

DAVID MARSHALL, Box 24635, St. Louis MO 63141. (314)423-1100. President: Marshall Gross. Art publisher/distributor/gallery handling and distributing sculpture, cast paper, silk screens, lithographs and sculpted paper. Clients: galleries, architects, designers and fine furniture stores. Distributes the work of 10-15 artists/year. Publishes/distributes the work of 25 artists/year. Pays flat fee of $15-50 for each item; royalties possible; payment method can be negotiated. Buys all rights. Provides insurance only while work is at firm, promotion and shipping from the firm. Send query letter with brochure showing art style or photographs. Samples are not filed. Samples not filed are returned only if requested by artist. Reports within 7 days. Call to schedule an appointment to show a portfolio, which should include roughs, slides and color photos.
Acceptable Work: Considers pastels, watercolor and cast paper. Prefers contemporary, impressionism, original themes and primitivism. Prefers individual works of art and unframed series; 36x40" maximum. "We will buy inexpensive canvasses if artist will reproduce.
Tips: "We prefer items that work with current home fashion color trends. Glass and mirror designs are given special consideration."

BRUCE MCGAW GRAPHICS, INC., 230 Fifth Ave., New York NY 10001. (212)679-7823. Acquisitions: Paul Liptak. Send query letter with brochure showing art style or resume, tear sheets, Photostats, photocopies, slides and photographs. Samples not filed returned by SASE. Reports within weeks. To show a portfolio, mail color, tear sheets and photographs. Considers skill and experience of artist, saleability of artwork, client's preferences and rights purchased when establishing contract.

METROPOLITAN ART ASSOCIATES, 346 New York Ave., Huntington NY 11743. (516)549-8300. President: Richard Greenberg. Distributor/gallery handling limited and unlimited editions, posters, and oils. Clients: galleries, auctioneers, retail. Payment method is negotiated. Send query letter with brochure showing art style, tear sheets, photocopies and slides. Samples are filed. Samples not filed are returned only if requested. Reports back only if interested. Write to schedule an appointment to show a portfolio, which should include final reproduction/product.

MITCH MORSE GALLERY INC., 334 E. 59th St., New York NY 10022. (212)593-1812. President: Mitch Morse. Art publisher and distributor. Produces limited edition handpulled originals for framers, galleries, interior designers, architects, hotels and better furniture stores. Publishes 8-10 artists/year; distributes the work of 15-20 artists/year. Negotiates payment. Offers advance. Provides promotion and shipping. Send query letter with resume, and slides and photographs. SASE. Reports within 1 week.
Acceptable Work: Unframed realistic, impressionistic and romantic paintings, lithographs, serigraphs and etchings; individual works; 4x6' maximum.
Tips: "There is continued emphasis on color as a major ingredient in the selection of art and greater interest in more traditional subject matter. Actively seeking additional artists who do original paintings on paper."

MYSTIC SEAPORT MUSEUM STORES, 39 Greenmanville Ave., Mystic CT 06355. (203)572-8551. Trade Sales Manager: Dot Hazlin. Art publisher of limited editions, offset reproductions, unlimited editions, handpulled originals, posters, cards and stationery items. Clients: galleries, poster shops. Publishes the work of 8 freelance artists/year. Pays royalties of 7-10%; payment is negotiated. Send query letter with photographs or transparencies. Samples not filed are returned. Reports back within 1 month. To show a portfolio, mail transparencies, final reproduction/product and color.
Acceptable Work: Considers pen & ink line drawings and oil paintings. Prefers maritime art. Prefers individual works of art.

THE NATURE COMPANY, 750 Hearst Ave., Berkeley CA 94710. (415)644-1337. Product Development Director: Lon Murphy. Art publisher/distributor of unlimited editions. Publishes work of 8-14 artists/year. Pays $250-800 flat fee or royalties; wholesale commission. Negotiates rights purchased. Provides in-transit insurance, insurance while work is at firm, promotion, shipping to firm, shipping from firm and a written contract. Send query letter with brochure showing art style or tear sheets, Photostats, photographs, slides and transparencies. Samples are filed. Samples not filed are returned only if requested. Reports back within 2 months. To show a portfolio, mail roughs, Photostats, tear sheets, slides, transparencies, color and b&w.
Acceptable Work: Will receive all media. Considers pen & ink line drawings, oil paintings, acrylic paintings, pastels, watercolor, tempera and mixed media. "Must be natural history subjects (i.e, plants, animals, landscapes). Avoid domesticated plants, animals, and people-made objects."

NEW DECO, INC., Suite A11, 10018 Spanish Isles Blvd., Boca Raton FL 33498. (305)482-6295. President: Brad Morris. Art publisher/distributor. Produces limited editions using offset lithography for galleries, also publishes/distributes unlimited editions. Publishes 1 freelance artist/year. Needs new designs for reproduction. Pays flat fee. Offers advance. Negotiates rights purchased. Provides promotion, shipping and a written contract. Negotiates ownership of original art. Send brochure, resume, and tear sheets, Photostats or photographs to be kept on file. Samples not kept on file are returned. Reports only if interested. Call or write for appointment to show portfolio, which should include tear sheets.
Acceptable Work: Prefers Art Deco, Art Nouveau themes and styles. Prefers individual works of art, pairs or series.

NEW ENGLAND GRAPHIC IMAGES, 5 Deer Brook Rd., Woodstock VT 05091. (802)672-3557. Publisher: J. Allmon. Estab. 1986. Art publisher of limited and open editions, offset reproductions and handpulled originals for galleries and interior designers. Works with 3-4 artists/year at present. Payment method is negotiated. Negotiates rights purchased. Provides a written contract. Send query letter with brochure showing art style or slides. Samples are filed. Samples not filed are returned. Reports back within 1 month. To show a portfolio, mail slides.
Acceptable Work: Considers oil paintings, acrylic paintings, watercolor and tempera. Prefers New England scenes.
Tips: "Don't send it unless it sells New England."

NEW YORK GRAPHIC SOCIETY, Box 1469, Greenwich CT 06836. (203)661-2400. Art & Production Manager: Caron Caswell. Art publisher/art distributor of offset reproductions, limited editions, posters and handpulled originals. Clients: galleries, frame shops, museums and foreign trade. Publishes 10 new freelance artists/year. Distributes work for 10 new artists/year. Pays flat fee or royalty of 1.2%. Offers advance. Buys all print reproduction rights. Provides in-transit insurance from firm to artist, insurance while work is at firm, promotion, shipping from firm and a written contract; provides insurance for art requested. Send query letter with slides or photographs. Write for artist's guidelines. All submissions returned to artists by SASE after review. Reports within 2 months.
Acceptable Work: Considers oils, acrylics, pastels, watercolors and mixed media; pencil drawings (colored). Distributes posters only. Publishes/distributes serigraphs, stone lithographs, plate lithographs and woodcuts.
Tips: "We publish a broad variety of styles and themes. However, we do not publish experimental, hard-edge, sexually explicit or suggestive material. Work that is by definition fine art and easy to live with, that is, which would be considered decorative, is what we are always actively looking for."

NORTH BEACH FINE ARTS, INC., 2565 Blackburn St., Clearwater FL 33575. President: James Cournoyer. Art publisher and art distributor handling limited edition graphics and posters. Clients: galleries, architects, interior designers and art consultants. Pays 50% or consignment, 50% commission. Negotiates rights purchased. Provides insurance when work is at firm, promotion, written contract and markets expressly-select original handmade editions of a small number of contemporary artists. Send query letter with brochure, resume, tear sheets, Photostats, photocopies, slides and photographs to be kept on file. Accepts any sample showing reasonable reproduction. Samples returned by SASE only if request-

ed. Reports within 2 months. To show a portfolio, mail original/final art, color, tear sheets, Photostats, photographs and b&w.
Acceptable Work: Considers pen & ink line drawings and mixed media; serigraphs, stone lithographs, plate lithographs, woodcuts and linocuts. Especially likes contemporary, unusual and original themes or styles.
Tips: Wants "original prints and posters by serious, experienced, career-oriented artists with a well developed and thought-out style.

OAKSPRINGS IMPRESSIONS, 6840 Sir Francis Dr., Forest Knolls CA 94933. (415)488-0194. General Manager: Michael Pettit. Art publisher/distributor of limited and unlimited editions, offset reproductions and handpulled originals. Publishes work of 2 artists/year and distributes the work of 6 artists/year. Payment method is negotiated. Buys first rights, one-time rights and all rights. Negotiates rights purchased. Requires exclusive representation. Provides promotion, shipping from firm and a written contract. Send query letter with brochure or resume, tear sheets, photographs and slides. Samples are not filed. Samples are returned by SASE. Reports back within 1 month. To show a portfolio, mail slides and 4x5 transparencies.
Acceptable Work: Considers acrylic paintings, pastels, watercolor, tempera and mixed media. Prefers individual works of art, pairs and unframed series.

***PANACHE EDITIONS LTD**, 234 Dennis Lane, Glencoe IL 60022. (312)835-1574. President: Donna MacLeod. Art publisher and distributor of offset reproductions and posters for galleries, frame shops, domestic and international distributors. Publishes/distributes the work of 5-8 artists/year. Pays royalties of 10%. Buys reprint rights; negotiates rights purchased. Requires exclusive representation of the artist. Provides in-transit insurance, insurance while work is at firm, promotion, shipping to and from firm and a written contract. Send query letter with brochure showing art style or photographs, photocopies and transparencies. Samples are filed. Reports back only if interested. To show a portfolio, mail roughs, original/final art, final reproduction/product and color.
Acceptable Work: Considers acrylic paintings, pastels, watercolor and mixed media. "Looking for contemporary compositions in soft pastel color palettes, also renderings of children on beach, in park, etc." Prefers individual works of art and unframed series.
Tips: "We are looking for artists who have not previously been published (in the poster market) with a strong sense of current color palettes. We want to see a range of your style and coloration."

PETERSEN PRINTS, 6725 Sunset Blvd., Los Angeles CA 90028. Director: William L. Cooksey. Produces limited editions (maximum 950 prints) using offset lithography for galleries, department stores and publishes sporting merchandisers. Publishes 15-25 freelance artists/year. Buys all rights. Requires exclusive representation of the artist. Provides in-transit insurance, insurance while work is at publisher, promotion, shipping from publisher and a written contract. Artist owns original art. Send query letter with brochure, resume, slides or photographs to be kept on file. Samples not kept on file are returned by SASE. Reports within 3 weeks. Write for appointment to show portfolio.
Acceptable Work: Considers oil and acrylic paintings, oils, gouache, mixed media, and watercolors. Prefers paintings of wildlife and outdoor subjects. Prefers individual works of art.
Tips: "We do not want to see newspaper clippings in a portfolio. However, there should be a complete biography."

***PORTFOLIO GRAPHICS INC.**, #2, 4120S 500 W., Salt Lake City UT 84123. (800)843-0402 or (801)266-4844. Vice President: Kent Barton. Estab. 1986. Art publisher and distributor of limited editions, offset reproductions, unlimited editions, handpulled originals and posters. Distributes the work of 15 freelance artists/year. Publishes/distributes the work of 20 artists/year. Pays royalties of 10%. Offers an advance when appropriate. Negotiates rights purchased. Provides promotion and a written contract. Send query letter with tear sheets, Photostats, photographs, slides and transparencies. Samples are filed. Samples not filed are returned. Reports back within 2 weeks. To show a portfolio, mail tear sheets, slides or transparencies.
Acceptable Work: Considers oil paintings, acrylic paintings, pastels, watercolor, tempera and mixed media. Prefers contemporary, original themes, photorealistic works, landscapes, abstract and literal work, colorful decorative art. Prefers individual works of art.
Tips: "Simply send samples first. Call in 3 days to assure it's been received. Ask for a letter of denial if it be the case. And be pushy about making a decision and yet accept what they say concerning future use. They may mean it."

***POSNER GALLERY**, 207 N. Milwaukee St., Milwaukee WI 53202. (414)273-3097. President: Judith L. Posner. Art publisher/distributor/gallery. Produces limited and unlimited editions of offset reproductions and original serigraphs and lithographs. Publishes 10 freelance artists/year. Distributes the work of

©1987 Petersen Prints

"Security, aloofness and the innate beauty of the cat" are the qualities artist Guy Coheleach of Bernardsville, New Jersey wanted to convey in his oil painting, which Peterson Prints reproduced as a limited edition print. "I just made it, and Peterson wanted to print it," says Coheleach, a leading wildlife artist. William Cooksey, director of the Los Angeles company, met the artist on a fishing trip. "In spite of his international reputation," says Cooksey, "he is always willing to exchange ideas and accept direction from a publisher." The artist sold reprint rights to the publisher.

25 freelance artists/year. Pays royalty, or works on consignment (50% commission). Buys all rights. Requires exclusive representation of artist. Provides promotion and shipping from firm. Send resume and slides. Samples are returned by SASE only if requested. Reports within 10 days.
Acceptable Work: Considers all media. Prefers individual works of art. Specializes in contemporary themes.
Tips: "Must be contemporary. No surrealist, space themes or strange subject matter."

***PREMIER EDITIONS INC**, Suite 534, 3808 Rosecrans St., San Diego CA 92110. (619)267-0909. Creative Director: Gary Cohen. Estab. 1986. Art publisher of offset reproductions and posters. Clients: galleries, department stores, decorators and distributors. Publishes/distributes the work of 4 artists/year. Pays royalties of 10%. Offers an advance when appropriate. Buys all rights or reprint rights. Provides promotion, shipping to and from firm and a written contract. Send query letter with brochure, resume, tear sheets, photographs or transparencies (35mm or 4x5). Samples are not filed. Samples not filed are returned by SASE. Reports back within 30 days. To show a portfolio, mail final reproduction/product and color.
Acceptable Work: Considers oil paintings, acrylic paintings, pastels, watercolor, mixed media and airbrush. Prefers impressionism and contemporary styles and abstracts, landscapes, florals. Prefers individual works of art and pairs. Maximum size proportional to 24x36".

PRESTIGE ART GALLERIES, INC., 3909 W. Howard St., Skokie IL 60076. (312)679-2555. President: Louis Schutz. Art publisher/dealer/gallery. Publishes limited editions and offset reproductions for retail professionals and galleries. Publishes 4 freelance artists/year. Works on consignment basis; firm charges 33% commission. Buys all rights or negotiates rights purchased. Provides insurance while work is at publisher, promotion and a written contract. Publisher owns original art. Send query letter with brochure, resume, prices, photos, and slides to be kept on file. Samples returned by SASE. Reports only if interested.
Acceptable Work: Considers oil and acrylic paintings, watercolor, oils and pastels. Prefers realism, and mother and child themes. Prefers individual works of art; unframed; 30x40" maximum.
Tips: "Be professional."

***QUEST FINE ARTS**, 626 Cypress Ave., Box 3850, Venice FL 34293. (813)485-7882. Contact: Art Director. Art publisher/distributor of offset reproductions and posters. Clients: framers for mass market, gift industry, and furniture industry. Publishes the work of 5+ freelance artists/year. Distributes the work of 10+ freelance artists/year. Publishes/distributes the work of 10+ artists/year. Payment method is negotiated. Offers an advance when appropriate. Negotiates rights purchased. Provides promotion, insurance while work is at firm, shipping from firm and written contract. Send query letter with brochure, tear sheets, photographs, slides and transparencies. Samples not filed are returned by SASE only if requested by artist. Reports back only if interested. To show a portfolio, mail slides, transparencies, final reproduction/product and color.
Acceptable Work: Considers oil paintings, acrylic paintings, pastels, watercolor, tempera and mixed media. Prefers current decorator colors, subjects. "We will work with an artist in creating a look or series." Prefers pairs; 24x36" maximum.
Tips: "Submit only outstanding work."

REECE GALLERIES INC., 24 West 57th St., New York NY 10019. (212)333-5830. Co-Directors: Shirley and Leon Reece. Art dealers and consultants to corporations and private collectors. Also distributes for other artists to galleries. Works with many freelance artists/year. Send query letter with resume, slides and photographs. Samples not filed returned by SASE. Reports within 14 days. Call to schedule an appointment to show a portfolio, which should include original/final art. Pays 50% of net proceeds.
Acceptable Work: Considers skill and experience of artist, saleability of artwork and clients' preferences when reviewing slides. Prefers urban, abstract landscapes, prints and other media. Accepts most media.
Tips: Artist should have "technical skill that must be obvious in the media worked overall quality; no offset work."

***REUBEN SAUNDERS GALLERY**, (a division of Reuben Saunders Inc.), 125 S. Washington, Wichita KS 67202-4721. (316)264-0572. Gallery Director: Jane L. Eby. Distributor and gallery handling original art, limited editions and posters. Reuben Saunders Inc. is a wholesale distributor of picture frames and supplies. Clients: designers, architects, interior decorators, corporations, individuals for office and home, art collectors. Distributes the work of 30 freelance artists/year. Pays on consignment basis: firm receives 40% commission. Offers an advance when appropriate. All rights remain with the artists unless negotiated for one-time project. Insurance, promotion, shipping and a written contract are negotiated based on the job or project. Send query letter with resume, slides, reviews or articles and a statement of intent. Slides are filed. Slides not filed are returned by SASE. Reports back within 3 months. Write to schedule an appointment to show a portfolio, or mail slides.
Acceptable Work: Prefers contemporary, original subjects; traditional, interpretive landscapes; abstract works; contemporary ceramics and sculpture. Prefers individual works of art, pairs and unframed series.
Tips: "Send slides of works that are available for sale. Make sure slides are of good quality and accurately represent the work. We prefer to work directly with artists rather than through agents of artists. Emphasis on regional Midwest artists but will consider others as well."

***ROSELAND PUBLISHING CO.**, 1423 Armour Blvd., Mundelein IL 60060. President: Mark Rowland. Art publisher of limited edition handpulled original serigraphs. Clients: galleries, decorators and a distributor of wall accessories. Publishes 6 freelance artists/year. Pays royalty of 10% or negotiates payment method. Negotiates rights purchased. Provides promotion and shipping from firm. Send query letter and samples to be kept on file unless requested otherwise. Write for appointment to show portfolio. Prefers slides or photographs as samples. Samples not filed returned by SASE. Reports only if interested.
Acceptable Work: Considers pen & ink drawings, oils, acrylics, pastels, mixed media and serigraphs.
Tips: "Submit work that lends itself well to serigraphic reproduction. It should incorporate current decor color schemes and a clear, crisp, professional look."

FELIX ROSENSTIEL'S WIDOW & SON LTD., 33-35 Markham St., London SW3 England. 44-1-352-3551. Also New York office. Director: David A. Roe. Art publisher handling limited and unlimited editions, offset reproductions, hand colored engravings. Clients: galleries, department stores and wholesale picture manufactures. Publishes approximately 30-40 freelance artists/year. Pays $200-1,000 flat fee or 8% royalties. Buys all rights or negotiates rights purchased. Provides in-transit insurance, insurance while work is at firm, promotion, shipping from firm and a written contract. Send query letter with slides and photographs. Samples returned by SASE (nonresidents include IRC). Reports within 30 days.
Acceptable Work: Considers oils, acrylics, pastels, watercolors and mixed media; etchings and engravings.

***ANDREA RUOFF ART ASSOC. LTD.**, 5 Lincoln Rd., Scarsdale NY 10583. (914)725-4928. President: Andrea Ruoff. Gallery/art publisher/distributor of limited editions. Clients: galleries, corporations and collectors. Publishes/distributes the work of 2 artists/year. Payment method is negotiated. Offers an advance when appropriate. Provides promotion and a written contract. Send query letter with brochure, resume, tear sheets, slides and transparencies. Samples are filed. Samples not filed are returned by SASE. Reports back within 1 month. To show a portfolio, mail appropriate materials.
Acceptable Work: Considers oil paintings, acrylic paintings, watercolor, tempera and mixed media. Prefers contemporary, original themes, primitivism and sophisticated humor. Prefers individual works of art or an unframed series.
Tips: "Send professional-quality only."

SCAFA-TORNABENE ART PUBLISHING CO. INC., 100 Snake Hill Rd., West Nyack NY 10994. (914)358-7600. Co-owner: Claire Scafa. Produces unlimited edition offset reproductions for framers, commercial art trade and manufacturers world-wide. Publishes 50-100 artists/year. Pays $200-350 flat fee for each accepted piece. Published artists (successful ones) can advance to royalty arrangements with advance against 5-10% royalty. Buys only reproduction rights (written contract). Artist maintains ownership of original art. Requires exclusive publication rights to all accepted work. Send query letter first with slides or photos and then arrange interview. SASE. Reports in about 2 weeks.
Acceptable Work: Unframed decorative paintings, watercolors, posters, photos and drawings; usually pairs and series. Prefers trendy, decorative art and inspirationals. Prefers airbrush, watercolor, acrylics, oils, gouache, collage and mixed media.
Tips: Always looking for something new and different. "Study the market first. See and learn from what stores and galleries display and sell. For trends we follow the furniture market as well as bath, kitchen and all household accessories."

***SHADOWLIGHT IMPRESSIONS**, Box 150706, Nashville TN 37215. President: Bill Barnes. Estab. 1986. Art publisher and distributor of offset reproductions, limited editions to 850 and open editions and posters. Clients: poster stores, galleries, corporate art buyers and frame shops. Publishes/distributes the work of 20 artists/year. Pays royalties of 8-15%. Negotiates rights purchased. Provides insurance while work is at firm and return shipment. Provides written contract. Samples are filed. Samples not filed are returned only if requested by artist. Reports back within 3 weeks. Write to schedule an appointment to show a portfolio or mail tear sheets, slides, or color prints.
Acceptable Work: Considers oil and acrylic paintings, pastels, watercolor, tempera and mixed media. Prefers original themes, impressionist, realistic, realistic but painterly, strong concepts, all themes. Maximum size of acceptable work: 30x40".
Tips: "Over the next few years our emphasis will be on increasing our limited editions. We will concentrate our efforts on those artists capable of producing consistent high-quality images. Our marketing efforts will be aimed at upscale national and international markets. In your portfolio, include theme pieces that run through the artist's work. I do not want to see cartoons or abstracts."

***SHAR/DECOR, INC.** Suite 404, 12423 62nd St. N, Largo FL 34643. (813)536-6019. President: Sharon Bailey. Estab. 1985. Distributor of offset reproductions, limited and unlimited editions, posters, handpulled originals and handmade paper. Clients: galleries, designers, decorators and furniture stores. Pays flat fee of $20 minimum. Does not require exclusive representation. Provides insurance while work is at firm and promotion. Send query letter with brochure or photographs. Samples not filed are returned. Reports back within 10 days. Call to schedule an appointment to show a portfolio, which should include final reproduction/product and color.
Acceptable Work: Prefers contemporary, original themes. Prefers individual works of art. Maximum size of acceptable work: 36x48".

***SHOWCASE SYSTEMS, INC.**, 540 N. Commercial, Manchester NH 03105. (603)627-8484. President: W. Duschatko. Contract/art publisher. Publishes hand-painted and hand-screened originals for architects, interior designers and specifiers for the contract furnishings market. Send query letter with contact sheets, slides or photos of art. Prefers out-of-town artists and photographers. Reports within weeks. Provides promotion, shipping from publisher and written agreement. Also needs "nostalgia photos-old trains, airplanes, automobiles and city scenes and lighthouse and sailboat photographs."
Acceptable Work: Line drawings and photos, primarily nature-oriented. "Our present line is primarily hard-edge geometric in nature (hand-painted by our own people in various sizes as specified by the purchaser). We have increased our screen printing department to include other themes and styles as required by the contract art market." Especially needs items that we can screen-print on fabric, one or two colors, large sizes. Negotiates pay.
Tips: "When designing for two or three colors, registrations is key concern since most items are in the 2x4' to 4x8' range."

Close-up

Claire Scafa

Scafa-Tornabene Art Publishing Co., Inc.
West Nyack, New York

It's easy to see why Claire Scafa enjoys art publishing. It's a profitable business—for both her and the artists she represents. "If artists publish several major series for our company, they can realize six-figure royalties and enormous exposure."

Her company, Scafa-Tornabene, publishes and distributes unlimited edition prints. Printed in runs of at least 5,000 a piece, Scafa's unlimited editions decorate the walls of our offices and homes. This means more exposure than a gallery could provide.

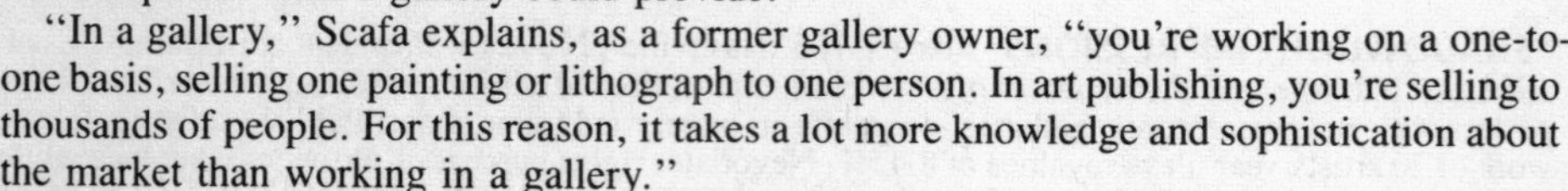

"In a gallery," Scafa explains, as a former gallery owner, "you're working on a one-to-one basis, selling one painting or lithograph to one person. In art publishing, you're selling to thousands of people. For this reason, it takes a lot more knowledge and sophistication about the market than working in a gallery."

Instead of selling her prints directly to the public, Scafa sells them to other outlets, who in turn sell them to the public. Among her clients are manufacturers of picture frames, who buy prints in order to fill the frames they sell. Therefore, Scafa must sell them prints that fit frames, both in size and styling. "If the frame is a French Provincial style, we usually match it with an impressionistic picture."

Since the framing industry closely follows furniture trends, so must Scafa, "We are definitely a trendy company. If the majority of people are furnishing their homes with traditional furniture, we publish traditional prints. If contemporary is in, we make airbrushed prints. But there always are prints like florals and landscapes that have a universal appeal."

In order to cover the many needs of frame manufacturers, Scafa sends a sample package of up to 250 prints to them two or three times a year. From these, the manufacturers can order what they need.

Offering such a variety of prints requires a large number of artists on call. Scafa works with 50-100 artists a year. Though their styles and subject matter vary, artists who work with her company must produce decorative images suitable for wall decor. "We ask for a great sense of current home furnishing colors. Color is important, and so is style and flair, coupled with expertise in the medium they work in."

Her best-selling artists are P.C. Chiu and Carlos Rios. Scafa attributes their popularity to their versatility. "They can change their styles to adapt to my needs. They also never get in a rut."

In her constant search for "new, professional talent," Scafa attends gallery openings and art shows, both here and abroad. Though she finds most artists through gallery shows, she realizes that what sells in a gallery does not necessarily make a good print or poster. "Our artists do not need a successful gallery record. Sometimes what passes for art in a gallery does not make a suitable art reproduction." Political or expressionistic themes, for example, don't fit into most living rooms.

Like most publishers, Scafa likes to review transparencies in order to see the artists' true color schemes. Though she reviews hundreds of samples each year, she sees a "glimmer of hope" in the work of a hundred or so artists, then narrows them down to 50 or 60. When she selects an artist, she asks for a series based on the sample she likes. "I'll ask the artist to create three or four pieces in the same series, like all different florals or all different landscapes." She has found that a series is much easier to sell to her clients because it covers so many decorative possibilities.

When sending work to a publisher, artists must remember that what's popular with a few friends might not work as an unlimited edition print. "Artists think that because a few people admired their work that it will become a smashing reproduction. They forget that they showed it to 20 people and 20 people loved it, whereas my initial run is 5,000 and 5,000 people have to love it."

—Susan Conner

Carlos Rios is one of Claire Scafa's best-selling artists. She says he is a versatile artist who is "mature and not in a rut." His work appeals to a diversity of tastes, which is important to an art publisher."

SOMERSET HOUSE PUBLISHING CORP., 10688 Haddington, Houston TX 77043. Contact: New Art Department. Clients: 5,000 retail art galleries. Publishes 15 artists/year. Payment method is negotiated. Send query letter with slides. Samples not filed returned. Reports within months. To show a portfolio, mail slides and photographs. Considers saleability of artwork when establishing payment. Buys first rights. Special interest: nautical/seascapes and wildlife themes.
Tips: "We do not want to see already printed samples of prints."

***SOUNDWORKS GALLERY**, Box 70014, Eugene OR 97407. (503)933-2562. Director: Kitrick Short. Works with 5 freelance artists/year. Works on assignment only. Prefers etchings, pen & ink and line drawings. Prefers religious and modern themes. Send query letter with brochure showing art style or resume and tear sheets, slides and photographs. Samples not filed are returned by SASE. Reports within 3 weeks. To show a portfolio, an artist should mail original/final art, color and tear sheets. Artist receives 50% of net proceeds. Pays on publication. Considers skill and experience of artist, saleability of artwork, clients' preferences and rights purchased when establishing payment. Buys all rights.
Acceptable Work: Prefers etchings and silkscreens; religious and modern themes.

***SOUTHEASTERN WILDLIFE EXPOSITION**, Box 71468, Charleston SC 29415. (803)723-1748. Art publisher, distributor and gallery handling limited editions, unlimited editions, handpulled originals and posters for galleries and representatives. Pays royalties of 30-50%; payment is negotiated. Offers an advance when appropriate. Negotiates rights purchased. Provides in-transit insurance, insurance while work is at firm, promotion and a written contract. Send query letter with resume and slides. Samples are filed. Samples not filed are returned only if requested. Reports only if interested. To show a portfolio, mail tear sheets and slides.
Acceptable Work: Considers pen & ink line drawings, oil paintings, acrylic paintings, pastels, watercolor and mixed media. Prefers wildlife art. Prefers individual works of art.

STRICTLY LIMITED EDITIONS, 1258 2nd Ave., San Francisco CA 94122. Contact: Jacob F. Adler. Art publisher/distributor of limited edition handpulled originals. Clients: galleries. Works with 8-10 artists/year. Negotiates payment method and rights purchased. Provides promotion and a written contract. Send query letter with brochure and samples to be kept on file. Write for appointment to show portfolio. Prefers to review original work. Samples are returned only if requested. Reports back only if interested.
Acceptable Work: Considers original graphics; serigraphs and etchings. Especially likes a variety of styles in figurative art.
Tips: "Have patience!"

STUDIO HOUSE EDITONS, 415 W. Superior, Chicago IL 60610. (312)751-0974. Director: Bill Sosin. Art publisher of offset reproductions. Clients: galleries. Publishes 7 freelance artists/year. Distributes 15 artists/year. Negotiates payment method and rights purchased. Provides promotion. Send query letter with brochure and slides to be kept on file. Samples not filed returned only if requested. Reports only if interested.
Acceptable Work: Photographs; stone lithographs and plate lithographs. Especially likes decor themes or styles.
Tips: "Send only high quality transparent duplicates of best work."

***SUMMERFIELD EDITIONS**, 2019 E. 3300 S., Salt Lake City UT 84109. (801)484-0700. Owner: Majid Omana. Estab. 1986. Art publisher, distributor and gallery handling offset reproductions, unlimited editions, posters and art cards for galleries, department stores, card stores and gift shops. Publishes the work of 12 freelance artists/year. Pays royalties of 10% plus signing fee. Offers an advance when appropriate. Negotiates rights purchased; prefers to buy all rights. Provides a written contract. Send query letter with brochure showing art style or resume, tear sheets, Photostats, photocopies, slides and transparencies. Samples are filed. Samples not filed are returned only if requested. Reports back within 1 month. Call or write to schedule an appointment to show a portfolio, or mail tear sheets, slides and transparencies.
Acceptable Work: Considers oil paintings, acrylic paintings, pastels, watercolor, mixed media or color photographs. Prefers Americana, country, Southwest and contemporary themes. Prefers individual works of art.
Tips: "Color photos or slides and/or finished art are preferred. We also like to see a resume. We do not want to see uncompleted, sloppy work."

JOHN SZOKE GRAPHICS INC., 164 Mercer St., New York NY 10012. Director: John Szoke. Produces limited edition handpulled originals for galleries, museums and private collectors. Publishes 10-25 artists/year. Charges commission or negotiates royalties. Provides promotion and written contract. Arrange interview or submit slides. SASE. Reports within 1 week.

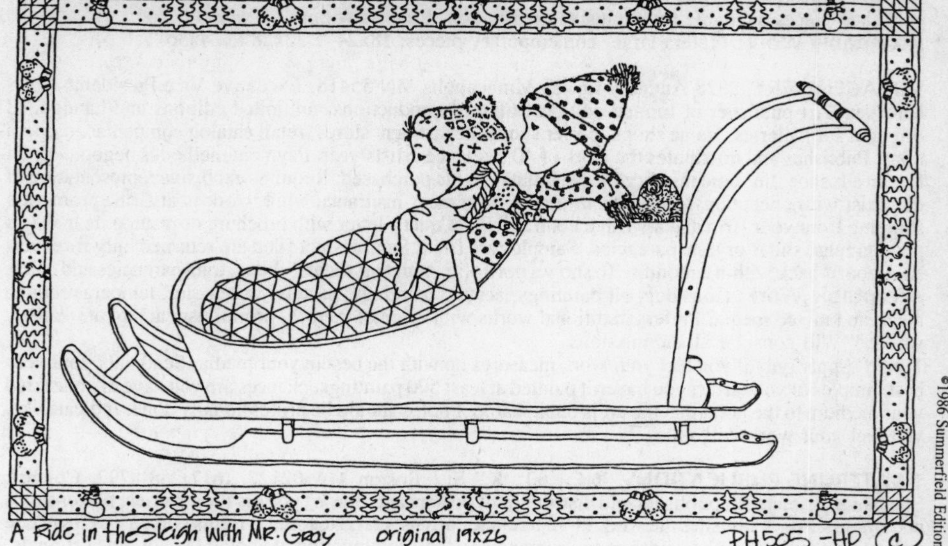

A Ride in the Sleigh with Mr. Gray
original 19x26
PH505 -HP ©
©1986 Summerfield Editions

Illustrator Peg Wheeler Hope of Salt Lake City, Utah brings back memories of a traditional Christmas with this greeting card, published by Summerfield Editions. Owner Kelly S. Omana found Hope at a local art show. "She has been easy to work with as well as very friendly. She meets deadlines and is always showing us new and fresh ideas." Hope sold all rights to the watercolor-and-ink piece.

TELE GRAPHICS, 607 E. Walnut St., Pasadena CA 91101. President: Ron Rybak. Art publisher/art distributor handling limited editions, offset reproductions, unlimited editions and handpulled originals. Clients: galleries, picture framers, interior designers and regional distributors. Publishes 1-4 freelance artists/year. Distributes work for 25 artists/ year. Works with 35-40 artists/year. Negotiates payment method. Offers advance. Negotiates rights purchased. Requires exclusive representation. Provide promotion, shipping from your firm and a written contract. Send query letter with resume and samples. Samples not filed returned only if requested. Reports within 30 days. Call or write to schedule an appointment to show a portfolio, which should include original/final art. Pays for design by the project. Considers skill and experience of artist, and rights purchased when establishing payment.
Tips: "Be prepared to show as many varied examples of work as possible. Show transparencies or slides plus photographs to show a particular style. We are not interested in seeing only 1 or 2 pieces."

TOH-ATIN GALLERY, 145 W. 9th St., Durango CO 81301. (303)247-8444. Vice President: Antonia Clark. Art publisher/distributor and gallery handling offset reproductions for galleries, gift shops, Indian art shops, interior design and decorators. Publishes work of 1-2 artists/year and distributes work of 10-12 artists/year. Pays royalties of 10%; payment method is negotiated. Negotiates rights purchased. Provides in-transit insurance, insurance while work is at firm and shipping from firm. Send query letter with brochure or resume, tear sheets, Photostats, photographs, slides and transparencies. Samples are filed. Samples not filed are returned by SASE. Reports within 2 months. Call or write to schedule an appointment to show a portfolio.
Acceptable Work: Considers oil paintings, acrylic paintings, pastels, watercolor and mixed media. Prefers Southwestern or Indian subjects. Prefers individual works of art. Maximum size 48x48".
Tips: "Send photos first—then call for an appointment. Don't use a company's toll-free lines to sell your images to them. If you have your own prints and want them marketed, price them reasonably."

***VALLEY COTTAGE GRAPHICS**, Box 564, Valley Cottage NY 10989. (914)358-7605 or 358-7606; or (800)431-2902. Contact: Ms. Claire Scafa or Ms. Sheila Berkowitz. Publishes "top of the line" unlimited edition posters and prints. Clients: galleries and custom frame shops nationwide. Buys reproduction rights (exclusively) and/or negotiates exclusive distribution rights to "special, innovative, existing

fine art publications." Query first; submit slides, photographs of unpublished originals, or samples of published pieces available for exclusive distribution. Reports within 2-3 weeks.
Acceptable Work: Prefers large, contemporary pieces; 18x24", 22x28", 24x36".

VOYAGEUR ART, 2828 Anthony Ln. S, Minneapolis MN 55418. Executive Vice President: James Knuckey. Art publisher of limited editions, offset reproductions, unlimited editions and handpulled originals for galleries, frame shops, poster shops, department stores, retail catalog companies, corporations. Publishes and distributes the work of 40 freelance artists/year. Payment method is negotiated. Offers an advance "in some instances." Negotiates rights purchased. Requires exclusive representation of the artist with exceptions. Provides in-transit insurance, insurance while work is at firm, promotion, shipping from your firm and a written contract. Send query letter with brochure or resume, tear sheets, photographs, slides or transparencies. Samples are filed. Samples not filed are returned only if requested. Reports back within 2 months. To show a portfolio, mail tear sheets, slides, transparencies and color.
Acceptable Work: Considers oil paintings, acrylic paintings, pastels, watercolor, tempera, scratch board and mixed media. Prefers traditional works with original themes, primitivism and photorealistic works. "Will consider all submissions."
Tips: "Apply only if you feel your work measures up with the best in your media. Send only your very best samples of your art. If you haven't painted at least 500 paintings, chances are you have not mastered your medium to the point that the art is publishable. Photos should be professionally done. Indicate why you feel your work will sell."

***WATERLINE PUBLICATIONS, INC.**, 60 "K" St., Boston MA 02127. (617)268-8792. Contact: Stephanie Cramer. Art publisher and distributor of posters and fine art posters for galleries, poster shops and frame shops. Publishes the work of 12 freelance artists/year. Negotiates rights purchased. Send query letter with photographs, slides or transparencies, "any combination of above. Do not send originals." Samples not filed are returned by SASE. Reports back within 2 months. Call to schedule an appointment to show a portfolio, after initially sending slides. Portfolio should include slides.
Acceptable Work: Considers oil paintings, acrylic paintings, pastels, watercolor, tempera, mixed media and photography. Prefers individual works of art.

***EDWARD WESTON EDITIONS**, 19355 Business Center Dr., Northridge CA 91324. (818)885-1044. Vice President/Secretary: Ann Weston. Art publisher, distributor and gallery handling limited and unlimited editions, offset reproductions and handpulled originals. Publishes 6 freelance artists/year. Distributes work for 30 artists/year. Pays flat fee; royalty of 10% of lowest selling price; or negotiates payment method. Sometimes offers advance. Buys first rights, all rights, reprint rights or negotiates rights purchased. Requires exclusive representation. Provides promotion and written contract. Send brochure and samples to be kept on file. Prefers original work as samples. Samples not filed returned by SASE. "Publisher is not responsible for returning art samples." Reports within 2 months. Write for appointment to show portfolio.
Acceptable Work: Considers all media. Especially likes "new, different, unusual techniques and style."

WINDY CREEK INC., 221 N. Scott, Bluffton IN 46714. (219)824-5666. President: Bob Hayden. Art publisher and distributor of limited editions, unlimited editions and posters for galleries, mail order and gift shops. Publishes/distributes the work of 3 artists/year. Payment method is negotiated. Offers an advance when appropriate. Negotiates rights purchased. Provides promotion. Send query letter with brochure showing art style or photocopies. Samples are filed. Samples not filed are returned only if requested. Reports back within weeks. Write to schedule an appointment to show a portfolio.
Acceptable Work: Considers pen & ink line drawings, oil paintings, acrylic paintings and watercolor. Prefers wildlife art. Prefers individual works of art and unframed series.

THE WINN CORPORATION, Box 80096, Seattle WA 98108. (206)763-9544. President: Larry Winn. Art publisher and distributor of limited editions, offset reproductions and handpulled originals. Clients: interior designers, art galleries, frame shops, architects, art consultants, corporations, hotels, etc. Publishes 10 freelance artists/year (prints). Distributes work for 120 artists/year (posters). Pays flat fee, $500-10,000; variable royalties; 50% commission; payment method is negotiated. Offers advance. Negotiates rights purchased. Requires exclusive representation. Provides in-transit insurance, insurance while work is at firm, promotion, shipping from firm and written contract. Send query letter with resume and slides. Slides returned by SASE. Reports within 1 month.
Acceptable Work: Considers pen & ink line drawings, oil and acrylic paintings, pastels, collage, watercolors and mixed media; serigraphs, stone lithographs, plate lithographs, woodcuts and linocuts. Especially interested in "good design and contemporary imagery."
Tips: "I look for printmaking skills, versatility, design sense, and fresh look."

Associations & Institutions

Service-oriented associations rely heavily on the print media to convey their messages, and on freelance help for the design and illustration of magazines, newsletters, posters, invitations, brochures and catalogs. Universities and colleges produce publications for their students and alumni, and they also use artists to spice up special reports.

Handling a diversity of projects, these groups have many art needs yet seldom employ large inhouse staffs. Thus they turn to freelancers, who can find opportunities in this category both locally and nationwide. Some projects such as layout and paste-up call for a local artist to facilitate quick turnaround time. However, other projects, such as magazine illustration, can be discussed, assigned and submitted through the mail.

Have patience. The fluctuating budgets of these organizations often determine how many art projects can be assigned. Keep this in mind when waiting to hear from them, because it often takes a while for a reply. Make sure you have samples on file in their offices so you will be called when the need arises.

Because of their budget restrictions, some groups ask artists to donate their work. You will have to weigh the pros and cons of a nonpaying assignment: Do you believe strongly in the organization's cause? Does the assignment give you a chance to explore a new medium or style? Will the widely-distributed literature give you exposure, leading to referrals and lucrative jobs?

For additional information, consult the *Encyclopedia of Associations*, *Barron's Profiles of American Colleges*, *Comparative Guide to American Colleges*, *Peterson's Annual Guide to Undergraduate Studies*, and the *Directory of World Museums*.

***ACCURACY IN MEDIA**, 1275 K St. NW, Washington DC 20005. (202)371-6710. Executive Secretary: Don Irvine. Nonprofit educational organization with 25,000 members dedicated to combatting media bias and inaccuracy.
Needs: Works with 1-2 freelance artists/year. Uses artists for advertising and brochure design, illustration and layout.
First Contact & Terms: Send query letter with brochure, resume, tear sheets, Photostats and photocopies. Samples are filed. Reports back within 7 days. Call to schedule an appointment to show a portfolio. Pays for design by the project, $100-500. Considers complexity of project, turnaround time and how work will be used when establishing payment. Buys all rights or reprint rights.
Tips: "Study organization materials. Must have a feel for what we do. Very few artists we have met can grasp our organization."

AESTHETICIANS INTERNATIONAL ASSOCIATION, INC., Suite D, 3606 Prescott, Dallas TX 75219. (214)526-0752. Chairman of the Board: Ron Renee. Promotes education and public awareness of skin care, make-up and body therapy. Produces seminars and holds an annual congress; produces a magazine, *Dermascope*, published bimonthly.
Needs: Works with 6 freelance artists/year. Works on assignment only. Uses artists for advertising design, illustration and layout, brochure and magazine/newspaper design, exhibits, displays and posters.
First Contact & Terms: Send query letter with brochure showing art style, tear sheets, Photostats, photocopies, slides or photographs to be kept on file. Samples not kept on file are returned by SASE. Reports only if interested. Call or write to schedule an appointment to show portfolio, which should include tear sheets, Photostats and photographs. Pays by the hour, $3.75-6 average. Considers available budget when establishing payment.
Tips: "Have something that is creative that reflects our profession."

AFFILIATE ARTISTS INC., 37 W. 65 St., New York NY 10023. Director, Communications: Katharine Walling. A national not-for-profit organization, producing residencies and concert series for performing artists of all disciplines. "Affiliate Artists supports the professional development of exceptionally talented performers and builds audiences for live performance. Residencies are sponsored by corporations and corporate foundations, and presented locally by arts institutions and community organizations. Roster represents every discipline."
Needs: Works with 3 freelance artists/year. Works on assignment only. Uses artists for advertising and brochure design and layout.
First Contact & Terms: Send query letter with resume and Photostats. Samples returned only if requested. Reports only if interested. Pays by the project. Considers available budget when establishing payment.

AFS INTERCULTURAL PROGRAMS, 313 E. 43rd St., New York NY 10017. (212)949-4242. Creative Director: Margaret Connelly. AFS is a nonprofit student and adult international exchange program. "Our International and U.S. headquarters is in New York. We have offices in 70 countries. Most of our exchanges are educational in nature, involving students, teachers, the school stystems."
Needs: Works with 5 freelance artists/year. Prefers local artists only. Works on assignment only. Uses artists for advertising and brochure illustration, magazine illustration and posters. "We are usually limited to black-and-white line work, although we might use color on occasion. We like to show an ethnically diverse situation, with people interacting in an educational situation."
First Contact & Terms: Send query letter with photocopies. Samples are filed. Samples not filed are not returned. Reports back only if interested. To show a portfolio, mail tear sheets, color and b&w. Pays for illustration by the project, $50 minimum. Considers available budget when establishing payment. Buys all rights.

AMERICAN ACADEMY OF PEDIATRICS, 141 Northwest Point Blvd., Elk Grove Village IL 60009-0927. Publications Editor: Michael Burke. "A professional organization serving more than 34,000 pediatricians who are dedicated to the health, safety and well-being of infants, children, adolescents and young adults."
Needs: Works with 6 freelance artists/year. "Local artists only, please." Works on assignment only. Quick turnaround necessary. Uses artists for newspaper illustration, and annual report design. Prefers pen & ink and charcoal/pencil. Especially needs themes related to child health care improvement.
First Contact & Terms: Send query letter with resume and tear sheets. Samples not filed are not returned. Reports only if interested. Write to schedule an appointment to show a portfolio, which should include thumbnails, roughs, original/final art, final reproduction/product, tear sheets, Photostats, photographs and b&w. Pays for illustration by the project, $100 minimum. "Payment varies considerably; will pay for talent." Considers complexity of project, client's budget, skill and experience of artist, how work will be used, turnaround time and rights purchased when establishing payment.
Tips: "No telephone calls please. Show me art that *communicates*. We have added to newspaper's editorial staff and more than doubled our editorial content. We're growing. In turn, we need more and more creative talent."

AMERICAN ASSOCIATION FOR ADULT CONTINUING EDUCATION, Suite 420, 1201 16th St. NW, Washington DC 20036. (202)463-6333. Contact: Jane Melton. Merger of 2 previous associations. Promotes the development of adult education for educational administrators, researchers and teachers.
Needs: Works with 2 freelance artists/year. Prefers local artists. Uses artists for brochure design and magazine covers.
First Contact & Terms: Send query letter with brochure, or resume and photocopies. Samples are filed. Samples not filed are not returned. Reports back only if interested. Call to schedule an appointment to show a portfolio. Pays for design and illustration by the project. Considers complexity of project when establishing payment.

***AMERICAN BONSAI SOCIETY, INC.**, Box 358, Keene NH 03431. (603)352-9034. Executive Secretary: Anne D. Moyle. Nonprofit educational corporation and organization of individuals interested in the art of miniature trees; a journal and newsletter published quarterly.
Needs: Works with 2-3 freelance artists/year.
First Contact & Terms: Send query letter to be kept on file.

The asterisk before a listing indicates that the listing is new in this edition. New markets are often the most receptive to freelance submissions.

AMERICAN CORRECTIONAL ASSOCIATION, Suite L-208, 4321 Hartwick Rd., College Park MD 20740. (301)699-7627. Publications Manager/Art Director: Alonzo L. Winfield. 14,000-member nonprofit association dealing primarily with correctional personnel and services to improve the correctional field.
Needs: Works with 3-5 freelance artists/year. Call for appointment to show portfolio. Works on assignment only. Uses artists for advertising, brochure, catalog and magazine/newspaper layout and pasteup. Prefers themes on corrections.
First Contact & Terms: Prefers primarily local artists; "however, there may be infrequent exceptions." Send query letter with resume to be kept on file. Reports only if interested. Call for appointment to show a portfolio. Pays by the hour, $6 minimum. Considers complexity of project, available budget, skill and experience of artist and turnaround time when establishing payment.
Tips: "Artists' work should be clean, concise, with quick turnaround." Abilities should not be too specialized. "Most clients are not interested in dividing their work among several artists. They prefer to work closely with only one or two artists."

AMERICAN FILM AND VIDEO ASSOCIATION, INC., Suite 152, 920 Barnsdale Rd., LaGrange IL 60525. (312)482-4000. Executive Director: Ron MacIntyre. "The leading professional association concentrating on 16mm films, video and other nonprint media for education and community use." Members include: public libraries, universities/colleges, museums, community groups, film programmers, filmmakers, film teachers, etc.
Needs: Works with 1 artist/year for all illustrations; 1 for ad design. "Artists must work within strict guidelines."
First Contact & Terms: Query by mail or write with samples. Works on assignment only. Samples returned by SASE. Reports back on future assignment possibilities. Provide resume, business card, brochure/flyer, tear sheet samples or "anything that gives a good idea of work experience" to be kept on file for future assignments. Pay is negotiable.
Tips: "Send samples that apply to film/video technology, film librarians, independent video and filmmakers."

AMERICAN GEM SOCIETY, 5901 West Third St., Los Angeles CA 90036. Contact: Editor. "AGS is a nonprofit professional organization of jewelers and educators which seeks to build consumer confidence in the retail jeweler through promotion of ethical business standards and continuing advancement of the gemological professional (nationwide) serving retail jewelers, jewelry suppliers and jewelry consumers."
Needs: Works with 5 freelance artists/year. Artist must have "ability to portray beauty and romance of jewelry." Uses artists for brochure design, illustration and layout; AV presentations and exhibits. Prefers "an effective blend of simplicity, quality, and the tastefulness exemplified by fine jewelry stores."
First Contact & Terms: Send query letter with brochure showing art style or resume and tear sheets. Samples not filed are returned by SASE. Reports only if interested. Write to schedule an appointment to show a portfolio, which should include roughs and final reproduction/product. "Bids are taken on projects." Considers available budget, bids and satisfaction with previous work when establishing payment.
Tips: "Visit AGS stores (listed in the Yellow Pages) to see the kind of clientele we serve."

AMERICAN INSTITUTE OF BIOLOGICAL SCIENCES, 730 11th St. NW, Washington DC 20001-4584. (202)628-1500. Managing Editor: Anne Meltzer. Umbrella organization representing over 40 affiliated societies and 70,000 life scientists dealing with the biological sciences. Members are individual biologists and libraries.
Needs: Works with 1-2 freelance artists/year. Uses artists for brochure design and magazine illustration. Prefers technical and biological illustration. Prefers pen & ink. "Artists redraw figures supplied by the author. We decide by researching general pricing for services."
First Contact & Terms: Send query letter with brochure or resume, photocopies and slides. Samples are filed. Samples not filed are returned. Reports back within 2-6 months. To show a portfolio, mail original/final art, final reproduction/product, photographs and slides. Pays for design by the project, $15-60. Pays for illustration by the project, $10-20. Considers complexity of project and client's budget when establishing payment.
Tips: Looks for "biological, technical subjects, ability to work in black & white. Include a lot of variety in portfolio. We do not want to see originals. Send copies or slides."

AMERICAN SCIENCE FICTION ASSOCIATION, Suite 95, 421 E. Carson, Las Vegas NV 89101. Vice President: M. Silvers. Promotion and publishing of *all* facets of science fiction and fantasy literature for science fiction fans mostly.
Needs: Works with 20-40 freelance artists/year. Uses artists for brochure and magazine design, illustration and layout; AV presentation, exhibits, displays, signage and posters. Prefers futuristic themes.

First Contact & Terms: Send query letter with resume and samples. Samples not filed are not returned. Reports back within 4 weeks. To show a portfolio, mail original/final art. Pays for design by the hour, $18.50 minimum; by the project, $500 minimum; by the day, $88 minimum. Pays for illustration by the project, $250 minimum. Considers complexity of project and rights purchased when establishing payment.
Tips: "Past experience seems to indicate that the more material submitted the better the chance of our using the artist's services."

AMERICAN SOCIETY FOR THE PREVENTION OF CRUELTY TO ANIMALS, 441 E. 92nd St., New York NY 10128. (212)876-7700. Contact: Editor of Publications. A nonprofit humane society which cares for 200,000 animals annually. Its members are animal lovers and those concerned about humane issues.
Needs: Often uses illustrations for posters, booklets and newsletters. Needs realistic depictions of animals, and cartoons.
First Contact & Terms: Write with samples. Samples returned by SASE. Provide resume, brochure/flyer and tear sheet samples to be kept on file for future assignments. Reports within 3 weeks. Pays $25/small illustration for a pamphlet. Pay for product design and illustration depends on job required and funds available.

***AMERICAN YOUTH SOCCER ORGANIZATION**, 5403 W. 138th St., Hawthorne CA 90250. (213)643-9236. Publications Manager: Kristen Kearney. National nonprofit organization dedicated to youth soccer. Publishes quarterly magazine (*Soccer Now*), semi-annual newsletter, monthly news bulletin. Serves 325,000 players, ages 5-18 and 125,000 volunteers.
Needs: Works with 2-3 freelance artists/year. Local artists only. Uses artists for advertisings, brochure, catalog and publication illustration and AV presentations. Prefers line art, cartoons depicting humorous soccer-playing situations or cover illustrations.
First Contact & Terms: Send query letter with tear sheets. Samples are filed. Samples not filed are returned only if requested by artist. Reports back within days. Portfolio which should include tear sheets and color or b&w work. Pays for illustration by the project, $50-150. Considers complexity of project, available budget and skill and experience of artist when establishing payment. Buys all rights or reprint rights.
Tips: "Illustrations must be positive, lively, upbeat and 'slice of life.' "

APPALACHIAN CONSORTIUM PRESS, University Hall, Boone NC 28608. (704)262-2064. Executive Director: Dr. Barry Buxton. A nonprofit educational organization dedicated to preserving the cultural heritage of Southern Appalachia. "Our 15 members are colleges and universities in the Southern Highlands, governmental agencies and organizations, a craft guild, and a folk school. Our service region covers 156 counties in seven states. We serve not only our member institutions but the local community in our 156 county service region."
Needs: Works with 3 freelance artists/year. Uses artists for brochure and catalog design and layout, exhibits and signage.
First Contact & Terms: Send query letter with brochure or resume and photographs. Samples are filed. Reports back only if interested. Call or write to schedule an appointment to show a portfolio. Pays for design by the project, $100 minimum. Considers complexity of project and turnaround time when establishing payment.

***ATLANTIC SALMON FEDERATION**, Suite 1030, 1435 St. Alexandre, Montreal Quebec H3A 2G4 Canada. Managing Editor: Terry Davis. Conservation organization representing 500,000 anglers and conservationists across North America. Dedicated to protect and conserve the Atlantic Salmon. Serves sportsmen, biologists and environmentalists.
Needs: Works with approximately 10-14 freelance artists/year. Uses artists for cartoons, advertising, brochure and publication design, illustration and layout, catalog design, exhibits, displays, signage and posters. Publishes *The Atlantic Salmon Journal*. "Illustrations are usually compatible with magazine topics. Read sample copy for direction."
First Contact & Terms: Send query letter with brochure, resume, tear sheets, Photostats, photocopies, slides and photographs; "do not send original material with unsolicited manuscript or query." Samples are filed. Samples not filed are returned by SASE only if requested. Reports back within 6-8 weeks. Call or write to schedule an appointment to show a portfolio, which should include photographs, tear sheets, slides, color or b&w work. Pays for design by the project, $75-500. Pays for illustration by the project, $75-250. Considers, complexity of project, client's budget, turnaround time, skill and experience of artist and rights purchased when establishing payment. Buys first rights.
Tips: "Read our magazine carefully. Illustrations must be scientifically accurate if animals or fish are depicted. Most assignments follow a query with samples. Quick turn-around is an asset."

BIKECENTENNIAL, INC., 113 W. Main, Missoula MT 59802. (406)721-1776. Editor: Daniel D'Ambrosio. Service organization for touring bicyclists; 15,000 members.
Needs: Works with 2 freelance artists/year. Works on assignment only. Uses artists for illustration. Prefers line art.
First Contact & Terms: Send query letter with brochure showing art style. Samples not filed are returned by SASE. Reports within 2 weeks. To show a portfolio, mail slides. Pays by the project, $30-100. Considers complexity of project, and skill and experience of artist when establishing payment. Buys one-time rights.

***BROWARD COMMUNITY COLLEGE**, 225 E. Las Olas Blvd., Ft. Lauderdale FL 33301. (305)761-7490. Director of Cultural Affairs: Dr. Ellen Chandler. Assigns 2 jobs/year.
Needs: Works with 1 illustrator and 1 designer/year. Mostly local artists. Works on assignment only. Seasonal illustration needs during concert season: October-March. Uses artists for exhibits/displays. Especially needs season brochure and/or poster.
First Contact & Terms: Send query letter with photographs or call for interview. Looks for "imaginative design and clean, clear work." Reports in 1 month. Samples returned by SASE. Pay varies. Considers complexity of project and available budget when establishing payment.
Tips: "Our own college art students and printing department have become more actively involved in our projects."

BUCKNELL UNIVERSITY, Lewisburg PA 17837. (717)523-3200. Director of Public Relations and Publications: Sharon Poff. 3,400-student university; public relations department serves students, alumni (31,000), donors and students' parents.
Needs: Works with 3-4 freelance artists/year. Prefers freelancers with strong experience in college/university graphics and located within a 3-hour drive from campus. Uses artists for brochure, catalog and magazine/newspaper design, illustration and layout; graphic design and posters. Prefers themes "appropriate to a university with a traditional design style." Prefers pen & ink, charcoal/pencil and collage.
First Contact & Terms: Send query letter with samples, brochure/flyer and resume. Accepts any type samples. Looks for innovation, appropriateness of design concept to target audience and "sensitivity to our particular 'look'—rather classic and dignified, but not boring" when reviewing artist's work. Samples returned by SASE. Call or write for appointment to show portfolio. Payment is by the project, $100-3,000 or by the hour, $30 average; method is negotiable. Considers complexity of project, available budget and turnaround time when establishing payment.
Tips: Artists should "be able to help me produce graphically strong and cost-effective pieces."

CALIFORNIA BAPTIST COLLEGE, 8432 Magnolia Ave., Riverside CA 92504. (714)689-5771. Vice President for Public Affairs: Dr. Jay P. Chance.
Needs: Assigns 3-5 jobs/year. Local artists only. Uses artists for annual reports, catalog covers/layouts, direct mail/publicity brochures, displays, newspaper ad layouts, lettering, recruitment literature and company publications.
First Contact & Terms: Send query letter with samples to Division of Public Information on campus. SASE. Reports in 3 weeks. Call to schedule an appointment to a show a portfolio, which should include final reproduction/product. Pays by the hour.
Tips: "Call for appointment with Ken Miller."

CALIFORNIA STATE UNIVERSITY, LONG BEACH, University Publications, 1250 Bellflower Blvd., Long Beach CA 90840. (213)498-5453. Director of University Publications: Maggie Lowe Tennesen. CSULB is one of the 19 campuses in the California State University system. It offers 128 baccalaureate programs and 72 master's programs. There are 33,000 students enrolled. Publications are mailed to over 100,000 alumni and friends of the University in the community.
Needs: Works with 5-10 freelance artists/year. Works on assignment only. Uses artists for advertising and brochure design, illustration and layout, catalog layout, magazine illustration and layout and posters.
First Contact & Terms: Send query letter with resume, tear sheets, Photostats or photocopies. Samples are filed. Reports back within 2 weeks. Call or write to schedule an appointment to show a portfolio. Pays for design and illustration by the project, $50-1,500. Considers complexity of project and turnaround time when establishing payment. Rights purchased vary according to project.

CCCO/An Agency for Military and Draft Counseling, 2208 South St., Philadelphia PA 19146. (215)545-4626. Publications Director: Robert A. Seeley. "The largest national draft and military counseling organization in the country; publishes an extensive line of literature, a quarterly newsletter reaching 45,000 people, and one other special-interest newsletter." Serves CCCO contributors and conscientious objectors registered with CCCO. "All are peace-oriented and interested in issues surrounding the draft and military."

Needs: Uses artists for brochure and magazine/newspaper illustration, and possibly for brochure design. Interested in war and peace themes particularly as they affect individuals; open to any style. Graphics and illustrations considered on a case by case basis; especially interested in cartoons.
First Contact & Terms: Send query letter with samples to be kept on file. Reviews any type of sample; finished artwork must be camera-ready. Samples not kept on file returned by SASE. Reports within 4 weeks. "We pay only in contributors' copies, but since our material reaches 45,000 people nationwide, including a number of magazines, we also offer exposure."
Tips: "Send several samples if possible."

***CHAPMAN COLLEGE**, 333 N. Glassell, Orange CA 92666. Director of Publications: Rosalinda M. Monroy. A 4-year private liberal arts college producing publications for use by donors and approximately 1,800 students enrolled on the home campus and the surrounding community.
Needs: Works with 2 full-time and 2 part-time artists and occasionally freelancers. Prefers artists who "live in the surrounding area to be available for meetings." Works on assignment only. Uses artists for catalog design, illustration and layout; exhibits, displays, signage and calligraphy. Especially needs freelance illustrations, photographs and production artists/designers.
First Contact & Terms: Send query letter, resume and business card with photos or photocopies to be kept on file; write for appointment. Looks for "quality, creative, clean and cost-conscious design" when reviewing artist's work. Samples not filed are returned by SASE. Payment varies according to job. Considers complexity of project, available budget, and skill and experience of artist when establishing payment.
Tips: CASE, The Council for the Advancement of Secondary Education, and UCDA, The University & College Designers Association, and local community organizations such as public relations societies or business associations are helpful organizations to join for education art contacts. "The ability to communicate clearly is important. Administrators at institutions are involved in so many meetings and other tasks that the opportunity to catch them anytime with questions is not always there. Artists need to be versatile and able to illustrate, design and have a working knowledge of production and printing processes." Artists should avoid "underselling themselves by asking for less than they deserve, or overselling by asking for much more than their experience shows."

***CHAROLAIS PUBLICATIONS, INC.**, Box 20247, Kansas City MO 64195. (816)464-5977. Manager: Amber E. Spafford. Publishes *Charolais Journal*, a monthly color and b&w 8½x11 magazine which is the "voice of the industry from east to west coasts and some foreign countries." Serves 4,500 members who are breeders of Charolais cattle or investors.
Needs: Prefers local artists. Uses freelance artists for advertising, brochure and catalog design, catalog illustration and catalog layout.
First Contact & Terms: Send query letter with resume. Write to schedule an appointment to show a portfolio.

CHILD AND FAMILY SERVICES OF NEW HAMPSHIRE, 99 Hanover St., Box 448, Manchester NH 03105. (603)668-1920. Contact: Development Director. "Our purposes are to reduce social problems, promote and conserve wholesome family life, serve children's needs and guard children's rights."
Needs: Works with 1 illustrator and designer/year; February-May only. Uses artists for annual reports, direct mail brochures, exhibits/displays, posters, publicity brochures and trademarks/logotypes. Prefers pen & ink. Especially needs b&w photos of children and/or families. Prefers realistic portrayals of family life.
First Contact & Terms: Query with business card and tear sheets to be kept on file or arrange interview. Looks for human interest appeal when reviewing artist's work. Reports in 2 weeks. Works on assignment only. Samples returned by SASE. Pays for design by the project, $100-1,000. Pays for illustration by the project, $25-250. Considers complexity of project and available budget when establishing payment.
Tips: "In black-and-white work, we look for a balance—nothing too stark or horrific—but a snapshot of real people, children, families."

CHILDREN'S ART FOUNDATION, Box 83, Santa Cruz CA 95063. (408)426-5557. Co-director: Gerry Mandel. "The Children's Art Foundation is a nonprofit educational organization. We operate a museum of international children's art and an art school for children. We also publish *Stone Soup*, a national magazine of writing and art by children. We currently have about 9,000 members. We serve schools, libraries, children, teachers, parents, and the general public."
Needs: Works with 5 freelance artists/year. Prefers children up to age 13 only. Uses artists for magazine illustration.
First Contact & Terms: Send query letter with Photostats, photocopies, slides, photographs, or original drawings. Samples are filed. Samples not filed are returned by SASE. Reports back within 8 weeks.

Pays $7.50 "for each illustration we publish." Buys all rights.
Tips: "We like illustrations that depict complete scenes and fill the entire page with detail."

COACHING ASSOCIATION OF CANADA, Department of Promotions and Communication, 333 River Rd., Ottawa, Ontario, K1L 8H9 Canada. (613)748-5624. Development Editor: Steve Newman. National nonprofit organization dedicated to coaching development and the profession of coaching.
Needs: Works with 4-5 freelance artists/year. Works on assignment only. Uses artists for advertising, brochure, catalog and magazine illustration. Prefers coaching (sport) themes in realistic styles.
First Contact & Terms: Send brochure and samples to be kept on file. Prefers slides or photographs as samples. Samples not kept on file are returned. Reports within 4 weeks. Pays by the project, $50-400 average. Considers how work will be used and rights purchased when establishing payment. Buys reprint rights.
Tips: "Artists must have a good understanding of sport. Humorous illustrations are helpful."

COLLEGE OF THE SOUTHWEST, 6610 Lovington Highway, Hobbs NM 88240. (505)392-6561. Contact: Public Information Officer. Privately supported, independently governed 4-year college offering professional studies on a foundation of arts and sciences, emphasizing Christian principles and the private enterprise system.
Needs: Works with varying number of freelance artists/year. Prefers to work with artists in the Southwest. Works on assignment only. Uses artists for advertising, brochure and graphic design; advertising and brochure illustration; and posters. Especially needs artwork "relating to Southwestern heritage."
First Contact & Terms: Send query letter; submit portfolio for review. Prefers 5-10 Photostats or slides as samples. Samples returned by SASE. Reports within 2 weeks. Provide resume and samples to be kept on file for possible future assignments. Negotiates payment.

THE CONTEMPORARY ARTS CENTER, 115 E. 5th St., Cincinnati OH 45202. (513)721-0390. Publications Coordinator: Carolyn Krause. The Center is a small organization (8-10 full-time positions) with changing exhibitions of contemporary art surveying individuals, movements, regional artists, etc., in all media. "We have a growing membership which is geared toward contemporary art and design."
Needs: Works with 2-5 freelance artists/year. Works on assignment only. Uses artists for advertising, brochure and catalog design, magazine/newspaper design and layout; signage and posters. Prefers contemporary styles.
First Contact & Terms: Send query letter with brochure and resume to be kept on file. Reports only if interested. Pays by the project; "other payment arrangements can be devised as needed." Considers complexity of project, available budget, skill and experience of artist, and turnaround time when establishing payment.

CORE PUBLICATIONS, 1457 Flatbush Ave., Brooklyn NY 11210. (718)434-3580. Communications Coordinator: George Holmes. Nonprofit association providing civil rights publications.
Needs: Works with 20-30 freelance artists/year. Works on assignment only. Uses artists for advertising and magazine/newspaper design, illustration and layout.
First Contact & Terms: Send query letter with samples and resume. Especially looks for artistic skill, imagination, reproduction ability and originality when reviewing work. Samples not filed returned by SASE. Reports within 6 weeks. Negotiates payment by the project.

COVENANT COLLEGE, Scenic Highway, Lookout Mountain GA 37350. (404)820-1560. Director of Publications: Rona Gary. "Convenant College is a four-year Christian liberal arts college affiliated with the Presbyterian Church in America."
Needs: Works with 2 freelance artists/year. Prefers local artists. Works on assignment only. Uses artist for AV presentations and displays.
First Contact & Terms: Send query letter with brochure and resume. Samples are filed. Samples not filed are returned only if requested by SASE. Reports back only if interested. To show a portfolio, mail final reproduction/product. Payment for design and illustration is negotiable. Considers client's budget when establishing payment. Buys all rights; rights purchased vary according to project.

CYSTIC FIBROSIS FOUNDATION, 6931 Arlington Rd., Bethesda, MD 20814. (301)951-4422. Manager, Publications: Joann Fallon. National, nonprofit organization. Bethesda office oversees activities of 60 chapters throughout the country.
Needs: Works with 3 freelance artists/year. "Because we're a nonprofit organization, cost is a crucial factor—we must contract with artist that gives lowest bid, but we still strive for quality." Uses artists for brochure design; newspaper design, and layout; AV presentations, and posters. Especially needs artwork for promotional, fund-raising pieces and for corporate solicitations. Prefers simple, yet professional styles.

First Contact & Terms: Send query letter with brochure showing art style or resume and samples. Samples not filed are returned only if requested. Reports only if interested. "No calls please." Pays for design and illustration by the hour, $50 maximum. Considers complexity of project, client's budget and turnaround time when establishing payment.
Tips: "We see more nonprofit origanizations competing for less dollars, which means fund-raising pieces will become slicker, more professional and business-oriented."

DISCOVERY: THE ARTS WITH YOUTH IN THERAPY, 3977 2nd Ave., Detroit MI 48201. (313)832-4357. Director: Fr. Russ Kohler. "We fund self-employed artists to work for 15 weekly house calls to youth with cancer and long-term illnesses."
Needs: Works with "artists as we need them upon referral of patients by physicians and medical social workers. We prefer artists who are somewhat isolated in their medium and willing to enter the isolation of the child overly identified with his disease. Prefer a minimum of psychological and medical jargon; emphasis on the language of art and visual expression and experience."
First Contact & Terms: Write with resume to be kept on file for future assignments.

DREXEL UNIVERSITY, Dept. of Public Relations, 32nd and Chestnut Sts., Philadelphia PA 19104. (215)895-2613. Director: Philip Terranova. Buys 10 illustrations/year.
Needs: Uses designers for books, pamphlets and posters; illustrators for covers, spot art, advertising, annual reports, charts, direct mail brochures, exhibits/displays, handbooks, publicity, recruitment literature, magazines, newsletters and trademarks/logos. Also uses mechanical artists for same as need permits.
First Contact & Terms: Send query letter with resume, b&w or color tear sheets (slides OK) or arrange interview. Looks for originality and sound production skills. SASE. Reports in 1 week. Pays for mechanicals by the hour, $7.50-10; for illustration by the project, $100-300. Considers available budget and skill and experience of artist when establishing payment.

EPILEPSY FOUNDATION OF AMERICA, Suite 406, 4351 Garden City Dr., Landover MD 20785. (301)459-3700. Director of Administrative Services: Hugh S. Gage. Nonprofit association providing direct and indirect programs of advocacy, public health education and information, research, government liaison and fundraising to persons with epilepsy, their families and professionals concerned with the disorder.
Needs: Works with 3-4 freelance artists/year. Prefers local artists "because of tight deadlines. Sometimes this is not a problem. However, it depends on the job." Works on assignment only. Uses artists for advertising layout, brochure design, illustration and layout; graphic design, exhibits, displays, signage, AV presentations, annual reports, illustrations and layouts for fundraising materials. Themes must be suitable to a publicly-funded, charitable organization.
First Contact & Terms: Provide business card to be kept on file. Looks for "diversity, taste, 'non-cute' approaches." Samples returned by SASE. Reports back on whether to expect possible future assignments. Call for appointment. Payment is by the project. Considers complexity of project and available budget when establishing payment.
Tips: "We're looking for the most value for our money. Don't bring banged-up, poorly printed samples."

ESSEX COMMUNITY COLLEGE, 7201 Rossville Blvd., Baltimore County MD 21237. (301)522-1269. Contact: Managing Director. Performing arts center; presents musicals, cabaret plays, open-air Shakespearean and other classical plays, children's theatre, and seminars. "Cockpit is in residence at Essex Community College. We try to use the services of the school graphics department as much as possible but sometimes must use freelance artists because the staff at the school is too overloaded or they are unable to give us what we want."
Needs: Works with 2 illustrators and 2 designers/year. "Our brochure is our most important tool for publicity as it creates an image for our theatre. Work on the brochure begins in early fall for the following summer season." Uses artists for advertising, billboards, designer-in-residence, direct mail brochures, flyers, graphics, posters, sets and technical art.
First Contact & Terms: Local artists only. Query with samples or arrange interview. SASE. Reports within 2 weeks. Works on assignment only. Samples returned by SASE; and reports back on future assignment possibilities. Provide resume, business card, brochure, flyer and tear sheet to be kept on file for future assignments. Negotiates payment.
Tips: "Cockpit in Court Summer Theatre is a rarity. We are self-supporting through subscription sales, box office receipts, grants and donations. We have started an apprenticeship program to supplement nearly every production area and seldom require the services of a freelance artist as college faculty and staff members can usually produce what we want." To those artists interested in working in the performing arts field, "keep artwork simple! Graphics and typeface must be reproducible, will most likely be reduced for flyers, newspapers ads, etc. The simpler the typeface the better."

EXOTIC WORLD, 29053 Wild Rd., Helendale CA 92342. President: Jennie Lee. Associated with Exotic Dancers League of North America. Members are exotic dancers, strippers and their fans.
Needs: Works with 1-2 freelance artists/year. Uses artists for advertising and brochure design, illustration and layout, catalog design, magazine design, displays, signage, posters, portraits and murals of dancers, strippers and figures.
First Contact & Terms: Send brochure or resume, tear sheets, Photostats, photocopies, photographs and SASE. Samples are filed. Samples not filed are returned by SASE only if requested. Reports back within 2 weeks only if interested. Write to schedule an appointment to show a portfolio or mail Photostats, tear sheets, photographs and color. Pays for design by the project, $20-100. Pays for illustration by the project, $20-200. Negotiates rights purchased; rights purchased vary according to project.
Tips: "We are mostly interested in posters and murals. Please submit your ideas for our new brochure, using design, printing and color photos, folded in thirds."

FEDERAL BAR ASSOCIATION, Suite 408, 1815 H St. NW, Washington DC 20006. (202)638-0252. Director of Publications: Monica Goldberg. "Our 15,000 + member association was founded in 1920 to further the goals of the federal legal profession." Serves lawyers, magistrates, judges, district attorneys and members of the Military Judge Advocates Generals Corps.
Needs: Works with 3 or more freelance artists/year. Uses artists for magazine illustration.
First Contact & Terms: Send query letter with resume and samples. Samples are not returned. Reports only if interested. Call or write to schedule an appointment to show a portfolio. Pays for illustration by the project, limited budget. Considers available budget when establishing payment.

THE FINE ARTS CENTER, CHEEKWOOD, Forrest Park Dr., Nashville TN 37205. (615)352-8632. Director: Kevin Grogan. Art museum; full-time staff of 9; collects, preserves, exhibits and interprets art with special emphasis on American painting. The Tennessee Botanical Gardens and Fine Arts Center, Inc., has a membership in excess of 8,000, drawn primarily from Nashville (Davidson County) and neighboring counties in the middle Tennessee, southern Kentucky region.
Needs: Works with 1-3 freelance artists/year. Prefers local artists. Uses artists for advertising, brochure and catalog design and layout; signage and posters.
First Contact & Terms: Send query letter with resume, business card, slides and photographs to be kept on file; "slides, if any, will be returned." Reports within 4 weeks. Write to schedule an appointment to show portfolio and for artists' guidelines. Pays by the hour, $5-20 average. Considers complexity of project, available budget, skill and experience of artist, how work will be used and turnaround time when establishing payment.

FISK UNIVERSITY, 1000 17th Ave. N., Nashville TN 37208-3051. (615)329-8536. Director Public Relations: Angelina Radcliff. Predominantly Black liberal arts college with enrollment of 650 students. Oriented towards pre-professional training with high academic standards.
Needs: Works with 3 freelance artists/year. Prefers local artists. Works on assignment only. Uses artists for brochure design, magazine design and illustration, AV presentations and posters.
First Contact & Terms: Send query letter with brochure or tear sheets, slides and photographs. Samples are filed. Samples not filed are returned only if requested by SASE. Reports back within 5 days. Call to schedule an appointment to show a portfolio, which should include original/final art, tear sheets, color and b&w. Pays for design by the hour, $20-35. Pays for illustration by the project, $35-50. Considers complexity of project, skill and experience of artist and how work will be used when establishing payment. Rights purchased vary according to project.

FLORIDA MEMORIAL COLLEGE, 15800 NW 42nd Ave., Miami FL 33054. (305)625-4141. Public Affairs Director: Nadine Drew. Baptist-related, 4-year, accredited liberal arts college located on a 77-acre site with enrollment of 2,200 multi-racial students.
Needs: Works with 2-3 freelance artists/year. Works on assignment only. Uses artists for advertising, brochure and catalog design, illustration and layout.
First Contact & Terms: Send brochure/flyer with printed material, tear sheets and actual work. Samples returned upon request only with SASE. Reports immediately.

FRANKLIN PIERCE COLLEGE, Communications Office, Rindge NH 03461. Director/Communications: Richard W. Kipperman.
Needs: Regional artists only. Uses artists for illustrations for brochure and magazine covers, occasionally for brochure design and layout.
First Contact & Terms: Query with previously published work. Looks for "quality, artistic ability" when reviewing samples. Works on assignment only. Samples returned by SASE; and reports back on future possibilities. Provide resume and business card to be kept on file for future assignments. Pays per completed assignment (includes concept/roughs/comps/mechanicals).

THE FREEDONIA GAZETTE, Darien 28, New Hope PA 18938. (215)862-9734. Director: Paul Wesolowski. The purpose of this organization is to gather information on the lives and careers of the Marx Brothers and their impact on the world. It is a membership organization with approximately 400 members. Members consist of anyone interested in the Marx Brothers: students, professionals, libraries, fans.
Needs: Works with 1 freelance artist/year. Uses artists for magazine illustration and layout of the *The Freedonia Gazette*. Prefers pen & ink and markers. Prefers illustrations which relate in some way to the Marx Brothers.
First Contact & Terms: Send query letter with tear sheets, photocopies and photographs. Samples are filed. Reports back within 3 weeks. To show a portfolio, mail thumbnails, roughs, original/final art, tear sheets, photographs and b&w. "Portfolio should suggest the ability to draw or caricature one or more Marx Brothers."
Tips: "TFG is a not-for-profit organization. All writers, artists and editors volunteer their services. The only payment we offer is a complimentary copy of any issue your work appears in. We're oblivious to trends. We've filled a niche and are happy here."

GEORGIA INSTITUTE OF TECHNOLOGY, Office of Publications, Wardlaw Bldg, Atlanta GA 30332-0183. (404)894-2450. Director: Thomas Vitale. University with 11,000 students; publications serving alumni, graduate and undergraduate students and faculty.
Needs: Works with 5 freelance artists/year. Works on assignment only. Uses artists for brochure design and illustration, magazine/newspaper illustration and posters. Themes and styles vary with each project.
First Contact & Terms: Send query letter with brochure and samples to be kept on file. Samples not filed are returned only if requested. Reports only if interested. Call or write for appointment to show portfolio. Pays by the hour, $25-100 average. Considers complexity of project, available budget, skill and experience of artist, how work will be used, turnaround time and rights purchased when establishing payment.
Tips: "We are a state school—budgets are tight, but the work is very high-quality."

HAMPDEN-SYDNEY COLLEGE, Hampden-Sydney VA 23943. (804)223-4382. Director of Publications: Dr. Richard McClintock. Nonprofit all-male liberal arts college of 850 students in a historic zone campus.
Needs: Works with 5-6 freelance artists/year. Works on assignment only. Uses artists for advertising, brochure, catalog and graphic design; brochure and magazine/newspaper illustration; brochure, catalog and magazine/newspaper layout; AV presentations and posters. Especially needs illustrations and mechanical preparations.
First Contact & Terms: Send query letter with resume and actual work. Write for appointment to show portfolio. Portfolio should include fine line b&w art, range of styles and subjects. Samples returned by SASE. Reports in 1 week. Pays for design by the project, $25-300. Pays for illustration by the project, $25-100.
Tips: "Changes in art and design include more formality, careful design and quality of 'look.' "

***INSTITUTE OF INTERNAL AUDITORS**, 249 Maitland Ave., Altamonte Spgs. FL 32701. (407)830-7600, ext. 312. Art Director: W.P. Dolle. Professional association for accountants and auditors with 30,000 members in 128 countries around the world.
Needs: Works with 8-10 freelance artists/year. Artist must have 3-5 years of experience. Works on assignment only. Regional artists used but it is not necessary to be local. Uses artists for advertising, brochure and catalog design and illustration; magazine design and illustration, and photography. Prefers business/international theme.
First Contact & Terms: Send query letter with resume, tear sheets, Photostats and photocopies. Samples not filed are returned by SASE. Reports within days. Call or write to schedule an appointment to show a portfolio, which should include roughs, comps original/finished art, final printed pieces; color and b&w. Pays for design and illustration by the project, $200-600. Considers complexity of project, client's budget, and skill and experience of artist when establishing payment.
Tips: "When deadline is established, work should be delivered by that date, no excuses."

INTERNATIONAL BLACK WRITERS CONFERENCE, INC., Box 1030, Chicago IL 60690. A writers' organization that provides annual workshops and an annual awards banquet for writers and aspiring writers. There are 500 members nationally.
Needs: Works with approximately 150 freelance artists/year. Uses artists for magazine design, exhibits and displays. Prefers subjects relevant to writers.
First Contact & Terms: Send query letter with resume and photocopies.

INTERNATIONAL FABRICARE INSTITUTE, 12251 Tech Rd., Silver Spring MD 20904. (301)622-1900. Division Director of Membership: Kathleen Mitchell. Trade association for drycleaners and launderers serving 11,500 members.
Needs: Works with 2-3 freelance artists/year. Uses artists for brochure and catalog design, illustration and layout; and posters.
First Contact & Terms: Local artists only; "must have references, be reachable by phone, reliable and honor schedules." Works on assignment only. Call or write for appointment to show portfolio. Especially looks for "neatness, appeal to my own aesthetics and suitability to our company image." Reports only if interested. Pay varies according to project; "typical #10 brochure, $500-800." Considers complexity of project, available budget, and skill and experience of artist when establishing payment.
Tips: "Call for an appointment; don't 'drop in.' Have your portfolio ready and references available. Follow up if necessary; I'm busy and may forget by the time a suitable project comes up."

INTERNATIONAL RACQUET SPORTS ASSOCIATION, 132 Brookline Ave., Boston MA 02215. (617)236-1500. Editor: Craig R. Waters.Design Director: W. Kevin Wells. Trade association for commercially operated, investor-owned racquet and fitness clubs.
Needs: Works with 6 freelance artists/year. Prefers local artists. Uses artists for advertising, brochure and magazine/newspaper design, illustration and layout; posters. Prefers fitness club operations, business scenes and club sports as themes.
First Contact & Terms: Send query letter with brochure showing art style. Samples not filed are returned by SASE. Reports only if interested. Call or write to schedule an appointment to show a portfolio. Pays for design by the project, $200 minimum. Pays for illustration by the project, $100 minimum. Considers complexity of project, client's budget, skill and experience of artist, and turnaround time when establishing payment.
Tips: "We have only begun budgeting for design and illustration work fairly recently, so our rates are low. We are looking to build a stable of contacts—if you start with us, you can probably take on work from a variety of sources within our organization: monthly magazine, marketing department, meeting planning, etc. Opportunity to grow with us (we've jumped from 8 staff and $500,000 budget 2 years ago to 30 employees and $2 million budget)."

***INTERNATIONAL SURFING LEAGUE (ISL)**, Box 1315, Beverly Hills CA 90213. President: Dr. Gary Filosa,II. Professional sports league composed of 24 teams competing in standup surfing and sailsurfing. Publishes *ISL Surfworld*.
Needs: Works with 15 freelance artist/year. Uses freelance artists for publication illustration.
First Contact & Terms: Send query letter only. Samples not filed are returned by SASE. Reports back within 2 weeks. Write to schedule an appointment to show a portfolio. Pays for design by the project, $250 minimum. Pays for illustration by the project, $500 minimum. Considers complexity of project, how work will be used and rights purchased when establishing payment. Buys all rights.

INTER-TRIBAL INDIAN CEREMONIAL ASSOCIATION, Box 1, Church Rock NM 87311. (505)863-3896. WATS Line: 1-800-233-4528. Executive Director: Laurance D. Linford. Teaches Indian culture to Indians and non-Indians.
Needs: Assigns 1 art job/year. Uses artists for direct mail brochures and posters. Indian artists only. Especially needs posters and advertising art. Prefers Indian motifs by Indian artists. Prefers watercolor, acrylics, oils and pastel.
First Contact & Terms: Send query letter with brochure showing art style. SASE. Reports within 1 month. Write to schedule an appointment to show a portfolio, which should include original/final art and photographs. Pays $500 maximum/job, design.

IPI ADVERTISING GROUP, 6930 Owensmouth Ave., Canoga Park CA 91303. (818)999-6515. Senior Art Director: Barbara Schultz. National agency serving over 3,500 financial institutions, and 3,500 auto dealers in over 180 cities. Works in areas of auto, loan promotion, travel promotion; also deals in incentives and sales promotion, credit card systems and insurance.
Needs: Works on assignment only. Uses artists for advertising, brochure, magazine/newspaper and catalog design, illustration and layout; exhibits, displays, signage, posters and retouching. Especially needs "life-style types, four-color illustrations and layouts for financial promotions, i.e. IRA, ATM, loans, savings and checking printed pieces." Prefers bold graphics, silhouettes, block-print styles. Prefers "any easily reproducible black-and-white applications."
First Contact & Terms: Send query letter with brochure showing art style or resume and tear sheets, Photostats and photocopies to be kept on file. "No originals." Samples not kept on file are returned. Reports within 1 week. Call or write to schedule an appointment to show portfolio, which should include thumbnails, roughs, final reproduction/product, color, tear sheets, Photostats, photographs, b&w and slides of work if available. Pays for design by the hour, $20-40. Pays for illustration by the project,

$100-1,500;by the project, rate varies, generally normal L.A. freelance rates. "Projects are generally quoted as a result of the scale; artists must work in a do-not-exceed price structure." Considers complexity of project, available budget, skill and experience of artist and turnaround time when establishing payment.
Tips: Artists should "make sure their books are concise and self-explanatory, and show as wide a range of work as possible. We look for versatility in style. Since we work with over 3,500 banks, savings & loans and credit unions, each piece must be unique. We will work with artists on a national basis because we use printing facilities in over 180 cities. We have rapidly expanded into fullscale advertising and marketing in the financial marketplace. There has been rapid deregulation, thus more advertising." Would like to see some package design in the portfolio. "Do not include anything that looks even remotely like a school project."

JEWISH VEGETARIAN SOCIETY, INC., Box 5722, Baltimore MD 21208-0722. (301)486-4948. Chairman: Izak Luchinsky. Membership organization with 1,300 members in North America. "Advocates of non-carnivorous life based on Old Testament precepts. Members are vegetarian Jews."
Needs: Works with 1 freelance artist/year. Prefers experienced Hebrew calligraphers and those artists who can design *original* vegetarian/Jewish graphics. Uses artists for displays, signage, posters, T-shirts, stationery and jewelry with logo. Prefers diet, religion, anti-vivisection, soil conservation as themes; modern and ancient Hebrew lettering as styles.
First Contact & Terms: Send query with photocopies. Samples are not filed. Samples not filed are returned by SASE. Reports back only if interested. To show a portfolio, mail thumbnails. Pays for design and illustration by the project, amount being negotiable. Considers originality and rights purchased when establishing payment. Rights purchased vary according to project.

***HELEN KELLER SERVICES FOR THE BLIND**, 57 Willoughby St., Brooklyn NY 11201. "Helen Keller Services for the Blind is a multi-service rehabilitation agency serving persons who are visually impaired, blind and deaf-blind living throughout Queens, Kings, Nassau and Suffolk counties."
Needs: Prefers local artists only-N.Y. City, Long Island and Brooklyn. Works on assignment only. Uses artists for advertising and publication design, illustration and layout and posters.
First Contact & Terms: Send query letter with brochure. Samples are filed. Reports back only if interested. Write to schedule an appointment to show a portfolio. Pays for design and illustration by the hour, $1-55. Considers complexity of project and turnaround time when establishing payment. Buys all rights.

KIWANIS INTERNATIONAL, 3636 Woodview Trace, Indianapolis IN 46268. Art Director: Jim Patterson. Organization for small-businessmen and professionals with 300,000 members worldwide.
Needs: Works with approximately 20 freelance artists/year. Works on assignment only. Uses artists for publication illustration for the *Kiwanis Magazine*, *Keynote* and *Circle K*.
First Contact & Terms: Send query letter with brochure, tear sheets and photocopies. Samples not filed are returned by SASE only if requested. Reports back only if interested. Write to schedule an appointment to show a portfolio, which should include thumbnails, roughs, original/final art, tear sheets, final reproduction/product, slides, color or b&w work. Pays for design by the project. Pays for illustration by the project, $200-1200. Considers complexity of project, client's budget, turnaround time and skill and experience of artist when establishing payment. Buys first rights or one-time rights.
Tips: "Show a variety of subjects and directions even if they are in the same style."

***KOFFLER GALLERY**, (Jewish Community Centre of Toronto), 4588 Bathurst St., North York, Ontario M2R 1W6 Canada. (416)636-1880. Contact: Director or Public Relations. "The Koffler Gallery is a public gallery, a non-profit organization whose mandate is to show the fine arts, decorative arts and design and judaica. It is an educational institution aimed on making the visual arts available to the public."
Needs: Needs freelance artists when a catalogue needs to be designed, for a major public relations campaign etc. "This is never known in advance." Works on assignment only. Uses artists for brochure and catalog design, illustration and layout, poster design and illustration and set design.
First Contact & Terms: Send query letter with resume, samples, tear sheets, Photostats, photocopies, slides and photographs to be kept on file. Write for an appointment to show a portfolio, which should include "everything an artist feels that would benefit us for our choice." Samples returned only if requested. Reports within 2 months. Pays for design and illustration according to "artist's quote for each job." Considers available budget when establishing payment.
Tips: "People are becoming more capable in design, not necessarily with a design background. Contemporary design is moving very fast and with an interesting outlook."

***LABAN GUILD**, 62 Walcot Rd., Swindon, Wiltshire SN3 IDA UK. Administrator: J. Fear. A guild of members who work in professional, recreative dance, education, therapy, industry and seek to advance

Close-up

Terry Brown

Director, Society of Illustrators
New York City

Illustration is where the money is, according to Terry Brown. "Fine artists are jealous, because graphic artists are making so much money." He explains that it's easier for illustrators to get established because they can develop a cushion of clients, while fine artists have, at best, a few exhibitions a year in a gallery or two. Also, illustrators are paid upfront, while fine artists rely on commissions.

"I hear this all the time," says the director, "A fine artist comes up to me and says, 'A schoolmate I knew 10-15 years ago who wasn't any good has a big house in New Rochelle. He's doing illustration now.' "

As director of the Society of Illustrators, Brown rubs elbows with our foremost illustrators. It is his job to further the Society's goal "to promote and stimulate interest in the art of illustration—past, present and future." To preserve the past, Brown curates the Society's Museum of Illustration. He talks with illustrators on a daily basis as they sit in the Society's upstairs "club," a haven in mid-Manhattan for illustrators to gather and talk about their craft. Brown also oversees the Society's annual shows. The Society's Student Scholarship Competition fosters the hope of the future.

"Students are now trained to be illustrators in schools like the School of Visual Arts, Pratt Institute and the Rhode Island School of Design," Brown notes, stating that in the past, fine artists often adapted their draftsmanship skills they learned in art academies to illustration. "Now, they usually begin in editorial illustration, then go into advertising after developing their own style. An art director at an ad agency has to know what to look for. You have to be able to deliver, because the agency has a lot riding on you."

He estimates that it takes an illustrator five to eight years after graduation to get established. "You have to develop contacts with art directors. They have their Rolodexes, and they like to rely on people they know can do the job."

In order to get your phone number in the Rolodex, Brown suggests targeting your marketing efforts to companies that use a style similar to yours. Then send samples, preferably 8x10 transparencies. "If you don't have published work, then do something of professional quality." Stripping in type and doing your own mechanicals for your sample will add even a more professional touch. "Make the job as easy as possible for the art director to choose you."

Most art directors who are seeking freelance help review portfolios. In New York City, those important bundles are usually "dropped-off" on the art director's doorstep in the morning and picked up in the evening or the next morning. Brown has a suggestion concerning the drop-off policy: "Leave a hair in the zipper. If it's gone when you pick it up, then you know it's been reviewed." If you're not showing your "book" in person, include in it a short note saying you'd like the art director to review the work, with a space at the bottom where he or she can write a note and return it to you. "That makes life easier for the art director, and that makes it easier to get hired."

When you make the decision to become an illustrator, do it right, says Brown. "Either do it as a hobby or invest in yourself and conduct business in a professional manner."

—*Susan Conner*

the principles of movement provided by the late Rudolph Laban.
Needs: Works with 500 freelance dance/movement artists/year. "The Laban Guild produces 1 magazine and 4 newsletters, various advertising brochures and exhibitions. These are 'inhouse'; only printing is contracted out."

***LANE COLLEGE**, 545 Lane Ave., Jackson TN 38301. (901)424-4600, ext. 241. Public Relations Director: Mrs. Pené C. Long. Predominantly black church-affiliated institution.
Needs: Assigns 5-10 jobs/year. Local artists only. Uses artists for advertising, exhibits/displays, publicity brochures, recruitment literature and trademarks/logos.
First Contact & Terms: Send query letter with brochure showing art style or resume, business card and samples to be kept on file. SASE. Reports within 2 weeks. To show a portfolio, mail appropriate materials. Payment by job: $10-75, design; $30-80, illustration; $40-100, layout; $40-80, production.

LOYOLA UNIVERSITY OF CHICAGO, 820 N. Michigan Ave., Chicago IL 60611. (312)670-2974. Assistant Vice President/University Public Relations: James Reilly. One of the largest private universities in Illinois providing higher education to 15,000 students on 3 Chicago-area campuses and one in Rome, Italy.
Needs: Works with 6-7 freelance artists/year. Works on assignment basis only. Uses artists for brochure and catalog design and layout; graphic design, exhibits, displays, signage, AV presentations and posters.
First Contact & Terms: Send query letter. Prefers original work as samples. Samples are returned. Reports in 6 weeks. Write for appointment to show portfolio. Payment varies according to job.
Tips: "Keep up with the latest trends."

MACALESTER COLLEGE, Office of Public Relations & Publications, 1600 Grand Ave., St. Paul MN 55105. (612)696-6203. Director: Nancy A. Peterson. Four-year liberal arts college "with reputation as one of the nation's finest." Produces materials for student recruitment, academic use, alumni relations, fundraising, etc.
Needs: Works with a few freelance artists/year. Works on assignment only. Uses artists for brochure and catalog design, illustration and layout; graphic design, magazine illustration; and posters. Prefers variety of themes and styles. Especially needs b&w illustrations and photographs.
First Contact & Terms: Send query letter with resume, tear sheets, photocopies, photographs and printed samples. Reports back on whether to expect possible future assignments. Call or write for appointment to show portfolio. Samples not kept on file are returned. Pays for design by the hour, $8 minimum and by the project, $50 minimum. Payment varies according to job and client's budget.
Tips: "We're conservative in our approach to design, but we like something fresh and clean." Looks for "clean design; well-organized format; eye catching; interesting/innovative use of two-color format; strong photographs with a photojournalistic flair."

McALLEN CHAMBER OF COMMERCE, Box 790, McAllen TX 78501. (512)682-2871. Public Relations Manager: Susan Dennis. Promotes conventions, tourism, community programs, industry and legislation for McAllen.
Needs: Assign 8-15 jobs and buys 12 illustrations/year. Uses artists for advertising, magazines, newsletters, publicity brochures, exhibits/displays and trademarks/logos. Especially needs economic/business-oriented artwork; international trade and commerce themes; and Hispanic-related art and information.
First Contact & Terms: Send query letter with samples. SASE. Reports in 1 week. Pays $10-20/illustration. Considers turnaround time when establishing payment.
Tips: "We have expanded our monthly newsletter to a monthly economic report."

MUSIC TEACHERS NATIONAL ASSOCIATION, Suite 2113, 441 Vine St., Cincinnati OH 45202. (513)421-1420. Advertising & Production Manager: Poppy Evans. Association of music teachers most of whom teach independently. MTNA publishes a bimonthly journal.
Needs: Works with 3 freelance artists/year. Prefers local artists. Works on assignment only. Uses artists for magazine design and illustration. Prefers b&w silhouette style, ususlly music-related; pen & ink and calligraphy.
First Contact & Terms: Send query letter with brochure or resume, tear sheets, Photostats, photocopies, slides and photographs. Samples are filed. Samples not filed are returned only if requested. Does not report back. Call to schedule an appointment to show a portfolio, which should include original/final art, Photostats, tear sheets, final reproduction/product, photographs, slides and b&w. Pays for design by the project, $40-1,200; pays for illustration by the project, $30-140. Considers complexity of project, turnaround time and skill and experience of artist when establishing payment. Negotiates rights purchased; rights purchased vary according to project.

THE NATIONAL ASSOCIATION FOR CREATIVE CHILDREN & ADULTS, 8080 Springvalley Dr., Cincinnati OH 45236. Editor: Ann Isaacs.
Needs: Works with 1 artist/year for advertising design. Also uses artists for books and brochures.
First Contact & Terms: Send query letter with samples. Samples returned by SASE. Reports back on future assignment possibilities. Provide business card, brochure and/or tear sheet samples to be kept on file for future assignments. Reports in 3 months. Payment is in copies of publications.

***NATIONAL ASSOCIATION OF EVANGELICALS**, Box 28, Wheaton IL 60189. (312)665-0500. Director of Information: Donald R. Brown. Voluntary fellowship of evangelical denominations, churches, schools, organizations and individuals; seeks to be a means of cooperative effort between its various members; provides evangelical identification for 50,000 churches and 5 million Christians.
Needs: Works with 1-5 freelance artists/year. Uses artists for advertising illustrations and layout, and brochure design. Themes are specified per project.
First Contact & Terms: Send query letter with Photostats, photocopies and photographs. Samples are returned by SASE. Reports within 2 months. Call or write to schedule an appointment to show a portfolio. Pay varies according to assignment. Considers complexity of project, available budget, skill and experience of artist, how work will be used, turnaround time and rights purchased when establishing payment.
Tips: Artists should have "an understanding of the National Association of Evangelicals: its history, current projects and ministries; and its objectives and purpose." Currently using more line art.

THE NATIONAL ASSOCIATION OF LIFE UNDERWRITERS, 1922 F St. NW, Washington DC 20006. (202)331-6070. Editor: Ian Mackenzie. Publishes *Life Association News*, the monthly official association magazine with a circulation of 140,000. Subscriptions are limited to members and affiliated organizations, schools and libraries. Also publishes numerous brochures and catalogs. Serves life underwriters (life insurance agents), financial brokers and consultants, and businesspersons associated with insurance in general.
Needs: Works with 5-10 freelance artists/year. DC metropolitan area artists only. Works on assignment only. Uses artists for brochure, catalog and magazine illustration. Prefers pen & ink, washes, drybrush and airbrush. Especially needs editorial calendar. Looks for "clarity, expression, realism and freshness" in themes and styles.
First Contact & Terms: Send query letter or telephone with resume, original work, Photostats or tear sheets to be kept on file. Material not filed returned by SASE only if requested. Reports only if interested. Write for appointment to show portfolio. Pays by the project, $50-75 average for spot art. Considers complexity of project and turnaround time when establishing payment.

NATIONAL ASSOCIATION OF TOWNS & TOWNSHIPS, Suite 730, 1522 K St. NW, Washington DC 20005. Director of Communications: Bruce G. Rosenthal. Professional association providing educational materials and representation for local elected officials from small communities.
Needs: Works with several freelance artists/year. Uses artists for brochure and magazine/newspaper design and illustration, brochure layout and signage.
First Contact & Terms: Prefers local artists with "references from similar associations and creative style/ideas for a relatively limited budget." Send query letter with brochure to be kept on file. Reports only if interested. Works on assignment only. Considers complexity of project, available budget, and skill and experience of artist when establishing payment.

NATIONAL BUFFALO ASSOCIATION, Box 565, Ft. Pierre SD 57532. (605)223-2829. Executive Director-Editor: Lila Houck. Breed organization representing commercial producers of buffalo (bison); also caters to collectors, historians, etc. Publishes bimonthly magazine of interest to buffalo enthusiasts, collectors and producers; circ. 1,400. Membership: 1,000.
Needs: Works with 4-5 freelance artists/year. "We feature artists in the magazine (must paint, sketch, sculpt, etc., buffalo); also feature artwork on cover." Prefers acrylics, oil, pastels, calligraphy and computer illustration.
First Contact & Terms: Send query letter with brochure and photographs. Material is kept on file until used, then it is returned to artist. Samples not kept on file are returned. Reports within 2-3 weeks. No pay; "we trade magazine exposure for use of photos and story about the artist in *Buffalo!* magazine.
Tips: Especially looks for "a good representation of the American buffalo, as well as a well-rounded subject portfolio. Awards and credentials are also looked at but not as primary criteria—talent and salability of the work is number one." Current trends include "a back-to-basics movement where artists are doing native animals rather than the exotics that were the vogue a few years ago."

NATIONAL CAVES ASSOCIATION, Rt. 9, Box 106, McMinnville TN 37110. (615)668-3925. Secretary/Treasurer: Barbara Munson. "The NCA is an organization of show caves owners and operators, es-

tablished to set and maintain standards of operation and to promote the visitation of show caves."
Needs: "As an organization, the NCA offers little opportunity for freelance artists."

NATIONAL COMMITTEE FOR CITIZENS IN EDUCATION, Suite 301, 20840 Little Patuxent Pkwy., Columbia MD 21044. (301)997-9300. Editor: Chrissie Bamber. Purpose is to improve the education of children by mobilizing and assisting citizens, including parents, to strengthen public schools; an advocate for citizens helping them gain and use information and skills to influence the quality of public education.
Needs: Works with 3-4 freelance artists/year. Local artists preferred except for newspaper illustration. Works on assignment only. Uses artists for advertising, brochure and catalog design and layout; brochure illustration, magazine/newspaper design and illustration, and AV presentations.
First Contact & Terms: Send query letter with Photostats and tear sheets to be kept on file. Write for artists' guidelines. Samples not kept on file returned by SASE. Reports within 2 weeks. Pays by the project, $25-50 average for single illustration for newspaper; rates for "design of book cover, brochure, AV aids, etc, are higher." Considers complexity of project, available budget, skill and experience of artist, how work will be used, turnaround time and rights purchased when establishing payment.
Tips: Artists should exhibit an "understanding of current education issues" in their work.

***NATIONAL DUCKPIN BOWLING CONGRESS**, 4609 Horizon Circle, Baltimore MD 21208. (301)636-2699. Executive Director: Manuel S. Whitman. National organization serving the needs of Duckpin bowlers. Publishes *The Duckpin News*.
Needs: Works with 3 or 4 freelance artists/year. Works on assignment only. Uses freelance artists for advertising and brochure design, illustration and layout, signage and posters.
First Contact & Terms: Send query letter with brochure showing art style or resume. Samples are filed. Reports back only if interested. Write to schedule an appointment to show a portfolio, or mail thumbnails. Pays for design and illustration by the project.
Tips: "Contact us through the mail with samples of work that you have done in the past."

NATIONAL INSTITUTE FOR AUTOMOTIVE SERVICE EXCELLENCE, 1920 Association Dr., Reston VA 22091. (703)648-3838. Director of Publications: Martin Lawson.
Needs: Uses artists for magazine graphics, audiovisual materials, recruitment literature and public information brochures. Prefers realistic style—also some technical illustrations; pen & ink, markers and calligraphy.
First Contact & Terms: Call or write. Looks at "quality and price" when reviewing artist's work. Pays for design by the project, $50 minimum. Pays for illustration by the project, $50-200. Buys all rights.
Tips: Wants to see " realistic bold stroke drawings of automotive related themes—mechanics, autos, trucks, tools, etc. Also technical, illustrations; modern fast style, etc." Finds most artists through talent sourcebooks and samples.

NATIONAL SAFETY COUNCIL, 444 N. Michigan, Chicago IL 60611. Publisher: Gordon Bieberle. Director of Art: Frank Waszak. Publications Designer: Kim Zarley. Non-governmental, not-for-profit public service organization aimed at saving lives in industry and private sectors through education serving manufacturing, business and environmental health areas.
Needs: Works with 24 freelance artists/year. Local artists preferred. "Contemporary style important. Superior technique and conceptual abilities essential." Uses artists for the design, illustration and layout of advertising, brochures, magazines and posters.
First Contact & Terms: To show a portfolio, call or write to schedule an appointment; portfolio should include thumbnails, roughs, final reproduction/product and color. Payment "determined solely on project size negotiated at time of assignment." Considers complexity of project and how work will be used when establishing payment.
Tips: "Interested artists should query with samples of work (tear sheets) by mail."

***NATIONAL SKEET SHOOTING ASSOCIATION**, Box 680007, San Antonio TX 78268. (512)688-3371. Editor, *Skeet Shooting Review* Magazine: Sandy Burgamy. Emphasizes shotgun target shooting, particularly "skeet" shooting; approximately 15,000 members.
Needs: Works with 3-6 freelance artists/year. Uses artists for brochure and magazine illustration. Prefers shooting sports themes; primarily b&w illustrations (pen & ink, charcoal, etc.).
First Contact & Terms: Send query letter. Reports within 1 week. Write for appointment to show portfolio. Pays by the project, $50-200 average. Considers available budget, and skill and experience of artist when establishing payment.
Tips: "This is an excellent opportunity for inexperienced artists to get published in a national publication."

***NATIONAL SKI AREAS ASSOCIATION**, Box 2883, 20 Maple St., Springfield MA 01101. Assistant Communications Director: Lynne C. Murphy. Association for the ski industry.
Needs: Uses artists for advertising design, illustration and layout, illustration and design of books, training manuals, and annual reports.
First Contact & Terms: Send query letter with brochure, tear sheets and photocopies. Samples are filed. Samples not filed are returned. Reports back within months. Write to schedule an appointment to show a portfolio, or mail appropriate materials. Pays $100 + for b&w cover; $50 + for b&w inside; on publication. Negotiates rights purchased.

***NATIONAL SUFFOLK SHEEP ASSN.**, 3316 Ponderosa, Columbia MO 65205. (314)442-4103. Executive Secretary: Kathy Krafka. "We promote interest in producing and marketing Suffolk Sheep, and in doing so, we record the records for some 50,000 new sheep registered annually and some 30,000 sheep transferred by our 10,000 members."
Needs: Works with 12 freelance artists/year. Uses freelance artists for brochure and publication design, illustration and layout, AV presentations, exhibits, displays, signage and posters. Prefers realistic-looking suffolk sheep in a clean, concise style.
First Contact & Terms: Send query letter with brochure showing art style or resume and tear sheets, Photostats, photocopies and photographs. Samples are filed. Samples not filed are returned only if requested by artist. Reports back only if interested. Call or write to schedule an appointment to show a portfolio, which should include thumbnails, original/final art, Photostats, photographs, tear sheets and final reproduction/product. Pays for design and illustration by the project, $25-500. Considers complexity of project, available budget, skill and experience of artist and rights purchased when establishing payment. Buys all rights or rights purchased vary according to project.
Tips: "We are seeking a new modern image for our association which portrays our breed in a stylish, up-to-date look."

NATIONAL THEATRE OF THE DEAF, 5 W. Main St., Chester CT 06412. (203)526-4971. Director of Publications: Laine Dyer. International touring theatrical company of deaf and hearing actors who perform using a combination of sign language and the spoken word at the same time. "Audiences hear and see every word. This medium has been hailed by critics as 'sculpture in the air.' " Audiences are both hearing and deaf.
Needs: Works with 4 freelance artists/year. Prefers artists in New York, Connecticut and Rhode Island. Works on assignment only. Uses artists for advertising and brochure layout, catalog design and layout, AV presentations, exhibits, displays and posters.
First Contact & Terms: Send query letter with brochure. Samples are filed. Samples not filed are returned by SASE only if requested. Reports back within 3 months. Call to schedule an appointment to show a portfolio. Payment varies. "We decide by fee basis on each job." Considers complexity of project when establishing payment. Buys all rights or reprint rights; rights purchased vary according to project.
Tips: "Looking for creative approach to marketing a theatrical company on a nonprofit budget; looking for very visual graphics to match our very visual medium of theatre; very interested in motion photography/illustrations."

THE NEW ALCHEMY INSTITUTE, 237 Hatchville Rd., E. Falmouth MA 02536. (617)564-6301. Publications: David A. Wills. A nonprofit research and educational institution working on ecologically sound methods of producing food, energy and shelter for about 2,000 members and another 5,000 visitors who come by each year to the demonstration site on Cape Cod.
Needs: Works with 0-3 freelance artists/year. Uses artists for brochure design and magazine/newspaper design and illustration; postcard designs. Prefers themes emphasizing alternative technology such as gardening, solar design, compost and greenhouses; prefers b&w line drawings, also schematics. Prefers pen & ink and computer illustration.
First Contact & Terms: Send query letter with brochure showing art style or photocopies. Samples not filed are returned by SASE. Reports only if interested. To show a portfolio, mail appropriate materials. Pays for design by the hour, $10 minimum; by the project, $25 minimum. Pays for illustrations by the hour, $10 minimum; by the project, $25 minimum. "We use donated skill whenever possible."
Tips: "We have to use mostly students and people who believe in us rather than pros."

NEW JERSEY ASSOCIATION OF OSTEOPATHIC PHYSICIANS & SURGEONS, 1212 Stuyvesant Ave., Trenton NJ 08618. (609)393-8114. Executive Director: Eleanore A. Farley. Nonprofit association serving a membership of approximately 1,000 osteopathic physicians and 295 medical students.
Needs: Works with 1 freelance artist/year. Works on assignment only. Uses artists for brochure and magazine/newspaper design, illustration and layout; graphic design, and signage. Prefers themes which are in keeping with the medical profession.

First Contact & Terms: Send query letter with Photostats of original work and actual work. Looks for "quality and originality" when reviewing artist's work. Samples returned by SASE. Reports in 1 month. Write for appointment. Negotiates payment according to client's budget.

***NORML**, National Organization for the Reform of Marijuana Laws, Suite 640, 2035 S St. NW, Washington DC 20009. (202)483-5500. National Director: Jon Gettman. Nonprofit consumer educational organization working for reform of marijuana laws.
Needs: Works on assignment only. Uses artists for advertising, brochure, catalog and magazine/newspaper design, graphic design, public service announcements, original artwork for auction, AV presentations and posters. Especially needs magazine ads. "Work should relate to issue of marijuana law reform."
First Contact & Terms: Send query letter with tear sheets to be kept on file. Reports within 1 week. Payment varies according to job and available budget.
Tips: "Opportunity for major national coverage at initial public interest group rate of pay."

NORTH AMERICAN NATIVE FISHES ASSOCIATION, 123 W. Mt. Airy Ave., Philadelphia PA 19119. (215)247-0384. President: Bruce Gebhardt. "A 400-member group dedicated to study of fishes (mostly non-game) native to North America. It serves ichthyologists, biologists, government officials, aquarists and naturalists."
Needs: Uses artists for magazine/newspaper illustration. "We need realistic b&w sketches of fishes (non-game, mostly, native to North America)." Prefers accuracy, realism. Prefers pen & ink.
First Contact & Terms: Send query letter with resume and photocopies; include SASE. Samples not filed are returned by SASE. Reports back within 1 week. "We can't commission artwork; however, if someone had drawn a particular fish for another assignment and could legally and ethically use it again, it would be a way to pick up a couple of bucks." Pays for illustration, $5-10 minimum.
Tips: "We may be expanding our operations and art needs in the next few years. We're no major market, but artists who draw fish and wildlife art for other clients might try us as a second user."

***NSTA**, 1742 Connecticut Ave., N.W., Washington DC 20009. (202)328-5800. Associate Editor: Loleta Gwynn. Association of science teachers. Publishes *Science and Children*.
Needs: Works with approximately 15-20 freelance artists/year. Prefers reliable and fast artists. Works on assignment only. Uses artists for publication illustration. Prefers line art, watercolors and acrylics depicting children and science activities.
First Contact & Terms: Send query letter with brochure, tear sheets, Photostats, photocopies, slides and photographs. Samples are filed. Samples not filed are returned only if requested by artist. Reports back within 2 weeks. Call or write to schedule an appointment to show a portfolio, which should include "whatever is appropriate." Pays for illustration by the project, $25-150. Considers complexity of project, turnaround time and how work will be used when establishing payment. Buys one-time rights all rights or reprint rights; rights purchased vary according to project.

OCCIDENTAL COLLEGE, 1600 Campus Rd., Los Angeles CA 90041. (213)259-2677. Contact: Director of Public Information and Publications. Educational institution with approximately 1,600 students providing a liberal arts education and serving current students, alumni, faculty, administration, trustees, staff and the community.
Needs: Publishes a quarterly magazine, currently ranked as one of the "Top Five College Magazines" in the country. Magazine often showcases a single illustrator, who provides artwork for cover and 4 feature articles related by a common theme. Excellent exposure for aspiring illustrators in need of impressive portfolio piece. Occasionally uses illustrators for other publications, such as catalogs and fund-raising brochures. "We mostly use students or alumni. Perhaps use freelancers three or four times a year." Works on assignment only.
First Contact & Terms: Send query letter with business card and original work or photocopies. Looks for "originality, nice clean layout and realistic renderings, as opposed to fantasy pieces" when reviewing artist's work. Samples not returned. Reports in 2 weeks. Submit portfolio for review. Magazine showcase illustrators are paid $400 for the series of cover and feature illustrations. For other publications, artists must be willing to furnish high-quality illustrations or photographs at very modest cost. Payment varies according to job and client's budget.
Tips: "Tight financial picture demands development of one comprehensive illustration/publication that has components which can be reproduced on their own throughout the publication."

***ORT**, 315 Park Ave. S., New York NY 10010. Editor: E. Faust Levy. Women's volunteer organization with 150,000 members—supports schools worldwide. Publishes the ORT Reporter.
First Contact & Terms: Send query letter with Photostats, photocopies or other sample. Samples are

not filed and returned by SASE only if requested. Reports back within 2-6 weeks. Considers complexity of project, available budget, how work will be used and rights purchased when establishing payment. Buys one-time rights.
Tips: "No calls!"

***PERFORMANCE COMMUNICATIONS, INC.**, 7227 W. 90th Pl., Bridgeview IL 60455. Manager: Kimberly Wetzel. Specializes in motorsports, emphasizing drag racing. Produces large tabloid about drag racing.
Needs: Prefers local artists; sports marketing/motorsports artists. Works on assignment only. Uses artists for advertising, brohcure, catalog and publication design, illustration and layout.
First Contact & Terms: Send query letter with resume, tear sheets, Photostats and photocopies. Samples are filed. Samples not filed are returned by SASE. Reports back only if interested. Write to schedule an appointment to show a portfolio, which can include thumbnails, roughs, original/final art, tearsheets, color or b&w work. Pays for design by the hour or by the project. Pays for illustration by the hour or by the project. Considers complexity of project, client's budget, turnaround time, skill and experience of artist, how work will be used, and rights purchased when establishing payment. Rights purchased vary according to project.

PLAN AND PRINT, Suite 104, 611 Butterfield Rd., Lombard IL 60148. (312)852-3055. Editor: Janet A. Thill. Serves architects, engineers, design/drafters/computer-aided design users, reprographic firm owners and managers.
Needs: Works with 7-10 artists/year. Works on assignment only. Uses magazine article illustrations. Especially needs cover art.
First Contact & Terms: Send query letter with brochure showing art style or samples. Samples not filed are returned. Reports back within 10 days. Call or write to schedule an appointment to show a portfolio, which should include final reproduction/product, color, tear sheets and b&w. Pays for illustration by the project, $300-500. Considers complexity of project, client's budget and rights purchased when establishing payment. Buys all rights.

POPAI, 66 N. Van Brunt St., Englewood NJ 07631. (201)585-8400. Public Relations Manager: L.Z. Eccles. Promotes and fosters the use of point-of-purchase advertisers to marketers of all consumer goods and services (this includes retailers). Members are producers, buyers and users of P-O-P.
Needs: Works with 4 freelance artists/year. Prefers local artists. Works on assignment only. Uses artists for advertising, brochure and catalog design, illustration and layout.
First Contact & Terms: Send query letter with brochure or Photostats. Samples are filed. Samples not filed are not returned. Reports back only if interested. Write to schedule an appointment to show a portfolio. Pays for design and illustration by the project, payment varies. Considers complexity of project and available budget when establishing payment.
Tips: "Be flexible and able to turn work around quickly."

QUEENS COLLEGE OF THE CITY UNIVERSITY OF NEW YORK, 65-30 Kissena Blvd., Flushing NY 11367. Director: Ron Cannava. Higher education institution serving 16,000 students as well as faculty, alumni and the general public.
Needs: Works with 11 freelance artists/year. Works on assignment basis only. Uses artists for advertising, brochure, graphic and magazine/newspaper design; advertising and magazine/newspaper layout; magazine/newspaper illustration, exhibits, displays, signage, AV presentations and posters. Prefers dramatic situation involving people learning from others, such as teacher/student relationships in many different backgrounds with various age and ethnic groups represented—usually on a one-to-one basis. Also office situations with white collar, college-educated staff in action in various backgrounds. Needs originality at minimal cost.
First Contact & Terms: Send query letter with samples, brochure/flyer and resume. Write for appointment to show portfolio. Samples returned by SASE. Reports in 5 weeks. Provide resume, business card, brochure and 1 sample to be kept on file for possible future assignments. Payment is by the project: $25-300 average; by the hour: $10-15 average. Negotiable and can vary according to available budget, restriction on limited tax-levy funding, complexity of project, skill and experience of artist, how work will be used, turnaround time and rights purchased.
Tips: "There will be more use of freelance work by colleges and universities, more promotional effort for higher education. This is a low-paying market with high expectations—a place to grow, but not to depend on."

RIPON COLLEGE, Box 248, Ripon WI 54971. (414)748-8115. Director of College Relations: Andrew G. Miller. Four-year, coeducational, liberal arts college serving 950 students, alumni and prospective students.

Needs: Works with 3-4 freelance artists/year. Works on assignment basis only. Uses artists for advertising, brochure and magazine/newspaper illustration; graphic design and AV presentations; photography. Especially needs graphic design and photography. "Largest need is for architectural drawings. Occasionally use 'loose' people scenes." Prefers pen & ink, watercolor and computer illustration.
First Contact & Terms: Send query letter with resume and samples. Samples returned by SASE. Reports back on whether to expect possible future assignments. Call for appointment to show portfolio. Negotiates payment. Pays for design by the hour, $10 minimum. Pays for illustration by the project, $50 minimum. Finds most artists through references/word-of-mouth, portfolio reviews and samples.

***ROWAN COUNTY HISTORICAL SOCIETY, INC.**, 104 Main St., Morehead KY 40351. (606)784-9145. Public Relations Director: Lloyd Dean. "A society that studies the history of Rowan County and Morehead and collects pictures, prints, histories, diaries and items of historical interest."
Needs: "We might need artists to draw pictures of historical places in Rowan County and Morehead."
First Contact & Terms: Send a query letter with resume, business card, brochure and flyer to be kept on file. SASE. Reports in 5 weeks.
Tips: There is a trend toward "more concern for the historical past."

ST. VINCENT COLLEGE, Latrobe PA 15650. (412)539-9761. Director/Publications and Publicity: Don Orlando.
Needs: Assigns 25 jobs/year. Uses artists for advertising, annual reports, direct mail brochures, exhibits, flyers, graphics, posters and programs.
First Contact & Terms: Send query letter with samples. SASE. Reports in 1 month. Pays $10 minimum/hour, design, illustration and layout.

***SAVE THE CHILDREN FEDERATION**, 54 Wilton Rd., Westport CT 06880. Manager, Print Production: Cheryl Donnelly. Community development agency which solicits funds through direct response advertising.
Needs: Works with 2-5 freelance artists/year. Works on assignment basis only. Uses artists for advertising, brochure and catalog design, illustration and layout.
First Contact & Terms: Send query letter with resume. Samples are not filed. Samples not filed are returned only if requested by artist. Reports back only if interested. Write to schedule an appointment to show a portfolio, which should include final reproduction/product. Considers complexity of project and client's budget when establishing payment.

SLOCUMB GALLERY, East Tennessee State University, Department of Art, Box 23740A, Johnson City TN 37614-0002. (615)929-4247. Gallery Director: M. Wayne Dyer. Nonprofit university gallery.
Needs: Works with 0-2 freelance artists/year. Works on assignment only. Uses artists for advertising design, illustration and layout; brochure and catalog design; exhibits, signage and posters.
First Contact & Terms: Send query letter with slides to be kept on file. Samples not filed are returned only if requested. Reports within 1 month. Negotiates payment. Considers complexity of project and available budget when establishing payment.

***SMALL PRESS WRITERS & ARTISTS ORGANIZATION (SPWAO)**, 1412 N.E. 35th St., Ocala FL 32670, (904)732-7781. President: Margaret Ballif Simon. "We have a membership of approximately 600, expected to double by 1989. Members include pros and semi-pros, amateurs in need of information and markets, etc." Serves "all artists, poets, writers who specialize in the SF/H/F and speculative fields."
Needs: Works with approximately 50+ freelance artists/year. "Must be SPWAO member for receiving aid, publications, etc." Uses artists for brochure and publication, design, illustration and layout, exhibits and displays. Prefers work that relates to the SF/F/H and speculative field.
Tips: "SPWAO provides services and advice to freelance artists to help them gain more exposure, direct information on markets open, aid to illustrators with market news which includes terms of contract/assignments, etc. Provides a directory for editors who are interested in last minute deadline work. Advice: if you want to have your work published, if you want a beginning on a career—join SPWAO. You must be the sort of artist that enjoys the genre (SF/H/F or speculative) as a primary qualification."

SOCIETY OF SCRIBES, LTD., Box 933, New York NY 10150. Corresponding Secretary: Will Farrington. "1,000 memberships of calligraphers, professional, amateur and calligraphiles (those interested in calligraphy). S.O.S. promotes through educational programs and exhibitions the enjoyment of calligraphy in the graphic arts. Members are professional calligraphers, typographers, publishers and educators.
Needs: Works with 15 freelance artists/year. Works on assignment only. Uses artists for advertising, brochure, catalog design, illustration and layout, magazine design, illustration and layout, AV presenta-

tions, exhibits, displays, signage and posters.
First Contact & Terms: Send query letter with brochure or resume and slides. Samples are not filed. Samples not filed are returned by SASE. Reports back only if interested.

SOROPTIMIST INTERNATIONAL OF THE AMERICAS, 1616 Walnut St., Philadelphia PA 19103. (215)732-0512. Editor: Darlene Friedman. 46,000-member classified service organization for professional and executive business women.
Needs: Uses artists for brochure and magazine/newspaper illustration.
First Contact & Terms: Send query letter with brochure, resume, business card and samples to be kept on file. Prefers copies of brochures, publications in which artwork has appeared as samples. Reports only if interested. Works on assignment only. Pays by the project, $50-300 average. Considers complexity of project and available budget when establishing payment.

SUNDAY SCHOOL BOARD OF THE SOUTHERN BAPTIST CONVENTION, 127 9th Ave. N., Nashville TN 37234. (615)251-2365. Supervisor, Special Ministries Design Section: Mrs. Doris Mae Adams. Religious publisher of periodicals, books, Bibles, records, kits, visual aids, posters, etc. for churches.
Needs: Works with 45-50 freelance artists/year. Artists must be "people with experience that meet our quality requirements." Works on assignment only. Uses artists for illustration. Especially needs four-color Biblical illustrations in a realistic style.
First Contact & Terms: Send query letter with brochure showing art style. Call or write for appointment to show portfolio, which should include original/final art, final reproduction/product and color. Originals are preferred, tear sheets are acceptable; do not send slides. Samples are returned. Reports within 2 weeks. Pays by the illustration, $80-200 average. "For the price range quoted here, we buy all rights and retain the work."

TECHNICAL ASSISTANCE PROGRAM (TAP), Suite 809, 270 Lafayette St., New York NY 10012. (212)966-8658. Director: Donna Brady. Nonprofit organization serving the performing arts community as well as film, TV, advertising and fashion through referrals of qualified production personnel (designers, stage managers and technicians). TAP also maintains information files with wide ranging details on hard-to-find equipment.
Needs: Works with 50 freelance artists/year. Uses freelance artists for AV presentation, displays, signage, posters and theatrical application.
First Contact & Terms: Send query letter with brochure showing art style or resume. Samples not filed are returned by SASE. Call to schedule an appointment to show a portfolio, which should include original/final art, final reproduction/product and color. Payment varies. Considers complexity of project, available budget, skill and experience of artist, how work will be used, turnaround time and rights purchased when establishing payment.

***TELECOMMUNICATIONS FOR THE DEAF INC.**, 814 Thayer Ave., Silver Springs MD 20770. Executive Director: Al Sonnenstral. Advocates and coordinates telecommunication systems for deaf users. Publishes the *International Directory of TDD Users*.
Needs: Works with 2-5 freelance artists/year. Uses freelance artists for advertising, brochure, catalog and publication design, illustration and layout.
First Contact & Terms: Send query letter with brochure showing art style or resume and Photostats or photocopies. Samples are filed. Reports back only if interested. Write to schedule an appointment to show a portfolio, which should include original/final art, Photostats and final reproduction/product. Pays for design and illustration by the project. Considers available budget when establishing payment. Rights purchased vary according to project.

THE TEXTILE MUSEUM, 2320 S St. NW, Washington DC 20008. (202)667-0441. Public Relations Manager: Joan Wessel. Private, nonprofit museum dedicated to the collection, study, preservation, education and exhibition of historic and handmade textiles and carpets.
Needs: Works with 1-2 freelance artists/year. Local artists only. Works on assignment only. Uses artists for brochure illustration and layout, catalog design and layout, exhibits, displays and posters.
First Contact & Terms: Send query letter with samples to be kept on file. Prefers original work as samples. Reports only if interested. Negotiates pay according to project.
Tips: "Send samples of newsletters, invitations, catalogs or posters as these are items most often used by the institution; keep in mind the low budget of client."

UNITED HOSPITAL, 333 N. Smith Ave., St. Paul MN 55102. (612)292-5531. Media Specialist: Mary Farr.
Needs: Works with 5 illustrators and designers/year. Local artists only. Works on assignment only.

Uses artists for brochure and newsletter design, programs and general publications artwork. Especially needs logo design, publication and brochure design and keyline.
First Contact & Terms: Query with resume. SASE. Looks for "fast service, reasonable price, and creative and well thought-out approaches to project goals" when reviewing artist's work. Reports in 2 weeks. Samples returned by SASE. Provide resume and business card to be kept on file for possible future assignments. Pays by the hour. Considers complexity of project, available budget and turnaround time when establishing payment.
Tips: Especially likes "clean, uncluttered, simple, striking design."

***U.S. COMMITTEE FOR UNICEF**, 331 E. 38th St., New York NY 10016. (212)686-5522. Editorial and Print Production Manager: Paula Donovan. Non-profit private citizens organization. "We are a fundraising/educational/information organization in support of the United Nations Children's Fund (an international voluntary agency that helps developing countries address the needs of children and mothers in conditions of extreme poverty or emergency)."
Needs: Works with 30-35 freelance artists/year. Assigns 30-35 jobs/year. Works on assignment only. Uses artists for advertising, brochure and catalog design, illustration and layout, posters and magazine layout.
First Contact & Terms: Send query letter with brochure, slides and photographs. Samples are filed. Samples not filed are returned by SASE. Reports back within 6 weeks only if interested. Pays for design by the project, $300-3,000. Considers complexity of project, client's budget, skill and experience of artist, turnaround time and rights purchased when establishing payment. Negotiates rights purchased.
Tips: FYI "much of the artwork used by the U.S. Committee for UNICEF is contributed by well-known artists. Fee-for-service contracts are arranged for smaller projects (brochures, pamphlets, etc. rather than annual trick or treat campaign, etc.)."

U.S. SPACE EDUCATION ASSOC., NEWS OPERATIONS DIV., 746 Turnpike Rd., Elizabethtown PA 17022-1161. Editor, *Space Age Times*: Stephen M. Cobaugh. International grassroots association dedicated to the promotion of the peaceful uses of outer space. Serves both laymen and professionals concerned with all aspects of space education and news.
Needs: Works with 3 freelance artists/year. "Artist should be able to demonstrate knowledge of current space issues—both domestic and foreign." Uses artists for magazine/newspaper design and illustration; exhibits; displays and particularly editorial cartoons. Prefers space-related topics; particularly space shuttle, space station, commercialization, spinoffs, etc.
First Contact & Terms: Send query letter with brochure showing art style or resume, tear sheets, Photostats and photocopies. Samples not filed are returned by SASE. Reports only if interested. To show a portfolio, mail roughs and original/final art. Pays for design and illustration by the project, $25 minimum. Considers complexity of project, client's budget, turnaround time and rights purchased when establishing payment.

***U.S. TROTTING ASSN.**, 750 Michigan Ave., Columbus OH 43215. (614)224-2291. Executive Editor: Dean A. Hoffman. 50,000-member organization serving record-keeping and regulatory role in harness racing. Serves owners, breeders, trainers, and patrons in harness racing. Publishes *Hoof Beats* magazine.
Needs: Works with 10 freelance artists/year. Works on assignment only. Uses freelance artists for advertising, catalog and publication illustration. Prefers illustrations of horses or harness racing.
First Contact & Terms: Send query letter with tear sheets. Samples are filed. Reports back in 1 week only if interested. Write to schedule an appointment to show a portfolio, or mail roughs, original/final art and tear sheets. Pays for illustration by the project, $50-300. Consider complexity of project and turnaround time when establishing payment. Buys one-time rights.
Tips: "Query first. Send samples."

***UNIVERSITY OF LOWELL, ART DEPARTMENT**, Lowell MA 01854. (617)452-5000. Chairperson Art Department: Dr. Liana Cheney. Teaching institution, granting a BA degree and BFA in graphic design and fine arts degrees.
Needs: Works with 2 freelance artists/year. Local artists only. Works on assignment only. Uses artists for advertising, brochure and catalog design, illustration and layout. Prefers college-related themes, single style.
First Contact & Terms: Send resume to be kept on file for 1 year; mail slides. Slides are returned. Reports within 1 month.Pays by the hour, $10 minimum. Considers available budget when establishing payment.
Tips: "Be patient."

UNIVERSITY OF NEW HAVEN, West Haven CT 06516. (203)932-7000. Acting Director: Jacqueline Church.
Needs: Uses illustrations of campus architecture, still life (books, lab equipment, etc.), occassionally people, for program brochures. Especially interested in those with map experience. Looks for "simplicity of reproduction. Prefers b&w line art for illustrations. Contemporary style that would appeal to students (18-34)." Works on assignment only.
First Contact & Terms: Query with samples (brochures and other publications, especially those for educational or service organizations; cover designs; illustrations). SASE. No samples returned. Provide resume if available, business card, fee structure, and samples of work to be kept on file for future assignments. Considers complexity of project, available budget, skill and experience of artist and turnaround time when establishing payment.
Tips: "Our budget is modest. Most pieces are one or two colors. We'd like to see work that would appeal to younger and older students. We're interested in variety of styles. Also interested in area talent."

***VERIFICATION GALLERY, MAYNARD LISTENER LIBRARY**, 171 Washington, Taunton MA 02780. (617)823-3783. Executive Director: Merrill A. Maynard. Nonprofit free service organization for the blind and physically handicapped, served through The Maynard Listener Library.
Needs: Prefers artist with "motivation." Uses artists for graphic design, exhibits and displays. Especially needs calendar material. Prefers mobility information theme.
First Contact & Terms: Send query letter with samples. Prefers Photostats or slides as samples. Samples returned by SASE. Reports within 2 months. Provide samples to be kept on file for possible future assignments. Negotiates payment.
Tips: "We are creating a demand for our product; therefore artists should realize its potential."

***VISUAL INDIVIDUALISTS UNITED**, 2261 Ocean Ave., Brooklyn NY 11229-2368. (718)336-8633. President: Marilyn Mark. "We are a mixed media group of contemporary professional artists. We are a global association and from a percentage from sales plus the fees from our shows we serve humanity. All our shows have fees for exhibiting. We exhibit in universities, libraries, museums, galleries, art centers, public buildings.
Needs: Works with approximately 27-70 freelance artists/year. Uses artists for advertising design, brochure design, illustration and layout, catalog design and layout, exhibits, displays, public relations and posters. If our members are unable to handle the assignment, then we hire an outsider.
First Contact & Terms: Send query letter with photographs, resume, slides and SASE. Samples are filed. Samples not filed are returned by SASE. Reports back within 1 month. "When we pay for an assignment it is usually a free space in our show and a fee." Considers complexity of project, client's and our budget, turnaround time, skill and experience of artist and how work will be used when establishing payment. Negotiates rights purchased.
Tips: "We are seeking to network with a press agent and to bring the high calibre works to the attention of corporate collectors. We are seeking to develop commissions for our artists. We network with many avenues in business seminars. We want to see one sheet of each media if you work in more than one. We want to see an updated resume and slides of the work that is professionally taken so that we can see the work clearly. We sometimes check into a part of the resume for verificaiton. We seek integrity and committment in our associations. All our shows are juried for selection."

WASHINGTON UNIVERSITY IN ST. LOUIS, Campus Box 1070, St. Louis MO 63110. Art Director: Suzanne Oberholtzer. Educational institution publication office serving alumni development (alumni magazines) and various schools' recruiting and promotional needs.
Needs: Works with 20 freelance artists/year. Works on assignment only. Uses artists for advertising, brochure, catalog and magazine/newspaper illustration. Especially needs layout and paste-up, some design *with* art direction and illustration. Looks for diversity, versatility.
First Contact & Terms: Send query letter with brochure, resume, Photostats, slides, photographs and tear sheets to be kept on file. Samples not filed are returned by SASE only if requested. Reports only if interested. Call for appointment to show portfolio, which should include original/final art, final reproduction/product, color, tear sheets and b&w. Pays by the project, $50 minimum. Considers complexity of project, available budget, skill and experience of artist, how work will be used, turnaround time and rights purchased when establishing payment.
Tips: "Present a neat and clean portfolio, showing as much diversity as possible. Better to have only five strong pieces than twenty-five weak ones."

WOLF TRAP FARM PARK FOR THE PERFORMING ARTS, The Wolf Trap Foundation, 1624 Trap Rd., Vienna VA 22180. The Foundation serves as the administrative arm of the Park with the National Park Service maintaining the Park grounds. Wolf Trap is the only national park for the performing arts. "As a national park, Wolf Trap serves the nation as well as international visitors."

Needs: Uses artists for the design, illustration and layout of advertising, brochures, and magazines plus AV presentations, exhibits and displays.
First Contact & Terms: Send a query letter with resume and tear sheets, which will be kept on file. Samples not filed are returned only if requested. Reports back within 3-4 weeks. Call or write for an appointment to show a portfolio. Pays by the project. Considers available budget, skill and experience of the artist, and turnaround time when establishing payment.
Tips: "We are a nonprofit organization and do not have a large budget for outside services."

***WOMEN'S INTERNATIONAL BOWLING CONGRESS**, 5301 S. 76th St., Greendale WI 53129. Editor: Karen L Sytsma. The *Woman Bowler* is the official publication of the Women's International Bowling Congress, the membership organization for women league bowlers.
Needs: Works with 5 freelance artists/year. Works on assignment only. Uses freelance artists for publication illustration and cover art. Prefers pen & ink, airbrush, acrylics and collage.
First Contact & Terms: Send query letter with brochure showing art style or resume and photocopies. Pays for design by the project, $50-500; pays for illustration by the project, $50-250. Considers complexity of project, available budget, skill and experience of artist and how work will be used when establishing payment. Buys all rights.

WORCESTER POLYTECHNIC INSTITUTE, 100 Institute Rd., Worcester MA 01609. (617)793-5609. Director of Publications: Kenneth McDonnell. Third oldest college of engineering and science in U.S. with 3,500 students in undergraduate and graduate programs.
Needs: Works with 10-15 freelance artists/year. Prefers local artists. Works on assignment only. Uses artists for advertising illustration; brochure design, illustration and layout; catalog illustration and layout; AV presentations, exhibits, displays, signage and posters.
First Contact & Terms: Send query letter with resume, Photostats, slides, photographs and tear sheets. Write for appointment to show portfolio. Samples are returned by SASE. Reports within 2 weeks. Negotiates payment. Considers complexity of project, available budget, skill and experience of artist, turnaround time and rights purchased when establishing payment.

"It helps to see one piece of work in all its developmental stages. It provides insight into your thought process."

—Ellen Stein Burbach, OHIO Magazine
Cincinnati, Ohio

Book Publishers

Publishers know that books are judged by their covers, and most freelance opportunities in book publishing are found in the illustration of jackets/covers. With shelf space in bookstores at a premium, a striking cover grabs attention. In order to get an edge on the competition, art directors have been using special effects such as foil, embossing, die cutting and holograms on covers. Read this section's Close-up of Jackie Meyer, art director and vice president of Warner Books, for more information on how artwork is integrated with the marketing of books.

Not every book is illustrated, but all books must be designed. Book design involves a whole package—type specification, chapter openings, placement of illustrations and diagrams, determining page count and the flow of the text. Design is usually done inhouse or by freelancers who specialize in this area. Book designers must be skilled in illustration, type specification and layout. Show your mastery of these areas by including in your portfolio samples of cover designs using type and illustration.

Trade books (scholarly works, instructional manuals and biographies) generally feature simple designs and straightforward, realistic artwork, but the trend is toward using a "looser" style of illustration. "There's a less commercial look to trade books," says Carol Buchanan, art director of Writer's Digest Books. "There's a more historical use of type; type is not as predominant as before. Also, covers are following trends in illustration, using more colored pencil and pastels."

Because they must compete with other books on newsstands as well as in bookstores, mass-market books require bold, eye-catching covers to grab potential customers. The covers of romances and historical novels usually focus on one or two of the story's main characters.

Textbooks, which have relied in the past on simple graphics and two-color printing, have begun to use extra color and more charts and diagrams.

Children's books are experiencing a renaissance. Production of children's books increased 76% from 1981 to 1986. Picture books, which tell stories through pictures, represent 50 to 60% of the juvenile market, which used to be divided equally among fiction, information and picture books. The Close-up of illustrator Uri Shulevitz provides more insights into this popular genre.

New laser technology has opened up the children's market to artists who are not trained in pre-separation. Before, illustrations were rendered in black-and-white, then received acetate overlays with color instructions. Now artists can render illustrations as they will appear in the book, while the laser completes the separation process.

The old saw, "It doesn't matter where you are, it's where you're at," applies to book illustrators. Work is done largely through the mail, with art directors requesting occasional meetings. The most frequent complaint from art directors about freelance artists is that artists often send samples of work that are inappropriate for their line of books. Eliminate this unnecessary waste of time by writing and requesting a catalog of the company's line of books. Select the houses that use artwork similar to yours. If you have worked with publishers before, send covers or jackets you have done. If you do not have any published covers to show, send samples of work you would like to do and perhaps a mock cover or two. For a book you both write and illustrate, submit a dummy to the editor. If you wish to illustrate manuscripts written by other authors, submit representative samples or slides to the art director. Increase your chances of being selected by stamping every sample with your contact information, so that the art director can store this in his files.

In the listings we've provided information on the types of books a house publishes. The particular style of art a publisher wants can't always be stated since it will vary according to the book. This is a good reason to have your samples on file with as many publishers as possible.

For further information on this market, refer to *Writer's Market, Fiction Writer's Market, Literary Market Place, Books in Print* and *International Directory of Little Magazines and Small Presses*. The trade magazine *Publisher's Weekly* provides weekly updates on the industry. A new title, *Children's Writer's and Illustrator's Market* is available, March 1989.

A.D. BOOK CO., 6th Floor, 10 E. 39th St., New York NY 10157-0002. (212)889-6500. Art Director: Doris Gordon. Publishes hardcover and paperback originals on advertising design and photography. Publishes 12-15 titles/year; 4-5 of which require designers, 1-2 use illustrators.
First Contact & Terms: Send query letter which can be kept on file and arrange to show portfolio (4-10 tear sheets). Samples returned by SASE. Buys first rights. Originals returned to artist at job's completion. Free catalog. Advertising design must be contemporary. Pays $100 minimum/book design.
Jackets/Covers: Pays $100 minimum.

ACROPOLIS BOOKS LTD., 2400 17th St. NW, Washington DC 20009. Production Manager: Lloyd Greene. Publishes how-to, self-help, educational, political and Americana.
Needs: Uses artists for jacket design and illustration and advertising layouts.
First Contact & Terms: Local artists only. Send query letter with information on your background and specialties.

AEOLUS PUBLISHING LTD., Box 2643, Vista CA 92084. (619)724-5703. President: Chuck Banks. Specializes in hardcover and paperback originals and reprints on militaria. Publishes 12 titles/year.
First Contact & Terms: Works with 3 freelance artists/year. Send query letter. "No calls from artist or artist's agent." Samples returned only if requested. Reports within 1 month. Return of original work after job's completion depends on contract. Considers complexity of the project, skill and experience of artist, project's budget, turnaround time and rights purchased when establishing payment. Rights purchased vary according to project.
Book Design: Assigns 3 freelance jobs/year. Negotiates payment.
Jackets/Covers: Assigns 3 freelance illustration jobs/year. Negotiates payment.
Text Illustration: Assigns 2 freelance jobs/year. Negotiates payment.

***AGLOW PUBLICATIONS**, Box I, Lynwood WA 98046-1557. (206)775-7282. Art Director: Kathy Boice. Specializes in self-help paperbacks and reprints; also publishes a magazine. Publishes 12 titles/year; 50% require freelance illustration.
First Contact & Terms: Works with 35 freelance artists/year. Send query letter with brochure showing art style or tear sheets and photographs. Samples are filed. Samples not filed are returned only if requested. Reports back within 2 weeks only if interested. Originals returned to artist at job's completion. Call or write to schedule an appointment to show a portfolio, or mail original/final art or tear sheets. Considers complexity of project, project's budget and rights purchased when establishing payment. Buys one-time rights.
Jackets/Covers: Assigns 4 freelance design jobs/year. Pays by the project, $325-700.
Text Illustration: Assigns 30 freelance jobs/year. Pays by the project, $125-325.

***AIRMONT PUBLISHING CO., INC.**, 401 Lafayette St., New York NY 10003. (212)598-0222. Editor: Barbara J. Brett. "Airmont Books are all reprints of classics. We are not at this time buying any cover art, but at any time in the future when we may need art, we will consider artists we have worked with on our Avalon Books, published by our Thomas Bouregy Company. See that listing."

ALLYN AND BACON INC., College Division, 160 Gould St., Needham MA 02194. (617)455-1200. Cover Administrator: Linda Knowles Dickinson. Publishes hardcover and paperback textbooks. Publishes 100*f* titles/year; 75% require freelance cover designers.
First Contact & Terms: Needs artists/designers experienced in preparing art and mechanicals for print production. Designers must be strong in book cover design and contemporary type treatment.
Jackets/Covers: Assigns 85 freelance design jobs/year; assigns 2-3 freelance illustration jobs/year. Pays for design by the project, $300-550. Pays for illustration by the project, $150-500. Prefers sophisticated, abstract style. Prefers pen & ink, airbrush, charcoal/pencil, watercolor, acrylics, oils, collage and calligraphy. "Always looking for good calligraphers."

Tips: "Keep stylistically and technically up to date. Learn *not* to over-design: read instructions, and ask questions. Introductory letter must state experience and include at least photocopies of samples of your work. We prefer designers/artists based in the Boston area."

ALYSON PUBLICATIONS, INC., 40 Plympton St., Boston MA 02118. Publisher: Sasha Alyson. Book publisher emphasizing gay and lesbian concerns. Publishes 15 titles/year. Circ. 800. Sample copy catalog free for SASE with 45¢ postage.
First Contact & Terms: Works on assignment only. Send query letter with brochure showing art style or tear sheets, Photostats, photocopies and photographs. Samples returned by SASE. Reports only if interested.
Jackets/Covers: Buys 10 cover illustrations/year. Pays $200-500, b&w, $300-500, color; on acceptance.

***AMERICAN ATHEIST PRESS, INC.**, 7215 Cameron Rd., Austin TX 78752. (512)458-1244. Editor: R. Murray-O'Hair. "The American Atheist Press, Inc., a nonprofit, nonpolitical, educational corporation, specializes in the publication of atheist and freethought paperbacks and reprints, as well as criticism of religion. It also publishes a monthly magazine, the American Atheist." Publishes 8 titles/year; 40% require freelance illustration.
First Contact & Terms: Works with 60 freelance artists/year. Prefers pen & ink and airbrush. Send query letter with brochure showing art style or "anything showing style is fine." Samples are filed. Reports back within 2 months on submissions only if interested. Does not report back on queries. Originals returned to artist at job's completion if artist requests. Call or write to schedule an appointment to show a portfolio, which should include roughs, original/final art, Photostats, tear sheets or final reproduction/product. Considers complexity of project, skill and experience of artist and project's budget when establishing payment. Negotiates rights purchased.
Book Design: Assigns 3 freelance illustration jobs/year. Pays by the project, $25-500.
Jackets/Covers: Assigns 3-6 freelance design and 3-6 freelance illustration jobs/year. Pays by the project, $50-500.
Text Illustration: Assigns 3 freelance jobs/year. Pays by the project, $25-500.

***ANASTACIA PRESS**, Box 834, Bethel Park PA 15102-9998. Editor: Stacey A. Harris. Specializes in chapbooks of poetry. Publishes 3 titles/year; 90% require freelance illustration.
First Contact & Terms: Works with 2 freelance artists/year. Works on assignment only. Send query letter with brochure, resume, tear sheets, Photostats and photographs. Samples ae filed. Reports back within 4 weeks. Originals sometimes returned at job's completion. To show a portfolio, mail Photostats, tear sheets, final reproduction/product and photographs.
Jackets/Covers: Assigns 3 freelance illustration jobs/year. Pays by the project, $50 minimum.
Text Illustration: Assigns 3 freelance jobs/year. Pays by the project, $25 minimum per drawing.
Tips: "We are also looking for fashion illustration, and we publish a literary magazine."

APPLEZABA PRESS, Box 4134, Long Beach CA 90804. (213)591-0015. Publisher: D.H. Lloyd. Specializes in paperbacks on poetry and fiction. Publishes 2-4 titles/year.
First Contact & Terms: Works on assignment only. Send query letter with brochure, tear sheets and photographs to be kept on file. Samples not filed are returned by SASE. Reports only if interested. Originals returned to artist at job's completion. Considers project's budget and rights purchased when establishing payment. Rights purchased vary according to project.
Jackets/Covers: Assigns 1 freelance design job/year. Prefers pen & ink and collage. Pays by the project, $30-100.

APRIL PUBLICATIONS, INC., Box 1000, Staten Island NY 10314. Art Director: Verna Hart. Specializes in paperback nonfiction. Publishes 25 titles/year.
First Contact & Terms: Works with 10 freelance artists/year. Works on assignment only. Send query

The asterisk before a listing indicates that the listing is new in this edition. New markets are often the most receptive to freelance submissions.

letter with samples to be kept on file. Prefers Photostats as samples. Samples not filed are returned by SASE. Reports only if interested. Considers project's budget and rights purchased when establishing payment. Buys all rights.

ARCsoft PUBLISHERS, Box 132, Woodsboro MD 21798. (301)845-8856. President: A.R. Curtis. Specializes in original paperbacks, especially in space science, computers, miscellaneous high-tech subjects. Publishes 12 titles/year.
First Contact & Terms: Works with 5 freelance artists/year. Works on assignment only. Send query letter with brochure, resume and non-returnable samples. Samples not filed are not returned. Reports back within 3 months only if interested. Original work not returned after job's completion. Considers complexity of project, skill and experience of artist, project's budget and turnaround time when establishing payment. Buys all rights.
Book Design: Assigns 5 freelance illustration jobs/year. Pays by the project.
Jackets/Covers: Assigns 1 freelance design and 5 freelance illustration jobs/year. Pays by the project.
Text Illustration: Assigns 5 freelance jobs/year. Pays by the project.
Tips: "Artists should not send in material they want back. All materials received become the property of ARCsoft Publishers."

ART DIRECTION BOOK CO., 6th Floor, 10 E. 39th St., New York NY 10157-0002. (212)889-6500. Art Director: Doris Gordon. Specializes in hardcover and paperback books on advertising art and design. Publishes 15 titles/year; 50% require freelance designers.
First Contact & Terms: Works with 5 freelance artists/year. Professional artists only. Call for appointment. Drop off portfolio. Samples returned by SASE. Originals returned to artist at job's completion. Buys one-time rights.
Book Design: Assigns 10 jobs/year. Uses artists for layout and mechanicals. Pays by the job, $100 minimum.
Jackets/Covers: Assigns 10 design jobs/year. Pays by the job, $100 minimum.

ARTIFACTS PRESS OF SPVVVA, Box 315, Ft. Ontario Park, Oswego NY 13126. Director: Carlos Steward. Specializes in hardcover and paperback reprints on environmental themes, art books and children's books. Publishes 4-5 titles/year.
First Contact & Terms: Works with 5-6 freelance artists/year. Prefers artists from NY state; offers residencies to NY state artists, at $1,200 per month. Send query letter with resume, slides and photographs. Samples are filed. Samples not filed are returned by SASE. Reports back within 3 months. Originals returned to artist at job's completion. To show a portfolio, mail photographs and slides. Considers complexity of project, skill and experience of artist and project's budget when establishing payment. Negotiates rights purchased.
Book Design: Assigns 5-6 freelance illustration jobs/year. Pays by the hour, $8 minimum; by the project, $75- 7,200.
Tips: "Interested in people working in residencies programs for $1,200 per month, workspace programs (materials furnished), and strong black-and-white photographs and artwork. Residencies available in art (all media), crafts, photography, film/video and animation."

ARTIST'S MARKET, Writer's Digest Books, 1507 Dana Ave., Cincinnati OH 45207. Contact: Editor. Annual hardcover directory of freelance markets for graphic artists. Send b&w samples—photographs, Photostats or good quality photocopies of artwork. "Since *Artist's Market* is published only once a year, submissions are kept on file for the next upcoming edition until selections are made. Material is then returned by SASE." Buys one-time rights.
Needs: Buys 50-60 illustrations/year. "I need examples of art that has sold to one of the listings in *Artist's Market*. Thumb through the book to see the type of art I'm seeking. The art must have been freelanced; it cannot have been done as staff work. Include the name of the listing that purchased the work, what the art was used for, and the payment you received." Pays $25 to holder of reproduction rights and free copy of *Artist's Market* when published.

***ARTS END BOOKS**, Box 162, Newton MA 02168. (617)965-2478. Editor and Publisher: Marshall Brooks. Specializes in hardcover and paperback originals and reprints of contemporary literature. Publishes 2 titles/year.
First Contact & Terms: Works with 2-3 freelance artists/year. Send query letter with photostats and tear sheets to be kept on file. Samples not filed are returned by SASE. Reports within a few days. Return of original work depends on arrangement with artist. Considers complexity of the project, skill and experience of artist, project's budget, turnaround time and rights purchased when establishing payment. Rights purchased vary according to project.
Book Design: Pays by the project.

Jackets/Covers: Assigns 2 freelance jobs/year. Pays by the project.
Text Illustration: Prefers pen and ink work. Pays by the project.
Tips: "We are mainly interested in artist's books project or work akin that explores book arts from more of a fine arts perspective than a commercial arts one. We are not, at this time, interested in buying commercial freelance artwork."

ASHLEY BOOKS INC., Box 768, Port Washington NY 11050. (516)883-2221. President: Billie Young. Publishes hardcover originals; controversial, medical and timely, fiction and nonfiction. Publishes 50 titles/year; 40% require freelance designers or freelance illustrators. Also uses artists for promotional aids.
First Contact & Terms: Metropolitan New York area residents only; experienced artists with book publisher or record album jacket experience. Arrange interview to show portfolio. Buys first rights. Negotiates payment. Free catalog. Send SASE.
Book Design: Assigns 35 jobs/year. Uses artists for layout and paste-up.
Jackets/Covers: Assigns 35 jobs/year. "Cover should catch the eye. A cover should be such that it will sell books and give an idea at a glance what the book is about. A cover should be eye catching so that it draws one to read further."
Tips: "As a result of an upsurge in consumer interest in cooking, more cookbooks will be produced generating more illustrations and more artwork."

THE ATHLETIC PRESS, Box 80250, Pasadena CA 91108. Contact: Donald Duke. Publishes sports training and conditioning books.
First Contact & Terms: Query.
Needs: "We are looking for line art of sport movements, anatomical drawings, etc."

AUGSBURG PUBLISHING HOUSE, Box 1209, 426 S. 5th St., Minneapolis MN 55440. (612)330-3300. Photo Editor/Designers. Publishes paperback Protestant/Lutheran books (45 titles/year); religious education materials; audiovisual resources; periodicals. Also uses artists for catalog cover design, advertising circulars, advertising layout, design and illustration. Negotiates pay, b&w and color.
First Contact & Terms: "We don't have a rule only to work locally, but the majority of the artists are close enough to meet here on assignments." Works on assignment only. Call, write, or send slides or photocopies. Reports in 5-8 weeks. Samples not filed are returned by SASE. Reports back on future assignment possibilities. Provide brochure, flyer, tear sheet, good photocopies and 35mm transparencies; if artist willing to have samples retained, they are kept on file. Buys all rights on a work-for-hire basis. May require artist to supply overlays on color work.
Book Design: Assigns 45 jobs/year. Uses artists primarily for cover design; occasionally inside illustration, sample chapter openers. Pays $600-1,000 for cover design.
Text Illustration: Negotiates pay, 1-, 2-, and 4-color.

AVON BOOKS, Art Department, 105 Madison Ave., New York NY 10016. (212)481-5663. Publisher: Rena Wolner. Art Director: Tom Egner. Publishes paperback originals and reprints—mass market, trade and juvenile. Publishes 300 titles/year; 80% require freelance illustrators.
First Contact & Terms: Works with 100 freelance artists/year. Works on assignment only. Send resume and samples to be filed. Drop-off portfolio. Accepts any type sample. Samples returned only by request. Reports within 1 month. Works on assignment only. Original work returned to the artist after job's completion. Considers complexity of the project, skill and experience of the artist and project's budget when establishing payment.
Book Design: Assigns 20 jobs/year. Uses artists for all aspects. Payment varies.
Jackets/Covers: Assigns 150 freelance design and 150 freelance illustration jobs/year.
Text Illustration: Assigns 20 freelance jobs/year.
Tips: "Look at our books to see if work is appropriate for us before submitting."

AZTEX CORP., Box 50046, 1126 N. 6th Ave., Tucson AZ 85703. (602)882-4656. President: W. R. Haessner. Publishes hardcover and paperback originals on transportation history, mainstream and how-to. Publishes 9-12 titles/year.
First Contact & Terms: Works on assignment only. Send query letter with resume and/or brochure showing art style and samples. Especially looks for realism and detail when reviewing samples. Reports in 6 weeks. Samples returned by SASE. Buys reprint or all rights. No originals returned to artist at job's completion. Free catalog.
Jackets/Covers: Assigns 4 jobs/year. "We need technical drawings and cutaways." Pays $50-150, opaque watercolors and oils.

BAKER BOOK HOUSE, 6030 E. Fulton Rd., Ada MI 49301. (616)676-9185. Art Director: Dwight Baker. Specializes in hardcovers, paperbacks, originals and reprints of religious trade and textbooks. Publishes 100 titles/year.
First Contact & Terms: Works with 10 freelance artists/year. Works on assignment only. Send query letter with brochure showing art style or resume, tear sheets, Photostats, photocopies, slides and photographs. Samples not filed are returned by SASE only if requested. Reports only if interested. Original artwork is returned after the job's completion if requested. Considers complexity of project, skill and experience of artist, and project's budget when establishing payment. Buys all rights. Finds most artists through references/word-of-mouth, portfolio reviews and samples received through the mail.
Jackets/Covers: Assigns 12 freelance design and 12 freelance illustration jobs/year. Pays by the project, $300 minumum.
Text Illustration: Assigns 2-4 freelance jobs/year. Prefers pen & ink cartoons and line drawings. Pays $15-35/spot drawing.
Tips: "Examine the cover designs in any bookstore—religious or general. Pay particular attention to the psychology, philosophy and religion sections. We are always looking for jacket designers who work primarily with type for our academic book covers. The most valuable illustrators are those who are able to envisage the completed cover design and compose their illustration to incorporate the type copy that will be added later. In presenting samples or portfolios the most common error we see is the tendency for artists to include weaker pieces that distract from their strong ones."

***BASCOM COMMUNICATIONS CO.**, 399 E. 72nd St., New York NY 10021. President: Betsy Ryan. Specializes in juvenile hardcover and paperback originals. Publishes 6 titles/year; 100% require freelance illustration.
First Contact & Terms: Works with 3 freelance artists/year. Works on assignment only. Send query letter with brochure showing art style. Samples are filed. Samples not filed are not returned. Does not report back. Originals returned to artist at job's completion. Write to schedule an appointment to show a portfolio, which should include original/final art, tear sheets and final reproduction/product. Considers complexity of project, project's budget and turnaround time.
Book Design: Assigns 5 freelance design and 5 freelance illustration jobs/year. Pays by the hour, $15 minimum.
Jackets/Covers: Assigns 5 freelance design and 5 freelance illustration jobs/year. Pays by the project, $1000 minimum.
Text Illustration: Assigns 5 freelance jobs/year. Pays by the project, $3,000 minimum.

***BEHRMAN HOUSE INC.**, 235 Watchuno Ave., West Orange NJ 07052. (201)669-0447. Art Director: Ruby G. Strauss. Specializes in textbooks/ "Jewish publications." Publishes 10 title/year. 90% require freelance illustration.
First Contact & Terms: Works with 8 freelance artists/year. Works on assignment only. Send query letter with brochure, tear sheets and Photostats. Samples are filed. Samples not filed are returned only if requested by artist. Reports back only if interested. Originals returned to artist at job's completion. To show a portfolio, mail Photostats, tear sheets and photographs. Considers complexity of project, project's budget and turnaround time when establishing payment. Negotiates rights purchased.
Book Design: Assigns 8 freelance design and 8 freelance freelance illustration jobs/year. Pays by the hour, $15-25; by the project $1,000-5,000.
Jackets/Covers: Assigns 8 freelance design and 8 freelance illustration jobs/year. Pays by the project, $100-500.
Text Illustration: Assigns 8 freelance jobs/year. Pays by the project, $1,000-5,000.

BENGAL PRESS, INC., 1885 Spaulding SE, Grand Rapids MI 49506. (616)949-8895. President: John Ilich. Specializes in paperback originals and reprints of nonfiction (business, history, law, how-to) and fiction (science fiction, religious, inspirational). Publishes 1-4 titles/year; 100% require freelance designers; 25% require freelance illustrators.
First Contact & Terms: Send query letter with samples to be kept on file. Accepts any samples the artist deems relevant to show quality and type of work. Reports only if interested. Works on assignment only. No originals returned to artist at job's completion. Considers complexity of project, skill and experience of artist and project's budget when establishing payment. Negotiates rights purchased.
Book Design: Assigns 1-3 freelance jobs/year. Pays by the project, $100-1,000.
Jackets/Covers: Assigns 1-3 freelance design and 1-4 freelance illustration jobs/year. Pays by the project, $100-1,000.
Text Illustration: Assigns 1-3 freelance jobs/year. Pays by the project, $100-1,000.
Tips: "Good samples should be sent for our company files, so that when a project comes up, we can seek an artist based upon the samples filed."

***THE BENJAMIN/CUMMINGS PUBLISHING CO.**, 2725 Sand Hill Rd., Menlo Park CA 94025. Contact: Production Manager. Specializes in college textbooks in biology, chemistry, computer science and mathematics. Publishes 40 titles/year; 90% require freelance design and illustration.
Illustration: Works with 25-75 freelance artists/year. Specializes in 1, 2, and 4 color illustrations, technical, biological and medical. "Our biologic texts require trained bio/med illustrators. Proximity to Bay Area is a plus, but not essential." Works on assignment only. Original artwork not returned to artist at job's completion. Send query letter with resume and samples. Samples returned only if requested. Pays by piece, $20-80 average and job maximum.
Book Design: Assigns 30 jobs/year. "From manuscript, designer prepares specs and layouts for review. After approval, final specs and layouts are required. On our books which are dummied, very often the designer is contracted as dummier at a separate per page fee." Pays per page $3-5.50.
Cover: Assigns 40 jobs/year. Pays by the job, $500-1,000.

BENNETT & MCKNIGHT PUBLISHING, 809 W. Detweiller, Peoria IL 61615. (309)691-4454. Director of Art/Design/Production: Donna M. Faull. Specializes in original hardcovers and paperbacks, especially in vocational education (industrial arts/high-tech/home economics/career education textbooks, filmstrips, software). Publishes over 100 titles/year.
First Contact & Terms: Works with over 30 freelance artists/year. Works on assignment only. Send query letter with brochure, resume and "any type of samples." Samples not filed are returned if requested. Reports back in weeks. Original work not returned after job's completion; work-for-hire basis with rights to publisher. Considers complexity of the project, skill and experience of the artist, project's budget, turnaround time and rights purchased when establishing payment. Buys all rights.
Book Design: Assigns over 30 freelance design and over 30 freelance illustration jobs/year. Pays by the hour, $10-40; pays by the project, $300-3,000 and upward (very technical art, lots of volume).
Jackets/Covers: Assigns over 50 freelance design jobs/year. Pays by the project, $200 for 1-color; 4,000 for complete cover/interiors for textbooks.
Text Illustration: Assigns over 50 freelance jobs/year. Pays by the hour, $10-40; amount varies.
Tips: "Try not to call or never drop in without an appointment."

***BERKLEY PUBLISHING GROUP**, 200 Madison Ave., New York NY 10016. (212)686-9820. Art Director: Joni Friedman. Publishes general interest fiction and nonfiction plus mass market and trade paperbacks for adults and young adults. Publishes 450 titles/year.
First Contact & Terms: Works with 50-100 freelance artists/year. Prefers realistic treatments. Works on assignment only. Send query letter. Call or write to schedule an appointment to show a portfolio, which should include original/final art, tear sheets, final reproduction/product and transparencies. "A concise and professional-looking portfolio makes more of an impression than many different pieces in various degrees of quality." Considers complexity of project, skill and experience of artist, project's budget, turnaround time and rights purchased when establishing payment.
Jackets/Covers: Works with 50-100 freelance artists/year. Prefers "realistic and correct autonomy, dramatic scenery and convincing skin." Payment negotiated.
Tips: "It's easier for a newcomer to approach the category romances, since so many are published. They are especially good for artists who have been working a while and are just getting recognized.

BKMK PRESS, College of Arts & Sciences, University of Missouri-Kansas City, 5100 Rockhill Rd., Kansas City MO 64110. (816)276-1305. Editor-in-Chief: Dan Jaffe. Specializes in paperback originals dealing with poetry, art, and quality short stories. Publishes 6 titles/year; 50% require freelance illustrators.
First Contact & Terms: Send query letter with photographs to be kept on file. "We want to see how things reproduce—no slides, please." Samples not kept on file are returned by SASE. Reports within 2 months only if interested. Works on assignment only. Originals returned to artist at job's completion. Write for appointment to show portfolio. Considers complexity of project, skill and experience of artist, project's budget, turnaround time and rights purchased when establishing payment. Negotiates rights purchased.
Jackets/Covers: Assigns 4-5 freelance design jobs/year.
Text Illustration: Pays by the project, $50 minimum.

BLACKTHORNE PUBLISHING INC., 1340 Hill St., El Cajon CA 92020. (619)588-2055 or Fax (619)588-4678. Art Director: Steven J. Schanes. Specializes in paperback originals and reprints, comic books, signed prints and trade books. Publishes 200 titles/year.
First Contact & Terms: Works with 50 freelance artists/year. "We look for professional standards in the artists we work with." Send query letter with brochure, resume, and samples to be kept on file; originals will be returned. Prefers slides and Photostats as samples. Samples not filed are returned. Reports within 3 weeks. Originals returned to artist after job's completion. Considers complexity of the project,

skill and experience of artist, project's budget and turnaround time when establishing payment. Rights purchased vary according to project.
Book Design: Assigns 50 jobs/year. Pays by the project, depending on the job, from $50 for a spot illustration to $15,000 for a complete comic book series.
Jackets/Covers: Assigns 15 freelance design and 30 freelance illustration jobs/year. Pays by the hour, $5-40 average; by the project, $50-10,000 average.
Text Illustration: Assigns 15 jobs/year. Prefers pen & ink. Pays by the hour, $5-40 average; by the project, $50-10,000 average.

BLACKWELL SCIENTIFIC PUBLICATIONS, INC., Suite 209, 3 Cambridge Center, Cambridge MA 02142. (617)225-0401. Production Manager: Julia M. Salas. Specializes in hardcovers of medical and nursing books. Publishes 12 titles/year.
First Contact & Terms: Artists must have experience in medical illustration. "However, 95% of our authors supply finished art. We have hired freelance illustrators once in 5 years."
Book Design: Pays by the project, $500-1,000.
Jackets/Covers: Some cover design work for experienced designers. Prefers pen & ink. Pays by the project, $350-500.
Tips: Artists should "investigate the potential purchaser to see if their work is even appropriate."

BONUS BOOKS, 160 E. Illinois, Chicago IL 60611. Production Editor: Kathy Wallen. Specializes in hardcover and paperback nonfiction trade books, including sports, careers, guidebooks, general interest. Publishes 10-15 titles/year.
First Contact & Terms: Works with 10-15 freelance artists/year. Prefers local artists. Works on assignment only. Send query letter with slides and a SASE. "Do not send originals." Samples are filed. Samples not filed are returned by SASE. Reports back within 2 weeks only if interested. Originals returned to artist at job's completion "depending on job." Local artists can call or write to schedule an appointment to show a portfolio, which should include roughs and original/final art. Considers complexity of project, skill and experience of artist, project's budget, turnaround time and rights purchased when establishing payment.
Jackets/Covers: Assigns 30 freelance design and 2 freelance illustration jobs/year. Pays by the project, $100 minimum.
Text Illustration: Assigns 2 freelance jobs/year. Prefers line art (pen & ink). Pays by the project, $10 minimum.
Tips: "Unless your illustrations are book cover material, we probably aren't interested. We're most interested in talented book cover designers with a strong type sense."

***BOOK DESIGN**, Box 193, Moose WY 83012. Art Director: Robin Graham. Specializes in hardcover and paperback originals of nonfiction, natural history. Publishes 3+ titles/year.
First Contact & Terms: Works with 16 freelance artists/year. Works on assignment only. Send query letter with "examples of past work and one piece of original artwork which can be returned." Samples not filed are returned by SASE if requested. Reports back within 10 days. Originals not returned to artist at job's completion. Write to schedule an appointment to show a portfolio. Considers complexity of project, skill and experience of artist, project's budget and turnaround time when establishing payment. Negotiates rights purchased.
Book Design: Assigns 6 freelance design jobs/year. Pays by the project, $50-3,500.
Jackets/Covers: Assigns 2 freelance design and 4 freelance illustration jobs/year. Pays by the project, $50-3,500.
Text Illustration: Assigns 26 freelance jobs/year. Prefers technical pen illustrations, maps (using airbrush, overlays etc.), watercolor illustrations for children's books, calligraphy and lettering for titles and headings. Pays by the hour, $5-20; by the project, $50-3,500.

***DON BOSCO MULTIMEDIA**, Box T, 475 North Ave., New Rochelle NY 10802. (914)576-0122. Production Manager: Gus Vibal. Specializes in religious hardcover and paperback originals, filmstrips and videotapes. Publishes 8 titles/year; 20% require freelance illustration/
First Contact & Terms: Works with 5 freelance artists/year. Works on assignment only. Send query letter with brochure showing art style. Samples are filed. Reports back within 3 weeks. Originals returned to artist at job's completion. Call to schedule an appointment to show a portfolio, which should include thumbnails, roughs, original/final art, tear sheets and slides. Considers complexity of project, skill and experience of artist and project's budget. Buys one-time rights.
Jackets/Covers: Assigns 8 freelance design jobs/year. Prefers religious, realistic style. Pays by the project, $200 minimum.

***THOMAS BOUREGY & CO., INC. (AVALON BOOKS)**, 401 Lafayette St., New York NY 10003. (212)598-0222. Editor: Barbara J. Brett. Specializes in hardcover originals of romances and westerns for young adults. Publishes 60 titles/year; 100% require freelance illustration.
First Contact & Terms: Works with many freelance artists/year. Prefers local artists "so that we can have personal contact and work quickly. We prefer that the artist have some professional experience." Works on assignment only. Send query letter with brochure showing art style or resume and tear sheets. Samples are filed. Samples not filed are returned by SASE only if requested. Reports back only if interested. Originals not returned to artist at job's completion. Pays a flat rate of $200. Buys all rights.
Jackets/Covers: Assigns 60 freelance illustration jobs/year. Prefers acrylics: "oils OK." Pays by the project, $200.

BOWLING GREEN UNIVERSITY POPULAR PRESS, Bowling Green University, Bowling Green OH 43403. (419)372-2981. Managing Editor: Pat Browne. Publishes hardcover and paperback originals on popular culture, folklore, women's studies, science fiction criticism, detective fiction criticism, music and drama. Publishes 15-20 titles and 8 journals/year.
First Contact & Terms: Send previously published work. SASE. Reports in 2 weeks. Buys all rights. Free catalog.
Jackets/Covers: Assigns 20 jobs/year. Pays $50 minimum, color washes, opaque watercolors, gray opaques, b&w line drawings and washes.

BRIARCLIFF PRESS, 11 Wimbledon Court, Jericho NY 11753. (516)681-1505. Editorial/Art Director: Trudy Settel. Publishes hardcover and paperback cookbook, decorating, baby care, gardening, sewing, crafts and driving originals and reprints. Publishes 18 titles/year; 100% require freelance designers and illustrators. Uses artists for color separations, lettering and mechanicals; assigns 25 jobs/year, pays $5-10/hour. Also assigns 5 advertising jobs/year for catalogs and direct mail brochures; pays $5-10/hour.
First Contact & Terms: Send query letter; no samples until requested. Artists should have worked on a professional basis with other firms of this type. SASE. Reports in 3 weeks. Buys all rights. No advance. Pays promised fee for unused assigned work.
Book Design: Assigns 25/year. Pays $6 minimum/hour, layout and type spec.
Jackets/Covers: Buys 24/year. Pays $100-300, b&w; $250-500, color.
Text Illustration: Uses artists for text illustrations and cartoons. Buys 250/year. Pays $10-30, b&w; $25-50, color.

BROADMAN PRESS, 127 9th Ave. N., Nashville TN 37234. (615)251-2630. Art Director: Jack Jewell. Religious publishing house.
First Contact & Terms: Artist must be experienced, professional illustrator. Works on assignment only. Send query letter with brochure and samples to be kept on file. Call or write for appointment to show portfolio. Send slides, tear sheets, Photostats or photocopies; "samples *cannot* be returned." Reports only if interested. Pays for illustration by the project, $250-1,000. Considers complexity of the project, client's budget and rights purchased when establishing payment. Negotiates rights purchased.
Needs: Works with 50 freelance artists/year. Uses artists for illustration. "We publish for all ages in traditional and contemporary styles, thus our needs are quite varied."
Tips: "The quality of art in the Christian book publishing market has greatly improved in the last five years. We actively search for 'realist' illustrators who can work in a style that looks contemporary." Looks for " the ability to illustrate scenes with multiple figures, to accurately illustrate people of all ages, including young children and babies, and illustrate detailed scenes described in text."

***BROOKS/COLE PUBLISHING COMPANY**, 511 Forest Lodge Rd., Pacific Grove CA 93950. Art Director: Vernon T. Boes. Specializes in hardcover and paperback college textbooks on technical and softside subjects. Publishes 60-100 titles/year. 90% require freelance illustration.
First Contact & Terms: Works with 25 freelance artists/year. Prefers talented, professional and prompt artists. Works on assignment only. Send query letter with brochure, resume, tear sheets, Photostats and photographs. Samples are filed. Samples not filed are returned by SASE. Reports back within 6 weeks. Write to schedule an appointment to show a portfolio, which should include thumbnails, roughs, original/final art, Photostats, tear sheets, final reproduction/product, photographs, slides and transparencies. Considers complexity of project, skill and experience of artist, project's budget and turnaround time. Buys all rights
Book Design: Assigns 15 freelance design and 40 freelance illustration jobs/year. Pays by the project, $100 minimum.
Jackets/Covers: Assigns 40 freelance design and 40 freelance illustration jobs/year. Prefers abstract of technical styles. Pays by the project, $150 minimum.
Text Illustration: Assigns 60-100 freelance jobs/year. Prefers ink. Pays by the project, $50 minimum.

***WILLIAM C. BROWN PUBLISHERS**, 2460 Kerper Blvd., Dubuque IA 52001. (319)588-1451. Vice President and Director, Production and Design: Beverly A. Kolz. Visual/Design Manager: Faye M. Schilling. Publishes hardbound and paperback college textbooks. Publishes 200 titles/year; 10% require freelance designers, 50% require freelance illustrators. Also uses artists for advertising. Pays $35-350, b&w and color promotional artwork.
First Contact & Terms: Works on assignment only. Send query letter with resume, brochure, tear sheets or 8½x11" photocopies or finished 11x14" or smaller (transparencies if larger) art samples or call for interview. Reports in 4 weeks. Samples returned by SASE if requested. Reports back on future assignment possibilities. Buys all rights. Pays half contract for unused assigned work.
Book Design: Assigns 10-15 freelance design jobs/year; assigns 75-100 freelance illustration jobs/year. Uses artists for all phases of process. Pays by the project, $500 minimum; varies widely according to complexity. Pays by the hour, mechanicals.
Jackets/Covers: Assigns 15-25 freelance design jobs and 20-30 freelance illustration jobs/year. Pays $100-350 average and negotiates pay for special projects.
Text Illustrations: Assigns 75-100 freelance jobs/year. Uses b&w and color work. Prefers mostly continuous tone, some line drawings; ink preferred for b&w. Pays $25-300. Artwork includes medical and geological illustration.
Tips: "In the field, there is more use of color. There is need for sophisticated color skills—the artist must be knowlegeable about the way color reproduces in the printing process. The designer and illustrator must be prepared to contribute to content as well as style. Tighter production schedules demand an awareness of overall schedules. *Must* be dependable."

ARISTIDE D. CARATZAS, PUBLISHER, Box 210, 30 Church St., New Rochelle NY 10802. (914)632-8487. Managing Editor: John Emerich. Publishes books about archaeology, art history, natural history and classics for specialists in the above fields in universities, museums, libraries and interested amateurs. Accepts previously published material. Send letter with brochure showing artwork. Samples not filed are returned by SASE. Reports only if interested. To show a portfolio, mail appropriate materials or call or write to schedule an appointment. Buys all rights or negotiates rights purchased.

CAREER PUBLISHING, INC., Box 5486, Orange CA 92613-5486. (714)771-5155. Secretary/Treasurer: Sherry Robson. Specializes in paperback original textbooks on trucking, medical office management, medical insurance billing, motorcycle dictionary, real estate dictionary, micro computer courses and guidance for jobs. Uses artists for advertising, direct mail and posters.
First Contact & Terms: Works with 3 freelance artists/year. Works on assignment only. Send query letter with brochure/flyer or resume, Photostats and line drawings or actual work to be kept on file. Submit portfolio for review. Guidelines given for each project. Samples returned by SASE. Reports in 2 months. No originals returned to artist at job's completion. Buys all rights.
Book Design: Assigns 12 jobs/year. Pays for design by the project, $50-300.
Jackets/Covers: Assigns 12 design and 150 illustration jobs/year. Prefers line drawings, paintings and cartoons for illustrations. Pays for illustration by the project, $50-100.
Text Illustration: Assigns approximately 10 jobs/year. Pays by the project, $50-100.
Tips: Uses some medical illustrations and technical drawings.

CARNIVAL ENTERPRISES, Box 19087, Minneapolis MN 55419. (612)870-0169. Art Director: Gloria Blockey. "Carnival is a book producer, not a publisher. The titles we create are for clients who market them in many outlets and editions. Produces juvenile fiction and nonfiction. Produces 25-45 titles/year.
First Contact & Terms: Works with 25-45 freelance artists/year. "Experience in children's literature is *crucial*, including past published children's books and experience in picture book design." Works on assignment only. Send query letter with brochure, resume, photocopies, slides, printed excerpts—anything except original work—to be kept on file. "Carnival uses a file system and only contacts artists on an assignment basis. No specific submissions will be accepted; no queries are followed upon by Carnival due to the volume of our mail. We literally match up artists with appropriate styles. All samples are welcome, but bulk should be kept to a minimum for easy filing." Samples not filed are returned *only* by request with a SASE. Does not report back to the artist. Considers complexity of the project, skill and experience of artist, project's budget, (vital) turnaround time, rights purchased and going rates when establishing payment. Rights purchased vary from client to client.
Text Illustration: Assigns 25-45 titles/year. Considers watercolor, markers, colored pencil and gouache—any "flexible" medium for laser separation. Pays by the project, $2,000-6,000 for color. B&w line art pays less.

CATHOLIC BOOK PUBLISHING CO., 257 W. 17th St., New York NY 10011. (212)243-4515. Manager: Robert W. Cavalero. Specializes in hardcover and paperback originals. Publishes 10 titles/year; 50% require freelance illustrators.

First Contact & Terms: Works with 6 freelance artists/year. Works on assignment only. Send samples and tear sheets to be kept on file. Reports within 1 week. Call or write for appointment to show portfolio. No originals returned to artist at job's completion. Considers skill and experience of artist when establishing payment. Buys all rights.
Text Illustration: Assigns 10 freelance jobs/year.

***CHELSEA HOUSE PUBLISHERS**, 95 Madison Ave., New York NY 10016. Art Director: Mariah Epf. Specializes in hardcover young adult non-fiction. Publishes 200 + titles/year. 40% require freelance illustration.
First Contact & Terms: Works with 200 freelance artists/year. Prefers local artists, "but have worked with artists from all over the country and Europe." Send query letter with tear sheets, Photostats, slides and photographs. Samples are filed. Samples not filed are returned only if requested by artist. Reports back only if interested. Originals returned at job's completion. Write to schedule an appointment to show a portfolio, which should include original/final art, Photostats, photographs and slides. Considers complexity of project, skill and experience of artist, project's budget primarily and turnaround time when establishing payment. Buys one-time rights.
Book Design: Assigns 5 freelance design jobs/year. Pays by the hour, $12-15. Pays by the project, $75-350.
Jackets/Covers: Assigns 5 freelance design and 100 freelance illustration jobs/year. Prefers color portrait paintings, realistic, yet painterly. Pays by the project, $350-700.
Text Illustration: Assigns 100 freelance jobs/year. Prefers both b&w technical and b&w "halftone realistic." Pays by size, $40/spot-200/full page.
Tips: "Because of tight deadlines and budgets, assignments must be given most often to artists who already have experience in the type of project I am assigning. From time to time, however, the right kind of painting style, coupled with a desire to fulfill an assignment, gives me the incentive to take a risk on an artist, regardless of his published experience."

***CHICAGO REVIEW PRESS**, 814 N. Franklin, Chicago IL 60610. (312)337-0747. Editor: Linda Matthews. Specializes in hardcover and paperback originals; trade nonfiction: how-to, travel, cookery, popular science, Midwest regional. Publishes 12 titles/year; 2% require freelance illustration and all require cover or jacket design.
First Contact & Terms: Works with 5 freelance artists/year. Send query letter with resume and tear sheets, or phone. Samples are filed. Samples not filed are returned by SASE. Reports back only if interested. Originals not returned to artist at job's completion "unless there are special circumstances." Call to show a portfolio, which should include tear sheets, final reproduction/product and slides. Considers project's budget when establishing payment. Buys one-time rights.
Book Design: Assigns 2 freelance design jobs/year. Pays by the project, $35-400.
Jackets/Covers: Assigns 10 freelance design and 5 freelance illustration jobs/year. Pays by the project, $400.

THE CHILD'S WORLD, INC., Box 989, Elgin IL 60120. Editor: Diane Dow Suire. Specializes in hardcover originals on early childhood education. Publishes 40 titles/year; 50% require freelance designers and 100% require freelance illustrators.
First Contact & Terms: Works with 20 freelance artists/year. Prefers artists who have experience illustrating for children. "We use both realistic and stylized art." Works on assignment only. Send samples and tear sheets to be kept on file except for original work. "Correspond please. Don't call." Prefers tear sheets, original art, or good photocopies. Prefers not to see slides. Reports only if interested. No originals returned to artist at job's completion. Considers complexity of project, skill and experience of artist, and project's budget when establishing payment. Buys all rights. Finds most artist through references/word-of-mouth and samples received through the mail.
Jackets/Covers: Assigns 4-6 (by series) freelance design jobs/year. Pays by the project for design and illustration, $100-2,500.
Text Illustration: "We do about 40 books in series format. We publish in full-color and use very little black-and-white art." Prefers watercolor, acrylics, oils and pastels. Pays by the project, $1,000-3,500.
Tips: Looks for "art geared for the very young child—there's a big demand for more quality books for preschool children. Request current catalog to review art styles currently used."

CHILTON BOOK CO., 201 King of Prussia Rd., Radnor PA 19089. (215)964-4711. Art Director: Edna H. Jones. Publishes hardbound and paperback arts and crafts, business, technical, trade and automotive books. Publishes 80 titles/year; 50% require freelance designers, fewer than 5% require freelance illustrators.
First Contact & Terms: Query. "I prefer to deal in person rather than through the mail." Reports within 3 weeks. Buys world rights. No originals returned at job's completion. Works on assignment only.

Samples returned by SASE. Provide resume, business card, flyer and tear sheet to be kept on file for future assignments. Artist sometimes supplies overlays for color work. Full payment for unused assigned work. Pays on acceptance.
Book Design: Assigns 20 jobs/year. Uses artists for layout, type spec and scaling art, castoffs. Pays by the project, $500-1,200 upon completion and acceptance. Price is discussed at beginning of the job with the designer.
Jackets/Covers: Assigns 40 freelance design and 10 freelance illustration jobs/year. Prefers oils and acrylics. Pays $850-1,400.
Text Illustration: Assigns 1-2 freelance jobs. Prefers pen & ink. Pays by the project, $500-1,200.
Tips: "I don't want to see art school class projects. I want to see a range of the artist's style, preferably in jobs he/she has done for similar clients. Also show knowledge of how to create art for reproduction."

CHRISTIAN BOARD OF PUBLICATION, Box 179, St. Louis MO 63166. Director of Product Development, Design and Promotion: Guin Stemmler. Publishes several paperbacks annually. Also publishes magazines, curriculum, catalogs and advertising pieces. Uses artists for design and illustration of curriculum, books, direct mail brochures and display pieces.
First Contact & Terms: Send query letter with resume, brochure or copies of work to be kept on file. SASE. Reports in 6-8 weeks. Buys all rights. Originals not usually returned to artist at job's completion. Works on assignment only. Samples returned by SASE.
Jackets/Covers: Assigns a few jobs/year. Pays $250 minimum, 2-color and 4-color.
Text Illustration: Assigns many jobs/year. Pays $40 minimum, 2-color; $55 minimum, 4-color.

***CHRISTIAN SCHOOLS INTERNATIONAL**, 3350 E. Paris SE, Grand Rapids MI 49508. Production Manager: Judy Bandstra. Specializes in textbooks and teacher editions on Bible, language, science, social studies, physical education, etc. Publishes 20-30 titles/year; 75% require freelance illustration.
First Contact & Terms: Works with 3-10 freelance artists/year. Works on assignment only. Send query letter with tear sheets. Samples are filed. Samples not filed are returned only if requested. Reports back only if interested. Originals not returned to artist at job's completion. Write to schedule an appointment to show a portfolio, which should include original/final art and tear sheets. Considers complexity of project, skill and experience of artist, project's budget and turnaround time. Buys all rights.
Jackets/Covers: Assigns 1-5 freelance design jobs/year. Pays by the project, $200-500.
Text Illustration: Assigns 5-10 freelance jobs/year. Pays by the project.

CHRONICLE BOOKS, Suite 806, One Hallidie Plaza, San Francisco CA 94102. (415)777-7240. Production and Art Director: David Barich. Publishes hardcover and paperback originals on California and the West Coast, how-to, architecture, contemporary fine art books and cookbooks, California history, urban living, guidebooks, art and photography; some paperback reprints. Publishes 60-70 titles/year; 50% require freelance designers, 10% require freelance illustrators.
First Contact & Terms: Personal contact required. Query with resume or arrange interview to show portfolio. SASE. Reports within 2 weeks. Buys various rights. Free catalog.
Book Design: Assigns 25 jobs/year. Uses artists for layout, type spec and design. Pays by the project, $400-600 average. Payment upon completion of project.
Jackets/Covers: Assigns 40 jobs/year. Pays by the project, $225-550 average for design; by the project, $125-400 average for illustrations, b&w line drawings, washes and gray opaques; $400-650, color washes and opaque watercolors.
Text Illustration: Pays by the project, $200 minimum.

CLIFFHANGER PRESS, Box 29527, Oakland CA 94604-9527. Editor: Nancy Chirich. Estab. 1986. Specializes in paperback mystery and suspense. Publishes 4 titles/year.
First Contact & Terms: Works with 4 freelance artists/year for covers only. Works on assignment only. Send query letter with brochure, tear sheets or samples showing b&w techniques. "All our covers are 2-color (i.e. black and red). We are interested in line drawings, wash, watercolor—whatever will reproduce with black and a color for the covers, with or without a halftone." Prefers artists who can also do mechanicals. Samples are filed. Samples not filed are returned by SASE only if requested. Reports back within 2-3 weeks. To show a portfolio, mail disposable samples, such as thumbnails, tear sheets, roughs and final reproduction/product. Considers project's budget and turnaround time when establishing payment. Buys one-time rights for time book is in print. "Artist keeps copyright to artwork, if product is result of his/her original idea. We welcome suggestions."
Jackets/Covers: Assigns 4 freelance design jobs/year. "Artist gets synopsis or copy of manuscript." Pays by the project, $200-250, including "cover design by . . ." on cover.
Tips: "We do not want to see slick, four-color work, since we don't use it." To retain their needs, "ask for Cliffhanger Press books in your library or stores."

CLIFFS NOTES INC., Box 80728, Lincoln NE 68501. Contact: Michele Spence. Publishes educational and trade (Centennial Press) books. Uses artists for educational posters.
First Contact & Terms: Works on assignment only. Samples returned by SASE. Reports back on future assignment possibilities. Send brochure, flyer and/or resume. No originals returned to artist at job's completion. Buys all rights. Artist supplies overlays for color art.
Jackets/Covers: Uses artists for covers and jackets.
Text Illustration: Uses technical illustrators for mathematics, science, miscellaneous.

COASTAR PUBLISHING, Subsidiary of Newtek Industries, Box 46116, Los Angeles CA 90046. (213)874-6669. Publisher: Jules Brenner. Publishes 1 original paperback—the *Brenner Restaurant Index*—each year. Also publishes a software program for home and office computers.
First Contact & Terms: "We are not yet working with artists, but would consider doing so." Send query letter with resume and samples to be kept on file. Accepts any type sample. Samples not filed are returned by SASE. Reports within 3 weeks. Original work returned to artist "if artist insists." Rights purchased vary according to project.
Jackets/Covers: Will probably assign 1 freelance illustration job/year. Pays 3 copies of book.
Text Illustration: Will consider using text illustration.

***COMPACT PUBLICATIONS, INC.**, 2131 Hollywood Blvd., Hollywood FL 33020. (305)925-5242. President: Donald L. Lessne. Specializes in hardcovers, paperbacks and magazines—mostly trade books. Publishes 20 titles/year.
First Contact & Terms: Works with 5 freelance artists/year. Prefers local artists only. Works on assignment only. Send brochure showing art style or photocopies. Samples not filed are returned only if requested. Reports within 30 days. No originals returned to artist at job's completion "unless specifically requested that they need it back." Considers rights purchased when establishing payment. Rights purchased vary according to project.
Book Design: Assigns 20 freelance design and 20 freelance illustration jobs/year. Pays by the project, $400-1,000.
Jackets/Covers: Assigns 20 freelance design and a variable amount of freelance illustration jobs/year. Pays by the project, $400-1,000.
Tips: "We are looking for fresh approaches to creative art in the trade area. We are looking for contemporary artists; we are looking for self-starters that are able to complete total job ready for typesetting."

COMPUTER SCIENCE PRESS INC., 1803 Research Blvd., Rockville MD 20850. (301)251-9050. Production Manager: Ilene Hammer. Publishes hardcover and paperback computer science, engineering, computers and math textbooks. Publishes 18 titles/year; 80% require freelance illustrators. Also uses artists for paste-up and for technical drawings using templates and form letters or Leroy lettering.
First Contact & Terms: Works on assignment only. Prefers local artists. Send query letter with template work, an illustration or line drawing as well as an upper and lower case alphabet and some words in Leroy or Berol lettering. Photocopy of work is OK. Samples not returned. Reports back only if interested. Buys all rights. No originals returned to artist at job's completion. Check for most recent titles in bookstores. Artist supplies overlays for cover artwork. Send artwork to the attention of Ilene Hammer.
Jackets/Covers: Assigns 12 freelance design jobs/year. Pays by the project, $100 minimum.
Text Illustration: Buys text illustrations (artist "reproduces our rough art"). Assigns 12 freelance text illustration jobs/year; prefers pen & ink drawings. Pays by the hour, $8 minimum.
Tips: "We would like to develop a file of freelance technical draftsmen familiar with Leroy or Berol lettering. Local artists preferred. We provide rough art to copy."

COMPUTER TECHNOLOGY RESOURCE GUIDE, Box 294, Rhododendron OR 97049. (503)622-4798. Editor: Michael P. Jones. Estab. 1986. Book about computers and computer accessories, computer services, books "and anything else related to computers" for beginners to advanced users of computers plus those involved with providing technical assistance to users. Circ. 2,500. Accepts previously published material. Original artwork returned to the artist after publication. Sample copy: $8. Art guidelines for SASE with 1 first class stamp.
Cartoons: Buys 1-3 cartoons/issue from freelancers. Prefers single-panel, double-panel and multi-panel with and without gagline; b&w line drawings, b&w washes and color washes. Send query letter with samples of style, roughs and finished cartoons. Samples are filed. Samples not filed are returned by SASE. Reports back within 2 weeks. Write for appointment to show a portfolio. Buys one-time rights. Pays in copies.
Illustrations: Buys 10 illustrations/issue from freelancers. "We want to see computers being used and featured in artwork." Send query letter with brochure or resume, tear sheets, Photostats, photocopies, slides and photographs. Samples not filed are returned by SASE. Reports back within 2 weeks. To show a portfolio, mail thumbnails, roughs, original/final art, final reproduction/product, color, tear sheets,

Photostats, photographs and b&w. Buys one-time rights. Pays in copies on publication.
Tips: "I am looking for good quality black-and-white sketches. Give me a good sample of what you can draw, even if you haven't done much in the way of computers. Send me whatever you have, and I'll be able to get a good idea from the samples. Color is in, but not with us."

DAVID C. COOK PUBLISHING COMPANY, Chariot Books, 850 N. Grove Ave., Elgin IL 60120. (312)741-2400. Managing Editor: Catherine L. Davis. Publishes religious children's books for ages infant-junior high. Publishes 65 titles/year; 100% require freelance illustrators. Work-for-hire and royalty arrangements.
First Contact & Terms: Prefers artists with publishing experience. Send photocopies of work or 35mm slides with return package and postage. Samples returned by SASE. Provide "anything that can be kept or photocopied" to be kept on file for future assignments. Check for most recent titles in bookstores. Artist sometimes supplies overlays on inside illustrations.
Book Design: Assigns 35-45/year. Buys realistic illustrations. Uses artists for layout and full-color art. Illustrated books usually have an advance and royalty.
Jackets/Covers: Assigns 35-45/year. Buys realistic illustrations; prefers b&w and full-color. Uses artists for layout and full-color art. Pays by the job.

THE COUNTRYMAN PRESS; BACKCOUNTRY PUBLICATIONS, Box 175, Woodstock VT 05091-0175. (802)457-1049. Production Manager: Louis Wilder. Specializes in hardcover, paperback originals and reprints on Vermont history and travel, outdoor recreation, contemporary fiction, how-to; reprints and originals of crime, suspense (Foul Play Press imprint). Publishes 25-30 titles/year.
First Contact & Terms: Works with 6-10 freelance artists/year. Works on assignment only. Send query letter with resume, tear sheets, Photostats, photographs and "relevant samples of work." Samples are filed. Samples not filed are returned by SASE if requested. Reports back within 1 month. Originals returned to artist at job's completion "if requested." Call or write to schedule an appointment. Considers complexity of project, budget, turnaround time and rights purchased. Negotiates rights purchased.
Book Design: Assigns 15-20 freelance design and 20-25 freelance illustration jobs/year. Pays by the hour, $10-35 "depending on dummies, paste-up and complexity."
Jackets/Covers: Assigns 14 freelance design jobs/year. Pays by the hour, $10-35.
Text Illustration: Assigns infrequent freelance jobs/year.
Tips: "Write for a catalogue. Take a preliminary look at some of our titles in a book shop or library. We are also interested in cartography."

CPI, 145 E. 49th St., New York NY 10017. (212)753-3800. Contact: Sherry Olan. Publishes hardcover originals, workbooks and textbooks for ages 4-14. Publishes 40 titles/year; 100% require freelance illustrators. Also uses artists for instructional software, workbooks, textbooks and scientific illustration.
First Contact & Terms: Works on assignment only. Send query letter with flyer, tear sheets and photocopies. Reports in 2 weeks. Samples returned by SASE. Reports back only for future assignment possibilities. No originals returned to artist at job's completion. Buys all rights. Free artist's guidelines.
Text Illustration: Assigns 100 freelance jobs/year. "Submit samples of b&w line and color action subjects. In general, realistic and representational art is required." Pays by the project, $35-200, opaque watercolors or any strong color medium except fluorescents.

***CRAFTSMAN BOOK COMPANY**, 6058 Corte del Cedro, Carlsbad CA 92008. (619)438-7828. Art Director: Bill Grote. Specializes in paperback technical construction books. Publishes 12 titles/year; 50% require freelance illustrators.
First Contact & Terms: Works with 6 freelance artists/year. Send query letter with brochure/flyer or resume, photocopies or tear sheets to be kept on file. Reports back on whether to expect future assignments. Originals returned to artist at job's completion. Buys all rights.
Book Design: Assigns 6 freelance design and 6 freelance illustration jobs/year. Pays by the project, $150 average.
Jackets/Covers: Assigns 6 freelance design and 6 illustration jobs/year. Prefers color comps for illustrations. Pays by the job, $50-350 average.
Tips: "List prices up front. We are using more 4-color. We need artists with full-color background and experience."

THE CROSSING PRESS, Box 207, 22-D Roache Road, Freedom CA 95019. (408)722-0711. Publishers: John and Elaine Gill. Publishes hardcover and paperback cookbooks, how-to, feminist/gay literature, and greeting cards and calendars. Publishes 20 titles/year.
First Contact & Terms: Send photocopies.
Jackets/Covers: Assigns 15 jobs/year. Payment varies up to $200, b&w line drawings and washes.
Text Illustration: Assigns 3-4 jobs/year. Pays $10 and up/illustration or $300-1,000/book for b&w line drawings and washes.

CROWN PUBLISHERS, INC., 225 Park Ave. S., New York NY 10003. Design Director: Ken Sansone. Specializes in trade—fiction, nonfiction and illustrated nonfiction. Publishes 250 titles/year.
First Contact & Terms: Works with 50 artists/year. Prefers local artists. Works on assignment only. Contact only through artist's agent, who should send query letter with brochure showing art style. Samples not filed are returned by SASE. Reports only if interested. Original work returned at job's completion. Considers complexity of project, skill and experience of artist, project's budget, turnaround time and rights purchased when establishing payment. Negotiates rights purchased; rights purchased vary according to project.
Book Design: Assigns 20-30 freelance design and very few freelance illustration jobs/year. Pays by the project.
Jackets/Covers: Assigns 100 freelance design and/or illustration jobs/year. Pays by the project.
Text Illustration: Assigns very few jobs/year.

***CUSTOMBOOK**, 77 Main St., Tappan NY 10983. (914)365-0414. Art Buyer: L. Kranston. Specializes in hardcover history, pictorial books. Publishes 30 titles/year; 40% require freelance illustration.
First Contact & Terms: Works with 30 freelance artists/year. Works on assignment only. Send query letter with brochure showing art style or resume. Samples are filed. Samples not filed are returned by SASE only if requested. Reports back within 1 month. Write to schedule an appointment to show a portfolio. Considers complexity of project and project's budget when establishing payment. Buys one-time rights.
Book Design: Assigns 10 freelance design and 10 freelance illustration jobs/year. Pays by the project, $200-500.
Jackets/Covers: Assigns 20 freelance design and 20 freelance illustration jobs/year. Pays by the project, $100-3,000.

CUSTOM COMIC SERVICES, Box 50028, Austin TX 78763. Art Director: Scott Deschaine. Estab. 1985. Specializes in educational comic books for promotion and advertising for use by business, education, and government. "Our main product is full-color comic books, 16-32 pages long." Prefers pen & ink, airbrush and watercolor. Publishes 12 titles/year.
First Contact & Terms: Works with 24 freelance artists/year. "We are looking for artists who can produce finished artwork for educational comic books from layouts provided by the publisher. They should be able to produce consistently high-quality illustrations for mutually agreeable deadlines, with no exceptions." Works on assignment only. Send query letter with business card and nonreturnable samples to be kept on file. *Samples should be of finished comic book pages*; prefers Photostats. Reports within 6 weeks; must include SASE for reply. Considers complexity of project and skill and experience of artist when establishing payment. Buys all rights.
Text Illustration: Assigns 18 freelance jobs/year. "Finished artwork will be black-and-white, clean, and uncluttered. Artists can have styles ranging from the highly cartoony to the highly realistic." Pays $100-250/page of art.

DATA COMMAND, Box 548, 329 E. Court, Kankakee IL 60901. (815)933-7735. Editor: Patsy Gunnels. Specializes in educational software, teacher's guides, supplements to school curriculum in the language arts, math, science and social studies. Publishes 6 titles/year.
First Contact & Terms: Works with 4 freelance artists/year. Prefers artists with experience in marketing and cover design. Works on assignment only. Send resume and tear sheets, photocopies, slides and photographs. Samples not filed are returned by SASE. Reports back within 3 weeks. Original work not returned after job's completion. Considers complexity of project, skill and experience of artist and project's budget when establishing payment. Buys all rights.
Book Design: Pays by the project.
Jackets/Covers: Assigns 3-4 freelance design and 1-2 freelance illustration jobs/year. Pays by the project, $100 minimum.
Text Illustration: Assigns 1-2 freelance jobs/year. Pays by the project.
Tips: "All our products are aimed at educators and students from kindergarten to twelfth grade."

DECALOGUE BOOK INC., Box 2212, Mount Vernon NY 10550. (914)664-7944. Art Director: Rosemary Campion. Publishes paperback educational materials. Publishes 10 titles/year. Also uses artists for posters, direct mail brochure illustration, catalog and letterhead design. Negotiates pay.
First Contact & Terms: Send resume and samples; local and experienced artists only. SASE. Works on assignment only. Reports back within 1 month on whether to expect future assignments. Provide business card, flyer and tear sheet to be kept on file for possible future assignments. Originals not returned after completing assignment. "Samples supplied to artists we wish to consider." Buys all rights unless negotiated.
Book Design: Assigns 5-10 jobs/year. Uses artists for layout and type spec. Negotiates pay.

Jackets/Covers: Assigns 2 jobs/year. Buys color washes, opaque watercolors, gray opaques, b&w line drawings and washes. Negotiates pay.
Text Illustration: Assigns 5 jobs/year. Buys opaque watercolors, color washes, gray opaques, b&w line drawings and washes. Negotiates pay.
Tips: Buys small number of cartoons for use as cover art in educational material. Negotiates pay.

***DELL PUBLISHING CO., INC.**, 1 Dag Hammerskjald Plaza, New York NY 10017. (212)605-3000. Assistant Art Director: Barbara VanBuskirk. Specializes in hardcover and paperback originals and reprints. Publishes fiction, mass-market paperbacks and original nonfiction. Genres include family sagas, historical romances, suspense, mysteries, children's book, thrillers, occult/horror. Publishes 500 titles/year.
First Contact & Terms: VanBuskirk works with a stable of artists, but she is willing to look at the work of new artists. Portfolio dropoff plicy. Works on assignment only.
Jackets/Cover: Usually prefers representational, realistic style. Pays $1,500-4,000.
Tips: Wants to see printed pieces in portfolios, no student work.

DELMAR PUBLISHERS INC., Box 15-015, 2 Computer Dr. W., Albany NY 12212. Contact: Karen Seebald. Specializes in original hardcovers and paperbacks, especially textbooks—science, computers, health, mathematics, professions and trades. Publishes 50 titles/year.
First Contact & Terms: Works with 35 freelance artists/year. Prefers artists with "professional technical art and photo preparation skills; dummy and page make-up skills; book publishing experience." Prefers technical and medical illustration. Works on assignment only. Send query letter with brochure, resume, tear sheets, Photostats, photocopies, slides and photographs. Samples not filed are returned by SASE. Reports back only if interested. Original work not returned after job's completion. Considers complexity of project, project's budget and turnaround time when establishing payment. Buys all rights.
Book Design: Assigns 15 freelance design and 4-5 freelance illustration jobs/year. Pays by the project, $100-750.
Jackets/Covers: Assigns 15 freelance design and 15 freelance illustration jobs/year. Pays by the project, $200-400.
Text Illustration: Assigns 35 freelance jobs/year. Prefers ink and mylar or vellum; simplified style (axonometrics, schematics, diagrams and anatomical art). Pays by the project, $100-450.
Tips: "Quote prices for samples shown."

***DIAL BOOKS FOR YOUNG READERS**, 2 Park Ave., New York NY 10016. (212)725-1818. Editor: Toby Sherry. Specializes in juveniles and young adult hardcovers. Publishes 40 titles/year. 40% require freelance illustration.
First Contact & Terms: Works with 20 freelance artists/year. Prefers artists with some book experience. Works on assignment only. Send query letter with brochure, tear sheets, Photostats, slides and photographs. Samples are filed. Samples not filed are not returned. Reports back only if interested. originals returned at job's completion. Call to schedule an appointment to show a portfolio, which should include original/final art and tear sheets. Considers complexity of project, skill and experience of artist and project's budget when establishing payment. Rights purchased "depend whether book or picture book, agented or not."
Book Design: Assigns 20 freelance design and 30 freelance illustration jobs/year.
Jackets/Covers: Assigns 2 freelance design and 8 freelance illustration jobs/year.

DILLON PRESS, 242 Portland Ave. S, Minneapolis MN 55415. (612)333-2691. Publisher: Uva Dillon. Specializes in hardcovers of juvenile nonfiction (Gemstone Books) and fiction for school library and trade markets. Publishes 40 titles/year.
First Contact & Terms: Works with 5 freelance artists/year. Works on assignment only. Send query letter with resume and samples to be kept on file. Call or write for appointment to show portfolio. Prefers slides and tear sheets as samples. Samples not filed are returned by SASE. Reports within 6 weeks. Originals not returned to artist. Considers complexity of the project, skill and experience of artist and project's budget when establishing payment. Rights purchased vary according to project.
Book Design: Assigns 10 jobs/year. Pays by the hour or by the project, negotiated so as competitive with other publishers in area.
Jackets/Covers: Assigns 10 freelance design and 10 freelance illustration jobs/year. Pays by the hour or by the project, negotiated so as competitive with other publishers in area.
Text Illustration: Assigns 10 jobs/year. Seeks a variety of media and styles. Pays by the hour or by the project, negotiated so as competitive with other publishers in area.

THE DONNING COMPANY/PUBLISHERS, 5659 Virginia Beach Blvd., Norfolk VA 23502. Publishes hardcover and paperback originals of pictorial histories, science fiction and fantasy, graphic

novels, illustrated cookbooks, general and regional. Publishes 30-35 titles/year. Sample catalog $1.
First Contact & Terms: Works on assignment only. Send query letter to be kept on file for future assignments. Samples returned by SASE. Reports in 4 weeks. Buys first rights. Originals returned to artist at job's completion. Artist supplies overlays for cover artwork. Pays for illustration by the project, $60-2,000.
Tips: "We are concentrating on our graphic novels (high quality, extended-length comics) at present, so we need illustrators who can tell a story in pictures. Actually, our greatest need at present is probably for inkers and colorists." Looks for "believability—even in creating fantastic creatures or scenes; character- or people- oriented art; unique vision rather than slick copies of someone else's style." Common mistakes freelancers make are "sending entire portfolios when we only want samples; sending old work that doesn't reflect current abilities; failing to indicate whether we may keep the samples or if they are expected back; failing to include return postage; omitting a cover letter."

DORCHESTER PUBLISHING CO., INC. (publishers of Leisure Books), Suite 900, 6 E. 39th St., New York NY 10016. (212)725-8811. Production Manager: Lesley Poliner. Specializes in paperbacks, originals and reprints, especially mass market category fiction—historical romance, contemporary women's fiction, western, adventure, horror, mystery, romantic suspense, war. Publishes 144 titles/year.
First Contact & Terms: Works with 24 freelance artists/year. "Should have experience doing paperback covers, be familiar with current design trends." Works on assignment only. Send brochure showing art style or resume, Photostats, slides and photographs. Samples not filed are returned by SASE. Reports within 2 weeks. Call for appointment to show portfolio. Original work returned after job's completion. Considers complexity of project and project's budget when establishing payment. Usually buys first rights, but rights purchased vary according to project.
Jackets/Covers: Pays by the project, $500 minimum.
Tips: "Talented new artists are welcome. Be familiar with the kind of artwork we use on our covers. If it's not your style, don't waste your time and ours."

DOUBLEDAY AND CO. INC., 245 Park Ave., New York NY 10167. (212)492-9780. Head Art Director: Alex Gotfryd. Publishes general adult, juvenile, western, science fiction, mystery, religious and special interest titles. Call Doug Bergstresser and Diana Klemin for interview.
Needs: Uses artists for jackets, inside illustrations.

WM. B. EERDMANS PUBLISHING COMPANY, 255 Jefferson Ave. SE, Grand Rapids MI 49503. (616)459-4591. Art Director: Willem Mineur. Specializes in hardcovers, paperbacks, originals and reprints. Publishes 70 titles/year.
First Contact & Terms: Works on assignment only. Send query letter with slides and photographs. Samples not filed are returned. Reports within 5 days. To show a portfolio, an artist should mail appropriate materials or call or write to schedule an appointment; portfolio should include original/final art. Buys one-time rights.
Jackets/Covers: Uses 40-50 freelance designs/year, 4 or 5 illustrations/year. Payment depends on the project.
Text Illustration: Payment depends on the project.

EMC PUBLISHING, 300 York Ave., St. Paul MN 55101. (612)771-1555. Editor: Eileen Slater. Specializes in educational books and workbooks for schools and libraries. Uses artists for book design and illustration.
First Contact & Terms: Works with 1-2 freelance artists/year. Prefers local artists with book experience. Works on assignment only. Send query letter with resume, business card and samples. Call for appointment to show a portfolio. Reports in 3 weeks. Buys all rights. Negotiates payment by the project.

ENSLOW PUBLISHERS, Box 777, Bloy St. & Ramsey Ave., Hillside NJ 07205. Production Manager: Brian Enslow. Specializes in hardcovers, juvenile young adult nonfiction; science, social issues, biography. Publishes 30 titles/year.
First Contact & Terms: Works with 3 freelance artists/year. Works on assignment only. Send query letter with brochure or photocopies. Samples not filed are not returned. Does not report back. Considers skill and experience of artist when establishing payment. Rights purchased vary according to project.
Book Design: Assigns 3 freelance design jobs/year. Pays by the project.
Text Illustration: Assigns 5 freelance jobs/year. Pays by the project.
Tips: "We're interested in b&w india ink work. We keep a file of samples by various artists to remind us of the capabilities of each."

Close-up

Uri Shulevitz

Children's book illustrator

New York City

"A picture book is a unique art form that requires a special way of visual thinking," says Uri Shulevitz, who has written and illustrated more than 25 children's books. "A picture book says in words only what pictures cannot show. It could not, for example, be read over the radio and be understood fully."

Because they both contain text and illustration, picture books are often confused with storybooks. Shulevitz explains that a story book tells a story with words, while a picture book tells a story mainly with pictures: Beatrix Potter's illustrations add to the story of *The Tale of Peter Rabbit*, but the story can be understood without them, whereas Maurice Sendak describes the 'wild rumpus' in *Where the Wild Things Are* by illustrations, not words.

Shulevitz has created both story and picture books, winning the coveted Caldecott Medal with *The Treasure* and *The Fool of the World and the Flying Ship*. "I take a very simple approach to telling a story," he explains. "I try to be as accurate as possible about what is happening." His book *Dawn* is a good example. The story describes in pictures the unfolding of a day. "I drove out to a lake and made a study of the dawn. I recorded what I felt about the dawn in a diary, organized those feelings, then composed them into a book."

In truth, the process of composing children's books is not that simple. "This type of book has special demands which must be met through sensitivity to the content and words. You as an illustrator must empathize with the text; you must take the text seriously. It must be so real to you that you can see it clearly." Shulevitz visualizes stories through introspection and intuition. "I don't try to remember what happened in my childhood, but I do fall back on my feelings. Those feelings never die out."

Born in Poland, Shulevitz says he started his career in the cradle. "I created abstract expressionism on the walls." Unlike other children, he didn't stop drawing. "I kept drawing because it was important to me. It seemed vital to me."

He began his career by taking his portfolio to Harper & Row, where he was rejected at first. "I took many projects to them, and they were turned down. But I kept trying. The editor criticized this and that, and I finally came up with my first book, *The Moon in My Room*. He published his first six books with Harper & Row and now works with Farrar Straus & Giroux. He feels you must develop a good relationship with your editor, because, as a team, you can help each other to produce a better book.

When submitting your work to a publisher, Shulevitz advises showing a variety of samples that show good draftsmanship and the ability to draw animals and people in different settings and moods. Include both black-and-white and color samples plus jackets you have designed for well-known stories. "Put in what you like to do. Include what you can live with and enjoy doing." He adds that editors choose material largely through "gut response," so your material must convey your joy in creating it. Picture books should be submitted in dummy form to show that you can handle telling a story pictorially, creating a rhythm to the sequence of the pictures.

Always leave samples for the art director's files, since they must match many authors with illustrators. There are three ways to illustrate a book: write your own; retell a story in the public domain; or illustrate someone else's story. If you're on file, you have a chance of being matched with an author whose story requires illustration.

You increase your chances of being published, says Shulevitz, by being both an author and illustrator, but he cautions against insisting upon a package deal at first. Accept assignments to illustrate other people's stories first. Then you can develop a good rapport with the editor and learn how the publishing industry works. But once a manuscript is offered to you, make sure the story interests you. "You must listen to your own feelings. Otherwise your work is not real or worthwhile. If it's not real, the story is just like packaging—no real substance."

If you are rejected by a publisher, Shulevitz advises you to try elsewhere. But first follow up on the rejection by asking the editor what he or she thought worked and what didn't. Editors know what makes successful and satisfying books, and they can offer positive advice that can help you in the future.

No matter if you're a novice or a pro, Shulevitz has these words of advice for you: "Do the best you can do. Don't make compromises. If you do, you won't be able to live with the book. A good book gives pleasure to both the reader and the author."

—Susan Conner

This illustration is from* The Treasure*, which won a Caldecott Award. The book is about a man who has a dream that he will find a treasure under a bridge. He travels far and wide just to find that the treasure was in his home. For this illustration Shulevitz used pen and ink and watercolor.

ENTELEK, Ward-Whidden House/The Hill, Box 1303, Portsmouth NH 03801. Editorial Director: Albert E. Hickey. Publishes paperback education originals; specializing in computer books and software. Clients: business, schools, colleges and individuals.
First Contact & Terms: Query with samples. Prefers previously published work as samples. SASE. Reports in 1 week. Free catalog. Works on assignment only. Provide brochure, flyer and tear sheets to be kept on file for possible future assignments. Pays $300, catalogs and direct mail brochures.
Needs: Works with 1 artist for ad illustrations; 1, advertising design; and 1, illustration, for use on 6 products/year. Especially needs cover designs/brochure designs.

FATHOM PUBLISHING COMPANY, Box 1960, Cordova AK 99574. (907)424-3116. President/Manager: Connie Taylor. Specializes in paperback originals, newsletters, flyers, and cards on commercial fishing, poetry and Alaska. Publishes 2+ titles/year; 100% require freelance illustrators.
First Contact & Terms: Works with 3 freelance artists/year. Prefers local artists. Send query letter with photocopies to be kept on file. No originals. Reports within 2 weeks. Works on assignment only. No originals returned at job's completion. Considers complexity of project and rights purchased when establishing payment. Negotiates rights purchased.
Text Illustration: Assigns 5-10 freelance jobs/year. Prefers pen & ink. Pays by the hour, $15 minimum; by the project, $10-65 average.
Tips: "Bring me an idea that I can sell to the public."

FOREIGN SERVICES RESEARCH INSTITUTE/WHEAT FORDERS, Box 6317, Washington DC 20015-0317. (202)362-1588. Director: John E. Whiteford Boyle. Specializes in paperback originals of modern thought; nonfiction and philosophical poetry.
First Contact & Terms: Works with 2 freelance artists/year. Artist should understand the principles of book jacket design. Works on assignment only. Send query letter to be kept on file. Reports within 15 days. No originals returned. Considers project's budget when establishing payment. Buys first rights or reprint rights.
Book Design: Assigns 1-2 freelance jobs/year. Pays by the hour, $25-35 average.
Jackets/Covers: Assigns 1-2 freelance design jobs/year. Pays by the project, $250 minimum.
Tips: "Submit samples of book jackets designed for and accepted by other clients. SASE, please."

THE FREE PRESS, A DIVISION OF MACMILLAN, INC., 866 Third Ave., New York NY 10022. Manufacturing Director: W.P. Weiss. Specializes in hardcover and paperback originals, concentrating on professional and tradebooks in the social sciences. Publishes 70 titles/year.
First Contact & Terms: Works with around 10 artists/year. Prefers artists with book publishing experience. Works on assignment only. Send query letter with brochure showing art style or resume and nonreturnable samples. Samples not filed are returned by SASE. Reports only if interested. Original work returned after job's completion. Considers complexity of project, skill and experience of artist, project's budget, turnaround time and rights purchased when establishing payment. Buys all rights.
Book Design: Assigns around 70 freelance design jobs/year. Pays by the project.
Jackets/Covers: Assigns around 70 freelance design jobs/year. Pays by the project.
Text Illustration: Assigns around 35 freelance jobs/year. "It is largely drafting work, not illustration." Pays by the project.

***FRIENDSHIP PRESS PUBLISHING CO.**, 475 Riverside Dr., New York NY 10115. (212)870-2280. Art Director: E. Paul Lansdale (Room 552). Specializes in hardcover and paperback originals, reprints and textbooks; "adult and children's books on social issues from an ecumenical perspective." Publishes 10+ titles/year; many require freelance illustration.
First Contact & Terms: Works with 10+ freelance artists/year. Works on assignment only. Send brochure showing art style or resume, tear sheets, Photostats, slides, photographs and "even black & white photocopies. Send nonreturnable samples." Samples are filed. Samples not filed are not returned. Reports back only if interested. Originals returned to artist at job's completion. To show a portfolio, call or write to schedule an appointment, or mail thumbnails, roughs, original/final art, Photostats, tear sheets, final reproduction/product, photographs, slides, transparencies or dummies. Considers skill and experience of artist, project's budget and rights purchased when establishing payment.
Jackets/Covers: Assigns 10 freelance design and 5+ freelance illustration jobs/year. Pays by the project, $300-500.
Text Illustration: Assigns 8+ freelance jobs/year. Pays by the project, $30-70, b&w.

***FROST PUBLISHING GROUP, LTD.**, 117 E. 24th St., New York NY 10010. (212)598-4280. President: Helena Frost. Specializes in textbooks. Publishes titles/year; 100% require freelance illustration.
First Contact & Terms: Works on assignment only. Send query letter with brochure showing art style or tear sheets. Samples are filed. Reports back only if interested. Originals returned to artist at job's

completion. Write to schedule an appointment to show a portfolio, which should include original/final art, tear sheets and slides. Considers complexity of project, project's budget, turnaround time and rights purchased when establishing payment. Buys first rights.
Text Illustration: Assigns many freelance jobs/year.

FUNKY PUNKY AND CHIC, Box 601, Cooper Sta., New York NY 10276. (212)533-1772. Creative Director: R. Eugene Watlington. Specializes in paperback originals on poetry, celebrity photos and topics dealing with new wave, high fashion. Publishes 4 titles/year; 50% require freelance designers; 75% require freelance illustrators.
First Contact & Terms: Works with 20 freelance artists/year. Send query letter with business card, photographs and slides. Samples not kept on file are returned by SASE. Reports only if interested. Write for appointment to show portfolio. No originals returned to artist at job's completion. Considers complexity of project and project's budget when establishing payment. Buys all rights.
Book Design: Assigns 1 freelance job/year. Pays by the project, $100-300 average.
Jackets/Covers: Assigns 3 freelance illustration jobs/year. Pays by the project, $50-75 average.
Text Illustration: Assigns 2 freelance jobs/year. Pays by the project, $50-75 average.

GENERAL HALL INC., 5 Talon Way, Dix Hills NY 11746. Editor, for editorial and advertising work: Ravi Mehra. Publishes hardcover and paperback originals; college texts and supplementary materials. Publishes 4-6 titles/year; 100% require freelance designers, 10% require freelance illustrators.
First Contact & Terms: Local artists only. Query. SASE. Reports in 1-2 weeks. No originals returned to artist at job's completion. Works on assignment only. Provide brochure/flyer to be kept on file for future assignment. Artist provides overlays for color artwork. Buys all rights. Free catalog and artist's guidelines.
Book Design: Assigns 4-6 jobs/year. Uses artists for layout. Pays on job basis.
Jackets/Covers: Assigns 3-5 jobs/year. Pays by the project, $50-100 for design; $25-50 for illustration, b&w line drawings, washes, gray opaques and color washes.
Text Illustration: Assigns 1-2 jobs/year. Pays by the project, $10-25, b&w line drawings, washes and gray opaques.

***C.R. GIBSON**, 32 Knight St., Norwalk CT 06856. (203)847-4543. Creative Services Coordinator: Marilyn Schoenleber. Publishes 100 titles/year. 95% require freelance illustration.
First Contact & Terms: Works with approximately 70 freelance artists/year. Works on assignment—"most of the time." Send tear sheets, Photostats, slides, photographs, sketches and published work. Samples are filed. Samples not filed are returned by SASE. Reports back within 1 month only if interested. Call to schedule an appointment to show a portfolio or mail tear sheets, slides and published samples. Considers complexity of project, project's budget and rights purchased when establishing payment. Negotiates rights purchased.
Book Design: Assigns at least 65 freelance design jobs/year. Pay by the project, $1200 minimum.
Jackets/Covers: Assigns 20 freelance design jobs/year. Pays by the project, $500 minimum.
Text Illustration: Assigns 20 freelance jobs/year. Pays by the hour, $15 minimum. Pays by the project, $1500 minimum.
Tips: "Submit by mail a cross-section of your work-slides, printed samples, finished art no larger than a mailing envelope. Enclosed SASE in the envelope."

GLENCOE PUBLISHING COMPANY, 15319 Chatsworth St., Mission Hills CA 91345. Design Director: Gary Hespenheide. Specializes in hardcover and paperback textbooks in all subjects. Publishes 120-150 titles/year.
First Contact & Terms: Works with 50-60 freelance artists/year. Looking for "quality work." Works on assignment only. Send resume and tear sheets. Reports back only if interested. Original work not returned after job's completion. Considers project's budget when establishing payment. Negotiates rights purchased but generally buys all rights.
Book Design: Assigns 20 freelance design and 50 freelance illustration jobs/year. Pays by the project, $300-1,500.
Jackets/Covers: Assigns 20 freelance design and 30 freelance illustration jobs/year. Pays by project, $200-600.
Text Illustration: Assigns 50 freelance jobs/year. Pays by the project, $50-200.

***GLOBE BOOK COMPANY**, 50 W. 23rd St., New York NY 10010. (212)741-0505. Assistant Art Director: Kathie Vaccaro. Specializes in high school level textbooks or social studies, language arts, science and health. Publishes 80 titles/year; 50% require freelance illustration.
First Contact & Terms: Works with 40 freelance artists/year. Works on assignment only. Send query letter with brochure showing art style or tear sheets, Photostats or any printed samples. Samples are

filed. Samples not filed are not returned. Reports back only if interested. Originals returned to artist at job's completion. Call to schedule an appointment to show a portfolio, or mail original/final art, tear sheets and photographs. Considers complexity of project, project's budget and turnaround time when establishing payment. Buys one-time rights.
Book Design: Assigns several freelance design jobs/year. Pays by the project.
Jackets/Covers: Assigns several freelance design jobs/year. Pays by the project.
Text Illustration: Assigns several freelance jobs/year. Does not want juvenile illustration. Pays by the project.
Tips: "Looking for individuals who can produce four-color, one-color or preseparated work, and four-color maps. We need technical and medical illustrators. Also, need freelance dummying and book and cover designers."

GOLDEN WEST BOOKS, Box 80250, San Marino CA 91108. Contact: Donald Duke. Publishes Americana railroad, steamship and transportation history books. Publishes 5 titles/year; 45% require freelance illustrators.
First Contact & Terms: Buys first rights. Catalog available.
Jackets/Covers: Uses artists for jacket design. Pays $250 minimum.

GREAT COMMISSION PUBLICATIONS, 7401 Old York Rd., Philadelphia PA 19126. (215)635-6515. Art Director: John Tolsma. Publishes paperback original educational and promotional materials for two Presbyterian denominations.
First Contact & Terms: Works with 6 freelance artists/year. Seeks experienced illustrators, usually local artists, but some may be from out-of-state. Works on assignment only. Send query letter with brochure, resume, business card and tear sheets to be kept on file. Material not filed is returned only if requested. Reports only if interested. No originals returned at job's completion. Considers complexity of project, skill and experience of artist, and the project's budget when establishing payment. Buys all rights.
Text Illustration: Assigns 100-150 jobs per year. Prefers stylized and humorous illustration, primarily figure work with some Biblical art; 1-, 2- and 4-color art. Pays by the project, $500 maximum. Assigns from 1-13 projects at one time.

***THE GREEN TIGER PRESS**, 1061 India St., San Diego CA 92101. Art Director: Christy Warwick. Specializes in original paperback gift and children's books with "imaginative plus unusual themes and illustrations." Publishes 10-12 titles/year.
First Contact & Terms: Works with 3-4 freelance artists/year. Works on assignment only. Send query letter with samples to be kept on file "only if it's work we're interested in." Write for artists' guidelines. Prefers slides and photographs as samples. Never send originals. Samples not filed are returned by SASE. Reports back to the artist within 3 months. Originals returned at job's completion. Considers project's budget and rights purchased when establishing payment. Rights purchased vary according to project.
Text Illustration: Assigns 3-6 freelance jobs/year. Payment is usually on a royalty basis.
Tips: "We are looking for artists who have a subtle style and imagination that reflect our aesthetic views. We look for art containing a romantic, visionary or imaginative quality. We also welcome notalgia and the 'world of child' themes. We do not publish science fiction. Artists should have a good variety of samples including animals and human figures."

GUERNICA EDITIONS, Box 633, Station N.D.G., Montreal, Quebec H4A 3R1 Canada. President: Antonio D'Alfonso. Specializes in hardcover and paperback originals of poetry, translations and essays. Publishes 8 titles/year.
First Contact & Terms: Works with 5 local freelance artists/year. Works on assignment only. Send query letter with brochure and photographs to be kept on file. Samples not filed are returned by Canadian SASE. Reports only if interested. Write for appointment to show portfolio. Originals returned to artist at job's completion depending on royalty agreement. Buys all rights.
Book Design: Assigns 3 freelance jobs/year. Pays by the project, $200-500 average.
Jackets/Covers: Assigns 3 freelance design and 3 freelance illustration jobs/year. Pays by the project, $200-500 average.
Text Illustration: Assigns 1-2 freelance jobs/year. Pays by the project, royalties, $200 maximum.

***HARCOURT BRACE JOVANOVICH, INC.**, 1250 Sixth Ave., San Diego CA 92101. (619)699-6443. Art Director: Trade Books: Joy Chu. Specializes in hardcover and paperback originals and reprints. Publishes "general books of all subjects (not including text, school or institutional books)." Publishes 250 titles/year. 100% require freelance illustration.
First Contact & Terms; Works with 200 freelance artists/year. Prefers "experienced artists from all

over the country." Works on assignment only. Send query letter with brochure, tear sheets and Photostats. Samples are filed. Samples not filed are returned by SASE. Reports back within 6 weeks. Originals returned to artist at job's completion. To show a portfolio, mail Photostats, tear sheets, final reproduction/product, photographs and photocopy of book dummy if it's a children's book. Considers complexity of project, skill and experience of art and project's budget when establishing payment. Buys all rights.
Book Design: Assigns 50 freelance design and 50 freelance illustration jobs/year. Pays by the project, $300-600.
Jackets/Covers: Assigns 250 freelance design and 200 freelance illustration jobs/year. Pays by the project, $750-$1,400.
Text Illustration: Assigns 50 freelance jobs/year.Prefers that all work should be rendered on flexible paper. Pays by the project, amount varies.
Tips: "Send samples along with a cover letter and background experience."

***HARLEQUIN BOOKS**, 225 Duncan Mill Rd., Don Mills Ontario M3B 3K9 Canada. (416)445-5860. Contact: Art Director. Publishes 60 titles/month.
First Contact & Terms: Works with 70-80 freelance artists/year. Prefers realistic treatment for covers. Works on assignment only. Send query letter with tear sheets, Photostats, slides or photographs. Samples not filed are returned by SASE. Reports back only if interested. Call or write to schedule an appointment to show a portfolio. Considers complexity of project and skill and experience of artist when establishing payment. Negotiates rights purchased.
Jackets/Covers: Works with 70-80 artists/year. Payment is negotiated.
Tips: "Research the line. We look for images that fit our books."

HARPER & ROW PUBLISHERS, INC., 10 East 53rd St., New York NY 10022. (212)207-7036. Art Director: Harriet Barton. Specializes in fiction and nonfiction hardcover, paperback and picture books for young adults and children. Publishes 165 hardcover and 69 paperback titles/year.
First Contact & Terms: Works with 40 freelance artists/year. Works on assignment only. Send query letter with resume and photocopies (no originals). Samples not filed returned only if requested. Reports only if interested. Originals returned to artist at job's completion. Buys all rights.
Jackets/Covers: Assigns 40 freelance illustration jobs/year. Pays by the project.
Tips: "If possible, visit publishers in person to show a portfolio or go to your library or bookstores to see which books are publishing your type of art. Your work has to hold up to competitor's work—and it has to hold up on its own. Remember, your art is for children."

HARVEST HOUSE PUBLISHERS, 1075 Arrowsmith, Eugene OR 97402. (503)343-0123. Production Editor: Nancy Olson. Specializes in hardcovers and paperbacks of adult nonfiction, children's books, adult fiction and youth material. Publishes 55 titles/year.
First Contact & Terms: Works with 5 freelance artists/year. Works on assignment only. Send query letter with brochure or resume, tear sheets and photographs. Samples are filed. Reports back only if interested. Originals sometimes returned to artist at job's completion. Call or write to schedule an appointment to show a portfolio, or mail tear sheets and final reproduction/product. Considers complexity of project, skill and experience of artist, project's budget and turnaround time when establishing payment. Buys all rights.
Jackets/Covers: Assigns 50 freelance design and 10 freelance illustration jobs/year.
Text Illustration: Assings 5 freelance jobs/year. Pays approximately $125/page.

HEMISPHERE PUBLISHING CORPORATION, 79 Madison Ave., New York NY 10016. Advertising & Promotion Manager: Suzan T. Mohamed. Specializes in hardcover originals, mainly technical and scientific books and journals. Publishes 70 titles/year.
First Contact & Terms: Works with 10-15 freelance artists/year. Prefers experienced direct mail and space ad artists, design through mechanicals. Works on assignment only. Send query letter with brochure, resume and tear sheets. Samples are filed. Samples not filed are not returned. Reports back only if interested. Originals are not returned to artist at job's completion. To show a portfolio, mail roughs, original/final art, tear sheets, final reproduction/product and dummies. Considers complexity of project, project's budget and turnaround time when establishing payment. Buys all rights.
Book Design: Assigns 0-5 freelance jobs/year. Pays by the project, $250.
Jackets/Covers: Assigns 0-5 freelance design jobs/year. Pays $300.
Tips: "Designer are becoming a rarity. Graphic artists nowadays have little or no ability to illustrate, and illustrators have little or no ability for mechanicals. All must become more diversified." Portfolio artists "must update portfolios continously. I don't want to see 10-year-old art."

HEMKUNT PRESS, A-78 Naraina Indl. Area Ph.I, New Delhi 110028 India. Phone: 505079. Director: Mr. G.P. Singh. Specializes in educational text books, illustrated general books for children and also books for adults. Subjects include religion and history. Publishes 30-50 titles/year.
First Contact & Terms: Works with 7-8 freelance artists/year. Works on assignment only. Send query letter with resume and samples to be kept on file. Prefers photographs and tear sheets as samples. Samples not filed are not returned. Reports only if interested. Originals not returned to artist. Considers complexity of the project, skill and experience of artist and project's budget when establishing payment. Buys all rights.
Book Design: Assigns 40-50 titles/year. Payment varies from job to job.
Jackets/Covers: Assigns 30-40 freelance design jobs/year. Payment varies.
Text Illustration: Assigns 30-40 jobs/year. Pays by the project, $50-600.

***T. EMMETT HENDERSON, PUBLISHER**, 130 W. Main St., Middletown NY 10940. (914)343-1038. Contact: T. Emmett Henderson. Publishes hardcover and paperback local history, American Indian, archaeology, and genealogy originals and reprints. Publishes 2-3 titles/year; 100% require freelance designers, 100% require freelance illustrators. Also assigns 5 advertising jobs/year; pays $10 minimum.
First Contact & Terms: Send query letter. No work returned. Reports in 4 weeks. Buys book rights. Originals returned to artist at job's completion. Works on assignment only. Send resume to be kept on file for future assignments. Check for most recent titles in bookstores. Artist supplies overlays for cover artwork. No advance. No pay for unused assigned work.
Book Design: Assigns 2-4 jobs/year. Uses artists for cover art work, some text illustration. Prefers representational style.
Jackets/Covers: Buys 2-4/year. Uses representational art. Pays $20 minimum, b&w line drawings and color-separated work.
Text Illustrations: Pays $10 minimum, b&w. Buys 5-15 cartoons/year. Uses cartoons as chapter headings. Pays $5-12 minimum, b&w.

HERALD PRESS, 616 Walnut Ave., Scottdale PA 15683. (412)887-8500, ext. 244. Art Director: James M. Butti. Specializes in hardcover and paperback originals and reprints of inspirational, historical, juvenile, theological, biographical, fiction and nonfiction books. Publishes 24 titles/year. Catalog available.
First Contact & Terms: Works with 3-4 freelance artists/year. Prefers oils, pen & ink, colored pencil, watercolor, and acrylics. Works on assignment only. Send query letter with brochure or resume, tear sheets, Photostats, slides and photographs. Samples are not filed. Samples not filed are returned by SASE. Reports back within 2 weeks. Originals not returned to artist at job's completion "except in special arrangements." To show a portfolio, mail original/final art, Photostats, tear sheets, final reproduction/product, photographs and slides. "Portfolio should include approximate times different jobs or illustrations had taken." Considers complexity of project, skill and experience of artist and project's budget when establishing payment. Buys all rights.
Jackets/Covers: Assigns 8 freelance design and 8 freelance illustration jobs/year. Pays by the project, $150 minimum.
Text Illustration: Assigns 6 freelance jobs/year. Pays by the project, $300-600 (complete project).
Tips: "We look for a light, free and easy style that will work well in children's books."

***HOLIDAY HOUSE**, 18 E. 53rd St., New York NY 10022. (212)688-0085. Vice President Design and Production: David Rogers. Specializes in hardcover children's books. Publishes 45 titles/year; 30% require freelance illustration.
First Contact & Terms: Works with 10-15 freelance artists/year. Prefers art suitable for children through young adult. Works on assignment only. Samples are filed. Samples not filed are returned by SASE. Reports back only if interested. Originals returned to artist at job's completion. Call to schedule an appointment to show a portfolio, which should include "whatever the artist likes to do and think's he does well." Considers complexity of project, skill and experience of artist and project's budget when establishing payment. Buys one-time rights.
Book Design: Pays by the hour, $15-20.
Jackets/Covers: Assigns 10-15 freelance illustration jobs/year. Prefers watercolor, then acrylics and charcoal/pencil. Pays by the project, $900.
Text Illustrations: Assigns 5-10 jobs/year. Pays royalty.
Tips: "Show samples of everything you do well and like to do."

HOLLOWAY HOUSE PUBLISHING COMPANY, 8060 Melrose Ave., Los Angeles CA 90046. (213)653-8060. President: Ralph Weinstock. Specializes in paperbacks directed to the black reader, i.e., romance books, biographies, fiction, nonfiction, gambling-game books. Publishes 30-50 titles/year.
Needs: Assigns 25-50 book design and jacket/cover illustration jobs/year.

First Contact & Terms: Works with 6-10 freelance artists/year. Professional artists only. Works on assignment only. Send query letter with resume, slides, photostats, photographs or tear sheets to be kept on file. Samples not filed are returned by SASE only if requested. Reports only if interested. Call for appointment to show portfolio. Considers project's budget when establishing payment. Rights purchased vary according to project.

***HENRY HOLT & CO.**, 115 W. 18th St., New York NY 10011. (212)886-9200. Art Director: Robert Reed. Specializes in hardcover and paperback originals and reprints on fiction and nonfiction. Publishes 150 titles/year. 25% require freelance illustration.
First Contact & Terms: Works with 20 freelance artists/year. Works on assignment only. Send query letter with resume and tear sheets. Samples are filed if interested. Reports back "when project suits particular artist." Originals returned to artist at job's completion. Call or write to schedule an appointment to show a portfolio or mail tearsheets, final/reproduction/product, photographs and slides. Considers project's budget and rights purchased when establishing payment.
Jackets/Covers: Assigns 1 or 2 freelance design and 70 freelance illustration jobs/year. Pays by the project, $700 minimum.
Tips: "Be sure you have samples of your art style that can be left with us."

HOMESTEAD PUBLISHING, Box 193, Moose WY 83012. Art Director: Carl Schreier. Specializes in hardcover and paperback originals of nonfiction, natural history, Western art and general Western regional literature. Publishes 3+ titles/year.
First Contact & Terms: Works with 16 freelance artists/year. Works on assignment only. Prefers pen & ink, airbrush, charcoal/pencil and watercolor. Send query letter with samples to be kept on file or write for appointment to show portfolio. Prefers to receive as samples "examples of past work, if available (such as published books or illustrations used in magazines, etc.). For color work, slides are suitable; for b&w technical pen, Photostats. And one piece of original artwork which can be returned." Samples not filed are returned by SASE only if requested. Reports within 10 days. No original work returned after job's completion. Considers complexity of project, skill and experience of artist, project's budget and turnaround time when establishing payment. Rights purchased vary according to project.
Book Design: Assigns 6 freelance jobs/year. Pays by the project, $50-3,500 average.
Jackets/Covers: Assigns 2 freelance design and 4 freelance illustration jobs/year. Pays by the project, $50-3,500 average.
Text Illustration: Assigns 26 freelance jobs/year. Prefers technical pen illustrations, maps (using airbrush, overlays, etc.), watercolor illustrations for children's books, calligraphy and lettering for titles and headings. Pays by the hour, $5-20 average; by the project, $50-3,500 average.
Tips: "We are using more graphic, contemporary designs."

HUMANICS LIMITED, Suite 370, 1389 W. Peachtree St., Atlanta GA 30309. (404)874-2176. Executive Editor: Melanie S. Baffes. Specializes in original paperback textbooks on early childhood education and development. Publishes 10 titles/year. Also uses artists for advertising, direct mail pieces, catalogs and posters.
First Contact & Terms: Works with 5 freelance artists/year. Prefers local artists. Send query letter with resume and business card to be kept on file. Call or write for appointment to show portfolio. Prefers line drawings, finished work, published ads and brochures as samples. Samples returned by SASE. Reports within 2 weeks. Works on assignment only. No originals returned after job's completion. Buys all rights.
Book Design: Assigns 10 freelance jobs/year. Pays by the job; $75 minimum.
Jackets/Covers: Assigns 10 illustration jobs/year. Prefers b&w line drawings and mechanical designs suitable for PMS colors. Pays for illustration by the project, $15-150 average.
Text Illustration: Assigns 10 jobs/year. Prefers line illustrations. Pays by the job; "we negotiate a per book rate; $150 minimum."
Tips: Looks for "excellent ability to draw children, and a childlike quality to artwork."

CARL HUNGNESS PUBLISHING, Box 24308, Speedway IN 46224. (317)244-4792. Editorial Director: Carl Hungness. Publishes hardcover automotive originals. Publishes 2-4 titles/year. Send query letter with samples. SASE. Reports in 2 weeks. Offers $100 advance. Buys book, one-time or all rights. No pay for unused assigned work. Free catalog.

HUNTER HOUSE PUBLISHERS, Box 1302, Claremont CA 91711. Production Manager: Paul J. Frindt. Specializes in hardcover and paperback originals on adult and young adult nonfiction, areas of health and psychology. Publishes 6-11 titles/year.
First Contact & Terms: Works with 2-3 freelance artists/year. Prefers local artists. Works on assignment only. Send query letter with resume, slides and photographs. Samples are filed. Samples not filed

are returned by SASE. Reports back within weeks. Originals not returned to artist at job's completion. Write to schedule an appointment to show a portfolio, which should include thumbnails, roughs, original/final art, photographs, slides, transparencies and dummies. Considers complexity of project, skill and experience of artist, project's budget, turnaround time and rights purchased when establishing payment. Buys all rights.
Book Design: Assigns 2-3 freelance design and 2-4 freelance illustration jobs/year. Pays by the hour, $7.50-15; by the project, $250-750.
Jackets/Covers: Assigns 3-6 freelance design and 4-8 freelance illustration jobs/year. Pays by the hour, $10-25; by the project, $250-750.
Text Illustration: Assigns 1-3 freelance jobs/year. Pays by the hour, $10-18; by the project, $150-450.
Tips: "We work closely with freelancers and prefer designers/illustrators/artists who are open to suggestion, feedback, and creative direction. Much of the time may be spent consulting; we don't appreciate impatient or excessively defensive responses. In book design we are conservative, in cover and illustration rather conceptual and somewhat understated but interested in originality."

HURTIG PUBLISHERS LTD., 10560 105th St., Edmonton, Alberta T5H 2W7 Canada. (403)426-2359. Contact: Editorial Dept. Specializes in hardcover and paperback originals of nonfiction, primarily on Canadian-oriented topics. Publisher of The Canadian Encyclopedia.
First Contact & Terms: Artists must have "considerable experience and be based in Canada." Send query letter to be kept on file; "almost all work is specially commissioned from current sources." Reports within 3 months. Considers complexity of project, skill and experience of artist, project's budget, turnaround time and rights purchased when establishing payment. Rights purchased vary according to project.

***IDEALS PUBLISHING CORP.**, Nelson Place at Elm Hill Pike, Nashville TN 37214. (615)885-8270. Vice President, Publishing: Patricia A. Pingry. Specializes in original children's books.
First Contact & Terms: Works with 10-12 freelance artists/year. Works on assignment only. Send query letter with brochure showing art style, tear sheets, Photostats, slides and photographs. Samples are filed. Samples not filed are returned by SASE only if requested. Does not report back. Originals not returned to artist at job's completion. To show a portfolio, mail appropriate materials. Considers skill and experience of artist and project's budget when establishing payment. Buys all rights.
Book Design: Pays by the project.

IGNATIUS PRESS, Catholic Publisher, 2515 McAllister St., San Francisco CA 94118. Production Editor: Carolyn Lemon. Art Editor: Roxanne Lum. Catholic theology and devotional books for lay people, priests and religious readers.
First Contact & Terms: Works on assignment only. Will send art guidelines "if we are interested in the artist's work." Accepts previously published material. Send brochure showing art style or resume and photocopies. Samples not filed are not returned. Reports only if interested. To show a portfolio, mail appropriate materials; "we will contact you if interested." Pays on acceptance.
Jackets/Covers: Buys cover art from freelance artists. Prefers Christian symbols/calligraphy and religious illustrations of Jesus, saints, etc. (used on cover or in text). "Simplicity, clarity, and elegance are the rule. We like calligraphy, occasionally incorporated with Christian symbols. We also do covers with type and photography." Prefers pen & ink, charcoal/pencil, and calligraphy. "Since we are a nonprofit Catholic press, we use 'donated' work."
Tips: "We are thinking of incorporating more fine art (pen & ink, sketches, whatever) into our cover designs. I do not want to see any schmaltzy religious art."

***INCENTIVE PUBLICATIONS INC.**, 3835 Cleghorn Ave., Nashville TN 37215. (615)385-2934. Art Director: Susan Eaddy. Specializes in supplemental teacher resource material. Workbooks and arts and crafts books for children K-8. Publishes 15-30 titles/year; 40% require freelance illustration.
First Contact & Terms: Works with 4-5 freelance artists/year. Works on assignment only primarily with local artist. Send query letter with brochure showing art style, resume, tear sheets and/or Photostats. Samples are filed. Samples not filed are returned by SASE. Reports back within 3 weeks. Originals not returned to artist at job's completion. Call or write to schedule an appointment to show a portfolio, which should include original/final art, Photostats, tear sheets and final reproduction/product. Considers complexity of project, project's budget and rights purchased when establishing payment. Buys all rights.
Jackets/Covers: Assigns 4-6 freelance illustration jobs/year. Prefers four-color covers—any medium. Pays by the project, $200-350.
Text Illustration: Assigns 4-6 freelance jobs/year. Black line art only. Pays by the project, $175-600.
Tips: "We look for a whimsical, *not* cartoony, style of line art that respects the integrity of the child."

***INNER TRADITIONS INTERNATIONAL**, One Park St., Rochester VT 05767. (802)767-3174. Art Director: Estella Arias. Specializes in hardcover and paperback originals and reprints on estoeric philosophy, religion, metaphysics, healing, health, cookbooks ("New Age Books"). Publishes 25 titles/year; all require freelance illustration.
First Contact & Terms: Works with 25 freelance artists/year. Works on assignment only. Send resume, slides and photographs. Samples are filed. Samples not filed are returned by SASe only if requested. Reports back within 2 weeks only if interested. Originals sometimes returned to artist at job's completion. Call to schedule an appointment to show a portfolio, or mail photographs, slides and transparencies. Considers project's budget when establishing payment. Buys all rights.
Book Design: Assigns 25 freelance design and 25 freelance illustration jobs/year. Pays by the project, $250-500.
Jackets/Covers: Assigns 25 freelance design and 25 freelance illustration jobs/year. Pays by the project, $250-600.
Text Illustration: Assigns 8 freelance jobs/year. Pays by the project.

INSTITUTE OF INTERNATIONAL EDUCATION, Communications Division, 809 United Nations Plaza, New York NY 10017. Senior Production Editor: Ellen Goodman. Specializes in information flyers, paperback catalogs and statistical analysis; also annual report. Publishes 15 titles/year.
First Contact & Terms: Work freelance artists. Send query letter with brochure, resume and samples to be kept on file. Write for appointment to show portfolio.
Book Design: Uses artists for various jobs depending on project. Pays by the project.
Text Illustration: Assigns "a few" jobs/year.

***INSTRUCTIONAL FAIR**, Box 1650, Grand Rapids MI 49501. Editor: Jackie Servis. Publisher of educational material, elementary level, all curriculum areas. These are supplemental materials. Clients: elementary school teachers.
First Contact & Terms: Works with several freelance artists/year. Works on assignment only. Send query letter with Photostats. Samples are filed. Samples not filed are returned only if requested by artists. Reports back within 1-2 months, only if interested. Write to schedule an appointment to show a portfolio, or mail original/final art and final reproduction/product. Pays by the project, amount negotiated. Considers client's budget and how work will be used when establishing payment. Buys all rights.

INTERNATIONAL MARINE PUBLISHING CO. Seven Seas Press, Box 220, Camden ME 04843. (207)236-4837. Production Director: Molly Mulhern. Specializes in hardcovers and paperbacks on marine (nautical) topics. Publishes 25 titles/year.
First Contact & Terms: Works with 12 freelance artists/year. Prefers local artists. Works on assignment only. Send resume and tear sheets. Samples are filed. Reports back only if interested. Originals are not returned to artist at job's completion. Write to schedule an appointment to show a portfolio, which should include roughs and tear sheets; "then follow with phone call." Considers project's budget when establishing payment. Buys one-time rights.
Book Design: Assigns 20 freelance design and 2 freelance illustration jobs/year. Pays by the project, $50-450.
Jackets/Covers: Assigns 15-25 freelance design and 3 freelance illustration jobs/year. Pays by the project, $200-700.
Text Illustration: Assigns 3 freelance jobs/year. Prefers technical drawings. Pays by the hour, $15-40.
Tips: "Write with a resume and sample; then follow with a call; then come by to visit."

JUDSON PRESS, American Baptist Churches USA, Board of Educational Ministries, Publishing Division, Valley Forge PA 19481. Senior Artist: David E. Monyer. Specializes in paperbacks on religious themes (inspirational, Christian education, church administration, missions). Publishes 10-12 titles/year; 90% require freelance cover designers.
First Contact & Terms: Works with 4 or more freelance artists/year. Artists with book cover experience only. Prefers realistic style "with a modern flair--but not too stylized." Prefers pen & ink, then airbrush, colored pencil, acrylics and markers. Send query letter, brochure/flyer, resume and samples to be kept on file. Prefers examples of book cover designs as samples. Samples not kept on file are returned by SASE. "We don't report on acceptance or rejection, but keep samples on file." Works on assignment only. No originals returned to artist at job's completion.
Jackets/Covers: Assigns 8-10 design and 1-2 illustration jobs/year. Prefers bold graphics, title dominant, for cover designs. Pays by the job, $400 average; "We pay for type and stats."
Text Illustration: Assigns 1-2 freelance jobs/year. Prefers realistic line drawings. Pays by the project, $40-100/illustration.
Tips: "In your portfolio, include bold graphics and realistic illustration with a contemporary style."

KALEIDOSCOPIX, INC., Children's Book Division, Box 389, Franklin MA 02038-0389. (617)528-6211. Editor: J.A. Kruza. "Kaleidoscopix, Inc. has two new divisions: book publishing and audio cassette publishing. The products of both are marketed to an upscale audience like tourists through seacoast gift stores. Titles include historical and nautical material relevant to the area, tourism guides, and children's books for ages 3-7." Our books feature stories which present a problem that is solved by the hero through his/her own effort."
First Contact & Terms: "We are reviewing manuscripts and/or illustrations. And we are contracting with effective communicators with either in-depth knowledge, or storytelling or singing ability."
Text Illustration: Send a summary letter with slides, photographs, Photostats and photocopies. Samples are filed. Samples not filed are returned by SASE. Reports back within 15-45 days. Call to schedule an appointment to show a portfolio, which should include original/final art, final reproduction/product and photographs. Buys all rights. Pays $25 and up, b&w; $50 and up, color, inside; on publication. Pays by the project, $300-1,000.
Tips: "Photocopies of representative style and technique show what your skills are. Sometimes an IBM full color photocopy or slide shows your sense for color. Send them."

KAR-BEN COPIES, INC., 6800 Tildenwood Lane, Rockville MD 20852. Editor: Madeline Wikler. Specializes in hardcovers and paperbacks on juvenile Judaica. Publishes 8 titles/year.
First Contact & Terms: Works with 3-5 freelance artists/year. Send query letter with Photostats or tear sheets to be kept on file or returned. Samples not filed are returned by SASE. Reports within 2 weeks only by SASE. Originals returned after job's completion. Considers skill and experience of artist and turnaround time when establishing payment. Buys all rights.
Text Illustration: Assigns 3-5 freelance jobs/year. Pays by the project, $500-1,500 average, or royalty.

B. KLEIN PUBLICATIONS INC., Box 8503, Coral Springs FL 33065. Editor: Bernard Klein. Publishes reference books, such as the *Guide to American Directories*. Publishes approximately 15-20 titles/year.
Needs: Uses artists for jacket design and direct mail brochures. Submit resume and samples. Pays $50-300.

KNEES PAPERBACK PUBLISHING CO., 4115 Marshall St., Dallas TX 75210. (214)948-3613. Managing Editor: Dorothy J. Watkins. Specializes in paperback originals on poetry, children's and prose books. Publishes 2 titles/year; 15% require freelance designers; 15% require freelance illustrators.
First Contact & Terms: Works with 2 freelance artists/year. Local artists only. Send query letter with business card to be kept on file. Prefers slides as samples. Reports within 2 weeks. Works on assignment only. No originals returned to artist at job's completion. Considers complexity of project, and skill and experience of artist when establishing payment. Buys one-time rights or negotiates.
Book Design: Assigns 7 freelance jobs/year. Pays by the hour, the project or negotiates.
Tips: Artists should "always adhere to the given schedule." Current trends in the field are toward "more abstract design." Especially looks for "creativity, form and projection" when reviewing samples.

LACE PUBLICATIONS, Box 10037, Denver CO 80210-0037. Managing Editor: Artemis OakGrove. Specializes in paperbacks of lesbian fiction. Publishes 5 titles/year.
First Contact & Terms: Works with 10-15 freelance artists/year. Lesbians or sexually-sensitive women only. Prefers realistic style. Prefers pen & ink, airbrush, charcoal/pencil and watercolor. Works on assignment only. Send query letter with resume, b&w photographs or photocopies to be kept on file except for "the ones I don't like." Samples not filed are returned by SASE. Reports within 1 month. Original work returned after the job's completion; cover art returned only if requested. Considers complexity of project, skill and experience of artist, and project's budget when establishing payment. Rights purchased vary according to project; all rights purchased on cover art.
Jackets/Covers: Assigns 5 freelance design and varying number of freelance illustration jobs/year. Pays by the project. $75-150.
Text Illustration: Pays $75 minimum.
Tips: "I wish trends would develop that quality female illustrators would concentrate on really good female figures."

***DAVID S. LAKE PUBLISHER INC.**, (formerly Fearon/Pitman Publishing Inc.,) 19 Davis Dr., Belmont CA 94002. Director of Design: Eleanor Mennick. Publishes special education, teacher-aid, professional and management training books. Query.
Covers and Text Illustration: Uses artists for 1, 2 and 4-color work. Also needs experienced book designers and production people.

LIBRARIES UNLIMITED, Box 3988 Englewood CO 80155-3988. (303)770-1220. Marketing Director: Shirley Lambert. Specializes in hardcover and paperback original reference books concerning library science and school media for librarians, educators and researchers. Publishes 45 titles/year.
First Contact & Terms: Works with 4-5 freelance artists/year. Works on assignment only. Send query letter with resume and photocopies. Samples not filed are returned only if requested. Reports within 2 weeks. No originals returned to artist at job's completion. Considers complexity of project, skill and experience of artist, and project's budget when establishing payment. Buys all rights.
Book Design: Assigns 2-4 freelance illustration jobs/year. Pays by the project, $100 minimum.
Jackets/Covers: Assigns 45 freelance design jobs/year. Pays by the project, $250 minimum.
Tips: "We look for the ability to draw or illustrate without overly-loud cartoon techniques. We need the ability to use two-color effectively, with screens and screen builds. We ignore anything sent to us that is in four-color. We also need a good feel for typefaces, and we prefer experience with books."

LIFE CYCLE BOOKS, Box 792, Lewiston NY 14092-0792. (416)690-5860. Manager: Paul Broughton. Specializes in reprint paperbacks, pamphlets and brochures. Publishes 4-8 titles/year.
First Contact & Terms: Works with 2-3 freelance artists/year. Works on assignment only. Send query letter with resume, tear sheets, Photostats, photocopies, slides and photographs. Samples not filed are returned by SASE. Reports back only if interested. Original work not returned after job's completion. Considers complexity of project, skill and experience of artist and project's budget when establishing payment. Negotiates rights purchased.
Jackets/Covers: Assigns 2-3 freelance illustration jobs/year. Pays by the project, $200-500.

LITTLE, BROWN AND COMPANY, 34 Beacon St., Boston MA 02106. (617)227-0730. Art Director: Steve Snider. Specializes in trade hardcover and paperback originals and reprints. Publishes 300 titles/year. 50% require freelance illustration.
First Contact & Terms: Works with approximately 50 freelance artists/year. Works on assignment only. Send query letter with brochure, resume, tear sheets, Photostats and photographs. Samples are filed. Samples not filed are returned only if requested by artist. Reports back only if interested. Originals returned to artist at job's completion. Call to schedule an appointment to show a portfolio, which should include original/final art, tear sheets, final reproduction/product and photographs. Considers complexity of project, project's budget and turnaround time when establishing payment.
Jackets/Covers: Assigns freelance design and illustration jobs/year. Pays by the project, $700 minimum.

***LIVING FLAME PRESS**, 325 Rabro Dr., Hauppauge NY 11788. (516)348-5251. Manager: Theresa Rinere. Specializes in paperback originals that deal with prayer, spiritual growth, family life and most topics that are relevant to contemporary Christians. Also branching out into other areas of publishing, such as fiction and children's books.
First Contact & Terms: Artists must have at least 1 year of experience. Works on assignment only. Send resume and samples. Samples not filed are returned only if requested. Reports back within 2 months only if interested. Originals sometimes returned to artist at job's completion. Call or write to schedule an appointment to show a portfolio, which should include original/final art, tear sheets and photographs. Considers project's budget when establishing payment. Negotiates rights purchased.
Tips: "We need artists who have the ability to listen and who are willing to work with use in creating book covers."

LLEWELLYN PUBLICATIONS, Box 64383, St. Paul MN 55164. Art Director: Terry Buske. Specializes in paperback originals. Publishes metaphysical, astrology and New Age books. Works with at least 6 freelance artists/year. Uses artists for book cover designs and inside art, color and b&w. Prefers realistic metaphysical themes—mostly people; airbrush, pen & ink, watercolors, acrylics and oils.
First Contact & Terms: Works on assignment only. Send query letter with samples to be kept on file. No preference regarding types of samples, but "must be professionally submitted. No roughs, fragments or photocopies of other than excellent quality. Do not send actual artwork." Samples not kept on file are returned by SASE only if requested. Reports within 2 weeks after receipt of submission if SASE is supplied. Negotiates payment. Considers project's budget, skill and experience of artist, and rights purchased when establishing payment. Negotiates rights purchased.
Jackets/Covers: Assigns 25 freelance illustration jobs/year. Pays by the project, $300-600.
Text Illustration: Assigns 15 freelance jobs/year. Prefers pen & ink. Pays per illustration, $20-40.
Tips: "People expect more of a high-tech, photorealistic or refined look for the product. We are interested in artists who express our themes in more general terms reaching a broad audience. We are interested in realistic (photorealism) art." Especially looks for "technique and professionalism" in artist's work. Uses many airbrush paintings.

©1985 Leslie Rogalski

Illustrator Leslie Rogalski sold first rights to Llewellyn Publications for use of her rendering of a Tarot card for The Magic of the Tarot. *Rogalski explains, "The artwork was done for myself. Art director Terry Buske bought it from my portfolio, since it related so directly to their reprinting of the book." The Havertown, Pennsylvania artist was the model for the piece, rendered in acrylic on illustration board. "I was even recognized in a book store which sold the book!" She learned of the St. Paul, Minnesota publisher through the* Artist's Market. *Buske notes that Rogalski "met her deadline, is always willing to work together with me on ideas and is very professional."*

LODESTAR BOOKS, imprint of E.P. Dutton, 2 Park Ave., New York NY 10016. (212)725-1818. Senior Editor: Rosemary Brosnan. Publishes young adult fiction (12-16 years) and nonfiction hardcovers, fiction and nonfiction for ages 9-11 and 10-14 years and nonfiction picture books. Publishes 20-22 titles/year.
First Contact & Terms: Send query letter with samples or drop off portfolio. Especially looks for "knowledge of book requirements, previous jackets, good color, strong design and ability to draw people and action" when reviewing samples. Prefers to buy all rights.
Jackets/Covers: Assigns approximately 10-12 jackets/year. Pays $600 minimum, color.
Tips: In young adult fiction, there is a trend toward "covers that are more realistic with the focus on one or two characters. In nonfiction, strong, simple graphic design, often utilizing a photograph. Three-color jackets are popular for nonfiction; occasionally full color is used."

LOLLIPOP POWER BOOKS, Box 277, Carrboro NC 27510. Contact: Anne Weston. Publishes alternative picture books for ages 2-8, nonsexist, multi-racial.
First Contact & Terms: Works with 1 freelance artist/year. Works on assignment only. Send brochure showing art style and photocopies. Samples are filed. Samples not filed are returned if accompanied by a SASE. "We file until we have a manuscript ready, then send out letters to all our artists to see if they want to submit illustrations for that book." Considers project's budget when establishing payment.
Book Design: Pays by the project.
Jackets/Covers: Pays by the project.
Text Illustration: Pays by the project.

***LOWELL MOSS PUBLISHING,INC.**, #1260, 870 Market, San Francisco CA 94102. (415)956-5966. President: Lowell Moss. Specializes in paperbacks emphasizing how-to, children, directories and guidelines. Publishes 100 titles/year. 10% require freelance illustration.
First Contact & Terms: Works with 10 freelance artists/year. Prefers prior successful book experience. Works on assignment only. Send brochure, resume, tear sheets, Photostats, slides, photocopies and photographs. Samples are filed. Samples not filed are returned by SASE. Reports back only if interested. Originals returned upon job's completion. To show a portfolio, mail thumbnails, original/final art and final reproduction/product. Considers complexity of project, skill and experience of artist, project's

budget, turnaround time, and rights purchased when establishing payment. Negotiates rights purchased.
Book Design: Assigns 10 freelance design and 15 freelance illustration jobs/year. Pays by the hour, $15-50; by the project, $200-2,500.
Jackets/Covers: Assigns 50 freelance design and 10 freelance illustration jobs/year. Pays by the hour, $15-50; by the project, $200-1,000.
Text Illustration: Assigns 10 freelance jobs/year. Pays by the hour, $15-50; by the project, $200-2,500.
Tips: "Projects can be any subject or style. When a book our regular artists cannot do is contracted for, we look through our files to match an artist's skills and experience with the project at hand."

MCDOUGAL, LITTELL & COMPANY, 1560 Sherman Ave., Evanston IL 60201. (312)869-2300. Senior Designer: Mary MacDonald. Specializes in elementary-high school textbooks.
First Contact & Terms: Send query letter with brochure or resume, tear sheets, Photostats, slides and photographs. Samples are filed. Samples not filed are returned. Call or write to schedule an appointment to show a portfolio. Considers complexity of project, skill and experience of artist and project's budget when establishing payment. Negotiates rights purchased.

MCGRAW-HILL SCHOOL DIVISION, 1200 N. W. 63rd St., Oklahoma City OK 73116. (405)840-1444. Contact: Louis Stewart. Specializes in hardcover and paperback original and reprint textbooks in the language arts (K-8th grade). Publishes 2,000 titles; 75% require freelance illustrators. Also uses artists for occasional posters and other teaching aids.
First Contact & Terms: Works with 100 artists/year. Works only with published artists experienced in book illustration. Send brochure/flyer and samples or actual work; submit portfolio for review. Prefers color illustrations, either originals or tear sheets, as samples. Samples returned by SASE. Reports in 2 weeks. Works on assignment only. No originals returned to artist at job's completion. Buys all rights.

MACMILLAN PUBLISHING CO., School Division, 866 Third Ave., New York NY 10022. (212)702-7925. Design Director: Zlata Paces. Publishes hardcover and auxiliary originals and reprints for elementary and high schools. Publishes 250 titles/year; 30% of which require freelance designers; 80% use freelance illustrators.
First Contact & Terms: Send letter of inquiry, resume and samples. Prefers pen & ink, watercolor, acrylics, collage and paper sculpture collage. Prefers tear sheets, stats, color photocopies, etc. as samples or drop off portfolio (overnight). Samples will be kept on file for future reference unless accompanied by SASE. Works on assignment only. Originals returned to artist at job's completion.
Book Design: Assigns 10 jobs/year. Uses freelance artists for layout and type specs. Pays by the hour, $15-20 average; also pays by the day.
Jackets/Covers: Assigns 30 jobs/year. Pays for illustration by the project; $200-400 average.
Text Illustration: Assigns 800-1,500 jobs/year. Pays by the project, "depends on assignment."

MARVEL BOOKS, 387 Park Ave. S., New York NY 10028. Art Director: Lillian Lovitt. Publishes liscened product children's books. Publishes 50-100 titles/year.
First Contact & Terms: Works with 50 freelance artists/year. Works on assignment only. Send query letter with tear sheets and photocopies. Samples not filed are not returned. Reports back only if interested. Originals are returned to the artist at job's completion. Considers complexity of project, skill and experience of artist, project's budget, turnaround time and rights purchased when establishing payment. Buys all rights.
Book Design: Assigns 10-20 freelance design and 50-100 freelance illustration jobs/year. Pays by the project, $2,000-8,000.
Jackets/Covers: Assigns 10-20 freelance design and 50-100 freelance illustration jobs/year. Pays by the project, $500-1,000.
Tips: "Send only your best work in photocopy form with card that has sample on it."

MASTERY EDUCATION, 85 Main St., Watertown MA 02172. Managing Editor: Elena Wright. Specializes in paperback originals of teacher-directed instruction books. Publishes 10 titles/year, K-8th grade materials.
First Contact & Terms: Works with 10 artists/year. Artists should have experience in educational textbooks. Works on assignment only. Send resume, tear sheets and photocopies. Samples not filed are returned by SASE. Reports only if interested. No originals returned to artist at job's completion. Considers complexity of project and project's budget when establishing payment. Buys all rights.
Book Design: Assigns 2 freelance design jobs/year. Pays by the project.
Text Illustration: Assigns many of jobs/year. Pays by the project.
Tips: "Look at what is good in children's trade book art and show how you can transplant that excitement into elementary textbooks. School books require realistic line art of children at exact proportions

for each year of age. No cartoon-style exaggerated features. We need real-looking kids, of all races, depicted to show their dignity and intelligence."

MECKLER PUBLISHING CORPORATION, 11 Ferry Ln. W., Westport CT 06880-5808. (203)226-6967. Marketing Director: Jim Wright. Specializes in hardcover and paperback textbooks on computers, libraries, information and publishing. Publishes 50 titles/year.
First Contact & Terms: Works with 3 or more freelance artists/year. Send query letter with brochure. Samples are not filed. Samples not filed are returned by SASE. Does not report back. Originals not returned to artist at job's completion unless requested. To show a portfolio, mail appropriate materials. Buys all rights.
Tips: "We buy promotion design as well as occasional covers, illustrations, etc."

MEDIA PROJECTS INCORPORATED, Suite 340, 305 2nd Ave., New York NY 10003. (212)777-4510. Contact: Art Director. Specializes in hardcover and paperback originals on juveniles, lifestyles and cookery. Publishes 15 titles/year.
First Contact & Terms: Works with 3-6 freelance artists/year. Works on assignment only. Send query letter with brochure showing art style or resume and tear sheets, Photostats, photocopies, slides and photographs. Samples not filed are returned by SASE. Reports within 2 weeks. Original work returned at job's completion. Considers project's budget when establishing payment. Negotiates rights purchased.
Book Design: Assigns 10 freelance design and 10 freelance illustration jobs/year. Pays by the project, negotiable amount.
Jackets/Covers: Assigns 10 freelance design and 10 freelance illustration jobs/year. Pays by the project, negotiable amount.
Text Illustration: Assigns 10 freelance jobs/year. Prefers line drawings. Pays by the project, negotiable amount.

***METAMORPHOUS PRESS INC.**, 3249 NW 29th Ave., Box 10616, Portland OR 97210. (503)228-4972. Publisher: David Balding. Specializes in hardcover and paperback originals, general trade books, mostly nonfiction. "We are a general book publisher for a general audience in North America." Publishes at least 12 titles/year.
First Contact & Terms: Works with a varying number of freelance artists/year. "We're interested in what an artist can do for us—not experience with others." Works on assignment only. Send query letter with brochure, business card, Photostats, photographs, and tear sheets to be kept on file. Samples not filed are returned by SASE. Reports within a few days usually. Originals returned to artist at job's completion if requested. Considers complexity of project and project's budget when establishing payment. Rights purchased vary according to project.
Book Design: Rarely assigns freelance jobs. "We negotiate payment on an individual basis according to project."
Jackets/Covers: Will possibly assign 5-10 jobs in both freelance design and freelance illustration this year. Payment would vary as to project and budget.
Text Illustration: Assigns 5-10 freelance jobs/year. Payment varies as to project and budget.

MILADY PUBLISHING CORP., 3839 White Plains Rd., Bronx, New York NY 10467. (800)223-8055. Editor: Mary Healy. Publishes textbooks and audiovisual aids for vocational schools.
First Contact & Terms: Works on assignment only. Send query letter with Photostats to be kept on file. Samples not filed are returned by SASE. Reports only if interested. Write for appointment to show portfolio. Pays by the hour, $5 minimum; by the project depending on nature of project and length of time needed for completion. Considers complexity of the project, client's budget and skill and experience of artist when establishing payment. Buys all rights. Catalog costs $1.
Needs: Works with 3 freelance artists/year during overloads. Especially important is ability to produce accurate and neat mechanicals and clean line illustrations. Uses technical and "fashion features and hairstyles" illustrations.
Tips: "Build up skills in illustrating hands and hair."

MODERN CURRICULUM PRESS, 13900 Prospect Rd., Cleveland OH 44136. (216)238-2222. Art Director: John K. Crum. Specializes in supplemental text books, readers and workbooks. Publishes 100 titles/year. Also needs local artists for advertising and mechanicals.
First Contact & Terms: All freelance. Works on assignment only. Send resume and tear sheets of children to be kept on file. Samples not kept on file are returned by SASE. Reports back only if interested. Buys all rights.
Book Design: Assigns 6-10 freelance jobs/year. Uses artists for layout, mechanicals, type specs. Pays by the project, on acceptance. Payment varies.
Covers: Pays by the project; payment varies.

Text Illustration: Prefers animated real life themes "nothing too cartoony; must be accurate." Pays by the project; payment varies.
Tips: Looks for "professional, serious illustrators who know production techniques. Don't drag in oil paintings, sculpture, etc."

MODERN PUBLISHING, 155 East 55th St., New York NY 10022. (212)826-0850. Art Director: Frank Stinga. Specializes in hardcovers and paperbacks and coloring books. Publishes approximately 20 titles/year.
First Contact & Terms: Works with 15 freelance artists/year. Works on assignment only. Send query letter with resume and samples. Samples not filed are returned only if requested. Reports only if interested. Original work not returned at job's completion. Considers turnaround time and rights purchased when establishing payment. Buys all rights.
Jackets/Covers: Pays by the project, $100-200 average per cover, "usually 4 books per series."
Text Illustration: Pays by the project, $15-20 average per page (line art), "48-382 pages per book, always 4 books in series."

***WILLIAM MORROW & CO. INC.**, (Lothrop, Lee, Shepard Books), 105 Madison Ave., New York NY 10016. (212)889-3050. Art Director: Cindy Simon. Specializes in hardcover originals and reprints. Publishes 70 titles/year. 100% require freelance illustration.
First Contact & Terms: Works with 30 freelance artists/year. Works on assignment only. Send query letter with resume and samples, "followed by call." Samples are filed. Reports back within 3-4 weeks. Originals returned to artist at job's completion. Portfolio should include original/final art and dummies. Considers complexity of project and project's budget when establishing payment. Negotiates rights purchased.
Book Design: "Most design is done on staff." Assigns 1 or 2 freelance design jobs/year. Pays by the project.
Jackets/Covers: Assigns 1 or 2 freelance design jobs/year. Pays by the project.
Text illustration: Assigns 70 freelance jobs/year. Pays by the project.
Tips: "Be familiar with our publications."

MOTT MEDIA INC., PUBLISHERS, 1000 E. Huron, Milford MI 48042. Contact: Geroge Mott. Publishes hardcover and paperback Christian books and textbooks. Publishes 20-25 titles/year. Also uses artists for posters and mailables.
First Contact & Terms: Works on assignment only. Reports back in one month on future assignment possibilities. Provide resume, flyer, tear sheet and letter of inquiry to be kept on file for possible future assignments. SASE. Buys all rights. No originals returned to artist at job's completion. Artist supplies all color overlays. Pays ½ on acceptance of sketch and ½ on submission of finished art. Free catalog.
Needs: Special need for book cover design, and internal illustration for children's books. Assigns 20-25 book design jobs/year. Minimum payment: $400 + for complete cover art and mechanicals; $150 for inside b&w sketch.

***MOUNTAIN LION, INC.**, Box 257, Route 206, Rocky Hill NJ 08553. (609)924-8369. Managing Editor: Martha Wickenden. Produces hardcover and paperback originals for publishers on sports, health, how-to, fitness and large format pictorials, 10-12 titles/year published; ⅓ require freelance illustration.
First Contact & Terms: Works with 4-5 freelance artists/year. Prefers artists who have some experience with books/publishing. Works on assignment only. Send query letter with resume, tear sheets, Photostats, duplicate slides and photographs or other samples. Samples are filed. Samples not filed are returned only if requested. Reports back within 1 week. Originals not returned to artist at job's completion. To show a portfolio, mail thumbnails, Photostats, tear sheets, final reproduction/product, duplicate photographs and slides. Considers complexity of project, skill and experience of artist, project's budget, turnaround time and rights purchased. Negotiates rights purchased.
Book Design: Assigns 10-12 freelance design and 4-5 freelance illustration jobs/year. Pays by the hour, $15.
Jackets/Covers: Assigns 10-12 freelance design and 4-5 freelance illustration jobs/year. Pays by the hour, $15.
Text Illustration: Assigns 4-5 freelance jobs/year. Pays by the hour, $12.
Tips: "Flexibility is a must. We work with individuals who are professional in their approach: meet deadlines, take direction, bring creativity, solve problems."

JOHN MUIR PUBLICATIONS, Box 613, Santa Fe NM 87504. (505)982-4078. President: Ken Luboff. Publishes trade paperback nonfiction. "We specialize in travel books and auto repair manuals and are always actively looking for new illustrations in these fields." Prefers pen & ink, colored pencil, acrylics and calligraphy. Publishes 26 titles/year.

First Contact & Terms: Works with 5-6 freelance artists/year. Prefers local artists. Send query letter with resume and samples to be kept on file. Write for appointment to show portfolio. Accepts any type of sample "as long as it's professionally presented." Samples not filed are returned by SASE. Reports within months; "it depends on how harried our schedule is at the time." Originals not returned at job's completion. Considers complexity of project, skill and experience of artist, project's budget, turnaround time and rights purchased when establishing payment. Buys all rights.
Jackets/Covers: Assigns 25-30 freelance design and freelance illustration jobs/year. Mostly 4 color. Negotiates payment, by the project, $250 minimum.
Text Illustration: Assigns 20 freelance jobs/year. Usually prefers pen & ink. Negotiates payment.

NAVPRESS, Box 6000, Colorado Springs CO 80934. (303)598-1212. Art Director: Wendy Reis or Naomi Trujillo. Publishes Christian books, Bible studies, and a bimonthly magazine, *Discipleship Journal*. Publishes 35 titles/year.
First Contact & Terms: Works with 15 freelance artists/year. Works on assignment only. Send query letter with brochure or tear sheets, slides and photographs. Samples are filed. Samples not filed are returned by SASE only if requested. Reports back within 1 month. Originals returned to artist at job's completion. Call or write to schedule an appointment to show a portfolio, which should include tear sheets, slides and transparencies. Considers complexity of project, skill and experience of artist, project's budget, turnaround time and rights purchased when establishing payment. Buys one-time rights.
Magazine Design: Assigns 15-20 freelance illustration jobs/year. Pays by the project, $350-1,000.
Jackets/Covers: Pays by the project, $350-1,000.
Tips: "Call or inquire by mail first. Include only what best represents your work. Sending updated samples as you get them is nice."

NBM PUBLISHING CO., 35-53 70th St., Jackson Heights NY 11372. (718)458-3199. Publisher: Terry Nantier. Publishes graphic novels including *The Mercenary*, *Corto Maltese* and *Roxanna* for an audience of 18-24 year olds. Genres: adventure, fantasy, mystery, science fiction, horror and social parodies. Themes: sf, fantasy, mystery and social commentary. Circ. 5-10,000. Original artwork returned after publication. Sample copies available.
Jacket Covers: Uses freelance artists for lettering, paste-up and covers. Prefers pen & ink, watercolor, and oils. Send query letter with resume and samples. Samples are filed. Samples not filed are returned by SASE. Reports back within 2 weeks. To show a portfolio, mail photocopies of original pencil art or inking. Pays by the project, $200 minimum.

THOMAS NELSON PUBLISHERS, Box 141000, Nashville TN 37214-1000. (615)889-9000. Vice President: Robert J. Schwalb. Specializes in hardcover and paperback originals, Bibles and textbooks on religious and inspirational subjects. Publishes 135 titles/year.
First Contact & Terms: Works with 100 freelance artists/year. Prefers decorative and realistic styles. Send query letter with brochure or tear sheets. Samples are filed. Samples not filed are returned by SASE if requested. Reports back within 2 weeks. Return of originals depends on rights purchased. Call or write to schedule an appointment to show a portfolio, which should include final reproduction/product and slides. Considers project's budget and rights purchased when establishing payment. Negotiates rights purchased.
Book Design: Assigns 15 freelance design and 50 freelance illustration jobs/year. Pays by the project, $15-1,500.
Jackets/Covers: Assigns 120 freelance design and 40 freelance illustration jobs/year. Pays by the project, $15-1,500.
Text Illustration: Assigns 20 freelance jobs/year. Pays by the project, $15-500.
Tips: "We also purchase art for advertising and newsletters." Prefers "people, Biblical scenes and artifacts, rendered in realistic style and interesting point of view. Prefer gouache, dyes, watercolor as well as pen & ink (Rapidograph style.)"

***THE NEW ENGLAND PRESS**, Box 575, Shelburne VT 05482. (802)863-2520. Managing Editor: Jeff Olson. Specializes in paperback originals—regional New England titles, nature. Publishes 12 titles/year; 60% require freelance illustration.
First Contact & Terms: Works with 6-8 freelance artists/year. Northern New England artists only. Send query letter with brochure showing art style or resume. Samples are filed. Reports back only if interested. Originals not usually returned to artist at job's completion, but negotiable. To show a portfolio, mail "anything that shows talent." Considers complexity of project, skill and experience of artist, project's budget and turnaround time when establishing payment. Negotiates rights purchased.
Book Design: Assigns 8-10 freelance design and 6-8 freelance illustration jobs/year. Payment varies.
Jackets/Covers: Assigns 4-5 freelance illustration jobs/year. Payment varies.
Text Illustration: Assigns 6-8 freelance jobs/year. Payment varies.

NEW SOCIETY PUBLISHERS, 4527 Baltimore Ave., Philadelphia PA 19143. (215)382-6543. Production Director: Barbara Hirshkowitz. Specializes in hardcover and paperback originals and reprints on nonviolent social change. Publishes 15 titles/year.
First Contact & Terms: Works with several freelance artists/year. Works on assignment only. Send query letter with samples to be kept on file. Call for appointment to show portfolio. Prefers Photostats and photographs as samples. Samples not filed are returned only by SASE. Reports only if interested. Original work may or may not be returned to the artist. Considers complexity of the project, project's budget and rights purchased when establishing payment. Negotiates rights purchased.
Covers: Assigns 8-10 freelance design jobs/year. Pays by the project, $50 for 3 sketches. If one is accepted then $200 for completed mechanicals. Additional must be negotiated—for complex jobs.
Text Illustration: Assigns 1-2 jobs/year. Prefers pen & ink line drawings. Pays by the hour, $5-10 or negotiated by the project.

***NEWBURY HOUSE PUBLISHERS**, 10 E. 53 St., New York NY 10022. (212)207-7373. Production Coordinator: Cynthia Funkhouser. Specializes in textbooks emphasizing English as a second language. Publishes 30 titles/year; 75% require freelance illustration.
First Contact & Terms: Works with 12 freelance artists/year. Works on assignment only. Send query letter with resume and photocopies. Samples are filed. Samples not filed are not returned unless SASE is enclosed. Reports back only if interested. Originals not returned at job's completion. Write to schedule an appointment to show a portfolio, which should include roughs, original/final art and final reproduction/product. Considers skill and experience of artist and project's budget when establishing payment. Buys all rights.
Book Design: Assigns 12 freelance design jobs/year. Pays by the project, $200 and up.
Text Illustration: Assigns 12 freelance jobs/year. Prefers line art and ink drawings. Pays per illustration or per project, $20 and up.
Tips: "Designers should have experience in el-hi and/or college book design with samples available to show. Artists should be able to show photocopies of published tear sheets. We use both cartoons and serious illustrations. We seek artists who are able to portray a broad range of ethnic identities in their drawings."

NICHOLS PUBLISHING COMPANY, Box 96, New York NY 10024. (212)580-8079. President: Linda Kahn. Specializes in hardcover professional and reference books in architecture, business, education, technology and energy. Publishes 35 titles/year.
First Contact & Terms: Works with 4 freelance artists/year. Works on promotion assignment only. Artists must be in New York area. Send query letter with brochure and resume. Samples not kept on file are returned only if requested. Reports only if interested. Call or write for appointment to show portfolio, which should include promotion brochures. Considers complexity of project, skill and experience of artist and project's budget when establishing payment. Rights purchased vary.

OCTAMERON PRESS, 4805A Eisenhower Ave., Alexandria VA 22304. President: Anna Leider. Specializes in paperbacks—college money and college admission guides. Publishes 10-15 titles/year.
First Contact & Terms: Works with 1 or 2 artists/year. Local artists only. Works on assignment only. Send query letter with brochure showing art style or resume and photocopies. Samples not filed are returned. Reports within 1 week. Original work returned at job's completion. Considers complexity of project and project's budget when establishing payment. Rights purchased vary according to project.
Jackets/Covers: Works with variable number of freelance designers/year. Pays by the project, $75-250.
Text Illustration: Works with variable number of freelance artists/year. Prefers line drawings from photographs. Pays by the project, $35-75.

ODDO PUBLISHING, INC., Box 68, Fayetteville GA 30214. (404)461-7627. Vice President: Charles W. Oddo. Specializes in hardcovers on juvenile fiction. Publishes 6-10 titles/year; 100% require freelance illustration. Prefers cartoon and/or realistic work; airbrush, watercolor, acrylics and oils.
First Contact & Terms: Works with 3 freelance artists/year. Send query letter with brochure, resume, business card, samples or tear sheets to be kept on file. Accepts "whatever is best for artist to present" as samples. Samples not kept on file are returned by SASE only if requested. Reports only if interested. Works on assignment only. Write for appointment to show portfolio. No originals returned to artist at job's completion. Buys all rights.
Book Design: Assigns 3 freelance jobs/year. Pays for illustration and design combined by the project, $250 minimum.
Text Illustration: Assigns 3 freelance jobs/year. Artwork purchased includes science fiction/fantasy.
Tips: Portfolio should include "human form to show that artist can illustrate accurately. Chances are if an artist can illustrate people that look real, his or her talents are highly refined. We also look for quality

cartoon-illustrating ability. We expect to see various styles to indicate the artist's versatility. Artists tend to want to show their entire portfolios without first determining what the publisher needs and what styles of art are in the portfolios that meet those needs."

ONCE UPON A PLANET, INC., 65-42 Fresh Meadow Lane, Fresh Meadows NY 11365. Art Director: Alis Jordan. Publishes trade paperback originals, greeting cards, pads and novelty books (humor). Uses artists for book design, cover and text illustration, mechanicals, displays, brochures and flyers.
First Contact & Terms: Prefers local artists. Send query letter with brochure showing art style or resume, tear sheets, photocopies and/or slides. Works on assignment only. If originals are sent, SASE must be enclosed for return. Reports in 3-5 weeks. Prefers to buy all rights, but will negotiate. Payment is negotiated.
Book Design: Assigns 8-12 jobs/year. Uses artists for layout, type specifications.
Jackets/Covers: Assigns 6 jobs/year. Uses 2-color art, occasionally 4-color art.
Text Illustration: Assigns 8-12 jobs/year. Uses b&w line drawings and washes.

ONESS PRESS, University Center, 1522 Orchard, Eugene OR 97403. (503)933-2034. Editor/Publisher:ll Sunanda. Specializes in paperback originals and reprints on children's liberation, natural sexual healing, wholistic health and group marriage and home dication. Sample copy of Kids Lib News available $1.
First Contact & Terms: Prefers parents, nature lovers, sufi, new artists. Send query letter with resume, tear sheets, Photostats, slides and photographs. Samples are filed. Samples not filed are returned only if requested. Reports back within 3 weeks only if interested. Originals returned to artist at job's completion if requested. To show a portfolio, mail thumbnails, roughs, Photostats, tear sheets and photographs. Considers complexity of project, skill and experience of artist and project's budget when establishing payment.
Book Design: Assigns 2-7 freelance design and 5-10 freelance illustration jobs/year. Pays by the hour, $5-15; by the project, $15-100.
Jackets/Covers: Prefers kids, nature, coupling, healing as themes. Pays by the hour, $5-15; by the project, $10-100.
Text Illustration: Assigns 3 freelance jobs/year. Prefers line drawing or collage. Pays by the hour, $5-15; by the project, $10-100.
Tips: "Submit photocopy sample of alternative themes, mostly of young people doing natural family trips, playful. Show only natural families or cartoons of kids playing, drawing, fearing, etc."

OTTENHEIMER PUBLISHERS, INC., 300 Reisterstown Rd., Baltimore MD 21208. (301)484-2100. Art Director: Diane Parameros Shea. Specializes in mass market-oriented hardcover and paperback originals and reprints—encyclopedias, dictionaries, self-help books, cookbooks, children's coloring and activity books, story books and novelty books. Publishes 200 titles/year.
First Contact & Terms: Works with 15-20 freelance artists/year. Local artists only, preferably professional graphic designers and illustrators. Works on assignment only. Send query letter with resume, slides, Photostats, photographs, photocopies or tear sheets to be kept on file, except for work style which is unsuitable for us. Samples not filed are returned by SASE. Reports only if interested. Call or write for appointment to show portfolio. "I do not want to see unfinished work, sketches, or fine art such as student figure drawings." Original work not returned at job's completion. Considers complexity of project, project's budget and turnaround time when establishing payment. Buys all rights.
Book Design: Assigns 20-40 freelance design jobs/year and 25 illustration jobs/year. Pays by the project, $50-2,000 average.
Jackets/Covers: Assigns 25+ freelance design and 25+ freelance illustration jobs/year. Pays by the project, $100-1,000 average, depending upon project, time spent and any changes.
Text Illustration: Assigns 30+ jobs/year. Prefers water-based color media and b&w line work. Prefers graphic approaches as well as very illustrative. "We cater more to juvenile market." Pays by the project, $25-2,000 average.
Tips: Prefers "art geared towards children. Cuteness and cuddliness are 'in' especially when animals are featured." Looks for "clean work that will reproduce well. I also look for the artist's ability to render children/people well, which is a problem for some. A sure control of one's media should also be present. Very few freelancers are able to present a nice resume. I like it when people have taken the time and effort to record their art history. It helps me know something more about the person than they might let on during an interview and I respect them more for it."

OUTDOOR EMPIRE PUBLISHING INC., Box C-19000, 511 Eastlake Ave. E., Seattle WA 98109. (206)624-3845. Vice President/General Manager: Alec Purcell. Publishes paperback outdoor and how-to books on all aspects of outdoor recreation. Publishes 40 titles/year: 10% require freelance designers, 50% require freelance illustrators. Also uses artists for advertising layout and illustration. Minimum

payment: $10-15, b&w; $25-50, color.
First Contact & Terms: Arrange interview or mail art. Especially looks for style, accuracy in rendering figures and technical illustrations when reviewing samples. Buys all rights. No originals returned at job's completion. Works on assignment only. Samples returned by SASE; and reports back within 3 weeks on future assignment possiblities. Send resume, flyer, business card, tear sheet, brochure and photocopies of samples that show style to be kept on file. Artist sometimes supplies overlays for color artwork. Gives minimum payment for unused assigned work. Pays on publication.
Book Design: Uses artists for layout and type spec. Pays by the hour, $10-35 average; by the project, $10-1,500; "depends upon project."
Jacket/Covers: Pays for design by the hour, $10-35 average; by the project, $50-1,000 average. Pays for illustration by the hour, $10-35 average; by the project, $10-500 average.
Text Illustration: Pays by the hour, $10-35 average; by the project, $10-100 average. Occasionally uses cartoons; buys 6 cartoons/year. Pays $10, b&w.
Tips: "Assignments sometimes depend upon timing—right style for the right project. Availability is important, especially with 'rush' projects. The competition is getting tougher. More people are trying to break into the field."

***OXFORD UNIVERSITY PRESS**, English Language Teaching (ELT), 200 Madison Ave., 9th Fl, New York NY 10016. Art Buyer: Paula Radding. Specializes in textbooks emphasizing English language teaching. Also produces wall charts, picture cards, etc.
First Contact & Terms: Works with 75 freelance artists/year. Works on assignment only. Send query letter with brochure, resume, tear sheets, Photostats, slides and photographs. Samples are filed. Reports back only if interested. Originals returned to artist at job's completion. To show a portfolio, mail orignal/final art, Photostats, tear sheets, final reproduction/product, slides and transparencies. Considers complexity of project, skill and experience of artist and project's budget when establishing payment. Buys all rights.
Text Illustration: Assigns 75-100 freelance jobs/year. "Line drawings are used most frequently, ranging from very realistic to more interpretive styles. But we also use half-tones and color work." Pays by the project, $100-2,500.
Tips: "Please wait for us to call you. You may send new samples to update your file at any time."

PALADIN PRESS, Box 1307, Boulder CO 80306. (303)443-7250. Art Director: Amy Lockard. Publishes hardcover and paperback originals and reprints; military-related (weaponry, self-defense, martial arts and survival) and titles of general interest. Publishes 40 titles/year. Catalog for SASE.
First Contact & Terms: Local artists only for book design. Works on assignment only. Send query letter with good quality photocopies of sample work to be kept on file. Samples returned by SASE. Artist supplies overlays for all color artwork. Buys all rights.
Text Illustration: Assigns 8/year. Uses "99% pen & ink, b&w. Often technical." Buys b&w line drawings, washes and color washes. Pays for illustration by the project, $20-200.
Tips: "We prefer working with artists who have a strong background in mechanical and production skills (have they ever worked with a printer?). There is continued expansion into the martial arts market, financial survival, outdoor skills, etc. Also an increased demand for high-caliber execution of how-to photo layouts."

***PARTNER PRESS**, Box 124, Livonia MI 48152. Vice President Sales/Marketing: John R. Faitel. Specializes in paperback preschool education materials. Publishes 3 titles/year.
First Contact & Terms: Works with 2 freelance artists/year. Artists must be good in drawing children's faces/bodies. Send query letter with samples to be kept on file. Prefers tear sheets as samples. Samples not filed returned by SASE. Reports only if interested. No originals returned after job's completion. Considers complexity of project and project's budget when establishing payment. Buys all rights.
Book Design: Assigns 2 freelance jobs/year. Pays by the project, $300 minimum.
Jackets/Covers: Assigns 2 freelance design jobs/year. Pays by the project, $100 minimum.
Text Illustration: Assigns 2 freelance jobs/year. Prefers b&w line drawings. Pays by the project, $300 minimum.

PEANUT BUTTER PUBLISHING, 329 2nd Ave. W., Seattle WA 98119. (206)281-5965. Specializes in paperback regional cookbooks and also speciality cookbooks for people who like to dine in restaurant and try the recipes at home. Publishes 30 titles/year.
First Contact & Terms: Works on assignment only. Send brochure showing art style or tear sheets, Photostats and photocopies. Samples not filed are returned only if requested. Reports only if interested. To show a portfolio, mail appropriate materials. Pays for design by the project, $400 minimum. Pays for illustration by the project, $100 minimum. Negotiates rights purchased.

PEGASUS ORIGINALS, INC., 129 Minnie Fallow Rd. Lexington SC 29072. (803)755-1141. Design Editor: Stephanie S. Hedgepath. Specializes in paperbacks on counted cross stitch and craft booklets. Publishes 10 titles/year.
First Contact & Terms: Works with variable freelance artists/year. Send query letter with chart and photo of model. Samples are filed. Reports back within 10 days. Originals not returned to artist at job's completion. Call to show a portfolio, which should include roughs and photos of any charted design work previously done, or charts, etc. Considers rights purchased and royalty.
Tips: "We prefer someone who is familiar with the counted cross stitch and craft market, but we are open to those artists who have never worked in charted design."

PELICAN PUBLISHING CO., Box 189, 1101 Monroe St., Gretna LA 70053. (504)368-1175. Assistant Production Manager: Dana Bilbray. Publishes hardcover and paperback originals and reprints. Publishes 40-50 titles/year.
First Contact & Terms: Works on assignment only. Send query letter and 3-4 samples. SASE. Samples are not returned. Reports back on future assignment possibilities. Originals are not returned at job's completion. Buys complete rights.
Book Design: Assigns variable number of freelance jobs. Payment varies.
Jackets/Covers: Assigns variable number of freelance jobs. Payment varies.
Text Illustration: Assigns variable number of freelance jobs. Payment varies.

PEN NOTES INC., 134 Westside Ave., Freeport NY 11520. (516)868-5753 or 868-1966. President: Lorette Konezny. Produces books for children ages 3 and up; calligraphy age 8 and up.
First Contact & Terms: Buys designs and illustrations from freelance artists. Prefers New York area artists with toy-book experience. Send letter with brochure or Photostats and photocopies. Samples are filed. Reports back within 5 days if requested. Call or write to schedule an appointment to show a portfolio or mail original/final art, Photostats, dummies, color and b&w. Original artwork is not returned to the artist after job's completion. Buys all rights.
Text Illustration: Also uses freelance artists for calligraphy, P-O-P displays, mechanicals and book illustrations. Prefers pen & ink. Pays by the project, $1,000 average.
Tips: Artists should "have strong experience in illustration for toy-book market and be able to complete work under deadline situation."

***PENNWELL PUBLISHING COMPANY (BOOK DIVISION)**, 1421 S. Sheridan, Tulsa OK 74112. Production Manager: Carol Schaefer. Specializes in hardcover technical books in petroleum, dentistry, high tech. Publishes 6-10 titles/year. 100% require freelance illustration.
First Contact & Terms: Works with 2-5 freelance artists/year. Prefers experience in book layout specifications and technical/mechanical rendering plus some cover illustration. Works on assignment only. Send query letter with brochure, resume and tear sheets. Samples are filed. Samples not filed are returned only if requested by artist. Reports back only if interested. Write to schedule an appointment to show a portfolio, which should include roughs and original/final art. Considers complexity of project and project's budget when establishing payment. Buys all rights.
Book Design: Assigns 2-5 freelance design and 2-5 freelance illustration jobs/year. Pays by the project, $100-5,000.
Jackets/Covers: Considers all styles; "need some computer artists." Pays by the project, $1,000 maximum.
Text Illustration: Assigns 2-5 freelance jobs/year. Prefers line art. Pays by the project, $3,000 maximum.
Tips: "Need fresh ideas on file. Prefer area artists, personal contact."

PERGAMON PRESS INC., Fairview Park, Elmsford NY 10523. (914)592-7700. Art Department Manager: Angela Langston. Publishes scientific, technical, scholarly, educational, professional and business books and journals. Publishes 50 titles/year: 75% require freelance designers, 15% require freelance illustrators. Also uses artists for jacket designs, cover designs, advertising design, mechanicals and direct mail brochures. Mostly needs artists for 1-2-color promotion pieces. Produces about 100 pieces per year. 80% need freelance artists.
First Contact & Terms: Prefers local artists. Works on assignment only. Call for interview. No originals returned at job's completion. Check for most recent titles in bookstores. Pays net 90 days.

PICTURE BOOK STUDIO, 10 Central St., Saxonville MA 01701. Publisher: Robert Saunders. Produces children's picture books. Publishes 25 books/year with 10-12 illustrations in each. "Request a catalog."
First Contact & Terms: Prefers artwork that is "fresh and original, with childlike spontanceity and warmth." Prefers watercolor, then pen & ink, colored pencil, pastels and college. Send query letter with

slides. Samples not filed returned by SASE. Reports within 1 month. "We always must see slides first. Do not call." Originals returned to artist at job's completion. Buys worldwide book rights.
Tips: "I want to see work which the illustator likes to do most."

PLAYERS PRESS, Box 1132, Studio City CA 91604. Associate Editor: Marjorie Clapper. Specializes in children's books, covers to books, jackets, etc.
First Contact & Terms: Buys up to 30 illustrations/year from freelancers. Works on assignment only. Send query letter with brochure showing art style or resume and samples. Samples not filed are returned by SASE. Reports only if interested. To show a portfolio, mail thumbnails, original/final art, final reproduction/product, tear sheets, photographs and as much information as possible. Buys all rights. Payment varies.

PLYMOUTH MUSIC CO., INC., 170 NE 33rd St., Ft. Lauderdale FL 33334. (305)563-1844. General Manager: Bernard Fisher. Specializes in paperbacks dealing with all types of music. Publishes 60-75 titles/year; 100% require freelance designers, 100% require freelance illustrators.
First Contact & Terms: Works with 10 freelance artists/year. Artists "must be within our area." Works on assignment only. Send brochure, resume and samples to be kept on file. Samples not kept on file file are returned. Reports within 1 week. Call for appointment to show portfolio. No originals returned to artist at job's completion. Considers complexity of project when establishing payment. Buys all rights.
Jackets/Covers: Assigns 5 freelance design and 5 freelance illustration jobs/year. Pays by the project.

POCKET BOOKS, Art Department, Simon & Schuster Bldg., 1230 Ave. of the Americas, New York NY 10020. (212)698-7000. Art Director: Bruce Hall. Publishes paperback romance, science fiction, Westerns, young adult, fiction, nonfiction and classics. Publishes 250 titles/year; 80% require freelance illustrators.
First Contact & Terms: Works with 30 freelance artists/year. "We prefer artists who live close enough that they are able to deliver and discuss their work in person. We judge them on their portfolio work. We prefer color illustration." Send brochure/flyer and color slides, transparencies and prints. Submit portfolio for review, no appointment necessary. Samples not kept on file are returned by SASE. Reports in weeks. Works on assignment only. Provide brochure/flyer, samples, tear sheets to be kept on file for possible future assignments. Originals returned to artist at job's completion. Buys all rights.
Jackets/Covers: Assigns 220 freelance illustration jobs/year. Prefers paintings and color washes. Pays by the job, $800-4,000 average.

PORTER SARGENT PUBLISHERS, INC., 11 Beacon St., Boston MA 02108. (617)523-1670. Coordinating Editor: Peter Casey. Specializes in hardcover and paperback originals and reprints of college texts in the social sciences, particularly political science, sociology and history. Publishes 4-5 titles/year; 20% require freelance designers, 20% require freelance illustrators.
First Contact & Terms: Works with 2-4 freelance artists/year. Local artists only. Works on assignment only. Send query letter with resume, business card and tear sheets to be kept on file; write for appointment to show portfolio. "We are basically looking for samples of dust jacket cover designs." Samples not kept on file returned by SASE. Reports only if interested. No originals returned at job's completion. Considers complexity of project, and skill and experience of artist when establishing payment. Buys all rights.
Jackets/Covers: Assigns 1-2 freelance design jobs/year. Pays by the project, $200 minimum; negotiates.

PRAEGER PUBLISHERS, 1 Madison Ave., New York NY 10010. (212)685-6267. Art Director: Carole A. Russo. Specializes in hardcover and paperback trade and academic books on political, medical, business, science, economics, psychology and sociology themes. Publishes 200 titles/year.
First Contact & Terms: Works with 10-12 freelance artists/year. Works on assignment only. Send query letter with tear sheets. Samples are filed. Samples not filed are not returned. Reports back only if interested. Originals not returned to artist at job's completion. Call or write to schedule an appointment to show a portfolio, which should include roughs, original/final art and final reproduction/product. Considers skill and experience of artist when establishing payment. Negotiates rights purchased.
Jackets/Covers: Assigns 45 freelance design jobs/year. Pays by the project, $350-550.
Tips: "Want to see type designs mainly; rarely use illustrations or photographs."

THE PRAIRIE PUBLISHING COMPANY, Box 2997, Winnipeg MB R3C 4B5 Canada. (204)885-6496. Publisher: Ralph E. Watkins. Specializes in paperback juvenile fiction and local history. Publishes 3 titles/year.
First Contact & Terms: Works with 3-4 freelance artists/year. Works on assignment only. Send query

letter with resume and tear sheets. Samples are filed. Samples not filed are returned. Reports back within weeks. Originals not returned to artist at job's completion. To show a portfolio, mail appropriate roughs. nsiders skill and experience of artist and project's budget when establishing payment. Negotiates rights prchased.
Book Design: Pays by the project, $100-150.
Jackets/Covers: Pays by the project, $100-150.
Text Illustration: Prefers line drawings. Pays by the project, $100-150.
Tips: "A freelancer should have other projects on which he is working. On the other hand, he must be able to carry out the work for which he has bid."

***BYRON PREISS VISUAL PUBLICATIONS, INC.**, 24 W. 25th St., New York NY 10010. (212)645-9870. Design Coordinator/Associate Editor: Randall Reich. Specializes in hardcover and paperback science fiction, fantasy, animal/and nature books, young adult and children's books. Publishes 100 titles/year; 85% require freelance illustration.
First Contact & Terms: Works with 50 freelance artists/year. Prefers pen & ink, airbrush, charcoal/pencil, colored pencil, watercolor, acrylics, oils, pastels and computer illustration. Works on assignment only. Send query letter with brochure showing art style or tear sheets, Photostats, slides, photographs or "color reproductions of any color art." Samples are filed. Samples not filed are returned by SASE only if requested. Reports back only if interested. Originals returned to artist at job's completion. Call or write to schedule an appointment to show a portfolio, which should include the "best samples possible." Considers complexity of project, skill and experience of artist, project's budget, turnaround time and rights purchased when establishing payment. Negotiates rights purchased.
Book Design: Assigns approximately 10 freelance design and approximately 50 freelance illustration jobs/year. Pays by the project, $1,500 minimum.
Jackets/Covers: Assigns approximately 20 freelance design and approximately 50 freelance illustration jobs/year. Pays by the project, $3,600 minimum.
Text Illustration: Assigns 50 freelance jobs/year. Pays by the project, $100-500.
Tips: "Please consider subject matter of our books when showing artwork."

PRICE/STERN/SLOAN PUBLISHERS, 410 N. La Cienega Blvd., Los Angeles CA 90048. (213)657-6100. Art Director: John Beach. Publishes books (children's and humor), greeting cards and calendars.
First Contact & Terms: Send query letter with samples to be kept on file. Prefers photocopies or Photostats as samples. Samples not filed are returned by SASE. Does not report back. Sometimes returns original art after reproduction. Negotiates rights purchased.
Illustrations: Buys 200+ illustrations/year from freelance artists. Seeks illustrations for children's books, inside and covers. Also uses artists for paste-up and mechanicals. Pay varies; "depends on illustration, book, size, colors, etc."

PRUETT PUBLISHING COMPANY, 2928 Pearl St., Boulder CO 80301. Project Editor: Jim Pruett. Specializes in hardcover and paperback originals on western history, outdoor themes, Americana and railroads. Publishes 20 titles/year. Also uses freelancers for brochure, catalog and advertising design. Assigns 20-25 projects/year. Pays by the project.
First Contact & Terms: Works with 4-5 freelance artists/year. Prefers local artists. Works on assignment only. Send query letter with brochure showing art style. Samples not filed are returned only if requested. Reports within 10 days. Original work returned at job's completion. Considers complexity of project, skill and experience of artist, project's budget and turnaround time when establishing payment. Rights purchased vary according to project.
Book Design: Assigns 20 freelance design and 0-1 freelance illustration jobs/year. Pays by the project, $150-400.
Jackets/Covers: Assigns 20 freelance design and 5-10 freelance illustration jobs/year. Pays by the project, $200-550.
Text Illustration: Assigns 0-1 freelance jobs/year. Pays by the project, $200-500.

PUBLISHERS ASSOCIATES, Box 160361, Las Colinas TX 75016. (817)478-8564. Chief Operating Officer: Nicholas Lashmet. Established 1985. A consortium of 14 independent academic presses. Specializes in paperback originals on feminist/liberal subjects. Publishes 20 titles/year.
First Contact & Terms: Works with 7 freelance artists/year. Send query letter with brochure showing art style or photocopies. Samples not filed are returned by SASE only if requested. Reports within 45 days. "Never send original work until requested." Considers skill and experience of artist, project's budget and rights purchased when establishing payment. Buys all rights.
Book Design: Works with 10 freelance designers and 10 freelance illustrators/year. Pays by the project, $50 on up.
Jackets/Covers: Works with 10 freelance designers and 10 freelance illustrators/year. Pays by the proj-

ect, $50 on up. "We need quality/realistic work for medieval books—primarily on women, some men illustrations."
Text Illustration: Works with 10 freelance artists/year. Prefers line drawings, ink only. Pays by the project, $100 on up. "We are in desperate need of artists who can draw men with/without clothing (no porno) in historic settings. Our preference is for realism; we do not wish da Vinci type males (small, effeminate, etc.) Will pay well. Our staff artists currently are capable only in area of women. Need freelance here, too."
Tips: "Never send original work. Write first, submit 2 or 3 examples in areas of our needs, include SASE. We do not use cartoons, unless commissioned first. Cartoons are political (liberal) in nature. All other work must be realistic in style. Our primary emphasis is women—we will not accept 'Gibson Girl' or 'clip art' style work. Historic/period brings top dollars."

***PULSE-FINGER PRESS**, Box 488, Yellow Springs OH 45387. Contact: Orion Roche or Raphaello Farnese. Publishes hardbound and paperback fiction, poetry and drama. Publishes 5-10 titles/year. Also uses artists for advertising design and illustrations. Pays $25 minimum for direct mail promos.
First Contact & Terms: Send query letter. "We can't use unsolicited material." SASE. "Inquiries without SASE will not be acknowledged." Prefers local artists. Works on assignment only. Reports in 6 weeks. Samples returned by SASE; reports back on future assignment possibilities. Send resume to be kept on file for future assignments. Artist supplies overlays for all color artwork. Originals returned to artist at job's completion. Buys first serial and reprint rights.
Jackets/Covers: "Must be suitable to the book involved; artist must familiarize himself with text. We tend to modernist/abstract designs. Try to keep it simple, emphasizing the thematic material of the book." Pays $25-100, b&w jackets, on acceptance.

G.P. PUTNAM'S SONS, (Philomel Books), 200 Madison Ave., New York NY 10016. (212)689-9200. Art Director, Children's Books: Nanette Stevenson. Publishes hardcover and paperback juvenile books. Publishes 100 titles/year.
First Contact & Terms: "We take drop-offs on Tuesday mornings. Please call in advance with the date you want to drop off your portfolio." Originals returned to artist at job's completion. Works on assignment only. Samples returned by SASE. Provide flyer, tear sheet, brochure and photocopy or stat to be kept on file for possible future assignments. Free catalog.
Jackets/Covers: "Full-color paintings, tight style."
Text Illustration: "A wide cross section of styles for story and picture books."

RAINTREE PUBLISHERS GROUP, INC., 310 W. Wisconsin Ave., Milwaukee WI 53203. (414)273-0873. Art Director: Suzanne Beck. Specializes in educational material for children. Publishes 40 titles/year; 90% require freelance illustrators.
First Contact & Terms: Works with 12 freelance artists/year. Send slides, tear sheets or photocopies or submit portfolio for review. Do not call in person. Provide samples to be kept on file for possible future assignments. Samples not kept on file are returned by SASE. Reports in 2-3 weeks. Works on assignment only. Originals sometimes returned to artist at job's completion. Buys all rights.
Jackets/Covers: Assigns 12 illustration jobs/year. Payment varies depending on job and artist's experience.
Text Illustration: Assigns 12 jobs/year. Payment varies depending on job and artist's experience.

***RANDOM HOUSE, INC., (Juvenile)**, 201 50th St., New York NY 10022. (212)751-2600. Art Director: Cathy Goldsmith. Specializes in hardcover and paperback originals and reprints. Publishes 300 titles/year. 100% require freelance illustration.
First Contact & Terms: Works with 100-150 freelance artists/year. Works on assignment only. Send query letter with resume, tear sheets and Photostats; no originals. Samples are filed. Samples not filed are returned. "No appointment necessary for portfolios. Come in on Wednesdays only, before noon." Considers complexity of project, skill and experience of artist, project's budget, turnaround time and rights purchased when establishing payment. Negotiates rights purchased.
Book Design: Assigns 50 freelance design and 50 freelance illustration jobs/year. Pays by the project.
Text Illustration: Assigns 300 freelance jobs/year. Pays by the project.

READ'N RUN BOOKS, Box 294, Rhododendron OR 97049. (503)622-4798. Publisher: Michael P. Jones. Estab. 1985. Specializes in fiction, history, environment, wildlife for children through adults. "Varies depending upon subject matter. Books for people who do not have time to read lengthy books." Publishes 2-6 titles/year. Accepts previously published material. Original artwork returned to the artist after publication. Sample copy: $6. Art guidelines for SASE with 1 first-class stamp.
Text Illustration: Buys 30 illustrations/year from freelancers. Prefers pen & ink, airbrush, charcoal/pencil, markers, calligraphy and computer illustration. Send query letter with brochure or resume, tear

sheets, Photostats, photocopies, slides and photographs. Samples not filed are returned by SASE. Reports back within 2 weeks. To show a portfolio, mail thumbnails, roughs, original/final art, final reproduction/product, color, tear sheets, Photostats, photographs and b&w. Buys one-time rights. Pays in copies, on publication.
Tips: "We publish books on wildlife, history and nature. We will be publishing short-length cookbooks." In portfolios, "I want to see a lot of illustrations showing a variety of styles. Then is little that I actually don't want to see."

RESOURCE PUBLICATIONS INC., Suite 290, 160 E. Virginia, San Jose CA 95112. Editorial Director: Kenneth Guentert. Publishes paperback originals related to celebration and the arts. Publishes 12 titles/year. Also uses artists for advertising and production. Assigns 4 advertising jobs/year. Pays $4-25/hour; catalogs, direct mail brochures, letterhead and magazines. Assigns 12-16 production jobs/year. Pays $5-10/hour, paste-up.
First Contact & Terms: Send query letter with samples. SASE. Reports in 6-8 weeks. No advance. Buys all rights. Free catalog.
Book Design: Assigns 1-4/year. Pays $5-25/hour, layout and type spec.
Jackets/Covers: Buys 1-4/year. Pays $45-125, b&w; $50-250, color.

ROYAL HOUSE PUBLISHING CO., INC., Book Division of Recipes-of-the-Month Club, Box 5027, Beverly Hills CA 90210. (213)277-3340. Director: Mrs. Harold Klein. Publishes paperbacks on entertaining, humor, sports and cooking. Publishes 10 titles/year. Also uses artists for brochures, ads, letterheads and business forms.
First Contact & Terms: Query with samples; local artists only. SASE. Reports in 4-6 weeks. Purchases outright. No originals returned to artist at job's completion. Works on assignment only. Provide brochure to be kept on file for future assignments. Check for most recent titles in bookstores. Negotiates pay.
Book Design: Assigns 8-12 jobs/year. Uses artists for layout and type spec.
Jackets/Covers: Assigns 8-12 jobs/year. Uses "4-color art; old-fashioned heirloom quality." Buys color washes, opaque watercolors and b&w line drawings.
Text Illustration: Assigns 8-12 jobs/year. Buys b&w line drawings.

WILLIAM H. SADLIER INC., 11 Park Place, New York NY 10007. (212)227-2120. Art Director: Grace Kao. Publishes hardcover and paperback Catholic adult education, religious, mathematics, social studies and language arts books. Publishes 60 titles/year. Also uses artists for direct mail pieces and catalogs. Pays $12-15/hour or $175-350/job.
First Contact & Terms: Query with samples. SASE. Reports within 2 weeks. Buys all rights.
Book Design: Assigns 40 jobs/year. Uses artists for layout, type spec and mechanicals. Pays $10-15/hour.
Text Illustration: Assigns 30 jobs/year. Pays $75-200, color washes and opaque watercolors; $60-200, gray opaques, b&w line drawings and washes.

SANTILLANA PUBLISHING CO. INC., 257 Union St., Northvale NJ 07647. (201)767-6961. President: Sam Laredo. Editorial Director: Bernice Randall. Specializes in hardcover and paperback juvenile and teen textbooks and workbooks. Publishes 35 titles/year.
First Contact & Terms: Works with 8-10 freelance artists/year. Prefers pen & ink, airbrush, colored pencil, watercolor, acrylics and computer illustration. Works on assignment only. Send query letter with brochure, tear sheets or "anything we don't have to return" to be kept on file. Call or write for appointment to show portfolio. Samples not filed are returned by SASE. Reports only if interested. No originals returned to artist at job's completion. Considers skill and experience of artist, project's budget and rights purchased when establishing payment. Buys all rights or negotiates rights purchased.
Text Illustration: All jobs assigned to freelancers. Pays by the project, $200-5,000 average.
Tips: Looks for "lots of details, strong lines, good color."

***C & J SAPP PUBLISHING COMPANY**, Drawer 610, Bokeelia FL 33922. (813)283-3800. Editor: Jean Sapp. Specializes in annual directories for hunters - editions for the forty-eight contiguous states.
First Contact & Terms: Works with several freelance artists/year. Send query letter with slides or photographs. Samples are filed. Samples not filed are returned only if requested. Reports back within 2 weeks only if interested. Originals not returned to artist at job's completion. To show a portfolio, mail photographs and slides (include phone number). Considers turnaround time and rights purchased when establishing payment. Buys all rights.
Jackets/Covers: "We are looking for 7 different covers for our hunting directories to be reproduced from original oil paintings (approx. 18"x22", September/October settings) of typical landscapes for these areas: Pacific coast, Rocky Mountains (should have snow on the mountains), plains, Midwest,

©1987 Michael Conway

The exuberance of four girls spills over in Michael Conway's illustration for the cover of **Sleepover Friends** *for Scholastic Inc. The illustration, rendered in watercolor and colored pencil, was one of a series of covers: Conway completed each one within two months. Art director David Tommasino told him that in the story the girls were visiting the city and stopped into an ice cream parlor overlooking the city. "I was familiar with the characters and had been using the same models from the beginning." Conway originally contacted the publisher by sending tear sheets of his work in the junior adult market. "I began by using the* **Artist's Market** *to see publishers in general." He was recommended to Tommasino by another publisher. Tommasino finds Conway "easy to work with. His sketches and finals are always on time. He is very creative with the composition of the piece and color." Conway was paid $2,300 for first rights.*

Southeast, Mid-Atlantic, New England. Several directories will be published with the same cover. No animals, birds, or buildings. A hunter should be able to paint himself into this landscape." Pays by the project, $150 minimum.

***SCHOLASTIC INC.**, 730 Broadway, New York NY 10003, Art Director: David Tommasino. Specializes in hardcover, paperback originals and reprints of young adult, biography, classics, historical romance, contemporary teen romance. Publishes 250 titles/year; 80% require freelance illustration.
First Contact & Terms: Works with 75 freelance artists/year. Prefers local artists with experience. Prefers oils, then airbrush and acrylics. Send query letter with brochure showing art style or tear sheets. Samples are filed. Samples not filed are returned only if requested. Reports back within 2 weeks only if interested. Originals returned to artist at job's completion. Considers complexity of project and skill and experience of artist when establishing payment. Buys first rights.
Jackets/Covers: Assigns 200 freelance illustration jobs/year. Pays by the project, $1,500-3,500.

***SCHOLIUM INTERNATIONAL INC.**, 99 Seaview Blvd., Port Washington NY 11050. (516)484-3290. President: A. L. Candido. Publishes scientific and technical books.
First Contact & Terms: Send photocopies or transparencies. Uses artists for jacket design, direct mail brochures and advertising layouts/art.

***SCIENCE TECH PUBLISHERS**, 701 Ridge St., Madison WI 53705. (608)238-8664. Managing Editor: Katherine M. Brock. Specializes in hardcover science and technical books. Also production services for other publishers. Publishes 5-6 titles/year; 90% require freelance illustration.
First Contact & Terms: Works with 3-6 freelance artists/year. Needs artists skilled in technical art. Works on assignment only. Send query letter with brochure showing art style or resume. Samples are filed. Samples not filed are returned only if requested. Reports back within 3 weeks. Originals not returned to artist at job's completion. Call to schedule an appointment to show a portfolio, which should include "a good selection" of work. Considers complexity of project, skill and experience of artist and project's budget when establishing payment. Buys all rights. Finds most artists through references/word-of-mouth, portfolio reviews and samples received through the mail.
Text Illustration: Assigns 3-6 freelance jobs/year. Prefers scientific illustration—graphs, line art, bar graphs, diagrams— in pen & ink, airbrush, collage and computer illustration with overlays. Pays by the hour, $8-45.
Tips: "Provide a good selection of work and especially final printed pieces in which the work was used."

SCOTT, FORESMAN AND CO., 1900 E. Lake Ave., Glenview IL 60025. Design Manager: John Mayahara. Specializes in hardcover and paperback originals and reprints on elementary and high school textbooks for major subject areas. Publishes over 100 titles/year.
First Contact & Terms: Works with over 200 artists/year. Works on assignment only. Send query letter with slides or "any material that can be filed; *no* original art." Samples not filed are returned by SASE. Reports within 1 month. No originals returned to artist at job's completion. Considers complexity of project, skill and experience of artist and project's budget when establishing payment. Buys all rights.

SIERRA CLUB BOOKS, 730 Polk St., San Francisco CA 94109. Publisher: Jon Beckmann. Editorial Director: Daniel Moses. Design Director: Eileen Max. Publishes books on natural history, science, ecology, conservation issues and related themes, calendars and guides.
First Contact & Terms: Send query letter with resume, tear sheets and/or business card to be kept on file.
Needs: Uses artists for book design and illustration (maps, juvenile art) and jacket design. Pays by the project, $600-900 for book design. Pays by the project, $450-1,000 for jacket/cover design; $175-500 for jacket/cover illustration; $1,000-2,000 average for text illustration. Buys U.S. or world rights.

***SIMON AND SCHUSTER BOOKS FOR YOUNG READERS**, 1230 Ave. of the Americas, New York NY 10020. Art Coordinator: Rose Lopez. Specializes in hardcover and paperback juvenile trade books, for ages 3-12. Publishes 50 hardcover and 20 paperbacks/year.
First Contact & Terms: Assigns 50 jobs/year "but only to artists we have previously met and selected. We do not look at portfolios and have a stable on whom we rely. We pay an advance or flat fee."

SINGER COMMUNICATIONS, INC., 3164 Tyler Ave., Anaheim CA 92801. (714)527-5650. Contact: Natalie Carlton. Licenses paperback originals and reprints; mass market, Western, romance, doctor/nurse, mystery, science fiction, nonfiction and biographies. Licenses 200 titles/year through affiliates, 95% require freelance designers for book covers. Also buys 3,000 cartoons/year to be internationally syndicated to newspaper and magazine publishers—also used for topical books. Pays 50% of syndication fee received; books, 15% USA, 20% foreign.
First Contact & Terms: Send query letter with photocopies and tear sheets to be kept on file. Do not send original work. Material not filed is returned by SASE. Reports in 2 weeks. Buys first and reprint rights. Originals returned to artist at job's completion. Artist's guidelines $1.
Book Design: Assigns "many" jobs/year. Uses artists for reprints for world market. Prefers clean, clear, uncluttered style.
Jackets/Covers: Popular styles include Western, romance, mystery, science fiction/fantasy, war and gothic. "We are only interested in color transparencies for paperbacks." Duplicates only. Offers advance.
Tips: "Study the market. Study first the best seller list, the current magazines, the current paperbacks and then come up with something better if possible or something new. We now utilize old sales for reprint." Looking for "new ideas, imagination, uniqueness. Every artist is in daily competition with the best artists in the field. A search for excellence helps. We get hundreds of medical cartoons, hundreds of sex cartoons. We are overloaded with cartoons showing inept office girls but seldom get cartoons on credit cards, senior management, aerobics, fitness, romance. We have plenty on divorce, but few on nice romance and love. We would like more positive and less negative humor. Can always use good travel cartoons around the world."

SOUTHERN HISTORICAL PRESS, INC., 300 South 1st St., Box 738, Easley SC 29641-0738. (803)859-2346. President: The Rev. Silas Emmett Lucas, Jr. Specializes in hardcover and paperback originals and reprints on genealogy and history. Publishes 40 titles/year.
First Contact & Terms: Works with 1 freelance artist/year. Works on assignment only. Send query letter and samples to be kept on file. Call or write for appointment to show portfolio. Prefers tear sheets or photographs as samples. Samples not filed are returned by SASE if requested. Reports back only if interested. Original work not returned after job's completion. Considers complexity of the project, skill and experience of artist, project's budget and turnaround time when establishing payment. Buys all rights.
Needs: Assigns 5 freelance book design, cover design and illustration, and text illustration jobs/year.

STANDARD PUBLISHING, 8121 Hamilton Ave., Cincinnati OH 45231. Advertising Manager: John Weidner. Art Director: Frank Sutton. Publishes religious, self-help and children's books.
First Contact & Terms: Artists with at least 4 years of experience. Send query letter with business card to be kept on file. SASE. Reports in 2 weeks. Buys all rights. Free catalog.
Needs: Art director uses artists for illustrations only. Advertising manager uses artists for advertising, books, catalogs, convention exhibits, decorative spots, direct mail brochures, letterheads, magazines, packages and posters.

STAR PUBLISHING, Box 68, Belmont CA 94002. Managing Editor: Stuart Hoffman. Specializes in original paperbacks and textbooks on science, art, business. Publishes 12 titles/year. 33% require freelance illustration.
First Contact & Terms: Works with 7-8 artists/year. Send query letter with resume, tear sheets and photocopies. Samples not filed are returned only by SASE. Reports back only if interested. Original work not returned after job's completion. Rights purchased vary according to project but does buy one-time rights.
Book Design: Assigns 12 freelance design and 20 freelance illustration jobs/year. Pays by the project.
Jackets/Covers: Assigns 5 freelance design jobs/year. Pays by the project.
Text Illustration: Assigns 6 freelance jobs/year.

STEIN AND DAY, Scarborough House, Briarcliff Manor NY 10510. Contact: Art Department. Publishes hardcover, paperback, original and reprint mass market fiction and nonfiction. Publishes 100 titles/year; 10% require freelance designers, 20% require freelance cover illustrators.
First Contact & Terms: Prefers local artists with experience with other publishers, but young unpublished artists are welcome to submit. Send query letter with brochure showing art style or resume and nonreturnable samples. Especially looks for clean, smooth art, good color design and layout; also a variety of technical skills. SASE. Works on assignment only. Reports back on future assignment possibilities. Portfolios accepted at Westchester office for review. Artist provides overlays for color covers. Buys all rights. 15% kill fee. Pays on publication. Free catalog.
Jackets/Covers: Assigns 15 freelance design and 25 illustration jobs/year. Pays by the project, $500-1,200 average; mass market cover illustration, $700-1,500 average.
Text Illustration: Assigns 3-5 jobs/year. Pays by the project, $150-500 average. "We use very little text illustration but on occasion we require maps or b&w line drawings."
Tips: "Our covers are very diversified. All styles and designs are considered. A book can make it or break it by its cover. Simple design executed properly is the best design. Artist is selected for the best style that matches my layout and concept."

STEMMER HOUSE PUBLISHERS, INC., 2627 Caves Rd., Owings Mills MD 21117. (301)363-3690. President: Barbara Holdridge. Specializes in hardcover and paperback fiction, nonfiction, art books, juvenile and design resource originals. Publishes 20 titles/year; 50% require freelance designers, 75% require freelance illustrators.
First Contact & Terms: Works with 10 freelance artists/year. Works on assignment only. Send brochure/flyer, tear sheets, photocopies or color slides to be kept on file; submission must include SASE. Do not send original work. Material not filed is returned by SASE. Call or write for appointment to show portfolio. Reports in 6 weeks. Works on assignment only. Originals returned to artist at job's completion on request. Negotiates rights purchased.
Book Design: Assigns 1 freelance design and 5 illustration jobs/year. Uses artists for design. Pays by the project, negotiable amount.
Jackets/Covers: Assigns 2 freelance design jobs/year. Prefers paintings. Pays by the project, $300 minimum.
Text Illustration: Assigns 8 jobs/year. Prefers full-color artwork for text illustrations. Pays by the project on a royalty basis.

Tips: Looks for "draftmanship, flexibility, realism, understanding of the printing process." A common mistake freelancers make in presenting samples or portfolios is "presenting original work only without printed samples."

STONE WALL PRESS INC., 1241 30th St. NW, Washington DC 20007. Publisher: Henry Wheelwright. Publishes paperback and hardcover environmental, backpacking, fishing, beginning and advanced outdoor originals, also medical. Publishes 1-2 titles/year; 10% require freelance illustrators.
First Contact & Terms: Prefers artists who are accessible. Works on assignment only. Send query letter with brochure showing art style. Samples returned by SASE. Reports in only if interested. Buys one-time rights. Originals returned to artist at job's completion.
Book Design: Assigns 1 job/year. Uses artists for composition, layout, jacket design. Prefers generally realistic style—photo, color or b&w. Artist supplies overlays for cover artwork. Pays cash upon accepted art.
Text Illustration: Buys b&w line drawings.

***SUPPORT SOURCE**, 420 Rutgers Ave., Swathmore PA 19081. Publisher: Jane Heald. Specializes in paperback originals on "caregiving to the elderly and spiritual life education.". Publishes 2 titles/year.
First Contact & Terms: Send brochure showing art style. Samples are filed. Samples not filed are returned by SASE. Reports back within weeks. Originals returned to artist at job's completion. To show a portfolio, mail Photostats, tear sheets, final reproduction/product and b&w. Considers complexity of project and project's budget when establishing payment. Negotiates rights purchased.
Text Illustration: Prefers line drawings. Pays by the project, $20 each.
Tips: "Build our file of samples so that we will have a selection of styles to choose from when planning each book."

TEN SPEED PRESS, Box 7123, Berkeley CA 94707. (415)845-8414. President: Phil Wood. Publishes hardcover and paperback cookbook, history, sports, gardening, career and life planning originals and reprints. Publishes 50 titles/year. Assigns 50 advertising jobs/year. Pays $1,500 maximum/job, catalogs; $1,000 maximum/job, direct mail brochures.
First Contact & Terms: Submit query. Reports within 4 weeks. Works on assignment only. Samples returned by SASE. Provide resume, flyer and/or sample art which may be kept on file for future assignments. Buys all rights, but may reassign rights to artist after publication. Pays flat fee. Offers advance. Pays promised fee for unused assigned work. Free catalog.
Book Design: Assigns 50 jobs/year. Pays by the project, $200 minimum.
Jackets/Covers: Assigns 50 freelance design jobs and 50 illustration jobs/year. Pays by the project, $200 minimum.
Text Illustration: Assigns 20 jobs/year. Pay varies.

TEXAS MONTHLY PRESS, Box 1569, Austin TX 78767. (512)476-7085. Design & Production Director: Cathy S. Casey. Specializes in hardcover and paperback originals and reprints on general trade books. Publishes 25-28 titles/year.
First Contact & Terms: Works with 15 freelance artists/year. Works on assignment only. Send resume, tear sheets and Photostats. Samples not filed are returned only if requested. Reports within 3 weeks. Originals returned at job's completion. Considers complexity of project and project's budget when establishing payment. Buys first rights.
Book Design: Assigns 25-28 freelance design and 3 freelance illustration jobs/year. Pays by the project, $350-1,000.
Jackets/Covers: Assigns 25-28 freelance design and 3 freelance illustration jobs/year. Pays by the project, $350-1,200.
Text Illustration: Assigns 2 freelance jobs/year. Pays by the project, $200-500.

THORNDIKE PRESS AND NORTH COUNTRY PRESS, Box 159, Thorndike ME 04986. (207)948-2962. Operations Manager: Charles Fortier. Specializes in hardcover and paperback originals and reprints—large print books for the visually impaired. Publishes 136 titles/year.
First Contact & Terms: Works with 15-18 freelance artists/year. "Demand experience in preparation of mechanicals for four-color process." Works on assignment only. Send query letter with tear sheets and slides. Samples not filed returned by SASE. Reports only if interested. Pays for design by the the project, $100-160. Pays for illustration by the project, $200. Considers project's budget when establishing payment. Rights purchased vary according to project.
Book Design: Assigns 12 freelance design jobs and 6 freelance illustration jobs/year. Payment is negotiable.
Jackets/Covers: Works with 16 freelance designers/year. Pays by the project, negotiable amount.
Text Illustration: Works with 6 freelance artists/year. Prefers pen & ink. Payment is negotiable.

Tips: "We are looking for artists/designers who have experience in four-color process on the trade book publishing level; textbook or magazine experience is *not* sufficient in most cases."

***TRAVEL KEYS BOOKS**, Box 160691, Sacramento CA 95816. (916)452-5200. Publisher: Peter B. Manston. Specializes in paperback originals on travel, antiques and home security. Publishes 4 titles/ year; 100% require freelance illustration.
First Contact & Terms: Works with 4 freelance artists/year. "We contract only on a work-for-hire basis. All books include between 15 and 60 illustrations, usually as pen & ink drawings." Works on assignment only. Send query letter with brochure showing art style or tear sheets and Photostats. Samples are filed. Samples not filed are returned. Reports back within 2 months. Originals not returned to artist at job's completion. Write to schedule an appointment to show a portfolio, which should include roughs, original/final art, Photostats, tear sheets and final reproduction/product. Considers skill and experience of artist, project's budget and rights purchased when establishing payment. Buys all rights.
Jackets/Covers: Assigns 2 freelance illustration jobs/year. Must fit in with Travel Keys series designs. Pays by the project, $150-800.
Text Illustration: Assigns 4 freelance jobs/year. Prefers representational pen & ink for most projects. Pays by the hour, $20; by the project, $1,000 maximum.
Tips: "Please query first, request catalog with SASE (1 first class stamp). Do not send production work for other clients."

TROLL ASSOCIATES, Book Division, 100 Corporate Dr., Mahwah NJ 07430. Vice President: Marian Frances. Specializes in hardcover and paperbacks for juveniles to 3 to 15 years. Publishes 100 + titles/ year; 30% require freelance designers and illustrators.
First Contact & Terms: Works with 30 freelance artists/year. Prefers artists with 2-3 years of experience. Send query letter with brochure/flyer or resume and tear sheets or Photostats. Samples "usually" returned by SASE only if requested. Reports in 1 month. Works on assignment only. Originals "usually not" returned to artist at job's completion. Write to schedule an appointment to show a portfolio, or mail original/final art, Photostats and tear sheets. Considers complexity of project, skill and experience of artist, project's budget and rights purchased when establishing payment. Buys all rights or negotiates rights purchased.

THE TRUMPET CLUB/DELL PUBLISHING COMPANY, 245 47th St., New York NY 10017. (212)605-3123. Art Director: Ann Hoffman. Establ. 1985. Mail-order school book club specializing in paperbacks and related promotional material. Publishes juvenile fiction and non-fiction.
First Contact & Terms: Works with 25 freelance artists/year. Prefers local mechanical people only. Prefers local illustrators, but out-of-towners okay. Send query letter with brochure, resume and tear sheets. Samples are filed. Samples not filed are not returned. Reports back only if interested. "We only report if we are interested or you can call for an appointment to show your portfolio. We prefer illustrators with children's experience, but we will consider others, too." Originals returned after job's completion. Call or write to schedule an appointment to show a portfolio, which should include Photostats, final reproduction/product, slides and transparencies. Considers complexity of project and project's budget when establishing payment.
Tips: "We are looking for freelance mechanical people, designers and illustrators. Designers and mechanical people may work on or off premises, depending on the complexity of the project. Designers must be able to carry a job through to production.

***TYNDALE HOUSE PUBLISHERS,INC.**, 336 Gundersen Dr., Wheaton IL 60189. (312)668-8300. Creative Director: Tim Botts. Specializes in hardcover and paperback originals on "Christian beliefs and their effect on everyday life." Publishes 80-100 titles/year; 25% require freelance illustration.
First Contact & Terms: Works with 15-20 freelance artists/year. Send query letter, tear sheets and slides. Samples are filed. Samples not filed are returned by SASE. Reports back only if interested. Negotiates whether originals returned to artist at job's completion. To show a portfolio, mail tear sheets and slides. Considers complexity of project, skill and experience of artist, project's budget and rights purchased. Negotiates rights purchased.
Jackets/Covers: Assigns 20 freelance illustration jobs/year. Prefers progressive but friendly style. Pays by the project, $400 and up.
Text Illustrations: Assigns 20 freelance jobs/year. Prefers progressive but friendly style. Pays by the project, $100 and up.
Tips: "Show your best work. We are looking for illustrators who can tell a story with their work and who can draw the human figure in action when appropriate."

***UNDERWOOD-MILLER**, 515 Chestnut St., Columbia PA 17512. (717)684-7335. Publisher: Chuck Miller. Specializes in hardcover originals and reprints on science fiction, fantasy, romance and popular

literature. Publishes 12-20 titles/year.
First Contact & Terms: Works with 5 freelance artists/year. Works on assignment only. Send query letter with Photostats, photos and tearsheets (not original art) to be kept on file. Samples not filed are returned by SASE. Reports only if interested. Original work returned to artist. Considers complexity of project, project's budget and rights when establishing payment. Usually buys one-time rights, but can vary according to project.
Book Design: Assigns 2 jobs/year. Pays by the project, $250 minimum.
Jackets/Covers: Assigns 15 freelance illustration jobs/year. Pays by the project, $250 minimum.
Text Illustration: Assigns 4 jobs/year. Prefers b&w line drawings. Pays by the project, $250 minimum.

UNIVELT INC., Box 28130, San Diego CA 92128. (619)746-4005. Manager: H. Jacobs. Publishes hardcover and paperback originals on astronautics and related fields; occasionally publishes veterinary first-aid manuals. Publishes 10 titles/year; all have illustrations.
First Contact & Terms: Prefers local artists. Send query letter with resume, business card and/or flyer to be kept on file. Samples not filed are returned by SASE. Reports in 4 weeks on unsolicited submissions. Buys one-time rights. Originals returned to artist at job's completion. Free catalog.
Jackets/Covers: Assigns 10 jobs/year. Uses artists for covers, title sheets, dividers, occasionally a few illustrations. Pays $50-100 for front cover illustration or frontispiece.
Tips: "Illustrations have to be space-related. We obtain most of our illustrations from authors and from NASA."

***THE UNIVERSITY OF ALABAMA PRESS**, Box 2877, Tuscaloosa AL 35487. (205)348-5180. Production Manager: A.F. Jacobs. Specializes in hardcover and paperback originals and reprints of academic titles. Publishes 40 titles/year; 33% require freelance design.
First Contact & Terms: Works with 4-6 freelance artists/year. Requires book design experience, preferably with university press work. Works on assignment only. Send query letter with resume, tear sheets and slides. Samples not filed are returned only if requested. Reports back within a few days. Originals not returned to artist at job's completion. To show a portfolio, mail tear sheets, final reproduction/product and slides. Considers project's budget when establishing payment. Buys all rights.
Book Design: Assigns 10-15 freelance design jobs/year. Pays by the project, $250 minimum.
Jackets/Covers: Assigns 10-15 freelance design jobs/year. Pays by the project, $250 minimum.

UNIVERSITY OF IOWA PRESS, University of Iowa, Iowa City IA 52242. Director: Paul Zimmer. Publishes scholarly works, short fiction series some trade books. Publishes 28 titles/year; 20 require freelance scholarly book designers, 2 require freelance illustrator or photographer.
First Contact & Terms: "We use freelance book designers." Query with "two or three samples; originals not required." Works on assignment only. Samples returned by SASE. Check for most recent titles in bookstores. Free catalog.
Book Design: Assigns 20 freelance jobs/year. Pays $300 to draw specifications and prepare layouts. Pays $300 minimum, book design; $300, jacket.

***UNIVERSITY OF NEBRASKA PRESS**, 901 N. 17th St., Lincoln NE 68588-0520. (402)472-3581. Designer: Richard Eckersley. Specializes in hardcover and paperback originals, reprints and textbooks on English and American literature, criticism and literature in translation, economics, political science, music, the American West, the American Indian, food production and distribution, agriculture, natural history, modern history of Western Europe, Latin American studies and Bison paperback reprints (ficton, memoirs, biography, etc.).
First Contact & Terms: Works with 6 freelance artists/year. "Work judged solely on merit and appropriacy." Works on assignment only. Send query letter with brochure showing art style or resume, tear sheets, Photostats, slides and photographs. Samples are filed. Samples not filed are returned by SASE. Reports back within 2 weeks. Originals returned to artist at job's completion. Call or write to schedule an appointment to show a portfolio, or mail Photostats, tear sheets, final reproduction/product, photographs, slides and transparencies. Considers complexity of project, skill and experience of artist and project's budget. Negotiates rights purchased. Finds most artists through references/word-of-mouth, portfolio review and samples received through the mail.
Book Design: Assigns 8 freelance design and 1 freelance illustration jobs/year. Pays by the project, $300-850.
Jackets/Covers: Assigns 12 freelance design jobs/year. Prefers pen & ink, airbrush, charcoal/pencil, watercolor, acrylics, oils, pastels and collage. "Both line and four-color process. Subjects very varied in main list; styles range from minimalist abstractions to naturalistic. Paperbacks mostly 19th century western subjects. We also require calligraphy on occasion." Pays by the project, $250-600.
Text Illustration: Assigns 2 freelance jobs/year. Prefers mostly line subjects (pen, woodcut, scratch-

Watercolor was used by illustrator Pete Catalanotto to convey the mood of a hot summer afternoon in Florida for a cover to Robert Peck's Hallapoosa*, published by Walker & Co., in New York City. Art director Laurie McBarnette told the Brooklyn artist to convey a feeling of loneliness, "of someone holding his dignity in a physically oppressive environment." Catalanotto drew upon his experience in advertising to complete the work within a week. "Pete is fast, clean and professional," remarks McBarnette, who bought all rights to the piece. "I knew he could render figures well, and I could trust him to bring out an understated elegance while still keeping the scene hot and heavy." Catalanotto was recommended by another editor.*

board, etc.) Pays by the project, $250-1,000.
Tips: "Illustrators should be conversant with graphic reproduction. Book designers are required to supply accurate tissues and detailed type specifications."

UNIVERSITY OF PENNSYLVANIA PRESS, Blockley Hall, 13th Floor, 418 Service Dr., Philadelphia PA 19104. Director: Thomas M. Rotell. Design & Production Manager: Carl E. Gross. Publishes scholarly books and texts; hardcover and paperback originals and reprints. Publishes 60-70 titles/year. Also uses artists for advertising layout, catalog illustration, direct mail design, book design and cover design. Assigns 30-40 advertising jobs/year. Prefers pen & ink, airbrush, acrylics and calligraphy. Minimum payment: $400, catalogs or direct mail brochures. Assigns 60-70 production jobs/year. Pays $9/hour minimum, mechanicals and paste-ups. Arrange interview; local artists only. SASE. Buys all rights. No advance. Negotiates payment for unused assigned work. Free catalog.
Book Design: Assigns 60-70 jobs/year. Uses artists for layout, type spec; all design shipped out-of-house. Pays $350-375/job, text layout; $75/job, type spec.
Jackets/Covers: Assigns 35-40 jobs/year. Pays for design by the job, $350-375 average; $300-350 b&w line drawings and washes, gray opaques and color-separated work.
Text Illustration: Pays $10-15/hour for maps, charts.
Tips: Production of books has doubled. Artists should have some experience in book and jacket design.

THE UNIVERSITY OF WISCONSIN PRESS, 114 N. Murray St., Madison WI 53715. (608)262-4978. Production Manager: Gardner R. Wills. Publishes scholarly hardcover and paperback books. Publishes 40-50 titles/year.
First Contact & Terms: Works on assignment only. Query first. Reports in 2 weeks. Buys all rights. No originals returned to artist at job's completion. Samples returned by SASE. Reports back on future assignment possibilities. Provide letter of inquiry and samples as agreed upon to be kept on file. "Printed samples are best." Check for most recent titles in bookstores. Designer supplies overlays for cover artwork. No advance. Finds most artists through references/word-of-mouth, portfolio reviews and samples received through the mail.
Book Design: Assigns 20-25/year. Pays upon completion of design. Pays by the project, $200-350.
Jackets/Covers: Assigns 30-40 freelance design jobs/year. Prefers "generally conservative" style; pen & ink, airbrush and calligraphy. Pays for design by the project, $175-250. "We do not purchase individual items of art."
Tips: "In presenting samples via mail, many freelancers do not personalize the presentation with either a cover letter or a note. So mechanical. Often, in-person presentations do not include work relevant to my needs."

VONGRUTNORV OG PRESS, INC., Box 411, Troy ID 83871. (208)835-4902. Publisher: Steve E. Erickson. Specializes in paperback originals on philosophy, metaphysics, poetry, creative fiction.
First Contact & Terms: Works with 1-2 freelance artists/year. Works on assignment only. Send query letter with Photostats or copies to be kept on file. Samples not filed not returned. Whether original work is returned after the job's completion "depends on the type of assignment and agreement or contract with the artist." Considers complexity of project, project's budget and rights purchased when establishing payment. Rights purchased vary according to project.

J. WESTON WALCH, PUBLISHER, Box 658, Portland ME 04104-0658. (207)772-2846. Managing Editor: Richard Kimball. Specializes in supplemental secondary school materials including books, poster sets, filmstrips and computer software. Publishes 120 titles/year.
First Contact & Terms: Works with 20 freelance artists/year. Works on assignment only. Send query letter with resume and samples to be kept on file unless the artist requests return. Write for artists' guidelines. Prefers Photostats as samples. Samples not filed are returned only by request. Reports within 6 weeks. Original work not returned to the artist after job's completion. Considers project's budget when establishing payment. Rights purchased vary according to project.
Jackets/Covers: Assigns 20 freelance design and 20 freelance illustration jobs/year. Pays by the hour, $12-20 and by the project, $100 minimum.
Text Illustration: Assigns 10 freelance jobs/year. Prefers b&w pen & ink. Pays by the hour, $12-20 and by the project, $100 minimum.

WALKER & COMPANY, 720 Fifth Ave., New York NY 10019. (212)265-3632. Cable address: REKLAWSAM. Art Director: Laurie McBarnette. Publishes hardcover originals and reprints on mysteries, regency romance, children's science, adult trade, etc. Publishes 200 titles/year; 60% require freelance designers, 60% require freelance illustrators. Also uses artists for catalog design and layout, educational and adult/juvenile.
First Contact & Terms: Works with 20-30 freelance artists/year. Illustrators must be within 2 hours of

New York; designers must have textbook experience. Works on assignment only. Send query letter with brochure showing art style or tear sheets, Photostats, slides and photographs. Samples not filed are returned by SASE. Reports only if interested. Buys all rights. Originals returned to artist at job's completion (except in special instances).

Book Design: Assigns 20 freelance design and 50 freelance illustration jobs/year. Uses freelance artists for complete follow-through on job, layout, type spec. Prefers classic style—modern conservative. Pays by the project, $400-1,750 average; 60 days upon completion.

Jackets/Covers: Assigns 50 freelance design and 10 freelance illustration jobs/year. Pays by the project, $100-1,200.

Text Illustration: Assigns 1 freelance job/year. Prefers b&w line drawings or pencil. Pays by the project $500 minimum.

Tips: "Send samples of work. Only see portfolios when project calls for freelancer. Use my files to contact illustrators/designers. No samples, no call."

WARNER BOOKS INC., 666 Fifth Ave., New York NY 10103. (212)484-3151. Vice President and Creative Director: Jackie Meyer. Publishes mass market paperbacks, adult trade hardcovers and children's books. Publishes 400 titles/year; 20% require freelance designers, 80% require freelance illustrators. Works with countless freelance artists/year. Buys hundreds of designs from freelance artists/year. Buys hundreds of illustrations from freelance artists/year.

First Contact & Terms: Works on assignment only. Send brochure or tear sheets and photocopies. Samples are filed. Samples not filed are returned by SASE. Reports back only if interested. To show a portfolio, mail appropriate materials. Originals returned to artist at job's completion (artist must pick up). Pays $650/design; $1,000/illustration. Negotiates rights purchased. Check for most recent titles in bookstores.

Jackets/Covers: Uses realistic jacket illustrations. Payment subject to negotiation.

Tips: Industry trends include "more graphics and stylized art. Looks for "photorealistic style with imaginative and original design and use of eyecatching color variations." Artists shouldn't "talk too much. Good design and art should speak for themselves."

***WATERFRONT BOOKS**, 98 Brookes Ave., Burlington VT 05401. (802)658-7477. Publisher: Sherrill N. Musty. Specializes in paperback textbooks; trade and academic books for children and adults. "Waterfront Books specializes in books dealing with mental health, education, family, parenting and learning possibilities." Publishes 2 titles/year.

First Contact & Terms: Works with 2 freelance artists/year. Prefers an artists with an interest in children's illustrations, "though at this point we would like to keep our options open." Works on assignment only. Send query letter with brochure, resume, tear sheets, Photostats, slides, photographs; and "A little of everything possible." Samples are filed. Samples not filed are returned by SASE. Reports back within 2 weeks. Originals not returned at job's completion. Write to schedule an appointment to show a portfolio, or mail, thumbnails, roughs, original/final art, Photostats, tear sheets, final reproduction/product, photographs, slides, transparencies, and dummies. Considers complexity of project, skill and experience of artist, slides, project's budget, and rights purchased when establishing payment. Buys one-time rights, reprint or all rights.

Book Design: Assigns 3 freelance design and 2 freelance illustration jobs/year. Pays by the project.

Jackets/Covers: Prefers pencil or wash expressive or active, for children. Pays by the project.

Text Illustration: Assigns 2 freelance jobs/year. Prefers pencil or wash. Pays by the project.

Tips: "Show samples right away, with your first submission."

SAMUEL WEISER INC., Box 612, York Beach ME 03910. (207)363-4393. Production Manager: Kathryn Sky-Peck. Specializes in hardcover and paperback originals, reprints and trade publications on metaphysics/oriental philosophy/occult. Publishes 20 titles/year.

First Contact & Terms: Works with 4 freelance artists/year. Send query letter with resume, slides, book covers and jackets. Samples are filed. Samples not filed are returned by SASE only if requested by artist. Reports back within 1 month only if interested. Originals returned to artist at job's completion. To show a portfolio, mail tear sheets and slides. Considers complexity of project, skill and experience of artist, project's budget, turnaround time and rights purchased when establishing payment. Buys one-time non-exclusive rights. Finds most artists through references/word-of-mouth, portfolio reviews and samples received through the mail.

Jackets/Covers: Assigns 20 freelance design jobs/year. Prefers airbrush, watercolor, acrylics and oils. Pays by the project, $200-600.

Tips: "We're interested in artists with professional experience with cover mechanicals—from inception of design to researching/creating image to type design, color-separated mechanicals to logo in place. Don't send us drawings of witches, goblins and demons, for that is not what the occult field is. You should know something about us before you send materials. Ask for catalog."

Close-up

Jackie Meyer

Vice President, Art Director
Warner Books
New York City

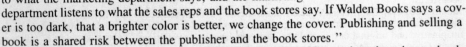

Even though she's under 30 years of age, Jackie Meyer is vice president and art director of one of the largest mass-market publishers in the country. She oversees the design and illustration of over 500 titles a year.

"I'm part of a publishing team," the young, energetic woman says. "As the art director, I have to be responsive to what the marketing department says, and the marketing department listens to what the sales reps and the book stores say. If Walden Books says a cover is too dark, that a brighter color is better, we change the cover. Publishing and selling a book is a shared risk between the publisher and the book stores."

Meyer has her own ideas—ideas which have won over 100 awards—about how a book cover or jacket should look. Both mass-market and trade books need, as Meyer points out, "a single poster image," an illustration which summarizes the plot and also sends out certain "messages" to consumers to make them reach out and buy the book. "Your books have to stand out on the racks," says Meyer. "A book's best advertisement is its cover, and it has to be a strong image."

As art director, Meyer must aim each cover towards the right audience. As she originates an idea for a cover, she must keep in mind the book's genre, whether it is a mystery, adventure, romance or a trade book. Different treatments must also be given to books by prominent authors, whose books usually receive larger marketing budgets because of their proven sales records. "The more variations you have to consider, the greater the stress is on getting a great cover idea."

Deciding on the right cover is a team effort. Every month, Meyer has "cover concept meetings," where she shows sketches of cover ideas to the editorial and marketing departments. "I show them what I'd like to do for a cover. I don't take their opinions as gospel. If I disagree with what's decided at this meeting, I'll take it to the publisher for approval."

Once the idea is approved, Meyer assigns the job to an illustrator. She works with about 150 to 200 freelancers a year. "It's a revolving door. I like to see new, fresh work; I don't like to eliminate any creative ideas. But I do have my favorite artists."

She reviews approximately 500 portfolios or "books" each year, and she also combs illustration annuals for possible candidates. She looks for various attitudes and techniques to fit specific genres. "Every book has a personality. So I look for an artist whose style fits that personality." Often, a best-selling author is identified by not only his own writing style but also by the cover art. "People recognize the name of the author and also the style of the illustrator," Meyer notes. "When that author has a major departure in his style or subject matter, I'll seek a new look to match it."

Like many publishers, Meyer has a drop-off policy on portfolios. She prefers to see 10 pieces or less. "Show only your best work. I'll remember you by the bad pieces. It would be my luck that that's what I'd get from you. Let go of those pieces. Always try to do your best on any job so you can put that piece in your portfolio."

Meyer likes to look at a variety of work in a portfolio. "If you're trying for the mass market, it can help to specialize, but it's better if you can show a variety of things." She noted that one artist who specialized in trade books included some samples of horror jackets in her portfolio. "I would have never thought of her for that genre, but I did use her for that after seeing those samples."

The best advice for aspiring book illustrators is to keep current, says Meyer. Look at the racks in your stores and order catalogs to get an idea of what books are being published by a certain company.

Book illustration can be lucrative for artists who can consistently meet deadlines and deliver the right message. Meyer offers this encouragement: "Don't worry about money. It'll come if you can deliver."

—Susan Conner

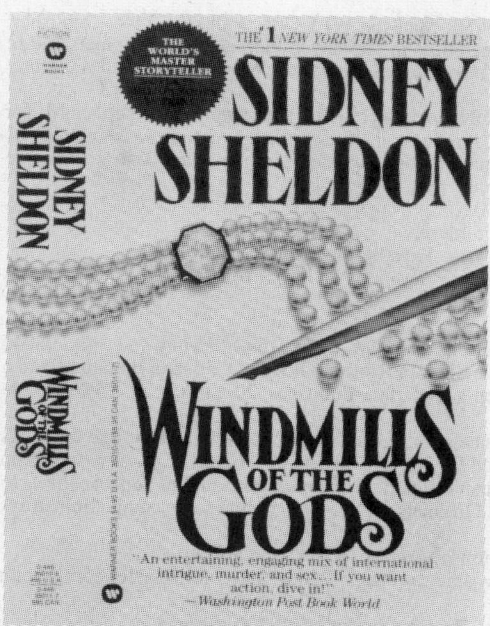

"This was a group project," Meyer says about the cover of the best-selling novel, **Windmills of the Gods,** *by Sidney Sheldon. "The lettering was done by Dave Gatti and the illustration by airbrush artist Stanislaw Fernandez, whom Meyer calls "a versatile illustrator/designer who's a great problem solver." Meyer conceptualized the cover, which has won numerous awards.*

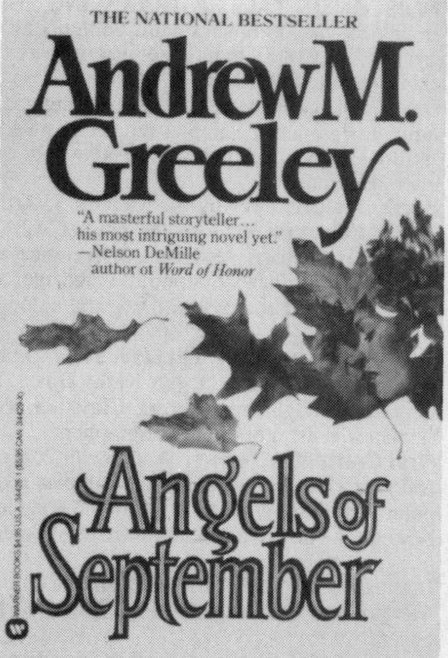

Meyer chose airbrush artist Max Ginsberg from New York City for this cover because his style fits the message of the cover. "He has a very painterly style that's realistic yet loose enough to be lyrical. I didn't want the piece to be too literal, but more poetic. I called Max because he is a great fine artist as well as an illustrator."

ALBERT WHITMAN & COMPANY, 5747 W. Howard St., Niles IL 60648. Editor: Kathleen Tucker. Specializes in hardcover original juvenile fiction and nonfiction—many picture books for young children. Publishes 21 titles/year; 100% require freelance illustrators.
First Contact & Terms: Works with 18 freelance artists/year. Prefers working with artists who have experience illustrating juvenile trade books. Works on assignment only. Send brochure/flyer or resume and "a few slides and photocopies of original art and tear sheets that we can keep in our files. Do *not* send original art through the mail." Samples not returned. Reports to an artist if "we have a project that seems right for him. We like to see evidence that an artist can show the same children in a variety of moods and poses." Original work returned to artist at job's completion "if artist holds the copyright." Rights purchased vary.
Cover/Text Illustration: Cover assignment is usually part of illustration assignment. Assigns 18 jobs/year. Prefers realistic art. Pays by flat fee or royalties.
Tips: Especially looks for "an artist's ability to draw people, especially children."

WILSHIRE BOOK CO., 12015 Sherman Rd., North Hollywood CA 91605. (213)875-1711 or (818)983-1105. President: Melvin Powers. Publishes paperback reprints on psychology, self-help, inspirational and other types of nonfiction. Publishes 25 titles/year.
First Contact & Terms: Local artists only. Call. Buys first, reprint or one-time rights. Negotiates pay. Free catalog.
Jackets/Covers: Assigns 25 jobs/year. Buys b&w line drawings.

***WISCONSIN TALES & TRAILS, INC.**, Box 5650, Madison WI 53705. (608)231-2444. Publisher: Howard Mead. Publishes adult trade books. Specializes in hardcover and paperback originals and reprints. "Only those that relate in some way to Wisconsin." 3 categories: Wisconsiana, guides, nature/environment. Publishes 1-2 titles/year.
First Contact & Terms: Works on assignment only. Send query letter and samples to be kept on file for future assignments. Samples returned by SASE "if requested." Reports back on future assignment possibilities. Buys one-time rights. Return of original artwork "depends on individual contract or agreement negotiated."
Book Design: Pays by the project, $300-1,000.
Jackets/Covers: Pays by the project, $200 minimum.
Text Illustration: Assigns 1-2 freelance jobs/year. Pays by the project, $300-1,000.
Tips: Also publishes bimonthly magazine, *Wisconsin Trails*. "We have been using freelance artwork regularly in our magazine, b&w and color."

WOMEN'S AGLOW FELLOWSHIP, Publications Division, Box 1548, Lynnwood WA 98046. (206)775-7282. Art Director: Kathy Boice. Specializes in Bible studies and Christian literature, and a bimonthly magazine offering Christian women's material. Publishes 20 titles/year; 25% require freelance illustrators and calligraphers.
First Contact & Terms: Works with 20 freelance artists/year. Send slides, Photostats, line drawings and reproduced art as samples. Samples returned by SASE. Reports in 6 weeks. Call or write for appointment to show portfolio. Provide resume, business card, brochure/flyer, samples and tear sheets to be kept on file for possible future assignments. Originals returned to artist at job's completion. Buys one-time rights.
Jackets/Covers: Pays for design and illustration by the job, $200 average.
Magazine Illustrations: Pays $80-175, b&w line drawings; $200-325, color, inside; $500, color, cover.
Text Illustration: Prefers b&w line drawings. Pays by the job, $35-200 average.
Tips: "Be aware of organization's emphasis. Be motivated to work for a women's organization."

WOODALL PUBLISHING COMPANY, Suite 100, 100 Corporate North, Bannockburn IL 60015-1253. (312)295-7799. Production Manager: Sue Hallwas. Specializes in paperback annuals on camping. Publishes 3 titles/year.
First Contact & Terms: Works with 4 freelance artists/year. Works on assignment only. Call for appointment to show portfolio. Reports within 4 weeks. No original work returned at job's completion. Considers complexity of project, skill and experience of artist, and project's budget when establishing payment. Rights purchased vary according to project.
Book Design: Assigns 3-4 jobs/year. Pays by the project.
Jackets/Covers: Assigns 2 freelance design and illustration jobs/year. Pays by the project.
Text Illustration: Pays by the project.

***WOODSONG GRAPHICS INC.**, PO Box 238, New Hope PA 18938. (215)794-8321. President: Ellen Bordner. Specializes in paperback originals covering a wide variety of subjects, "but no textbooks or

technical material so far." Publishes 3-6 titles/year.
First Contact & Terms: Works with 1-5 freelance artists/year depending on projects and schedules. Works on assignment only. Send query letter with brochure and samples to be kept on file. Any format is acceptable for samples, except originals. Samples not filed are returned by SASE. Reports only if interested. Originals returned to artist at job's completion. Considers complexity of the assignment, skill and experience of artist, project's budget and turnaround time when establishing payment. Rights purchased vary according to project.
Book Design: Assigns 2-3 freelance jobs/year. Pays by the project, $400 minimum.
Jackets/Covers: Assigns 3-6 freelance illustration jobs/year. Pays by the project, $100 minimum.
Text Illustration: Assigns 2-3 freelance jobs/year. Medium and style vary according to job. Pays by the project, $250 minimum.

WRITER'S DIGEST BOOKS/NORTH LIGHT, F&W Publishing, 1507 Dana Ave., Cincinnati OH 45207. Art Director: Carol Buchanan. Publishes 25-30 books annually for writers, artists, photographers, plus selected trade titles. Send photocopies of printed work to be kept on file. Works on assignment only.
Text Illustration: Uses artists for text illustration and cartoons.
Tips: Uses artists for ad illustration and design, book jacket illustration and design, and direct mail design.

YANKEE PUBLISHING INC., BOOK DIVISION, Main St., Dublin NH 03444. Assistant to Editorial Director: Rebecca Robinson. Specializes in hardcover and paperback originals on New England topics; cookbooks. Publishes 14 titles/year; 30% require freelance illustrators.
First Contact & Terms: Works with 4-8 freelance artists/year. Send query letter with resume and slides or photocopies to be kept on file. Samples not kept on file are returned by SASE. Works on assignment only. Originals returned to the artist at job's completion if stated in contract. Considers complexity of project, project's budget and rights purchased when establishing payment. Negotiates rights purchased.
Jackets/Covers: Pays by the project, $200-600 average, usually full color.
Text Illustration: Pays by the project, $50-500 average, usually b&w line art.

YE GALLEON PRESS, Box 25, Fairfield WA 99012. (509)283-2422. Editorial Director: Glen Adams. Publishes rare western history, Indian material, antiquarian shipwreck and old whaling accounts, and town and area histories; hardcover and paperback originals and reprints. Publishes 30 titles/year; 20% require freelance illustrators.
First Contact & Terms: Query with samples. SASE. No advance. Pays promised fee for unused assigned work. Buys book rights. Free catalog.
Text Illustration: Buys b&w line drawings, some pen & ink drawings of a historical nature; prefers drawings of groups with facial expressions and some drawings of sailing and whaling vessels. Pays for illustration by the project, $10-35.
Tips: " 'Wild' artwork is hardly suited to book illustration for my purposes. Many correspondents wish to sell oil paintings which at this time we do not buy. It costs too much to print them for short edition work."

"I don't want to see art school class projects. I want to see a range of the artist's styles, preferably in jobs done for similar clients."

—Edna H. Jones, Chilton Book Co.
Radnor, Pennsylvania

Businesses

The variety of businesses listed in this section—t-shirt manufacturers, a broadcasting station, collectible plate manufacturers, insurance companies and resorts, to name a few—calls for artists who are versatile in both illustration and design. Their talents are used in annual reports, print ads, brochures, point-of-purchase displays and product illustration.

In a survey of freelance artists conducted by the *Artist's Market* last year, over half of the respondents said they worked with small businesses in their communities. Locally, there are hundreds of assignments from small businesses awaiting you. Your doctor may need informational brochures, and the tuxedo rental shop downtown may need some ads a month before prom time. Keep in mind that you will probably oversee the job from start to finish—conceptualizing and rendering the piece as well as supervising the printing. (Doctors and tuxedo shops don't have art directors.) Consult the listings in this section and in the Yellow Pages for businesses in your area. By building a good reputation and a strong portfolio with them, you will be in demand with other businesses nationwide. Read the special feature, "How to Work with a Small Business," by illustrator Michael Fleishman to see how local contacts are made.

Businesses generally need realistic artwork to render their products accurately. They most often need illustrations for newspaper ads and catalogs. For this reason, most listings in this section prefer work done in pen and ink, airbrush and watercolor. The business world also has needs for fine art for the illustration of collectible plates. Collectible manufacturers can be found in this section and also in *The Bradford Book of Collector's Plates* and in *Plate World*. This year's Business section also includes architectural firms, which seek architectural renderers, modelmakers and interior design illustrators.

The art needs of fashion firms (which are singled out at the end of this section) revolve around the illustration and design of clothing and accessories. Catalogs and retail advertisements call for realistic treatments, because consumers want to see details in the clothing they might buy. Fine artists often apply their skills to fashion editorial, which entails a freer, more expressionistic touch in articles on trends. Fashion demands you look months ahead in your artwork. To keep up with trends, refer to *Women's Wear Daily* or *W*.

While many businesses rely on references and word-of-mouth to find freelance artists on the local level, they also review portfolios and refer to their files for samples artists send them through the mail. In your initial package and portfolio, include samples of both black-and-white and color work. Show your versatility with examples of logos, letterhead design and print advertisements you have done.

If you are interested in a particular type of business, check the Yellow Pages and ask at your local library for suggestions of trade periodicals dealing with that type of business. Also consult the *Thomas Register of Manufacturers*, which lists companies alphabetically and according to product. Trade shows showcase the latest developments within a certain field. Check trade magazines for dates and times of these shows. When you attend, bring along brochures and business cards, because there are many valuable contacts to be made. Also obtain a directory of exhibitors, which usually lists the names and addresses of manufacturers at the show.

***ABBEY ASSOCIATES-LANDSCAPE ARCHITECTS**, Suite A, 3337 Highland Rd., Baton Rouge LA 70802. (504)383-6078. Contact: Austin Abbey. Interior and landscape design firm specializing in museum design and commercial landscape architecture. Clients: government, industrial and commercial.
Needs: Works with 1 freelance artist/year. Must be experienced. Works on assignment only. Uses freelance artists for interior renderings, landscape renderings, architectural renderings and design consulting. "Should be able to work with Apple Macintosh and Mac II."
First Contact & Terms: Send query with brochure showing art style. Samples are filed. Samples not

filed are not returned. Reports back within 3 weeks. Call to schedule an appointment to show a portfolio. Negotiates fee or salary. Considers complexity of project, skill and experience of artist, turnaround time and client's budget when establishing payment. Buys all rights.

ABBEY PRESS, Hill Dr., St. Meinrad IN 47577. Creative Director: Jo Anne Calucchia. Manufacturer/distributor/mail order catalog providing Christian products, greeting cards, wall decor and sculpture. Clients: Christian bookstores and retail catalog.
Needs: Works with 50 freelance artists/year. Buys 200-300 freelance designs/illustrations/year. Artist must have knowledge of art preparation for reproduction; prefers 3 years experience in greeting cards. Works on assignment only. Uses artists for 3-dimensional product design, illustration on product and model making. "Quick turnaround time is required."
First Contact & Terms: Send query letter with resume, tear sheets, slides and photographs. Samples not filed are returned by SASE. Reports back within 1 month. Pays for design by the project, $75 minimum. Pays for illustration by the project, $200 minimum.
Tips: "Our products are of a religious and/or inspirational nature. We need full-color illustrations from experienced artists who know how to prepare art for reproduction. Familiarize yourself with current looks and trends in the Christian market."

ABRACADABRA MAGIC SHOP, Box 450, Dept. AM87, Scotch Plains NJ 07076. (201)668-1313. President: Robert Bokor. Manufacturer/mail order specializing in fun products for boys, marketed via mail order. Clients: boys, as well as hobby and magic shops.
Needs: Works with 2-3 freelance artists/year. Local artists only. Works on assignment only. Uses artists for advertising and catalog design, illustration and layout; packaging design and layout.
First Contact & Terms: Send query letter with resume and photocopies. Samples not filed are returned by SASE. Reports back within 1 month. To show a portfolio, mail appropriate materials. Pays for design by the project, $50-1,000. Considers client's budget when establishing payment.
Tips: "Freelancers with past experience designing products/ads for boys and cartooning."

***ACI MARKETING SERVICES**, 600 W. Fulton, Chicago IL 60606. Production Manager: Janet Lumley. Third party insurance administrator. Clients: alumni association, insurance companies, business and social organizations.
Needs: Prefers local artists. Works on assignment only. Uses artists for advertising and brochure design and layout, production design, posters, magazine design and layout.
First Contact & Terms: Send query letter with resume. Samples are not filed. Samples not filed are returned. Reports back only if interested. Write to schedule an appointment to show a portfolio, which should include thumbnails, roughs and original/final art. Pays for design by the hour, $12-18. Considers complexity of project, skill and experience of artist and turnaround time when establishing payment.

ADELE'S II, INC., 2832 Angelo Dr., Los Angeles CA 90077. (213)276-5566. Contact: Shirley Margulis. Franchisor and retailer of personalized gifts including acrylic and oak desk accessories, stained glass boxes, novelty clocks, personalized gift items from any medium. Sells to "high-quality-conscious" customers.
Needs: Works with 100-150 freelance artists/year. Uses artists for product design, model making and lettering. "We always will consider any type of item that can be personalized in some way, shape or form."
First Contact & Terms: Send query letter with brochure or photocopies and photos to be kept on file. Samples not filed are returned by SASE. Reports only if interested. Write for appointment to show portfolio, which should include thumbnails b&w photographs or actual samples. Pays for design by the hour, $10-15; by the project, $10-300. Considers rights purchased when establishing payment.
Tips: "Consider first that we only purchase items we or you can personalize. A beautiful picture can't be personalized. Common mistakes freelancers make in presenting samples or portfolios is to "talk too much and show sloppy samples. Also, they don't know how to cost out their item. We require a firm price and commitment."

***ADVANCE SPECTACLE CO., INC.**, 3710 Commercial Ave., Northbrook IL 60062. President: S.F. Levine. Mail order business offering eyeglasses and products for senior citizens.
Needs: Works with 1 freelance artist/year. Assigns 20 jobs/year. Prefers local artists. Works on assign-

The asterisk before a listing indicates that the listing is new in this edition. New markets are often the most receptive to freelance submissions.

ment only. Uses artists for advertising, brochure and catalog design, illustration and layout.
First Contact & Terms: Send query letter with brochure. Samples are filed. Reports back only if interested. Write to schedule an appointment to show a portfolio. Pays for design and illustration by the project, $25/hour. Considers complexity of project and client's budget when establishing payment. Negotiates rights purchased.

AERO PRODUCTS RESEARCH INC., 11201 Hindry Ave., Los Angeles CA 90045. (213)641-7242. Director of Public Relations: J. Parr. Aviation training materials producer. Produces line of plastic credit and business cards.
Needs: Works with about 2 illustrators/month. Prefers local artists. Uses artists for brochures, catalogs, advertisements, graphs and illustrations.
First Contact & Terms: Send query letter with brochure/flyer, resume and tear sheets to be kept on file. No originals returned to artist at job's completion. Negotiates pay according to experience and project.

AHPA ENTERPRISES, Box 506, Sheffield AL 35660. Marketing Manager: Allen Turner. Media products producer/marketer. Provides illustrations, fiction, layouts, video productions, computer-printed material, etc. Specializes in adult male, special-interest material. Clients: limited-press publishers, authors, private investors, etc.
Needs: Seeking illustrators for illustration of realistic original fiction or concepts. Wants only those artists "who are in a position to work with us on an intermittent but long-term basis." Prefers a tight, realistic style. Prefers pen & ink, airbrush, colored pencil and watercolor. Works on assignment only.
First Contact & Terms: Send query letter with resume and photocopies or tear sheets, Photostats, photographs and new sketches to be kept on file. Samples not filed are returned by SASE only if requested. Reports back only if interested (within 3-7 days). Pays for illustration by the project, $40-1,000 average. Considers complexity of the project and number and type of illustrations ordered when establishing payment. Buys all rights.
Tips: "This is an excellent place for capable amateurs to 'turn pro' on a part-time, open-end basis. We are most inclined to respond to artists whose cover letters indicate a willingness to adapt to our particular market needs."

AK INTERNATIONAL, 1116 Marshall Ave., Lancaster PA 17601. (717)394-0202. President: O. Ali Akincilar. Full line of photo frames including brass, chrome and brass, exotic woods and aluminum. Clients: the gift industry, premium, department stores, photo stores.
Needs: Buys approximately 20 designs/year from freelance artists. Prefers line drawings for illustrations. Artists must have a knowledge of photo etching. Works on assignment only.
First Contact & Terms: Send query letter with brochure, resume and photographs to be kept on file. Samples not filed are returned only if requested. Reports only if interested. Call for appointment to show portfolio. Original art not returned after reproduction. Pays by the project, $50-500 average. Buys all rights.
Tips: Looks for "eye for proportion and exactness, feel for proper color, knowledge of current market trends."

ALBEE SIGN CO., 561 E. 3rd St., Mt. Vernon NY 10553. (914)668-0201. President: William Lieberman. Produces interior and exterior signs and graphics. Clients are commercial accounts, banks and real estate companies.
Needs: Works with 6 artists for sign design, 6 for display fixture design, 6 for P-O-P design and 6 for custom sign illustration. Local artists only. Works on assignment only.
First Contact & Terms: Query with samples (pictures of completed work). Previous experience with other firms preferred. SASE. Reports within 2-3 weeks. No samples returned. Reports back as assignment occurs. Provide resume, business card and pictures of work to be kept on file for future assignments. Pays by job.

ALL-STATE LEGAL SUPPLY CO., One Commerce Dr., Cranford NJ 07016. (201)272-0800. Advertising Manager: Paul Ellman. Manufacturer and distributor of supplies, stationery, engraving, printing. Clients: lawyers.
Needs: Works with 6 freelance artists/year. Experienced, local artists and designers only. Works on assignment only. Uses artists for advertising, brochure and catalog design, illustration and layout; display fixture design, and illustration on product. Especially needs cover illustrations and catalog work.
First Contact & Terms: Send query letter with Photostats to be kept on file. Reports only if interested. Call for appointment to show portfolio. Pays by the project, $350-1,500 average. Considers complexity of project, skill and experience of artist and turnaround time when establishing payment.

ALMOST HEAVEN HOT TUBS, LTD, Attention: Art Dept., Route 5, Renick WV 24966. (304)497-3163. Art Director: Barry Glick. Manufacturer of hot water leisure products, i.e., hot tubs, spas, whirlpools, saunas. Clients: distributors, dealers, retailers, consumers.
Needs: Works with 5 freelance artists/year. Uses artists for advertising, brochure and catalog design, illustration and layout; product and display fixture design, illustration on product, P-O-P displays, posters, model making and signage.
First Contact & Terms: Send query letter with brochure, resume, business card, samples and tear sheets to be kept on file. Reports within 1 week. Pay varies. Considers complexity of project, skill and experience of artist, how work will be used, turnaround time and rights purchased when establishing payment.

ALVIMAR MANUFACTURING CO., INC., 51-02 21st St., Long Island City NY 11101. (718)937-0404. President: Alan P. Friedlander. Display firm and manufacturer of plastic inflatable swim toys, such as beach balls, rings, pools, mats. Also premium items, such as product replicas. Like Little Green Sprout and Wrigley Spearmint Chewing Gum. Clients: service advertising agencies, food and cosmetic manufacturers, "any category as we make product replicas."
Needs: Uses artists for product and P-O-P design and model making.
First Contact & Terms: Call for appointment. Prefers to see originals or Photostats of work. Samples returned by SASE. Reports in 4 months. Provide resume and tear sheets to be kept on file for possible future assignments. Payment method is negotiable and varies according to client's budget.

AMERICAN ARTISTS, Division of Graphics Buying Service, 225 W. Hubbard St., Chicago IL 60610. (312)828-0555. Advertising Coordinator: Lorraine Light. Manufacturer of limited edition plates and figurines. Specializes in horse, children, and cat themes, but considers others. Clients: wholesalers and retailers.
Needs: Works with 3 freelance artists/year. Uses artists for plate and figurine design and illustration; brochure design, illustration and layout. Open to most art styles.
First Contact & Terms: Send query letter with resume and samples to be kept on file unless return is requested or artwork is unsuitable. Prefers transparencies or slides but will accept photos—color only. Samples not filed are returned only if requested or if unsuitable. Reports within 1 month. Call or write for appointment to show portfolio. Payment varies and is negotiated. Rights purchased vary. Considers complexity of project, skill and experience of artist, how work will be used and rights purchased when establishing payment.

AMERICAN BOOKDEALERS EXCHANGE, Box 2525, La Mesa CA 92041. Editor: Al Galasso. Publisher of *Book Dealers World* targeted to self-publishers, writers and mail order book dealers. Clients: self-publishers, writers, business opportunity seekers.
Needs: Works with 3 freelance artists/year. Prefers artists with at least a year's experience. Works on assignment only. Uses artists for advertising, brochure and catalog design and illustration.
First Contact & Terms: Send query letter with Photostats to be kept on file. Samples not kept on file are returned only if requested. Reports only if interested. Pays by the project, $25-200 average. Considers complexity of project, skill and experience of artist, turnaround time and rights purchased when establishing payment.

AMERICAN EAGLE COMPANY, 1130 E. Big Beaver, Troy MI 48083. (313)689-9458. Creative Director: Diane Chownyk. Provides teaching aid products and marketing products/programs for hospitals and nurses and foreign language teachers.
Needs: Works with 6 freelance artists/year. Works on assignment only. Uses artists for advertising, brochure and catalog design, illustration and layout; product design, illustration on product, posters and model making. Prefers pen & ink, colored pencil, watercolor, markers and calligraphy.
First Contact & Terms: Send query letter with resume and photocopies. Samples not filed are not returned. Reports only if interested. To show a portfolio, mail appropriate materials or call or write to schedule an appointment. Pays for design and illustration by the hour, $10-20. Considers complexity of project, skill and experience of artist, and how work will be used when establishing payment.
Tips: Artist should "show their best samples—our interview time is limited. Have a resume if possible."

AMERICAN MANAGEMENT ASSOCIATION, 135 W. 50th St., New York NY 10020. (212)903-8157. Art Director: Dolores Wesnak. Provides educational courses, conferences and topical briefings to business managers and support staff. Clients: business executives, managers and supervisors.
Needs: Works with 6-10 freelance artists/year. Uses artists for brochure design and layout, catalog design and layout, and posters.
First Contact & Terms: Prefers local artists experienced in 2-color brochures, full-time professionals.

The ability to conceptionally develop ideas is important. Works on assignment only. Call for appointment to show portfolio. Pays by the project, $450 minimum. Considers complexity of project and skill and experience of artist when establishing payment.
Tips: Artists "must have a knowledge of design for direct mail and of postal regulations."

AMERICAN PERMANENT WARE, INC. (APW), 729 Third Ave., Dallas TX 75226. (214)421-7366. Director of Advertising and Marketing: Mary M. Cardone. Manufacturer of stainless steel food service equipment for dealers, distributors and national accounts.
Needs: Works with 4 freelance artists/year. Prefers local artists. Works on assignment only. Uses artists for the design, illustration and layout of advertising brochures and catalogs plus P-O-P displays and trade publication ad layouts.
First Contact & Terms: Send query letter with brochure showing art style or photocopies. Samples not filed are returned only if requested. Reports back only if interested. Write to schedule an appointment to show a portfolio, which should include final reproduction/product and color. Considers complexity of project and client's budget when establishing payment. Buys all rights.
Tips: "See more sophistication in the field."

ANNIS-WAY SIGNS LTD., 595 West St. S., Orillia, Ontario Canada L3V 6K5. (705)835-3121. Contact: Lloyd H. Annis.
Needs: Uses artists for exhibit, trademark and display design, sign redesign and lettering.
First Contact & Terms: Send resume.

***ARCHITECTURE BY SCHLOH**, 213 Bean Ave., Los Gatos CA 95030. (408)354-4551. Architectural firm providing architectural services for high-end custom homes. Clients: residential.
Needs: Works with 2 artists/year. Local artists preferred. Works on assignment only. Uses artists for advertising and brochure design, architectural renderings and model making.
First Contact & Terms: Send query letter with brochure and photocopies. Samples are filed. Reports back within 2 weeks. Write to schedule an appointment to show a portfolio, which should include photographs. Pays for illustration by the project, $600-2000. Considers complexity of project and client's budget when establishing payment. Buys first rights.

ARTISTS OF THE WORLD, 2915 N. 67th Place, Scottsdale AZ 85251. (602)946-6361. National Sales Manager: Thomas R. Jackson. Producer of plates, figurines and miniature plates and figurines. Clients: wholesalers and retailers.
Needs: Works with a variable number of freelance artists/year. Works on assignment only. Uses artists for the design and illustration of plates and figurines.
First Contact & Terms: Send query letter with brochure showing art style. Samples not filed are returned only if requested. Reports back within 2 weeks. To show a portfolio, mail appropriate materials, which should include original/final art, final reproduction/product and color. Pays for design by the project. Considers how work will be used when establishing payment.

THE ASHTON-DRAKE GALLERIES, 9333 Milwaukee Ave., Niles IL 60648. (312)966-2770, ext. 300. Product Development: Ed Bailey-Mershon. Direct response marketer of limited edition collectibles, such as porcelain dolls, figurines, ornaments, and other uniquely executed artwork sold in thematic series. Clients: Collectible consumers, represent all age groups.
Needs: Works with 200 freelance doll artists, costume designers, illustrators, artists, sculptors a year. Works on assignment only. Uses artists for concept illustrations, collectible designs, prototype specifications and construction. Prior experience in giftware design, doll design, greeting card and book illustration a plus. Subject matter is children and mothers, animals, nostalgia scenes. Prefers "cute, realistic, and naturalistic human features."
First Contact & Terms: Send query letter with resume, copies of samples to be kept on file, except for copyrighted slides which are duplicated and returned. Prefers slides, photographs, tear sheets, or Photostats (in that order) as samples. Samples not filed are returned. Reports within 45 days. Concept illustrations are done "on spec" to $200 maximum. Contract for length of series on royalty basis with guaranteed advances. Considers complexity of the project, project's budget, skill and experience of the artist, and rights purchased when establishing payment.

***ASSOCIATES DESIGN GROUP**, 6283 Walnut Lake Rd., W. Bloomfield MI 48322. (313)661-2825. Architect/Designer: Arnold Sabaroff. Architectural and interior design firm with specialties in shop and stores, commercial 8-industrial buildings and custom residential. Works with 2 freelance artists/year. Prefers local people with some experience. Works on assignment only. Uses freelance artists for interior renderings and architectural renderings.

AVALON LTD., 12217 Woodbine, Redford MI 48239. (517)332-4902. Vice President: Eric Fromm. Importer/distributor/retailer of rattan and bamboo home furnishings and furniture. Directed toward ages 20-45.
Needs: Works with 2-4 freelance artists/year. Uses artists for brochure and catalog design, illustration and layout; P-O-P displays, posters and direct mail. Prefers pen & ink, charcoal/pencil and colored pencil.
First Contact & Terms: Send query letter with resume and samples. Samples not filed are returned only if requested. To show a portfolio, mail roughs, original/final art, color and tear sheets. Pays for design and illustration by the project, $10-100. Considers complexity of project and budget when establishing payment. Finds most artists through samples.

BANCROFT-SAGE PUBLISHING, (formerly Baker Street Productions Ltd.), Box 1968, 112 Marshall St., Mankato MN 56001. (507)625-2482. Contact: Karyne Jacobsen. Service-related firm providing juvenile books to publishers.
Needs: Works with 2 freelance artists/year. Artists must be able to meet exact deadlines. Works on assignment only. Uses artists for illustration on product and book illustration. Prefers realistic style.
First Contact & Terms: Send query letter with resume and tear sheets. Reports back within 3 months. Write to schedule an appointment to show a portfolio, which should include roughs, final reproduction/product, color and photographs. Fee is determined by the size of the project involved. Pays for design and illustration by the project. Considers complexity of the project and how work will be used when establishing payment. Buys all rights.

BANKERS LIFE & CASUALTY COMPANY, 1000 Sunset Ridge Rd., Northbrook IL 60062. (312)498-1500. Manager-Communications/Graphics: Charles S. Pusateri. Insurance firm.
Needs: Works with 3-4 freelance artists/year. Works on assignment only. Uses artists for advertising and brochure displays, illustration and layout; posters and signage. Prefers pen & ink, airbrush, pencil, markers and calligraphy.
First Contact & Terms: Send query letter with resume and printed pieces to be kept on file. Samples returned only if requested. Reports within 2 weeks only if interested. Write to schedule an appointment to show a portfolio, which should include thumbnails, roughs and final reproduction/product. Pays for design by the project, $50-100. Pays for illustration by the project, $25-75. Considers complexity of project, skill and experience of artist, and turnaround time when establishing payment. Rights purchased vary according to project.
Tips: "Follow rules but don't give up. Timing is essential."

***BARBIZON INTERNATIONAL, INC.**, 3 E. 54th St., New York NY 10022. Marketing Director: Debra Heitmann. Service-related firm. Modeling school franchisor; advertising is directed to teenagers.
Needs: Works with 100 freelance artists/year. Assigns 25 jobs/year. Prefers local artists. Works on assignment only. Uses artist for advertising, brochure and catalog design, illustration and layout.
First Contact & Terms: Send query letter with brochure, tear sheets and resume. Samples are filed. Samples not filed are returned only if requested by artist. Reports back within 10 days; only if interested. To show a portfolio, mail final reproduction/product and tear sheets. Pays for design and illustration by the project $50 minimum. Negotiates rights purchased.
Tips: "Creative, fashion-oriented individuals should submit works for consideration."

***BAXTER HODELL DONNELLY PRESTON, INC. ARCHITECTS**, 3500 Red Bank Rd., Cincinnati OH 45227. Marketing Coordinator: Cynthia A. Jackson. "BHDP offers comprehensive services in programming, planning, design and construction administration. The company has earned a national reputation for quality and innovation-especially on large buildings with complex functional requirements. Our experience covers a broad range of projects, including office buildings, manufacturing facilities, research & development laboratories, schools, major department stores."
Needs: Uses freelance artists for interior renderings, architectural renderings and model making.
First Contact & Terms: Send query letter with brochure showing art style or resume and sample. Samples are filed. Samples not filed are returned only if requested by artist. Reports back within days. Write to schedule an appointment to show a portfolio, or mail a sample. Considers complexity of project, skill and experience of artist, turnaround time, client's budget and rights purchased when establishing payment. Negotiates rights purchased.
Tips: "We don't have a lot of time for meetings. Prefer contact by mail, and it's best to include a sample of work. All contacts are kept in files for future resources. Tight budgets are a considered factor, but quality does not always come cheap and that is also considered. Both the Marketing coordinator and the Manager of Business Development are relatively new to the firm and are unfamiliar with past contacts/projects. We are developing new ones and working with our own past ones. New standards are being set."

ARF/ARF!
"I wish I knew how to organize my wardrobe."
©Amy Huelsman

A fashion-conscious teen having trouble organizing her closet is the message of the illustration artist Amy Huelsman completed for Barbizon International. The Hastings, New York freelancer sold one-time rights for a series of pen-and-ink illustrations for a public relations campaign. Art director Debra Heitmann called Huelsman after seeing her ad in R.S.V.P.

BAY AREA RAPID TRANSIT (BART), 800 Madison St., Oakland CA 94619. (415)465-4100. Manager Passenger Service: Kay Springer. Transportation service firm providing passenger brochures, flyers, signs, information, advertising.
Needs: Works with 4-6 freelance artists/year. Uses artists for advertising and brochure design, illustration and layout; posters and signage.
First Contact & Terms: Local artists only (San Francisco Bay area). Send query letter with brochure, resume, business card and original work to be kept on file. Reports only if interested. Works on assignment only. Pays by the hour or by the project. Considers complexity of project and turnaround time when establishing payment.

***THE BECKER GROUP**, 901 Cathedral St., Baltimore MD 21201. Art Department: April Goetze. Designs, manufactures and installs Christmas decor for shopping malls. "We are the leading company offering these services in North America."
Needs: Works with 3-6 freelance artists/year. Prefers local artists with Christmas designing experience. Works on assignment only. Uses freelance artists for brochure design, illustration and layout, interior design, landscape design and renderings, architectural renderings and model making.
First Contact & Terms: Send query letter with brochure showing art style or resume and available samples. Samples are not filed. Samples not filed are returned only if requested by artist. Reports back within 2 weeks. Call or write to schedule an appointment to show a portfolio, which should include roughs, original/final art and color. Pays for design by the hour, $8-12. Considers complexity of project, skill and experience of artist and turnaround time when establishing payment. Buys all rights.
Tips: "Prepare a good presentation showing how you develop a Christmas program in color."

BERMAN LEATHERCRAFT INC., 25 Melcher St., Boston MA 02120. (617)426-0870. President: Robert S. Berman. Manufacturer/importer/mail order firm providing leathercraft kits and leather supplies, diaries and notepads. Clients: shops, hobbyists, schools and hospitals. "We mail to 5,000-25,000 people every six weeks."
Needs: Works with 2-4 freelance artists/year. Local artists only "for the convenience of both parties." Uses artists for brochure design, illustration and layout; "we produce two- to four-page fliers." Especially needs line drawings with dimension.
First Contact & Terms: Send query letter with printed brochures; "follow up with a phone call three to five days later." Samples not filed are returned by SASE only if requested. Pays by the project. Considers complexity of project, and skill and experience of artist when establishing payment. Buys all rights.

BEROL USA, 105 Westpark Dr., Box 2248, Brentwood TN 37024-2248. (615)371-1199. Art Product Group Manager: Lance Hopkins. Manufactures writing instruments, drawing materials and art supplies (Prismacolor Art Pencils, Art Markers and Art Stix ® artist crayons).

Needs: Uses artists for illustrations and layout for catalogs, ads, brochures, displays, packages. Artists must use Prismacolor and/or Verithin products only.
First Contact & Terms: Query with photographs and slides to be kept on file. Samples returned only by request. Reports within 2 weeks. Call or write to schedule an appointment to show a portfolio; portfolios not necessary. Pays by the project, $300 maximum. Rights purchased vary according to project.
Tips: "Hand-colored photographs (with Prismacolor® Art Pencils) becoming very popular."

***BLUE CHIP GIFTS/THE GIFT HORSE**, Box 6748, Lubbock TX 79493-6748. President: A. Edwin Fowler. Executive gift catalogs for the investment, oil & horse industries.
Needs: Works with 2 freelance artists/year. Assigns 2 jobs/year. Uses artists for advertising, brochure and catalog design and layout; and product design.
First Contact & Terms: Send query letter with brochure showing art style. Samples not filed are returned only if requested. Write to schedule an appointment to show a portfolio. Considers complexity of project, how work will be used and turnaround time when establishing payment.

THE BRADFORD EXCHANGE, 9333 Milwaukee, Niles-Chicago IL 60648. (312)966-2770, ext. 302. Artist Liaison: Janet Jensen. Marketers of collectible plates. Clients: plate collectors in all age groups and income groups.
Needs: Works with 200 freelance artists/year. Works on assignment only. Uses artists for plate design; interested in all media, especially watercolor, acrylics and oils, 2-D, 3-D. Subject matter includes people, wildlife, scenery, still life and movie themes. Especially needs professional artists of portraiture, landscape, sculptors, still life, wildlife, fantasy, nautical and religious. "Quality painting reproduced on plate."
First Contact & Terms: Send query letter with brochure, 18-20 slides, resume and samples to be kept on file. Prefers slides, photographs, photocopies, tear sheets or Photostats (in that order) as samples. Slides are returned within 15 days. Call or write for appointment to show portfolio; portfolio should include roughs, original/final art, final reproduction/product, tear sheets, photographs and slides or transparencies. Pays "on spec." Contract negotiated for series. Considers complexity of the project, project's budget, skill and experience of the artist and rights purchased when establishing payment.
Tips: "Need good portfolio. Poor slides or photographs often results in exclusion or are sometimes misjudged. Include a resume or biography."

***C.W.S.E. INC.**, Box 164, Elkhart Lake WI 53020. (414)876-3209. President: Steve Weller. Designs, manufactures, installs retail stores.
Needs: Works with 3 freelance artists/year. Works on assignment only. Uses freelance artists for brochure design, interior design and renderings, and color/materials specs.
First Contact & Terms: Send query letter with resume and photocopies. Samples are filed. Reports back within 5 days. To show a portfolio, mail photographs/blueprints. Pays for design by the hour, $25-60; by the project, $75-1,000+. Considers complexity of project, skill and experience of artist, turnaround time and client's budget when establishing payment. Buys all rights.
Tips: Looking for "store front design experience and interior decor design experience."

CANTERBURY DESIGNS, INC.. Box 4060, Martinez GA 30907. (800)241-2732 or (404)860-1674. President: Angie A. Newton. Publisher and distributor of charted design books; counted cross stitch mainly. Clients: needlework specialty shops, wholesale distributors (craft and needlework), department stores and chain stores.
Needs: Works with 12-20 freelance artists/year. Uses artists for product design.
First Contact & Terms: Send query letter with samples to be returned. Prefers stitched needlework, paintings, photographs or charts as samples. Samples not filed are returned. Reports within 1 month. Call for appointment to show portfolio. Payment varies. "Some designs purchased outright, some are paid on a royalty basis." Considers complexity of project, salability, customer appeal and rights purchased when establishing payment.
Tips: "When sending your work for our review, be sure to photocopy it first. This protects you. Also, you have a copy from which to reconstruct your design should it be lost in mail. Also, send your work by certified mail. You have proof it was actually received by someone."

CENIT LETTERS, INC., 7438 Varna Ave., North Hollywood CA 91605. (818)983-1234 or (213)875-0880. President: Don Kurtz. Sign firm producing custom cutout letters. Clients: building managers and their tenants (high rise), designers and architects. Assigns 25 jobs/year.
Needs: Local artists only. Works with artists for sign design, exhibit design, P-O-P design, and custom sign artwork. Also uses artists for layout and gold leaf work.
First Contact & Terms: Send query letter with resume. SASE. Reports in 1 week. Samples returned by SASE. Call to schedule an appointment to show a portfolio, which should include original/final art

and photographs. Pays $100 minimum gold leaf. Pays for design and illustration by the hour, $15 or more.
Tips: Especially looks for "proficiency in hand lettering and accurate full-scale layouts. Find an end-user for your artwork (e.g. a buyer for 3-dimensional graphics) and we could produce the end product."

***RONALD CHARLES ASSOCIATES**, 3900 N. Miami Ave., Miami FL 33127. Secretary/Treasurer: Charles Schwartz. Manufacturer, distributor, converter, wholesaler. "We manufacture and convert fabrics and wallcoverings suitable for residential and contract jobs."
Needs: Works with many freelance artists/year. Assigns 1-10 jobs/year. Uses artists for product design.
First Contact & Terms: Send query letter with brochure. Reports back within 1 week. Call or write to schedule an appointment to show a portfolio, which should include original/final art. Considers skill and experience of artist and how work will be used when establishing payment. Buys all rights; negotiates rights purchased.

CMA MICRO COMPUTER, Box 2080, 55888 Yucca Trail, Yucca Valley CA 92286-2080. (619)365-9718. Director/Advertising: Phyllis Wattenbarger. Manufacturer/distributor of computer software. Clients: computer software manufacturers and distributors.
Needs: Works with 10 freelance artists/year. Uses artists for advertising and brochure design and illustration.
First Contact & Terms: Send query letter with Photostats, photographs, photocopies or tear sheets to be kept on file. Samples not filed returned only if requested. Reports only if interested. To show a portfolio, mail appropriate materials, which should include tear sheets and Photostats. Pays for design by the hour, $8 minimum. Considers complexity of project, skill and experience of the artist, how work will be used and turnaround time ("very important") when establishing payment. Buys all rights.
Tips: "Just mail material appropriate to the computer industry. If we wish to respond, we will call or write."

COLLINS-LACROSSE SIGN CORP., 222 Pine St., LaCrosse WI 54601. (608)784-8200. President/Manager: Charles C. Collins. Outdoor advertising sign firm. Clients: food manufacturers, beer and soft drink bottlers, oil companies; "any commercial enterprise."
Needs: Works with artists for sign design and custom sign illustration. Works on assignment only. Also uses artists for billboards, displays, neon signs and sign redesign.
First Contact & Terms: Send brochure showing art style, resume, tear sheets or photographs. Write to schedule an appointment to show a portfolio, which should include thumbnails, roughs, original/final

Need Diskettes?

Ken Ascher, chairman and CEO of Communications Electronics, Inc., paid illustrator Deborah Kerschbaum $150 for all rights to her pen-and-ink illustration of a man thinking about purchasing computer diskettes. Kerschbaum, from Ann Arbor, Michigan, originally sent the company (also located in Ann Arbor) samples of her work and a resume.

art and photographs. Reports in 3 days. Samples returned by SASE. Pays $25-75, full color sketches; $6, rough pencil-$30, accurate pencil; by the hour, $8-12 average. Considers complexity of project, skill and experience of artist, and turnaround time when establishing payment. Rights purchased vary according to project.
Tips: "There is a trend toward animation. Freelance artists need to be able to provide fast service. Determine a need, supply roughs to start and get an okay for precise work."

COLORSCAN SERVICES, INC., 241 Stuyvesant Ave., Lyndhurst NJ 07071. (201)438-6729. President: J. Principato. Graphic services firm providing separations and printing services. Clients: ad agencies, printers, manufacturers and publishers.
Needs: Works with 3 freelance artists/year. Works on assignment only. Uses artists for advertising, brochure and catalog design, illustration and layout; product design; illustration on product; P-O-P displays; display fixture design; posters; model making; and signage.
First Contact & Terms: Send resume and tear sheets to be kept on file. Samples not filed are returned by SASE. Reports only if interested. Write for appointment to show portfolio. Pays by the project. Considers complexity of the project and rights purchased when establishing payment.

COLORTEX CO., One Cape May St., Harrison NJ 07029. (201)482-5500. Product Manager: Judy Gross. Manufacturer of needlecraft kits; counted and stamped cross-stitch, plastic canvas; line-work designs for wholesalers, shops and mass merchandiser.
Needs: Works with 15 freelance artists/year. Prefers artists with experience with stamped and counted cross stitch.
First Contact & Terms: Send query letter with brochure or tear sheets, Photostats and photographs. Samples not filed are returned. Reports back within 1 week. Call or write to show a portfolio, which should include thumbnails, roughs and original/final art. Pays for design by the project, $75-450. Pays for illustration (color charts) by the project, $25-150. Considers complexity of project when establishing payment. Buys all rights.
Tips: "I do not have enough artists for amount of development we would like to do. Look for overall design attractiveness and design balance. Need overall feeling of being filled out without undue complexity. Please, experienced designers only! We'll review all work. Please call before sending and/or bringing."

COMMUNICATIONS ELECTRONICS, Dept. AM, Box 1045, Ann Arbor MI 48106-1045. (313)973-8888. Editor: Ken Ascher. Manufacturer, distributor and ad agency (10 company divisions). Clients: electronics, computers.
Needs: Works with 300 freelance artists/year. Uses artists for advertising, brochure and catalog design, illustration and layout; product design, illustration of product, P-O-P displays, posters and renderings. Prefers pen & ink, airbrush, charcoal/pencil, watercolor, acrylics, markers and computer illustration.
First Contact & Terms: Send query letter with brochure, resume, business card, samples and tear sheets to be kept on file. Samples not kept on file returned by SASE. Reports within 1 month. Call or write for appointment to show portfolio. Pays for design and illustration by the hour, $15-100; by the project, $10-15,000; by the day, $40-800. Considers complexity of project, skill and experience of artist, how work will be used, turnaround time and rights purchased when establishing payment.

CONIMAR CORPORATION, Box 1509, Ocala FL 32678. (904)732-7235. Creative Director: Ray Mayer. Manufactures placemats, coasters, table hot pads, calendars, recipe cards, note cards, postcards.
Needs: Buys 10-15 designs/year. Designs include floral, abstract, Christmas and children's. Especially needs illustrations. Artist quotes price to be considered by Conimar. "Our designs are based a lot on designs of dinnerware, glassware and stationery items." Works on assignment only.
First Contact & Terms: Send query letter, resume and tear sheets, photocopies, slides and photographs. Reports in 1 week. Samples returned by SASE. To show portfolio, mail color, tear sheets, Photostats and photographs. Pays for design by the hour, $15-25; pays for illustration by the project, $50-350. Buys all rights.

MAURICE COURLAND & SON/ARCHITECTS-ENGINEERS-PLANNERS, Central Savings Bank Building, 2112 Broadway, New York NY 10023. (212)362-7018. Contact: R.H. Courland or N.M. Courland. Architecture/engineering/space planning/design firm. Clients: industrial, banks, residential, commercial, restaurants, corporate, financial institutions, government, public and semi-public, institutional and educational.
Needs: Buys 2-6 renderings of new buildings and building restoration work/year. Works on assignment only. Uses artists for architectural and interior renderings, murals/graphics and scale models. Occasionally purchases artwork (paintings; sculpture; etc.).

First Contact & Terms: Send query letter with brochure, resume, business card, and tear sheets to be kept on file. Portfolio should include color photos. SASE. Reports within "weeks." Negotiates pay/project. Certain projects require design and execution; murals; sculpture; paintings; graphics; logos; presentation (color) renderings; exteriors and interiors. Considers complexity of project, client's budget, skill and experience of artist and how work will be used when establishing payment.

CREATE YOUR OWN, INC., R.R. #2, 57 Hickory Corner Rd., Milford NJ 08848. (201)479-4015. Contact: Lynne McGarry or Susan Hollenbeck. Manufactures needlework and craft kits, including needlepoint, crewel, fabric dolls, crochet, stamped cross stitch and counted cross stitch, plastic canvas, candlewicking, lace net darning and a finished gift line. Clients: catalog houses, department store chains, needlework chains, retail stores, etc.
Needs: Works with 2-3 freelance artists/year. Prefers local artists with some experience in needleworking design, if possible. Works on assignment only. Uses artists for product design in needlework area only and model making.
First Contact & Terms: Send query letter with brochure, resume, business card and samples to be kept on file, except for original art work. Prefers photographs or tear sheets as samples. Samples returned only if requested. Pays by the project, $25-300. Considers skill and experience of the artist, how work will be used, turnaround time and rights purchased when establishing payment.
Tips: Looks for "designs suitable for silk screening (maximum 4 colors), possibly accented with minimum embroidery, designs for counted cross stitch, crewel embroidery, or finished gift ideas involving minimum assembly."

CREATIVE AWARDS BY LANE, 1575 Elmhurst Rd., Elk Grove IL 60007. (312)593-7700. President: Don Thompson. Distributor of recognition incentive awards consisting of trophies, plaques, jewelry, crystal, ad specialties and personalized premiums. Clients: companies, clubs, associations, athletic organizations.
Needs: Works with 3-4 freelance artists/year. Local artists only. Uses artists for advertising, brochure and catalog design, illustration and layout; and signage.
First Contact & Terms: Send query letter to be kept on file. Write for appointment to show portfolio, which should include Photostats, photographs or photocopies. Reports within 10 days. Pays by the project. Considers complexity of project when establishing payment.

JERRY CUMMINGS ASSOCIATES INC., Suite 301, 420 Boyd St., Los Angeles CA 90013. (213)621-2756. Contact: Jerry Cummings. Landscape architecture firm. Clients: commercial and residential.
Needs: Assigns 20-30 freelance renderings/year. Works on assignment only. Works with artists for landscape architectural renderings. Prefers loose yet realistic landscape illustration. Prefers markers, then pen & ink.
First Contact & Terms: Send query letter with brochure showing art style or resume and photographs. Reports within 2 weeks. Samples returned by SASE. Reports back on future possibilities. Call or write to schedule an appointment to show portfolio, which should include original/final art. Pays for illustration by the hour, $25-35. Considers complexity of project, client's budget, and skill and experience of artist when establishing payment.
Tips: "Include landscape renderings in your portfolio. Do not include portraits or abstract art designs."

***CUSTOM HOUSE**, Box 448, Crescent City CA 95531. Owners: George Thompson and Alice Thompson. Fine art bronzes and custom wood carving. Wildlife, bird and animal casting for fountains, light fixtures and sculptures, bronze doors, gates, fences, archictural ornaments for doors, walls, ceilings and mantels. Clients: architects, interior decorators, galleries, contractors and private commissions.
Needs: Works with 5-6 freelance artists/year. Uses artists for product design, model making, and/or pattern makers.
First Contact & Terms: Send query letter with brochure showing art style or resume, photographs or model. Reports back within 30 days only if interested. Call or write to schedule an appointment to show a portfolio, which should include photographs and b&w.

CUSTOM HOUSE OF NEEDLE ARTS, INC., Box 1128, Norwich VT 05055. (802)649-3261. Owner/President: Carolyn Purcell. Manufacturer of traditional crewel embroidery kits. Clients: needlework shops and catalogs.
Needs: Uses artists for product design. "We hope the artist is a crewel stitcher and can produce sample model."
First Contact & Terms: Send query letter with samples and any pertinent information to be kept on file. Prefers colored drawings or photos (if good closeup) as samples. Samples not filed are returned by SASE only if requested. Reports within 1 month. Pays royalty on kits sold.

Tips: "We emphasize *traditional* designs; use *some* current 'cutesy' type designs, but only if exceptional, for pictures, pillows, bellpulls, chair seats and clock faces."

CUSTOM STUDIOS INC., 1337 W. Devon Ave., Chicago IL 60660. (312)761-1150. President: Gary Wing. Custom T-shirt manufacturer. "We specialize in designing and screen printing of custom T-shirts for schools, business promotions, fundraising and for our own line of stock."
Needs: Works with 4 illustrators and 4 designers/month. Assigns 50 jobs/year. Especially needs b&w illustrations (some original and some from customer's sketch). Uses artists for direct mail and brochures/flyers, but mostly for custom and stock T-shirt designs.
First Contact & Terms: Send query letter with resume, Photostats, photocopies or tear sheets; "do not send originals as we will not return them." Reports in 3-4 weeks. Call or write to schedule an appointment to show a portfolio, or mail tear sheets, Photostats and b&w to be kept on file. Pays by the hour, $5-25 average. Considers turnaround time and rights purchased when establishing payment. On designs submitted to be used as stock T-shirt designs, pays 5-10% royalty. Rights purchased vary according to project.
Tips: "Send good copies of your best work. Do not get discouraged if your first designs sent are not accepted."

DISCOVERIES INC., 235 W. 1st St., Bayonne NJ 07002. Contact: Frank Latino. Submit tear sheets. Reports in 2-3 weeks.
Needs: Buys ideas for department store window and interior display props. Pays 10% of sales ($40-10,000) for display sold to individual store; 5% of sales ($1,000-100,000) for display purchased by chain. Pays when idea is sold.

DISPLAYCO, 2055 McCarter Hwy., Newark NJ 07104. (201)485-0023. Creative Art Director: Chris Byrd. Designers and producers of P-O-P displays in all materials. Clients: "any consumer products manufacturers."
Needs: Works with 12 freelance artists/year. Prefers artists experienced in P-O-P or display/exhibit. Works on assignment only. Uses artists for advertising layout, brochure illustration and layout, display fixture and P-O-P design, and model making. Especially needs P-O-P designers with excellent sketching and rendering skills.
First Contact & Terms: Send samples, brochure/flyer and resume. Submit portfolio for review or call for appointment. Prefers renderings, models, produced work, photos of models, work, etc., as samples. Samples not returned. Reports back on whether to expect possible future assignments. Provide resume, business card, brochure, flyer or tear sheets to be kept on file for possible future assignments. Payment is determined by the project; method is negotiable and varies according to job.
Tips: There is a "need for greater creativity and new solutions. Freelancers should have knowledge of P-O-P materials (plastics, wire, metal, wood) and how their designs can be produced."

DUKE'S CUSTOM SIGN CO., 601 2nd St. NE, Canton OH 44702. (216)456-2729. Marketing/Art Director: Diana Klaasen. Clients: banks, merchants, architects, hospitals. schools and construction firms.
Needs: Assigns 5-10 jobs/year. Works with 1-2 artists/year for sign design. Prefers local artists. Works on assignment only. Especially needs sign shapes for outdoor and free-standing displays.
First Contact & Terms: Send query letter with resume to be kept on file. SASE. Reports within 2 weeks. Call to schedule an appointment to show a portfolio, which should include thumbnails. Pays for design by the hour, $4.50-10. Considers complexity of project, skill and experience of artist, and how work will be used when establishing payment.
Tips: "Please bring samples of what you think are quality sign displays. Know current graphic designing."

***DU-SAY'S LTD.**, Box 1036, Picayune MS 39466. President: Richard Dusse. Retail mail order firm for pet supplies and pet-motif personal items.
Needs: Works with 3 freelance artists/year. Assigns 50-60 jobs/year. Works on assignment only. Uses artists for advertising and catalog design, illustration and layout and product design.
First Contact & Terms: Send query letter with brochure showing art style. Samples are filed. Samples not filed are returned. Reports back within 10 days. To show a portfolio mail appropriate materials.

***EARTHWARE COMPUTER SERVICES**, Box 30039, Eugene OR 97403. (503)344-3383. President: Donna J. Goles. Manufacturer of software for home and school. The educational products are geared for jr. high through college ages.
Needs: Works with 2 freelance artists/year. Prefers local or regional artists. Works on assignment only. Uses artists for advertising design, illustration and layout; and product design.
First Contact & Terms: Send query letter with brochure, resume, business card, Photostats, photo-

graphs, photocopies, slides or tear sheets to be kept on file. Samples not filed are returned. Reports within 1 month. Pays by the project. Considers complexity of project when establishing payment.
Tips: "Do not over supply us with samples."

EMBOSOGRAPH DISPLAY MFG. CO., 1430 W. Wrightwood, Chicago IL 60614. (312)472-6660. Specializes in "complete creative art services and manufacturing in litho, silk screen, plastic molding of all kinds, spray, hot stamping, embossing, die cutting, metal work and assembly." Clients: brewery, beverage, food, automotive, hardware, cosmetics, service stations, appliances, clocks, plus consumer wall decor plus retail merchandisers.
Needs: Assigns 50-100 jobs/year. Works with 15 artists for sign design, display fixture design, costume design, model-making, P-O-P design, print advertising and custom sign illustration. Especially needs P-O-P design. Works on assignment only.
First Contact & Terms: Query with resume or call. Prefers roughs and previously published work as samples. Reports in 2 weeks. Samples returned by SASE. Provide resume and brochure to be kept on file for possible future assignments. Pays $25-45/hour.
Tips: "We have added consumer items, mostly wall decor." There is a trend toward "counter and wall cases and stands" in this business field.

ENVIRONMENTAL TECTONICS CORP., County Line Industrial Park, Southhampton PA 18966. (215)355-9100. Art Director: Larry Keffer. Manufacturer of environmental systems, hospital and industrial sterilizers, hyperbaric systems, aeromedical physiological training systems for clients in medicine, industry and government.
Needs: Works with a various amount of freelance artists/year. Works on assignment only. Uses artists for the design and illustration of advertising, brochures, and catalogs, plus technical illustration.
First Contact & Terms: Send query letter with brochure, resume, tear sheets, Photostats and photocopies. Samples not filed are returned if requested. Reports back within 2 weeks. Call or write to schedule an appointment to show a portfolio or mail roughs, original/final art, final reproduction/product, color, tear sheets and Photostats. Pays for design by the hour, $20 minimum; pays for illustration by the project, $75 minimum. Considers complexity of project, client's budget, skill and experience of artist, how work will be used, turnaround time and rights purchased when establishing payment.
Tips: Looking for "strong, clean, well-executed design and illustration shouting superior quality and originality capable of competing in high-tech international market. The particular subject or style is not important in judging the artist's capabilities. It is the concept and execution of the piece that is important. If the artist is successful in those areas, matching that style to fit the requirements of a project is a matter of judgement on the part of the art director."

EPSILON DATA MANAGEMENT, INC., 50 Cambridge St., Burlington MA 01803. (617)273-0250. Creative Director, Design: Thomas Flynn. Full-service direct response advertising and direct mail for commercial and not-for-profit organizations. Clients: 250 diversified clients nationwide, nonprofit and commercial.
Needs: Works with 40 freelance artists/year. Uses artists for direct mail packaging; advertising, brochure and catalog design, illustration and layout; and signage.
First Contact & Terms: Local artists generally with three years direct response experience, plus "must work fast and accurately on very tight deadlines." Send query letter with brochure, resume, business card, samples and tear sheets to be kept on file. Considers Photostats, slides, photographs or original work as samples. Samples not kept on file are not returned. Reports only if interested. Works on assignment only. Pays by the hour, $50-80 average; by the project, $150-3,000 average; by the day, $150-300 average. Considers complexity of project, skill and experience of artist and turnaround time when establishing payment.
Tips: "Be well experienced in direct response advertising."

EVERTHING METAL IMAGINABLE, INC. (E.M.I.), 401 E. Cypress, Visalia CA 93277. (209)732-8126. Vice President: Dru McBride. Wholesale manufacturer. "We manufacture lost wax bronze sculpture. We do centrifugal white metal casting; we do resin casting (cold cast bronze, alabaster walnut shell, clear resin etc.). Clients: wholesalers, premium incentive consumers, retailers.
Needs: Works with "inummerable" freelance artists/year. Prefers artists that understand centrifugal casting, bronze casting and the principles of mold making. Works on assignment only. Uses artists for figurine and illustration and model making. Prefers a tight, realistic style.
First Contact & Terms: Send query letter with brochure or resume, tear sheets, Photostats, photocopies and slides. Samples not filed are returned only if requested. Reports back only if interested. Call to show a portfolio, which should include original/final art and photographs "or any samples." Pays for design by the project, $100 minimum. Considers complexity of project, client's budget, how work will be used, turnaround time and rights purchased. Buys all rights.

Tips: "Artists must be conscious of detail in their work, be able to work expediently and under time pressure. Must be able to accept criticism of work from client and price of program must include completing work to satisfaction of customers."

EXHIBIT BUILDERS INC., 150 Wildwood Rd., Deland FL 32720. (904)734-3196. Contact: J.C. Burkhalter. Produces custom exhibits, displays, scale models, dioramas, sales centers and character costumes. Clients: primarily manufacturers, ad agencies and tourist attractions.
Needs: Works on assignment only. Uses artists for exhibit/display design and scale models.
First Contact & Terms: Provide resume, business card and brochure to be kept on file. Samples returned by SASE. Reports back on future possibilities. Considers complexity of project, skill and experience of artist, how work will be used, turnaround time and rights purchased when establishing payment.
Tips: "Wants to see examples of previous design work for other clients; not interested in seeing school-developed portfolios."

***GEORGE E. FERN CO.**, 1100 Gest St., Cincinnati OH 45203. (513)621-6111. General Manager: George J. Budig. Exposition service contractor/display firm.
Needs: Very limited art needs; "almost zero." Works on assignment only. Sometimes uses artists for backdrop displays, trade show exhibit/design, convention entrances and special room decorations.
First Contact & Terms: Query by phone. Reports in 1 week. Samples returned by SASE. Pays by the hour, $20-35; by the project, $100-500. Considers complexity of project, skill and experience of artist, how work will be used and turnaround time when establishing payment.
Tips: "We need some names, addresses and phone numbers so we can call."

***FISHER/MORRIS AND ASSOCIATES**, #209, 5567 Reseda Blvd., Tarzana CA 91356. (818)344-3045. Associate Designer: Reza Ahmadi. Architectural and interior design firm providing architectural interior design for commercial, office and residential.
Needs: Works with 5 freelance artists/year. Works on assignment only. Uses artists for interior and architectural renderings, design consulting and model making.
First Contact & Terms: Send query letter with resume, slides or photographs. Samples not filed are returned only if requested. Reports back within 10 days. Write to schedule an appointment to show a portfolio, which should include final reproduction. Pays for design by the project, $200 minimum. Considers complexity of project, skill and experience of artist, client's budget and how work will be used when establishing payment. Negotiates rights purchased.

FRANKLIN ELECTRIC, 400 Spring St., Bluffton IN 46714. Manager of Corporate Communications: Mel Haag. Manufacturer of submersible and fractional H.P. motors for original equipment manufacturers and distributors.
Needs: Works with 8 freelance artists/year. "Freelance artists must be proven." Works on assignment only. Uses artists for the design, illustration and layouts of advertising and brochures, the design and layout of catalogs and for posters.
First Contact & Terms: Send query letter with brochure showing art style or resume, tear sheets, slides and photographs. Samples not filed are returned only if requested. Reports only if interested. Call to schedule an appointment to show a portfolio, which should include roughs, original/final art, final reproduction/product, color and tear sheets. Pays for design and illustration by the hour, $30 minimum; payment is negotiated.
Tips: "I look for all styles and subjects. I am very interested in new techniques and styles."

***FREELANCE VISUAL PRODUCTIONS, INC.**, Box #843, Philadelphia PA 19105. (215)342-1492. Contact: Art Submissions Director. Clients include producers of special photo and art decor products.
Needs: Considers all mediums and subjects which the artists can submit to be filed. Send slides,color and b&w contact sheets, prints up to 8x10. "Our art/design department is searching for a certain look which can be adapted to very special products. We are especially interested in artists who can produce their own art photography, or have access to a Photo-Art photographer."
First Contact & Terms: Send query letter with samples which may be filed. Include a SASE. Reports back within 4-6 weeks. "For all samples which are held for potential placement and marketing a fee for usage will be paid depending where and how many items are produced. In the event that one of your visuals is selected for production, you will be contacted with the details. Usage fees can range from $1 per use and up. The more items produced with your visual, the more you will receive." Negotiates rights purchased.
Tips: "We are looking for artists with vision, selling your creations to a very special marketplace will require time and patience. If you are willing to invest same, we can find a potential future for your works."

How to Work With Small Businesses

by Michael Fleishman

"How do I find clients?" That's the big question for artists who are just starting out. The answer is simple: "Right in your own backyard." Small businesses in your city or town offer a variety of jobs from logo design for your physician to advertising illustration for the bank. Freelance illustrator Michael Fleishman tells how he established roots in his town by working with professionals and small businesses, then branched out regionally and nationally.

"You can find enough work to make a good living by working with local businesses. My town, Yellow Springs, Ohio, is not a high-tech town, but it does support businesses and professionals who have based themselves here.

There are a number of ways to find out who is in need of freelance help. Networking is one of the best ways. You have to keep in touch with friends, relatives, teachers, professionals, whomever, to keep your name in circulation. Let people know you're interested and capable. Once I owed money to a doctor for some minor surgery. When I mailed him the check, I drew on the envelope, like I always do. When he received it, he called me and said he liked the drawing so much that he wanted me to do a logo for him.

There's also the phone book. Look up businesses you'd like to work for. Make a mailing list of the ones you're interested in; you can probably see their ads or posters around town and find out the type of work they're looking for. Then send samples of your work to the ones you'd like to work for.

Check the Chamber of Commerce for businesses just starting up, because they'll need logos, letterhead design and so forth. Yellow Springs has what's called a Small Business Incubator, which helps people start their own businesses. I'm able to look over its client list to see who's starting a business. The whole idea is to locate names, numbers and addresses for a mailing list.

I don't think each type of business requires a different approach. I don't alter my promotion for each client, although I do tailor a submission or portfolio to the individual client. For example, you wouldn't send risqué material to a Christian publisher. A little prior fact-finding can often cut many corners on the path to an assignment.

I'm a firm believer in marketing and self-promotion. It requires organization, discipline and a financial investment, but it's worth it! Most of my business is a direct result of my continuing marketing and self-promotion.

When I started out, I gave myself a complete graphic look—logo, letterhead, envelopes and business card. Right off the bat, as soon as a potential client sees anything with my name on it, I *look* like I mean business.

I send out a four-color flyer as my initial sample, no matter if it's a local or national business. It shows off my style and is generic enough to cover a lot of territory. With the flyer I also send a stamped reply card. I follow with a black-and-white promo piece (usually a postcard) every month; this serves as a continual reminder of who I am and what I do. If I get a positive response, I then target a submission to that client.

When you get a job, it's best to get written documentation of it. I don't always get a purchase order or contract on a job, but I do send a letter of confirmation. This can simply be a short thank-you note outlining the terms of the agreement and job specifications. It's not filled with legalese, just plain, polite talk spelling out the arrangement.

It's best to be clear about terms right from the start. Take good notes over the phone or at the meeting. If the client is slow with the paperwork, do it from your end.

A word about bids and estimates. Don't be pressured into taking money or cutting the deal on the spot. When you need the time, take it. Say, 'I'll call you back in an hour.' If you're meeting in person, excuse yourself for ten minutes. Take time to work out a realistic bid.

Don't be afraid to ask for what you really need to do the job. Be prepared to say 'no' and maybe lose the job. Approach all negotiations with open eyes and mind. Negotiation is a bit of a game, and it's all a learning process.

Many businesses ask for a buy-out. If you can't negotiate out of one you can proceed in three ways. First you can say, 'No thank-you,' and walk away from a bad deal. Or you can accept a trade-off. Ask yourself, 'Is it a good client to have? A great vehicle for my work? Will it be a dynamite portfolio piece? Is it an entry into a new market?' Or can you make it worth your while by getting a good pay-off. The more rights you sell, the higher the price should be.

When you're working with any type of business, small or large, be down-to-earth, be yourself. Above all, be dependable, on time and flexible. Do your best work at all times. The only thing left to say is to have fun!"

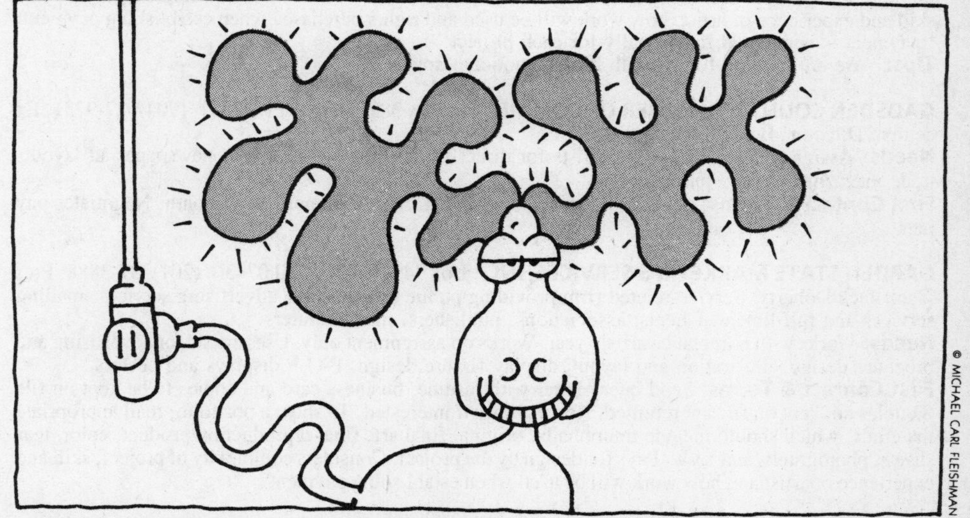

When Fleishman began his career as a freelance illustrator, he mailed a few self-promotion pieces, but he found most of his jobs from word-of-mouth or referrals. "At first I wasn't serious about self-promotion. Now I have a total self-promotion package from letterhead to mailers." This mailer is an example of reminder cards he send to clients on his mailing list.

FRELINE, INC., Box 889, Hagerstown MD 21740. Art Director: Mark Kretzer. Manufacturer and developer of library promotional aids—posters, mobiles, bookmarks, t-shirt transfers, reading motivators and other products to promote reading, library services and resources. Clients: school and public libraries, classroom teachers.
Needs: Works with 10-15 freelance artists/year. Works on assignment only. Uses artists for illustration and graphics design and promotional materials. Prefers pen & ink, airbrush, colored pencil, watercolor, acrylics, pastels, collage and gouache. Most assignments for 4-color process.
First Contact & Terms: Experienced designers or illustrators only. Send query letter with resume and tear sheets to be kept on file. Slides sent for review will be returned. Reports within 15 days. Pays by the project, $250-800. Considers complexity of the project, skill and experience of the artist, turnaround time and rights purchased when establishing payment.
Tips: "Portfolios with a emphasis on illustration suit our needs best. Our market caters to library usage and education, grade school level up to college."

G.A.I. INCORPORATED, Box 30309, Indianapolis IN 46230. (317)257-7100. President: William S. Gardiner. Licensing agents. "We represent artists to the collectibles and gifts industries. Collectibles include high-quality prints, collector's plates, figurines, bells, etc. There is no up-front fee for our services. We receive a commission for any payment the artist receives as a result of our efforts." Clients: manufacturers of high-quality prints and lithographs, porcelain products.
Needs: Works with 30-40 freelance artists/year. Works on assignment only. "We are not interested in landscapes, still lifes, or modern art. We are looking for 'people-oriented' art that will appeal to the average person."
First Contact & Terms: Send query letter with resume and color photographs; do *not* send original work. Samples not kept on file are returned by SASE. Reports in 1-3 months. Payment: "If we are successful in putting together a program for the artist with a manufacturer, the artist is usually paid a royalty on the sale of the product using his art. This varies from 4%-10%." Considers complexity of project, skill and experience of artist, how work will be used and rights purchased when establishing payment; "payment is negotiated individually for each project."
Tips: "We are looking for art with broad emotional appeal."

GADSDEN COUNTY CHAMBER OF COMMERCE, Box 389, Quincy FL 32351. (904)627-9231. Executive Director: Ben Ellinor.
Needs: Assigns 2 jobs/year. Uses artists for direct mail/publicity brochures, newspaper ad layouts, trade magazine ads and publications.
First Contact & Terms: Arrange interview or mail art. SASE. Reports in 1 month. Negotiates payment.

GARDEN STATE MARKETING SERVICES, INC., Box 343, Oakland NJ 07436. (201)337-3888. President: Jack Doherty. Service-related firm providing public relations and advertising services, mailing services and fulfillment. Clients: associations, publishers, manufacturers.
Needs: Works with 6 freelance artists/year. Works on assignment only. Uses artists for advertising and brochure design, illustration and layout; display fixture design, P-O-P displays and posters.
First Contact & Terms: Send query letter with resume, business card and copies to be kept on file. Samples not kept on file are returned. Reports only if interested. To show a portfolio, mail appropriate materials, which should include thumbnails, original/final art, final reproduction/product, color, tear sheets, photographs and b&w. Pays for design by the project. Considers complexity of project, skill and experience of artist and how work will be used when establishing payment.

GARON PRODUCTS INC., 1924 Highway 35, Wall NJ 07719. (201)449-1776. Marketing Manager: Christy Karl. Industrial direct marketers of maintenance products, i.e., concrete repair, roof repair. Clients: maintenance departments of corporations, government facilities, small businesses.
Needs: Works with 3 freelance artists/year. Uses artists for brochure and catalog design, illustration and layout. Seeks "local artists and ones who will work within the organization so that corrections and additions can be done on the spot."
First Contact & Terms: Send query letter with brochure, resume, business card, photographs or Photostats to be kept on file. Reports only if interested. Pays by the page or by the project. Considers complexity of project, and skill and experience of artist when establishing payment.
Tips: "Professionalism is a must! Work should be camera-ready for commercial printing upon completion. I need experienced catalog artists with creative ideas."

GARTH PRODUCTS, INC., 32-4 Littell Rd., East Hanover NJ 07936. (201)887-8487. President: Garth Patterson. Manufacturer of silkscreened ceramic and glass souvenirs. Clients: banks, museums, amusement parks, restored villages, tourist attractions, resorts, hotels and retail stores.

Needs: Works with 5 artists/year. Uses artists for illustrations on products. Especially needs line drawings of buildings, statues, flowers and songbirds.
First Contact & Terms: Send query letter, Photostats, brochure/flyer or actual work. Samples returned by SASE. Reports within 3-4 weeks. Provide business card, brochure and samples to be kept on file for possible future assignments. Payment is by the project, $25-100 average. Considers complexity of job and skill and experience of artist when establishing payment.
Tips: "Understand the type of line work needed for silkscreening. We now also use pencil work. Better artwork is more appreciated."

***DANIEL E. GELLES ASSOC., INC.**, Mohonk Rd., High Falls NY 12440. (914)687-7681. Vice President: Robert S. Gelles. Interior design firm which also designs and manufactures visual merchandise, display fixtures, etc. "We design custom fixturing for both manufacturers and stores (retailers). We do store floor layouts, plans, etc. We also maintain a stock fixturing line which requires updating consistently. Clients: both large and small hard and soft goods manufacturers (Black Flag insecticide to Maidenform lingerie, Sears, Penney's, Bloomingdales, etc.)".
Needs: Works with 3-4 freelance artists/year. Prefers artists with some experience in the field of visual merchandising or P-O-P display. Uses artists for interior deisgn and renderings and renderings and concepts for display ideas, fixturing, P-O-P displays, etc.
First Contact & Terms: Send resume and "any clear facsimile that would indicate artist's style and technique." Samples are filed. Call or write to schedule an appointment to show a portfolio, which should include thumbnails, roughs, original/final art, actual renderings (color) and original concepts. Pays for illustration by the hour, $15-35. Considers complexity of project and skill and experience of artist when establishing payment. Negotiates rights purchased.

GENERAL MOTORS CORP., 3044 W. Grand Blvd., Detroit MI 48202. (313)556-2017. Contact: Art Director, Public Relations Staff. Manufactures cars and trucks. Call for interview or send fees and samples for files; local artists only. SASE. Buys all rights.
Needs: Uses artists for annual reports, employee/student handbooks, technical charts/illustrations and company publications. Pay varies.

***GOES LITHOGRAPHING CO.**, 42 W. 61st St., Chicago IL 60621. Marketing Director: W.J. Goes. Manufacturer of all-year letterheads and holiday letterheads. Clients: printers and businesses.
Needs: Uses artists for letterheads.
First Contact & Terms: Send pencil sketches or thumbnail sketches. Samples not filed are returned by SASE. Reports back only if interested. Portfolio should include thumbnail sketches. "No final work should be sent at this time." Considers how work will be used when establishing payment. Buys reprint rights.
Tips: "Listen to what we want and are looking for. Thumbnail work is the first step for use. Call for some of our samples."

***GOFF ASSOCIATES ARCHITECTURE**, 180 Meeting St., Charleston SC 29401. Director of Marketing: Mark W. Sheehan. Full-service architectural design firm with in-house computer-added design and drafting; developer-oriented. Clients: commercial, retail, office space, hospital plus elderly facilities, governmental projects.
Needs: Works with 8 freelance artists/year. works on assignment only. Uses freelance artists for brochure design, interior renderings, landscape and architectural renderings, maps and model making. Prefers pen & ink, airbrush, watercolor, acrylics and oils.
First Contact & Terms: Send query letter with brochure showing art style or resume. Samples are filed. Samples not filed are returned with a SASE only if requested. Reports back within 2 weeks. Write to schedule an appointment to show a portfolio. Pays for design by the hour, $25-100; by the project, $500-1,500. Considers complexity of project, skill and experience of artist, turnaround time, client's budget and rights purchased when establishing payment. Negotiates rights purchased; all rights preferred.
Tips: "Our office does 10-15 large projects a year (for this market) and turnaround and minimal handholding are necessary. Artists who can fully understand our needs, do high-quality work and get the job done will get the jobs."

GOLDBERGS' MARINE, 201 Meadow Rd., Edison NJ 08818. (201)819-3500. Vice President Marketing: Richard Goldberg. Produces 9 mail order catalogs of pleasure boating equipment and water-sport gear for the active family.
Needs: Works with 6 freelance artists/year. Artists must be "flexible with knowledge of 4-color printing, have a willingness to work with paste-up and printing staff, and exhibit the ability to follow up and take charge." Uses artists for brochure and catalog design, illustration and layout; retail events and

signage. "Seasonal freelance work also available."
First Contact & Terms: Send query letter with brochure, business card, printed material and tear sheets to be kept on file. "Original work (mechanicals) may be required at portfolio showing." Reports only if interested. Call for appointment to show portfolio. Pays by the project. Considers complexity of project, how work will be used and turnaround time when establishing payment.
Tips: "Boating experience is helpful and a willingness to do research is sometimes necessary. Long-term relationships usually exist with our company. We have plenty of work for the right people."

***GREAT AMERICAN AUDIO CORP., INC.**, 33 Portman Rd., New Rochelle NY 10801. President: Nina Joan Mattikow. Audio publishers: products range from old time radio, self-help, humor, children's, books-on-tape, etc.
Needs: "We do not buy actual work. All artwork is commissioned by us." Uses artists for product and P-O-P design, advertising illustration and layout. Prefers full-color inks or tempera for product illustrations. "Art must be customized to suit us. We do not purchase any work, but look for a particular style of work."
First Contact & Terms: Artists must be in New York metropolitan area. Send query letter with brochure and resume to be kept on file. Do not send samples. Write for appointment to show portfolio. Finished original art seen by appointment only. Reports only if interested. Works on assignment only. No originals returned to artist at job's completion. Pays by the project, $200-500 average. Buys all rights.

THE GREAT MIDWESTERN ICE CREAM COMPANY, Box 1717, 209 N. 16 St., Fairfield IA 52556. (515)472-7595. President: Fred Gratzon. Manufacturer and franchiser. "We manufacture an excellent ice cream which we feel is the new standard in the industry. We sell it through supermarkets, restaurants and our beautiful franchise stores." Clients are grocery shoppers and ice cream lovers.
Needs: Works with 15+ freelance artists/year. Uses freelance artists for the design, illustration and layout of advertising, brochures and catalogs plus product design, illustration of the product, P-O-P displays, display fixture design, posters, model making, signage, and fashion clothing design for franchise employees and customers (t-shirts, etc.).
First Contact & Terms: Send query letter with resume and samples. Samples not filed are returned with SASE. Reports back only if interested. Call to schedule an appointment to show a portfolio. Pays for design by the project, $3,000; pays for illustration by the project, $1,000. Considers complexity of project, client's budget, skill and experience of artists, how work will be used and rights purchased when establishing payment.
Tips: "We are a highly creative company that prefers art on the cutting edge. We are looking for all types of art—from painting to cartoons—that uses ice cream as the theme."

GUILFORD PUBLICATIONS INC., 72 Spring St., New York NY 10012. (212)431-9800. Art Director: Denise Adler. Produces professional, educational and industrial audiovisuals and books.
Needs: Assigns 20 jobs/year. Local artists only. Uses artists for catalog design, book jackets and ads.
First Contact & Terms: Query. SASE. Reports within 4 weeks. Pays by job.

THE HAMILTON COLLECTION, Suite 1000, 9550 Regency Square Blvd., Jacksonville FL 32211. (904)723-6000. Vice President, Product Development: Melanie Hart; Senior Design and Production Director (for commercial art/advertising): Deorah Levine. Direct marketing firm for collectibles: limited edition art, plates, sculpture, and general gifts. Clients: general public, specialized lists of collectible buyers and retail market.
Needs: Works with 5 freelance artists in creative department and 15 in product development/year. Only local artists with three years of experience for mechanical work. For illustration and product design, "no restrictions on locality, but must have *quality* work and flexibility regarding changes which are sometimes necessary. Also, a 'name' and notoriety help." Uses artists for advertising mechanicals, brochure illustration and mechanicals, product design and illustration on product.
First Contact & Terms: Send query letter with samples to be kept on file, except for fine art which is to be returned (must include a SASE or appropriate container with sufficient postage). Samples not kept on file are returned only if requested by artist. Reports within 2-4 weeks. Call or write for appointment to show portfolio. Pays for design by the hour, $10-50. Pays for illustration by the project, $50-5,000. Pays by the hour for mechanicals, $20 average. Considers complexity of project, skill and experience of artist, how work will be used and rights purchased when establishing payment.
Tips: Prefers conservative, old fashioned, realistic style. "Attitude and turnaround time important." In presenting portfolio, don't "point out mistakes, tell too much, tell not enough, belittle work or offer unsolicited opinions. Be prepared to offer sketches on speculation."

HAMPSHIRE PEWTER COMPANY, Box 1570, 9 Mill St., Wolfeboro NH 03894-1570. (603)569-4944. Vice President: J.H. Milligan. Manufacturer of handcast pewter tableware, accessories, and

Christmas ornaments. Clients: jewelry stores, department stores, executive gift buyers, tabletop and pewter speciality stores, churches, and private consumers.
Needs: Works with 3-4 freelance artists/year. "We prefer New-England based artists for convenience." Works on assignment only. Uses artists for brochure and catalog design, product design, illustration on product and model making.
First Contact & Terms: Send brochure or slides and photographs. Samples are not filed. Samples not filed are returned only if requested. Reports back to the artist within weeks. Call to schedule an appointment or mail roughs, photographs and b&w. Pays for design and illustration by the project. Considers complexity of project, client's budget and rights purchased. Buys all rights.
Tips: "Inform us of your capabilities. We commission work by the project. For artists who are seeking a manufacturing source, we will be happy to bid on manufacturing of designs, under private license to the artists, all of whose design rights are protected. If we commission a project, we intend to have exclusive rights to the designs by contract as defined in the Copyright Law and we intend to protect those rights."

HANSEN LIND MEYER, Suite 1100, 800 N. Magnolia, Orlando FL 32803. (305)422-7061. Director of Design: Charles W. Cole, Jr. Architectural/interior design firm providing complete architecture and engineering services. Clients: commercial, health care, justice and government.
Needs: Works with 6 freelance artists/year. Works on assignment only. Uses artists for interior, landscape and architectural renderings, maps and model making.
First Contact & Terms: Send query letter with resume and samples. Samples not filed are returned only if requested. Reports only if interested. To show a portfolio, mail thumbnails, final reproduction/product, color and photographs. Pays for illustrations by the project, $400-3,500. Considers complexity of project, client's budget, skill and experience of artist, and turnaround time when establishing payment.

HERFF JONES, Box 6500, Providence RI 02940-6500. (401)331-1240. Art Director: Fred Spinney. Manufacturer of class ring jewelry; motivation/recognition/emblematic awards—service pins, medals, medallions and trophies. Clients: high-school and college-level students; a variety of companies/firms establishing recognition programs.
Needs: Works with 6 freelance artists/year. "Previous experience in this field helpful but not necessary. Must be strong in illustration work." Works on assignment only. Uses artists for illustration of product.
First Contact & Terms: Send query letter with brochure, resume, business card, slides and photos to be kept on file; originals will be returned if sent. Samples not kept on file returned by SASE. Reports only if interested. Write for appointment to show portfolio. Pays by the project, $25-100 average. Considers complexity of project, skill and experience of artist, and turnaround time when establishing payment.
Tips: Artists approaching this firm "should be of a professional level. The artist should have a good versatile background in illustrating as well as having some mechanical drawing abilities, such as hand lettering."

HUTCHESON DISPLAYS, INC., 517 S. 14th St., Omaha NE 68102. (402)341-0707. President: Jim Lynch. Manufacturer of screen printed display materials. Clients: advertisers.
Needs: Works with 6 freelance artists/year. Uses artists for advertising layout. Especially needs graphic design.
First Contact & Terms: Send query letter with brochure showing art style. Samples returned. Portfolio should include photographs. Pays by the project. Pays for design and illustration by the project. Considers complexity of project when establishing payment. Buys one-time rights.

IGPC, 460 W. 34th St., 10th Floor, New York NY 10001. (212)869-5588. Contact: Art Department. Agent to foreign governments; "we produce postage stamps and related items on behalf of 40 different foreign governments."
Needs: Works with more than 100 freelance artists/year. Artists must be within metropolitan (NY) or tri-state area. "No actual experience required except to have good tight art skills (four-color) and excellent design skills." Works on assignment only. Uses artists for postage stamp design. Prefers tight, realistic style and technical illustration. Prefers airbrush, watercolor and acrylics.
First Contact & Terms: Send samples. Reports back within 5 weeks. Portfolio should contain "4-color illustrations of realistic, tight flora, fauna, technical subjects, autos or ships. Also include reduced samples of original artwork." Pays by the project, $500-1,500 average. Considers government allowance per project when establishing payment.
Tips: "Artists considering working with IGPC must have excellent 4-color abilities (in general or specific topics, i.e., flora, fauna, transport, famous people, etc.); sufficient design skills to arrange for and position type; the ability to create artwork that will reduce to postage stamp size and still hold up to clari-

ty and perfection. All of the work we require is realistic art. In some cases, we supply the basic layout and reference material; however, we appreciate an artist who knows where to find references and can present new and interesting concepts. Initial contact should be made by phone for appointment, (212)629-7979."

THE IMAGE GROUP, 398 S. Grant Ave., Columbus OH 43215. (614)221-1016. Contact: Richard Henry Eiselt. Architecture/interior design firm. Clients: commercial.
Needs: Uses artists for restaurant design, architectural and full-color renderings, graphic and interior design, paintings, sculpture, signs and wall art.
First Contact & Terms: Mail photos or transparencies. Pay varies according to client's budget, and skill and experience of artist.

***INFO VIEW CORPORATION, INC.**, (formerly Personal Leather Design, Inc.), Box 9155, Wethersfield CT 06109. (203)721-0270. President: Larry Bell. Designs interactive video presentations for trade shows and retail accounts.
Needs: Works on assignment only. Work with computer graphic artists in New York and New England for business/broadcast graphics. Buys 40 + sketches/year. Uses graphics for video stills and special effects. Looks for unique style. Prefers artists that have a feeling for current Euro/American trends.
First Contact & Terms: Query. SASE. Reports in 2 weeks. Provide photocopy of recent work to be kept on file for future assignments. Pays by the project.

INTERNATIONAL RESEARCH & EVALUATION, 21098 Ire Control Ctr., Eagan MN 55121. (612)888-9635. Art Director: Ronald Owon. Private, nonpartisan, interdisciplinary research firm that collects, stores and disseminates information on line, on demand to industry, labor and government on contract/subscription basis.
Needs: Works with 30-40 freelance artists/year. Works on assignment only. Uses artists for advertising, brochure and catalog design, illustration and layout; product design and P-O-P displays.
First Contact & Terms: Artists should request "Capabilities Analysis" form from firm. Reports only if interested. Pays by the hour, $50-250 average. Considers how work will be used when establishing payment.

JAMES ARCHITECTS & ENGINEERS, INC., Suite 122, 120 Monument Cir., Indianapolis IN 46204. (317)631-0880. Director Corporate Communications: Theresa Thompson. Architectural/interior design firm providing architectural, engineering, interior design, planning design and construction administration. Clients: government, corporate, institutional, criminal justice, commercial and industrial.
Needs: Works with 3-4 freelance artists/year. "Some projects/clients would prefer local artists." Works on assignment only. Uses artists for advertising design, brochure design and illustration, architectural renderings, photographs, environmental art and sculpture.
First Contact & Terms: Send query letter with brochure showing art style or resume, tear sheets, Photostats, slides and photographs. Samples filed, returned only if requested. Reports only if interested. Call to schedule an appointment to show a portfolio, which should include roughs, final reproduction/product, color and photographs. Pays for design by the hour, $15-70. Pays for illustration by the hour, $15-70. Considers complexity of project, client's budget, skill and experience of artist, and turnaround time when establishing payment.

***JB PROMOTIONS**, 13A E. Main St., Salem VA 24153. President: Julie Becker. Estab. 1986. "Promotions company producing advertising, promotions and public relations through print, broadcast and also special events." Serves retail stores, wholesale distributors and contractors.
Needs: Prefers local artists. Works on assignment basis. Uses artists for advertising, brochure and catalog illustration, rendering of product, posters and magazine illustration.
First Contact & Terms: Send query letter with Photostats. Samples are not filed returned by SASE. Reports back only if interested. Write to schedule an appointment to show a portfolio. Pays for design by the project, $25-500. Pays for illustration by the project, $25-100. Considers complexity of project, client's budget, skill and experience of artist, how work will be used, turnaround time and rights purchased when establishing payment. Buys all rights.

JEWELITE SIGNS, LETTERS & DISPLAYS, INC. 154 Reade St., New York NY 10013. (212)966-0433. Vice President: Bobby Bank. Produces signs, letters, silk scrrening, murals, hand lettering, displays and graphics.
Needs: Works with 12 freelance artists/year. Works on assignment only. Uses artists for signs, interior design, architectural renderings, design consulting and model making. Prefers airbrush and lettering.
First Contact & Terms: Call or send query letter. Call to schedule an appointment to show a portfolio, which should include photographs. Pays for design and illustration by the project, $75 and up. Considers complexity of project and skill and experience of artist when establishing payment.

***J. JOSEPHSON, INC.**, 20 Horizon Blvd., S. Hackensack NJ 07606. Director of Marketing: Leslie Meisner. Manufacturer of wallcoverings. "We also provide them to the public in the form of sample books." Serves wallcovering and paint stores, interior designers and architects.
Needs: Works with many artists/year. Uses artists for advertising, catalog and product design, P-O-P displays and display fixture design.
First Contact & Terms: Send tear sheets. Samples are filed. Samples not filed are returned only if requested by artist. Reports back only if interested. Call to schedule an appointment to show a portfolio which should include original/final art and final reproduction/product. Pays for design by the project. Considers complexity of project, skill and experience of the artist and rights purchased when establishing payment. Negotiates rights purchased.

***ARLAN KAY & ASSOCIATES**, 110 King St., Madison WI 53703. (608)251-7515. Architect: Arlan Kay. Architectural firm offering architecture and construction management. Clients: commercial, residential, and institutional with 70% of work in recycling/restoration of existing buildings.
Needs: Works with 1-2 freelance artists/year. Prefers local artists. Works on assignment only. Uses artists for brochure design and architectural renderings.
First Contact & Terms: Send query letter with brochure to be kept on file. Reports only if interested. Pays for illustration by the hour, $7-25 average; by the project, $100-500 average; or by the day, $50-150 average. Considers complexity of project, client's budget, and skill and experience of artist when establishing payment.

KELCO, Division of Merck & Co., Inc., 8355 Aero Dr., San Diego CA 92123. (619)292-4900. Advertising and Communications: Yoland Nunez. Specialty chemical firm. Clients: food companies, industrial users and oil field companies.
Needs: Works with 1-2 freelance artists per year. Works on assignment only. Uses artists for advertising and brochure design and illustration; employee annual report, and AV presentations.
First Contact & Terms: Send query letter. Reports in 3 weeks. Negotiates payment.

***KELSEY NATIONAL CORP.**, 3030 S. Bundy, Los Angeles CA 90066. Marketing Manager: Susan Stepan. Service-related firm providing small group health and life insurance products. Clients: small businesses of under 100 employees nationwide.
Needs: Works with 3-4 freelance artists/year. Assigns 50 + jobs/year. Prefers local artists. Works on assignment only. Uses artists for advertising and brochure design, illustration and layout, posters and signage.
First Contact & Terms: Send query letter. Samples are filed. Reports back only if interested. Call or write to schedule an appointment to show a portfolio, which should include original/final art, final reproduction/product and tear sheets. Pays for illustration by the project. "We ask for an estimate by job and have no specific hourly rate in mind." Considers client's budget, skill and experience of artist and turnaround time when establishing payment. Buys all rights.
Tips: "Exceptional creativity is not wanted by the company. We need someone to take much information and put it in clear, clean, readable materials."

KLITZNER IND., INC., 44 Warren St., Providence RI 02901. (401)751-7500, ext. 242. Design Director: Louis Marini. Manufacturer; "four separate divisions that serve uniquely different markets: ad specialty, fraternal, direct mail and retail."
Needs: Works with "several" freelance artists/year. Artists must be "qualified to provide the desired quality of work within our time frame." Works on assignment only. Uses artists for product design, illustration on product and model making. Prefers pen & ink, airbrush, markers and computer illustration.
First Contact & Terms: Send query letter with resume to be kept on file. Reviews Photostats, photographs, photocopies, slides or tear sheets; "they must clearly illustrate the quality, detail, etc. of artist's work." Materials not filed are returned by SASE. Reports back only if interested. Write for appointment to show portfolio. Portfolio should include "only professional, commerical samples of work. Do not have need to see school projects." Pays for design by the project, $100 minimum; "a mutually agreed upon figure *before* the project is undertaken." Finds most artists through references/word-of-mouth.
Tips: "Turn-around time on most projects has been virtually cut in half. More competitive market warrants quick, dependable service. This change has created a bigger need for outside assistance during heavy backlog periods."

KOZAK AUTO DRYWASH, INC., 6 S. Lyon St., Box 910, Batavia NY 14020. (716)343-8111. President: Ed Harding. Manufacturer and direct marketer of automotive cleaning and polishing cloths and related auto care products distributed by direct mail and retail. Clients: stores with car care lines, consumers and specialty groups.
Needs: Works with up to 2 freelance artists/year. Uses artists for advertising design and illustration, P-

Klitzner Industries' art director Louis Marini commissioned illustrator/architectural renderer Wallace A. Young, Jr. of Lincoln, Rhode Island to illustrate a cache for a world currency series. The pen-and-ink rendering depicts a native of Maldives gathering coral from the sea, which represents the country's main source of employment. Marini says that Young "has the reputation of being one of the finest artists in New England. He is equally proficient at full-color airbrush illustrations, black-and-white line art and architectural renderings." The Providence, Rhode Island manufacturer bought all rights to the work.

O-P displays, packaging design and direct response advertising.
First Contact & Terms: Prefers artist located within a convenient meeting distance with experience in desired areas (P-O-P, packaging, direct response). Works on assignment only. Send query letter with brochure, resume and business card to be kept on file. Material not filed returned only if requested. Reports within 2 weeks. Pays by the project. Considers complexity of project, skill and experience of artist, and how work will be used when establishing payment.

***KRAFTBILT**, Box 800, Tulsa OK 74101. General Manager: Mike Goldberg. Distributor or art, photos, gift items for the petroleum industry, personalized note pads, craft-type products.
Needs: Works with 5 freelance artists/year. Assigns 3-5 jobs/year. Uses artists for product design, model making and product manufacturing.
First Contact & Terms: Send query letter with brochure showing art styles or photographs. Samples are filed. Reports back within weeks. Write to schedule an appointment to show a portfolio, which should include roughs and final reproduction/product. Pays for illustration by the hour, $35-65.
Tips: "We look for commercial potential and realistic cost."

KRISCH HOTELS, INC., Box 14100, Roanoke VA 24022. (703)342-4531. Director of Communications: Julie Becker. Estab. 1985. Service-related firm providing all advertising, in-room and P-O-P pieces for camping (inhouse department). Clients: hotel/motels and restaurants/lounges.
Needs: Works with 10-20 freelance artists/year. Prefers local artists. Works on assignment only. Uses artists for advertising and brochure illustration; illustration on product, P-O-P displays, posters and signage. Prefers pen & ink, airbrush, charcoal/pencil and computer illustration.

First Contact & Terms: Send query letter with resume and photocopies. Samples not filed are not returned. Reports only if interested. Call or write to schedule an appointment to show a portfolio, which should include roughs, original/final art, tear sheets and Photostats. Pays for design and illustration by the hour, $10 minimum; by the project, $25 minimum; by the day, $100 minimum. Considers complexity of project, client's budget, how work will be used, turnaround time and rights purchased when establishing payment. Finds most artists through references/word-of-mouth.
Tips: "Increased competition in all markets leads to more sophisticated work attitudes on the part of our industry. Artists should know their own abilities and limitations and be able to interact with us to achieve best results."

KVCR—TV/FM RADIO, 701 S. Mount Vernon Ave., San Bernardino CA 92410. (714)888-6511 or 825-3103. Program Director: Lew Warren. Specializes in public and educational radio/TV.
Needs: Assigns 1-10 jobs/year. Uses artists for graphic/set design, set design painters and camera-ready cards.
First Contact & Terms: Query and mail photos or slides. Reports in 2 weeks. Samples returned by SASE. Pays $20-30, camera-ready cards.

LABUNSKI ASSOCIATES ARCHITECTS, Suite A3, 3301 S. Expressway 83, Harlingen TX 78550. (512)428-4334. President: R.A. Labunski. Architectural firm providing architecture, planning, construction, management, design, space planning, interiors, advertising. Clients: commercial, retail, residential, corporate, banks, hotel/motel/restaurant and schools.
Needs: Works with 5 freelance artists/year. Works on assignment only. Uses artists for advertising design, illustration and layout; brochure design, interior and architectural renderings, design consulting, furnishings and model making.
First Contact & Terms: Desires "affordable, practical" artists with referrals/references. Send query letter with brochure, resume and business card to be kept on file; also send samples. Samples returned by SASE. Reports within 2 weeks. Call or write for appointment to show portfolio. Pays by the project. Considers complexity of project, client's budget, and skill and experience of artist when establishing payment.

LANE & ASSOCIATES, ARCHITECTS, 1318 N. "B", Box 3929, Fort Smith AR 72913. (501)782-4277. Owner: John E. Lane, AIA-ASID. Architectural and interior design firm providing architecture and interiors for remodeling and new construction; also art consultant. Clients: residential, religious, commercial, institutional and industrial.
Needs: Works with 10-12 freelance artists/year. Works on assignment only. Uses artists occasionally for architectural renderings, charts, graphic design and advertising illustration; selects or commissions art pieces for clients; paintings, drawings, sculpture, photographs, macrame, tapestry (all mediums). Arranges art exhibits for large local bank—"would like sources of talent for various mediums, painting, sculptures, photography, drawings, etc." Prefers pen & ink, watercolor, acrylics, oils, pastels and collage.
First Contact & Terms: Prefers to be able to meet in person with artist. Send query letter with brochure showing art style or resume and tear sheets, slides or photographs. Samples returned by SASE, but "would prefer to retain." Payment varies. Considers complexity of project, client's budget, skill and experience of artist, how work will be used, turnaround time and rights purchased when establishing payment.

LARAMI CORPORATION, 340 North 12 St., Philadelphia PA 19107. (215)923-4900. Director of Research & Development: Mel Mednick. Produces toys.
Needs: Uses local artists only. Works on assignment only. Uses artists for mechanicals.
First Contact & Terms: Send query letter with brochure showing art style and/or resume and samples. Samples not filed are not returned. Reports only if interested. To show a portfolio, mail thumbnails, roughs, original/final art, final reproduction/product, color, tear sheets, Photostats, photographs and b&w.

LEISURE AND RECREATION CONCEPTS INC., 2151 Fort Worth Ave., Dallas TX 75211. (214)942-4474. President: Michael Jenkins. Designs and builds amusement and theme parks.
Needs: Assigns 200 jobs/year. Uses artists for exhibits/displays and sketches of park building sections and bird's eye views of facilities.
First Contact & Terms: Query with samples or previously used work, or arrange interview. SASE. Reports in 1 week. Pay determined by job.

LILLIAN VERNON CORP., 510 S. Fulton Ave., Mount Vernon NY 10550. (914)699-4131. Vice President: David Hochberg. Direct mail giftware firm that produces greeting cards, giftwrap, calendars, sta-

tionery and paper tableware products. Also produces toiletries, housewares, textiles, dinnerware and toys.
Needs: Buys 250 designs and 100 illustrations/year from freelance artists. Only artists within 250 miles "for ease in communication." Works on assignment only. Considers all types of media for illustrations. "We are heavily oriented toward Christmas merchandise"; submit seasonal artwork in January or February.
First Contact & Terms: Send query letter with brochure, resume, Photostats, photographs or tear sheets to be kept on file. "Please don't call!" Samples not filed are returned only if requested. Reports within 2 weeks. Original art not returned after reproduction. Pays flat fee. Buys first rights.
Tips: "We are *always* on the lookout for good talent!"

LIVING ARTS, INC., 250 West 57th St., New York NY 10019. Director: Peter Klein. Theatrical agency. Clients: musicians, Broadway productions, and major ballet and dance companies.
Needs: Buys 10-15 illustrations/year. Uses artists for catalog layouts, stationery design, posters and publicity brochures.
First Contact & Terms: Query. SASE. Reports in 2 weeks. Provide brochures/flyers and tear sheets to be kept on file for future assignments. Originals returned to artist at job's completion. Minimum payment: $1,000, brochure design; $500, poster design.

LOON MOUNTAIN RECREATION CORP., Kancamagus Hwy., Lincoln NH 03251. (603)745-8111. Marketing Director: Rick Owen. Ski resort with hotel, restaurants and lounges.
Needs: Works with 2 advertising designers/year. Assigns 6 jobs and buys 2 illustrations/year. Uses artists for design and illustration of brochures, signs, displays, mailings and other promotional materials. Especially needs renderings of future projects.
First Contact & Terms: Arrange interview. SASE. Reports within 2 weeks. Negotiates pay; pays by the hour, $10 average. Considers skill and experience of artist, and turnaround time when establishing payment.

***THE LUCKMAN PARTNERSHIP, INC.**, 9220 Sunset Blvd., Los Angeles CA 90069. (213)274-7755. Assistant Director of Design: John Janulaw. Architectural firm. Clients: office buildings, hotels, educational facilities, sports facilities, theaters and entertainment centers.
Needs: Works with 3-4 freelance artists/year. Prefers local artists. Works on assignment only. Uses freelance artists for interior renderings, architectural renderings and model making.
First Contact & Terms: Send query letter with resume, tear sheets and photocopies. Samples are filed. Samples not filed are returned only if requested by artist. Call to schedule an appointment to show a portfolio, which should include roughs, photographs and color. Pays for illustration by the project, $500-20,000. Considers complexity of project, skill and experience of artist, turnaround time and client's budget when establishing payment. Buys all rights.

McALLEN CHAMBER OF COMMERCE, Box 790, McAllen TX 78502. (512)682-2871. Public Relations Director: Susan Dennis. Promotes conventions, tourism, community programs, industry and legislation for McAllen.
Needs: Assigns 8-15 jobs and buys 12 illustrations/year. Uses artists for advertising, magazines, newsletters, publicity brochures, exhibits/displays and trademarks/logos. Especially needs economic/business oriented artwork; international trade and commerce themes; and Hispanic-related art and information.
First Contact & Terms: Query with samples. SASE. Reports in 1 week. Pays $10-20/illustration. Considers turnaround time when establishing payment.
Tips: "We have expanded our monthly newsletter to a monthly economic report."

MARBURG WALL COVERINGS, 7601 Cicero, Chicago IL 60652. General Manager: Mike Vukosavich. Manufacturer and distributor which designs, styles and manufactures decorative wall coverings. Clients: wholesale distributors, contractors and architects.
Needs: Works with 2 freelance artists/year. Prefers bilingual English/German artists. Works on assignment only. Uses artists for product design.
First Contact & Terms: Send query letter with brochure or tear sheets. Samples are filed. Samples not filed are returned only if requested. Reports back only if interested. To show a portfolio, mail thumbnails, tear sheets and color. Payment is negotiable. Considers client's budget and skill and experience of artist when establishing payment. Buys first rights or reprint rights.

MARTIN & DETHOFF REGISTERED ARCHITECTS, 422 Franklin St., Reading PA 19602. Contact: Robert S. Martin. Architectural/interior design firm providing architectural, engineering and interior design. Clients: commercial.

Needs: Works with 4 freelance artists/year. Works on assignment only. Uses artists for architectural renderings and furnishings.
First Contact & Terms: Send query letter with resume to be kept on file. Reports back only if interested. Pays for design by the hour, $25-50. Pays for illustration by the project, $500-1,000. Considers complexity and size of project when establishing payment.
Tips: Needs illustrators who are "fast and not expensive." Looks for "strong delineation and color."

METROPOLITAN WATER DISTRICT OF SOUTHERN CALIFORNIA (MWD), Box 54153, 1111 Sunset Blvd., Los Angeles CA 90054. (213)250-6496. Graphic Arts Designer: Mario Chavez. Supplies water for southern California. "MWD imports water from the Colorado River and northern California through the state water project, it imports about half of all the water used by some 14 million consumers in urban southern California from Ventura to Riverside to San Diego counties. MWD wholesales water to 27 member public agencies which, along with about 130 subagencies, deliver it to homes, businesses and even a few farms in MWD's 5,200-square-mile service area."
Needs: Works with 4-6 freelance artists/year. "Color artwork for publication is separated on scanner, it should be flexible; final agreement (contract) is purchase order, based upon verbal agreement of artist accepting assignment. All artwork is vested in Metropolitan Water Distict unless agreed upon." Works on assignment only. Uses artists for brochure/publications design, illustration and layout.
First Contact & Terms: Send query letter with brochure showing art style. Samples not filed are returned by SASE. Reports only if interested. Call to schedule an appointment to show a portfolio, which should include roughs, original/final art, color, tear sheets and b&w. Pays for design by the project, $100 minimum. Pays for illustration by the project, $50 minimum. Considers complexity of project, client's budget, skill and experience of artist, how work will be used, turnaround time and rights purchased when establishing payment.
Tips: "Phone calls should be kept short and to a minimum. Public affairs of MWD is interested in skillful execution of conceptual artwork to illustrate articles for its publication program. Number of projects is limited."

MEYER SCHERER AND ROCKCASTLE, LTD., 325 Second Ave. N., Minneapolis MN 55401. Principal: Garth Rockcastle. Architecture/interior and landscape design firm providing design, document preparation and construction supervision. Clients: residential, commercial, institutional and industrial.
Needs: Works with 5-6 freelance artists/year. Works on assignment only. Uses artists for exterior, interior and landscape design; brochure design and layout, design consulting. "We occasionally enter national competitions in partnership with artists of our choosing without reimbursement to the artist unless we are winners. Contact for details. We also collaborate with artists on special projects such as stained glass or building furniture."
First Contact & Terms: Send query letter with resume and slides. Samples not filed are returned by SASE. Reports only if interested. Write to schedule an appointment to show a portfolio, which should include roughs, original/final art and color. Pays for design and illustration by the hour, $15-40; or by the project. Considers complexity of project, client's budget, skill and experience of artist, how work will be used, turnaround time and rights purchased when establishing payment.
Tips: Looks for "innovation and understanding of architecture. Don't ask questions about what we might be particularly interested in."

J. MICHAELS INC., 182 Smith St., Brooklyn NY 11201. (718)852-6100. Advertising Manager: Lance Davis. Retailer of furniture and home furnishings for young married couples ages 20-45.
Needs: Works with 5-6 freelance artists/year. Uses artists for advertising illustration, P-O-P displays, calligraphy, paste-up, mechanicals and posters. "We use a lot of line, ink furniture illustrations." Prefers tight, realistic style.
First Contact & Terms: Send query letter with brochure or nonreturnable samples, such as photocopies. Samples are filed. Samples not filed are not returned. Reports back only if interested. "Mail photocopies. If I want to see more, I will call." Pays for illustration by the project, $50 for items like charts on TV. Considers complexity of project and skill and experience of artist when establishing payment. Buys all rights.
Tips: "We are a furniture retailer. Show me furniture illustrations that can print in newspapers."

MILWAUKEE SIGNS CO., 1964 Wisconsin Ave., Grafton WI 53024. (414)377-8920. Director of Marketing: Bob Aiken.
Needs: Local artists only. Works on assignment only. Works with 3 artists for sign design and P-O-P design. Also uses artists for custom sign faces, brochure and ad design.
First Contact & Terms: Arrange interview to show portfolio. Samples returned by SASE. Reports back on future possibilities. Send resume, business card and brochure to be kept on file. Considers complexity of project, skill and experience of artist, and how work will be used when establishing payment.

MURPHY INTERNATIONAL SALES ORGANIZATION, 11444 Zelzah Ave., Granada Hills CA 91344. (818)363-1410. President: F.S. Murphy. Distributor and service-related firm providing retrofit, covering materials, new products and patents. Clients: building and home owners.
Needs: Works with 2 freelance artists/year. Uses artists for advertising, brochure and catalog design, and illustration on product. Prefers loose, impressionistic style. Prefers calligraphy and computer illustration.
First Contact & Terms: Send samples to be kept on file. Write for art guidelines. Prefers photocopies as samples. Samples not filed are not returned. Reports back only if interested. Pays by the hour, $25 minimum. Considers how work will be used when establishing payment.
Tips: "Design should be realistic. Art is becoming more simple and less dramatic."

MURRAY HILL PRESS, 56 Central Dr., Farmingdale NY 11735. (516)454-0800. President: Ralph Ceisler. Printer. Clients: paint manufacturers, window treatment magazines and general commercial.
Needs: Assigns 12 jobs/year; uses mostly local artists. Uses artists for catalogs, direct mail brochures, flyers and P-O-P displays. Especially needs P-O-P displays in retail stores, paint and hardware stores in particular. "Need good catalog-brochure art. Must be creative. We compete with originals by supplying full package. Artist preferably should be from Long Island for better access."
First Contact & Terms: Send query letter with tear sheets. SASE. Reports in 2 weeks. Call or write to schedule an appointment to show a portfolio, which should include thumbnails, roughs, original/final art and final reproduction/product. Pays for design and illustration by the project, $100 minimum. Pay depends strictly on job and is negotiable. Considers complexity of project, skill and experience of artist, and how work will be used when establishing payment. Rights purchased vary according to project.
Tips: "Have samples showing rough thru completion."

NEIBAUER PRESS, INC., 20 Industrial Dr., Warminister PA 18974. (215)322-6200. Contact: Nathan Neibauer. Publishers and printers of religious publications.
Needs: Works with 12 freelance artists/year. Works on assignment only. Uses artists for advertising, brochure and catalog design, illustration and layout; illustration on product, and posters.
First Contact & Terms: Send query letter with photocopies. Reports only if interested. Write for appointment to show portfolio. Pays by the hour, $12 minimum; or by the project. Considers skill and experience of artist when establishing payment.

NOE & NOE ARCHITECTS, 539 Cooke St., Honolulu HI 96813-5235. (808)533-7836. Contact: Joyce or Leon Noe. Architectural/interior design firm providing planning, design, special services, and consultant services. Clients: commercial, institutional, governmental.
First Contact and Terms: Artists must be "technically competent in their chosen field and able to provide accurate drawings and budgets to demonstrate adequately how their work fits in with the project." Send query letter with resume and samples to be kept on file. Call or write for appointment to show portfolio. Prefers to see original work. Samples returned if not kept on file. Reports within 2 weeks. Works on assignment only. Payment figures "are negotiated with each artist individually and privately." Pays for design by the hour, $10 minimum; by the project, $100 minimum; by the day, $320 minimum. Pays for illustration by the hour, $8 minimum; by the project, $80 minimum; by the day, $320 minimum. Considers complexity of project, client's budget, skill and experience of artist, how work will be used, and turnaround time when establishing payment.

NORTHWIND STUDIOS INTERNATIONAL, Suite 2, 295 Mobile Ave. Camarillo CA 93010. (805)493-1661. Contact: John J. Tobin. Syndicates characters to magazines and book publishers.
Needs: Buys from 8-10 freelance artists/year. Considers single panel cartoons. Prefers pen & ink line drawings. "Our current needs include cute animal and character cartoons that appeal to both women and children. Any any wholesome concepts with similar appeal."
First Contact & Terms: Prefers experienced artists. Send resume or samples for consideration to be kept on file. Artists guidelines will be sent after review of resume and samples. Prefers photocopies as samples. Samples returned by SASE. Reports within 2 weeks. Pay artists on acceptance. Considers skill and experience of artist, salability of artwork and rights purchased when establishing payment. Buys all rights.
Tips: "Northwind Studios International has a commitment of quality to all its subscribers, therefore we ask all artists who are applying for a position to be aware of these rules: 1) production of good wholesome cartoons; 2) maintain a 'Disney' style. Because of this criteria it is necessary that we ask only qualified and talented Disney-style artists apply. The right artists will find a long term and pleasant relationship with our studio."

NORTON OUTDOOR ADVERTISING, 5280 Kennedy Ave., Cincinnati OH 45213. (513)631-4864. Contact: Tom Norton. Outdoor advertising firm.

Needs: Assigns 30-60 jobs/year. Local artists only. Uses artists for billboards.
First Contact & Terms: Call for interview. Pays $25 minimum, roughs; $75-100, finished sketch.

OHIO PRODUCTS, INC., 2554 Needmore, Dayton OH 45414. (513)276-392. President: J.E. Ryan. Manufacturer of custom plastic displays and parts for many clients, including department stores, art stores, museums, malls.
Needs: Works with 2 freelance artists/year. Works on assignment only. Uses artists for advertising, brochure and catalog design, illustration and layout, illustration on product, P-O-P displays and display fixture design.
First Contact & Terms: Send query letter with brochure. Samples are not filed. Samples not filed are returned only if requested. Reports back only if interested. To show a portfolio, mail appropriate materials; portfolio should include final reproduction/product and photographs. Payment is negotiable. Considers complexity of project, skill and experience of artist and turnaround time when establishing payment. Negotiates rights purchased.
Tips: "We can only use two artists at a time. Have patience."

O'KEEFFE'S INC., 75 Williams Ave., San Francisco CA 94124. (415)822-4222. Marketing Manager: Bill Fisher. Manufacturer of skylights, aluminum building products and fire-rated glass door, window and wall systems for architects, contractors and builders.
Needs: Works with 1-5 freelance artists/year. Works on assignment only. Uses artists for advertising, brochure and catalog design, illustration and layout.
First Contact & Terms: Reports back only if interested. Call or write for appointment to show portfolio. Pays by the hour, $25-50 average. Considers complexity of the project, skill and experience of artist, and turnaround time when establishing payment.
Tips: "Work more on planning, not necessarily on the finished piece—that's the printer's art."

OSSIPOFF, SNYDER & ROWLAND (ARCHITECTS) INC., 1210 Ward Ave., Honolulu HI 96814. President: Sidney E. Snyder, Jr., AIA. Architecture/interior design firm. Clients: commercial (offices), residential, institutional and religious.
Needs: Works with 5-10 freelance artists/year. Artist should be in Hawaii for this contact. Works on assignment only. Uses artists for interior design, architectural renderings, furnishings, model making and fine arts in building projects.
First Contact & Terms: Send query letter with brochure showing art style. Reports back. Write to schedule an appointment to show a portfolio. Payment determined by job.
Tips: "Interested in high quality."

PDT & COMPANY ARCHITECTS/PLANNERS, 7434 Montgomery Rd., Cincinnati OH 45236. (513)891-4605. Project Architect: Mark Tilsley. Clients: commercial, institutional and multi-family residential.
Needs: Works with 10+ artists per year. Uses artists for brochure layout, architectural and interior renderings, landscape design and model making. Works on assignment only. Especially needs brick and stone sculptors and renderers.
First Contact & Terms: Send query letter with brochure showing art style or resume and photographs. Samples are filed, or returned if requested by artist. Reports back in 3 weeks. Call or write to schedule an appointment so show a portfolio, or mail photographs. "All fees negotiable." Considers skill and experience of artist, client's budget and rights purchased when establishing payment. Negotiates rights purchased.

P.O.P. DISPLAYS, INC., 11-12 30 Drive Astoria, New York NY 11102. (212)721-6700. Creative Director: Tom Haas. Display/P-O-P firm. Clients: distillers, cosmetic firms and various others.
Needs: Assigns 400-500 jobs/year. Works with six artists for P-O-P design.
First Contact & Terms: Query with samples. SASE. Reports in 1 week. Works on assignment only. Samples returned by SASE. Provide resume and brochure to be kept on file for future assignments.

PALMLOOM CO., Box 1541, New York NY 10017. (212)688-8797. Advertising Manager: N. Tyler. Direct response (mail order) marketer (magazines) and catalogs.
Needs: Works with 2-3 freelance artists/year. Uses artists for advertising design (mail order), brochure and catalog design and layout, and paste-up.
First Contact & Terms: Send query letter with samples to be kept on file. Prefers tear sheets (nonreturnable printed matter) as samples. Reports back only if interested. Pays $10/hour for paste-up; $20/hour for design and layout.

***PEN NOTES, INC.**, 134 Westside Ave., Freeport NY 11520-5499. (516)868-1966/5753. President: Lorette Konezny. Produces children's learning books and calligraphy kits for children ages 3 and up, teenagers and adults.
Needs: Works with freelance artists. Prefers New York artists with book or advertising experience. Works on assignment only. Also uses freelance artists for calligraphy, P-O-P displays and mechanicals. Prefers pen and ink. Prefers realistic style with true perspective and color.
First Contact & Terms: Send query letter with brochure, Photostats and photocopies. Samples are filed. Samples not filed are returned only if requested by artist. Reports back within 10 days if requested. Call or write to schedule an appointment to show a portfolio or mail original/final art, final reproduction/product, tear sheets, Photostats, color and b&w. Original artwork is not returned after job's completion. Pays by the project, $100-1,000. Buys all rights.
Tips: "Work must be clean, neat and registered for reproduction. The style must be geared for children's toys. You must work on deadline schedule set by printing needs."

PERFECT PEN & STATIONERY CO. LTD., #42, 1241 Denison St., Markham, Ontario L3R 4B4 Canada. (416)474-1866. President: S. Szlrtes. Distributor of advertising specialties, office specialties and gifts. Clients: "all businesses across Canada."
Needs: Works with 6 freelance artists/year. Artists must have a minimum of 5 years of experience and references. Works on assignment only. Uses artists for advertising, brochure and catalog design and layout; photography and film work.
First Contact & Terms: Send query letter with brochure to be kept on file. Prefers tear sheets as samples. Samples not filed are not returned. Reports back only if interested. Write for appointment to show portfolio. Pays by the project. Considers complexity of the project when establishing payment.
Tips: "Apply only if you're experienced in direct mail advertising or a closely related area."

PHILADELPHIA T-SHIRT MUSEUM, 235 N 12th St., Philadelphia PA 19107. (215)625-9230. President: Marc Polish. Manufacturer and distributor of imprinted t-shirts and sweatshirts for retail shops and national mail order firms.
Needs: Uses artists for imprinted sportwear.
First Contact & Terms: Send query letter with brochure showing art style or photocopies. Samples not filed are returned. Reports within 1 week. To show a portfolio, mail roughs and Photostats. Pays in percent of sales or outright purchase.

PICKARD, INC., 782 Corona Ave., Antioch IL 60002. Director of Marketing: Patti Kral. Manufacturer of fine china dinnerware and collector plates. Clients: retailers.
Needs: Works with 3-4 freelance artists/year. Works on assignment only. Uses artists for patterns for dinnerware and fine art for collector plates. Prefers realistic and classical styles. Seeks "fine art as opposed to illustration for our limited edition plates." Prefers acrylics, colored pencil and watercolor.
First Contact & Terms: Send query letter with brochure, resume and slides. Samples are returned only if requested. Reports within 1 month. Write to schedule an appointment to show a portfolio, which should include color, b&w, photographs, slides and transparencies. Negotiates payment; generally a flat fee and/or royalties. Considers complexity of project, project's budget, skill and experience of the artist, how work will be used, turnaround time and rights purchased when establishing payment. Negotiates rights purchased.

PICKHARDT & SIEBERT USA, 700 Prince Georges Blvd., Upper Marlboro MD 20772. (301)249-7900. Director of Design: Barbara Brower. Manufacturer/importer of wallcoverings. "We sell to distributors, who service retail wallcoverings stores."
Needs: Uses artists for product design and styling, and "purchases wallpaper designs from freelancers on an ongoing basis."
First Contact & Terms: Send query letter with resume. Samples are filed. Samples not filed are returned only if requested. Reports back only if interested. Write to schedule an appointment to show a portfolio, which should include roughs, original/final art, slides and color. Pays by the project, $200-900.
Tips: "Designs need to be right scale and layout to appear in repeat on a wall."

PICTURESQUE PRODUCTS, Box 41630, Tucson AZ 85717. President: B.B. Nelson. Mail order firm of general gift items. Clients: consumers.
Needs: Works with 2 freelance artists/year. Uses artists for advertising, brochure and catalog design, illustration and layout; and P-O-P displays.
First Contact & Terms: Send query letter to be kept on file. Reports only if interested. Pays by the project, $100-500 average. Considers skill and experience of artist, how work will be used and rights purchased when establishing payment.
Tips: "Originality in the presentation sells me."

PLANET-TRANS, INC., 5 Blake Ave., Brooklyn NY 11212. (718)773-3332. President: Marino Bonilla. Manufacturer of iron-on heat transfers in all types of designs—adults, children, souvenir, babies—with worldwide distribution.

Needs: Works with 10 freelance artists/year. Works on assignment only. Uses artists for advertising illustration. Prefers airbrush.

First Contact & Terms: Send query letter with original work, slides or photos to be kept on file. Samples not filed are returned by SASE. Reports only if interested. Call or write for appointment to show portfolio. Pays for design by the project, $50-200 average. Considers skill and experience of artist when establishing payment.

Tips: "Prefers airbrush artwork on boards."

POURETTE MFG. INC., 6910 Roosevelt Way NE, Seattle WA 98115. (206)525-4488. President: Don Olsen. Manufacturer and distributor specializing in candle making supplies and soap making supplies. Clients: anyone interested in selling candle making supplies or making candles.

PRECISION GRAPHIC SERVICES INC., 119 W. Washington St., Champaign IL 61820. (217)359-6655. President: Jeff Mellander. Specializes in technical illustration for book publishers.

Needs: Works with 1-5 freelance artists/year. Uses artists for one-color, two-color and four-color work including airbrush illustration.

First Contact & Terms: Seeks artists experienced in drawing with technical pens and with highly developed skills in the area of technical illustration. Send query letter with brochure showing art style or resume, tear sheets, Photostats, photocopies and slides to be kept on file. Samples not filed are returned by SASE only if requested. Reports only if interested. Write for appointment to show portfolio, which should include original/final art. Pays according to accepted job bid of artist. Considers complexity of project, skill and experience of artist, and turnaround time when establishing payment.

Tips: Looks for "quality—not quantity—and consistency" when reviewing work. "Beginning artists just out of school tend to show too much; try to hit on too many areas. Show what you *like* to do and what you do best."

PRESTIGELINE, INC., 5 Inez Dr., Brentwood NY 11717. (516)273-3636. Director of Marketing: Ken Golden. Manufacturer of lighting products.

Needs: Buys various illustrations from freelance artists/year. Uses artists for advertising and catalog design, illustrations and layout; and illustration on product. Prefers b&w line drawings. Produces seasonal material for Christmas, Mother's Day, Father's Day, Thanksgiving, Easter, back-to-school and graduations; submit work 3-4 months before season.

First Contact & Terms: Send resume, business card and Photostats. Call for appointment to show a portfolio. Samples returned by SASE. Reports within 2 weeks. Buys all rights. Payment method is negotiable.

Tips: "There is an increased demand for b&w line art for newspaper advertisements."

PRISS PRINTS, INC., (a subsidiary for ISSC), 3002 Jeremes Landing, Garland TX 75043. (800)543-4971; Texas (214)278-8276. President: Toni Fischer Morath. Manufacturer. "We manufacture pressure sensitive wall decorations used primarily in children's rooms." Clients: retail stores selling wallcoverings and/or children's products to the parents of infants and children.

Needs: Works with 4-5 freelance artists/year. Uses artists for advertising and brochure design, illustration and layout, product design, illustration on product and signage.

First Contact & Terms: Send query letter with Photostats. Samples are filed. Samples not filed are returned. Reports back only if requested; if not interested, all submissions returned. To show a portfolio, mail Photostats. Pays for design and illustration by the project, $100 minimum. Considers complexity of project and interpretation of instructions when establishing payment. Buys all rights.

Tips: "Don't overwhelm me with long letters and too many samples. Don't send any originals unless requested."

PULPDENT CORPORATION OF AMERICA, 75 Boylston St., Brookline MA 02147. (617)232-2380. Director of Product Information: Jane Hart Berk. Manufacturer/distributor of dental supplies including instruments, pharmaceuticals, X-ray supplies, sterilizers, needles, articulating paper, etc. Clients: dental supply dealers and dentists.

Needs: Works with 3-5 freelance artists/year. Prefers local artists. Works on assignment only. Uses artists for advertising, brochure and catalog design, illustration and layout; photography and technical illustration.

First Contact & Terms: Send query letter with business card, Photostats and tear sheets. Samples returned by SASE if not kept on file. Reports within 6 weeks. Call or write for appointment to show portfolio. Pays by the project, $40 minimum. Considers complexity of project, and skill and experience of

artist when establishing payment; "how much our product is worth determines to some extent the amount we are willing to invest in designing, etc."
Tips: "We prefer simple, not-too-trendy designs aimed at the dental professional."

***DAVID C. RACKER ASLA & ASSOCIATES**, 3120 S. 950 E., Bountiful UT 84010. (801)295-5335. Contact: Dave Racker. Landscape architecture/land planning firm, providing consulting services. Clients: commercial, residential and industrial.
Needs: Assigns 20-30 jobs/year. Works with artists for renderings, graphic design and scale models.
First Contact & Terms: Send a query letter. SASE. Reports in 2 weeks. Pays for illustration by the hour, $12.50 minimum.

***DARIAN RAITHEL & ASSOCIATES**, 8623 Old Perry Hgwy., Pittsburgh PA 15237. (412)367-4357. President: Darian Raithel. Architectural, interior design and landscape design firm providing total planning and design of retail stores, restaurants, offices and some residential.
Needs: Works with 5 freelance artists/year. Uses freelance artists for interior design and renderings, design consulting and furnishings. Especially needs drafting on a freelance basis.
First Contact & Terms: Send brochure showing art style or resume. Samples are filed. Samples not filed are returned. Reports back within 2 weeks. Call or write to schedule an appointment to show a portfolio, which should include thumbnails, roughs, photographs and color. Pays for design by the hour, $5-15; by the day, $35-105. Pays for illustration by the hour, $5-15; by the day, $35-105. Considers skill and experience of artist when establishing payment. Buys one-time rights.
Tips: "Looks for creativity and neatness."

REALTORS NATIONAL MARKETING INST., Suite 500, 430 N. Michigan, Chicago IL 60611-4092. (312)670-3780. Editorial Assistant: Paula Ludman. Trade organization for real estate brokers.
Needs: Works with 4-8 freelance artists/year. Prefers local artists. Works on assignment only. Uses artists for advertising and brochure illustration. Prefers pen & ink and charcoal/pencil.
First Contact & Terms: Send query letter with resume, tear sheets and photocopies. Samples not filed are not returned. Reports only if interested. Call or write to schedule an appointment to show a portfolio, which should include original/final art, final reproduction/product and b&w. Pays for illustration by the hour, $10-50; by the project, $25-250. Considers complexity of project, how work will be used and turnaround time when establishing payment. Finds most artists through references/word-of-mouth.
Tips: "We would like to see simple, black and white pieces done for non-profit organizations and trade associations. We do not want to see airbrush, acrylics, oils, pastel, collage, etc., because we have no use for this artwork. We rarely print in four-color or complex pieces. Production is now accomplished via computer. We may be looking for computer art."

RECO INTERNATIONAL CORPORATION, Collector's Division, Box 951, 138-150 Haven Ave., Port Washington NY 11050. (516)767-2400. Manufacturer/distributor of limited editions collectors plates, lithographs and figurines. Clients: stores.
Needs: Works with 4 freelance artists/year. Uses artists for plate and figurine design, and limited edition fine art prints. Prefers romantic and realistic styles.
First Contact & Terms: Send query letter and brochure to be filed. Write for appointment to show a portfolio. Reports within 3 weeks. Negotiates payment.

RECO INTERNATIONAL CORPORATION, Kitchen Gourmet Accessories Division, 138-150 Haven Ave., Port Washington NY 11050. (516)767-2400. President: Heio W. Reich. Publisher and manufacturer.
Needs: Designers to design houseware and kitchen utensils on an exclusive basis for production according to designs. Works on assignment only.
First Contact & Terms: Send query letter and brochure showing art style or resume; submit portfolio for review. Prefers to see "anything that will show artist's ability." Reports "when needed." Negotiates payments.
Tips: "In a portfolio, I like to see a good representation of the types of art you're best at and a biography."

***RILEY & TURVILLE ARCHITECTS**, Suite 107, 10 Thacher St., Boston MA 02113. (617)367-3460. Partner: William S. Turville. Office Manager: Ms. Kim E. Sears. Provides full services for architectural and interior design for multi and single family residential, commercial/retail buildings and stores, historic renovation/restoration, theatres, exhibits and other special environments.
Needs: Works with 3-6 freelance artists/year. Prefers expert specialists with broad knowledge of their general fields. Works on assignment only. Uses freelance artists for advertising design and illustration, brochure design, illustration and layout, interior design and renderings, landscape design and render-

ings, architectural renderings, design consulting, furnishings, model making and graphic/signage/logo design.
First Contact & Terms: Send query letter with brochure showing art style or resume and tear sheets. Samples are filed or returned only if requested by artist. Reports back within 7-10 days. Write to schedule an appointment to show a portfolio, or mail tear sheets, Photostats, photographs, b&w or color. Pays for design by the hour, $15 minimum, or negotiates payment by the project. Considers complexity of project, skill and experience of artist, turnaround time, client's budget, how work will be used and rights purchased when establishing payment. Also considers level of completeness (final, sketch, etc.) required. Negotiates rights purchased.
Tips: "Call, then write, then please be patient as we develop various projects where your skills may be useful."

BOB ROBINSON MARKETING INC., 963 Brush Hollow Rd., Westbury NY 11590. (516)334-8600. President: Bob Robinson.
Needs: Assigns 100 jobs/year. Uses artists for display/P-O-P design and scale models.
First Contact & Terms: Arrange interview to show portfolio. SASE. Reports in 2 weeks. Pays $50-300/sketch or $100-1,000/job for design of permanent displays.

ROCKING HORSE, Box 306, Highland NY 12528. (914)691-2927. Convention center, ranch-resort. Clients: social vacationers—business meeting executives, senior citizens, couples, families.
Needs: Works with 2 ad illustrators, 2 ad designers, 2 or 3 product designers and 2 illustrators for products/year. Uses artists for descriptive brochures, exhibits, signs and meeting room decorations. Especially needs caricatures, brochures, rate schedule line work or design as samples.
First Contact & Terms: Send published samples (resort ads around a western scene). Prefers "bartering" as payment method.
Tips: "Foresees more use of artists" in the field. Artists should "make their abilities and offerings known to potential clients."

ROCKY POINT PARK, Warwick RI 02889. (401)737-8000. General Manager: David Cascioli. Clients: general public.
Needs: Uses artists for direct mail brochures, programs, trade magazine ads, bumper stickers, and pennants.
First Contact & Terms: Submit photos, roughs or tear sheets of published work. Pays going rates.

***RODOLPH, INC.**, Box 1249, 999 W. Spain St., Sonoma CA 95476. Marketing Director: Francine Allyn. Importer/wholesaler of home furnishing fabric. "We import/wholesale/market very sophisticated high-end home furnishing fabrics. Presently, the collections are silk and wool." Clients: interior designers and architects.
Needs: Works with freelance artists for both print/weave designs product development. Uses artists for advertising, brochure and catalog design and layout.
First Contact & Terms: Send query letter with brochure. Reports back within 1 month. To show a portfolio, mail final reproduction/product. Pays for design by the project. Considers complexity of project and rights purchased when establishing payment.
Tips: "Keep in mind that designs we'd be interested in would be used for fabric. Therefore designs should be applicable and sophisticated. With prints there may be technical limitations but we can direct artist to overcome these."

S. ROSENTHAL & CO. INC., 9933 Alliance Rd., Cincinnati OH 45242. (513)984-0710. Creative Director: Steven Brown. Clients: publishers, manufacturers, associations and schools.
Needs: Works with 1-3 artists/month for paste-up. Uses artists for layout and retouching for direct mail, magazines, catalogs and brochures.
First Contact & Terms: Local artists only. Query by mail. No originals returned to artist at job's completion. Pay varies.

THE ROSENTHAL JUDAICA COLLECTION, by Rite Lite, 260 47th St., Brooklyn NY 11220. (718)439-3030. President: Alex Rosenthal. Manufacturer and distributor of a full range of Judaica ranging from mass-market commercial goods to exclusive numbered pieces. Clients: gift shops, museum shops and jewelry stores.
Needs: Works with 3-4 freelance artists/year. Works on assignment only. Uses artists for brochure and catalog design, illustration and layout and product design.
First Contact & Terms: Send query letter with brochure or resume, tear sheets and photographs. Samples are filed. Reports back only if interested. Call to schedule an appointment to show a portfolio,

which should include original/final art, tear sheets, photographs, slides and color. Pays for design by the project, $500 minimum. Considers complexity of project, client's budget, skill and experience of artist and turnaround time when establishing payment. Buys all rights.

ROYALEIGH DESIGNS, LTD., 1784 Pitkin Ave., Brooklyn NY 11212. (718)495-3700. President: Rubin B. Leigh. General Manager: Ian Leigh. Manufacturer of handprinted wallcoverings. Clients: wallcovering distributors and interior designers.
Needs: Works with 3-4 freelance artists/year. Prefers local artists only.
First Contact & Terms: Send query letter with tear sheets or "call." Samples are not filed. Samples are returned only if requested. Reports back within 10 days. Call to schedule an appointment to show a portfolio, which should include roughs and original/final art. Pays for design by the project. Considers client's budget, skill and experience of artist and rights purchased when establishing payment. Buys all rights.
Tips: Artists should "have wallcovering or fabric design experience."

RSVP MARKETING, Suite 5, 450 Plain St., Marshfield MA 02050. (617)837-2804. President: Edward C. Hicks. Direct marketing consultant services—catalogs, direct mail and telemarketing. Clients: primarily industry and distributors.
Needs: Works with 7-8 freelance artists/year. Desires "primarily local artists; must have direct marketing skills." Uses artists for advertising, copy brochure and catalog design, illustration and layout.
First Contact & Terms: Send query letter with resume and finished, printed work to be kept on file. Reports only if interested. Pays for design by the job, $400-5,000. Pays for illustration by the hour, $25-85. Considers skill and experience of artist when establishing payment.

***SAFETY INDUSTRIES, INC.**, Box 1137, McGill NV 89318. President: Arthur Bruyere. "Direct mail company that specializes in small unique markets. We manufacture 75% of our products and purchase the balance outside. Product lines consist of driver education supplies, rural mail carrier supplies, promotional supplies for dentists and fire department supplies." Serves schools, dentists, municipalities and letter carriers.
Needs: Works with 2 freelance artists/year. Assigns 4-6 jobs/year. Works on assignment only. Uses artists for advertising, brochure and catalog design, illustration and layout, rendering of product and posters.
First Contact & Terms: Send query letter with brochure or resume. Samples not filed are returned. Call to schedule an appointment to show a portfolio, or mail thumbnails and final reproduction/product. Pays for design and illustration by the day, $100 minimum. Considers complexity of project, turnaround time and rights purchased when establishing payment. Negotiates rights purchased.

SANTA FE PARK SPEEDWAY, 9100 S. Wolf Rd., Hinsdale IL 60521. (312)839-1050. Public Relations: Mary Lou Tiedt. Stock car racetrack. Clients: "We are a public family entertainment establishment and service a wide variety of manufacturers, patrons and small businesses locally. A large portion of advertisers, which need the work of our artists, are auto shops, motorcycle shops and restaurants."
Needs: Works with 2 artists/year for advertising design. Uses artists for advertising, direct mail brochures, posters, publicity brochures, yearly programs, bumper stickers and road signs. "We are looking for new original layouts and designs for racing." Especially needs speedway logo to be used on t-shirts, mailings and the program cover.
First Contact & Terms: Mail art. Will review basic pencil sketches or photos; previously published work is preferred. SASE. Reports in 2-4 weeks. Provide business card to be kept on file for possible future assignments. Call or write to schedule an appointment to show a portfolio, which should include original art, final reproduction, color or photographs. Negotiates pay. Considers how work will be used, turnaround time and rights purchased when establishing payment. Rights purchased vary according to project.
Tips: "Artist must keep up to date on the car models on the market for designs as we run a 'late model stock car' division; also on trends in t-shirt design and what will work well for printing (silkscreen). Keep in touch and be persistent, as we get very busy. Send samples with envelope to return work in-...this allows a quick return and response to work. The best time to contact us for work is in November or late January. The spring season is much too late. By March, we are already set for the summer season."

THE J.H. SCHULER CO., 1649 Broadway, Hanover PA 17331. (717)632-5000. Director of Product Development: John H. Schuler. Distributor of giftware for fundraising. Clients: nonprofit groups.
Needs: Uses illustrators and dimensional designers.
First Contact & Terms: Send query letter with samples. Prefers printed pieces as samples. Samples returned by SASE only if requested.

SINCLAIR ASSOCIATES, INC., 15 N. Ellsworth Ave., San Mateo CA 94401. (415)348-6865. Principal Architect: George L. Sinclair. Estab. 1985. Architectural firm providing full architectural design services. Clients: residential, commercial, retail, public and industrial.
Needs: Works with 2-5 freelance artists/year. Works on assignment only. Uses artists for advertising and brochure design and layout; brochure illustration; interior and landscape design, and architectural renderings.
First Contact & Terms: Send query letter with brochure showing art style or resume and photocopies. Samples not filed are not returned. Reports only if interested. Call or write to schedule an appointment to show a portfolio. Considers complexity of project, client's budget, skill and experience of artist, and how work will be used when establishing payment.

SLADE CREATIVE MARKETING, Box 484, Santa Barbara CA 93102. (805)687-5331. President: S. Richard Slade. Service-related firm providing graphics, brochures, technical drawings, collateral material and general advertising. Clients: technical and consumer.
Needs: Works with 10-12 freelance artists/year. Artists must be able to communicate directly with company. Works on assignment only. Uses artists for advertising, brochure and catalog design, food illustration, illustration and layout; illustration on product, P-O-P displays, signage, photography and technical writing.
First Contact & Terms: Send query letter with resume, Photostats, photographs, photocopies, slides or tear sheets to be kept on file. Samples not filed are returned by SASE only if requested. Reports only if interested. Write for appointment to show portfolio. Pays by project, $100-750 average. Considers complexity of project, how work will be used and rights purchased when establishing payment.
Tips: "Be flexible and open to any job within your range."

***SMETHPORT SPECIALTY CO.**, 1 Magnetic Ave., Smethport PA 16749. Director of Product Development: Reid Matteson. Produces games for children 4 to adult.
Needs: Works with 6 freelance artists/year. Buys 100 designs from freelance artists/year. Buys 10 illustrations from freelance artists/year. Prefers experienced artists. Works on assignment only. Also uses freelance artists for mechanicals.
First Contact & Terms: Send brochure showing art style. Samples not filed are returned only if requested. Reports back within 2 weeks. Call or write to schedule an appointment to show a portfolio. Original artwork is not returned to the artist after job's completion. Buys all rights.

SNAP-ON TOOLS CORP., 1801 80th St., Kenosha WI 53140-2801. (414)656-5348. Advertising Manager: William Tower. Manufacturer of tools and provides retouching of hand tool photos for dealers and marketing needs.
Needs: Works with 5 freelance artists/year on a daily basis, 5 outside freelancers. Prefers artists with three years of experience. Uses artists for the design, illustration and layout of advertising brochures and catalogs plus product design, illustration on product, P-O-P displays, display fixture design, posters, model making and signage.
First Contact & Terms: Contact only through artist's agent. Samples not filed are not returned. Reports back only if interested. Call or write to schedule an appointment to show a portfolio, which should include thumbnails, roughs, original/final art, final reproduction/product, color, tear sheets, Photostats, photographs and b&w. Pays for design by the hour, $15-55. Pays for illustration by the hour, $15-55. Considers complexity of project, client's budget, skill and experience of artist, how work will be used, turnaround time and rights purchased when establishing payment.

TOM SNYDER PRODUCTIONS, INC., 90 Sherman St., Cambridge MA 02140. Art Director: Annette Donnelly. Developer of educational computer software for ages 5-adult; develops software, documentation, ancillary materials (music, art, books). Clients: schools, department stores, program stores.
Needs: Works with several freelance artists/year. Uses artists for b&w and color work, brochure design, illustration and layout; illustration on product and package design and computer graphics. Prefers pen & ink, charcoal/pencil, watercolor, oils, computer illustration and woodblocks.
First Contact & Terms: Works on assignment only. Send query letter with resume and samples to be kept on file. Prefers photocopies as samples. Samples not filed are returned by SASE only if requested. Reports back only if interested. Pays by the hour, $15-25 average. Considers complexity of the project, skill and experience of the artist, how work will be used and turnaround time when establishing payment.
Tips: "Let your work speak for itself. Just send photocopies and be patient. When an appropriate job comes up and your work is on file, we'll call you. A confident style and ability is important, but creativity is what I really look for in a portfolio."

SOFTSYNC, INC., 162 Madison Ave., New York NY 10016. (212)685-2080. President: Sue Currier. Manufacturer of software for a variety of home computers. Subject matter includes education, personal productivity. Clients: computer and mass market retail stores.
Needs: Works with 5 freelance artists/year. Works on assignment only. Uses artists for advertising and brochure design, illustration and layout; illustration on product, P-O-P displays and posters.
First Contact & Terms: Send query letter with brochure and photographs, slides or tear sheets to be kept on file. Samples not filed are returned only if requested. Reports within days. Call or write for appointment to show portfolio. Pays by the hour, $10-15 average, or by the project, $350-1,000 average. Considers complexity of project, skill and experience of artist and how work will be used when establishing payment.
Tips: "For mechanical artists, we need people who are quick and accurate. For illustrators, bring us samples that are colorful, zippy and innovative."

SPENCER GIFTS, INC., 1050 Black Horse Pike, Pleasantville NJ 08232. (609)645-5526. Art Director: James Stevenson. Retail gift chain located in approximately 440 malls in 43 states; gifts range from wall decorations to 14k gold jewelry.
Needs: Assigns 35-50 jobs/year. Prefers artists with professional experience in their field of advertising art. Uses artists for package design illustration, hard line art, fashion illustration, newspaper ads and toy, poster, package and product design, T-shirt design and other soft goods.
First Contact & Terms: Query with samples, previously published work or arrange interview to show portfolio. With samples, enclose phone number where you can be reached during business hours. Reports within 2 weeks. Negotiates pay.

STAMP COLLECTORS SOCIETY OF AMERICA, Box 3, W. Redding CT 06896. Executive Vice President and Creative Director: Malcolm Decker. Philatelic marketing firm. Develops mail order/direct response buyers of stamps using publications and mailing lists.
Needs: Works with 6 freelance designers/year. Prefers local (Westchester, New Haven, Fairfield County and New York City) designers; "experience requirement is determined by the job complexity." Works on assignment only. Uses designers for advertising and brochure design, illustration and layout; product design, album and editorial design, and "full-dress" direct mail packages.
First Contact & Terms: Send query letter and resume; "if interested, we'll call you. Show your portfolio and leave behind or send in samples or photocopies as requested." Pays by the hour, by the project, or offers a retainer. Considers complexity of project, and skill and experience of the designer when establishing payment.
Tips: "Send a comprehensive, detailed resume listing all the clients served, noting those for whom the most work was done."

STUDIO 38 DESIGN CENTER, (formerly Galaxie Handprints, Inc.), 38 William St., Amityville NY 11701. (516)789-4224. Vice President: Andrea Reda. Self-contained manufacturer of wallpaper for national clients.
Needs: Uses artists for wallpaper. Prefers pen & ink, airbrush, colored pencil, watercolor, pastels, and markers.
First Contact & Terms: Portfolio should include colors, geometrics and florals. No figures.

***SUN HILL INDUSTRIES, INC.**, 48 Union St., Stamford CT 06906. Art Director: Amy Wintering; Product Development Manager: Nancy Mimoun. Manufacturer of Easter egg decorating kits, plastic home-office stationery items, health and beauty aids (organizers and novelties). Clients: discount chain and drug stores and mail order catalog houses.
Needs: Works with 2-3 freelance artists/year. Assigns 5-6 jobs/year. Works on assignment only. Uses artists for product design, rendering of product, model making and package design.
First Contact & Terms: Send query letter with brochure and resume. Samples are filed. Samples not filed are returned only if requested by artist. Reports back only if interested. Call to schedule an appointment to show a portfolio. Pays for design by the hour, $25 minimum, or by the project, $350 minimum. Pays for illustration by the hour, $25 minimum, or by the project, $350 minimum. Considers complexity of project and turnaround time when establishing payment. Buys all rights.

SUNDBERG, CARLSON AND ASSOCIATES, INC., 914 West Baraga Ave., Marquette MI 49855. (906)228-2333. Designer/Illustrator: Mike Lempinen. Architectural/interior design/engineering firm providing architectural design, interior design, graphic design, illustration architectural renderings, and model making. "We are interested in seeing artwork for brochures, advertising, and architectural rendering services, and are especially interested in beginning a file on available art services; freelance, art houses, publication firms, etc."
First Contact & Terms: Send query letter with brochure showing art style or resume, tear sheets,

Photostats and printed pieces. Samples not filed are not returned. Reports only if interested. To show a portfolio, mail appropriate materials. Pays for design by the hour, $8-50. Pays for illustration by the hour, $10-50. Considers complexity of project, client's budget, and skill and experience of artist when establishing payment.
Tips: "Please do not send returnable pieces, slides or photos. We can not return unsolicited materials."

***SUNDESIGNS ARCHITECTS**, 901 Blake Ave., Glenwood Springs CO 81601. Architect: D.K. Moffatt. Architectural/interior and landscape design/land planning firm providing commercial and residential architectural design and land planning of residential P.U.D.'s and resorts. Clients: bank buildings, office buildings, resorts and housing developers.
Needs: Works with 6 freelance artists/year. Local, experienced and innovative artists only. Uses artists for advertising illustration, brochure and interior design, landscape, interior and architectural renderings.
First Contact & Terms: Send query letter with brochure showing art style to be kept on file. Reports within 1 month. Write to schedule an appointment to show a portfolio, which should include thumbnails, roughs, final reproduction/product, color and photographs. Pays by the hour, $45 minimum; by the project, $500 minimum. Considers complexity of project, client's budget, and skill and experience of artist, how work will be used and turnaround time when establishing payment.

PHILLIPS SWAGER ASSOCIATES, 3622 N. Knoxville, Peo IL 61603. (309)688-9511. Vice President/Design Coordinator: Jim Matarelli. Full-service architectural/engineering/interiors firm serving governmental, health care, education, general practice clients.
Needs: Works with 2-3 freelance artists/year. Works on assignment only. Uses freelance artists for brochure design and architectural renderings.
First Contact & Terms: Send resume and slides. Samples are filed. Samples not filed are not returned. Reports back only if interested. Call or write to schedule an appointment to show a portfolio, which should include thumbnails, color, Photostats, photographs and b&w. Pays for illustration by the hour, $10-20 minimum; by the project, $200 minimum. Considers complexity of project, client's budget, skill and experience of artist, how work will be used and turnaround time when establishing payment.

TEACH YOURSELF BY COMPUTER SOFTWARE, INC., Suite 1000, 349 W. Commercial St., East Rochester NY 14445. (716)381-5450. President: Lois B. Bennett. Publisher of educational software for microcomputers. Clients: schools, individuals, stores.
Needs: Local artists only. Works on assignment only. Uses artists for advertising, brochure and catalog design, illustration and layout; and illustration on product.
First Contact & Terms: Send query letter with brochure, resume, Photostats, photographs, photocopies, slides or tear sheets to be kept on file. Samples not filed are returned by SASE. Reports within 6 weeks. Write for appointment to show portfolio, which should include roughs, Photostats and photographs. Pays for design and illustration by the hour. Considers complexity of project, skill and experience of artist, how work will be used, turnaround time and rights purchased when establishing payment. Buys all rights.

THOG CORPORATION, Box 424, Tallmadge OH 44278. Sales Manager: Don Martin. Provides equipment for the graphic arts industry.
Needs: Works with 2-3 freelance artists/year. Uses freelance artists for advertising, brochure and catalog design, illustration and layout; and product design.
First Contact & Terms: Send query letter. Samples are filed. Reports back only if interested. Write to schedule an appointment to show a portfolio, which should include roughs and Photostats. Pays for design and illustration by the project, $25 minimum. Considers complexity of project, client's budget and rights purchased when establishing payment. Buys all rights.
Tips: "We use a lot of custom line art."

THOMAS NELSON PUBLISHERS, Box 141000, Nelson Place, Elm Hill Pike, Nashville TN 37214. (615)889-9000. Vice President Advertising and Marketing: Robert J. Schwalb. Manufacturer and distributor of religious materials, Bibles, Christian books; also secular markets from subsidiary companies. Clients: retailers, book stores.
Needs: Works with 60 freelance artists/year. Works on assignment only. Uses artists for advertising, brochure and catalog design, illustration and layout; product and display fixture design; illustration on product; P-O-P displays; posters; model making and signage.
First Contact & Terms: Send query letter with brochure showing art style or tear sheets, Photostats, photocopies, slides and photographs. Samples not kept on file are returned. Reports only if interested. Call or write to schedule an appointment to show a portfolio, which should include original/final art, final reproduction/product and photographs. No set pay range; "project budget sets price." Payment

terms of 10 days or 30-day turnaround. Firm reserves publishing rights. Buys all rights.
Tips: Industry trends are toward "a clean-cut motif with simple design." When reviewing work, evaluates "presentation of work, cleaness and creative concept." Artists should "research the type of work or creative needs of the business they interview with."

***TRANSAMERICA LIFE COMPANIES**, 1150 South Olive St., Los Angeles CA 90015. Graphic Design Director: Paul Ushijima. Provides financial services.
Needs: Works with 15 + freelance artists/year. Assigns 100 + jobs/year. Prefers local artists. Works on assignment only. Uses artists for brochure design, illustration, and layout, P-O-P displays, display fixture design, magazine design, illustration and layout.
First Contact & Terms: Send query letter with resume. Samples are not filed and are not returned. Reports back only if interested. Write to schedule an appointment to show portfolio, which should include thumbnails, roughs, original/final art, and final reproduction/product. Pays for design by the hour, $15 minimum. Pays for illustration by the project, $50 minimum. Considers complexity of project, client's budget and skill and experience of artist when establishing payment. Buys all rights.

TREASURE CRAFT/POTTERY CRAFT, 2320 N. Alameda, Compton CA 90222. Director of Design and Marketing: Nina Dooley. Manufacturer of earthenware and stoneware housewares and gift items. Clients: department stores and gift shops.
Needs: Works with 3 freelance artists/year. Uses artists for advertising and product design, illustrations, layout and model making.
First Contact & Terms: Prefers local area artists. Send query letter. Reports in 3 weeks. Works on assignment basis only. Provide business card and flyer to be kept on file for possible future assignments. Payment determined by the project.

TURNROTH SIGN CO., 1207 E. Rock Falls Rd., Rock Falls IL 61071. (815)625-1155. Contact: R. Neil Turnroth. Clients: banks, business, retail and industry.
Needs: Works with artists for billboards ($25-50), neon signage ($20-75), sign redesign ($20-100). Works primarily with out-of-town artists. Assigns 15-20 jobs/year.
First Contact & Terms: Send query letter with samples. SASE. Reports within 1 week. Payment by the job.
Tips: "Artists should have some nice photos of sketch work."

UARCO, INC., 121 N. Ninth St., Dekalb IL 60115. Advertising Manager: Ed Beckmann. Direct mail catalog providing computer supplies and business forms to businesses with computers.
Needs: Works with 4-5 freelance artists/year. Works on assignment only. Uses artists for brochure design and layout and cover designs.
First Contact & Terms: Send query letter with resume, tear sheets and photocopies. Samples not filed are returned only if requested. Reports only if interested. To show a portfolio, mail roughs, final reproduction/product and tear sheets. Pays for design by the project, $100 minimum. Considers complexity of project, skill and experience of artist, and turnaround time when establishing payment.

THE UNGAME COMPANY, 761 Monroe Way, Placentia CA 92670. (714)993-9800. Vice President Marketing: Martin H. Magdaleno. Manufacturer and distributor of educational and entertainment games and toys with the theme "games and toys with a heart." Clients: chain toy stores, department stores, specialty stores and christian bookstores.
Needs: Works with 4-6 freelance artists/year. Prefers local artists. Works on assignment only. Uses artists for advertising, brochure and catalog design, illustration and layout, product design, illustration on product, P-O-P displays, posters and magazine design.
First Contact & Terms: Send query letter with brochure. Samples are not filed. Samples are returned only if requested. Reports back only if interested. Call or write to schedule an appointment to show a portfolio. Pays for design and illustration by the project, $100-5,000. Considers complexity of project, client's budget, skill and experience of artist, turnaround time and rights purchased when establishing payment. Negotiates rights purchased.

***UNIQUE INDUSTRIES, INC.**, 2400 S. Weccacoe Ave., Philadelphia PA 19148. Director of New Products: Martin Moshel. (215)336-4300. Manufacturer. "We publish a complete line of children's party supplies. We also produce an extensive line of everyday party supplies." Products include paper plates, napkins, tablecovers, giftwrap. party hats, blowouts, invitations, games, hanging decorations, etc.
Needs: Works with 15-20 freelance artists/year. Assigns 50-100 jobs/year. "Purchased birthday and party designs and graphics. Frequently after reviewing artist's style and capabilities, we will offer a specific assignment." Uses artists for product design, rendering of product and model making. "Art must

be prepared to be printed in four flat colors. Existing art can be presented in any size. New art created for our party supplies must be in a 9' circle."
First Contact & Terms: Send query letter with resume, tear sheets, Photostats, photographs and SASE. Samples are filed. Reports back with 2-4 days. Call or write to schedule an appointment to show a portoflio, which should include roughs, final reproduction/product, tear sheets and Photostats. Pays for design by the project, $50 minimum. Pays for illustration by the project, $50-250. Considers complexity of project, how work will be used and rights purchased when establishing payment. Buys all rights. "All art used becomes the exclusive property of Unique Industries, Inc."
Tips: "Visit large party goods stores and major toy chains which have large party goods departments. Artwork submitted to us must be cheerful and upbeat. Our catalog is available if you send a 9x12 SASE."

VERMONT T'S, Main St., Chester VT 05143. (802)875-2091. President: Thomas Bock. Commercial screen printer, specializing in t-shirts and sweatshirts. Vermont T's produces custom as well as tourist-oriented silkscreened sportwear. Does promotional work for businesses, ski-resorts, tourist attractions and events.
Needs: Works with 6 freelance artists/year. Uses artists for graphic designs for t-shirt silkscreening. Prefers pen & ink, calligraphy and computer illustration.
First Contact & Terms: Send query letter with brochure. Samples are filed. Samples not filed are returned only if requested. Reports back within 10 days. Mail Photostats. Pays for design by the project, $75-250. Considers complexity of project, client's budget, skill and experience of artist and how work will be used when establishing payment. Negotiates rights purchased. Finds most artists through portfolio reviews and samples.
Tips: "Have samples showing rough through completion. Understand the type of linework needed for silkscreening."

VISUAL AID/VISAID MARKETING, Box 4502, Inglewood CA 90309. (213)473-0286. Manager: Lee Clapp. Distributes sales promotion (aids), marketing consultant (service)—involved in all phases. Clients: manufacturers, distributors, publishers and graphics firms (printing and promotion) in 23 SIC code areas.
Needs: Works with 3-5 freelance artists/year. Uses artists for advertising, brochure and catalog design, illustration and layout; product design, illustration on product, P-O-P displays, display fixture design and posters. Buys some cartoons and humorous and cartoon-style illustrations. Additional media: fiber optics, display/signage, design/fabrication.
First Contact & Terms: Works on assignment only. Send query letter with brochure, resume, business card, Photostats, duplicate photographs, photocopies and tear sheets to be kept on file. Originals returned by SASE. Reports within 2 weeks. Write for appointment to show a portfolio. Pays for design by the hour, $5-75. Pays for illustration by the project, $100-500. Considers complexity of project, skill and experience of artist and turnaround time when establishing payment.
Tips: "Do not say 'I can do anything.' We want to know best media you work in (pen/ink, line, illustration, layout, etc.)."

WELLS CONCRETE PRODUCTS, PRESTRESSED BUILDINGS DIV., Box 308, Hwy. 109 E., Wells MN 56097. Marketing Communications Manager: Bruce Borkenhagen. Manufacturer of commercial/industrial/office buildings, building components and bridges. Clients: business owners, developers, architects and government.
Needs: Works with 6 freelance artists/year. Works on assignment only. Uses artists for advertising, brochure and catalog design, illustration and layout; illustration on product and signage. Prefers pen & ink.
First Contact & Terms: Send query letter. Samples not filed are returned by SASE. Reports only if interested. Call or write to schedule an appointment to show a portfolio, which should include roughs. Pays for design and illustration by the hour, $10 minimum; by the project, $30 minimum. Considers complexity of project when establishing payment. Finds most artist through references/word-of-mouth and this listing.
Tips: "Outside work would be primarily doing line perspective drawings by photographs supplied by us (work on buildings by quote)."

***WILDERNESS LOG HOMES, INC.**, Route 2, Plymouth WI 53073. President: Paul Maxon. Manufactures and distributes log homes.
Needs: Prefers artist "who is self-motivated and willing." Works on assignment only. Uses freelance artists for advertising and catalog design, advertising and brochure illustration and layout, rendering of product, P-O-P displays, model making, signage, magazine design and illustration.
First Contact & Terms: Send query letter with brochure showing art style or resume. Samples are

filed. Reports back only if interested. Call to schedule an appointment to show a portfolio. Considers skill and experience of artist when establishing payment.
Tips: "Be ready and willing for lots of hard work with some changes."

***WIN-TEX INC.**, #202, 9011 Carpenter Freeway, Dallas TX 75247. Design Director: Kathryn Inman. Manufacturer/importer of kitchen textiles. Needs designs with *broad* market appeal.
Needs: Works with 5 freelance artists/year. Uses artists for advertising, brochure and catalog design, illustration and layout; product, accessory, textile, pattern, and package design, P-O-P displays, paste-up, mechanicals, direct mail, package inserts and photography.
First Contact & Terms: Send query letter with brochure showing art style or resume, tear sheets and Photostats. Pays for design by the hour, $15 minimum. Prefers quotes by artist/agent for specific job. Considers complexity of project, client's budget, skill and experience of artist, how work will be used and marketability of design when establishing payment.
Tips: Artist should have "knowledge of our market by researching the market on their own—knowing who is doing what."

WINDSOR ART PRODUCTS, INC., 9101 Perkins St., Pico Rivera CA 90660. (213)723-6301. Design Director: Pauline Raschella. Manufacturer of decorative framed artwork and mirrors for retail stores.
Needs: Works with 5 freelance artists/year. Prefers local artists. Works on assignment only. Uses artists for product design.
First Contact & Terms: Send query letter with brochure showing art style and photographs. Samples not filed are returned only if requested. Reports only if interested. Call or write to schedule an appointment to show a portfolio, which should include roughs, original/final art, final production/product and photographs. Pays for design by the project, $300 minimum. Pays for illustration by the project, $100 minimum. Considers complexity of project when establishing payment.

WOODMERE CHINA INC., Box 5305, New Castle PA 16105. (412)658-1630. President: L.E. Tway. Manufacturer and importer of all types of collectible plate and porcelain figurines, dinnerware and giftware. Clients: wholesalers, retailers and corporations.
Needs: Works with 6-12 freelance artists/year. Works on assignment only. Uses artists for plate and figurine design; mechanicals; advertising, brochure and catalog design, illustration and layout.
First Contact & Terms: Send query letter with resume and samples to be filed unless return requested. Accepts any type sample. Reports within 2 weeks. Pays by the project, $1,000-10,000 or on an advance and royalty basis. Considers complexity of the project, skill and experience of the artist and reputation of artist in market when establishing payment.
Tips: Be professional. Seeks "only art styles that fit our markets and that are good, tight quality work."

CLIFFORD N. WRIGHT ASSOC. ARCHITECTS, 4066 W. Maple, Birmingham MI 48010. (313)647-2022. President: William L. Baldner A.I.A. Vice President: William D. Shiels A.I.A. Architectural firm providing total architectural services. Clients: residential, commercial, light industrial.
Needs: Works with 10 freelance artists/year. Works on assignment only. Uses artists for landscape and interior design, interior and architectural renderings, design consulting and furnishings.
First Contact & Terms: Send brochure and resume to be kept on file. Reports only if interested. Call for appointment to show portfolio. Pays by the project for design and illustration. Considers complexity of project, client's budget, and skill and experience of artist when establishing payment.

***ZANE YOST & ASSOCIATES, INC.**, 144 Island Brook Ave., Bridgeport CT 06606. (203)384-2201. Marketing Director: Joanne Carroll. Architectural firm. Clients: residential developers (multi-family housing), banks and commercial developers.
Needs: Works with 4-6 freelance artists/year. Works on assignment only. Uses artists for advertising illustration, brochure design, architectural renderings and model making.
First Contact & Terms: Send query letter with brochure showing art style or resume, tear sheets, photocopies and slides. Samples not filed are not returned. Reports only if interested. To show a portfolio, mail appropriate materials. Pays for illustration by the hour, $40 minimum; by the project, $800-1,500. Considers complexity of project, client's budget, and skill and experience of artist when establishing payment.

Fashion

ACT YOUNG IMPORTS INC., 49 W. 37th St., New York NY 10018. (212)354-8894. Executive Vice President: Joe Hafif. Manufacturers and importers of printed totes, diaper bags, knapsacks, school bags, ladies handbags, clutches made of canvas, vinyl, oxford, nylon, etc.
Needs: Buys 300-600 designs/year. Especially needs experienced designers. Local artists only.
First Contact & Terms: Query with samples. Designs on paper only, no sample manufacturing necessary.

ADVERTIR, LTD., 990 Avenue of the Americas, New York NY 10001. (212)629-8755. President: Eve Denbaum.
Needs: Works with many freelance artists/year. Local artists only. Works on assignment only. Uses artists for illustrations, brochures, catalogs, magazines, newspapers, mechanicals, retouching, airbrushing and advertisements.
First Contact & Terms: Send query letter with brochure showing art style or samples. Samples not filed are returned only if requested. Reports only if interested. Call to schedule an appointment to show a portfolio, which should include final reproduction/product, color, tear sheets and b&w. Pays by the project. Considers complexity of project, client's budget, skill and experience of artist, and how work will be used when establishing payment.
Tips: "Respond only if professional."

AFRICAN FABRIC PRINTS/AFRICAN GARMENTS INC., Box 91, New York NY 10108. (212)725-1199. Contact: Vince Jordan.
Needs: Uses artists for fashion and textile design and ready-to-wear patterns.
First Contact & Terms: Mail tear sheets, original art or design ideas. Reports in 5-6 weeks. Pays $50 minimum.

***AMRUN SALES, INC.**, 18 W. 33rd St., New York NY 10001. (212)564-3656. President: Stuart Edelman. Manufacturer and importer of mens, boys and ladies leather jackets and accessories for ages 28-40. Labels: U2-Wear Me Out; Butter; and Wear Me Out.
Needs: Works with 2 freelance artists/year. Prefers experienced artists only. Works on assignment only. Uses artists for advertising design, illustration and layout; bruchre, catalog, product, fashion and accessory design.
First Contact & Terms: Send query letter with brochure. Samples are filed. Samples not filed are returned only if requested. Reports back within 1 week. Call or write to schedule an appointment to show a portfolio. Pays for design and illustration by the project, $100 minimum. Considers complexity of project and skill and experience of artist when establishing payment. Buys all rights.

BAIMS, 408 Main, Pine Bluff AR 71601. (501)534-0121. Contact: David A. Shapiro. Retailer. Carries Haggar, Van Heusen and other labels.
Needs: Works with 2-3 illustrators/designers/year. Assigns 25-100 jobs/year. Uses artists for ad illustrations.
First Contact & Terms: Send a query letter with resume, business card and samples to be kept on file. Reports in 2 weeks. Call or write to arrange an appointment to show a portfolio. Pays $5-20/job.

BODY FASHIONS/INTIMATE APPAREL, 545 5th Ave., New York NY 10017. (212)503-2910. Editor/Associate Publisher: Jill Gerson. Information for merchandise managers, buyers, manufacturers and suppliers about men's and women's hosiery and underwear and women's intimate apparel and leisurewear. Monthly. Circ. 13,500.
Illustrations: Interested in fashion illustrations of intimate apparel. Do not mail artwork. Arrange interview to show portfolio. Works on assignment only. Keeps file consisting of editor's comments on portfolio review and samples of work. Reports in 4 weeks. Pays on publication.

***BRADMILL USA**, 1900 Oakdale Ave., San Francisco CA 94124. (415)282-9100. Designer: Lyda Cort. Manufacturer of active beachwear for men boys and infants. Labels: Stubbies (men and boys), Koala kids (children and toddlers) and Tony Hawk Skate Board Collection.

Needs: Works with 10-15 freelance artists/year. Prefers local artists. Works on assignment only. Uses artists for advertising, brochure and catalog design, illustration and layout, fashion illustration, textile, pattern and package design and posters.
First Contact & Terms: Send query letter with brochures, resume, tear sheets, Photostats, photocopies and slides. Samples are filed. Reports back only if interested. Call to schedule an appointment to show a portfolio. Pays for design by the project, $250-2,000. Pays for illustration by the project, $50-1,000. Considers complexity of project, skill and experience of artist, client's budget and how work will be used when establishing payment. Buys first rights, reprint rights or all rights.

***CALIFORNIA APPAREL NEWS**, 945 S. Wall St., Los Angeles CA 90015. (213)626-0411. Art Director: Jim Yousling. Trade publication emphasizing women's fashion. Weekly. Circ. 75,000. Accepts previously published material. Original artwork is returned to the artist after publication. Sample copies available. Buys 2,000 illustrations/year from freelancers. Works on assignment ony. Send query letter with brochures, resume, tear sheets and photocopies. Samples are filed. Samples not filed are returned only if requested by artist. Reports back only if interested. Call or write to schedule an appointment to show a portfolio which should include roughs, original/final art, tear sheets, Photostats, photographs, color and b&w. Negotiates rights purchased. Pays $35-175 color, cover. Pays on publication.

CATALINA/Division of Kayser Roth, 6040 Bandini Blvd., Los Angeles CA 90815. (213)726-1262, ext. 281. Art Director: Jaye Pape. Manufacturer of women's, men's, juniors, and girls' swimwear and sportswear; Catalina.
Needs: Works with 10 freelance artists/year. Local artists only. Uses artists for brochure design and illustration, catalog illustration and fashion illustration, paste-up and mechanicals. Seeks "contemporary but not 'high' fashion look" in art styles. Prefers b&w work or wash with charcoal pencil line. Watercolors and markers are generally used in color work.
First Contact & Terms: Send Photostats and photocopies to be kept on file. Reports back only if interested. Call for appointment to show portfolio, which should include original/final art. Pays by the hour, $10-25 for production; by the project, $100-250 for illustration/per figure. "For catalogs that are totally illustrated, we would like to make arrangements according to budget." Considers complexity of project, available budget and how work will be used when establishing payment.

***H. COTLER CO., INC.**, 10 W. 33rd St., New York NY 10001. Director of Marketing: Pamela Gelson. Manufacture of menswear and boys, prep, kids' wear. Prefers contemporary, high fashion, youthful style. Directed towards men (18-34), kids (4-7), boys/prep (8-20). Labels: COTLER, Kamikaze, Blues Alley, Direzion.
Needs: Works with 4 freelance artists/year. Prefers local artist with an updated, trendy style. Uses freelance artists for fashion illustration, package design, calligraphy, paste-up and mechanicals. Needs paste-up artists on continuous basis year-round.
First Contact & Terms: Send query letter with photocopies. Samples are filed. Samples not filed are not returned. Reports back only if interested. Write to schedule an appointment to show a portfolio, which should include Photostats. Pays for illustration by the project, $100-2,000. Pays for mechanicals by the hour, $20. Considers complexity of project when establishing payment. Buys all rights.

EARNSHAW'S REVIEW, 225 W. 34th St., New York NY 10001. (212)563-2742. Publisher: Thomas Hudson. Managing Editor: Catherine Connors. Art Director: Bette Gallucci. For designers, manufacturers, buyers and retailers in the children's fashion industry. Monthly. Circ. 10,000.
Needs: Buys 180 illustrations/year on fashion (infants to pre-teenagers). Works with 12-15 illustrators/year. Especially needs color fashion sketches.
First Contact & Terms: Send tear sheets with an SASE or call. Reports in 1 week. Call to schedule an appointment to show a portfolio, which should include original/final art, color, tear sheets, photographs and b&w. Pays for design by the project, $20-250; for illustration by the project, $15-250.
Tips: "There is more fashion orientation and color in the field. We are interested in new people. Know children's body shapes, size, and age differences."

***EXECUTIVE APPAREL, INC.**, "A" & Lippincott Sts., Philadelphia PA 19134. (215)634-6668. President: Robert Singer. Manufacturer of uniform designs.
Needs: Local artists only, "knowledge of historical clothing a plus." Works on assignment. Uses artists for advertising, brochure and catalog design and layout, fashion illustration, mechanicals and direct mail. "Artists must be capable of developing presentation boards."
First Contact & Terms: Send query letter with resume and samples. Samples are filed. Samples not filed are returned only if requested by artist. Reports back within 7 days. Call to schedule an appointment to show a portfolio, which should include roughs, original/final art and color. Pays $75-100/figure. Considers complexity of project when establishing payment. Buys all rights.

Artist: Pat Jones Birenbaum

Marker and pencil were used by freelance illustrator Pat Jones Birenbaum of Woodland Hills, California to complete ad slicks for Catalina Swimwear. Birenbaum, who originally answered the company's advertisement for a freelance artist in a trade paper, says the company "always strives for a clean-cut image." The artwork for ad slicks is usually done in a simple, conservative style suitable for use by a variety of stores. Jaye Pape, Catalina's art director, says the artist meets deadlines and uses a conservative style appropriate to the assignment. Catalina bought all rights for $150.

***FABIL MFG. CORP**, 521 W. 57th St., New York NY 10019. (212)757-6100. Vice President: Ron Reinisch. Manufacturer and importer of boys' and girls' outerwear, rainwear, boys' sportswear, swim wear and shirts. Labels: Members Only, Coca-Cola (jackets and rainwear only).
Needs: Works with 5 freelance artists/year. Local artists only, experience with children's wear. Uses artists for catalog design, illustration and layout, fashion design and fashion illustration.
First Contact & Terms: Send query letter with samples. Samples are filed. Samples not filed are returned only if requested. Reports back wihtin 3 weeks, only if interested. Write to schedule an appointment to show a portfolio, or mail appropriate materials. Pays for illustration by the project, $50-75. Considers complexity of project, skill and experience of artist and client's budget when establishing payment. Buys all rights.

GELMART INDUSTRIES, INC., 180 Madison Ave., New York NY 10016. (212)889-7225. Vice President and Head of Design: Ed Adler. Manufacturer of high fashion socks, gloves, headwear, scarves, and other knitted accessories. "We are prime manufacturers for many major brands and designer names."
Needs: Uses artists for fashion accessory design. Prefers pen & ink, colored pencil, watercolor, acrylics, collage and markers.

First Contact & Terms: Call for appointment to show a portfolio. Pays by the project.
Tips: "Keep the products in mind and show us how your ideas can adapt."

JOHN PAUL GOEBEL, 10 Park Ave., New York NY 10016. (212)696-0444. Vice President: Suzette Lynch. Specializes in fashion. Clients: fibers, textiles and ready to wear.
Needs: Works with 2-6 freelance artists/year. Uses artists for illustrations, brochures, catalogs, newspapers and model making.
First Contact & Terms: Works on assignment only. Send query letter with brochure, business card and samples to be kept on file. Write for appointment to show portfolio, which should include Photostats, photocopies or tear sheets. Reports back only if interested. Pays for illustration by the project, $100-5,000 average. Considers complexity of project, client's budget and how work will be used when establishing payment.
Tips: "Submit examples of your fashion illustrations. We deal primarily with men's apparel."

***GUAVAS INC.**, 7633 Varna Ave., Unit I, N. Hollywood CA 91605. (818)901-0720. Purchasing Agent: Rosanna Locke. Manufacturer and distributor of men's activewear clothing for ages 15-30.
Needs: Works with 5 freelance artists/year. Uses artists for product, fashion and accessory design, window design and T-shirt illustration design. Prefers simplistic, original designs.
First Contact & Terms: Send query letter with brochure, resume, tear sheets, Photostats, photocopies and slides. Samples are filed. Samples not filed are returned by SASE only if requested by artist. Reports back within weeks only if interested. Write to schedule an appointment to show a portfolio, which should include roughs. Pays for design by the project, $50-250. Considers complexity of project, skill and experience of artist, client's budget, how work will be used, turnaround time and rights purchased when establishing payment. Buys all rights; negotiates rights purchased.
Tips: "Enjoy your work. It makes all the difference to the purchaser."

HOSIERY AND UNDERWEAR, 545 Third Ave., New York NY 10017. (212)503-2910. Managing Editor: Lynn Rhodes. Emphasizes hosiery; directed to hosiery buyers (from department and specialty stores; mass merchandisers, etc.) and hosiery manufacturers nationwide. Monthly. Circ. 10,000. Returns original artwork after publication if requested. Sample copy for SASE; art guidelines available.
Illustrations: Considers illustrations of hosiery; "we look for a clean style that pays attention to detail, but has a fresh, '80s look." Works on assignment only. Send query letter with brochure, resume and samples to be kept on file. Accepts Photostats, tear sheets or photocopies as samples; no slides and photographs. Samples not filed are returned only if requested. Reports back. Write for appointment to show portfolio. Buys all rights. Pays $8/b&w figure; $75-100 for color spread. Pays on acceptance.

KICK BACK SPORTWEAR INC., 5058 Venice Blvd., Los Angeles CA 90019. (213)937-5007. President: Craig Hiller. Manufacturer of beach wear for young men and boys. Label: Kick Back.
Needs: Works with many freelance artists/year. Prefers local artist from Orange County or Los Angeles. Works on assignment only. Uses artists for fashion design and illustration, textile and pattern design and paste-up.
First Contact & Terms: Samples not filed are returned. Reports back within 7 days. Call to schedule an appointment to show a portfolio, which should include thumbnails, roughs, original/final art and color. Pays for design by the project, $200-1,000. Pays for illustration by the project, $150-750. Considers complexity of project, turnaround time and rights purchased when establishing payment. Buys all rights.
Tips: Artists should have "confidence, skill and ability to accept advice."

KNITTING TIMES, 386 Park Ave. S., New York NY 10016. (212)683-7520. Editor: David Gross. Official publications of the National Knitwear and Sportwear Association emphasizing apparel manufacturing, management and marketing. It covers the latest trends in fabrics, color and technology. Monthly. Circ. 11,000.
Needs: Local artists with a knowledge of fashion to do interpretive work in the editorial area. "Artists must be able to do interpretive work, to use their imagination. If I tell them I want a long dress or a tunic sweater over a short skirt, they have to know what I need. If you can only work with figure models, you can't work with me." Prefers an "interesting" contemporary look but no avant garde.
First Contact & Terms: Send a query letter with photocopies. Samples are filed for future reference. "Artists must show the ability to meet tight deadlines." Call to schedule an appointment to show a portfolio.

***MAIDENFORM, INC.**, 90 Park Ave., New York NY 10016. (212)953-1441. Art Director: Rhonda Cohen. Manufacturer of women's intimate apparel (bras, lingerie and panties). "Intimate apparel that is fashion oriented, feminine and contemporary in style for women 18-60 years." Label: Maidenform.

1986 Mariah Graham

Illustrator Mariah Graham of New York City was given five days to illustrate lingerie hangtags for Maidenform, Inc. In order to render the garments with accurate detail, Graham worked with live models. Art director Rhonda Cohen, who found Graham through the Advertising Directions trade show, says, "She has no objections to changes when they are necessary, follows instructions well and meets all deadlines." For the hangtags, rendered in marker and ink, Graham sold all rights for $250 for two figures and $125 for one figure.

Needs: Works with 5 freelance artists/year. Prefers professional talent. "For *ongoing* projects, local artists are preferred." Uses artists for advertising design and illustration, catalog illustration, fashion illustration and calligraphy. "Contemporary but not high fashion style." Prefers color and/or b/w renderings. Attention to detail in lace rendering extremely important. Medium depends on specific project needs (medium must reproduce well in color).
First Contact & Terms: Send query letter with brochure, resume and tear sheets. Samples are filed. Samples not filed are returned only if requested by artist. Reports back only if interested. Call to schedule an appointment to show a portfolio. Pays for design by the project, $150 minimum. Pays for illustration by the project, $100/figure minimum. Considers complexity of project, client's budget and size and scope of entire project when establishing payment. Buys all rights.
Tips: "Artist must be completely professional and willing to make changes on artwork based on client's needs. Artists must be responsible for meeting all deadlines."

MAYFAIR INDUSTRIES INC., 1407 Broadway, New York NY 10018. President: Robert Postal. Manufacturer of T shirts, sweat shirts and sportswear. Prefers screen printed tops and bottoms (fun tops). Directed towards ages 2 to 21. B. J. Frog, Jane Colby and Rrribbit Rrribbit labels.
Needs: Works with 10 freelance artists/year. Uses artists for pattern design. Prefers cartoon style, young in look.
First Contact & Terms: Send query letter with brochure showing art style. Samples not filed are returned only if requested. Reports only if interested. To show a portfolio, mail appropriate materials. Pays for illustrations by the project, $100-500. Considers complexity of project when establishing payment.

***MILACA MILLS**, 10401 Bren Rd. E., Minnetonka MN 55343. (612)935-8440. Vice President: Richard Green. Manufacturer of ladies and junior lingerie for ages 14-40. Labels: Demis Jrs; Jordache and G-Gee.
Needs: Works with 1 freelance artist/year. Uses artist for product, textile and pattern design.
First Contact & Terms: Send query letter with resume and samples. Samples are filed. Samples not filed are returned only if requested by artist. Reports back within 1 week. Call or write to schedule an appointment to show a portfolio, which should include oringal/final art and final reproduction/product. Pays for design and illustration by the project, fee is negotiable. Considers complexity of project, skill and experience of artist and client's budget when establishing payment. Negotiates rights purchased.
Tips: "We are very willing to listen to new ideas. A freelance artist will receive an initial review."

MS. LIZ, 61 W. 68th St., New York NY 10023. Contact: Ms. Barbara Slate. Design studio providing designs for apparel, gifts; television production and advertising (animation).
Needs: Works with 10 freelance artists/year. Uses artists for advertising and brochure design, illustration, and layout; fashion design, fashion accessory design, package design, graphics, illustration on product and animation. Prefers "cartoon art—high fashion—adult appeal."
First Contact & Terms: Artists with heavy experience, New York City area only. Send query letter with brochure, resume, samples and tear sheets to be kept on file. Write for appointment to show portfolio. Accepts "anything but original work" as samples. Samples returned by SASE if not kept on file. Reports within 2-3 weeks. Pays for design by the hour, $10-25 average; by the project, $100-5,000 average; by the day, $75-200 average. Pays for illustration by the hour, $10-25 average; by the project, $200-1,000 average; by the day $75-150 average. Considers complexity of project, available budget, and skill and experience of artist when establishing payment.
Tips: "Show a complete spectrum of skills."

NETWORK IND./CLASS KID LTD., 350 Fifth Ave., New York NY 10118. Design Director: Debbie Kuhfahl. Importer of men's and boy's sportswear. Labels: Laguna, Pro-Keds, Evenkeel.
Needs: Works with 4-6 seasonal freelance artists/year. Uses artists for fashion, textile, and graphic screen print design. Prefers markers, then pen & ink, charcoal/pencil, colored pencil and computer illustration.
First Contact & Terms: Send query letter with resume and photocopies. Samples not filed are not returned. Reports back only if interested. To show a portfolio, mail appropriate materials; portfolio should include roughs (concepts), original/final art and color. Pays for design by the hour, $10-20; by the project, $15-100. Pays for illustration by the hour, $10-15; by the project, $10-100. Considers complexity of project and skill and experience of artist when establishing payment.

LOUIS NICHOLE, INC., Office and showroom location 105 E 29th St., New York NY 10016. (212)685-0395. Design studio location 54 New Haven Rd., Prospect CT 06712. (203)758-3160. President: Louis Nichole. Design company for home furnishings and decorative arts products providing very detailed romantic European 18th and 19th century designing of wallcovering, fabrics, dinnerware, glassware, stationery, greeting cards, dolls, furniture lace, bridal and children apparel.
Needs: Works with 20 freelance artists/year. Uses artists for product design, illustration on product, posters, signage and illustration. Pen & ink with watercolor preferred, muted old world colors "antique" looks, French/English 18th century style."
First Contact & Terms: Send query letter with brochure, resume, samples and tear sheets to be kept on file or call for appointment to show a portfolio. Samples returned by SASE only if requested by artist. Reports within 1 week. Pays by the hour, $10-50 average. Considers complexity of project, skill and experience of artist, and turnaround time when establishing payment.

PENDLETON WOOLEN MILLS, 218 SW Jefferson, Portland OR 97201. (503)226-4801. Menswear Communications Manager: Carolyn A. Zelle; Womenswear Communications Manager: Pat McKevitt. Manufacturer of men's and women's sportswear, blankets and piece goods; all 100% pure virgin wool. Pendleton Woolen Mills.
Needs: Works with 1 or 2 freelance artists/year directly and "through our agency more." Seeks local artist for line art. Uses artists for advertising illustration.
First Contact & Terms: Send query letter with samples to be kept on file. Call for appointment to show portfolio. Reports to the artist within 3 weeks. Considers complexity of project, available budget and how work will be used when establishing payment. Pays for illustration by the project, $40 minimum.

PINEHURST TEXTILES INC., Box 1628, Asheboro NC 27204. (919)625-2153. Contact: Bonna R. Leonard. Manufactures ladies' lingerie, sleepwear and leisurewear; nylon tricot, 100% cotton, woven satin, woven polyester/cotton, brushed polyester and fleece; Pinehurst Lingerie label.
Needs: Works with 2 illustrators/year. Seasonal needs: spring and summer due September 1; fall and winter due March 1. Prefers pen & ink, watercolor and acrylics.
First Contact & Terms: Pays for illustration by the project, $75 minimum.

PLYMOUTH MILLS, INC., 330 Tompkins Ave., Staten Island NY 10304. (718)447-6707. President: Alan Elewson. Manufacturer of imprinted sportswear—t-shirts, sweatshirts, fashionwear, caps, aprons, and bags. Clients: mass merchandisers/retailers.
Needs: Works with 6 freelance artists/year. Uses freelance artists for advertising and catalog design, illustration and layout; product design.
First Contact & Terms: Send brochure and resume. Reports back only if interested. Pays for design and illustration by the hour, $10; by the project, $100.. Considers complexity of the project and how work will be used when establishing payment.

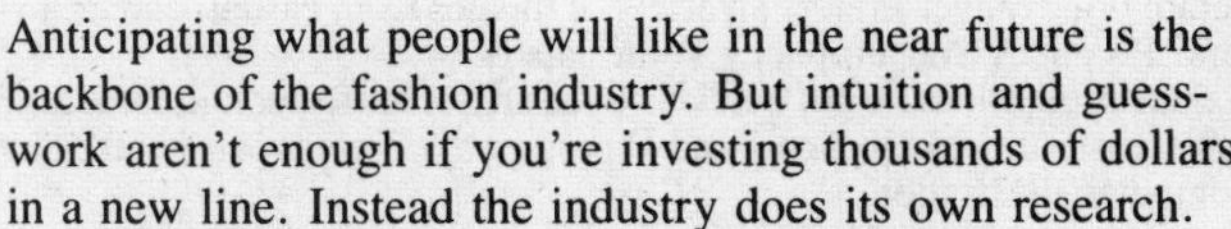

Debbie Kuhfahl
Network Industries/Class Kid Ltd.
New York City

Anticipating what people will like in the near future is the backbone of the fashion industry. But intuition and guesswork aren't enough if you're investing thousands of dollars in a new line. Instead the industry does its own research.

"Before we plan a line of clothes," explains Debbie Kuhfahl, design director at Network, which produces men's and boys' sportswear, "we send representatives to look at clothes in all the shops in Europe." The trends there are modified here a year later. The company also sends representatives to Singapore, where much sportswear is produced for importers. Debbie has to keep up with the yearly trade shows, such as the one sponsored by the National Association of Men's Sportswear Buyers (NAMSB), where manufacturers display their latest fashions. The fabric shows not only feature the hottest cottons and twills but also colors that will fill the racks for the next season. Must reading is trade periodicals such as *Women's Wear Daily* and the *Daily News Record*, plus *Vogue* and European fashion magazines. Debbie says skiing magazines also supply color trends. "I also look at biker clothes, because they're not afraid to be different."

She also subscribes to forecasting services. One such service sends Debbie boxes of pompons colored with the season's most popular hues. She stores them in a cabinet along with color cards sent by fabric companies. Debbie matches these colors to her design specifications when she develops the next season's line.

Debbie explains how a line is developed: "After looking at all the magazines and the forecasts, I have a pretty good idea of the look and the colors I want to use. I sketch the new lines and then color them in coordinating groups." For example, one board will show a sweatshirt with blue and green stripes on the sleeve, while another board shows the same sweatshirt with red and yellow stripes on the sleeves.

After Debbie sketches her ideas, she gives them to a freelance artist, who draws them on presentation boards. The artist follows Debbie's specifications, coloring in the details while keeping the drawing simple and easy to comprehend. After the presentation boards are finished, Debbie attaches exact measurements to the drawings so that sample clothing can be made. The samples are then shown by sales representatives to potential buyers.

The fashion industry works on a tight schedule, because new lines must be shown at the right shows. Also, since much manufacturing is done overseas, deadlines have to be met in order to avoid costly late shipments. Therefore, the art director must deliver the goods on time. Debbie expects her freelance help to keep the same deadlines. "I can't afford to put up with somebody who can't produce on time. It's too costly."

By looking through a portfolio, Debbie can spot reliable and talented help. "I have to see a good design sense, first, not just a photographic rendering. I also like to see creativity, that the artist isn't afraid to do something different." She favors artists who are open to suggestions, those who can give and take constructive criticism. Debbie is emphatic about what she doesn't want to see. "I don't want to see an unorganized portfolio with messy sketches. That shows me you're going to produce sloppy work."

Her advice to anyone interested in pursuing fashion as a career is to attend a school devoted to fashion such as the Fashion Institute of Technology. Located in New York City, FIT is in the heart of the garment district, where students can gain experience in the industry while going to school. Fellow students also prove to be good connections in later years.

After graduating, take any job related to fashion, Debbie advises. "Stick in there. If you're just out of school, keep knocking on doors. Take any little thing to keep you in the business."

—Susan Conner

PROPHECY CORP., 1302 Champion Circle, Carrollton TX 75006. (214)247-1900. Director of Advertising: Jayme Stoutt. Manufacturer of misses and petite fashions: jackets, blouses, skirts, sweaters, pants and dresses in the upper moderate price range. Prefers a variety of themes from casual, career, to dressy. Directed toward 35-60 years. Prophecy and Prophecy Petite labels.
Needs: Artists must constantly produce professional work quickly. Uses artists for fashion illustration, textile and pattern design, calligraphy, paste-up, mechanicals and photography. Prefers pen & ink, airbrush, markers, calligraphy and computer illustration.
First Contact & Terms: Send query letter with any type of sample that does not need to be returned. Samples not filed are not returned. Reports only if interested. Call to schedule an appointment to show a portfolio. Pays for design by the project. Pays for illustration by the project. Considers complexity of project, skill and experience of artist, and turnaround time when establishing payment.
Tips: "I look for a portfolio that specializes in fashion illustration or textiles. Many artists feel that it is important to show how versatile they are, however, when I look at a portfolio, I look for consistency of style. I want to know what I will be getting. Too many times I have requested a style in a portfolio that the artist could not duplicate."

PROTECH LEATHER APPAREL, INC., 155 Webster St., Hanover MA 02339. (617)871-5227. Advertising/PR: James Goodson. Manufacturer and importer of leather outerwear "with a youthful sporty appeal," mostly a motorcycle-type theme for ages 18-35. Labels: Protech Leather Apparel.
Needs: Works with 3-4 freelance artists/year. Prefers artists experienced in fashion or experience with models. Uses artists for advertising and brochure design and layout, catalog design, illustration and layout, product design and direct mail.
First Contact & Terms: Send query letter with resume, tear sheets, Photostats and photocopies. Samples are filed. Reports back only if interested. To show a portfolio, mail roughs, original/final art, color, Photostats and photographs. Pays for design and illustration by the project, $50-200. Considers complexity of project, skill and experience of artist and client's budget when establishing payment. Negotiates rights purchased.

R-TEX DECORATIVES CO., INC., 59 Sea Cliff Ave., Glen Cove NY 11542. (516)671-7600. President: Lillian Sturm. Manufacturer of high-fashion decorative yard goods, posters, panels and banners. Clients: department stores.
Needs: Works with 3-4 freelance artists/year. Works on assignment only. Uses artists for product design and posters.
First Contact & Terms: Send query letter with brochure and samples to be kept on file. Call or write for an appointment to show a portfolio. Accepts any type sample. Samples not filed are returned only if requested. Reports back only if interested. Pays by the project. Considers complexity of the project and artist's bid when establishing payment.

SAMPLE, THE, 1927 Elmwood Ave., Buffalo NY 14207. (716)874-1730. Director of Advertising: Bruce Barber. Retailer (fashion specialty stores).
Needs: Prefers local experienced artists. Works on assignment only. Uses artists for retail illustration.
First Contact & Terms: Send query letter with brochure or tear sheets. Samples are filed. Reports back only if interested. Call or write to schedule an appointment to show a portfolio. Pays for illustration by the hour, $8-25. Considers skill and experience of artist when establishing payment. Buys all rights.

SEW NEWS, News Plaza, Box 1790, Peoria IL 61656. (309)682-6626. Art Director: Denise M. Koch Parr. Tabloid emphasizing home sewing and fashion primarily for women, average age 49. Monthly. Does not accept previously published material. Original artwork is not returned to the artist after publication. Sample copy and art guidelines are not available.
Needs: Buys up to 10 illustrations per issue. Works on an assignment basis only.
First Contact & Terms: Send query letter with resume. Write for an appointment to show a portfolio. Reports back to the artist only if interested. Purchases all rights. Pays on acceptance.

***SHERRY MFG. CO., INC.**, 3287 N.W. 65 St., Miami FL 33147. Art Director: Jeff Seldin. Manufacturer of silk-screen t-shirts with beach and mountain souvenir themes. Label: Sherry's Best.
Needs: Works with 10 freelance artists/year. Prefers artists that know the T-shirt market and understand the technical aspects of T-shirt art. Uses freelance artists for T-shirt design. Prefers colorful graphics or highly-stippled detail.
First Contact & Terms: Send query letter with brochure showing art style or resume and Photostats and photocopies. Samples are not filed. Samples are returned only if requested. Reports back within 2 weeks. Call or write to schedule an appointment to show a portfolio, which should include thumbnails, roughs, original/final art, final reproduction/product, color, tear sheets, Photostats and photographs. Pays for design and illustration by the project, $150-400 ($400 figure includes separations). Considers complexity of project, skill and experience of artist and volume of work given to artist when establishing payment. Buys all rights.
Tips: "Know the souvenir T-shirt market and have previous experience in T-shirt art preparation."

***SPORTAILOR, INC.**, 6501 N.E. 2nd Ct., Miami FL 33138. (305)754-3255. Director of Marketing: Stan Rudman. Manufacturer and distributor of men's and boys' apparel (mostly sportswear) for toddlers through senior citizens. Labels: Sun Country Surfwear, Hawaiian County Lines, Weekender (mature men), and Maui Valley Lines.
Needs: Works with 3 freelance artists/year. Works on assignment only. Uses artists for advertising design, fashion design and illustration.
First Contact & Terms: Send query letter with brochure showing art styles or samples and photocopies. Samples are usually filed. Samples not filed are returned only if requested. Reports back within 1 week. Call to schedule an appointment to show a protfolio, which should include roughs, original/final art and color. "Show all the work you can do." Payment depends on the size of project; it can be a $25 job or a $200 job. Considers client's budget when establishing payment.
Tips: "We are looking for an artist who can easily sketch from photographs for catalog work as well as a fashion designer who understands the surf market and knows how to come up with a boys' and young men's look."

PRESTON STUART ART SERVICES, 69 W. 9th St., New York NY 10011. Director: Preston Stuart. Specializes in corporate presentations. Clients: fashion and corporate companies and ad agencies.
Needs: Works with 10 freelance artists/year. Desires "a professional relationship and good work." Works on assignment only. Uses artists for design and illustration, mechanicals and retouching.
First Contact & Terms: Send query letter with samples and tear sheets to be kept on file. "Photocopied samples are best." Reports only if interested. Pays for illustration by the project, $150-800 average. Considers client's budget, skill and experience of artist, how work will be used, turnaround time and rights purchased when establishing payment.

UFO, 466 Bloome St., New York NY 10013. (212)925-5477. Vice President: Lorna Brody. Manufacturer of contemporary sportswear for ages 16 to 40. Labels: UFO jeans and sportswear; Surplus by UFO.
Needs: Works with 4-5 freelance artists/year. Prefers local artists only. Works on assignment only. Uses artists for advertising design and illustration, brochure design and layout, catalog design, illustration and layout, fashion illustration, package design and direct mail.
First Contact & Terms: Send query letter with resume, tear sheets, Photostats and photocopies. Samples are filed. Reports back only if interested. Write to schedule an appointment to show a portfolio. Pays for design and illustration by the project. Considers complexity of project, skill and experience of artist, client's budget, how work will be used and turnaround time when establishing payment. Negotiates rights purchased.

U.S. SHOE CORPORATION, One Eastwood Dr., Cincinnati OH 45227. (513)527-7000. Promotion Services Director: Philip Gleeson. Manufacturer of shoes featuring current fashion trends; Red Cross, Socialités, Cobbies, Joyce, Selby, Pappagallo and Capezio.
Needs: Works with 3 freelance artists/year. "Experience is normally necessary." Uses artists for advertising, brochure and catalog design, illustration and layout; fashion design and illustration; paste-up and mechanicals.
First Contact & Terms: Send query letter with samples to be kept on file. Call or write for an appointment to show a portfolio. Accepts any type sample. Samples not kept on file are returned only if requested by artist. Reports to the artist only if interested. Pays by the hour, $25-30 for design; $30-35 for illustration. Considers complexity of project, available budget and turnaround time when establishing payment.

Galleries

To many artists, being represented in a gallery equals "making it." Acceptance in a gallery means you have accumulated a consistent body of work which shows a definite style and technique.

Thousands of galleries exist, but, if you're searching for your first gallery, try your own backyard. Most likely, you've already established a reputation in your vicinity, which means that local gallery owners may already know of your work. Also, it's much easier to keep a local gallery supplied with artwork and to keep tabs on their sales.

Finding the right gallery

Begin your search for a gallery by defining what type of gallery is right for you and your work. There are retail galleries which either buy your work outright or take it on consignment in order to sell to private collectors or other businesses. Retail galleries are in business to *sell* and will aggressively promote your work; the more money you make, the more they make. Most retail galleries work on consignment, that is, they are middlemen between the buyer and the artist for the sale of the work. Both the artist and the buyer benefit from this arrangement. You can devote more time to the creative side of your craft by being freed from the commercial aspect. Also, you will receive more exposure and publicity through a gallery than from private sales or even art shows. In exchange for selling, promoting and publicizing your work, the gallery receives a commission on sales of your work, ranging from 40 to 60 percent. If your work sells for $3,000, and the gallery receives a 50 percent commission, then you and the gallery receive $1,500 each from its sale.

Retail galleries are only one type of commercial gallery. Cooperatives—galleries in which you become a member in exchange for exhibit space—offer display time and promotion if you have the time to commit to the gallery's maintenance. Some take small commissions (20 to 30 percent), others do not. Many museums sell work through their shops; they often "rent" artwork for a specified amount of time, after which the work is returned. Avoid vanity or subsidy galleries, in which you will not only pay for exhibition space but also for promotion.

When you decide on the type of gallery that suits your needs, find out what individual galleries have to offer. If you are seeking a local gallery, ask your art-related friends if they can provide any inside information about a particular gallery. Attend the gallery's openings, where you can see firsthand how well artists are promoted. Visit the gallery during regular hours, but do so as a potential buyer. Investigate the following aspects:

- How long the gallery has been in business. If it's been around for years, you can expect it to continue. Galleries which have recently opened are more receptive to accepting artists, but they may be financially unstable.
- The gallery's hours. If they are limited to only a few hours during the weekend, then your work is not going to receive much attention. Also note if the gallery is open only during certain seasons, as are many galleries located in tourist towns.
- The gallery's specialty. If the artwork displayed is representational and your work is not, this is not the place for you.
- If the gallery features emerging artists. If not, the gallery is probably only interested in established artists. Also ask how many group shows there are annually, because they are the best introductions for new artists.
- Price range. If your prices don't match the price range of the works currently shown, then your work would probably not be saleable in this gallery.
- Knowledgeability of the sales staff. If the gallery employees are well-versed on the works displayed, then your work will probably receive the same treatment.

After you've chosen the galleries you want to approach, call the gallery director (address him by name, not title) and set up an appointment to show your work. If the gallery is not reviewing new work, ask if you can send a cover letter, brochure or sample to be kept on file. If you get an interview, gear your presentation to that particular gallery, keeping in mind the medium or genre it leans toward. Bring 15 to 20 transparencies or duplicate slides, some leave-behinds (brochure, resume and business card) and two or three originals. Think through your presentation so you will give a smooth, professional impression.

Setting terms

Be prepared, however, for either outcome: acceptance or rejection. If your work is not accepted, you will have benefitted from the experience of showing your work; you will also have a better grasp of your strengths and weaknesses. Ask for a referral to another gallery which might be more suited to your style.

If you're accepted, make sure you know all the terms before you agree on the representation. Here is a checklist of questions you should ask:

- Is the work sold on consignment, and, if so, what is the gallery's commission?
- What is the gallery's extent of representation? Does it ask for exclusive representation? If so, in what area—100 miles or the whole state? Will the agreement cover only the sale of works exhibited in the gallery or also works sold in your studio?
- How long will this agreement last? A lifetime deal might sound good now, but it won't when your career is established.
- Who pays for promotion, insurance and shipping? The gallery generally foots the bill for promotion and inhouse insurance, but shipping costs may be shared.
- Will the gallery provide you with names and addresses of people who buy your work through the gallery? Buyers are the name of the game, and you want to keep in contact with them. The gallery director may want to keep this information to himself. If this is the case, ask him to provide the names of past buyers, while he can keep confidential the names of prospective buyers.
- Who sets the retail price, the gallery or you? Often it's a compromise, but you should be consulted.
- How much publicity will the gallery provide? This is crucial in establishing your reputation. The more the gallery invests in publicizing your work and/or show, the better your sales will be. Make sure your show will be noted in press releases. Also determine how much display time your work will receive in a show.
- What happens if the gallery folds? You are guaranteed the return of your artwork under the Uniform Commercial Code, but make sure your agreement acknowledges this.
- Does the gallery provide a statement of accounts on a regular basis? If not, you will not be able to know if the gallery is selling your work and how much it owes you.
- Will you receive name credit on any reproductions of your work such as gallery brochures?
- Will you be able to remove your work during the extent of your contract? You might enter some of your pieces in a juried show or need to take down a piece to photograph it; make sure you clear this with the gallery director before you sign the contract. Also, to be prepared, photograph the pieces before you turn them over to the gallery.

Bring along your own agreement in case the gallery does not provide a contract. (Refer to North Light Books' *The Artist's Friendly Legal Guide* for contracts and agreements you can use.) Don't leave any work without a signed receipt. Iron out all the details before you make a commitment, and confirm all verbal agreements in writing the following day.

Moving on

If you're an already established artist and have had many local gallery shows, then broaden your scope by querying galleries within your region, then farther away. You probably have developed a second sense as to what type of gallery is right for you. Send these galleries the same package that you did before, only emphasize your successful shows and sales record. Make sure you update your brochure to include your most recent works.

The most complete list of galleries (though it lacks marketing information) is found in *Art in America's Guide to Galleries, Museums and Artists*. Other directories include *Art Now/ U.S.A's The National Art Museum and Gallery Guide, The Artist's Guide to Philadelphia Galleries*, and *Washington Art*. Keep up with the national and international art scene in *ARTnews*. Regional publications such as *U.S.A. Art, Southwest Art, Art New England, West Art*, and *Artweek* list gallery exhibitions in their areas. Also check with your local or state arts council for more information on galleries in your area.

Alabama

WHITING ART CENTER, 401 Oak St., Fairhope AL 36532. (205)928-2228. Director: Claiborne Walsh.
Profile: Nonprofit gallery. Estab. 1952. Clientele: tourists, schools, decorators, etc; 95% private collectors, 5% corporate clients. Represents 15-20 artists. Sponsors 9-10 solo and 2-3 group shows/year. Average display time 1 month. Overall price range: $10-2,500 or 3,000; most work sold at $50-250.
Media: Considers oils, acrylics, watercolor, pastels, pen & ink, drawings, mixed media, collage paper, sculpture, ceramics, fibers and photography. Most frequently exhibited media: watercolors, oils, ceramics/sculpture. Considers color and b&w limited edition offset reproductions.
Style: Exhibits painterly abstraction, conceptual, surrealism, impressionism, photorealism and realism. Genres include landscapes, florals, Americana, Western, portraits, and figurative work. "Our records indicate that sales of oils, acrylics, watercolors, etc. lean towards soft watercolors, oils, etc. with a realistic approach."
Terms: Accepts artwork on consignment (25% commission). Retail price set by gallery. Exclusive area representation not required. Gallery provides insurance (negotiated), promotion and a contact.
Submissions: Send query letter, resume, slides, brochure, photographs and SASE. Write to schedule an appointment to show a portfolio, which should include originals and slides. All material is filed "unless otherwise specified."

Arizona

ARTISTIC GALLERY, 7077 E. Main St., Scottsdale AZ 85241. (602)945-6766. Owner: Carole and Jay Rosenblatt.
Profile: Retail gallery. Estab. 1981. Clientele: Affluent tourists; 99% private collectors. Represents 12-14 artists. All work hangs 12 months a year. Overall price range: $750; most work sold at $1,000-2,000.
Media: Considers oils, acrylics, watercolors, pastels, drawings, sculpture and ceramics.
Style: Exhibits contemporary, abstract, figurative and south western works. "We carry watercolors, oils, acrylics, bronzes, marble and alabaster sculptures, Gorman lithographs and drawings."
Terms: Accepts work on consignment or buys outright. Gallery and artist sets retail price. Gallery provide insurances and promotion; artist pays for promotion.
Submissions: Send query letter, resume, brochure, and photographs. Write to schedule an appointment to show a portfolio.

EL PRADO GALLERIES, INC., Tlaquepaque Village, Box 1849, Sedona AZ 86336. (602)282-7390. President: Don H. Pierson.
Profile: Retail Gallery. Estab. 1976. Clientele: tourists, 90% private collectors, 10% corporate clients.

Represents 93 artists. Sponsors 4 solo and 3 group shows/year. Overall price range: $150-30,000; most artwork sold at $2,500.
Media: Considers oils, acrylics, watercolors, pastels, mixed media, collage, paper, sculpture, ceramics and crafts. Most frequently exhibited media: oils, acrylics and watercolor. Considers unlimited edition original handpulled prints and offset reproductions.
Style: Exhibits impressionism, photorealism, expressionism, neo-expressionism and realism. Genres include landscapes, florals, Americana, western and figurative work. Prefers "works reflecting Americana."
Terms: Accepts work on consignment (45% commission). Retail price set by gallery and artist. Exclusive area representation required.
Submissions: Send query letter, resume, brochure and photographs. Write to schedule an appointment to show a portfolio, which should include originals, slides and transparencies. "Artist information we may accept" is filed.

FAGEN-PETERSON FINE ART, INC., 7077 Main St., Scottsdale AZ 85251. (602)941-9989. Owners: Eleanor or Gene Fagen.
Profile: Retail Gallery. Estab. 1980. Clientele: "Young professionals interested in very modern art;" 100% private collectors. Represents 12 artists. Sponsors 8 solo and 2 group shows. Interested in emerging artists. Overall price range: $50-6,000.
Media: Considers oils, acrylics, watercolors, pastels, drawings, mixed media, collage, paper, sculpture, glass and original handpulled prints. Considers acrylics, watercolors and clay.
Style: Exhibits hard-edge/geometric abstraction, painterly abstraction, post-modern, primitivism and expressionistic works. Genres exhibited: landscapes and figurative work. "We prefer to represent emerging modern artists, artists that stretch the medium to its greatest. Artists that are professional and hard working and continuously creating new and exciting works of art. They have to be artists whose works are affordable, and want to see the pieces move into collections."
Terms: Accepts work on consignment (40% commission). Retail price set by gallery and artist. Exclusive area representation required.
Submissions: Send query letter, resume, slides, photographs and SASE. Call or write for an appointment to show a portfolio, which should include: originals, resumes, slides and all P.R. on the artist.

GALERIA MESA, 155 N. Center, Mesa AZ 85201. (602)834-2056. Curator: Michael Costello.
Profile: Nonprofit gallery. Estab. 1981. Clientele: residents, tourists and students; 100% private collectors. Sponsors 7 group shows/year. Average display time is 4 weeks. Interested in emerging and established artists. Overall price range: $500-1,500; most artwork sold at $100-300.
Media: Considers all media and original handpulled prints.
Style: Exhibits contemporary works. "Each exhibit is directed toward a specific theme or medium. All work is contemporary, by American artists and is selected by slides. Artists submit slides for acceptance based on the theme or mediums required for the particular exhibit."
Terms: Accepts work on consignment (15% commission). Exclusive area representation not required. Gallery provides insurance, promotion and contract; shipping costs are shared.
Submissions: Send query letter, resume, slides, and brochure. Resume, brochure and photographs are filed.

ELAINE HORWITCH GALLERIES, 4211 N. Marshall Way, Scottsdale AZ 85251. (602)945-0791. Arizona Director: Victoria Boyce.
Profile: Retail gallery. Estab. 1962. Clientele: tourists, corporations and residents. Represents 25+ artists. Sponsors 6 solo and 6 group shows/year. Average display time is 2 weeks. Interested in emerging and established artists. Overall price range: $1,000-15,000; most artwork sold at $4,000.
Media: Considers oils, acrylics, watercolor, pastels, mixed media, collage, paper, sculpture, ceramics, crafts and glass. Most frequently exhibited media: painting, sculpture and ceramics.
Terms: Accepts artwork on consignment (50% commission). Retail price set by gallery and artist. Exclusive area representation required. Gallery provides promotion; shipping costs are shared.
Submissions: Send query letter, resume, slides, brochure, business card, photographs and SASE. Call or write to schedule an appointment to show a portfolio, which should include slides and transparencies. Slides, resume and biographical information filed.

MARS GALLERY, 1201 S. First Ave., Phoenix, AZ 85003. (602)253-3541. Director: Rudy Guglielmo.
Profile: Cooperative gallery. Estab. 1978. Clientele: 10% private collectors. Represents 10 artists. Sponsors 12 solo and 12 group shows/year. Average display time is 1 month. Accepts Mexican-American and Mexican artists. Overall price range: $200-700; most artwork sold at $300.

Media: Considers all media.
Style: Exhibits contemporary, abstract, landscape, floral, non-representational, neo-expressionistic and post-pop. "MARS provides an alternative artspace for art, conceptual and performance art and encompasses the cultrual diversities of the Southwest region. MARS is a nonprofit artist cooperative whose goal is to serve as a vital resource and networking center for communities and artists."
Terms: Accepts artwork on consignment (10% commission from co-op member artists, 20% others); co-op membership fee plus donation of time. Retail price set by gallery and artist. Exclusive area representation not required. Gallery provides insurance, promotion and contract; shipping costs are shared.
Submissions: Send query letter, resume and slides. Call or write to schedule an appointment to show a portfolio. "All important material is filed. We will return artists' materials if they will enclose a samped self-addressed envelope."

SAVAGE GALLERIES, 7112 Main St., Scottsdale, AZ 85251. (602)945-7114. Director: Gwen Gunstead.
Profile: Retail gallery. Estab. 1960. Located downtown on gallery row. Clientele: tourists and locals; 75% private collectors, 25% corporate clients. Represents 28 artists. Total space devoted to hanging the work of gallery artists. Average display time is 3 months. Interested in emerging and established artists. Overall price range: $1,000-12,000; most artwork sold at $2,000-3,000.
Media: Considers oils, acrylics, watercolor and sculpture. Most frequently exhibited media: watercolor, oils, acrylics and bronze sculpture.
Style: Exhibits impressionism, expressionism and realism. Genres include landscapes, Western and portraits. Prefers realism. "Our gallery specializes in those works which depict the historical and contemporary cowboy and also the landscapes of the Western and Southwestern regions."
Terms: Accepts artwork on consignment. Retail price set by gallery and artist. Exclusive area representation required. Gallery provides insurance and promotion; artist pays for shipping.
Submissions: Send query letter, slides, photographs and SASE. Call to schedule an appointment to show a portfolio, which should include originals, slides and photos. Biographies and resumes filed.

TEMPE ARTS CENTER, Box 549, Tempe AZ 85281. (602)968-0888. Executive Director: John E. Coraor.
Profile: Nonprofit organization. Estab. 1982. Average display time is 5 weeks. "Current program focuses on local and regional artists with some juried exhibitions. Also places outreach exhibitions of local artists in satellite locations in the community."
Media: Considers oils, acrylics, watercolors, pastels, pen & ink, drawings, sculpture, ceramics, fibers, photography, crafts, mixed media, performance, collage, glass, installations and original handpulled prints.
Style: Exhibits "a diverse selection of contemporary works in all media."
Terms: Accepts artwork on consignment (25% commission). Artist sets retail price. Exclusive area representation not required. Gallery provides insurance, publicity and reception.
Submissions: Send query letter, resume, slides and SASE. Proposals reviewed periodically throughout the year. Exhibit schedule booked one year in advance; less in advance for outreach exhibits.

UNION GALLERIES, UNIVERSITY OF ARIZONA, Box 10,000, Tucson AZ 85720. Arts Coordinator: Tina McNearney.
Profile: Nonprofit gallery. Estab. 1982. Clientele: 100% private collectors. Represents 300 artists. Sponsors 3 solo and 10 group shows/year. Average display time is 3 weeks. Interested in emerging and established artists. Overall price range: $40-5,000; most artwork sold at $40-300.
Media: Considers oils, acrylics, watercolors, pastels, pen & ink, drawings, mixed media, collage, paper, sculpture, ceramics, crafts, fibers, glass, installations, photography, performance and prints. Most frequently exhibited media: photography, watercolors and clay.
Style: Exhibits hard-edge/geometric abstractions, color field, painterly abstraction, conceptualism, post-modern, surrealism, expressionism, neo-expressionism and realism. Genres include landscapes, figurative and nonobjective work. Prefers painterly abstraction, realism and post-modern works. "We do not cater to any specific style of artwork. We are interested in a well-rounded schedule of exhibitions of art, culture, history and information."
Terms: Accepts work on consignment (25% commission). Retail prices set by artist. Exclusive area representation not required. Gallery provides insurance, promotion and contract; artist pays for shipping.
Submissions: Send query letter and clippings. "Since we jury once a year, artists are notified *when* to send materials. Write to have name put on mailing list to announce annual slide review. Slides are reviewed in the spring."

California

A.R.T./BEASLEY GALLERY, 2802 Juan St., San Diego CA 92110. (619)295-0075. Director: Murray Tarleton.
Profile: Retail gallery. Establ. 1980. Represents 150 artists. Sponsors 4 solo and 4 group shows/year. Average display time is 6 weeks. Interested in emerging and established artists. Overall price range: $300-3,000; most artwork sold at $800-1,500.
Media: Considers oils, acrylics, watercolors, pastels, pen & ink, drawing, sculpture ceramics, fibers, crafts, mixed media, collage, glass, original handpulled prints and posters.
Style: Exhibits contemporary, abstract, impressionistic, figurative, landscape, floral and non-representational work. Prefers contemporary and abstract works. "We feature works in all media with contemporary subject matter."
Terms: Accepts work on consignment (50% commission). Gallery and artist sets retail price. Gallery provides insurance, promotion and contract; artist pays for shipping to gallery, gallery returns.
Submissions: Send query letter, resume, brochure, slides and SASE. Slides, biographical material (resume, published articles, brochures) artist's statement about the work, black-and-white photos are filed. "All slides must be labeled with artists' name, title of work, media and size."

CABRILLO GALLERY, 6500 Soquel Dr., Ceptos CA 95003. (408)479-6308. Director: Jane Gregorius.
Profile: Nonprofit gallery. Estab. 1975. Clientele: students, some collectors; 100% private collectors. Sponsors 7 solo shows/year. Average display time is 4 weeks. Interested in emerging and established artists. Overall price range: $250-7,000; most artwork sold at $250.
Media: Considers oils, acrylics, watercolor, pastels, pen & ink, drawings, mixed media, collage, paper, sculpture, ceramics, crafts, fibers, glass, installations, photography, performance and original handpulled prints. Most frequently exhibited media: painting, drawings, fibers, ceramics and sculpture.
Style: Exhibits color field, painterly abstraction, minimalism, conceptual, post-modern, pattern painting, primitivism, impressionistic, photo-realistic, expressionistic, and surrealism. "No protest or message art. We also try to steer clear of awful work." Prefers abstract and realistic work. "We try to exhibit as many different styles in as many media as possible. We're part of an art department in a college and feel that we need to inform our visitors; to show them something they may never have seen."
Terms: Retail price set by artist. Gallery provides insurance and contract; shipping costs are shared.
Submissions: Send resume, slides and SASE. Write to schedule an appointment to show a portfolio, which should include slides.

CENTER FOR THE VISUAL ARTS, 519 17th St., Oakland CA 94612. (415)451-6300. President, Board of Directors: Alton Jelks.
Profile: Nonprofit gallery. Clientele: gallery owners, consultants, collectors and general public. Sponsors 6 solo and 6 group shows/year. Average display time is 6 weeks-2 months.
Media: Considers oils, acrylics, watercolors, pastels, pen & ink, drawings, sculpture, ceramics, fibers, photography, crafts, mixed media, collage and glass.
Style: Exhibits a wide variety of styles. "CVA is a nonprofit artists membership organization. We are not a commercial gallery."
Terms: Nonprofit membership fee plus donation of time and referral. Retail price set by artist. Exclusive area representation not required. Gallery provides insurance, promotion and contract; artist pays for shipping.
Submissions: Send query letter.

EVA CHAN GALLERY, 7427 Girard Ave., La Jolla CA 92037. (619)-459-4343. Director: Eva Chan.
Profile: Retail gallery and art consultancy. Estab. 1985. Clientele: 100% private collectors. Represents 12 artists. Sponsors 6 solo and 6 group shows/year. Average display time is 1 month. Interested in emerging and established artists. Overall price range: $1,000-20,000; most artwork sold at $2,000-10,000.
Media: Considers oils, acrylics, mixed media, collage, paper sculpture, and original handpulled prints. Most frequently exhibited media: watercolors, batik, oil and acrylics.
Style: Exhibits painterly abstraction, post-modern impressionistic and realistic works. Genres include landscapes and figurative work.
Terms: Accepts work on consignment. Retail price set by gallery and artist. Exclusive area representation required. Gallery provides insurance, promotion and contract; artist pays for shipping.
Submissions: Send query letter, resume, brochure, slides, photographs and SASE. Write to schedule an appointment to show a portfolio, which should include originals and slides. Resume, slides and related information are filed.

COLLECTOR'S CHOICE, 20352 Laguna Canyon Rd., Laguna Beach CA 92651-1137. Director: Beverly Inskeep.
Profile: Art consultancy. Estab. 1976. Clientele: 78% collectors and tourists, 15% corporate clients. Represents 15 artists. Accepts only artists from southern California. Interested in emerging and established artists. Most artwork sold at $1,000.
Media: Considers all media and limited edition original handpulled prints. Most frequently exhibited media: sculpture, painting and photography. Looking for crafts: chairs and furnishings, toys and whirligigs.
Style: Exhibits color field, painterly abstraction, minimalism, conceptual, post-modern, surrealism, impressionism, photorealism, expressionism, neo-expressionism, realism and magic realism. Genres include landscapes, florals, portraits and figurative work. Features "sculpture and paintings with unusual subject matter and execution in a contemporary mode."
Terms: Accepts work on consignment (40% commission). Retail price set by gallery and artist. Exclusive area representation not required.
Submissions: Send query letter with resume, brochure, slides and SASE. Write to schedule an appointment to show a portfolio, which should include originals, slides and transparencies. Material is filed for corporate clients.

SUSAN CUMMINS GALLERY, 32 Miller Ave., Mill Valley CA 94941. (415)383-1512. Owner: Susan Cummins and Beth Changstrom.
Profile: Retail gallery. Estab. 1983. Clientele: Local and serious artwork collectors; 100% private collectors. Represents 50 artists. Sponsors 9 solo and 2 group shows/year. Average display time is 3 months. Interested in emerging and established artists. Overall price range: $300-3,000.
Media: Considers drawings and ceramics. Most frequently exhibited media: ceramics, painting and jewelry.
Style: Exhibits painterly abstraction, primitivism and expressionism. Genres include landscapes, portraits, florals and figurative work. "Our gallery specializes in narrative, figurative paintings and ceramic sculpture."
Terms: Accepts work on consignment (50% commission). Retail price set by gallery and artist. Exclusive area representation not required. Gallery provides promotion and contract; shipping costs are shared.
Submissions: Send resume, slides and SASE. Write to schedule an appointment to show a portfolio, which should include slides.

CUNNINGHAM MEMORIAL ART GALLERY, 1930 R St., Bakersfield CA 93301. (805)323-7219. Director: Patricia Archer.
Profile: Estab. 1956. 100% percentage of sales to private collectors. Sponsors 3 solo and 7 group shows/year. Average display time is 4 weeks. Interested in emerging and established artists. Overall price range: $100-100,000.
Media: Considers oils, acrylics, watercolors, pastels, drawing, sculpture, ceramics fibers, photography crafts, mixed media, performance, collage, glass, installations, original handpulled prints and posters.
Style: Exhibits contemporary, abstract, Americana, impressionistic, figurative, landscape, floral primitive, non-representational, photo-realistic, realism, neo-expressionistic and post-pop.
Terms: Juried works only, 20% commission. Retail price set by artist. Exclusive area representation not required. Gallery provides insurance, promotion and contract.
Submissions: Send query letter, resume, slides or photography. Resumes, slides and photos are filed.

DJUROVICH GALLERY, 727½ J St., Sacramento CA 95814. (916)446-3806. Director: Mark Orewyler.
Profile: Retail gallery and art consultancy. Estab. 1985. Clientele: young professionals, corporations and collectors; 25% private collectors, 25% corporate clients. Represents 35 artists. Sponsors 4 solo and 10 group shows/year. Average display time is 4 weeks. Interested in emerging and established artists. Overall price range: $300-3,000; most artwork sold at $500-1,000.
Media: Considers oils, acrylics, watercolor, pastels, pen & ink, drawings, mixed media, collage, paper, sculpture, ceramics, crafts, fibers and glass. Most frequently exhibited media: sculpture, oil on canvas and works on paper.

EATON/SHOEN GALLERIES, INC., 315 Sutter St., 94108 and 500 Paul Ave., San Francisco CA 94124. (415)788-3476.
Profile: Retail gallery. Estab. 1980. Clientele: private, corporate and institutional clients; 70% private collectors, 10 corporate and 20% institutions. Represents 16 artists. Sponsors 10 solo and 10 group shows/year. Average display time is 6 weeks. Interested in established artists. Overall price range:

$300-20,000; most artwork sold at $2,000-10,000.
Media: Considers all media.
Style: Exhibits contemporary works. "Our gallery exhibits painting, sculpture, photographs and graphics by regional, national and international artists whose career is considered established, mid-career or emerging."
Submissions: Send query letter and SASE.

FRESNO ART MUSEUM, 2233 North First St., Fresno CA 93703. (209)485-4810. Manager: Jerrie Peters.
Profile: Nonprofit gallery. Estab. 1957. Clientele: general public and students; 100% sales to private collectors. Sponsors 13 solo and 12 group shows/year. Average display time is 2 months. Interested in emerging and established artists. Overall price range: $250-25,000; most artwork sold at $300-1,000.
Media: Considers all media.
Style: Considers all styles. "Our museum is a forum for new ideas yet attempts to plan exhibitions coinciding within the parameters of the permanent collection."
Terms: Accepts work on consignment (40% commission). Retail price set by gallery and artist. Exclusive area representation not required. Gallery provides insurance, promotion and contract; shipping costs are shared.
Submissions: Send query letter, resume, slides, and SASE. Query letter, resume, slides and photos are filed.

GALLERY WEST, 107 S. Robertson Blvd., Los Angeles CA 90048. (213)271-1145. Director: Roberta Feuerstein.
Profile: Retail gallery. Estab. 1971. Located near showrooms catering to interior design trade and several restaurants. Represents 25 artists. Sponsors 5 solo and 3 group shows/year. Average display time is 5 weeks. Interested in emerging and established artists. Overall price range: $500-25,000; most artwork sold at $3,500.
Media: Considers oils, acrylics, watercolor, pastels, mixed media, collage, paper, sculpture, ceramics, crafts, fibers and limited edition original handpulled prints. Prefers paintings.
Style: Exhibits color field, painterly abstraction, photo-realistic and realistic works. Prefers abstract expressionism, trompe l'oeil and realism.
Terms: Accepts work on consignment (50% commission). Retail price set by gallery and artist. Exclusive area representation required. Gallery provides insurance, promotion and contract; shipping costs are shared.
Submissions: Send query letter, resume, slides and SASE. Slides and biography are filed.

GRAPHICS GALLERY, 2140 Bush St., San Francisco CA 94115. (415)921-7677. Director: R. Strauss.
Profile: . Retail gallery. Estab. 1968. Clientele: 50% private collectors. Represents approximately 100 artists. Average display time is 2 months. Interested in mature emerging and established artists. Overall price range: $100-6,000; most artwork sold at $100-1,000.
Media: Considers oils, acrylics, watercolors, mixed media, collage and original handpulled prints.
Style: Exhibits contemporary, abstract, landscape, representational and non-representational, photo-realistic, realistic and post-pop works. Features "the finest and largest collection of works on paper, unique works and original prints."
Terms: Accepts work on consignment (50% commission). Retail price is set by gallery and artist. Gallery provides insurance, promotion and contract; artist pays for shipping.
Submissions: Send query letter, with resume, brochure, slides and SASE. Bios and slides are filed.

INTERNATIONAL GALLERY, 643 G St., San Diego CA 92101. (619)235-8255. Director: Stephen Ross.
Profile: Retail gallery. Estab. 1980. Clientele: 99% private collectors. Represents 50 + artists. Sponsors 1 solo and 3 group shows/year. Average display time is 2 months. Interested in emerging and established artists. Overall price range: $15-10,000; most artwork sold at $25-200.
Media: Considers sculpture, ceramics, crafts, fibers, glass and jewelry.
Style: "Gallery specializes in contemporary crafts (traditional and current) folk and primitive art as well as naif art."
Terms: Accepts work on consignment. Retail price is set by gallery and artist. Exclusive area representation not required. Gallery provides insurance, promotion and contract; shipping costs are shared.
Submissions: Send query letter, resume, slides and SASE. Call or write to schedule an appointment to show a portfolio, which should include slides and transparencies. Resumes, work description and sometimes slides are filed.

LIZARDI/HARP GALLERY, 290 W. Colorado Blvd., Pasadena CA 91105. (818)792-8336. Director: Grady Harp and Armando Lizardi.
Profile: Retail gallery and art consultancy. Estab. 1982. Clientele: 90% private collectors, 10% corporate clients. Represents 15 artists. Sponsors 10 solo and 2 group shows/year. Average display time is 4 weeks. Interested in emerging and established artists. Overall price range: $400-20,000; most artwork sold at $2,000-8,000.
Media: Considers oils, acrylics, watercolor, pastels, pen & ink, drawings, mixed media, collage, sculpture, installations and original handpulled prints. Most frequently exhibited media: oils, pastels and sculpture.
Style: Exhibits surrealism, primitivism, impressionism, expressionism, neo-expressionism and realistic works. Genres include landscapes and figurative work. "Our gallery emphasizes quality of craftmanship no matter the style or medium. Works musts show evidence of sophistication of technique. We mix established and emerging artists and are less interested in 'leading edge or fad' than quality."
Terms: Accepts work on consignment (50% commission). Retail price is set by gallery and artist. Exclusive area representation required. Gallery provides insurance, promotion and contract; artist pays for shipping.
Submissions: Send query letter, resume, brochure, slides, photographs and SASE. Write to schedule an appointment to show a portfolio, which should include slides and transparencies. A completed application is filed.

LOS ANGELES MUNICIPAL ART GALLERY, Barnsdall Art Park, 4804 Hollywood Blvd., Los Angeles CA 90027. (213)485-4581. Curator: Marie de Alcuaz.
Profile: Nonprofit gallery. Estab. 1971. Sponsors 6 solo and 6 group shows/year. Average display time is 6 weeks. Accepts primarily Los Angeles artists. Interested in emerging and established artists.
Media: Considers oils, acrylics, watercolors, pastels, pen & ink, drawings, sculpture, ceramics, fibers, photography, crafts, mixed media, performance, collage, glass, installations, original handpulled prints and offset reproductions.
Style: Exhibits contemporary works. "The Los Angeles Municipal Art Gallery organizes and presents exhibitions which primarily illustrate the significant developments and achievements of living Southern California artists. Highlighting the gallery's programs are exhibitions of emerging, mid-career and well-established Los Angeles artists. The gallery strives to present works of the highest quality in a broad range of media and styles. We seek to provide a national and international forum for Los Angeles artists by participating in exchange and travelling shows. Our programs are to be significant for Southern California and are reflective of the unique spirit of this region and the grand wealth and diversity of the cultural activities in the visual arts in the city of Los Angeles."
Terms: Gallery provides insurance, promotion and contract.
Submissions: Send query letter, resume, brochure, slides and photographs. Write to schedule an appointment to show a portfolio. Slides and resumes are filed.

BURNETT MILLER GALLERY, 964 North La Brea Ave., Los Angeles CA 90038. (213)874-4757. Director: Burnett Miller.
Profile: Retail gallery. Estab. 1985. Clientele: 80% private collectors. Represents 8 artists. Sponsors 7 solo and 3 group shows/year. Average display time is 5 weeks. Interested in emerging and established artists. Overall price range: $1,000-70,000; most artwork sold at $3,000-10,000.
Media: Considers oils, acrylics, watercolors, pastels, pen & ink, drawings, sculpture, photography, mixed media, performance, collage and installations. Most frequently exhibited media: sculpture, paintings and drawings.
Style: Exhibits contemporary, abstract, non-representational and minimalist works. Features "sculpture, painting and photography with a contemporary theme."
Terms: Accepts work on consignment (50% commission). Retail price is set by gallery and artist. Exclusive area representation required. Gallery provides insurance, promotion and contract.
Submissions: Send query letter, resume, brochure, business card, slides and SASE. Biography, brochures, slides and photographs are returned.

MODERNISM, 685 Market St., San Francisco CA 94105. (415)541-0461. Director: Katya Slavenska.
Profile: Retail gallery. Estab. 1979. Located in downtown San Francisco. Clientele: 60% private collectors, 40% corporate clients. Represents 30 artists. Sponsors 4 solo and 1 group shows/year. Average display time is 6 weeks. Interested in emerging and established artists. Overall price range: $500-3,000,000; most artwork sold at $10,000.
Media: Considers oils, acrylics, watercolor, pastels, pen & ink, drawings, mixed media, collage, paper, sculpture and ceramics. Most frequently exhibited media: painting on canvas, watercolor on paper and 3-D mixed media.
Style: Exhibits hard-edge/geometric abstraction, painterly abstraction, minimalism, post-modern,

photo-realistic, realistic and 20th century historical works. "Modernism is a gallery with a program of 20th century exhibitions including contemporary and early-century works. The trends of the century are represented in turn, from Russian avant-garde to the neo-expressionist art of the 80's."
Terms: Accepts work on consignment. Retail price is set by gallery. Exclusive area representation required. Gallery provides insurance, shipping and promotion.
Submissions: Send query letter, slides and SASE. Slides are filed or returned.

MONTEREY PENINSULA MUSEUM OF ART, 559 Pacific St., Monterey CA 93940. (408)372-5477. Director: Jo Farb Hernandez.
Profile: Nonprofit museum. Estab. 1969. Features nine galleries. Sponsors approximately 32-35 exhibitions/year. Average display time is 4-12 weeks.
Media: Considers all media.
Style: Exhibits contemporary, abstract, impressionistic, figurative, landscape, primitive, non-representational, photo-realistic, western, realism, neo-expressionistic and post-pop works. "Our mission as an educational institution is to present a broad range of all types of works."
Terms: No sales. Museum provides insurance, promotion and contract; shipping costs are shared.
Submissions: Send query letter, resume, slides and SASE. Resume and cover letters are filed.

TOBEY C. MOSS, 7321 Beverly Blvd., Los Angeles CA 90036. (213)933-5523. Owner: Tobey C. Moss.
Profile: Retail gallery. Estab. 1979. Clientele: 50% private collectors. Represents 10 artists. Sponsors 2 solo and 6 group shows/year. Average display time is 4 weeks. Interested in emerging and established artists. Overall price range: $25-50,000; most artwork sold at $5,000-10,000.
Media: Considers oils, acrylics, watercolors, pastels, pen & ink, drawings, collage and original handpulled prints.
Style: Exhibits abstract and non-representational work. Specializes in "Modernism, 1910-1960."
Terms: Accepts work on consignment or buys outright. Retail price is set by gallery and artist. Exclusive area representation not required. Gallery provides insurance, promotion and contract; shipping costs are shared.
Submissions: Send query letter, resume, slides and SASE. Call or write to schedule an appointment to show a portfolio.

NEW LANGTON ARTS, 1246 Folsom St., San Francisco CA 94103. (415)626-5416. Program Coordinator: Wayland Blake.
Profile: Nonprofit gallery. Estab. 1975. Clientele: artists and art patrons. Sponsors 10 solo shows/year. Average display time is 4 weeks. Interested in emerging and established artists.
Media: Considers sculpture, installations, photography and performance. Most frequently exhibited media: installations, video and performance.
Style: Exhibits conceptual and post-modern works. "We present contemporary, experimental artwork in a variety of media. The emphasis is on work that is noncommercial."
Terms: Gallery provides promotion and contract; shipping costs are shared.
Submissions: Send query letter, resume, slides and SASE. "Specific proposal videotape for a performance and video." Call or write to schedule an appointment to show a portfolio, which should include: slides and transparencies.

ORANGE COUNTY CENTER FOR CONTEMPORARY ART, 3621 W. MacArthure Blvd., Space 111, Santa Ana CA 92706. (714)549-4989. Director: Darrell Montague.
Profile: Nonprofit gallery. Estab. 1979. Exhibits work of 27 individuals and 3 groups/year. 1 juried show with 70 artists and 2 curated shows with 30 artists. Average display time is 4 weeks. Interested in emerging artists.
Media: Considers original handpulled prints.
Style: Exhibits contemporary, abstract, primitive, non-representational and neo-expressionistic works. Prefers contemporary work. "Orange County Center for Contemporary Art is a nonprofit organization providing Orange County, California, with a forum for contemporary art. All positions are filled by volunteer artists who in turn have been juried into affiliate membership by their peers. Membership is limited to thirty-five. The Director is elected from among the affiliate artist membership. OCCCA provides community services in the form of lectures, performances, and an annual juried show open to the entire state of California. In addition, one outside guest artist each month is invited to exhibit with two affiliate artist members. At least twice yearly the gallery invites someone from the artists community in Los Angeles or Orange County to curate an exhibition dealing with specific concerns in the contemporary art world. There is no 'ideal' concept of artwork shown at OCCCA. Each artist is entirely free to show any work with the only criteria being that of professional excellence in execution and presentation."

Terms: Retail price is set by artist. Exclusive area representation not required. Gallery provides insurance, promotion and contract; artist pays for shipping.
Submissions: Send query letter, resume and slides.

ORLANDO GALLERY, 14553 Ventura Blvd., Sherman Oaks CA 91403. (818)789-6012. Co-Director: Robert Gina.
Profile: Retail gallery. Estab. 1958. Represents 30 artists. Sponsors 22 solo shows/year. Average display time is 4 weeks. Accepts only Los Angeles artists. Interested in emerging and established artists. Overall price range: up to $10,000; most artwork sold at $2,500.
Media: Considers oils, acrylics, watercolors, pastels, pen & ink, drawing, mixed media, collage, paper, sculpture, ceramics and photography. Most frequently exhibited media: oils, watercolors and acrylics.
Style: Exhibits painterly abstraction, conceptual, primitivism, impressionistic, photo-realistic, expressionistic, neo-expressionistic, realistic and surrealistic works. Genres include landscapes, florals, Americana, figurative work and fantasy illustration. Prefers impressionism, surrealism and realism.
Terms: Accepts work on consignment. Retail price is set by artist. Exclusive area representation required. Gallery provides insurance and promotion; artist pays for shipping.
Submissions: Send query letter, resume and slides. Portfolio should include slides and transparencies.

PALO ALTO CULTURAL CENTER, 1313 Newell Rd., Palo Alto CA 94303. (415)329-2366. Curator: Dyana Chadwick.
Profile: Nonprofit gallery. Estab. 1971. Clientele: adults and senior citizens; organized tour groups of school children. Exhibits the work of 100 individuals and 3 groups/year. Sponsors 3 solo and 12 group shows/year. Average display time is 6-8 weeks. Interested in established or emerging artists who have worked for at least 3 years in their medium. Overall price range: $150-10,000; most artwork sold at $200-800.
Media: Considers oils, acrylics, watercolors, pastels, pen & ink, drawings, sculpture, ceramics, fibers, photography, mixed media, collage, glass, installations, decorative art (i.e., furniture, handcrafted textiles etc.) and original handpulled prints. "All works on paper must be suitably framed and behind plexiglass." Most frequently exhibited media: ceramics, photography and mixed media.
Style: Exhibits contemporary, abstract, Americana, figurative, landscape, primitive, non-representational, photo-realistic, realism, neo-expressionistic, post-pop, and architectronic works. "Our shows are thematic and range from realism to conceptual art. Our gallery specializes in contemporary, historic and ethnic art which addresses pertinent issues in Californian and American art."
Terms: Accepts work on consignment (10-30% commission). Retail price is set by gallery and artist. Exclusive area representation not required. Gallery provides insurance, promotion and contract; artist pays for shipping.
Submissions: Send query letter, resume, slides, business card, and SASE. Resume and 1 slide are filed.

THE JOHN PENCE GALLERY, 750 Post St., San Francisco CA 94109. (415)441-1138. Proprietor/Director: John Pence.
Profile: Retail gallery or art consultancy. Estab. 1975. Clientele: collectors, designers, businesses and tourists, 85% private collectors, 15% corporate clients. Represents 16 artists. Sponsors 7 solo and 2 group shows/year. Average display time is 4 weeks. Interested in emerging and established artists. Overall price range: $450-65,000; most artwork sold at $4,500-8,500.
Media: Primarily considers oils and pastels. Will occasionally consider watercolor and bronze.
Style: Exhibits painterly abstraction, impressionism, realism and academic realism. Genres include landscapes, florals, Americana, portraits, figurative work and still life. "We deal eclecticly. Thus we may accept someone who is the best of a field or someone who could become that. We are *actively involved* with the artist, not merely reps."
Terms: Accepts work on consignment (50% commission) or buys outright (33% markup). Retail price is set by gallery and artist. Exclusive area representation required. Gallery provides insurance and promotion.
Submissions: Send Query letter, resume and slides. "No appointments. Send for application/instructions." Resumes are filed.

SAN FRANCISCO ART INSTITUTE, 800 Chestnut St., San Francisco CA 94133. (415)771-7020. Gallery Coordinator: Richard Pinegar.
Profile: Nonprofit gallery. Estab. 1968. Clientele: audience of general art community, artists, teachers and students. Exhibits the work of 3 individuals and 7 groups of between 2 and 8 artists/year. Average display time is 5 weeks. "We review and exhibit work by artists of any nationality, creed, gender, ⅔ Bay area, ⅓ elsewhere. We do not offer works for sale."

Media: Considers all media.
Style: Exhibits contemporary, abstract and figurative works. "We exhibit all media and styles, but the galleries are especially suitable for performance, installation, painting, sculpture and photography."
Terms: Retail price is set by artist. Exclusive area representation not required. Gallery provides insurance, shipping, promotion and contract.
Submissions: Send query letter, resume and slides. Call or write to schedule an appointment to show a portfolio. Resumes and slides of artists passing review are filed.

THE SAN FRANCISCO MUSEUM OF MODERN ART RENTAL GALLERY, Building A, Fort Mason, San Francisco CA 94123. (415)441-4777. Director: Marian Parmenter.
Profile: Nonprofit gallery and art consultancy. Estab. 1978. Amount of exhibition space (in square feet) 1,500. Clientele: Corporations and private collectors; 40% private collectors, 60% corporate clients. Represents 70% of our stable. Sponsors 3 person or 2 group shows/year. "All work is stored, not really 'displayed' in racks except sculpture and the exhibiting artists." Interested in emerging and established artists. Overall price range: $100-15,000; most artwork sold at $1,000-5,000.
Media: Considers oils, acrylics, watercolor, pastels, drawings, mixed media, collage, sculpture, installations, photography and original handpulled prints. Most frequently exhibited media: painting, sculpture and photography.
Style: Exhibits hard-edge/geometric abstraction, painterly abstraction, minimalism, post-modern, pattern painting, surrealism, primitivism, photorealism, expressionism, neo-expressionism and realism. Genres include landscapes and figurative work. "Work chosen to be exhibited is chosen for quality, not style or theme."
Terms: Accepts work on consignment (40% commission). Retail price is set by gallery. Exclusive area representation not required. Gallery provides insurance, promotion and contract; artist pays for shipping.
Submissions: Send query letter, resume, slides and SASE.

SAN JOSE ART LEAGUE/DOWNTOWN GALLERY, 66 N. Market St., San Jose CA 95113. (408)287-8435. Director: Helen Mackinlay.
Profile: Nonprofit gallery. Estab. 1960. Clientele: private collectors and corporate clients. Average display time is 6 weeks. Interested in emerging and established artists. "We also do at least 3 International Exchange shows a year, and we also have juried competitions." Overall price range: $120-3,000.
Media: Considers oils, acrylics, watercolors, pastels, sculpture, ceramics, fibers, photography, mixed media, collage, galls and original handpulled prints.
Style: Exhibits contemporary, abstract, impressionistic, figurative, landscape, floral, non-representational, photo-realistic, realistic and neo-expressionistic works. "Our gallery specializes in contemporary work by both emerging and established artists."
Terms: Retail price is set by artist. Exclusive area representation not required. Gallery provides contract; artist pays for shipping.
Submissions: Call or write to schedule an appointment to show a portfolio.

SAXON-LEE GALLERY, 7525 Beverly Blvd., Los Angeles CA 90036. (213)933-5282. Co-Principal: Daniel Saxon.
Profile: Retail gallery. Estab. 1986. Clientele: 85% private collectors, 15% corporate clients. Represents 15 artists. Sponsors 8 solo and 6 group shows/year. Average display time is 1 month. Interested in emerging and established artists. Overall price range: $2,000-70,000; most artwork sold at $10,000.
Media: Considers oils, acrylics, watercolor, pastels, drawings, mixed media, collage, sculpture and performance. Most frequently exhibited media: oils, acrylics and sculpture.
Style: Exhibits painterly abstraction, conceptual and neo-expressionism. Prefers abstract, representational and conceptual works.
Terms: Accepts work on consignment (50% commission) or buys outright (50% markup). Retail price is set by gallery and artist. Gallery provides insurance, shipping, promotion and contract.
Submissions: Send resume and slides. Slides are filed.

BARCLAY SIMPSON FINE ARTS, 3669 Mt. Diablo Blvd., Lafayette CA 94549. (415)284-7048. Assistant Director: Sharon Simpson.
Profile: Retail gallery. Estab. 1981. Clientele: 70% private collectors, 30% corporate clients. Sponsors 6 solo and 3 group shows/year. Average display time is 5 weeks. Interested in emerging and established artists. Overall price range: $150-10,000; most artwork sold at $1,500.
Media: Considers oils, acrylics, watercolors, mixed media, collage, paper, sculpture and original handpulled prints. Most frequently exhibited media: watercolors, acrylic on canvas and paper and monotypes or prints.
Style: Exhibits color field, painterly abstraction, impressionism and realism. Genres include land-

scapes and western works. Prefers painterly abstraction, impressionism and color field. "We specialize in 'emerging' artists and have no hard and fast rules as to style, although the tendency is toward abstraction. Right now we are looking for art to sell to corporate clients, i.e., soft abstract colors, modern landscapes—both acrylics and prints. We also have a continuing interest in any artist of exceptional talent, whatever the medium."
Terms: Accepts work on consignment (50% commission). Retail price is set by gallery and artist. Exclusive area representation required. Gallery provides insurance, promotion and contract; artist pays for shipping.
Submissions: Send query letter with resume, slides and photographs. Write to schedule an appointment to show a portfolio; send slides first. "We either send back the slides or keep them pending receipt of original work or a look at it by appointment."

SOUTHERN CALIFORNIA CONTEMPORARY GALLERY, 825 N. La Ceienga Blvd., Los Angeles CA 90069. (213)652-8272. Director: Helen Wordemann.
Profile: Nonprofit gallery. Estab. 1924. Clientele: 95% private collectors, 5% corporate clients. Represents 500 members. Sponsors 2 solo and 10 group shows/year. Average display time is 4 weeks. Accepts only Los Angeles area artists. Interested in emerging and established artists. Overall price range: $200-2,500; most artwork sold at $500-1,000.
Media: Considers oils, acrylics, watercolors, pastels, pen & ink, drawings, mixed media, collage, paper, sculpture, photography and original handpulled prints. Most frequently exhibited media: watercolor, prints and acrylics.
Style: Exhibits hard-edge/geometric abstraction, color field, painterly abstraction, minimalism, conceptual, post-modern, pattern painting, feminist/political, primitivism, impressionistic, photo-realistic, expressionistic, neo-expressionistic, realistic and surrealistic work. Genres include landscapes, florals, figurative work and fantasy illustration. Prefers "contemporary art in all styles."
Terms: Accepts work on consignment (33% commission). Retail price is set by artist. Exclusive area representation not required.
Submissions: Call to schedule an appointment to show a portfolio, which should include: originals. Biographical information and slides are filed.

JEREMY STONE GALLERY, 23 Grant Ave., San Francisco CA 94108. (415)298-6535. Gallery Director: Jeremy Stone.
Profile: Retail gallery. Estab. 1982. Clientele: young professionals; 75% private collectors, 25% corporate clients. Represents 25 artists. Sponsors 8-9 solo and 2-3 group shows/year. Average display time is 4 weeks. Overall price range: $500-15,000; most artwork sold at $1,000-8,000.
Media: Considers oils, acrylics, drawings, mixed media and collage.
Style: Exhibits painterly abstraction, expressionism and realism. Features "contemporary paintings and drawings by younger emerging artists. High quality is sought rather than any particular style."
Terms: Accepts work on consignment (50% commission). Retail price is set by gallery and artist. Exclusive area representation required. Gallery provides insurance and promotion; shipping costs are shared.
Submissions: Send query letter, resume, slides and SASE.

TARBOX GALLERY, 1202 Kettner Blvd., San Diego CA 92101. (619)234-5020. Owner-Director: Ruth R. Tarbox.
Profile: Retail gallery. Estab. 1969. Clientele: 60% collectors, 40% corporate clients. Represents 42 artists. Sponsors 5 or 6 solo and group shows alternately/year. Average display time is 3 weeks. Overall price range: posters to $6,000; average sale $800.
Media: Considers oils, acrylics, watercolors, pastels, mixed media, collage, sculpture and ceramics. Most frequently exhibited media: watercolors, oils, acrylics, pastels and airbrush.
Style: Exhibits painterly abstraction, primitivism, impressionism and realism. Genres include landscapes, florals, southwestern, and figurative work. Prefers landscapes. "Our gallery already has some excellent watercolorists, and we would like to augment these with artists in oil working in contemporary themes."
Terms: Accepts work on consignment (50% commission). Retail price is set by gallery and artist. Exclusive area representation required within 10-mile radius. Gallery provides insurance, promotion and contract; shipping costs are shared.
Submissions: Send query letter, resume, slides and SASE. Call or write to schedule an appointment to show a portfolio, which should include originals (at least 1) and slides. Resumes of promising artists are filed. Slides are returned.

TOPAZ UNIVERSAL, 4632 W. Magnolia Blvd., Burbank CA 91505. (818)766-8660. Director: Diane Binder.
Profile: Retail gallery. Estab. 1982. Located in the center of movie studio and metro media area. Clien-

tele: 60% private collectors. Represents 8 artists. Sponsors 2 solo and 4 group shows/year. Average display time is 3 months. Interested in established artists. Overall price range: $2,000-100,000; most artwork sold at $6,000-25,000.
Media: Considers oils, acrylics, watercolors, pastels, pen & ink, drawings, sculpture, mixed media, performance and original handpulled prints.
Style: Exhibits contemporary, impressionistic, figurative and neo-expressionistic works. Specializes in contemporary, figurative and expressionistic works.
Terms: Accepts work on consignment (50% commission). Buys outright. Retail price is set by gallery and artist. Exclusive area representation not required. Gallery provides insurance, promotion and contract; shipping costs are shared.
Submissions: Send query letter with resume and brochure.

UNIVERSITY ART GALLERY (CALIFORNIA STATE UNIVERSITY, HAYWARD), (415) 881-3111. Director: Jeanne Howard.
Profile: Nonprofit gallery. Estab. 1970. Exhibits the work of 2 individuals and 5-8 groups/year. Average display time is 4-6 weeks. Overall price range: $100-10,000; most artwork sold at under $500.
Media: Considers oils, acrylics, watercolors, pastels, pen & ink, drawings, sculpture, ceramics, fibers, photography, crafts, mixed media, collage, installations and original handpulled prints.
Style: Exhibits contemporary, abstract, impressionistic, figurative, realistic, works and landscapes. General exhibition program—all media shown. "We are primarily interested in contemporary art. Shipping costs limit our ability to show artists from other areas."
Terms: Accepts work on consignment (20% commission). Retail price is set by artist. Exclusive area representation not required. Gallery provides insurance, promotion and contract; artist pays for shipping.
Submissions: Send query letter, resume, slides and SASE. Resume and slides are filed "if possible."

VORPAL GALLERY, 393 Grove St., San Francisco CA 94102. (415)397-9200. Director: David Love.
Profile: Retail gallery. Estab. 1962. Gallery hosts films, lectures, performance art, concerts—extremely large space for varied exhibitions. Clientele: private and corporate. Sponsors 8-10 shows/year. Average display time varies. Interested in emerging and established artists.
Media: Considers works in all media.
Style: Exhibits contemporary.
Terms: Terms vary.
Submissions: Send query letter and slides with SASE.

Colorado

KYLE BELDING GALLERY, 1110 17th St., Denver CO 80202. (303)825-2555. Contact: Director.
Profile: Retail gallery. Estab. 1985. Clientele: tourists and Colorado collectors; 60% private collectors, 40% corporate clients. "We work with architects, interior decorators and independent art advisors." Represents 20 artists. Sponsors 3 solo and 9 group shows/year. Average display time is 3 weeks. Interested in emerging and established artists. Overall price range: $200-20,000; most artwork sold at $800-5,000.
Media: Considers oils, acrylics, watercolor, pastels, pen & ink, drawings, mixed media, collage, paper, sculpture, fibers, installations, performance and original handpulled prints. Most frequently exhibited media: oil, sculpture and acrylics.
Style: Exhibits painterly abstraction, photorealism, expressionism and realism. Genres include landscapes and figurative work. "Our gallery specializes in contemporary painting and sculpture with an expressionistic, abstract or realistic style."
Terms: Accepts work on consignment (50% commission). Retail price is set by gallery and artist. Exclusive area representation required. Gallery provides insurance, promotion and contract; shipping costs are shared.
Submissions: Send query letter, resume, slides, brochure, photographs and SASE. Slides, resume and reviews are filed.

BOULDER CENTER FOR THE VISUAL ARTS, 1750 13th St., Boulder CO 80302. (303)443-2122. BCVA Board of Directors: Exhibitions Committee.
Profile: Nonprofit gallery. Estab. 1976. Exhibits the work of 60 individuals and 10 groups/year. Sponsors 4 solo and 8 group shows/year. Average display time is 6 weeks. "Emphasis is on Colorado artists." Interested in emerging and established artists. Overall price range: $200-17,000; most artwork sold at $850-2,500.
Media: Considers all media.

Style: Exhibits contemporary, abstract, figurative, non-representational, photo-realistic, realistic and neo-expressionistic works.
Terms: Accepts work by invitation only. Retail price is set by artist. Exclusive area representation not required. Gallery provides insurance, promotion and contract; artist pays for shipping.
Submissions: Send query letter, resume, slides and SASE. Press and promotional material, slides and BCVA history are filed.

SANDY CARSON GALLERY, 2601 Blake St., Denver CO 80205. (303)297-8585. Director: Jodi Carson.
Profile: Retail gallery and art consultancy. Estab. 1974. Clientele: individuals and corporations; 10% private collectors, 90% corporate clients. Represents 300 artists. Sponsors 6-8 group and solo shows/year. Average display time is 6 weeks. Interested in emerging and established artists. Overall price range: $125-10,000; most artwork sold at $2,000.
Media: Considers oils, acrylics, watercolor, pastels, pen & ink, drawings, mixed media, paper, sculpture, creamics, fibers, glass, photography and original handpulled prints.
Style: Exhibits hard-edge geometric abstraction, color field, painterly abstraction, minimalism, conceptual, post-modern, pattern painting, surrealism, primitivism, impressionism, photorealism, expressionism, neo-expressionism and realism. "We carry all types of art to accommodate both individuals and corporations. We have the capability of carrying large scale pieces."
Terms: Accepts work on consignment (50% commission). Retail price is set by gallery and artist. Exclusive area representation required. Gallery provides insurance, promotion and contract; artist pays for shipping.
Submissions: Send query letter, resume and slides. Call or write to schedule an appointment to show a portfolio, which should include: originals, slides and transparencies. Resumes are filed.

DRISCOL GALLERY LTD., 555 17th St., Denver CO 80202. (303)292-5520. Gallery Director: Pam Driscol.
Profile: Retail gallery. "We also have galleries in Vail and Beaver Creek." Estab. 1979. Clientele: 70% private collectors, 30% corporate. Represents 30 artists. Sponsors 3 solo and 2 group shows/year. Average display time is 3 weeks. Interested in emerging and established artists. Overall price range: $300-65,000; most artwork sold at $1,500-10,000.
Media: Considers oils, acrylics, watercolors, pastels and sculpture.
Style: Exhibits impressionistic, figurative, landscapes and Southwestern styles. "We are looking for fresh approaches to life today in watercolor or oil or acrylic. We especially like artists that have graduated from the American Academy, Chicago. We are interested in life size or heroic sculpture (traditional)."
Terms: Accepts work on consignment (40% commission). Retail price is set by artist. Exclusive area representation required. Gallery provides insurance, promotion and contract; artist pays for shipping.
Submissions: Send query letter, resume, brochure, slides or photographs. Call or write to schedule an appointment to show a portfolio.

THE FOOTHILLS ART CENTER, INC., 809 15th St., Golden CO 80401. (303)279-3922. Director of Exhibitions: Regina Hogan.
Profile: Nonprofit gallery. Estab. 1968. Clientele: 75% of sales to private collectors. Exhibits the work of 600 individuals and 80 groups/year. Sponsors 40 solo and 16 group shows/year. Average display time is 1 month. Accepts only Colorado artists except in NASE & RMN Competitions. Overall price range: $25-10,000; most artwork sold at $100-600.
Media: Considers oils, acrylics, watercolors, pastels, pen & ink, drawings, sculpture, ceramics, fibers, photography, crafts, mixed media, performance, collage, glass, installations and original handpulled prints.
Style: Exhibits contemporary, abstract, Americana, impressionistic, figurative, landscape, floral, primitive, non-representational, photo-realistic, Western, realistic, neo-expressionistic and post-pop work.
Terms: Accepts work on consignment (30% commission). Retail price is set by artist. Exclusive area representation not required. Gallery provides insurance, promotion and contract; artist pays for shipping.
Submissions: Send query letter, resume, brochure, slides and SASE.

JOANNE LYON GALLERY, INC., 525 E. Cooper Ave., Aspen CO 81611. (303)925-9044. Director: Joanne Lyon.
Profile: Retail gallery and art consultancy. Estab. 1978. Clientele: 95% private collectors, 5% corporate clients. Represents 36 artists. Sponsors 6 solo and 2 group shows/year. Average display time is 3 weeks. Interested in emerging and established artists. Overall price range: $50-400,000; most artwork

sold at $5,000-25,000.
Media: Considers oils, acrylics, watercolor, pastels, pen & ink, drawings, mixed media, collage, paper, sculpture, ceramics, glass and original handpulled prints. Most frequently exhibited works: paintings, works on paper and sculpture.
Style: Genres exhibited: landscapes americana and western. "This gallery is quite eclectic."
Terms: Buys outright. Retail price is set by gallery and artist. Exclusive area representation required. Gallery provides insurance, promotion and contract; shipping costs are shared.
Submissions: Send query letter, resume, slides and SASE. Write to schedule an appointment to show a portfolio, which should include originals, slides and transparencies. Bios and slides are filed.

TAOS CONNECTIONS OF DENVER, 162 Adams St., Denver CO 80206. (303)393-8267. Owner: Robert J. Covlin.
Profile: Retail gallery. Estab. 1983. Clientele: 90% private collectors, 10% corporate clients. Represents 20 artists. Sponsors 6 solo shows/year. Average display time is 3 months. Accepts only regional artists (Southwest contemporary). Interested in emerging and established artists. Overall price range: $150-8,000; most artwork sold at $500-1,000.
Media: Considers oils, acrylics, watercolor, pastels, drawings, mixed media, sculpture and original handpulled prints. Most frequently exhibits oils, watercolors and mixed media.
Style: Exhibits impressionistic, expressionistic and realistic works. Genres exhibited include landscapes, florals and figurative work. "Taos Connections of Denver features Southwestern contemporary art for the art collector, home, office or gift-giving pleasures; including oils, watercolors and other media, metal and stone sculptures, hand-painted furniture, pottery and glassware. Art by respected regional and Southwestern artists."
Terms: Accepts work on consignment (40% commission). Retail price is set by gallery and artist. Exclusive area representation required. Gallery provides insurance and promotion; shipping costs are shared.
Submissions: Send query letter, resume and photographs. All received material is filed.

THE WESTERN COLORADO CENTER FOR THE ARTS, 1803 North 7th St., Grand Junction CO 81501. (303)243-7337. Director: David M. Davis.
Profile: Nonprofit community art center. Estab. 1954. Sponsors various numbers of shows/year. Average display time is 1 month.
Media: Considers oils, acrylics, watercolor, pastels, pen & ink, drawings, mixed media, collage, paper, sculpture, ceramics, crafts, fibers, glass, installations, photography, performance, original handpulled prints and posters.
Style: Exhibits hard-edge geometric abstraction, color field, painterly abstraction, minimalism, conceptual, post-modern, pattern painting, feminist/political, primitivism, impressionistic, photo-realistic, expressionistic, neo-expressionistic, realistic and surrealistic works. Genres exhibited include landscapes, florals, Americana, Western, portraits, figurative work and fantasy illustration. Specializes in realism and impressionism. "We are completely unlimited."
Terms: Accepts work on consignment (25% commission). Rental fee for space. Retail price is set by artist. Exclusive area representation not required. Gallery provides insurance, promotion and contract; artist pays for shipping.
Submissions: Send query letter, resume, brochure, business card, slides, photographs and SASE. Call or write to schedule an appointment to show a portfolio, which should include slides and transparencies. "Slides are returned, all other material is copied, and copies are filed."

Connecticut

MONA BERMAN FINE ARTS, 78 Lyon St., New Haven CT 06511. (203)562-4720. Director: Mona Berman.
Profile: Retail gallery and art consultancy. Estab. 1979. Clientele: 25% private collectors, 75% corporate clients. Represents 30 artists. Sponsors 4-6 shows/year. Average display time is 4-8 weeks. Interested in emerging and established artists. Overall price range: $200+; most artwork sold at $300-2,000.
Media: Considers oils, acrylics, watercolor, pastels, drawings, mixed media, collage, paper, sculpture, photography and limited edition original handpulled prints. Exhibited media: all except large sculpture.
Style: Exhibits variety of styles. Prefers "fine contemporary and ethnographic art."
Terms: Accepts work on consignment (50% commission). Retail price is set by gallery and artist. Exclusive area representation required. Gallery provides insurance, promotion and contract; artist pays for shipping.

Submissions: Send query letter, resume, brochure, slides and SASE. "Appointments only after preliminary slide review." Various material is filed.

BROOKFIELD/SONO CRAFT CENTER, Brookfield Alley at 127 Washington St., South Norwalk CT 06854. (203)853-6155. Gallery Manager: Debra Porter.
Profile: Nonprofit gallery. Estab. 1984. Clientele: 90% private collectors, 10% corporate clients. Represents 300+ artists. Sponsors 6 solo and 2 group shows/year. Interested in emerging and established artists. Overall price range: $25-1,500; most artwork sold at $25-100.
Media: Considers mixed media, paper, sculpture, ceramics, crafts, fibers, glass and original handpulled prints. Most frequently exhibited media: furniture, glass and ceramics.
Terms: Accepts work on consignment (40% commission). Retail price is set by artist. Gallery provides insurance and promotion; artist pays for shipping.
Submissions: Send query letter, resume, brochure, business card, slides, photographs and SASE. Write to schedule an appointment to show a portfolio.

IN SEARCH OF ART, INC., Box 216, Greenwich CT 06831. (203)622-6434. President: Phyllis Schreiber.
Profile: Retail gallery. Estab. 1981. Represents 40 artists. Sponsors ongoing solo and 3-5 group shows/year. Average display time is months. Overall price range: from $100 for original signal prints and up; Vanguard Russian is much higher."
Media: Considers oils, acrylics, watercolor, pen & ink, drawings, mixed media, collage, sculpture, fibers, glass and original handpulled prints. Most frequently exhibits: acrylic and sculpture.
Style: Exhibits color field, painterly abstraction, impressionism and realism. Genres exhibited: landscapes, florals and portraits.
Terms: Accepts work on consignment or buys outright (50% markup); net "payable at once." Retail price is set by gallery and artist. Exclusive area representation required. Gallery provides insurance and contract; artist pays for shipping.
Submissions: Send query letter, resume, brochure, slides and photographs. Write to schedule an appointment to show a portfolio, which should include originals, slides, artists price, and transparencies. "We keep a file on each artist we accept and keep it updated."

THE OLD STATE HOUSE, 800 Main St., Hartford CT 06103. (203)522-6766. Executive Director: Wilson H. Faude.
Profile: Nonprofit gallery. Estab. 1979. Sponsors 6-7 shows/year. Average display time is 4 weeks. "Shows generally limited to those not shown before in Connecticut." Interested in emerging and established artists.
Media: Considers all media and prints. Most frequently exhibited media: oils, acrylics and sculpture.
Style: Exhibits all styles and genres. "Our gallery space is devoted to bringing to the state of Connecticut collections of works that have not been organized and shown in the state before."
Terms: Accepts work on consignment (10% commission). Retail price is set by artist. Gallery provides insurance, promotion and contract; artist pays for shipping.
Submissions: Send query letter, resume, brochure, business card and photographs. Write to schedule an appointment to show a portfolio which should include originals, slides and photos. Resumes, brochures and photos "unless required returned" are filed.

REAL ART WAYS, 94 Allyn St., Hartford CT 06103. (203)525-5521. Curator: Leslie Tonkonow.
Profile: Nonprofit gallery. Estab. 1975. Sponsors solo and group shows. Average display time is 1 month. Interested in emerging artists.
Media: Considers all media.
Style: Exhibits contemporary works. Prefers new and experimental work.
Terms: Exclusive area representation not required. Gallery provides insurance, promotion and contract; shipping costs are shared.
Submissions: Send query letter with resume, slides and SASE. Slides and resume are filed.

Delaware

DELAWARE CENTER FOR THE CONTEMPORARY ARTS, 103 E. 16th St., Wilmington DE 19801. (301)656-6466. Director: Izzy Mead.
Profile: Nonprofit gallery. Estab. 1979. Clientele: Mostly middle to upper middle class locals; 100% private collectors. Represents 250 artists. Sponsors 1 solo and 11 group shows/year. Average display time is 3 weeks. Interested in emerging and established artists. "Lean towards emerging artists." Overall price range: $50-4,000; most artwork sold at $50-600.

Media: Considers all media and original handpulled prints.
Style: Exhibits contemporary, abstract, impressionistic, figurative, landscape, floral, non-representational, photo-realistic, Western, realism and neo-expressionistic works. Prefers regional contemporary works.
Terms: Accepts work on consignment (35% commission). Retail price is set by gallery and artist. Exclusive area representation not required. Gallery provides insurance, promotion and contract; shipping costs are shared.
Submissions: Send query letter, resume, slides and photographs. Write to schedule an appointment to show a portfolio. Slides are filed.

DOVER ART LEAGUE, 59 S. Governor Ave., Dover DE 19901. (302)674-9070. Director: Jean Francis.
Profile: Cooperative gallery. Estab. 1984. Clientele: 3% private collectors. Represents 45 artists but expanding. Sponsors 8 solo and 12-14 group shows/year. Average display time is 1-3 months. Overall price range: $45-1,500; most artwork sold at $100-300.
Media: Considers oils, acrylics, watercolors, pastels, pen & ink, drawings, sculpture, fibers, mixed media, collage, glass, installations and original handpulled prints.
Style: Exhibits contemporary, landscape, florals and realism. "Our gallery represents original art in a broad spectrum of both style and media, be it contemporary or not. Our second concept, or reason for existing, is that an organization such as ours in which many of the artists in the area meet and socialize at least once a month bridges the isolation gap many of us experience."
Terms: Accepts work on consignment (30% commission). Retail price is set by artist. Exclusive area representation not required. Gallery provides some promotion and a contract; shipping costs paid by artist.
Submissions: Send query letter, resume and slides. Call or write to schedule an appointment to show a portfolio. Resume, slides, brochure and card are filed.

UNIVERSITY GALLERY, UNIVERSITY OF DELAWARE, 301 Old College, Newark DE 19716. (302)451-1251. Director/Curator: Belena S. Chapp.
Profile: Nonprofit university museum. Estab. 1978. Clientele: students, faculty, regional and national. Sponsors 1-2 solo and 1-2 group shows/year. Average display time is 6 weeks. Interested in emerging and established artists.
Media: Considers all media. Most frequently exhibits printmaking, painting and sculpture.
Style: Considers all styles. Genres include landscapes, Americana, portraits, figurative work and fantasy illustration. "As an educational institution, we make an effort to exhibit a broad range of contemporary and historical exhibitions and do not make a practice of focusing on one special area."
Submissions: Send query letter, resume, brochure, business card, slides, photographs and SASE. Write to schedule an appointment to show a portfolio, which should include originals, slides and transparencies. Resume and materials are filed. "Slides are filed if the artist allows us to keep them."

District of Columbia

AARON GALLERY, 1717 Connecticut Ave. NW, Washington DC 20009. (202)234-3311. Assistant Director: Annette Aaron.
Profile: Retail gallery and art consultancy. Estab. 1970. Clientele: 60% private collectors, 40% corporate clients. Represents 18 artists. Sponsors 12 solo and 16 group shows/year. Average display time is 2-4 weeks. Interested in emerging and established artists. Overall price range: $500 and up; most artwork sold at $4,000-8,000.
Media: Considers oils, acrylics, watercolor, pastels, pen & ink, drawings, mixed media, collage, paper, sculpture, ceramics, glass installations and original handpulled prints. Most frequently exhibits sculpture, acrylic, acrylic on paper or canvas and original prints.
Style: Exhibits hard-edge/geometric abstraction, color field, post-modern, primitivism, expressionistic and neo-expressionistic works. Prefers post-expressionistic work. "Our gallery specializes in abstract expression in painting on canvas—fine colorist, luminescence and sculpture—intense in very contemporary themes."
Terms: Accepts work on consignment (40-50% commission). Retail price is set by gallery and artist. Exclusive area representation required. Gallery provides insurance, promotion and contract; shipping costs are shared.
Submissions: Send query letter, resume, brochure, business card, slides, and SASE. Write to schedule an appointment to show a portfolio, which should include originals and photographs. Slides, resume and brochure are filed.

AFR FINE ART, 2030 R St., Washington DC 20009. (202)265-6191. Director: Andrea F. Ruggieri.
Profile: Retail gallery. Estab. 1986. Clientele: 40% private collectors, 10% corporate clients. Represents 7 artists. Sponsors 6 solo and 4 group shows/year. Average display time is 1 month. Interested in emerging and established artists. Overall price range: $300-20,000; most artwork sold at $1,500-3,000.
Media: Considers oils, watercolor, pastels, pen & ink, drawings, mixed media, sculpture and original handpulled prints. Most frequently exhibits oil, charcoal and watercolor.
Style: Exhibits representational, abstraction and minimalism. "We specialize in contemporary painting, works on paper and sculpture. Works displays strong formalist interests."
Terms: Accepts work on consignment (50% commission). Retail price is set by gallery and artist. Exclusive area representation required. Gallery provides all promotion and contract; artist pays for 50% of shipping.
Submissions: Send letter, resume, brochure, slides and SASE. "Slides of artists we are interested in are given consideration over a period of one month."

ATLANTIC GALLERY, INC., 1055 Thomas Jefferson St. NW, Washington DC 20007. (202)337-2299. Director: Virginia Smith.
Profile: Retail gallery. Estab. 1976. Clientele: 70% private collectors, 30% corporate clients. Represents 10 artists. Sponsors 5 solo shows/year. Average display time is 3 months. Interested in emerging and established artists. Overall price range: $100-25,000; most artwork sold at $250-4,000.
Media: Considers oils, watercolor, pen & ink, drawings and limited edition prints. Most frequently exhibits oils, watercolor and limited edition prints.
Style: Exhibits realism. Prefers marine art and landscapes.
Terms: Accepts work on consignment (40% commission). Retail price is set by gallery and artist. Exclusive area representation required. Gallery provides insurance, promotion and contract; artist pays for shipping.
Submissions: Send query letter and slides. Portfolio should include originals and slides.

BIRD-IN-HAND BOOKSTORE & GALLERY, 323 Seventh St. SE, Washington DC 20003. (202)543-0744. Owner: Christopher Ackerman.
Profile: Retail gallery. Estab. 1983. Clientele: mostly private collectors. Represents 40 artists. Sponsors 4 solo and 8 group shows/year. Average display time is 3 weeks. Interested in emerging and established artists. Overall price range: $60-650; most artwork sold at $200-300.
Media: Considers oils, watercolor, pastels, pen & ink, drawings, photography and original handpulled prints. Most frequently exhibits prints, watercolor and photography.
Style: Exhibits landscapes and florals. Prefers landscapes, abstracts and photography.
Terms: Accepts work on consignment (40% commission). Retail price is set by gallery and artist. Exclusive area representation not required. Gallery provides insurance, promotion and contract; shipping costs are shared.
Submissions: Send query letter, resume, slides and SASE. Write to schedule an appointment to show a portfolio. Resumes are filed.

ROBERT BROWN CONTEMPORARY ART, 1005 New Hampshire Ave. NW, Washington DC 20037. (202)822-8737. Director: Robert Brown.
Profile: Retail gallery. Estab. 1981. Represents 12 artists. Sponsors 6 solo and/or group shows/year. Interested in emerging and established artists. Overall price range: $300-30,000.
Media: Considers oils, acrylics, watercolors, pastels, pen & ink, drawings, sculpture, mixed media and original handpulled prints.
Style: Exhibits contemporary works.
Terms: Accepts work on consignment. Retail price is set by gallery and artist. Exclusive area representation may be required. Gallery provides insurance and promotion.
Submissions: Send query letter, resume and brochure.

THE COLLECTOR, 1630 V St. NW, Washington DC 20009. (202)745-1825. President: Bill Wooby.
Profile: Retail gallery. Estab. 1987. Clientele: 90% private collectors, 10% corporate clients. Represents 9 artists. Sponsors 8 solo and 8 group shows/year. Average display time is 1 month. Interested in emerging and established artists. Overall price range: $500 and up; most artwork sold at up range.
Media: Considers pastels, pen & ink, drawings, collage, paper, sculpture, ceramics, crafts, fibers, glass, installations, photography, performance, original handpulled prints, offset reproductions and posters. Most frequently exhibits acrylics, oils, sculpture and collage. High quality crafts.
Style: Exhibits hard-edge/geometric abstraction, color field, painterly abstraction, minimalism, conceptual, post-modern, pattern painting, feminist/political, primitivism, impressionistic,

photo-realistic, expressionistic, neo-expressionistic, realistic and surrealistic works. Genres exhibited are landscapes, florals, Americana, portraits, figurative work and fantasy illustration. Prefers post-modern, abstract and neo-expressionist works. "The Collector has shown work ranging from photography to large figurative sculpture. The focus is on contemporary art and often emerging artists. We represent DC artists as well as artists from the rest of the country, though we are not necessarily limited to work from the United States."
Terms: Accepts work on consignment (50% commission). Retail price is set by gallery and artist. Exclusive area representation not required. Gallery provides insurance and promotion; shipping costs are shared.
Submissions: Send query letter and slides. Write to schedule an appointment to show a portfolio, which should include: originals and slides.

FOXHALL GALLERY, 3301 New Mexico Ave. NW, Washington DC 20016. (202)966-7144. Associate Director: Caryl D. Brody.
Profile: Retail gallery. Sponsors 6 solo and 6 group shows/year. Average display time is 3 months. Interested in emerging and established artists. Overall price range: $250-20,000; most artwork sold at $1,500-6,000.
Media: Considers oils, acrylics, watercolors, pastels, sculpture, mixed media, collage and color original handpulled prints (small editions).
Style: Exhibits contemporary, abstract, impressionistic, figurative, landscape, photo-realistic and realism.
Terms: Accepts work on consignment (50% commission). Retail price is set by gallery and artist. Exclusive area representation required. Gallery provides insurance.
Submissions: Send resume, brochure, slides, photographs and SASE. Call or write to schedule an appointment to show a portfolio.

GALLERY K, 2010 R St. NW, Washington DC 20009. (202)234-0339. Director: Mr. Komei Wachi.
Profile: Retail gallery. Estab. 1975. Clientele: 90% private collectors, 10% corporate clients. Represents 38 artists. Sponsors 25 solo and 3 group shows/year. Average display time is 3 weeks. Overall price range: $500-5,000; most artwork sold at $2,000.
Media: Considers oils, acrylics, watercolor, pastels, pen & ink, drawings, mixed media, collage, paper, sculpture, ceramics, installations and original handpulled prints. Most frequently exhibits oil, sculpture and drawing.
Style: Exhibits hard-edge/geometric abstraction, color field, painterly abstraction, minimalism, primitivism, photo-realistic, expressionistic, neo-expressionistic, realistic and surrealistic works. Genres exhibited are landscapes and figurative work. Prefers surrealism, realism and photo-realism.
Terms: Accepts work on consignment (50% commission). Retail price is set by gallery and artist. Exclusive area representation required. Gallery provides insurance, promotion and contract; artist pays for shipping.
Submissions: Send resume, brochure, slides, photographs and SASE. Resume and brochure are filed.

ZENITH GALLERY, 413 7th St. NW, Washington DC 20004. (202)783-2963. Gallery Director: Margery Goldberg.
Profile: Retail gallery. Estab. 1978. Clientele: corporate, interior designers; 25% private collectors, 50% corporate clients. Sponsors 8 solo and 4 group shows/year. Average display time is 1 month. Interested in emerging and established artists. Overall price range: $500-3,500; most artwork sold at $200-6,000.
Media: Considers oils, acrylics, watercolor, pastels, pen & ink, drawings, mixed media, collage, paper, sculpture, ceramics, tapestry, photography and color and b&w limited edition prints. Most

"I sent photographs of my graphite drawings to Visions. The art director chose a piece that had already been published. So she assigned me a cover. Literary magazines don't pay much, but they give you the opportunity to publish your work."

—Adam Niklewicz
Moberly, Missouri

frequently exhibited media: sculpture, mixed media and acrylics.
Style: Exhibits humor, sculptured furniture, neon, painterly abstraction, conceptual, post-modern, impressionistic, photo-realistic and realism. Genres include landscapes, Western, figurative work and fantasy illustration. Prefers realism, expressionism and abstraction.
Terms: Accepts work on consignment (50% commission). Retail price is set by gallery. Exclusive area representation required. Gallery provides insurance, promotion and contract; shipping costs are shared.
Submissions: Send query letter, resume, slides and SASE. Call to schedule an appointment to show a portfolio, which should include originals and slides. Slides and resumes are filed.

Florida

THE ART PLACE AT CAULEY SQUARE, 22400 Old Dixie Hwy., Miami FL 33170. (305)258-4222. Owner, Director: Sonde Garcia.
Profile: Retail gallery and art consultancy. Estab. 1980. Clientele: Mixed; 40% private collectors, 60% corporate clients. Represents 50-75 artists. Sponsors 4 solo and 4 group shows/year. Average display time is 2-3 months. Interested in emerging and established artists. Overall price range: up to $10,000; most artwork sold at under $2,000.
Media: Considers all media. Most frequently exhibits watercolor, mixed media and ceramics. Currently looking for ceramics, sculpture, (all media, especially wood), oil or acrylics and prints.
Style: Considers all styles. Genres include landscapes, florals, Americana, portraits and figurative work. Currently seeking primitivism, abstraction, realism and impressionism.
Terms: Accepts work on consignment (50% commission). Retail price is set by gallery or artist. Exclusive area representation not required, "but some boundaries." Gallery provides insurance, promotion and contract; shipping costs are shared.
Submissions: Send query letter, resume, brochure (if available), slides and photographs. Resume, slides, photos and brochures are filed.

BACARDI ART GALLERY, 2100 Biscayne Blvd., Miami FL 33137. (305)573-8511. Director, Coordinator of the Advisory Committee: Juan Espinosa.
Profile: Nonprofit gallery. Estab. 1963. Sponsors 4 solo and 6 group shows/year. Average display time is 5 weeks. Interested in emerging and established artists.
Media: Considers all media.
Style: Considers all styles. "As a community service in the visual arts, we seek to bring important artists or collections to our community, as well as present notable examples of either from our own resources in South Florida."
Terms: "We do not charge fee, commission, or buy works." Gallery provides insurance, promotion and contract.
Submissions: Send query letter with resume, slides and SASE. Resume and slides are filed "if given permission to retain them."

DUNEDIN ART CENTER, 1143 Michigan Blvd., Dunedin FL 33528. (813)733-4446. Executive Director: Nancy J. McIntyre.
Profile: Nonprofit gallery. Estab. 1975. Clientele: general public, art buyers, artists. Sponsors 5 solo and 7 group shows/year. Average display time is 1 month. Accepts only local or regional artists. "Must consider fact that we have large number of families and children." Interested in emerging and established artists. Overall price range: $85-500; most artwork sold at $85-200.
Media: Considers any media, except performance art.
Style: Exhibits 180 contemporary, abstract, Americana, impressionistic, landscape, floral, primitive, non-representational, photo-realistic and realistic works.
Terms: Accepts work on consignment (30% commission). Retail price is set by artist. Exclusive area representation not required. Gallery provides insurance, promotion and contract.
Submissions: Send query letter with resume and slides. Files 1-2 slides of artist's work and resume.

GALLERY L, 1750 University Dr., Coral Springs FL 33071. (305)753-1552. Director: Lorna Herńandez.
Profile: Retail gallery, studio and art consultancy. Estab. 1987. Clientele: young, upscale, new home buyers, designers; 50% private collectors, 50% corporate clients. Represents 10-20 artists. Sponsors 2 solo and 6 group shows/year. Average display time is 2-6 months. Interested in emerging and established artists. Overall price range: $150-2,000.
Media: Considers oils, acrylics, watercolor, pastels, mixed media, collage, paper, ceramics, crafts, fibers, limited edition handpulled prints, fabric arts and commissioned works. Most frequently exhibits clay, painting, and mixed media.

Style: Exhibits hard-edge/geometric abstraction, color field, painterly abstraction, expressionism, neo-expressionism and realism. Genres include figurative work. Most frequently exhibited styles; abstraction, figurative expression and realism. Currently seeking large abstract canvases; painterly abstraction.
Terms: Accepts work on consignment (commission varies). Retail price is set by gallery or artist. Exclusive area representation not required. Gallery provides insurance, promotion and contract.
Submissions: Send query letter with brochure, slides, photographs and SASE. Call to schedule an appointment to show a portfolio, which should include originals and slides. Slides, resumes, color and b&w brochures, other exhibition notices (postcards, invitations, brochures) are filed.

THE HANG-UP, INC., 3850 South Osprey Ave., Sarasota FL 34239. (813)953-5757. President: Frank T. Troncale.
Profile: Retail gallery. Estab. 1971. Clientele: affluent and business personnel; 75% private collectors, 25% corporate clients. Represents 15 artists. Sponsors 4 solo and 2 group shows/year. Average display time is 6-8 weeks. Interested in emerging and established artists. Overall price range: $400-3,000; most artwork sold at $300-500.
Media: Considers oils, acrylics, mixed media, collage, paper, sculpture, fibers, glass, limited edition offset reproductions, and graphics. Most frequently exhibits acrylics, graphics and sculpture.
Style: Exhibits painterly abstraction, conceptual, surrealism and impressionistic. Genres include landscapes and figurative work.
Terms: Accepts work on consignment (40% commission) or buys outright (net 30 days). Retail price is set by gallery or artist. Exclusive area representation required. Gallery provides insurance, promotion and contract; shipping costs are shared.
Submissions: Send query letter with resume, brochure, slides and photographs. Write to schedule an appointment to show a portfolio, which should include originals and slides. Brochures and/or slides and resumes are filed.

IMAGE GALLERY, 500 N. Tamiami Trail, Sarasota FL 34236. (813)366-5097. Director: Ruth Katzman.
Profile: Retail gallery. Estab. 1977. Clientele: specializes in fine crafts, jewelry and wearable art. Represents 50 artists. Sponsors 4 solo and 3 group shows/year. Average display time is 1 month. Interested in emerging and established artists. Overall price range: $50-5,000; most artwork sold at $500-2,500.
Media: Considers sculpture, ceramics, fibers, crafts, mixed media and glass.
Style: Exhibits contemporary works. Currently seeking "good work—exciting and new."
Terms: Accepts work on consignment (50% commission) or buys outright (net 30 days). Retail price is set by gallery or artist. Exclusive area representation required. Gallery provides insurance and promotion; shipping costs are shared.
Submissions: Send query letter with resume, brochure, business card, slides, photographs and SASE if return is requested. Call or write to schedule an appointment to show a portfolio.

NAPLES ART GALLERY, 275 Broad Ave. S., Naples FL 33940. (813)262-4551. Owners: Warren C. Nelson and William R. Spink.
Profile: Retail gallery. Estab. 1965. Clientele: 95% private collectors, 5% corporate clients. Represents 63 artists. Sponsors 13 solo and 20 group shows/year. Average display time is 3 weeks. Interested in emerging and established artists. Overall price range: $2,000-30,000; most artwork sold at $2,000-15,000.
Media: Considers oils, acrylics, watercolor, drawings, mixed media, collage, paper, sculpture and glass. Most frequently exhibits oils, acrylics and glass. Currently looking for glass and paintings.
Style: Exhibits primitivism, impressionistic, photo-realistic, expressionistic and realism. Genres include landscapes, florals, Americana, figurative work and fantasy. Most frequently exhibited styles: realism, impressionistic and abstract. Currently seeking abstract.
Terms: Accepts work on consignment. Retail price is set by artist. Exclusive area representation required. Gallery provides insurance, promotion and agreement; shipping costs are shared.
Submissions: Send query letter with resume and slides. Write to schedule an appointment to show a portfolio, which should include slides and transparencies.

O.K. SOUTH, WORKS OF ART, #312, 5701 Sunset S., Miami FL 33143. (305)665-4500. Art Director: Ethan Karp.
Profile: Retail gallery. Estab. 1986. Clientele: 60% private collectors, 40% corporate clients. Represents 50+ artists. Sponsors 11 solo shows/year. Average display time is 1 month. Interested in emerging and established artists. Overall price range: $575-125,000; most artwork sold at $6,000-10,000.
Media: Considers oils, acrylics, watercolor, pastels, pen & ink, drawings, mixed media, collage,

paper, sculpture and ceramics. Most frequently exhibits acrylics, watercolor and oils.
Style: Exhibits hard-edge/geometric abstraction, color field, painterly abstraction, minimalism, photo-realistic and realism. Most frequently exhibits: photo-realism, trompe l'oeil and material illusion.
Terms: Accepts work on consignment (50% commission). Retail price is set by gallery or artist. Exclusive area representation required. Gallery provides insurance, shipping costs, promotion and contract.
Submissions: Send resume, brochure, slides and photographs. Bios and slides are filed.

ORMOND MEMORIAL ART MUSEUM & GARDENS, 78 E. Granada Blvd., Ormond Beach FL 32074. (904)677-1857. Curator: C.W. Johnson.
Profile: Nonprofit gallery. Estab. 1946. Clientele: mostly tourist; 100% private collectors. Sponsors 2 solo and 9 group shows/year. Average display time is 3 weeks. Interested in emerging and established artists. Overall price range: $100-2,000; most artwork sold at $100-200.
Media: Considers all media, except performance art. Most frequently exhibits mixed media, ceramics and oils.
Style: Considers all styles.
Terms: Accepts work on consignment (30% commission). Retail price is set by artist. Exclusive area representation not required. Gallery provides insurance, promotion and contract.
Submissions: Send query letter with slides and brochure. All material filed, "but return slides after exhibit."

THE THOMAS CENTER GALLERY, 302 NE 6th Ave., Gainesville FL 32602. (904)374-2197. Visual Arts Coordinator: Mallory McCane O'Connor.
Profile: Nonprofit gallery. Estab. 1980. Clientele: "serves the community as a cultural center." Sponsors 3 solo and 8 group shows/year. Average display time is 1 month. "We concentrate on regional artists." Interested in emerging and established artists.
Media: Considers all media.
Style: Considers all styles.
Terms: Accepts work on consignment (20% commission). Retail price is set by artist. Exclusive area representation not required. Gallery provides insurance, promotion and contract; shipping costs may be shared.
Submissions: Send query letter with resume, brochure, slides and SASE. Write to schedule an appointment to show a portfolio. Resume and 2 slides are filed.

THE UPHAM GALLERY, 348 Corey Ave., St. Petersburg Beach FL 33706. (813)360-5432. Owner/Director: Carol Upham.
Profile: 3 connected retail galleries, a workshop/classroom area, darkroom and studio. Estab. 1985. Clientele: local residents and tourists; 80% private collectors, 20% corporate clients. Represents 50 artists. Sponsors 6 solo and 6 group shows/year. Average display time is 1 month. Specializes in Florida artists, but will consider artists from all regions. Overall price range: $10-4,000; most artwork sold at $100-400.
Media: Considers all media except crafts and performance art. Most frequently exhibits photography, mixed media and oils.
Style: Exhibits hard-edge/geometric abstraction, color field, painterly abstraction, conceptual, primitivism, impressionistic, photo-realistic, expressionistic, neo-expressionistic, realism and surrealism. Genres include landscapes, florals, Americana, portraits, figurative work, fantasy illustration. Most frequently exhibits: multi-image photo, mixed-media paintings and photo lithographs.
Terms: Accepts work on consignment (40% commission). Retail price is set by gallery or artist. Gallery provides insurance, promotion and contract; shipping costs are shared.
Submissions: Send query letter with resume, brochure, slides and SASE. Slides, resumes, brochures, articles are filed.

VALENCIA COMMUNITY COLLEGE ART GALLERIES, 701 N. Econlockhatchee Trail, Orlando FL 32807. (305)299-5000. Gallery Curator: Judith Page.
Profile: Nonprofit gallery. Estab. 1982. Clientele: 100% private collectors. Sponsors 1 solo and 5 group shows/year. Average display time is 6 weeks. Interested in emerging and established artists.
Media: Considers all media. Most frequently exhibits sculpture, painting and drawing.
Style: Considers all styles.
Terms: Accepts work on consignment (no commission). Retail price is set by artist. Exclusive area representation not required. Gallery provides insurance, shipping costs, promotion and contract.
Submissions: Send query letter with resume, slides, photographs and SASE. Write to schedule an appointment to show a portfolio, which should include slides and transparencies. Resumes and other biographical material are filed.

Georgia

ABSTEIN GALLERY OF ART AND FRAMING, 1139 Spring St. NW., Atlanta GA 30309. (404)872-9020. Gallery Director: Maralics Kiernan.
Profile: Retail gallery. Estab. 1973. Clientele: corporations, interior designers; 25% private collectors. Represents 40 artists. Average display time is 2 months. Interested in emerging and established artists. Overall price range: $100-2,300; most artwork sold at $350-750.
Media: Considers oils, acrylics, watercolors, pastels, fibers, photography, mixed media, collage, color original handpulled prints and posters.
Style: Exhibits contemporary, abstract, impressionistic, landscape, floral, non-representational and realism. Currently seeking impressionism. "We prefer original work that is basically contemporary, non-controversial and colorful."
Terms: Accepts work on consignment (40% commission). Retail price is set by gallery or artist. Exclusive area representation not required. Gallery provides insurance and promotion; shipping costs are shared.
Submissions: Send query letter with resume, slides and photographs. Write to schedule an appointment to show a portfolio. All correspondence is filed; slides are returned to artist after review.

ALIAS STUDIO/GALLERY, 1574-B Piedmont Ave. NE, Atlanta GA 30324. President: Sara A. Hatch. (404)874-4465.
Profile: Retail gallery. Estab. 1985. Clientele: all great art appreciators—artist to upper middle class; 90% private collectors, 10% corporate clients. Represents 10 artists. Sponsors 4 solo and 5 group shows/year. Average display time is 4-8 weeks. "My standards for quality work are very high." Interested in emerging and established artists. Overall price range: $75-3,500; most artwork sold at $250-500.
Media: Considers oils, acrylics, watercolor, pastels, mixed media, collage, sculpture, ceramics, installations, photography and limited edition handpulled prints. Most frequently exhibits paintings, pastels and photography. Currently looking for sculpture.
Style: Exhibits painterly abstraction, conceptual, primitivism, expressionistic work. Genres include landscapes, figurative work and fantasy illustration. "The ideal work is the true vital expression of the artist and his or her ability to create a work which stands on its own merits. It has a 'life' of its own. Am always looking for the new idea."
Terms: Central gallery space is rented, 4'x8' area for $25/month and 20% commission. Accepts some work on consignment (40% commission). Retail price is set by gallery or artist. Gallery provides insurance, promotion and contract.
Submissions: Send resume, slides brochure, photographs and SASE. Call or write to schedule an appointment to show a portfolio, which should include originals, slides and photographs. Resume and brochures are filed.

FRANCES ARONSON GALLERY, 56 E. Andrews Dr. NW, Atlanta GA 30305. (404)262-7331. President: Frances Aronson. Vice President: Laura Aronson.
Profile: Retail and rental gallery and art consultancy. Estab. 1968. Clientele: collectors, corporate appraisal clients. Represents 15 artists. Sponsors 7 solo and 1 group shows/year. Average display time is 2 to 3 weeks. Interested in established artists and "unusually fine new artists." Overall price range: $150-150,000; most artwork sold at $2,500.
Media: Considers oils, acrylics, watercolor, pastels, pen & ink, drawings, mixed media, collage, paper and sculpture. Most frequently exhibits oils, watercolors, pastels. Currently looking for oils.
Style: Exhibits painterly abstraction, impressionistic, expressionistic and realism. Genres include landscapes, florals and figurative work. Most frequently exhibited styles: impressionistic, expressionistic and realistic.
Terms: Accepts work on consignment (50% commission). Retail price is set by gallery and artist. Exclusive area representation required. Gallery provides promotion and a consignment form; shipping costs are shared.
Submissions: Send query letter with resume and slides. Slides and resumes are filed.

THE ATLANTA COLLEGE OF ART GALLERY, 1280 Peachtree Street NE, Atlanta GA 30309. (404)898-1157. Director: Lisa Tuttle.
Profile: Nonprofit gallery. Estab. 1984. Clientele: general public and art students. Sponsors 10 group shows/year. Average display time is 5 weeks. Interested in emerging and established artists.
Media: Considers all media. Most frequently exhibits painting and drawing, sculpture, prints, photo, and installations.
Style: Considers all styles. "We primarily sponsor group exhibitions which are organized in a variety of

ways: curated, juried, invitational, rentals, etc."
Terms: Accepts work on consignment (30% commission). Retail price is set by artist. Exclusive area representation not required. Gallery provides insurance, promotion and contract; shipping costs are shared.
Submissions: Send query letter with resume, slides and SASE. Write to schedule an appointment to show a portfolio, which should include slides.

CHASTAIN ARTS CENTER GALLERY, 135 W. Wieuca Rd. NW, Atlanta GA 30342. (404)252-2927. Gallery Director: James Berry.
Profile: Nonprofit gallery. Estab. 1976. Sponsors 6 group shows/year. Average display time is 4-6 weeks. Interested in emerging and established artists. Overall price range: $100-1,000; most artwork sold at $300-600.
Media: Considers all media.
Style: Considers all styles.
Terms: Accepts work on consignment (20% commission). Retail price is set by artist. Exclusive area representation not required. Gallery provides insurance, promotion and contract.
Submissions: Write for an appointment to show a portfolio. Resumes and slides are filed.

EXHIBIT A, 342 Bull St., Savannah GA 31401. (912)238-2480. Gallery Director: Ruth L. Cohen. Assistant Director: Layne Brightwell.
Profile: Nonprofit gallery and art consultancy. Estab. 1979. Clientele: varied, locals, tourists, work with designers and architects; 80% private collectors, 20% corporate clients. Represents 45 artists. Sponsors 12 solo and 4 group shows/year. Average display time is 3 months. Interested in emerging and established artists. Overall price range: $100-1,000; most artwork sold at $200-400.
Media: Considers oils, acrylics, watercolor, pastels, pen & ink, drawings, mixed media, collage, paper, sculpture, ceramics, fibers, glass, installations, photography and limited edition handpulled prints. Most frequently exhibits creamics, acrylics and pastels. Currently looking for mixed medias, fiber and constructions.
Style: Exhibits primitivism, conceptual, neo-expressionistic and realism. Genres include landscapes, figurative work and fantasy illustration. "We wish to show new and innovative works showing talent, creativity, and originality."
Terms: Accepts work on consignment (40% commission). Retail price is set by artist. Exclusive area representation required. Gallery provides insurance, promotion and contract.
Submissions: Send query letter with resume, slides and photographs. Call or write to schedule an appointment to show a portfolio, which should include originals, slides and resume. Letters, resumes and slides are filed. "We do return slides, though we request duplicates for our file of artists that we represent."

THE GERTRUDE HERBERT INSTITUTE OF ART, 506 Telfair St., Augusta GA 30901. (404)722-5495. Director: Linda Vlcek.
Profile: Nonprofit gallery. Estab. 1937. Clientele: art patrons; 100% private collectors. Sponsors 6-8 solo shows/year. Average display time is 1-2 months. Interested in emerging and established artists. Average range: $500; most artwork sold at $300-500.
Media: Considers oils, acrylics, watercolors, pastels, pen & ink, drawings, sculpture, ceramics, fibers, photography, crafts, mixed media, collage, glass and color original handpulled prints.
Style: Exhibits contemporary, impressionistic, figurative, landscape, realism, neo-expressionistic works. "Each exhibit either introduces one regional artist or a group show."
Terms: Accepts work on consignment (20% commission). Retail price is set by gallery or artist. Exclusive area representation not required. Gallery provides insurance, promotion and contract.
Submissions: Send query letter with resume, brochure, slides and photographs. Write to schedule an appointment to show a portfolio. Resumes are filed; slides are returned.

LAGERQUIST GALLERY, 3235 Paces Ferry Place NW, Atlanta GA 30305. (404)261-8273. President: Evelyn Lagerquist.
Profile: Retail gallery. Estab. 1971. Clientele: metro Atlantians and from southeastern U.S.; 60% private collectors. Represents 30 artists. Sponsors 5 solo and 1 group shows/year. Average display time is 2-4 months. Interested in emerging and established artists. Overall price range: $200-5,000; most artwork sold at $1,000-2,000.
Media: Considers oils, acrylics, watercolors, pastels, pen & ink, drawings, sculpture, mixed media, collage and color and b&w limited edition original handpulled prints.
Style: Exhibits contemporary, abstract, impressionistic, figurative, landscape, floral, primitive, realism and sculpture.
Terms: Accepts work on consignment (40-50% commission). Retail price is set by gallery or artist.

Exclusive area representation required. Gallery provides insurance, promotion and contract.
Submissions: Send query letter with resume, slides and photographs. "Complete artist and work information" is filed.

Hawaii

HALE O KULA GOLDSMITH GALLERY, Box 416, Holualoa HI 96725. (808)324-1688. Owner: Sam Rosen.
Profile: Retail gallery. Estab. 1981. Clientele: tourist and local trade; 100% private collectors. Represents 6 artists. Specializes in miniature art. Overall price range: $100-3,000; most artwork sold at $100-1,000.
Media: Considers oils, acrylics, watercolors, pastels, pen & ink, drawings, sculpture, ceramics, fibers, photography, crafts, mixed media, collage, glass, and color and b&w original handpulled prints.
Style: Exhibits contemporary, abstract, impressionistic, floral, realism, neo-expressionistic works.
Terms: Accepts work on consignment (40% commission). Retail price is set by artist. Exclusive area representation not required. Gallery provides promotion and contract; shipping costs are shared.
Submissions: Send query letter with resume and slides. Write to schedule an appointment to show a portfolio.

IMAGES INTERNATIONAL OF HAWAII, Hyatt Regency Waikiki, Hemmeter Center, Honolulu HI 96815. (808)531-7051. Gallery Director/Vice President: Andrew P. Fisher.
Profile: Retail gallery. Estab. 1977. Clientele: international; 80% private collectors; 20% corporate clients. Represents 10 artists. Sponsors 8 solo shows/year. Interested in emerging and established artists. Overall price range: $1,000-60,000; most artwork sold at $1,000-10,000.
Media: Considers oil, acrylic, watercolor, mixed media and egg tempera. Most frequently exhibits oil, acrylic and watercolor.
Style: Exhibits contemporary, abstract, impressionistic, figurative, floral, primitive, photo-realistic, realism and Oriental works. Most frequently exhibited styles: Japanese, realism and abstract. Specializes in Japanese and other Oriental. Currently seeking work of high quality, craftsmanship, in upper-level price range. Seeks "beautiful art that inspires people to want to own a piece of paper for its beauty alone."
Terms: Accepts work on consignment (commission negotiable), or works with artist on exclusive basis. Retail price is set by gallery. Exclusive area representation required. Gallery provides insurance, shipping costs, promotion and contract.
Submissions: Send query letter with resume, brochure, business card, slides, photographs and SASE.

QUEEN EMMA GALLERY, 1301 Punchbowl St., Honolulu HI 96813. (808)547-4397. Director: Masa Morioka Taira.
Profile: Nonprofit gallery located in the main lobby of The Queen's Medical Center. Estab. 1977. Clientele: M.D.s, staff personnel, hospital visitors, community-at-large; 90% private collectors. Sponsors 8 solo and 4 group shows/year. Average display time is 3-3½ weeks. Interested in emerging and established artists. Overall price range: $50-1,000; most artwork sold at $100-300.
Media: Considers all media.
Style: Exhibits contemporary, abstract, impressionistic, figurative, landscape, floral, primitive, non-representational, photo-realistic, realism, neo-expressionistic works. Specializes in humanities-oriented interpretive, literary, cross-cultural and cross-disciplinary works. Interested in folk art, miniature works and ethnic works. "Our goal is to offer a variety of visual expressions by regional artists, including emergent and thesis shows by honors students and MFA candidates."
Terms: Accepts work on consignment (30% commission). Retail price is set by artist. Exclusive area representation not required. Gallery provides promotion and contract.
Submissions: Send query letter with resume, brochure, business card, slides, photographs and SASE. Call or write to schedule an appointment to show a portfolio. "Prefer brief proposal or statement or proposed body of works."

VOLCANO ART CENTER, Box 189, Volcano HI 96785. (808)967-7511. Gallery Manager: Margo Griffith.
Profile: Nonprofit gallery. Estab. 1974. Clientele: visitors to Hawaii Volcanoes National Park, from all over the world. Represents 150 artists. Monthly shows, 2 special exhibits annually. Average display time is 3 weeks-3 months. "We look for works that spring from an artist's relationship with the landscapes and/or cultures of Hawaii (regional)." Interested in emerging and established artists. Overall price range: $9-4,000; most artwork sold at $10-500.
Media: Considers all media.

Style: Exhibits contemporary, abstract, landscape, floral, primitive, non-representational, photo-realistic works. "We are looking for work that at once celebrates Hawaii as a source of creative inspiration and which pushes the artist and viewer into new ways of seeing. At the same time, we exhibit fine craft which celebrates Hawaii's rich ethnic mix and heritage."
Terms: Accepts work on consignment (50% commission). Retail price is set by artist. Exclusive area representation not required. Gallery provides promotion and contract.
Submissions: Send query letter with resume, brochure, business card, slides, photographs and SASE. Files "supporting materials for artists that have been accepted for display, such as resumes, statements, slides.

Illinois

MARY BELL GALLERIES, 361 West Superior, Chicago IL 60610. (312)642-0202. Director/Owner: Mary Bell.
Profile: Retail gallery and arts consultancy. Estab. 1981. Clientele: 30% private collectors, 70% corporate clients. Represents approximately 65 artists. Sponsors 10 group shows/year. Average display time is 1½ months. Interested in emerging and established artists. Overall price range: $200-500 for monoprints/graphics; $500-4,000 for unique paper works/paintings; most artwork sold at $300-1,500.
Media: Considers oils, acrylics, watercolor, pastels, mixed media, collage, paper, sculpture, ceramics, fibers and original handpulled prints. Most frequently exhibited media: watercolors, paper, pastels and acrylics.
Style: Exhibits color field, painterly abstraction, photo-realism, expressionism, neo-expressionism and realism. Genres include landscapes and florals. "My gallery exhibits contemporary paintings and paper works with an emphasis on color and surface beauty; they can be abstract or realistic."
Terms: Accepts work on consignment or buys outright. Retail price is set by gallery. Exclusive area representation not required. Gallery provides promotion and contract.
Submissions: Send query letter, resume, slides and SASE. Write to schedule an appointment to show a portfolio, which should include slides. Slides, biographies and brochures are filed.

WALTER BISCHOFF GALLERY, 340 W. Huron, Chicago IL 60610. (312)266-0244. Director: Oskar Friedl.
Profile: Retail gallery. Estab. 1985. Clientele: mostly those with large collections and young collectors; 80% private collectors. Represents 12-14 artists. Sponsors 9 solo and 2 group shows/year. Average display time is 5 weeks. Interested in emerging and established artists. Overall price range: $850-25,000; most artwork sold at $5,000.
Media: Considers oils, acrylics, sculpture mixed media, installations and original handpulled prints.
Style: Exhibits contemporary, abstract, figurative, non-representational, realism, neo-expressionistic works. Specializes in "mostly neo-expressionistic and abstract—very painterly works." Specializes in presenting European art in America with 1-2 shows of American artists/year.
Terms: Accepts work on consignment (50% commission). Retail price is set by gallery or artist. Exclusive area representation required. Gallery provides shipping costs, promotion and contract.
Submissions: Send query letter with resume, brochure, business card, slides and SASE. Call or write to schedule an appointment to show a portfolio "after sending above information." Files resume with slides "if interested for future project."

CONTEMPORARY ART WORKSHOP, 542 W. Grant Place, Chicago IL 60614. (312)472-4004. Administration Director: Lynn Kearney.
Profile: Nonprofit gallery. Estab. 1949. Clientele: art conscious public, well informed on art; 75% private collectors, 25% corporate clients. Sponsors 8 solo and 2 group shows/year. Average display time is 3½ weeks "if it's a show, otherwise we can show the work for an indefinite period of time." Interested in emerging and established artists. Overall price range: $300-5,000; most artwork sold at $1,500.
Media: Considers oils, acrylics, watercolor, mixed media, paper, sculpture, and original handpulled prints. Most frequently exhibits paintings, sculpture and works on paper.
Style: "Any good work" is considered.
Terms: Accepts work on consignment (⅓ commission). Retail price is set by gallery or artist. Exclusive area representation not required. Gallery provides insurance and promotion.
Submissions: Send query letter with resume, slides and SASE. Slides and resume are filed.

DEBOUVER FINE ARTS, 15-109 Merchandise Mart, Chicago IL 60654. (312)527-0021. President: Ronald V. DeBouver.
Profile: Wholesale gallery and art consultancy. Estab. 1981. Clientele: interior designers and

wholesale trade. Represents over 200 artists. Overall price range: $50-8,000; most artwork sold at $500.
Media: Considers oils, acrylics, watercolor, drawings, mixed media, collage, paper and posters. Most frequently exhibits oils, watercolors, graphics.
Style: Exhibits hard-edge/geometric abstraction, color field, painterly abstraction, primitivism, impressionistic, photo-realistic and realism. Genres include landscapes, florals, Americana, Western and figurative work. Most frequently exhibits: impressionistic, landscapes and floral. Currently seeking impressionistic, realism and abstract work.
Terms: Accepts work on consignment (1/3 to 1/2 commission). Retail price is set by gallery or artist. Exclusive area representation not required.
Submissions: Send resume, slides and photographs. Call to schedule an appointment to show a portfolio, which should include originals, slides and transparencies. Resume and photos are filed.

GILMAN/GRUEN GALLERIES, 226 W. Superior St., Chicago IL 60610. (312)337-6262. Director: Mack Gilman.
Profile: Rental gallery. Estab. 1959. Represents over 20 artists. Sponsors 9 solo and 3 group shows/year. Average display time is 4 weeks. Interested in emerging and established artists. Overall price range: $500-25,000; most artwork sold at $2,500-5,000.
Media: Considers oils, acrylic, paper and sculpture. Most frequently exhibited media: acrylic, oils and handmade paper.
Style: Exhibits painterly abstraction. Genres include landscapes and figurative work.
Terms: Accepts work on consignment (50% commission). Retail price is set by gallery or artist. Exclusive area representation required. Gallery provides insurance and promotion; shipping costs are shared.
Submissions: Send query letter, resume, slides and SASE. Call or write to schedule an appointment to show a portfolio, which should include slides and photos.

HYDE PARK ART CENTER, 1701 E. 53rd St., Chicago IL. (312)324-5520. Program Director: Barbara K. Saniie.
Profile: Nonprofit gallery. Estab. 1939. Clientele: general public. Sponsors 1 solo and 9 group shows/year. Average display time is 4-6 weeks. "Restricted to Illinois artists not currently affiliated with a retail gallery." Overall price range: $100-10,000.
Media: Considers all media.
Style: Considers all contemporary media.
Terms: Accepts work on consignment
Terms: Accepts work "for exhibition only." Retail price is set by artist. Exclusive area representation not required. Gallery provides insurance and a contract.
Submissions: Send query letter with resume, slides and SASE.

ILLINOIS ARTISANS SHOP, State of Illinois Center, 100 W. Randolph St., Chicago IL 60601. (312)917-5321. Administrative Manager: Ellen Gantner.
Profile: Retail gallery operated by the nonprofit Illinois State Museum Society. Estab. 1985. Clientele: tourists, conventioneers, business people, Chicagoans. Represents 350 artists. Average display time is 6 months. "Accepts only juried artists living in Illinois." Overall price range: $2-4,000; most artwork sold at $250.
Media: Considers all media. "The finest examples in all mediums by Illinois artists."
Style: Considers all styles. "Seeks contemporary, traditional folk and ethnic arts from all regions of Illinois."
Terms: Accepts work on consignment (50% commission), Retail price is set by gallery or artist. Exclusive area representation not required. Gallery provides promotion and contract.
Submissions: Send resume and slides. Accepted works are selected by a jury. Resume and slides are filed.

LAKEVIEW MUSEUM SALES/RENTAL GALLERY, 1125 W. Lake Ave., Peoria IL 61614. (309)686-7000. Museum Shop & Gallery Manager: Sally Stone.
Profile: Retail and rental gallery and art consultancy. Estab. 1965. Clientele: the community of Peoria; 40% private collectors, 60% corporate clients. Represents 100 artists. Sponsors 3 group shows/year. Average display time is 12. Accepts only midwest artists. Overall price range: $50-3,000; most artwork sold at $300.
Media: Considers all media except performance art. Most frequently exhibits watercolor, oil and acrylic. Currently looking for glass and jewelry.
Style: Exhibits painterly abstraction, impressionistic, photo-realistic, expressionistic, neo-expressionistic and realism. Genres include landscapes, florals, Americana and figurative work. Most frequently exhibited styles: impressionistic, realistic and expressionistic.

Terms: Accepts work on consignment (35% commission). Retail price is set by artist. Exclusive area representation not required. Gallery provides promotion and contract.
Submissions: Send query letter with resume and slides. Call or write to schedule an appointment to show a portfolio, which should include slides. Contract, resume, slides are filed.

PETER MILLER GALLERY, 356 W. Huron, Chicago IL 60610. (312)951-2628. Assistant Director: Natalie R. Domohenko.
Profile: Retail gallery. Estab. 1979. Clientele: 80% private collectors, 20% corporate clients. Represents 15 artists. Sponsors 9 solo and 3 group shows/year. Average display time is 1 month. Interested in emerging and established artists. Overall price range: $500-15,000; most artwork sold at $5,000.
Media: Considers oils, acrylics, pen & ink, drawings, mixed media, collage, sculpture, installations and photography. Most frequently exhibits oil on canvas, acrylic on canvas and mixed media.
Style: Exhibits painterly abstraction, conceptual, post-modern, expressionistic, neo-expressionistic, realism and surrealism.
Terms: Accepts work on consignment (50% commission). Retail price is set by gallery or artist. Exclusive area representation not required. Gallery provides insurance, promotion and contract; "if requested."
Submissions: Send slides and SASE. Slides, show card are filed.

PHYLLIS NEEDLMAN GALLERY, 1515 N. Astor, Chicago IL 60810. (312)612-7929. Proprietor: Phyllis Needlman.
Profile: Retail gallery. Estab. 1976. Clientele: 70% private collectors; 30% corporate clients. Represents 6 artists. Sponsors 4 solo and 2 group shows/year. Average display time is 1 month. Interested in emerging and established artists. Overall price range: $500-20,000; most artwork sold at $2,000-3,000.
Media: Considers oils, acrylics, drawings, mixed media, paper, sculpture and glass.
Terms: Retail price is set by gallery or artist. Exclusive area representation required. Gallery provides insurance and promotion.
Submissions: Send query letter with resume and slides. Call or write to schedule an appointment to show a portfolio, which should include originals and slides.

NORTHERN ILLINOIS UNIVERSITY ART GALLERIES, School of Art, Northern Illinois University, DeKalb IL 60115. (815)753-1936. Gallery Director: E. Michael Flanagan.
Profile: Nonprofit gallery. Estab. 1968. Clientele: campus and local community. Sponsors 7 solo and 13 group shows/year. Average display time is 3½ weeks. Interested in emerging and established artists.
Media: Considers all media. Most frequently exhibits paintings, photographs and prints.
Style: Considers all styles. Prefers "contemporary painting with good, intellectual content and sophisticated technique."
Terms: Gallery provides insurance, promotion and contract; shipping costs are shared.
Submissions: Send query letter with resume, brochure, slides, photographs and SASE. Call to schedule an appointment to show a portfolio, which should include originals. Resumes and correspondence are filed.

NINA OWEN, LTD., 620 N. Michigan Ave., Chicago IL 60611. (312)664-0474. Director: Audrey Owen.
Profile: Retail gallery and art consultancy. Estab. 1985. Clientele: professionals—designers, architects, developers; 33% private collectors, 67% corporate clients. Represents 100 artists. Sponsors 3 solo and 3 group shows/year. Average display time is 2 months. Accepts sculptors only. Overall price range: $150-25,000; most artwork sold at $4,500-5,000.
Media: Considers sculpture—metal, wood, mixed media, ceramics, fiber and glass. Most frequently exhibits steel, glass and wood sculptures. Currently looking for glass sculpture.
Style: Prefers "finely-executed abstract sculpture."
Terms: Accepts work on consignment (50% commission). Retail price is set by gallery or artist. Exclusive area representation not required. Gallery provides insurance, promotion and contract; shipping costs are shared.
Submissions: Send query letter with resume, slides and SASE. Call or write to schedule an appointment to show a portfolio, which should include originals, slides or maquette (optional). Files slides and printed material of sculptors in our slide registry (approximately 50 artists not exhibited in gallery, but submitted for commissions).

RANDOLPH ST. GALLERY, 756 N. Milwaukee, Chicago IL 60622. (312)666-7737. Contact: Exhibition Committee or Time Arts Committee.

Profile: Nonprofit gallery. Estab. 1979. Sponsors 10 group shows/year. Average display time is 1 month. Interested in emerging and established artists.
Media: Considers all media. Most frequently exhibits mixed media and performance.
Style: Exhibits hard-edge geometric abstraction, painterly abstraction, minimalism, conceptual, post-modern, feminist/political, primitivism, photo-realistic, expressionistic, neo-expressionistic works. "We curate exhibitions which include work of diverse styles, concepts and issues, with an emphasis on works relating to social and critical concerns."
Terms: Accepts work on consignment (20% commission). Retail price is set by artist. Exclusive area representation not required. Gallery provides shipping costs, promotion and contract.
Submissions: Send resume, brochure, slides, photographs and SASE. "Live events and exhibitions are curated by a committee which meets monthly." Resumes, slides and other supplementary material are filed.

LAURA A. SPRAGUE ART GALLERY, Joliet Junior College, 1216 Houbolt Ave., Joliet IL 60436. (815)729-9020. Gallery Director: Joe B. Milosevich.
Profile: Nonprofit gallery. Estab. 1978. Sponsors 4 solo and 5 group shows/year. Average display time is 3-4 weeks. Interested in emerging and established artists.
Media: Considers all media except performance. Most frequently exhibits painting, drawing and sculpture (all mediums).
Style: Considers all styles.
Terms: Gallery provides insurance and promotion; shipping costs are shared.
Submissions: Send query letter with resume, brochure, slides, photographs and SASE. Call or write to schedule an appointment to show a portfolio, which should include originals and slides. Query letters and resumes are filed.

A. MONTGOMERY WARD GALLERY AND CHICAGO GALLERY, Chicago Circle Center, 750 S. Halsted, Chicago IL 60607. (312)413-5070. Gallery Director: Pat Cagney/Campus Programs.
Profile: Nonprofit gallery. Estab. 1965. Clientele: diverse student population, faculty, staff and Chicago cultural community. Sponsors 9 solo and 3 group shows/year. Average display time is 1 month. Interested in emerging and established artists.
Media: Considers all media. Most frequently exhibits painting, photography, sculpture.
Style: Exhibits painterly abstraction, minimalism, conceptual, post-modern, pattern painting, feminist/political, primitivism, impressionistic, photo-realistic, expressionistic, neo-expressionistic, realism and surrealism. "We are expecially interested in new developments in art, we will consider anyone who is doing something new and is willing to take chances. We are not necessarily looking for the professional or 'established artist.' "
Terms: Accepts work on consignment (20% commission). Retail price is set by artist. Exclusive area representation not required. Gallery provides insurance, promotion and contract.
Submissions: Send query letter with resume, slides and SASE.

ZAKS GALLERY, 620 N. Michigan Ave., Chicago IL 60611. (312)943-8440. Director: Sonia Zaks.
Profile: Retail gallery. Represents 25 artists. Sponsors 10 solo and 2 group shows/year. Average display time is 1 month. Interested in emerging and established artists. Overall price range: $350-10,000, sculpture commisions higher prices."
Media: Considers oils, acrylics, watercolors, pastels, pen & ink, drawings, sculpture and mixed media. Specializes in paintings, works on paper and sculpture.
Style: Exhibits contemporary.
Terms: Accepts work on consignment. Retail price is set by gallery and artist. Exclusive area representation required. Gallery provides insurance and contract.
Submissions: Send query letter with resume and slides. Write to schedule an appointment to show a portfolio.

Indiana

ARTLINK CONTEMPORARY ARTSPACE, 1126 Broadway, Ft. Wayne IN 46802. (219)424-7195. Artist Panel Chairperson: Rick Cartwright.
Profile: Nonprofit gallery. Estab. 1976. Clientele: the general public; 25% private collectors; 75% corporate clients. Represents 150 artists. Sponsors 1 solo and 9 group shows/year. Average display time is 6 weeks. Interested in emerging and established artists. Overall price range: $300-45,000; most artwork sold at $100-500.
Media: Considers all media. Most frequently exhibits photography, oils and acrylics and work on paper.

Style: Exhibits hard-edge/geometric abstraction, painterly abstraction, post-modern, sculpture, feminist/political, neo-expressionistic and surrealism.
Terms: Accepts work on consignment (30% commission). Retail price is set by artist. Exclusive area representation not required. Gallery provides insurance, promotion and contract.
Submissions: Send query letter with resume, slides, photographs and SASE. Files resume, 6 slides, photographs, which are updated every 6 months.

EDITIONS LIMITED GALLERY, INC., Suite 132, 272 E. 86th St., Indianapolis IN 46240. (317)848-7878. Director: Bridget Webster.
Profile: Retail gallery. Estab. 1970. Clientele: 50% private collectors, 50% corporate clients. Represents 40 artists. Sponsors 5 solo and 2 group shows/year. Average display time is 6 weeks. Interested in emerging and established artists. Overall price range: $350-2,000; most artwork sold at $550.
Media: Considers oils, acrylics, watercolors, pastels, sculpture, ceramics, fibers, photography, mixed media and original handpulled prints.
Style: Exhibits contemporary works. Specializes in unique works by regional artists and craftspeople.
Terms: Accepts work on consignment (50% commission). Retail price is set by gallery or artist. Exclusive area representation required. Gallery provides insurance, promotion and contract.
Submissions: Send resume. Write to schedule an appointment to show a portfolio.

THE FORT WAYNE MUSEUM OF ART SALES AND RENTAL GALLERY, 311 E. Main St., Ft. Wayne IN 46802. (219)424-1461, ext. 26. Gallery Business Manager: Jean Fabish.
Profile: Retail and rental gallery. Estab. 1983. Clientele: 50% private collectors, 50% corporate clients. Represents 175 artists. "We stress Indiana, Ohio, Illinois and Kentucky artists. Interested in emerging and established artists. Overall price range: $150-2,000; most artwork sold at $300-400.
Media: Considers oils, acrylics, watercolors, pastels, pen & ink, drawings, sculpture, ceramics, fibers (non-functional), photography, mixed media, collage, glass and original handpulled prints.
Style: "We try to show the best regional artists available. We jury by quality, not saleability."
Terms: Accepts work on consignment (30% commission). Retail price is set by artist. Exclusive area representation not required. Gallery provides insurance, promotion and contract.
Submissions: Send query letter with resume, brochure, slides and photographs. Write to schedule an appointment to show a portfolio. Slides and resumes are filed.

PATRICK KING CONTEMPORARY ART, 427 Massachusetts Ave., Indianapolis IN 46204. (317)634-4101. Director: Patrick King.
Profile: Retail gallery. Estab. 1981. Clientele: private, corporate, museum. Represents 30 artists. Sponsors 4 solo and 5 group shows/year. Average display time is 5 weeks. "Gallery consigns works from exhibition to inventory for sales and presentations." Accepts only artists with 5-8 years of professional experience. Overall price range: $300 and up; most artwork sold at $600-3,500.
Media: Considers oils, acrylics, pastels, sculpture, ceramics, fibers, crafts, mixed media and installations. Specializes in painting, sculpture and textile.
Style: Exhibits contemporary, abstract, figurative, landscape, non-representational and realism.
Terms: Accepts work on consignment (50% commission). Retail price is set by gallery. Exclusive area representation required. Gallery provides promotion; shipping costs are shared.
Submissions: Send query letter with resume, slides, photographs and SASE. Files "correspondence, resumes, slides, photographs of all artists accepted for representation. All other portfolios returned provided artist sends SASE with intial query."

NEW HARMONY GALLERY OF CONTEMPORARY ART, 506 Main St., New Harmony IN 47631. (812)682-3156. Director: Connie Weinzapfel.
Profile: Nonprofit gallery. Estab. 1975. Clientele: 80% private collectors, 20% corporate clients. Represents approximately 130 artists. Sponsors 3 solo and 7 group shows/year. Average display time is 6 weeks. Accepts only Midwest artists. Interested in emerging and established artists. Overall price range: $50-5,000; most artwork sold at $100-500.
Media: Considers all media and original handpulled prints. Most frequently exhibited media: painting (oil and acrylic), mixed media and sculpture.
Style: Considers all contemporary styles.
Terms: Accepts work on consignment (35% commission). Retail price is set by artist. Exclusive area representation not required. Gallery provides insurance, promotion and contract.
Submissions: Send query letter, resume, brochure, slides and SASE. Call to schedule an appointment and to show a portfolio, which should includ originals. Slides and resumes are filed or returned, and reviewed quarterly.

Iowa

BLANDEN MEMORIAL ART MUSEUM, 920 Third Ave. S., Fort Dodge IA 50501. (515)573-2316. Director: Margaret Carney Xie.
Profile: Nonprofit municipal museum. Estab. 1931. Clientele: school children, senior citizens, tourists; 75% private collectors, 25% corporate clients. Sponsors 8 solo and 3 group shows/year. Average display time is 1 month. Interested in emerging and established artists.
Media: Most frequently exhibits painting, printmaking, and sculptureal works.
Style: Exhibits painterly abstraction. Genres include landscapes and florals.
Submissions: Send query letter with resume, brochure, slides and SASE. Write to schedule an appointment to show a portfolio, which should include originals and slides. Slides, resumes, brochures are filed.

PERCIVAL GALLERIES, INC., 520 Walnut, Valley National Bank Bldg., Des Moines IA 50309-4104. (515)243-4893. Director: Bonnie Percival.
Profile: Retail gallery. Estab. 1969. Clientele: corporate, private collectors, beginning collectors; 50% private collectors. Represents 20 artists. Sponsors 7 solo and 1 group shows/year. Average display time is 3 weeks. Interested in emerging and established artists. Most artwork sold at $500-1,000.
Media: Considers oils, acrylics, watercolors, pastels, pen & ink, sculpture, mixed media, collage, glass, installations, original handpulled prints and posters.
Style: Exhibits contemporary, abstract and realism. "Must meet our standards of high quaility."
Terms: Accepts work on consignment (40% commission). Retail price is set by gallery or artist. Exclusive area representation required. Gallery provides insurance and promotion.
Submissions: Send query letter with resume, brochure, slides, photographs, business card and SASE. Call or write to schedule an appointment to show a portfolio. Biographies and slides are filed.

Kansas

THE WICHITA GALLERY OF FINE ART, Fourth Financial Center, 100 N. Broadway KS 67202. (316)267-0243. Co-owner: Robert M. Riegle.
Profile: Retail gallery. Estab. 1977. Clientele: affluent business prfessionals; 80% private collectors, 20% corporate clients. Represents 25 artists. Sponsors 3 group shows/year. Average display time is 6 months. Interested in emerging and established artists. Overall price range: $100-10,000; most artwork sold at $500-1,500.
Media: Considers oils, acrylics, watercolor, pastels, sculpture and original handpulled prints. Most frequently exhibits oil, watercolor and sculpture. Currently looking for watercolor.
Style: Exhibits impressionistic, expressionistic and realism. Genres include landscapes, florals and figurative work. Most frequently exhibited styles: impressionism, realism and expressionism. "Style is secondary to quality."
Terms: Accepts work on consignment (40% commission). Retail price is set by gallery or artist. Exclusive area representation required. Gallery provides insurance, promotion and contract; shipping costs are shared.
Submissions: Send query letter with resume, brochure, slides, photographs and SASE. Call or write to schedule an appointment to show a portfolio, which should include originals. Letters are filed.

Kentucky

GEORGETOWN COLLEGE GALLERY, Mulberry St., Georgetown College, Georgetown KY 40324. (502)863-8106. Chairman, Art Department: James McCormick.
Profile: Nonprofit gallery. Estab. 1940. Clientele: area, faculty, student. Sponsors 4 or 5 solo and 1 or 2 group shows/year. Average display time is 3 weeks. Interested in emerging and established artists. Overall price range: $100-800.
Media: Considers all media.
Style: Considers all styles.
Terms: Accepts work on consignment. Retail price is set by artist. Exclusive area representation not required. Gallery provides insurance and promotion; shipping costs are shared.
Submissions: Send query letter with resume and slides.

LOUISVILLE ART GALLERY, 301 York St., Louisville KY 40203. (502)561-8635. Executive Director: Roberta L. Williams.

Profile: Nonprofit gallery. Estab. 1950. Clientele: general public. Sponsors 5 group theme exhibits/year. Past themes include: "The Artist and the Computer," "One-of-a-Kind Prints" and "Contemporary Quilts." Average display time is 6 weeks. Interested in emerging and established artists.

Media: Considers all media.

Style: Considers all styles. "Looking for contemporary artwork—all media. Must have high aesthetic and technical qualities. Professional artists only."

Terms: Accepts work on consignment (40% commission). "Prices are printed on a price sheet, but not posted on labels." Retail price is set by artist. Exclusive area representation not required. Gallery provides insurance, shipping costs, promotion and contract.

Submissions: Send query letter with resume and slides. Resumes, slides if available, and other materials showing artists' work are filed.

PADUCAH ART GUILD, INC., 200 Broadway, Paducah KY 42001. (502)442-2453. Executive Director: Dan Carver.

Profile: Nonprofit gallery. Estab. 1957. Clientele: tourists, artists, educators; 50% private collectors, 50% corporate clients. Sponsors 5 solo and 3 group shows/year. Average display time is 6 weeks. Interested in emerging and established artists. Overall price range: $50-5,000; most artwork sold at $50-500.

Media: Considers all media except performance art.

Style: Considers all styles.

Terms: Accepts work on consignment (25% commission). Retail price is set by artist. Exclusive area representation not required. Gallery provides insurance, promotion and contract; shipping costs are shared.

Submissions: Send query letter with resume, brochure, business card, slides, photographs and SASE. Call or write to schedule an appointment to show a portfolio, which should include originals and slides. Resumes and sample slides are filed.

PARK GALLERY, 3936 Chenoweth Square, Louisville KY 40207. (502)896-4029. Owners: Ellen Guthrie and Lucy Marret.

Profile: Retail gallery. Estab. 1973. Clientele: 80% private collectors. Represents 20 artists. Sponsors 6 solo and 1 group shows/year. Average display time is 1 month. Interested in emerging and established artists. Overall price range: $100-3,000; most artwork sold at $300-1,000.

Media: Considers oils, acrylics, watercolors, pastels, sculpture, ceramics, fibers, crafts, mixed media, glass and numbered limited-edition original handpulled prints.

Style: Exhibits contemporary, landscape, floral, primitive works.

Terms: Accepts work on consignment (40% commission) or buys outright (net 30 days). Retail price is set by gallery or artist. Gallery provides insurance, promotion and contract; shipping costs are shared.

Submissions: Send query letter with resume, brochure, slides and photographs. Call or write to schedule an appointment to show a portfolio. All materials are filed.

JB SPEED ART MUSEUM RENTAL AND PURCHASE GALLERY, 2035 South 3rd St., Louisville KY 40208. (502)636-2893. Administrator: Gerri Samples.

Profile: Retail and rental gallery. Estab. 1957. Clientele: collectors, major corporations. Represents 100 artists. Sponsors 4-6 group shows/year. Average display time is 2-3 months. "We do not accept students." Interested in emerging and established artists. Overall price range: $200-3,000; most artwork sold at $200-800.

Media: Considers oils, acrylics, watercolor, pastels, pen & ink, drawings, mixed media, collage, paper, sculpture, ceramics, fibers, glass, photography and original handpulled prints.

Style: Exhibits hard-edge/geometric abstraction, painterly abstraction, conceptual, surrealism, photorealism, expressionism, neo-expressionism and realism. Genres include landscapes, figurative work and Americana. Most frequently exhibited styles: geometric abstraction, conceptual and neo-expressionism.

Terms: Accepts work on consignment (40% commission). Retail price is set by artist. Exclusive area representation not required. Gallery provides insurance and contract.

Submissions: Send query letter with resume, slides and SASE. Write to schedule an appointment to show a portfolio, which should include originals. All materials are filed for archival use.

SWEARINGEN GALLERY, 4806 Brownsboro Center, Louisville KY 40207. (502)893-5209. Director/Owner: Carol Swearingen.

Profile: Retail gallery. Estab. 1971. Clientele: 98% private collectors. Represents 30 artists. Sponsors

8 group shows/year. Average display time is 6 weeks. Interested in emerging and established artists. Overall price range: up to $10,000.
Media: Considers all media.
Terms: Accepts work on consignment (50% commission). Retail price is set by gallery. Exclusive area representation required. Gallery provides insurance and promotion.
Submissions: Send query letter with resume and slides. Call or write to schedule an appointment to show a portfolio.

T.M. GALLERY, Thomas More College, Crestview Hills KY 41017. (606)344-3419. Director: Barbara Rauf.
Profile: Nonprofit gallery. Estab. 1978. Sponsors 7-8 shows/year. Average display time is 3-4. Interested in emerging and established artists. Overall price range: $50-5,000.
Media: Considers all media.
Style: Considers all styles.
Terms: Accepts work on consignment (no commission). Retail price is set by artist. Exclusive area representation not required. Gallery provides insurance, promotion and contract; shipping costs are shared.
Submissions: Send query letter with resume, slides and SASE.

Louisiana

LSU UNION ART GALLERY, Box 16316, Louisiana State University, Baton Rouge LA 70893. (504)388-5162. Gallery Director: Judith R. Stahl.
Profile: Nonprofit gallery. Estab. 1964. Clientele: university and Baton Rouge community. Sponsors 2 solo and 6 group shows/year. Average display time is 4-6 weeks. "Primary emphasis on local artists unless show is specialized, such as a metalsmith show." Interested in emerging and established artists. Overall price range: $50-500; most artwork sold at $100.
Media: Considers all media.
Style: Exhibits contemporary, abstract, Americana, impressionistic, figurative, landscape, non-representational, photo-realistic, realistic, neo-expressionistic, post-pop works. "The primary focus of the LSU Union Gallery is contemporary art. The LSU Union Art Advisory Board selects the shows for the gallery one year in advance of the exhibitions. The annual shows selected include a balance of photography shows and group shows. Two student shows are hosted annually."
Terms: Accepts work on consignment (25-40% commission). Market price is set by artist. Exclusive area representation not required. Gallery provides insurance, promotion and contract; shipping costs are shared.
Submissions: Send letter with resume; "request artist index file application form. No portfolios/slides accepted unless at the request of the Board."

POSSELT-BAKER GALLERY, 822 St. Peter, New Orleans LA 70116. (504)524-7252. Director/Owner: Rita Posselt.
Profile: Retail gallery. Estab. 1984. Clientele: tourists and some local; 97% private colletors, 3% corporate clients. Represents 15 artists. Sponsors 2 solo or group shows/year. Average display time is 11 months. Interested in emerging and established artists. Overall price range: $75-6,200; most artwork sold at $500-1,500.
Media: Considers oils, acrylics, watercolor, pastels, pen & ink, drawings, mixed media, collage, paper, sculpture and small-edition handpulled prints. Most frequently exhibits oils, acrylics, mixed media.
Style: Exhibits hard-edge/geometric abstraction, painterly abstraction, post-modern, primitivism, photo-realistic, expressionistic, neo-expressionistic, realism and surrealism. Genres include landscapes, figurative work and fantasy illustration. Most frequently exhibited styles: semi-figurative, realism/photo realism and hard-edge abstraction.
Terms: Accepts work on consignment (50% commission). Retail price is set by gallery and artist. Exclusive area representation required. Gallery provides some promotion; shipping costs are shared.
Submissions: Send query letter with resume, brochure, photographs and SASE. Write to schedule an appointment to show a portfolio, which should include originals and slides. Bios, photos or slides are filed.

STONER ARTS CENTER, 516 Stoner Ave., Shreveport LA 71101. (318)222-1780. Director: Katherine Kavanaugh.
Profile: Nonprofit gallery. Estab. 1972. Clientele: 95% private patrons, 5% grants. Sponsors 7 solo or 2-person shows/year. Average display time is 6 weeks. Interested in emerging and established artists.

Most artwork sold at $300-3,000 for large paintings; $100 or less for craft items in sales gallery.
Media: Considers oils, acrylics, watercolor, pen & ink, drawings, mixed media, collage, paper, sculpture, ceramics, fibers, glass, installations, photography and original handpulled prints. Most frequently exhibits oils, acrylics, mixed media and sculpture.
Style: Exhibits painterly abstraction, minimalism, conceptual, surrealism, primitivism, impressionism, neo-expressionism.
Terms: Accepts work on consignment (30% commission) in sales gallery. Retail price is set by artist. Exclusive area representation not required. Gallery provides insurance, promotion and contract.
Submissions: Send query letter with resume, slides and SASE.

Maryland

HOLTZMAN ART GALLERY, Towson State University, Towson MD 21204. (302)321-2808. Director: Christopher Bartlett.
Profile: Nonprofit gallery. Estab. 1973. Clientele: students and general Baltimore public; private collectors. Sponsors 2 solo and 5 group shows/year. Average display time is 3 weeks. Interested in established artists. Overall price range: $50-10,000; most artwork sold at $100-1,000.
Media: Considers oils, acrylics, watercolor, pastels, pen & ink, drawings, mixed media, collage, paper, sculpture, ceramics, crafts, fibers, glass, installations, photography, performance, original handpulled prints and silkscreens. Most frequently exhibits painting, watercolor and sculpture.
Style: Considers all styles and genres. "We exhibit a broad range of contemporary styles and media which also encompass diverse subject matter or themes as an educational resource to students and as displays of both traditional and avante-garde contemporary work."
Terms: Retail price is set by artist. Exclusive area representation not required. Gallery provides insurance, promotion and contract.
Submissions: Send query letter and resume. Resumes are filed. Slides are requested after initial contact.

Massachusetts

ANDOVER GALLERY, 68 Park St., Andover MA 01810. (617)475-7468. Director: Howard J. Yezerski.
Profile: Retail gallery. Estab. 1962. Represents 20 artists. Sponsors 16 solo and 8 group shows/year. Average display time is 3 weeks. Interested in emerging and established artists. Overall price range: $100-10,000; most artwork sold at $500.
Media: Considers oils, acrylics, watercolors, pastels, pen & ink, drawings, sculpture, ceramics, photography, collage, installations and original handpulled prints.
Style: Exhibits abstract and figurative works. Prefers "interesting and challenging work by emerging artists, whose work is relevant to our society."
Terms: Accepts work on consignment (40% commission). Retail price is set by gallery and artist.
Submissions: Send query letter, resume and slides. Slides and bios "of people we represent" are filed.

ALPHA GALLERY, 121 Newbury St., Boston MA 02116. (617)536-4465. Directors: Joanna E. Fink and Alan Fink.
Profile: Estab. 1967. Clientele: 70% private collectors, 25% corporate clients. Represents 15 artists. Sponsors 8-9 solo and 1-3 group shows/year. Average display time is 3½ weeks. Interested in emerging and established artists. Overall price range: $500-500,000; most artwork sold at $1,000-10,000.
Media: Considers oils, acrylics, watercolor, pastels, pen & ink, drawings, mixed media, sculpture and original handpulled prints. Most frequently exhibits oil on canvas, prints and works on paper.
Style: Exhibits painterly abstraction, expressionistic and realism. Genres include landscapes and figurative work. Most frequently exhibited styles: figurative, expressionistic and new-image. Prefers "strong, figurative, non-decorative oils, in which the paint itself is as important as what is portrayed."
Terms: Accepts work on consignment (50% commission). Retail price is set by gallery and artist. Exclusive area representation required. Gallery provides insurance, promotion mailing costs; shipping costs are shared.
Submissions: Send query letter with resume, slides and SASE.

CAMBRIDGE ART ASSOCIATION, 25 Rear Lowell St., Cambridge MA 02138. (617)876-0246. Director: Roberta Gould. Assistant Director: Cynthia Lewis.
Profile: Nonprofit gallery. Estab. 1944. Clientele: 20% private collectors, 80% corporate clients.

Represents 400 artists. Sponsors 1 solo and 8-10 group shows/year. Average display time is 3½ weeks. Interested in emerging and established artists. Overall price range: $150-3,000; most artwork sold at $150-500.

Media: Considers oils, acrylics, watercolors, pastels, pen & ink, drawings, mixed media, collage, paper, sculpture, ceramics, crafts, fibers, glass, installations, photography, performance, original handpulled prints, offset reproductions and posters. Most frequently exhibits painting, watercolors and collage.

Style: Exhibits hard-edge/geometric abstraction, color field, painterly abstraction, post-modern, pattern painting, impressionistic, photo-realistic, expressionistic and realistic works. Genres include landscapes, florals, Americana, portraits and figurative work. "The art exhibited here has a meaning and a content. We emphasize all styles."

Terms: Accepts work on consignment (40% commission). Retail price is set by artist. Exclusive area representation not required. Gallery provides insurance, promotion and contract; shipping costs are shared.

Submissions: Send query letter, resume and slides. Call or write to schedule an appointment to show a portfolio, which should include originals. Slides and resumes are filed.

GALLERY EAST, THE ART INSTITUTE OF BOSTON, 700 Beacon St., Boston MA 02215. (617)262-1223. Exhibitions Director: Catherine L. Smith.

Profile: Nonprofit gallery. Estab. 1911. Clientele: students and private individuals. Sponsors 1 solo and 6 group shows/year. Average display time is 1 month. Interested in emerging and established artists.

Media: Considers oils, acrylics, watercolor, pastels, pen & ink, drawings, mixed media, collage, paper, sculpture, ceramics, installations, photography and original handpulled prints. Most frequently exhibits photography, oil/acrylic and graphic design.

Style: Exhibits landscapes, portraits and figurative work. "The AIB is *not* a commercial gallery. It is an educational nonprofit gallery."

Terms: Accepts work on consignment (33% commission). Retail price is set by gallery and artist. Gallery provides insurance, promotion and contract; shipping costs are shared.

Submissions: Send query letter, resume, brochure, slides and SASE. Portfolio should include slides and transparencies. Resumes are filed.

ROCKPORT ART ASSOCIATION, 12 Main St., Rockport MA 01966. (617)546-6604. Executive Director: Ann Fisk.

Profile: Nonprofit gallery. Estab. 1921. Clientele: 95% private collectors, 5% corporate clients. Represents approximately 200 artists. Sponsors 20 solo and 14 group shows/year. Average display time is 4-6 weeks. Accepts only Cape Ann artists. Interested in emerging and established artists. Overall price range: $50-8,000; most artwork sold at $200-2,000.

Media: Considers original handpulled prints.

Style: Exhibits painterly abstraction, impressionistic and realistic works. Genres include landscapes, florals, portraits and figurative work. Prefers realistic New England scenes, impressionism and semi-abstract works. "We prefer quality work with a somewhat traditional theme presented by artists who have spent time on Cape Ann."

Terms: Accepts work on consignment (33⅓% commission). Retail price is set by artist. Gallery provides insurance and promotion.

SOUTH SHORE ART CENTER, 119 Ripley Rd., Cohasset MA 02025. (617)383-9548. Executive Director: Joel Conrad.

Profile: Nonprofit gallery. Estab. 1955. Clientele: Boston, South Shore and New England. Represents 100 artists. Sponsors 5 solo and 10 group shows/year. Average display time is 4 weeks. Overall price range: $50-2,000; most artwork sold at $500-700.

Media: Considers oils, acrylics, watercolor, pastels, pen & ink, drawings, mixed media, collage, paper, sculpture, ceramics, crafts, fibers, glass, installations, photography, limited edition offset reproductions and posters. Most frequently exhibits oils, acrylic and watercolor.

Style: Exhibits color field, painterly abstraction, impressionistic and realistic works. Genres include landscapes, florals, portraits and figurative work. Prefers realism, impressionism and abstraction. "Artists apply to become gallery members. Work for this membership is juried in February and in May. Gallery members hang artwork each month in a group show; they are eligible to be juried for a one person show in the second (invitational) gallery."

Terms: Accepts work on consignment (40% commission). Retail price is set by artist. Exclusive area representation not required. Gallery provides insurance, promotion and contract; artist pays for shipping.

Submissions: Send query letter, resume and slides.. "Submit original work to be juried." Resumes and slides are filed.

KENNETH TAYLOR GALLERY, Straight Wharf, Nantucket MA 02554. (617)228-0722.
Profile: Nonprofit gallery. Estab. 1945. Clientele: tourists; 90% private collectors, 10% corporate clients. Represents approximately 150 active artists. Sponsors 21 solo and 11 group shows/year. Average display time is 2 weeks. Accepts only Nantucket artists. Interested in emerging and established artists. Overall price range: $160-2,500; most artwork sold at $400 for originals, $60 for prints.
Media: Considers oils, acrylics, watercolor, pastels, pen & ink, drawings, mixed media, collage, paper, sculpture, ceramics, crafts, fibers, photography, original handpulled prints, offset reproductions and posters.
Style: Exhibits all styles. "As an artist's association, we are open to all styles and media. We encourage new genre work."
Terms: Accepts work on consignment (35% commission); membership fee plus donation of time. Retail price is set by gallery and artist. Gallery provides insurance, promotion and membership agreement; artist pays for shipping.
Submissions: Call to schedule an appointment to show a portfolio.

Michigan

ART CENTER OF BATTLE CREEK, 265 E. Emmett St., Battle Creek MI 49017. (616)962-9511. Director: A.W. Concannon.
Profile: Nonprofit and rental gallery. Estab. 1948. Clientele: individuals, businesses and corporations; 90% private collectors, 10% corporate clients. Represents 150 artists. Sponsors 13 solo and 8 group shows/year. Average display time for shows: 1 month; for rental gallery artists: 6 months. Interested in emerging and established artists. Overall price range: $5-1,000; most artwork sold at $5-300.
Media: Considers oils, acrylics, watercolor, pastels, pen & ink, drawings, mixed media, collage, paper, sculpture, ceramics, crafts, fibers, glass, photography and original handpulled prints. Most frequently exhibited media: watercolor, oil and acrylic painting.
Style: Exhibits painterly abstraction, minimalism, impressionistic, photo-realistic, expressionistic, neo-expressionistic and realistic works. Genres include landscapes, florals, Americana, portraits and figurative work. Prefers "work by Michigan artists that reflects contemporary trends."
Terms: Accepts work on consignment (33⅓% commission). Retail price is set by artist. Exclusive area representation not required. Gallery provides insurance, promotion and contract; artist pays for shipping.
Submissions: Send query letter, resume, brochure, slides and SASE. All material is filed "except slides which are returned. Michigan artists receive preference."

ART TREE SALES GALLERY, 461 E. Mitchell, Petoskey MI 49770. (616)347-4337. Manager: Audrey Collins.
Profile: Retail gallery of a nonprofit arts council. Estab. 1982. Clientele: heavy summer tourism; 99% private collectors, 1% corporate clients. Represents 70 artists. Sponsors 8 solo and 12 group shows/year. Average display time varies 2 weeks to 1 month. Prefers Michigan artists. Interested in emerging and established artists. Overall price range: $6-2,000; most artwork sold at $20-300.
Media: Considers oils, acrylics, watercolor, pastels, mixed media, collage, paper, sculpture, ceramics, fibers, glass, original handpulled prints, offset reproductions and posters.
Style: Exhibits painterly abstraction, impressionism, photo realism, expressionism and realism. Genres include landscapes, florals, Americana and figurative work. "The gallery is operated by a nonprofit arts council which seeks to exhibit works representing the spectrum of contemporary creativity encompassing the realm of media. We especially concentrate on theme shows or single-medium shows, or small solo exhibitions. Our audience tends to be conservative, but we enjoy stretching that tendency from time to time. We exhibit the work of Michigan artists who show and sell on a consignment basis."
Terms: Accepts work on consignment (33⅓% commission), Retail price is set by gallery and artist. Exclusive area representation not required. Gallery provides insurance and promotion; artist pays for shipping.
Submissions: Send query letter, resume, brochure, photographs and SASE. Write to schedule an appointment to show a portfolio, which should include originals, slides and photos.

JESSE BESSER MUSEUM, 491 Johnson St., Alpena MI 49707. (517)356-2202. Director: Dennis R. Bodem. Chief of Resources: Robert E. Haltiner.
Profile: Nonprofit gallery. Estab. 1962. Clientele: 80% private collectors; 20% corporate clients. Sponsors 5 solo and 16 group shows/year. Average display time is 1 month. Prefers northern Michigan artists, but not limited. Interested in emerging and established artists. Overall price range: $10-2,000; most artwork sold at $50-150.

Media: Considers oils, acrylics, watercolor, pastels, pen & ink, drawings, mixed media, collage, paper, sculpture, ceramics, crafts, fibers, glass, installations, photography, original handpulled prints and posters. Most frequently exhibited media: prints, watercolor and acrylic.
Style: Exhibits hard-edge/geometric abstraction, color field, painterly abstraction, pattern painting, primitivism, impressionism, photo realism, expressionism, neo-expressionism, realism and surrealism. Genres include landscapes, florals, Americana, portraits, figurative work and fantasy illustration.
Terms: Accepts work on consignment (25% commission). Retail price is set by gallery and artist. Exclusive area representation not required. Gallery provides insurance, promotion and contract.
Submissions: Send query letter, resume, brochure, slides and photographs. Write to schedule an appointment to show a portfolio, which should include slides. Letter of inquiry and brochure are filed.

FIELD ART STUDIO, 2646 Coolidge, Beckley MI 48072. (313)399-1320. Director: Jerome Feig.
Profile: Retail gallery and art consultancy. Estab. 1950. Represents 4 artists. Average display time is 1 month. Interested in emerging and established artists. Overall price range: $10-600; most artwork sold at $50-300.
Media: Considers watercolor, pastels, pen & ink, mixed media, collage, paper, fibers and original handpulled prints. Genres include aquatints, watercolor and acrylic paintings. Specializes in etchings and lithographs.
Style: Exhibits landscapes, florals and figurative work.
Terms: Accepts work on consignment (40% commission). Retail price is set by gallery and artist. Exclusive area representation not required. Gallery provides insurance, promotion and contract; shipping costs are shared.
Submissions: Send query letter, resume, slides or photographs. Write to schedule an appointment to show a portfolio, which should include originals and slides. Biography and resume are filed.

KALAMAZOO INSTITUTE OF ARTS, 314 South Park St., Kalamazoo MI 49007. (616)349-7775. Curator: Helen Sheridan.
Profile: Nonprofit gallery. Estab. 1924. Clientele: broad cross section of the general public and tourists; 90% private collectors; 2% corporate clients. Sponsors 12 solo and 20 group shows of 2 or more artists/year. Average display time is 4 weeks. Interested in emerging and established artists. Overall price range: $100-5,000; most artwork sold under $500.
Media: Considers oils, acrylics, watercolor, pastels, pen & ink, drawings, mixed media, collage, paper, sculpture, ceramics, crafts, fibers, glass, installations, photography and original handpulled prints.
Style: Exhibits hard-edge/geometric abstraction, color field, painterly abstraction, post-modern, pattern painting, surrealism, photo realism, expressionism, neo-expressionism and realism. Genres include landscapes, portraits and figurative work.
Terms: Accepts work on consignment (30% commission in sales from gallery; museum shop shows only Michigan artists and takes 40% commission). Retail price is set by artist. Gallery provides insurance, promotion and contract; artist pays for shipping.
Submissions: Send query letter, resume, slides, reviews and catalogs. Call or write to schedule an appointment to show a portfolio, which should include originals and slides. Resume and supporting materials are filed. "Works are reviewed by an exhibition committee once a month."

ROBERT L. KIDD GALLERY, 107 Townsend St., Birmingham MI 48011. (313)642-3909. Associate Director: Sally Parsons.
Profile: Retail gallery and ad consultancy. Estab. 1976. Clientele: 50% private collectors; 50% corporate clients. Represents approximately 125 artists. Sponsors 8 solo and 3 group shows/year. Average display time is 4 weeks. Interested in emerging and established artists. Overall price range: $200-18,000; most artwork sold at $800-5,000.
Media: Considers oils, acrylics, watercolor, pastels, mixed media, paper, sculpture, ceramics, fibers and glass. Most frequently exhibited media: acrylic, oil and sculpture.
Style: Exhibits color field, painterly abstraction, photo realism and realism. Genres include landscapes. "We specialize in original contemporary paintings, sculpture, fiber, glass, clay and handmade paper by American and Canadian artists."
Terms: Accepts work on consignment. Retail price is set by gallery and artist. Exclusive area representation required. Gallery provides insurance and promotion; shipping costs are shared.
Submissions: Send query letter, resume, slides and SASE.

ARNOLD KLEIN GALLERY, 4520 N. Woodward Ave., Royal Oak MI 48072. (313)647-7709. Director: Arnold Klein.
Profile: Retail gallery. Estab. 1971. Clientele: upper middle class, 95% private collectors; 5% corporate clients. Represents 10 artists. Sponsors 2 solo and 2 group shows/year. Average display time is

3 months. Interested in emerging and established artists. Overall price range: $75-2,500; most artwork sold at $250-750.
Media: Considers oils, acrylics, watercolors, pastels and original handpulled prints. Most frequently exhibited media: watercolors, color pencil and etchings.
Style: Exhibits impressionism and realism. Genres include landscapes and figurative work. Prefers romantic realism and impressionism. "The gallery avoids works done after photographs, which always appear photographic and thus vitiated in spirit and effect."
Terms: Accepts work on consignment (40% commission). Retail price is set by gallery and artist. Exclusive area representation not required. Gallery provides insurance; artist pays for shipping.
Submissions: Send query letter, resume, slides and SASE. Write to schedule an appointment to show a portfolio, which should include originals and slides. Resumes are filed.

KRASL ART CENTER, 707 Lake Blvd., St. Joseph MI 49085. (616)983-0271. Director: Dar Davis.
Profile: Retail gallery of a nonprofit arts center. Estab. 1980. Clientele: community residents and summer tourists. Sponsors 30 solo and group shows/year. Average display time is 1 month. Interested in emerging and established artists. Most artwork sold at $100-500.
Media: Considers oils, acrylics, watercolor, pastels, pen & ink, drawings, mixed media, collage, paper, sculpture, ceramics, crafts, fibers, glass, installations, photography and performance.
Style: Exhibits all styles. "The works we select for exhibitions reflect what's happening in the art world. We display works of local artists as well as major traveling shows from SITES. We sponsor annual regional art and photography competitions and construct significant holiday shows each December."
Terms: Accepts work on consignment (25% commission or 50% markup). Retail price is set by artist. Exclusive area representation required. Gallery provides insurance, promotion, shipping and contract.
Submissions: Send query letter, resume, slides, and SASE. Call to schedule an appointment to show a portfolio, which should include originals.

RUBINER GALLERY, 7001 Orchard Le., Rt. #430A, West Bloomfield MI 48322. (313)626-3111. President: Allen Rubiner.
Profile: Retail gallery. Estab. 1964. Clientele: 60% private collectors; 40% corporate clients. Represents 25 artists. Sponsors 5 solo and 3 group shows/year. Interested in emerging and established artists. Overall price range: $300-6,000; most artwork sold at $300-3,000.
Media: Considers oils, acrylics, watercolor, pastels, mixed media, collage, paper, sculpture and original handpulled prints.
Style: Exhibits painterly abstraction, impressionism and realism. Genres include landscapes, florals and figurative work. Prefers realism and abstraction.
Terms: Accepts work on consignment (50% commission). Retail price is set by gallery and artist. Exclusive area representation required. Gallery provides insurance and promotion; shipping costs are shared.
Submissions: Send query letter, slides and photographs. Call or write to schedule an appointment to show a portfolio, which should include originals. Resumes and slides are filed.

XOCHIPILLI GALLERY, 568 N. Woodward, Birmingham MI 48011. (313)645-1905. Manager: Lisa Konikow.
Profile: Retail gallery and art consultancy. Estab. 1970. Clientele: large businesses in Detroit; 60% private collectors, 40% corporate clients. Represents 30 artists. Interested in emerging and established artists. Overall price range: $500-5,000; most artwork sold at $2,000-3,000.
Media: Considers oils, acrylics, watercolor, pastels, pen & ink, drawings, mixed media, collage, paper, sculpture, ceramics, fibers and installations. Most frequently exhibited media: oils, acrylics and drawings.
Style: Exhibits all styles. "Our gallery specializes in contemporary themes with emphasis placed on exhibiting local artists."

Minnesota

ARTBANQUE GALLERY, 300 First Ave. N., Minneapolis MN 55401. (612)342-9300. Director: Richard Halonen.
Profile: Retail gallery and consultancy. Estab. 1982. Clientele: 60% private collectors, 40% corporate clients. Represents 15-20 artists. Sponsors 9 solo and 11 group shows/year. "The gallery space is divided on two levels. The upper level features shows six weeks long and the lower level is for gallery artists." Average display time is 6 weeks. Interested in emerging and established artists. Overall price range: $500-5,000; most artwork sold at $1,000-3,000.

Media: Considers oils, acrylics, watercolor, pastels, pen & ink, drawings, mixed media, collage, paper, sculpture, ceramics, fibers, glass, installations, photography, original handpulled prints and mono prints.
Style: Exhibits painterly abstraction, post modern, primitivism, expressionism and eno-expressionism. Genres include landscapes and figurative work. "The exhibitions of gallery artists, which includes primarily painters, sculptors and photographers, feature current work with a seemingly 'cutting edge.' "
Terms: Accepts work on consignment (50% commission). Retail price is set by gallery and artist. Exclusive area representation required. Gallery provides insurance, promotion and contract; shipping costs are shared.
Submissions: Send query letter, resume, slides and SASE. Call or write to schedule an appointment to show a portfolio, which should include slides and transparencies. Resume, bio and slides are filed.

BOCKLEY GALLERY, 400 N. 1st Ave., Minneapolis MN 55401. (612)339-3139. Directors: Mark or Todd Bockley.
Profile: Retail gallery. Estab. 1984. Clientele: 60% private collectors, 40% corporate clients. Represents 10 artists. Sponsors 6 solo and 3 group shows/year. Average display time is 6 weeks. Interested in emerging artists. Overall price range: $3,000-5,000.
Media: Considers all media. Most frequently exhibited media: acrylics, sculpture and drawings.
Style: Exhibits hard-edge/geometric abstraction, painterly abstraction, minimalism, conceptual and neo-expressionistic works.
Terms: Accepts work on consignment. Retail price is set by gallery and artist. Exclusive area representation required. Gallery provides insurance and promotion; shipping costs are shared.
Submissions: Send query letter, resume, brochure, slides, photographs and SASE.

FINGERHUT GALLERY, Suite 232, 400 1st Avenue N., Minneapolis MN 55401. (612)371-9530. Director: Allan Fingerhut.
Profile: Retail gallery. Clientele: 99% private collectors; 1% corporate clients. Represents 50 + artists. Sponsors 1 solo and 4 group shows/year. Average display time is 3 months. Interested in emerging and established artists. Overall price range: $560 for serigraphs to $15,000 for paintings; most work sold at $9,000.
Media: Considers oils, acrylics, mixed media and sculpture. Most frequently exhibited media: serigraphs, mixed media on hand made rice paper and oils.
Style: Exhibits painterly abstraction, impressionism and figurative work. "We are looking for artwork that would translate well into a limited edition media, either serigraphs or lithographs. The artwork must show outstanding mass appeal to all levels of collectors while not being either too sophisticated or too trite in its nature."
Terms: Accepts work on consignment (50% commission). Retail price is set by gallery. Exclusive area representation required. Gallery provides insurance, promotion and contract; shipping costs are shared.
Submissions: Send query letter, resume, slides and photographs. Write to schedule an appointment to show a portfolio, which should include originals, slides and transparencies.

MCGALLERY, 400 1st Ave., Minneapolis MN 55401. (612)339-1480. Gallery Director: M.G. Anderson.
Profile: Retail gallery. Estab. 1984. Clientele: collectors and art consultants; 60% private collectors, 40% corporate clients. Represents 30 artists. Sponsors 8 two-person shows/year. Average display time is 6 weeks. Interested in emerging and established artists. Overall price range: $800-4,000; most artwork sold at $1,500.
Media: Considers oils, acrylics, pastels, drawings, mixed media, collage, paper, sculpture, ceramics, photography, original handpulled prints and monotypes. Most frequently exhibited media: works on paper, sculpture and mixed media.
Style: Exhibits painterly abstraction, post-modern, pattern painting, expressionism and neo-expressionism. Prefers "artists that deal with art in a new perspective and approach art emotionally. They usually have an excellent color sense and mastery of skill."
Terms: Accepts work on consignment (50% commission). Retail price is set by artist. Exclusive area representation required. Gallery provides promotion and contract; artist pays for shipping.
Submissions: Send query letter, resume, slides and photographs. Call or write to schedule an appointment to show a portfolio, which should include originals, slides and/or transparencies.

THE WOMEN'S ART REGISTRY OF MINNESOTA, 414 First Ave. N., Minneapolis MN 55401. (612)332-5672. Membership Coordinator: Lynnea Forness.
Profile: Cooperative gallery. Estab. 1976. Exhibits the work of 24 members. Sponsors 8 2-person shows and 2 group shows/year. Average display time is 4 weeks. Accepts only women artists. "Must be

members of the collective or associate members." Interested in emerging and established artists. Overall price range: $150-5,000. "The Women's Art Registry of Minnesota (WARM Gallery) is a women's art collective that shows the work of the gallery members. We also have opportunities for artists to join as associate members who are then eligible to submit slides for special shows. Associate members also submit up to two pages of slides to be kept on file in our Slide Registry. Slides are cross-indexed by artist and medium. The Slide Registry is used by designers, curators, collectors and other artists."

Mississippi

THE CAPITOL STREET CRAFTS GALLERY, Box 15454, Jackson MS 39210. (601)969-2830. Executive Director of External Affairs: Martha Garrott.
Profile: Nonprofit gallery. Estab. 1984. Clientele: 90% private collectors, 10% corporate clients. Represents 285 artists and guest artists. Sponsors up to 24 solo and 1-2 group shows/year. Average display time is 1 month. Interested in emerging and established artists. Overall price range: $25-5,000; most artwork sold at $75-150.
Media: Considers oils, acrylics, watercolor, pastels, pen & ink, drawings, mixed media, collage, paper, sculpture, ceramics, crafts, fibers, glass, installations, photography, wood, native American art and original handpulled prints. Most frequently exhibited media: clay, fiber and glass.
Style: Exhibits all styles.
Terms: Accepts work on consignment (30% commission). Retail price is set by artist. Exclusive area representation not required. Gallery provides insurance, promotion and contract; exhibitor pays shipping or arranges delivery and pick up.
Submissions: Send resume, slides and SASE. Write to schedule an appointment to show a portfolio, which should include slides.

MERIDIAN MUSEUM OF ART, 628 25th Ave., Box 5773, Meridian MS 39302. (601)693-1501. Director: John Marshall.
Profile: Nonprofit gallery. Estab. 1970. Sponsors solo and group shows. Average display time is 4-6 weeks. Interested in emerging and established artists. Overall price range: $200-5,000; most artwork sold at $200-600.
Media: Considers oils, acrylics, watercolor, pastels, pen & ink, drawings, mixed media, collage, paper, sculpture, ceramics, fibers, glass, installations, photography, performance and original handpulled prints. Most frequently exhibited media: painting, drawing, sculpture, oil, pencil and wood.
Style: Exhibits color field, painterly abstraction, post-modern, neo-expressionism, realism and surrealism. Genres include landscapes, figurative work and fantasy illustration.
Terms: Accepts work on consignment (20% commission). Retail price is set by gallery and artist. Exclusive area representation not required. Gallery provides insurance, promotion and contract; artist pays for shipping.
Submissions: Send query letter, resume, brochure, slides, photographs and SASE. Write to schedule an appointment to show a portfolio, which should include originals and slides. Biographical and object-related material are filed.

MISSISSIPPI MUSEUM OF ART, 201 E. Pascagoula St., Jackson MS 39201. (601)960-1515. Associate Curator: Elise Smith.
Profile: Nonprofit museum. Estab. 1911. Clientele: all walks of life/diverse.
Media: Considers oils, acrylics, watercolor, pastels, pen & ink, drawings, mixed media, collage, paper, sculpture, ceramics, crafts, fibers, glass, installations, photography, performance and original handpulled prints. Most frequently exhibited media: painting, watercolor and photography.
Style: Exhibits all styles and genres.
Submissions: Send query letter, resume, slides and SASE. Slides and resumes are filed.

Missouri

ART RESEARCH CENTER, Lower Lobby Lucas Place, 323 W. 8th St., Kansas City MO 64105. (816)561-2006. Coordinator: Thomas M. Stephens.
Profile: Nonprofit gallery. Estab. 1966. Clientele: students, designers, architects, interested public. Sponsors 5-8 shows/year. Average display time is 6-8 weeks. Interested in emerging and established artists. Overall price range: $25-10,000.
Media: Considers oils, acrylics, watercolor, pastels, pen & ink, drawings, mixed media, collage,

paper, sculpture, fibers, glass, installations, photography and lectures, symposia, screenings and experimental theatre. Considers color and b&w original handpulled prints, posters, lithography and serigraphy.
Style: Exhibits hard-edge/geometric abstraction and constructionist, systematic and structural art. Seeks "multi-disciplinary experiment in constructive arts, exploring the relationships between art, science and technology."
Terms: Accepts work on consignment (no commission). "We do take 20-40% commission on multiples." Retail price is set by artist. Exclusive area representation not required. Gallery provides insurance and promotion; shipping costs are shared.
Submissions: Send query letter with resume, brochure, slides, photographs and SASE. Write to schedule an appointment to show a portfolio, which should include originals, slides, 2x2 transparencies or video/sound cassettes. Slides, resumes, brochures, catalogs, photographs, cassettes are filed.

BARUCCI'S ORIGINAL GALLERIES, 13496 Clayton Rd., St Louis MO 63131. (314)878-5090. President: Shirley Schwartz.
Profile: Retail gallery and art consultancy. Estab. 1977. Clientele: affluent young area; 70% private collectors, 30% corporate clients. Represents 25 artists. Sponsors 3-4 solo and 1 group shows/year. Average display time is 2 months. Interested in emerging and established artists. Overall price range: $500-2,000.
Media: Considers oils, acrylics, watercolors, pastels, collage and paper. Most frequently exhibited media: watercolors, oil and acrylics.
Style: Exhibits painterly abstraction, primitivism and impressionistic works. Genres include landscapes and florals. Currently seeking impressionistic landscapes.
Terms: Accepts work on consignment (50% commission). Retail price is set by gallery or artist. Gallery provides a contract.
Submissions: Send query letter with resume, slides and SASE. Write to schedule an appointment to show a portfolio, which should include originals and slides. Slides, bios and brochures are filed.

BEDYK GALLERY, 903 Westport Rd., Kansas City MO 64111. (816)561-3800. Director: Virginia Hillix.
Profile: Retail gallery. Estab. 1979. Clientele: locals, tourists, corporations; 40% private collectors, 60% corporate clients. Represents 35 artists. Sponsors 10 solo and 1 group shows/year. Average display time for a one-person show: 4 weeks; for consignment: 6 months. Prefers midwest artists. Interested in emerging and established artists.
Media: Considers oils, acrylics, watercolor, pastels, collage, paper, smaller sculpture, one-of-a-kind ceramics, fibers and original handpulled prints.
Style: Exhibits hard-edge/geometric abstraction, color field, painterly abstraction, impressionism, photo realism and realism. Genres include landscapes and florals. "We are seeking a price range not over $3,000 (retail); work in the 36x48 inch and upward range; seeking impressionist landscapes, gestural abstractions in soft colors."
Terms: Accepts work on consignment (50% commission). Retail price is set by gallery and artist. Exclusive area representation required. Gallery provides insurance, promotion and contract; plus shipping costs one way.
Submissions: Send query letter, resume, slides and SASE. Call or write to schedule an appointment to show a portfolio, which should include originals and slides. Slides and resumes are filed.

BOODY FINE ARTS, INC., 1425 Hanley Industrial Court, St. Louis MO 63144.
Profile: Retail gallery and art consultancy. "Gallery territory includes 15 Midwest/South Central states. Staff travels on a continual basis, to develop collections within the region." Estab. 1978. Clientele: 30% private collectors, 70% corporate clients. Represents 100 artists. Sponsors 6 group shows/year. Interested in established artists. Overall price range: $500-200,000.
Media: Considers oils, acrylics, watercolor, pastels, drawings, mixed media, collage, sculpture, ceramics, fibers, glass, handmade paper, photography, neon and original handpulled prints.
Style: Exhibits color field, painterly abstraction, minimalism, impressionism and photorealism. Prefers non-objective, figurative work and landscapes.
Terms: Accepts work on consignment or buys outright. Retail price is set by gallery and artist. Exclusive area representation required. Gallery provides insurance, promotion and contract; shipping costs are shared.
Submissions: Send query letter, resume and slides. Write to schedule an appointment to show a portfolio, which should include originals, slides and transparencies. All material is filed.

CHARLOTTE CROSBY KEMPER/KANSAS CITY ART INSTITUTE, 4415 Warwick, Kansas City MO 64111. (816)561-4852. Exhibitions Director: Sherry Cromwell-Lacy.

Profile: Nonprofit gallery. Clientele: collectors, students, faculty, general public. Sponsors 8-10 shows/year. Average display time is 4-6 weeks. Interested in emerging and established artists.
Media: All types of artwork are considered.
Submissions: Send query letter.

LEEDY-VOULKOS GALLERY, 1919 Wyandotte, Kansas City MO 64108. (816)474-1919. Director: Sherry Leedy.
Profile: Retail gallery. Estab. 1985. Clientele: 50% private collectors, 50% corporate clients. Represents 25-30 artists. Sponsors 6 2-person, 1 group and 2 solo shows/year. Average display time is 6 weeks. Interested in emerging and established artists. Overall price range: $500-25,000; most artwork sold at $5,000.
Media: Considers oils, acrylics, watercolor, pastels, pen & ink, drawings, mixed media, collage, paper, sculpture, ceramics, fibers, glass, installations, photography and original handpulled prints. Most frequently exhibited media: clay, painting and sculpture.
Style: Exhibits painterly abstraction, primitivism, expressionism and realism. "I am interested in quality work in all media. At the present I am interested in some good realistic work and work appropriate for corporate situations."
Terms: Accepts work on consignment (50% commission). Retail price is set by gallery and artist. Exclusive area representation not required. Gallery provides insurance, promotion and contract; shipping costs are shared.
Submissions: Send query letter, resume, slides, prices and SASE. Call or write to schedule an appointment to show a portfolio, which should include originals, slides and transparencies. Bio, vita, slides, articles, etc. are filed.

UNIVERSITY OF MISSOURI, KANSAS GALLERY OF ART, 5100 Rockhill Rd., Kansas City MO 64110—2499. (816)276-1502. Gallery Director: Assistant Professor Craig Subler.
Profile: Nonprofit gallery. Sponsors 2 solo and 6 group shows/year. Average display time is 7 weeks. Interested in established artists.
Media: Seeks "quality works, all media."
Submissions: "Send no slides, work on brochures. Slides, brochures and photgraphs will not be returned."

Montana

CASTLE GALLERY, 622 N. 29th St., Billings MT 59101. (406)259-6458. Owner: Jane W. Deschner.
Profile: Retail gallery. Estab. 1979. Clientele: 80% private collectors, 20% corporate clients. Represents approximately 30 artists. Sponsors 1 solo and 8 group shows/year. Average display time is 6 weeks for shows; 6 months otherwise. Interested in emerging and established artists. Overall price range: $5-1,500; most artwork sold at $50-300.
Media: Considers oils, acrylics, watercolor, pastels, pen & ink, drawings, mixed media, collage, paper, sculpture, ceramics, crafts, fibers, glass installations, photography, original handpulled prints and posters. Most frequently exhibited media: oil, acrylics and photos.
Style: Exhibits painterly abstraction, post-modern and impressionistic works. Genres include landscapes and figurative work.
Terms: Accepts work on consignment (40% commission) or buys outright (50% markup). Retail price is set by artist. Exclusive area representation required. Gallery provides insurance, promotion and contract; shipping costs are shared.
Submissions: Send resume, brochure, slides, photographs and SASE. Write to schedule an appointment to show a portfolio, which should include originals and slides. Resumes and brochures are filed.

CUSTER COUNTY ART CENTER, Box 1284, Pumping Plant Rd., Miles City MT 59301. (406)232-0635. Executive Director: Suzanne Katzanek.
Profile: Nonprofit gallery. Estab. 1977. Clientele: 90% private collectors, 10% corporate clients. Sponsors 10 group shows/year. Average display time is 4-6 weeks. Interested in emerging and established artists. Overall price range: $200-10,000; most artwork sold at $300-500.
Media: Considers oils, acrylics, watercolor, pastels, pen & ink, drawings, mixed media, collage, paper, sculpture, ceramics, fibers, glass, installations, photography and original handpulled prints. Most frequently exhibited media: paintings, sculpture and photography.
Style: Exhibits painterly abstraction, conceptualism, primitivism, impressionism, expressionism, neo-expressionism and realism. Genres include landscapes, florals, Americana, Western, portraits and

figurative work. "Our gallery is seeking artists working with traditional and non-traditional Western subjects in new, contemporary ways."
Terms: Accepts work on consignment (30% commission). Retail price is set by gallery and artist. Exclusive area representation not required. Gallery provides insurance, promotion and contract; shipping expenses are shared.
Submissions: Send query letter, resume, brochure, slides, photographs and SASE. Write to schedule an appointment to show a portfolio, which should include originals and slides. Slides and resumes are filed.

HAYNES FINE ARTS GALLERY, MSU School of Art, Bozeman MT 59717. (406)994-2562. Director: John Anacker.
Profile: Nonprofit gallery. Estab. 1974. Clientele: students and community. Sponsors 1 solo and 11 group shows/year. Average display time is 4 weeks. Interested in emerging and established artists.
Media: Considers all media and original handpulled prints. Most frequently exhibited media: painting, ceramics and sculpture.
Style: Exhibits painterly abstraction, conceptualism, post-modern, expressionism, neo-expressionism, realism and figurative work. Prefers contemporary work.
Terms: Accepts work on consignment (20% commission). Gallery provides insurance, promotion and contract; shipping costs are shared.
Submissions: Send query letter and resume. Write to schedule an appointment to show a portfolio. Resumes are filed.

LEWISTON ART CENTER, 801 W. Broadway, Lewiston MT 59457. (406)538-8278. Contact: Director.
Profile: Retail gallery of an art center. Estab. 1971. Clientele: a cross section. Exhibits the work of 17 individuals and 8 groups/year. Sponsors 24 solo and 17 group shows/year. Average display time is 6 months. "We would like for the artists to be in the Northwest, that consign to the Signature Shop." Interested in established artists. Most artwork sold at up to $1,500.
Media: Considers all media.
Style: Considers all styles. "As an Art Center we try to exhibit works of unusual mediums and textures different ways of expressing art for learning experience. In other words we want our people to see that the world has art beyond watercolor, oils, etc."
Terms: Accepts work on consignment (30% commission). Retail price is set by gallery and artist. Exclusive area representation not required. Gallery provides insurance, promotion and contract; artist pays for shipping.
Submissions: Send query letter, resume, slides and photographs. The letters and resumes are filed.

WESTERN MONTANA COLLEGE GALLERY MUSEUM, Dillon MT 59725. (406)683-7232. Gallery Director: Jim Corr.
Profile: Nonprofit gallery. Estab. 1970. Clientele: students, locals and tourists. Sponsors 5 solo and 5 group shows/year. Average display time is 4 weeks. Interested in emerging and established artists.
Media: Considers all media and all prints. Most frequently exhibited media: photography, painting and prints.
Style: Exhibits all styles and genres. "We don't sell. We are the community, college and artist resource for our area. We book traveling shows and provide space for our students and those who just wish to show for a future resume. Most professionals can't afford that, but our viewers really benefit."
Submissions: Send query letter. "Information about the show" is filed.

Nebraska

GALLERY 72, 2709 Leavenworth, Omaha NE 68105. (402)345-3347. Director: Robert D. Rogers.
Profile: Retail gallery and art consultancy. Estab. 1972. Clientele: individuals, museums, corporations; 75% private collectors, 25% corporate clients. Represents 10 artists. Sponsors 4 solo and 4 group shows/year. Average display time is 3 weeks. Interested in emerging and established artists. Overall price range: $750 and up.
Media: Considers oils, acrylics, watercolor, pastels, pen & ink, drawings, mixed media, collage, sculpture, ceramics, installations, photography, original handpulled prints and posters. Most frequently exhibited media: paintings, prints and sculpture.
Style: Exhibits hard-edge/geometric abstraction, color field, minimalism, impressionistic and realism. Genres include landscapes and figurative work. Most frequently exhibited style: colorfield/geometric, impressionistic and realism.
Terms: Accepts work on consignment (commission varies), or buys outright. Retail price is set by

gallery or artist. Gallery provides insurance and promotion; shipping costs are shared.
Submissions: Send query letter with resume, slides and photographs. Call to schedule an appointment to show a portfolio, which should include originals, slides and transparencies. Vitae and slides are filed.

HAYMARKET ART GALLERY, 119 S. 9th St., Lincoln NE 68508. (402)475-1061. Director: Lisa Cyriacks.
Profile: Retail gallery. Estab. 1968. Clientele: "established clientele built over 20 years." Represents over 100 artists. Sponsors 6-8 solo and/or group shows/year. Interested in emerging and established artists. Overall price range: $4.50-2,000; most artwork sold at $250.
Media: Considers original artwork of all media and original handpulled prints.
Style: "Our ideal concept is to display at all times the widest possible variety of works produced by artists of this region, with focusing on the emerging artist."
Terms: Accepts work on consignment (40% commission). Retail price is set by gallery and artist. Exclusive area representation not required. Gallery provides promotion and contract; artist pays for shipping.
Submissions: "Resueme and slides are considered by Exhibition Committee. Phone calls welcome."

Nevada

DONNA BEAM FINE ART GALLERY, Department of Art, University of Nevada, 4505 Maryland Pkwy., Las Vegas NV 89154. (702)739-3893. Exhibitions Curator: Michele Fricke.
Profile: Nonprofit gallery. Estab. 1960. Clientele: students and community members as well as tourists. Sponsors few solo and 6-8 group shows/year. Average display time is 1 month. Interested in emerging and established artists.
Media: Considers all media and original handpulled prints.
Style: Exhibits all styles and genres. "Our gallery is concentrating on group exhibitions featuring artists with national and, in some cases, international reputations. These artists work in all media."
Terms: "If an artist sells a work exhibited in our gallery we request that they donate 10% to us. This is not, however, required." Retail price is set by artist. Exclusive area representation not required. Gallery provides shipping and promotion.
Submissions: Send query letter, resume, slides, photographs and SASE. Call or write to schedule an appointment to show a portfolio, which should include originals, slides and transparencies. "Only the material of artists who we are going to exhibit" is filed.

MINOTAUR GALLERY, 3200 Las Vegas Blvd. S., Las Vegas NV 89109. (702)737-1400. President: R.C. Perry.
Profile: Retail gallery and art consultancy. Estab. 1980. Clientele: 95% private collectors, 5% corporate clients. Represents 2,000 artists on a rotating basis. Sponsors 5 solo and 3 group shows/year. Interested in emerging and established artists. Overall price range: $1,000-100,000; most artwork sold at $2,000-10,000.
Media: Considers oils, acrylics, watercolor, pastels, pen & ink, drawings, mixed media, paper, sculpture, ceramics, crafts, glass and original handpulled prints. Most frequently exhibited media: prints, paintings and sculpture.
Style: Exhibits painterly abstraction, impressionism, expressionism, realism and surrealism. Genres include landscapes, florals, Americana, Western, portraits, figurative work and fantasy illustration. "We are a department store of fine art covering a wide range of styles and taste levels."
Terms: Accepts work on consignment or buys outright. Retail price is set by gallery and artist. Exclusive area representation required. Gallery provides insurance, shipping, promotion and contract.
Submissions: Send query letter, resume, brochure, slides and photographs.

THE OFFICE GALLERY, 178 S. Maine St., Fallon NV 89406. (702)577-2701. Show Director: Darlene G. Novy-Zuelke.
Profile: Alternative space. Estab. 1979. Paintings are displayed in office furnishings department. Sponsors 6 2-or 3-person shows/year. Average display time is 2 months. Interested in emerging and established artists. Overall price range: $35-450; most artwork sold at $45-100.
Media: Considers oils, acrylics, watercolor, pastels, pen & ink, drawings, mixed media, collage, fibers, photography and original handpulled prints.
Style: Considers all styles and genres. "Medium is not too important. However, paintings and work depicting northern Nevada and near Northwest subject matter seems to draw the most interest along with interesting and unusual animal renditions."
Terms: Accepts work on consignment. Retail price is set by artist. Artist pays shipping costs both ways. No commission fees charged. Gallery provides insurance, promotion and contract.

Submissions: Send query letter, resume, brochure, business card, 4 slides and SASE. Two slides, resumes, brochure and business card "of artists who qualify for showing," are filed. "Unaccepted artists will have all material returned."

New Jersey

ARC-EN-CIEL, 64 Naughright Rd., Long Valley NJ 07853. (201)876-9671. Owner: Ruth Reed.
Profile: Retail gallery and art consultancy. Estab. 1980. Clientele: 50% private collectors; 50% corporate clients. Represents 20 artists. Sponsors 3 group shows/year. Average display time is 6 weeks-3 months. Interested in emerging and established artists. Overall price range: $50-8,000; most artwork sold at $250-1,500.
Media: Considers oils, acrylics, papier mache and sculpture. Most frequently exhibited media: acrylics, painted irons and oils.
Style: Exhibits surrealism, primitivism and impressionism. "I exhibit country-style paintings, naif art from around the world. The art can be on wood, iron or canvas. I also have some papier mache."
Terms: Accepts work on consignment or buys outright (50% markup). Retail price is set by gallery and artist. Exclusive area representation required. Gallery provides insurance, shipping costs are shared.
Submissions: Send query letter, resume, photographs and SASE. Call or write to schedule an appointment to show a portfolio. Photographs are filed.

THE ART GALLERIES OF RAMAPO COLEGE, 505 Ramapo Valley Rd., Mahwah NJ 07430. (201)825-9108. Gallery Director: Louise Murray Pocock.
Profile: Nonprofit gallery. Estab. 1979. Clientele: community, staff, students. Sponsors 6-8 solo and 8 group shows/year. Average display time is 1 month. Interested in emerging and established artists.
Media: Considers all types of media, including performance.
Style: Exhibits contemporary, abstract, Americana, impressionistic, figurative, landscape, floral, primitive, non-representational and photo-realistic styles.
Terms: Gallery provides insurance, promotion and contract; shipping costs are shared.
Submissions: Send query letter with resume, slides and SASE. Call or write to schedule an appointment to show a portfolio. Slides and resume are filed.

BARRON ARTS CENTER, 582 Rahway Ave., Woodbridge NJ 07095. (201)634-0413. Director: Linda Samsel.
Profile: Nonprofit gallery. Estab. 1977. Clientele: culturally minded individuals mainly from the central New Jersey region, 80% private collectors, 20% corporate clients. Represents 2 artists. Sponsors several solo and group shows/year. Average display time is 1 month. Interested in emerging and established artists. Overall price range: $500-5,000.
Media: Considers oils, acrylics, watercolor, pastels, pen & ink, drawings, mixed media, collage, paper, sculpture, ceramics, crafts, fibers, glass, installations, photography, performance and original handpulled prints. Most frequently exhibited media: acrylics, photography and mixed media.
Style: Exhibits painterly abstraction, impressionism, photo-realism, realism and surrealism. Genres include landscapes and figurative work. Prefers painterly abstraction, photorealism and realism.
Terms: Accepts work on consignment. Retail price is set by artist. Exclusive area representation not required. Gallery provides insurance, promotion and contract; shipping costs are shared.
Submissions: Send query letter, resume and slides. Call to schedule an appointment to show a portfolio. Resumes and slides are filed.

HOLMAN HALL ART GALLERY, Hillwood Lakes, CN 4700, Trenton NJ 08650-4700. (609)771-2189. Chairman Art Department: Dr. Howard Goldstein.
Profile: Nonprofit gallery and art consultancy. Estab. 1973. Clientele: students, educators, friends and general public. Represents 125 artists. Sponsors 7 solo and group shows, plus national printmaking exhibitions and national drawing exhibition on alternate years. Average display time is 5 weeks. Interested in emerging and established artists. Overall price range: $100-5,000; most artwork sold at $1,000 and up.
Media: Considers all media, original handpulled prints and offset reproduction. Most frequently exhibited media: photography, mixed media, sculpture, prints painting and drawing.
Style: Exhibits hard-edge/geometric abstraction, painterly abstraction, conceptualism, photorealism and expressionism. Genres include landscapes, Americana and figurative work. "Our gallery specializes in any type, style or concept that will best represent that type, style or concept. Being on a college campus we strive not only to entertain but to educate as well."
Terms: Retail price is set by gallery and artist. Exclusive area representation not required. Gallery provides insurance, promotion and contract; artist pays for shipping.

Submissions: Send query letter. Write to schedule an appointment to show a portfolio, which should include originals. Slides, letters and resume are filed.

THE KORBY GALLERY, 479 Pompton Ave., Cedar Grove NJ 07009. (201)239-6789. Owner: Alfred Korby.
Profile: Retail gallery. Estab. 1958. Clientele: upper income private buyers, upper-end designers; 70% private collectors. Represents 10 artists. Sponsors 4 solo and 4 group shows/year. Average display time is 4 weeks, 2 months. Interested in emerging and established artists. Overall price range: $200-2,500; most artwork sold at $1,500.
Media: Considers oils, acrylics, watercolors, sculpture, ceramics, fibers, collage, glass and color original handpulled prints. Specializes in lithos, serigraphs, etchings. Currently looking for oils.
Style: Exhibits contemporary, abstract, landscape, floral, primitive and miniature. Specializes in contemporary; currently seeking realism.
Terms: Accepts work on consignment (40% commission). Retail price is set by gallery and artist. Exclusive area representation required.
Submissions: Send query letter with resume, slides, photographs and SASE. Call or write to schedule an appointment to show a portfolio.

SIDNEY ROTHMAN—THE GALLERY, 21st on Central Ave., Barnegat Light NJ 08006. (609)494-2070. Owner: Sidney Rothman.
Profile: Retail gallery. Estab. 1958. Located on the seashore. Clientele: residents, tourists and summer home owners; 98% private collectors, 2% corporate clients. Represents 50 or more artists. Average display time is 3 months. Interested in emerging and established artists. Overall price range: $50-15,000; most artwork sold at over $1,000.
Media: Considers oils, acrylics, watercolor, pastels, pen & ink, drawings, mixed media, collage, paper, sculpture, ceramics and original handpulled prints. Most frequently exhibited media: watercolor, prints and oils/acrylics.
Style: Exhibits hard-edge/geometric abstraction, color field, painterly abstraction, conceptual, post-modern, surrealism, impressionism, expressionism and realism. Genres include landscapes, florals and figurative work. "The gallery is open during summer months for tourists and vacationers as well and second home owners. We present all styles of work, subject matter and with an inventory of over 500 works of art on hand."
Terms: Accepts work on consignment (33⅓% commission). Retail price is set by gallery and artist. Exclusive area representation required. Gallery provides insurance, promotion and contract.
Submissions: Send query letter, resume, brochure and slides. Call or write to schedule an appointment to show a portfolio, which should include originals, slides and transparencies. All material is filed.

SCHERER GALLERY, 93 School Rd. W., Marlboro NJ 07746. (201)536-9465. Owner: Marty Scherer.
Profile: Retail gallery. Estab. 1968. Clientele: 80% private collectors, 20% corporate clients. Represents over 40 artists. Sponsors 4 solo and 3 group shows/year. Average display time is 2 months. Interested in emerging and established artists. Overall price range: $200-25,000; most artwork sold at $1,000-3,000.
Media: Considers oils, acrylics, watercolor, pen & ink, drawings, mixed media, collage, paper, sculpture, glass and original handpulled prints. Most frequently exhibited media: paintings, original graphics and sculpture.
Style: Exhibits hard-edge/geometric abstraction, color field, painterly abstraction, minimalism, conceptualism, surrealism, impressionism, expressionism and realism. "Scherer Gallery is looking for artists who employ creative handling of a given medium(s) in a contemporary manner."
Terms: Accepts work on consignment (50% commission). Retail price is set by gallery and artist. Exclusive area representation required. Gallery provides insurance, promotion and contract; shipping costs are shared.
Submissions: Send query letter, resume, brochure, slides and photographs. Call or write to schedule an appointment to show a portfolio, which should include originals, slides and transparencies.

BEN SHAHN GALLERIES, William Paterson College, 300 Pompton Rd, Wayne NJ 07470. (201)595-2654. Director: Nancy Eireinhofer.
Profile: Nonprofit gallery. Estab. 1968. Clientele: college, local and New Jersey metropolitan-area community. Sponsors 5 solo and 10 group shows/year. Average display time is 6 weeks. Interested in emerging and established artists.
Media: Considers all media.
Style: Specializes in contemporary and historic styles, but will consider all styles.
Terms: Accepts work for exhibition only. Gallery provides insurance, promotion and contract; shipping costs are shared.

Submissions: Send query letter with resume, brochure, slides, photographs and SASE. Write to schedule an appointment to show a portfolio.

SPARTA GALLERY, 14 Winona Parkway, Sparta NJ 07871. (201)729-8075. Director: Mary Lewis.
Profile: Retail gallery. Clientele: upwardly mobile individuals; businesses, corporations. Represents 20 artists. Sponsors 1 solo and 4 group shows/year. Average display time is 3 months. Interested in emerging and established artists. Overall price range: $500-4,000; most artwork sold at $500.
Media: Considers oils, acrylics, watercolors, pastels, drawings, sculpture, ceramics, fibers, photography, mixed media, glass and color and b&w offset reproductions. Currently looking for collage, mixed media, oil and/or acrylic paintings.
Style: Exhibits contemporary, abstract, landscape, non-representational and realism. Seeking "artists from the U.S. who are seriously pursuing their careers in art, and who want the support and benefit of a good gallery."
Terms: Accepts work on consignment (40% commission). Retail price is set by gallery or artist. Gallery provides insurance, promotion and contract.
Submissions: Send query letter with resume, slides, photographs and SASE. Call or write to schedule an appointment to show a portfolio. Slides, resume, correspondence, news releases, etc. are filed.

New Mexico

THE ALBUQUERQUE MUSEUM, 2000 Mountain Rd., N.W., Albuquerque NM 87104. (505)243-7255. Curator of Art: Ellen Landis.
Profile: Nonprofit museum. Estab. 1967. Location: Old Town (near downtown). Sponsors mostly group shows/year. Average display time is 3-6 months. Interested in emerging and established artists.
Media: Considers all media.
Style: Exhibits all styles. Genres include landscapes, florals, Americana, Western, portraits, figurative and nonobjective work. "Our shows are from our permanent collection or are special traveling exhibitions originated by other museums or exhibition services."
Submissions: Send query letter, resume, slides, photographs and SASE. Call or write to schedule an appointment to show a portfolio.

ALBUQUERQUE UNITED ARTISTS, INC., Box 1808, Albuquerque NM 87103. (505)243-0531. Executive Director: Canoe Gandilhon.
Profile: Nonprofit gallery. Estab. 1978. Clientele: theater attendants and local people. Represents over 400 artists. Sponsors 8 group shows/year. Average display time is 4 weeks. Accepts only New Mexico artists. Interested in emerging artists. Overall price range: $150-2,500; most artwork sold under $200.
Media: Considers oils, acrylics, watercolor, pastels, pen & ink, drawings, mixed media, collage, paper, sculpture, ceramics, crafts, fibers, glass, installations, photography and original handpulled prints. Most frequently exhibited media: mixed media, acrylics and ceramics.
Style: Exhibits hard-edge/geometric abstraction, color field, painterly abstraction, conceptual works, post-modern, photo realism and expressionism. Genres include landscapes and florals. "Albuquerque United Artists does not specialize in any specific concept as long as the artwork is contemporary."
Terms: Accepts work "only for shows" on consignment (25% commission) or co-op membership fee plus donation of time. Retail price is set by artist. Exclusive area representation not required. Gallery provides insurance and contract; shipping costs are shared.
Submissions: Send resume and slides. Write to schedule an appointment to show a portfolio, which should include slides and transparencies. Slides and resumes are filed.

THE LEDOUX GALLERY, One Ledoux St., Box 2418, Taos NM 87571. (505)748-9101. Director/Owner: Lawrence Kaplan.
Profile: Retail gallery. Estab. 1976. Clientele: quality collectors; 90% private collectors, 10% corporate clients. Represents 26 artists. Accepts only Southwest artists. Interested in emerging and established artists. Overall price range: $200-7,500; most artwork sold at $500-1,000.
Media: Considers oils, acrylics, watercolor, pastels, mixed media, collage, ceramics and original handpulled prints. Most frequently exhibited media: oils, watercolors and prints.
Style: Exhibits painterly abstraction, minimalism, impressionism, expressionism and neo-expressionism. Genres include landscapes and figurative work. "I am concerned with all that connects to timelessness."
Terms: Accepts work on consignment (40% commission). Retail price is set by gallery and artist. Exclusive area representation not required. Gallery provides insurance, promotion and contract; artist pays for shipping.

Submissions: Send query letter. Write to schedule an appointment to show a portfolio. Names and addresses of potential artsts are filed. "Artists from Southwest a requisite."

MAGIC MOUNTAIN GALLERY, INC., 107A N. Plaza, Box 1267, Taos NM 87471. (505)758-9604. Owner/Director: Kathleen Decker.
Profile: Retail gallery. Estab. 1980. Clientele: tourists; 90% private collectors and some corporate clients. Represents 30 artists. Average display time is 6 months. Prefers Southwestern subject matter. Exclusive area representation required. Overall price range: up to $10,000; most artwork sold at $2,500-5,000.
Media: Considers oils, acrylics, watercolors, pastels, sculpture, ceramics, crafts, mixed media, collage and original handpulled prints.
Style: Exhibits contemporary, abstracts, landscapes and Southwestern works. Prefers contemporary Southwestern work. "Ours is a diverse gallery. We exhibit paintings, graphics, sculpture (stone & bronze), traditional Pueblo pottery, contemporary ceramics, turned wood bowls, large inlaid wood boxes and designer jewelry."
Terms: Accepts work on consignment (40% commission). Retail price is set by artist. Exclusive area representation required. Gallery provides insurance, promotion and contract; shipping costs are shared.
Submissions: Send query letter, resume, brochure, slides and photography. Write or phone to schedule an appointment to show a portfolio. "A wide variety of materials relating to the artists in the gallery including resumes, brochures, slides, etc. are filed."

ERNESTO MAYANS GALLERIES, 601 Canyon Rd., Santa Fe NM 87501; also at 310 Johnson St., Box 1889, Santa Fe NM 87504. (505)983-8068. Director: Maria Martinez and Ondine McRoberts.
Profile: Retail gallery and art consultancy. Estab. 1977. Clientele: 70% private collectors, 30% corporate clients. Represents 25 artists. Sponsors 4 solo and 4 group shows/year. Average display time is 1 month. Interested in emerging and established artists. Overall price range: $450-18,000; most artwork sold at $2,500-5,000.
Media: Considers oils, acrylics, watercolor, pastels, pen & ink, drawings, mixed media, sculpture, photography, original handpulled prints. Most frequently exhibited media: oils, photography, and lithographs.
Style: Exhibits painterly abstraction, post-modern, impressionism, expressionism, neo-expressionism and realism. Genres include landscapes and figurative work.
Terms: Accepts work on consignment. Retail price is set by gallery and artist. Exclusive area representation required. Gallery provides insurance; shipping costs are shared.
Submissions: Send query letter, resume, business card, slides and SASE. Write to schedule an appointment to show a portfolio, which should include slides and transparencies. Resume and business card are filed.

SANTA FE EAST GALLERY, 200 Old Santa Fe Trail, Santa Fe NM 87501. Associate Director: Joe Atteberry.
Profile: Retail gallery. Estab. 1980. Clientele: 98% private collectors, 2% corporate clients. Represents 100 artists. Sponsors 4 solo and 8 group shows/year. Average display time is 1 month. Interested in emerging and established artists. Overall price range: $150-35,000; most artwork sold at $900-3,500.
Media: Considers oils, acrylics, watercolor, pastels, mixed media, collage, sculpture and jewelry. Most frequently exhibited media: oils, sculpture and jewelry.
Style: Exhibits impressionism, expressionism and realism. Genres include landscapes and figurative work. Prefers American impressionism and contemporary realism. "We feature museum quality exhibitions of large nineteenth and early twentieth century American art, contemporary Southwest artists and one-of-a-kind designer jewelry."
Terms: Accepts work on consignment (40-50% commission). Retail price is set by gallery and artist. Exclusive area representation required. Gallery provides insurance, promotion and contract; artist pays for shipping and supplies professional quality photographs.
Submissions: Send query letter, resume, slides, photographs and SASE. Write to schedule an appointment to show a portfolio, which should include originals, slides and resume. Letters and resumes are filed.

SAVAGE GALLERIES, 102 E. Water, Santa Fe NM 87501. (505)982-1640. Art Director: James H. Bottorff.
Profile: Retail gallery. Estab. 1960. Clientele: 90% private collectors, 10% corporate clients. Represents 25 artists. Interested in emerging and established artists. Overall price range: $500 and up; most artwork sold at $2,000-3,000.
Media: Considers oils, acrylics, and watercolor. Most frequently exhibited media: oil, watercolor and acrylics.

Style: Genres include landscapes, florals, Americana, Western and portraits. Prefers Southwestern realism.
Terms: Accepts work on consignment (40% commission). Retail price is set by gallery and artist. Exclusive area representation required. Gallery provides insurance and promotion; artist pays for shipping.
Submissions: Send slides and photographs. Write to schedule an appointment to show a portfolio, which should include slides and photographs.

SHIDONI GALLERY, Box 250, Tesuque NM 87574. (505)988-8008. Director: Colette Hosmer.
Profile: Retail gallery. Estab. 1985. Clientele: 50% private collectors, 50% corporate clients. Represents 12 artists. Sponsors 7 solo and 12 group shows/year. Average display time is 1 month. Interested in emerging and established artists. Overall price range: $100-50,000; most artwork sold at $2,000-5,000.
Media: Considers oils, acrylics, drawings, mixed media, collage, sculpture, installations, performance and monotypes. Most frequently exhibited media: sculpture, acrylics and mixed media.
Style: Exhibits painterly abstraction, expressionism and neo-expressionism. Genres include figurative work. "The ideal artwork is new, exciting, original, unpretentious and honest. We look for artists who are totally devoted to art, artists who display a deep passion for the process of making art and who are driven by a personal and spiritual need to satisfy an inventive mind."
Terms: Accepts work on consignment (50% commission on 2-dimensional work; 45% on 3-dimensional work). Retail price is set by artist. Exclusive area representation required. Gallery provides insurance and promotion; artist pays for shipping.
Submissions: Send query letter, resume, slides and SASE. Write to schedule an appointment to show a portfolio, which should include slides and transparencies, resume, catalogs and clippings. Letters and resumes are filed.

YUCCA ART GALLERY, 1919 Old Town Rd. NW, Albuquerque NM 87111. (505)247-8931. Director: Margaret Mills.
Profile: Cooperative gallery. Estab. 1964. Clientele: tourists and local; 20% private collectors, 30% corporate clients. Represents 22 artists. Sponsors 8 solo and 4 group shows/year. Average display time is 2 months. Interested in emerging and established artists. Overall price range: $10-500; most artwork sold at $80.
Media: Considers oils, acrylics, watercolor, pastels, pen & ink, drawings, mixed media, sculpture, ceramics, fibers, glass, jewelry and wood. Most frequently exhibited media: watercolors, oils and clay.
Style: Exhibits impressionism, expressionism and realism. Genres include landscapes and florals.
Terms: Co-op membership fee plus donation of time and plus 10% commission. Retail price is set by artist. Exclusive area representation not required. Gallery provides contract; artist pays for shipping.
Submissions: Send query letter, resume, brochure and photographs. Write to schedule an appointment to show a portfolio.

New York

ADIRONDACK LAKES CENTER FOR THE ARTS, Route 29, Blue Mt. Lake NY 12812. (518)352-7715. Director: Elizabeth Folwell.
Profile: Nonprofit gallery. Estab. 1967. Clientele: tourists and summer residents. Sponsors 3 solo shows/year. Average display time is 1 month. Prefers artists from upstate New York, Vermont and New Hampshire. Interested in emerging and established artists. Overall price range: $3-750; most artwork sold at under $100.
Media: Considers oils, acrylics, watercolors, pastels, pen & ink, drawings, smaller sculpture, ceramics, fibers, photography, crafts, mixed media, collage, glass and original handpulled prints.
Style: Exhibits Americana, impressionism, landscapes, primitive works and photo realism. Specializes in styles "that reflect the area—woods, wilderness, water—but not necessarily representational. Our gallery is extremely small, yet raises about $12,000 annually to help support visual arts workshops, films, concerts, plays, etc. The clientele is not sophisticated yet has certain expectations of what they'd find in an Adirondack shop/gallery—quality art and crafts that reflect this lovely, unspoiled area."
Terms: Accepts work on consignment (35% commission) or buys outright (50% markup; net 10 days). Retail price is set by artist. Exclusive area representation required, "within 15 miles only." Gallery provides insurance, promotion and contract; shipping costs are shared.
Submissions: Send query letter, brochure, slides, photographs and SASE. Do not call or write to schedule an appointment to show a portfolio. Brochures, resumes, etc. are filed.

ELAINE BENSON GALLERY, INC., Montauk Highway, Box AJ, Bridgehampton NY 11932. (516)537-3233. Director: Elaine Benson.
Profile: Retail gallery. Estab. 1964. Clientele: rural, resort area, New Yorkers with second homes; 90% private collectors, 10% corporate clients. Represents about 100 artists. Sponsors 6 solo and some group shows/year. Average display time is 3 weeks. Interested in emerging and established artists. Overall price range: $200-20,000; most artwork sold at $500-1,000.
Media: Considers oils, acrylics, watercolor, pastels, pen & ink, drawings, mixed media, collage, paper, sculpture, ceramics, crafts, fibers, glass photography and limited edition original handpulled prints.
Style: Exhibits all styles. Prefers abstract expressionism, landscapes and realism.
Terms: Accepts work on consignment (50% commission). Retail price is set by gallery and artist. Exclusive area representation required. Gallery provides insurance, promotion and contract; artist pays for shipping.
Submissions: Send query letter, resume, slides and SASE. Write to schedule an appointment to show a portfolio, which should include slides. Slides and bios are filed.

BURCHFIELD ART CENTER, State University College, 1300 Elmwood Ave., Buffalo NY 14222. (716)878-6012. Director: Anthony Bannon.
Profile: Nonprofit gallery. Estab. 1966. Clientele: urban and suburban adults, college students, corporate clients, all ages in touring groups. Sponsors solo and group shows. Average display time is 4-8 weeks. Interested in emerging and established artists who have lived in western New York State.
Media: Considers oils, acrylics, watercolors, pastels, pen & ink, drawings, sculpture, ceramics, fibers, photography, crafts, mixed media, performance, collage, glass, installations and original handpulled prints.
Style: Exhibits contemporary, abstract, impressionistic, figurative, landscape, floral, primitive, non-representational, photo-realistic, realistic, neo-expressionistic and post-pop works. "We show both contemporary and historical work by western New York artists, Charles Burchfield and his contemporaries. The museum is not oriented toward sales."
Terms: Accepts work on craft consignment for gallery shop (50% commission). Retail price is set by gallery and artist. Exclusive area representation not required. Gallery provides insurance, promotion and contract; shipping costs are shared.
Submissions: Send query letter, resume, slides and photographs. Call or write to schedule an appointment to show a portfolio. Biographical and didactic materials about artist and work, slides, photos, etc. are filed.

CHAPMAN ART CENTER GALLERY, Cazenovia College, Cazenovia NY 13036. (315)655-9446. Chairman, Center for Art and Design Studies: John Aistars.
Profile: Nonprofit gallery. Estab. 1978. Clientele: the greater Syracuse community. Sponsors 3 solo and 4 group shows/year. Average display time is 3 weeks. Interested in emerging and established artists. Overall price range: $50-3,000; most artwork sold at $100-200.
Media: Considers oils, acrylics, watercolors, pastels, pen & ink, drawings, sculpture, ceramics, fibers, photography, crafts, mixed media, collage, glass and prints.
Style: Exhibits all styles. "Exhibitions at the Chapman Art Center Gallery are scheduled for a whole academic year at once. The selection of artists is made by a committee of the art faculty in early spring. The criteria in the selection process is to schedule a variety of exhibitions every year to represent different media and different stylistic approaches; other than that our primary concern is quality. Any artist interested in exhibiting at the gallery is asked to submit to the committee by March 1 a set of slides or photographs and a resume listing exhibitions and other professional activity."
Terms: Retail price is set by artist. Exclusive area representation not required. Gallery provides insurance and promotion; works are usually not shipped.
Submissions: Send query letter, resume, slides or photographs.

CHAUTAUQUA ART ASSOCIATION GALLERIES, Box 1365 Wythe Ave., Chautauqua NY 14722. Director: William Waite.
Profile: Nonprofit gallery. Estab. 1953. Seasons for exhibitions: June, July and August. Sponsors 7-10 solo and 4 group shows/year. Average display time is 4 weeks.
Media: Considers all media and original handpulled prints.
Style: Exhibits all styles and genres.
Terms: Accepts work on consignment (30% commission). Retail price is set by artist. Exclusive area representation not required. Gallery provides insurance, promotion and contract; shipping costs are shared.
Submissions: Send query letter and slides during only the months of June and July. Slides and resumes are filed.

COUNTRY ART GALLERY, 198 Birch Hill Rd., Locust Valley NY 11560. (516)676-6880. Director: Clarissa H. Watson.
Profile: Retail gallery. Estab. 1953. Clientele: 100% private collectors. Represents approximately 130 artists. Sponsors 7 solo and 5 group shows/year. Average display time is 4 weeks. Interested in emerging and established artists. Overall price range: $300-15,000; most artwork sold at $900-3,000.
Media: Considers oils, acrylics, watercolors, pastels and sculpture.
Style: Exhibits impressionism, landscapes, primitives and realism. "The emphasis in this gallery is on contemporary American realism."
Terms: Accepts work on consignment (45% commission). Retail price is set by gallery and artist. Exclusive area representation required. Gallery provides insurance and promotion; artist pays for shipping.
Submissions: Send query letter, resume and SASE. Biography and photographs are filed.

HANOVER GALLERY, 401 Irving Ave., Syracuse NY 13210. (315)474-0476. Director/Owners: Dolores and Henry Gernhardt.
Profile: Retail gallery. Estab. 1976. Clientele: coporations. Represents 250 artists. Sponsors 5 solo and 2 group shows/year. Interested in emerging and established artists. Overall price range: $150-5,000; most artwork sold at $300-500.
Media: Considers contemporary oils, acrylics, watercolors, pastels, pen & ink, drawings, sculpture, ceramics, fibers, glass, wood, jewelry and original handpulled prints.
Style: Exhibits contemporary, abstract and non-representational works. "The Gallery specializes in contemporary American art and crafts."
Terms: Accepts work on consignment (40% commission). Retail price is set by gallery and artist. Exclusive area representation required. Gallery provides insurance, promotion and contract; shipping costs are shared.
Submissions: Send query letter, resume and SASE.

HILLWOOD ART GALLERY, Long Island University, C.W. Post Campus, Brookville NY 11548. (516)299-2788. Director: Judy Collischan Van Wagner. Assistant Director: Carol Becker Davis.
Profile: Nonprofit gallery. Estab. 1974. Clientele: Long Island residents and university students. Sponsors 1-2 solo and 6-7 group shows/year. Average display time is 4-6 weeks. "We prefer area artists because of transportation costs." Overall price range: $2,000-80,000.
Media: Considers oils, acrylics, watercolor, pastels, pen & ink, drawings, mixed media, collage, paper, sculpture, ceramics, fibers, photography, performance and limited edition prints. Most frequently exhibited media: sculpture, paintings, drawing and photography.
Style: "Our gallery specializes in work representing the original ideas of artists dedicated to perceiving their world and experiences in a unique and individual manner."
Terms: Accepts work "in the context of invitational/exhibition." Retail price is set by artist. Gallery provides insurance, promotion and contract; shipping costs are shared.
Submissions: Send query letter, resume and slides. Selected slides and resumes are filed.

ISLIP ART MUSEUM, 50 Irish Ln., East Islip NY 11730. (516)224-5402. Director: Madeleine Burnside.
Profile: Nonprofit museum gallery. Estab. 1973. Clientele: contemporary artists, Long Island, New York City and abroad. Sponsors 8 group shows/year. Average display time is 6 weeks. Interested in emerging and established artists.
Media: Considers oils, acrylics, watercolor, pastels, pen & ink, drawings, mixed media, collage, paper, sculpture, ceramics, crafts, fibers, glass, installations, photography, performance and original handpulled prints. Most frequently exhibited media: installations, oils, and sculpture.
Style: Exhibits all styles. Genres include landscapes, Americana, portraits, figurative work and fantasy illustration. "We consider many forms of modern work by Long Island, New York City area and artists from abroad when organizing exhibitions. Our shows are based on themes, and we only exhibit group work. Museum expansion within the next two years will allow for one and two person exhibits to occur simultaneously with the ongoing group shows."
Terms: Retail price is set by artist. Exclusive area representation not required. Gallery provides insurance, promotion, contract and shipping.
Submissions: Send resume, brochure, slides and SASE. Slides, resumes, photos and press information are filed.

KIRKLAND ART CENTER, East Park Row, Clinton NY 13323. (315)853-8871. Director: Dare Thompson.
Profile: Nonprofit gallery. Estab. 1960. Clientele: general public and art lovers; 95% private collectors, 5% corporate clients. Sponsors 6 solo and 6 group shows/year. Average display time is 3-4

weeks. Interested in emerging and established artists. Overall price range: $60-4,000; most artwork sold at $200-600.
Media: Considers oils, acrylics, watercolor, pastels, pen & ink, drawings, mixed media, collage, paper, sculpture, ceramics, crafts, fibers, glass installations, photography, performance and original handpulled prints. Most frequently exhibited media: watercolor, oil/acrylic and prints.
Style: Exhibits painterly abstraction, conceptualism, impressionism, photo-realism, expressionism, realism and surrealism. Genres include landscapes, florals and figurative work.
Terms: Accepts work on consignment (25% commission). Retail price is set by artist. Exclusive area representation not required. Gallery provides insurance, promotion and contract; artist pays for shipping.
Submissions: Send query letter, resume, slides and SASE or write to schedule an appointment to show a portfolio. Resumes are filed.

BOLOGNA LANDI GALLERY, 49 Sag Harbor Rd., East Hampton NY 11937. (516)324-9775. Director: Joseph Landi.
Profile: Retail gallery and art consultancy. Estab. 1981. Clientele: nationwide; 90% private collectors, 10% corporate clients. Represents 40 artists. Sponsors 6 solo and 4 group shows/year. Average display time is 3 weeks; 1 winter show of gallery artists that lasts 4 months. Interested in emerging artists. Overall price range: $1,200-10,000; most artwork sold at $6,500.
Media: Considers oils, acrylics, watercolor, mixed media, sculpture, fibers, glass and original handpulled prints. Most frequently exhibited media: oils, acrylics and sculpture.
Style: Exhibits painterly abstraction, impressionism, expressionism, neo-expressionism and realism. Genres include landscapes and figurative work. "Bologna Landi is partial to painterly styles in any category. We are also interested in outdoor sculpture."
Terms: Accepts work on consignment (40% commission). Retail price is set by gallery and artist. Exclusive area representation required. Gallery provides insurance and promotion; artist pays for shipping.
Submissions: Send query letter, resume, brochure, slides, photographs and SASE. Write to schedule an appointment to show actual work. "Slides only O.K. after call. We only file material on the artists that we show."

MARI GALLERIES OF WESTCHESTER, LTD., 133 E. Prospect Ave., Mamaroneck NY 10543. (914)698-0008. Owner/Director: Carla Reuben.
Profile: Retail gallery. Estab. 1966. Located in a 200-year old red barn. Exhibits the work of 50-60 individuals/year. Sponsors 8 solo shows/year. Average display time is 4-5 weeks. Interested in emerging artists.
Media: Considers all media and prints.
Style: Exhibits all styles.
Terms: Accepts work on consignment (40-50% commission). Retail price is set by gallery and artist. Exclusive area representation required. Gallery provides insurance and promotion; shipping costs are paid by artist to and from gallery.
Submissions: Send query letter with resume, brochure, slides and SASE. Write to schedule an appointment to show a portfolio. "I keep a file on all my artists."

PETRUCCI GALLERY, 25 Garden Circle at Rt. 9W, Saugerties NY 12477. (914)246-9100. Owner: W.F. Petrucci.
Profile: Retail gallery. Estab. 1975. Clientele: 98% private collectors, 2% corporate clients. Represents 75 artists. Sponsors 12 solo shows/year. Average display time is 4 weeks. Interested in emerging and established artists. Overall price range: $1,000-25,000.
Media: Considers all media and original handpulled prints.
Style: Exhibits all styles.
Terms: "Terms are discussed with artist after acceptance." Retail price is set by gallery and artist. Exclusive area representation required. Gallery provides promotion and contract; artist pays for shipping.
Submissions: Send query letter with resume and photographs. Call to schedule an appointment to show a portfolio, which should include originals and slides. Resumes and photographs are filed.

PLATTSBURGH STATE ART GALLERIES, State University of New York at Plattsburgh NY 12901. (518)564-2178. Director: Edward Brohel.
Profile: Nonprofit gallery. Estab. 1974. "The galleries include the Myers Fine Arts, Lobby Gallery, Winkel Sculpture Courtyard and the Rockwell Kent." Clientele: 100% private collectors. Sponsors 8 solo and 12 group shows/year. Average display time is 2 months. Interested in emerging and established artists. Overall price range: $75-10,000; most artwork sold at $100-500.

Media: Considers oils, acrylics, watercolor, pastels, pen & ink, drawings, mixed media, collage, paper, sculpture, ceramics, fibers, glass and original handpulled prints. Most frequently exhibited media: oils, sculpture and works on paper.
Style: Exhibits all styles. "The Rockwell Kent Gallery concentrates on small shows (in addition to the permanent collection). We like one 'Adirondack' artist each year. Exhibits in Myers vary as much as we can, and the Winkel is a permanent installation."
Terms: Accepts work on consignment (25% commission). Retail price is set by artist. Exclusive area representation not required. Gallery provides insurance, promotion and contract; shipping costs are shared.
Submissions: Send query letter, resume, brochure, slides and photographs. "Work under future consideration" is filed.

SCHWEINFURTH ART CENTER, Box 916, 205 Genesee St., Auburn NY 13021. (315)255-1553. Director: James R. Dungey.
Profile: Nonprofit gallery. Estab. 1981. Clientele: local and regional children and adults, specialized audiences for fine art, architecture, photography and folk art. Sponsors 6 solo and 6 group shows/year. Average display time is 2 months. Interested in emerging and established artists. Overall price range: $25-7,500; most artwork sold at $100-500.
Media: Considers oils, acrylics, watercolors, pastels, pen & ink, drawings, sculpture, ceramics, fibers, photography, crafts installations, original handpulled prints and posters.
Style: Exhibits contemporary, impressionistic, figurative, landscape, primitive, photo-realism and realism.
Terms: Accepts work on consignment (20% commission). Retail price is set by artist. Exclusive area representation not required. Gallery provides insurance, promotion and contract; shipping costs are shared.
Submissions: Send query letter, resume, brochure, slides, photographs and SASE. Call to schedule an appointment to show a portfolio. "Slides, resumes, reviews and promotional materials for past exhibitions, all correspondence and notes" are filed.

THE STUDIO GALLERY, 133 S. Salina St., Syracuse NY 13202. (315)472-0805. Owner: Gail B. Wiltshire.
Profile: Retail gallery. Estab. 1980. Clientele: 90% private collectors, 10% corporate clients. Represents 200-250 artists. Sponsors 3 solo and constant group shows/year. Average display time is 6-10 weeks. Interested in emerging and established artists. Overall price range: $8-1,400; most artwork sold at $100-300.
Media: Considers oils, acrylics, watercolor, pastels, pen & ink, drawings, mixed media, collage, paper, sculpture, ceramics, crafts, fibers, glass, original handpulled prints and offset reproductions.
Style: Exhibits all styles. "We have an emphasis on three-dimensional, functional and decorative art. We look for outstanding quality in craftsmanship and artists vision."
Terms: Accepts work on consignment or buys outright (net 30 days). Retail price is set by artist. Exclusive area representation required. Gallery provides insurance, promotion and contract; shipping costs are shared.
Submissions: Send query letter, resume, brochure, photographs and SASE. Write to schedule an appointment to show a portfolio, which should include originals.

STUDIO K GALLERY, 10-63 Jackson Ave., Long Island City NY 11101. (718)784-0491. Owner/Director: Kenneth Bernstein.
Profile: Retail gallery. Estab. 1983. Clientele: 90% private collectors, 10% corporate clients. Represents 6 artists. Sponsors 2 solo and 2 group shows/year. Average display time is 5 weeks. Accepts

"My first assignment was from the Pig Iron Press in Youngstown, Ohio. I sent a letter plus slides, and they chose two of my samples. As a fine artist, I found it difficult to get published at first. However, I didn't give up. I would like to tell others to be confident and keep submitting work."

—Bob Crouch
Pittsburg, Kansas

only regional artists. Interested in emerging and established artists. Overall price range: $300-10,000; most artwork sold at $1,000-3,000.
Media: Considers oils, acrylics, watercolor, pastels, pen & ink, drawings, mixed media, collage, paper, sculpture, installations and original handpulled prints. Most frequently exhibited media: oil, sculpture and water media.
Style: Genres include landscapes and figurative work.
Terms: Accepts work on consignment (50% commission). Retail price is set by gallery and artist. Exclusive area representation not required.
Submissions: Send query letter with slides. Slides are filed.

New York City

ALTERNATIVE MUSEUM, 17 White St., New York NY 10013. (212)966-4444. Exhibitions Coordinator: David Donihue.
Profile: Nonprofit gallery. Estab. 1975. Clientele: artists, critics, collectors, dealers, curators and others. Exhibits the work of 80-100 individuals/year. Sponsors 8 solo and 5 group shows/year. Average display time is 4 weeks. Interested in emerging and established artists.
Media: Considers all media.
Style: Exhibits contemporary works. "The Alternative Museum presents thematic group exhibitions concerned with current issues in contemporary art as well as three other ongoing exhibition series."
Terms: Accepts work on consignment (25% commission). Retail price is set by artist. Exclusive area representation not required. Gallery provides insurance, promotion and contract; shipping costs are shared.
Submissions: Send resume, slides and SASE. "Only materials which may be used for scheduled upcoming exhibitions" are filed.

ARCH GALLERY, 644 Broadway, New York NY 10012. (212)260-5847. Director: Daniela Montana.
Profile: Retail gallery and art consultancy. Estab. 1982. Clientele: international; 30% private collectors, 30% corporate clients. Represents 5 artists. Sponsors 4 solo and 4 group shows/year. Average display time is 1 month. Interested in emerging and established artists. Overall price range: $1,500-5,000; most artwork sold at $2,000.
Media: Considers oils, acrylics, drawings, mixed media, collage, paper, sculpture, installations, performance, graphics and original handpulled prints. Most frequently exhibited media: painting, graphics and sculpture.
Style: Exhibits hard-edge/geometric abstraction, painterly abstraction, feminist/political, expressionistic and contemporary Latin American art. Genres include landscapes and figurative work. "Arch Gallery specializes in contemporary Latin American art."
Terms: Accepts work on consignment (40% commission). Retail price is set by gallery and artist. Exclusive area representation not required. Gallery provides promotion and contract; artist pays for shipping.
Submissions: Send query letter, resume, slides and SASE. Write to schedule an appointment to show a portfolio, which should include slides. Resumes, 5 slides and catalogs/reviews are filed.

BLUE MOUNTAIN GALLERY, 121 Wooster St., New York NY 10012. (212)226-9402. Director: Jackie Lima.
Profile: Cooperative gallery. Estab. 1980. Clientele: art lovers, collectors and artists; 90% private collectors, 10% corporate clients. Represents 25 artists. Sponsors 12 solo and 1 group shows/year. Average display time is 3 weeks. Interested in emerging and established artists. Overall price range: $100-8,000; most artwork sold at $100-3,000.
Media: Considers oils, acrylics, watercolor, pastels, pen & ink, drawings, mixed media, collage, paper, sculpture, installations, photography and original handpulled prints. Most frequently exhibited media: oil, watercolor and drawing mediums.
Style: Exhibits feminist/political, impressionism, expressionism, neo-expressionism and realism. Genres include landscapes, florals, portraits, figurative work and fantasy. "We like large, bold statements in imagery."
Terms: Co-op membership fee plus donation of time. Retail price is set by artist. Exclusive area representation not required. Gallery provides insurance, promotion and contract; artist pays for shipping.
Submissions: Send query letter and SASE.

BROADWAY WINDOWS, New York University, 80 Washington Square East, New York NY 10033. Viewing address: Broadway at E. 10th St. (212)998-5751. Director or Assistant Director: Marilynn Karp or Ruth D. Newman.

Profile: Nonprofit gallery. Estab. 1984. Clientele: the metropolitan public. On view to vehicular and pedestrian traffic 24 hours a day. Represents 30 artists. Sponsors 9 solo shows/year. Average display time is 5 weeks. Interested in emerging and established artists.
Media: Considers all media. "We are particularly interested in site specific installations."
Terms: Accepts work on consignment (20% commission). Retail price is set by artist. Exclusive area representation not required. Gallery provides insurance, promotion and contract; artist pays for shipping.
Submissions: Send query letter, resume, slides, photographs and SASE. "Proposals are evaluated once annually in response to an ad calling for proposals. Jurors look for proposals that make the best use of the 24 hour space."

CHRISTIE'S CONTEMPORARY ART, 799 Madison Ave., New York NY 10021. (212)535-4422. Gallery Manager: Myles Cooke.
Profile: Retail gallery. Estab. 1981. Clientele: 30% private collectors. Average display time is 1 month. Interested in emerging and established artists. Overall price range: $200-2,000; most artwork sold at $250.
Media: Considers sculpture and prints.
Style: Exhibits contemporary, figurative, landscapes and non-representational work.
Terms: Accepts work on consignment or buys outright. Retail price is set by gallery and artist. Exclusive area representation not required. Gallery provides insurance and promotion; shipping costs are shared.
Submissions: Send query letter, resume and slides.

CITY GALLERY, New York City Department of Cultural Affairs, 2 Columbus Circle, New York NY 10019. (212)974-1150. Director: Elyse Reissman.
Profile: Nonprofit gallery. Estab. 1980. Sponsors 8 group shows/year. Average display time is 4 weeks. Prefers New York City artists. Interested in emerging and established artists.
Media: Considers all media.
Style: Considers all styles and genres. "City Gallery is the official gallery of the City of New York. It presents exhibits that highlight the cultural diversity of New York City's many artistic and ethnic communities. Proposals for group shows from nonprofit arts organizations are reviewed twice each year and selected by a panel of artists and arts administrators."
Terms: Gallery provides promotion and contract.
Submissions: Send proposal, resume, slides and SASE. "Call and request a copy of application guidelines."

LEONARDA DI MAURO, 49 E. 96th St., New York NY 10128. (212)360-5049. Contact: Owner.
Profile: Retail gallery. Estab. 1982. Represents 6 artists. Sponsors 6 solo and 4 group shows/year. Average display time is 1 month. Interested in emerging and established artists. Overall price range: $300-25,000.
Media: Considers oils, acrylics, watercolor, pastels, pen & ink, drawings, mixed media, collage, paper and original handpulled prints. Most frequently exhibited media: oil, watercolor and pastel.
Style: Exhibits painterly abstraction, conceptualism, post-modern, primitivism, expressionism, neo-expressionism and surrealism. Genres include figurative work.
Terms: Accepts work on consignment (50% commission). Retail price is set by gallery and artist. Exclusive area representation required. Gallery provides insurance, promotion and contract; shipping costs are shared.
Submissions: Send resume, slides and SASE. Portfolio shoud include slides.

DORSKY GALLERY, 578 Broadway, New York NY 10012. (212)838-3423. Director: Samuel Dorsky.
Profile: Retail gallery. Estab. 1963. Represents 10 artists. Average display time is 4 weeks. Interested in emerging and established artists. Overall price range: most work sold at $3,000-10,000.
Media: Considers oils, acrylics, watercolor, pastels, pen & ink, drawings, mixed media, collage, paper, sculpture, ceramics, photography and limited edition prints. Most frequently exhibited media: watercolors, drawings and lithographs.
Style: Exhibits color field, painterly abstraction, post-modern, primitivism and surrealism. Genres include landscapes, figurative work and fantasy illustration. Prefers figurative work and surrealism.
Terms: Accepts work on consignment (50% commission) or buys outright. Retail price is set by gallery and artist. Exclusive area representation required. Gallery provides insurance and promotion; shipping costs are shared.
Submissions: Send resume. Write to schedule an appointment to show a portfolio, which should include originals, slides and transparencies.

DYANSEN GALLERY, 3 E. 54th St., New York NY 10022. (212)644-5100. Director of Merchandising: Ellen Salpeter.
Profile: Retail gallery. Clientele: 95% private collectors. Represents 20 artists. Average display time is 4 weeks. Interested in emerging and established artists. Overall price range: $1,500-20,00; most artwork sold at $4,000.
Media: Considers oils, acrylics and sculpture. Most frequently exhibited media: oil, acrylic and bronze.
Style: Exhibits color field. impressionism and realism. Genres include landscapes, figurative work and fantasy illustration. "Our galleries specialize in beautiful appealing figurative and landscape, architectural imagery."
Terms: Accepts work on consignment (60% commission) or buys outright. Retail price is set by gallery. Exclusive area representation required. Gallery provides insurance, promotion and contract; shipping costs are shared.
Submissions: Send query letter, resume, brochure, slides, photographs and SASE. Resume and brochure are filed.

55 MERCER, 55 Mercer St., New York NY 10013. (212)226-8513. President: Betti-Sue Hertz.
Profile: Cooperative gallery. Estab. 1970. Clientele: artists and critics. Represents 18 artists. Sponsors 28 solo and 4 group shows/year. Average display time is 3 weeks. "We tend to exhibit artists from New York City metropolitan area. The logistics are more complicated for out-of-town artists." Interested in emerging and established artists. Most artwork sold at $1-2,000.
Media: Considers oils, sculpture, mixed media and photography.
Style: Exhibits contemporary, abstract and neo-expressionistic work. "We are noted for our large sculptural, site-oriented installations. We lately have shown the current styles in neo-expressionist painting."
Terms: Co-op membership fee plus donation of time. Retail price is set by artist. Exclusive area representation not required. Gallery provides promotion.
Submissions: Send query letter with resume, slides and SASE. "We maintain a record of artists' work who exhibit with us for documentation for grant application."

GRACIE MANSION GALLERY, 167 Avenue A, New York NY 10009. (212)477-7331. Director: Gracie Mansion.
Profile: Retail gallery. Estab. 1981. Clientele: serious fine art collectors; 80% private collectors, 20% corporate clients. Represents 15 artists. Sponsors 8 solo and 2 group shows/year. Average display time is 4 weeks. Interested in emerging and established artists. Overall price range: $200-30,000; most artwork sold at $5,000-10,000.
Media: Considers oils, acrylics, watercolor, pastels, collage, paper, sculpture, installations and photography. Most frequently exhibited media: installations.
Style: Exhibits painterly abstraction, conceptual, post-modern, primitivism, expressionism, neo-expressionism and realism. "We are interested in serious, innovative, original artists."
Terms: Accepts work on consignment (50% commission). Retail price is set by gallery and artist. Exclusive area representation not required.
Submissions: Send query letter, resume, slides, photographs and SASE. "We do not set up appointments with artists for reviewing work. We only look at slides/photographs in order to get acquainted with an artist's work."

GRAND CENTRAL ART GALLERIES, 24 W. 57th St., New York NY 10019. (212)867-3344. Contact: Exhibitions Committee.
Profile: Retail gallery. Estab. 1922. Clientele: private, museum, corporate and industrial; 80% private collectors, 10% corporate clients. Represents 60 artists. Sponsors 5 solo and 5 group shows/year. Interested in emerging and established artists. Overall price range: $1,000-1,000,000; most artwork sold at $10-40,000.
Media: Considers oils, watercolor and pastels.
Style: Exhibits impressionism and realism. Genres include landscapes, portraits and figurative work. "Grand Central Art Galleries exhibits a mix of contemporary realism (oil, watercolor, sculpture) and late nineteenth- and early twentieth-century works."
Terms: Accepts work on consignment (40% commission). Retail price is set by gallery and artist. Exclusive area representation required. Gallery provides promotion and contract; shipping costs are shared.
Submissions: Send resume, slides and SASE.

HUDSON GUILD ART GALLERY, 441 W. 26th St., New York NY 10001. (212)760-9800. Gallery Director: Haim Mendelson.

Profile: Nonprofit gallery. Estab. 1948. Clientele: community. Represents 12 artists. Sponsors 1 solo and 5 group shows/year. Average display time is 3 weeks. Interested in emerging and established artists. Overall price range: $100-12,000.
Media: Considers oils, acrylics, watercolors, pastels, pen & ink, drawings, collage and original handpulled prints.
Style: Exhibits contemporary, figurative, landscapes and realism. "Our gallery shows the works of talented contemporary artists of professional status. Traditionally the gallery has been the showcase for emerging artists; John Sloan's first one-man show was at Hudson Guild Art Gallery. The gallery continues to exhibit the work of young artists of promise together with seasoned professionals. The exhibits include all media which can be hung on the walls. There are no facilities for free standing sculpture. Most exhibitors are from the New York City area."
Terms: Accepts work on consignment (15% commission). Retail price is set by artist. Exclusive area representation not required. Gallery provides insurance and contract; artist pays for shipping.
Submissions: Send query letter, resume, brochure, slides, photographs and SASE. Call or write to schedule an appointment to show a portfolio.

MICHAEL INGBAR GALLERY, 578 Broadway, New York NY 10012. (212)334-1100. Director: Michael Ingbar.
Profile: Retail gallery and art consultancy. Estab. 1977. Clientele: 1% private collectors, 99% corporate clients. Represents 27 artists. Sponsors 2 solo and 9 group shows a year on a co-op basis with the artists. Average display time is 1 month. Interested in emerging and established artists. Overall price range: $600-12,000; most artwork sold at $1,000-2,000.
Media: Considers oils, acrylics, paper, fibers and original handpulled prints.
Style: Exhibits hard-edge/geometric abstraction, impressionism, realism and surrealism. Genres include landscapes and figurative work. "We feel that we are one of the few solo galleries that show 'pleasing and pretty' works that have a soothing or uplifting effect on the viewer. All works should communicate to the generally uneducated public we sell to, which is primarily corporations with no current colections and are looking for art to be decorative as well as of a high quality."
Terms: Accepts work on consignment (50% commission). Retail price is set by gallery and artist. Exclusive area representation not required.
Submissions: Send query letter, slides and SASE. Slides are filed.

JADITE GALLERIES, 415 W. 50th St. New York NY 10019. (212)315-2740. Director: Roland Sainz.
Profile: Retail gallery. Estab. 1985. Clientele: 80% private collectors, 20% corporate clients. Represents 80 artists. Sponsors 6 solo and 12 group shows/year. Average display time is 2 weeks. Interested in emerging and established artists. Overall price range: $250-2,500; most artwork sold at $500-1,200.
Media: Considers oils, acrylics, watercolor, pastels, pen & ink, drawings, mixed media, collage, sculpture and original handpulled prints. Most frequently exhibited media: oils, acrylics, pastels and sculptures.
Style: Exhibits minimalism, post-modern, impressionism, neo-expressionism, realism and surrealism. Genres include landscapes, florals, portraits, Western collages and figurative work. Features "national and international emerging artists dealing with contemporary works."
Terms: Accepts work on consignment (40% commission). Retail price is set by gallery and artist. Exclusive area representation not required. Gallery provides insurance, promotion and contract; shipping and exhibition costs are shared.
Submissions: Send query letter, resume, brochure, slides, photographs and SASE. Call or write to schedule an appointment to show a portfolio, which should include originals, slides or photos. Resume, photographs or slides are filed.

MIDTOWN GALLERIES, 11 E. 57th St., New York NY 10022. (212)758-1900. Director: Bridget Moore.
Profile: Retail gallery. Estab. 1932. Represents 30 artists. Sponsors 6 solo and 4 group shows/year. Interested in emerging and established artists.
Media: Considers painting and sculpture.
Style: Features contemporary American artists.
Terms: Retail price is set by gallery and artist. Exclusive area representation required.
Submissions: Send query letter, resume, brochure, slides, photographs and SASE.

ALEXANDER F. MILLIKEN INC., 98 Prince St., New York NY 10012. (212)966-7800.
Profile: Retail gallery. Estab. 1976. Represents 16 artists. Sponsors 6 solo and 2 group shows/year. Average display time is 4-6 weeks. Interested in emerging and established artists. Overall price range: $500-250,000; most artwork sold at $10,000-25,000.

Media: Considers paintings, sculpture, drawings and prints.
Style: Exhibits contemporary, abstract, figurative work and realism.
Submissions: Send query letter, resume, slides and SASE.

MUSEUM OF HOLOGRAPHY, 11 Mercer St., New York NY 10013. (212)925-0581. Registrar: Larry Sheldon.
Profile: Nonprofit museum. Estab. 1976. Clientele: 95% private collectors, 5% corporate clients. Sponsors 4 group shows/year. Average display time is 3-4 months. Accepts only holography. Interested in emerging and established artists. Overall price range: $15-7,000; most artwork sold at $60-200.
Media: Considers only holograms.
Style: Exhibits hard-edge/geometric abstraction, color field, minimalism and surrealism. "Our museum specializes in all forms of holography, artistic, commercial, scientific and its applications. Style is not a consideration with our institution."
Terms: Accepts work on consignment. Retail price is set by gallery and artist. Exclusive area representation not required. Gallery provides insurance and promotion; shipping costs are shared.
Submissions: Send query letter, resume and slides. Write to schedule an appointment to show a portfolio, which should include originals and slides. Resumes and slides are filed.

NOVO ARTS, 57 E. 11th St., New York NY 10003. (212)674-3093. Fine Art Consultant: Lynda Deppe.
Profile: Fine arts consultants for private collectors and corporations. Sponsors 5 group shows/year. Average display time is 2 months. Interested in emerging and established artists. Overall price range: $200 and up; most artwork sold at $500-5,000.
Media: Considers all mediums.
Style: Exhibits all styles.
Terms: Accepts work on consignment. Retail price is set by gallery and artist. Exclusive area representation not required.
Submissions: Send query letter, resume, slides, price the artist would like to receive and SASE. Call or write to schedule an appointment to show a portfolio, which should include originals and slides. Slides, resume and price list are filed.

NOW GALLERY, 430 E. 9th St., New York NY 10009. (212)674-3211. Director: Jacek Tylicki.
Profile: Retail gallery. Estab. 1984. Represents 15 artists. Sponsors 8 solo and 3 group shows/year. Average display time is 3½ weeks. Interested in emerging and established artists. Overall price range: $1,000-5,000; most artwork sold at $1,500.
Media: Considers oils, acrylics, watercolor, pastels, pen & ink, drawings, mixed media, collage, paper, sculpture, installations, photography and performance. Most frequently exhibited media: painting, sculpture and installations.
Style: Exhibits conceptualism, neo-expressionism, anticonceptual and East Village art. Prefers "the now in contemporary art."
Terms: Accepts work on consignment (50% commission). Retail price is set by gallery and artist. Gallery provides insurance, promotion and contract; shipping costs are shared.
Submissions: Send query letter, resume, slides and SASE. Call to schedule an appointment to show a portfolio, which should include slides. Resumes and slides are filed.

PHOENIX GALLERY, 568-578 Broadway, New York NY 10012. (212)226-8711. Director: Linda Handler.
Profile: Cooperative gallery. Estab. 1950s. Clientele: 70% private collectors, 30% corporate clients. Represents 27 artists. Sponsors 11 solo and 3 group shows/year. Average display time is 4 weeks. Interested in emerging and established artists. Overall price range: $500-5,000; most artwork sold at $1,000.
Media: Considers oils, acrylics, watercolor, pastels, pen & ink, drawings, mixed media, collage, paper, sculpture, ceramics, fibers, glass, photography, original handpulled prints and offset reproductions. Most frequently exhibited media: oils, acrylics and mixed media.
Style: Considers all styles. Genres include landscapes, florals, portraits and figurative work. Prefers abstract expression, geometric and figurative works.
Terms: Co-op membership fee plus donation of time 30% commission. Retail price is set by gallery and artist. Exclusive area representation not required. Gallery provides insurance, promotion and contract.
Submissions: Send query letter and SASE. Write to schedule an appointment to show a portfolio, which should include slides.

PRINTED MATTER, INC., 7 Lispenard St., New York NY 10013. (212)925-0325. Director: John Goodwin.
Profile: Nonprofit gallery. Estab. 1976. Clientele: international. Represents 2,500 artists. Interested in

emerging and established artists. Overall price range: 50 cents-$3,500; most artwork sold at $20.
Media: Considers only artwork in book form in multiple editions.
Terms: Accepts work on consignment (50% commission). Retail price is set by artist. Exclusive area representation not required. Gallery provides promotion and contract; artist pays for shipping.
Submissions: Send query letter and review copy of book.

NATHAN SILBERBERG GALLERY, 16 E. 79th St., New York NY 10021. (212)861-6192. Also at: 832 W. Broadway, New York NY 10012. (212)861-6192. Owner: Nathan Silberberg.
Profile: Retail gallery. Estab. 1973. Clientele: collectors and galleries. Represents 10 artists. Sponsors 3 solo and 1 group shows/year. Average display time is 1 month. Interested in emerging and established artists. Overall price range: $5,000-100,000.
Media: Considers oils, watercolor, pastels, pen & ink, drawings, mixed media, collage, paper and sculpture.
Terms: Retail price is set by gallery and artist. Gallery provides insurance and contract; shipping costs are shared.
Submissions: Send query letter and resume. Call or write to schedule an appointment to show a portfolio.

SOHO CENTER FOR VISUAL ARTISTS, 114 Prince St., New York NY 10012. (212)226-1995. President: Larry Aldrich.
Profile: Nonprofit gallery. Estab. 1973. Clientele: 75% private collectors, 25% corporate clients. "We offer one-time group shows." Sponsors 7 group shows/year. Average display time is 5 weeks. Accepts only New York City artists. Interested in emerging artists. Overall price range: $1,000-3,000.
Media: Considers oils, acrylics, drawings, mixed media, collage and sculpture.
Style: "The Soho Center for Visual Artists is a nonprofit exhibition gallery sponsored by the Aldrich Museum of Contemporary Art, CT and the Mobil Foundation. Established in 1973, the Center sponsors group exhibitions of emerging New York City-based artists who are not represented by commercial galleries in New York."
Terms: Accepts work on consignment (No commission). Retail price is set by artist. Exclusive area representation not required. Gallery provides promotion and contract; artist pays for shipping.
Submissions: Send 20 slides of recent work, resume and SASE. Portfolio should include slides and transparencies. "Contact the Center for times for slide review."

STUX GALLERY, 155 Spring St., New York NY 10012. (212)219-0010. Director: Stefan Stux.
Profile: Retail gallery. Clientele: 80% private collectors, 20% corporate clients. Represents 10 artists. Sponsors 10 solo and 2 group shows/year. Average display time is 3½ weeks. Interested in emerging and established artists. Overall price range: $1,000-10,000; most artwork sold at $2,500-10,000.
Media: Considers oils, acrylics, watercolor, pastels, mixed media, paper sculpture, ceramics, photograph and original handpulled prints.
Style: Open to any style.
Terms: Accepts work on consignment (50% commission). Retail price is set by gallery and artist. Exclusive area representation required. Gallery provides insurance, promotion and contract.
Submissions: "The Director/Owner views materials with the artist present by appointment. Portfolio should include slides and transparencies. For artist unable to view materials with Director/Owner, send resume, slides, transparencies etc. and SASE."

JOHN SZOKE GRAPHICS, INC., 164 Mercer St., New York NY 10012. (212)219-8300. Director: John Szoke.
Profile: Retail gallery. Estab. 1973. Represents 50 artists. Sponsors 4 solo and 4 group shows/year. Average display time is 1 month. Accepts only prints. Interested in emerging and established artists. Overall price range: $200-1,000; most artwork sold at $500.
Media: Considers limited edition prints. Most frequently exhibited media: silkscreens, etchings and mezzotints.
Style: Exhibits painterly abstraction and realism. Genres include landscapes, florals, Americana, Western and figurative work. "John Szoke Graphics specializes in limited editions of contemporary prints."
Terms: Work bought outright. Retail price is set by gallery and artist. Exclusive area representation required. Gallery provides promotion and contract; artist pays for shipping.
Submissions: Send query letter, slides and SASE. Call or write to schedule an appointment to show a portfolio, which should include originals and slides. Query letter and visuals are filed.

TERNE GALLERY, 38 East 57th St., New York NY 10022. (212)593-1881. Director: John Michael.
Profile: Retail gallery. Estab. 1986. Clientele: art collectors; 50% private collectors, 50% corporate cli-

ents. Represents 20 artists. Sponsors 5 solo and 1 group shows/year. Average display time is 1 month. Interested in emerging and established artists. Overall price range: $2,500-200,000; most artwork sold at $5,000-10,000.
Media: Considers oils, acrylics, watercolor, pastels, pen & ink, drawings, mixed media, collage, paper, sculpture, glass and installations. Most frequently exhibited media: oil, acrylic and watercolor.
Style: Exhibits color field, painterly abstraction, conceptualism, post-modern, impressionism and neo-expressionism.
Terms: Accepts work on consignment (50% commission). Retail price is set by gallery and artist. Exclusive area representation required. Gallery provides insurance, promotion, contract and shipping.
Submissions: Send resume, slides and photographs. Call to schedule an appointment to show a portfolio, which should include originals, slides and transparencies. Slides, photographs and literature are filed.

ALTHEA VIAFORA GALLERY, 568 Broadway, New York NY 10012. (212)925-4422. Director: Althea Viafora.
Profile: Retail gallery. Estab. 1981. Clientele: 75% private collectors, 25% corporate clients. Represents 10 artists. Sponsors 8 solo and 3 group shows/year. Average display time is 1 month. Interested in emerging and established artists. Overall price range: $2,500-25,000; most artwork sold at $3,000-10,000.
Media: Considers oils, acrylics, watercolor, pastels, pen & ink, drawings, mixed media, collage, paper, sculpture, installations, photography and original handpulled prints. Most frequently exhibited media: acrylic on canvas, oil on canvas and photography.
Style: Exhibits painterly abstraction, conceptualism, surrealism and expressionism. Genres include landscapes and figurative work.
Terms: Accepts work on consignment. Retail price is set by gallery and artist. Gallery provides insurance and promotion.

VIRIDIAN GALLERY, 52 W. 57 St., New York NY 10019. (212)245-2882. Director: Paul Cohen.
Profile: Cooperative gallery. Estab. 1970. Clientele: consultants, corporations, private collectors; 50% private collectors, 50% corporate clients. Represents 31 artists. Sponsors 13 solo and 2 group shows/year. Average display time is 3 weeks. Interested in emerging and established artists. Overall price range: $1,000-15,000; most artwork sold at $2,000-8,000.
Media: Considers oils, acrylics, watercolors, pastels, pen & ink, drawings, mixed media, collage, paper, sculpture, installations, photography and limited edition prints. Most frequently exhibited media: oil, sculpture and mixed media.
Style: Exhibits hard-edge/geometric abstraction, color field, painterly abstraction, conceptualism, post-modern, primitivism, impressionism, photorealism, expressionism, neo-expressionism and realism. Genres include landscapes, florals, portraits and figurative work. "Eclecticism is Viridian's policy. The only unifying factor is quality. Work must be of the highest technical and aesthetic standards."
Terms: Accepts work on consignment (20% commission). Retail price is set by gallery and artist. Exclusive area representation not required. Gallery provides insurance, shipping, promotion and contract.
Submissions: Send query letter and SASE.

VORPAL GALLERY, 411 W. Broadway, New York NY 10012. (212)334-3939. Contact: Alicia Restrepo.
Profile: Estab. 1961. Clientele: 80% private collectors, 20% corporate clients. Represents 75 artists. Sponsors 15 solo and 19 group shows/year. Average display time is 4-5 weeks. Interested in emerging and established artists. Overall price range: $1,000-30,000; most artwork sold at $3,500-18,000.
Media: Considers oils, acrylics, watercolors, pastels, pen & ink, drawings, sculpture, collage and original handpulled prints.
Style: Exhibits contemporary, abstract, impressionism, figurative, landscapes, non-representationaism, realism, and neo-expressionism.
Terms: Accepts work on consignment. Retail price is set by gallery. Exclusive area representation required. Gallery provides insurance, promotion and contract; shipping costs are shared.
Submissions: Send query letter, resume, brochure, business card, slides, photographs and SASE. Responds in 6-8 weeks.

WIESNER GALLERY, 8812 Third Ave., Brooklyn NY 11209. (718)748-1322. Director: Nikola Vizler.
Profile: Retail gallery and art consultancy. Estab. 1985. Clientele: 50% private collectors, 50% corporate clients. Represents 30 artists. Sponsors 5 solo and 5 group shows/year. Average display time is 4 weeks. Interested in emerging and established artists. Overall price range: $200-15,000; most artwork sold at $1,200.
Media: Considers oils, acrylics, watercolor, pastels, pen & ink, drawings, mixed media, collage, pa-

per, sculpture, installations, photography and limited edition prints. Most frequently exhibited media: oils, acrylics and photography.
Style: Exhibits color field, painterly abstraction, minimalism, conceptual, post-modern, feminist/political, neo-expressionism, realism and surrealism. Genres include landscapes, Americana and figurative work. Seeks "strong contemporary works regardless of medium, with artist's statement about his/her viewpoint, philosophy, personal or universal message."
Terms: Accepts work on consignment (50% commission). Retail price is set by gallery and artist. Exclusive area representation not required. Gallery provides insurance and promotion; artist pays for shipping.
Submissions: Send resume, slides and SASE. Write to schedule an appointment to show a portfolio, which should include slides and transparencies. Resumes, slides, photographs, brochures and transparencies are filed.

North Carolina

ART ROOM, Box 53856, 1304 Fort Bragg Rd. Fayetteville NC 28305. (919)486-9111. Gallery Owner/Agent: Nancy Renfrow.
Profile: Retail gallery and art consultancy. Estab. 1987. Clientele: private collectors. Represents approximately 25 artists. Sponsors 4 group shows/year. Average display time is 3-6 months. Accepts Southern artists. Interested in emerging and established artists. Overall price range: $7-7,000; most artwork sold at $300-500.
Media: Considers oils, acrylics, watercolor, pastels, pen & ink, mixed media, fabri-collage, sculpture, ceramics, photography, wearable art, pottery, stained glass, jewelry and original handpulled prints.
Style: Exhibits abstractions, impressionism, photo realism, expressionism and realism. Genres include landscapes, florals, Americana, portraits and figurative work. "Our gallery specializes in quality professional-level original artworks done by Southern artists. "I am particuliaryly interested in uplifting artists of the Southern culture. I do not represent anyone who is currently exhibiting/selling in another business in Fayetteville."
Terms: Accepts work on consignment (30% commission). Retail price is set by gallery and artist. Exclusive area representation required. Gallery provides promotion and contract; artist pays for shipping.
Submissions: Send query letter, resume, business card, photographs and SASE. Call or write to schedule an appointment to show a portfolio. Inventory sheet, consignment agreement and photographs are filed.

CASE ART GALLERY, Atlantic Christian College, Lee St., Wilson NC 27893. (919)237-3161, ext. 365. Gallery Director: Edward Brown.
Profile: Nonprofit gallery. Estab. 1965. Clientele: students, faculty, townpeople, area visitors. Sponsors 3 solo and 4 group shows/year. Average display time is 3½ weeks. Interested in emerging and established artists. Most artwork sold at $350.
Media: Considers oils, acrylics, watercolor, pastels, pen & ink, drawings, mixed media, collage, paper, sculpture, ceramics, crafts, fibers, glass, installations, photography and original handpulled prints. Most frequently exhibited media: fibers, pottery and paintings.
Style: Considers all styles. Genres include landscapes, Americana, figurative work and fantasy illustration. Most frequently exhibited styles: abstract and photo-realistic. Looks for "good craftsmanship, professionally presented, strong design, originality and a variety of styles and subjects."
Terms: "We take no commission on possible sales." Retail price is set by gallery or artist. Gallery provides insurance, promotion and contract; shipping costs are shared.
Submissions: Send query letter with resume. Write to schedule an appointment to show a portfolio, which should include slides. Resumes are filed.

THE JUDGE GALLERY, 905 West Main St., Durham NC 27701. (919)688-8893. Director: Liza Freeze.
Profile: Retail gallery. Estab. 1981. Clientele: "very posh"; 75% private collectors, 25% corporate clients. Represents 50 artists. Sponsors 6 solo shows/year. Interested in emerging and established artists. Overall price range: $1,000-100,000. Average price: $2,000.
Media: Considers all media. Most frequently exhibited media: graphics, oils and acrylics.
Style: Considers all styles. Prefers abstracts and figurative work.
Terms: Accepts work on consignment (50% commission). Retail price is set by gallery or artist. Exclusive area representation required. Gallery provides insurance and promotion.
Submissions: Send query letter with resume, slides and SASE. Include on every slide your name, title, technique, dimensions and retail price. Write to schedule an appointment to show a portfolio. Resumes, brochures and other artist information are filed.

UNION COUNTY PUBLIC LIBRARY, 316 E. Windsor St., Monroe NC 28110. (704)283-8184. Director: Barbara M. Johnson.
Profile: Estab. 9165. Sponsors 8 solo and 6 group shows/year. Average display time is 3 weeks. Interested in emerging and established artists. Overall price range: $50-5,000; most artwork sold at $150-250.
Media: Prefers oil and watercolor; will consider other media.
Style: Exhibits americana, figurative, landscape, floral and realism.
Terms: Accepts work on consignment (10% commission). Retail price is set by gallery and artist. Exclusive area representation not required. Gallery provides promotion and contract.
Submissions: Send query letter with brochure and photographs. Call or write to schedule an appointment to show a portfolio. Artist information and publicity are filed.

WILKES ART GALLERY, 800 Elizabeth St., N. Wilkesboro NC 28659. (919)667-2841. Director: Ms. Marty Moore.
Profile: Nonprofit gallery. Estab. 1962. Clientele: middle-class, 75% private collectors, 25% corporate clients. Represents 71 artists. Sponsors 3 solo and 11 group shows/year. Average display time is 3-4 weeks. Interested in emerging and established artists. Overall price range: $200-9,000; most artwork sold at $500-1,500.
Media: Considers oils, acrylics, watercolor, pastels, pen & ink, mixed media, collage, paper, sculpture, ceramics, fibers, glass, photography and color and b&w limited edition prints and posters. Most frequently exhibited media: watercolor, oil and acrylic.
Style: Exhibits conceptual, primitivism, impressionistic, photo-realistic, expressionistic, realism and surrealism. Genres include landscapes, florals, Americana and figurative work. Most frequently exhibited styles: impressionism, realism and abstract. Currently seeking impressionism.
Terms: Accepts work on consignment (25% commission). Retail price is set by artist. Exclusive area representation not required. Gallery provides insurance, promotion and contract; shipping costs are shared.
Submissions: Send query letter with resume, brochure, slides and SASE. Resumes and brochures are filed.

North Dakota

ARTMAIN, 13 S. Main, Minot ND 58701. (701)838-4747. Partner/Owner: Beth Kjelson and Becky Piehl.
Profile: Retail gallery. Estab. 1981. Represents 12-15 artists. Sponsors 6 solo and 2 group shows/year. Average display time is 4-6 weeks. Interested in emerging artists. Overall price range: $100-500; most artwork sold at $100-300.
Media: Considers oils, acrylics, watercolors, pastels, pen & ink, drawings, ceramics, fibers, photography, crafts, mixed media, collage, original handpulled prints and posters.
Style: Exhibits contemporary, abstract, Americana, impressionistic, landscapes, primitives, non-representational and realistic works. "We specialize in Native American works."
Terms: Accepts work on consignment (30% commission). Retail price is set by gallery and artist. Exclusive area representation required. Gallery provides insurance, promotion and contract; shipping costs are shared.
Submissions: Send query letter, resume, slides or photographs. May call to schedule an appointment to show a portfolio.

THE ARTS CENTER, Box 363, 115 2nd St. SW, Jamestown ND 58402. (701)251-2496. Director: Joan Curtis.
Profile: Nonprofit gallery. Estab. 1981. Sponsors 8 solo and 4 group shows/year. Average display time is 1 month. Interested in emerging and established artists. Overall price range: $50-600; most artwork sold at $50-350.
Style: Exhibits contemporary, abstract, Americana, impressionistic, figurative, landscape, florals, primitives, photo-realistic and realistic work.
Terms: 20% commission on sales from regularly scheduled exhibitions. Retail price is set by artist. Gallery provides insurance, promotion and contract; shipping costs are shared.
Submissions: Send query letter, resume, brochure, slides, photograph and SASE. Write to schedule an appointment to show a portfolio. "Invitation to have an exhibition is extended by Arts Center curator, Jan Berg."

HUGHES FINE ARTS CENTER ART GALLERY, Dept. of Visual Arts, University of North Dakota, Grand Forks ND 58202-8134. (701)777-2257. Director: Brian Paulsen.

Profile: Nonprofit gallery. Estab. 1979. Clientele: students, faculty, staff and tourists. Sponsors 9 solo and 3 group shows/year. Average display time is 3 weeks. Interested in emerging and established artists. Overall price range: $25-1,000; most artwork sold at $25-200.
Media: Considers all media and original handpulled prints. Most frequently exhibited media: photographs, paintings and prints.
Style: Exhibits all styles. Features "unpretentious works which reveal the artists' process, ideas, thoughts, efforts. We avoid slick, gimmicky, overly facile work of established, 'big selling' persons who repeat predictable, shallow, predigested realism or decorative 'artworks' which present nothing new, personal or thought-provoking."
Terms: Retail price is set by artist. Exclusive area representation not required. Gallery provides insurance, shipping and contract.
Submissions: Send query letter and 12-20 slides. Resumes and 6 duplicate slides are filed.

MIND'S EYE GALLERY, Dickinson State University, Dickinson ND 58601. (701)227-2312. Professor of Art, Director: Dennis Navrat.
Profile: Nonprofit gallery. Estab. 1972. Clientele: 100% private collectors. Sponsors 5 solo and 6 group shows/year. Average display time is 3 weeks. Interested in emerging and established artists. Overall price range: $10-3,000; most artwork sold at $10-150.
Media: Considers oils, acrylics, watercolor, pastels, pen & ink, drawings, mixed media, collage, paper, sculpture, ceramics, crafts, fibers, photography and original handpulled prints. Most frequently exhibited media: oil and watercolor paintings and prints.
Style: Exhibits hard-edge/geometric abstraction, color field, painterly abstraction, post-modern, surrealism, impressionism, photo realism, expressionism, neo-expressionism and realism. Genres include landscapes, florals, Americana, Western, portraits and figurative work. "We program diverse exhibits of original visual art in all media. We sponsor a biennial 'Emerging Artists National Art Invitational' in which we welcome the opportunity to review slides and professional resumes of any interested artists. Ten to fifteen artists are invited for this group show. Slides are returned within six months of submission and invitations are extended year-round."
Terms: Retail price is set by artist. Exclusive area representation not required. Gallery provides insurance, promotion and contract; shipping costs are shared.
Submissions: Send query letter, resume, brochure, business card and slides. Write to schedule an appointment to show a portfolio, which should include originals and slides. Artist's names and resumes are filed; slides returned.

Ohio

ALAN GALLERY, 325 Front St., Berea OH 44017. (216)243-7794. President: Alan Boesger.
Profile: Retail gallery and arts consultancy. Estab. 1983. Clientele: 20% private collectors, 80% corporate clients. Represents 25-30 artists. Sponsors 4 solo shows/year. Average display time is 6-8 weeks. Interested in emerging and established artists. Overall price range: $700-6,000; most artwork sold at $1,500-2,000.
Media: Considers all media and limited edition prints. Most frequently exhibited media: watercolor, paper and mixed media.
Style: Exhibits color field, painterly abstraction and surrealism. Genres include landscapes, florals, Western and figurative work.
Terms: Accepts work on consignment (40% commission). Retail price is set by gallery and artist. Exclusive area representation not required. Gallery provides insurance, promotion and contract; shipping costs are shared.
Submissions: Send resume, slides and SASE. Call or write to schedule an appointment to show a portfolio, which should include originals and slides. All material is filed.

TONI BIRCKHEAD GALLERY, 324 W. Fourth St., Cincinnati OH 45202. (513)241-0212. Director: Toni Birckhead.
Profile: Retail gallery and arts consultancy. Estab. 1979. Clientele: 5% private collectors, 95% corporate clients. Represents 80-110 artists. Sponsors 4 solo and 2 group shows/year. Average display time is 6-7 weeks. Interested in emerging and established artists. Overall price range: $500-5,000; most artwork sold at $500-1,000.
Media: Considers oils, acrylics, watercolor, pastels, pen & ink, drawings, mixed media, collage, paper, sculpture, ceramics, installations, photography and original handpulled prints. Most frequently exhibited media: painting, sculpture and works on paper.
Style: Exhibits hard-edge/geometric abstraction, color field, painterly abstraction, minimalism, conceptual post-modern, neo-expressionism and realism.

Terms: Accepts work on consignment (50% commission). Retail price is set by gallery and artist. Exclusive area representation required. Gallery provides insurance, promotion and contract; shipping expenses are shared.
Submissions: Send query letter, resume, slides and SASE. Call or write to schedule an appointment to show a portfolio, which should include originals and slides. Slides, resumes and reviews are filed.

C.A.G.E., 344 W. 4th St., Cincinnati OH 45202. (513)381-2437. Contact: Programming Committee.
Profile: Nonprofit gallery. Estab. 1978. Clientele: mixed, 99.9% private collectors, .1% corporate clients. Sponsors 7-12 group shows/year. Average display time is 1 month. Interested in emerging and established artists. Overall price range: $100-5,000; most artwork sold at $100-500.
Media: Considers all media. Most frequently exhibited media: paintings, mixed media, installation.
Style: Considers all styles; "experimental, conceptual, political, media/time arts, public art and artists' projects encouraged." Most frequently exhibited styles: figurative, photographic and expressionist. "Proposals from artists are accepted and reviewed in January (deadline January 15) for exhibition 14-20 months from deadline. A panel of peer artists selects the exhibitions, and facilitates the showings."
Terms: Retail price is set by artist. Exclusive area representation not required. Gallery provides insurance, promotion and contract.
Submissions: Send query letter with SASE. Resumes, statements, reviews are filed.

THE CANTON ART INSTITUTE, 1001 Market Ave. N., Canton OH 44702. (216)453-7666. Associate Director: M.J. Albacete.
Profile: Nonprofit gallery. Estab. 1935. Sponsors 25 solo and 5 group shows/year. Average display time is 6 weeks. Overall price range: $50-3,000; few sales above $300-500.
Media: Considers all media. Most frequently exhibited media: oils, watercolor and photography.
Style: Considers all styles. Most frequently exhibited styles: painterly abstraction, post-modern and realism.
Terms: "While every effort is made to publicize and promote works, we cannot guarantee sales, although from time to time sales are made, at which time a 25% charge is applied."

CLEVELAND INSTITUTE OF ART GALLERY, 11141 E. Blvd., Cleveland OH 44106. (216)229-0970.
Profile: Nonprofit gallery. Estab. 1957. Clientele: primarily art students, but free and open to the public. Sponsors 2 outside group shows/year. Average display time is 3-4 weeks. Interested in emerging and established artists.
Media: Considers all media.
Style: "We show all styles; excellence is the criterium. On a rotating basis, we attempt to show exhibits representing the 15 disciplines of one studio majors (fine arts, applied design, crafts). On occasion we feature 'distinguished alumnus' work, sometimes contemporary regionsal art, or important movements."
Terms: "Work shown in annual faculty exhibit and annual student show is for sale. (15% commission for the institute)." Gallery provides insurance.

THE A.B. CLOSSON JR. CO.,401 Race St., Cincinnati OH 45202. (513)762-5564. Director: Phyllis Weston.
Profile: Retail gallery. Estab. 1866. Clientele: general. Average display time is 3 weeks. Overall price range: $600-75,000.
Media: Considers oils, watercolor, pastels, mixed media, sculpture, original handpulled prints and limited offset reproductions.
Style: Exhibits all styles and genres.
Terms: Accepts work on consignment or buys outright. Retail price is set by gallery and artist. Exclusive area representation required. Gallery provides insurance and promotion; shipping costs are shared. Portfolio should include originals.

EMILY DAVIS GALLERY, School of Art, University of Akron OH 44235. (216)384-2623. Director: Michael Jones.
Profile: Nonprofit gallery. Estab. 1974. Clientele: persons interested in contemporary/avant-garde art. Sponsors 8 solo and 4 group shows/year. Average display time is 3½ weeks. Interested in emerging and established artists. Overall price range: $100-65,000; "no substantial sales."
Media: Considers all media.
Style: Exhibits contemporary, abstract, figurative, non-representational, photo-realistic, realistic and neo-expressionistic works. Work must be "conceptually rigorous."
Terms: Retail price is set by artist. Exclusive area representation not required. Gallery provides insurance, shipping costs, promotion and contract.
Submissions: Send query letter with resume, brochure, slides, photographs and SASE. Write for an appointment to show a portfolio. Resumes are filed.

IMAGES GALLERY, 4324 W. Central Ave., Ottawa Hills Shopping Center, Toledo OH 43615. (419)537-1400. Owner/Director: Frederick D. Cohn.
Profile: Retail gallery. Estab. 1970. Clientele: 75% private collectors, 25% corporate clients. Represents 40+ artists. Sponsors 9 solo and 3 group shows/year. Average display time is 3-4 weeks. Accepts American artists usually. Interested in emerging and established artists. Most work sold at $750-3,000.
Media: Considers oils, acrylics, watercolor, pastels, pen & ink, drawings, mixed media, collage, paper, sculpture, glass, color and b&w limited edition prints and posters. Most frequently exhibited media: painting, sculpture and graphics.
Style: Exhibits hard-edge/geometric abstraction, color field, painterly abstraction, pattern painting, photo-realistic and realism. Genres include landscapes, florals, Americana, portraits and figurative work.
Terms: Accepts work on consignment (commission varies). Gallery provides insurance and promotion; shipping costs are shared. Will provide contract if required.
Submissions: Send query letter with slides. Call or write for an appointment to show a portfolio, which should include slides.

MILLER GALLERY, 2715 Erie Ave., Cincinnati OH 45208. (513)871-4420. Co-Directors: Barbara and Norman Miller.
Profile: Retail gallery. Estab. 1960. Located in affluent suburb. Clientele: 70% private collectors, 30% corporate clients. Represents about 50 artists. Sponsors 4 solo and 3 group shows/year. Average display time 3 months. Interested in emerging and established artists. Overall price range: $25-15,000; most work sold at $300-3,500.
Media: Considers, oils, acrylics, mixed media, collage, paper, ceramics, fiber, glass and original handpulled prints. Most frequently exhibited media: oils or acrylics, original etchings, lithographs and blown glass.
Style: Exhibits painterly abstraction, impressionism and realism. Genres include landscapes, florals and figurative work. "The ideal artworks for us are those executed in a sure, authoritative technique, not overworked, and not trite. We especially seek both fine realism and nonsubjective paintings; the realism must not include covered bridges or sentiment. Landscapes preferred and must have depth, substance and fine technique. Nonsubjective works must be handled with assurance and not be overworked or busy. We prefer medium to large paintings."
Terms: Accepts artwork on consignment (50% commission); buys outright when appropriate (50% markup). Retail price set by artist and gallery. Exclusive area representation is required. Gallery provides insurance, promotion and contract; shipping costs are shared.
Submissions: Send query letter with resume, brochure, slides or photographs, wholesale (artist) and selling price and SASE. "All material is filed if we're interested, none if not."

GRETA PETERSON GALERIE, 7696 Camargo Rd., Cincinnati OH 45243. (513)561-6785. Director: Mrs. Peterson.
Profile: Retail gallery and art consultancy. Estab. 1956. Clientele: 80% private collectors, 20% corporate clients. Represents 15 artists. Sponsors 4 solo and 4 group shows/year. Average display time is 1-2 months. Interested in emerging and established artists. Overall price range: $200-2,000; most artwork sold at $500-1,200.
Media: Considers oils, acrylics, watercolors, pastels, pen & ink, drawings, mixed media, collage, sculpture and fibers. Most frequently exhibited media: acrylics, watercolors and fiber.
Style: Exhibits color field, conceptual and impressionism. Genres include landscapes, florals and figurative work. Prefers impressionism.
Terms: Accepts work on consignment. Retail price is set by gallery and artist. Exclusive area representation not required. Gallery provides promotion and contract; artist pays for shipping.
Submissions: Send slides. Call or write for an appointment to show a portfolio, which should include originals, slides and transparencies. Slides are filed.

SARAH SQUERI GALLERY, Box 14059, Cincinnati OH 45250. (513)621-1650. Director: Sarah Squeri.
Profile: Retail gallery. Estab. 1984. Clientele: private as well as corporate. Represents 200 artists. Sponsors 6-9 group shows/year. Average display time is 6 weeks. Interested in emerging and established artists. Overall price range: $300-10,000; most artwork sold at $300-2,000.
Media: Specializes in 3-D work, especially glass. Considers oils, acrylics, collage, paper, ceramics, fibers and glass.
Style: Exhibits color field, painterly abstraction and architectural works. Genres include landscapes and figurative work.
Terms: Retail price is set by gallery or artist. Exclusive area representation required. Gallery provides

Close-up

Barbara and Norman Miller

Miller Gallery
Cincinnati, Ohio

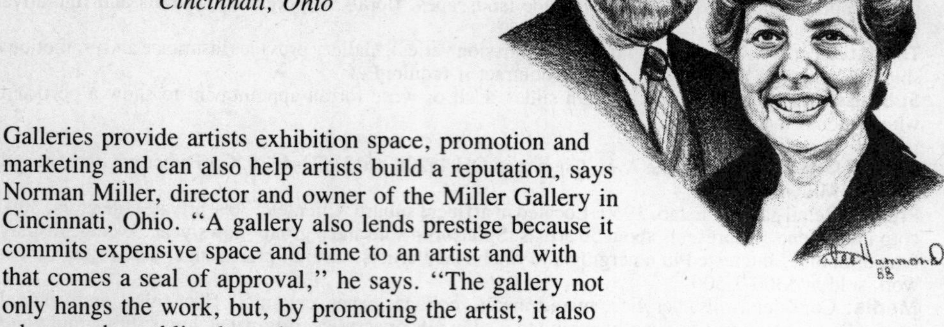

Galleries provide artists exhibition space, promotion and marketing and can also help artists build a reputation, says Norman Miller, director and owner of the Miller Gallery in Cincinnati, Ohio. "A gallery also lends prestige because it commits expensive space and time to an artist and with that comes a seal of approval," he says. "The gallery not only hangs the work, but, by promoting the artist, it also educates the public about that artist's work."

Barbara and Norman Miller opened their gallery in a "comfortable" suburb of Cincinnati 28 years ago and have built a reputation for handling both well-known and new artists. They take on from 5 to 10 new artists each year. Although the gallery does not show experimental or avant garde works, the Millers are not afraid to take risks—Miller Gallery was the first in the country to show contemporary art glass and has been a leader in the exhibition of animation cells and fine crafts. The gallery mainly exhibits paintings, prints and sculpture in both realistic and abstract styles.

"We look for quality, originality, beauty and skill—what we call a sure hand," says Barbara, "and we don't select just one kind of look but choose a variety of works for wide audience appeal."

The Millers advise artists to visit galleries in which they are interested, if at all possible. Artists should do a "thorough browsing" to determine the gallery's philosophy and approach to art before contacting the gallery director. Next, says Norman, make an appointment to show a portfolio. Although a visit is ideal, artists could also mail their slides, photographs or originals. Include a résumé or short biography—most directors like to get to know their artists, he says.

"It's vital to establish a rapport between gallery owners and artists," say the Millers, who see up to 10 portfolios each week. "We try to treat our artists like family—we're honest with them and we never ask them to change their style or approach. This is something gallery directors should never do." They say they try to keep aware of their artists' available work and feel a good working relationship will encourage an artist to show their new and different work.

The Millers recently purchased a videotape player, because they've noticed a number of artists have approached them with videotapes of their work in addition to slides. The videotapes, says Barbara, enable people to see the artist in action. Most include a voiceover describing the artist's methods and philosophy. The tapes can also be shown to customers and make an excellent marketing tool. In the future the Millers plan to make their own videos of featured artists for use in their solo exhibitions.

Miller Gallery holds six to eight shows each year divided evenly between group and solo exhibitions. It's easier for new artists to participate in group shows, says Norman, but these are sometimes built around a theme. In addition to the special exhibitions, the gallery also promotes artists with radio ads on a local classical music station and in local papers. "Word of mouth and mailers are also good promotional tools," he says. "We've built a long list of contacts over the years."

In addition to promotion and exposure, another benefit galleries can provide is a serious art-buying audience. The Millers notice that at many art fairs, most people come to look but not to buy, whereas, most of the Millers' clientele come to purchase artwork. Galleries provide the serious art buyer with information on the artist, an expert opinion on the value of a particular piece and a variety of work from which to choose.

—Robin Gee

"Yellow Tulip," an acrylic on linen, demonstrates artist Anne Shreve's virtuosity as a color impressionist. The Millers discovered her work at an invitational exhibit in Ohio eight years ago. Two of her paintings are now in the new National Museum of Women in the Arts in Washington, D.C.

insurance, promotion and contract; shipping costs are shared.
Submissions: Send query letter with resume and slides. Call or write to schedule an appointment to show a portfolio, which should include slides and resume.

Oklahoma

DAPHNE ART & FRAME GALLERY, INC., 115 N. Main, Sand Springs OK 74063. (918)245-8005. Secretary-Treasurer: Daphne Loyd.
Profile: Retail gallery. Estab. 1967. Clientele: 5% private collectors. Represents 20 artists. Sponsors 1 solo and 2 group shows/year. Average display time is 2 months. Interested in emerging and established artists. Overall price range: $50-2,500; most artwork sold at $150-250.
Media: Considers oils, acrylics, watercolor, pastels, mixed media, collage, sculpture and limited edition prints. Most frequently exhibited media: oils, watercolor and acrylics.
Style: Exhibits post-modern works and impressionism. Genres include landscapes, florals, Americana, Western and Indian art.
Terms: Accepts work on consignment (33⅓% commission) or buys outright (50% markup). Retail price is set by gallery and artist. Exclusive area representation required. Gallery provides insurance, promotion and contract; shipping costs are shared.
Submissions: Send query letter, brochure, slides and photographs. Call for an appointment to show a portfolio, which should include originals and slides.

ALEXANDRE HOGUE, University of Tulsa, 600 S. College Ave., Tulsa OK 74104. (918)592-6000. Associate Professor of Art: C.B. Tomlins.
Profile: Nonprofit gallery. Clientele: students, community members and tourists. Sponsors 4 solo and 2 group shows/year. Average display time is 1 month. Interested in emerging and established artists.
Media: Considers all media and original handpulled prints. Most frequently exhibited media: painting, sculpture and prints.
Style: Exhibits all styles and genres. "Our gallery exhibits all types of work. Selections are made by invitation only."
Terms: Gallery provides insurance, promotion and contract; shipping costs are shared.
Submissions: Send query letter, resume and slides. Write to schedule an appointment to show a portfolio, which should include slides and transparencies.

Oregon

LANE COMMUNITY COLLEGE ART GALLERY, 4000 E. 30th Ave., Eugene OR 97405. (503)747-4501. Gallery Director: Harold Hoy.
Profile: Nonprofit gallery. Estab. 1970. Sponsors 7 solo and 2 group shows/year. Average display time is 3 weeks. Interested in emerging and established artists. Most artwork sold at $100-1,500.
Media: Considers all media.
Style: Exhibits contemporary works.
Terms: Retail price is set by artist. Exclusive area representation not required. Gallery provides insurance, promotion and contract; shipping costs are shared.
Submissions: Send query letter, resume and slides. Resumes are filed.

LAWRENCE GALLERY, 842 S.W. First Ave., Portland OR 97204. (503)224-9442. Director: Kathleen Johnson-Kuhn.
Profile: Retail gallery and art consultancy. Estab. 1982. Clientele: corporate, tourists and collectors; 50% private collectors, 50% corporate clients. Represents 75 artists. Sponsors 11 solo and 1 group shows/year. Average display time is 1 month. "Special shows monthly, always revolving work." Interested in emerging and established artists. Overall price range: $200-10,000; most artwork sold at $1,000-2,000.
Media: Considers oils, acrylics, watercolor, pastels, pen & ink, drawings, mixed media, collage, paper, sculpture, ceramics, fibers, glass, photography and original handpulled prints. Most frequently exhibited media: oils, acrylics, ceramics and glass.
Style: Exhibits painterly abstraction, impressionism and photo realism. Genres include landscapes and figurative work.
Terms: Accepts work on consignment (50% commission). Retail price is set by gallery and artist. Exclusive area representation required. Gallery provides insurance, promotion and contract; artist pays for shipping.

Submissions: Send query letter, slides and photographs. Call to schedule an appointment to show a portfolio, which should include originals, slides and transparencies. All material is filed.

LAWRENCE GALLERY, Box 187, Sheridan OR 97378. (503)943-3633. Director: Anna Eason.
Profile: Retail gallery and art consultancy. Estab. 1977. Clientele: tourists, Portland and Salem residents; 80% private collectors, 20% corporate clients. Represents 150 artists. Sponsors 7 2-person and 1 group shows/year. Interested in emerging and established artists. Overall price range: $10-10,000; most artwork sold at $250-1,500.
Media: Considers oils, acrylics, watercolor, pastels, pen & ink, drawings, mixed media, collage, sculpture, ceramics, fibers, glass, jewelry and original handpulled prints. Most frequently exhibited media: oils, watercolor, metal sculpture and ceramics.
Style: Exhibits painterly abstraction, impressionism, photo realism and realism. Genres include landscapes, florals and Americana. "Our gallery features beautiful art-pieces that celebrate life."
Terms: Accepts work on consignment (50% commission). Retail price is set by artist. Exclusive area representation required. Gallery provides insurance, promotion and contract; artist pays for shipping.
Submissions: Send query letter, resume, brochure, slides and photographs. Write for an appointment to show a portfolio. Resumes, photos of work, newspaper articles, and other informative pieces and artist's statement about his work are filed.

LITTMAN GALLERY, Portland State University, Box 751, 1925 SW Broadway, Portland OR 97207. (503)464-4452. Director: Lonnie Feather.
Profile: Nonprofit gallery. Estab. 1972. Clientele: university students and local business people. Sponsors 6 solo and 2 group shows/year. Average display time is 4 weeks. Interested in emerging and established artists. Overall price range: $200-12,000; most artwork sold at $200-300.
Media: Considers oils, acrylics, watercolor, pastels, pen & ink, drawings, mixed media, collage, paper, sculpture, ceramics, crafts, fibers, glass, installations, performance and original handpulled prints. Most frequently exhibited media: oils and sculpture.
Terms: Accepts work on consignment. Retail price is set by artist. Exclusive area representation not required. Gallery provides insurance and promotion; artist pays for shipping.
Submissions: Send query letter, resume, slides and SASE. Call to schedule an appointment to show a portfolio, which should include slides.

NORTHVIEW GALLERY, 12000 SW 49th, Portland OR 97219. (503)244-6111. Director: Robert R. Dozono.
Profile: Nonprofit gallery. Sponsors 9-10 shows/year. Average display time is 3 weeks. Interested in emerging and established artists. Overall price range: $100-3,000; most artwork sold at $100-600.
Media: Considers oils, acrylics, watercolor, pastels, pen & ink, drawings, mixed media, collage, sculpture, ceramics, crafts, fibers, glass, installations, photography, color and b&w original handpulled prints and posters.
Style: Exhibits all styles and genres.
Terms: Accepts work on consignment; no commission. Retail price is set by artist. Exclusive area representation not required. Gallery provides insurance, promotion and contract; shipping costs are shared.
Submissions: Send query letter with resume, slides, photograph and SASE.

ROGUE GALLERY, 40 S. Bartlett, Medford OR 97501. (503)772-8118. Executive Director: Deborah Dozier.
Profile: Nonprofit sales and rental gallery. Estab. 1960. Clientele: valley residents and tourists; 95% private collectors, 5% corporate clients. Represents 375 artists. Main gallery sponsors 12 exhibits/year; "rental gallery changes monthly." Average display time is 6 months. Interested in emerging and established artists. Overall price range in rental shop: $50-1,200; most artwork sold at $300-600.

> ***"My first assignment was to illustrate an article for the* Boston Globe. *Fresh out of Boston University, I showed my portfolio to one of the editors. After looking through my portfolio, he took a manuscript from his desk and said, 'If you can come up with something good, we'll use it."***
>
> ***—Tom Swick***
> ***San Francisco, California***

Media: Considers all media and original handpulled prints.
Style: Exhibits all styles and genres.
Terms: Accepts work on consignment (35% commission) in rental gallery. Retail price is set by artist. Exclusive area representation not required. Gallery provides insurance and promotion; artist pays for shipping.
Submissions: Send resume and slides. Call or write to schedule an appointment to show a portfolio, which should include originals, slides and transparencies. Resumes are filed, slides returned.

Pennsylvania

CONCEPT ART GALLERY, 1031 S. Braddock Ave., Pittsburgh PA 15218. (412)242-9200. Director: Sam Berkovitz.
Profile: Retail gallery. Estab. 1971. Clientele: 50% private collectors, 50% corporate clients. Represents 40 artists. Sponsors 4 solo and 4 group shows/year. Average display time is 1 month. Interested in emerging and established artists. Overall price range: $50-25,000; most artwork sold at $300-1,000.
Media: Considers oils, acrylics, watercolor, pastels, pen & ink, drawings, mixed media, collage, paper, sculpture, ceramics, crafts, fibers, glass and limited edition original handpulled prints. Most frequently exhibited media: watercolors, prints and paintings.
Style: Exhibits hard-edge/geometric abstraction, color field, painterly abstraction, impressionistic, photo-realistic, expressionistic and neo-expressionistic works. Genres include landscapes and florals.
Terms: Accepts work on consignment (25-50% commission) or buys outright. Retail price is set by gallery. Exclusive area representation required. Gallery provides insurance and promotion; shipping costs are shared.
Submissions: Send query letter with resume, brochure, slides, photographs and SASE. Slides and biographies are filed.

DORIS FORDHAM GALLERY, INC., 421 S. State St., Clarks Summit PA 18411. (717)586-0088. President: Doris Fordham.
Profile: Retail gallery and art consultancy. Estab. 1980. Clientele: 50% private collectors, 50% corporate clients. Represents 15 artists/year. Sponsors 6 solo shows/year. Average display time is 3-6 weeks. Interested in professional artists only. Overall price range: $250-5,000; most artwork sold at $500-1,500.
Media: Considers oils, acrylics, watercolor, pastels, mixed media, collage and limited edition original handpulled prints. Most frequently exhibited media: watercolor, oils and pastels.
Style: Exhibits painterly abstraction, impressionistic, expressionistic, neo-expressionistic, realism, surrealism and naif works. Genres include landscapes, florals, portraits, figurative work and still life. Most frequently exhibited styles: landscape, floral and still life.
Terms: Accepts work on consignment (40% commission). Buys limited edition multiples outright (net 30 days). Retail price is set by gallery or artist. Exclusive area representation not required. Gallery provides insurance, promotion and contract; shipping costs are shared.
Submissions: Send query letter with resume and slides "then write for arrangements to show original work." Resume and "my notations concerning the work" are filed.

FREEDMAN GALLERY, ALLBRIGHT COLLEGE, Box 15234, Reading PA 91612-5234. (215)921-2381. Director: David S. Rubin.
Profile: Nonprofit gallery. Estab. 1976. Clientele: college community and general public. Sponsors 5 solo and 3 group shows/year. Average display time is 4-6 weeks. Interested in emerging and established artists.
Media: Considers oils, acrylics, watercolor, pastels, pen & ink, drawings, mixed media, collage, paper, sculpture, ceramics, fibers, installations, photography, performance, video and prints. Most frequently exhibited media: painting, sculpture and photography.
Style: Considers all styles. Seeks "work that is substantive in content, innovative in form, and provocative in impact."
Terms: Retail price is set by artist. Exclusive area representation not required. Gallery provides insurance, shipping costs, promotion and contract.
Submissions: Send query letter with resume, slides and SASE. Resume and slides are filed "when appropriate."

THE KLING GALLERY, 2301 Chestnut St., Philadelphia PA 19103. (215)569-2900. Director: Susan Cavanaugh.
Profile: Nonprofit gallery. Clientele: 70% private collectors, 30% corporate clients. Sponsors 10 solo

and 2 group shows/year. Average display time is 1 month. Interested in emerging and established artists. Overall price range: $300-10,000; most artwork sold at $500-1,000.
Media: Considers oils, acrylics, watercolors, pastels, pen & ink, drawings, mixed media, collage, photography and color original handpulled prints. Most frequently exhibited media: oils, acrylics and watercolors.
Style: Exhibits painterly abstraction, conceptual, impressionistic, photo-realistic, expressionistic and realism. Genres include landscapes, florals, Americana, portraits, figurative work and fantasy illustration. Most frequently exhibited styles: portraits, figurative and landscapes/floral.
Terms: Retail price is set by artist. Exclusive area representation not required. Gallery provides insurance and promotion.
Submissions: Send query letter with resume, brochure, slides and photographs. Write for an appointment to show a portfolio, which should include originals and slides. Bios and press clippings are filed.

PHILADELPHIA ART ALLIANCE, 251 S. 18th St., Philadephia PA 19103. Director: Dr. Marilyn Goodman.
Profile: Nonprofit gallery. Estab. 1915. Clientele: members and public; 50% private collectors, 50% corporate clients. Sponsors 14 solo and 7 group shows/year. Average display time is 6 weeks. Interested in emerging and established artists. Overall price range: $100 and up; most artwork sold at $500.
Media: Considers all media. Most frequently exhibited media: oils, acrylics, and drawings.
Style: Exhibits contemporary, abstract, primitive and non-representational.
Terms: Accepts work on consignment (40% commission). Retail price is set by gallery or artist. Exclusive area representation not required. Gallery provides insurance, promotion and contract; shipping costs are shared.
Submissions: Send query letter with resume and slides. One color slide with resume are filed.

Rhode Island

ARNOLD ART, 210 Thames, Newport RI 12840. (401)847-2273. President: Bill Rommel.
Profile: Retail gallery. Estab. 1870. Clientele: tourists and Newport collectors; 95% private collectors, 5% corporate clients. Represents 10-20 artists. Sponsors 6-8 solo or group shows/year. Average display time: 2 weeks. Overall price range: $150-12,000; most artwork sold at $150-750.
Media: Considers oils, acrylics, watercolor, pastels, pen & ink, drawings, mixed media, limited edition offset reproductions, color prints and posters. Most frequently exhibited media: oils, acrylics and watercolors.
Style: Exhibits painterly abstraction, primitivism, photo-realistic and realism. Genres include landscapes and florals. Specializes in marine art and local landscapes.
Terms: Accepts work on consignment. Retail price is set by gallery or artist. Exclusive area representation not required. Gallery provides insurance, promotion and contract.
Submissions: Send query letter with resume and slides. Call for an appointment to show a portfolio, which should include originals. Resume and slides are filed.

LENORE GRAY GALLERY, INC., 15 Meeting St., Providence RI 02903. (401)274-3900. Director: Lenore Gray.
Profile: Retail gallery. Estab. about 1970. Sponsors 6 solo and 6 group shows/year. Average display varies. Interested in emerging and established artists.
Media: Considers oils, acrylics, watercolors, pastels, drawings, sculpture, photography, mixed media, glass, installations and color and b&w original handpulled prints.
Style: Exhibits contemporary, abstract, Americana, impressionistic, figurative, landscape, primitive, non-representational, photo-realistic, realistic, neo-expressionisitic and post-pop works.
Terms: Accepts work on consignment. Retail price is set by gallery or artist. Exclusive area representation required. Gallery provides insurance.
Submissions: Send query letter with resume, slides, photographs or SASE. Write for an appointment to show a portfolio.

South Carolina

ARTISTIC SASS, INC., 14 Greenwood Dr., Hilton Head SC 29928. (803)785-8442. Director: Richard L. Tarchinski.
Profile: Retail gallery. Estab. 1979. Clientele: upscale; 90% private collectors. Represents 35 artists.

Sponsors 3 solo and 8 group shows/year. Average display time is 3 months. Accepts contemporary American artists only. Overall price range: $10-2,500; most artwork sold at $500 and under.
Media: Considers oils, acrylics, pastels, sculpture, ceramics, fibers, photography, crafts, mixed media, collage and glass. Currently looking for glass, clay and furniture.
Style: Exhibits contemporary, abstract and nonrepresentational works. Currently seeking contemporary. Looks for "excellent craftsmanship and design."
Terms: Accepts work on consignment. Retail price is set by gallery or artist. Exclusive area representation required. Gallery provides insurance, promotion and contract; shipping costs are shared.
Submissions: Send query letter with resume, slides, photographs and SASE. Call or write to schedule an appointment to show a portfolio. Letters, resumes, slides and photographs are filed.

CECELIA COKER BELL GALLERY, College Ave., Hartsville, SC 29550. (803)332-1381. Director: Kim Chalmers.
Profile: "The Cecelia Coker Bell Gallery is a campus-located teaching gallery which exhibits a great diversity of media and style to the advantage of exposing students and the community to the breadth of possibility for expression in art. Primarily exhibiting regional artists with an emphasis on quality. Features international shows of emerging artists, and sponsors competitions." Estab. 1984. Sponsors 8 solo and 2 group shows/year. Average display time is 3 weeks. Interested in emerging and established artists.
Media: Considers oils, acrylics, drawings, mixed media, collage, paper, sculpture, installations, photography, performance, graphic design and printmaking. Most frequently exhibited media: painting, sculpture/installation and mixed media.
Style: Considers all styles.
Terms: Retail price is set by artist. Exclusive area representation not required. Gallery provides insurance, promotion and contract; shipping costs are shared.
Submissions: Send query letter with resume, slides and SASE. Write for an appointment to show a portfolio, which should include slides. Resumes are filed.

THE GALLERY (sponsored by Spartanburg County Art Association), Arts Center, 385 S. Spring St., Spartanburg SC 29301. (803)582-7616. Curator: Pamela Nienhuis.
Profile: Nonprofit gallery. Estab. 1967. Clientele: Art Association membership, local visitors and vacationers. Sponsors 4-5 solo and 8-9 group shows/year and annual crafts show. Average display time for "special exhibits one month; permanent sales rotated, but no time limit involved. "For permanent display, usually only local or area artists are represented because of the inconvenience in shipping. Overall price range: $50-2,500; most artwork sold at $100-600 "at special shows, from permanent exhibit usually less."
Media: Considers oils, acrylics, watercolors, pastels, pen & ink, drawings, sculpture, ceramics, fibers, photography, crafts, mixed media, collage, glass and original handpulled prints.
Style: Exhibits contemporary, abstract, impressionistic, landscape, primitive, non-representational, photo-realistic, realistic and neo-expressionistic works. "We have a varied schedule representing most styles, but for sales traditional, realistic works are most popular."
Terms: Accepts work on consignment (⅓ commission). Retail price is set by artist. Exclusive area representation not required. Gallery provides insurance, promotion and contract; gallery sometimes pays return shipping costs.
Submissions: Send query letter with resume, brochure, slides, photographs SASE and prices.

South Dakota

DAHL FINE ARTS CENTER, 713 7th St., Rapid City SD 47701. (605)394-4101. Executive Director: Ruth Brennan.
Profile: Nonprofit gallery. Estab. 1974. Clientele: general public; 100% private collectors. Sponsors 16 solo and 8 group shows/year. Average display time is 4 weeks. Interested in emerging and established artists. Overall price range: $100-2,000; most artwork sold at $400 and under.
Media: Considers all media and original handpulled prints.
Style: Exhibits contemporary, impressionistic, figurative, non-representational and realistic works. Specializes in impressionistic realism. "Because our operation is an art center with two galleries, each with a different focus, our thrust leans toward education and therefore does not specialize more narrowly than the broad style of 'contemporary'."
Terms: Accepts work on consignment (33% commission). Retail price is set by gallery or artist. Exclusive area representation not required. Gallery provides insurance, promotion, contract and shipping.

Submissions: Send query letter, resume, slides and SASE. Call or write to schedule an appointment to show a portfolio. "We return most information to the artist, but we are beginning to build an artists' file of resumes and slides. The cost of duplicating slides limits this project."

THE HERITAGE CENTER, INC., Red Cloud Indian School, Pine Ridge SD 47770. (605)867-5491. Director: Brother Simon.
Profile: Nonprofit gallery. Estab. 1984. Clientele: 80% private collectors. Sponsors 6 group shows/year. Average display time is 10 weeks. Accepts only Native Americans. Overall price range: $50-1,500; most artwork sold at $100-400.
Media: Considers oils, acrylics, watercolors, pastels, pen & ink, drawings, sculpture and original handpulled prints.
Style: Exhibits contemporary, impressionistic, primitive, Western and realistic works.
Terms: Accepts work on consignment (20% commission). Retail price is set by artist. Exclusive area representation not required. Gallery provides insurance and promotion; artist pays for shipping.
Submissions: Send query letter, resume, brochure and photographs.

Tennessee

THE PARTHENON, Centennial Park, Nashville TN 37201. (615)259-6358. Museum Director: Miss Wesley Paine.
Profile: Nonprofit gallery in a full-size replica of the Greek Parthenon. Estab. 1931. Clientele: general public, tourists; 50% private collectors, 50% corporate clients. Sponsors 15 solo and 8 group shows/year. Average display time is 1 month. Interested in emerging and established artists. Overall price range: $300-1,000; most artwork sold at $400.
Media: Considers "nearly all" media.
Style: Exhibits contemporary, impressionistic and American expressionism. Currently seeking contemporary works.
Terms: Accepts work on consignment (20% commission). Retail price is set by artist. Exclusive area representation not required. Gallery provides a contract and limited promotion.
Submissions: Send query letter with resume and slides.

SLOCUMB GALLERY, East Tennessee State University, Department of Art, Box 23740A, Johnson City, TN 37614-0002. (615)929-4247. Director: M. Wayne Dyer.
Profile: Nonprofit gallery. Estab. 1960. Sponsors 2-3 solo and 5 group shows/year. Average display time is 1 month. Interested in emerging and established artists.
Media: Considers all media.
Style: Exhibits contemporary, abstract, figurative, landscape, primitive, non-representational, photo-realistic, realism, neo-expressionistic and post-pop styles.
Submissions: Send query letter with resume and slides. Call or write to schedule an appointment to show a portfolio. Slides and resumes are filed.

MARGARET FORT TRAHERN GALLERY, State University, Box 4677, Clarksville TN 37044. (615)648-7333. Gallery Director: Dr. James Diehr.
Profile: Nonprofit gallery. Estab. 1964. Clientele: cities and university community including Nashville, TN. Sponsors 6 + solo and 4 + group shows/year. Average display time is 3-4 weeks. Prefers Tennessee and southern regional artists. Overall price range: $300 average.
Media: Considers oils, acrylics, watercolors, pen & ink, drawings, sculpture, ceramics, photography, crafts, mixed media, original handpulled prints. and posters. "Media is not important, but quality is important."
Style: Exhibits contemporary, Americana, primitive, photo-realistic, Western and realism.
Terms: Accepts work on consignment. Exclusive area representation not required. "Our budget, insurance and security is very limited." Gallery provides shipping costs and promotion for some exhibits.
Submissions: Send query letter with resume, brochure and business card. "Then if really considered, send slides or photograph."

Texas

ADAMS-MIDDLETON GALLERY, 3000 Maple Ave., Dallas TX 75201. (214)871-7080. Director: Victoria Gaumer.
Profile: Retail gallery. Estab. 1980. Clientele: new and seasoned collectors, large and small

corporations ahd interior designers. Represents 25 artists. Sponsors 9 solo and 3 group shows/year. Average display time is 1 month. Interested in emerging and established artists. Overall price range: $500-100,000; most artwork sold at $4,000-5,000.
Media: Considers oils, acrylics, pastels, drawings, sculpture mixed media, collage and original handpulled prints.
Style: Exhibits contemporary, abstract, figurative, landscapes, non-representational, photo-realistic realistic and post-pop works.
Terms: Accepts work on consignment (50% commission). Retail price is set by gallery and artist. Exclusive area representation required. Gallery provides contract; shipping costs are shared.
Submissions: Send query letter, resume, brochure and slides. Call or write to schedule an appointment to show a portfolio. Slides, resumes, prices "on any artists we might need for presentations or future representation" are filed.

ALTERNATE GALLERY, 3406 Main St., Dallas TX 75226. (214)939-0245. Gallery Directors: Elona or Thomas McCaslin.
Profile: Retail gallery. Estab. 1983. Clientele: private collectors, consultants and artists; 70% private collectors, 30% other. Represents 10 artists. Sponsors 6 solo and 4 group shows/year. Average display time is 5 weeks. Exclusive area representation required. Overall price range: $300-4,000; most artwork sold at $1,000-2,500.
Media: Considers oils, acrylics, drawings, sculpture, ceramics, mixed media and original handpulled prints.
Style: Exhibits contemporary, figurative, landscape, primitive and neo-expressionistic works. Prefers contemporary figurative work.
Terms: Accepts work on consignment (50% commission). Retail price is set by gallery or artist. Exclusive area representation required. Gallery provides promotion and contract; artist pays for shipping.
Submissions: Send query letter, resume, brochure, business card, slides and SASE. Write for an appointment to show a portfolio. Resume, slides and other information are filed; "we return slides upon artist request with a SASE."

ART COMMUNITY CENTER, 902 Park Ave., Corpus Christi TX 78401. (512)884-6406. Director: Alley Josey.
Profile: Nonprofit gallery. Estab. 1972. Clientele: 90% private collectors, 10% corporate clients. Has 350 members. Sponsors 9 solo and 26 group shows/year. Average display time is 1 month. Interested in emerging artists. Overall price range: $100-1,000.
Media: Considers oils, acrylics, watercolor, pastels, pen & ink, drawings, mixed media, collage, sculpture, fibers and photography. Most frequently exhibited media: oil, acrylics, and watercolor.
Style: Exhibits painterly abstraction, impressionism and realism. Genres include landscapes, florals and portraits. "Our exhibits are competitive with the artist determining the concept of the artwork to be entered. The same applies to our one-artist exhibits. To show in our gallery the artist must be a member."
Terms: Retail price is set by artist. Exclusive area representation not required. Gallery provides insurance and promotion; artist pays for shipping.
Submissions: Send query letter. "We are interested in those artists who want to become members of the center."

ART LEAGUE OF HOUSTON, 1953 Montrose Blvd., Houston TX 77006. (713)523-9530. Exhibitions Coordinator: Jack Boynton.
Profile: Nonprofit gallery. Estab. 1948. Clientele: general; 60% private collectors. Sponsors 20+ group shows/year. Average display time is 4-5 weeks. Interested in emerging and established artists. Overall price range: $10-10,000; most artwork sold at $100-1,000.
Media: Considers all media and original handpulled prints.
Style: Exhibits contemporary work. Features "high-quality artwork reflecting serious aesthetic investigation and innovation. The work should additionally have a sense of personal vision."
Terms: Accepts work on consignment (20% commission, optional). Retail price is set by artist. Exclusive area representation not required. Gallery provides insurance, promotion and contract; shipping costs are shared.
Submissions: Send query letter, resume and slides. Slides, resumes and brochure are filed.

THE BARRETT GALLERY, 2717 N. Stanton, El Paso TX 79902. (915)545-1415. Owner: Elizabeth Barrett Edmunds.
Profile: Retail gallery. Estab. 1979. Represents 15 artists. Sponsors 4 group shows/year. Average display time is 8 months. Interested in emerging and established artists. Overall price range:

$300-1,500; most artwork sold at $400-500.
Media: Considers drawings, ceramics, fibers, crafts, mixed media, collage and original handpulled prints. Most frequently exhibited media: serigraphs, lithographs and intaglio prints.
Style: Exhibits contemporary, abstract, impressionistic, landscapes, primitives, non-representational works and still lifes.
Terms: Accepts work on consignment (40% commission) or buys outright (50% markup; net 30 days). Retail price is set by gallery and artist. Exclusive area representation required. Gallery provides insurance, promotion and contract; shipping costs are shared.
Submissions: Send query letter, resume, slides or photographs. "Anything the artist doesn't have to have back" is filed.

CONTEMPORARY GALLERY, 4152 Shady Bend Dr., Dallas TX 75244. (214)247-5246. Director: Pasty C. Kahn.
Profile: Retail gallery. Estab. 1964. Clientele: collectors and retail. Interested in emerging and established artists.
Media: Considers oils, acrylics, drawings, sculpture, mixed media and original handpulled prints.
Style: Contemporary, twentieth century art—paintings, graphics and sculpture.
Terms: Accepts work on consignment or buys outright. Retail price is set by gallery and artist. Gallery provides insurance, promotion and contract; shipping costs are shared.
Submissions: Send query letter, resume, slides and photographs. Write for an appointment to show a portfolio.

EAGLE'S NEST GALLERY, 1202 San Antonio St., Austin TX 78701. (512)453-2012. Director: Carole Gollhofer.
Profile: Retail gallery. Estab. 1977. Represents 35 artists. Sponsors 2-3 solo and 6-8 group shows/year. Average display time is 4 weeks. Interested in emerging and established artists. Overall price range: $200-2,500; most artwork sold at $300-500.
Media: Considers oils, acrylics, watercolors, pastels, pen & ink, drawings, sculpture, ceramics, fibers, crafts, mixed media, collage, glass, installations and original handpulled prints. Specializes in works on paper and art glass.
Terms: Accepts work on consignment (40% commission) or occasionally buys outright (50% markup). Retail price is set by gallery and artist. Exclusive area representation required. Gallery provides insurance, promotion and contract; shipping costs are shared.
Submissions: Send query letter, resume, brochure, slides, photographs and SASE. Write for an appointment to show a portfolio. Resumes, brochures and slides are filed.

GALLERY 1114, 1114 North Big Spring, Midland TX 79701. (915)685-9944. Exhibits Chairman: Michael Banschbach.
Profile: Cooperative gallery. Estab. 1983. Clientele: 95% private collectors, 5% business. Represents 15 artists. Sponsors 7 solo and 2 group shows/year. Average display time is 5 weeks. Interested in emerging and established artists. Overall price range: $20-1,000; most artwork sold at $20-200.
Media: Considers oils, acrylics, watercolors, pastels, pen & ink, drawings, sculpture, ceramics, fibers, photography, mixed media and collage.
Style: Exhibits contemporary, abstract, landscapes and primitives. "We are a contemporary artists cooperative. Therefore, we try to present artwork that is new, fresh and non-southwestern; however, we do handle work that is somewhat traditional but with a contemporary flair."
Terms: Accepts work on consignment (40% commission) and co-op membership fee plus donation of time. Retail price is set by artist. Exclusive area representation not required. Gallery provides promotion and contract; shipping costs are shared.
Submissions: Send query letter, resume, brochure, business card, slides, photographs and SASE. Call or write for an appointment to show a portfolio. Resume and slides are filed.

GRAHAM GALLERY, 1431 W. Alabama, Houston TX 77006. (713)528-4957. Director: William Graham.
Profile: Retail gallery. Estab. 1981. Clientele: 70% private collectors, 30% corporate clients. Represents 18 artists. Sponsors 9 solo and 2 group shows/year. Average display time is 1 month. Interested in emerging and established artists. Overall price range: $100-15,000; most artwork sold at $500-2,500.
Media: Considers oils, acrylics, watercolor, pastels, pen & ink, drawings, mixed media, collage, paper, sculpture, ceramics, crafts, fibers, glass, installations, photography and original handpulled prints. Most frequently exhibited media: oils, photos and sculpture.
Terms: Accepts work on consignment (50% commission). Retail price is set by gallery and artist. Exclusive area representation required. Gallery provides insurance, promotion and contract; artist pays for shipping.

JAN PIERCE, INC., Box 331748, Ft. Worth TX 76163-1748. (817)292-3498. President: Jan Pierce.
Profile: Retail gallery and art consultancy. Estab. 1986. Clientele: international; 50% private collectors, 50% corporate clients. Sponsors 2 solo and 2 group shows/year. Average display time is 2 months. Interested in emerging and established artists. Most artwork sold at $3,000-50,000.
Media: Considers oils, acrylics, watercolor, pastels, pen & ink, drawings, mixed media, collage, paper, sculpture, installations, photography and original handpulled prints. Most frequently exhibited media: sculpture, paintings and prints.
Style: Exhibits all styles.
Terms: Accepts work on consignment (25-50% commission). Retail price is set by gallery and artist. Exclusive area representation not required. Gallery provides promotion and contract; shipping costs are shared.
Submissions: Send query letter, resume, brochure, business card, slides, photographs and SASE. Write for an appointment to show a portfolio, which should include originals, slides and transparencies. Resumes, slides (extensive registry), brochures, photographs, business cards, etc. are filed.

VALLEY HOUSE GALLERY, INC., 6616 Spring Valley Rd., Dallas TX 75240. (214)239-2441. Vice President: Kevin Vogel.
Profile: Retail gallery. Estab. 1950. Clientele: 80% private collectors. Represents 8 artists. Sponsors 3-4 solo and 2 group shows/year. Interested in emerging and established artists. Overall price range: $90 and up; most artwork sold at $3,000-10,000.
Media: Considers oils, watercolors, pastels, pen & ink, drawings, sculpture, mixed media, collage and original handpulled prints.
Style: Exhibits contemporary, impressionistic, figurative, landscapes, florals, primitives, nonrepresentational and realistic works. Features "good solid painters specializing in landscapes or using the landscape as an element in their work."
Terms: Accepts work on consignment (50% commission) or buys outright (50% markup). Retail price is set by gallery and artist. Exclusive area representation required. Gallery provides insurance and promotion.
Submissions: Send query letter, resume, slides, photographs and SASE. "Usually any printed material is filed; we return slides."

Utah

APPLE YARD ART, 3096 S. Highland Ave., Salt Lake City UT 84106. (801)467-3621. Manager: Sue Valentine.
Profile: Retail gallery. Estab. 1981. Clientele: 80% private collectors, 20% corporate clients. Represents 10 artists. Sponsors 3 solo shows/year. Average display time is 6 weeks. Overall price range: $50-750; most artwork sold at $225.
Media: Most frequently exhibited media: watercolor, serigraphs and handmade paper.
Style: Exhibits impressionisim. Genres includelandscapes and florals. Prefers impressionistic watercolors.
Terms: Accepts work on consignment (40% commission). Retail price is set by artist. Exclusive area representation required. Gallery provides insurance, promotion and contract; artist pays for shipping.
Submissions: Send query letter, resume and slides. Write for an appointment to show a portfolio, which should include originals.

Vermont

PARADE GALLERY, Box 245, Warren VT 05674. (802)496-5445. Owner: Jeffrey S. Burnett.
Profile: Retail gallery. Estab. 1982. Clientele: tourist and upper middle class second home owners; 98% private collectors. Represents 15-20 artists. Interested in emerging and established artists. Overall price range: $20-2,500; most artwork sold at $50-300.
Media: Considers oils, acrylics, watercolor, pastels, mixed media, collage, paper, sculpture and original handpulled prints. Most frequently exhibited media: etching, silkscreen and watercolor. Currently looking for oil/acrylic and watercolor.
Style: Exhibits primitivism, impressionistic and realism. "Parade Gallery deals primarily with representational works with country subject matter. The gallery is interested in unique contemporary pieces to a limited degree."
Terms: Accepts work on consignment (1/3 commission) or buys outright (net 30 days). Retail price is set by gallery or artist. Exclusive area representation required. Gallery provides insurance and promotion.

Submissions: Send query letter with resume, slides and photographs. Write for an appointment to show a portfolio, which should include originals or slides. Biographies and background are filed.

WOODSTOCK GALLERY AND DESIGN CENTER, Route 4 E., Woodstock VT 05091. (802)457-1900. Gallery Director: Charles E.H. Fenton.
Profile: Retail and rental gallery and art consultancy. Estab. 1971. Clientele: knowledgeable collectors; 75% private collectors, 25% corporate clients. Represents 30-40 artists. Sponsors 3 solo and 6 group shows/year. Average display time is 12 weeks. Interested in emerging and established artists. Overall price range: $250-5,000; most artwork sold at $250-2,000.
Media: Considers all media. Most frequently exhibited media: paint, print and photography. Currently looking for oils and sculptures.
Style: Exhibits painterly abstraction, conceptual, primitivism, impressionistic, expressionistic and realism. Genres include landscapes, florals, Americana, figurative work and fantasy illustration. Most frequently exhibited styles: impressionistic, realistic and conceptual. Currently seeking abstraction and conceptual.
Terms: Accepts work on consignment (40% commission). Retail price is set by gallery or artist. Exclusive area representation required, "with exceptions." Gallery provides insurance, promotion and contract.
Submissions: Send query letter with resume, brochure, slides, photographs and SASE. Write for an appointment to show a portfolio, which should include originals, slides and transparencies. Resume and slides are filed if interested.

Virginia

FINE ARTS CENTER FOR NEW RIVER VALLEY, 21 W. Main St., Pulaski VA 24301. (703)980-7363. Director: Nancy Newhard.
Profile: Nonprofit gallery. Estab. 1978. Clientele: general public, corporate, schools; 80% private collectors, 20% corporate clients. Represents 75 artists and craftspeople (consignment basis only). Sponsors 10 solo and 2 group shows/year. Average display time is 1 month (gallery); 3-6 months (Art Mart). Interested in emerging and established artists. Overall price range: $20-500; most artwork sold at $20-100.
Media: Considers all media. Most frequently exhibited media: oils, watercolors and ceramics. Currently looking for good quality work—media not important.
Style: Exhibits hard-edge/geometric abstraction, painterly abstraction, minimalism, post-modern, pattern painting, feminist/political, primitivism, impressionistic, photo-realistic, expressionistic, neo-expressionistic, realism and surrealism. Genres include landscapes, florals, Americana, western, portraits and figurative work. Most frequently exhibits: landscapes, abstracts, Americana.
Terms: Accepts work on consignment. Interested in emerging and established artists (25% commission). Retail price is set by gallery or artist. Exclusive area representation not required. Gallery provides insurance (80% of value), promotion and contract.
Submissions: Send query letter with resume, brochure, slides, photographs and SASE. Write for an appointment to show a portfolio, which should include slides. Slides and resumes are filed.

SAWHILL GALLERY, Art Department, Ames Madison University, Harrisonburg VA 22807. (703)568-6216. Director: Stuart Downs.
Profile: Nonprofit gallery. Estab. 1966. Clientele: university and regional community. Sponsors 6 solo and 6 group shows/year. Average display time is 3 weeks. Interested in emerging and established artists. Overall price range: $100-2,000; most artwork sold at $100-2,000.
Media: Considers all media.
Style: Exhibits contemporary, abstract, primitive, non-representational, photo-realistic, realism and neo-expressionistic works.
Terms: No fees. Retail price is set by artist. Exclusive area representation not required. Gallery provides insurance, shipping costs, promotion and a contract.
Submissions: Send query letter with resume, slides and SASE. Resumes and 2-3 slides are filed; annual review, late spring.

Wisconsin

FOSTER GALLERY, University of Wisconsin-Eau Claire, Eau Claire WI 54702.
Profile: Nonprofit gallery. Estab. 1967. Clientele: university community. Sponsors 2 solo and 7 group

shows/year. Average display time is 3 weeks. Interested in emerging and established artists. Overall price range: $50-20,000; most artwork sold at $100-1,000.
Media: Considers oils, acrylics, watercolor, pastels, pen & ink, drawings, mixed media, collage, paper, sculpture, ceramics, crafts, fibers, glass, installations, photography, limited edition original handpulled prints and posters. Most frequently exhibited media: oils, drawing and photography. Currently looking for graphic design, video, light, illustration.
Style: Exhibits hard-edge/geometric abstraction, color field, painterly abstraction, minimalism, conceptual, feminist/political and impressionistic works. Genres include landscapes, figurative work and fantasy illustration. Currently seeking conceptual, photo-realistic and minimalism.
Terms: Retail price is set by artist. Exclusive area representation not required. Gallery provides insurance, shipping, costs and promotion.
Submissions: Send query letter with resume, brochure, slides, photographs and SASE.

ALLEN PRIEBE GALLERY, University of Wisconsin-Oshkosh, Oshkosh WI 54901. (414)424-2222. Gallery Director/Advisor: David Hodge.
Profile: Nonprofit gallery. Estab. 1975. Sponsors 5 group shows/year. Average display time is 1 month. Interested in emerging and established artists.
Media: Considers all media and prints.
Style: Exhibits contemporary, abstract, Americana, impressionistic, figurative, landscapes, primitive, non-representational, realistic, neo-expressionistic and post-pop works. "We try to offer a variety of shows which cater to the emphasis offered by the university art department."
Terms: Exclusive area representation not required. Gallery provides insurance, promotion and contract.
Submissions: Send resume, slides and photographs. Resumes and articles are filed.

VALPERINE GALLERY, 1719 Monroe St., Madison WI 53711. (608)256-4040. Director: Valerie Kazamias.
Profile: Retail gallery and art consultancy. Estab. 1983. Clientele: professionals, corporations and designers; 60% private collectors, 40% corporate clients. Represents 70 artists. Sponsors 2 solo and 4 group shows/year. Interested in emerging and established artists. Overall price range: $300-5,000; most artwork sold at $500-2,500.
Media: Considers oils, acrylics, watercolors, pastels, collage, paper, sculpture, ceramics, glass and prints. Most frequently exhibited media: watercolors, prints and acrylics/oils.
Style: Exhibits hard-edge/geometric abstraction, post-modern, impressionism, realism and surrealism. Genres include landscapes, florals, and fantasy illustration.
Terms: Accepts work on consignment (40% commission). Retail price is set by gallery and artist. Exclusive area representation required. Gallery provides return shipping, promotion and contract.
Submissions: Send query letter, resume, brochure, slides and photographs. Write for an appointment to show a portfolio, which should include slides, transparences and photographs. Inventory, contracts, resumes, slides and correspondence are filed.

Wyoming

ARTWEST GALLERY, 105 E. Broadway, Jackson WY 83001. (307)733-6379. Director: Karla Swiggum.
Profile: Retail gallery. Clientele: 90% private collectors, 10% corporate clients. Represents 55 artists. Sponsors 3 solo and 8 group shows/year. Average display time is 3 weeks. Accepts primarily artists from Rocky Mountain states. Interested in emerging and established artists. Overall price range: $20-600; most artwork sold at $200.
Media: Considers watercolor, pastels, pen & ink, drawings, mixed media, collage, paper, sculpture, ceramics, crafts, fibers, glass, installations, photography, performance and posters. Most frequently exhibited media: ceramics and watercolor painting.
Style: Exhibits all styles. Genres include landscapes, florals and figurative work. "Our gallery specializes in local and regional art with contemporary emphasis. We feature a wide variety of mediums."
Terms: Accepts work on consignment (40% commission). Retail price is set by artist. Exclusive area representation not required. Gallery provides insurance, promotion and contract; shipping costs are shared.
Submissions: Send query letter, resume, slides and SASE. Resumes, bios, and any other pertinent information is filed.

Greeting Cards and Paper Products

The greeting card industry continues to provide some of the best opportunities for freelance artists. Sales have almost doubled since 1980, and this year the industry expects to top the $4 billion mark in sales. Some 7.1 billion cards are expected to be sold and, according to industry leaders, about 40 percent of those cards will require freelance artwork.

Large firms have extensive inhouse art staffs but they also work with hundreds of freelancers each year. Hallmark, for example, works with so many freelance artists and writers each year they have a special department exclusively designed to handle freelance work. Smaller firms are experiencing the most rapid growth within the industry and many rely solely on freelance artwork.

Most cards can be placed in one of three very broad categories—traditional, studio and alternative. Traditional cards are generally sent for personal occasions, such as anniversaries or birthdays and for Christmas and other holidays. Styles vary, but most popular subjects include children, animals, holiday symbols and outdoor scenes. With the increased attention on alternative card lines since 1980, traditional cards appeared to be slipping in popularity (with the exception of Christmas cards), but greeting card firms report a renewed interest in traditional designs. Most have updated their listings to reflect a need for more traditional illustrations.

Studio cards are often vertical, oversized cards with humorous or cartoony illustration. Messages are light in tone; most of these cards are sent for birthdays, friendship and to wish someone good luck or a speedy recovery. In other words, studio cards are meant to cheer.

Alternative cards have been growing in popularity steadily in recent years. The target audience is somewhat sophisticated and the age range is young—from age 15 to 40. Most alternative cards are upbeat in tone, but styles can range from the offbeat and risqué to fine art designs. Although these cards are sent for traditional occasions, they are also sent to commemorate a divorce, a raise or trip overseas. Sparked by the success of alternative greetings, a few of the larger companies have introduced their own alternative lines.

Stationery and paper product companies, especially those that produce giftwrap, also have been influenced by the growing alternative market. The most common revision for these listings is an increased need for sophisticated and offbeat lines for a young audience. Color plays an important part—many giftwrap companies said they are seeking both unusual soft and vibrant colors. One company also noted a trend toward "more process-intensive designs," such as die cuts, embossing and application of foil.

Before contacting a greeting card or stationery firm, research the company by visiting a local card or gift shop to find which firm's products fit your style. Some firms will also supply a catalog—usually for a SASE. The next step is to contact the art director or freelance department by mail. Since greeting card art is colorful, send color samples—either slides, photographs, tear sheets or final art.

Card firms buy greeting card material in a variety of ways. While most will buy illustrations alone, artists who can design an entire card or write verse copy have a definite advantage. Even if you are not a writer, suggested copy will help sell your card idea. Think also in terms of card lines and related gift items. Many greeting card artists also work with licensing agents to market their ideas to a variety of gift manufacturing firms.

Payment rates for greeting card illustrations and design can be as high as payment for some magazine and book illustration. Unlike most publications, however, greeting card firms usually buy all rights (with an eye toward future use). Payment for additional uses such as mugs or calendars should be reflected in the initial price.

For more information on illustration and design of greeting cards see *The Complete Guide to Greeting Card Design and Illustration*, by Eva Szela or *The Art and Craft of Greeting Cards*, by Susan Evarts. *Step by Step Graphics* magazine and *The Artist's Magazine* also feature articles on the art of greeting card illustration. Industry publications such as *Greetings Magazine* and *Giftware News* provide news and information on market trends. For lists of stationery firms see the *Thomas Register of Manufacturers*.

—Robin Gee

***A.F.B. MFG & SALES CORP.**, 990 Old Dixie Hwy #2, Lake Park FL 33403. (305)848-8721. President: A.L. Brooks.
Needs: Buys illustrations from freelance artists. Also uses freelance artists for paste-up and mechanicals. Prefers watercolors, small size, 2½x2¾. Produces material for holidays. Submit 12 months before holiday.
First Contact & Terms: Send query letter with slides and photocopies. Samples not filed are returned only if requested. Reports back within 10 days, only if interested. Portfolio should include thumbnails.

AFRICA CARD CO. INC., Box 91, New York NY 10108. (212)725-1199. President: Vince Jordan. Publishes greeting cards and posters.
Needs: Buys 25 designs/year.
First Contact & Terms: Mail art, or arrange interview. SASE. Reports in 6 weeks. Pays $50 minimum, greeting cards and posters. Buys all rights.

AGENT ANDY, INC., 221 Orient Way, Lyndhurst NJ 07071. (201)933-0917. President: Andrew Abrams. Licenses new product concepts to manufacturers of games, toys, calendars, posters, stationery, paper tableware, mugs, novelties, housewares, desk accessories, home decor items, plush toys, pens, ceramics, and musical giftware.
Needs: New product concepts submitted on 8½"x11" format. "We work with non-artists who have an original, marketable concept as well as top designers." We are looking for conceptual work leading to lines of products, i.e., greeting cards and coffee mugs. etc.
First Contact & Terms: Send query letter with brochure or resume and photocopies. Samples are filed. Samples not filed are returned only if requested by artist. Reports back only if interested. "Nondisclosure forms are signed to protect new concepts." Call or write to schedule an appointment to show a portfolio. Negotiates royalties of 5-10%, $1,000 to $10,000 advance plus guarantees $5,000-25,000/year.
Tips: "We're more concerned with subject matter that shows creativity as opposed to technical skills. Concepts leading to extensive lines of product are most important. We're not interested in terrific technique without creative conceptual themes."

ALASKA MOMMA, INC., 303 Fifth Ave., New York NY 10016. (212)679-4404. President: Shirley Henschel. "We are a licensing company representing artists, illustrators and designers with regard to design concepts and cartoon characters. We license artwork to boy, clothing, giftware, stationery, housewares and novelty manufacturers of consumer products."
Needs: "An artist must have a distinctive and unique style that a manufacturer can't get from his own art department. We prefer art that can be applied to the product. We are not successful at licensing cartoon art."
First Contact & Terms: "Artists may submit work in any way they choose, as long as it is a fair representation of their style." Henschel prefers to see several multiple color samples in a mailable size. No originals. Charges royalties of 7-10% with an advance mandatory. Earned royalties "depend on whether the products sell."
Tips: "We are interested in the work of freelance artists whose work is suitable for licensing programs. We do not want to see black and white art. We do not want to see drawings. What we need to see are slides or color photographs or color photocopies of finished art. We need to see a consistent style in a fairly extensive package of art. Otherwise, we don't really have a feeling for what the artist can do."

ALBION CARDS, Box 102, Albion MI 49224. Owners: Maggie and Mike LaNoue. Produces greeting cards, prints, note cards, postcards, catalogues and brochures. Uses b&w, line art, realistic, detailed, old-fashioned, clear; must hold line quality when reduced—to "jump out"—high contrast. Directs

products to women, older people, tourists, nostalgia buffs and sports enthusiasts.
Needs: Buys approximately 50 designs from freelance artists/year. Considers pen & ink and watercolors. Size of originals 9x12 or proportionate; important elements of design and artist's signature should be one inch from all edges of the drawing. Produces material for Christmas and summer (skiing, golfing, bicycling, boating); other subjects: animals (cats & ducks especially), landscapes, wild flowers and herbs. Catalog $2; art guidelines free for SASE. Theme must be "upbeat" and positive, but not cutesy.
First Contact & Terms: Send query letter with brochure, showing art style and photocopies. Samples not filed are not returned. Reports back within 3 months if interested. Do not send originals. Send color photographs, b&w and photocopies. Pays for illustration by the project, 5% minimum. Payment depends entirely on sales; artists can boost sales and earn sales commission as well. Buys copyright outright to be used for cards only and prints; artist retains some rights for other items. Buys only scenes that have not been published as cards to date. "Looking for artists who seek long-term arrangement not fast cash."
Tips: "We are interested in producing series of cards relating to scenic tourist areas, seascapes, street scenes and landmarks. Need scenes of Washington D.C. for 1988. We can help promote other artists' works in their own locale. The card market is expanding; nostalgia is gaining in popularity. Our needs for freelance work have increased dramatically. There is a greater appreciation of quality work—we can no longer produce all the new card scenes that our customers would like to purchase—so we are using more freelance work. We are interested in serious artists. Please do not send quick sketchy work or designs that display bad taste. Work must reproduce well and give the viewer a good feeling."

***ALL IMAGES, INC.**, #10, 616 Washington, Denver CO 80203. (303)839-9666. Principals: Lark Birdsong and Anne Price. Estab. 1987. Produces greeting cards. "We produce custom-designed card packages for specific organizations."
Needs: Works with approximately 24 freelance artists/year. "This varies, but we may produce about 50 different cards this year." Prefers 8x10 size. "We will probably do a December season's greetings package."
First Contact & Terms: Send query letter with brochure, samples and SASE. Samples not filed are returned by SASE. Reports back within 4 weeks. Original artwork is not returned to artist after job's completion. Pays average flat fee of $150-200/design; $150-200/illustration. Buys all rights.

AMBER LOTUS DESIGNS, (formerly Dharmart Designs), 1241 21st. St., Oakland CA 94607. (415)839-3931. Director of Sales: Rima Tamar. Specializes in calendars and cards. Publishes 10 calendars.
Needs: Works on assignment only. Works with 2-6 freelance artists/year. Prefers local artists, but not necessary. Prefers airbrush, watercolor, acrylics, pastels, calligraphy and computer illustration. Buys approximately 12 computer illustrations from freelancers/year.
First Contact & Terms: Send query letter with brochure or small sampling. Samples are filed. Samples not filed are returned by SASE. Reports back within 6 weeks only if interested. Originals returned to artist at job's completion. Call or write to schedule an appointment to show a portfolio, which should include photographs. Considers skill and experience of artist, project's budget and rights purchased when establishing payment.

AMBERLEY GREETING CARD CO., 11510 Goldcoast Dr., Cincinnati OH 45249-1695. Art Director: Ned Stern. Publishes studio, humorous, and everyday greeting cards.
Needs: Assigns 200 jobs/year. Local artists only. Uses freelance artists for product illustration. Especially needs humorous cards. Prefers airbrush and acrylics.
First Contact & Terms: Call first. Buys all rights. No original work returned at job's completion. Call or write to schedule an appointment to show a portfolio, which should include original/final art and final reproduction/product. Pays for design and illustration by the project, $60; on acceptance. Finds most artists through references/word-of-mouth.
Tips: Visit greeting card shops to get a better idea of the types of cards published by Amberley. When reviewing an artist's work, "the first thing I look for is the professionalism of the presentation, i.e. samples neatly displayed (no loose drawings, scraps of paper, etc.); creativity—what has the artist done differently and effectively; use of color, and lettering." An artist's biggest mistake is having a sloppy portfolio; "I'd rather see 5 good examples of work than 25 poorly done."

The asterisk before a listing indicates that the listing is new in this edition. New markets are often the most receptive to freelance submissions.

AMCAL, 1050 Shary Ct., Concord CA 94518. (415)689-9930. Publishes calendars and greeting cards. Markets to all major gift, book and department stores throughout U.S. Some sales to Europe and Japan. Rapidly expanding company looking for distinctive card and gift ideas for growing market demand. "All subjects considered that fit our quality image."
Needs: Prefers work in 5x7 vertical card format. Send photos, slides or published work.
First Contact & Terms: Responds within 2 weeks. Send samples or call for appointment to show a portfolio. Pays for design by the hour, $20-50. Pays for illustration by the project, $200-700.
Tips: "Know the market. Go to gift shows and visit lots of stationery stores. Read all the trade magazines. Talk to store owners to find out what's selling and what isn't."

AMERICAN GREETINGS CORP., 10500 American Rd., Cleveland OH 44102. (216)252-7300. Director Creative Recruitment: Lynne Boswell. Publishes humorous, studio and conventional greeting cards, calendars, giftwrap, posters, stationery and paper tableware products. Manufactures candles and ceramic figurines.
First Contact & Terms: Query with resume. Forms for submitting portfolio will be mailed. Portfolios received without necessary paperwork will be returned unreviewed.
Tips: "We are staffed to generate our own ideas internally, but we will review portfolios for full-time or freelance employment."

***ARGUS COMMUNICATIONS, INC.**, Division of DLM, One DLM Park, Allen TX 75002. Managing Art Director: June Boisseau. Produces greeting cards, postcards, calendars, posters, etc.
Needs: Works with hundreds of freelance artists/year. Must be professional artist. Works on assignment only. Uses artists for roughs, layouts and final art. Particularly interested in new approaches to greeting card illustrations.
First Contact & Terms: Send query letter with resume and samples to be kept on file. Samples not filed are returned by SASE. Reports only if interested. To show a portfolio, mail thumbnails, roughs, tear sheets, Photostats and photographs. Payment depends on project. Considers complexity of the project and turnaround time when establishing payment.
Tips: "Be familiar with our product line before contacting us. Remember that greeting cards are a consumer product and must meet a consumer need to be successful."

ARTFAIRE, 600 E. Hancock St., Appelton WI 54911. (414)738-4284. Art Director: Marilyn Wolf. Produces giftwrap and paper tableware products.
Needs: Works with 25 freelance artists/year. Buys 100 designs from freelance artists/year. Buys 100 illustrations from freelance artists/year. Prefers artists experienced in giftwrap and party goods designing. Prefers watercolors, acrylics, etc. Produces material for everyday, Christmas, Valentine's Day and Halloween.
First Contact & Terms: Send query letter with brochure or tear sheets. Samples not filed are returned by SASE. Reports back within 2 months. To show a portfolio, mail original/final art, tear sheets, photographs and b&w. Original artwork is not returned after job's completion. Pays for design by the project, $100-700. Pays for illustration by the project, $250-700. Buys all rights.
Tips: Looks for "newness, strong style and excellence in execution. Also, knowledge of our product and the application of design to meet our products' needs."

***ATHENA INTERNATIONAL**, Box 13, 13-14 Raynham Rd., Bishop's Stortford, Hertsfordshire CM23 5PQ England. Group Publishing Director: Mr. Roger Watt. Produces greeting cards and posters.
Needs: Works with numerous freelance artists/year. Also uses freelance artists for P-O-P displays, paste-up and mechanicals. Produces material for everyday, special occasions, Christmas, Valentine's, Mother's Day, Father's Day and Easter.
First Contact & Terms: Send query letter with brochure, Photostats, photocopies, and slides. Samples not filed are returned. Reports back within 30 days. To show a portfolio, mail roughs, Photostats and photographs. Original artwork is returned to artist after job's completion. Negotiates rights purchased.

BARNSTABLE ORIGINALS, 50 Harden Ave., Camden ME 04843. (207)236-8162. Art Director: Marsha Smith. Produces greeting cards, posters, and paper sculpture cards. Directed toward tourists travelling in New England, and sailors or outdoors people—"nature and wildlife lovers."
Needs: Buys 50 designs and illustrations from freelance artists/year. Prefers 5x7 cards, vertical or horizontal. Prefers traditional style; watercolor, acrylics and oils.
First Contact & Terms: Send query letter with brochure showing art style, Photostats, photocopies, slides or photographs. Samples not filed are returned by SASE. Reports back within 1 month. To show a portfolio, mail Photostats, color photographs or slides of originals. No originals returned to artist at job's completion. Pays $50 minimum per design/illustration. Pays on acceptance. Buys all rights. Finds most artists through samples received through the mail.

Tips: "We're looking for quality art work—any creative and fresh ideas. The artist must display a sound background in art basics, exhibiting strong draftsmanship in a graphic style. Colors must be harmonious and clearly executed. Don't want to see resumes, letters of how great the artist is, etc. It is the artwork we're interested in—not where the artist has been. Very few artists are enclosing postage for return of materials."

BARTON-COTTON INC., 1405 Parker Rd., Baltimore MD 21227. (301)247-4800. Contact: Creative/Art Department. Produces religious greeting cards, commercial Christmas cards, wildlife designs and spring note cards. Free guidelines and sample cards; specify area of interest: religious, Christmas, spring, etc.
Needs: Buys 150-200 illustrations each year. Submit seasonal work "any time of the year."
First Contact & Terms: Send query letter with resume, tear sheets, photocopies, Photostats, slides and photographs. Previously published work and simultaneous submissions accepted. Reports in 4 weeks. To show a portfolio, mail original/final art, final reproduction/product, color and tear sheets. Submit full-color work only (watercolors, gouache, pastels, oils and acrylics); pays $150-500/illustration; on acceptance.
Tips: "Good draftsmanship is a must, particularly with figures and faces. Spend some time studying market trends in the greeting card industry to determine current market trends." There is an increased need for creative ways to paint traditional Christmas scenes with up-to-date styles and techniques."

BEACH PRODUCTS, 1 Paper Pl., Kalamazoo MI 49001. (616)349-2626. Creative Director: Gabrielle Runza. Publishes paper tableware products; general and seasonal, birthday, special occasion, invitations, announcements, stationery, wrappings and thank you notes for children and adults.
Needs: Buys designs from freelance artists. Uses artists for product designs and illustration. Sometimes buys humorous and cartoon-style illustrations. Prefers flat 4-color designs; 5¼ wide x 5½ high for luncheon napkins. Produces seasonal material for Christmas, Mother's Day, Thanksgiving, Easter, Valentine's Day, St. Patrick's Day, Halloween and New Year's Day. Submit seasonal material before June 1; everyday (not holidays) material before March.
First Contact & Terms: Send query letter with 9x12 SASE so catalog can be sent with response. Disclosure form must be completed and returned before work will be viewed. Call or write to schedule an appointment to show a portfolio, which should include original/final art and final reproduction/product. Previously published work OK. Originals not returned to artist at job's completion; "all artwork purchased becomes the property of Beach Products. Items not purchased are returned." Buys all rights. Pays average flat flee of $100/design; on acceptance. Considers product use when establishing payment.
the catalog, for example a 9x12 SAE. Artwork should have a clean, professional appearance and be the specified size for submissions, as well as a maximum of four flat colors."

CAROLYN BEAN PUBLISHING, LTD., 2230 W. Winton Ave., Hayward CA 94545. (415)957-9574. Art Director: Ande Axelrod. Publishes alternative and traditional greeting cards and stationery; diverse themes.
Needs: Buys 100-150 designs/illustrations per year from freelance artists. Uses artists for product design. Produces greatly expanded occasions and holiday images; submit material 12-18 months in advance. Prefers pen & ink, airbrush, colored pencil, watercolor, acrylics, pastels, markers and calligraphy.
First Contact & Terms: Send query letter with slides or photocopies. Samples returned only if accompanied by SASE. Reports in 4-8 weeks. Originals returned to artist at job's completion. Do not call or write to schedule an interview. Provide samples, business card and tear sheets to be kept on file for possible future assignments. Negotiates rights purchased; royalty arrangement if possible. Payment is made according to time schedule established in contract.
Tips: "Think about *cards*. I see good work all the time, but rarely things that have been created with greeting cards in mind. Do something different! We are not interested in seeing more of what is already available on the market."

***BRAZEN IMAGES**, 269 Chatterton Parkway, White Plains NY 10606. (914)949-2605. Art Director: Kurt Abraham. Produces greeting cards "for anyone over 18; we make adult sexually-oriented cards."
Needs: Works with 5-10 freelance artists/year. Buys 20-50 illustrations from freelance artists/year. Prefers airbrush. "We like a wide range of styles." Artwork must be proportional to a 5x7 greeting card with extra for tirm. Both vertical and horizontal are OK. Produces material for Christmas, Halloween, Valentine's, birthdays, and weddings. "We look for material all year long—we store it up until presstime if it doesn't make it in one year's printing, it'll make it the next."
First Contract & Terms: Send query letter with brochure, slides, SASE and any clear copy of non-published work plus SASE. Samples are filed. Samples not filed are returned by SASE only if requested

©1987 Carolyn Bean Publishing, Ltd.

Jacquie Marie Vaux originally sold this watercolor painting for $3,500. Then the Santa Rosa, California artist reproduced it as a limited edition print. "In the Artist's Market I discovered the greeting card listings. I sent several companies transparencies, posters and prints." After reviewing her work, Carolyn Bean's creative director Andrea Axelrod requested original art to use in a series of notecards. "I will eventually do designs that are more specifically geared to the greeting card market. Now, I feel a flat fee is a better arrangement for me, based on what my designs do in the marketplace. As I learn more about the greeting card industry, I will produce images that will have a longer life in reprint. Then I will go for a royalty arrangement."

by artists. Reports back within 1 month. Call or write to schedule an appointment to show a portfolio or mail original/final art, slides, photographs, color and b&w. Original artwork is returned to the artist after job's completion, "in most cases." Pays average flat fee of $200-300/illustration; by the project, $200-300 average. Buys one-time rights.
Tips: "As our name implies, we expect work to be brazen and very upfront sexually. Subtlety is not for us!"

BRILLIANT ENTERPRISES, 117 W. Valerio St., Santa Barbara CA 93101. Art Director: Ashleigh Brilliant. Publishes postcards.
Needs: Uses up to 300 designs/year. Artists may submit designs for word-and-picture postcards, illustrated with line drawings.
First Contact & Terms: Submit 5½x3½ horizontal b&w line drawings. SASE. Reports in 2 weeks. Buys all rights. "Since our approach is very offbeat, it is essential that freelancers first study our line. Ashleigh Brilliant's books include *I May Not Be Totally Perfect, But Parts of Me Are Excellent* and *Appreciate Me Now and Avoid the Rush*. We supply a catalog and sample set of cards for $2." Pays $40 minimum, depending on "the going rate" for camera-ready word-and-picture design.
Tips: "Since our product is highly unusual, freelancers should familiarize themselves with it by sending for our catalog ($2 plus SASE). Otherwise, they will just be wasting our time and theirs."

***BROOM DESIGNS INC.**, 16180 Meyers Rd., Detroit MI 48235. (313)863-6158. President: Edward M. Broom. Produces greeting cards.
Needs: Buys 10-15 illustrations from freelance artists/year. Seeks very good illustrators. Works on assignment only. Prefers poster color, 8x11. Produces material for Christmas; submit 7 months before holiday.
First Contact & Terms: Send query letter with Photostats and photocopies. Samples not filed are returned only if requested. Reports back within 2 weeks only if interested. Portfolio should include color and photographs. Original artwork is returned to the artist after job's completion. Pays by the project. Buys all rights.
Tips: "We are a *Black* greeting card company. Make sure that art work submitted to Broom designs is well done and realistic."

BURGOYNE, INC., (formerly Sidney J. Burgoyne & Sons Inc.), 2030 E. Byberry Rd., Philadelphia PA 19116. (215)677-8000. Art Director: Jon Harding. Publishes greeting cards and calendars; Christmas, winter and religious themes.
Needs: Buys 75-100 designs/year. Prefers artists experienced in greeting card design. Uses freelance artists for products design and illustration, and calligraphy. Will review any media; prefers art proportional to 5¼x7⅛. Produces seasonal material for Christmas; will review new work at any time.
First Contact & Terms: Send query letter with original art or published work or actual work. Samples

returned by SASE. Simultaneous submissions OK. Reports in 2 weeks. No originals returned to artist at job's completion. To show a portfolio, mail appropriate materials or call to schedule an appointment; portfolio should include original/final art and final reproduction/product. Pays for design by the project, $100-300. Buys all rights; on acceptance.
Tips: "Familiarize yourself with greeting card field. Spend time in card stores."

CAPE SHORE, INC., 42A N. Elm St., Box 537, Yarmouth ME 04096. Art Director: Anne W. Macleod. Produces notes, giftwrap, stationery products and giftware for both year round and Christmas markets. Predominantly nautical in theme. Directs products to gift and stationery stores/shops.
Needs: Buys 25-50 designs and illustrations/year from freelance artists. Prefers watercolor, acrylics, cut paper and gouache. June deadline for finished artwork.
First Contact & Terms: "Please send sample artwork so we can judge if style is compatible. All samples and reports will be returned within several weeks." Pays by the project, $25-200. Pays average flat fee of $125/design.Prefers to buy all rights. Originals returned to artist if not purchased.
Tips: "We do not use black-and-white artwork, photographs, greeting card prose. We do not want to see pen & ink work."

CARING CARD CO., Box 90278, Long Beach CA 90809. President: Shirley Hassell. Produces greeting cards, especially contemporary cards and "significant loss" cards for Hospice Programs for all ages and groups.
Needs: Buys 90% of designs used from freelance artists. Buys illustrations from freelance artists. Also uses artists for P-O-P displays. Prefers watercolors, acrylics, oils, pastels and computer illustrations; looks for "simplicity and elegance."
First Contact & Terms: Send brochure or Photostats, photocopies and slides. Samples are filed. Samples not filed are returned only if requested by artist. Reports back only if interested. To show a portfolio, mail slides, tear sheets, Photostats, photographs, color and b&w. Original artwork is not returned after job's completion. Pays royalties of 2-7%. Buys all rights.
Tips: "Include in your portfolio one set of slides, a price list, resume and a cover letter, plus a SASE. Before sending art on approval, mail a contract."

CARLTON CARDS, Box 660270, Dallas TX 75266-0270. (214)638-4800. Creative Coordinator: Laurel Milton. Produces greeting cards, calendars and paper tableware products. Produces announcemnts, general cards, informal cards, inspirational cards, invitations, contemporary cards, juvenile cards, soft line cards and studio cards.
Needs: Prefers 3 years of experience in the industry. Works on assignment only. Prefers pastels, then airbrush, watercolor and acrylics. Produces material for all seasons.
First Contact & Terms: Send query letter with SASE. Samples are filed. Samples not filed are returned by SASE. Reports back within 30 days. To show a portfolio, mail final reproduction/product, slides, photographs and color. Original artwork is not returned after job's completion. Pays average flat fee of $250/illustration. Buys all rights.
Tips: "We would like to see a portfolio that has been geared toward the greeting card industry. I want to see less advertising/graphic art."

CASE STATIONERY CO., INC., 179 Saw Mill River Rd., Yonkers NY 10701. (914)965-5100. President: Jerome Sudwow. Vice President: Joyce Blackwood. Produces stationery and tins for mass merchandisers in stationery and housewares departments.
Needs: Buys 50 designs from freelance artists/year. Works on assignment only. Uses artists for mechanicals and ideas. Produces materials for Christmas; submit 6 months in advance.
First Contact & Terms: Send query letter with resume and tear sheets, Photostats, photocopies, slides and photographs. Samples not filed are returned. Reports back. Call or write to schedule an appointment to show a portfolio. Original artwork is not returned. Pays a flat fee, by the hour, by the project or by royalties. Buys first rights or one-time rights.
Tips: "Get to know us. We're people who are creative and who know how to sell a product."

H. GEORGE CASPARI, INC., 225 Fifth Ave., New York NY 10010. (212)685-9726. President: Douglas H. Stevens. Publishes greeting cards, Christmas cards, invitations, giftwrap and paper napkins. The line maintains a very traditional theme.
Needs: Buys 80-100 illustrations/year from freelance artists. Prefers watercolors, color pencil and other color media. Produces seasonal material for Christmas, Mother's Day, Father's Day, Easter and Valentine's Day.
First Contact & Terms: Arrange an appointment with Lucille Andirola to review portfolio. Prefers unpublished original illustrations as samples. Reports within 4 weeks. Negotiates payment on acceptance; pays for design by the project, $300 minimum.

Tips: "Caspari and many other small companies rely on freelance artists to give the line a fresh, overall style rather than relying on one artist. We feel this is a strong point of our company."

***CERES DESIGNS-FINE ART CARDS**, Box 100 Marrimac MA 01860. (508)346-8969. Contact: Lucy E. Crocker. Estab. 1987. Produces fine art notecards.
Needs: Works with 2-4 freelance artists/year. Buys 8-10 designs from freelance artists/year. Prefers watercolors, colored pencil, and other full-color work. Prefers natural images, wildlife, gardens, and country scenes. Minimum size 4½x6½ Produces material for Christmas; submit seasonal material 6 months before holiday.
First Contact & Terms: Send query letter with brochure, tearsheets and slides. Samples are not filed. Samples not filed are returned. Reports back within 3 weeks. Call or write to schedule an appointment to show a portfolio or mail original/final art, final reproduction/product, slides, tearsheets, and photographs. Original artwork is returned to the artist after job's completion. Pays average flat fee of $50 minimum. Negotiates rights purchased.
Tips: "Our notecoards are museum-quality fine art reproductions. We enjoy working with freelance artists to promote their quality work. We prefer unpublished illustrations and designs, and we're always looking for new refreshing images."

CLASSICO SAN FRANCISCO INC., 16 Golden Gate Dr., San Rafael CA 94901. (415)459-3830. Vice President: Dolores Dietz. Produces contemporary postcards, cartoon postcards and art photography postcards.
First Contact & Terms: Send query letter with brochure or Photostats and photocopies. Samples are filed. Samples not filed are returned only if requested. Reports back within 2 weeks. Call or write to schedule an appointment to show a portfolio, which should include slides, tear sheets and photographs. Pays royalties of 5%. Negotiates rights purchased.
Tips: "Art must be applicable to postcard size."

THE COLORTYPE COMPANY, 1640 Market St., Coronua CA 91720. (714)734-7410. Vice President/Marketing: Mike Gribble. Produces greeting cards, stationery, mugs and bulletin boards.
Needs: Buys 150 designs from freelance artists/year. Experienced artists only. Uses artists for P-O-P displays, paste-up and mechanicals. Prefers pen & ink, watercolors and acrylics.
First Contact & Terms: Send query letter with brochure showing art style or samples. Samples not filed are returned by SASE. Reports back within 2 weeks. To show a portfolio, mail appropriate materials. No originals returned to artist at job's completion. Pays average flat fee of $120/design and illustration.
Tips: Artist should "be knowledgeable about the card business."

***CONFETTI GRAPHICS CORP.**, Suite #106, 408 N. Bishop, Dallas TX 75208. (214)943-4013. President: John Mooring. Produces greeting cards.
Needs: Prefers 5x7 greeting cards. Produces material for Christmas, Easter, Mother's Day, Valentine's Day; submit 10 months before holiday. Prefers pen & ink, colored pencil, watercolor, acrylics, pastels, collage, markers and calligraphy.
First Contact & Terms: Send query letter with resume, tear sheets, photocopies and slides. Samples are filed. Samples not filed are returned only if requested. Reports back within 2 months. Call or write to schedule an appointment to show a portfolio, or mail roughs, slides, tear sheets, Photostats, photographs, dummies, color and b&w. Original artwork is sometimes returned to the artist after job's completion. Pays royalties of 3-7%. Buys all rights.
Tips: Artist "should have 15-20 designs with copy per card line submitted."

***CONTENOVA GIFTS, INC.**, 1239 Adanac St., Vancouver, BC V6A 2C8 Canada. (604)253-4444. Creative Director: Jeff Sinclair.
Needs: Buys 100 illustrations from freelance artists/year. Local artists only. Works on assignment only. Prefers watercolor, acrylics. Prefers humorous or cutesy; 4x9 and 6x9 for greeting cards. Produces material for Christmas and Valentine's Day; submit 6 months before the holiday.
First Contact & Terms: Send query letter with Photostats. Samples are not filed; samples not filed are returned by SASE. Reports back within 6 weeks. Call or write to schedule an appointment to show a portfolio, which should include roughs and dummies. Original artwork is not returned after job's completion. Payment depends on size, colors required and many other factors. Buys all rights.

CREATIF LICENSING, Suite 106, 587 Main St., New Rochelle NY 10801. (914)632-2232. President: Stan Cohen. Licensing manager. "We handle artists and their properties with the purpose of licensing their art and concepts to companies that produce products compatible to those art styles." Serves gift, stationery, clothing and toy companies.

Needs: Works with 12 freelance artists/year. "We are looking for creative artists who have a unique, distinguishable style which lends itself to merchandise licensing." Prefers simple line drawings depicting children, animals or cartoon characters.
First Contact & Terms: Send query letter with brochure, photocopies and SASE. Samples are filed except for "styles we feel are not applicable for licensing." Samples not filed are returned by SASE. Reports back within 2 weeks. Call or write for appointment to show portfolio. "We work on 50% commission on all royalties our company receives."

CREATIVE DIRECTIONS, INC., Suite W-268, 323 S. Franklin Bldg., Dept G., Chicago IL 60606. (219)949-5000. Director: Barbara A. Woods. Establ. 1986. Produces greeting cards, which include announcements, invitation, all-occasion, general, informal, inspirational, contemporary, juvenile soft line and studio cards.
Needs: Works with a maximum number of freelance artists/year. Needs artwork "which is suitable for fine art framed display." Buys 100 designs and 100 illustrations from freelancers/year. "We welcome. new artists." Material will be cropped to 8½x5½. Produces material for all occasions; submit 12 months before holiday. Uses all media except computer illustration.
First Contact & Terms: Send query letter with resume, photocopies, slides, transparencies, photocopies and SASE. Samples are filed; samples not filed are returned by SASE. Reports back within 6 weeks. Original artwork is returned by SASE. Pays royalties of 5%. Buys first rights or reprint rights; negotiates rights purchased.

CREATIVE PAPER PRODUCTS, INC., 1523 Prudential, Dallas TX 75235. (214)634-1283. President: David Hardenbergh. Novelty pens, pencils, costume jewelry etc. for children 6-14 years old. "Hello Kitty"-type merchandise. Everyday themes for women.
Needs: Buys "simplistic flat art that is very colorful" from freelance artists. Uses artists for product design and illustration. Produces seasonal material; submit art 6 months before holiday.
First Contact & Terms: Send samples. Prefers Photostats and slides as samples. Samples returned on request. Reports within 3 weeks. Provide samples to be kept on file for possible future assignments. Material not copyrighted. Negotiates payment on acceptance.

CREATIVE PAPERS BY C.R. GIBSON, The C.R. Gibson Co., Knight St., Norwalk CT 06856. (203)847-4543. Vice President Creative Papers: Steven P. Mack. Publishes stationery, note paper, invitations and silk-screened and gravure giftwrap. Interested in material for stationery collections or individual notes and invitations. "Two to three designs are sufficient to get across a collection concept. We don't use too many regional designs. Stationery themes are up-to-date, fashion oriented. Designs should be somewhat sophisticated without being limiting. Classic designs and current material from the giftware business do well."
Needs: Buys 100-200 designs/year. Especially needs new 4-color art for note line and invitations; "we need designs that relate to current fashion trends as well as a wide variety of illustrations suitable for boxed note cards. We constantly update our invitation line and can use a diverse selection of ideas." Uses some humorous illustrations but only for invitation line. "We buy a broad range of artwork with assorted themes. The only thing we don't buy is very comtemporary or avant-garde." Prefers colored pencil, watercolor, acrylics, oils and collage. Speculation art has no size limitations. Finished size of notes is 4x5½ and 3¾x5; folded invitations, 3¾x5; card style invitations 4¾x6; and giftwrap repeat, 8x8 minimum.
First Contact & Terms: Send query letter with brochure showing art style or resume, photocopies and slides. Prefers 4-6 samples (slides or chromes of work or originals), published or unpublished. Previously published, photocopied and simultaneous submissions OK, if they have not been published as cards and the artist has previous publishers' permissions. SASE. Reports in 6 weeks. Call or write to schedule an appointment to show a portfolio, which should include thumbnails, roughs, original/final art and tear sheets. Pays $35 for rough sketch. Pays average flat fee of $175/design; $200/illustration; by the hour, $20-25 average; royalties of 6%. Negotiates payment. Considers complexity of project, skill and experience of artist, reproduction expense and rights purchased. Usually buys all rights; sometimes buys limited rights.
Tips: "Almost all of the artists we work with or have worked with are professional in that they have a background of other professional assignments and exhibits as well as a good art education. We have been fortunate to make a few 'discoveries,' but even these people have been at it for a number of years and have a very distinctive style with complete understanding of printing specifications and mechanicals. More artists are asking for royalties and are trying to develop licensed characters. Most of the work is not worthy of a royalty and people don't understand what it takes to make a 'character' sell. Keep your presentation neat and don't send very large pieces of art. Keep the submission as varied as possible. I am not particularly interested in pen and ink drawings. Everything we print is in full color."

"This is a simple, clean design which makes you smile to look at it," says James E. Alden, president of the Crockett Collection. Albany, New York artist Maria Vaci originally submitted the Christmas card design through the mail, after finding the company listed in the* Artist's Market *and then requested guidelines. Vaci used flat tempera colors for silkscreen printing. The design not only led to other assignments from Crockett but also work with other companies who use flat color designs.

THE CROCKETT COLLECTION, Rt. 7, Box 1428, Manchester Center VT 05255. (802)362-2913. President: James Alden. Publishes mostly traditional, some contemporary, humorous and whimsical Christmas and everyday greeting cards, postcards, note cards. Christmas themes geared to sophisticated, upper-income individuals. Free artist's guidelines.
Needs: Buys up to 100 designs/year from freelance artists. Produces products by silkscreen method exclusively.
First Contact & Terms: Send query letter. Request guidelines which are mailed out once a year in January, one year in advance of printing. Submit unpublished, original designs only. Art should be in finished form. Art not purchased returned by SASE. Buys all rights. Pays $80-130 per design.
Tips: "Designs must be suitable for silkscreen process. Airbrush and watercolor techniques are not amenable to this process. Bold, well-defined designs only. Our look is traditional, mostly realistic, and graphic. A serious artist will find out what a company specializes in and submit only appropriate work."

DECORAL INC., 232 Route 109, Farmingdale NY 11735. In NY (516)752-0076; outside NY (800)645-9868. President: Walt Harris. Produces decorative, instant stained glass plus sports and wildlife decals.
Needs: Buys 50 designs from freelance artists/year; buys 50 illustrations from freelance artists/year. Uses artists for P-O-P displays. Prefers watercolors.
First Contact & Terms: Send query letter with brochure showing art style or resume and samples. Samples not filed are returned. Reports back within 30 days. To show a portfolio, mail appropriate materials or call or write to schedule an appointment; portfolio should include original/final art, final reproduction/product and Photostats. Original artwork is not returned. Pays average flat fee. Buys all rights.

DESIGNER GREETINGS, INC., Box X, Staten Island NY 10314. (718)981-7700. Art Director: Fern Gimbelman. Produces greeting cards, general cards, informal cards, inspirational cards, invitations, contemporary cards, juvenile cards, soft line cards and studio cards.

Needs: Works with 16 freelance artists/year. Buys 100-150 designs and illustrations from freelance artists/year. Works on assignment only. Also uses artists for calligraphy, P-O-P displays and airbrushing. Prefers pen & ink, airbrush. No specific size. Produces material for all seasons; submit 6 months before holiday.
First Contact & Terms: Send query letter with brochure or tear sheets, Photostats or photocopies. Samples are filed. Samples not filed are returned only if requested. Reports back within 3-4 weeks. Call or write to schedule an appointment to show a portfolio, which should include original/final art, final reproduction/product, tear sheets and Photostats. Original artwork is not returned after job's completion. Pays average flat fee. Buys all rights.
Tips: "We are willing to look at any work through the mail, (photocopies, etc.). Appointments are given after I personally speak with the artist (by phone)."

DICKENS COMPANY, 59-47 Fresh Meadow Lane, Flushing NY 11365. (718)357-5700, (800)445-4632. Vice President/Art Director: James Chou. Produces greeting cards including musical greetings.
Buys: Buys 300 designs from freelance artists/year; also buys illustrations. Prefers watercolors mainly. Final art size 5¾x8. Produces material for everyday, Valentine's Day, Mother's Day, Father's Day and Christmas; submit 9 months in advance.
First Contact & Terms: Prefers local artists with experience in greeting card design. Send resume and photographs or slides to be kept on file. Prefers photographs or slides as samples. Samples not filed are returned only if requested. "No return postage is necessary, please." Reports within 1 month. Call or write for appointment to show portfolio. Originals are not returned to artist at job's completion unless agreed differently in advance. Pays average flat fee of $100-500/design; $20-300/illustration; or royalties. Negotiates rights purchased.
Tips: "We need experienced artists for greeting card artwork badly."

EARTH CARE PAPER CO., 100 S. Baldwin, Madison WI 53703. (608)256-5522. Art Director: Carol Magee. Produces greeting cards, giftwrap, notecards and stationery. "All of our products are printed on recycled paper and are targeted toward nature enthusiasts and environmentalists."
Needs: Buys 25-40 illustrations from freelance artists/year. Considers all media. Prefers watercolor, pen & ink, airbrush, colored pencil, acrylics, oils, pastels, collage, markers and calligraphy. Produces Christmas cards; seasonal material should be submitted 12 months before the holiday.
First Contact & Terms: "For initial contact, artists should submit samples which we can keep on file." Reports back within 1 month. Original artwork is usually returned after publication. Pays 5% royalties plus a cash advance on royalties or a flat fee, $75 minimum. Buys reprint rights.
Tips: "We primarily use a nature theme but will consider anything. We consider graphic or traditional designs. We would like to develop a humor line based on environmental and social issues, and a cute or whimsical animal line. We are primarily mail order."

EISNER ADVERTISING, 2421 Traymore Rd., University Heights OH 44118. (216)932-2669. President: Adele Eisner. Produces greeting cards, calendars, posters and stationery. Publishes announcements, general cards, informal cards, invitations and judaica.
Needs: Works with 10 freelance artists/year. Buys 10 illustrations, from freelance artists/year. Prefers local artists. Also uses artists for P-O-P displays, paste-up and mechanicals. Prefers pen & ink, markers and calligraphy. Produces material for mostly Jewish holidays and nonseasonal, informal, get well, thank you's, etc.; submit 4 months before holiday.
First Contact & Terms: Send query letter with tear sheets. Samples are filed. Samples not filed are not returned. Reports back only if interested. "If interested we will contact artist" to schedule an appointment to show a portfolio, which should include final reproduction/product, tear sheets, Photostats, photographs and dummies. Original artwork is not returned to the artist after job's completion. Pays average flat fee of $50/design; or by the hour, $10. Negotiates rights purchased.
Tips: "Wait until I contact. Looking for clean work with good proportion-of-letter sense."

***KRISTEN ELLIOTT, INC.**, 6 Opportunity Way, Newburyport MA 01950. (617)465-1899. Contact: Charles F. Elliott, Jr., and Barbara Elliott. Produces all-occasion greeting cards, boxed notes and hangups, correspondence cards for everyday and Christmas, Christmas cards and giftwrap.
Needs: Works with freelance artists on speculation and assignment basis. Prefers watercolor "with clear, bright colors; other media accepted. Designs range from traditional florals to contemporary humor and graphics. Greeting card designs should include copy."
First Contact & Terms: Send query letter with samples and roughs. Samples are returned by SASE. Reports back within 2 weeks. Call or write to schedule an appointment to show a portfolio, which should include original/final art, final reproductions or slides; "or send facsimile by mail." Color is preferred. Original artwork is generally not returned to the artist after job's completion. Pays average flat fee of $100/design. Buys reprint or all rights.

THE EVERGREEN PRESS, INC., 3380 Vincent Rd., Pleasant Hill CA 94523. (415)933-9700. Art Director: Malcolm K. Nielsen. Publishes greeting cards, giftwrap, and stationery; high quality art reproductions, Christmas cards and Christmas postcards.
Needs: Buys 200 designs/year from freelance artists. Uses artists for product design (any design that can be used to produce greeting cards, giftwrap, stationery and other products sold through book, stationery, card and gift stores). Uses only full-color artwork in any media in unusual designs, sophisticated art and humor or series with a common theme. No super-sentimental Christmas themes, single greeting card designs with no relation to each other, or single color pen or pencil sketches. Roughs may be in any size to get an idea of work; final art must meet size specifications. Produces seasonal material for Christmas, Easter and Valentine's Day; "we examine artwork at any time of the year to be published for the next following holiday."
First Contact & Terms: Send query letter with brochure showing art style or slides and actual work; write for art guidelines. Samples returned by SASE. Reports within 2 weeks. To show a portfolio, mail roughs and original/final art. Originals returned at job's completion. Negotiates rights purchased. "We usually make a cash down payment against royalties; royalty to be negotiated. Royalties depend upon the type of product that is submitted and the state of readiness for publication." Considers product use and reproduction expense when establishing payment. Pays on publication.

EXCLUSIVE HANDPRINTS INC., 96 NW 72nd St., Miami FL 33150. (305)751-0281. Vice President: Stanley Bercovitch. Wallpaper firm.
Needs: Buys 12 designs from freelance artists/year. Artists who are "well experienced in wallpaper and fabric designs" only. Uses artists for wallpaper and fabric patterns. If design is repeated, accepts 18" repeat pattern; will also consider nonrepeated designs.
First Contact & Terms: Call or write for appointment to show portfolio. No originals returned at job's completion. Pays flat fee/design. Buys all rights.

FRAVESSI-LAMONT INC., 11 Edison Place, Springfield NJ 07081. Art Director: Helen M. Monahan. Publishes greeting cards; general, cute and some humorous.
Needs: Buys "thousands" of designs and "few" illustrations/year from freelance artists. Uses artists for greeting card design and illustration. Especially needs seasonal and everyday designs; prefers color washes or oil paintings for illustrations. Pays $50 minimum.
First Contact & Terms: Send query letter and samples of work. Prefers roughs as samples. Produces seasonal material for Christmas, Mother's Day, Father's Day, Thanksgiving, Easter, Valentine's Day and St. Patrick's Day; submit art 10 months before holiday. SASE. Reports in 2-3 weeks. No originals returned to artist at job's completion. Provide samples to be kept on file for possible future assignments. To show a portfolio, mail roughs and color. Buys all rights. Negotiates payment; pays $75 minimum; pays on acceptance. Considers product use and reproduction expense when establishing payment. Free artist's guidelines.
Tips: "Just send a few samples of type of work to see if it fits in with our line."

FREEDOM GREETINGS, Box 715, Bristol PA 19007. (215)945-3300. Vice President: Jay Levitt. Produces greeting cards featuring flowers and scenery.
Needs: Buys 100 designs from freelance artists/year. Works on assignment only. Considers watercolors, acrylics, etc. Call for size specifications. Produces material for all seasons and holidays; submit 14 months in advance.
First Contact & Terms: Send query letter with resume and samples. Samples are returned by SASE. Reports within 10 days. To show a portfolio, mail roughs and original/final art. Originals returned to artist at job's completion. Pays for design by the project, $150-200. Buys all greeting and stationery rights.

***G.N.I. INC.**, 266 Beacon St., Boston MA 02116. Art Director: Betsey Cavallo. Produces giftwrap, tags and bows for both holiday and everyday use, but the emphasis is on Christmas designs for all age groups.
Needs: "Art work should incorporate contemporary elements into traditional holiday designs." Prefers to work with artists with some greeting card or giftwrap experience. Also uses freelance artists for mechanicals. Pattern repeats should be even division of 20½" (with denominators of ⅝", 10" or 20½"). Submit holiday material 18 months before holiday.
First Contact & Terms: Send query letter wih brochure, resume, tear sheets, color roughs and SASE. Samples are not filed. Reports back with 1 month. Original artwork is not returned to the artists after job's completion. Pays by the project. Buys all rights.

***GIBSON GREETING CARDS**, Box 371804, 2100 Section Rd., Cincinnati OH 45222-1804. (513)841-6693. Director of Creative Control: Bill Luckman. Assistant Vice President and Creative Director: Sandy Jones. Produces greeting cards and calendars.

Close-up

Sandy Jones

Creative Director, Assistant Vice President
Gibson Greeting Cards
Cincinnati, Ohio

A veteran of the greeting card industry has some simple advice for freelance artists interested in the market.

"Get yourself a job at a greeting card company," says Sandy Jones, assistant vice president and creative director at Gibson Greeting Cards in Cincinnati. "Work there for a year or two, find out what it's all about. That's the quickest, easiest way."

Jones, who has worked 19 years in the greeting card industry, explains that many greeting card artists who have made it on their own worked in the industry before freelancing, learning the way cards are made and marketed. They apply what they learned from the pros to their own creative and marketing efforts.

What qualities does she look for in a greeting card artist?

"We look for people who have good drawing skills and a fairly well-developed color sense. Then we figure that we can train them," says Jones. "To make good greeting cards, those are two qualities you cannot be without."

Jones says that Gibson always asks artists for original drawings and likes to review sketchbooks to see how well they can draw. Her company will look at anything, says Jones, but she asks people not to send framed paintings. "They do it. You'd be surprised how often they do." Developing a line of cards is an involved process. "We work with fairly tight specifications given to us from product management. A line planner, who is in charge of a season or project, gives us the price, the sending situation, the size, the color and the subject matter.

"It then goes through the editorial department to get a verse applied. So, we're designing something pretty tight when we get to that point. We do a concept first, it's reviewed and then we go to a finished piece of art."

Jones says an idea that comes from a freelance artist may be unusable for a number of reasons. The style may be inappropriate for their lines, and the artwork may not reproduce well because of the medium used. Additionally, the basic concept may not fit with an appropriate verse or message. Jones says that her company usually purchases the idea and asks the artist to adapt it to their specifications.

In the past, many of the top greeting card companies such as Gibson and Hallmark relied on an inhouse staff to supply the creative work. However, the popularity of alternative cards changed their minds. The whimsical and off-beat humor of the alternative cards came largely from freelance artists. While their own staffs are capable of producing similar types of cards, the companies opened their mail boxes to the fresh outlook of other creative people.

A good greeting card, Jones feels, is one that carries a message that is meaningful to the consumer. "I think that's all there is. The message the artwork and the verse carry is the important part."

—Bob Firestone

Needs: "A total of 5,000 new items are added to the Gibson line each year. Of that number, freelance artwork is used for about 40 percent." Works with 100 + freelance artists/year. Prefers artists who have had experience with giftwrap or wallpaper. "The best route for those interested in working with us is to work in-house for at least one year." Works on assignment only.
First Contact & Terms: Send query letter with slides. Reports back within 2 weeks. Write to request to send in a portfolio, which should include a resume and a variety of work. "Portfolios will be returned in about three weeks." Pays average fee of $200-400. "Payment for large, four-color fold cards or calendars can go higher." Buys all rights.

THE C.R. GIBSON CO., 32 Knight St., Norwalk CT 06856. (203)847-4543. Director of Creative Services: Gary E. Carpenter. Publishes stationery, baby and wedding books, paper tableware and other gift products. SASE. Reports in 6 weeks. No finished art, paid for, is returned. Buys all rights.
Needs: Buys 200 designs/year. Uses artists for illustration and calligraphy. Assigns specific art needs for individual projects. Does not usually buy unsolicited finished art.
First Contact & Terms: Send query letter with samples to the attention of Creative Services Coordinator: Marilyn Schoenleber.

THE C.R. GIBSON CO., Creative Papers/Greeting Cards, 32 Knight St., Norwalk CT 06856. (203)847-4543. Product Manager: John C.W. Carroll. Produces greeting cards.
Needs: Buys 100-200 designs and illustrations from freelance artists/year. Considers most media except collage. Prefers airbrush, colored pencil, watercolor, acrylics, oils, pastels and markers. Scale work to a minimum of 4 7/8x6 3/4. Prefers vertical image. Submit seasonal material 12 months before the holiday. Will send guidelines on request.
First Contact & Terms: Send query letter and samples showing art style and or resume and tear sheets, Photostats, photocopies, slides, photographs and other materials. Prefers samples, not originals. Samples not filed are returned by SASE. Reports in 2 months. Call or write for appointment to show portfolio, which should include final reproduction/product, color, tear sheets, photographs and transparencies along with representative originals. Original artwork returned at job's completion. Pays $200 minimum per illustration/design. Negotiates rights purchased.
Tips: "If your images are appropriate for card use ("sendability"), then accompanying text should follow relatively easily; artists *can* write . . . it's a complete concept. Our orientation is toward fashion. "Pretty" as a category has become tremendously important; it includes florals and general styling of a line, by illustration and design. Our line has grown more traditional, because this is what our customers perceive as appropriate coming from C.R. Gibson/Creative Papers."

GRAND RAPIDS CALENDAR CO., 906 S. Division Ave., Grand Rapids MI 49507. (616)243-1732. Art Director: Rob Van Sledright. Publishes calendars; pharmacy, medical and family themes.
Needs: Buys approximately 15 designs/year. Uses artists for advertising art and line drawings.
First Contact & Terms: Send query letter and SASE for information sheet. Reports in 2 weeks. Previously published, photocopied and simultaneous submissions OK. Pays $10 minimum.

***GRAPHICALLY SPEAKING**, Box 17067, Denver CO 80217. President: Wanda Hocker. Estab. 1987. Produces greeting cards, giftwrap, games, calendars and posters. "Our target group is the black consumer, although designs should be distinctive enough to be enjoyed by all."
Needs: Buys over 100 illustrations from freelance artists/year. Works on assignment only. Considers all media. "We are interested in art that conveys positive imagery and upbeat designs." Prefers designs no larger than 15x21, vertical card format. Produces material for everyday, Christmas, Mother's Day, Father's Day, Easter, Valentine's Day; submit 12 months before holiday.
First Contact & Terms: Send query letter with brochure, resume, tear sheets, Photostats, photocopies, slides and SASE. Samples not filed are returned by SASE. Reports back within 2 months. To show a portfolio, mail slides, tear sheets, Photostats, photographs and color. Original artwork is not returned to the artist after job's completion. Negotiates payment on acceptance. Buys all rights.
Tips: "We are a fresh and new art company interested in designs with one or two subjects geared toward the black consumer. We are looking for clean, full-color creative designs. You will find it helpful to familiarize yourself with the varying degrees of black skin tones."

GREAT LAKES CONCEPTS DESIGNED, Box 2107, Traverse City MI 49685. (616)941-1372. General Manager: Ardana J. Titus. Estab. 1983. Produces note cards. Seeks "creative, romantic and humorous designs with one or two subjects. We need colorful and imaginative designs for all-occasion notecard line." No landscapes. Sample cards $3.
Needs: Buys 12 designs from freelance artists/year. Currently working with Michigan artists only. Considers primarily watercolor—bright, distinct colors and designs—no washes. Final art size 8x11; allow ¼" on all sides for trim. Prefers vertical designs but will consider horizontal.

First Contact & Terms: Prefers Michigan artists. Send query letter with samples to be kept on file. Write for art guidelines with SASE. Prefers photographs or originals as samples. Samples not filed are returned by SASE. Reports back within 3 months. Original art returned after reproduction. Pays flat fee of $50 for design. Purchases first rights and/or reprint rights.
Tips: "When submitting material, send bright designs using imaginative approaches. An example is a white lily on a bright yellow background. We will consider a series. We're looking for designs of one or two children as subjects. Designs must be of easily recognizable subjects. Customers want designs of distinct subject work, landscapes don't seem to do well on stationery cards."

GREAT NORTHERN PUBLISHING, INC., 116 W. Denny Way, Seattle WA 98119. (206)285-6838. President: Jeffrey Ross. Produces calendars and stationery.
Needs: Works with 6 freelance artists/year. Buys 12 designs and 40 illustrations from freelance artists/year. Works on assignment only. Prefers calendar format, 11¾x16½ or 9½x12. "We feature entertainment (music, TV and movie) related licensed properties or ideas."
First Contact & Terms: Send query letter with brochure or photocopies and slides. Samples are filed. Samples not filed are returned only if requested. Reports back within 1 month only if interested. Call or write to schedule an appointment to show a portfolio, which should include original/final art, slides, photographs, thumbnails and roughs. Original artwork is returned to artist after job's completion. Pays average flat fee of $400+/design; $100+/illustration; by the project, $800-1400; royalties of 8-10%. Buys one-time rights.

THE GREAT NORTHWESTERN GREETING SEED COMPANY, Box 776, Oregon City OR 97045. (503)631-3425. Art Director: Betty Barrett. Produces greeting cards. Uses pastel watercolor, black overlay; whimsical, botanical and natural themes.
Needs: Works on assignment with local artists only. Uses artists for calligraphy, P-O-P displays, paste-up and mechanicals. Prefers pen & ink and watercolor. Prefers final size of art to be equal to 150% of product. Produces material for Christmas, Mother's Day, Father's Day and Valentine's Day. Submit 6 months in advance.
First Contact & Terms: Send query letter with resume and samples to be kept on file. Accepts slides, Photostats, photographs, photocopies and tear sheets as samples. Samples not filed are returned by SASE only. Call or write to schedule an appointment to show a portfolio, which should include thumbnails, roughs, original/final art, final reproduction/product and color. Reports within several weeks. No originals returned to artist at job's completion. Buys all rights.

GREEN TIGER PRESS, 1061 India St., San Diego CA 92101. (619)238-1001. Art Director: Christy Warwick. Publishes greeting cards, giftwrap, calendars, posters, stationery products and picture books.
Needs: Uses artists for cards, book and calendar illustration. Prefers oils, then pen & ink, airbrush, charcoal/pencil, colored pencil, watercolor, acrylics, pastels, collage and calligraphy.
First Contact & Terms: Send color slides. Provide samples to be kept on file for possible future assignments. Samples not kept on file are returned by SASE. Reports in 3 months. Originals returned to artist at job's completion. Negotiates rights purchased. Negotiates payment.
Tips: Artists should have a "good variety of samples; include human figures, especially children if available. "We do not use cartoon-style work or science fiction. We look for art containing a romantic, visionary or imaginative quality, often with a mythic quality. Never send originals."

GREETWELL, D-23, M.I.D.C., Satpur, Nasik 422 007 India. Chief Executive: H.L. Sanghavi. Produces greeting cards, calendars and posters. Specializes in wildlife, flowers, landscapes; general purpose only.
Needs: Buys 50 designs from freelance artists/year.
First Contact & Terms: Send color photos and samples to be kept on file. Samples not filed are returned only if requested. Reports within 4 weeks. Original art returned after reproduction. Pays flat fee of $50/design. Buys reprint rights.
Tips: "We will supply 5,000 greeting cards at twelve cents each of your selected design."

***HALLMARK CARDS, INC.**, Box 419580, 2501 McGee, Kansas City MO 64141-6580, Mail Drop 276. Contact: Carol King. Produces greeting cards, giftwrap, calendars, stationery and gift items.
Needs: Works with 300 freelance artists/year. Assigns approximately 1,500 design and illustration jobs/year. Buys artwork for a diversified product offering. "Freelancers must display a unique concept, innovative technique or unusual point of view. We look for strong concepts and imaginative layouts and an eye for trends." Works on assignment only. Looks for "artwork designed to compete within the industry and not for self-expression." Send query letter and SASE to request an information sheet. "Once contacted by the company, you may be asked to send samples such as slides, tear sheets or prints." Reports back within 5 weeks. Illustrations are purchased alone, in a series or along with editorial material

The whimsical humor of Nadine Bernard Westcott earmarks the cards produced by Hartland Cards. Westcott, who lives in Woodstock, Vermont, uses watercolor and pen and ink to create her cards. After graduating from Syracuse University, she worked for Hallmark Cards, where she learned to illustrate cards. She left Hallmark to form Hartland Cards. "The greeting card industry depends on freelance artists," she says. "Companies can't afford not to use them." Westcott has applied her sense of "pure nonsense" found in her cards to children's books.

as a package. Buys all rights.
Tips: "Study the lines. Hallmark has a large and prolific creative staff. Freelancers must show exceptional skills and originality to interest our product lines who are used to creating the very best."

HARTLAND CARDS, Box 210, Woodstock VT 05091. (802)457-3905. General Manager: Jack Anderson. Produces greeting cards, announcements, invitations and humorous cards for ages 18 to 65.
Needs: Works on assignment only. Prefers pen & ink, watercolors and acrylics. Prefers 4⅞x7⅜, vertical format mostly; horizontal OK. Produces material for Christmas, Valentines, Easter, Mother's Day and Father's Day, Graduation, St. Patrick's Day; submit 1 year before holiday. Also produces all-occasion, everyday cards.
First Contact & Terms: Send query letter with photocopies or card roughs and SASE. Samples are not filed. Samples not filed are returned by SASE. Reports back only if interested. "We need an adjunct line or lines to market in concert with that of the company's major artist, Nadine Westcott. Primarily looking for humor, but will look at other themes. Would like to see at least 12-24 cards in a line to start with a commitment to building the line. Humor should be "cute," not "sappy" or "raunchy." Slightly risque is OK. Occasions and themes should address real life, contemporary situations. Colorful cartooned styles preferred." Original artwork is returned after job's completion. Pays royalties of 3-5%, with usual advancement on royalties of $50-100 per design. All payments negotiated.
Tips: "Send cover letter and 12 cards at least roughed out, final art work is not necessary. Reports only if interested. Originals or slides will be treated carefully and returned with SASE."

MARIAN HEATH GREETING CARDS, INC., 9 Kendrick Rd., Wareham MA 02175. (617)291-0766. Art Director: Susan Bint. Produces greeting cards, giftwrap, stationery and children's books. Produces announcements, general cards, informal cards, inspirational cards, invitations and juvenile cards.
Needs: Works with 12 freelance artists/year. Buys 100 designs from freelance artists/year. Prefers full color. Produces material for Christmas, Valentine, Easter, Thanksgiving; submit 1 year before holiday.
First Contact & Terms: Send query letter with brochure or Photostats, photocopies, slides and SASE. Samples are filed. Samples not filed are returned by SASE only if requested. Reports back within 3 weeks. Call or write to schedule an appointment to show a portfolio or mail thumbnails, roughs, original/final reproduction/product and slides. Original artwork is sometimes returned to artist after job's completion. Pays average flat fee of $150/design. Negotiates rights purchased.
Tips: "We look for tight rendering especially. Will consider roughs if accompanied by a finished piece of work, either original or reproduction; color important."

INTERCONTINENTAL GREETINGS LTD., 176 Madison Ave., New York NY 10016. (212)683-5830. Creative Marketing Director: Robin Lipner. Sells reproduction rights on a per country per product basis. Licenses and syndicates to 4,500-5,000 publishers and manufacturers in 50 different countries. Industries include greeting cards, calendars, prints, posters, stationery, books, textiles, heat transfers, gift-

ware, china, plastics, toys and allied industries, scholastic items and giftwrap.
Needs: Assigns 400-500 jobs and 1,500 designs and illustrations/year. "The trend is to more graphic—clean, modern work." Uses some humorous and cartoon-style illustrations. Prefers airbrush and watercolor, then colored pencil, acrylics, pastels, markers and computer illustration.
First Contact & Terms: Send query letter and/or resume, tear sheets, slides and photographs. SASE. To show a portfolio, mail appropriate materials or call or write to schedule an appointment; portfolio should include original/final art, color, tear sheets, photographs and originals. Pays by average flat fee of $225/design. Pays by the project, design and illustration. Pays 20% royalties upon sale of reproduction rights on all selected designs. Contractual agreements made with artists and licensing representatives, will negotiate reasonable terms. Considers skill and experience of artist, product use, turnaround time and rights purchased when establishing payment. Provides worldwide promotion, portfolio samples (upon sale of art) and worldwide trade show display.
Tips: "More and more of our clients need work submitted in series form, so we have to ask artists for work in a series or possibly reject the odd single designs submitted. Make as neat and concise a presentation as possible with commerical application in mind. Show us color examples of at least one finished piece as well as roughs."

JOLI GREETING CARD CO., 2520 W. Irving Park Rd., Chicago IL 60618. (312)588-3770. President: Joel Weil. Art Director: Mindy Katz. Produces greeting cards and stationery.
Needs: Number of designs and illustrations bought/year varies. Artists must not have worked for Joli's immediate competition. Uses artists for P-O-P displays. Considers airbrush for product illustration. Prefers finished art of 4x9 for studio cards and 5x7 for 5x7 line. Publishes seasonal material for Christmas, St. Valentine's Day, Mother's Day, Father's Day.
First Contact & Terms: Send query letter with samples to be kept on file. Accepts "whatever is available" as samples. Samples not filed are returned by SASE. Reports within 1 month. Sometimes returns original art after reproduction. Pays flat fee; "open, depending on project." Buys all rights.
Tips: "We are looking for a 'today-look', primarily in the medium of airbrushing and cartooning. In a portfolio, include a resume, printed samples and comprehensives. No sketches or loose roughs."

KOGLE CARDS, INC., Suite 212, 5575 S. Sycamore St., Littleton CO 80120. President: Patty Koller. Produces greeting cards.
Needs: Buys 50 designs from freelance artists/year; buys 50 illustrations from freelance artists/year. Works on assignment only. Considers all media for illustrations. Prefers 5x7" for final art. Produces material for Christmas and all major holidays plus birthdays; material accepted all year round.
First Contact & Terms: Send resume and slides. Samples not filed are returned by SASE. Reports back within 2 weeks. To show a portfolio, mail original/final art, color, Photostats, photographs and b&w. Original artwork is not returned. Pays on royalty basis. Buys all rights.

***LEAVERLY GREETING**, 10502 Magnolia Blvd., N. Hollywood CA 91601. Creative Director: Kim Tucker. Estab. 1987. Produces photographic greetings cards, stationery, calendars, and posters.
Needs: Works with 2 freelance photographers/year. Buys 100 + designs from freelance photographers/year. Buys no illustrations from freelance artists. Prefers photography only. Also uses freelance artists for calligraphy, P-O-P displays, paste-up, and mechanicals. "Prefers sophisticated themes for an adult market—no humor." Produces material for Christmas, Valentine's and Mother's Day.
First contact & Terms: "Inquire only by mail with a query letter." Samples are not filed and not returned.
Tips: "We work with local artists, who are used for mechanicals."

PAUL LEVY-DESIGNER, 2993 Lakewood Lane, Hollywood FL 33021. (305)981-9550. President: Paul Levy. Produces wallpaper and fabrics.
Needs: Buys 12-24 designs from freelance artists/year. Uses artists for original designs for wallcovering and fabric. Prefers gouache - watercolor designers colors for illustrations; side repeats divisible into 27" and down repeats 18" to 27"
First Contact & Terms: Send resume and original sketches. Call or write to schedule an appointment to show a portfolio, which should include original/final art, final reproduction/product and color. Pays for design by the hour, $10-12; "price depends on experience of artist."
Tips: "Designs in fabrics and wall covering will continue in a contemporary fashion with a modest blending of 'transitional' which is a combination of traditional and contemporary. It is most critical to be as original as possible. Designs of 'me too' nature will not be acceptable in marketplace. Have eyes everywhere as design is universal. Search out the unusual and try to apply it to the medium and field you are designing for. Keep up with color trends as color is as important if not more so than design."

LIFE GREETINGS, Box 468, Meeting House Lane, Little Compton RI 02837. (401)635-8535. Art Director: Kathy Brennan. Produces greeting cards, specialized religious announcements and inspirational cards.

Needs: Works with 12 freelance artists/year. Buys 200 designs from freelance artists/year. Buys 200 illustrations from freelance artists/year. Prefers pen & ink, pencil, charcoal and some watercolor. Produces material for Christmas, Mother's Day, Father's Day, graduation, First Communion, Confirmation and all occasion; submit 6 months before holiday. "Open to ideas and new lines of artwork from freelance artists."

First Contact & Terms: Send query letter with brochure; "would like some representation of type of work." Samples are filed. Samples not filed are returned by SASE only if requested by artist. Reports back within 1 month. Negotiates pay with artist. Buys all rights.

MAINE LINE COMPANY, Box 418, Rockport ME 04856. (207)236-8536 or 1-800-624-6363. Contact: Liz Stanley or Marjorie MacClennen. Publishes greeting cards for contempory men and women from college age up, with primary concentration on people in their 30s. Most of the cards are humorous and deal with contemporary concerns. Also publishes humorous postcards and notepads, and other gift products.

Needs: Buys 300 illustrations a year from freelance artists; most work is commissioned. "We're looking for illustrators with a sense of humor, whose style is contemporary, funky and colorful. You need not write your own copy to illustrate cards for us, but we're also looking for illustrators who write as well." Prefers "humorous illustrated work with a sophisticated style." Accepts all media except oils. Commissions a group or series of cards, rather than a single card. Also reviews artists or designers concepts for greeting card and postcard series. Other products: button, mugs.

First Contact & Terms: Send query letter with photocopies, Photostats, tearsheets, slides or photographs. SASE needed for return of samples. Sample card $1 each; creative guidelines for SASE with 60¢ postage. Turnaround time 6 weeks. To show a portfolio, mail appropriate materials, which should include final reproduction/product, color, tear sheets, photographs, b&w and slides.

Tips: "We are using more and more full-color art and have more need for illustrators and designers. Please send organized work, labeled, with SASE. I do not want to see original art."

MARCEL SCHURMAN CO. INC., 954 60th St., Oakland CA 94608. (415)428-0200. Art Director: Sandra McMillan. Produces greeting cards, giftwrap and stationery. Specializes in "very fine art work with many different looks: traditional, humorous, graphic designs, photography, juvenile designs, etc."

Needs: Buys 800-1000 designs/year from freelance artists. Prefers colored pencil, watercolor, oils, pastels, collage and calligraphy. Prefers final art sizes proportionate to 5x7", 4x6"; Produces seasonal material for Valentine's Day, Easter, Mother's Day, Father's Day, graduation, Halloween, Christmas, Hanukkah and Thanksgiving. Submit art by March for Valentine's Day and Easter, end of June for Mother's and Father's Day, graduation; November for Christmas, Halloween, Thanksgiving and Hanukkah. Interested in all-occasion cards also.

First Contact & Terms: Send query letter with slides, printed material or photographs showing a variety of styles. "No bios, news clippings or original art, please." Reports within 1 month. Returns original art after reproduction. Pays average flat fee of $250/illustration; royalites of 5%. Buys all rights.

Tips: "There is more process intension design (foils, diecuts, tripanels, etc.). There is also more attention paid to paperstock."

MARK I INC., 1733 W. Irvine Park Rd., Chicago IL 60613. (312)281-1111. Creative Director: Alex H Cohen. Publishes greeting cards and stationery products for adult and juvenile markets.

Needs: Buys 1000 designs from freelance artists/year. Will work on assignment. Uses artists for calligraphy. Prefers contemporary and traditional designs. Prefers total line concept of 18-36 pieces. Considers all media. Categories in humorous and sensitivity; everyday, Christmas, Valentine's Day Mother's Day, Father's Day, Easter and Graduation.

First Contact & Terms: Send query letter to be kept on file. Write for art guidelines. Samples not filed are returned by SASE. Reports within 2 weeks. Originals returned to artist at job's completion. Write for appointment to show portfolio. Pays for design by the project, terms negotiable. Pays by the project, $100/design-$250/design. Buys exclusive world-wide rights for greeting cards. Will pay usage fee against a royalty.

Tips: "We look for images that are neutral enough to be sold to an unlimited portion of this buying market."

MICHEL'S DESIGNS, INC.,—DIVISION OF THE VIOLA GROUP, INC., 8 Engineers Lane, Farmingdale, Long Island NY 11735. (212)585-1577. Creative Coordinator: Arthur D. Viola. Produces period and high fashion (contemporary) hand-silk screen wallcoverings for interior designers/interior decorators; home-furnishings; showrooms; and major wallcovering distribution companies. Works with wallcovering artists only.

Needs: Buys 18-36 designs from freelance artists/year. Priority to local artists having contacts and a presence in the home furnishings and/or Interior Decorator/Interior Designer markets. Ability to create artwork; produce color separations on acetate, thus creating camera-ready artwork. Uses artists for paste-up and mechanicals. "Prefers watercolor or color pencils initially, and subsequently reproduction on acetates to produce the wallcovering design samples at our factory. Prefers 28" to 32" pattern repeat, initially on notepaper, and subsequently reproduced on acetate in color separations by creative freelance artists. Coloring of designs must be current and applicable to the season the line is launched—which is usually fall or spring."
First Contact & Terms: Contact only through artist's agent, who should send query letter with resume, tear sheets, Photostats, photocopies and photographs. Samples not filed are returned by SASE. Reports back within 4 weeks. To show a portfolio, mail appropriate materials or call or write to schedule an appointment. Portfolio should include thumbnails, original/final art, final reproduction/product, color, Photostats and photographs. No originals returned to artist at job's completion. Payment is reimbursement of reasonable expenses, a royalty arrangement which includes publicly trading common stock in our parent company; and if the line (you help create) goes, a permanent creative consulting position in the division created to house your line and others. Buys all rights.
Tips: "We are looking for a freelancer with sufficient business acumen and commitment to act as manager of a division of a small public company. This division of our parent company will be created around the line her artwork helps to create. A block of stock in the company may be available at the "insider" price to the right candidate should her creative ability produce a profitable line. She will gain through capital gains on the stock and through profit-sharing percentage on the line created."

***MILES KIMBALL COMPANY**, 41 W. 8th Ave., Oshkosh WI 54901. Vice President-Christmas Card Design and Sales: Alfred F. Miyamoto. Produces greeting cards. "We sell cards by direct mail to people who are looking for a 'custom' look—cards designed around the personalized theme."
Needs: Buys 2-20 designs with copy from freelance artists/year. "We are looking for designers for personalized Christmas cards. Our look is more 'cozy' than high-tech or sophisticated. We want someone able to create a whole concept: design and copy." Considers idea roughs on vellum stock in almost any media. "We are looking for ideas more than technique." Standard greeting card sizes; "4¼x5½" is the most popular folded size." Produces material for Christmas only; "best time to submit material is early spring; but material is accepted year round."
First Contact & Terms: "We need experienced artists who can write the text for their cards, too." Send query letter with samples to be kept on file; write for art guidelines. "As we are looking for ideas mainly, roughs are accepted for preliminary evaluation. We prefer not to have slides or photographs sent." Samples not filed are returned by SASE only. Reports within 2 months. No originals returned to artist at job's completion. Pays flat fee. Buys all rights.
Tips: "Since our cards are sold imprinted with customer's name, we are looking for designers who can create a total card concept, that looks as if each was made especially for the buyer. Studio card humor and ultra-sophistication does not work for us. We will give guidelines after previewing samples."

NATIONAL ANNOUNCEMENTS INC., 34-24 Collins Ave., Flushing NY 11753. (718)353-4002. Vice President: David Rosner. Produces wedding invitations (blank stock, ready for printing) for women ages 18 up.
Needs: Works with freelance artists/year. Prefers local artists with greeting card background.
First Contact & Terms: Send query letter with brochure. Samples are not filed. Samples not filed are returned only if requested by artist. Reports back only if interested. Call or write to schedule an appointment to show a portfolio, which should include final reproduction/product. Original artwork is not returned to the artist after job's completion. Pays by the project, $50-250. Buys all rights.
Tips: "Greeting card experience is necessary plus it's helpful to understand the graphic arts process."

***NEW DECO, INC.**, #A11, 10018 Spanish Isles Blvd., Boca Raton FL 33498. (305)482-6295. Vice-President: Brad Hugh Morris. Produces greeting cards and posters.
Needs: Works with 5-10 freelance artists/year. Buys 8-10 designs from freelance artists/year. Buys 5-10 illustrations from freelance artists/year. Prefers art deco, contemporary and figurative styles.
First Contact & Terms: Send query letter with brochure, resume, tear sheets, slides and SASE. Samples not filed are returned by SASE. Reports back within 10 days only if interested. To show a portfolio, mail slides, color. Original artwork is returned after job's completion. Pays royalties of 10%. Buys all rights; negotiates rights purchased.

OATMEAL STUDIOS, Box 138, Rochester VT 05767. (802)767-3171. Art Director: Helene Lehrer. Publishes greeting cards; creative ideas for everyday cards and holidays.
Needs: Buys 100-150 designs/illustrations per year from freelance artists. Uses artists for greeting card design and illustration. Considers all media; prefers 5x7, 6x8½, vertical composition. Produces season-

al material for Christmas, Mother's Day, Father's Day, Easter, Valentine's Day and Hanukkah. Submit art in August for Christmas and Hanukkah, in January for other holidays.
First Contact & Terms: Send query letter with slides, roughs, printed pieces, brochure/flyer to be kept on file; write for artists' guidelines. "If brochure/flyer is not available, we ask to keep one slide or printed piece." Samples returned by SASE. Reports in 2-4 weeks. Negotiates payment arrangement with artist.
Tips: "We're looking for exciting and creative illustrations and graphic design for greeting cards. Also, light humor with appeal to college age and up."

OUTREACH PUBLICATIONS, Box 1010, Siloam Springs AR 72761. (501)524-9381. Creative Art Director: Darrell Hill. Produces greeting cards, calendars and stationery. Produces announcements, general cards, informal cards, inspirational cards, invitations, contemporary cards, soft line cards and studio cards plus calendars and stationery.
Needs: Works with 12 freelance artists/year. Buys 30 designs from freelance artists/year. Prefers experienced greeting card artists. Works on assignment only. Also uses artists for calligraphy. Prefers designers gouache colors and watercolors. "Greeting card sizes range from 4½x6½ to 5½x8½, prefer same size, but not more than 200% size." Produces material for Valentine's, Easter, Mother's Day, Father's Day, Confirmation, Graduation, Thanksgiving, Christmas; submit 1 year before holiday.
First Contact & Terms: Send query letter with brochure or photocopies, slides and SASE. Samples are not filed. Samples not filed are returned by SASE. Reports back within 4-6 weeks. To show a portfolo, mail original/final art, final reproduction/product, slides, photographs and color. Original artwork is not returned after job's completion. Pays average flat fee of $100-325/design. Buys all greeting card rights.
Tips: "Outreach Publications produce Dayspring Greeting cards, a Christian card line. Suggest interested artists request our guidelines for freelance artists. Experienced greeting cards artists preferred. Submissions should include no more than 12 selections."

PACIFIC PAPER GREETINGS, INC., (formerly Snap Dragon Floral Design), Box 2249, Sidney British Columbia V8L 3S8 Canada. (604)656-0504. President: Louise Rytter. Produces greeting cards,stationery and related items.
Needs: "Prefers experience and artists that will develop a theme to their artwork thus creating a series for greeting cards." Uses artists for paste-up and also verse writing. Prefers romantic style, fantasy and humor. Prefers watercolor and acrylics. Prefers greeting cards of stand-up size, 5x7. Produces material for Christmas, Mother's Day, Easter, Father's Day, Valentine's Day and all general occasions; submit 1 year before holiday.
First Contact & Terms: Send query letter with brochure showing art style or resume, tear sheets, Photostats, photocopies, slides and photographs. Samples not filed returned by SASE. Reports within 1 month. To show a portfolio, mail appropriate materials such as slides and a brief bio. Negotiates payment and rights purchased.
Tips: "Remember we are looking for a theme artist to create a card line. Not cutsey."

PAPEL, INC., Box 9879, North Hollywood CA 91609. (818)765-1100. Art Coordinator: Helen Scheffler. Produces souvenir and seasonal ceramic giftware items: mugs, photo frames, greeting plaques.
Needs: Buys 300 illustrations from freelance artists/year. Artists with minimum 3 years of experience in greeting cards only; "our product is ceramic but ceramic experience not necessary." Uses artists for product and P-O-P design, illustrations on product, calligraphy, paste-up and mechanicals. Produces material for Christmas, Valentine's Day, Easter, St. Patrick's Day, Mother's and Father's Day; submit 1 year before holiday.
First Contact & Terms: Send query letter with brochure, resume, Photostats, photocopies, slides, photographs and tear sheets to be kept on file. Samples not kept on file are returned by SASE if requested. Reports within one month. No originals returned to artist at job's completion. To show a portfolio, mail appropriate materials, which should include final reproduction/product, color, tear sheets, Photostats, photographs and b&w. Pays by the project, $50-350. Buys all rights.
Tips: "I look for an artist who has realistic drawing skills but who can temper everything with a decorative feeling. I look for a 'warm' quality that I think will be appealing to the consumer. We still depend a tremendous amount on freelance talent. Send samples of as many different styles as you are capable of doing well. Versatility is a key to having lots of work."

PAPER ART COMPANY INC., 3500 N. Arlington Ave., Indianapolis IN 46218. (800)428-5017. Creative Director: Jo Anne Madry. Produces paper tableware products, invitations and party decor.
Needs: Buys 25% of line from freelance artists/year. Prefers flat watercolor, designer's gouache for designs. Prefers 5x5 design area for luncheon napkin designs; 4x4 for cocktail napkins; 9¼ for plate design. Produces general everyday patterns for birthday, weddings, casual entertaining, baby and bridal showers; St. Patrick's Day, Easter, Valentine's Day, Fall, Halloween, Thanksgiving, Christmas and New Year.

First Contact & Terms: Send query letter with brochure showing art style, photocopies and printed samples. Samples are not returned. Reports back within 2 weeks. Call to schedule an appointment to show a portfolio, which should include original/final art, final reproduction/product, color and designs. Original artwork is not returned if purchased. Pays by the project, $150-250.
Tips: "Color coordinating and the mixing and matching of patterns are prevalent. Need sophisticated designs. In paper products, the biggest change is in non-drinking type cocktail napkins. For us, we require professional, finished art that would apply to our product."

PAPER PEDDLER, INC., 1201 Pennsylvania Ave., Richmond CA 94801. Produces postcards. "Our postcards have a variety of subject matter. Humor, fine arts, black-and-white, and contemporary. The postcards are generally directed towards the younger, more style-conscious crowd."
Needs: Buys 15-20 designs and illustrations from freelance artists/year. Prefers 4 1/8x5 7/8 or proportional for postcards.
First Contact & Terms: Send query letter with slides or originals. Samples are filed. "Please include SASE." Reports back within 4-6 weeks. To show a portfolio, mail original/final art, photographs or slides. Original artwork is returned after job's completion. Pays average of $50-150/design; $50-150/illustration; advance against royalties of 5%. Buys reprint rights.
Tips: "Paper Peddler, Inc. is largely an importer of postcards. However, we also do our own publishing. Our postcard line covers a variety of subject matter including humor, black-and-white photo, fine arts, Americana, and nature images, and the market tends to be the younger, more style-conscious crowd."

PECK INC., 3963 Vernal Pike, Box 1148, Bloomington IN 47402. Art Director: Jane Ackerman. Manufactures Christmas tags; Christmas, Halloween, Valentine and Easter cutouts; and educational bulletin board aids.
Needs: Uses artists for product design and illustrations. Specific needs include juvenile characters, animals, traditional Christmas, Halloween and/or all occasion design.
First Contact & Terms: Send a query letter with color or b&w samples.SASE. Reports in approximately 2 weeks. Pays by the project; negotiates payment according to complexity of project and product use.
Tips: Especially looks for "full-color work and emphasis on clarity of color and design. It would be helpful if the artist has worked with a large format."

***PICKHARDT & SIEBERT (USA) INC.**, 16201 Trade Zone Ave., Upper Marlboro MD 20772. (301)249-7900. Produces wallcovering and companion fabrics.
Needs: Uses artists for product design, illustration on product, calligraphy, paste-up and mechanicals. "Wallcovering manufacturing being done in Germany; some wallcovering textile designs are purchased in the US. We do find the need for *local* freelance artists."
First Contact & Terms: Send query letter with resume; tear sheets and Photostats to be kept on file. Reports only if interested. To show a portfolio, mail original/final art or call or write to schedule an appointment. Negotiates pay.
Tips: "Need complete package as soon as possible—prefer approach with total concept."

***PINEAPPLE PRESS**, Suite 207, 8300 Delongpre Ave., Los Angeles CA 90069. (213)656-7124. President: Shelley A. Piña. Estab. 1986. Produces posters and limited editions.
Needs: Works with 8 freelance artists/year. Buys 5 designs from freelance artists/year. Buys 20 illustrations from freelance artists/year. Prefers "artists who understand a deadline." Works on assignment only. Also uses freelance artists for paste-up, mechanicals and lettering. Prefers acrylics, but will consider the artist's style and technique. Prefer contemporary look.
First Contact & Terms: Send query letter with resume, slides and SASE. Samples are filed. Samples not filed are returned by SASE. Reports back within 2 months. Call or write to schedule an appointment to show a portfolio. Original artwork is returned to artist after job's completion. Pays by the project, $200-1,000 average; royalties of 5-10%. Negotiates rights purchased.
Tips: "Be professional. New emerging artists should not be afraid to submit their work."

PLUM GRAPHICS INC., Box 136, Prince Station, New York NY 10012. President: Yvette Cohen. Produces greeting cards for all ages, male and female.
Needs: Needs illustrations from freelance artists. Prefers local artists, but not a requirement. Prefers tight watercolors, oil, airbrush. Illustrations must be colored in reproducible colors. Prefers 5x7 or larger to be reproduced in 5x7 format.
First Contact & Terms: Send query letter with slides or tear sheets or photocopies. Samples are filed. Samples not filed are returned by SASE or not returned. Reports back within 2 months only if interested. "If we're interested artist will be contacted" to schedule an appointment to show a portfolio, which should include original/final art, final reproduction/product, tear sheets and color. Original artwork is

returned after job's completion. Pays average flat fee of $150-200/illustration; by the project; or may provide negotiable flat fee for future reprints. Buys greeting card rights.
Tips: "In a sample package, I must see some photocopies. A query letter alone with no indication of style is useless."

PLYMOUTH INC., 361 Benigno Blvd., Bellmawr NJ 08031. Art Director: Nancy Yarnall. Produces posters, stationery and paper products, such as 3x5 wire-bound memo books, wire-bound theme books, porfolios, scribble pads, book covers, pencil tablets, etc., all with decorative covers for school, middle grades and high school. "We use contemporary illustrations. Some of our work is licensed. We are expanding into the gift trade with various paper products aimed toward an older age group 19 and up."
Needs: Buys 300 designs and 300 illustrations from freelance artists/year. Works on assignment only. Uses artists for illustration, logo design, design, paste-up and mechanicals. Prefers full color and airbrush. Prefers "very graphic designs and illustration."
First Contact & Terms: Send query letter with brochure showing art style or resume, tear sheets, Photostats, photocopies, slides and photographs. Samples returned by SASE. Reports only if interested. Mail appropriate materials or write to schedule an appointment to show a portfolio, which should include final reproduction/product, color and tear sheets. Pays according to project and based upon experience. Buys all rights or negotiates rights purchased.
Tips: "Plymouth is looking for professional illustrators and designers. The work must be top notch. It is the art that sells our products. We use many different styles of illustration and design and are open to new ideas. Portfolio should include slides, we do not use black-and-white illustration or cartoons."

POPSHOTS, INC., 167 East Ave., Norwalk CT 06851. (203)838-5777. Art Director: Paul Zalon. Produces pop-up greeting cards for women ages 18 to 32, college-educated.
Needs: Works with 50 freelance artists/year. Buys 50 designs from freelance artists/year. Buys 50 illustrations from freelance artists/year. Works on assignment only. Prefers airbrush, then acrylics and oils. Job specs given. Produces material for Valentine's Day, Christmas, birthday, get well; submit 1 year before holiday.
First Contact & Terms: Contact only through artist's agent or send query letter with brochure or Photostats and photocopies. Samples are filed. Samples not filed are returned by SASE. Reports back only if interested. To show a portfolio, mail tear sheets and Photostats. Original artwork is sometimes returned after job's completion. Pays average flat fee of $1,500-2,000 illustration. Negotiates rights purchased.
Tips: "We look for realistic yet humorous illustration."

***POTPOURRI PRESS**, 6210 Swiggett Rd., Greensboro NC 27410; mailing address: Box 19566, Greensboro NC 27419. (919)852-8961. Director: of New Product Development: Janet Pesther. Produces paper products including bags, boxes and tableware, tins, stoneware, fragrance and fabric items for giftshops, the gourmet shop trade, and department stores.
Needs: Buys 10-20 designs from freelance artists/year; buys 10-20 illustrations from freelance artists/year. Works on assignment only. Uses artists for calligraphy, mechanicals and art of all kinds for product reproduction. Prefers watercolor, acrylics, markers and mechanical work. Produces everyday and seasonal products; submit material 1-2 years in advance.
First Contact & Terms: Send query letter with resume and tear sheets, Photostats, photocopies, slides and photographs. Samples not filed are returned by SASE. Reports back as soon as possible. Call or write to schedule an appointment to show a portfolio, which should include anything to show ability. "Artist must have good portfolio showing styles the artist is comfortable in." Original artwork not returned. Pays for illustration by the project $150-1,200. Buys all rights.
Tips: "Business is booming. Our art needs are increasing. We need artists who are flexible and willing to meet deadlines. Provide references that can tell us if you meet deadlines, are easy, medium or tough to work with, etc."

PRELUDE DESIGNS, 1 Hayes St., Elmsford NY 10523. Art Director: Madalyn Grano. Produces wallpaper/fabric/T-shirts.
Needs: Buys 10 designs and 1-5 illustrations from freelance artists/year. Local artists only. Works on assignment only. Uses artists for paste-up and color paint-ups. Prefers tempera, watercolor and acrylic. Prefers 36x27 (or fractions thereof).
First Contact & Terms: Send query letter with resume. Samples not filed are returned. Reports within 7 days. To show a portfolio, which should include original/final art, final reproduction/product, color and photographs. Originals sometimes returned to artist at job's completion. Pays average flat fee of $200-500. Negotiates rights purchased.

THE PRINTERY HOUSE OF CONCEPTION ABBEY, Conception MO 64433. Art Director: Rev. Norbert Schappler. A publisher of religious greeting cards; religious Christmas and all occasion themes for people interested in religious yet contemporary expressions of faith. "Our card designs are meant to touch the heart and feature strong graphics, calligraphy and other appropriate styles."
Needs: Works with 25 freelance artists/year. Uses artists for product illustrations. Prefers acrylics, pastels, cut paper, silk-screen, oil, watercolor, line drawings; classical and contemporary calligraphy. Produces seasonal material for Christmas and Easter.
First Contact & Terms: Send query letter with brochure showing art style or resume, tear sheets, Photostats, photocopies, slides and photographs. Samples returned by SASE. Reports within 3 weeks. To show a portfolio, mail appropriate materials only after query has been answered. Portfolio should include final reproduction/product, color, tear sheets and photographs. "In general, we continue to work with artists year after year once we have begun to accept work from them." Pays by the project; $150-250. Usually purchases exclusive reproduction rights for a specified format, occasionally buys complete reproduction rights.
Tips: "Abstract or semi-abstract background designs seem to fit best with religious texts. Color washes and stylized flowers sometimes appropriate. Simple designs and fresh, clean calligraphy are looked for. Computerized graphics are beginning to have an impact in our field; multi-colored calligraphy is a new development. Remember our specific purpose of publishing greeting cards with a definite Christian/religious dimension but not piously religious. Wedded with religious dimension, it must be good quality artwork. We sell mostly via catalogs so artwork has to reduce well for catalog."

PRODUCT CENTRE-S.W. INC./THE TEXAS POSTCARD CO., Box 708, Plano TX 75074. (214)423-0411. Art Director: Susan Hudson. Produces greeting cards, calendars, posters, melamine trays, coasters and postcards. Themes range from nostalgia to art deco to pop/rock for contemporary buyers.
Needs: Buys 100 designs from freelance artists/year. Uses artists for P-O-P display, paste-up and mechanicals. Considers any media, "we do use a lot of acrylic/airbrush designs." Prefers contemporary styles. Final art must not be larger than 8x10. "Certain products require specific measurements; we will provide these when assigned."
First Contact & Terms: Send resume, business card slides, Photostats, photographs, photocopies and tear sheets to be kept on file. Samples not filed are returned only by request with SASE including return insurance. Reports within 16 weeks. No originals returned to artist at job's completion. Call or write for appointment to show portfolio. Pays by the project, $50-100. Buys all rights.
Tips: "Artist should be able to submit camera-ready work and understand printer's requirements. The majority of our designs are assigned. We do not want to see crafty items or calligraphy."

***P.S. GREETINGS, INC.**, 4345 W. Division St., Chicago IL 60651. Art Director: Kevin Lahvic. Produces greeting cards.
Needs: Works with 15-20 freelance artists/year. Buys 65 illustrations from freelance artists/year. Prefers 5x7 cropped. Produces material for Christmas and everyday.
First Contact & Terms: Send query letter with "pieces for sale." Samples not filed are returned by SASE. Reports within 1 month. Original artwork is sometimes returned after job's completion. Pays $75-150/illustration. Buys all rights.
Tips: "Send artwork for sale at our payment rate. At this time we do not produce humorous work."

RAINBOWORLD CARDS, 319 A St., Boston MA 02210. (617)350-0260. Art/Marketing: Deborah Landy.Publishes die cut, stamped and embossed greeting cards, stationery and invitations. General themes, all occasions. Upscale market.
Needs: Buys 50 designs and 100 illustrations/year from freelance artists. Works on assignment only. Considers any color media with graphic orientation sized 10x14 or larger. No Photography. Produces seasonal material for Christmas, Spring (Easter, Mother's Day, Father's Day, Graduation) and Valentine's Day; submit art 6-12 months before holiday.
First Contact & Terms: Send resume and samples. No originals or slides. "If work is suitable, we will arrange to review portfolio and other work." Reports as soon as possible. Originals returned to artist at job's completion. Buys first rights and reprint rights. Negotiates payment, $250 and up/project; on publication. Considers complexity of project, skill and experience of artist, product use and rights purchased when establishing payment.
Tips: "For initial contact, artists should submit copies of their work which we can *keep* on file—even photocopies. This allows us to keep a 'review' file to use as projects develop and allows us to quickly discover which artists are suitable for our market with a minimum of inconvenience to both parties. Do not send resumes without samples and do not bother to write asking for further information on firm. Send samples. This is a visual medium, not verbal. We are an alternative company selling into upscale, trendy card and gift stores. Our target market is 20-50 years old. The humor market and the kids' market are the two areas that are always expanding in the marketplace. Do not solicit all greeting card companies. Look for those that fit your style."

RECYCLED PAPER PRODUCTS INC., 3636 N. Broadway, Chicago IL 60613. Art Director: Melinda Gordon. Publishes greeting cards, calendars, mugs, magnets, post-it notes and buttons; unique subjects. Artist's guidelines available.

Needs: Buys 1,000-2,500 designs and illustrations/year from freelance artists. Uses artists for product design and illustrations. Considers b&w line and color—"no real restrictions." Looking for "any theme or style executed in a fresh, unique manner," any media. Prefers 5x7 vertical format for cards, 10-14 maximum. "Our primary concern is card design." Produces seasonal material for all major and minor holidays including Jewish holidays. Submit seasonal material 18 months in advance; everyday cards are reviewed throughout the year.

First Contact & Terms: Send query letter with roughs and printed pieces or actual work. Samples returned by SASE. Reports in 2 months. Original work usually not returned at job's completion, but "negotiable." Buys all rights. Average flat fee is currently under review; also negotiates payment "if we have major interest."

Tips: "Study our product before submitting work. Remember that a greeting card is primarily a message sent from one person to another. The art must catch the customer's attention, and the words must deliver what the front promises. We are looking for unique points of view and manners of expression whether the themes are traditional or very contemporary. Our artists must be able to do concepts, art and messages. The must be able to work with a minimum of direction, and meet deadlines."

RED FARM STUDIO, 334 Pleasant St., Box 347, Pawtucket RI 02862. (401)728-9300. Creative Director: Mary M. Hood. Produces greeting cards, giftwrap, coloring books, paper dolls, story coloring books, paper party ware, playing cards, Christmas cards, gift enclosures, notes, invitations, postcards and paintables. Specializing in nautical and country themes and fine watercolors. Art guidelines available upon request if SASE is provided.

Needs: Buys approximately 200 designs and illustrations/year from freelance artists. Considers watercolor artwork. Prefers final art of 6¾x8⁷⁄₁₆ (³⁄₁₆ bleed) for Christmas cards; 4¾x6¾ (⅛ bleed) for everyday cards; and 6³⁄₁₆x8¹³⁄₁₆ (³⁄₁₆ bleed) for notes. Submit Christmas artwork 1 year in advance.

First Contact & Terms: Send query letter with printed pieces, photographs, or original art. Call for appointment to show portfolio. Portfolio should include "good examples, either printed or originals of finished product. Do not send sketches. Important—always include an SASE." Samples not filed are returned by SASE. Reports within 2 weeks. Original artwork not returned after reproduction. "Pays for illustration by the project, $175 minimum. Buys all rights. Finds most artists through references/word-of-mouth, samples received through the mail and portfolio reviews.

Tips: "We are interested in realistic, fine art watercolors of traditional subjects like country and nautical scenes, flowers, birds, shells and baby animals. We do not reproduce photography."

C.A. REED, INC., 99 Chestnut St., Box 3128, Williamsport PA 17701-0128. Art Director: Carol Cillo. Publishes paper tableware products; birthday, everyday, seasonal and holiday.

Needs: Buys 100-150 designs/year. Uses artists for product design and illustration. Interested in material for paper tableware, i.e. plates, napkins, cups, etc. Some invitations. Prefers "largely traditional special occasion or birthday or seasonal subject matter. Style should be cognizant of current trends and styles."

First Contact & Terms: Query with samples or photocopies. SASE. Reports in 6-8 weeks. Photocopied and simultaneous submissions OK. "Buys all rights within our field of publication." Pays for design by the project,$100-200. Pays for illustration an average flat fee of $150. "Requests for artist's guidelines only granted with SASE and review of samples."

Tips: "Artist should visit stationery shops, party stores and discount store party goods sections. There is a greater expansion of the party goods field. We need more variation within traditional subject parameters. There is trend towards more sophistication in design. Portfolios should contain a full range of artists' techniques and media. Tearsheets of printed samples are preferred, followed by slides and photocopies."

REEDPRODUCTIONS, 1102 Church St., San Francisco CA 94114. (415)282-8752. Partner/Art Director: Susie Reed. Produces postcards, stationery, notebooks, address books, etc.

Needs: Works with few freelance artists/year. Buys various number of design and illustrations from freelance artists/year. Prefers local artists with experience. Works on assignment only. Also uses artists for paste-up and mechanicals. Prefers color or b&w illustrations.

First Contact & Terms: Send query letter with brochure or resume, tear sheets, Photostats, photocopies or slides and SASE. Samples are filed. Samples not filed are returned by SASE. Reports back within 1 month only if interested. Call or write to schedule an appointment to show a portfolio, which should include original/final art, final reproduction/product, slides, tear sheets, photographs, color and b&w. Original artwork is returned after job's completion. Pays royalties of 2-10%. Negotiates rights purchased.

Tips: "We specialize in products related to Hollywood memorabilia."

REGENCY & CENTURY GREETINGS, 1500 W. Monroe St., Chicago IL 60607. (312)666-8686. Art Director: David Cuthbertson. Publishes Christmas cards; traditional and some religious Christmas.
Needs: Buys 200 illustrations and designs/year. Prefers pen & ink, airbrush, watercolor, acrylics, oils, collage and calligraphy.
First Contact & Terms: Send query letter with samples. Submit seasonal art 8 months in advance. Reports in 6 weeks. Previously published work OK. Buys *exclusively Christmas* card reproduction rights. Originals can be returned to artist at job's completion. Pays $100 minimum, b&w; $150, color design. Pays on acceptance. Finds most artists through references/word-of mouth, samples received through the mail and galleries.
Tips: "Artist should visit stationery shops for ideas, and request artist's guidelines to become familiar with the products. Portfolio should include published samples. Does not want to see college projects. Traditional still sells best in more expensive lines but will review contemporary designs for new lines."

RENAISSANCE GREETING CARDS, Box 845, Springvale ME 04083. Creative Director: Robin Kleinrock. Publishes greeting cards; "current approaches" to all occasion cards, seasonal cards, Christmas cards and nostalgic Christmas themes.
Needs: Buys 200 illustrations/year from freelance artists. Full-color illustrations only. Prefers art proportional to 8½x11 and 5x7. Produces everyday occasions—birthday, Get Well, friendship and seasonal material for Christmas, Valentine's Day, Mother's Day, Father's Day, Easter, graduation, St. Patrick's Day, Halloween, Thanksgiving, Passover, Jewish New Year and Hanukkah; submit art 18 months in advance for Christmas material; approximately 1 year for other holidays.
First Contact & Terms: Send query letter with printed pieces, tear sheets and/or slides; write for artists' guidelines. Samples returned by SASE. Reports in 3 months. To show a portfolio, mail appropriate materials, which should include original/final art, color tear sheets and slides or transparencies. Originals returned to artist at job's completion. Pays for design by the project, $200-500. Pays for illustration by the project, $125-500, plus royalties.
Tips: "Start by sending a small (10-12) sampling of 'best' work, preferably printed samples or slides of your best work (with SASE for return). This allows a preview for possible fit, saving time and expense."

REPRODUCTA CO. INC., 11 E. 26th St., New York NY 10010. Art Director: Thomas B. Schulhof. Publishes stationery, postcards and greeting cards; religious and general.
Needs: Buys 750 designs/year. Works with all occasions—religious plus floral, wildlife and "cutes."
First Contact & Terms: Mail art. SASE. Seasonal: Christmas, Mother's Day, Easter and Father's Day themes. No originals returned to artist at job's completion. Request artist's guidelines. Buys all rights. Pays $50-200; payment negotiated.

RIVERSIDE PAPER COMPANY, Box 179, Appleton WI 54912-0179. (414)733-6651. Marketing Manager: John Mund. Produces fine printing papers.
Needs: Buys 10 designs from freelance artists/year; buys 4-5 illustrations from freelance artists/year. Works on assignment only. Prefers brochures, top sheets, etc.

RUBY STREET, INC., 16 E. 23rd St., New York NY 10010. (212)529-0400. Art Director: Ann Perrini. Produces calendars and Christmas card for ages 18-45, college-educated.
Needs: Works with freelance artists. Will buy 10 calendars for 1990. Works on assignment only. Also uses artists for calligraphy, paste-up and mechanicals. Produces material for Christmas; submit 12 months before holiday.
First Contact & Terms: Send query letter with brochure or tear sheets, Photostats and slides. Samples are not filed. Samples not filed are returned by SASE. Reports back within 1 month only if interested. To show a portfolio, mail slides, final reproduction/product, tear sheets, Photostats and photographs. Original artwork is returned after job's completion. Pays royalties. Negotiates rights purchased.
Tips: "Develop general audience calendar concepts."

SACKBUT PRESS, 2513 E. Webster Place, Milwaukee WI 53211. Contact: Angela Peckenpaugh. Publishes poem postcards and notecards.
Needs: "A few line drawings for very specific themes."
First Contact and Terms: Send query letter with Photostats. Samples returned. Reports in 1 month. Buys one-time rights. Pays for illustration by the project, $10; on publication, plus 25 cards.
Tips: "I went from publishing a literary magazine to publishing poem postcards and notecards. I have little time or money to market my product. I sell at fairs. Produce sporadic direct mail ads and classifieds. Usually my prices only appeal to beginners or hobbyists."

Close-up

Mary "Ching" Walters

Greeting card artist
St. Louis, Missouri

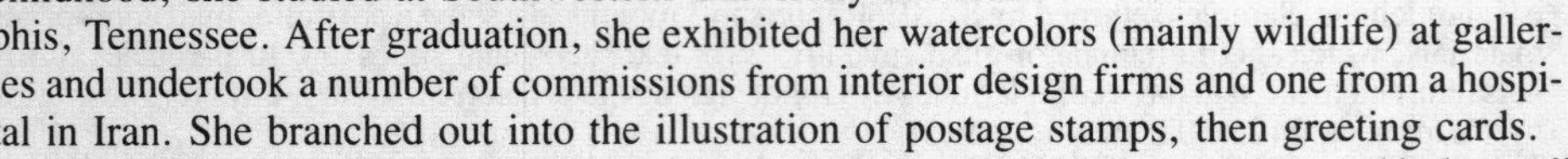

"You have to be a self-motivated person to succeed as a freelancer," says Mary "Ching" Walters, a greeting card artist who has freelanced for 26 years. "You need self-discipline, professionalism, determination, and the ability to get along with people."

Walters was trained as a fine artist. Gifted in art since childhood, she studied at Southwestern University in Memphis, Tennessee. After graduation, she exhibited her watercolors (mainly wildlife) at galleries and undertook a number of commissions from interior design firms and one from a hospital in Iran. She branched out into the illustration of postage stamps, then greeting cards.

"I always felt my ability to vary my style would fit in well with the greeting card industry," notes Walters. She likes the fact that greeting cards are a "renewable source," that they constantly need new designs and illustrations. "The fast turnover of designs is very challenging."

When she first decided to try her hand at greeting cards, she purchased a copy of the *Artist's Market*, studied the needs of various companies and submitted samples of original artwork along with her resume. "Naturally, not every company I contacted was willing to publish my work, but I was persistent and continued to submit my designs until I received my first commission." After about four months of queries, Walters received her first commission from Carole Smith Gallery in Salem, Oregon.

She makes most initial contacts with greeting card companies through the mail and follows up with telephone calls. "I send original artwork, slides and published samples. I have rarely been asked to show my portfolio. A commission is often the result of a piece that was sent as a sample."

She sends a variety of work because she feels the industry itself is based on variety. "It's nice to have your own style and look, but I think a company likes to see that you're not a 'one-trick pony.' " For the same reason, she doesn't feel that a static promotional piece fits the bill for card companies because it doesn't display an artist's versatility.

She adds that art skills are important in working for a greeting card company, but they are not the only factors. "Your actual art skills often count for less than you might think. As a freelancer, both in fine art and greeting card design, you must be able to sell yourself over and over again."

Working with a greeting card company also requires using your listening skills. The company specifies how the card will be used and the card's basic concept. Walters says it's most important for a freelancer to listen to what the company's asking for and to ask the art director questions in order to clarify the concept. "Once you understand the concept, then you must let your creative juices flow, but stay with the concept." After discussing the idea with the art director, she quickly sketches many variations of the concept, then rates them to narrow her selections. "Often a company will request a series of roughs; other companies want finished artwork only."

Keeping up with trends keeps her style fresh and appealing to greeting card companies. She visits card shops and subscribes to various trade publications such as *Greetings Magazine*. "There are styles in the card industry, like any other, and it's important to be aware of what's in." She also experiments with new styles and materials, sometimes inadvertently. "But it's always fun to try something new. It keeps the mind fresh."

Having fun is also profitable. Between new commissions and royalties, Walters makes about $50,000 to $60,000 a year. "That's not bad for an artist in St. Louis."

Just as a greeting card company is selective about the artists it chooses, Walters is picky about the companies she works with. "I place the most value on a good working relationship with a company. It is also very important to me that my work will be reproduced as a quality product. The pay varies so much from company to company that its importance falls short of harmonious business dealings. You have to have a little fun!"

Besides being creative and cooperative, freelancers must conduct themselves in a professional manner, Walters believes. "Meet all your deadlines promptly and with a smile. Be prepared to put your ego on the shelf. Believe in yourself and you cannot lose. Roll up your sleeves and go to work!"

—Susan Conner

Walters sold this watercolor-and-ink barnyard scene to Carole Smith Galleries in Salem, Oregon for $160. The gallery was representing Walters when Smith asked her for a notecard design "with wide appeal and charm." Smith notes, "Ching is very responsible and professional to work with. She is a great communicator."

ST. CLAIR-PAKWELL PAPER PRODUCTS, Box 800, Wilsonville OR 97070. (503)638-9833. Art Director: Anna Mack. Publishes gift boxes, giftwrap and various packaging.
Needs: Buys many designs/year. Uses artists for product design and illustration. "For use in department stores as courtesy packaging or used for pre-wrapped box coverings."
First Contact & Terms: Send query letter with resume and tear sheets, Photostats, photocopies, slides, photographs and "anything available." Prefers 15" repeat and even divisions thereof for giftwrap. SASE. Reports in 2 weeks. Call or write to schedule an appointment to show a portfolio, which should include original/final art and final reproduction/product. No originals returned to artist at job's completion. Pays for design and illustration by the project, $50-500. Buys all rights.
Tips: "Work should be geared toward the resale market—not the fine arts."

***SANDECOR INC.**, 430 Pike Rd., Southhampton PA 18966. (215)355-2410. Operations Manager: Dan Griffin. Produces greeting cards, calendars and posters.
Needs: Also uses freelance artists for calligraphy, P-O-P displays and mechanicals.
First Contact & Terms: Samples not filed are returned. Call or write to schedule an appointment to show a portfolio, which should include slides, Photostats, photographs and color. Original artwork is sometimes returned to the artist after job's completion. Negotiates rights purchased.

***SECOND NATURE, LTD.**, 10 Malton Rd., London, W105UP England. (01)960-0212. Art Director: Rod Shrager. Produces greeting cards and giftwrap. "High-end, higher-priced product for 15-40 year old (mainly women)."
Needs: Prefers airbrush or acrylics; contemporary styles. Produces material for Christmas, Valentine's day, Mother's Day, and Father's Day; submit 18 months before holiday.
First Contact & Terms: Send query letter with brochure showing art style. Samples not filed are returned only if requested by artist. Reports back within 2 months. Call or write to schedule an appointment to show a portfolio. Original artwork is not returned after job's completion. Negotiates payment and rights purchased.
Tips: "We are interested in all forms of paper engineering."

***SELECT DIRECT**, 125 5th Ave., 8th Floor, New York NY 10011. Manager: Mary White. Produces giftwrap and games.
Needs: Works with 10 freelance artists/year. Buys 20 designs from freelance artists/year.
First Contact & Terms: Send brochure, tear sheets, Photostats, and slides. Samples are filed. Samples not filed are returned. Reports back within 2 weeks only if interested. To show a portfolio, mail original/final art, slides, tear sheets, Photostats, photographs and color. Pays by the hour, $25-35; by the project, $500 average; royalties of 2-4%. Buys all rights.

***W.N. SHARPE LTD.—CLASSIC CARDS**, Bingley Rd., Bradford, West Yorkshire BD9 6SD England. 44-02-744-1365. Publishing Director: Roger Hutchings. Produces greeting cards and giftwrap.
Needs: Buys 800 designs from freelance artists/year. Considers watercolors and acrylics for illustrations. Prefers final art size of 9⅛x6⅜. Produces seasonal material for St. Valentine's Day, Christmas; submit artwork 6 months in advance.
First Contact & Terms: Artists must have a minimum of 3 years of experience in greeting cards. Works on assignment only. Send query letter with resume and samples; write for art guidelines. Prefers printed cards or finished art as samples. Samples not filed are returned. Reports within 2 weeks. Original art not returned after reproduction. Pays flat fee of $250/design. Buys all rights.
Tips: "Send samples similar to those published by the three main USA publishers. We are a part of the Hallmark group and require designs in a similar vein suitable for the 'popular' market."

***CAROLE SMITH GALLERY**, 456 Court St. N.E., Salem OR 97301. (503)362-9185. Estab. 1985. Produces greeting cards for "upper-middle income, educated professional women, ages 20-40. Also sell to increasing number of men."
Needs: Works with 40 artists/year. Buys 80 designs from artist/year. "I do not work with graphic designers. I only buy copyright use from professional artists with gallery representation. I do not buy illustration. I prefer watercolor paintings of floral and animal subject matter. I do not use artwork with black or solid color backgrounds." Prefers color-correct slides or transparencies. Produces material for Christmas and everyday only; submit in January prior to Christmas.
First Contact & Terms: Send query letter with resume, slides and SASE. Samples are not filed. Samples not filed are returned by SASE. Reports back within 1 month. To show a portfolio, mail slides and resume. Original artwork is returned to artist after job's completion. Pays average flat fee of $100/design. Buys reprint rights.
Tips: "We only work with the fine artists whose work is sold through galleries for at least three to five years. A resume must list galleries. We print full-color only. No photographs."

STONEWAY LTD., Box 548, Southeastern PA 19399. (215)272-4400. Art Director: RoseAnne Flynn. Publishes coloring books and brochures, children cartoon themes for 2-8 year-olds.
Needs: Buys 20 designs and 250 illustrations/year from freelance artists. Needs artists experienced in children's illustration line. Uses artists for product design and illustrations plus advertising and catalog design, illustration and layout. Prefers b&w line drawings and color washes; 17x22 and 8½x11,for 11x14 coloring books. Children's craft books 9x12; 8½x11. Also produces seasonal material.
First Contact & Terms: Send query letter with roughs and resume to be kept on file. Samples not kept on file are returned by SASE. Reports in 4 weeks. No originals returned to artist at job's completion. Write for appointment. Buys all rights. Payment varies per type of job or project. Pays on acceptance *only*.

STUART HALL CO., INC., Box 419381, Kansas City MO 64141. Director of Advertising and Art: Judy Riedel. Produces stationery, school supplies and office supplies.
Needs: Buys 40 designs and illustrations from freelance artists/year. Artist must be experienced—no beginners. Works on assignment only. Uses artists for design, illustration, calligraphy, paste-up and mechanicals. Considers pencil sketches, rough color, layouts, tight comps or finished art; watercolor, gouache, or acrylic paints are preferred for finished art. Avoid fluorescent colors. "All art should be prepared on heavy white paper and lightly attached to illustration board. Allow at least one inch all around the design for notations and crop marks. Avoid bleeding the design. In designing sheet stock, keep the design small enough to allow for letter writing space. If designing for an envelope, first consult us to avoid technical problems."
First Contact & Terms: Send query letter with resume, tear sheets, Photostats, slides and photographs. Samples not filed returned by SASE. Reports only if interested. To show a portfolio, mail roughs, original/final art, final reproduction/product, color, tear sheets, Photostats and photographs. No originals returned to artist at job completion. "Stuart Hall may choose to negotiate on price but generally accepts the artist's price." Buys all rights.

SUNRISE PUBLICATIONS INC., Box 2699, Bloomington IN 47402. (812)336-9900. Vice President, Creative Services: Lorraine Merriman Farrell. Publishes greeting cards and other paper products. Art guidelines available.
Needs: Generally works on assignment but also picks up existing pieces. Purchases 500-600 designs and illustrations/year. Considers any medium. Full-color illustrations scaled to 5x7 vertical, but these can vary. Produces seasonal material for Christmas, New Years, Hanukkah, Valentine's Day, St. Patrick's Day, Easter, Mother's Day, Father's Day, graduation, Halloween and Thanksgiving.
First Contact & Terms: Send query letter with slides as samples. "Indicate whether or not samples may be kept on file." Reports in 3 weeks. Samples returned only by SASE. Originals returned to artist at job's completion. Offers an advance against royalty program.

TAYLOR CORPORATION, 1725 Roe Crest Dr., North Mankato MN 56002.Design Director: Margaret Nelson.Produces stationery, greeting cards, Christmas cards and wedding invitations.
Needs: Buys 50 designs/year. Needs contemporary and traditional designs. Wedding invitation and Christmas card designs usually involue embossing and foil treatments. Also use artists skilled in color illustration in these catagories. Prefers airbrush, colored pencil, watercolor, acrylics, oils and pastels.
First Contact & Terms: Submit 4-5 illustrations. Prefers unpublished samples. SASE. Reports within 1 month. No originals returned at job's completion. Pays $250-300 for illustration. Buys all rights. Terms negotiable.
Tips: "Send samples of your work—published or unpublished. When we select an artist, it is because of his/her style. Then we'll work with them on a specific project."

TEXAN HOUSE, INC., 40214 Industrial Park Circle. Georgetown TX 78626. (512)863-9460. President: Joan K. Davis. Produces greeting cards, giftwrap, stationery and paper tableware products. Publishes general cards and invitations.
Needs: Works with 7 freelance artists/year. Works on assignment only. Also uses artists for calligraphy. Produces material for Christmas; submit 8 months before holiday.
First Contact & Terms: Send query letter with brochure or Photostats and photocopies. Samples are returned. Reports back within 2-4 weeks. Call or write to schedule an appointment to show a portfolio, which should include thumbnails, original/final art and photographs. Original artwork is not returned after job's completion. Pays flat fee. Buys all rights.

ARTHUR THOMPSON & COMPANY, 1260 S. 16th St., Omaha NE 68108. (402)342-2162. Vice President: Jim Ogden. Publishes greeting cards and letterheads; holiday and special occasion designs.
Needs: Uses 6 freelance artists/year for product illustrations. Prefers oils, acrylic paintings or mixed media; fall and winter scenes, Christmas and Thanksgiving background designs, birthday and special occasion designs.

First Contact & Terms: Write and send samples if possible. Prefers transparencies, slides of original art or original art as samples. Samples returned. Reports in 6 weeks. Provide sample and tear sheets to be kept on file for possible future assignments. Pays flat fee or negotiates payment. Considers product use and rights purchased when establishing payment.

TO COIN A PHRASE, 104 Forrest Ave., Narberth PA 19072. (215)664-3130. Owner: Gerri Rothman. Produces stationery, general cards, informal cards, invitations, contemporary cards and juvenile cards for 30 upwards in age and affluent.
Needs: Uses freelance artists for calligraphy.
First Contact & Terms: Send query letter with photocopies or call. Samples not filed are returned only if requested. Reports back only if interested. Call or write to schedule an appointment to show a portfolio. Pays for calligraphy, $10 per hour or by the piece.

VAGABOND CREATIONS INC., 2560 Lance Dr., Dayton OH 45409. (513)298-1124. Art Director: George F. Stanley, Jr. Publishes stationery and greeting cards with contemporary humor. 99% of artwork used in the line is provided by staff artists working with the company.
Needs: Works with 4 freelance artists/year. Buys 120 finished illustrations from artists/year. Prefers local artists; line drawings, washes and color-separations; material should fit in standard size envelope.
First Contact & Terms: Query. Samples returned by SASE. Reports in 2 weeks. Submit (everyday, graduation, Christmas, Mother's Day, Father's Day and Valentine's Day) material at any time. Originals only returned upon request. Payment negotiated.
Tips: "Important! Important! Currently we are *not* looking for additional freelance artists because we are very satisfied with the work being submitted by those individuals working directly with us. We do not in any way wish to offer false hope to anyone . . . but it would be foolish on our our part not to give consideration. Our current artists are very, very experienced and have have been associated with us for many years, in some cases over 30 years."

WILDCARD©, Box 3960, Berkeley CA 94703-0960. Art Director: Leal Charonnat. Publishes greeting cards and stationery; current, avant-garde themes for 20-40 year olds—"young, upwardly mobile urbanites." Send $2.50 for sample cards and submittal pack. Many designs die-cut. Specializes in animals (graphic), cats, zoo, dinosaurs, etc.
Needs: Imaginative die-cut designs that fit the basic greeting card market themes (birthday, Christmas, Valentine's, friendship, etc.); must be very graphic as opposed to illustrated. Specializes in die-cut, 3-D cards."
First Contact & Terms: Please "submit after receiving our guidelines. Cannot review submittals that have not received our guidelines." Send submittal pak, and brochure/flyer or resume to be kept on file. All materials 8½x11 only. Prefers brochure of work with nonreturnable pen & ink Photostats or photocopies as samples; do not send original work. "If your project is accepted, we will contact you. But we cannot always promise to contact everyone who submits." Pays for design by the project or royalties, $75-250; flat fee of $75-250/illustration. Also pays royalties for card line ideas. Considers complexity of project, product use and reproduction expense when establishing payment. "We will have all publishing rights for any work published. Artist may retain ownership of copyright." Pays on publication.
Tips: "Present only commercially potential examples of your work. Prefer to see only die-cut ideas. *Do not* present work that is not of a professional nature or what one would expect to see published. Know what is already in the market and have a feeling for the subjects the market is interested in. Go out and look at *many* card stores before submitting. Ask the owner or buyer to 'review' your work prior to submitting."

CAROL WILSON FINE ARTS, INC., Box 17394, Portland OR 97217. (503)283-2338 or 281-0780. Contact: Gary Spector. Produces greeting cards, postcards, posters and stationery that range from contemporary to nostalgic. "At the present time we are actively looking for unusual humor to expand our contemporary humor line. We want cards that will make people laugh out loud! Another category we also wish to expand is fine arts."
Needs: Uses artists for product design and illustration. Considers all media. Produces seasonal material for Christmas, Valentine's Day and Mother's Day; submit art preferably 1 year in advance.
First Contact & Terms: Send query letter with resume, business card, tear sheets, Photostats, photocopies, slides and photographs to be kept on file. No original artwork on initial inquiry. Write for an appointment to show portfolio or for artists' guidelines. "All approaches are considered but, if possible, we prefer to see ideas that are applicable to specific occasions, such as birthday, anniversary, wedding, new baby, etc. We look for artists with creativity and ability." Samples not filed are returned by SASE. Reports within 2 months. Negotiates return of original art after reproduction. Payment ranges from flat fee to royalties. Buys all rights.
Tips: "We have noticed an increased emphasis on humorous cards for specific occasions, specifically, feminist and 'off-the-wall' humor. We are also seeing an increased interest in fine arts cards."

Magazines

There are several reasons magazines are one of the best and most consistent markets for freelance illustrators and cartoonists. First, there are about 11,000 magazines published in the U.S., and most of them use illustrations and/or cartoons. Secondly, magazines are usually published monthly or bimonthly, meaning they have art needs that must be filled consistently. Most magazine art directors work with contributing artists entirely through the mail. If you can follow directions and meet deadlines, plus produce quality work, you can submit your work to the magazines listed in this section.

Study magazines on the newsstands and in libraries so that you can gear your work to the appropriate market. You'll find successful magazines target their editorial content to specific audiences. Consumer magazines appeal to the general public, but they, too, find their own niche, such as women's or men's magazines. Here, illustration serves to enrich the editorial message by attracting attention to the article and capsulizing its essence. Trade or business publications focus on a certain profession. The busy professionals who read them look for high-access, quick-read information. Therefore, graphic images must communicate their messages quickly through charts and graphs and illustrations that focus on a simple, direct image. Inhouse (or company) publications are produced by businesses for their employees or stockholders. For some, they serve as a bulletin for employee activities, while others reach customers, shareholders and community leaders as prime image builders. Literary magazines combine fiction, poetry, essays and artwork to make an alternative statement apart from the mainstream of thought. They feature lithographic and somewhat abstract artwork to accompany fiction and thought-provoking articles.

Before you send samples, consider the needs of magazine art directors. Their challenge is to hold the reader's attention by creating some "magic" throughout a magazine. The magical ingredient is often artwork, which the art director chooses in a subjective manner. Some prefer a homogeneous look and work with either the same illustrators or those who can produce the same look. Others opt for a variety of styles and are constantly looking for new talent. Compare several magazines and examine how they use artwork—to accompany fiction, as spot art or a cover illustration. Examine the style and media a magazine uses, and see if your artwork would fit in. Also check if cartoons are used.

Most art directors want to see samples of your work that are geared to the magazine's purpose. For example, the art director at a children's magazine does not want to see how well you draw nudes. Instead, he wants to review how well you handle children, adults and animals in a variety of situations. Your samples should exhibit a distinctive style and show a range of drawing abilities. Specialists, such as medical or scientific illustrators, have a good chance of developing unique approaches to esoteric subjects. Their work suits specialized publications where artwork requires their expertise. And generalists can play the field, using their adaptability and versatility for a variety of magazines.

Submit nonreturnable or photocopied samples for black-and-white work, slides for color. Make it clear in your cover letter that the art director can keep your samples on file, that they do not have to be returned unless you specify otherwise.

If you are a newcomer, start with the less-circulated and more focused publications to increase your chances for a sale. Consider non- or low-paying magazines, because they accept new talent readily and foster experimental work. The tear sheets you gather from them will give your portfolio a professional boost.

Cartoonists should submit 10 to 12 finished or rough cartoons, each cartoon labeled on the back with your name, address and phone number, plus a cartoon reference number. When an art director selects a cartoon from the batch you submit, he can refer to the cartoon by the number on the caption. Try to send both gag and pantomime cartoons to show your mastery. Gear your samples to the magazine; editors resent packages that show no knowledge of their magazine's focus.

Payment for editorial illustration and cartoons varies according to the type and circulation of the magazine, the size of the artwork, your reputation and the use of color. Magazines usually purchase one-time or first rights, since many illustrations and cartoons can be sold to other markets. Even though publications copyright their contents, always place your copyright notice on the front of your artwork so you will be protected.

In addition to the listings offered in this section, check your library for the following directories, which furnish names and addresses but no marketing information: the *Standard Periodical Directory*, the *Internal Publications Directory*, *The Gebbie Press All-in-One Directory of Publications* and *Ulrich's International Periodical Directory*. To keep current with industry trends, read *Folio* and *Magazine Design and Production*. Cartoonists can find valuable information by reading *Cartoon World*, *Witty World*, *The Gag Recap*, and *Trade Journal Recap*.

***AB BOOKMAN WEEKLY**, Box AB, Clifton NJ 07015. Contact: Jacob L. Chernofsky. For professional and specialist booksellers, acquisitions and academic librarians, book publishers book collectors, bibliographers, historians, etc. Query with resume.
Cartoons: Buys cartoons on bookselling, books, libraries, and book collecting. Also uses artists for layout and pasteup.

ABORIGINAL SF, Box 2449, Woburn MA 01888-0849. Editor: Charles C. Ryan. Estab. 1986. Science fiction magazine for adult science fiction readers. Bimonthly. Circ. 13-15,000. Sample copy $3; art guidelines for SASE with 1 first-class stamp.
Cartoons: Buys 2-8 cartoons from freelancers. Prefers science fiction, science and space themes. Prefers single panel or double panel with or without gagline; b&w line drawings, b&w washes and color washes. Send finished cartoons. Samples are filed. Samples not filed are returned by SASE. Reports back within 2 months. Buys first rights and nonexclusive reprint rights. Pays $15, b&w; $15, color.
Illustrations: Buys 8-16 illustrations/issue from freelancers. Works on assignment only. Prefers science fiction, science and space themes. "Generally, we prefer art with a realistic edge, but surrealistic art will be considered." Prefers watercolor, acrylics, oils and pastels. Send query letter with photocopies and slides. Samples not kept on file are returned by SASE. Reports back within 2 months. To show a portfolio, mail photocopied samples and/or color slides. Buys first rights and nonexclusive reprint rights. Pays $300, color, cover; $250, color, inside; on publication.
Tips: "Show samples of color art showing a range of ability."

***ABYSS**, 1402 21st St. NW, Washington DC 20036. Editor: David F. Nalle. Digest-sized magazine emphasizing fantasy and adventure games for adult game players with sophisticated and varied interests. Bimonthly. Circ. 1,300. Does not accept previously published material. Returns original artwork after publication. Sample copy for $2. Art guidelines free for SASE with first-class postage.
Cartoons: Buys up to 2/issue. Prefers humorous, game or fantasy-oriented themes. Prefers single, double or multiple panel with or without gagline; b&w line drawings. Send query letter with roughs. Write for appointment to show portfolio. Material not filed is returned by SASE. Reports within 6 weeks. Buys first rights. Pays $3-8, b&w; on publication.
Illustrations: Buys 8-12/issue. Prefers fantasy, dark fantasy, horror or mythology themes. Send query letter with samples. Write for appointment to show portfolio. Prefers photocopies or photographs as samples. Samples not filed are returned by SASE. Reports within 1 month. Buys first rights. Pays $20-30, b&w, and $30-50, color, cover; $3-8, b&w, inside; on publication.

***ACA JOURNAL OF CHIROPRACTIC**, 8229 Maryland Ave., St. Louis MO 63105. Editor: Dean Denton. Emphasizes chiropractic for doctors of chiropractic in US who are members of the American Chiropractic Association. Monthly. Circ. 23,000. Accepts previously published material and simultaneous submissions. Original artwork returned after publication. Sample copy and art guidelines available.
Illustrations: Uses 3 illustrations/issue. Prefers chiropractic or general themes. Send query letter to be kept on file or write for appointment to show portfolio. Prefers photographs as samples. Samples returned if not kept on file. Reports within 30 days.

***ACCENT**, Box 10010, Ogden UT 84409. (801)394-9446. Editor: Robyn Walker. Articles on travel. Circ. 90,000.
First Contact & Terms: Sample copy $1. Buys color transparencies to accompany articles. Send query letter with resume, tear sheets and photocopies. Samples returned by SASE. Reports in 6 weeks. Pays $35 color, inside; $50 color, cover; on acceptance.

ACCENT ON LIVING, Box 700, Bloomington IL 61702. Editor: Betty Garee. Emphasis on success and ideas for better living for the physically handicapped. Quarterly. Original artwork returned after publication, if requested. Sample copy $2.
Cartoons: Buys approximately 12 cartoons/issue from freelancers. Receives 5-10 submissions/week from freelancers. Interested in people with disabilities in different situations. Send finished cartoons. SASE. Reports in 2 weeks. Buys first-time rights (unless specified). Pays $20 b&w; on acceptance.
Illustrations: Uses 3-5 illustrations/issue. Interested in illustrations that "depict articles/topics we run." Works on assignment only. Provide samples of style to be kept on file for future assignments. Samples not kept on file are returned by SASE. Reports in 2 weeks. To show a portfolio, mail color and b&w. Buys all rights on a work-for-hire basis. Pays $250-300, color, cover; on acceptance.
Tips: "Send a sample and be sure to include various styles of artwork that you can do."

ACROSS THE BOARD, 845 Third Ave., New York NY 10022. (212)759-0900. Art Director: Josef Kozlakowski. Emphasizes business-related topics for Chief Executive Officers in the business field and industry. Monthly. Returns original artwork after publication. Sample copy for SASE.
Illustrations: Buys 4-6 illustrations/issue from freelancers. Works on assignment only. Send brochure and samples to be kept on file. Prefers tear sheets or photocopies as samples. Samples not filed are returned by SASE. Reports back only if interested. Call for appointment to show portfolio. Buys first rights. Pays $400 for color cover; $200 for b&w inside; on publication.

ACTION, 901 College Ave., Winona Lake IN 46590. (219)267-7656. Contact: Vera Bethel. For ages 9-11. Circ. 25,000. Weekly. SASE. Reports in 1 month.
Cartoons: Buys 1/issue on school, pets and family. Pays $10, b&w; on publication. Send finished artwork.
Illustrations: Uses color illustrations on assignment. Send samples or slides. Pays $75 for full-color drawings (no overlays); on acceptance.

ADIRONDAC, 174 Glen St., Glens Falls NY 12801. (518)793-7737. Editor: Neal Burdick. Emphasizes the Adirondack Mountains and conservation for members of Adirondack Mountain Club, conservationists and outdoor-oriented people in general. Published 10 times/year. Circ. 9,000. Accepts previously published material and simultaneous submissions. Original artwork returned after publication. Sample copy $1.75; art guidelines free for SASE.
Cartoons: Interested in environmental concerns, conservation, outdoor activities as themes. Prefers single panel with gagline; b&w line drawings. Send query letter to be kept on file. Reports within 4 weeks. Negotiates rights purchased. No payment.
Illustrations: Prefers maps, specific illustrations for articles. Send query letter to be kept on file. Reports within 4 weeks. No payment.

AIM, Box 20554, Chicago IL 60620. (312)874-6184. Editor-in-Chief: Ruth Apilado. Managing Editor: Dr. Myron Apilado. Art Director: Bill Jackson. Readers are those "wanting to eliminate bigotry and desiring a world without inequalities in education, housing, etc." Quarterly. Circ. 16,000. Sample copy $3; artist's guidelines for SASE. Reports in 3 weeks. Previously published, photocopied and simultaneous submissions OK. Receives 12 cartoons and 4 illustrations/week from freelance artists. Finds most artists through references/word-of-mouth and samples received through the mail.
Cartoons: Uses 1-2 cartoons/issue; all from freelancers. Interested in education, environment, family life, humor through youth, politics and retirement; single panel with gagline. Especially needs "cartoons about the stupidity of bigotry." Mail finished art. SASE. Reports in 3 weeks. Buys all rights on a work-for-hire basis. Pays $5-15, b&w line drawings; on publication.
Illustrations: Uses 4-5 illustrations/issue; half from freelancers. Prefers pen & ink. Interested in current events, education, environment, humor through youth, politics and retirement. Provide brochure to

The asterisk before a listing indicates that the listing is new in this edition. New markets are often the most receptive to freelance submissions.

be kept on file for future assignments. No samples returned. Reports in 4 weeks. Prefers b&w for cover and inside art. Buys all rights on a work-for-hire basis. Pays $25 for b&w illustrations, cover; on publication.

Tips: "For the most part, artists submit material omitting black characters. We would be able to use more illustrations and cartoons with people from all ethnic and racial backgrounds in them. We also use material of general interest. Artists should show a representative sampling of their work and target their samples magazine's specific needs; nothing on religion."

THE ALTADENA REVIEW, Box 212, Altadena CA 91001. Editor: Robin Shectman. Literary magazine emphasizing poetry. "We publish poetry, reviews of books of poetry, occasional interviews with poets." Published 1-2 times/year. Circ. 250-300. Original artwork returned after publication if requested. Sample copy $2.50.

Illustrations: Buys 4-12 illustrations/year from freelancers. Prefers pen & ink, then charcoal/pencil, markers and calligraphy. "Black-and-white work only; no halftones." Send query letter with camera-ready b&w artwork; prefer 4x5 or smaller. Samples are not filed. Samples not filed are returned by SASE. Reports back within 5 weeks by SASE. To show a portfolio, mail original/final art, final reproduction/product or b&w. "These should be things we could actually publish, not samples." Buys first rights. Pays 2 copies on publication.

Tips: "We like to see four to six drawings that relate to each other to form a series. Artwork we publish should be able to stand alone—we do not use 'illustrations'."

***ALTERNATIVE HOUSING BUILDER MAGAZINE**, 16 1st Ave., Corry PA 16407. Managing Editor: Charles Mancino. Emphasizes industrialized housing: log homes, modular, panelized, post & beam construction and any other type of building systems housing for kit package manufacturers and builder-dealers of these homes. Published 13 times/year. Circ. 28,000. Original artwork returned after publication if requested. Sample copy and art guidelines free for SASE.

Cartoons: Buys 1-2 cartoons/issue from freelancers. Considers anything pertaining to log homes, modular, panelized, post & beam construction or the problems faced by the men and women who are building these homes. Prefers single panel with or without gagline; b&w line drawings or b&w washes. Send query letter with finished cartoons, slides and photographs to be kept on file. Material not filed is returned only if requested. Reports within 2 weeks. Buys all rights. Pays on publication.

Illustrations: Buys illustrations/issue. Send query letter with slides, photographs and illustrations. To show a portfolio, mail appropriate materials.

Tips: "We focus on making our readers more profits throught sales, housing trends and marketing articles. Any art which could relate to these topics would be considered."

AMAZING HEROES, Suite 101, 1800 Ridgegate St., Westlake Village CA 91361. (805)379-1881. Art Director: Dale Crain. Magazine emphasizing news and features on popular comic books. Circ. 20,000. Original artwork is returned to the artist after publication. Sample copy $3.50.

Illustrations: Prefers b&w spot illustrations and gags dealing with comics. Send query letter with samples to Mr. Kim Thompson. Buys one-time North American rights. Pays $2.50 +, b&w; inside; on publication.

AMELIA, 329 "E" St., Bakersfield CA 93304. (805)323-4064. Editor: Frederick A. Raborg, Jr. Magazine; also publishes 2 supplements—*Cicada* (haiku) and *SPSM&H* (sonnets) and illustrated postcards. Emphasizes fiction and poetry for the general review. "Our readers are drawn from a cross-section of reading tastes and educational levels, though the majority tend to be college-educated." Quarterly. Circ. 1,250. Accepts some previously published material from illustrators. Original artwork returned after publication if requested with SASE. Sample copy $5.95; art guidelines for SASE.

Cartoons: Buys 3-5 cartoons/issue from freelancers for *Amelia*. Prefers sophisticated or witty themes (see Cynthia Darrow's or Jessica Finney's work). Prefers single panel with or without gagline (will consider multi panel on related themes); b&w line drawings, b&w washes. Send query letter with finished cartoons to be kept on file. Material not filed is returned by SASE. Reports within 1 week. Buys first rights or one-time rights; prefers first rights. Pays $5-25, b&w; on acceptance.

Illustrations: Buys 80-100 illustrations and spots annually from freelancers for *Amelia;* 24-30 spots for *Cicada*; 15-20 spots for *SPSM&H*; and 50-60 spots for postcards. Considers all themes; "no taboos except no explicit sex; nude studies in taste are welcomed, however." Prefers pen & ink, pencil, watercolor, acrylics, oils, pastels, mixed media and calligraphy. Send query letter with resume, Photostats and/or photocopies to be kept on file; unaccepted material returned immediately by SASE. "See work by James Michael Dorsey, Richard Dahlstrom, Adam Niklowicz, Gregory Powell, Steve Delmonte, Cliff Johnson, Melinda Giordano, Jay Moon, Carol Gale Anderson." Reports in 1 week. Portfolio should contain "one or two possible cover pieces (either color or black and white); several b&w sports, plus several more fully realized b&w illustrations. Cartoonists ought to include 'toons from several different

themes in a good showing of techniques used--line, wash etc. Benday is fine for emphatic shading." Buys first rights or one-time rights; prefers first rights; Pays $25, b&w, $100, color, cover; $5-25, b&w, inside; on acceptance, "except spot drawings which are paid for on assignment to an issue."
Tips: "We use virtually every subject and style that would fit into a literary quarterly's range. Above all we look for skill and sophistication with wit. Wit and humor above all in cartoons. In illustrations, it is very difficult to get excellent nude studies (such as one we used by Carolyn G. Anderson to illustrate a short story by Judson Jerome in our Fall 1986 issue.) Everyone seems capable of drawing an ugly woman; few capture sensuality, and fewer still draw the nude male tastefully."

AMERICAN AGRICULTURIST, Box 370, Ithaca NY 14851. (607)273-3507. Art Director: Elise Gold. Emphasizes agriculture in the Northeast, specifically New York, New Jersey and New England. Monthly. Circ. 72,000. Artwork returned after publication. Art guidelines for SASE.
Cartoons: Buys 3 cartoons/issue from freelancers. Prefers agriculture theme. Single panel, 2⅛" wide by 2¾-3¼" high or similar proportions, with gagline; b&w line drawings. Send query letter with finished cartoons. Material not returned. Reports within 3 weeks. Buys one-time rights. Pays $10, b&w; on acceptance.

***AMERICAN ARTIST**, 1515 Broadway, New York NY 10036. (212)764-7300. Emphasizes the American artist—realistic, naturalistic and fine art for artists, students and teachers. Monthly. Circ. 170,000. Sample copy $2.50; art guidelines for SASE.
Needs: Does not assign or use freelancers. If an artist wants to be the subject of a feature article, he should contact the editor. Wants to see slides or b&w glossies of artist's work for possible feature articles.

THE AMERICAN ATHEIST, Box 2117, Austin TX 78768. (512)458-1244. Editor: R. Murray-O'Hair. For atheists, agnostics, materialists and realists. Monthly. Circ. 30,000. Simultaneous submissions OK. Free sample copy, send 9x12 envelope or label.
Cartoons: Buys 10 cartoons/issue. Cartoons, $15 each. Especially needs 4-seasons art for covers and greeting cards. Send query letter with resume and samples.
Illustrations: Buys 1 illustration/issue on acceptance. "Illustrators should send samples to be kept on file. We do commission artwork based on the samples received. All illustrations must have bite from the atheist point of view and hit hard." Prefers pen & ink, then airbrush, charcoal/pencil and calligraphy. To show a portfolio, mail original/final art, final reproduction/product, photographs and b&w. Pays $75-100, cover and $25 inside.
Tips: "*The American Atheist* looks for clean lines, directness and originality. We are not interested in side-stepping cartoons and esoteric illustrations. Our writing is hard-punching and we want artwork to match. The mother press of the *American Atheist*, the American Atheist Press, buys book cover designs and card designs. I would like to see a sample of various styles, but since we can't print in color, I need to know if the artist can design/illustrate for offset printing."

AMERICAN BANKERS ASSOCIATION-BANKING JOURNAL, 345 Hudson St., New York NY 10014. (212)620-7256. Art Director: Rob Klein. Emphasizes banking for middle and upper level-banking executives and managers. Monthly. Circ. 42,000. Accepts previously published material. Returns original artwork after publication.
Illustrations: Buys 4 illustrations/issue from freelancers. Themes relate to stories, primarily financial; styles vary, realistic, cartoon, surreal. Works on assignment only. Send query letter with brochure and samples to be kept on file. Prefers tear sheets, slides or photographs as samples. Samples not filed are returned by SASE. Negotiates rights purchased. Pays $350-500 for color cover and $75-100 for b&w or color inside; on acceptance.

THE AMERICAN BAPTIST MAGAZINE, Box 851, Valley Forge PA 19482-0851. (215)768-2441. Managing Editor: Ronald Arena. Executive Editor: Philip Jenks. Manager of Print Media Services: Richard Schramm. National publication of American Baptist Churches in the USA. Contains feature articles, news, and commentary of interest to the American Baptist (1.5 million) constituency. Circ. 100,000. Bimonthly. Guidelines available.
Illustrations: All artwork on assignment for specific themes/subjects. (May make occasional use of freelance line art and cartoons.) Compensation negotiable. Portfolio samples and resume welcomed; enclose SASE for material to be returned.
Tips: "Artists should be willing to work promptly and creatively within stated guidelines for both specific and thematic art work."

AMERICAN BIRDS, National Audubon Society, 950 3rd Ave., New York NY 10022. (212)546-9189. Associate Editor: Manuela Soares. Emphasizes ornithology—migration, distribution, breeding and be-

havior of North and Middle American birds, including Hawaii and the West Indies for amateur and professional birders, scientists, researchers, schools and libraries. Published 5 times/year (seasonal and Christmas Bird Count issue). Circ. 11,000. Original artwork returned after publication. Sample copy $3. Art guidelines for SASE with 1 first-class stamp.
Illustrations: Buys 5-10 illustrations/issue from freelancers. Prefers "detailed drawings of birds of the Americas; drawings to aid in identification (anatomically correct a must); artistic renderings for inside material; outstanding artwork for cover." Send query letter with Photostats and slides. Samples not filed are returned only if requested. Reports back within 4 months. Buys first rights. Pays up to $100, b&w or color, cover; $10-25, b&w or color, inside; on publication.

AMERICAN BOOKSELLER, Booksellers Publishing Inc., 137 W. 25th St., New York NY 10001. Editor-in-Chief: Ginger Curwen. Art Director: Joan Adelson. For booksellers interested in trends, merchandising, recommendations, laws and industry news. Monthly. Circ. 8,700. Original artwork returned after publication. Sample copy $3.
Cartoons: Uses 2 cartoons/year; buys all from freelancers. Receives 5-10 submissions/week from freelancers. Interested in bookselling, authors and publishing; single panel with gagline. Send finished cartoons. SASE. Reports in 4 weeks. Buys first North American serial rights.
Illustrations: Uses 4 illustrations/issue; buys 4/issue from freelancers. Prefers local artists due to tight deadlines. Receives 10 submissions/week from freelancers. Looks for strong concepts and an original style. Interested in books, inventory or material for specific assignments. Works on assignment only. Send query letter with samples. Provide business card, flyer and tear sheet to be kept on file for future assignments. SASE. Reports back only if interested. Call to schedule an appointment to show or drop-off a portfolio, which should include Photostats, tear sheets and final reproduction/product. Considers project's budget and rights purchased when establishing payment. Buys first North American serial rights. Pays $50 minimum for b&w line drawings, washes and gray opaques; on acceptance.
Tips: "I have a greater and greater need for strong conceptual work. Yet the mailing pieces I get don't give me enough sense of the artist's ability to solve a visual problem with a visual idea. Please send more than one sample of work, as it gives me a sense of the artist's range and aids in the decision-making process."

AMERICAN DEMOGRAPHICS, Box 68, Ithaca NY 14851. (607)273-6343. Managing Editor: Caroline Arthur. Emphasizes demographics and population trends. Readers are business decision makers, advertising agencies, market researchers, newspapers, banks and professional demographers and business analysts. Monthly. Circ. 35,000. Original artwork returned after publication. Sample copy $6.
Cartoons: Uses 1-3 cartoons/issue, all from freelancers. Receives 5-10 submissions/week from freelancers. Interested in population trends including moving, aging, families, birth rate, the census, surveys, changing neighborhoods, women working, data (use, computers, etc.), market research, business forecasting and demographers. Format: single panel b&w line drawings and b&w washes with gagline. Prefers to see finished cartoons. SASE. Reports in 2 weeks. Buys one-time rights. Pays $50-100 on publication.
Illustrations: Uses 2 illustrations/issue. Interested in demographic themes. Needs "styles that reproduce best in b&w. Spare statements with a light approach to the subject." Prefers to see portfolio; contact Caroline Arthur. SASE. Provide photocopies of work to be kept on file for future needs. Reports in 1 month. Buys one-time rights. Inside: pays $50, under ½ page; $75, ½ page; $100, full page.

AMERICAN FILM AND VIDEO ASSOCIATION, (formerly Sightlines), Suite 152, 920 Barnsdale Rd., La Grange Park IL 60525. (312)482-4000. Publisher: Ron MacIntrye. Editor: Ray Rolff. Emphasizes film and video for the nontheatrical film/video world, including librarians in university and public libraries, independent filmmakers, film teachers on the high school and college levels, film programmers in the community, universities, religious organizations and film curators in museums." Quarterly magazine for the membership. Circ. 3,000. Previously published material OK; simultaneous submissions "OK if not with competitor." Original artwork returned after publication. Sample copy $3.50 plus $2 shipping.
Cartoons: "We sometimes buy cartoons which deal with library and film/video issues that relate to educational and community use of media"; b&w line drawings. Send query letter with samples of style and resume. Samples returned by SASE. Buys one-time rights. Pays approximately $25 (but negotiable), b&w; on publication.
Tips: "We use very little freelance artwork."

AMERICAN FITNESS,Suite 310, 15250 Ventura Blvd., Sherman Oaks CA 91403. (818)905-0040. Editor: Peg Angsten. Magazine emphasizing fitness, health and exercise for sophisticated, college-educated, very active lifestyles. Bimonthly. Circ. 30,000. Accepts previously published material. Original artwork returned after publication. Sample copy $1.

Cartoons: Buys 1 cartoon/issue from freelancers. Material not kept on file is returned if requested. Buys one-time rights. Pays $35.
Illustrations: Buys 1-2 illustrations/issue from freelancers. Works on assignment only. Prefers very sophisticated line drawings. Send query letter with brochure showing art styles and tear sheets. Reports back within 2 months. To show a portfolio, mail thumbnails and roughs. Buys one-time rights. Pays $50; on publication.

***AMERICAN JOURNAL OF NURSING**, 555 W. 57th St., New York NY 10019. Graphic Arts Director: Charles Volpe. Magazine for nurses and student nurses dealing with geriatrics or pediatrics. Bimonthly. Circ. 100,000. Original artwork is returned to the artist after publication. Sample copies available.
Cartoons: Send samples of style. Samples are filed. Samples not filed are returned if requested. Reports back within 2 weeks only if interested. Negotiates rights purchased.
Illustrations: Works on assignment only. Call to schedule an appointment to show a portfolio, which should include original/final art, tear sheets and final reproduction/product. Negotiates rights purchased. Pays on acceptance.
Tips: "Portfolio must consist of work that would relate to our magazine. Elderly people (geriatric nursing), children (maternal child nursing) and maybe nurses.

THE AMERICAN LEGION MAGAZINE, Box 1055, Indianapolis IN 46206. Contact: Cartoon Editor. Emphasizes the development of the world at present and milestones of history; general-interest magazine for veterans and their families. Monthly. Original artwork not returned after publication.
Cartoons: Uses 2-3 cartoons/issue, all from freelancers. Receives 100 submissions/week from freelancers. Especially needs general humor in good taste. "Generally interested in cartoons with broad appeal. Prefer action in the drawing, rather than the illustrated joke-type gag. Those that attract the reader and lead him to read the caption rate the highest attention. No-caption gags purchased only occasionally. Because of tight space, we're not in the market for the spread or multipanel cartoons but use both vertical and horizontal single-panel cartoons. Themes should be home life, business, sports and everyday Americana. Cartoons that pertain only to one branch of the service may be too restricted for this magazine. Service-type gags should be recognized and appreciated by any ex-service man or woman. Cartoons that may offend the reader are not accepted. Liquor, sex, religion and racial differences are taboo. Ink roughs not necessary but desirable. Finish should be line, Ben-day." Usually reports within 30 days. Buys first rights. Pays $125-150; on acceptance.
Tips: "Artists should submit their work as we are always seeking new slant and more timely humor. Black-and-white art is primarily what we seek. Note: Cartoons are separate from the art department."

AMERICAN LIBRARIES, American Library Association, 50 E. Huron St., Chicago IL 60611. (312)944-6780. Editor-in-Chief: Arthur Plotnik. Managing Editor: Thomas M. Gaughan. Senior Editor/Production: Edith McCormick. For professional librarians, library employees and individuals in business-related fields. Published 11 times/year. Circ. 47,000. Sample copy $4. Free artist's guidelines.
Cartoons: Buys 4-10/year on libraries and library-patron interaction; single panel with gagline. Avoid stereotypes. Query with samples or with resume and portfolio. SASE. Reports only if interested. Buys first North American serial rights. Pays $30-75, b&w line drawings and washes, depending on assignments.
Illustrations: Buys 4-8/year on libraries, library-patron interaction and assigned themes. Query with samples or with resume and portfolio. SASE. Reports only if interested. Buys first North American serial rights. Cover: Pays $50-200, b&w; $300 maximum, color. Inside: Pays $15-200, color and b&w; on acceptance.
Tips: "Review a few issues of our magazine at your public library so you are familiar with the type of articles we illustrate and sophistication of audience being addressed. Avoid stereotypical images of librarians."

AMERICAN MOTORCYCLIST, American Motorcyclist Association, Box 6114, Westerville OH 43081-6114. (614)891-2425. Executive Editor: Greg Harrison. Managing Editor: Bill Wood. Associate Editor: Roger T. Young. Monthly. Circ. 130,000. For "enthusiastic motorcyclists, investing considerable time and money in the sport." Sample copy $1.50.
Cartoons: Uses 1-2 cartoons/issue; all from freelancers. Receives 5-7 submissions/week from freelancers. Interested in motorcycling; "single panel gags." Prefers to receive finished cartoons. SASE. Reports in 2 weeks. Buys all rights on a work-for-hire basis. Pays $15 minimum, b&w washes; on publication.
Illustrations: Uses 1-2 illustrations/issue, almost all from freelancers. Receives 1-3 submissions/week from freelancers. Interested in motorcycling themes. Send query letter with resume and tear sheets to be

kept on file. Prefers to see samples of style and resume. Samples returned by SASE. Reports in 3 weeks. Buys first North American serial rights. Pays $75 minimum, color, cover; $30-100, b&w and color, inside; on publication.

AMERICAN SALON, 7500 Old Oak Blvd., Cleveland OH 44130. Editor: Jody Byrne. Concerns the art of cosmetology and related fashions; for beauty salons. Monthly. Cir. 158,000. Simultaneous submissions OK "if trade exclusive." Receives 1-2 cartoons and 2-3 illustrations/month.
Illustrations: Buys themes on hairstyling. Especially needs drawings of men and women with current or avante garde hairstyles. Uses b&w line drawings and photos. Query with resume and samples or arrange interview to show a portfolio. SASE. Reports only if interested. Negotiates pay. Buys all rights.
Tips: "In your portfolio include printed pieces—art that has already been separated and commerical pieces, not fine art."

THE AMERICAN SPECTATOR, Box 10448, Arlington VA 22210. Managing Editor: Wladyslaw Pleszczynski. Concerns politics and literature. Monthly. Circ. 43,000. Original artwork returned after publication. Sample copy.
Illustrations: Uses 2-3 illustrations/issue, all from freelancers. Interested in "caricatures of political figures (for portraits with a point of view)." Works on assignment only. Samples returned by SASE. Reports back on future assignment possibilities. Provide resume, brochure and tear sheets to be kept on file for future assignments. Prefers to see portfolio and samples of style. Reports in 2 weeks. Buys first North American serial rights. Pays $150 minimum, b&w line drawings, cover. Pays $35 minimum, b&w line drawings, inside; on publication.

AMERICAN SPORTS, Box 6100, Rosemead CA 91770. Art Director: Michael Harding. Magazine emphasizing prep, collegiate, professional and recreational sports. Features general interest, historical, how-to, inspirational, interview/profile, personal experience, travel articles and experimental fiction (all sports-related). Monthly. Circ. 400,500. Accepts previously published material. Original artwork returned after publication.
Illustrations: Buys 5 illustrations/issue from freelancers. Buys 60 illustrations/year from freelancers. Send query letter with resume, tear sheets, slides and photographs. Samples are filed. Samples not filed are returned. Reports back within 1 week. To show a portfolio mail tear sheets, final reproduction/product, photographs, slides, color and b&w. Buys first rights, one-time rights, reprint rights and all rights. Pays on acceptance.
Tips: "Be consistent in style and quality."

AMERICAN SQUAREDANCE, Box 488, Huron OH 44839. Editors: Stan and Cathie Burdick. For squaredancers, callers and teachers. Emphasizes personalities, conventions and choreography. Monthly. Original artwork returned after publication if requested. Free sample copy.
Cartoons: Uses 1 cartoon/issue; buys 6/year from freelancers. Interested in dance theme; single panel. Send finished cartoons. SASE. Reports in 1 week. Buys all rights on a work-for-hire basis. Pays $10-20, halftones and washes; on publication.
Illustrations: Uses 5 illustrations/issue; buys 1/issue from freelancers. Interested in dance themes. Send finished art. SASE. Reports in 1 week. Buys all rights on a work-for-hire basis. Pays $25-50, b&w line drawings, washes and color-separated art, cover; $5-15, b&w line drawings and washes inside; on publication.

***AMERICAS 2001**, #5, 5313 E. Beverly Blvd., Los Angeles CA 90022. (213)727-2046. Managing Editor: Beatrice Echaveste. Magazine. "The primary focus of *Americas 2001* magazine is to encourage debate on the wide range of national issues that affect the Latino community on a daily basis. These issues include race relations, equal representation in politics, fair representation in media, voter registration, poverty, assimilation, bilingual education, culture and art, civil rights, immigraion, employment and the education dropout crisis, to name a few." Bilingual format. Bimonthly. Circ. 20,000. Original artwork is not returned to the artist after publication. Sample copies free for SASE with 90¢ postage.
Cartoons: Buys cartoons/issue from freelancers. Prefers themes which reflect the future; advancement, as well as those that portray Hispanics in positive manners. "Cartoons should be either humorous about daily life or make some type of political or social statement." Prefers multiple panels. Send query letter with samples of style. Samples are filed. Samples not filed are not returned. Reports back within 6 days. Buys all rights. Pays $50, b&w.
Illustrations: Buys illustrations/issue from freelancers. Works on assingment only. Prefers artwork about daily life or political/social issues. Send query letter with tear sheets, photocopies, slides and photographs. Samples are filed. Samples not filed are not returned. Reports back within 6 days. Call or write to schedule an appointment to show a portfolio, which should include tear sheets, photographs, slides and b&w. Buys all rights. Pays $100, color, cover; $50, b&w; $100, color, inside; on publication.
Tips: "Be familiar with the magazine and its objective provided upon request."

AMIGA WORLD AND RUN MAGAZINES, C W Communications/Peterborough, 80 Pine St., Peterborough NH 03458. (603)924-9471. Art Director: Rosslyn A. Frick. Emphasizes computing for business and families who own and operate Commodore computers. Monthly. Circ. 225,000. Original artwork returned after publication.
Illustrations: Prefers exciting, creative styles and Amiga-generated artwork. Works on assignment only. Send tear sheets, photographs, or promotional material. Reports only if interested. Negotiates rights purchased. Pays $300-600, b&w; $500-1,000, color, cover; $300-600 b&w; $500-1,000, color, inside; on acceptance.

ANIMALS, 350 S. Huntington Ave., Boston MA 02130. Photo Researcher: Laura Ten Eyck. "*Animals* is a national full-color, bimonthly magazine published by the Massachusetts Society for the Prevention of Cruelty to Animals. We publish articles on and photographs of wildlife, domestic animals, conservation, controversies involving animals, animal-welfare issues, pet health and pet care. Circ. 50,000. Original artwork usually returned after publication. Sample copy $2.50.
Illustrations: Buys 5 illustrations/year from freelancers. Prefers pets or wildlife illustrations relating to a particular article topic. Prefers pen & ink, then airbrush, charcoal/pencil, colored pencil, watercolor, acrylics, oils, pastel, and mixed media. Send query letter with brochure or tear sheets. Samples are filed. Samples not filed are returned by SASE. Reports back within 1 month. Write to schedule an appointment to show a portfolio, which should include roughs, original/final art, tear sheets, final reproduction/product and color. Negotiates rights purchased. Pays minimum $50, b&w; minimum $100, color, inside; on acceptance.
Tips: "In your samples, include work showing animals, particularly dogs and cats or humans with cats or dogs. Show a representative sampling."

***ANOTHER CHICAGO MAGAZINE**, Box 11223, Chicago IL 60611. Art Editor: Mary Sherman. Magazine emphasizing poetry and fiction for people interested in contemporary literature and art. Published twice a year. Circ. 1,000. Original artwork returned after publication. Sample copy $5.
Illustrations: Buys 8 illustrations/issue from an individual artist. Send query letter with resume, photocopies and photographs. Samples not filed are returned by SASE. Reports within 2 months. Buys one-time rights. Pays $25-50; on acceptance.

ANTIC, The Atari Resource, 544 Second St., San Francisco CA 94107. (415)957-0886. Production Manager: Linda Tapscott. Magazine emphasizing computers for Atari enthusiasts. Monthly. Circ. 100,000. Original artwork returned after publication.
Illustrations: Buys 3-5 illustrations/issue from freelancers. Works on assignment only. Prefers sophisticated, highly realistic styles using airbrush, colored pencil, pastels, or acrylics. Send brochure showing art style or resume and tear sheets, Photostats, photocopies, slides and photographs; "color work should be in color though." Samples not filed are returned. Reports back only if interested. To show a portfolio, mail appropriate materials, which should include original/final art, final reproduction/product, color and tear sheets. Buys one-time rights. Pays $800-1,000, color, cover; $50-150, b&w; $75-700, color, inside; 30 days from acceptance date.

THE ANTIQUARIAN, Box 798, Huntington NY 11743. (516)271-8990. Editors: Marguerite Cantine and Elizabeth Kilpatrick. Concerns antiques, arts, shows and news of the market; for dealers and collectors. Monthly. Circ. 15,000.
Illustrations: Receives 2 illustrations/week from freelance artists. "We are one magazine that hates the use of photography but it's more available to us than good illustrations. We ran a complete history of the teddy bear and would have used all drawings if we could have found an illustrator. Instead we had to use photos. We've also recently started using many illustrations of colonial and Victorian buildings." Buys b&w line drawings. Especially needs illustration for ad designs. Query with resume, samples and SASE. "No phone calls, please!" Include 8½x11" SASE with $1.25 if sample copy is requested. Reports in 4-8 weeks. Buys all rights. Pay "depends on the size of the article. We commission the entire article or issue if possible to one artist. I like for the artist to quote his/her rates." Pays $10 maximum, b&w; on acceptance.
Tips: "Our covers are us. They are children's illustrations from fine, usually German, books circa 1850-1875. If an artist can get the feel of what we're trying to convey with our covers, the rest is easy. We specialize in totally designed magazines. I think we're a leader in the antiques trade field and people will follow the trend. We are heavily illustrated—we use few photos. Send 5-10 illustrations *after* reviewing the publication. Suggest a price range. If the illustration is good, needed, usable, the price is never a problem. So suggest one. Only the artist knows the time involved. We buy *all rights only*. Please quote prices accordingly."

AOPA PILOT, 421 Aviation Way, Frederick MD 21701. (301)695-2353. Emphasizes general aviation (no military or airline) for aircraft owners and pilots. Monthly. Circ. 270,000. Original artwork returned after publication. Sample copy $2.
Illustrations: Buys 1-3 illustrations/issue. Uses illustrations specifically for manuscripts. Works on assignment only. Send query letter with tear sheets, Photostats, photocopies, slides and photographs. Samples returned by SASE. Reports only if interested. Call to schedule an appointment to show a portfolio, which should include original/final art and tear sheets. Buys first rights. Pays for illustration by the project,$250-2,500. Pays on acceptance.
Tips: Looks for "strong conceptual abilities, technical competence, solid design and confidence." Don't include pencil drawings in samples or portfolio. "Avoid duplicating photographs, as such an illustration is an unnecessary extra step. If I can use photography, I will."

***APALACHEE QUARTERLY**, Box 20106, Tallahassee FL 32304. Editor: Barbara Hamby, Pam Ball, Bruce Boehrer, Claudia Johnson and Paul McCall. Literary magazine emphasizing fine arts for a well-educated, literary audience. Quarterly. Circ. 500. Accepts previously published material. Original artwork returned after publication. Sample copy $3.50; art guidelines available.
Illustrations: Buys 5-10 illustrations/issue from freelancers. "We're very open on themes and styles. We like playful, technically accomplished work." Send samples to be kept on file. Prefers Photostats, photographs or photocopies as samples. Samples not filed are returned by SASE. Reports within 2 months. Buys one-time rights. Pays in 2 copies, b&w; cover and inside. "We pay as we receive grants."

APPALACHIAN TRAILWAY NEWS, Box 807, Harpers Ferry WV 25425. (304)535-6331. Editor: Judith Jenner. Emphasizes the Appalachian Trail for members of the Appalachian Trail Conference. 5 issues/year. Circ. 22,000. Sometimes accepts previously published material. Returns original artwork after publication. Sample copy $1 for serious inquiries; art guidelines for SASE with first-class postage. Finds most artists through references/word-of-mouth and samples received through the mail.
Cartoons: Buys 0-1 cartoon/issue from freelancers. Prefers themes on hikers and trailworkers on Appalachian Trail. Open to all formats. Send query letter with roughs and finished cartoons. Only materials pertinent to Appalachian Trail are considered. Material not filed is returned by SASE. Reports within 1 month. Negotiates rights purchased. Pays $25-50 for b&w; on acceptance.
Illustrations: Buys 2-5 illustrations/issue from freelancers. Prefers pen & ink, charcoal/pencil, colored pencil, watercolor, acrylics, oils, pastels and calligraphy. Themes/styles are assigned to particular story ideas. Send query letter with samples to be kept on file. Prefers Photostats, photocopies or tear sheets as samples. Samples not filed are returned by SASE. Reports within 1 month. Negotiates rights purchased. Pays $75-150, b&w and $150 up, color (watercolor only) for covers; $25-100, b&w for inside; pays on acceptance.

***AQUA-FIELD PUBLICATIONS**, 656 Shrewsbury Ave., Shrewsbury NJ 07701. (201)842-8300. Art Director: Anita Schettino. Magazine emphasizing outdoor recreation: hunting, fishing, scuba, gold and camping. "Geared to the active outdoors-oriented adult, mid-to-upper income area. There is some family material. Publishes annuals. Circ. 200,000 per magazine. Accepts previously published material. Original artwork is returned to the artist after publication. Sample copies and art guidelines free for SASE with first-class postage.
Illustrations: Buys 4-8 illustrations/issue from freelancers. Buys approximately 200 illustrations/year from freelancers. Works on assignment only. Send query letter with Photostats and slides. Samples are filed. Samples not filed are returned by SASE. Reports back within 1 month. Call or write to schedule an appointment to show a portfolio, which should include original/final art, tear sheets, photographs, slides, color and b&w. Buys one-time rights; negotiates rights purchased. Pays $35-50, b&w spots; $300 and up (negotiable), color, cover; $75, ½ and full page, color, inside. Pays on publication.

ARIZONA LIVING MAGAZINE, Suite C, 5046 N. 7th St., Phoenix AZ. (602)264-4295. Art Director: Margie Diguiseppe. Magazine emphasizing Arizona lifestyle and strong issues for 28-45 age group; salary of $30,000 or more a year; yuppie type. Monthly. Circ. 18,000. Accepts previously published material. Original artwork returned after publication. Sample copy for SASE with 95¢ postage.
Illustrations: Buys 3 illustrations/issue from freelancers. Works on assignment only. Prefers themes dealing with people and subjects pertaining to story. Send query letter with resume, tear sheets and Photostats. Samples not filed returned only if requested. Reports only if interested. Call or write to schedule an appointment to show a portfolio, which should include original/final art, tear sheets and Photostats. Buys one-time rights. Pays by project, $50-400.

***ARIZONA TREND**, 3003 N. Central Ave., Phoenix AZ 85012. (602)230-1117. Art Director: Katherine McGee. Estab. 1986. Magazine emphasizing business and finance. This is a business/finance magazine directed to upper management of Arizona (statewide) companies. Monthly. Circ. 25,000. Ac-

cepts previously published material. Original artwork is returned to the artist after publication. Samples and art guidelines available.
Illustrations: Buys 8-10 illustrations/issue from freelancers. Buys 96 illustrations/year from freelancers. Works on assignment only. Send query letter with tear sheets, Photostats, photocopies, slides and photographs. Samples are filed. Samples not filed are returned only if requested. Reports back only if interested. Call or write to schedule an appointment to show a portfolio, or mail tear sheets, photographs, slides color and b&w. Buys one-time rights. Pays $50, b&w; $300, color, cover; $50, b&w; $100, color inside; on acceptance.

ART BUSINESS NEWS, 60 Ridgeway Plaza, Stamford CT 06905. (203)356-1745. Editor: Jo Yanow-Schwartz. Trade journal emphasizing the business of selling art and frames, trends, new art editions, limited editions, posters and framing supplies. Features general interest, interview/profile and technical articles. Weekly. Circ. 25,000. Original artwork returned after publication. Sample copy available. Art guidelines available for SASE.
Cartoons: Buys some cartoons/issue from freelancers. Prefers "sophisticated, light business orientation." Prefers single panel, b&w line drawings and b&w washes. Send query letter with samples of style. Samples are filed. Samples not filed are returned. Reports back within weeks. Pays $35-50, b&w; $50-100, color.
Illustrations: Works on assignment only. Send query letter with brochure showing art style, tear sheets and slides. Samples are filed (excluding slides). Samples not filed are returned. Reports back within weeks. Write to schedule an appointment to show a portfolio or mail tear sheets, photographs, color and b&w. Buys one-time rights. Pays by the project, $35-100.

ART DIRECTION, 10 E. 39th St., 6th Floor, New York NY 10016. (212)889-6500. Editor: Hedi Levine. Emphasizes advertising for art directors. Monthly. Circ. 12,000. Original work not returned after publication. Sample copy $3.50. Art guidelines available. Receives 7 illustrations/week from freelance artists.
Illustrations: Uses 2-3 illustrations/issue; all from freelancers. Works on assignment only. Interested in themes that relate to advertising. Send query letter with brochure showing art styles. Samples are not filed and returned only if requested. Reports in 3 weeks. Write to schedule an appointment to show a portfolio, which should include tear sheets. Negotiates rights purchased. Pays $350, b&w; $1,000, color, cover; on publication.
Tips: "Must be about current advertising.

ART MATERIAL TRADE NEWS, 6255 Barfield Rd., Atlanta GA 30328. (404)256-9800. Editor: Anthony Giometti. Emphasizes art material business, merchandising and selling trends, products, store and manufacturer profiles for dealers, manufacturers, wholesalers of artist supplies. Monthly. Circ. 11,500. Accepts previously published material. Original artwork returned after publication. Sample copy $2.
Cartoons: Themes and styles open. Send query letter with samples of style to be kept on file "if desired by artist." Write for appointment to show portfolio. Material not kept on file returned by SASE. Reports "ASAP." Negotiates rights purchased. Payment negotiable. Pays on publication.
Illustrations: Works on assignment only. Send brochure, resume, samples and tear sheets to be kept on file. Write for an appointment to show portfolio. Prefers "anything but originals" as samples. Samples returned by SASE if not kept on file. Reports "ASAP." Negotiates rights purchased. Pays on publication.

THE ARTIST'S MAGAZINE, 1507 Dana Ave., Cincinnati OH 45207. Editor: Mike Ward. Emphasizes the techniques of working artists for the serious beginning and amateur artist. Published 12 times/year. Circ. 185,000. Occasionally accepts previously published material. Returns original artwork after publication. Sample copy $2 with SASE and 50¢ postage.
Cartoons: Contact Mike Ward, editor. Buys 2-3 "top-quality" cartoons/issue from freelancers. Most cartoons bought are single-panel finished cartoons with or without gagline; b&w line drawings, b&w washes. "We're also on the lookout for color, multi panel (4-6 panels) work with a theme to use on our 'P.S.' page. Any medium." All cartoons should be artist-oriented, appeal to the working artist and should not denigrate art or artists. Avoid cliche situations. For single panel cartoon submissions, send cover letter with 4 or more finished cartoons. For "P.S." submissions, query first with samples of your artwork. Material not filed is returned only by SASE. Reports within 1 month. Pays $50 and up for b&w single panels; pays $200 and up for "P.S." work. Buys first North American serial rights. Pays on acceptance.
Illustrations: Contact Carole Winters, Art Director. Buys 2-3 illustrations/issue from freelancers. Works on assignment only. Send query letter with brochure, resume and samples to be kept on file. Prefers Photostats or tear sheets as samples. Samples not filed are returned by SASE. Buys first rights. Pays on acceptance.

ATLANTIC CITY MAGAZINE, 1637 Atlantic Ave., Atlantic City NJ 08401. (609)348-6886. Art Director: Jeff Roth. Emphasizes the growth, people and entertainment of Atlantic City for residents and visitors. Monthly. Circ. 50,000.

Illustrations: Buys 2-4 illustrations/issue. Mainly b&w, some 4-color. Works on assignment only. Send query letter with brochure showing art style and tear sheets, slides and photographs to be kept on file. Call or write to schedule an appointment to show a portfolio, which should include original/final art, final reproduction/product, color, tear sheets, photographs and b&w. Buys first rights. Pays $50-250, b&w, $150-400, color; on publication.

Tips: "We are looking for intelligent, reliable artists who can work within the confines of our budget and time frame. Deliver good art and receive good tear sheets."

ATLANTIC SALMON JOURNAL, Suite 1030, 1435 St. Alexandre, Montreal, Quebec H3A 2G4 Canada. (514)842-8059. Managing Editor: Terry Davis. Emphasizes conservation and angling of Atlantic salmon; travel, biology and cuisine for educated, well-travelled, affluent and informed anglers and conservationists, biologists and professionals. Quarterly. Circ. 20,000. Does not accept previously published material. Returns original artwork after publication. Sample copy free for SAE. Art guidelines available.

Cartoons: Uses 2-4/issue. Prefers environmental or political themes, specific to salmon resource management, travel and tourism—light and whimsical. Prefers single panel with or without gagline; b&w line drawings. Send query letter with samples of style to be kept on file. Material not filed is returned. Reports within 8 weeks. Buys first rights and one-time rights. Pays $25-50, b&w; on publication.

Illustrations: Uses 4-6/issue. Prefers themes on angling, environmental scenes and biological drawings. Prefers spot pencil sketches, watercolors and acrylics. Send query letter with samples to be kept on file. Prefers Photostats, tear sheets, slides or photographs as samples. Include SAE and IRC. Samples not filed are returned. Reports within 8 weeks. Buys first rights and one-time rights. Pays $50-150, b&w, and $100-250, color, inside; on publication.

***AURA LITERARY/ARTS REVIEW**, Box 76, University Center, UAB, Birmingham AL 35210. (205)934-3216. Editor: Randy Blythe. Magazine emphasizing literature and art for largely academic, literary minded and artistic people. Biannually. Circ. 500. Does not accept previously published material. Original artwork returned after publication. Sample copy $2.50. Art guidelines free for SASE with first-class postage.

Illustrations: "We use art that is thematic in its own right; it is not illustration."

***AUSTRALIAN WOMEN'S WEEKLY**, 54 Park St., Sydney Australia 2000. A.C.P. Designer-in-Chief: Phil Napper. Readers are average to highly sophisticated women. Monthly. Circ. 1 million +. Original artwork not returned after publication. Art guidelines with SASE (nonresidents include IRC's).

Illustrations: Uses 2 illustrations/issue; buys all from freelancers. Interested in action illustration in traditional style; good anatomy, any medium. Works on assignment only. Provide tear sheets to be filed for possible future assignments. Send samples of style. No samples returned. Reports in 2 weeks. Buys all rights. Pays with Australian dollars; $300-400/mono; on acceptance.

Tips: Artists "must be good enough for national publication."

AUTO TRIM NEWS, 1623 Grand Ave., Baldwin NY 11510. Contact: Nat Danas. "For the small businessman." Does not return original artwork after publication.

Cartoons: Buys 2/issue from freelancers. Prefers to see roughs; reports in 2 weeks. Pays on publication.

Illustrations: Buys 1/issue from freelancers. Works on assignment only. Send query letter with roughs and samples of style; samples returned. Reports in 2 weeks. Buys all rights on a work-for-hire basis. Pays $10, spot drawings; $25-50, cover design; on publication.

Tips: Artists should "visit a shop" dealing in this field.

AXIOS, The Orthodox Journal, 800 S. Euclid Ave., Fullerton CA 92632. (714)526-2131. Editor: David Gorham. Emphasizes "challenges in ethics and theology, some questions that return to haunt one generation after another, old problems need to be restated with new urgency. *Axios* tries to present the 'unthinkable.' " Works from an Orthodox Catholic viewpoint. Monthly. Circ. 6,478. Accepts previously published material and simultaneous submissions. Original artwork returned after publication. Sample copy $2.

The asterisk before a listing indicates that the listing is new in this edition. New markets are often the most receptive to freelance submissions.

Illustrations: Buys 5-10 illustrations/issue from freelancers. Prefers bold line drawings, seeks icons, b&w; "no color *ever*; use block prints—do not have to be religious, but must be *bold*!" Send query letter with brochure, resume, business card or samples to be kept on file. Samples not filed are returned by SASE. Reports within 5 weeks. To show a portfolio, mail final reproduction/product and b&w. Buys one-time rights. Pays $100, b&w cover and $50-75, b&w inside; on acceptance.
Tips: "Realize that the Orthodox are *not* Roman Catholics, nor Protestants. We do not write from those outlooks. Though we do accept some stories about those religions, be sure *you* know what an Orthodox Catholic is. Know the traditional art form—we prefer line work, block prints, lino-cuts."

B.C. OUTDOORS, 202-1132 Hamilton St., Vancouver, British Columbia V6B 2S2 Canada. (604)687-1581. Editor: George Will. Emphasizes fishing, hunting, RV camping, wildlife/conservation. Published 10 times/year. Circ. 36,000. Original artwork returned after publication unless bought outright. Free sample copy.
Cartoons: Uses 3-4 cartoons/issue; buys all from freelancers. Cartoons should pertain to outdoor recreation: fishing, hunting, camping, wildlife in British Columbia. Format: single panel b&w line drawings with or without gagline. Prefers finished cartoons. SAE (nonresidents include IRC). Pays on acceptance. Reports in 2 weeks. Buys one-time rights.
Illustrations: Uses 12 illustrations/year. Interested in outdoors, creatures and activities as stories require. Freelancers selected "generally because I've seen their work." Format: b&w line drawings for inside, rarely for cover; b&w washes for inside; and color washes for inside and cover. Works on assignment only. Samples returned by SAE (nonresidents include IRC). Reports back on future assignment possibilities. Arrange personal appointment to show portfolio or send samples of style. When reviewing samples, especially looks at how their subject matter fits the publication and the art's quality. Reports in 2-6 weeks. Buys first North American serial rights or all rights on a work-for-hire basis. Payment negotiable, depending on nature of assignment. Pays on acceptance.

BAJA TIMES, Box 755, San Ysidro CA 92073. (706)612-1244. Editorial Consultant: John W. Utley. Emphasizes Baja California, Mexico for tourists, other prospective visitors and retirees living there. Monthly. Circ. 50,000. Accepts previously published material. Original artwork returned after publication. Sample copy for 9x12 or larger SASE with 85¢ postage.
Cartoons: All must be Baja California-oriented. Prefers single panel with gagline; b&w line drawings. Send query letter with sample of style to be kept on file. Material not filed returned by SASE. Reports within 1 month. Buys one-time rights. Payment not established. Pays on publication.
Illustrations: Theme: Baja California. Send query letter with samples, tear sheets or photocopies to be kept on file. Samples not filed are returned by SASE. Reports within 1 month. Buys one-time rights. Payment not established. Pays on publication.
Tips: "We have not used art, mostly because it has not been offered to us. If properly oriented to our theme (Baja California), we would consider on an occasional basis."

BAKERSFIELD LIFESTYLE MAGAZINE, 123 Truxtun Ave., Bakersfield CA 93301. (805)325-7124. Editor: Steve Walsh. City magazine aimed at local lifestyles of college-educated males/females, ages 25-65. Monthly. Circ. 5,000. Accepts previously published material. Original artwork returned after publication. Sample copy $3; art guidelines free for SASE.
Cartoons: Buys 4 cartoons/issue from freelancers. No political humor. Prefers single panel with gagline; b&w line drawings or b&w washes. Send finished cartoons to be kept on file. Material not filed is returned by SASE. Reports only if interested. Buys one-time rights or reprints rights. Pays $5, b&w; on publication.
Illustrations: Buys 6 illustrations/issue from freelancers. Prefers realistic style. Prefers pen & ink, airbrush and charcoal/pencil. Send Photostats, tear sheets or photocopies to be kept on file. Write for appointment to show portfolio. Samples not filed are returned by SASE. Reports only if interested. Buys one-time rights or reprint rights. Pays $100, b&w and $150, color, cover; $50, b&w and $75, color, inside; on publication.
Tips: "I do not want to see original art or slides in a portfolio." Has less need for freelancers but a greater need for graphic services.

BALLOON LIFE MAGAZINE, 3381 Pony Express Dr., Sacramento CA 95834. (916)922-9648. Editor: Tom Hamilton. Estab. 1985. Monthly magazine emphasizing the sport of ballooning. This is a "four-color magazine covering the life of sport ballooning, contains current news, feature articles, calendar and more. Audiences is sport balloon enthusiasts." Circ. 2,500. Accepts previously published material. Original artwork returned after publication. Sample copy for SASE with $1.25 postage.
Cartoons: Buys 10-15 cartoons/year from freelancers. Prefers gag cartoons, editorial or political cartoons, caricatures and humorous illustrations. Prefers single panel with or without gaglines; b&w line drawings. Send query letter with samples, roughs and finished cartoons. Samples are filed. Samples not

filed are returned. Reports back within 2 weeks. Buys first rights. Pays $25, b&w; on publication.
Illustrations: Buys 1-3 illustrations/year from freelancers. Send query letter with business card and samples. Samples are filed. Samples not filed are returned. Reports back within 2 weeks. Buys first rights. Pays $50, color, cover; $40, color, inside; on publication.

BALTIMORE JEWISH TIMES, 2104 North Charles St., Baltimore MD 21218. (301)752-3504. Art Director: Kim Muller-Thym. Assistant Art Director: Carol Steuer. Tabloid emphasizing special interest to the Jewish community for largely local readership. Weekly. Circ. 20,000. Returns original artwork after publication, if requested. Sample copy available.
Illustrations: Buys 2-3 illustrations/issue from freelancers. Works on assignment only. Prefers high-contrast b&w illustrations. Send query letter with brochure showing art style or tear sheets and photocopies. Samples not filed are returned by SASE. Reports back only if interested. To show a portfolio, mail appropriate materials or write to schedule an appointment; portfolio should include original/final art, final reproduction/product, color, tear sheets and Photostats. Buys first rights. Pays $100-150, b&w, cover and $200-300, color, cover; $30-100, b&w, inside; on publication.

BANJO NEWSLETTER, INC., Box 364, Greensboro MD 21639. (301)482-6278. Editor/Publisher: Hub Nitchie. Emphasizes banjo 5-string music for musicians and instrument collectors. Monthly. Circ. 7,000. Accepts previously published material. Original artwork returned after publication. Sample copy $1; deductible on subscription..
Cartoons: Buys 1 cartoon/issue from freelancers 5-string banjo related. Prefers single panel; b&w line drawings. Send query letter with sample of style to be kept on file. Material not filed is returned by SASE. Reports within 2 weeks. To show a portfolio, mail thumbnails. Buys one-time rights. Pays $20-25, b&w; on publication.
Illustrations: Buys 1-2 illustrations/issue from freelancers. Send query letter to be kept on file. Samples returned by SASE. Reports within 2 weeks. Buys one-time rights. Pays approximately $30, b&w, cover; $20-30, b&w, inside; on publication.

BAY AND DELTA YACHTSMAN, Recreation Publications, 2019 Clement Ave., Alameda CA 94501. (415)865-7500. Editor: Dave Preston. Concerns boating and boat owners in northern California. Monthly. Circ. 20,000. Previously published and simultaneous submissions OK (if not published in northern California). Original artwork returned after publication if requested. Sample copy $1.50.
Cartoons: Buys 4-5/year on boating. Prefers to see roughs. SASE. Reports in 2 weeks. Buys all rights on a work-for-hire basis. Pays $5 minimum, b&w line drawings; on publication.
Illustrations: Uses 2-3 charts and technical drawings/issue on boating. Prefers to see roughs. SASE. Send query letter with resume to be kept on file. Reports in 2 weeks. Buys all rights on a work-for-hire basis. Pays $5 minimum, b&w line drawings; on publication.

Freelance artist Donna Bair achieved dramatic contrasts by using pen and ink to highlight the tensions of a story excerpted in the* Baltimore Jewish Times*. Art director Kim Muller-Thym gave Bair a week to complete the piece, buying first rights for $60. The Holland, Pennsylvania illustrator originally sent a self-promotion piece and samples after learning of the publication in the* Artist's Market*. "Her pieces were not slick or expensive," says Thym, " but they were clever and comprehensive, all based on concept." Bair has included this assignment in her resume and uses it as a portfolio piece.

BEND OF THE RIVER ® MAGAZINE, 143 W. Third St., Box 239, Perrysburg OH 43551. Editors-in-Chief: Chris Raizk Alexander and R. Lee Raizk. For local history enthusiasts. Monthly. Circ. 3,000. Previously published and photocopied submissions OK. Original artwork returned after publication. Sample copy $1.
Cartoons: Buys 12 cartoons/issue from freelancers. Interested in early Americana; single panel with gagline. SASE. Buys first North American serial rights or all rights on a work-for-hire basis. Pays $1-3, b&w line drawings.
Illustrations: Buys 20 illustrations/year. Interested in "historic buildings for ads." Works on assignment only. Prefers to see roughs. SASE. No samples returned. Reports in 6 weeks. Buys first North American serial rights or all rights on a work-for-hire basis. Pays $10-15, b&w line drawings, inside. Especially needs antiques, nostalgic items, landscapes and riverscapes.

THE BERKELEY MONTHLY, 1301 59th St., Emeryville CA 94710. (415)658-9811. Art Director: Renete Woodbury. Tabloid emphasizing art/ad mix and exciting graphics for Bay area residents. Monthly. Circ. 90,000. Accepts previously published material. Original artwork returned after publication. Sample copy for SASE.
Cartoons: Buys 1-2 cartoons/issue from freelancers. Prefers single, double or multiple panel; b&w line drawings. Send samples of style to be kept on file. Material not filed is returned by SASE. Reports only if interested. Buys one-time rights. Pays $50-75.
Illustrations: Buys 5 illustrations/issue from freelancers. Works on assignment only. Send query letter. Samples not filed are returned by SASE. Reports only if interested. To show a portfolio, mail final reproduction/product, tear sheets and photographs. Buys one-time rights. Pays $200, color, cover; $50-100, b&w, and $100, color, inside; on publication.

BETTER HOMES & GARDENS, Meredith Corp., 1716 Locust, Des Moines IA 50336. Contact: Cartoon Editor. For "middle-and-up income, homeowning and community-concerned families." Monthly. Circ. 8,000,000. Original artwork not returned after publication. Free artist's guidelines.
Cartoons: Uses 2 cartoons/issue; buys all from freelancers. Receives 50-75 submissions/week from freelancers. Interested in current events, education, environment, family life, humor through youth, politics, religion, retirement, hobbies, sports and businessmen; single panel with gag line. Prefers finished cartoons. SASE. Reports in 2 weeks. Buys concurrent rights. Fees negotiable. Pays $300 minimum, b&w line drawings; on acceptance.

BEVERAGE WORLD MAGAZINE, 150 Great Neck Rd., Great Neck NY 11021. (516)829-9210. Art Director: Alice Cosby. Managing Editor: Jeanne Lukasick. Emphasizes beverages (beers, wines, spirits, bottled waters, soft drinks, juices) for soft drink bottlers, breweries, bottled water/juice plants, wineries and distilleries. Monthly. Circ. 30,000. Accepts simultaneous submissions. Original artwork returned after publication if requested. Sample copy $2.50.
Illustrations: Uses 5 illustrations/issue; buys 3-4 illustrations/issue from freelancers. Works on assignment only. Send query letter with Photostats, slides or tear sheets to be kept on file. Write for appointment to show portfolio. Reports only if interested. Negotiates rights purchased. Pays $350 color, cover; $30, b&w, inside; on acceptance. Uses color illustration for cover. Usually black-and-white for sport illustrations inside.

BIKEREPORT, Box 8308, Missoula MT 59807. (406)721-1776. Editor: Daniel D'Ambrosio. Magazine. Emphasizes long-distance bicycle touring for bicycle enthusiasts. Circ. 18,000. Accepts previously published material. Original artwork returned after publication. Sample copy and art guidelines free for SASE.
Illustrations: Uses 3-6 illustrations/issue. Themes/styles are open. Works on assignment only. Send query letter with samples to be kept on file. Samples not kept on file are returned. Reports within 1 month. To show a portfolio, mail tear sheets and Photostats. Buys first rights. Pays $75, b&w, cover; $20-50, b&w, inside; on publication.

***BIOSCIENCE**, 730 11th St., NW, Washington DC 20001-4584. (202)628-1500. Managing Editor: Anne Meltzer. "A review journal for the professional biologist containing peer-reviewed articles, features, announcements and a variety of departments." Monthly. Circ. 12,000. Accepts previously published material. Original artwork is sometimes returned to artist after publication. Sample copies available.
Cartoons: Buys 0-2 cartoons/year from freelancers. Prefers single panel with or without gagline, b&w line drawings. Send query letter with samples of style. Samples are filed. Samples not filed are returned if requested. Reports back only if interested. Negotiates rights purchased. Pays $20-30, b&w.
Illustrations: Buys 0-5 illustrations/year from freelancers. Prefers biological, realistic illustration. Prefers pen & ink. Send query letter with brochure showing art style. Samples are filed. Samples not

filed are returned only if requested. Reports back only if interested. "Portfolio requested only if interested." Negotiates rights purchased. Pays $30-100, color cover; $50, b&w, inside; on publication.
Tips: Portfolio should contain "lots of pen & ink. I do not want to see too much abstract art, but a diveristy of talent is important."

BIRD WATCHER'S DIGEST, Box 110, Marietta OH 45750. (614)373-5285. Editor: Mary B. Bowers. Emphasizes birds and bird watchers for "bird watchers and birders (backyard and field; veteran and novice)." Bimonthly. Circ. 60,000. Previously published material OK. Original work returned after publication. Sample copy $3.
Cartoons: Uses 1-3 cartoons/issue; buys all from freelancers. Interested in themes pertaining to birds and/or bird watchers. Single panel with or without gagline, b&w line drawings. Send roughs. Samples returned by SASE. Reports in 1 month. Buys one-time rights and reprint rights. Pays $20, b&w; on publication.

BLACK BEAR PUBLICATIONS, 1916 Lincoln St., Croydon PA 19020-8026. (215)788-3543. Editor: Ave Jeanne. Associate Editor: Ron Zettlemoyer. Magazine emphasizing social, political, ecological, environmental subjects for a mostly well-educated audience, any age group. Semiannual. Circ. 400. Accepts previously published material. Original artwork returned after publication with SASE. Sample copy $2 (for back issues); art guidelines for SASE with first-class postage. Current copy $3 postpaid in U.S. and Canada.
Illustrations: Buys 12 illustrations/issue from freelancers. Prefers collage, woodcuts, pen & ink. Send query letter with SASE, resume and photocopies. Samples not filed returned by SASE. Reports within 10 days. To show a portfolio, mail photocopies. Buys one-time rights or reprint rights. Pays in copies; on publication, for the magazine. Pays cash on acceptance for chapbook illustrators.

***THE BLACK COLLEGIAN MAGAZINE**, 1240 S. Broad St., New Orleans LA 70125. Art Director: Tom Dennis. Magazine emphasizing "career, job and self-development information for black college students entering the world of work." Bimonthly. Circ. 120,000. Original artwork is sometimes returned to the artist after publication. Sample copies $4; art guidelines free for SASE with first-class postage.
Illustration: Buys about 5 illustrations/issue from freelancers. Buys about 10 illustrations/year from freelancers. Prefers artwork featuring black students and professionals in positive work settings. Write to schedule an appointment to show a portfolio, which should include thumbnails, roughs and original/final art. Pays $50, b&w; $100, color cover; $25, b&w; $100, color inside; on publication.
Tips: "Study previous issues to know format and audience."

***THE BLACK WARRIOR REVIEW**, University of Alabama, Box 2936, Tuscaloosa AL 35487. (205)348-4518. Editor: Amber Vogel. For general literary audience. Published semiannually. Circ. 2,000. Sample copy $3.50.
Illustrations: Needs b&w or color illustrations for covers. SASE. Reports in 4 weeks. Buys all rights, but may reassign rights to artist after publication. Pays $25-100, b&w or color; on publication.

THE BLADE "TOLEDO" MAGAZINE, 541 Superior St., Toledo OH 43660. Editor: Sue Stankey. Weekly. Circ. 210,000. Query. Previously published and simultaneous submissions OK. Free sample copy.
Illustrations: Buys 1 or 2 on local or regional themes. "Most of our original art is done by staff artists or Toledo-area people. We currently use very little outside freelance illustration" Query. SASE. Buys one-time rights. Cover: Pays $50-150, color. Inside: Pays $35-50, color; $20-30, b&w; on publication.

BLUE COMET PRESS, 1708 Magnolia Ave., Manhattan Beach CA 90266. (213)545-6887. President/Publisher: Craig Stormon. Estab. 1986. Publishes limited edition comic books. Genres: adventure, fantasy, science fiction, animal parodies and social parodies. Themes: outer space, future science and social commentary. "Our comics are for everybody—for kids and grown ups. We have PG rating." Bimonthly and quarterly. Circ. 10-20,000. Original artwork returned after publication. Sample copy $2.50. Art guidelines for SASE with 1 first-class stamp.
Illustrations: Uses freelance artists for inking, lettering, pencilling, color work, posters and covers. Send query letter with resume and photocopies of work, story form 4-8 pages. Samples not filed are returned by SASE if requested. Reports back within 1 month. Call or write to schedule an appointment to show a portfolio, or mail 4-8 pages of pencil or ink drawings, 4-8 pages of action continuity, 4-8 photocopies of original pencil art or inking and 4-8 pages of lettering. Rights purchased vary. Pays $10-35/page for pencilling, $15-25/page for inking and $5-10 for lettering. Pays on publication "or after."
Tips: "I don't need cartoony art. Need realistic art, good anatomy. Must be top quality."

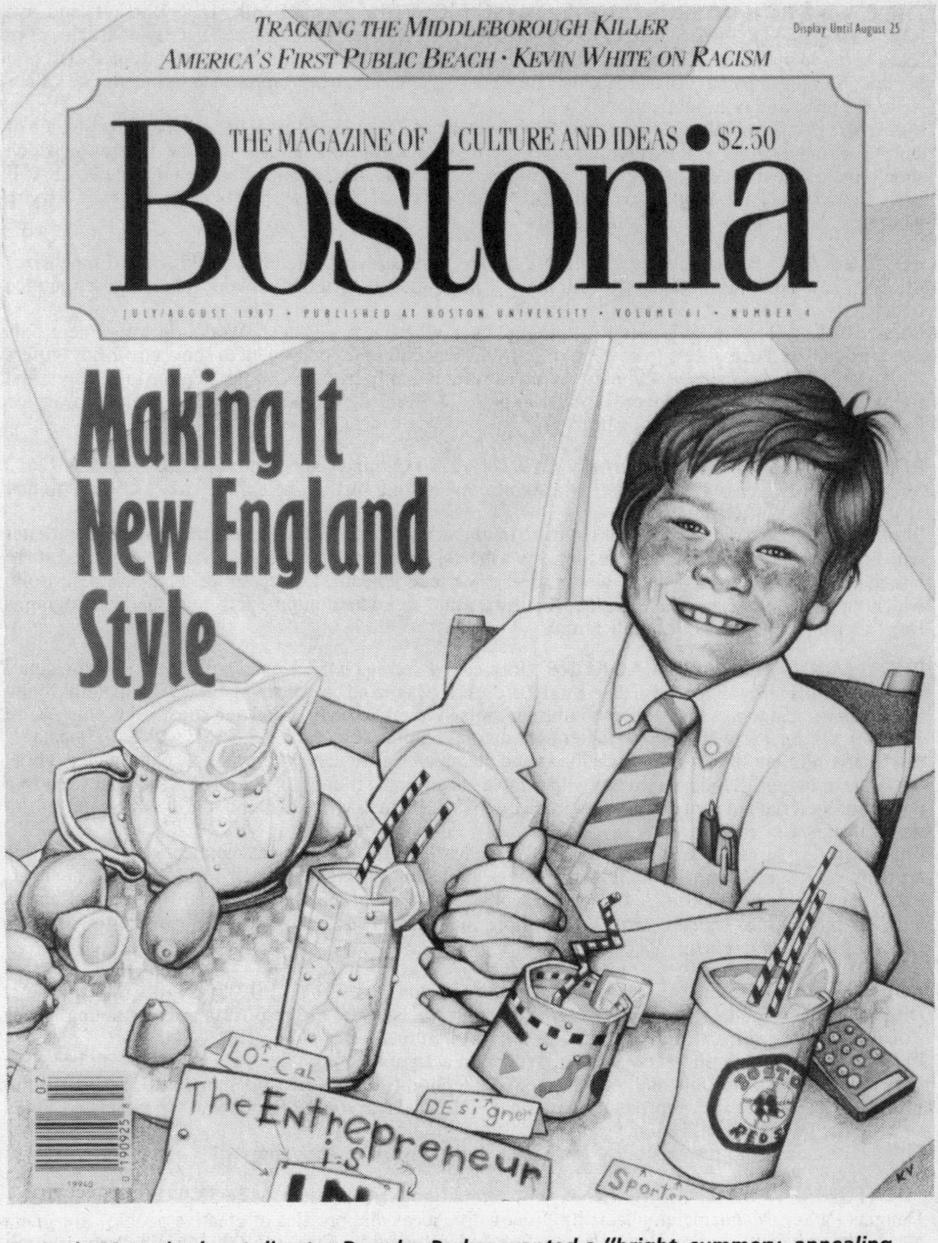

TRACKING THE MIDDLEBOROUGH KILLER
AMERICA'S FIRST PUBLIC BEACH • KEVIN WHITE ON RACISM

Display Until August 25

THE MAGAZINE OF CULTURE AND IDEAS • $2.50

Bostonia

JULY/AUGUST 1987 • PUBLISHED AT BOSTON UNIVERSITY • VOLUME 61 • NUMBER 4

Making It New England Style

©1987 Kathleen Volp

Bostonia Magazine's art director Douglas Parker wanted a "bright, summery, appealing look," explains illustrator Kathleen Volp. He wanted the boy to be appealing yet also slightly precocious and imaginative." The Somerville, Massachusetts artist was given three weeks to conceptualize and complete the piece, using Winsor & Newton liquid watercolor and Prismacolor. The magazine bought first North American serial rights. Volp, who originally sent mailers to the magazine, received much exposure through the piece. "This is a hot new magazine on the Boston scene. They are very cooperative and pay well. They also provide 100 tear sheets. Since I was just breaking into the color market, this job proved to other art directors that they could use my color work."

THE B'NAI B'RITH INTERNATIONAL JEWISH MONTHLY, B'nai B'rith, 1640 Rhode Island Ave. NW, Washington DC 20036. (202)857-6645. Editor: Marc Silver. Emphasizes a variety of articles of interest to the Jewish family. Published 10 times/year. Circ. 200,000. Original artwork returned after publication. Sample copy $1. Also uses artists for "design, lettering, calligraphy on assignment. We call or write the artist, pay on publication."
Illustrations: Buys 2 illustrations/issue from freelancers. Theme and style vary, depending on tone of story illustrated. Works on assignment only. Write or call for appointment to show portfolio, which should include tear sheets, slides or photographs. Reports within 3 weeks. Samples returned by SASE. Buys first rights. Pays $150, b&w and $250, color, cover; $100, b&w and color, inside; rates vary regarding size of illustration; on publication.

BOATING, 1515 Broadway, New York NY 10036. Art Director: Victor Mazurkiewicz. Emphasizes lifestyle, new products and boat test. Monthly. Circ. 180,000. Original artwork returned after publication.
Illustrations: Occasionally uses illustrations; buys all from freelancers. Works on assignment only. Send samples and tear sheets to be kept on file. Write or call for appointment to show portfolio. Prefers Photostats or photographs as samples. Samples returned only by SASE if not kept on file. Buys first rights. Pays $1,000, color, cover. Pays $100-500, b&w, inside; $1,000, color, 2-page spread, inside. Pays 30 days after submission of bill.

BODYBOARDING, (formerly *Surfing Magazine*), 2720 Camino Capistrano, San Clemente CA 92672. Managing Art Director: Dave Vecker. Magazine emphasizing surfing. Monthly. Circ. 27,500. Original artwork returned after publication.
Illustrations: Buys 1 illustration/issue from freelancers. Works on assignment only. Send query letter with brochure showing art style or resume, tear sheets, slides and photographs. Samples not filed are returned by SASE. Reports within 3 weeks. Call or write to schedule an appointment to show a portfolio, which should include roughs, original/final art, final reproduction/product, color and photographs. Buys reprint rights. Pays on publication.

BODY, MIND AND SPIRIT MAGAZINE, (formerly *Psychic Guide Magazine*), Box 701, Providence RI 02901. (401)351-4320. Publisher: Paul Zuromski. Magazine emphasizing New Age, natural living and metaphysical topics for people looking for tools to improve body, mind and spirit. Bimonthly. Circ. 150,000. Original artwork returned after publication. Sample copy for 9x12 SASE with $1.07 postage.
Cartoons: Prefers New Age, natural living and metaphysical themes. Prefers single panel with gagline; b&w line drawings. Send query letter with samples of style and roughs to be kept on file. Write to show a portfolio. Material not kept on file is returned by SASE. Reports within 3 months. Buys one-time reprint rights. Negotiates payment.
Illustrations: Buys 5-10 illustrations/issue from freelancers. Works on assignment only. Prefers line art with New Age, natural living and metaphysical themes. Send query letter with resume, tear sheets, Photostats, photocopies, slides and photographs. Samples not filed are returned by SASE. Reports within 3 months. To show a portfolio, mail original/final art and tear sheets. Buys one-time reprint rights. Negotiates payment. Pays on publication.

BOSTON MAGAZINE, 300 Massachusetts Ave., Boston MA 02115. (617)262-9700. Associate Art Director: Steven Banks. Emphasizes regional/city subjects/issues of the Boston area for young professionals. Monthly. Circ. 110,000. Original artwork returned after publication.
Illustrations: Uses 8 illustrations/issue. Works on assignment only. Send query letter with brochure showing art style or resume and tear sheets to be kept on file. Call for appointment to show portfolio, which should include final reproduction/product, color and tear sheets. Reports only if interested. Buys first rights. Pays on publication.
Tips: "We accept no responsibility for unsolicited art work or photographs."

***BOSTONIA MAGAZINE**, 10 Lenox St., Brookline MA 02146. (617)353-9711. Art Director: Douglas Parker. Magazine emphasizing "innovative ideas and profiles of creative people" for graduates of the university and residents of New England. Bimonthly. Circ. 145,000. Original artwork is returned to the artist after publication. Sample copies $2.50.
Cartoons: "Haven't used but would be interested in creative ideas." Send query letter with samples of style. Samples are filed. Reports back wihtin weeks only if interested. Buys first rights.
Illustrations: Buys 25 illustrations/issue from freelancers. Buys 150 illustrations/year from freelancers. Works on assignment only. Send resume, tear sheets, Photostats, photocopies, slides and photographs. Samples are filed. Reports back within weeks only if interested. To show a portfolio, mail thumbnails, roughs, original/final art, tear sheets, final reproduction/product, Photostats, photographs, slides, color and b&w. Buys first rights. "Payment depends on final use and publication size." Pays on acceptance.

BOTH SIDES NOW, Rt. 6, Box 28, Tyler TX 75704. (214)592-4263. Contact: Editor. Magazine emphasizing the new age for people seeking holistic alternatives in spiritual, lifestyle and politics. Irregular publication. Circ. 2,000 printed. Accepts previously published material. Original artwork returned by SASE. Sample copy 75¢.
Cartoons: Buys various number of cartoons/issue from freelancers. Prefers fantasy, political satire, religion and exposes of hypocrisy as themes. Prefers single or multi panel; b&w line drawings. Send query letter with samples of style such as good photocopies. Samples not filed are returned by SASE. Reports within 3 months. Pays in copies only.
Illustrations: Buys variable amount of illustrations/issue from freelancers. Prefers fantasy, surrealism, spirituality and realism as themes. Send query letter with resume and photocopies. Samples not filed are returned by SASE. Reports back within 3 months. Pays in copies; on publication.

BOW & ARROW MAGAZINE, Box HH, Capistrano Beach CA 92624. (714)493-2101. Editorial Director: Roger Combs. Emphasizes bowhunting and bowhunters. Bimonthly. Original artwork not returned after publication.
Cartoons: Uses 2-3 cartoons/issue; buys all from freelancers. Prefers single panel, with gag line; b&w line drawings. Send finished cartoons. Material not kept on file returned by SASE. Reports within 2 months. Buys all rights. Pays $7.50-$10, b&w. Pays on acceptance.
Illustrations: Uses 1-2 illustrations/issue; buys all from freelancers. Prefers live animals/game as themes. Send samples. Prefers photographs or original work as samples. Especially looks for perspective, unique or accurate use of color and shading, and an ability to clearly express a thought, emotion or event. Samples returned by SASE. Reports in 2 months. Buys all rights or negotiates rights purchased. Pays $100-150, color, cover; payment for inside b&w varies. Pays on acceptance.

BOWHUNTER, Editorial Offices, 3720 S. Calhoun, Fort Wayne IN 46807. (219)456-3580. Editor-in-Chief: M.R. James. For "readers of all ages, background and experience. All share two common passions—hunting with the bow and arrow and a love of the great outdoors." Bimonthly. Circ. 180,000.
Cartoons: Uses few cartoons; but considers all submissions. Interested in "bowhunting and wildlife. No unsafe hunting conditions; single panel." Prefers to see roughs. SASE. Reports in 6 weeks. Buys all rights on a work-for-hire basis; will reassign rights. Pays $20-25, line drawings; on acceptance.
Illustrations: Buys b&w and color illustrations/issue, all from freelancers. Interested in "wildlife-bowhunting scenes." Send query letter with slides and photographs. SASE. Reports in 6 weeks. To show a portfolio, mail roughs. Buys first rights. Pays $200 color, cover; $20 + b&w and $50 + color, inside; on acceptance.
Tips: "We are presently overstocked with cartoons but need good wildlife art." Artist must convey "a feeling and understanding for the game represented. Call it atmosphere or mood, or whatever, it's something that is either there or not. The art we select for publication has this extra something the viewer immediately senses. We are using more color on inside pages. This opens up additional possibilities for freelance artists with good wildlife art. Study the magazine before contacting us. Know what we use before making suggestions or submitting ideas. Know the subject down to the finest details."

BOWLING DIGEST, 1020 Church St., Evanston IL 60201. Art Director: Thomas M. Miller. Emphasizes pro and amateur bowling. Bimonthly. Circ. 115,000. Original artwork returned after publication.
Cartoons: Considers sports themes. Prefers single panel; b&w line drawings or color washes. Send query letter. Write for appointment to show portfolio. Material not filed is returned by SASE. Reports only if interested. Pays on publication.
Illustrations: Considers sports—bowling themes. Works on assignment only. Send query letter. Write for appointment to show portfolio. Samples returned by SASE. Reports only if interested. Pays on publication.

***BOY'S LIFE**, 1325 Walnut Hill Ln., Irving TX 75038-3096. Design Director: Joseph Connolly. Magazine emphasizing fiction and articles on scout-related topics such as camping, nature lore, history and science. Monthly. Circ. 1,400,000.
Cartoons: Buys 5 cartoons/issue from freelancers.
Illustrations: Buys 6 b&w and 5 color illustrations/issue from freelancers. Prefers b&w work. Send query letter with photocopies and slides. Reports back within 10 days. Buys first rights. Pays $1,250-1,500 color, cover; $175-200, b&w; $950, color inside.
Tips: "Artwork for this magazine should not be simplistic or crude and should not be geared down to kids."

BREAD, 6401 The Paseo, Kansas City MO 64131. (816)333-7000. Editor-in-Chief: Karen DeSollar. Christian leisure reading magazine for ages 12-17 with denominational interests. Monthly. Circ. 25,000. Previously published and simultaneous submissions OK. Free sample copy and artist's guide-

lines *with* SASE.
Illustrations: Uses 15 illustrations/year. Works on assignment only. Prefers to see samples. Pays $150-200, color, cover; $25-30, b&w, inside; on acceptance.

BREAKFAST WITHOUT MEAT, Room 188, 1827 Haight St., San Francisco CA 94117. Art Director: G. Obo. Magazine emphasizing music and satire. "We want outrageous stuff only; please no mainstream cartoons!" We have world-wide distribution, mainly to fans of humor and punk music. Quarterly. Circ. 1,000. Sample copy $1.25. Art guidelines free for SASE with first-class postage.
Cartoons: Buys 2 cartoons/issue from freelancers. Prefers single or multi panel with gagline; b&w line drawings. Send query letter with finished cartoons. Samples not filed are returned by SASE. Reports back within 4 weeks. Negotiates rights purchased. Pays in copies and unusual gifts.
Tips: "We are looking for unusual minds, not bland guys that sit around trying to figure out what people want. Our ideal portfolio would contain candy, money and free drinks. It would not contain feeble attempts at mainstream humor."

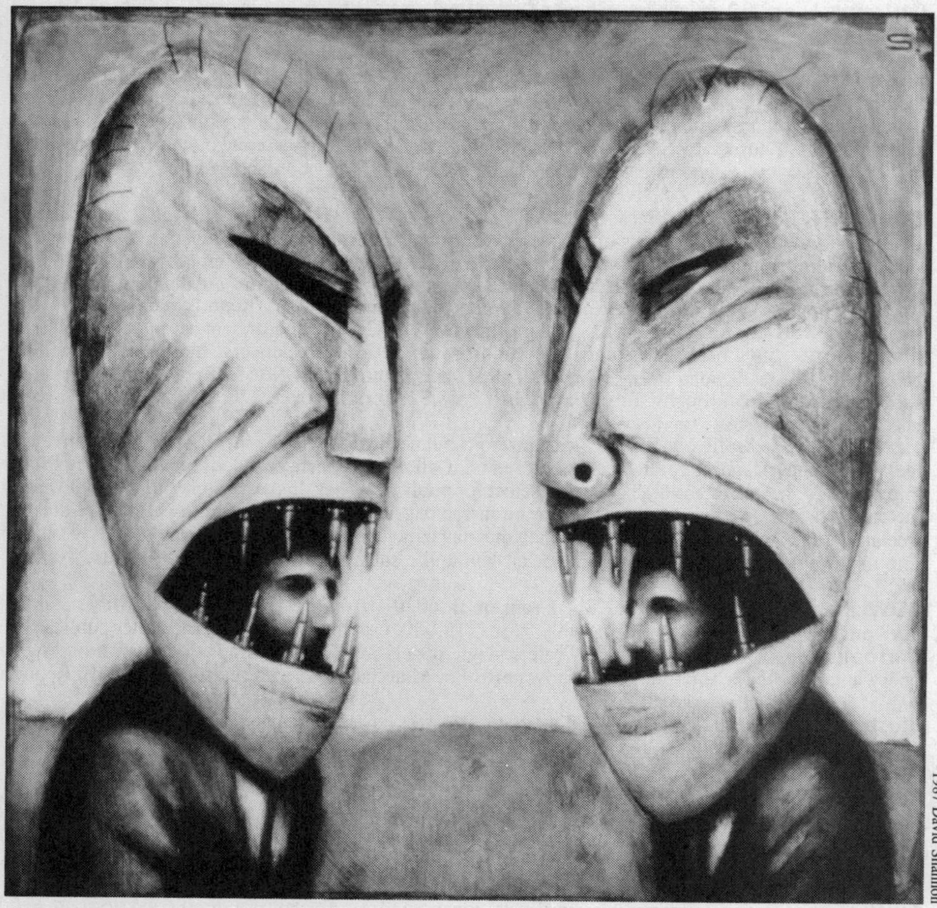

Art director Lisa Grayson of the Bulletin of Atomic Scientists *bought first rights to this piece by New York City illustrator David Shannon. The dramatic piece, rendered with acrylics, highlights an article on U.S.-Soviet relations and "each country's distorted perceptions of each other." Grayson contacted Shannon after seeing his work in other magazines. She gave him two weeks to complete sketches and the final piece. "I thought the manuscript reflected a lot of murky psychological undertones, and Shannon is a master of m.p.u.'s" Shannon now includes the piece in his portfolio.*

BRIGADE LEADER, Box 150, Wheaton IL 60189. (312)665-0630. For Christian laymen and adult male leaders of boys enrolled in the Brigade man-boy program. Circ. 12,000. Published 4 times/year. Original artwork returned after publication. Sample copy for $1.50 and large SASE; artist's guidelines for SASE.
Cartoons: Contact: Cartoon Editor. Uses 1 cartoon/issue, all from freelancers. Receives 3 submissions/week from freelancers. Interested in sports, nature and youth; single panel with gagline. "Keep it clean." SASE. Buys first rights only. Pays $20, b&w line drawings; on publication.
Illustrations: Art Director: Lawrence Libby. Uses 2 illustrations/issue. Prefers bold, clean line & wash. Prefers pen & ink, airbrush, charcoal/pencil and watercolor. Interested in man and boy subjects, sports, camping—out of doors, family. Works on assignment only. Samples returned by SASE. Reports back on future assignment possibilities. Provide resume and flyer to be kept on file for future assignments. Prefers to see portfolio and samples of style. Reports in 2 weeks. Pays $85-100, for inside use of b&w line drawings and washes; on publication.
Tips: Looks for "good crisp handling of black & white line work, clean washes and skill in drawing. Portfolios should have printed samples of work. We are moving toward desk-top publishing for some of our publications work. We like to see original concepts and well-executed drawings. We nee more work on sports of all kinds."

BUILDER/DEALER, (formerly Alternative Builder), 16 1st Ave., Corry PA 16407. Production Director: William Stright. Emphasizes log, dome, modular, timber, post and beam, component, precut and panelized construction and any other type of housing for kit package manufacturers and builder-dealers of these homes. Monthly. Circ. 28,500. original artwork returned after publication if requested. Sample copy and art guidelines for SASE.
Cartoons: Buys 1-2 cartoons/issue from freelancers. Considers anything pertaining to the industrialized housing industry or the problems faced by the men and women who are building or selling these homes. Prefers single panel with or without gagline; b&w line drawings or b&w washes. Send query letter with finished cartoons, slides and photographs to be kept on file. Material not filed is returned only if requested. Reports within 2 weeks. Buys all rights. Pays $15-25, b&w; on publication.
Illustrations: Buys 1-2 illustrations/issue. Send query letter with slides, photographs and illustrations. To show a portfolio, mail appropriate materials.
Tips: "We're sprucing up the appearance of our magazine and, as such, may be more receptive to freelancer's work.

BUILDER MAGAZINE, Suite 475, 655 15th St. NW, Washington DC 20005. (202)737-0717. Art Director: Karen Polard. Emphasizes the housing industry for the National Association of Home Builders members and subscriptions. Monthly. Circ. 185,000. Original artwork not returned after publication unless requested. Sample copy and art guidelines available.
Illustrations: Uses 4-7 illustrations/issue. Works on assignment only. Send query letter with samples to be kept on file. Prefers tear sheets, Photostats or photocopies as samples. Looks for "originality, a distinct style and creativity" when reviewing samples. Reports only if interested. Buys one-time rights. Call for appointment to show portfolio. Pays $75-150, b&w; payment negotiable for color, inside. Pays on acceptance.

BULLETIN OF THE ATOMIC SCIENTISTS, 6042 S. Kimbark, Chicago IL 60637. (312)702-2555. Art Director: Lisa Grayson. Emphasizes arms control; science and public affairs for audience of 40% scientists, 40% politicians and policy makers, and 20% interested, educated citizens. Monthly. Circ. 25,000. Original artwork returned after publication. Sample copy $2.50; free artist's guidelines for SASE. Finds artists through talent sourcebooks, references/word-of-mouth, portfolio reviews, samples received through the mail and artist representatives.
Cartoons: Buys about 5-10 cartoons/issue including humorous illustrations from freelancers. Considers arms control and international relations themes. "We are looking for new ideas. Please, no mushroom clouds or death's heads." Prefers single panel without gagline; b&w line drawings. Send finished cartoons. Cartoon portfolios are not reviewed. Material returned by SASE. Reports within 1 month. Buys first rights. Pays $25, b&w; on acceptance.
Illustrations: Buys 2-8 illustrations/issue from freelancers. Prefers serious conceptual b&w art with political or other throughtful editional themes; pen & ink, airbrush, charcoal/pencil, acrylics, oils, and collage. "Do not even consider sending work until you have viewed a few issues. The name of the magazine misleads artists who don't bother to check; they wind up wasting time and postage." Works on assignment only. Send query letter with brochure and tearsheets or Photostats to be kept on file, except for completely unsuitable work which is returned promptly by SASE. Artist may write or call for appointment to show portfolio but prefers mailed samples. Reports within 1 month. Buys first world-wide rights. Pays $300, b&w, cover; $100/¼ page, $150/½ page, $250/full page, b&w, inside; on acceptance.

Tips: "Don't show design, advertising, calligraphy samples—just editional illustration. It helps to show printed pieces within the published text so I can see how the artist interpreted the article. Also, don't bother with nude figure studies. Come on, look at the titles of the magazines you send to! A representative sampling of work is OK. Our needs are so specific that artists usually try too hard to match them-with little success."

BUSINESS & COMMERCIAL AVIATION, (Division of McGraw Hill), Hangar C-1, Westchester City Airport, White Plains NY 10604. Art Director: Mildred Stone. Technical publication for corporate pilots and owners of business aircraft. Monthly. Circ. 55,000.
Illustrations: Especially needs full-page spot art of a business-aviation nature. "We generally only use artists with a fairly realistic style. This is a serious business publication—graphically conservative. We have a monthly section for the commuter industry and another for the helicopter industry. These magazines will have a more consumer-magazine look and will feature more four-color illustration than we've used in the past. Need artists who can work on short deadline time." Query with samples. SASE. Reports in 4 weeks. Photocopies OK. Buys all rights, but may reassign rights to artist after publication. Negotiates payment. Pays on acceptance.
Tips: "Send or bring samples. I like to buy based more on style than whether an artist has done aircraft drawings before."

BUSINESS TODAY, Aaron Burr Hall, Princeton NJ 08540. (609)921-1111. Contact: Production Manager. For college undergraduates interested in business, politics and careers in those fields. Published 3 times/academic year. Circ. 205,000. Receives 10 cartoons and 2 illustrations/week from freelance artists. Especially needs illustrations and political cartoons. Query with samples to be kept on file; do not send originals, photocopies only. Will contact artists as needed. Previous work as magazine illustrator preferred. Reports in 2 months. Previously published, photocopied, and simultaneous submissions OK. Buys one-time, reprint or simultaneous rights. Pays on publication. Original artwork returned after publication. Sample copy $2.
Cartoons: Buys 4-5/issue on current events, education, environment, politics, business, college life and careers. "Keep the student readership in mind; *no typical scenes with executives and secretaries*."
Illustrations: Buys 4-5/issue on current events, education, environment, politics, college life and careers. Prefers pen & ink, watercolor, pastels, markers and mixed media. "We like the style of *The New Yorker* and op-ed cartoons in *The New York Times*." Prefers to have samples of style and topic areas covered. Provide business card and letter of inquiry to be kept on file for future assignments. Cover: Pays $50 minimum, color; $10-20, b&w. Inside: Pays $20 minimum, color; $10 minimum, b&w; on publication.
Tips: There is a trend toward "more quality, less quantity of artwork; we like to have artwork that says something. We need both concrete and abstract photos, as long as they are of quality and in sharp focus."

BUTTER FAT MAGAZINE, Box 9100, Vancouver B.C., V6B 4G4 Canada. (604)420-6611. Managing Editor: Carol A. Paulson. Editor: Grace Hahn. Emphasizes dairy farming, dairy product processing, marketing and distribution for dairy cooperative members and employees in British Columbia. Monthly. Circ. 3,500. Free sample copy and art guidelines. Finds most artists through references/word-of-mouth and portfolio reviews.
Cartoons: Uses 2 cartoons/issue; buys all from freelancers. Receives 10 submissions/week from freelancers. Interested in agriculture, dairy farming, farming families and Canadian marketing systems. No cartoons unrelated to farming, farm family life or critical of food prices. Prefers single panel b&w line drawings or washes with gagline. Send query letter with finished cartoons. Reports in 2 weeks. Negotiates rights purchased. Pays $10, b&w; on acceptance.
Illustrations: Uses 1 illustration/issue; buys mostly from freelancers. Prefers charcoal/pencil, watercolor, pastels, markers and mixed media. Interested in making assignments for specific issues—variable technical, food. Works on assignment only. Send brochure. Samples not kept on file are returned. Provide resume and samples to be kept on file for possible future assignments. Reports in 2 weeks. To show a portfolio, mail original/final art. Portfolio should include color work. Negotiates rights purchased. Pays $75-150 minimum for b&w inside; on acceptance.
Tips: "We prefer to meet artists as well as see their work. Target your samples to our need—dairying. Most assignments are short notice: 10-14 days." Prefers "gentle, nostalgic" style.

THE CALIFORNIA FIREMAN, Suite 1, 2701 K St., Sacramento CA 95816. (916)441-4153. Editor: Gary Giacomo. Fire service related magazine. "Our publication is geared towards our association's members. They are all firefighters from throughout California." Monthly. Circ. 30,000. Accepts previously published material. Original artwork sometimes returned after publication if requested. Sample copies available, for $1.50, editorial calendar for SASE.
Cartoons: Prefers fire service/safety related. Send query letter with samples of style. Samples are not

filed. Samples not filed are returned if requested. Reports back only if interested. Pays $5-10.
Illustrations: Prefers fire service/safety related. Prefers line drawings and graphic symbols. Send query letter. Samples not filed are returned only if requested. Reports back only if interested. Pays $10-20.
Tips: "Send clear, crisp samples; no dull photocopies."

CALIFORNIA GARDEN, San Diego Floral Association, Casa del Prado, Balboa Park, San Diego CA 92101-1619. (619)232-5762. Editor: Elizabeth B. Glover. Magazine emphasizing horticulture. Bimonthly. Circ. 3,000. Accepts previously published material. Original artwork returned after publication. Sample copy $1.
Illustrations: "Anything pertaining to horticulture." Send query letter with photographs or illustrations. Samples not filed are returned if requested. Reports back within 15 days. Pays in 3 contributor's copies.

CALLI'S TALES, Box 1224, Palmetto FL 34220. Editor: Annice E. Hunt. Magazine emphasizing wildlife and pets for animal lovers of all ages. Quarterly. Circ. 100#. Accepts previously published material. Sample copy $2. Art guidelines free for SASE with first-class postage.
Cartoons: Buys 1 cartoon/issue from freelancers. Prefers animals, wildlife and environment in good taste as themes. Prefers pen & ink. Prefers single panel with gagline; b&w line drawings. Send query letter with samples of style and finished cartoons to be kept on file. Samples not filed are returned by SASE. Reports back within 8 weeks. Buys one-time rights. Payment is one free copy of issue.
Illustrations: Buys 5-6 illustrations/issue from freelancers. Prefers wildlife, pets and nature scenes as themes. Send query letter with resume and tear sheets. Samples not filed are returned by SASE. Reports within 8 weeks. Payment is one free copy of issue.

CAMPUS LIFE, 465 Gundersen Dr., Carol Stream IL 60188. Art Director: Jeff Carnehl. For high school and college students. "Though our readership is largely Christian, *Campus Life* reflects the interests of all kids—music, activities, photography and sports." Monthly. Circ. 175,000. Original artwork returned after publication. "No phone calls, please. Show us what you can do."
Cartoons: Uses 3-5 single-panel cartoons/issue plus cartoon features (assigned). Receives 5 submissions/week from freelancers. Buys 50/year on high school and college education, environment, family life, humor through youth, and politics; apply to 13-23 age groups; prefers single panel, both horizontal and vertical format. Prefers to receive finished cartoons. Reports in 4 weeks. Pays $50 minimum, b&w; on acceptance.
Illustrations: Uses 2 illustrations/issue; buys all from freelancers. Receives 5 submissions/week from freelancers. Styles vary from "literal traditional to very conceptual." Prefers pen & ink and watercolor. Works on assignment only. "Show us what you can do, send photocopies, transparencies or tearsheets. Samples returned by SASE." Reporting time varies; is at least 6 weeks. Buys first North American serial rights; also considers second rights. Pays $250-400, color; $50, b&w; on acceptance.
Tips: "I do like to see a variety in styles, but I don't want to see work that 'says' grade school or 1965."

CANADIAN FICTION MAGAZINE, Box 946, Station F, Toronto, Ontario M4Y 2N9 Canada. Editor: Geoffrey Hancock. Anthology devoted exclusively to contemporary Canadian fiction. Quarterly. Canadian artists or residents only. Sample copy $5.50.
Illustrations: Uses 16 pages of art/issue; also cover art. SAE (nonresidents include IRC). Reports in 4-6 weeks. Pays $10/page; $25, cover. Uses b&w line drawings, photographs.
Tips: "Portraits of contemporary Canadian writers in all genres are valuable for archival purposes."

***CANADIAN RESEARCH**, 777 Bay St., Toronto, Ontario M5W 1A7 Canada. (416)596-5728. Managing Editor: Tom Gale. Emphasizes research science. Monthly. Circ. 15,000. Original artwork is returned to the artist after publication. Sample copies available.
Cartoons: Buys 2 cartoons/issue from freelancers. Prefers double panel with gagline. Send query letter with roughs. Samples are not filed and not returned. Reports back only if interested. Pays $90, b&w; $150, color.
Illustrations: Buys 2 illustrations/issue from freelancers. Works on assignment only. Send query letter with brochure showing art style or photocopies. Samples are not filed, and returned only if requested. Reports back only if interested. Call or write to schedule an appointment to show a portfolio. Buys first rights. Pays $500, color, cover; $200, color inside; on acceptance.
Tips: "Examine sample issue first."

CAR CRAFT, Petersen Publishing Co., 8490 Sunset Blvd., Los Angeles CA 90069. (213)657-5100. Editor-in-Chief: Cameron Benty. Managing Editor: Anne Lubow. Art Director: Todd Westover. "We feature articles on automotive modifications and drag racing. Monthly. Circ. 425,000. Original artwork not returned unless prior arrangement is made. Free sample copy and artist's guidelines.

"Continuous work" is the result of cartoonist/illustrator Kevin Pope's "column" in* Campus Life. *The Bloomington, Indiana artist found the magazine listed in the* Artist's Market *and then mailed photocopies and tear sheets. Art director Jeff Carnehl liked his sense of humor so much that he created a special feature for him called "Pope-pourri." Pope was paid $75 for one-time rights to the pen-and-ink cartoons. Pope is still a regular contributor as an editorial artist. "Kevin's work borders on the bizarre and seems to fit with styles teens are bombarded with in music videos and other markets."

Illustrations: Uses 1 or more illustrations/issue; buys 1/issue from freelancers. Interested in "automotive editorial illustration and design with a more illustrative and less technical look." Works on assignment only. Query with business card, brochure, flyer and tear sheet to be kept on file for future assignments. SASE. Reports in 2 weeks. Pays for design and illustration by the project, $100-1,000. Buys all rights on a work-for-hire basis.

CAROLINA QUARTERLY, Greenlaw Hall 066A, University of North Carolina, Chapel Hill NC 27514. Editor: Allison Bulsterbaum. Magazine emphasizing literature for libraries and readers all over the U.S. who are interested in contemporary poetry and fiction. Publishes 3 issues/year. Circ. 1,000. Returns original artwork after publication. Sample copy $5 (includes postage and handling). Art guidelines free for SASE with first-class postage.
Illustrations: Buys up to 5/issue. Prefers small b&w sketches. Send query letter with samples. Prefers photographs as samples. Reports within 2 months. Buys first rights. Pays $10, b&w, covers; and $5, b&w inside; on publication.

CARTOONS, 8490 Sunset Blvd., Los Angeles CA 90069. Contact: Dennis Ellefson. For young males who like cars and bikes.
Cartoons: Buys 150 pages of cartoon stories and 60 single panel cartoons annually. Should be well-drawn, identifiable, detailed cars. Prefers to see roughs. SASE. Reports in 2-4 weeks. Pays $100 minimum/page; $25/single panel; $25, spot drawings.
Tips: "Check out the automotive scene in *Hot Rod* and *Car Craft* magazines. And then look at *Cartoons*."

CAT FANCY, Fancy Publications Inc., Box 6050, Mission Viejo CA 92690. (714)855-8822. Editor: Linda W. Lewis. For cat owners, breeders and fanciers. Readers are men and women of all ages interested in all phases of cat ownership. Monthly. Circ. 200,000. Simultaneous submissions and previously published work OK. Sample copy $3; free artist's guidelines.
Cartoons: Buys 12/year; single, double and multi panel with gagline. "Central character should be a cat." Send query letter with Photostats or photocopies as samples. SASE. Reports in 6 weeks. Pays $20-50, b&w line drawings; on publication. Buys first rights.
Illustrations: Uses 2-5 b&w spot illustrations per issue. Prefers to work with local artists. Pays $20 for spots. Article illustrations assigned. Pays $50-100 for b&w illustrations.
Tips: "We need good cartoons."

CATHOLIC FORESTER, 425 W. Shuman Blvd., Naperville IL 60566. (312)983-4920. Editor: Barbara Cunningham. Magazine. "We are a fraternal insurance company but use general interest art and photos. Audience is middle-class, many small town as well as big city readers, patriotic, somewhat conservative. We are distributed nationally." Bimonthly. Circ. 150,000. Accepts previously published material. Original artwork returned after publication if requested. Sample copy for SASE with 73¢ postage.
Cartoons: Considers "anything *funny* but it must be clean." Prefers single panel with gagline; b&w line drawings. Send query letter with roughs. Material returned by SASE if requested. Reports within 3 months; "we try to do it sooner." Buys one-time rights or reprint rights. Pays $25, b&w; on acceptance.
Illustrations: Prefers watercolor, pen & ink, aribrush, oils and pastels. Send query letter with Photostats, tear sheets, photocopies, slides, photographs, etc. to be kept on file. Samples not filed are returned by SASE. Reports within 3 months. Write for appointment to show portfolio. Buys one-time rights or reprint rights. Payment depends on work and negotiation with artist. "We have large and small needs, so it's impossible to say." Pays on acceptance.

CATHOLIC SINGLES MAGAZINE, Box 1920, Evanston IL 60204. (312)731-8769. Founder: Fred C. Wilson. Magazine for single, widowed, separated and divorced Catholic persons. Circ. 10,000. Accepts previously published material. Original artwork returned after publication by SASE. Sample copy $3. Art guidelines free for SASE with first-class postage.
Cartoons: Buys variable amount of cartoons/issue from freelancers. Prefers anything that deals with being single (no porn) as themes. Uses all media. Send query letter with finished cartoons to be kept on file. Write or call to schedule an appointment to show a portfolio. Material not filed returned by SASE only if requested. Reports only if interested. Buys one-time rights. Pays on publication.
Illustrations: Works on assignment only. Prefers anything dealing with singledom as themes. Send query letter with samples. Samples not filed returned by SASE. Reports only if interested. To show a portfolio, mail original/final art. Buys one-time rights. Pays $25, b&w cover; $10, b&w inside; on publication.
Tips: "We would like to go four-color. We review everything but smut! Show a representation sampling of your work."

CATS MAGAZINE, Box 37, Port Orange FL 32029. Editor: Linda J. Walton. Emphasizes household pet cats and show cats. Monthly. Circ. 138,000. Returns original artwork after publication on request. Sample copy and art guidelines for SASE.
Cartoons: Buys 1-2 cartoons/issue from freelancers. Considers line work suitable for b&w publication with or without gaglines. Send finished cartoons to be kept on file. Material not filed is returned by SASE. Does not report back. Buys first rights. Payment varies; made on publication.
Illustrations: Buys 3-5 illustrations/issue from freelancers. Prefers pen & ink and charcoal/pencil. Prefers cats or cat-oriented themes. Send samples; copies are not returned, originals are returned by SASE. Does not report back. Buys first rights. Payment varies; made on publication.
Tips: "I do not want to see photocopies of art with a note that I can request originals if I want."

THE CATTLEMAN, 1301 W. Seventh St., Fort Worth TX 76102. (817)332-7155. For Southwestern cattle producers and cattlemen. Monthly. Circ. 19,169. Sample copy $2.
Cartoons: Contact Carolyn Brimer. Uses 3 cartoons/issue. Receives 10 submissions/week from freelancers. Interested in beef cattle raising and the Old West. Prefers single panel with gagline. Prefers to see finished cartoons. SASE. Reports in 1 month. Buys first North American serial rights. Pays $10 minimum, b&w line drawings; on acceptance.
Illustrations: Contact Lionel Chambers, editor. Buys limited number of illustrations. Interested in beef cattle, raising cattle and horses, western art. Send query letter with resume and samples to be kept on file. Samples not kept on file are returned by SASE. Reports in 2 weeks. Buys first North American serial rights or buys all rights on a work-for-hire basis. Pays $100 minimum, color washes, cover. Pays $15-25, color washes and opaque watercolors; $15-20, b&w line drawings, washes and gray opaques, inside; on acceptance.

CAVALIER, Dugent Publishing Corp., 2355 Salzedo St., Coral Gables FL 33134. Contact: Nye Willden. "For young men and college students interested in good fiction, articles and sex." Monthly. Circ. 250,000. Sample copy $3; guidelines free. Receives 50-75 cartoons and 3-4 illustrations/week from freelance artists. Original work only; no simultaneous submissions.
Cartoons: Buys 5/issue on erotica; single panel with gagline. Send query letter with samples. SASE. Reports in 2 weeks. Buys first rights. Pays $50-100, b&w line drawings and washes; 30 days before publication.
Illustrations: Buys 3/issue on erotica and assigned themes, including some humorous and cartoon-style illustrations. Works on assignment only. Send query letter with samples. SASE. Reports in 2 weeks. Buys first rights. Pays $150 minimum, b&w line drawings and washes; $200/page, $300/spread, color washes and full-color work, inside; 30 days before publication.
Tips: "Send 35mm slide samples of your work that art director can *keep* in his file, or tear sheets of published work. We have to have samples to refer to when making assignments. Large portfolios are difficult to handle and return. Also send samples *related* to our publication, i.e., erotica or nude studies. We are an excellent market for unpublished but very talented artists and cartoonists. Many of the top people in both fields — Mort Drucker, Peter Max, Ed Arno, Sid Harris—started with us, and many of them still work for us. Study *our* magazine for samples of acceptable material. *Do not submit* original artwork for our evaluation; slides, photos or stats only."

CHAIN STORE AGE, 425 Park Ave., New York NY 10022. (212)371-9400. Emphasizes retail stores. Readers are buyers, retail executives, merchandise managers, vice presidents of hard lines and store personnel. Monthly. Circ. 30,000.
Cartoons: Occasional use of line art *by assignment only*. Send samples of style to art director. SASE. Keeps file on artists. Pays $50-125 on publication for b&w cartoons. Buys all rights on a work-for-hire-basis.
Illustrations: Uses 1-2 illustrations/issue, all from freelancers. We "keep samples on file; must be in NY area. Must see portfolio." Uses inside b&w line drawings and washes, four-color cover. Send roughs, tear sheets and samples of style, and/or arrange personal appointment to show portfolio to art director. SASE. Reports in 1 week. Pays $50-125 on publication for inside b&w, $300 maximum for color cover, $150-250 for inside color. Buys all rights.

***CHALLENGES**, Box 299, Carthage IL 62321-0299. (217)357-3981. Art Director: Tom Sjoerdsma. Magazine for gifted children. Published five times/year.
Illustrations: Works with 20 freelance artists/year. Prefers pen & ink. "I am open to cartoon and realistic treatment of kids and to typical storybook illustrations using children and animals." Send query letter with photocopies. Samples are filed. Reports back within 2 weeks only if interested. Buys all rights. Pays $5/hour.

***CHANNELS MAGAZINE**, Suite 812, 19 W. 44th St., New York NY 10036. (212)302-2680. Contact: Art Director. "Controlled circulation for the decisionmakers in the broadcasting business." Monthly. Circ. 32,000. Original artwork is returned to the artist after publication.
Illustrations: Send query letter with brochure showing art style or tear sheets. Samples are filed. Does not report back. Call to schedule an appointment to show portfolio. Negotiates rights purchased. Payment varies. Pays on acceptance.

CHARIOT, Ben Hur Life Association, Box 312, Crawfordsville IN 47933. Editor: Loren Harrington. Emphasizes fraternal activities and general interest for members of the Association, a fraternal life insurance benefit society. Quarterly. Circ. 10,000. Accepts previously published material. Original artwork returned after publication if requested. Sample copy for 9x12 SASE with 88¢ postage; art guidelines for #10 SASE with first-class postage.
Cartoons: Rarely buys cartoons from freelancers. Considers humor and some satire. Prefers single panel with gagline; b&w line drawings or washes. Send finished cartoons to be kept on file. Material not filed is returned by SASE. Reports within 1 month. Negotiates rights purchased. Pays $1-20; on acceptance.
Illustrations: Rarely buys illustrations from freelancers but may work on assignment basis. Prefers line and wash, b&w only. Send query letter with resume and samples to be kept on file. Write for appointment to show portfolio. Accepts any type of sample that portrays quality of work. Reports in 1 month. Negotiates rights purchased and payment. Pays by the project $5-200. Pays on acceptance, sometimes on publication.

***CHATTANOOGA LIFE & LEISURE**, 1085 Bailery Ave., Chattanooga TN 37404. (615)629-5375. Managing Editor: Ted Betts. Magazine. "We are a city magazine that serves the greater Chattanooga area. Our motto is entertaining, informative, and productive. Our readers are newcomers and natives

who have an interest in the region and want the inside story." Monthly. Accepts previously published material. Original artwork is returned to the artist after publication. Sample copies $2.50.
Cartoons: Buys some cartoons/year from freelancers. Prefers creative, colorful and detailed cartoons, although we use some b&w line drawings. Prefers b&w line drawings, b&w and color washes. Samples are not filed. Samples not filed are returned by SASE. Reports back within 3 months. Buys first rights or one-time rights. Pays $20 minimum, b&w; $20 minimum, color.
Illustrations: Buys 1-2 illustrations/issue from freelancers. Buys 12-24 illustrations/year from freelancers. Works on a ssignment only. Prefers architectural, creative, and thematic illustration plus portraits. Send query letter with brochure, resume and tear sheets. Samples are not filed. Samples not filed are returned by SASE. Reports back within 3 months. Call to schedule an appointment to show portfolio, or mail original/final art, tear sheets, final reproduction/product, color and b&w. Buys first rights and one-time rights. Negotiates rights purchased. Pays $20 minimum, b&w; $20, minimum, color, cover; $20, minimum, b&w; $20, minimum, color, inside; on publication.
Tips: "Have a decent portfolio. Be confident that you are able to meet the deadlines. Remember, we are a regional magazine that covers Chattanooga. I do not need sunsets over Miami. Be creative. Too many artists do landscapes that don't interest us."

CHESS LIFE, 186 Route 9W, New Windsor NY 12550. (914)562-8350. Art Director: Jami Anson. Official publication of the United States Chess Federation. Contains news of major chess events with special emphasis on American players, plus columns of instruction, general features, historical articles, personality profiles, cartoons, quizzes, humor and short stories. Monthly. Circ. 60,000. Accepts previously published material and simultaneous submissions. Sample copy for SASE with $1.07 postage; art guidelines for SASE with first-class postage.
Cartoons: Buys 1-2 cartoons/issue from freelancers. All cartoons must have a chess motif. Prefers single panel, with gagline; b&w line drawings. Send query letter with brochure showing art style. "We may keep a few cartoons on hand, but most are either bought or returned." Material not kept on file returned by SASE. Reports within 2-4 weeks. Negotiates rights purchased. Pays $10-25, b&w; on publication.
Illustrations: Buys 1-2 illustrations/issue from freelancers. All must have a chess motif; uses some humorous and occasionally cartoon-style illustrations. "We use mainly b&w." Works on assignment, but will also consider unsolicited work. Send query letter with Photostats or original work for b&w; slides for color, or tear sheets to be kept on file. Reports within 4 weeks. Call to schedule an appointment to show a portfolio, which should include roughs, original/final art, final reproduction/product and tear sheets. Negotiates rights purchased. Pays by the project, $25-150. Pays on publication.

***CHIC**, Larry Flynt Publications, Suite 300, 9171 Wilshire Blvd., Beverly Hills CA 90210. (213)858-7100. Cartoon/Humor Editor: Dwaine and Susan Tinsley. For affluent men, 25-30 years of age, college-educated and interested in current affairs, luxuries, investigative reporting, entertainment, sports, sex and fashion. Monthly. Returns original art.
Cartoons: Publishes 20/month; 10 full-page color, 4 color spots and 6 b&w spots. Receives 300-500 cartoons from freelancers. Especially needs "outrageous material. Mainly sexual, but politics, sports OK. Topical humor and seasonal/holiday cartoons good." Mail samples. Prefers 8½x11" size; avoid crayons, chalks or fluorescent colors. Also avoid, if possible, large, heavy illustration board. Samples returned by SASE only. Place name, address and phone number on back of each cartoon. Reports in 3 weeks. Buys first rights with first right to reprint. Pays $150, full page color; $75 spot color; $50 spot b&w. Pays on acceptance.
Tips: Especially needs more cartoons, cartoon breakaways or one-subject series. "Send outrageous humor—work that other magazines would shy away from. Pertinent, political, sexual, whatever. We are constantly looking for new artists to complement our regular contributors and contract artists. An artist's best efforts stand the best chance for acceptance!"

CHICAGO, 414 N. Orleans, Chicago IL 60610. (312)222-8999. Editor: Hillel Levin. Art Director: Kathy Kelley. For active, well-educated, high-income residents of Chicago's metropolitan area concerned with quality of life and seeking insight or guidance into diverse aspects of urban/suburban life. Monthly. Circ. 204,000. Original artwork returned after publication.
Illustrations: Uses 7-8 illustrations/issue, all from freelancers. Interested in "subjective approach often, but depends on subject matter." Works on assignment only. Query with brochure, flyer and tear sheets, Photostats, photocopies, slides and photographs to be kept on file. Accepts finished art, transparencies or tear sheets as samples. Samples not filed are returned by SASE. Reports in 4 weeks. Call to schedule an appointment to show a portfolio, which should include original/final art, tear sheets and Photostats. Buys first North American serial rights. Negotiates pay for covers, color-separated and reflective art. Inside: Pays $600, color; $400 minimum, b&w ($100-200 for spot illustrations); on publication.

CHIEF FIRE EXECUTIVE, 33 Irving Place, New York NY 10003. (212)475-5400. Managing Editor: A. Saly. Art Director: Michael B. Delia. Estab. 1986. Magazine emphasizing management issues relative to community fire protection for fire chiefs, corporate safety officers, fire marshals, architects and engineers. Bimonthly. Circ. 42,000. Accepts previously published material. Sample copy and art guidelines for SASE.
Cartoons: Uses various cartoons/issue. Send query letter with finished cartoons. Call to schedule an appointment to show a portfolio. Material not filed is returned by SASE. Reports only if interested. Buys one-time rights.
Illustrations: Buys various illustrations/issue from freelancers. Works on assignment only. Send query letter with resume and tear sheets. Samples not filed are not returned. Reports only if interested. Call to schedule an appointment to show a portfolio, which should include tear sheets. Buys one-time rights. Pays $100-800; on publication.
Tips: "I prefer realistic over a cartoon or looser style. I like very tight drawings."

CHILD LIFE, 1100 Waterway Blvd., Box 567, Indianapolis IN 46206. (317)636-8881. Art Director: Janet K. Moir. For children 7-9. Monthly except bimonthly February/March, April/May, June/July and August/September. Receives 3-4 submissions/week from freelance artists. Sample copy 75¢.
Illustrations: Buys 30 (average)/year on assigned themes. Especially needs health-related (exercise, safety, nutrition, etc.) themes, and stylized and realistic styles of children 7-9 years old. Send query letter with brochure showing art style or resume and tear sheets, Photostats, photocopies, slides, photographs and SASE. Especially looks for an artist's ability to draw well consistently. SASE. Reports in 4 weeks. To show a portfolio, mail appropriate materials or call or write to schedule an appointment; portfolio should include original/final art, b&w and 2-color and/or 4-color pre-separated art. Buys all rights. Pays $225/illustration, color, cover. Pays for illustrations inside by the job, $60-125 (4-color), $50-100 (2-color), $25-65 1 page (b&w); thirty days after completion of work. "All work is considered work for hire."
Tips: "Children's magazines are using a lot more photography. They are willing to experiment with new styles in illustration to keep up with changing culture. Our biggest competition is TV-kids want to see brighter colors, strange shapes. They spend less time reading so what they do read needs to be very accessible visually. We are starting to use more art in proportion to copy. I need to see how an illustrator handles a strory, i.e. a series of illustrations rather than a single illustration. Many of my stories involve group situations so I like to see children interacting with each other, with adults and with animals. I don't want to see fine art, ie. drawings, paintings, prints. Artists can rarely transfer their talents to a more commerical field like editorial illustration. Most of the work should be targeted to my needs, but I like to see other styles. How a piece is designed tells me a lot about the artist even though I just buy illustration. A good design sense is important."

CHILDREN'S DIGEST, Box 567, Indianapolis IN 46206. (317)636-8881. Art Director: Lisa A. Nelson. Special emphasis on health, nutrition, safety and exercise for boys and girls 8-10 years of age. Monthly except bimonthly February/March, April/May, June/July and August/September. Accepts previously published material and simultaneous submissions. Sample copy 75¢; art guidelines free for SASE.
Illustrations: Uses 25-35 illustrations/issue. Works on assignment only. Send query letter with brochure, resume, samples and tear sheets to be kept on file. Write for appointment to show portfolio. Prefers Photostats, slides and good photocopies as samples. Samples returned by SASE if not kept on file. Reports within 4 weeks. Buys all rights. Pays $225, color, cover; $25-65, b&w; $50-100, 2-color; $60-125, 4-color, inside. Pays on acceptance. "All artwork is considered work for hire."
Tips: Likes to see situation and story-telling illustrations with more than 1 figure. When reviewing samples, especially looks for artists' ability to bring a story to life with their illustrations. "Contemporary artists, by and large, are more experimental in the use of their mediums, and are achieving a greater range of creativity. We are aware of this and welcome the artist who can illustrate a story that will motivate a casual viewer to read."

CHILDREN'S PLAYMATE, Box 567, Indianapolis IN 46206. (317)636-8881. Art Director: Steve Miller. For ages 5-7; special emphasis on health, nutrition, exercise and safety. Published 8 times/year. Sample copy sent if artist's work might be used.
Illustrations: Uses 25-35 illustrations/issue; buys 10-20 from freelancers. Interested in "stylized, humorous or realistic themes; also nature and health." Prefers pen & ink, airbrush, charcoal/pencil, colored pencil, watercolor, acrylics, oils, pastels, collage and computer illustration. Especially needs b&w and 2-color artwork for line or halftone reproduction; text and full-color cover art. Works on assignment only. Prefers to see portfolio and samples of style; include illustrations of children, families, animals—targeted to children. SASE. Provide brochure or flyer, tear sheet, stats or good photocopies of sample art to be kept on file. Buys all rights on a work-for-hire basis. Pays $225, 4-color, cover; $25-65, b&w; $50-100, 2-color; $60-125, full-color inside. Will also consider b&w art, camera-ready for puzzles, such as

dot-to-dot, hidden pictures, crosswords, etc. Payment will vary. "All artwork is considered work for hire."
Tips: "Look at our publication prior to coming in; it is for *children*. Also, gain some experience in preparation of two-color and four-color overlay separations."

CHINA PAINTER, 2641 N.W. 10th St., Oklahoma City OK 73107. (405)521-1234 or (405)943-3841. Founder/Trustee: Pauline Salyer. Emphasizes porcelain china painting for those interested in the fine art. Bimonthly. Circ. 9,000. Original artwork returned after publication. Sample copy $2.75 plus 95¢ postage.
Illustrations: Send query letter. Prefers art designs in color or photographs of hand-painted porcelain china art as samples. Prefers pen & ink. Samples returned by SASE only if requested.

THE CHRISTIAN CENTURY, 407 S. Dearborn St., Chicago IL 60605. (312)427-5380. Production Coordinator:Matthew Giunti. Emphasizes religion and comments on social, political and religious subjects; includes news of current religious scene, book reviews, humor. Weekly. Circ. 38,000. Original artwork not returned after publication. Sample copy free for SASE. Finds most artists through references/word-of-mouth.
Cartoons: Occasionally uses cartoons. Prefers social, political, religious (non-sexist) issues. Prefers single panel with gagline; b&w line drawings. Send query letter with finished cartoons to be kept on file unless "we can't possibly use them." Material not filed is returned only if requested. Reports only if interested. Buys one-time rights. Pays $20, b&w; on publication.
Illustrations: Uses 4 illustrations/issue; buys 1-2 from freelancers. Prefers pen & ink, charcoal/pencil, colored pencil and collage. Prefers religious and general scenes, people at various activities, books. Send query letter with resumes and photocopies to be kept on file. Samples not filed are returned by SASE. Reports only if interested. Buys one-time rights. Pays $50, cover and $20, inside b&w; on publication.
Tips: "Because of our newsprint, bold, uncluttered styles work the best. Too much detail gets lost. We need more inclusive illustrations—non-sexist." Target samples to magazine's specific needs.

CHRISTIAN HERALD, 40 Overlook Dr., Chappaqua NY 10514. (914)769-9000. Editor: Dean Merrill. Grassroots magazine for Christian adults (30 and up); specializes in people stories, real-life examples. Monthly. Circ. 180,000. Original artwork returned after publication. Receives 3 illustrations/week from freelance artists. Sample copy $2.
Cartoons: Should have religious flavor.
Illustrations: Uses 2-3 illustrations/issue; buys all from freelancers. Prefers "more realistic and figurative styles due to the 'real people in action' format of our publication." Prefers colored pencil, then collage, mixed media, calligraphy, pen & ink, airbrush, washes, oils, acrylics. Works on assignment only. Send query letter with resume and tear sheets, Photostats and slides. Samples not kept on file are returned by SASE. Reports in 4 weeks or less. Negotiates rights purchased. Pays $75-200 inside, b&w line drawings or b&w washes; $100-350 inside, color washes; upon publication.
Tips: "I want to see work that shows the artist's ability to interpret. Show a variety of work, but include a couple of pieces geared especially to our needs."

CHRISTIAN HOME & SCHOOL, 3350 E. Paris Ave. SE, Grand Rapids MI 49508. (616)957-1070. Associate Editor: Judy Zylstra. Emhasizes current, crucial issues affecting the Christian home for parents who support Christian education. Published 8 times/year. Circ. 10,000. Original artwork returned after publication. Sample copy for SASE with 75¢ postage; art guidelines for SASE with first-class postage. Finds most artists through references/word-of-mouth, portfolio reviews, samples received through the mail and artist representative.
Illustrations: Buys approximately 2 illustrations/issue from freelancers. Prefers pen & ink, charcoal/pencil, colored pencil, watercolor, collage, markers, mixed media and calligraphy. Prefers family or school life themes. Works on assignment only. Send query letter with resume, tear sheets, photocopies or photographs. Show a representative sampling of work. Samples returned by SASE. Reports only if interested. Buys first rights. Pays on publication.

THE CHRISTIAN MINISTRY, 407 S. Dearborn St., Chicago IL 60605. (312)427-5380. For the professional clergy (primarily liberal Protestant). Bimonthly. Circ. 12,000.
Cartoons: Buys 3 cartoons/issue on local church subjects. Send query letter with brochure showing art style or resume, tear sheets, Photostats, photocopies and photographs. SASE. Reports in 2 weeks. Pays $20 minimum, b&w; on publication.
Illustrations: Uses 4 spot drawings/issue on local church issues; preaching, counseling, teaching, etc. Illustrations and cartoons should reflect the diversity of professional clergy—male, female, black, white, young, old, etc. To show a portfolio, mail thumbnails, original/final art, final reproduction/prod-

uct, Photostats, photographs and b&w. Pays $50, b&w, cover; $20, b&w, inside; on publication.
Tips: "We tend to use more abstract than concrete artwork. We insist on a balance between portrayals of male and female clergy."

THE CHRONICLE OF THE HORSE, Box 46, Middleburg VA 22117. Editor: John Strassburger. Emphasizes horses and English horse sports for dedicated competitors who ride, show and enjoy horses. Weekly. Circ. 22,000. Occasionally accepts previously published material. Sample copy available.
Cartoons: Buys 1-2 cartoons/issue from freelancers. Considers anything about English riding and horses. Prefers single panel with or without gagline; b&w line drawings or b&w washes. Send query letter with finished cartoons to be kept on file if accepted for publication. Material not filed is returned. Reports within 2 weeks. Buys first rights. Pays $20, b&w; on publication.
Illustrations: "We use a work of art on our cover every week. The work must feature horses, but the medium is unimportant. We do not pay for this art, but we always publish a short blurb on the artist and his or her equestrian involvement, if any." Send query letter with samples to be kept on file until published. If accepted, insists on high-quality, b&w 8x10 photographs of the original artwork. Samples are returned. Reports within 2 weeks.

***CHRONICLES, A MAGAZINE OF AMERICAN CULTURE**, 934 N. Main St., Rockford IL 61103. (815)964-5813. Art Director: Anna Mycek-Wodecki. Literary magazine. Monthly. Original artwork is returned to the artist after publication. Sample copies available.
Illustrations: Buys 6-7 illustrations/issue from freelancers. Prefers fine art drawings. "No commercial drawings." Prefers pen & ink, airbrush, colored pencil, watercolor, acrylics, oils and pastels. Send query letter with portfolio. Samples are filed. Samples not filed are returned. Reports back only if interested. Write to schedule an appointment to show a portfolio, or mail original/final art, slide, color and b&w. Buys first rights. Pays $250 for 7-9 b&w drawings; $400, color cover; on publication.
Tips: "I do not want to see any 'commercial' drawings."

***CHURCH MANAGEMENT—THE CLERGY JOURNAL**, Box 162527, Austin TX 78716. (512)327-8501. Editor: Manfred Holck Jr. For professional clergy and church business administrators. Circ. 30,000. Original artwork returned after publication if requested. Monthly (except June and December).
Cartoons: Uses 4 single panel cartoons/issue on religious themes. SASE. Reports in 2 months. Pays $10, b&w; on publication.

THE CHURCHMAN, 1074 23rd Ave. N., St. Petersburg FL 33704. (813)894-0097. Editor: Edna Ruth Johnson. Published 9 times/year. Circ. 10,000. Original artwork returned after publication. Sample copy available.
Cartoons: Uses 2-3 cartoons/issue. Interested in religious, political and social themes. Prefers to see finished cartoons. SASE. Reports in 1 week. Pays on acceptance.
Illustrations: Uses 2-3 illustrations/issue. Interested in themes with "social implications." Prefers to see finished art. Provide tear sheet to be kept on file for future assignments. SASE. Reports in 1 week. Pays $5, b&w spot drawings; on acceptance.
Tips: "Read current events news so you can apply it humorously."

CINCINNATI MAGAZINE, Suite 300, 35 E. 7th St., Cincinnati OH 45202. (513)421-4300. Editor: Laura Pulfer. Art Director: Thomas Hawley. Emphasizes Cincinnati living. For college-educated, ages 25+ with an excess of $35,000 incomes. Monthly. Circ. 30,000. Previously published and simultaneous submissions OK. Original artwork returned after publication. Buys all rights. Pays on acceptance.
Cartoons: Uses 2 cartoons/issue, all from freelancers. Receives 3 submissions/week from freelancers. Interested in current events, education and politics; single panel. Send finished cartoons. SASE. Reports in 3 weeks. Buys all rights on a work-for-hire basis. Pays $15-25, b&w washes; on acceptance.
Illustrations: Uses 3 illustrations/issue, all from freelancers. Receives 3 illustrations/week from freelance artists. Buys cover art and article illustrations on assigned themes. Works on assignment only. Prefers to see portfolio or samples of style. Samples returned by SASE. Reports in 3 weeks. Buys all rights on a work-for-hire basis.

CINEFANTASTIQUE, Box 270, Oak Park IL 60303. Editor-in-Chief: Frederick S. Clarke. Emphasizes science fiction, horror and fantasy films for "devotees of 'films of the imagination.'" Bimonthly. Circ. 20,000. Original artwork not returned after publication. Sample copy $6.
Cartoons: Buys 0-1 cartoon/issue; buys all from freelancers. Interested in a variety of themes suited to magazine's subject matter; formats vary. Send query letter with resume and samples of style. Samples not returned. Reports in 3-4 weeks. Buys all rights. Pays $75/page or proportionally for fraction thereof; b&w; on publication.
Illustrations: Uses 1-2 illustrations/issue; buys all from freelancers. Interested in "dynamic, powerful

styles, though not limited to a particular look." Works on assignment only. Send query letter with resume, brochure and samples of style to be kept on file. Samples not returned. Reports in 3-4 weeks. Buys all rights. Pays $75 maximum, inside b&w line drawings; $75 maximum, inside b&w washes; $150 maximum, cover color washes; $75 maximum, inside color washes; on publication.

CIRCLE TRACK MAGAZINE, 8490 Sunset Blvd., Los Angeles CA 90069. (213)854-2350. Art Director: Mike Austin. Magazine emphasizing oval-track racing for enthusiasts, ages 18-40. Monthly. Circ. 110,000. Original artwork returned after publication. Sample copy and art guidelines available.
Cartoons: Buys 1-2 cartoons/issue from freelancers. Prefers technical, automotive themes. Prefers single panel, b&w line drawings. Send samples of style to be kept on file. Call for appointment to show portfolio. Material not filed is returned. Reports only if interested. Negotiates rights purchased. Pays $75, b&w; $150, color.
Illustrations: Buys 0-1 illustrations/issue from freelancers. Works on assignment only. Prefers automotive themes. Send resume. Samples not filed are returned. Reports only if interested. Call to schedule an appointment to show a portfolio, which should include original/final art. Negotiates rights purchased. Pays $200, b&w; $400, color, inside; on publication.

***CLASSIC TOY TRAINS**, 1027 N. Seventh St., Milwaukee WI 53233. Art Director: Lawrence Luser. Magazine emphasizing collectible toy trains. Quarterly. Circ. 73,000. Accepts previously published material. Original artwork is sometimes returned to the artist after publication. Sample copies and art guidelines available.
Illustrations: Buys various illustrations/issue from freelancers. Send query letter with brochure. Samples are filed. Samples not filed are returned only if requested. Reports back only if interested. Write to schedule an appointment to show a portfolio, or mail original/final art, final reproduction/product, photographs, color and b&w. Negotiates rights purchased.

CLAVIER, 200 Northfield Rd., Northfield IL 60093. Editor: Barbra Barlow Kreader. For teachers and students of keyboard instruments. Published 10 times/year. Buys all rights. Sample copy available with magazine-sized SASE.
Cartoons: Buys 10-20/year on music, mostly keyboard music. Receives 1 set of cartoons/week from freelance artists. Pays $15 on acceptance.

***CLEARWATER NAVIGATOR**, 112 Market St., Poughkeepsie NY 12603. (914)454-7673. Graphics Coordinator: Nora Porter. Emphasizes sailing and environmental matters for middle-upper income Easterners with a strong concern for environmental issues. Bimonthly. Circ. 8,000. Accepts previously published material. Original artwork returned after publication. Sample copy free with SASE.
Cartoons: Buys 1 cartoon/issue from freelancers. Prefers editorial lampooning—environmental themes. Prefers single panel with gaglines; b&w line drawings. Send query letter with samples of style to be kept on file. Material not filed is rturned only if requested. Reports within 1 month. Buys first rights. Pays negotiable rate, b&w; on publication.

CLEVELAND MAGAZINE, Suite 730, 1422 Euclid Ave., Cleveland OH 44115. (216)771-2833. City magazine emphasizing local news and information. Monthly. Circ. 50,000.
Illustrations: Buys 5-6 editorial illustrations/issue on assigned themes. Sometimes uses humorous illustrations. Send query letter with brochure showing art style or samples. Call or write to schedule an appointment to show a portfolio, which should include original/final art, final reproduction/product, color, tear sheets and photographs. Payment varies.
Tips: "Artists used on the basis of talent. We use many talented college graduates just starting out in the field. We do not publish gag cartoons but do print editorial illustrations with a humorous twist. Full page editorial illustrations usually deal with local politics, personalities and stages of general interest. Generally, we are seeing more intelligent solutions to illustration problems and better techniques."

***CLIFTON MAGAZINE**, 204 Tangeman University Center, University of Cincinnati, Cincinnati OH 45221. (513)556-6379. Editor-in-Chief: Lewis Wallace. General interest publication for the university community and neighborhood. Published 4 times/academic year. Circ. 10,000. Copy available for SASE.
Illustrations: Contact Art Director. Uses illustrations and photography for feature stories; art photos published. Reports in 6-8 weeks. Acquires first serial rights.

CLUBHOUSE, Box 15, Berrien Springs MI 49103. (616)471-9009. Editor: Elaine Meseraull. Art Director: Jim Bowser. Magazine emphasizing stories, puzzles and illustrations for children ages 9-15. Published 10 times/year. Circ. 17,000. Accepts previously published material. Returns original artwork after publication if requested. Sample copy for SASE with postage for 3 oz. Finds most artist through

The pen-and-ink work of Anni Matsick of State College, Pennsylvania, added a lighter touch to the serious story of a girl adjusting to the death of her brother published in* Clubhouse. *"The comic book outlines make it intriguing to the magazine's young readers without being 'down,' " says Matsick. Art director Jim Bowser says Matsick "has the ability to convey expression with tight, powerful strokes. She is easy to work with, complies with specific assignments, yet feels free to offer alternative suggestions." The magazine, which Matsick found in the* Artist's Market, *purchased first rights.

references/word-of-mouth and samples received through the mail.
Cartoons: Buys 2/issue. Prefers animals, kids and family situation themes; single panel with gagline, vertical format; b&w line drawings. Accepts previously published material. Pays $10-12 on acceptance.
Illustrations: Buys 19-20/issue on assignment only. Prefers pen & ink, charcoal/pencil and all b&w. Assignments made on basis of samples on file. Send query letter with resume and samples to be kept on file. Samples returned by SASE within 1 month. Portfolio should include final reproduction/product, tear sheets, Photostats and b&w. Usually buys one-time rights. Pays according to published size: $30 b&w, cover; $25 full page, $18 half page, $15 third page, $12 quarter page, b&w inside; on acceptance.
Tips: Prefers "natural, well-proportioned, convincing expressions for people, particularly kids. Children's magazines must capture the attention of the readers with fresh and innovative styles--interesting forms. Bright colors are also very important. I continually search for new talents to illustrate the magazine and try new methods of graphically presenting stories. Samples illustrating children and pets in natural situations are very helpful. Tearsheets are also helpful. I do not want to see sketchbook doodles, adult cartoons, or any artwork with an adult theme."

COAST & COUNTRY, (formerly Lynn, the North Shore Magazine), Sutie 43, 644 Humphrey St., Swampscott MA 01907. CEO: Paula R. Hastings. Magazine emphasizing the general consumer, some emphasis on local geographical area (North Shore of Boston) for upscale homeowners, age 30 and up. Bimonthly. Circ. 75,000. Accepts previously published material. Original artwork returned after publication if requested. Sample copy for SASE with $2.50 postage.
Cartoons: Prefers lifestyle themes, human issues, sports or the ocean and wildlife. Prefers single panel with gagline; b&w line drawings and b&w washes. Send query letter with samples of style and finished cartoons. Samples not filed are returned by SASE. Reports only if interested. Buys one-time rights. Pays $50, b&w.

COBBLESTONE MAGAZINE, 20 Grove St., Peterborough NH 03458. (603)924-7209. Editor: Carolyn Yoder. Emphasizes American history; features stories, supplemental nonfiction, fiction, biographies, plays, activities, poetry for children between 8 and 14. Monthly. Circ. 45,000. Accepts previously published material and simultaneous submissions. Sample copy $3.95. Material must relate to theme of issue; subjects/topics published in guidelines which are available for SASE.
Illustrations: Uses variable number of illustrations/issue; buys 1-2/issue from freelancers. Prefers historical theme as it pertains to a specific feature. Works on assignment only. Send query letter with bro-

chure, resume, business card, photocopies or tear sheets to be kept on file. Samples not kept on file are returned by SASE. Write for appointment to show portfolio. Buys all rights. Payment varies. Artists should request illustration guidelines. Pays on publication.
Tips: "Study issues of the magazine for style used. Send samples and update samples once or twice a year to help keep your name and work fresh in our minds."

***COLLECTIBLE AUTOMOBILE MAGAZINE**, 7373 N. Cicero Ave., Lincolnwood IL 60646. (312)676-3470. Publisher: Frank E. Peiler. Estab. 1984. Emphasizes collectible cars, 1930-present. Bimonthly. Circ. 100,000. Sometimes returns original artwork after publication. Sample copy $2.10; art guidelines available.
Cartoons: Prefers single panel with or without gagline; color washes. Send samples of styles or roughs to be kept on file. Material not filed is returned only if requested. Reports back only if interested. Buys all rights. Payment varies; pays on acceptance.
Illustrations: Works on assignment only. Send query letter and samples to be kept on file. Write or call for appointment to show portfolio. Prefers slides or photographs as samples. Samples not filed are returned only if requested. Reports back only if interested. Buys all rights. Payment varies; pays on acceptance.

COLLEGIATE MICROCOMPUTER, Rose-Hulman Institute of Technology, Terre Haute IN 47803. (812)877-1511. Managing Editor: Brian J. Winkel. Emphasizes uses of microcomputers in *all* areas of college life, teaching, administration, residence, recreation, etc. for college libraries, college faculty and college students. Quarterly. Circ. 5,000. Original artwork returned after publication. Accepts previously published material and simultaneous submissions.
Cartoons: Plans to use 8-10 cartoons/issue. Prefers activities surrounding microcomputers and the educational environment—spoofs of uses—as themes. Prefers single, double, or multi panel, with or without gagline; b&w line drawings or b&w washes. Query with samples of style, roughs or finished cartoons to be kept on file. Material not kept on file is returned by SASE. Reports within 2 weeks. Negotiates rights purchased and payment. Pays on acceptance.

COLLISION MAGAZINE, Box M, Franklin MA 02038. (617)528-6211. Editor: Jay Kruza. Has an audience of new car dealers, auto body repair shops, and towing companies. Articles are directed at the managers of these small businesses. Monthly. Circ. 24,000. Prefers original material but may accept previously published material. Sample copy $4. Art guidelines free for SASE with first-class postage.
Cartoons: Cartoon Editor: Brian Sawyer. Buys 3 cartoons/issue. Prefers themes that are positive or corrective in attitude. Prefers single panel with gagline; b&w line drawings. Send rough versions or finished cartoons. Reports back in 2 weeks or samples returned by SASE. Buys all rights and reprint rights. Pays $15/single panel b&w line cartoon.
Illustrations: Buys about 2 illustrations/issue from freelancers based upon a 2-year advance editorial schedule. Send query letter with brochure, tear sheets, Photostats, photocopies, slides and photographs. Samples are returned by SASE. Reports back within 15-30 days. "Payment is for assigned artwork ranging form $25 for spot illustrations up to $200 for full page material" on acceptance.
Tips: "Show us your style and technique on a photocopy. Include phone number and time to call. We'll suggest material we need illustrated if your work seems appropriate. We prefer clean pen and ink work but will use color."

THE COLORADO ALUMNUS, Koenig Alumni Center, University of Colorado, Boulder CO 80309. (303)492-8484. Editor: Ronald A. James. For university administrators, alumni, librarians and legislators. Published 6 times/year. Circ. 100,000. Previously published work and simultaneous submissions OK. Original artwork not returned after publication. Free sample copy.
Cartoons: Uses 1 cartoon/issue from freelancers. Receives 2-3 submissions/month from freelancers. Interested in sports, humor through youth, environment, campus and problems in higher education. Prefers to see finished cartoons. SASE. Reports in 2 weeks. "Work becomes the property of the University of Colorado." Pays $25 minimum, line drawings and halftones; on acceptance.
Illustrations: Uses 2-3 illustrations/issue from freelancers. Receives 1-2 submissions/week from freelancers. Interested in sports, campus and higher education. Send query letter with samples, SASE. Reports in 2 weeks. "Work becomes the property of the University of Colorado." Call or write to schedule an appointment to show a portfolio, which should include roughs, original/final art and final reproduction/product. Pays $25 minimum, b&w line drawings cover and inside; on acceptance.

***COLORADO HOMES & LIFESTYLES MAGAZINE**, Suite 154, 2550 31st St., Denver CO 80216. (303)455-1944. Art Director: Karen Polaski. Magazine emphasizing homes and people of Colorado. "It attempts to showcase model homes and unique designs, profile interesting people in their home or engaged in their favorite activity, and capture the natural beauty of Colorado." Bimonthly. Circ. 20,000. Sample copies available.

Illustrations: Buys 4-6 illustrations/year from freelancers. Works on assignment only. Send query letter with resume, tear sheets, Photostats and photocopies. Samples are filed. Samples not filed are returned only if requested by artist. Reports back only if interested. Write to schedule an appointment to show a portfolio, or mail b&w original/final art. Buys all rights. Pays $25-35, b&w, inside; on acceptance.

COLUMBIA, Drawer 1670, New Haven CT 06507. (203)772-2130, ext. 263-64. Editor: Richard McMunn. Art Director: John Cummings. Fraternal magazine of the Knights of Columbus; indepth interviews on family life, social problems, education, current events and apostolic activities as seen from the Catholic viewpoint. Monthly. Circ. 1,405,411. Sample copy available.

Cartoons: Buys cartoons from freelancers. Interested in pungent, captionless humor. Send roughs or finished cartoons to be kept on file. SASE. Reports in 2 weeks. Pays $50; on acceptance.

Illustrations: Buys cover illustrations. Prefers a realistic style. Prefers acrylics, then airbrush, watercolor, oils, pastels, collage, markers, mixed media and calligraphy. Send query letter with tear sheets or slides to be kept on file for future assignments. SASE. Reports in 4 weeks. To show a portfolio, mail color, tear sheets and photographs. Pays up to $1,000, full-color cover design; on acceptance.

Tips: "We are completely open to new styles and ideas. We do not want to see anything that is not designed with reproduction in mind."

COLUMBUS MONTHLY, Columbus Monthly Publishing Corp., 171 E. Livingston Ave., Columbus OH 43215. (614)464-4567. Editor: Max S. Brown. Art Director: Jane Fuller. Regional/city publication. Emphasizes subjects of general interest primarily to Columbus and central Ohio. Circ. 40,000. Sample copy $1.75.

Illustrations: Uses 4-6 illustrations/month; buys most from freelancers. Interested in contemporary editorial illustration. Prefers pen & ink, then airbrush, charcoal/pencil, colored pencil, watercolor, acrylics, oils, pastels, collage and mixed media. Works on assignment only. Samples returned with SASE. Provide resume, business card, letter of inquiry and brochure or tear sheets to be kept on file for future assignments. Prefers to see portfolio (finished art). Buys publication rights. Pays $200-350, color washes and full-color art, cover; $75 minimum, b&w line drawings and washes, inside.

Tips: "In a portfolio, include only your very best work. Weed out all those old samples you're not sure of anymore. Samples should show what type of work you do and something about your creativity."

COMICO THE COMIC COMPANY, 1547 DeKalb St., Norristown PA 19401. Editor-in-Chief: Diana Schutz. Publishes limited edition comic books and graphic novels. Titles include *Elementals*, *Grendel*, *Jonny Quest*, *Justice Machine*, *Robotech The Macross Saga*, *Star Blazers*, *Gumby*, *Rocketeer Adventure Magazine*, *The World of Ginger Fox*, *Space Ghost*, *Night and the Enemy* and *Rio*. "We are not restrictive in our choice of material and are willing to look at any and all genres. All of our publications strive to maintain a high degree of quality, both in art and writing. Comico is presently publishing an eclectic assortment of comic book titles, with a wide audience appeal—from the very young to the elderly." Circ. 70,000. Original artwork returned 90 days after publication.

Illustrations: Uses vertical panels, horizontal panels, inset panels, borderless panels, circular panels, double-page spreads and sequential narrative (any form). Uses freelance artists for inking, lettering, pencilling, color work, posters, covers and cover paintings and pin-ups. Prefers pen & ink, airbrush, watercolor, oils, collage and markers. Send query letter with resume and samples. Samples are filed. Samples not filed are returned by SASE. Reports back within 6 weeks. To show a portfolio, an artist should mail photocopies of original pencil art or inking. Rights purchased vary. Negotiates payment. Pays on acceptance.

Tips: "We are looking for the artist's ability to tell a story through pictures. We want to see storytelling samples, not single illustrations. Due to the comic book market's preference for realism coupled with highly detailed renderings, we also look for the artist's abilities in anatomy, perspective, proportion, composition, good use of negative space. Artists should never send original art, unless they want to risk losing it. We are not responsible for unsolicited submissions. Don't send single illustrations instead of storytelling samples. Don't send more than five pages. Generally, the thicker a submissions package is, the longer it takes the editor to get around to looking at it."

THE COMICS JOURNAL, 4359 Cornell Rd., Agoura CA 91301. (818)706-7606. Art Director: Dale Crain. Magazine emphasizing the news and people of the world of comic books and strips. Circ. 8,000. Original artwork is returned to the artist after publication. Sample copy $4.50.

Illustrations: Prefers b&w spot illustrations and gags dealing with comics. Send query letter with samples. Buys one-time North American rights. Pays $2.50+, b&w, inside; on publication.

***COMMERCIAL FISHERIES NEWS**, Box 37, Main St., Stonington ME 04681. (207)367-2396. Production Manager: Susan Hawkins. "We are a commercial fishing trade publication covering all areas of the industry from legislative information to fishing trends, new products, market reports, etc. Our readership consists of those involved in the industry." Monthly. Circ. 10,000. Accepts previously published material. Original artwork is returned to the artist after publication. Sample copies and art guidelines available.
Cartoons: Cartoon Editor: William McKinnley. Prefers single panel, b&w line drawings. Send query letter with samples of style and finished cartoons. Samples are filed. Samples not filed are returned if requested. Reports back within 1 month. Buys reprint rights. Pays $40, b&w.
Illustrations: Works on assignment only. Prefers "subjects of the fishing industry. Often idea described by editor." Send query letter with photocopies. Samples are filed. Samples not filed are returned only if requested. Reports back in 1 month. Call or write to schedule an appointment to show a portfolio, which should include final reproduction/product. Buys reprint rights. Pays $15, b&w, inside. Photos are used for cover.

COMMON LIVES/LESBIAN LIVES, Box 1553, Iowa City IA 52264. Contact: Editorial Collective. Magazine emphasizing lesbian lives for lesbians of all ages, races, nationalities, and sizes. Quarterly. Circ. 2,000. Original artwork returned if requested and if SASE provided. "Otherwise, all submissions sent to the Lesbian Herstory Archives." Sample copy $4.
Cartoons: Prefers lesbian themes. Prefers vertical format 8½x5½ page. Send finished cartoons to be kept on file. Material not kept on file is returned only if SASE provided. Reports within 4 months.
Illustrations: Prefers lesbian themes. Prefers vertical format 8½x5½ page. Samples not filed are returned only if SASE provided. Reports back within 3 months.

COMMUNICATION WORLD, Suite 940, 870 Market St., San Francisco CA 94102. (415)433-3400. Editor: Gloria Gordon. Emphasizes communication, public relations (international) for members of International Association of Business Communicators: corporate and nonprofit businesses, hospitals, government communicators, universities, etc. who produce internal and external publications, press releases, annual reports and customer magazines. Monthly except June/July combined issue. Circ. 14,000. Accepts previously published material. Original artwork returned after publication. Art guidelines available.
Cartoons: Buys 6 cartoons/year from freelancers. Considers public relations, entrepreneurship, teleconference, editing, writing, international communication and publication themes. Prefers single panel with gagline; b&w line drawings or washes. Send query letter with samples of style to be kept on file. Material not filed is returned by SASE only if requested. Reports within 2 months only if interested. Write or call for appointment to show portfolio. Buys first rights, one-time rights or reprint rights; negotiates rights purchased. Pays $25-50, b&w; on publication.
Illustrations: Buys 6-8 illustrations/issue from freelancers. Theme and style are compatible to individual article. Send query letter with samples to be kept on file; write or call for appointment to show portfolio. Accepts tear sheets, photocopies or photographs as samples. Samples not filed are returned only if requested. Reports back within 1 year only if interested. Buys first rights, one-time rights or reprint rights; negotiates rights purchased. Pays $100, b&w and $300, color, cover; $75 maximim, b&w and $250, color, inside; on publication.
Tips: Artwork "must be professionally displayed. Show understanding of subject, discipline in use of media, general knowledge of working with editorial design problems."

***COMPUTER CURRENTS**, 5720 Hollis St., Emeryville CA 94608. Art Director: Bill Bexis. "A newsmagazine which delivers timely and topical information of a national/regional nature to business/professional PC users." Published twice a month in San Francisco Bay are, monthly in Los Angeles, Boston, Washington DC. Circ. San Francisco: 120,000; Los Angeles: 70,000; Boston: 40,000; Washington, DC: 55,000. Accepts previously published material. Original artwork is returned to the artist after publication.
Cartoons: Cartoon Editor: Lynne Werbeek. Buys 2 cartoon/issue from freelancers. Buys 12-15 cartoons/year from freelancers. Prefers high-tech style and microcomputer themes. Prefers single panel with gagline; b&w line drawings. Send query letter with samples of style. Samples are filed. Samples not filed are returned by SASE if requested. Reports back only if interested. Buys first rights. Pays $25, b&w.
Illustrations: Buys 15-20 illustrations/year from freelancers. Prefers high-tech style and microcomputer themes. Send query letter with brochure showing art style or tear sheets and photocopies. Samples are filed. Reports back only if interested. Call to schedule an appointment to show a portfolio, which should include roughs, original/final art, tear sheets and final reproduction/product. Negotiates rights purchased. Pays $150, b&w; $150, color, inside; on acceptance.
Tips: "Work from manuscript without much direction. Work fast in styles easily reproducible for open web printing."

COMPUTER DECISIONS, Glenpointe Centre East, DeGraw NJ 07666. Art Director: Janine Gevas. For computer-involved management in industry, finance, academia, etc.; well-educated, sophisticated and highly-paid. Monthly. Circ. 110,000.
Illustrations: Buys 5-9/issue. Assigned to illustrate columns and some feature stories. Prefers mixed media, then airbrush, colored pencil, watercolor, acrylics, oils, pastels, collage and computer illustration. Works on assignment only. Prefers to see portfolio or samples of style. Send query letter with brochure or samples to be kept on file. Reports in 1 week. Call or write to schedule an appointment to show a portfolio, which should include original/final art, final reproduction/product, color and tear sheets. Buys all rights. Pays $300-1,250, color, inside; $1,500, cover; on acceptance.
Tips: "Conceptual thinkers are needed for sophisticated readers. Art must be high quality and well-executed. I don't want to see very tight advertising-style or product illustration."

CONFIDENT LIVING, Box 82808, Lincoln NE 68501. Managing Editor: Norman Olson. Interdenominational magazine for adults ages 16 and up. Monthly. Circ. 125,000. Previously published work OK. Original artwork returned after publication. Sample copy $1.50.
Illustrations: Interested in themes that are "serious, related to the subjects of the articles about the Christian life." Works on assignment only. Send query letter with brochure showing art style. Samples returned by SASE. "Helps to know if person is a Christian, too, but not necessary." Reporting time varies. Buys first North American serial rights. Pays $80 color, cover; $20 b&w and $50 color, inside; on publication.

CONNECTICUT MAGAZINE, 789 Reservoir Ave., Bridgeport CT 06606. (203)374-3388. Art Director: Joan Barrow. Emphasizes issues and entertainment in Connecticut for "upscale, 40-50's, Connecticut residents." Monthly. Circ. 92,000. Accepts previously published material. Original artwork returned after publication.
Illustrations: Uses 1-3 illustrations/issue; buys all from freelancers. Works on assignment only. Send query letter with brochure, business card, samples or tear sheets to be kept on file. Drop off portfolios on Wednesday morning, pick up on Thursday afternoon. Call before dropping portfolio off. Samples not filed are not returned. Pays $200-600, color, cover; $75-400, b&w, $200-600, color, inside; on publication.

CONSTRUCTION EQUIPMENT OPERATION AND MAINTENANCE, Construction Publications, Inc., Box 1689, Cedar Rapids IA 52406. (319)366-1597. Editor-in-Chief: C.K. Parks. Concerns heavy construction and industrial equipment for contractors, machine operators, mechanics and local government officials involved with construction. Bimonthly. Circ. 67,000. Original artwork not returned after publication. Free sample copy.
Cartoons: Uses 8-10 cartoons/issue, all from freelancers. Interested in themes "related to heavy construction industry" or "cartoons that make contractors and their employees 'look good' and feel good about themselves"; multiple panel. Send finished cartoons. SASE. Reports within 2 weeks. Buys all rights but may reassign rights to artist after publication. Pays $10-15, b&w.
Illustrations: Uses 20+ illustrations/issue; "very few" are from freelancers. Pays $80-125; on acceptance.

THE CONSTRUCTION SPECIFIER, 601 Madison St., Alexandria VA 22314. (703)684-0300. Editor: Kimberly C. Smith. Emphasizes commercial (*not* residential) design and building for architects, engineers and other A/E professionals. Monthly. Circ. 18,000. Returns original artwork after publication if requested. Sample copy for SASE.
Illustrations: Buys 1-2 illustrations/issue from freelancers. Works on assignment only. Send query letter with Photostats, tear sheets, photocopies, slides or photographs. Samples not filed are returned by SASE. Reports back only if interested. Buys one-time rights. Pays on publication.

" ***I submitted cartoons to a market I found in the Artist's Market. My first effort was not a success, but second and all other attempts since then have been fruitful to the point that my cartoons are appearing regularly in the magazine.*** **"**

—Lawrence Ray Raimonda
El Cajon, California

CONSUMER GUIDE MAGAZINE, (A Division of Publication International), 7373 N. Cicero, Lincolnwood IL 60646. (312)676-3470. Art Directors: Terry Kolodziej and Mike Johnson. Emphasizes publications from cookbooks to medical journals. Does not return original artwork after publication.
Illustrations: Works on assignment only. Send samples to be kept on file. "Photocopies are fine as samples, whatever the artist usually sends." Samples not filed are returned only if requested. Reports back only if interested. Write for appointment to show portfolio. Buys all rights. Payment varies according to project; pays on acceptance.

CONTEMPORARY CHRISTIAN MAGAZINE, Box 6300, Laguna Hills CA 92653. (714)951-9106. Art Director: Lynn Schrader. Reviews and comments on personalities, music, arts, entertainment and issues relevant to Christian adults. Emphasis on music. Monthly. Circ. 40,000. Accepts previously published material and simultaneous submissions if specified with which publications. Originals returned to artist after publication only if requested and accompanied by required postage. Sample copy $1.95.
Cartoons: Interested in using cartoons as editorial fillers. Should be music oriented. Prefers single panel with hand-lettered gagline; *New Yorker* style. Mail prints or reproducible photocopies of finished cartoons to be kept on file; do not call. Material not kept on file is not returned. Reports only if cartoon is used. Buys one-time rights or negotiates. Pays $15-25, b&w; 30 days after publication. Return address, phone and credit information must be on the back of each cartoon.
Illustrations: Buys 1 illustration/issue from freelancers. Works on assignment only. Send query letter with brochure showing art style or photocopies to be kept on file. Samples not kept on file are returned by SASE. Reports only if interested. Call to schedule an appointment to show a portfolio, which should include original/final art, final reproduction/product and b&w. Buys one-time rights or negotiates. Pays $25-150, b&w, inside; 30 days after publication.
Tips: "Include a self-addressed stamped postcard as a response card. That way it will be sent back (usually right away). Type inquiries, it looks more professional."

CONTRACT, Gralla Publications, 1515 Broadway, New York NY 10036. (212)869-1300. Editor: Len Corlin. Provides "ideas for interior installations, product information, and news on developments in the commercial interior design industry." Monthly. Circ. 35,000.
Illustrations: Buys 10-15/year on interior design; all on assignment only. Mail art or samples, or arrange interview to show portfolio. SASE. Reports in 3 weeks. Buys one-time rights. Negotiates payment. Pays on publication.
Tips: "Illustrators should not be shy. Call editor(s) to show portfolio."

DAVID C. COOK PUBLISHING CO., 850 N. Grove Ave., Elgin IL 60120. (312)741-2400. Director of Design Services: Randy R. Maid. Publisher of magazines, teaching booklets, visual aids and film strips. For Christians, "all age groups."
Illustrations: Buys about 30 full-color illustrations/week from freelancers. Send tear sheets, slides or photocopies of previously published work; include self-promo pieces. No samples returned unless requested and accompanied by SASE. Reports in 2-4 weeks to personal queries only. Works on assignment only. Pays on acceptance $50 minimum for inside b&w; $275-300, for color cover and $100 minimum for inside color. Considers complexity of project, skill and experience of artist and turnaround time when establishing payment. Buys all rights. Originals can be returned in most cases.
Tips: "We do not buy illustrations or cartoons on speculation. We welcome those just beginning their careers, but it helps if the samples are presented in a neat and professional manner. Our deadlines are generous but must be met. We send out checks as soon as final art is approved, usually within 2 weeks of our receiving the art. We want art radically different from normal Sunday School art. Fresh, dynamic, the highest of quality is our goal; art that appeals to preschoolers to senior citizens; realistic to humorous, all media."

CORVETTE FEVER MAGAZINE, Box 44620, Fort Washington MD 20744. (301)839-2221. Editor: Patricia Stivers. For "Corvette owners and enthusiasts, ages 25-55." Bimonthly. Circ. 35,000. Original artwork not returned after publication. Sample copy $2; general art guidelines for SASE.
Cartoons: Uses 2 cartoons/issue; buys 2-4 from freelancers. Themes "must deal with Corvettes"; single panel with gagline, b&w line drawings. Send roughs. Samples returned by SASE. Reports in 6 weeks. Buys first rights and reprint rights. Pays $15-35, b&w; on publication.
Illustrations: Uses 4-6 illustrations/issue; buys 3-6 from freelancers. Themes "must deal with Corvettes." Provide resume, brochure and tear sheets to be kept on file for possible future assignments. Send roughs with samples of style. Samples returned by SASE. Reports in 6 weeks. Buys first rights and reprint rights. Pays $10-75, inside, b&w line drawings; on publication.

COSMOPOLITAN, 224 W. 57th St., New York NY 10019. (212)649-3547. Cartoon Editor: Parker Reilly. For career women, ages 18-34.
Cartoons: Works largely with extensive present list of cartoonists. Receives 200 cartoons/week from freelance artists. Especially looks for "light, sophisticated, female-oriented cartoons."
Tips: "Less and less freelance work is purchased—the competition is tougher. Choose your topics and submissions carefully. We buy only sophisticated cartoons that stress a *positive* view of women—females as the subject of the cartoon but not the butt of the joke. Please read the magazine—there are only about 20 cartoonists who really understand our needs. I can't stress this enough." When reviewing an artist's work, "appropriateness to the magazine comes first. Sense of humor comes next, then quality of art. We like pretty people to be featured in our magazine—even in the cartoons. Be aware of *all* the outlets available to you—papers, ad agencies—then study the market *you're* trying to break into. Every magazine has its own slant. Read half a dozen issues and then ask yourself—can I describe, in two or three sentences, a typical reader's concerns, interests, age and economic background?"

THE COVENANT COMPANION, 5101 N. Francisco Ave., Chicago IL 60625. (312)784-3000. Editor: James R. Hawkinson. Emphasizes Christian life and faith. Monthly. Circ. 25,500. Original artwork returned after publication if requested. Sample copy $1.50.
Illustrations: Uses b&w drawings or photos about Easter, Advent, Lent, and Christmas. Works on assignment only. Write or submit art 10 weeks in advance of season. SASE. Reports "within a reasonable time." Buys first North American serial rights. Pays in month after publication.

***CREATIVE CHILD & ADULT QUARTERLY**, The National Association for Creative Children and Adults, 8080 Spring Valley, Cincinnnati OH 45236. Publisher: Anne Fabe Isaacs. Editor: Dr. Wallace D. Draper. Emphasizes creativity in *all* its applications for parents, teachers, students, administrators in the professions. Quarterly. Original artwork returned after publication if SASE is enclosed. Sample copy $10.
Cartoons: Uses 1 + cartoon/issue. Prefers single panel; b&w line drawings. Send samples of style or finished cartoons to be kept on file. Material not kept on file is returned by SASE. Reports within weeks. Pays in copies of publication.
Illustrations: Uses various number of illustrations/issue, including some humorous and cartoon-style illustrations. Send query letter and original work. Samples returned by SASE. Reports within weeks. Pays in copies of publication.

CREATIVE IDEAS FOR LIVING, 820 Shades Creek Pkwy., Birmingham AL 35209. (205)877-6469. Art Director: Lane Gregory. Magazine emphasizing lifestyle for women 28-40. Monthly. Circ. 800,000. Original artwork returned after publication. Sample copy for a large manila SASE.
Illustrations: Buys 3-4 illustrations/issue from freelancers. Works on assignment only. Prefers watercolors, colored pencil and pen & ink. Send query letter with brochure showing art style or resume and samples. Samples returned only if requested. Reports only if interested. Call or write to schedule an appointment to show a portfolio, which should include tear sheets, slides, color and b&w. Buys one-time rights. Pays $200, b&w; $300 color, inside; on acceptance.
Tips: In a portfolio include "four to five best pieces to show strengths and/or versatility. Smaller pieces are much easier to handle than large. Its best not to have to return samples but to keep them for reference files."

CRICKET, The Magazine for Children, Box 300, Peru IL 61354. Art Director: Maryann Leffingwell. Emphasizes children's literature for children, ages 6-12. Monthly. Circ. 140,000. Accepts previously published material. Original artwork returned after publication. Sample copy $1; art guidelines free for SASE.
Illustrations: Uses 70 illustrations/issue; buys 45 illustrations/issue from freelancers. Prefers realistic styles (animal or human figure); occasionally accepts caricature. Works on assignment only. Send query letter with brochure, samples and tear sheets to be kept on file, "if I like it." Prefers Photostats, tear sheets as samples. Samples are returned by SASE if requested or not kept on file. Reports within 6-8 weeks. Buys reprint rights. Pays $500, color, cover; $150/full page, b&w. Pays on publication.
Tips: "Very little chance of cartoon sales at *Cricket*."

CROSSCURRENTS, 2200 Glastonbury Rd., Westlake Village CA 91361. (818)991-1694. Graphic Arts Editor: Michael Hughes. "This is a literary quarterly that uses graphic art as accompaniment to our fiction and poetry. We are aimed at an educated audience interested in reviewing a selection of fiction, poetry and graphic arts." Circ. 3,000. Original artwork returned after publication. Sample copy $5; art guidelines available for SASE.
Illustrations: Uses 5-7 illustrations/issue; buys 75% from freelancers. Considers "any work of high quality and in good taste that will reproduce b&w, 5x7", with clarity, including but not limited to line

drawings, charcoal sketches, etchings, lithographs, engravings; vertical format. No pornography." Send brochure, resume, tear sheets, Photostats, slides and photographs. No simultaneous submissions or previously published material. SASE. Reports in 3 weeks. To show a portfolio, mail appropriate material. Buys first rights. Pays $10 minimum cover or inside b&w line drawings and b&w washes; $15 minimum cover, color washes; on publication.
Tips: "Study a sample copy of our publication and read our guidelines to understand what it is that we use, and what styles we publish." When reviewing an artist's work, "we look for technical excellence, strength of style, something of worth. A professional, neat submission is a must, of course."

CROW, (formerly *Afta—The Alternative Magazine*), 147 Crater Ave., Wharton NJ 07885. (201)828-5467. Editor: Bill-Dale Marcinko. Emphasizes rock music, films, TV and books for young (18-35) male readers who are regular consumers of books, records, films and magazines; and socially and politically aware. 60% are gay; 50% are college educated or attending college. Quarterly. Circ. 25,000. Receives 10 cartoons and 30 illustrations/week from freelance artists. Previously published material and simultaneous submissions OK. Original work returned after publication. Sample copy $3.50. Especially needs political satire; rock and film illustrations, surreal, erotic work.
Cartoons: Uses 10 cartoons/issue; buys all from freelancers. Interested in satires on social attitudes, current political events, films, TV, books, rock music world, sexuality; single and multiple-panel with gagline, b&w line drawings. No color work accepted. Send query letter with samples of style. Samples returned. Buys one-time rights. Pays in contributor copies; on publication.
Illustrations: Uses 75 illustrations/issue; buys all from freelancers. Interested in illustrations from films, rock music stars, books and TV programs. No color work accepted. Send query letter with samples of style to be kept on file. Samples not kept on file are returned. Reports in 1 week. Buys one-time rights. Pays in contributor copies; on publication.
Tips: "Read a sample copy of *CROW* before submitting work."

CRUISING WORLD, 524 Thames St., Newport RI 02840. (401)847-1588. Assistant Art Director: Rachel Cocroft. Magazine emphasizing cruising sailboats for audience with a $98,000 average income, most own their own boat, approx. 40-50 years old. Circ. 125,000. Finds most artists through references/word-of-mouth, portfolio reviews and samples received through the mail.
Illustrations: Buys 10 or more illustrations/issue from freelancers. Prefers pen & ink, airbrush, colored pencil, watercolor, acrylics, oils, pastel, mixed media and calligraphy. Works on assignment only. Prefers b&w or four-color marine, boat-oriented editorial illustrations as well as b&w technical line illustrations. Send query letter with brochure showing art style or tear sheets, Photostats, photocopies, slides and photographs. To show a portfolio, mail color tear sheets, Photostats, photographs, b&w. Buys first rights. Pays $100-300, b&w; $200-800, color, inside; on publication.
Tips: "Freelance artists must be familiar with the magazine, and with boats, what they look and feel like when sailing. An artist must have ability to render human anatomy accurately in scale with marine equipment and also to interpret editorial matter creatively. We are using more airbrushed material, more four-color and we are looking for diversity of styles. We are, also, increasingly interested in spot illustrations that are not necessarily marine-oriented." Artists should show a representative sampling of their work and target their samples magazine's specific needs.

CRUSADER, Baptist Brotherhood Commission, 1548 Poplar, Memphis TN 38104. (901)272-2461. Art Director: Herschel Wells. Christian-oriented mission magazine for boys grades 4-6. Monthly. Circ. 100,000. Photocopied and simultaneous submissions OK. Original artwork returned after publication, if requested.
Illustrations: Uses 10 illustrations/issue; buys 2/issue from freelancers. Interested in boys' activities. Prefers pen & ink, airbrush, charcoal/pencil, colored pencil, watercolor and acrylics. Works on assignment only. Sample copy provided "if we consider using the artist after we've seen samples." Send roughs or samples of style, which may be returned or duplicated to be kept on file. Samples not filed are returned by SASE. Reports in 3 weeks. To show a portfolio, mail original/final art, tear sheets and Photostats. Buys first North American serial rights. Pays $100, b&w, and up to $250, color, cover; $35-$120, b&w, inside; on acceptance.
Tips: "Please send several samples if you have more than one style. We must see human figure work as most of our art requires this."

CRYPTOLOGIA, Rose-Hulman Institute of Technology, Terre Haute IN 47803. (812)877-1511. Managing Editor: Brian J. Winkel. Emphasizes all aspects of cryptology: data (computer) encryption, history, military, science, ancient languages, secret communications for scholars and hobbyists. Quarterly. Circ. 1,000. Accepts previously published material and simultaneous submissions. Original artwork returned after publication.
Cartoons: Uses 1-2 cartoons/issue. Prefers plays on language, communication (secret), ancient lan-

guage decipherment, computer encryption. Prefers single, double or multi panel, with or without gagline; b&w line drawings or b&w washes. Send query letter with samples of style, roughs, or finished cartoons to be kept on file. Material not kept on file is returned by SASE. Reports within 2 weeks. Negotiates rights purchased. Pays on acceptance.

CURRENTS, Box 6847, 314 N. 20th St., Colorado Springs CO 80904. Editor: Eric Leeper. Magazine emphasizing whitewater river running for kayakers, rafters and canoeists; from beginner to expert; middle-class, college-educated. Bimonthly. Circ. 10,000. Accepts previously published material. Original artwork returned after publication. Sample copy 75¢. Art guidelines for SASE with first-class postage.
Cartoons: Buys 0-1 cartoon/issue from freelancers. Themes *must* deal with whitewater rivers or river running. Prefers single panel with gagline; b&w line drawings. Send query letter with roughs of proposed cartoon(s) to be kept on file. Samples not kept on file are returned by SASE. Reports within 6 weeks. Buys one-time rights. Pays $10-35, b&w.
Illustrations: Buys 0-2 illustrations/issue from freelancers. Prefers pen & ink. Works on assignment only. Themes must deal with rivers or river running. Send query letter with proposed illustrations. Samples not filed returned by SASE. Reports within 6 weeks. To show a portfolio, mail appropriate materials, which should include "whatever they feel is necessary." Buys one-time rights. Pays $10-35, b&w; inside. Pays on publication.
Tips: "Make sure you have seen a sample copy of *Currents* and our guidelines. Be sure you know about rivers and whitewater river sports. Art must pertain to whitewater river running."

CWC/PETERBOROUGH, 80 Elm St., Peterborough NH 03458. (617)924-9471. Creative Director: Christine Destrempes. "We publish 5 microcomputing monthlies and various quarterlies: *AmigaWorld*, *Computers in Science*, *CD-ROM Review*, *80 Micro*, *RUN*, and *inCider*." Circ. 100,000-550,000. Accepts previously published material. Returns original artwork after publication. Sample copy for SASE.
Cartoons: Minimal number of cartoons purchased from freelancers. Prefers single panel without gaglines; b&w line drawings, b&w washes or color washes. "I don't use light cartoons." Send query letter with samples of style or finished cartoons to be kept on file. Material not filed is returned only if requested. Reports within 5 weeks. Rights purchased and payment varies; pays within 30 days.
Illustrations: Buys 8-20 illustrations/issue from freelancers. Uses airbrush, charcoal/pencil, watercolor, acrylics, oils, collage and computer illustration. Buys 2-3 computer illustrations/year from freelancers. Works on assignment only. Send query letter with resume and tear sheets to be kept on file. Samples not filed are returned only if requested. Reports within 5 weeks. To show a portfolio, mail final reproduction/product, color and b&w or call or write to schedule an appointment. Rights purchased and payments vary; pays on acceptance.
Tips: "Artists must understand technical manuscripts. They must be very creative and must do excellent work. I like to see what artists perceive as their best work, but samples targeted to our specific needs are most helpful."

CYCLE WORLD, 1499 Monrovia Ave., Newport Beach CA 92663. (714)720-5300. For active motorcyclists who are "young, affluent, educated, very perceptive." Monthly. Circ. 375,000. "Unless otherwise noted in query letter, we will keep spot drawings in our files for use as future fillers." Free sample copy and artist's guidelines.
Illustrations: Art Director: Elaine Anderson. Uses 7-8 illustrations/issue, all from freelancers. Receives 25-30 submissions/week from freelancers. Interested in motorcycling and assigned themes. Works on assignment only. Prefers to see resume and samples. Samples returned, if originals; kept if photocopies. Reports back on future assignment possibilities to artists who phone. Does not report back to artists who contact through mail. Call or write to schedule an appointment to show a portfolio, which should include original/final art, final reproduction/product, color, tear sheets and b&w. Provide brochure, tear sheet, letter of inquiry and business card to be kept on file for future assignments. Buys all rights. Pays $300-500, cover. Pays $25-150, b&w; $100-400, color; $75, spot drawings, on publication.
Tips: "We use a lot of spot drawings as fillers. black-and-white motorcyle illustrations used mostly. Call or write. Do not send original art or unsolicited art."

DC COMICS INC., 666 Fifth Ave., New York NY 10103. Executive Editor: Dick Giordano. Super-hero and adventure comic books for mostly boys 7-14, plus an older audience of high school and college age. Monthly. Circ. 6,000,000. Original artwork is returned after publication.
Illustrations: Buys 22 pages/comic. Works on assignment only. Send query letter with resume and photocopies. Do not send original artwork. Samples not filed are returned if requested and accompanied by SASE. Reports back within 2 months. Write to schedule an appointment to show a portfolio, which should include thumbnails and original/final art. Buys all rights. Payment varies on acceptance.
Tips: "Work should show an ability to tell stories with sequential illustrations. Single illustration are not particularly helpful, since your ability at story telling is not demonstrated."

DEATH RATTLE, Kitchen Sink Enterprises, No. 2 Swamp Rd., Princeton WI 54968. (414)295-6922. Story Editor: Dave Schreiner. Serious comic book emphasizing science fiction and horror for serious readers and collectors of quality fantasy, science fiction and horror comics. Bimonthly. Circ. 20-25,000. Does not accept previously published material unless obscure publications. Original artwork returned after publication. Sample copy $2.50 postpaid; art guidelines for SASE with first-class postage.
Cartoons: "We *never* buy "gag" or single panel cartoons. This is a comic book featuring fully developed graphic stories." Prefers b&w line drawings. Send query letter with samples of style, roughs or photocopies of finished cartoons to be kept on file. Samples not filed are returned only by SASE. "Do not send original art for consideration. Reports within 2 weeks. Negotiates rights purchased. Payment variable; generally $50-200/page, paid on royalty basis. "Higher earnings possible."
Illustrations: For cover only; "balance is fully-developed graphic stories." Generally works on assignment only. Preferred style is simplified realism. Send query letter with brochure showing art styles or tear sheets, Photostats and photocopies. Samples returned by SASE. Reports within 2 weeks. "Portfolio presentations unrealistic for geographic reasons." Negotiates rights purchased. Pays $200-400, b&w, cover. Pays one-half on acceptance, one-half on publication.

DECOR, 408 Olive, St. Louis MO 63102. (314)421-5445. Associate Editor: Sharon Shinn. "Trade publication for retailers of art, picture framing and related wall decor. Subscribers include gallery owners/directors, custom and do-it-yourself picture framers, managers of related departments in department stores, art material store owners and owners of gift/accessory shops." Monthly. Circ. 20,000. Simultaneous submissions and previously published work OK. Original artwork not returned after publication. Sample copy $4.
Cartoons: Uses 6-10 cartoons/year; buys all from freelancers. Receives 5-10 submissions/week from freelancers. Interested in themes of galleries, frame shops, artists and small business problems; single panel with gagline. "We need cartoons as a way to 'lighten' our technical and retailing material. Cartoons showing gallery owners' problems with shows, artists and the buying public, inept framing employees, selling custom frames to the buying public and running a small business are most important to us." Send finished cartoons. SASE. Reports in 1 month. Buys various rights. Pays $20, b&w line drawings and washes; on acceptance.
Tips: "Most of our cartoons fill one-quarter-page spaces. Hence, cartoons that are vertical in design suit our purposes better than those which are horizontal. Send good, clean drawings with return envelopes; no more than 6 cartoons at a time."

DELAWARE TODAY MAGAZINE, 120A Senatorial Dr., Wilmington DE 19807. (302)656-1809. Art/Design Director: Ingrid Hansen-Lynch. Magazine emphasizing regional interest in and around Delaware. Features general interest, historical, humorous, interview/profile, personal experience and travel articles. "The stories we have are about people and happenings, in and around Delaware. They are regional interest stories. Our audience is middle-aged (40-45) people with incomes around $60,000, mostly educated." Monthly. Circ. 18,000. Accepts previously published material. Original artwork returned after publication. Sample copy available.
Cartoons: Buys 1 cartoon every other month from freelancers. Buys approximately 6 cartoons/year from freelancers. Open to all styles. Prefers no gagline; b&w line drawings, b&w and color washes. Send query letter with samples of style. Samples are filed. Reports back only if interested. Buys first rights or one-time rights. Pays $50 small; $100 large.
Illustrations: Buys 2 illustrations/issue from freelancers. Buys 24 illustrations/year from freelancers. Works on assignment only. Open to all styles. Send query letter with resume, tear sheets, slides and whatever pertains. Samples are filed. Reports back only if interested. Call to schedule an appointment to show a portfolio, which should include original/final art, tear sheets, final reproduction/product, color and b&w. Buys first rights and one-time rights. Pays $50, small b&w and color; $100 large b&w and color, inside; $250, cover; on publication.
Tips: "The most appropriate way to contact us is to send a resume, cover letter and a promo card or brochure showing black-and-white and color samples and different styles of the artist's work."

DENTAL HYGIENE, Suite 3400, 444 N. Michigan, Chicago IL 60611. (312)440-8900. Contact: Staff Editor. Emphasizes "professional concerns and issues involving dental hygienists and scientific topics concerning dental hygiene" for "a primarily female audience of dental hygienists." Monthly. Circ. 35,000. Original artwork returned after publication. Sample copy available.
Illustrations: Uses 1 cover illustration/issue; buys 1/issue from freelancers. Prefers a variety of styles. "The theme depends on the individual issue." Works on assignment only. Send query letter with brochure, resume, samples and tear sheets to be kept on file. Prefers slides or photographs of color work. Reports within 1 month. Write for appointment to show portfolio. Buys one-time rights. Payment depends on the artwork. Pays on publication.

DETROIT MAGAZINE, 321 W. Lafayette, Detroit MI 48231. (313)222-6446. Contact: Art Director: Patrick Mitchell. Sunday magazine of major metropolitan daily newspaper emphasizing general subjects. Weekly. Circ. 800,000. Original artwork returned after publication. Sample copy available.
Illustrations: Buys 1-2 illustrations/issue from freelancers. Uses a variety of themes and styles, "but we emphasize fine art over cartoons." Works on assignment only. Send query letter with samples to be kept on file unless not considered for assignment. Send "whatever samples best show artwork and can fit into 8½x11 file folder." Samples not filed are not returned. Reports only if interested. Buys first rights. Pays $350-600, color, cover; up to $350, color and up to $175, b&w, inside; on publication.

DETROIT MONTHLY MAGAZINE, 1400 Woodbridge, Detroit MI 48207. Design Director: Michael Ban. Emphasizes "features on political, economic, style, cultural, lifestyles, culinary subjects, etc., relating to Detroit and region" for "middle and upper-middle class, urban and suburban, mostly college-educated professionals." Monthly. Circ. approximately 100,000. "Very rarely" accepts previously published material. Sample copy for SASE.
Illustrations: Uses 10 illustrations/issue; buys 10/issue from freelancers. Works on assignment only. Send query letter with samples and tear sheets to be kept on file. Write for appointment to show portfolio. Prefers anything *but* original work as samples. Samples not kept on file are returned by SASE. Reports only if interested. Pays $600, color, cover, $300-400, color, full page, $200-300, b&w, full page, $100, sport illustrations; on publication.

***DIABETES SELF-MANAGEMENT**, 42-15 Crescent St., Long Island City, NY 11101. (718)937-4283. Production Director: Maryanne Schott. Estab. 1983. Magazine. Emphasizes diabetes self-care. Bi-monthly. Circ. 250,000. Original artwork not returned after publication. Sample copy $3.
Cartoons: Buys 6-8 cartoons/issue from freelancers. Themes or styles dependent on editorial content. Prefers single panel or multi-panel; b&w washes, color washes. Send query letter with samples of style to be kept on file. Material not filed is returned by SASE. Reports only if interested. Buys all rights. Pays on publication.
Illustrations: Buys 20-30 illustrations/issue from freelancers. Themes or styles vary from issue to issue based on editorial. Send query letter with tear sheets, Photostats, slides and photos to be kept on file. Samples not filed are returned by SASE. Reports only if interested. Buys all rights. Pays on publication.

***DIABLO MAGAZINE**, 2520 Camino Diablo, Walnut Creek CA 94596. (415)943-1111. Art Director: Scot Kambic. City magazine "reflecting the affluent lifestyle of the central Contra Costa County/Diablo Valley area east of San Francisco." Monthly. Circ. 70,000. Accepts previously published material. Original artwork is returned to the artist after publication. Sample copies available.
Cartoon: Buys 2-5 cartoons/issue from freelancers. Buys 24 cartoons/year from freelancers. Prefers "dining themes, but open to anything showing sophisticated wit." Prefers single panel with gagline; b&w line drawings. Send query letter with samples of style. Samples are filed. Samples not filed are returned by SASE if requested by artist. Reports back only if interested. Buys one-time rights. Pays $25-50, b&w.
Illustrations: Buys 2-5 illustrations/issue from freelancers. Buys 30 illustrations/year from freelancers. Works on assignment only. Send query letter with brochure, resume, tear sheets, Photostats, photocopies, slides and photographs. Samples are filed. Samples not filed are returned by SASE if requested by artist. Reports back only if interested. Call or write to schedule an appointment to show a portfolio, or mail original/final art, tear sheets, final reproduction/product, color and b&w. Buys one-time rights. Pays $200-300, color, cover; $75-150, b&w; $150-250, color inside; on publication.

DIRT RIDER MAGAZINE, Petersen Publishing, 8490 Sunset, Los Angeles CA 90069. (213)854-2390. Art Director: John Thomas Sutton. Consumer magazine emphasizing dirt bike riding, riders and maintenance. Features how-to, humor, interview/profile, personal experience, technical, travel and humorous fiction. "Caters to athletic, younger readers." Monthly. Circ. 160,000. Original artwork not returned after publication. Sample copy $2.
Cartoons: Buys 12 cartoons/issue from freelancers. Buys 150 cartoons/year from freelancers. Prefers single panel, double panel or multi panel with or without gaglines; b&w line drawings, b&w or color washes. Send query letter with samples of style and roughs. Samples are filed. Samples not filed are not returned. Does not report back. Buys all rights. Pays $50, b&w.
Illustrations: Buys 12 illustrations/issue from freelancers. Buys 150 illustrations/year from freelancers. Send query letter with brochure showing art style or tear sheets, photocopies, slides and photographs. Samples are filed. Samples not filed are not returned. Does not report back. To show a portfolio, mail tear sheets, final reproduction/product, Photostats, photographs, color and b&w. Buys all rights. Pays $50, b&w; on acceptance or publication.

Stippling creates the right mood for this spot used in* Dog Fancy. *Art director Linda Lewis says the piece by illustrator Christine Palmer "conveys a sense of the holiday season, the dog waiting for the family to come home with the Christmas tree, perhaps." This was Palmer's first published piece, selling first rights. "I bought the* Artist's Market *and successfully sold on the first try. I chose editorial illustration because your book recommended it for first timers. Once I was published, I could send tear sheets along with my next try."

THE DISCIPLE, Christian Board of Publication, Box 179, St. Louis MO 63166. Editor: James L. Merrell. For ministers and laypersons. Monthly. Circ. 51,000. Photocopied and simultaneous submissions OK. Original artwork returned after publication, if requested. Sample copy $1.50; free artist's guidelines.

Cartoons: Buys 1 cartoon/issue from freelancers. Receives 10 submissions/week from freelancers. Interested in family life and religion; single panel. Church material only. "Originality in content and subject matter stressed. No clergy collars—ties or robes preferred." Especially needs "good religious cartoons along the lines of those which appear in the New Yorker." Prefers to see finished cartoons. SASE. Reports in 4 weeks. Buys first North American serial rights. Pays $15 minimum, b&w line drawings and washes; on acceptance.

Illustrations: Uses 2 illustrations/issue; buys 1/issue from freelancers. Receives 10 submissions/week from freelancers. Interested in "seasonal and current religious events/issues." Also uses 4 cartoon-style illustrations/year. Send query letter with tear sheets, photocopies and photographs. SASE. Reports in 2 weeks. To show a portfolio, mail tear sheets, Photostats and photographs. Buys first North American serial rights. Payment depends on quality. Pays on acceptance.

Tips: "We would be very happy to look at samples of artists' work (covers), in case we want to commission. Read the magazine before submitting material. Send seasonal art, especially Easter and Christmas, at least six months in advance. Do not send 'dial-a-prayer' cartoons."

DISTRIBUTOR, Box 745, Wheeling IL 60090. (312)537-6460. Editorial Director: Steve Read. Emphasizes heating, air conditioning, ventilation and refrigeration wholesaling for executives at management level in the wholesale field. Monthly. Circ. 11,600. Accepts previously published materials. Returns original artwork sometimes after publication. Sample copy $4. Art guidelines available.

Illustrations: Buys 4-6 illustrations/year from freelancers. Works on assignment only. Send query letter with brochure, Photostats, tear sheets, photocopies, slides or photographs, to be kept on file; *no* original work. Reports within 3 weeks only if interested. Call or write to schedule an appointment to show a portfolio, which should include thumbnails, roughs, original/final art, final reproduction/production, tear sheets, photographs and color. Buys first rights. Pays $300, color, cover; $100 color, inside; on publication.

Tips: "Order a sample copy of the magazine to learn what issues we cover and what our general style is. We would like to see more illustration on our covers."

DIVER MAGAZINE, Suite 295, 10991 Shellbridge Way, Richmond, British Columbia V6X 3C6 Canada. (604)273-4333. Editor: Neil McDaniel. Emphasizes scuba diving, ocean science and technology (commercial and military diving) for a well-educated, outdoor-oriented readership. Published 9 times yearly. Circ. 25,000. Sample copy $3; art guidelines for SAE (nonresidents include IRC).

Cartoons: Buys 1 cartoon/issue from freelancers. Interested in diving-related cartoons only. Prefers single panel b&w line drawings with gagline. Send samples of style. SAE (nonresidents include IRC). Reports in 2 weeks. Buys first North American serial rights. Pays $15 for b&w; on publication.

Illustrations: Interested in diving-related illustrations of good quality only. Prefers b&w line drawings for inside. Send samples of style. SAE (nonresidents include IRC). Reports in 2 weeks. Buys first North American serial rights. Pays $7 minimum for inside b&w; $100 minimum for color cover and $15 minimum for inside, color. Payment 1 month after publication.

DOG FANCY, Box 6050, Mission Viejo CA 92690. (714)240-6001. Editor: Linda Lewis. For dog owners and breeders of all ages, interested in all phases of dog ownership. Monthly. Circ. 150,000. Simultaneous submissions and previously published work OK. Sample copy $3.; free artist's guidelines with SASE.

Cartoons: Buys 12 cartoons/year; single, double or multiple panel. "Central character should be a dog." Mail finished art. SASE. Prefers Photostats or photocopies as samples. Reports in 6 weeks. Buys first rights. Pays $20-50, b&w line drawings; on publication.

Illustrations: Uses 2-5 spots/issue. Prefers local artists. Works on assignment only. Buys one-time rights. Pays $20/spot, $50-100 for b&w illustrations, on publication.

Tips: "Spot illustrations are used in nearly every issue. I need dogs in action (doing just about anything) and puppies. Please send a selection that we can keep on file. We pay $20 for each spot drawing used. Drawings should be scaled to reduce to column width (2¼)"

DOLLS—THE COLLECTOR'S EDITION, 170 5th Ave., New York NY 10010. (212)989-8700. Art Director: Diane Lemonides. Magazine emphasizing antique and collectible dolls for doll collectors. Bimonthly. Circ. 52,500. Original artwork returned after publication. Sample copy $2. Art guidelines for SASE with first-class postage.

Illustrations: Buys 3 illustrations/issue from freelancers. Works on assignment only. Prefers realistic presentations. b&w line art or full-color for covers and how-to type drawings. Send query letter with re-

sume, tear sheets, Photostats and photocopies. Samples not filed returned by SASE. Reports only if interested. Call to schedule an appointment to show a portfolio, which should include roughs, original/final art, final reproduction/production, color, tear sheets, photographs and b&w. Buys first rights; negotiates rights purchased. Pays by the project, $100-1,000. Pays 30 days after submission.
Tips: Also accepts illustration for *Dollmaking*, quarterly magazine emphasizing doll projects and plans (circ. 50,000) and *Teddy Bear Review*, quarterly magazine emphasizing antique and collectible bears (circ. 30,000)

THE DOLPHIN LOG, The Cousteau Society, 8440 Santa Monica Blvd., Los Angeles CA 90069. (213)656-4422. Editor: Pamela Stacey. Educational magazine covering "all areas of science, history and the arts related to our global water system, including marine biology, ecology, the environment, and natural history" for children ages 7-15. Bimonthly. Circ. 60,000. Original artwork returned after publication. Sample copy for $2 and SASE with 56¢ postage; art guidelines for SASE with first-class postage.
Cartoons: Buys 2 cartoons/year from freelancers. Considers themes or styles related to magazine's subject matter. Prefers single panel with or without gagline; b&w line drawings. Send query letter with samples of style. Samples are not filed, but are returned by SASE. Reports within 1-2 months. Buys one-time rights, reprint rights and translation rights. Pays $25-75, b&w and color; on publication.
Illustrations: Buys 1-2 illustrations/issue from freelancers. Uses simple, biologically and technically accurate line drawings and scientific illustrations. Subjects should be carefully researched. Prefers pen & ink, aribrush and watercolor. Send query letter with tear sheets and photocopies or brochure showing art style. "No portfolios. We review only tearsheets and/or photocopies. No original artwork, please." Samples are not filed and returned by SASE. Reports within 1-2 months. Buys one-time rights and worldwide translation rights. Pays $25-150 on publication.
Tips: "Artists should first request a sample copy to familiarize themselves with our style. Do not send art which is not water-oriented."

DOWN EAST, Box 679, Camden ME 04843. (207)594-9544. Art Director: F. Stephen Ward. Concerns Maine's people, places, events and heritage. Monthly. Circ. 85,000. Buys first North American serial rights. Sample copy $2. Finds most artists through talent sourcebooks, references/word-of-mouth and portfolio reviews.
Illustrations: Buys 50/year on current events, environment, family life and politics. Prefers pen & ink, airbrush, watercolor, oils, markers and computer illustration. Query with resume and samples or arrange interview to show portfolio. SASE. Reports in 4-6 weeks. Inside: Pays $75-400, b&w or color; on publication.
Tips: "Neatness in presentation is as important as the portfolio itself. Show me a style you do well and easily."

DRAGON MAGAZINE, TSR, Inc., Box 110, Lake Geneva WI 53147. (414)248-8044. Editor: Roger E. Moore. Art Director: Roger Raupp. For readers interested in role-playing games, particularly Dungeons and Dragons. Circ. 90,000. Query with samples. SASE. Usually buys first rights only. Pays within 60 days after acceptance.
Cartoons: Buys 40-60/year on fantasy role-playing. Pays $35-80, b&w only.
Illustrations: Buys at least 100/year on fantasy and science fiction subjects. Pays $250/page, b&w; $700 and up for color cover art.
Tips: "Commissions are not likely unless the artist provides a sampling of work which demonstrates his ability to render realistic fantasy art. The more particular the work is to the Dungeons & Dragons game the better."

DRAMATIKA, 429 Hope St., Tarpon Springs FL 34689. Editor: J. Pyros. For persons interested in the performing arts, avant garde and traditional. Published semiannually. Sample copy $4.
Illustrations: Query first. SASE. Reports in 1 month. Cover: Pays $15, b&w. Inside: Pays $5, b&w line drawings; on acceptance.

***EAP DIGEST**, #103, 2145 Crooks Rd., Troy MI 48084. (313)643-9580. Art Director: Grace Young. Trade journal emphasizing employee assistance programs. "We focus on problems people face that can interfere with job performance. Emphasis is on alcoholism and drug addiction; but the gamut is covered—marital, financial, child care problems, etc. Also, we cover how employee assistance professionals can and do deal with these issues." Bimonthly. Circ. 20,000. Accepts previously published material. Original artwork is not returned to the artist after publication. Sample copy available.
Cartoons: Prefers single panel with gagline; b&w line drawings. Send query leter with samples of style. Samples are filed. Samples not filed are returned if requested by artist. Reports back within 2 weeks. Negotiates rights purchased. Pays $15, b&w.

Illustration: Buys about 2 illustrations/year from freelancers. Works on assignment only. Send query leter with brochure. Samples are filed. Samples not filed are returned only if requested by artist. Reports back wihtin 2 weeks. Call to schedule an appointment to show portfolio, which should include roughs, original/final art and final reproduction/product. Negotiates rights purchased. Pays $200, b&w; $300, color cover; $200, b&w; $100, color inside. Pays on acceptance.

***EAST WEST—The Journal of Natural Health & Living**, 17 Station St., Box 1200, Brookline MA 02147. Art Director: Betsy Woldman. Magazine emphasizing current alternative natural health and lifestyle issues. "We cover topics on holistic health, whole foods cooking, natural lifestyles, organic gardening, and spirituality." Monthly. Circ. 80,000. Accepts previously published material. Original artwork is returned to the artist after publication. Sample copies $2.50. Art guidelines free for SASE with first-class postage.
Illustrations: Buys 10 illustrations/issue from freelancers. Buys 120 illustrations/year from freelancers. Works on assignment only. "We use whole range of styles." Prefers pen & ink, airbrush, charcoal/pencil, collage, mixed media and calligraphy. Send query letter with brochure, resume, tear sheets, Photostats and photocopies. Samples are filed. Does not report back. To show a portfolio, mail final reproduction/product, original/final art, tear sheets, Photostats and b&w. Buys one-time rights. Pays $75-250, b&w; $500-650, color cover; on publication.
Tips: "We use mainly black-and-white work. Please look at the magazine before you approach us. We do not want to see artwork that is inappropriate to our magazine. Show editorial work so we can tell how a person works out a story idea, how they think out a problem."

ECLIPSE COMICS, Box 1099, Forestville CA 95436. Editor-in-Chief: Catherine Yronwode. Publishes comic books and graphic albums. "All our comics feature fictional characters in action-adventures. Genres include super-heroes, science fiction, weird horror, western, detective adventure, funny-animal, etc. The emphasis is on drawing the human figure in action. Audience is adolescent to adult. The age varies with each series. (For instance, adolescents prefer *Airboy*, a teen hero, while adults prefer *Scout*, a post-holocaust science fiction series with strong romantic and political overtones.)" Publishes 24 comics/month on average. Most are monthlies, some bi-monthly; others are one-shots or mini-series. Circ. 30,000-80,000, depending on title. Does not accept previously published material except for reprint collections by famous comic book artists. Original artwork returned after publication. Sample copy $1.75; art guidelines for SASE.
Cartoons: "We buy entire illustrated stories, not individual cartoons. We buy approximately 6,250 pages of comic book art by freelancers/year—about 525/month." Interested in realistic illustrative comic book artwork—drawing the human figure in action; good, slick finishes (inking); ability to do righteous 1-, 2- and 3-point perspective required. "The bulk of our material continues to be color comics in the realistic action vein." Formats: b&w line drawings or fully painted pages with balloon lettering on overlays. Send query letter with samples of style to be kept on file. "Send minimum of 4-5 pages of full-size (10x15) photocopies of pencilled *storytelling* (and/or inked too)—no display poses, just typical action layout continuities." Material not filed is returned by SASE. Reports within 2 months by SASE only. Buys first rights and reprint rights. Pays $100-200/page, b&w; "price is for pencils plus inks; many artists only pencil for us, or only ink."; on acceptance (net 30 days). Pays $25-35/page for painted or airbrushed coloring of greylines made from line-art; on acceptance (net 30 days).
Illustrations: "We buy 12-15 cover paintings for science fiction and horror books per year." Science fiction paintings: fully rendered science fiction themes (e.g. outer space, aliens); horror paintings: fully rendered horror themes (e.g. vampires, werewolves, etc.). Send query letter with business card and samples to be kept on file. Prefers slides, color photos or tear sheets as samples. Samples not filed are returned by SASE. Reports within 2 months by SASE only. Buys first rights or reprint rights. Pays $200-500, color; on acceptance (net 30 days).
Tips: Prefers "comic book art with perfect figure drawing, expressive anatomy, accurate use of perspective and good layouts which help continuity along." In comic book illustration, "the trend is towards greater individuality of style and less 'comic-booky' looking art."

***EDUCATIONAL OASIS**, Box 299, Carthage IL 62331-0299. (217)357-3981. Art Director: Tom Sjoerdsma. Magazine for children in grades 5-8. It is sent to teachers who reproduce the artwork for classroom use. Published 5 times/year. Combined circ. 100,000.
Illustrations: "Art is 60% freelanced. Art must be easily reproduced. It should use clean, black line." Prefers pen & ink. "Two- and three-color overlays are also used." Send query letter with photocopies. Samples are filed. Reports back within 2 weeks only if interested. Buys all rights. Work-for-hire. Pays $5/hour.

EIDOS MAGAZINE: Erotic Entertainment for Women, Box 96, Boston MA 02137-0096. (617)262-0096. Editor: Brenda L. Tatelbaum. Magazine emphasizing erotica and erotic entertainment

for women and men. Quarterly. Original artwork returned after publication.
Illustrations: Works with 12-15 artists/year. Send query letter with resume, tear sheets, Photostats and photographs. Samples are filed. Samples not filed are returned by SASE. Reports back within 2 months. Write to schedule an appointment to show a portfolio, which should include original/final art, Photostats and photographs. Buys first rights. "We have standard payment terms."
Tips: "We look for sensuous, sensitive, sophisticated erotica depicting mutually respective sexuality and images of the human form. Alternative to commercial mainstream men's and women's magazines. More images of men and couples are published in *Eidos* than female images. We do not want to see the kind of art published in commercial, mainstream monthlies."

ELECTRICAL APPARATUS, 400 N. Michigan Ave., Chicago IL 60611-4198. (312)321-9440. Managing Editor: Kevin N. Jones. Magazine. Readers include electrical engineers and technicians who maintain and service electrical equipment, particularly industrial motors, generators, transformers and related controls. Monthly. Circ. 15,000. Original artwork is not returned to the artist after publication. Sample copies $4.
Cartoons: Cartoon Editor: Horden Barr. Buys 3-4 cartoons/issue from freelancers.

***ELECTRICAL CONTRACTOR**, 7315 Wisconsin Ave., Bethesda MD 20814. (301)657-3110. Managing Editor: Walt Albro. Trade journal emphasizing management of electrical construction businesses. "We are a controlled-circulation magazine distributed to the owners and key employees of all electrical construction businesses in the U.S. We publish features and news of interest to the entire electrical construction industry." Monthly. Circ. 66,000. Original artwork is sometimes returned to the artist after publication. Sample copies available.
Illustrations: Buys 6-8 illustrations/year from freelancers. Works on assignment only. Prefers "a sophisticated look, suitable for a management magazine." Send query letter with resume. Samples are filed. Reports back only if interested. Call or write to schedule an appointment to show a portfolio, which should include original/final art. Buys one-time rights or reprint rights. Pays $100, color, cover; $25, b&w; $50, color, inside; on publication.

***ELECTRICAL WHOLESALING MAGAZINE & ELECTRICAL MARKETING NEWSLETTER**, 1221 6th Ave., New York NY 10020. (212)512-2181. Art Director: Jackie Sirvio. Trade magazine for white and blue collar workers in the electrical industry. Monthly. Circ. 18-20,000. Original artwork is returned to the artist after publication. Samples copies available.
Cartoons: Buys 5 cartoons/issue from freelancers. Prefers single panel, double panel or multiple panel without gagline; b&w line drawings or b&w washes. Call or send query letter. Samples are filed. Samples not filed are not returned. Reports back only if interested. Buys reprint rights or one-time rights. Negotiates payment.
Illustrations: Works on assignment only. Prefers pen & ink, airbrush, watercolor, oils and computer illustration. Call or send query letter with tear sheets. Samples are filed. Samples not filed are not returned. Reports back only if interested. Call to schedule an appointment to show a portfolio, which should include tear sheets, final reproduction/product, slides, color and b&w. Buys one-time rights or reprint rights. Negotiates payment. Pays on acceptance.
Tips: "We also buy computer graphics—illustrations and cartoons without gaglines. Pays by the project. We negotiate rights purchased."

ELECTRICAL WORLD, McGraw-Hill Inc., 11 W. 19TH St., New York NY 10011. (212)512-2440. Art Director: Kiyo Komoda. Emphasizes operation, maintenance and use of electric utility facilities. For electric utility management and engineers. Monthly. Original artwork returned after publication, on request. Pays $50-150 b&w, $80-200 color; on acceptance.
Cartoons: Buys 1 cartoon/issue from freelancers, works on assignment only. Interested in industry-related situation cartoon, usually related to editorial articles. Buys one-time and reprint rights. Pays on acceptance.
Illustrations: Uses 15 illustrations/issue, buys 9 from freelancers. Interested in energy systems; 90% are mechanical line drawings, maps, flow designs, graphs and charts. Works on assignment only. Samples returned by SASE. Provide resume or business card to be kept on file for future assignments. Prefers to see portfolio or finished art. Reports in 1 week. Buys one-time and reprint rights. Cover: Pays $100-200, b&w line drawings, $200-300 full color; on acceptance.
Tips: "We prefer artists with clean and crisp line work. They should know about color separation and overlays. Young artists welcomed."

***ELECTRONIC BUSINESS**, 275 Washington St., Newton MA 02101. Art Director: Bill Cooke. "*Electronic Business* is written for corporate managers in the electronics industry. It presents news, trends and analysis of events that impact the industry." Published twice a month. Circ. 64,000. Accepts previously

published material. Original artwork is returned to the artist after publication. Sample copies available. Art guidelines not available.
Illustrations: Buys 1-3 illustrations/issue from freelancers. Buys 60-70 illustrations/year from freelancers. Prefers watercolor, then pen & ink, airbrush, colored pencil, acrylics, pastels, mixed media, and computer illustration. Works on assignment only. Send query letter with brochure showing art style or tear sheets, Photostats and photocopies. Samples are filed. Samples not filed are returned by SASE only if requested. Reports back only if interested. Write to schedule an appointment to show a portfolio, which should include original/final art, tear sheets, final reproduction/product and Photostats. Negotiates rights purchased.
Tips: "In a portfolio, show conceptual, editorial style illustration. I do not want to see children's book stuff."

ELECTRONIC COMMUNICATION, INC., Suite 220, 1311 Executive Center Dr., Tallahasee FL 32301. (904)878-4178. Art Director: Faye Howell. Three publications emphasizing educational technology for kindergarten to high school principals, teachers, and administrators and also college and upper educational teachers and administrators. Monthly, bimonthly and quarterly. Circ. 275,000; 70,000; 34,000. Original material not returned after publication. Sample copy for SASE with postage for three ounces.
Illustrations: Buys 0-3 illustrations/issue from freelancers. Works on assignment only. Send query letter with brochure showing art style. Samples not filed are returned only if requested. Reports only if interested. To show a portfolio, mail appropriate materials, which should include final reproduction/product, color and tear sheets. Negotiates rights purchased. Payment "varies widely;" pays on publication.

***ELECTRONIC MEDIA**, 740 Rush St., Chicago IL 60611. (312)649-5293. Contact: Susan Graening. "Our editorial content includes coverage of the broadcast industry and all its avenues." Weekly. Circ. 28,000. Original artwork is sometimes returned to the artist after publication. Sample copies available. Art guidelines not available.
Illustrations: Buys 20 illustrations/year from freelancers. Send query letter with brochure showing art style. Samples are filed. Reports back within 2-3 days. Call or write to schedule an appointment to show a portfolio, which should include original/final art, color and b&w (anything would be fine). Negotiates rights purchased. Pays on acceptance.
Tips: "Call/write early in the week. Our busiest season is September-February."

ELECTRONICS, McGraw-Hill Publishing Co., 1221 Avenue of the Americas, New York NY 10020. (212)512-2430. Art Director: Fred Sklenar. Emphasizes electronic technology, news and new products—very high-tech, for the trade only. For electronics engineers, marketing people and executives. Biweekly. Circ. 150,000. Original artwork returned after publication. Photocopied and simultaneous submissions OK.
Cartoons: "Cartoons illustrations are on assignment to illustrate a specific article. All types might be considered." Call to scheudle an appointment to show a portfolio. Samples are filed. Reports back only if interested. Buys first rights. Pays $150, b&w.
Illustrations: Buys 10 illustrations/issue from freelancers. Receives 20-30 illustrations/week from freelance artists. Buys 26 covers/year on assigned conceptual themes. Uses all media and all styles. Prefers airbrush, acrylics and pen & ink. Works on assignment only. "Personal interview would be best way to contact." Samples returned by SASE. Provide tear sheet and sample art to be kept on file for future assignments. Prefers finished art, portfolio, samples of style, or tear sheets as samples. Buys all first-time world rights. Cover: Pays $1,000 minimum, color. Inside: Pays $150, b&w; $1,000, color.
Tips: "Prepare portfolio professionally and have samples ready to leave so they may be kept on file. Include a variety of subjects and concepts, not only 'people'."

EMERGENCY MEDICINE MAGAZINE, 249 W. 17th St., New York NY 10011. (212)645-0067. Art Director: Lois Erlacher. Emphasizes emergency medicine for primary care physicians, emergency room personnel, medical students. Bimonthly. Circ. 129,000. Returns original artwork after publication.
Illustrations: Buys 3-4 illustrations/issue from freelancers. Prefers all media except markers and computer illustration. Works on assignment only. Send tear sheets, transparencies, original art or Photostats to be kept on file. Samples not filed are not returned. To show a portfolio, mail appropriate materials. Reports only if interested. Buys first rights. Pays $750 for color, cover; $250-500, b&w and $500-600, color, inside; on acceptance.
Tips: "Portfolios may be dropped off any day of the week. Art Director prefers to keep overnight—call first. Show a representative samplier of work."

***ENTREPRENEUR MAGAZINE**, 2392 Morse Ave., Box 19787, Irvine CA 92714-6234. Editor: Rieva Lesonsky. Design Director: Richard R. Olson. Magazine offers how-to information for starting a busi-

ness plus ongoing information and support to those already in business. Monthly. Circ. 250,000. Original artwork returned after publication. Sample copy $3.
Illustrations: Uses varied number of illustrations/issue; buys varied number/issue from freelancers. Works on assignment only. Send query letter with resume, samples and tear sheets to be kept on file. Write for appointment to show portfolio. Buys all rights. Payment varies; on publication.

ENVIRONMENT, 4000 Albemarle St. NW, Washington DC 20016. (202)362-6445. Production Graphics Editor: Ann Rickerich. Emphasizes national and international environmental and scientific issues. Readers range from "high school students and college undergrads to scientists, business and government leaders and college and university professors." Circ. 12,500. Published 10 times/year. Original artwork returned after publication if requested. Sample copy $4.50; cartoonist's guidelines available.
Cartoons: Uses 0-1 cartoon/issue; buys all from freelancers. Receives 2 submissions/week from freelancers. Interested in single panel b&w line drawings or b&w washes with or without gagline. Send finished cartoons. SASE. Reports in 2 months. Buys first North American serial rights. Pays $35, b&w cartoon; on publication.
Illustrations: Buys 0-5/year from freelance artists. Send query letter, brochure, tear sheets and photocopies. To show a portfolio, mail original/final art or reproductions. Pays $200 b&w, cover; $50-200 b&w, inside; on publication.
Tips: "Regarding cartoons, we prefer the witty to the slapstick." For illustrations, "we are looking for an ability to communicate complex environmental issues and ideas in an unbiased way."

***EQUILIBRIUM 10**, Box 162, Golden CO 80402. Graphic Coordinator: Gary Eagle. Magazine emphasizing equilibrium: balance, opposites and antonyms for all ages. Monthly. Accepts previously published material.
Cartoons: Buys 20 cartoons/issue from freelancers. Accepts any format. Send query letter with samples and finished cartoons. Samples not filed are returned by SASE. Reports back within 3 months. Rights purchased vary. Pays $10-20, color; on publication.
Illustrations: Buys 10 illustrations/issue from freelancers. Send query letter with brochure and samples. Samples are filed. Samples not filed are returned by SASE. Reports back within 3 months. Negotiates rights purchased. Pays $45, b&w cover; on publication.
Tips: "Letters and queries arriving at our office become the property of our firm and may and will be published 'as is'."

ESQUIRE, 1790 Broadway, New York NY 10019. (212)459-7500. Art Director: Ms. Wendall Harrington. Emphasizes politics, business, the arts, sports and the family for American men.
Illustrations: Buys 1-10 illustrations/issue, depending on special sections. Send brochure showing art style or resume and tear sheets. To show a portfolio, mail original/final art, final reproduction/product, color, tear sheets, photographs and b&w. Pays on acceptance.

ETERNITY MAGAZINE, 1716 Spruce St., Philadelphia PA 19103. (215)546-3696. Art Director: Teresa J. Hill. Emphasizes news and news trends from a Christian viewpoint 20-70 years of age. Monthly. Circ. 38,000. Accepts previously published material. Original artwork returned after publication. Sample copy $2; art guidelines available.
Illustrations: Buys 5-7 illustrations/year from freelancers. Themes range from sports to politics to environment to family. Usually prefers a traditional style. Prefers pen & ink. Works on assignment only. Send query letter with resume, tear sheets, Photostats, photocopies, slides and photographs. "Please do not send original work." Samples returned by SASE. Reports only if interested. Call or write to schedule an appointment to show a portfolio, which should include original art, final reproduction/product, color, tear sheets and b&w. Buys one-time rights. Pays $75-250, color only on cover; $35-75, b&w or color, inside; on acceptance.
Tips: "Illustrations should be strong with good tonal variations and are on a project basis. Portfolio should include mechanicals, roughs and different styles."

EUROPE, MAGAZINE OF THE EUROPEAN COMMUNITY, Seventh Floor, 2100 M St. NW, Washington DC 20037. (202)862-9500. Editor: Webster Martin. Emphasizes European affairs, US-European relations—particularly economics, trade and politics. Readers are businessmen, professionals, academics, government officials and consumers. Published 10 times/year. Circ. 65,000. Free sample copy.
Cartoons: Occasionally uses cartoons, mostly from a cartoon service. "The magazine publishes articles on US-European relations in economics, trade, business, industry, politics, energy, inflation, etc." Considers single panel b&w line drawings or b&w washes with or without gagline. Send resume plus finished cartoons and/or samples. SASE. Reports in 3-4 weeks. Buys one-time rights. Pays $25; on publication.
Illustrations: Uses 3-5 illustrations/issue. "At present we work exclusively through our designer and

set up charts and graphs to fit our needs. We would be open to commissioning artwork should the need and opportunity arise. We look for economic graphs, tables, charts and story-related statistical artwork"; b&w line drawings and washes for inside. Send resume and photocopies of style. SASE. Reports in 3-4 weeks. To show a portfolio, mail original/final art. Buys all rights on a work-for-hire basis. Payment varies; on publication.

EVANGEL, 901 College Ave., Winona Lake IN 46590. (219)267-7656. Contact: Vera Bethel. Readers are 65% female, 35% male; ages 25-31; married; city-dwelling; mostly non-professional high school graduates. Circ. 35,000. Weekly.
Cartoons: Buys 1/issue on family subjects. Pays $10, b&w; on publication. Mail finished art.
Illustrations: Buys 1/issue on assigned themes. Pays $40, 2-color; on acceptance. Query with samples or slides. SASE. Reports in 1 month.

EVENT, Douglas College, Box 2503, New Westminster, British Columbia V3L 5B2 Canada. (604)520-5400. Editor: Dale Zieroth. For "those interested in literature and writing." Published 3 times/year. Circ. 1,000. Original artwork returned after publication. Sample copy $4.
Illustrations: Buys approximately 3/year. "Interested in drawings and prints, b&w line drawings, photographs and lithographs for cover and inside, and thematic or stylishic series of 12-20 works. Work must reproduce well in one color." SAE (non residents include IRC). Reporting time varies; at least 2 months. Buys first North American serial rights. Pays honorarium plus complimentary copy on publication.

THE EXCEPTIONAL PARENT, 605 Commonwealth Ave., Boston MA 02215. (617)536-8961. Editor: Stanley Klein. "A national consumer publication for parents and professionals who are concerned with the education of children and young adults with disabilities. We publish on a wide range of topics: health care, education, technology, recreation, employment, etc." 8 issues/year. Circ. 40,000. Accepts previously published material. Original artwork returned after publication. Sample copy and editorial guidelines $5 with SASE.

EXPECTING MAGAZINE, 685 Third Ave., New York NY 10017. (212)878-8700. Art Director: Azade Erhun. Emphasizes pregnancy, birth and care of the newborn; for pregnant women and new mothers. Quarterly. Circ. 1.2 million distributed through obstetrician and gynecologist offices nationwide. Original artwork returned after publication.
Illustrations: Buys approximately 6/issue. Color only. Works on assignment. "We have a drop-off policy for looking at portfolios; include a card to be kept on file." Buys one-time rights. Pays within 30 days after publication.

THE EYE MAGAZINE, 11th & Washington Sts., Wilmington DE 19801. (302)571-6978. Art Director: Paul A. Miles. Tabloid for high school students; all writing, cartoons, photographs, etc. are produced by high-school age cartoonists and artists. Monthly October through May. Circ. 25,000. Accepts previously published material. Original artwork returned after publication. Sample copy for SASE with 37¢ postage.
Cartoons: Uses 1 cartoon/issue. Prefers single panel with gagline; b&w line drawings. Prefers themes showing resourcefulness of young people. "We prefer ones that do not show teens in a derogatory manner." Send query letter with samples of style to be kept on file. Material not kept on file is returned by SASE. Reports within 30 days. Buys one-time rights.
Illustrations: Buys 1 illustration/issue from freelancers. Works on assignment only. Primary theme is teenagers; artist must be 14-19 years old. Prefers b&w high-contrast or pen & ink drawing; or charcoal/pencil, markers and computer illustration. Send query letter with resume and photocopies. Samples not filed are returned by SASE. Reports within 30 days. "We do not see portfolios." Buys one-time rights. Pays $25, b&w, cover; $10, b&w, inside. "Our publication is a nonprofit publication to give students a voice to their peers and adults. We are a training ground and as such do not pay very much for editorial or artwork. We will gladly give copies of publication and letters of recommendations to high school students interested in getting something published."
Tips: "Don't expect very much from us. We are small and like to help artists; not monetarily, but through public work."

***F.O.C.U.S. (Focus in Coaching and Understanding Sport),** Published by Coaching Association of Canada, 333 River Rd., Ottawa, Ontario K1L 8H9 Canada. (613)748-5624. Editor: Steve Newman. Continuing series of 16-20 page booklets concentrating on one topic. Geared to coaches working with teenage athletes. Especially needs good practical applied information that is original; creative illustration; sport specific and life-like illustration. Original artwork returned after publication. Free sample copy.

Illustrations: Buys 2-8 illustrations/issue from freelancers. Illustrations should be in the style of "creative realism . . . depicting athletes in action." Prefers color washes for cover and inside; b&w line drawings for inside. Reports in 2 weeks. Call to schedule an appointment to show a portfolio, which should include color, tear sheets, Photostats and b&w. Negotiates payment.
Tips: There is a trend toward "realistic illustration showing coaching techniques. Read the magazine before sending in work."

***FAMILY CIRCLE**, 110 5th Ave., New York NY 10011. Art Director: Doug Turshen. Circ. 7,000,000. Supermarket-distributed publication for women/homemakers covering areas of food, home, beauty, health, child care and careers. 17 issues/year. Does not accept previously published material. Original artwork returned after publication. Sample copy and art guidelines not available.
Cartoons: No unsolicited cartoon submissions accepted. Reviews in office first Wednesday of each month. Uses 1-2 cartoons/issue. Prefers themes related to women's interests, feminist viewpoint. Uses limited seasonal material, primarily Christmas. Prefers single panel with gagline, b&w line drawings or washes. Buys all rights. Pays $325 on acceptance. Contact Christopher Cavanaugh, (212)463-1000, for cartoon query only.
Illustrations: Uses 20 illustrations/issue, all from freelancers. Works on assignment only. Reports only if interested. Provide query letter with samples to be kept on file for future assignments. Prefers slides or tear sheets as samples. Samples returned by SASE. Prefers to see portfolio (finished art). Submit portfolio on "portfolio days," every Wednesday. All art is commissioned for specific magazine articles. Reports in 1 week. Buys all rights on a work-for-hire basis. Pays on acceptance.

FAMILY MOTOR COACHING, 8291 Clough Pike, Cincinnati OH 45244. (513)474-3622. Editor: Pamela Wisby Kay. Emphasizes self-contained motor homes for families who own or enjoy the recreational use of such vehicles. Monthly. Circ. 50,000. Original artwork returned after publication, "if requested." Sample copy $2.50; art guidelines available with SASE.
Cartoons: Uses 1-5 cartoons/issue; buys all from freelancers. Themes "must pertain to motorhoming, RV lifestyle, travel, or the outdoors. No trailers." Prefers single, double, or multi panel with or without gagline, b&w line drawings, b&w washes. Send finished cartoons. Samples returned by SASE. Reports in 4-6 weeks. Buys first rights. Pays $20, b&w; on publication.

FAMILY PLANNING PERSPECTIVES, 111 5th Ave., New York NY 10003. (212)254-5656. Production Manager: Diana Nolan. Trade journal emphasizing family planning and contraceptive technology for health-care providers. Features technical articles. Bimonthly. Circ. 16,000. Original artwork returned after publication. Sample copy available.
Cartoons: Buys 1 cartoon/year from freelancers. Prefers single panel, without gagline; b&w line drawings. Send query letter with finished cartoons. Samples are filed. Samples not filed are returned by SASE. Reports back only if interested. Buys one-time rights. Pays $50, b&w.
Illustrations: Buys 1-2 illustrations/year from freelancers. Send query letter with brochure or resume. Samples are filed. Samples not filed are returned by SASE. Reports back only if interested. Call to schedule an appointment to show a portfolio, which should include original/final art, tear sheets and photographs. Buys one-time rights. Pays $250-400, b&w; $350-550, color, cover; $80-125, b&w, inside; on publication.

FANFARE, Box 720, Tenafly NJ 07670. (201)567-3908. Editor: Joel Flegler. Magazine emphasizing classical record reviews for classical record collectors. Bimonthly. Circ. 20,000. Accepts previously published material. Original artwork returned after publication. Sample copy $5.
Illustrations: Buys 1 illustration/issue from freelancers. Prefers anything to do with music as themes. Send query letter with resume and samples. Samples not filed are returned by SASE. Reports only if interested. Call to discuss artwork; no appointments. Buys one-time rights. Pays $100, color, cover; on acceptance.

FANTAGRAPHIC BOOKS, Suite 101, 1800 Bridgegate St., West Lake Village, CA 91361. (805)379-1881. Contact: Gary Groth or Kim Thompson. Publishes comic books and graphic novels. Titles include *Love and Rockets*, *Amazing Heroes*, *Los Tejanos*, *Anything Goes*, *Lloyd Llewelyn*, *Neat Stuff* and *Critters*. All genres except superheroes. Monthly and bimonthly depending on titles. Circ. 8-30,000. Sample copy $2.50.
Illustrations: Fantagraphic is looking for artists who can create an entire product or who can work as part of an established team. Most of the titles are black and white. Send query letter with samples which display storytelling capabilities, or submit a complete package. All artwork is creator-owned. Buys one-time rights usually. Payment terms vary. Creator receives an advance upon acceptance and then royalties after publication.

FARM SUPPLIER, Watt Publishing Co., Mount Morris IL 61054. Editorial Director: Clayton Gill. Editor: Karen McMillan. For retail farm suppliers and dealers throughout the U.S. Monthly (except June and July).
Illustrations: "We use color slides that match editorial material. They should relate to the farm supply retail business, including feed, custom application of chemicals and fertilizers." Send query letter with slides. To show a portfolio, mail photographs and slides. Pays $150 color, cover; on acceptance.

THE FIDDLEHEAD, Old Arts Bldg., University of New Brunswick, Frederiction, New Brunswick E3B 5A3 Canada. (506)453-3501. Editor: Michael Taylor. Emphasizes poetry, short stories, essays and book reviews for a general audience. Quarterly. Circ. 1,050. Original artwork returned after publication. Sample copy U.S. $4.25 plus postage (nonresidents include IRC).
Illustrations: Buys 3-5 illustrations/issue from freelancers. Prefers pen & ink. Send query letter with tear sheets, Photostats and photocopies to be filed "if considered suitable." Samples returned by SAE (include Canadian stamps or IRC). Reports within 6-8 weeks. Buys first rights. Pays $50, b&w and $75, color, cover; $20, b&w, inside; on publication.
Tips: "I want to see drawings which show skill, originality and concepts which can stand on their own—ie, not illustration. I do not want to see cartoons, doodles, copies or illustrations."

FIELD & STREAM MAGAZINE, 1515 Broadway, New York NY 10036. (212)719-6552. Art Director: Victor J. Closi. Magazine emphasizing wildlife hunting and fishing. Monthly. Circ. 2 million. Original artwork returned after publication. Sample copy and art guidelines for SASE.
Illustrations: Buys 9-12 illustrations/issue from freelancers. Works on assignment only. Prefers "good drawing and painting ability, realistic style, some conceptual and humorous styles are also used depending on magazine article." Send query letter with brochure showing art style or tear sheets and slides. Samples not filed are returned only if requested. Reports only if interested. Call or write to schedule an appointment to show a portfolio, which should include roughs, original/final art, final reproduction/product and tear sheets. Buys first rights. Payment varies: $75-300 on simple spots; $500-1,000 single page; $1,000 and up on spreads, and $1,500 and up on covers; on acceptance.

THE FINAL EDITION, Box 294, Rhododendron OR 97049. (503)622-4798. Editor: Michael P. Jones. Estab. 1985. Investigative journal that deals "with a variety of subjects—environment, wildlife, crime, etc. for professional and blue collar people who want in-depth reporting." Monthly. Circ. 1,500. Accepts previously published material. Original artwork is returned after publication. Art guidelines for SASE with 1 first-class stamp.
Cartoons: Buys 1-18 cartoons/issue from freelancers. Prefers single panel, double panel, multi panel, with or without gagline; b&w line drawings, b&w or color washes. Send query letter with samples of style, roughs or finished cartoons. Samples are filed. Samples not filed are returned by SASE. Reports back within 2 weeks. Buys one-time rights. Pays in copies.
Illustrations: Buys 10 illustrations/issue from freelancers. Prefers pen & ink, aribrush, pencil, markers, calligraphy and computer illustration. Send query letter with brochure showing art style or resume and tear sheets, Photostats, photocopies, slides or photographs. Samples not filed are returned by SASE. Reports back within 2 weeks. To show a portfolio, mail thumbnails, roughs, original/final art, final reproduction/product, color, tear sheets, Photostats, photographs or b&w. Buys one-time rights. Pays in copies.
Tips: "We have a real need for nonfiction illustrations. *The Final Edition* deals with real things and real events, not science fiction. The type of illustrations we are looking for must deal with the subject matter of *The Final Edition* for that month, it may be on Bison, wolves, wild horses, wiretapping, environmental social justice issues, or profiling the life history of an individual. I want to see everything from wilderness to urban scenes. I want to know the wide range of topics an artist can illustrate."

***THE FINGER LAKES MAGAZINE**, 108 S. Albany St., Ithaca NY 14850. (607)272-3470. Editor: Linda McCandles. Magazine emphasizing Finger Lakes region of New York state. "We are a regional magazine published seasonally (four times a year) that covers the people and places of interest in the Finger Lakes." Quarterly. Circ. 18,000. Original artwork is returned after publication. Sample copies $2.
Cartoons: Buys 1 cartoon/issue from freelancers. Buys 4 cartoons/year from freelancers. Prefers single or multi panel; b&w line drawings. Send query letter with samples of style. Samples are filed. Samples not filed are returned by SASE. Reports back within 4 weeks. Buys first rights. Pays $50-100, b&w.
Illustrations: Buys 1 illustration/issue from freelancers. Buys 4-6 illustrations/year from freelancers. Works on assignment only. Send query letter with tear sheets. Samples are filed. Samples not filed are returned by SASE. Reports back within 4 weeks. Write to schedule an appointment to show portfolio, or mail thumbnails, tear sheets, color and b&w. Buys first rights. Pays $150-200, color, cover; $25-50, b&w; $50-100, color, inside; on publication.
Tips: "The artist should be from the Finger Lakes region."

FIRST HAND LTD., 310 Cedar Ln., Teaneck NJ 07666. (201)836-9177. Art Director: Laura Patricks. Emphasizes homoerotica for a male audience. Monthly. Circ. 60,000. Sample copy $3; art guidelines available for SASE.
Cartoons: Buys 5 cartoons/issue from freelancers. Prefers single panel with gagline; b&w line drawings. Send finished cartoons to be kept on file. Material not filed is returned by SASE. Reports within 2 weeks. Buys first rights. Pays $15 for b&w; on acceptance.
Illustrations: Buys 20 illustrations/issue from freelancers. Prefers "nude men in a realistic style; very basic, very simple." Send query letter with Photostats or tear sheets to be kept on file. Samples not filed are returned. Reports within 2 weeks. Call or write for appointment to show portfolio. Buys all magazine rights. Pays for design by the hour, $10. Pays $25-50 for inside b&w; on acceptance.
Tips: "I like to see current work, not work that is too old. And I prefer to see printed samples if that is possible."

FIRST PUBLISHING, 435 N. LaSalle, Chicago IL 60610. (312)670-6770. Art Director: Alex Wald. Publishes comic books and graphic novels including *Badger* and *American Flagg*.
Illustrations: Prefers comic storytelling with well-realized figures. Uses freelance artists for inking, lettering, pencilling, color work and covers. Send query letter with photocopies of original art, which should be proportional to 10x15; include your name, address and phone number on every sample page. Samples are sometimes filed. Call to schedule an appointment to show a portfolio. Negotiates rights purchased and payment. All material is invoiced. Payment is upon receipt. 30-60 days after acceptance.

FISH BOAT, Box 2400, Covington LA 70434. Managing Editor: Robert Carpenter. Trade journal emphasizing commercial fishing. Features general interest and technical articles. Monthly. Circ. 19,500. Accepts previously published material. Original artwork returned after publication. Sample copy $3. Finds most artists through samples received through the mail.
Illustrations: Buys 2 illustrations/issue from freelancers. Buys 10 illustrations/year from freelancers. Prefers mixed media and computer illustration. Send query letter with slides and photographs. Artists should target their samples to the magazines needs. Samples are filed. Samples not filed are returned. To show a portfolio, mail slides, color and b&w. Buys all rights. Pays $125, color, cover. Pays on acceptance.

FISHING WORLD, 51 Atlantic Ave., New York NY 11001. (516)352-9700. Editor: Keith Gardner. Emphasizes angling. Readers are adult male U.S. sport fishermen. Editorial content is a mix of how-to and where-to with emphasis on the former, that is, on advanced use of tackle and techniques. Bimonthly. Circ. 350,000. Original artwork returned after publication. Sample copy $1.
Illustrations: Buys 3-6 illustrations/year from freelancers. Interested in realistic illustrations. Uses inside color washes. Works on assignment only. Send query letter with slides. Samples are filed. Samples not filed are returned only if requested by artist. SASE. Reports in 3 weeks. Buys first North American serial rights. Pays $300 for color, cover; $200 color, inside; on acceptance.
Tips: "Know the sport and milieu."

FLING, Relim Publishing Co., 550 Miller Ave., Mill Valley CA 94941. (415)383-5464. Editor: Arv Miller. Bimonthly. Emphasizes sex, seduction, sports, underworld pieces, success stories, travel, adventure and how-to for men, 18-34. Sample copy for $5.
Cartoons: Prefers sexual themes. "The female characters must be pretty, sexy and curvy, with extremely big breasts. Styles should be sophisticated and well-drawn." Pays $30, b&w, $50-100, color; on acceptance.

FLORIST, Florists Transworld Delivery Association, Box 2227, Southfield MI 48037. (313)355-9300. Editor-in-Chief: William Golden. Production Manager: Margaret Baumgarten. Managing Editor: Susan Nicholas. Emphasizes information pertaining to the operation of the floral industry. For florists and floriculturists. Monthly. Circ. 24,000. Reports in 1 month. Accepts previously published material. Does not return original artwork after publication.
Cartoons: Buys 3 cartoons/issue. Interested in retail florists and floriculture themes; single panel with gagline. Mail samples or roughs. SASE. Buys one-time rights. Pays $20, b&w line drawings; on acceptance.
Illustrations: Works on assignment only. Send query letter with Photostats, tear sheets, photocopies, slides or photographs. Samples not filed are returned by SASE. Reports within 3 months. To show a portfolio, mail final reproduction/product, tear sheets, Photostats and photographs. Buys first rights.

FLOWER AND GARDEN, 4251 Pennsylvania, Kansas City MO 64111. (816)531-5730. Editor: Rachel Snyder. Emphasizes "gardening for avid home gardeners." Bimonthly. Circ. 630,000. Sample copy $2.

Cartoons: Uses 1 cartoon/issue. Receives about 10 submissions/week. Needs cartoons related to "indoor or outdoor home gardening." Format: single panel b&w line drawings or washes with gagline. Prefers to see finished cartoons. SASE. Reports in 4 weeks. Buys one-time rights. Pays $20, b&w cartoon; on acceptance.

THE FLYFISHER, 1387 Cambridge Dr., Idaho Falls ID 83401. (208)523-7300. Editor: Dennis G. Bitton. For members of the Federation of Fly Fishers. Concerns fly fishing and conservation. Quarterly. Circ. 10,000. Buys first North American serial rights. Sample copy $3 from Federation of Fly Fishers main office, Box 1088, West Yellowstone, MT 59758.
Cartoons: Buys 3-4 cartoons/issue. Pays $25 b&w; $25-150 color.
Illustrations: Interested in fly-fishing themes. Send query letter with tear sheets, Photostats and photocopies. Samples returned by SASE. Reports in 2 weeks. To show a portfolio, mail appropriate materials. Buys first North American serial rights. Pays $150-200 b&w and; $150-200 color, cover; $25-150 b&w and; $35-150 color, inside; on publication.
Tips: "We always encourage freelancers to submit material. The possibility for a sale is good with good material. We especially look for an artist's ability to illustrate an article by reading the copy. See a current issue of the magazine. In general there is better line art."

FOOD & SERVICE NEWS,Box 1429, Austin TX 78767. (512)444-6543. Editor: Bland Crowder. Art Director: Neil Ferguson. Official trade publication of Texas Restaurant Association. Seek materials dealing with business problems of restaurant owners and foodservice operators, primarily in Texas, and including managers of clubs, bars and hotels. Published 11 times/year. Circ. 5,000. Simultaneous submissions OK. Sample copy for SASE.
Cartoons: Not used.
Illustrations: Seeks high-quality b&w or color artwork in variety of styles (airbrush, watercolor, pastel, pen & ink, etc.). Seeks versatile artists who can illustrate articles about foodservice industry, particularly business aspects. Works on assignment only. Query with resume, samples and tear sheets. Call for appointment to show portfolio. Pays for illustration by the project $50-400. Negotiates rights and payment upon assignment. Returns original artwork after publication.
Tips: "We try to provide business solutions in *Food & Service*, and illustrations are often surreal depictions of the problems or solutions. I look for innovative, professional and unique styles."

FOOD & WINE, 1120 Avenue of the Americas, New York NY 10036. (212)382-5702. Art Director: Elizabeth Woodson. Emphasizes food and wine for "an upscale audience who cook, entertain and dine out stylishly." Monthly. Circ. 750,000.
Illustrations: Buys all from freelancers. Interested in sophisticated style; if humorous, not cartoony. Prefers colored pencil, pen & ink, watercolor and pastels. Works on assignment and pick up. Send brochure and samples of style to be kept on file; drop portfolio off on third Tuesday of the month only. Reports when assignment is available. Buys one-time rights. Pays $100 minimum, inside, b&w line drawings; on acceptance.
Tips: "I do not want to clip-art style black and white food drawings. We never use renderings of food."

FOOD PROCESSING, Putman Publishing Co., 301 E. Erie, Chicago IL 60611. (312)644-2020. Editor/Publisher: Roy Hlavacek. Emphasizes equipment, new developments, laboratory instruments and government regulations of the food processing industry. For executives and managers in food processing industries. Monthly. Circ. 64,000. Photocopied submissions OK. Original artwork not returned after publication. Free sample copy and artist's guidelines.
Cartoons: Buys 1-2 cartoons/issue, from freelancers. Receives 10-15 submissions/week from freelancers. Interested in "situations in and around the food plant (e.g., mixing, handling, transporting, weighing, analyzing, government inspection, etc.)"; single panel with gagline. Prefers to see finished cartoons. SASE. Reports in 1 week. Buys all rights. Pays $20 minimum, b&w line drawings.
Tips: "Avoid most 'in-the-home' and all retailing cartoon situations. Stick to in-the-food-plant situations—meat packing, vegetable and fruit canning, candymaking, beverage processing, bakery, dairy—including any phase of processing, inspecting, handling, quality control, packaging, storage, shipping, etc."

***FORECAST FOR HOME ECONOMICS**, 730 Broadway, New York NY 10003. (212)505-3000. Art Editor: Roe Lobretto. Used as a teaching guide for *Choices* magazine. Circ. 78,000. Monthly (September-June). SASE. Pays on publication.
Illustrations: Occasionally needs story illustrations. Pays $50-450, b&w; $50-1,000, color; varies according to size. Arrange interview to show portfolio.

FOREIGN SERVICE JOURNAL, 2101 E St. NW, Washington DC 20037. (202)338-4045. Contact: Assistant Editor. Emphasizes foreign policy for foreign service employees. Monthly. Circ. 9,000. Accepts previously published material. Returns original artwork after publication. Sample copy for SASE with 87¢ postage.
Cartoons: Write or call for appointment to show portfolio. Buys first rights. Pays on publication.
Illustrations: Buys 1-2 illustrations/issue from freelancers. Works on assignment only. Write or call for appointment to show portfolio. Buys first rights. Pays on publication.

FOREST NOTES, 54 Portsmouth St., Concord NH 03301. (603)224-9945. Editor: Richard Ober. Magazine emphasizing conservation and environmental news. "*Forest Notes* offers news of conservation, forestry and environmental issues in New Hampshire and New England. Quarterly. Circ. 8,000. Accepts previously published material. Original artwork sometimes returned after publication. Sample copy available.
Cartoons: Buys 1 cartoon/issue from freelancers. Buys 4 cartoons/year from freelancers. Prefers people-oriented, nonsensational art for upscale readers. Prefers single panel without gagline; b&w line drawings. Send query letter with samples of style. Samples are filed. Samples not filed are returned. Reports back within 3 weeks. Buys first or reprint rights. Pays $50 maximum, b&w.
Illustrations: Buys 1 illustration/issue from freelancers. Buys 4 illustrations/year from freelancers. Works on assignment only. Send query letter with brochure or tear sheets. Samples are filed. Reports back within 3 weeks. To show a portfolio, mail Photostats. Buys first or reprint rights. Pays $50, b&w. Pays on acceptance.
Tips: "Live and work in New Hampshire or New England."

4 WHEEL & OFF-ROAD MAGAZINE, 8490 Sunset Blvd., Los Angeles CA 90069. (213)854-2222. Art Director: Karen Hawley. Magazine emphasizing 4-wheel drive vehicles for males aged 16-35. Monthly. Circ. 350-400,000.
Cartoons: Buys 1-3 cartoons/issue from freelancers. Prefers single or multiple panel; b&w line drawings. Send samples of style to be kept on file. Call to schedule an appointment to show a portfolio. Material not kept on file is returned only if requested. Reports only if interested. Buys all rights.
Illustrations: Buys 0-3 illustrations/issue from freelancers. Works on assignment only. Send query letter with resume, tear sheets, Photostats and photocopies. Samples not filed are returned only if requested. Reports only if interested. Call or write to schedule an appointment to show a portfolio, which should include original/final art and final reproduction/product. Buys all rights. Pays on publication.

FREEWAY, Box 632, Glen Ellyn IL 60138. (312)668-6000. Designer: Mardelle Ayers. Sunday School paper emphasizing Christian living for high school and college age teens from a conservative, evangelical Christian upbringing. Published 4 quarters/year, 13 issues/quarter. Circ. 60,000. Accepts previously published material. Returns originals after publication. Sample copy for SASE with first-class postage.
Cartoons: Buys 4-5 cartoons/quarter. Prefers any style or theme that appeals to teens. Prefers single, double or multi panel with gagline; b&w line drawings or b&w washes. Send query letter with finished cartoons. Material not kept on file is returned by SASE. Reports within 4 weeks. Buys first rights. Pays $15, b&w.
Illustrations: Buys 1-3 illustrations/issue from freelancers. Works on assignment only. Prefers any theme or style appealing to teens. Send query letter with resume, Photostats and photocopies. Samples not filed are returned by SASE if requested. Reports only if interested. To show a portfolio, mail Photostats and b&w photos. Payment is variable; on acceptance.

***FRETS MAGAZINE, THE MAGAZINE FOR ACOUSTIC STRING MUSICIANS**, 20085 Stevens Creek, Cupertino CA 95014. (408)446-1105. Art Director: Courtney Granner. Magazine emphasizing acoustic string instrument playing, building and teaching for acoustic string instrument builders, players, teachers and salesmen. Monthly. Circ. 55,000. Accepts previously published material. Original artwork returned after publication if requested. Sample and/or art guidelines for SASE with first-class postage.
Cartoons: Rarely buys cartoons from freelancers. Send query letter with samples of style to be kept on file. Material not kept on file is returned only if requested. Does not report back. Buys one-time or reprint rights. Pays $45-150, b&w."

FRONT PAGE DETECTIVE, RGH Publications, 20th Floor, 460 W. 34th St., New York NY 10001. Editor: Rose Mandelsberg. For mature adults—law enforcement officials, professional investigators, criminology buffs and interested laymen. Monthly.
Cartoons: Must have crime theme. Submit finished art. SASE. Reports in 10 days. Buys all rights. Pays $25; on acceptance.
Tips: "Make sure the cartoons submitted do not degrade or ridicule law enforcement officials. Omit references to supermarkets/convenience stores."

***FUTURIFIC MAGAZINE**, Suite 1210, 280 Madison Ave., New York NY 10016. Publisher: B. Szent-Miklosy. Emphasizes future-related subjects for highly educated, upper income government, corporate leaders of the community. Monthly. Circ. 10,000. Previously published material and simultaneous submissions OK. Original artwork returned after publication. Free sample copy for SASE with $2 postage and handling.
Cartoons: Buys 5/issue from freelancers. Prefers positive, upbeat, futuristic themes; no "doom and gloom." Prefers single, double or multiple-panel with or without gagline, b&w line drawings. Send finished cartoons. Samples returned by SASE. Reports within 4 weeks. Will negotiate rights and payment. Pays on publication.
Illustrations: Buys 5 illustrations/issue from freelancers. Prefers positive, upbeat, futuristic themes; no "doom and gloom." Send finished art. Samples returned by SASE. Reports within 4 weeks. Call or write to schedule an appointment to show a portfolio. Will negotiate rights and payment. Pays on publication.
Tips: "Only optimists need apply. Looking for good, clean art. Interested in future development of current affairs, but not sci-fi."

THE FUTURIST, 4916 St. Elmo Ave., Bethesda MD 20814. (301)656-8274. Art Director: Cynthia Fowler. Managing Editor: Timothy H. Willard. Emphasizes all aspects of the future for a well-educated, general audience. Bimonthly. Circ. 30,000. Accepts simultaneous submissions. Return of original artwork following publication depends on individual agreement. Sample copy available.
Illustrations: Buys 3-4 illustrations/issue from freelancers. Uses a variety of themes and styles "usually line drawings, often whimsical. We like an artist who can read an article and deal with the concepts and ideas." Works on assignment only. Send query letter with brochure, samples or tear sheets to be kept on file. Call or write for appointment to show portfolio. "Photostats are fine as samples; whatever is easy for the artist." Reports only if interested. Rights purchased negotiable. Pays $300-500, color, cover; $100-125, b&w, inside; on acceptance.

GALLERY MAGAZINE, 800 2nd Ave., New York NY 10017. (212)986-9600. Creative Director: Michael Monte. Emphasizes sophisticated men's entertainment for the middle-class, collegiate male. Monthly. Circ. 700,000. No art guidelines, editorial content dictates illustration style.
Cartoons: Buys 5 cartoons/issue from freelancers. Interested in sexy humor; single, double, or multiple panel with or without gagline, color and b&w washes, b&w line drawings. Send finished cartoons. Reports in 1 month. Buys first rights. Pays on publication. Enclose SASE. Contact: J. Linden.
Illustrations: Buys 4-5 full-page illustrations monthly from freelancers. Works on assignment only. Interested in the "highest creative and technical styles." Especially needs slick, high quality, 4-color work. Send flyer, samples and tear sheets to be kept on file for possible future assignments. Send samples of style or submit portfolio. Samples returned by SASE. Reports in several weeks. Negotiates rights purchased. Pays $1,000 maximum for inside color washes; on publication.

GAMBLING TIMES, 1018 N. Cole Ave., Hollywood CA 90038. (213)466-5261. Editor-in-Chief: Len Miller. Art Director: David Gardner. Emphasizes gambling techniques and personalities in gambling. Monthly. Circ. 100,000. Original artwork returned after publication. Sample copy $1; free artist's guidelines.
Cartoons: Buys approximately 20/year on topic directly related to gambling. Prefers finished cartoon, full-page, single panel; b&w line drawings. SASE. Reports in 2 weeks. Buys all rights. Pays $25-100; on publication.
Illustrations: Uses 6-7 illustrations/issue; buys 5/issue from freelancers. Interested in simple and clean b&w line drawings; satirical or humorous visuals used occasionally. Works on assignment only. Samples returned by SASE. Provide business card or tear sheet to be kept on file for future assignments. Prefers to see portfolio. Reports in 1 week. Buys all rights on a work-for-hire basis. Pays $25-100; on publication.

GAMES, 810 Seventh Ave., New York NY 10019. (212)246-4640. Contact: Art Director. Emphasizes games, puzzles, mazes, brain teasers, etc. for adults interested in paper and pencil games. Bimonthly. Circ. 600,000.
Cartoons: Buys 1 cartoon/issue from freelancers. Pays $100 b&w and $200 color.
Illustrations: Buys 5-15 illustrations/issue from freelancers. Illustrations should be lighthearted but not childish. Send query letter with brochure showing art style or tear sheets. To show a portfolio, drop off on Wednesdays or mail tear sheets. Buys one-time rights. Pays $1,500 b&w; $2,500 color, cover.
Tips: "We encourage artists to create games or puzzles that they can execute in their own style after editorial approval. Illustrations are often required to be based on specific puzzles but can also be conceptual in nature."

GARDEN, New York Botanical Garden, Bronx NY 10458. Associate Editor: Jessica Snyder. Emphasizes all aspects of the plant world—botany, horticulture, the environment, etc. for "members of botanical gardens and arboreta—a diverse readership, largely college graduates and professionals, with a common interest in plants." Bimonthly. Circ. 30,000. Accepts previously published material. Original artwork returned after publication. Sample copy $3.
Illustrations: Works on assignment only. Send query letter with Photostats, photographs, tear sheets, slides or photocopies. Especially looks for "quality, botanical accuracy and style." Samples not kept on file are returned by SASE. Reports only if interested. To show a portfolio, mail appropriate materials. Buys one-time rights. Pays $35 minimum, color, inside; $150, color, cover; on publication.

GENERAL LEARNING CORPORATION, 60 Revere Dr., Northbrook IL 60062-1563. (312)564-4070. Photo and Graphics Editor: Cecily Rosenwald. Produces *Current Health 1*, *Current Health 2*, *Career World*, *Writing!* and *Current Consumer & Lifestudies* published monthly during the school year. Readership is 7-12th grade students. *Your Health & Fitness* is published bimonthly, *Energy Sense*, *Health Report*, *Money Plan* are quarterly. The readership is a general audience. Accepts previously published material. Original artwork returned after publication. Sample copy for 8x10 SASE.
Illustrations: Occasionally commissions original illustration. Prefers pen & ink, airbrush, watercolor, acrylics, oils, pastels, collage, markers, mixed media and computer illustration. Medical illustrator sought. Pays on publication. Negotiates rights purchased and payment for general magazines; on acceptance.
Tips: "Target your samples around medical illustration or on the topic of safe exercising. I do not want to see fashion pieces or anything sexy.

***GENESIS**, 770 Lexington Ave., New York NY 10021. (212)486-8430. Emphasizes celebrities, current events, issues and personal relationships. For the young male "celebrating all that is in the good life." Monthly. Circ. 300,000.
Cartoons: Contact Cartoon Editor. Uses 2-8 cartoons/issue, all from freelancers. Interested in erotic themes. Prefers finished cartoons. SASE. Reports in 2-4 weeks. Buys first North American serial rights. Pays $75-200, b&w or color; 30 days from acceptance.
Tips: "There is no need for any more black-and-white cartoons since we have enough in inventory for a number of years."

GENT, Dugent Publishing Co., 2355 Salzedo St., Coral Gables FL 33134. Publisher: Douglas Allen. Editor: Bruce Arthur. Managing Editor: Nye Willden. For men "who like big-breasted women." Sample copy, $5.
Cartoons: Buys humor and sexual themes; "major emphasis of magazine is on large D-cup-breasted women. We prefer cartoons that reflect this slant." Mail cartoons. Buys first rights. Pays $50, b&w spot drawing; $75/page.
Illustrations: Buys 3-4 illustrations/issue on assigned themes. Submit illustration samples for files. Buys b&w only. Buys first rights. Pays $125-150.
Tips: "Send samples designed especially for our publication. Study our magazine. Be able to draw erotic anatomy. Write for artist's guides and cartoon guides *first*, before submitting samples, since they contain some helpful suggestions."

GLAMOUR, 350 Madison Ave., New York NY 10017. (212)880-8800. Art Director: George Hartman. Emphasizes fashion, beauty, travel, lifestyle for women ages 18-35. Query with resume and arrange to show portfolio.
Needs: "All work done here is freelance." Pays $225/page.

GLASS DIGEST, 310 Madison Ave., New York NY 10017. Editor: Charles B. Cumpston. For management in the distribution, merchandising, and installation phases of the flat glass, architectural metal, and allied products industry (including stained, art glass and mirrors). Original artwork not returned after publication. Free sample copy.
Cartoons: Uses 0-3 cartoons/issue; buys about 2/issue from freelancers. Receives 5 submissions/week from freelancers. Interested in storefront and curtain wall construction and automotive glass industry. Prefers to see finished cartoons. SASE. Reports in 1 week. Pays $7.50; on acceptance.
Illustrations: Works on assignment only. Prefers to see roughs. Samples returned by SASE. Reports in 1 week. Buys first North American serial rights. Pays on acceptance.
Tips: "Stick to the subject matter."

GLASS NEWS, Box 7138, Pittsbrugh PA 15213. (412)362-5136. Manager: Liz Scott. Emphasizes glass manufacturing and industry news for glass manufacturers, dealers, and others involved in making, buying, and selling glass items and products. Semimonthly. Circ. 1,600. Sample copy for SASE with 56¢ postage.

Cartoons: Uses 1 cartoon/issue. Receives an average of 1 submisson/week from freelancers. Cartoons should pertain to glass manufacturing (flat glass, fiberglass, bottles and containers; no mirrors). Prefers single and multiple panel b&w line drawings with gagline. Prefers roughs or finished cartoons. SASE. Reports in 1-3 months. Buys all rights. Pays $25; on acceptance.
Tips: "Learn about making glass of all kinds."

GLENFED TODAY, 700 N. Brand Blvd., 11th floor, Box 1709, Glendale CA 91209. (818)500-2732. Editor-in-Chief: Lisa Jason. Emphasizes the savings and loan industry and company events for employees of Glendale Federal. Monthly. Circ. 8,000.
Cartoons: Buys from one freelancer each issue.
Illustrations: Uses 1-2 illustrations/issue; buys 1-2 from freelancers. Interested in conservative themes. No anti-establishment themes. Prefers conceptual art addressing serious subjects. Prefers pen & ink, airbrush, charcoal/pencil and computer illustration. Works on assignment only; reports back whether to expect possible future assignments. Send query letter "that we can keep. Do not phone. Do not send unsolicited photos. We cannot return them." Reporting time "depends on work load." Buys all rights. Negotiates pay; pays on publication.
Tips: "We are becoming comprehensive family financial centers with a housing orientation. Changes within our operation include the introduction of interest-bearing checking accounts, credit cards, etc. Freelance artists should be sure to query first and send SASE. We prefer to deal with local artists as we do not ususally buy pre-made art. We usually conceptualize and hire an artist to meet our needs. Close locations allows for quick and easy revision."

GOLDEN YEARS MAGAZINE, 233 E. New Haven Ave., Melbourne FL 32901. (305)725-4888. Art Director: Debbie Billington. Statewide magazine for the mature market (50 and over). Monthly. Circ. 700,000. Accepts previously published material. Sample copy $1. Art guidelines available.
Illustrations: Pays $25-150.
Tips: Looks for "ability to illustrate an article in a way that isn't obvious, i.e., with a sense of humor or maybe looking at the subject from a different perspective. Photocopies aren't very impressive. Printed pieces attract attention."

***GOLF ILLUSTRATED**, 3 Park Ave., New York NY 10016. (212)340-4803. Art Director: Steven Adams. "First full-service golf magazine. It helps readers improve their game and stay on top of events on the pro tour. Also additional coverage of travel, fitness and fashion." Published 10 times a year. Circ. 350,000. Original artwork is sometimes returned to the artist after publication. Sample copies free for SASE with first-class postage.
Cartoons: Buys 10 cartoons/year from freelancers. Prefers "not your typical golf cartoon." Prefers single or double panel with or without gagline; b&w line drawings. Send query letter with finished cartoons. Samples are filed. Samples not filed are returned by SASE. Returns unusable cartoons within 2 weeks. Does not report back on kept cartoons until used. Buys first rights. Pays $50, b&w.
Illustrations: Buys 5-10 illustrations/issue from freelancers. Works on assignment only. Prefers all styles. Send query letter with samples. Samples are filed. Samples not filed are not returned. Does not report back. Call or write to schedule an appointment to show a portfolio, which should include tear sheets or final reproduction/product, color and b&W. Buys first rights. Pays $200 and up, b&w; $300 and up, color, inside; on publication.
Tips: "While style is important for an Art Director to visualize what he is purchasing, I am more interested in seeing an artist's own concepts and way of thinking.

GOLF JOURNAL, Golf House, Far Hills NJ 07931. (201)234-2300. Managing Editor: George Eberl. Readers are "literate, professional, knowledgeable on the subject of golf." Published 8 times/year. Circ. 155,000. Original artwork not returned after publication. Free sample copy.
Cartoons: Buys 2-3 cartoons/issue from freelancers. Receives 50 submissions/week from freelancers. "The subject is golf. Golf must be central to the cartoon. Drawings should be professional, and captions sharp, bright and literate, on a par with our generally sophisticated readership." Formats: single or multiple panel, b&w line drawings with gagline. Prefers to see finished cartoons. SASE. Reports in 1 month. Buys one-time rights. Pays $25, b&w cartoons; on acceptance.
Illustrations: Buys several illustrations/issue from freelancers. "We maintain a file of samples from illustrators. Our needs for illustrations—and we do need talent with an artistic light touch—are based almost solely on assignments, illustrations to accompany specific stories. We would assign a job to an illustrator who is able to capture the feel and mood of a story. Most frequently, it is light-touch golf stories that beg illustrations. A sense of humor is a useful quality in the illustrator; but this sense shouldn't lapse into absurdity." Uses color washes. Send samples of style to be kept on file for future assignments. SASE. Reports in 1 month. Buys all rights on a work-for-hire basis. Payment varies, "usually $300/page.

Tips: "We often need illustrations supporting a story. Knowledge of the game and a light touch, however, are imperative and, too often, sadly lacking. I can't call it a trend, but at times it seems that self-expression supersedes the ability and willingness to underscore a point artistically."

GOLF MAGAZINE, Times Mirror Magazines, 380 Madison Ave., New York NY 10017. Art Director: Ron Ramsey. Emphasizes golf. Monthly. Circ. 850,000. Original artwork returned after publication. Art guidelines for SASE.
Illustrations: Uses 3-6 illustrations/issue; buys 2-3/issue from freelancers. Works on assignment only. Send 35mm photographs or tear sheets to be kept on file. Samples not kept on file are returned by SASE. Reports only if interested. Buys first or all rights. Write for appointment to show portfolio; drop off policy. Pays $700, b&w and $1,000, color, cover; $300, b&w and $700, color, inside; on acceptance.

GOLF SHOP OPERATIONS, 5520 Park Ave., Trumbull CT 06611. (203)373-7000. Contact: Lori Wendin. Art Director: Nancy Graham. For golf professionals at public and private courses, resorts and driving ranges. Published 8 times/year. Circ. 13,200. Original artwork returned after publication. Free sample copy.
Illustrations: Buys 4-6 illustrations/issue. Works on assignment only. Soft goods oriented. Illustrations often used for conceptual pieces. Send query letter with brochure showing art style or tear sheets, slides and photographs. Samples returned by SASE. Reports back on future assignment possibilities. Reports in 2 weeks. Call to schedule an appointment to show a portfolio, which should include thumbnails, roughs, original/final art, final reproduction/product, color, tear sheets and b&w. Buys one-time reproduction rights on a work-for-hire basis. Payment is negotiated. Pays on acceptance.

GOOD HOUSEKEEPING, Hearst Corp., 959 8th Ave., New York NY 10019. (212)649-2000. Editor-in-Chief: John Mack Carter. Contact: Art Director. For homemakers. Emphasizes food, fashion, beauty, home decorating, current events, personal relationships and celebrities. Monthly. Circ. 5,000,000.
Cartoons: Buys 150/year on family life, animals and humor through youth; single panel. Arrange an interview to show portfolio. Buys all reproduction rights. Pays $250 maximum, b&w line drawings and washes; on acceptance.
Illustrations: Buys 15 illustrations/issue on romantic themes. "Drop off" policy for portfolios. Reports in 3 weeks. Buys all reproduction rights. Inside: pay for b&w line drawing and washes depends on complexity of job, $1,000-2,000, color washes and full-color renderings; on acceptance.

GOOD READING MAGAZINE, Box 40, Litchfield IL 62056. (217)324-3425. "Nonfiction magazine which emphasizes travel, business, human interest and novel occupations." Monthly. Circ. 8,000. Original artwork returned after publication, only if requested.
Cartoons: Buys 1 cartoon/issue from freelancers. Receives 10 submissions/week from freelancers. Interested in "business, points of interest, people with unusual hobbies and occupations, and wholesome humor." Prefers to see finished cartoons. SASE. Reports in 6-8 weeks. To show a portfolio, mail original/final art. Buys first North American serial rights. Pays $20 b&w; on acceptance.

GORHAM, 800 S. Euclid Blvd., Fullerton CA 92632. (714)526-2131. Publisher/Editor: Daniel J. Gorham. Emphasizes genealogy and history for people interested in their family's history. Monthly. Circ. 2,083. Accepts previously published material and simultaneous submissions. Original artwork returned after publication. Sample copy $2.
Illustrations: Uses 15-45 illustrations/issue; buys 20-30/issue from freelancers. Themes and styles are open, but desires "good, serious work." Send query letter with samples to be kept on file. Samples not kept on file are returned by SASE. Reports within 2 months. Write for appointment to show portfolio. Buys first rights. Pays $500-1,000, b&w, cover; $75-500, b&w, inside; on publication.
Tips: Seeks *neat* work, with a "timeless aspect."

***GOURMET**, Conde Nast Publications, Inc., 560 Lexington Ave., New York NY 10022. (212)371-1330. Art Director: Irwin Glusker. Magazine "for those interested in all aspects of good living, preparation of food, wine, dining out and travel." Monthly. Circ. 700,000. Sample copies $2.50 and SASE.
Cartoons: Buys one-time rights. Pays $300, b&w.
Illustrations: "Larger issues include work from 15 artists. We are open to new artists, especially for black-and-white work." Columns are illustrated by regular freelancers, but restaurants in other cities are sometimes featured, and those areas' local artists are generally used. Send query letter with photocopies and SASE. Samples are filed. Reports "as soon as possible." Buys one-time rights. Pays $200-400, b&w.

GRADUATING ENGINEER, 1221 Avenue of the Americas, New York NY 10020. (212)512-3796. Art Director: Vincent Lomonte. Directed to the young engineer in the last year of school, who is about to en-

ter the job market. Quarterly with 3 special issues: computer, women, minority. Circ. 83,000. Returns original artwork after publication. Art guidelines available.
Illustrations: Buys 10-15 illustrations/issue from freelancers. Works on assignment only. Send brochure and business card to be kept on file. Will review Photostats, tear sheets, photocopies, slides or photographs. Reports back only if interested. Call art director for appointment to show portfolio. Negotiates rights purchased. Pays $200-300 for b&w and $500 for color, cover; $125-225 for b&w inside; on acceptance.

GRAND RAPIDS MAGAZINE, Gemini Publications, Suite 1040, Trust Building, 40 Pearl St. NW, Grand Rapids MI 49503. (616)459-4545. Editor: Ronald E. Koehler. Managing Editor: Carole Vallade Smith. For greater Grand Rapids residents. Monthly. Circ. 13,500. Original artwork returned after publication. Local artists only.
Cartoons: Buys 2-3 cartoons/issue from freelancers. Prefers Michigan, Western Michigan, Lake Michigan, city, issue or consumer/household themes. Send query letter with samples. Samples not filed are returned by SASE. Reports within 1 month. Buys all rights. Pays $25-35 b&w.
Illustrations: Buys 2-3 illustrations/issue from freelancers. Prefers Michigan, Western Michigan, Lake Michigan, city, issue or consumer/household themes. Send query letter with samples. Samples not filed are returned by SASE. Reports within 1 month. To show a portfolio, mail original/final art and final reproduction/product or call to schedule an appointment. Buys all rights. Pays $100 color, cover; $20-30 b&w and $30-50 color, inside; on publication.
Tips: "Approach only if you have good ideas."

GRAPHIC ARTS MONTHLY, 249 W. 17th St., New York NY 10011. (212)463-6834. Editor: Roger Ynostroza. Managing Editor: Peter Johnston. For management and production personnel in commercial and specialty printing plants and allied crafts. Monthly. Circ. 94,000. Sample copy $5.
Cartoons: Buys 15 cartoons/year on printing, layout, paste-up, typesetting and proofreading; single panel. Mail art. SASE. Reports in 3 weeks. Buys first rights. Pays on acceptance.

GRAY'S SPORTING JOURNAL, 205 Willow St., So. Hamilton MA 01982. (617)468-4486. Editor-in-Chief: Ed Gray. Art Director: DeCourcy Taylor. Concerns the outdoors, hunting and fishing. Published 4 times/year. Circ. 35,000. Sample copy $6.50; artist's guidelines for SASE.
Illustrations: Buys 10 illustrations/year, 2-6/issue, on hunting and fishing. Send query letter with tear sheets or slides. SASE. Reports in 4 weeks. To show a portfolio, mail tear sheets and photographs. Buys one-time rights. Pays $350, color art; $75-200, b&w line drawings, inside.
Tips: "Will definitely not accept unsolicited original art."

***GREEN FEATHER MAGAZINE**, Box 2633, Lakewood OH 44107. Editor: Gary S. Skeens. Emphasizes fiction and poetry for general audience. Published 4 times a year (March, June, September, December). Circ. 150-200. Accepts previously published material. Original artwork returned after publication. Sample copy $1.50; art guidelines for SASE.
Cartoons: Buys 1 cartoon/issue from freelancers. Prefers single panel with gagline; b&w line drawings. Send query letter with samples of style to be kept on file. Material not filed is returned by SASE. Reports in 1 month. Buys first rights or reprint rights. Negotiates payment, $5 maximum; on publication.
Illustrations: Buys 1 illustration/issue from freelancers. Send query letter with resume, tear sheets or photocopies to be kept on file. Samples not filed are returned by SASE. Reports within 1 month. To show a portfolio, mail tear sheets and b&w. Buys first rights or reprint rights. Negotiates payment. Pays on publication.

THE GRENADIER MAGAZINE, 3833 Lake Shore, Oakland CA 94610. (415)763-0928. Publisher: Jeffry Tibbetts. Emphasizes military simulation and its historical context for military professionals, war gamers and game theorists. Bimonthly. Circ. 7,500. Original artwork not returned after publication. Sample copy for 9x12 SASE with $1.41postage; art guidelines for SASE with first-class postage.
Cartoons: Buys 0-1 cartoon/issue from freelancers. Military simulation theme. Prefers single panel with gagline; b&w line drawings or b&w washes. Send query letter with samples of style or finished cartoons to be kept on file. Material not filed is returned by SASE. Reports within 1 month. To show a portfolio, mail appropriate materials. Buys all rights. Pays $10-5, b&w; open rate, color; on acceptance.
Illustrations: Buys 0-12 illustration/issue from freelancers. Works on assignment only. Send query letter with brochure and samples to be kept on file. Photocopies OK as samples if they show the artist's style and capability. Samples not filed are returned by SASE. Reports within 1 week. To show a portfolio, mail appropriate materials. Buys all rights. Pays $250 +, color, cover; $10-25, b&w, inside; on acceptance.

***GROCERY DISTRIBUTION MAGAZINE**, Suite 924, 307 N. Michigan Ave., Chicago IL 60601. (312)263-1057. Editor/Publisher: Richard Mulville. Trade journal emphasizing warehousing and transportation in the food industry. "The editorial content concerns itself with plant development activities and physical distribution procedures at these facilities. The circulation universe includes food warehouses operated by supermarket chains, food wholesalers, food-service distributore, specialty food distributior, food manufacturers, convenience store chains, frozen food distributors and public warehouses serving the food distribution system. Additional circulation is directed toward materials handling equipment/fixture dealers and distributors." Bimonthly. Circ. 16,000. Original artwork is sometimes returned to the artist after publication. Sample copies free for SASE with first-class postage. Art guidelines available.

Illustrations: Works on assignment only. Send query letter. Samples are filed. Samples not filed are returned by SASE. Call or write to schedule an appointment to show a portfolio. *"All fees subject to negotiation, the assignment, what kind of work and travel may be involved."

Tips: "While Grocery Distribution Magazine does not often make use of freelance artists or photographers, there is occasional need for this type of contribution to our magazine. The best advice for a freelancer would be to write to us, inquiring about our possible need for his or her type of service. Depending on our editorial schedule and other factors, we can then guide the freelancer in the appropriate direction."

GROUP PUBLISHING, 2890 N. Monroe, Loveland CO 80538. (303)669-3836. Director of Design: Jean Bruns. Publications include *Group Magazine* (8 issues/year; circ. 62,000), and *Group's Jr. High Ministry Magazine* (5 issues/year) for adult leaders of Christian youth groups; *Group Members Only Magazine* (8 issues/year) for members of high-school-age Christian youth groups; and *Parents & Teenagers Newsletter* (bimonthly) for families with teenagers. Also produce books, audiovisual material and printed marketing material. Previously published, photocopied and simultaneous submissions OK. Original artwork returned after publication, if requested. Sample copy $1.

Illustrations: Buys 2-5 illustrations/issue from freelancers. Prefers a loose, lighthearted pen & ink and/or color style. Send query letter with brochure showing art style or samples to be kept on file for future assignments. Reports in 1 month. To show a portfolio, mail Photostats, slides, color, b&w. Cover: Pays $350 minimum, color. Inside: Pays $25-350, from b&w/spot illustrations (line drawings and washes), to full-page color illustrations. Pays on acceptance. Buys first publication rights and sometimes reprint rights.

Tips: "We seek black-and-white illustrations of a serious, more conceptual nature as well as humorous illustrations in styles appropriate to our Christian adult audience (mature, not childish). We look for evidence of maturity and a well-developed style in the illustrator. We are also attracted to good, artistically-sound renderings, particularly of people and the ability to conceptualize well and approach subjects in an unusual way. We do not want to see amateurish work nor work that is crude, gross or delibrately offensive. We want to see work that shows thought, care, good technique and craftsmanship."

GUIDEPOSTS, 747 3rd Ave., New York NY 10017. (212)754-2200. Contact: Design Director. "*Guideposts* is an inspirational monthly magazine for all faiths in which men and women from all walks of life tell how they overcame obstacles, rose above failures, not sorrow, learned to master themselves, and became more effective people through the direct application of the religious principles by which they live." Monthly. Original artwork returned after publication. Free sample copy.

Illustrations: Uses 2-3 illustrations/issue; buys 2-3/month from freelancers. Receives 15 samples/month from freelancers. Works on assignment only. Call Larry Laukhuf for portfolio dropoff dates. Provide business card, brochure, flyer and tear sheet to be kept on file for future assignments. Buys one-time rights on a work-for-hire basis. Buys full-color illustrations, and washes.

***GUITAR WORLD**, 8th Floor, 1115 Broadway, New York NY 10010. (212)807-7100. Group Design Director: Skip Bolen. "Directed to musicians playing and interested in guitar playing, learning new techniques, and such." Monthly. Circ. 165,000. Original artwork is returned to the artist after publication. Sample copies free for SASE with first-class postage. Art guidelines not available.

Cartoons: Buys 1-2 cartoons/issue from freelancers. Buys 12-18 cartoons/year from freelancers. Prefers artwork related to keyboard, guitar musicians, music theory, and such. Prefers single panel, double panel or multiple panel with gagline. Send query letter with samples of style. Samples are filed. Samples not filed are returned if requested. Reports back only if interested. Buys one-time rights. Pays $150, b&w; $200, color.

Illustrations: Buys 1-4 illustrations/issue from freelancers. Buys 60-100 illustrations/year from freelancers. Works on assignment only. "Nothing safe or corporate—I'm looking for new and experimental work, with an edge to it." Send query letter with brochure showing art style or tear sheets, Photostats, photocopies, slides, photographs, and portfolio. Samples are sometimes filed. Samples not filed are returned only if requested. Reports back only if interested. Call to schedule an appointment to show a portfolio, which should include final reproduction/product, Photostats, photographs, slides, color and b&w. Buys one-time rights. Pays $150, b&w; $200, color, inside; on publication

GULFSHORE LIFE MAGAZINE, 2975 S. Horseshoe Dr., Naples FL 33942. (813)643-3933. Creative Director: Alyce Mathias. Magazine emphasizing lifestyle of southwest Florida for an affluent, sophisticated audience. Monthly. Circ. 20,000. Accepts previously published material. Original artwork returned after publication. Sample copy $3.
Illustrations: Send query letter with brochure, resume, tear sheets, Photostats and photocopies. Samples not filed are returned by SASE. Reports back only if interested. Write to schedule appointment to show a portfolio, which should include thumbnails, original/final art, final/reproduction/product and tear sheets. Negotiates rights purchased. Payment negotiated; pays on publication.

***GUN WORLD**, Box HH, Capistrano Beach CA 92624. Contact: Managing Editor. For shooters and hunters. Monthly. Circ. 136,000. Mail art. SASE. Reports in 8 weeks. Buys all rights, but may reassign rights to artist after publication. Pays on acceptance.
Cartoons: Buys 3-4 cartoons/issue on shooting and hunting. Pays $10-15, halftones.
Illustrations: Buys assigned themes.

HADASSAH MAGAZINE, 50 W. 58th St., New York NY 10019. (212)355-7900. Editor-in-Chief: Alan M. Tigay. Advertising Director: Robert Kinney. Art Director: Meyer Fecher. For American Jewish families; deals with social, economic, political and cultural developments in Israel and Jewish communities in the U.S. and elsewhere. Monthly. Circ. 353,000. Sample copy $2.50. SASE. Reports in 6 weeks. Buys first rights. Pays on publication.

HAM RADIO, Greenville NH 03048. (603)878-1441. Editor-in-Chief: T.H. Tenney, Jr. Managing Editor: Terry Northup. Art Director: Susan Shorrock. Address inquiries to Terry Northup. For licensed amateur radio operators and electronics experimenters. Monthly. Circ. 40,000.
Illustrations: Buys drafting (on assignment), cover art, illustration. Prefers charcoal/pencil, mixed media and computer illustration. Prefers to see photocopied samples; do not send original art unless requested to do so. Reports in 30 days. Minimum payment: cover art, $100; illustration, $20; on publication.
Tips: "On our covers we favor strong graphic interpretations of concepts in electronics. The use of bright, bold colors sets us apart from other publications in our field. We prefer to see work targeted toward the amateur radio field. We are a very specialized publication."

HANDS-ON ELECTRONICS, 500 B Bi-County Blvd., Farmingdale NY 11735. (516)293-3000. Editor: Julian Martin. Magazine emphasizing hobby electronics for consumer and hobby-oriented electronics buffs. Monthly. Circ. 120,000. Original artwork not returned after publication. Sample copy free.
Cartoons: Buys 3-5 cartoons/issue from freelancers. Prefers single panel with or without gagline; b&w line drawings and b&w washes. Send finished cartoons; "we purchase and keep! Unused ones returned." Samples are returned. Reports within 1 week. Buys all rights. Pays $25 b&w.
Illustrations: Does not buy illustrations currently, "but would like to start." Works on assignment only. Send query letter with brochure showing art style. Samples not filed are returned. Reports within 1 week. Write to schedule an appointment to show a portfolio, which should include thumbnails, roughs, original/final art, final reproduction/product, color, tear sheets, photographs and b&w. Buys all rights. Pays $300, color, cover; payment depends on usage for inside; on acceptance.

HARROWSMITH, Camden House Publishing Ltd., Ontario K0K 1J0 Canada. (613)378-6661. Art Director: Pamela McDonald. Concerns alternative lifestyles, energy sources and architecture, the environment, country living and gardening. Publishes 6 issues/year. Circ. 164,000. Sample copy $5. Receives 4 cartoons and 6 illustrations/week from freelance artists.
Cartoons: Uses 2-3 cartoons/issue, all from freelancers. Single panel with gagline. Prefers roughs, samples for files and business card; SAE (nonresidents include IRC). Reports in 6 weeks. Pays $25-100 on acceptance.
Illustrations: Uses 12 illustrations/issue, all from freelancers. Interested in "high-quality color, drawings and some fine art on country living theme. Many have won awards." Works on assignment only. Likes to have samples on file. Reports back on future assignment possibilities; SAE (nonresidents include IRC). Reports in 6 weeks. Buys first North American serial rights. Cover: pays $500-1,200, color. Inside: pays $250-1,000 color; $150-500, b&w; on acceptance.

HARROWSMITH MAGAZINE, The Creamery, Charlotte VT 05445. (802)425-3961. Editor: Tom Rawls. Estab. 1986. Magazine emphasizing country living in the northern U.S. for sophisticated, well-educated, between 25-45 years of age interested in country living. Bimonthly. Circ. 225,000. Original

artwork returned after publication. Sample copy $4. Art guidelines for SASE with postage for two ounces.
Cartoons: Buys 1 cartoon/issue from freelancers. Prefers b&w line drawings. Send query letter with samples of style to be kept on file. Samples not filed returned by SASE. Reports within 4 weeks. Buys first or reprint rights. Negotiates payment.

***HEALTH EDUCATION**, 1900 Association Dr., Reston VA 22091. Managing Editor: Patricia Steffan. "For school and community health professionals, keeping them up-to-date on issues, trends, teaching methods, and curriculum developments in health." Bimonthly. Circ. 10,000. Original artwork is returned to the artist after publication if requested. Samples copies available. Art guidelines not available upon request.
Illustrations: Buys 10-20 illustrations/year from freelancers. Wants health-related topics, any style. Prefers watercolor, pen & ink, airbrush, acrylics, oils and computer illustration. Works on assignment only. Send query letter with brochure showing art style or Photostats, photocopies, slides or photographs. Samples are filed. Samples not filed are returned by SASE. Reports back within weeks only if interested. Write to schedule an appointment to show a portfolio, which should include thumbnails, roughs, original/final art, Photostats, photographs, slides, color and b&w. Negotiates rights purchased. Pays $200, color, cover; $40, b&w, inside; on acceptance.

***HEALTH EXPRESS**, (formerly Good Health), Davis Communications, 19701 8 Miles Rd., Cleveland OH 44128. (216)662-6969. Managing Editor: Suzanne Pelisson. Estab. 1988. Magazine emphasizing health and fitness. "*Health Express* is edited for busy men and women who take an active role in staying mentally and physically fit." Bimonthly. Circ. 100,000+. Accepts previously published material. Original artwork is returned to the artist after publication. Sample copies available. Art guidelines free for SASE with first-class postage.
Cartoons: Cartoon Editor: Michael Cohen. Buys 5-10 cartoons/issue from freelancers. Prefers health-oriented themes, working moms, career families and diet/nutrition. Prefers single panel with gagline; b&w line drawings. Send query letter with samples of style. Samples are filed. Samples not filed are returned if requested by artist. Reports back only if interested. Buys reprint rights. Pays $10, b&w; $25, color.
Illustrations: Buys 8-10 illustrations/year from freelancers. Works on assignment only. Prefers health-oriented themes. Send query letter with brochure. Samples are filed. Samples not filed are returned only if requested by artist. Reports back only if interested. Write to schedule an appointment to show a portfolio, which should include original/final art and tear sheets. Buys one-time rights. Pays $75, b&w; $125, color, cover; $50, b&w; $75, color, inside on publication.

HEALTH MAGAZINE, 41st Floor, 3 Park Ave., New York NY 10016. (212)340-9200. Art Director: Maxine Davidowitz. Circ. 1,000,000. Original artwork returned after publication.
Illustrations: Uses 10 illustrations/issue. Works on assignment only. Send samples to be kept on file. Buys first rights. Payment varies; pays on acceptance.

***HEALTH WORLD**, 1477 Rollins, Burlingame CA 94010. (415)343-1637. President: Kumar Pati. Estab. 1986. Magazine emphasizing health and nutrition. "*Health World* is an open forum for discussion of a wide variety of health sciences, news, and health products available around the world." Bimonthly. Circ. 60,000. Accepts previously published material. Original artwork is returned to the artist after publication. Samples copies $2.50. Art guidelines available.
Cartoons: Prefers b&w line drawings and b&w and color washes. Send samples of style. Samples not filed are returned. Pay is negotiable.
Illustrations: Works on assignment only. Send query letter with brochure or tear sheets, photocopies and photographs. Call or write to schedule an appointment to show a portfolio. "Bill proper invoice." Pays on publication.

THE HERB QUARTERLY, Box 275, Newfane VT 05345. (802)365-4392. Editor and Publisher: Sally Ballantine. Magazine emphasizing horticulture for middle to upper class, affluent men and women with an ardent enthusiasm for herbs and all their uses—gardening, culinary, crafts, etc. Most are probably home-owners. Quarterly. Circ. 30,000. Accepts previously published material. Original artwork returned after publication if requested. Sample copy $5. Art guidelines available.
Illustrations: Prefers pen & ink illustrations, heavily contrasted. Illustrations of herbs, garden designs, etc. Artist should be able to create illustrations drawn from themes of manuscripts sent to them. Send query letter with brochure showing art style or resume, tear sheets, photocopies, slides and photographs. Samples not filed are returned by SASE only if requested. Reports within weeks. To show a portfolio, mail original/final art, final reproduction/product, photographs or b&w. Buys reprint rights. Pays on publication.

HIBISCUS MAGAZINE, Box 22248, Sacramento CA 95822. Editor: Margaret Wensrich. Estab. 1985. Magazine for "people who like to read poetry and short stories." Published three times/year. Circ. 2,000. Original artwork returned after publication if requested. Sample copy $3; art guidelines for SASE with 39¢ postage.
Cartoons: Uses all subjects. Pays $5 on acceptance.
Illustrations: Buys 3-4 illustrations/issue from freelancers. Works on assignment only. Send query letter with resume and samples. Samples not filed are returned by SASE. Reports back only if interested. To show a portfolio, mail original/final art or photocopy of finished work. "We use pen & ink drawings only. No color, slides, etc." Buys first rights. Pays for design and illustration by the project $10-25; on acceptance.
Tips: "We need clean pen & ink or pencil that can be reproduced exactly by printer. Subjects are assigned. The portfolio gives us an idea of artist's work."

HIGHLIGHTS FOR CHILDREN, 803 Church St., Honesdale PA 18431. Art Director: John R. Crane. Cartoon Editor: Kent Brown. For ages 2-12. Monthly, bimonthly in July/August. Circ. 2,300,000.
Cartoons: Buys 2-4 cartoons/issue from freelancers. Receives 20 submissions/week from freelancers. Interested in upbeat, positive cartoons involving children, family life or animals; single or multiple panel. Send roughs or finished cartoons. SASE. Reports in 4-6 weeks. Buys all rights. Pays $20-40, line drawings; on acceptance. "One flaw in many submissions is that the concept or vocabulary is too adult, or that the experience necessary for its appreciation is beyond our readers. Frequently, a wordless self-explanatory cartoon is best."
Illustrations: Uses 30 illustrations/issue; buys 25 from freelancers. Works with freelancers on assignment only. "We are always looking for good hidden pictures. We require a picture that is interesting in itself and has the objects well hidden. Usually an artist submits pencil sketches. In no case do we pay for any preliminaries to the final hidden prictures." Also needs "original ideas and illustrations for covers and 'What's Wrong' illustrations for back cover. Prefers "realistic and stylized work, very little cartoon." Prefers pen & ink, colored pencil, watercolor, markers and mixed media. Send samples of style and flyer to be kept on file. SASE. Reports in 4-6 weeks. Buys all rights on a work-for-hire basis. Pays on acceptance.
Tips: "I want to see if and how an illustrator can draw people, especially children. We have a wide variety of needs, so I would prefer to see a representative sample of an illustrator's style or styles."

HISTORIC PRESERVATION, 1785 Massachusetts Ave. NW, Washington DC 20036. Editor: Thomas J. Colin. For members of the National Trust for Historic Preservation; concerns national preservation of architectural and cultural heritage. Bimonthly. Circ. 200,000. No simultaneous submissions or previously published work. Artist's guidelines available.
Illustrations: Buys 12 illustrations/year on education, architecture, folk art and historical subjects. Query with previously published work. SASE. Reports in 2 weeks. Buys one-time rights. Inside: Pays $150 maximum, color washes; $75 minimum, b&w line drawings and washes; on publication.

ALFRED HITCHCOCK MYSTERY MAGAZINE, Davis Publications, 380 Lexington Ave., New York NY 10017. (212)557-9100. Art Director: Terry Czeczkr. Art Editor: Ron Kuliner. Emphasizes mystery fiction.
Illustrations: Line drawings, minimum payment: $100.
First Contact & Terms: Call for interview. Reports in 1 week. Pays on acceptance. Buys first rights.

THE HORROR SHOW, 14848 Misty Springs Ln., Oak Run CA 96069-9801. (916)472-3540. Editor: David B. Silva. Magazine emphasizing short horror fiction for "anyone who enjoys a good chill up their spine." Quarterly. Circ. 4,000. Original artwork not returned after publication. Sample copy $4.95; art guidelines for SASE with first-class postage.
Cartoons: Buys 1-2 cartoons/issue. Pays $5 b&w; on acceptance.
Illustrations: Buys 13-20 b&w illustrations/issue from freelancers. Works on assignment only. Send query letter with tear sheets and photocopies to be kept on file, except for slides, which will be returned. Samples not filed are returned by SASE. Reports within 2 weeks. Buys first rights or reprint rights. To show a portfolio, mail tear sheets, photographs and b&w. Pays $15, color, cover; $10, b&w, inside; on acceptance.

HORSE ILLUSTRATED, Box 6050, Mission Viejo CA 92690. (714)855-8822. Editor: Jill-Marie Jones. For people of all ages who own, show and breed horses, and who are interested in all phases of horse ownership. Monthly. Circ. 80,000. Sample copy $3; art guidelines for SASE.
Cartoons: Buys several cartoons/issue. Prefers single or double panel. "Central character should be a horse." Send finished art. SASE. Reports within 6 weeks. Buys one-time rights. Pays $25-50, b&w line drawings; on publication.

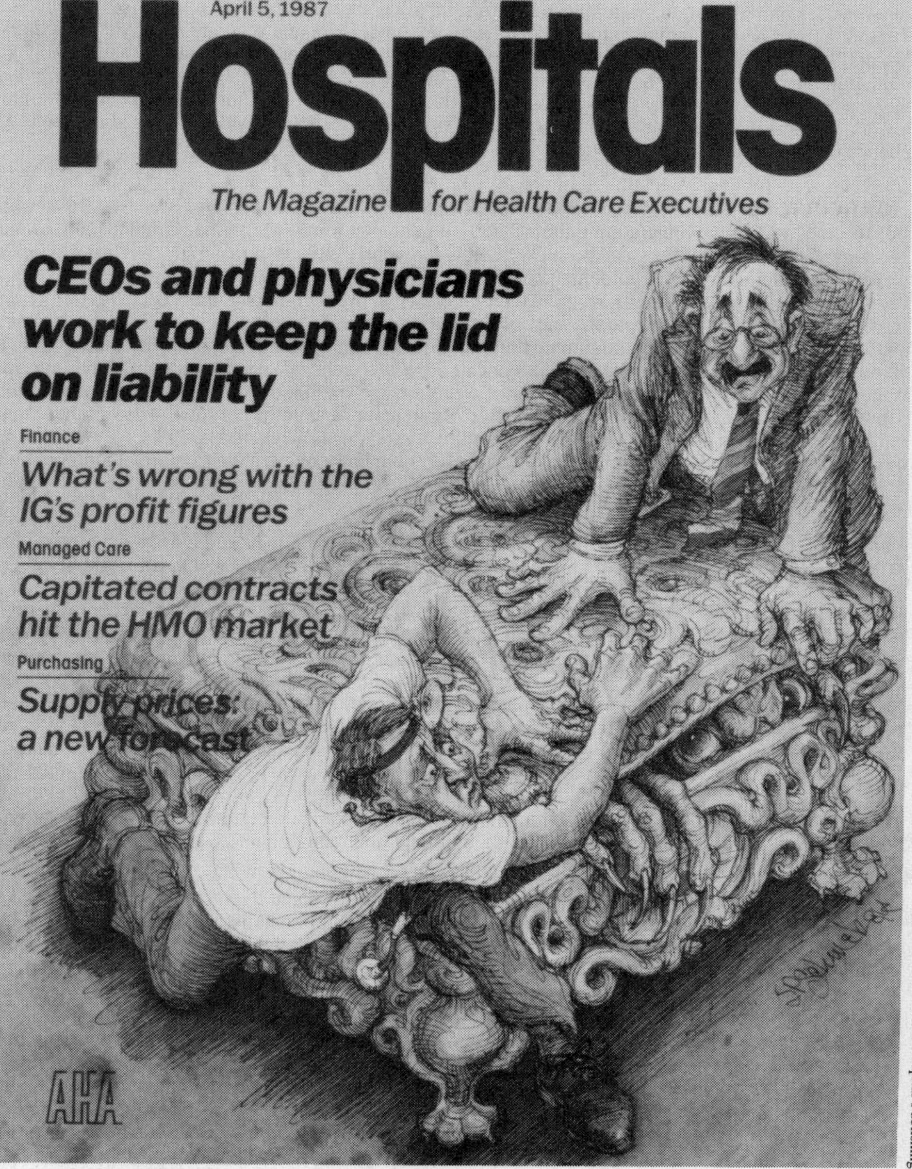

April 5, 1987
Hospitals
The Magazine for Health Care Executives
CEOs and physicians work to keep the lid on liability
Finance
What's wrong with the IG's profit figures
Managed Care
Capitated contracts hit the HMO market
Purchasing
Supply prices: a new forecast
AHA

Freelance illustrator John Schmelzer of Oak Park, Illinois was commissioned to do this cover of Hospitals Magazine by Marcia Kuhr, director of graphic design of American Hospital Publishing in Chicago, Illinois. "The lead story was about CEO's and physicians working to keep the lid on liability," explains Schmelzer. "The drawing was to take up a triangular area on the bottom right of the cover to allow for subheads." Kuhr, who had worked with Schmelzer before, knew his style was appropriate to the slightly humorous touch she wanted. Schmelzer, who was paid $700 for first rights, proved his "good conceptual skills, flexibility and ability to meet deadlines" by completing the piece in two weeks. It was rendered in pen and ink and wash.

Illustrations: Buys several illustrations/year of horses. Send query letter with resume and samples or send finished art. SASE. Reports within 6 weeks. Buys one-time rights. Pays $20-100, b&w line drawings, inside; on publication. Rate depends on use and whether illustrator was assigned.
Tips: When reviewing an illustrator's work, "we look for realism and accurate portrayal of the horse. We don't use 'fantasy' or 'surrealistic' art. For cartoons, we look for drawing ability and humor. We will, however, accept good humor with adequate illustration over good illustration with poor humor. Generally, we use free-standing illustrations as art rather than going to the illustrator and commissioning a work, but this is impossible if the artist sends us poor reproductions. Naturally, this also lessens his chance of our seeking out his services."

HORTICULTURE, THE MAGAZINE OF AMERICAN GARDENING, 755 Boylston St., Boston MA 02116. (617)482-5600. Illustration Editor: Sarah Boorstyn Schwartz. Magazine geared to homeowners. Monthly. Circ. 140,000. Very occasionally accepts previously published material. Original artwork returned after publication. Art guidelines available.
Illustrations: Buys 15 illustrations/issue from freelancers. Works on assignment only. Prefers gardening as a theme, 'how-to' illustrations and color floral pieces. Send query letter with tear sheets, Photostats, photocopies, slides or photographs. Samples not filed are returned. Reports within 2 months. To show a portfolio, mail appropriate materials or call or write to schedule an appointment. Buys one-time rights. Fee schedule depends on complexity of piece and the amount of material; pays on publication.
Tips: "Show as many different styles as possible. Bring in (or send in) lots of work—doesn't have to be only gardening or horticulture material. Besides illustrating plants and gardens, I look for ability to render hand manipulations and figures. We are doing far more how-to, step-by-step sorts of illustration to gear ourselves to the new gardeners."

HOSPITAL PRACTICE, 10 Astor Place, New York NY 10003. (212)477-2727. Design Director: Robert S. Herald. Emphasizes clinical medicine and research for practicing physicians throughout the U.S. 18 issues/year. Circ. 200,000. Original artwork returned after publication if requested.
Illustrations: Uses 40-50 illustrations/issue; buys 15-20 illustrations/issue from freelancers. Uses only non-symbolic medical and scientific (conceptual) illustrations in a style similar to *Scientific American*. Also charts and graphs. Prefers "an elegant, if traditional, visual communication of biomedical and clinical concepts to physicians." Prefers pen & ink, airbrush, watercolor and acrylics. Works on assignment only. Send query letter with brochure showing art style, resume, Photostats, photographs/slides and/or tear sheets to be kept on file. Does not report unless called. Call for appointment to show portfolio, which should include original/final art, color, tear sheets, Photostats and b&w. Returns material if SASE included. Negotiates rights purchased. Pays $900, color, cover; $100 and up, b&w, inside; on publication.
Tips: "Our specific editorial approach limits our interest to physician-oriented, 'just-give-us-the-facts' type of medical and scientific illustrations, though they, too, can be done with creative imagination."

***HOSPITALS MAGAZINE**, 7th Floor, 211 E. Chicago Ave., Chicago IL 60611. Design Director: Marcia Kuhr. "Primary audience for *Hospitals* is the hospital CEO or administrator. Issues include: reporting/analysis of various industry trends; healthcare legislation in Washington; marketing and business; social issues; medical staff issues and economics." Biweekly. Circ. 100,000. Original artwork is usually returned to the artist after publication. Sample copies available. Art guidelines not available.
Illustrations: Buys 1 illustration/issue from freelancers. Works on assignment only. Send query letter with brochure showing art style, tear sheets or photocopies. Samples are filed. Samples not filed are returned by SASE only if requested. Reports back only if interested. Call to schedule an appointment to show a portfolio, which should include original/final art, tear sheets, final reproduction/product, color and b&w. Buys first rights. Pays $500, color, cover; $150, b&w; $250, color, inside.
Tips: "Most of the artwork purchased is for the cover of *Hospitals*. You should have good conceptual skills and be able to work within tight deadlines (published every two weeks!)."

HOUSE & GARDEN, 350 Madison Ave., New York NY 10017. (212)880-6693. Art Director: Karen Lee Grant. Readers are upper income home owners or renters. Monthly. Circ. 500,000.
Illustrations: Uses minimum number of illustrations/issue; all of which are commissioned by the magazine. Selection based on "previous work, samples on file, and from seeing work in other publications. Illustrations are almost always assigned to fit specific articles." Themes "vary with our current format and with article we want illustrated." Format: b&w line drawings or washes. Portfolios viewed on first Tuesday of every month. Send samples of style to art director. SASE. Reports "from immediately to 4 weeks." Payment on acceptance "varies depending on artist, size and type of illustration." Buys one-time rights.

HUMPTY DUMPTY'S MAGAZINE, Box 567, Indianapolis IN 46206. (317)636-8881. Art Director: Lawrence Simmons. Special emphasis on health, nutrition, safety and exercise for girls and boys, ages 4-6. Monthly except bimonthly February/March, April/May, June/July and August/September. Sample copy 75¢; art guidelines for SASE.
Illustrations: Uses 25-35 illustrations/issue. Works on assignment only. Send query letter with resume, Photostats, slides, good photocopies or tear sheets to be kept on file. Samples returned by SASE if not kept on file. Reports within 8-12 weeks. Buys all rights. To show a portfolio, mail original/final art, final reproduction/product, color, b&w and 2-color. Include SASE for return. Pays $225, cover; and $25-65, b&w; $50-100, 2-color; $60-125, 4-color, inside; on publication.
Tips: Illustrations should be figurative and should be composed of story-telling situations. "Be familiar with the magazines before submitting artwork or samples that are completely inappropriate."

***THE HUNGRY YEARS**, Box 7213, Newport Beach CA 92660. (714)548-3324. Editor/Publisher: Les Brown. Small press publication emphasizing fiction, nonfiction, poetry and the work of new talent for creative people of all ages and interests. Biannually. Circ. 1,000. Previously published material OK. Original artwork returned after publication. Free sample copy and art guidelines for SASE.
Cartoons: Uses 2-4 cartoons/issue. "Basically we ask for good taste"; can be in abstract, avant garde style; no pornography or religious themes. Send query letter with roughs or samples of style. Samples returned by SASE. Reports in 6 months. Material not copyrighted. Pays in copies; on publication.
Illustrations: Prefers b&w pen and ink. Artwork is matched with written compositions to mutually complement both works whether poetry, fiction or essays. Will send sample copy to serve as example of styles wanted. Provide samples to be kept on file for possible future assignments. Send query letter with roughs or samples of style. Samples returned by SASE. Reports in 6 months. Material not copyrighted. Pays in copies; on publication.

***HUSTLER**, Larry Flynt Publications, Suite 300, 9171 Wilshire Blvd., Beverly Hills CA 90210. (213)858-7100. Cartoon/Humor Editor: Dwaine and Susan Tinsley. For middle income men, 18-35 years of age, interested in current affairs, luxuries, investigative reporting, entertainment, sports, sex and fashion. Monthly. Original artwork returned after publication.
Cartoons: Publishes 23 cartoons/month; 10 full-page color, 4-color spots, 8 b&w and 1 "Most Tasteless." Receives 300-500 cartoons/week from freelance artists. Especially needs "outrageous material, mainly sexual, but politics, sports acceptable. Topical humor and seasonal/holiday cartoons good." Mail samples. Prefers 8½xll" size; avoid crayons, chalks or fluorescent colors. Prefers original art submissions to roughs. Avoid, if possible, large, heavy illustration board. Samples returned by SASE only. Place name, address and phone number on back of each cartoon. Reports in 3 weeks to 1 month. Adheres to Cartoonists Guild guidelines. Pays $300, full- page color; $125 ¼-page color; $100 ¼-page b&w; $100, ¼-page "Most Tasteless." Pays on acceptance.
Tips: Especially needs more cartoons, cartoon breakaways or one-subject theme series. "Send outrageous humor—work that other magazines would shy away from. Pertinent, political, sexual, whatever. We are constantly looking for new artists to compliment our regular contributors and contract artists. Let your imagination and daring guide you. We will publish almost anything as long as it is funny. Remember, we are 'equal-opportunity offenders'."

***HUSTLER HUMOR MAGAZINE**, Larry Flynt Publications, Suite 300, 9171 Wilshire Blvd., Beverly Hills CA 90210. (213)858-7100. Cartoon/Humor Editor: Dwaine and Susan Tinsley. Bimonthly. Circ. 150,000.
Cartoons: Uses 150-180 cartoons/issue; buys 30% from freelancers. Prefers "outrageous sexual, social, political" themes. Prefers single or multiple panel, with or without gag line; b&w line drawings, b&w washes. Send finished cartoons to be kept on file. Material not kept on file returned by SASE. Reports within 1 month. Buys first rights. Pays $7.50 b&w spot, $75 b&w strips/page. Original artwork returned after publication. Payment on acceptance.
Illustrations: Uses 2 covers, full-color sight gags. Prefers soft sexual themes; realistic cartoon styles. Send samples and tear sheets to be kept on file. Reports within 2 weeks. Pays $500, front; $200, back. Pays on acceptance.
Tips: This is a "humor magazine consisting of jokes and cartoons exclusively. The material is primarily sexual in nature—but the scope is wide-ranging. We need work *badly* to build our inventory."

IDEALS MAGAZINE, Box 140300; Nelson Place at Elm Hill Pike, Nashville TN 37214. (615)885-8270. Editor: Peggy Schaefer. Magazine emphasizing poetry and light prose. Published 8 times/year. Accepts previously published material. Sample copy $3.95.
Illustrations: Buys 6-8 illustrations/issue from freelancers. Prefers seasonal themes rendered in a realistic style. Prefers pen & ink, airbrush, charcoal/pencil, watercolor and pastels. Send query letter with brochure showing art style or tear sheets and slides. Samples not filed are returned by SASE. Reports

within 2 months. To show a portfolio, mail appropriate materials; portfolio should include final reproduction/product and tear sheets. Do not send originals. Buys artwork outright. Pays on publication.
Tips: "In portfolios, target our needs as far as style is concerned, but show representative subject matter."

IN BUSINESS, Box 323, Emmaus PA 18049. (215)967-4135. Managing Editor: Nora Goldstein. Emphasizes small business start-up and management. Bimonthly. Circ. 50,000. Original artwork returned after publication. Sample copy $2.50; art guidelines for SASE.
Cartoons: Uses 2-3 cartoons/issue; buys all from freelancers. Prefers single panel, with gagline; b&w line drawings. Send query letter with roughs. Material not kept on file is returned by SASE. Reports within 4 weeks. Buys first rights. Pays $35, b&w; on publication.
Illustrations: Uses 5-6 illustrations/issue; buys all from freelancers. Uses themes related to article subject. Works on assignment only. Send query letter with brochure and tear sheets to be kept on file; call for appointment to show portfolio. Reports within 4 weeks. Buys first rights. Pays $35, b&w, inside; on publication.

INDEPENDENT AGENT MAGAZINE, 100 Church St., New York NY 10007. (212)285-4255. Art Director: Bette Cowles. Trade journal emphasizing insurance. Features general interest, interview/profile, technical and travel articles. "*Independent Agent* is a trade publication promoting the interests of the independent insurance agent." Monthly. Circ. 62,000. Accepts previously published material. Original artwork is sometimes returned to artist after publication. Sample copy $5.
Cartoons: Buys 2-6 cartoons/year from freelancers. Uses various themes. Prefers color washes, pen & ink, airbrush, watercolor, acrylics, oils, pastels, collage, mixed media and computer illustration. Send query letter with samples of style. Samples are filed. Samples not filed are not returned. Reports back only if interested. Negotiates rights purchased. Pays $500 cover, color.
Illustrations: Buys 15 illustrations/year from freelancers. Works on assignment only. Uses various themes. Send query letter with brochure or photocopies. Samples are filed. Samples not filed are not returned. Reports back only if interested. Call to schedule an appointment to show a portfolio which should include original/final art and tear sheets. Negotiates rights purchased. Pays $500, color, cover; $100, b&w; $250, color, inside; on publication.
Tips: "Bring a card or photocopy with a sample to leave for our files. Also, show a representative sampling of your work in your portfolio."

INDIANAPOLIS 500 YEARBOOK, Box 24308, Speedway IN 46224. (317)244-4792. Publisher: Carl Hungness. Emphasizes auto racing for auto racing fans. Annually. Circ. 50,000. Previously published material OK. Original artwork returned after publication. Sample copy $14.95.
Illustrations: Works on assignment only. Send query letter plus information to be kept on file for possible future assignments. Samples returned by SASE. Reports in 2 weeks. Buys one-time rights. Pays on publication.

INDUSTRIAL MACHINERY NEWS, division of Hearst Business Media Corp., Box 5002, 29516 Southfield Rd., Southfield MI 48086. (313)557-0100. Publisher: L.D. Slate. For those in the metalworking industry responsible for manufacturing, purchasing, engineering, metalworking, machinery, equipment and supplies.
Illustrations: Contact publisher for guidelines.

INSIDE, 226 S. 16th St., Philadelphia PA 19102. (215)893-5760. Contact: Art Director. Quarterly. Circ. 70,000. Original artwork returned after publication.
Illustrations: Buys 3 or more illustrations/issue from freelancers. Prefers color and b&w drawings. Works on assignment only. Send samples and tear sheets to be kept on file; call for appointment to show portfolio. Samples not kept on file are not returned. Reports only if interested. Buys first rights. Pays from $100, b&w, and from $300 full-color, inside; on acceptance. Prefers seeing sketches.

INSIDE DETECTIVE, RGH Publications, 20th Floor, 460 W. 34th St., New York NY 10001. (212)947-6500. Editor: Rose Mandelsberg. For mature adults—law enforcement officials, professional investigators, criminology buffs and interested laymen. Monthly.
Cartoons: Receives approximately 20 cartoons/week from freelance artists. Must have crime theme. Submit finished art. SASE. Reports in 10 days. Buys all rights. Pays $25; on acceptance.
Tips: "Make sure that the humor in the cartoons is *not* at the expense of police officers or law enforcement officials. Omit references to supermarket/convenience stores."

INSIDE SPORTS, 990 Grove St., Evanston IL 60201. Art Director: Thomas M. Miller. Emphasizes sports. Monthly. Circ. 475,000. Original artwork returned after publication.

Cartoons: Considers sports themes. Prefers single panel; b&w line drawings or color washes. Send 4-color sample tear sheets (no original artwork). Material not filed is returned by SASE. Pays on acceptance.
Illustrations: Considers sports themes. Works on assignment only. Send 4-color sample tear sheets (no original art). Prefer caricatures and conceptual pieces. Samples not filed are returned by SASE. Pays on acceptance.

***INSIDE TEXAS RUNNING**, 9514 Bristlebrook, Houston TX 77083. "Information, features and calendar for runners, triatheletes and bicyclists in the state of Texas. Slant is on healthy competition and exercise." Monthly. Circ. 10,000. Accepts previously published material. Original artwork is not returned to the artist after publication. Sample copy $1.50. Finds most artists through references/word-of-mouth and samples received through the mail.
Cartoons: Buys 6 cartoons/year from freelancers. Prefers single panel with gagline; b&w line drawings. Send roughs and finished cartoons. Samples are not filed and not returned. Reports back within 6 weeks. Buys reprint rights, one-time rights or all rights. Pays $10, b&w.
Illustrations: Buys 6 illustrations/year from freelancers. Prefers pen & ink. Send query letter with brochure showing art style or tear sheets, Photostats, photocopies or photographs. Samples are not filed, but returned by SASE. Reports back within 6 weeks. To show a portfolio, mail appropriate materials. Buys one-time rights, reprint rights or all rights. Negotiates rights purchased. Pays $10, b&w; $25, color, cover.

THE INSTRUMENTALIST, 200 Northfield Rd., Northfield IL 60093. (312)328-6000. Contact: Elaine Guregian. Emphasizes music education for "school band and orchestra directors and teachers of the instruments in those ensembles." Monthly. Circ. 24,000. Original artwork may be returned after publication. Sample copy $2.
Cartoons: Buys 3 cartoons/issue; buys all from freelancers. Interested in postive cartoons; no themes stating "music is a problem"; single panel with gagline, if needed; b&w line drawings. Send finished cartoons. Samples not returned. Reports in 1-2 months. Buys all rights. Pays $20, b&w; on acceptance.
Illustrations: Buys Kodachrome transparencies or slides for covers. Query about suitable subjects. Pays $50-100 on acceptance.
Tips: Looks for "realistic or abstract closeups of performers and musical instruments. Style should be modern, with clean lines and sharp focus that will reproduce well. Black-and-white glossy photos are best; color slides for covers should be Kodachrome film. Inexperienced freelancers sometimes attach long lists of fees or policies, not understanding that each magazine sets its own acceptance and payment policies."

INSURANCE SALES, Rough Notes Publishing Co. Inc., Box 564, Indianapolis IN 46206. (317)634-1541. Editor: Roy Ragan. For life and health insurance salespeople; "emphasis on sales and marketing methods, and on the uses of life and health insurance to solve personal and business financial situations." Monthly. Circ. 27,000. Sample copy $1. Receives 15-20 cartoons/week from freelance artists.
Cartoons: Buys 50-60 cartoons/year from freelancers. Interested in life and health insurance salesmanship, tax payer and IRS situations, inflation, recession, vagaries of bankers and stock market; single panel. "No cartoons which show salesman holding prospect on ground, twisting arm, knocking doors down, etc." Send finished cartoons with SASE. Reports in 1 week. Buys all rights. Pays $15, b&w line drawings; on acceptance.

INTERRACIAL BOOKS FOR CHILDREN BULLETIN, 1841 Broadway, New York NY 10023. Contact: Editor. Emphasizes "bias-free children's literature and learning materials" for teachers, librarians, parents, authors, and others concerned with children's materials. Published 8 times/year. Circ. 5,000. Accepts previously published material. Original artwork returned after publication. Sample copy $3.50; art guidelines for SASE.
Cartoons: Rarely uses cartoons. Prefers b&w line drawings. Send query letter with samples of style; samples will be kept on file if relevant. Material not kept on file is returned by SASE. Reports within 2 months.
Illustrations: Uses up to 15 illustrations/issue. Send query letter with Photostats and photographs; material will be kept on file if relevant. Samples returned by SASE if not kept on file. Reports within 4 weeks. Buys one-time rights. Pays $50, b&w, cover; $25, b&w, inside; on publication.

IOWA MUNICIPALITIES, League of Iowa Municipalities, Suite 209, 100 Court Ave., Des Moines IA 50309. Editor-in-Chief: B.J. Reed. Executive Director: Peter B. King. Magazine for city officials. Monthly. Circ. 10,000. Previously published, photocopied and simultaneous submissions OK. Sample copy $1.50.
Cartoons: Would run for no fee. Political orientation relating to cities or issues concerning cities. Buys none.

Illustrations: Buys none. Will consider illustrations if accompanied by an article. Pays $100, cover; "two-color art is acceptable." Pays upon publication.
Tips: "Have a good idea? Try us. Just looking for work? Don't try us. We rarely need freelancers without ideas of their own."

JACK AND JILL, Box 567, 1100 Waterway Blvd., Indianapolis IN 46206. (317)636-8881. Art Director: Edward F. Cortese. Emphasizes entertaining articles written with the purpose of developing the reading skills of the reader. For ages 6-8. Monthly except bimonthly February/March, April/May, June/July and August/September. Buys all rights. Original artwork not returned after publication (except in case where artist wishes to exhibit the art. Art must be available to us on request.) Sample copy 75¢.
Illustrations: Buys 25 illustrations/issue; buys 10-15/issue from freelancers. Receives 3-4 submissions/week from freelancers. Interested in "stylized, realistic, humorous, mystery, adventure, science fiction, historical and also nature and health." Prefers mixed media. Work on assignment only. Send query letter with brochure showing art style or resume, tear sheets, Photostats, photocopies, slides and photographs to be kept on file; include SASE. Reports in 1 month. To show a portfolio, mail appropriate materials or call or write to schedule an appointment; portfolio should include original/final art, color, tear sheets, b&w and 2-color pre-separated art. Buys all rights on a work-for-hire basis. Pays $225 cover, $125 full page, $80 ½ page, $60 spot for 4-color. Pays $200 full page, $70 ½ page, $50 spot for 2-

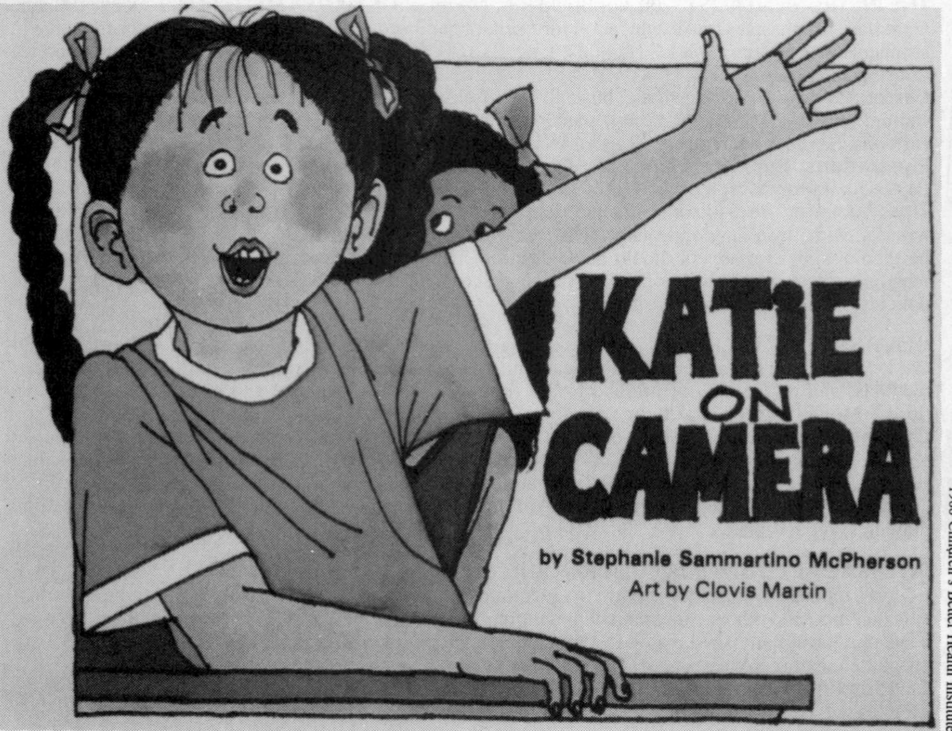

Executive art director Edward Cortese assigned Clovis Martin of Cleveland Heights, Ohio this editorial illustration of a story series called "Katie on Camera" for Jack and Jill *Magazine in Indianapolis, Indiana. Cortese says, "I told Clovis that the story ran for five pages, and the art would be in full color. The deadlines for sketches were due in three weeks and, for finishes, an additional three weeks." Martin, who was also responsible for layout and position of type, sold all rights to the piece, drawn with markers and watercolor. Martin originally contacted the magazine after seeing it listed in the* Artist's Market. *He now works on a regular basis with the magazine.*

color. Pays $65 full page, $50 1/2 page, $25 spot for b&w. "Kill fees rarely occur. If they should, they will be handled on a case-by-case basis." Pays 30 days after completion of work.
Tips: Portfolio should include "illustrations composed in a situation or storytelling way, to inhance the text matter. I do not want to see samples showing *only* single figures, portraits or landscapes, sea or air."

JAPANOPHILE, Box 223, Okemos MI 48864. (517)349-1795. Editor: Earl R. Snodgrass. Emphasizes cars, bonsai, haiku, sports, etc. for educated audience interested in Japanese culture. Quarterly. Circ. 800. Accepts previously published material. Original artwork not returned after publication. Sample copy $4; art guidelines free for SASE.
Cartoons: Buys 1 cartoon/issue from freelancer. Prefers single panel with gagline; b&w line drawings. Send finished cartoons. Material returned only if requested. Reports only if interested. Buys all rights. Pays $5; on publication.
Illustrations: Buys 1-5 illustrations/issue from freelancers. Prefers sumie or line drawings. Send Photostats or tear sheets to be kept on file if interested. Samples returned only if requested. Reports only if interested. Buys all rights. Pays $15, cover and $5, inside, b&w; on publication.

JEMS JOURNAL OF EMERGENCY MEDICAL SERVICES, Box 1026, Solana Beach CA 92075. (619)481-1128. Managing Editor: Rick Minerd. Emphasizes emergency medical services for emergency room physicians, nurses, paramedics, emergency medical technicians and administrators. Monthly. Circ. 33,000. Accepts previously published material. Original artwork returned after publication. Sample copy for SASE with $1.07 postage; art guidelines for SASE with 22¢ postage.
Illustrations: Buys 3-5 illustrations/issue from freelancers. Works on assignment only. Send query letter with Photostats, tear sheets, photocopies, slides or photos to be kept on file. Samples not filed are returned by SASE. Reports within 2 weeks. Buys one-time rights. Pays $150-200, color, cover; $35-50, b&w, and $50-75, color, inside; on publication.

JOURNAL OF ACCOUNTANCY, 1211 Avenue of the Americas, New York NY 10036. (212)575-5268. Art Coordinator: Jeryl Costello. Magazine emphasizing accounting for certified public accountants. Monthly. Circ. 300,000. Original artwork returned after publication.
Illustrations: Buys 2 illustrations/issue from freelancers. Prefers business, finance and law themes. Prefers mixed media, then pen & ink, airbrush, colored pencil, watercolor, acrylics, oils and pastels. Works on assignment only. Send query letter with brochure showing art style. Samples not filed are not returned. Reports only if interested. Call to schedule an appointment to show a portfolio, which should include original/final art, color, tear sheets and b&w. Buys first rights. Pays $1,200, color, cover; $150-600, color (depending on size), inside; on publication.
Tips: "I look for indications that an artist can turn the ordinary into something extraordinary, whether it be through concept or style. In addition to illustrators, I also hire freelancers to do charts and graphs. In portfolios, I like to see tear sheets showing how the art and editorial worked together."

JOURNAL OF THE NATIONAL TECHNICAL ASSOCIATION, 1240 S. Broad St., New Orleans LA 70125. (504)821-5694. Art/Production Director: Thomas Dennis. Emphasizing engineering and science. "Audience is the experienced black technical professional. We feature technical papers, career opportunity articles and scientific profiles." Quarterly. Circ. 10,000. Original artwork is sometimes returned to the artist after publication. Sample copies $5 and $1.50 postage.
Illustrations: Buys 4 illustrations/issue from freelancers. Works on assignment only. Send query letter with brochure, resume and tear sheets. Samples are filed. Samples not filed are returned only if requested by artist. Reports back within 30 days. Call or write to schedule an appointment to show a portfolio which should include original/final art, final reproduction/product, color and b&w. Buys one-time rights. Pays $200, b&w; $350, color, cover; $50, b&w; $150, color, inside; on publication.

JOURNAL OF READING, Int'l Reading Assn., Box 8139, Newark DE 19714-8139. (302)731-1600. Graphic Design Co-ordinator: Boni Nash. Magazine emphasizing teaching for teachers, reading specialists and professors. Published monthly Oct.-May (8 issues/year). Circ. 19,000. Sample copy for SASE with 60¢ postage. Art guidelines available.
Cartoons: Buys 1 cartoon/issue from freelancers. Prefers double panel with or without gagline; b&w line drawings. Send finished cartoons. "We buy what we want immediately and return the rest." Reports within 14 days. Buys one-time rights. Pays $20, b&w. Prefers themes about schools and reading.
Tips: " I like to see a series of artwork dedicated to a theme, preferably educational. I do not want to see wildlife."

JOURNAL OF THE WEST, 1531 Yuma, Box 1009, Manhattan KS 66502. (913)532-6733. Editor: Robin Higham. Emphasizes the West for readers in public libraries and classrooms. Quarterly. Circ. 4,500 (readership). Original artwork returned after publication. Sample copy available.

©1987 Dave Bailey

Freelance illustrator David Bailey of Wilmington, Delaware received $250 for first rights to this cover illustration for the* Journal of Reading, *located in Newark, Delaware. Graphics design coordinator Larry Husfelt asked for a pencil illustration of a past president of a reading association, and also overlays for a halftone silhouette. This was one of an eight-piece series, with a month to complete each part. Bailey says, "A series is always nice to have in your portfolio, because it helps to show continuity of style." Husfelt contacted Bailey after receiving a recommendation.

Illustrations: Uses cover illustrations only; artist supplies 4-color separations. Send query letter with brochure or samples and/or tear sheets to be kept on file. Prefers either photographs, prints or preferably duplicate slides as samples. Samples not filed are returned only if requested. Reports within 4 days. Negotiates rights purchased. Payment: exchange cover art for advertising space.
Tips: There is a trend toward "pastels with sometimes interesting and eye-catching results in Western scenes." Looks for work that is "original and not copied from a photograph; and is evidence of artistic talent and ability. We also are attempting to concentrate on the twentieth century, but other material will be considered. Please ask for a sample issue before submitting."

JUDICATURE, Suite 1600, 25 E. Washington, Chicago IL 60602. Contact: David Richert. Journal of the American Judicature Society. Published 6 times/year. Circ. 22,000. Accepts previously published material. Original artwork returned after publication. Sample copy for SASE with $1.07 postage.
Cartoons: Buys 1-2 cartoons/issue. Interested in "sophisticated humor revealing a familiarity with legal issues, the courts and the administration of justice." Send query letter with samples of style. SASE. Reports in 2 weeks. Buys one-time rights. Pays $35 for unsolicited cartoons.
Illustrations: Buys 2-3 illustrations/issue. Works on assignment only. Interested in styles from "realism to light cartoons." Prefers subjects related to court organization, operations and personnel. Send query letter with brochure showing art style. SASE. Reports within 2 weeks. Write to schedule an appointment to show a portfolio, which should include roughs and original/final art. Buys one-time rights. Negotiates payment. Pays $250, b&w, cover; $175, b&w, inside.

KEYBOARD WORLD, 8th Floor, 1115 Broadway, New York NY 10010. Group Design Director: Skip Bolen. "Keyboard World is directed to musicians interested in very contemporary music, keyboard setups, style, techniques and such." Monthly. Circ. 165,000. Original artwork is returned to the artist after publication. Samples copies for SASE with first-class postage. Art guidelines not available.
Cartoons: Buys 1-2 cartoons/issue from freelancers. Buys 12-18 cartoons/year from freelancers. Prefers artwork related to keyboard or guitar musicians, music theory, etc. Prefers single panel, double panel or multiple panel with gagline. Send query letter with samples of style. Samples are sometimes filed. Samples not filed are returned if requested. Reports back only if interested. Buys one-time rights. Pays $150, b&w; $200, color.
Illustrations: Buys 1-4 illustrations/issue from freelancers. Buys 60-100 illustrations/year from freelancers. Works on assignment only. Prefers "nothing safe or corporate. I'm looking for new and experi-

mental work, with an edge to it." Send query letter with brochure showing art style or tear sheets, Photostats, photocopies, photographs and portfolio. Samples are sometimes filed. Samples not filed are returned only if requested. Reports back only if interested. Call to schedule an appointment to show a portfolio, which should include tear sheets, final reproduction/product, Photostats, photographs, slides, color and b&w. Buys one-time rights. Pays $150, b&w; $200, color, inside; on publication.

KEYNOTER, Kiwanis International, 3636 Woodview Trace, Indianapolis IN 46268. (317)875-8755. Executive Editor: Jack Brockley. Art Director: Jim Patterson. Official publication of Key Club International, nonprofit high school service organization. Published 7 times/year. Copyrighted. Circ. 130,000. Previously published, photocopied and simultaneous submissions OK. Original artwork returned after publication. Free sample copy.
Illustrations: Buys 3 illustrations/issue from freelancers. Works on assignment only. "We only want to work with illustrators in the Indianapolis area; it is otherwise too inconvenient because of our production schedule." SASE. Reports in 2 weeks. "Freelancers should call our Production and Art Department for interview." Buys first rights. Pays by the project, $100-500. Pays on publication.

***KID CITY MAGAZINE**, 1 Lincoln Plaza, New York NY 10023. (212)595-3456, ext. 512. Art Director: Mecca Culbert. For ages 6-11.
Illustrations: Buys 60/year. Query with photocopied samples. SASE. Reports in 2 weeks. Buys one-time rights. Pays $300 minimum/page, b&w; $450/page, $600/spread, color; on acceptance.

KIWANIS, 3636 Woodview Trace, Indianapolis IN 46268. (317)875-8755. Executive Editor: Chuck Jonak. Art Director: James Patterson. Magazine emphasizing civic and social betterment, business, education, religion and domestic affairs for business and professional persons. Uses cartoons, illustrations, and photos from freelancers. Original artwork returned after publication. Published 10 times/year. Finds artists through talent sourcebooks, references/word-of-mouth and portfolio reviews.
Cartoons: Buys 1-2 cartoons/issue, all from freelancers. Interested in "daily life at home or work. Nothing off-color, no silly wife stuff, no blue-collar situations." Prefers finished cartoons. Send query letter with brochure showing art style or tear sheets, slides and photographs. SASE. Reports in 3-4 weeks. Pays $50, b&w; on acceptance.
Illustrations: Buys 6-8 illustrations/issue from freelancers. Prefers pen & ink, airbrush, colored pencil, watercolor, acrylics, mixed media, calligraphy and paper sculpture. Interested in themes that correspond to themes of articles. Works on assignment only. Keeps material on file after in-person contact with artist. Prefers portfolio, "anything and everything." SASE. Reports in 2 weeks. To show a portfolio, mail appropriate materials (out of town/state) or call or write to schedule an appointment; portfolio should include roughs, original/final art, final reproduction/product, color, tear sheets, Photostats, photographs and b&w. Buys first North American serial rights or negotiates. Pays $1,000, full-color, cover; $400-800, full-color, inside; $50-75, spot drawings; on acceptance.
Tips: "We deal direct—no reps. Have plenty of samples, particulary those that can be left with us. I see too much student or unassigned illustration in many portfolios."

LACMA PHYSICIAN, Box 3465, Los Angeles CA 90054. (213)483-1581. Managing Editor: Howard Bender. "Membership publication for physicians who are members of the Los Angeles County Medical Association; covers association news and medical issues." Published 20 times/year, twice monthly except January, July, August and December. Circ. 11,000. Does not accept previously published material. Original artwork returned after publication "if requested." Sample copy for SASE with $1.75 postage.
Illustrations: "Occasionally use illustrations for covers." These are "generally medical, but can relate to a specific feature story topic." Works on assignment only. Send query letter with business card and samples to be filed. Samples not kept on file are returned by SASE. Reports only if interested. Call or write for appointment. Negotiates payment; pays on acceptance. Buys all rights.

***LANDSCAPE TRADES**, 1293 Matheson Blvd., Mississauga, Ontario Canada. (416)629-1184. Rosemary Dexter. Readers are landscapers, nursery garden centers, grounds maintenance firms, wholesale growers, suppliers of goods to the landscaping industry, parks and recreation officials, horticulturists and others. Monthly. Circ. 5,086. Free sample copy.
Cartoons: Uses 1 cartoon/issue which should relate to the industry and have appeal to readers mentioned above. Prefers single or multiple panel b&w line drawings or washes with or without gag line but will also consider color cartoons. Send finished cartoons or samples of style. Buys one-time rights. Pays $20 (Canadian), b&w; on publication. "Please include phone number when writing."
Illustrations: Uses 1 illustration/issue; buys 0-1 from freelancers. "I'd be happy to keep samples on file and request illustrations when a particular need or idea comes up." Prefers b&w line drawings or washes for inside. Send finished art or samples of style. Pays $20 (Canadian) for inside b&w on publication. "Please include phone number when writing."

THE LEATHERNECK MAGAZINE, Magazine of the Marines, Box 1775, Quantico VA 22134. (703)640-6161. Art Director: Cheryl North. Emphasizes activities of Marines—air, land, sea ships, tanks, aircraft, physical fitness, etc. for Marines, dependents, retired, friends of the Corps, plus former Marines. Monthly. Circ. 105,000. Occasionally accepts previously published material. Sample copy available.
Cartoons: Uses 8 cartoons/issue; buys all from freelancers. Marine-related subjects only and "correctly pictured uniforms particularly." Prefers single panel with gagline; b&w line drawings. Send query letter with samples of style. Material not kept on file is returned by SASE. Reports within 30 days. Buys first rights. Pays $25, b&w; on acceptance.

***LEGAL ASSISTANT TODAY**, #534, 6060 N. Central Expressway, Dallas TX 75206. (214)369-6868. Editorial Assistant: Kyle Groves. Magazine emphasizing paralegal/legal assistants. "We give a general portrayal of the profession of legal assistants." Bimonthly. Circ. 20,000. Accepts previously published material. Original artwork is sometimes returned to the artist after publication. Sample copies $2.
Illustrations: Buys 3-4 illustrations/issue from freelancers. Send query letter.

LEGAL ECONOMICS, A Magazine of the Section of Economics of Law Practice of the American Bar Association, Box 11418, Columbia SC 29211. (803)754-3563 or 359-9940. Managing Editor/Art Director: Delmar L. Roberts. For the practicing lawyer. Published 8 times/year. Circ. 23,817. Previously published work rarely used. Pays on publication.
Cartoons: Primarily interested in cartoons "depicting situations inherent in the operation and management of a law office, e.g., operating word processing equipment and computers, interviewing, office meetings, lawyer/office staff situations, and client/lawyer situations. We are beginning to use 1-2 cartoons/issue. We never use material about courtroom situations." Send query letter with resume. Reports in 90 days. Usually buys all rights. Pays $50 for all rights; on acceptance.
Illustrations: Uses inside illustrations and, infrequently, cover designs. Prefers pen & ink, then airbrush, charcoal/pencil, watercolor, acrylics, oils, collage and mixed media. Send query letter with resume. Reports in 90 days. Usually buys all rights. Pays $75-125; more for covers and for 4-color; on publication.
Tips: "There's an increasing need for artwork to illustrate high-tech articles on technology in the law office. We're also interested in computer graphics for such articles."

LEGION, 359 Kent St., Ottawa, Ontario K2P 0R6 Canada. (613)235-8741. Editor-in-Chief: Mac Johnston. Contact: Art Director. For Royal Canadian Legion members. Published 10 times/year. Circ. 528,908. Original artwork returned after publication. Free sample copy.
Illustrations: Buys 6-8 illustrations/issue from freelancers. Interested in "various techniques." Works on assignment only. "Because of the invariable loss of time clearing illustrations through Canada Customs, Canadian artists are used to illustrate most stories." Provide 35mm slides to be kept on file for possible future assignments. Prefers to see portfolio. Reports immediately. Buys various rights. Cover: Pays $450-1,500, color. Inside: Pays $100-1,200, b&w; $100-1,500, color; on acceptance.

LEISURE WHEELS, Box 7302, Station E, Calgary, Alberta T3C 3M2 Canada. (403)263-2707. Publisher: Murray Gimbel. Emphasizes recreational vehicles, travel and outdoors for upper income, ages 30-65. Yearly. Circ. 100,000. Sample copy 50¢; free art guidelines.
Cartoons: Uses 4 cartoons/issue; buys all from freelancers. Receives 1 submission/month from freelancers. Especially needs cartoons. Subject matter should concern traveling and camping as it relates to trailering, motorhoming, fishing or hiking. Prefers b&w line drawings with gag line. Send samples of style. SASE (nonCanadians include International Reply Coupons). Reports in 2 weeks. Cartoons can appear in other publications. Pays $25 for b&w.
Illustrations: Uses 4 illustrations/issue; buys all from freelancers. Receives 1 submission/week from freelancers. Usually works on assignment. Illustration needs identical to cartoons. Prefers b&w line drawings for inside. Send samples of style. SASE (nonCanadians include International Reply Coupons). Reports in 3 weeks. "Prefer illustrations not appear in a similar magazine." Pays $50-100 for inside b&w on publication.
Tips: "We now feature a broader range of editorial content. Basically, any subject that applies to recreational activity outdoors."

PETER LI, INC./PFLAUM PRESS, 2451 E. River Rd., Dayton OH 45439. (513)294-5785. Art Director: Jim Conley. Publishes three monthly magazines—*The Catechist*, *Classroom Computer Learning* and *Today's Catholic Teacher*.
Illustrations: Works with 20 freelance artists/year. "Local artists are, of course, more preferable but it's not an absolute." Uses artists for 4-color cover illustrations and b&w and 2-color spot illustrations.

"We are only interested in *professional* illustrators, especially those with fresh, innovative styles. Experience a plus but not necessary." Works on assignment only. Send query letter with Photostats, photographs, slides or tear sheets. Samples returned by SASE. Reports only if interested. Pays by the project, $100-600 average. Considers complexity of the project when establishing payment. Buys all rights.

LIGHT & LIFE, 303 Potero St., #29-106, Santa Cruz CA 95060. (408)426-1537. Art Director: Emiline Secaur. "Emphasizes evangelical Christianity with Wesleyan slant for a cross-section readership." Readers are mostly of Free Methodist denomination. Monthly. Circ. 43,500. Original artwork returned after publication, if requested and postage included. Sample copy $1.50. Finds most freelance artists through references/word-of-mouth, portfolio reviews and samples received through the mail.
Cartoons: Rarely used. Interested in religious themes. Format: single panel b&w line drawings with or without gagline. Prefers finished cartoons. SASE. Reports in 4 weeks. Buys all rights. Pays $5-20; on acceptance.
Illustrations: Buys 2-4 illustrations/issue from freelancers. Prefers contemporary style; pen & ink, airbrush, charcoal/pencil, watercolor, markers, mixed media and calligraphy. Interested in art that illustrates themes of articles. Works on assignment only. Send query letter with brochure showing art style or resume and tear sheets. Reports in 4 weeks. To show a portfolio, mail original/final art, final reproduction/product, color and tear sheets. Artists should show a representative sampling of their work. Buys all rights on a work-for-hire basis. Pays $25 and up, inside b&w and 2-color; on publication.
Tips: "Does the artwork have freshness rather than an overworked appearance? I look for an obvious use of adequate resources (models) to avoid human body distortion, and for consistency within a piece of artwork. Consider the media used; will it reproduce well? Use quality drawing paper or appropriate type of illustration board. Freelancers don't go to enough trouble and expense to 'show off' their work; they use cheap photo albums, photocopies. I would encourage availability of a list of their employment in the art field as well as their educational background, and the use of tear sheets of published work."

LOG HOME GUIDE FOR BUILDERS & BUYERS, Rt. 32 & 321, Cosby TN 37722. (615)487-2256. Editor: Allan Muir. Emphasizes buying and building log homes; energy-efficiency. Audience: ages 25-60, college educated, middle- upper-middle income; prefer country life. Quarterly. Circ. 150,000. Sometimes accepts previously published material. Original artwork returned after publication. Sample copy $3.50; art guidelines for SASE.
Cartoons: Buys occasional cartoons/issue from freelancers. Themes include renderings of log homes; warmth of log home living; amusing aspects of building with logs; and country living. Prefers single panel without gagline; b&w line drawings, b&w and color washes. Send query letter with samples of style or roughs to be kept on file. Material not filed is returned if accompanied by SASE. Reports within 6 weeks. Negotiates rights purchased. Pays $10-25, b&w; $25-50, color; on publication.
Illustrations: Buys occasional illustrations/issue from freelancers. Themes include log home renderings; log homes in rural scenes; and beavers and badgers in natural settings. Send query letter with brochure, resume, business card and samples to be kept on file. Prefers tear sheets, slides and photographs as samples. Samples not filed are returned by SASE. Reports within 6 weeks. Negotiates rights purchased. Pays $15-35, b&w and $25-50, color, inside; on publication.

LOLLIPOPS, Box 299, Carthage IL 62321-0299. (217)357-3981. Art Director: Tom Sjoerdsma. Magazine for children in pre-school through second grade. Published 5 times/year.
Illustrations: Works with 20 freelance artists/year. Prefers pen & ink. "I am open to cartoon and realistic treatment of kids and to typical storybook illustrations using children and animals." Send query letter with photocopies. Samples are filed. Reports back within 2 weeks. Buys all rights. Work-for-hire. Pays $5/hour.

LONE STAR HUMOR, Lone Star Publications of Humor, Suite 103, Box 29000, San Antonio TX 78229. Editor/Publisher: Lauren Barnett. "Book-by-subscription" (magazine-type format). Audience: "comedy connoisseurs," and "others who like to laugh." Published about 3 times/year. Circ. 1,200. Sometimes accepts previously published material. Original artwork returned after publication. Inquire for update on sample copy; art guidelines for SASE with first-class postage.
Cartoons: Buys 20-25 cartoons/issue from freelancers. Prefers single, double or multiple panel with or without gagline; b&w line drawings. Send roughs or finished cartoons. Material returned by SASE. Reports within 3 months. Negotiates rights purchased. Pays on publication ("but we try to pay before"). Inquire for update on pay scale.

THE LOOKOUT, 8121 Hamilton Ave., Cincinnati OH 45231. (513)931-4050. Editor-in-Chief: Mark A. Taylor. For conservative Christian adults and young adults. Weekly. Circ. 140,000. Original artwork not returned after publication, unless requested. Sample copy and artists' guidelines available for 50¢.
Cartoons: Uses 1 cartoon/issue; buys 20/year from freelancers. Interested in church, Sunday school

and Christian family themes. Send roughs or finished cartoons. Samples returned by SASE. Reports in 2 weeks. Buys one-time rights. Pays $15-35.
Illustrations: Buys 3-4 illustrations/issue. Interested in "adults, families, interpersonal relationships; also, graphic treatment of titles." Works on assignment only. Send query letter with brochure, flyer or tear sheets to be kept on file for future assignments to Frank Sutton, art director, at above address. Reporting time varies. Buys all rights but will reassign. Inside: Pays $125 for b&w, $150 for full-color illustrations, firm; on acceptance. Cover: "Sometimes more for cover work."

LOS ANGELES, 1888 Century Park E, Los Angeles CA 90067. (213)557-7592. Design Director: William Delorme. Emphasizes lifestyles, cultural attractions, pleasures, problems and personalities of Los Angeles and the surrounding area. Monthly. Circ. 170,000. SASE. Reports in 2-3 weeks. Especially needs very localized contributors—custom projects needing person-to-person concepting and implementation. Previously published work OK. Pays on publication. Sample copy $3.
Cartoons: Contact Geoff Miller, editor-in-chief. Buys 5-7/issue on current events, environment, family life, politics, social life and business; single, double or multi panel with gagline. Mail roughs. Pays $25-50, b&w line or tone drawings.
Illustrations: Buys 10/issue on assigned themes. Send or drop off samples showing art style (tear sheets, Photostats, photocopies and dupe slides). Pays $300-500, color, cover; $150-500, b&w and $200-800, color, inside; on publication.
Tips: "Show work similar to that used in the magazine—a sophisticated style. Study a particular publication's content, style and format. Then proceed accordingly in submitting sample work." There is a trend toward "imaginative imagery and technical brilliance with computer-enhanced art being a factor. Know the stylistic essence of a magazine at a gut level as well as at a perceptive level. Identify with Los Angeles or Southern California."

***LOST TREASURE**, Box 937, Bixby OK 74008. (918)496-8169. Managing Editor: Kathryn L. Dyer. Emphasizes treasure hunting for treasure hunters, coinshooters, metal detector owners. Monthly. Circ. 50,000. Sample copy for 9x12 SASE.
Cartoons: Buys "some horizontal cartoons;" all from freelancers. Receives 10 cartoons from freelancers/month. Cartoons should pertain to treasure hunting, people using metal detectors, prospecting, etc. Prefers single, panel b&w line drawings or b&w washes with gagline. Send query letter with finished cartoons. SASE. Reports in 6-8 weeks. Pays $5 on publication. Buys first North American serial rights.
Tips: "Cartoon should be very treasure hunting-oriented and funny. Prefer irony to slap stick."

***LOTUS**, 1 Broadway, Cambridge MA 02142. Art Director: Deborah Flynn-Hanrahan. "For task-oriented professionals who look to their personal computers and software for a quick, powerful solution to a variety of their business problems. It includes tutorials, product reviews, industry overviews, explorations of vertical markets, etc." Monthly. Circ. 300,000. Original artwork is returned to the artist after publication. Art guidelines available.
Illustrations: Buys 22 illustrations/issue from freelancers. Works on assignment only. Prefers conceptual content combined with unique images. (Computer-related imagery not necessary.) Send query letter with brochure showing art style or tear sheets, slides or photographs. Samples are filed. Samples not filed are returned only if requested. Reports back only if interested. To show a portfolio, mail original/final art, tear sheets, final reproduction/product, Photostats, photographs, slides, color and b&w. Buys first rights or reprint rights. Pays $1,000, color, cover; $250, b&w; $300, color, inside (spot, 1/4 page); on acceptance.
Tips: "Be familiar with the publication and its subject matter. (Do not send obviously inappropriate material like fashion or juvenile). Be aware that *LOTUS* uses a very sophisticated, oblique, almost fine-arts approach to its visuals. It is *not* a trade publication for visual illiterates."

LOUISIANA LIFE MAGAZINE, 4200 S. I-10 Service Rd., Metairie LA 70002. (504)456-2220. Art Director: Julie Dalton Gourgues. Emphasizes the lifestyle of Louisiana (food, entertainment, work, etc.) for the upper-income Louisianian, "proud of the state and its diversity." Bimonthly. Circ. 50,000. Original artwork returned after publication. Sample copies available.
Illustrations: Buys 3 illustrations/issue from freelancers. Works on assignment only. Send query letter with brochure and tear sheets to be kept on file. Samples not kept on file are returned by SASE. Reports only if interested. Call or write to schedule an appointment to show a portfolio, which should include original/final art (if possible), final reproduction/product, slides and tear sheets. Buys one-time rights. Pays $85, b&w; $250, color, cover; $185, color, inside; on publication.
Tips: "Do your homework. Explore the magazine before you submit any work. Tailor your selection based on your research."

THE LUTHERAN, 8765 W. Higgins Rd., Chicago IL 60631. (312)380-2540. Editor-in-Chief: Edgar R. Trexler. General interest magazine of the Evangelical Lutheran Church in America. Published 18 times a year. Circ. 1.2 million. Previously published work OK. Original artwork returned after publication on request. Free sample copy.
Cartoons: Buys 1 cartoon/issue from freelancers. Receives 30 submissions/week from freelancers. Interested in humorous or thought-provoking cartoons on religion or about issues of concern to Christians; single panel. Prefers roughs or finished cartoons. SASE. Reports usually within a week. Buys first rights. Pays $25-50, b&w line drawings and washes; on publication.
Illustrations: Buys 2 illustrations/issue from freelancers. Interested in church-related family scenes, Christmas, Advent, Baptism, Communion, Confirmation, church entering, leaving, interior, exterior, choirs, funerals, Easter and Lent. Works on assignment only. Send samples of style to keep on file for future assignments. Buys all rights on a work-for-hire basis. Samples returned by SASE if requested. Buys 30-40/year on assigned themes. Pays $150, b&w and 2-color; on publication.

THE LUTHERAN JOURNAL, 7317 Cahill Rd., Edina MN 55435. Contact: J.W. Leykom. Family magazine for Lutheran Church members, middle aged and older. Previously published work OK. Free sample copy.
Illustrations: Seasonal 1-, 2- or full-color covers. Mail art with price. Buys one-time rights. Pays on publication.

MADE TO MEASURE, 600 Central Ave., Highland Park IL 60035. (312)831-6678. Publisher: William Halper. Emphasizes uniforms, career clothes, men's tailoring and clothing. Magazine distributed to retailers, manufacturers and uniform group purchasers. Semiannually. Circ. 24,000. Art guidelines available.
Cartoons: Buys 15 cartoons/issue from freelancers. Prefers themes relating to subject matter of magazine; also general interest. Prefers single panel with or without gagline; b&w line drawings. Send query letter with samples of style or finished cartoons. Any cartoons not purchased are returned to artist. Reports back. Buys first rights. Pays $20-25 b&w, on acceptance.

MAGIC CHANGES, 2S424 Emerald Green Dr., Warrenville IL 60555. (312)393-7856. Editor: John Sennett. Emphasizes fantasy and poetry for college students, housewives, teachers, artists and musicians: "People with both an interesting and artistic slant." Annually. Circ. 500. Accepts previously published material. Original artwork returned after publication. Sample copy $4; art guidelines for SASE.
Cartoons: Buys 2 cartoons/issue from freelancers. Considers space, art, animals and street activity themes. Single, double, or multi panel with or without gagline; b&w line drawings. Send query letter with finished cartoons. Material returned by SASE. Reports within 2 weeks. Acquires first rights. Pays $0-10.
Illustrations: Buys 10 illustrations/issue from freelancers. Considers city, wilderness, bird, space and fantasy themes. Prefers pen & ink, then charcoal/pencil and computer illustration. Send query letter with samples. Samples returned by SASE. Reports within 2 weeks. To show a portfolio, mail original/final art, final reproduction/product or b&w. Acquires first rights. Pays $0-10.
Tips: "I want to see black-and-white drawings, no larger than 8½x11. I do not want to see slides. Target your samples to our needs."

MAGICAL BLEND, Box 11303, San Francisco CA 94101. Art Editor: Jeff Fletcher. Emphasizes spiritual exploration, transformation and visionary arts. Quarterly. Circ. 75,000. Original artwork sometimes returned after publication. Sample copy $4; art guidelines for SASE.
Cartoons: Buys 1 cartoon/issue from freelancers. Buys 4 cartoons/year from freelancers. Send query letter with Photostats.
Illustrations: Buys 5 illustrations/issue from freelancers. Receives 1 submission/week from freelancers. "We keep samples on file and work by assignment according to the artists and our time table and workability. We accept b&w line drawings, also pencil and pre-separated color work. We look for pieces with occult, psychic and spiritual subjects with positive, inspiring, uplifting feeling." Especially needs Oriental themes and strong cultural themes, i.e., African, Latin American, Zen brush work, Indian, etc. Send query letter with brochure or tear sheets, final reproduction/product, Photostats, photographs and slides. SASE. Reports in 6 months. Buys first North American serial rights. Rights revert to artist. Pays in copies.

The asterisk before a listing indicates that the listing is new in this edition. New markets are often the most receptive to freelance submissions.

Tips: "We are basically a print works from San Francisco's Visionary School, although we also print occasional abstract surreal, expressionist/impressionistic works. We want work that is energetic and thoughtful, and that has a hopeful outlook on the future. Our page size is 8½x11, although few full-page works are printed. Please send a SASE with your slides or artwork if you want them returned. High-quality, camera-ready reproductions are preferable over originals. The best way to see what we need is to send $4 for a sample copy of *Magical Blend*. If you are doing work of quality, that is positive and inspiring, we would like to see it."

***MANAGEMENT ACCOUNTING**, 10 Paragon Dr., Montvale NJ 07645. (201)573-6269. Managing Editor: Robert F. Randall. Emphasizes management accounting for management accountants, controllers, chief accountants, treasurers. Monthly. Circ. 85,000. Accepts simultaneous submissions. Original artwork not returned after publication. Sample copy free for SASE.
Cartoons: Buys 1 cartoon/issue from freelancers. Prefers single panel with gagline; b&w line drawings. Send finished cartoons. Material not kept on file is returned by SASE. Reports within 2 weeks. Buys one-time rights. Pays $15-25, b&w; on acceptance.
Illustrations: Buys 1 illustration/issue.

***MANAGING**, Graduate School of Business, University of Pittsburgh, Pittsburgh PA 15260. (412)648-1644. Editor: Charles W. Shane. Emphasizes business for "middle- to upper-level managers, primarily in the Pittsburgh area." Published 4 times/year. Circ. 15,000. Previously published material OK.
Cartoons: Interested in business-related themes; single panel with or without gagline, b&w line drawings. Send query letter with roughs and samples of style. Samples returned on request. Reports in 2 months. Buys one-time rights and reprint rights. Pays $10-30, b&w; on acceptance.
Tips: "We don't publish much freelance artwork."

MARRIAGE AND FAMILY LIVING, Abbey Press, St. Meinrad IN 47577. (812)357-8011. Contact: Art Director. For Christian families. Monthly. Circ. 40,000. Buys one-time rights and exclusive rights. Pays on publication.
Illustrations: Buys 20 illustrations/year.

MARVEL COMICS, 387 Park Ave. S., New York NY 10016. (212)696-0808. Contact: appropriate editors. Publishes comic books and graphic novels. Created superheroes like Spider Man and the Incredible Hulk. Produces up to 50 titles/month.
Illustrations: Uses freelance artists for inking, lettering, pencilling and color work. Most artists work in-house. Pencillers should send 4-5 samples of sketches one-and-one-half times up on kid-finish Bristol paper, which demonstrate skills at figure drawing and narration; there should be some continuity. "Draw any character you want, but show a variety of settings and situations. Prove that you can draw ordinary people, superheroes, action and quiet scenes." Inkers should submit 4-5 pages of pencil work which has been inked. Submit both the inked pencil drawing and the photocopy of the original pencil art. Letterers should submit samples of lettering one-and-one-half times up with sound effects, titles, and display lettering. Letter your samples in India ink on kid-finish Bristol paper. Colorists should photocopy pages of b&w comic book pages on bond paper, then color appropriate areas with Dr. Martin's watercolor dyes. Most in-house work is work-for-hire, with the artist receiving a royalty after a certain number of sales. Graphic novels are creator-owned, the artist retaining the copyright. Pays $70-100/page for pencilling and $45-70/page for inking.
Tips: "Before sending us anything, take time to give your work a long hard objective look. Is it really in the same league with the very best work you see printed in our publications? Be honest with yourself. If it isn't as good or better than our best, don't send it. Practice, study and work to get better instead."

***MB NEWS**, 1612 Central St., Evanston IL 60201. (312)869-2031. Managing Editor: Ronnveig Ernst. "A trade publication that goes to members of the Monument Builders of North America trade association—wholesalers, retailers, manufacturers, service-related businesses, i.e., diamond saws, abrasives—emphasizing monument building, mostly cemetary monuments, some war memorials, some building cladding, for marble, granite, bronze and brass. Monthly. Circ. 2,000. Sometimes accepts previously published material. Original artwork is sometimes returned to the artist after publication. Sample copies available.
Illustrations: Buys 2-3 illustrations/issue from freelancers. Works on assignment only. Send query letter with brochure showing art style or tear sheets, Photostats or photocopies. Samples are filed. Samples not filed are returned by SASE, or not returned. Reports back only if interested. Write to schedule an appointment to show a portfolio. Negotiates rights purchased. Pays $10-25, b&w; on acceptance.
Tips: "Need artists that are looking for exposure rather than reasonable amounts of money (our acquisition budget is 0.00) and have a fresh, clean style, neither 'trendy' nor imitative."

MEDIA & METHODS, 1429 Walnut St., Philadelphia PA 19102. (215)563-3501. Emphasizes the methods and technologies of teaching for all school teachers and administrators. Bimonthly. Circ. 40,000 +. Accepts previously published material. Returns original artwork after publication. Sample copy for SASE.
Illustrations: Buys 1-2 illustrations/issue from freelancers. Send query letter with brochure, business card, tear sheets, photocopies or photographs. Material not filed is returned by SASE. Reports back only if interested. To show a portfolio, mail original/final art, final reproduction/product, color, tear sheets, Photostats, photographs and b&w. Buys first rights or reprint rights. Pays $175 for b&w and $250 for color, cover; $150 for b&w and $175 for color, inside; on publication.
Tips: "We like to see consistency in artwork so that if we commission some art we have an idea of what we'll get."

MEDICAL ECONOMICS FOR SURGEONS, 680 Kinderkamack Rd., Oradell NJ 07649. (201)267-3030. Art Administrator: Mrs. Donna DeAngelis. Magazines for physicians, surgeons and financial specialists. Monthly. Circ. 45,000. Accepts previously published material. Original artwork returned after publication.
Cartoons: Buys 5-7 cartoons/issue from freelancers. Prefers medically-related themes. Prefers single panel with gagline; b&w line drawings and b&w washes. Send query letter with finished cartoons. Samples not filed are returned by SASE. Reports within 2 months. Buys all rights. Pays $50, b&w.
Illustrations: Buys 5-10 illustrations/issue from freelancers. Works on assignment only. Send query letter with resume, tear sheets, and slides. Samples not filed are returned by SASE. Reports back only if interested. Call to schedule an appointment to show a portfolio, which should include original/final art (if possible) and tear sheets. Buys one-time rights. Pays $300-1,000, color, cover; $50-300, b&w, $200-500, color, inside; on acceptance.

MEDICAL ECONOMICS MAGAZINE, 680 Kinderkamack Rd., Oradell NJ 07649. (201)599-8442. Art Administrator: Mrs. Donna DeAngelis. Magazine for those interested in the financial and legal aspects of running a medical practice. Bimonthly. Circ. 182,000. Accepts previously published material. Original artwork returned after publication.
Cartoons: Buys 10 cartoons/issue from freelancers. Prefers medically-related themes. Prefers single panel, with gagline; b&w line drawings and b&w washes. Send query letter with finished cartoons. Material not filed is returned by SASE. Reports within 8 weeks. Buys all rights. Pays $50, b&w.
Illustrations: Buys 10-12 illustrations/issue from freelancers. Prefers pen & ink, airbrush, charcoal/pencil, colored pencil, watercolor, acrylics, oils, pastels, collage, mixed media and 3-D illustration. Works on assignment only. Send query letter with resume and samples. Samples not filed are returned by SASE. Reports only if interested. Call to schedule an appointment to show a portfolio, which should include original/final art (if possible) and tear sheets. Buys one-time rights. Pays $350-1,200, color, cover; $80-400, b&w and $300-850, color, inside; on acceptance.
Tips: "In a portfolio, include original art and tear sheets, showing conceptualization. I do not want to see work copied from another source."

MEDICAL TIMES, 80 Shore Rd., Port Washington NY 11050. Executive Editor: Anne Mattarella. Emphasizes clinical medical articles. Monthly. Circ. 120,000. Sample copy $5.
Cartoons: Buys 5-6 cartoons/year from freelancers. Prefers medical themes, "but nothing insulting to our audience. Jokes about doctors' fees are *not* funny to doctors." Accepts single panel with gagline; b&w line drawings. Send query letter with finished cartoons; "we'll either accept and pay or return them within one month." Negotiates rights purchased. Pays $25, b&w; on acceptance.
Illustrations: Buys 2 or 3 illustrations/issue, 24-36/year from freelancers. Works on assignment only. Send query letter with resume and medical samples such as tear sheets, Photostats, photocopies, slides

"My first assignment was for a piece of spot art for CATS Magazine. I sent a resume and letter asking for a sample copy. Knowing my style would fit, I submitted an illustration to be used as spot art. I kept to a general theme to broaden its possibilities of uses."

—Audrey Przybylski
New Castle, Pennsylvania

and photographs. Samples not filed are returned. Reports within 1 month. Write to schedule an appointment to show a portfolio, which should include original art (1 or 2 pieces only) and printed material "so we can see how the artist's work reproduces. Most of the portfolio should consist of printed pieces." Negotiates rights purchased. Payment varies; pays on acceptance.
Tips: "With the ever-increasing number of medical journals competing for the same ad budgets, competition and cost controls are becoming fierce. This may mean a cutback in the amount of artwork purchased by some of the marginally successful journals."

MEMCO NEWS, Box 1079, Appleton WI 54912. Editor: Richard F. Metko. Emphasizes "welding applications as performed with Miller Electric equipment. Readership ranges from workers in small shops to metallurgical engineers." Quarterly. Circ. 44,000. Previously published material and simultaneous submissions OK. Original artwork not returned after publication.

MEN'S LOOK, Suite 3800, 2029 Century Park E., Los Angeles CA 90067-3054. (213)556-1173. Art Director: Dot Dakota. Estab. 1987. Magazine emphasizing lifestyle trends, fashion and career-oriented tips for men ages 18-34. "We're more accessible to younger men than is *Esquire* , and we have more information than GQ." Circ. 200,000.
Illustration: Prefers "young, fresh and modern" illustrations. Humorous and spot illustrations are used to highlight features. Send query letter with tear sheets, Photostats, photocopies, slides and photographs. Samples are filed. Reports back only if interested. Portfolios are dropped off; portfolio should include thumbnails, roughs, original/final art, tear sheets, Photostats, photographs and slides. Negotiates rights purchased. Pays $125-400, color, inside; on acceptance.

THE MERCEDES-BENZ STAR, 1235 Pierce St., Lakewood CO 80214. (303)235-0116. Editor: Frank Barrett. Magazine emphasizing new and old Mercedes-Benz automobiles for members of the Mercedes-Benz Club of America and other automotive enthusiasts. Bimonthly. Circ. 25,000. Does not usually accept previously published material. Returns original artwork after publication. Sample copy for SASE with $2 postage.
Illustrations: Buys 1-5/issue. Prefers Mercedes-Benz related themes. Looks for authenticity in subject matter. Prefers pen & ink, airbrush and oils. Send query letter with resume, slides or photographs to be kept on file except for material requested to be returned. Write for appointment to show portfolio. Samples not filed are returned by SASE. Reports within 3 weeks. Buys first rights. Pays $100-1,500; pays on publication.
Tips: " In a portfolio, include subject matter similar to ours."

MICHIGAN OUT OF DOORS, Box 30235, Lansing MI 48909. Contact: Kenneth S. Lowe. Emphasizes outdoor recreation, especially hunting and fishing; conservation; and environmental affairs. Sample copy $1.50.
Illustrations: "Following the various hunting and fishing seasons we have a need for illustration material; we consider submissions 6-8 months in advance." Reports as soon as possible. Pays $15 for pen & ink illustrations in a vertical treatment; on acceptance.
Tips: "Our magazine has shifted from newsprint to enamel stock. We have our own art department and thus do not require a great deal of special material."

***MID ATLANTIC COUNTRY MAGAZINE**, #305, 300 N. Washington St., Alexandria VA 22314. Art Director: Karol Keane. Magazine emphasizing travel/leisure, home/entertaining and gardening. "We are a travel/leisure magazine for the Mid-Atlantic region; we are the only magazine of this kind in this market. We use illustrations in our feature stories as well as regular columns such as our gardening column." Monthly. Accepts previously published material. Art guidelines free for SASE with first-class postage.
Illustrations: Buys 2-4 illustrations/issue from freelancers. Buys 25-100 illustrations/year from freelancers. Works on assignment only. Prefers New Yorker style. Contact only through artist's agent who should send brochure and resume. Samples are not filed. Samples not filed are not returned. Does not report back. Write to schedule an appointment to show a portfolio, which should include tear sheets, color and b&w. Buys one-time rights. Pays $50, b&w; $75, color, inside; on publication.
Tips: "We very rarely use people shots. Moreover, we use landscape and still-life, mostly soft pencil work, but occasionally pen and ink, no marker work."

MILITARY LIFESTYLE MAGAZINE, 1732 Wisconsin Ave. NW, Washington DC 20007. Art Director: Judi Connelly. Emphasizes active-duty military lifestyles for military families. Published 10 times/year. Circ. 530,000. Original artwork returned after publication.
Illustrations: Buys 2-6 illustrations/issue from freelancers. Theme/style depends on editorial content. Works on assignment only. Send brochure and business card to be kept on file. Accepts Photostats, tear

sheets, photocopies, slides, photographs, etc. as nonreturnable samples. Samples returned only if requested. Reports only if interested. Buys first rights. Payment depends on size published, cover and inside; pays on publication.

MILITARY MARKET MAGAZINE, Springfield VA 22159-0210. (703)750-8676. Editor: Nancy M. Tucker. Emphasizes "the military's PX and commissary businesses for persons who manage and buy for the military's commissary and post exchange systems; also manufacturers and sales companies who supply them." Monthly. Circ. 10,000. Simultaneous submissions OK. Original artwork not returned after publication.
Cartoons: Buys 3-4 cartoons/issue from freelancers. Interested in themes relating to "retailing/buying of groceries and general merchandise from the point of view of the store managers and workers"; single panel with or without gagline, b&w line drawings. Send finished cartoons. Samples returned by SASE. Reports in 6 months. Buys all rights. Pays $25, b&w; on acceptance.
Tips: "We use freelance cartoonists only—*no* other freelance artwork."

MILLER/FREEMAN PUBLICATIONS, 500 Howard St., San Francisco CA 94105. (415)397-1881. Associate Art Director: thomas E. Dorsaneo. Business magazines on paper and pulp, computers and medical subjects. Monthly. Circ. 100,000+. Returns original artwork after publication.
Illustrations: Buys 2 illustrations/month from freelancers. Works on assignment only. Send query letter with samples to be kept on file. Samples not filed are returned by SASE. Reports back only if interested. Negotiates rights purchased. Payment varies; on acceptance.

MPLS. ST. PAUL MAGAZINE, Suite 1030, 12 S. 6th St., Minneapolis MN 55402. (612)339-7571. Contact: Tara Christopherson. City/regional magazine. For "professional people of middle-upper income levels, college educated, interested in the arts, dining and the good life of Minnesota." Monthly. Circ. 48,000. Original artwork returned after publication.
Illustrations: Uses 12 illustrations/issue. Works on assignment only. Arrange interview to show portfolio. Provide business card, flyer or tear sheet to be kept on file for future assignments. Reports in 2 weeks. Buys first North American serial rights, and all rights on a work-for-hire basis. Pays $75-200, b&w; $600 maximum/full-page, color; on acceptance.

MISSOURI LIFE, Suite 7, 4825 Everhart, Corpus Christi TX 78413. (512)857-7293. Editor: Debra Gluck. Magazine about Missouri. Readers are people interested in where to go, what to do in the state, and the beauty and fascination of Missouri places and faces. Bimonthly. Circ. 30,000. Original artwork returned after publication. Sample copy $3; art guidelines for SASE.
Cartoons: Used to illustrate some departments and features.
Illustrations: Uses original artwork depicting Missouri places or people. Receives 2 illustrations/week from freelance artists. Especially needs variety of b&w and color line art and other types of art for illustration of specific stories, on assignment; interested in a variety of styles. Format: b&w, color cover washes, inside and cover color washes and original art that will reproduce for offset printing/web. Samples returned by SASE. Provide letter of inquiry, tear sheet, proposal and sample of work to be kept on file for future assignments. Reports in 4 weeks. Buys first North American serial rights. Pays $25-50 for b&w, on publication.
Tips: "Send samples of work that show the styles and media you are experienced and good at."

MODERN DRUMMER, 870 Pompton Ave., Cedar Grove NJ 07009. (201)239-4140. Editor-in-Chief: Ronald Spagnardi. Art Director: David Creamer. For drummers, all ages and levels of playing ability with varied interests within the field of drumming. Monthly. Circ. 85,000. Previously published work OK. Original artwork returned after publication. Sample copy $2.95.
Cartoons: Buys 3-5 cartoons/year. Uses 1 cartoon/every other issue. Interested in drumming; single and double panel. "We want strictly drummer-oriented gags." Prefers finished cartoons or roughs. SASE. Reports in 3 weeks. Buys first North American serial rights. Pays $5-25; on publication.

***MODERN LITURGY**, #290, 160 E. Virginia St., San Jose CA 95112. Editor: Kenneth Guentert. For religious artists, musicians and planners of worship services for Catholic and Protestant liturgical traditions. Published 9 times/year. Circ. 15,000. Sample copy $4.
Illustrations: Holds two contests each year for liturgical artists. Features liturgical art and artists in every issue. Send query with samples. SASE. Reports in 4-6 weeks. Buys all rights but may reassign rights to artist after publication. Pays with subscription, copies, advertising credit.

MODERN MATURITY, 3200 East Carson, Lakewood CA 90712. (213)496-2277. Picture Editor: Ms. M.J. Wadolny. Emphasizes health, lifestyles, travel, sports, finance and contemporary activities for members 50 years and over. Bimonthly. Previously published work OK. Original artwork returned after

publication. Sample copy available.
Cartoons: Uses 4 cartoons/issue; buys 2/issue from freelancers. Receives 50 submissions/week from freelancers. Interested in general interest themes. Send finished cartoons, color and b&w. SASE. Reports in 2 months. Buys all rights on a work-for-hire basis. Pays $200, 8x10" finished cartoons.

MODERN PLASTICS, 1221 Avenue of Americas, New York NY 10020. (212)512-3491. Art Director: Bob Barravecchia. Trade journal emphasizing technical articles for manufacturers of plastic parts and machinery. Monthly. Circ. 60,000. Original artwork is sometimes returned after publication.
Illustrations: Prefers pen & ink. Works on assignment only. Send brochure. Samples are filed. Does not report back. Call to schedule an appointment to show a portfolio, which should include tear sheets, photographs, slides, color and b&w. Buys all rights. Pays $800, color, cover; $75, color, inside; on acceptance.

MONEY MAKER, 5705 N. Lincoln Ave., Chicago IL 60659. Art Director: Debora Clark. Magazine emphasizing financial investments. Bimonthly. Circ. 300,000. Accepts previously published material. Original artwork returned after publication.
Illustration: Buys 15 illustrations/issue. Works on assignment only. Prefers financial themes in any art style. Prefers pen & ink, airbrush, charcoal/pencil, colored pencil, watercolor, acrylics, oils and mixed media. Send query letter with brochure showing art style, tear sheets, Photostats, photocopies and slides. Samples are filed or returned by SASE. Reports only if interested. To show a portfolio, mail appropriate materials or write to schedule an appointment; portfolio should include original/final art and tear sheets. Buys reprint rights or negotiates rights purchased. Payment is negotiable.
Tips: "Show a bit of everything in your portfolio."

THE MORGAN HORSE, Box 1, Westmoreland NY 13490. (315)735-7522. Production Manager: Carol Misiaszek. Emphasizes all aspects of the Morgan horse breed including educating Morgan owners, trainers and enthusiasts on breeding and training programs; the true type of the Morgan breed, techniques on promoting the breed, how-to articles, as well as preserving the history of the breed. Monthly. Circ. 10,000. Accepts previously published material and simultaneous submissions. Original artwork returned after publication. Sample copy $5.
Illustrations: Uses 2-5 illustrations/issue. "Line drawings are most useful for magazine work. We also purchase art for promotional projects dealing with the Morgan horse—horses should look like *Morgans*." Send query letter with samples and tear sheets. Accepts "anything that clearly shows the artist's style and craftsmanship" as samples. Samples are returned by SASE. Reports within 6-8 weeks. Call or write for appointment to show portfolio. Buys all rights or negotiates rights purchased. Pays $50 minimum, color cover; $10 minimum, b&w inside; on acceptance.

THE MOTHER EARTH NEWS, 80 Fifth Ave., New York NY 10010. Art Directors: Will Hopkins, Ira Friedlander. Associate Art Director: John Baxter. Magazine emphasizing self-reliant living, do-it-yourself products, natural foods, organic gardening, etc. for suburban, rural, small town, upper-middle income, family folks. Bimonthly. Circ. 700,000. Accepts previously published material. Original artwork returned after publication.
Illustrations: Buys 1-4 illustrations/issue from freelancers. Works on assignment only. Send query letter with brochure showing art style or tear sheets, Photostats and photocopies. Samples not filed are returned by SASE. Reports only if interested. Negotiates rights purchased. Pays $200-400, b&w, and $300-500, color, inside; on acceptance.

MOTOR MAGAZINE, 555 W. 57th St., New York NY 10019. (212)399-5671. Art Director: Harold A. Perry. Emphasizes automotive technology, repair and maintenance for auto mechanics and technicians. Monthly. Circ. 135,000. Accepts previously published material. Original artwork returned after publication if requested. Never send unsolicited original art.
Illustrations: Buys 5-15 illustrations/issue from freelancers. Works on assignment only. Prefers realistic/technical line renderings of automotive parts and systems. Send query letter with resume and photocopies to be kept on file. Will call for appointment to see further samples. Samples not filed are not returned. Reports only if interested. Buys one-time rights. Write to schedule an appointment to show a portfolio, which should include final reproduction/product, color and tear sheets. Payment negotiable for cover, basically $300-1,500; pays $50-500, b&w, inside; on acceptance.
Tips: "*Motor* is an educational, technical magazine and is basically immune to illustration trends because our drawings *must* be realistic and technical. As design trends change we try to incorporate these into our magazine (within reason). Though *Motor* is a trade publication, we approach it, design-wise, as if it were a consumer magazine. We make use of white space when possible and use creative abstract and impact photographs and illustration for our opening pages and covers. But we must always retain a 'technical look' to reflect our editorial subject matter. There are more and more *Folio* and *Forbes* clones.

A few of the elite say what is good and the rest fall into line. Publication graphics is becoming like TV programming, more calculating and imitative and less creative."

***MOTOR TREND**, 8490 Sunset Blvd., Los Angeles CA 90069. (213)854-2222. Art Director: William Claxton. Emphasizes automobiles, world-wide automotive field. Monthly. Circ. 900,000. Sometimes returns original artwork after publication; depends on agreement with artist. Sample copy available.
Cartoons: Buys 1-2 cartoons/issue from freelancers. Prefers any automotive theme, sophisticated style. Considers single or double panel with gagline; b&w line drawings, b&w washes. Send roughs to be kept on file. Material not filed is returned only if requested. Reports only if interested. Negotiates rights purchased. Payment varies; pays on acceptance.
Illustrations: Buys 3-4 illustrations/issue from freelancers. Themes are automotive (both technical and general illustrations); personality portraits. Send query letter with samples to be kept on file. Accepts "only high-quality samples and examples" to review. Samples not filed are returned only if requested. Reports only if interested. Call for appointment to show portfolio. Negotiates rights purchased. Payment varies; pays on acceptance.

MOUNTAIN FAMILY CALENDAR, Box 294, Rhododendron OR 97049. (503)622-4798. Editor: Michael P. Jones. Newspaper emphasizing family activities, recreation, history, wildlife, environment. Monthly. Circ. 3,000. Accepts previously published material. Original artwork returned after publication. Sample copy for SASE with 50¢ postage. Art guidelines for SASE with first-class postage.
Cartoons: Buys 1-8 cartoons/issue from freelancers. Prefers single panel, double panel, multi panel with or without gagline; b&w line drawings, b&w or color washes. Send query letter with samples of style, roughs or finished cartoons. Samples are filed. Samples not filed are returned by SASE. Reports back within 2 weeks. Buys one-time rights. Pays in copies.
Illustrations: Buys 10 illustrations/issue from freelancers. Themes include wildlife, outdoor recreation, nature and family activities. Prefers pen & ink, airbrush, charcoal/pencil, markers, calligraphy and computer illustration. Send query letter with brochure showing art style or resume, tear sheets, Photostats, photocopies, slides or photographs. Samples not filed are returned by SASE. Reports back within 2 weeks. To show a portfolio, mail thumbnails, roughs, original/final art, final reproduction/product, color, tear sheets, Photostats, photographs or b&w. Buys one-time rights. Pays in copies.
Tips: "Include a lot of samples in your portfolio. Also, sample illustrations in different sizes. I do not want to see just two or three samples, but I will look at them if that is all that the artist has to show. I want to really get to know the individual's talent."

MUSCLE MAG INTERNATIONAL, Unit 2, 52 Bramsteele Rd., Brampton, Ontario L6W 3M5 Canada. (416)457-3030. Editor-in-Chief: Robert Kennedy. For 16- to 50-year-old men and women interested in physical fitness and overall body improvement. Published 12 times/year. Circ. 210,000. Previously published work OK. Original artwork not returned after publication. Sample copy $4.
Cartoons: Buys 6 cartoons/issue from freelancers. Receives 30 submissions/week from freelancers. Interested in weight training and body building; single panel; "well-drawn work—professional." Send finished cartoons. SAE (nonresidents include IRC). Send $3 for return postage. Reports in 3 weeks. Buys all rights on a work-for-hire basis. Pays $15-25, color; $10-20, b&w; on acceptance. More for superior work.
Illustrations: Uses 2 illustrations/issue; buys 1/issue from freelancers. Receives 20 submissions/week from freelancers. Interested in "professionally drawn exercise art of body builders training with apparatus." Prefers pen & ink, pastels and collage. Send query letter with tear sheets, photocopies, slides, photographs, and preferably finished art. SAE (nonresidents include IRC). Send $4 for return postage. Reports in 2 weeks. Call to schedule an appointment to show a portfolio, which should include original/final art. Buys all rights on a work-for-hire basis. Pays $300, color, cover; $100, color and $80, b&w, inside; on acceptance. "Pay can be triple for really professional or outstanding artwork."
Tips: "We only want to see top line work—we want only the best. We do not want to see amateur stuff by untrained hopefuls."

MUSIC OF THE SPHERES, Box 1751, Taos NM 87571. (505)758-0405. Editor: John Patrick Lamkin. Emphasizing new age art and music. Quarterly. Circ. 10,000. Accepts previously published material. Original artwork is returned to the artist after publication. Sample copy $4.50. Art guidelines available for SASE with first class postage.
Illustrations: Buys varied number of illustrations/issue from freelancers. Prefers "New Age"/visionary/spiritual/fantasy/future (positive) themes. Send query letter with resume, tear sheets, slides and photographs. Samples are filed. Samples not filed are returned by SASE. Reports back within 30 days. To show a portfolio, mail original/final art, final reproduction/product, photographs, slides, color and b&w. Buys one-time rights. Pays $100, color, cover; $25, b&w; $50, color, inside; on publication.
Tips: "We accept only positive/visionary/spiritual/etc. work. We also publish articles and short sketches on artists. For this we need photos, bio and articles about the artist, etc."

MUSICIAN MAGAZINE, 31 Commercial St., Gloucester MA 01930. (617)281-3110. Art Director: Gary Koepke. Consumer magazine emphasizing music. Features interview/profile. Monthly. Circ. 110,000. Original artwork returned after publication. Sample copy for SASE.
Cartoons: Send query letter with samples of style. Samples are filed. Reports back only if interested. Buys one-time rights. Pays $50, b&w; $100, color.
Illustrations: Buys 2 illustrations/issue from freelancers. Buys 24 illustrations/year from freelancers. Works on assignment only. Send query letter with brochure showing art style or slides. Samples are filed. Samples not filed are returned by SASE. Reports back only if interested. To show a portfolio, mail tear sheets, slides, color and b&w. Buys one-time rights. Pays $250, b&w; $500, color, cover; $50, b&w; $350, color, inside. Pays on publication.

***MY WEEKLY, "THE MAGAZINE FOR WOMEN EVERYWHERE"**, 80 Kingsway East, Dundee 0D4 8SL Scotland. Editor: Stewart D. Brown. Magazine emphasizing women's interests for family-oriented women of all ages. Weekly. Circ. 696,275. Accepts previously published material. Original artwork returned after publication. Art guidelines free for SASE with postage.
Illustrations: Buys 2 illustrations/issue from freelancers. Prefers romantic, family . . . "up-dated Rockwell" themes. Send query letter with brochure showing art style or resume, tear sheets and photographs. Samples not filed are returned only if requested. Reports within 2 months. Buys British rights. Pays on acceptance.

***NAIL & BEAUTY TRENDS MAGAZINE**, 457 Busse Rd., Elk Grove IL 60607. (312)956-1040. Executive Director: John J. Savas. Publications covering manicure, pedicure, skin care cosmetics.
Illustrations: Works with 3 freelance artists/year. Works on assignment only. Uses artists for advertising design and illustrations, displays, signage and posters. Prefers line drawings.
First Contact & Terms: Send brochure showing art style or photostats or original work ot be kept on file. Samples not filed returned by SASE. Reports only if interested. Write for appointment to show portfolio., Considers available budget when establishing payment.

THE NATIONAL FUTURE FARMER, Box 15130, Alexandria VA 22309. (703)360-3600. Editor-in-Chief: Wilson W. Carnes. For members of the Future Farmers of America who are students of vocational agriculture in high school, ages 14-21. Emphasizes careers in agriculture/agribusiness and topics of general interest to youth. Bimonthly. Circ. 422,528. Reports in 3 weeks. Buys all rights. Pays on acceptance. Sample copy available.
Cartoons: Buys 15-20 cartoons/year on Future Farmers of America or assigned themes. Receives 30 cartoons/week from freelance artists. Pays $15, cartoons; more for assignments.
Illustrations: "We buy a few illustrations for specific stories; almost always on assignment." Send query letter with tear sheets or photocopies. Write to schedule an appointment to show a portfolio, which should include final reproduction/product, tear sheets and Photostats. Negotiates payment.
Tips: "We suggest you send samples of work so we can keep your name on file as the need arises. We prefer b&w line art. Please include rates. We are a bimonthly publication and buy very little art. Study back issues and offer suggestions for improvement through the use of art. We need more youthful cartoons."

NATIONAL GEOGRAPHIC, 17th and M Sts. NW, Washington DC 20036. (202)857-7000. Contact: Art Director. Monthly. Circ. 10,500,000. Original artwork returned after publication, in some cases.
Illustrations: Number of illustrations bought/issue varies. Interested in "full-color, representational renderings of historical and scientific subjects. Nothing that can be photographed is illustrated by artwork. No decorative, design material. We want scientific geological cut-aways, maps, historical paintings." Works on assignment only. Prefers to see portfolio and samples of style. Samples are returned by SASE. "The artist should be familiar with the type of painting we use." Provide brochure, flyer or tear sheet to be kept on file for future assignments. Reports in 2 weeks. Minimum payment: Inside: $1,000, color; $200, b&w; on acceptance.

NATIONAL MOTORIST, 188 The Embarcadero, San Francisco CA 94105. (415)777-4000. Graphic Artist: Lana Peters. Editor: Jane Offers. Emphasizes travel on the West Coast for all members of the National Automobile Club in California. Bimonthly. Circ. 205,000. Original artwork returned after publication. Sample copy 50¢ postage.
Illustrations: Uses very few illustrations/issue. Prefers auto- or travel-related themes. Send query letter with samples to be kept on file. Prefers original work as samples. Samples not kept on file are returned. Buys first rights. Pays "all on request"; on acceptance.

THE NATIONAL NOTARY, 8236 Remment Ave., Box 7184, Canoga Park CA 91304-7184. (818)713-4000. Contact: Production Editor. Emphasizes "notaries public and notarization—goal is to impart knowledge, understanding, and unity among notaries nationwide and internationally." Readers are notaries of varying primary occupations (legal, government, real estate and financial), as well as state and federal officials and foreign notaries." Bimonthly. Circ. 80,000. Original artwork not returned after publication. Sample copy $5.

Cartoons: May use. Cartoons "must have a notarial angle"; single or multi panel with gagline, b&w line drawings. Send samples of style. Samples not returned. Reports in 4-6 weeks. Call to schedule an appointment to show a portfolio. Buys all rights. Negotiates pay; on publication.

Illustrations: Uses about 5 illustrations/issue; buys all from local freelancers. Works on assignment only. Themes vary, depending on subjects of articles. Send business card, samples and tear sheets to be kept on file. Samples not returned. Reports in 4-6 weeks. Call for appointment. Buys all rights. Negotiates pay; on publication.

Tips: "We are very interested in experimenting with various styles of art in illustrating the magazine. We generally work with Southern California artists, as we prefer face-to-face dealings."

NATIONAL REVIEW, 150 E. 35th St., New York NY 10016. (212)679-7330. Production Editor: Ione Whitlock. Emphasizes world events from a conservative viewpoint. Bimonthly. Original artwork returned after publication.

Cartoons: Buys 15 cartoons/issue from freelancers. Interested in "political, social commentary." Prefers to receive finished cartoons. SASE. Reports in 2 weeks. Buys first North American serial rights. Pays $25 b&w; on publication.

Illustrations: Contact: Pat Sarch. Uses 15 illustrations/issue. Especially needs b&w ink illustration, portraits of political figures and conceptual editorial art (b&w line plus halftone work). "I look for a strong graphic style; well-developed ideas and well-executed drawings." Works on assignment only. Send query letter with brochure showing art style or tear sheets and photocopies. No samples returned. Reports back on future assignment possibilities. Call to schedule an appointment to show a portfolio, which should include original/final art, final reproduction/product, tear sheets and b&w. SASE. Also buys small decorative and humorous spot illustrations in advance by mail submission. Buys first North American serial rights. Pays $15, small spots, $35, larger spot, $40 assigned illustration; $40 b&w, inside; $300 color, cover; on publication.

Tips: "Tear sheets and mailers are helpful in remembering an artist's work. Artists ought to make sure their work is professional in quality, idea and execution. Printed samples alongside originals help. Changes in art and design in our field include fine art influence and use of more halftone illustration."

NATIONAL RURAL LETTER CARRIER, Suite 100, 1448 Duke St., Alexandria VA 22314. (703)684-5545. Managing Editor: RuthAnn Saenger. Emphasizes news and analysis of federal law and current events. For rural letter carriers and family-oriented, middle-Americans; many are part-time teachers, businessmen and farmers. Weekly. Circ. 70,000. Mail art. SASE. Reports in 4 weeks. Original artwork returned after publication. Previously published, photocopied and simultaneous submissions OK. Buys first rights. Sample copy 24¢. Receives 1 cartoon and 2 illustrations/month from freelance artists.

Illustrations: Buys 12 covers/year on rural scenes, views of rural mailboxes and rural people. Buys 1 illustration/issue from freelancers. Interested in pen & ink or pencil on rural, seasonal and postal matter. Especially needs rural mailboxes and sketches of scenes on rural delivery. Works on assignment only. Send query letter with brochure showing art style or resume, tear sheets, photocopies, slides and photographs. Samples returned by SASE. Reports in 1 week, if accepted; 1 month if not accepted. Write to schedule an appointment to show a portfolio, which should include original/final art, final reproduction/product, color, tear sheets, Photostats, photographs and b&w. Buys all rights on a work-for-hire basis. Pays by the project, $60-150; on publication.

Tips: "Please send in samples when you inquire about submitting material." Have a definite need for "realistic painting and sketches. We need a clean, crisp style. Subjects needed are scenic, mailboxes, animals and faces. We need fine black-and-white, pen-and-ink, and watercolor."

NATURAL HISTORY, American Museum of Natural History, Central Park W. and 79th St., New York NY 10024. (212)769-5500. Editor: Alan Ternes. Designer: Tom Page. Emphasizes social and natural sciences. For well-educated professionals interested in the natural sciences. Monthly. Circ. 500,000. Previously published work OK.

Illustrations: Buys 23-25 illustrations/year; 25-35 maps or diagrams/year. Works on assignment only. Query with samples. Samples returned by SASE. Provide "any pertinent information" to be kept on file for future assignments. Reports in 1 week. Buys one-time rights. Inside: Pays $200 and up for color illustrations; on publication.

Tips: "Be familiar with the publication. Always looking for accurate and creative scientific illustrations, good diagrams and maps."

NEW AGE JOURNAL, 342 Western Ave., Brighton MA 02135. (617)787-2005. Art Director: Howie Green. Emphasizes alternative lifestyles, holistic health, ecology, personal growth, human potential, planetary survival. Bimonthly. Circ. 150,000. Accepts previously published material and simultaneous submissions. Original artwork returned after publication by request. Sample copy $3.
Illustrations: Uses 8 illustrations/issue. Illustrations accompany specific manuscripts. Send query letter with samples or tear sheets to be kept on file. Prefers Photostats, photocopies or slides as samples. Samples returned by SASE if not kept on file. Buys one-time rights.

***NEW BODY MAGAZINE**, 888 Seventh Ave., New York NY 10106. (212)541-7100. Editorial Assistant: Heather Batting. Magazine emphasizng health and fitness aimed at women age 18-49. "Readers are interested in diet, exercise, health, nutrition and psychology." Monthly. Circ. 320,000. Accepts previously published material. Sample copies free for SASE with first-class postage. Art guidelines available.
Illustrations: Works on assignment only. Send query letter with resume and tear sheets. Samples are filed. Samples not filed are returned by SASE. Reports back within 2 weeks. Write to schedule an appointment to show a portfolio, or mail tear sheets, final reproduction/product, photographs, color and b&w. Buys all rights.

***NEW DIMENSIONS MAGAZINE**, Box 811, 111 NE Evelyn St., Grants Pass OR 97526. (503)479-0549. Managing Editor: David Masters. Published by The Foundation of Human Understanding.Focuses on both spiritual and practical in direction, content focuses on helping people deal with stresses and pressures of everyday life. Emphasis is on resolving problems and conflicts through becoming objective to them.
Needs: Works with 100 freelance artists/year. Uses artists for advertising and brochure design and illustration; magazine design, illustration and layout. Prefers thought-provoking, iconolastic, controversial b&w, pen & ink, photos, cartoons, modern, classic, etc; variety of artwork designed to provoke or stimulate ideas surrounding article content.
First Contact & Terms: Send query letter with tear sheets, Photostats, photocopies, slides, photographs and original artwork. Samples not filed are not returned. Reports within 2 weeks. To show a portfolio, mail thumbnails, roughs, original/final art, final reproduction/product, color, tear sheets, Photostats, photographs and b&w. Pays $25-30.
Tips: "Submit all types of art."

***NEW ENGLAND BUILDER**, Box 5059, Burlington VT 05402. (802)864-3680. Art Director: Theresa Sturt. Tabloid, trade journal emphasizing residential and light commercial building and remodeling. Emphasizes the practical aspects of building technology and small-business management. Monthly. Circ. 25,000. Accepts previously published material. Original artwork is returned to the artist after publication. Samples copy $3.
Illustrations: Buys 10 illustrations/issue from freelancers. Buys 120 illustrations/year from freelancers. "Lots of how-to illustrations are assigned on various construction topics." Send query letter with brochure, resume, tear sheets, Photostats and photocopies. Samples are filed. Samples not filed are returned only if requested by artist. Reports back within 2 weeks. Call or write to schedule an appointment to show a portfolio, which should include original/final art, tear sheets, final reproduction/product and b&w. Buys one-time rights. Pays $300, color, cover; $50 b&w, inside; on acceptance.
Tips: "Write for a sample copy. We are unusual in that we have drawings illustrating construction techniques. We prefer artists with construction and/or architectural experience."

***NEW ENGLAND MONTHLY**, 132 Main St., Haydenville MA 01039. (413)268-7262. Art Director: Mark Danzig. "A general interest magazine focusing on contemporary matters that affect the lives of the residents of New England. Covers all subjects, people, politics, recreation, arts, the outdoors, business, food, and often a photo-heavy article or portfolio. Monthly. Circ. 100,000. Original artwork is returned to the artist after publication. Sample copies and art guidelines available.
Illustrations: Works on assignment only. Send query letter with brochure, tear sheets, slides and photographs. Samples are filed. Samples not filed are returned only if requested by artist. Reports back within weeks. Call to schedule an appointment to show a portfolio, which should include tear sheets, final reproduction/product, photographs and slides. Pays $700, color, cover; $300, b&w; $450, color, inside; on acceptance or publication.

THE NEWFOUNDLAND HERALD, Box 2015, St. John's, Newfoundland A1C 5R7 Canada. (709)726-7060. 130-page informative entertainment magazine with TV listings for the province. Paid circ. 40,000. Weekly. Simultaneous submissions and previously published work OK. "Our publication is copyrighted."
Cartoons: Buys TV, movie, entertainment and Hollywood themes. Send roughs. Pays on publication.

***NEW LETTERS**, 5216 Rockhill Rd., University of Missouri, Kansas City MO 64110. "Innovative" small magazine with an international scope. Quarterly. Sample copy $4.
Illustrations: Uses camera-ready spot drawings, line drawings and washes; "any medium that will translate well to the 6x9" b&w printed page." Also needs cover designs. Submit art. Reports in 2-8 weeks. Buys all rights. Pays $5-10, pen & inks, line drawings and washes. Must include SASE for return of work.
Tips: "Fewer pieces of freelance art being accepted; we consider only work of the highest quality. Artwork does not necessarily have to relate to content."

NEW MEXICO MAGAZINE, 1100 St. Francis Dr., Santa Fe NM 87503. (505)827-0220. Art Director: Mary Sweitzer. Emphasizes the state of New Mexico for residents, and visiting vacationers. Monthly. Circ. 100,000. Accepts previously published material and simultaneous submissions. Original artwork returned after publication. No printed artists' guidelines, but may call for information. Also interested in calligraphers.
Cartoons: Uses 12-15 cartoons/year, 1-2/issue. Prefers single panel; b&w line drawings, b&w washes. Send resume, tear sheets, Photostats, photocopies and slides. Call to schedule an appointment to show a portfolio, which should include original/final art, final reproduction/product, color, tear sheets, photographs and b&w. Material not kept on file is returned only if requested. Reports only if interested. Buys one-time rights. Pays $50-100, b&w; $50-100, color; two weeks after acceptance, on publication for stock material.
Illustrations: Uses 2 illustrations/issue. Works on assignment only. Send query letter with samples to be kept on file. Samples not kept on file are returned only if requested. Reports only if interested. Buys one-time rights. Pays for design $7-15; $40 for small illustrations to $300 for 4-color work, usually all inside; on acceptance.
Tips: Contact verbally or with written material first. Send appropriate materials and samples.

NEW ORLEANS, SEM Publishing Co., 6666 Morrison Rd., New Orleans LA 70126. (504)831-3731. Editor: Sherry Spear. Emphasizes entertainment, travel, sports, news, business and politics in New Orleans. For readers with high income and education. Monthly. Circ. 44,000. Previously published and photocopied submissions OK. Sample copy $2.50.
Illustrations: Query with samples. SASE. Buys assigned illustrations and cartoons on current events, education and politics. Especially needs assigned feature illustrations "specifically relating to and illustrating a concept in one of our main feature stories." Pays $40-100, spot drawings; $75-200, feature illustrations; on publication.
Tips: "Do not send unassigned, unsolicited work on speculation. It creates a burden for me to sift through work and return it. However, do send nonreturnable photocopies or stats of work so I can keep them on file when work becomes available."

NEW ORLEANS REVIEW, Box 195, Loyola University, New Orleans LA 70118. (504)865-2294. Editor: John Mosier. Journal of literature and culture. Published 4 times/year. Sample copy $9.
Illustrations: Uses 5-10 illustrations/issue. Cover: uses color, all mediums. SASE. Reports in 4 months. Inside: uses b&w line drawings, photos/slides of all mediums.

NEW REALITIES, Heldref Publications, 4000 Albemarle St. NW, Washington, D.C. 20016. Editor/Publisher: Neal Vahle. Managing Editor: Joy O'Rourke. Concerns "holistic health and personal growth." Bimonthly. Pays on publication.
Illustrations: Buys 2-3 illustrations/issue on assigned themes. Prefers New Age themes (spirituality, transformation). "We want abstract concepts rather than technical representations." Prefers pen & ink, then airbrush, charcoal/pencil, colored pencil, watercolor, acrylics, collage and mixed media. Inside: $75-150, b&w.
Tips: "In your portfolio, show a wide assortment of sujects, ones that can be applied to more than one idea, meaning we don't want to see very specific personality/represtational work."

***the new renaissance**, 9 Heath Rd., Arlington MA 02174. Contact: Louise T. Reynolds. Magazine emphasizing literature, arts and opinion for "the general, literate public which has an aesthetic sensibility and which has an interest in provocative ideas or opinion pieces." Bi-annual (Spring & Fall). Circ. 1,600. Returns original artwork after publication if SASE is enclosed. Sample copy $4.95.
Illustrations: Buys 5-8 illustrations/issue from freelancers and "occasional art pieces." Works mainly on assignment. Send resume, samples, photos and SASE. No slides. Samples not filed are returned by SASE. Reports within 1-2 months. To show a portfolio, mail appropriate materials; portfolio should include roughs, photographs, b&w and SASE. Buys one-time rights. Pays $25, b&w, after publication.

THE NEW REPUBLIC, 1220 19th St. NW, Washington DC 20036. (202)331-7494. Assistant Editor: Leona Hiraoka Roth. Emphasizes politics and culture for a "well-educated, well-off audience with a median age of 40." Weekly. Circ. 100,000. Accepts previously published material and simultaneous submissions. Original artwork returned after publication.
Cartoons: Buys 1 cartoon/month from freelancers. Send query letter with samples of style, finished cartoons and color work, if possible, to be kept on file. Material not kept on file returned only if requested and only if accompanied by SASE. Write for appointment to show portfolio. Reports only if samples are accompanied by cover letter or written inquiry. Negotiates rights purchased. Pays $50 b&w; on publication.
Illustrations: Uses 1 illustration/issue. Prefers political, literary themes. Works on assignment only. Send query letter with brochure, resume, business card, samples and tear sheets to be kept on file. Write for appointment to show portfolio. Negotiates rights purchased and payment. Pays on publication.

NEW WOMAN MAGAZINE, 215 Lexington Ave., New York NY 10016. (212)685-4790. Magazine emphasizing emotional self-help for women ages 25-34, 50% married. Most have attended college. Published monthly. Circ. 1.2 million. Accepts previously published material. Returns original artwork to the artist upon request.
Cartoons: Uses approximately 10 freelance cartoons/issue. Prefers single panel, with or without gagline; b&w line drawings. "We have changed quite a bit. We are still pro-women, but not as hard-hitting or as sexist in putting men down. We need cartoons every month for our word power quiz, Pin-ups and letters to the editor column. Look at recent issues of the magazine." Contact Rosemarie Lennon, cartoon editor, for more information, or to be added to the monthly mailing list, which tells which articles in upcoming issues will require cartoons. Cartoons are matched with editorial. Send finished cartoon and SASE. Purchases all serial rights. Pays $225 on acceptance.
Illustrations: Uses 3-4 freelance illustrations/issue. Works on assignment only. Send query letter with tear sheets and photocopies to be kept on file to Caroline Bowyer, art director. Samples not kept on file are not returned. Reports only if interested. Payment varies. Pays on acceptance.

NEW YORK MAGAZINE, 755 Second Ave., New York NY 10017. (212)880-0700. Design Director: Robert Best. Art Director: Josh Gosfield. Emphasizes New York City life; also covers all boroughs for New Yorkers with upper-middle income and business people interested in what's happening in the city. Weekly. Original artwork returned after publication.
Illustrations: Works on assignment only. Send query letter with tear sheets to be kept on file. Prefers Photostats as samples. Samples returned if requested. Call or write for appointment to show portfolio (drop-offs). Buys first rights. Pays $1,000, b&w and color, cover; $600 for 4-color, $400 b&w full page, inside; $225 for 4-color, $150 b&w spot, inside. Pays on publication.

THE NEW YORKER, 25 W. 43rd St., New York NY 10036. Contact: Art Editor. Emphasizes news analysis and lifestyle features.
Cartoons: Buys cartoons and cover designs. Receives 3,000 cartoons/week. Mail art or deliver sketches on Wednesdays. SASE. Strict standards regarding style, technique, plausibility of drawing. Especially looks for originality. Pays $500 minimum, cartoons; top rates for cover designs. "Not currently buying spots."
Tips: "Familiarize yourself with your markets."

NINE TO FIVE, TEAMWORK, SUCCESSFUL SUPERVISOR, CUSTOMERS, EFFECTIVE EXECUTIVE, Dartnell Corporation, 4660 N. Ravenswood Ave., Chicago IL 60640. Art Director: G.C. Gormaly, Jr. Emphasize salesmanship. Monthly. Previously published material OK.
Cartoons: Uses 1 cartoon/issue. Prefers single panel with or without gagline, b&w line drawings or b&w washes. Send query letter and samples of style. Samples returned. Reports in 1 month. Negotiates rights purchased. Pays $20-50, b&w; on acceptance.
Illustrations: Uses illustrations occasionally; seldom buys from freelancers. Send query letter and samples of style to be kept on file for possible future assignments. Samples not kept on file are returned. Reports in 2 months. Buys reprint rights. Pays $100-600 cover, $100-300 inside, b&w line or tone drawings; on acceptance.

NJEA REVIEW, 180 W. State St., Box 1211, Trenton NJ 08607. (609)599-4561. Editor-in-Chief: Martha O. DeBlieu. Nonprofit, for New Jersey public school employees. Monthly. Circ. 123,000. Previously published work OK. Original artwork not returned after publication. Free sample copy.
Cartoons: Buys 3-4/year from freelancers. Receives 20 submissions/week from freelancers. Interested in b&w cartoons with an "education theme—do not make fun of school employees or children"; single panel. Prefers to see finished cartoons. Buys all rights on a work-for-hire basis. Pays on acceptance. Limited budget.

Illustrations: Buys 1-2 illustrations/issue from freelancers. Receives 1-2 submissions/week from freelancers. Especially needs education-related spot art. Send query letter with brochure showing art style or resume, tear sheets, Photostats, photocopies and photographs. Reports as soon as possible. To show a portfolio, mail appropriate materials, which should include original/final art, tear sheets, photographs and b&w. Buys all rights on a work-for-hire basis. Pays $25 b&w, cover; $7.50-10 b&w, inside; on acceptance.
Tips: "Like bigger and bolder art rather than intricate work. Too much artwork we see is too finely detailed or on the other extreme, too simplistic, amateur looking. Look at our magazine and don't send us material not related to our type of magazine."

NORTH AMERICAN HUNTER, Box 35557, Minneapolis MN 55435. (612)941-7654. Managing Editor: Bill Miller. Publishes hunting material only for avid hunters of both small and big game in North America. Bimonthly. Circ. 155,000. Accepts previously published material. Original artwork returned after publication unless all rights are purchased. Sample copy $2; art guidelines available.
Cartoons: Buys 36 cartoons/year from freelancers. Considers humorous hunting situations. "Must convey ethical, responsible hunting practices; good clean fun." Prefers single panel with gagline; b&w line drawings or washes. 8½x11 vertical or horizontal format. Send query letter with roughs or finished cartoons. Returns unpurchased material immediately. Reports within 2 weeks. Buys all rights. Pays $15, b&w; on acceptance.
Illustrations: Buys 2 illustrations/issue from freelancers; usually includes 1 humorous illustration. Prefers line art, mostly b&w, occasionally color. "Work should be close to being photographically real in most cases." Works on assignment only. Send query letter with samples. Samples not filed are returned. Reports within 2 weeks. Buys one-time rights. Pays $250, color, cover; $75-100, b&w or color, inside; on acceptance.
Tips: "Send only art that deals with hunting, hunters, wildlife or hunting situations. North American big and small game only. We accept only detailed and realistic-looking pieces—no modern art."

NORTHEAST OUTDOORS, Box 2180, Waterbury CT 06722-2180. (203)755-0158. Editor: Camilo Falcon. For camping families in the Northeastern states. Monthly. Circ. 14,000. Original artwork returned after publication, if requested. Previously published material and simultaneous submissions OK if noted in cover letter. Editorial guidelines for SASE with 1 first-class stamp; sample copy for 9x12 SASE with 6 first-class stamps.
Cartoons: Buys 1 cartoon/issue on camping and recreational vehicle situations. Send query letter with samples. Reports in 2 weeks. Pays $10, b&w; on acceptance.
Illustrations: Buys 2-3 illustrations/year with manuscripts. To show a portfolio, mail appropriate materials. Pays $40 b&w, cover; $10-30 b&w, inside; on publication.
Tips: "Make it neat. Felt-tip pen sketches won't make it in this market any more. Query or send samples for illustration ideas. We occasionally buy or assign to accompany stories. Artists who have accompanying manuscripts have an extra edge, as we rarely buy illustrations alone."

THE NORTHERN LOGGER & TIMBER PROCESSOR, Northeastern Loggers Association Inc., Box 69, Old Forge NY 13420. (315)369-3078. Editor: Eric A. Johnson. Emphasizes methods, machinery and manufacturing as related to forestry. "For loggers, timberland managers and processors of primary forest products." Monthly. Circ. 13,000. Previously published material OK. Free sample copy; guidelines sent upon request.
Cartoons: Uses 1 cartoon/issue, all from freelancers. Receives 1 submission/week from freelancers. Interested in "any cartoons involving forest industry situations." Send finished cartoons with SASE. Reports in 1 week. Pays $10 minimum, b&w line drawings; on acceptance.
Tips: "Keep it simple and pertinent to the subjects we cover. Also, keep in mind that on-the-job safety is an issue that we like to promote."

NORTHWEST REVIEW, 369 PLC, University of Oregon, Eugene OR 97403. (503)686-3957. Editor: John Witte. Art Editor: George Gessert. Emphasizes literature. "We publish material of general interest to those who follow American/world poetry and fiction." Original artwork returned after publication. Published 3 times/year. Sample copy $3.
Illustrations: Uses b&w line drawings, graphics and cover designs. Receives 20-30 portfolios/year from freelance artists. Arrange interview or mail slides. SASE. Reports as soon as possible. Acquires one-time rights. Pays in contributor's copies. Especially needs high-quality graphic artwork. "We run a regular art feature of the work of one artist, printed in b&w, 133-line screen on quality coated paper. A statement by the artist often accompanies the feature."
Tips: "We are presently engaged in an ongoing series of features exploring the artist's book, in each issue reproducing in its entirety one such book."

NOTRE DAME, University of Notre Dame, 415 Main Bldg., Box M, Notre Dame IN 46556. Art Director: Don Nelson. For university alumni. Quarterly. Circ. 100,000. Uses 6 illustrations/issue, all from freelancers. Professional artists only. "Please don't request sample copies." Accepts previously published material. Original artwork returned after publication.
Illustrations: Seeks " 'graphic' solutions to communication problems." Prefers pen & ink, airbrush, charcoal/pencil, colored pencil, watercolor, acrylics, oils, pastels and collage. Send brochure showing art style or tear sheets, Photostats and photocopies. Works on assignment only. Samples returned by SASE. Buys one-time rights. Pays on acceptance.
Tips: "Do not show unprofessional work."

NOW COMICS/THE NOW LIBRARY, Box 8042, Chicago IL 60680-8042. (312)786-9013. Contact: Fred Schiller. Estab. 1985. Publishes limited edition comic books and graphic novels. Titles include *Ralph Snart Adventures*, *Valor Thunderstar*, *Syphons*, *Vector* and *EB'NN*. Genres: adventure, mystery, science fiction, animal parodies and superheroes. Themes: outer space, future science and teenage exploits. "We are a 'creator-oriented' company which reaches males and females from age 13-34. We're looking for educated writers." Monthly and bimonthly. Average circ. 25,000. Original artwork returned after publication. Sample copy and art guidelines for SASE with 50¢ postage.
Illustrations: Uses freelance artists for inking, lettering, pencilling, color work and covers. Send query letter with photocopies of work. Samples are filed. Samples not filed are returned by SASE if requested. Reports back within 1 month. Call or write to schedule an appointment to show a portfolio, which should include 10 pages of pencil or ink drawings one-and-one half times up, 5 pages of action continuity and 3 pages of lettering—one-and-one-half up with sound effects. Creators retain own rights. Pays $25-30/page for pencilling, $15-30/page for inking, $8-15/page for lettering and $10-30/page for coloring. Negotiates payment for graphic novels. Pays on publication.
Tips: Looks for "storytelling talent and capability in drawing anatomy. A common mistake freelancers make is sending or showing too many samples."

***NSBE JOURNAL**, 1240 S. Broad St., New Orleans LA 70125. (504)822-3533. Art and Production Director: Thomas Dennis. Magazine emphasizing engineering studies and careers. "NSBE Journal is the official publication of the National Society of Black Engineers, a student run organization of more than 5,000. The Journal provides information on employment, financial assistance, coping in academic and corporate environements, and cultural awareness." Published 5 times/year. Circ. 15,000. Original artwork is sometimes returned to artist after publication. Sample copies $3.50. Art guidelines free for SASE with first-class postage.
Illustrations: Buys 10 illustrations/year from freelancers. Send query letter with brochure, photocopies and photographs. Samples are filed. Samples not filed are returned by SASE. Reports back within 3 weeks. Write to schedule an appointment to show a portfolio, which should include original/final art, photographs, color and b&w. Negotiates rights purchased. Pays $200, b&w and $350, color cover; $50, b&w and $75, color, inside; on publication.

NUCLEAR TIMES MAGAZINE, Suite 300, 1601 Connecticut Ave., NW, Washington DC 20009. (202)332-9222. Art Director: Elliott Negin. Provides straight news coverage of U.S.-Soviet relations, U.S. foreign policy, and the anti-nuclear weapons movement. Bimonthly. Circ. 70,000. Accepts previously published material. Returns original artwork after publication. Sample copy $4.
Illustrations: Buys 5 illustrations/issue from freelancers.Primarily works on assignment. Write for appointment to show portfolio. Prefers to review photocopies and tear sheets in mail submissions. Samples not filed are returned by SASE only if requested. Reports within 2 weeks. Buys one-time rights. Pays $500 for four-color cover; $50-300 for b&w and color inside; on publication.
Tips: "I like to see printed pieces. I don't want to see any work from more than three years before. Gear your samples to our specific needs. I don't want to see childrens book illustrations, for example."

NUGGET, Dugent Publishing Co., 2355 Salzedo St., Coral Gables FL 33134. Editor: Jerome Slaughter. Illustration Assignments: Nye Willden. For men and women with fetish interests.
Cartoons: Buys 10 cartoons/issue, all from freelancers. Receives 50 submissions/week from freelancers. Interested in "funny fetish themes." B&w only for spots, b&w and color for page. Prefers to see finished cartoons. SASE. Reports in 2 weeks. Buys first North American serial rights. Pays $50, spot drawings; $75, page.
Illustrations: Buys 4 illustrations/issue from freelancers. Interested in "erotica, cartoon style, etc." Works on assignment only. Prefers to see samples of style. No samples returned. Reports back on future assignment possibilities. Send brochure, flyer or other samples to be kept on file for future assignments. Buys first North American serial rights. Pays $125-150, b&w.
Tips: Especially interested in "the artist's anatomy skills, professionalism in rendering (whether he's

published or not) and drawings which relate to our needs." Current trends include "a return to the 'classical' realistic form of illustration which is fine with us because we prefer realistic and well-rendered illustrations."

NUTRITION TODAY, 428 E. Preston St., Baltimore MD 21202. (301)528-8520. Art Director: James R. Mulligan. Trade journal emphasizing nutrition in the public and private sector directed to the practicing dietitian. Features general interest and technical articles. Bimonthly. Circ. 16,000. Accepts previously published material. Original artwork returned after publication. Sample copy available. Art guidelines for SASE with 50¢ postage.
Illustrations: Buys 8 illustrations/year from freelancers. Works on assignment only. Prefers technical illustrations of diverse topics. Send query letter with brochure or resume and photocopies. Samples are filed. Samples not filed are not returned. Reports back only if interested. Write to schedule an appointment to show a portfolio, which should include original/final art, final reproduction/product, slides, color and b&w. Buys all rights. Pays $200, b&w; $400, color, cover; $100, b&w; $300, color, inside; on acceptance.
Tips: "Have a strong background in technical art, such as graphs and flow charts incorporating graphics."

OCEANS, 2001 W. Main St., Stanford CT 06902. (203)359-8626. Editor: Michael W. Robbins. "For those interested in the beauty, science, adventure and conservation of the oceans and the life therein." Bimonthly. Circ. 55,000. Original artwork returned after publication. Sample copy $3.50; free contributor guidelines.
Cartoons: Interested in sea-oriented themes. Uses very few authors. Prefers roughs. SASE. Buys first North American serial rights.
Illustrations: By assignment only, based on editorial need.

***ODYSSEY**, Kalmbach Publishing Co., 1027 N. Seventh St., Milwaukee WI 53233. (414)272-2060. Art Director: Jane Borth Lucius. Magazine designed to teach and entertain children ages 8-14 about space topics. Monthly. Circ. 96,480.
Illustrations: "Artwork accompanies speculative topics such as the future of space exploration." Send query letter with tear sheets and slides. "Please note any scientific background or experience in technical illustration." Reports back within 4-6 weeks. Buys first rights. Pays up to $400/illustration.
Tips: "This is a very, very hard market to break into, but it is open to new artists if they can handle the technical accuracy."

OFF DUTY, Suite C-2, 3303 Harbor Blvd., Costa Mesa CA 92626. Art Director: John Wong. Three editions: Europe, Pacific and America. Emphasizes general interest topics for military Americans stationed around the world. Combined circ. 708,000. Accepts previously published material and simultaneous submissions if not submitted to other military magazines. Assignment artwork returned after publication. Sample copy $1.
Cartoons: Uses occasional cartoons in two categories. First must relate to military personnel, families and military life. Off-duty situations preferred. Send to Bruce Thorstad, U.S. Editor. Second category relates to hobbies of audio, video, computers or photography. "A military angle in this category is ideal, but not necessary." Send to Gary Burch, Technical Editor. "Keep in mind that all readers are active duty military, not retirees or vets." Pays $40 minimum b&w; more by negotiation.
Illustrations: *Off Duty*'s America edition uses illustrations by assignment only. Accepts photocopies or tear sheets of previous work that can be kept on file, but does not want originals or anything that must be returned. Pays $50-150 on acceptance for assignments.

OFFICIAL DETECTIVE STORIES, 20th Floor, 460 W. 34th St., New York NY 10001. Editor: Art Crockett. For readers of factual crime stories and articles. Monthly.
Cartoons: Buys crime genre themes. "Avoid cliche situations such as 2 convicts conversing in cell; cute, mild sex." Submit roughs. SASE. Reports in 2 weeks. Buys all rights. Pays $25; on acceptance.

OHIO MAGAZINE, 40 S. Third St., Columbus OH 43215. (614)461-5083. Managing Editor: Ellen Stein Burbach. Emphasizes feature material of Ohio for an educated, urban and urbane readership. Monthly. Circ. 110,000. Previously published work OK. Original artwork returned after publication. Sample copy $3.
Illustrations: Buys 1-3/issue from freelancers. Interested in Ohio scenes and themes. Prefers fine art versus 'trendy' styles. Prefers pen & ink, charcoal/pencil, colored pencil, watercolor, acrylics, oils, pastels, collage, markers, mixed media and calligraphy. Works on stock and assignment. Send query letter with brochure showing art style or tear sheets, dupe slides and photographs. SASE. Reports in 4 weeks. On assignment: pays $75-150, b&w; $100-250, color, inside; on publication. Buys one-time publication rights.

Tips: "It helps to see one work in all its developmental stages. It provides insight into the artist's thought process. Some published pieces as well as non-published pieces are important. A representative sampling doesn't hurt, but it's a waste of both parties' time if their work isn't even close to the styles we use."

OLD WEST, Box 2107, Stillwater OK 74076. (405)743-0130. Editor: John Joerschke. Emphasizes American western history from 1830 to 1910 for a primarily rural and suburban audience, middle-age and older, interested in Old West history, horses, cowboys, art, clothing and all things western. Quarterly. Circ. 90,000. Accepts previously published material and considers some simultaneous submissions. Original artwork returned after publication. Sample copy $1. Art guidelines for SASE.
Illustrations: Uses 5-10 illustrations/issue, including 2 or 3 humorous illustrations; buys all from freelancers. "Inside illustrations are usually, but need not always be, pen & ink line drawings; covers are western paintings." Send query letter with samples to be kept on file; "we return anything on request." Call or write for appointment to show portfolio. "For inside illustrations, we want samples of artist's line drawings. For covers, we need to see full-color transparencies." Reports within 1 month. Buys one-time rights. Pays $100-150 for color transparency for cover; $15-40, b&w, inside. "We're paying about twelve months after acceptance but are slowly speeding that up."
Tips: We think the mainstream of interest in Western Americana has moved in the direction of fine art, and we're looking for more material along those lines."

***ONLINE ACCESS**, Suite 1750, 53 W. Jackson Blvd., Chicago IL 60604. (312)922-9292. Art Director: Leslie Bodenstein. Estab. 1986. Consumer/business magazine emphasizing online services. "We are a national magazine dedicated to keeping the readers up-to-speed in the expanding world of online services. The magazine bridges the gap of understanding high-tech information, in a non-high-tech format." Bimonthly. Circ. 150,000. Accepts previously published material. Original artwork is returned to the artist after publication. Sample copies available. Art guidelines available.
Cartoons: Cartoon editor: Lisa Jordan. Samples are filed. Buys first rights or reprint rights.
Illustrations: Prefers a creative, stylized and imaginative style. Prefers pen & ink, airbrush, colored pencil, acrylics, oils, pastels, collage, mixed media and computer illustration. Send query letter with brochure, resume, tear sheets, photocopies and slides. Samples are filed. Reports back only if interested. To show a portfolio, call to schedule an appointment or mail original/final art, slides and tear sheets. Buys first rights, one-time rights or reprint rights. Pays on publication.
Tips: "We prefer stylized illustration, non-computer oriented images. We like images that create a metaphor to explain the information in a new and exciting way."

ONTARIO OUT OF DOORS, 7th Floor, 777 Bay St., Toronto, Ontario M5W 1A7 Canada. (416)596-5022. Editor-in-Chief: Burton Myers. Emphasizes hunting, fishing, camping and conservation. Published 10 times/year. Circ. 55,000. Previously published work OK. Original artwork not returned after publication. Free sample copy and artist's guidelines.
Cartoons: Buys 2 cartoons/issue, all from freelancers. Receives 10-20 cartoons/month from freelance artists. Interested in fishing, hunting and camping themes; single panel. Send roughs. SASE (nonresidents include IRC). Reports within 6 weeks. Buys one time rights. Pays $50, b&w line drawings; 4 weeks after acceptance.
Illustrations: Uses 1-2 color illustrations plus 2-4 b&w line drawings/issue, all from freelancers. Interested in wildlife and fish themes. Especially needs cover artwork. Prefers to see roughs. SAE (nonresidents include IRC). Provide business card to be kept on file for future use. Reports in 6 weeks. Pays $250-500, color, cover; 4 weeks after acceptance.
Tips: "Strive for realism. Take the time to research the publication. Ask for a sample copy first before sending submissions." Especially looks for "the ability to depict nature or an activity in a clear-cut, informative fashion that supports the article."

***OPEN WIDE**, University of Illinois, 284 Illini Union, 1401 W. Green St., Urbana IL 61801. Contact: Iris Chang. Magazine emphasizing fiction and poetry. "*Open Wide* is a literary magazine that publishes creative writing, artwork and music. It is edited and published by University of Illinois students. Therefore, our audience consists of intelligent, college-educated people. We need unique, talented artwork to complement the stories." Published semi-annually. Circ. 700. Accepts previously published material. Sample copies $3.
Cartoons: Cartoon Editor: Joe Marciniak. Buys 0-3 cartoons/issue from freelancers. Buys 0-10 cartoons/year from freelancers. Prefers b&w line drawings. Send finished cartoons. Samples are filed. Samples not filed are returned by SASE. Reports back within 2 months only if interested. Negotiates rights purchased. Pays $5, b&w.
Illustrations: Buys 10-30 illustrations/issue from freelancers. Buys 20-60 illustrations/year from freelancers. Prefers surrealism or abstract art. Prefers pen & ink, then markers and calligraphy. Send query

letter with resume, photocopies and photographs. Samples are filed. Samples not filed are returned by SASE. Reports back within 2 months only if interested. To show a portfolio, mail Photostats, photographs and b&w. Negotiates rights purchased. Pays $5, b&w; cover or inside; on publication.
Tips: "We look for black and white artwork that would fit on an 8½ by 11" page. Art that photocopies well would reproduce well on our magazine. No color, pencil, charcoal or watercolor pictures, please."

OPPORTUNITY MAGAZINE, 6 N. Michigan Ave., Chicago IL 60602. Editor: Jack Weissman. Features articles dealing with direct (door-to-door) selling and on ways to start small businesses. For independent salesmen, agents, jobbers, distributors, sales managers, flea market operators, franchise seekers, multi-level distributors, route salesmen, wagon jobbers and people seeking an opportunity to make money full- or part-time. Monthly. Original artwork not returned after publication. Sample copy free for SASE with 50¢ postage.
Cartoons: Buys 2-3 cartoons/issue from freelancers. Interested in themes dealing with humorous sales situations affecting door-to-door salespeople. Considers single panel with gagline; b&w line drawings. Prefers roughs or finished cartoons. SASE. Buys all rights. Pays $5 on publication.
Tips: "Get sample copy beforehand and have an idea of what is appropriate."

THE OPTIMIST MAGAZINE, 4494 Lindell Blvd., St. Louis MO 63108. (314)371-6000. Editor: James E. Braibish. Emphasizes activities relating to Optimist clubs in U.S. and Canada (civic-service clubs). "Magazine is mailed to all members of Optimist clubs. Average age is 42, most are management level with some college education." Circ. 160,000. Accepts previously published material. Sample copy for SASE.
Cartoons: Buys 3 cartoons/issue from freelancers. Prefers themes of general interest; family-oriented, sports, kids, civic clubs. Prefers single panel, with gagline. No washes. Send query letter with samples. Submissions returned by SASE. Reports within 1 week. Buys one-time rights. Pays $30/b&w; on acceptance.

ORANGE COAST MAGAZINE, Suite 8, 245-D Fischer Ave, Costa Mesa CA 92626. (714)545-1900. Art Director: Leslie Freidson Lawicki. General interest regional magazine. Monthly. Circ. 35,000. Returns original artwork after publication. Sample copy and art guidelines available. Contact Linda Crook, Associate Art Director for guidelines.
Illustrations: Buys 3 illustration/issue from freelancers. Considers airbrush. Works on assignment only. Send brochure showing art style or tear sheets, slides or transparencies to be kept on file. Samples not filed are returned only if requested. Reports only if interested. To show a portfolio, mail original/final art, final reproduction/product, color, tear sheets and photographs. Buys one-time rights. Pays for design by the hour, $5-10. Pays for illustration by the project, $50-500; on publication.
Tips: There is a need for "fluid free-style illustration and for more photojournalistic expression within an artists mode—i.e. the art meets needs to express a story exactly, yet in a creative manner and executed well. Please send samples soon."

OREGON RIVER WATCH, Box 294, Rhododendron OR 97049. (503)622-4798. Editor: Michael P. Jones. Estab. 1985. Books published in volumes emphasizing "fisheries, fishing, camping, rafting, environment, wildlife, hiking, recreation, tourism, mountain and wilderness scenes and everything that can be related to Oregon's waterways." Monthly. Circ. 2,000. Accepts previously published material. Original artwork returned after publication. Art guidelines for SASE with first-class postage.
Cartoons: Buys 1-3 cartoons/issue from freelancers. Prefers single panel, double panel, multiple panel with or without gagline; b&w line drawings, b&w or color washes. Send query letter with samples of style, roughs or finished cartoons. Samples are filed. Samples not filed are returned by SASE. Reports back within 2 weeks. Buys one-time rights. Pays in copies.
Illustrations: Buys 10-20 illustrations/issue from freelancers. Send query letter with brochure showing art style or resume and tear sheets, Photostats, photocopies, slides or photographs. Samples not filed are returned by SASE. Reports back within 2 weeks. To show a portfolio, mail thumbnails, roughs, original/final art, final reproduction/product, color, tear sheets, Photostats, photographs or b&w. Buys one-time rights. Pays in copies.
Tips: "We need b&w or pen & ink sketches. We have a lot of projects going on at once but cannot always find an immediate need for freelancer's talent. Being pushy doesn't help. I want to see examples of the artist's expanding horizons, as well as their limitations."

***ORGANIC GARDENING**, 33 E. Minor St., Emmaus PA 18098. Art Director: Scott M. Stephens. Magazine emphasizing gardening. Monthly. Circ. 1.2 million. Original artwork is sometimes returned to the artist after publication. Sample copies free for SASE with first-class postage.
Cartoons: Buys 6-8 cartoons/year by assignment only. B&w line drawings or b&w washes. Send query letter with samples of style. Samples are filed. Samples not filed are returned by SASE. Reports back

within 1 month. Buys all rights. Pays per assignment.
Illustrations: Buys 20 illustrations/issue from freelancers. Buys 250 illustrations/year from freelancers. Works on assignment only. Prefers botanically accurate plants and, in general, very accurate drawing and rendering. Send query letter with brochure, tear sheets, slides and photographs. Samples are filed. Samples not filed are returned by SASE. Reports back within 1 month. Call or write to schedule an appointment to show a portfolio, which should include final reproduction/product, color and b&w. Buys first rights one-time rights.
Tips: "Work should be very accurate and realistic. Detailed and fine rendering quality is very important."

THE ORIGINAL NEW ENGLAND GUIDE, Historical Times, Inc., Box 8200, 2245 Kohn Rd., Harrisburg PA 17105. Editor: Howard Crise. Art Director: Jeanne Collins. Emphasizes New England travel of all kinds. Readers are "those planning on going on vacation trips, weekend jaunts, mini-holidays, day trips. For North American and overseas visitors to New England." Annually. Circ. 160,000. Sample copy $5.
Illustrations: "*The Guide* is almost always able to make its few assignments for artwork locally. However, we are certainly happy to know about freelancers and their special abilities, and welcome letters and/or samples (clips are fine)." Pays $50 and up on publication for inside artwork, depending on use. Send correspondence to Art Director.

THE OTHER SIDE, 300 W. Apsley St., Philadelphia PA 19144. (215)849-2178. Editor: Mark Olson. Art Director: Cathleen Boint. "We are read by Christians with a radical commitment to social justice and a deep allegiance to Biblical faith. We try to help readers put their faith into action." Published 10 times/year. Circ. 15,000. Receives 3 cartoons and 1 illustration/week from freelance artists. Sample copy $3.
Cartoons: Buys 6 cartoons/year on current events, environment, economics, politics and religion; single and multiple panel. Pays $25, b&w line drawings; on publication. "Looking for cartoons with a radical political perspective."
Illustrations: Especially needs b&w line drawings illustrating specific articles. Send query letter with tear sheets, photocopies, slide, photographs and SASE. Reports in 6 weeks. Photocopied and simultaneous submissions OK. To show a portfolio, mail appropriate materials or call to schedule an appointment; portfolio should include roughs, original/final art, final reproduction/product and photographs. Pays "within 4 weeks of publication." Pays $125-200, 4-color. Pays $40-150, b&w line drawings inside, on publication.
Tips: "We're looking for illustrators who share our perspective on social, economic and political issues, and who are willing to work for us on assignment."

OTTAWA MAGAZINE, 192 Bank St., Ottawa, Ontario K2P 1W8 Canada. (613)234-7751. Art Director: Peter de Gannes. Emphasizes lifestyles for sophisticated, middle and upper income, above average education professionals; ages 25-50. Monthly. Circ. 50,000. Accepts previously published material. Sample copy available; include $2 Canadian funds to cover postage (nonresidents include 4 IRCs).
Illustrations: Buys 6-8 illustrations/issue from freelancers. Receives 3-4 submissions/week from freelancers. "Illustrations are geared to editorial copy and run from cartoon sketches to *Esquire*, *New York* and *D* styles. Subjects range from fast-food franchising to how civil servants cope with stress. Art usually produced by local artists because of time and communication problems." Open to most styles including b&w line drawings, b&w and color washes, collages, photocopy art, oil and acrylic paintings, airbrush work and paper sculpture for inside. Also uses photographic treatments. Send query letter with resume and photocopies. "Do not send original artwork." No samples returned. Reports in 1 month. To show a portfolio, mail appropriate materials, which should include tear sheets and Photostats. Buys first-time rights, or by arrangement with artist. Pays $35-150 for inside b&w; and $75-250 for inside color; on acceptance.
Tips: Prefers "work that shows wit, confidence in style and a unique approach to the medium used. Especially in need of artists who can look at a subject from a fresh, unusual perspective. There is a trend toward more exciting illustration, use of unusual techniques like photocopy collages or collages combining photography, pen & ink and watercolor. Freedom given to the artist to develop his treatment. Open to unusual techniques. Have as diversified a portfolio as possible."

OUTDOOR AMERICA MAGAZINE, Suite 1100, 1701 N. Ft. Meyer Dr., Arlington VA 22209. Editor: Carol Dana. Emphasizes conservation and outdoor recreation (fishing, hunting, etc.) for sportsmen and conservationists. Quarterly. Circ. 45,000. Accepts previously published material. Original artwork returned after publication. Sample copy $1.50.
Illustrations: Buys 2-3 illustrations/issue from freelancers. Rarely commissions original work from non-local artists, but will occasionally purchase one-time or reprint rights to existing wildlife or recrea-

tion illustrations. Send query letter with samples to be kept on file. Prefers tear sheets or photocopies as samples. Samples not filed are returned. Reports within 2 months. Buys one-time rights or reprint rights. Pays on publication.

OUTDOOR CANADA MAGAZINE, 801 York Mills Rd., Don Mills, Ontario M3B 1X7 Canada. Editor: Teddi Brown. Emphasizes wildlife and active people enjoying the Canadian outdoors. Stories for anglers, hikers, canoeists, campers, hunters, conservationists and the adventurous. Readers are 81% male. Publishes 7 regular issues a year, a fishing special in April and a hunting special in August. Circ. 150,000. Finds most artists through references/word-of-mouth.
Illustrations: Buys approximately 10 drawings/issue. Prefers pen & ink, airbrush, acrylics, oils and pastels. Buys all rights. Pays up to $400. Artists should show a representative sampling of their work.

OUTDOOR LIFE, 380 Madison Ave., New York NY 10017. (212)687-3000. Art Director: Jim Eckes. Emphasizes hunting, fishing, boating and camping for "male and female, young and old who enjoy the outdoors and what it has to offer." Monthly. Circ. 1.5 million. Original artwork returned after publication "unless we buy all rights." Sample copy available "if work is going to be published."
Cartoons: Very seldom uses cartoons. Send finished cartoons to be kept on file, except for "those we won't ever use." Material not kept on file is returned by SASE. Reports only if interested. Buys first rights. Pays on publication.
Illustrations: Uses 1-2 illustrations/issue. Prefers "realistic themes, realistic humor." Works on assignment only. Send query letter with samples and tear sheets to be kept on file except "those which do not meet our standards." Prefers slides, tear sheets and originals as samples. Samples not kept on file are returned. Reports only if interested. Call for appointment to show portfolio. Negotiates rights purchased. Pays for design by the hour, $10-15. Pays for the illustration by the project, $400-1,200 for 4-color ink on publication. Payment "depends on size and whether it is a national or regional piece."
Tips: "First of all, we're looking for 'wildlife, realists'—those who know how to illustrate a species realistically and with action."

OUTSIDE, 1165 N. Clark St., Chicago IL 60610. (312)951-0990. Managing Editor: John Rasmus. Design Director: John Askwith. Concerns enjoyment and participation in the great outdoors. Published 12 times/year. Circ. 275,000+.
Illustrations: Uses 60 illustrations/year; buys 60/year from freelancers. Works on assignment only. Receives 5-10 submissions/week from freelancers. Prefers contemporary editorial styles. Ask for artists' guidelines. Especially needs spot (less than ½ page) 4-color art; "contemporary, communicative, powerful illustration. We are also interested in seeing any contemporary stills for assignment purposes." Send "good slides" or previously published work as samples. SASE. Reports in 2 weeks. Send samples or tear sheet to be kept on file for future assignments. Buys one-time rights. Pays $100-1,000, b&w line drawings, washes and full-color renderings, inside; on publication.
Tips: "In a portfolio include lots of samples (tearsheets) or slides showing one or two strenghts."

OVERSEAS!, Kolpingstr 1, 6906 Leimen, West Germany. Editorial Director: Charles L. Kaufman. Managing Editor: Greg Ballinger. "*Overseas!* is the leading lifestyle magazine for the U.S. military male stationed throughout Europe. Primary focus is on European travel, with regular features on music, sports, video, audio and photo products, and men's fashion. The average reader is male, age 24." Sample copy for SAE and 4 IRCs; art guidelines for SAE and 1 IRC.
Cartoons: Buys 3-5 cartoons/issue. Prefers single and multiple panel cartoons. "Always looking for humorous cartoons on travel and being a tourist in Europe. Best bet is to send in a selection of 5-10 for placement of all on one-two pages. Looking for more *National Lampoon* or *Playboy*-style cartoons/humor than a *Saturday Evening Post*-type cartoon. Anything new, different or crazy is given high priority. On cartoons or cartoon features don't query, send nonreturnable photocopies. Pay is negotiable, $25-75/cartoon to start."
Illustrations: Uses 3-5 illustrations/month. Prefers pen & ink, charcoal/pencil and mixed media. Send query letter with nonreturnable photocopies. "We will assign when needed." To show a portfolio, mail appropriate materials or call or write to schedule an appointment. Pays $75-200, negotiable.
Tips: "We are very interested in publishing new young talent. Previous publication is not necessary."

PACIFIC COAST JOURNAL, Box 254822, Sacramento CA 95865. Editor-in-Chief: Jill Scopinich. For horse breeders, trainers and owners interested in performance, racing and showing of quarter horses. Monthly. Circ. 7,800. Previously published and simultaneous submissions OK "if we are notified."
Cartoons: Buys 24 cartoons/year on horses; single panel. Send query letter with samples. SASE. Reports in 4 weeks. Buys first, reprint, all or simultaneous rights. Pays $7.50-20, washes; on acceptance.

PAINT HORSE JOURNAL, Box 18519, Fort Worth TX 76118. (817)439-3400. Editor: Bill Shepard. Art Director: Vicki Day. Official publication of breed registry for Paint horses. For people who raise, breed and show Paint horses. Monthly. Circ. 12,000. Receives 4-5 cartoons and 2-3 illustrations/week from freelance artists. Original artwork returned after publication if requested. Sample copy $2; artist's guidelines free for SASE.
Cartoons: Buys 1 or 2 cartoons/issue, all from freelancers. Interested in *Paint* horses; single panel with gagline. Material returned by SASE only if requested. Reports in 1 month. Buys first rights. Pays $10, b&w line drawings; on acceptance.
Illustrations: Uses 1-3 illustrations/issue; buys few/issue from freelancers. Receives few submissions/week from freelancers. Send business card and samples to be kept on file. Prefers snapshots of original art or Photostats as samples. Samples returned by SASE if not kept on file. Reports within 1 month. Send query letter with brochure showing art style or photocopies and finished art. Buys first rights. Pays $5-25, b&w, inside; $50 color, cover; on publication.
Tips: "We use a lot of different styles of art, but no matter what style you use-you *must* include Paint horses with acceptable (to the APHA) conformation. As horses are becoming more streamlined-as in race-bred Paints, the older style of horse seem so out dated. We get a lot of art from older artists who still draw the Paint as stocky and squatty—which they are not."

PALM BEACH LIFE, 265 Royal Poinciana Way, Palm Beach FL 33480. (305)837-4762. Design Director: Anne Wholf. Emphasizes culture, cuisine, travel, fashion, decorating and Palm Beach County lifestyle. Readers are affluent, educated. Monthly. Circ. 35,000. Sample copy $4.18; art guidelines for SASE.
Illustrations: Uses 3-4 illustrations/issue; all from freelancers. Only assigned work. Uses line drawings to illustrate regular columns as well as features. Format: color washes for inside and cover; b&w washes and line drawings for inside. "Any technique that can be reproduced is acceptable." Send samples or photocopies and/or arrange appointment to show portfolio. No original artwork returned "unless special arrangements are made." SASE. Reports in 4-6 weeks. Buys all rights on a work-for-hire basis. Pays $300-500 on acceptance for color cover; $100-350 for inside color; $30-200 for inside b&w. Top price on covers only paid to established artists; "the exception is that we are looking for super-dramatic covers." Subjects related to Florida and lifestyle of the affluent. Price negotiable. Send slides or prints; do not send original work. *Palm Beach Life* cannot be responsible for unsolicited material.
Tips: "Look at magazines to see what we are like—make an appointment."

PANDORA, #12, 609 E. 11 Mile, Royal Oak MI 48067. Editor: Meg MacDonald. Emphasizes science fiction and fantasy. Semiannually. Circ. 500. Accepts previously published material. Original artwork returned after publication if requested but prefers Photostat. Sample copy $3.50.
Cartoons: Buys 1-2 cartoons/year from freelancers. Considers science fiction themes. Prefers single panel; b&w line drawings. Send query letter with samples to be kept on file. Material not filed is returned by SASE. Reports within 8 weeks. Rights negotiated individually; prefers all rights on in-house generated ideas. Pays $2 and up, b&w; on publication.
Illustrations: Buys 5-7 illustrations/issue from freelancers. Style should suit story. Prefers pen & ink, then charcoal/pencil markers, calligraphy and computer illustration. Will consider unsolicited work for art portfolio section as well. Send query letter with tear sheets or photocopies to be kept on file. Samples not filed are returned by SASE. Reports in 8 weeks. Buys first North American serial rights; buys all rights on cover. Pays $7 and up, b&w, cover and inside; on publications.
Tips: "We lean somewhat more toward fantasy art than hard sf--we're not about hardware, we're about people of all races and biological makeup. As as digest-sized magazine, we cannot use extremely detailed or busy work...consider final size when sending samples. We highly recommend artists study issues before submitting. Tell us you want a good representation of our current art needs when you order back issues. We like to see versatility of content and style in samples, as well as a good grasp of anatomy, contrast, and composition. We use anything from action scenes to portraits (usually for story illustrations) to cartoons, border designs, and filler doodles. No horror!"

***PARACHUTIST**, 1440 Duke St., Alexandria VA 22314. (703)836-3495. Editor: Larry Jaffe. Emphasizes sport parachuting. Monthly. Circ. 18,000. Accepts previously published material. Returns original artwork after publication. Sample copy available.
Cartoons: Prefers skydiving-related themes. Material not filed is returned. Reports within weeks.
Illustrations: Prefers skydiving-related themes. Samples not filed are returned. Reports within weeks.

PARADE MAGAZINE, 750 Third Ave., New York NY 10017. (212)573-7187. Director of Design: Ira Yoffe. Photo Editor: Brent Petersen. Emphasizes general interest subjects. Weekly. Circ. 31 million (readership is 60 million). Original artwork returned after publication. Sample copy and art guidelines available.

Illustrations: Uses varied number of illustrations/issue. Prefers various themes. Works on assignment only. Send query letter with brochure, resume, business card and tear sheets to be kept on file. Call or write for appointment to show portfolio. Reports only if interested. Buys first rights, and occasionally all rights.
Tips: "Provide a good balance of work."

PARAPLEGIA NEWS, Suite 111, 5201 N. 19th Ave., Phoenix AZ 85015. Art Director: Carol Beiriger. Magazine emphasizing wheelchair living for wheelchair users, rehabilitation specialists. Monthly. Circ. 24,000. Accepts previously published material. Original artwork not returned after publication. Sample copy free for SASE with 96¢ postage; art guidelies free for SASE with first-class postage.
Cartoons: Buys 1 cartoon/issue from freelancers. Prefers line art with wheelchair theme. Prefers single panel with or without gagline; b&w line drawings. Send query letter with samples of style or finished cartoons to be kept on file. Write for appointment to show portfolio. Material not kept on file is returned by SASE. Reports only if interested. Buys all rights. Pays $10, b&w.
Illustrations: Buys 1 illustration/issue from freelancers. Prefers wheelchair living or medical and financial topics as themes. Send query letter with brochure showing art style or tear sheets, Photostats, photocopies and photographs. Samples not filed are returned by SASE. Reports only if interested. To show a portfolio, include final reproduction/product, color, tear sheets, Photostats, photographs and b&w. Negotiates rights purchased. Pays on acceptance.

PARENT'S CHOICE, Box 185, Waban MA 02168. (617)965-5913. Editor: Diana Huss Green. Reviews children's media. Designed to alert parents to the best books, TV, records, movies, music, toys, computer software, rock-n-roll, home video cassettes. Quarterly. Original artwork returned after publication. Sample copy $2.50.
Illustrations: Uses 4 illustrations/issue, 2 from freelancers. Uses "work of exceptional quality." Format: b&w line drawings for inside and cover; no pencil. Works on assignment only. Send samples or arrange appointment to show portfolio. Samples returned. Prefers to see portfolio. SASE. Reports in 4-6 weeks. Pays on publication.

PASTORAL LIFE, The Magazine for Today's Ministry, Rt. 224, Canfield OH 44406. (216)533-5503. Editor: Rev. Jeffrey Mickler. Emphasizes religion and anything involving pastoral ministers and ministry for Roman Catholic priests (70%); the remainder are sisters, brothers, laity and ministers of other denominations. Monthly. Circ. 5,000. Original artwork returned after publication. Sample copy available.
Illustrations: Prefers religious, pastoral themes. Works on assignment only. Send query letter with photographs. Call or write for appointment to show portfolio, which should include b&w or photographs. Samples not kept on file are returned by SASE only if requested. Reports within 3 weeks. Buys first rights. Payment varies; on publication.

***PC RESOURCE**, 80 Elm St., Peterborough NH 03458. (603)924-9471. Art Director: Anne Fleming. Practical guide to MS-DOS computing. Circ. 150,000. Original artwork returned after publication. Art guidelines available. Finds most artists through talent sourcebooks, samples received through the mail and artist representatives.
Illustrations: Buys 1-3 illustrations/issue from freelancers. Works on assignment only. Prefers creative, original and new themes and styles. Send query letter with brochure showing art style or tear sheets, Photostats and photocopies. Artists should show a representative sampling of their work. Samples not filed are returned only if requested. Reports back only if interested. Call or write to schedule an appointment to show a portfolio, which should include original/final art, final reproduction/product and tear sheets. Buys first rights. Pays $175, b&w; $100-800, color,inside; on acceptance.

PEDIATRIC ANNALS, 6900 Grove Rd., Thorofare NJ 08086. (609)848-1000. Managing Editor: Sandra L. Patterson. Emphasizes pediatrics for practicing pediatricians. Monthly. Circ. 33,000. Original artwork returned after publication. Sample copy and art guidelines available.
Illustrations: Buys 4-5 illustrations/issue from freelancers. Prefers technical and conceptual medical illustration which relate to pediatrics. Prefers watercolor, acrylics, oils, pastels and mixed media. Send query letter with tear sheets, slides and photographs to be kept on file except for those specifically requested back. Reports within 2 months. Buys one-time rights or reprint rights. Pays $150, b&w and $250-450, color, cover; $25-30, b&w and $50-100, color, inside; on publication.
Tips: "*Pediatric Annals* continues to require that illustrators be able to treat medical subjects with a high degree of accuracy. We need people who are experienced in medical illustration, who can develop ideas from manuscripts on a variety of topics, and who can work independently (with some direction) and meet deadlines. Nonmedical illustration is also used occasionally. We anticipate that our needs for illus-

tration will continue to increase. We deal with medical topics specifically related to children. Include color work, previous medical illustrations and cover designs in a portfolio, show a representative sampling of work."

PENNSYLVANIA MAGAZINE, Box 576, Camp Hill PA 17011. (717)761-6620. Editor-in-Chief: Albert Holliday. For college-educated readers, ages 35-60+, interested in self-improvement, history, travel and personalities. Bimonthly. Cir. 50,000. Query with samples. SASE. Reports in 3 weeks. Previously published, photocopied and simultaneous submissions OK. Buys first serial rights. Pays on publication or on acceptance for assigned articles/art. Sample copy $2.95.
Illustrations: Buys 50-75 illustrations/year on history and travel-related themes. Minimum payment for cover, $100, inside color, $25-50; inside b&w, $5-50. "I would like to see small *New Yorker*-type pen & ink sketches for spot art."

***PENNY POWER**, 256 Washington St., Mount Vernon NY 10553. Art Director: Robert Jenter. Magazine emphasizing stories, puzzles, how-to articles and product ratings for children age 8-14. Bimonthly. Circ. 140,000.
Illustrations: Works with 10-20 artists/year. Buys artwork for 3-4 stories/issue. "We tend toward realism, but not necessarily—work can be primitive and fun, but must be sophisticated." Send query letter with photocopies and an SASE. Samples are filed. Reports back only if interested. Call to schedule an appointment to show a portfolio. Buys first rights. Pays $250-1,000; payment is on a per story basis. Pays on acceptance.

PERINATOLOGY-NEONATOLOGY, Macmillan Professional Journals, 1640 5th St., Santa Monica CA 90401. Publisher: Curt Pickelle. Art Director: Ron Tammerillo. Emphasizes technological, medical and professional news.
Illustrations: Submit brochure/flyer to be kept on file for possible future assignments. Reports only when assignment available. Buys all rights. Pays $60 and up, spot art; $400, full-color cover; on acceptance.

***PERSONAL SELLING POWER**, Box 5467, Fredericksburg VA 22403. Editor-in-Chief: Laura B. Gschwandtner. Tabloid-size trade magazine emphasizing sales and marketing executives. "*Personal Selling Power* is designed to train, educate, and motivate sales and marketing executives." Published 8 times/per year. Circ. 135,000. Original artwork is sometimes returned to the artist after publication. Sample copies and art guidelines available.
Cartoons: Buys 4-5 cartoons/issue from freelancers. Buys 35-45 cartoons/year from freelancers.

PERSONNEL JOURNAL, Suite B2, 245 Fischer, Costa Mesa CA 92626. (714)751-1883. Art Director: Susan Overstreet. Emphasizes the hiring, firing, training, recruiting of employees. Directed to directors or managers of corporate personnel departments in organizations with 500 or more employees. Monthly. Circ. 20,000. Original artwork returned after publication.
Cartoons: Buys 1 cartoon/issue; buys 1/issue from freelancer. Prefers theme of the world of work, jobs, careers. "Please, no sexist or racist cartoons." Prefers single panel with gagline; b&w line drawings or b&w washes. Send query letter with samples of style to be kept on file. Reports within 3 weeks. Buys one-time rights. Pays $50, b&w; on acceptance.
Illustrations: Buys 3 illustrations/issue; buys all from freelancers. Prefers professional themes such as the workplace, office equipment, professionals (line drawings). Works on assignment; will also accept previously published material. Send query letter with resume, business card and Photostats to be kept on file. Call or write for appointment to show portfolio. Samples not kept on file are returned only if requested. Reports only if interested. Negotiates payments and rights purchased.

PET BUSINESS, 5400 N.W. 84th Ave., Miami FL 33166. Editor: Amy Jordan Smith. A monthly news magazine for the pet industry (retailers, distributors, manufacturers, breeders, groomers). Circ. 15,500. Sample copy $3.
Cartoons: Pet-related themes; single panel. SASE. Pays $10; on publication.
Illustrations: Anatomically correct line drawings of pet animals. Pays $10; on publication.
Tips: "Send two or three samples and a brief bio, only."

PETERSENS HUNTING MAGAZINE, Petersen Publishing Co., 8490 Sunset Blvd., Los Angeles CA 90069. (213)854-2222. Editor: Craig Boddington. Art Director: C. A. Yeseta. Emphasizes sport hunting for hunting enthusiasts. Monthly. Circ. 300,000. Sometimes returns originals after publication. Sample copy $2. Occasionally uses production paste-up artists on an hourly wage.
Cartoons: Uses 1-2 cartoons/year from freelancers on hunting scenes and wildlife. Prefers to see finished cartoons. Reports in 1 week. Pays on publication.

Illustrations: Buys 8-10 illustrations/year on "very realistic wildlife themes and action hunting scenes"; some "how-to" drawings. Works on assignment only. Prefers to see finished art, roughs, portfolio, samples of style or previously published work. Arrange interview to show portfolio. Samples returned by SASE. Provide resume, business card, letter of inquiry; also brochure or flyer containing examples of work to be kept on file for future assignments. Reports in 4 weeks. Buys various rights. Inside: Pays $75-250, b&w line drawings; on publication.

PGA MAGAZINE, 100 Avenue of the Champions, Palm Beach Gardens FL 33418. (305)626-3600. Assistant Editor: Pete Wofford. Circulates to 16,000 golf club professionals and 14,000 amateur golfers nationwide.
Needs: Works with 2 artists/year for magazine illustrations for *PGA Magazine*. Artists "should know something about golf and golf tournaments." Interested in title page art and golf tip illustrations. Works on assignment most of the time.
First Contact & Terms: Write with tear sheets to be kept on file. Samples returned by SASE. Reports in 2 weeks. Reports back on future assignment possibilities. Negotiates pay by prior agreement.
Tips: "Read our magazine and read and check the artwork in golf's two major national publications: *Golf Magazine* and *Golf Digest*."

PHI DELTA KAPPAN, Box 789, Bloomington IN 47402. Editor-in-Chief: Pauline Gough. Design Director: Kristin Herzog. Emphasizes issues, policy, research findings and opinions in the field of education. For members of the educational organization Phi Delta Kappa and subscribers. Published 10 times/year. Circ. 150,000. SASE. Reports in 2 weeks. "We return cartoons after publication." Sample copy $2.50—"the journal is available in most public and college libraries."
Illustrations: Uses 1 b&w illustrations/issue, all from freelancers, who have been given assignments from upcoming articles. Most illustrations depict teachers or principals. Samples returned by SASE. To show a portfolio, mail a few slides or photocopies with SASE. Buys one-time rights. Payment varies.

PHILADELPHIA MAGAZINE, 1500 Walnut St., Philadelphia PA 19102. Contact: Art Director. For a professional, upper-middle-income audience. Monthly. Circ. 142,000. Simultaneous submissions OK. Original artwork returned after publication.
Cartoons: Buys 0-1 cartoons/issue.
Illustrations: Uses 10-16 illustrations/issue; buys all from freelancers. Interested in a variety of themes and styles. Works on assignment only. Send query letter with resume and tear sheets, Photostats, photocopies, slides and photographs to be kept on file. Samples not returned. Buys one-time rights. Pays $75-375 b&w; $100-500 color, inside; on acceptance.
Tips: "Variety is the key word. Accurate and intelligent interpretation of the editorial message is essential. Look at several issues of the magazine in the library. Understand the level of work expected."

PHYSICIAN'S MANAGEMENT, 7500 Old Oak Blvd., Cleveland OH 44130. (216)243-8100, ext. 808. Editor: Robert A. Feigenbaum. Art Director: David Komitau. Published 12 times/year. Circ. 110,000. Emphasizes business, practice management and legal aspects of medical practice for primary care physicians.
Cartoons: Receives 50-70/week from freelancers. Buys 10 cartoons/issue. Themes typically apply to medical and financial situations "although we do publish general humor cartoons." Prefers single and double panel; b&w line drawings with gagline. Uses "only clean-cut line drawings." Send query letter with brochure showing art style or resume and tear sheets, Photostats, photocopies, slides and photographs. SASE. Reports in 2 weeks. Call or write to schedule an appointment to show a portfolio, which should include final reproduction/product and photographs. Buys one-time rights. Pays $80 for b&w; on acceptance. No previously published material and/or simultaneous submissions.
Illustrations: Buys 5 illustrations/issue. Accepts b&w and color illustrations. All work done on assignment. Send a query letter to editor or art director first or send examples of work. Fees negotiable. Buys first rights. No previously published and/or simultaneous submissions.
Tips: "First, become familiar with our publication, second, query the art director. Cartoons should be geared toward the physician—not the patient. No cartoons about drug companies or medicine men. No sexist cartoons. Illustrations should be appropriate for a serious business publication. We do not use cartoonish or comic book styles to illustrate our articles. We work with artists nationwide."

PIG IRON, Box 237, Youngstown OH 44501. (216)783-1269. Editors-in-Chief: Jim Villani and Rose Sayre. Emphasizes literature/art for writers, artists and intelligent lay audience with emphasis in popular culture. Annually. Circ. 1,000. Previously published and photocopied work OK. Original artwork returned after publication. Sample copy $2.50.
Cartoons: Uses 1-15 cartoons/issue, all from freelancers. Receives 1-3 submissions/week from freelancers. Interested in "the arts, political, science fiction, fantasy, alternative lifestyles, psychology, hu-

mor"; single and multi panel. Especially needs fine art cartoons. Prefers finished cartoons. SASE. Reports in 1 month. Buys first North American serial rights. Pays $2 minimum, b&w halftones and washes; on acceptance.
Illustrations: Uses 15-30 illustrations/issue, all from freelancers. Receives 1-3 submissions/week from freelancers. Interested in "any media: pen & ink washes, lithographs, silk screen, charcoal, collage, line drawings; any subject matter." B&w only. Prefers finished art or velox. Reports in 2 months. Buys first North American serial rights. Minimum payment: Cover: $4, b&w. Inside: $2; on publication.
Tips: "*Pig Iron* is a publishing opportunity for the fine artist; we publish art in its own right, not as filler or story accompaniment. The artist who is executing black-and-white work for exhibit and gallery presentations can find a publishing outlet with *Pig Iron* that will considerably increase that artist's visibility and reputation." Current themes: Labor in the Post-Industrial Age and Epistolary Fiction and the Letter as Artifact.

PITTSBURGH MAGAZINE, 4802 5th Ave., Pittsburgh PA 15213. (412)622-1360. Art Director: Michael Maskarinec. Emphasizes culture, feature stories and material with heavy Pittsburgh city emphasis; public broadcasting television and radio schedule. Monthly. Circ. 58,000. Sample copy $2.
Illustrations: Uses 5-10 illustrations/issue; all from freelancers; inside b&w and 4-color illustrations. Works on assignment only. Prefers to see roughs. SASE. Buys one-time rights on a work-for-hire basis. Pays on publication.

PLAN AND PRINT, International Reprographic Association, Suite 104, 611 E. Butterfield Rd., Lombard IL 60148. Editor: Janet Thill. For commercial reproduction company owners, managers and dealers in architects', engineers' and draftsmen's supplies and equipment, in-plant reproduction department supervisors, in-plant design and drafting specialists, computer-aided design users and architects. Monthly. Circ. 29,000. Originals not returned after publication. Free sample copy and artist's guidelines.
Illustrations: Buys 1 spot illustration/issue. Especially needs spots related to the industry. Interested in reprographics and design/drafting. Works on assignment only. Send samples of style. SASE. Keeps files of information on artists for future assignment possibilities. Reports in 1 week. Buys all rights on a work-for-hire basis. Pays $7.50-10, b&w spots. Payment for article illustrations and 4-color cover art varies from $50-450.
Tips: "Heavy use of computer-aided design."

PLANNING, American Planning Association, 1313 E. 60th St., Chicago IL 60637. (312)955-9100. Editor-in-Chief: Sylvia Lewis. Art Director: Richard Sessions. For urban and regional planners interested in land use, housing, transportation and the environment. Monthly. Circ. 25,000. Previously published work OK. Original artwork returned after publication, upon request. Free sample copy and artist's guidelines.
Cartoons: Buys 2 cartoons/year on the environment, city/regional planning, energy, garbage, transportation, housing, power plants, agriculture and land use. Prefers single, double and multi panel with gaglines ("provide outside of cartoon body if possible"). SASE. Reports in 2 weeks. Buys all rights. Pays $25 minimum, b&w line drawings; on publication.
Illustrations: Buys 20 illustrations/year on the environment, city/regional planning, energy, garbage, transportation, housing, power plants, agriculture and land use. Prefers to see roughs and samples of style. SASE. Reports in 2 weeks. Buys all rights. Pays $200 maximum, b&w drawings, cover. Pays $25 minimum, b&w line drawings inside; on publication.

PLAYBILL, Suite 320, 71 Vanderbilt Ave., New York NY 10169. (212)557-5757. Editor-in-Chief: Joan Alleman. Concerns theater in New York City. Monthly. Circ. 1,040,000.
Cartoons: Buys b&w line drawings on New York City theater. SASE. Reports in 4 weeks. Buys all rights. Pays on acceptance.
Illustrations: Assigns work on New York City theater. SASE. Reports in 4 weeks. Buys all rights. Pays on acceptance.

PLAYBOY, 919 Michigan Ave., Chicago IL 60611. Executive Art Director: Tom Staebler. Emphasizes celebrities, beautiful women, dining, humor and fiction. For the sophisticated, urban male. All work generally done on assignment. Reports in 3-4 weeks.
Cartoons: Submit roughs with one finished drawing to Michelle Urry, cartoon editor. Buys 40/month on satirical, sophisticated, and other situations. Prefers cartoons that deal with sex and are slanted toward young, urban male market. "Style and technique very important." Pays $350, b&w; $600, full-page color.
Illustrations: Submit samples to Kerig Pope, managing art director. Pays $1,200/page or $2,000/spread; $200-250, spot drawings.

POCKETS, Box 189, 1908 Grand Ave., Nashville TN 37202. (615)340-7333. Associate Editor: Janet Bugg. Devotional magazine for children 6 to 12. Monthly magazine except January/February. Circ. 68,000. Accepts previously published material. Original artwork returned after publication. Sample copy for SASE with 73¢ postage.
Illustrations: Uses variety of styles; 4-color, 2-color, flapped art appropriate for children. Realistic fable and cartoon styles. We will accept tear sheets, Photostats and slides. Samples not filed are returned by SASE. Reports only if interested. Buys one-time or reprint rights. Pays $50-500 depending on size. Pays on acceptance. Decisions made in consultation with out-of-house designer.
Tips: "We forward artists' samples to our out-of-town designer. He handles all contacts with illustrators."

PODIATRY MANAGEMENT MAGAZINE, 401 N. Broad St., Philadelphia PA 19108. (215)925-9744. President: Scott Borowsky. Emphasizes practice management for podiatrists, faculty and students. Published 8 times/year. Circ. 11,000. Original artwork returned after publication. Also uses paste-up artists; pays $7-8/hour.
Illustrations: Buys 2-3 b&w illustrations/issue from freelancers. Themes tie in with stories. Works on assignment only. Send query letter with resume to be kept on file; write for appointment to show portfolio. Prefers Photostats and tear sheets as samples. Samples returned by SASE. Reports only if interested and if SASE is included. Buys all rights. Pays $100-175, b&w and $250, color, cover; $100, b&w, inside; on publication.

POPULAR PHOTOGRAPHY, 1 Park Ave., New York NY 10016. (212)719-6000. Art Director: Steven Powell. Magazine emphasizing photography with how-to and technical articles. Monthly. Circ. 800,000. Original artwork is returned after publication. Sample copy for SASE.
Illustrations: Buys 5 illustrations/issue from freelancers. Buys 60 illustrations/year from freelancers. Works on assignment only. Prefers line drawings to illustrate photo techniques and equipment. Send brochure or tear sheets and photocopies. Samples are filed. Samples not filed are not returned. Reports back only if interested. Call to schedule an appointment to show a portfolio which should include original/final art, tear sheets, color and b&w. Buys one-time rights. Pays $75, b&w; $150, color, inside; on acceptance.
Tips: "Nearly all assigned work will pertain to photographic techniques or related equipment utilized."

POPULAR SCIENCE, Times Mirror Magazines, Inc., 380 Madison Ave., New York NY 10017. (212)687-3000. Art Director: David Houser. For the well-educated adult male, interested in science, technology, new products. Receives 3 illustrations/week from freelance artists. Original artwork returned after publication.
Illustrations: Uses 30-40 illustrations/issue; buys 30/issue from freelancers. Works on assignment only. Interested in technical 4-color art and 2-color line art dealing with automotive or architectural subjects. Especially needs science and technological pieces as assigned per layout. Samples returned by SASE. Reports back on future assignment possibilities. Provide tear sheet to be kept on file for future assignments. "After seeing portfolios, I photocopy or Photostat those samples I feel are indicative of the art we might use." Reports whenever appropriate job is available. Buys first publishing rights.
Tips: "More and more scientific magazines have entered the field. This has provided a larger base of technical artists for us. Be sure your samples relate to our subject matter, i.e., no rose etchings, and be sure to include a tear sheet for our files."

POWER, McGraw-Hill, Inc., 11 W. 19th St., New York NY 10020. (212)337-4086. Art Director: Kiyo Komoda. Emphasizes the systems and equipment for the use and conservation of energy for power generation and plant energy systems. Monthly plus 2 annuals. Original artwork returned after publication, on request only.
Illustrations: Uses 30 illustrations/issue on energy systems. Buys 30%/issue from freelancers; most are graphs, charts and mechanical line drawings. Especially needs "graphs, charts, diagrams with more imagination or creative dramatization of what they represent." Works on assignment only. Send query letter with brochure showing art style or tear sheets and Photostats. Samples returned by SASE. Reports in 1 week. Call to schedule an appointment to show a portfolio, which may include original/final art, final reproduction/product and tear sheets. Buys one-time and reprint rights. Cover: Pays $150-500, color. Inside: Pays $30-300, color; $10-200, b&w line drawings; on acceptance.
Tips: "We prefer artists with clean and crisp line works. They should know about color separation and the use of Zipatone. Young artists welcomed. Follow the specs—especially those arts with deadlines. I'll never recall any artist if he or she fails to meet specs or deadlines."

PRAYING, Box 410335, Kansas City MO 64141. (816)531-0538. Editor: Arthur N. Winter. Emphasizes spirituality for everyday living for lay Catholics and members of mainline Protestant churches; pri-

marily Catholic, non-fundamentalist. "Starting point: The daily world of living, family, job, politics, is the stuff of religious experience and Christian living." Bimonthly. Circ. 20,000. Accepts previously published material. Original artwork not returned after publication. Sample copy and art guidelines available.
Cartoons: Buys 1-2 cartoons/issue from freelancers. Especially interested in cartoons that spoof fads and jargon in contemporary spirituality, prayer and religion. Prefers single panel with gagline; b&w line drawings. Send query letter with samples of style to be kept on file. Material not filed is returned by SASE. Reports within 2 weeks. Buys one-time rights. Pays $25, b&w; on acceptance.
Illustrations: Buys 2-3 illustrations/issue from freelancers. Prefers contemporary interpretations of traditional Christian symbols to be used as incidental art; also drawings to illustrate articles. Send query letter with samples to be kept on file. Prefers Photostats, tear sheets and photocopies as samples. Samples returned if not interested or return requested by SASE. Reports within 2 weeks. Buys one-time rights. Pays $25, b&w; on acceptance.

***PRELUDE MAGAZINE**, Box 4628, Carmel CA 93921. (408)375-5711. Art Director: Johathan Drake. Magazine emphasizing fine arts, classical, music and entertainment for the northwestern United States. Monthly. Circ. 25,000. Accepts previously published material. Original artwork is returned to the artist after publication. Sample copies free for SASE with first-class postage. Art guidelines free for SASE with first-class postage.
Cartoons: Cartoon Editor: Jeffrey Parks. Buys 3 cartoons/issue from freelancers. Buys 40 cartoons/year from freelancers. Prefers single, double or multiple panel with gagline; b&w line drawings. Send roughs. Samples are filed. Samples not filed are returned. Reports back within 6 weeks. Pays $15 + up, b&w.
Illustrations: Buys 3-6 illustrations/issue from freelancers. Buys 30-60 illustrations/year from freelancers. Prefers b&w editorial illustrations in all media. Works on assignment only. Send query letter with brochure, resume, tear sheets, photocopies, slides and photographs. Samples are filed. Samples not filed are returned. Reports back within 6 weeks. To show a portfolio, mail thumbnails, roughs, tear sheets, Photostats, photographs, slides, color and b&w. Buys first rights. Pays $50, b&w, cover; on publication.

THE PRESBYTERIAN RECORD, 50 Wynford Dr., Don Mills, Ontario M3C 1J7 Canada. (416)441-1111. Production and Design: Mary Visser. Published 11 times/year. Deals with family-oriented religious themes. Circ. 71,444. Original artwork returned after publication. Simultaneous submissions and previously published work OK. Free sample copy and artists' guidelines.
Cartoons: Buys 1-2 cartoons/issue; buys from freelancers. Interested in some theme or connection to religion. Send roughs. SAE (nonresidents include IRC). Reports in 1 month. Pays on publication.
Illustrations: Buys 1 illustration/year on religion. "We use freelance material, and we are interested in excellent color artwork for cover." Any line style acceptable— should reproduce well on newsprint. Works on assignment only. Send query letter with brochure showing art style or tear sheets, photocopies and photographs. Samples returned by SAE (nonresidents include IRC). Reports in 1 month. To show a portfolio, mail appropriate materials; portfolio should include original/final art, color, tear sheets and b&w. Buys all rights on a work-for-hire basis. Pays $50, color washes and opaque watercolors, cover; pays $20-30, b&w line drawings, inside; on publication.
Tips: "We don't want any 'cute' samples (in cartoons). Prefer some theological insight in cartoons; some comment on religious trends and practices."

PRESBYTERIAN SURVEY, 341 Ponce de Leon Ave. NE, Atlanta GA 30365. (404)873-1549. Art Director: Richard Brown. Emphasizes Presbyterian-related features and news, issues facing the church, Christian life. Monthly. Circ. 180,000. Sample copy for SASE.
Cartoons: Runs 1/issue on topics which speak to the issues of the day. Prefers finished cartoons. Reports in 6 weeks. Pays $20, b&w.
Illustrations: Buys 2/issue. Works on assignment only. Send query letter with brochure showing art style or tear sheets and photocopies. Samples not returned. Reports only if interested. To show a portfolio, mail final reproduction/product, tear sheets and Photostats. Negotiates rights purchased.

PREVENTION, 33 E. Minor St., Emmaus PA 18049. (215)967-5171. Executive Art Director: Wendy Ronga. Emphasizes health, nutrition, fitness, cooking. Monthly. Circ. 3,500,000. Returns original artwork after publication.
Cartoons: Buys 2-3 cartoons/issue from freelancers. Prefers themes of health, pets, fitness. Considers single panel with gagline; b&w line drawings, b&w washes. Samples of style are filed; unused roughs or finished cartoons are returned by SASE within 2 weeks. Reports back only if interested. Buys one-time rights.
Illustrations: Buys about 20 illustrations/issue from freelancers. Themes are assigned on editorial ba-

sis. Works on assignment only. Send samples to be kept on file. Prefers tear sheets or slides as samples. Samples not filed are returned by SASE. Reports back only if interested. Buys one-time rights. Pays $100-3,000.

PRIMAVERA, University of Chicago, 1212 E. 59th St., Chicago IL 60637. (312)324-5920. Contact: Editorial Board. Emphasizes art and literature by women for readers interested in contemporary literature and art. Annual. Circ. 800. Original artwork returned after publication. Sample copy $4; art guidelines available for SASE.
Illustrations: Buys 15-20 illustrations/issue from freelancers. Receives 5 illustrations/week from freelance artists. "We are open to a wide variety of styles and themes. Work must be in b&w with strong contrasts and should not exceed 7" high x 5" wide." Send finished art. Reports in 1-2 months. "If the artist lives in Chicago, she may call us for an appointment." Acquires first rights. "We pay in 2 free copies of the issue in which the artwork appears"; on publication.
Tips: "It's a good idea to take a look at a recent issue. Artists often do not investigate the publication and send work which may be totally inappropriate. We publish a wide variety of women artists. We have increased the number of graphics per issue. Send us a *variety* of prints. It is important that the graphics work well with the literature and the other graphics we've accepted. Our decisions are strongly influenced by personal taste and the work we know has already been accepted. Will consider appropriate cartoons and humorous illustrations."

PRIVATE PILOT/AERO/KITPLANES, Box 6050, Mission Viejo CA 92690. (714)855-8822. Contact: Editor. For owners/pilots of private aircraft, student pilots and others aspiring to attain additional ratings and experience. Circ. 105,000. Monthly. Receives 5 cartoons and 3 illustrations/week from freelance artists.
Cartoons: Buys 2-4 cartoons/issue on flying. Send finished artwork. SASE. Reports in 3 months. Pays $35, b&w; on publication.
Illustrations: Send query letter with samples. SASE. Reports in 3 months. Pays $50-100, b&w; $75-150, color. "We also use spot illustrations as column fillers; buys 1-2 spot illustrations/issue. Pays $25/spot."
Tips: "Know the field you wish to represent; we get tired of 'crash' gags submitted to flying publications."

PRIVATE PRACTICE, Suite 470, 3535 NW 58th St., Oklahoma City OK 73112. (405)943-2318. Art Director & Design Director: Rocky C. Hails. Editorial features "maintenance of freedom in all fields of medical practice and the effects of socioeconomic factors on the physician." Monthly. Circ. 180,000. Free sample copy and artists' guidelines.
Cartoons: Send query letter with resume and samples or arrange interview to show portfolio. SASE. Reports in 2-3 weeks. Negotiates pay; pays on acceptance.
Illustrations: Buys 1-4 illustrations/issue on politics, medicine and finance. Also uses artists for 4-color cover illustration. Uses some humorous illustrations and occasionally cartoon-style illustrations. Especially looks for "craftsmanship, combined with an ability to communicate complex concepts." Send a brochure showing art style or tear sheets, Photostats, slides and photographs. Call to schedule an appointment to show a portfolio, which should include original/final art, final reproduction/product, color, tear sheets, Photostats, photographs and b&w. Buys first and reprint rights. Pays $200-400, unlimited to media, all forms, cover; pays $60-110, color washes and opaque watercolors; $40-100, b&w line drawings and washes inside; on acceptance.
Tips: "Provide rproductions of several illustrations (that demonstrate the uniqueness of your style) to leave with the art director. Include a postcard requesting my response to the applicability of your work to *Private Practice*. This is efficient for both the art director and artist. It is encouraging to see the wide variety of 'accepted' styles and the design revisions going on in major journals. There is a rapid movement toward interactive production techniques freeing the designer for greater experimentation and creativity."

PROBE, Baptist Brotherhood Commission, 1548 Poplar, Memphis TN 38104. (901)272-2461. Art Director: Herschel Wells. Christian-oriented mission magazine for boys grades 7-9. Monthly. Original artwork returned after publication, if requested. Circ. 50,000. Previously published, photocopied and simultaneous submissions OK.
Illustrations: Uses 3 illustrations/issue; buys 1/issue from freelancers. Interested in family life with emphasis on boys and their interests. "Our freelance needs are usually directed toward a specific story; we frequently use humorous illustrations and sometimes use cartoon-style illustrations; we very seldom use art submitted on spec." Prefers pen & ink, airbrush and charcoal/pencil. Send brochure showing art style or resume and roughs to be kept on file. Reports in 3 weeks. Samples returned by SASE. Buys first North American serial rights. Cover: Pays $200-250, full-color; $100-180, b&w line drawings, washes and gray opaques. Inside: Pays $45-120, b&w line drawings, washes and gray opaques. Pays on acceptance.

***PROCEEDINGS**, U.S. Naval Institute, Annapolis MD 21402. (301)268-6110. Art Director: LeAnn Bauer. Magazine emphasizing naval and maritime subjects. "Proceedings is an independent forum for the sea services." Monthly. Circ. 110,000. Accepts previously published material. Sample copies and art guidelines available.
Cartoons: Buys 1 cartoon/issue from freelancers. Buys 23 cartoons/year from freelancers. Prefers cartoons assigned to tie in with editorial topics. Send query letter with samples of style to be kept on file. Material not filed is returned if requested by artist. Reports within 1 month. Negotiates rights purchased. Payment varies.
Illustrations: Buys 1 illustration/issue from freelancers. Buys 12 illustrations/year from freelancers. Works on assignment only. Prefers illustrations assigned to tie in with editorial topics. Send query letter with brochure, resume, tear sheets, Photostats, photocopies and photographs. Samples are filed. Samples not filed are returned only if requested by artist. Reports within 1 month. Write to schedule an appointment to show a portfolio or mail appropriate materials. Negotiates rights purchased. Payment varies. "Contact us first to see what our needs are."

PROFESSIONAL AGENT, 400 N. Washington St., Alexandria VA 22314. (703)836-9340. Editor: Eric R. Wassyng. For independent insurance agents and other affiliated members of the American Agency System. Monthly. Circ. 40,000. Original artwork returned after publication. Free sample copy.
Illustrations: Buys 3/issue from freelancers. Local artists preferred. Prefers a "light-hearted, amusing, style." Prefers pen & ink, then charcoal/pencil, colored pencil, watercolor, acrylics and mixed media. Provide samples to be kept on file for future assignments. Pays by the project, $75-500. Buys first-time North American rights.
Tips: Conceptual approach often required. Trends are toward "more humorous with message." Include in your portfolio "originals of printed pieces, a list of former clients, award-winning pieces and tear sheets. I do not want to see fine art paintings (landscapes, still lifes, etc.)." Prefers to see a representative sampling.."

PROFESSIONAL ELECTRONICS, 2708 W. Berry St., Ft. Worth TX 76109. (817)921-9062. Editor-in-Chief: Wallace S. Harrison. For professionals in electronics, especially owners, technicians and managers of consumer electronics sales and service firms. Bimonthly. Circ. 10,000. Samples of previously published cartoons furnished on request.
Cartoons: Buys themes on electronics sales/service, association management, conventions and directors' meetings. Prefers single panel with gagline. Submit art with SASE. Reports in 2 weeks. Buys first rights. Pays $10, b&w line drawings; on acceptance.
Illustrations: Buys assigned themes. Submit art and SASE. Reports in 2 weeks. Buys first rights. Pays $30-60, b&w line drawings, cover. Pays $10-15, b&w line drawings, inside; on acceptance.
Tips: "We need more diversity in subject matter. Most freelancers submit TV-only gags or computer-only. What might be funny to a consumer isn't necessarily funny to a professional (our market)."

PROFILES MAGAZINE, 533 Stevens Ave., Solana Beach CA 92075. (619)481-3934. Art Director: Goss/Keller/Martinez, Inc. Magazine emphasizing computers. Monthly. Circ. 80,000. Original artwork returned after publication. Sample copy available.
Cartoons: Buys 4 cartoons/issue. Prefers single panel, with gagline; b&w line drawings. Send finished cartoons to be kept on file. Samples not filed are not returned. Does not report back. Buys first rights.
Illustrations: Buys 4 illustrations/issue from freelancers. Works on assignment only. Send tear sheets, Photostats, photocopies, slides and photographs. Samples not filed are not returned. Reports only if interested. To show a portfolio, mail original/final art, final reproduction/product, color, tear sheets, Photostats, photographs and b&w to Goss/Keller/Martinez, Inc., 853 Camino del Mar, Del Mar CA 92014. Buys first time rights. Payment varies.

PROFIT, Box 1132, Studio City CA 91604. (818)789-4980. Associate Editor: Marjorie Clapper. Magazine emphasizing business news for the business community. Circ. 10,000. Monthly. Original artwork not returned after publication. Sample copy $1.
Cartoons: Prefers single panel; b&w line drawings or b&w washes. Send query letter with samples of style to be kept on file if acceptable. Write for appointment to show portfolio. Samples not filed are returned by SASE. Reports only if interested. Buys all rights. Payment varies.
Illustrations: Buys 0-12 illustrations/issue from freelancers. Works on assignment only. Send query letter with brochure showing art style or resume and samples. Samples returned by SASE. Reports only if interested. To show a portfolio, mail thumbnails, original/final art, final reproduction/product, tear sheets, b&w photographs and as much information as possible. Buys all rights. Payment varies. Pays on publication.

THE PROGRESSIVE, 409 E. Main St., Madison WI 53703. (608)257-4626. Art Director: Patrick JB Flynn. Monthly. Circ. 50,000. Free sample copy and artists' guidelines.
Illustrations: Buys 10 b&w illustrations/issue from freelancers. Works on assignment only. Send query letter with tear sheets and/or photocopies. Samples returned by SASE. Reports in 2 months. Cover pays $300, b&w. Inside pays $100-200, b&w line or tone drawings/paintings, inside; on publication, cover. Buys first rights.
Tips: Do not send original art. Send appropriate return postage. "The most obvious trend in editorial work is toward more artistic freedom in ideas and style. The successful art direction of a magazine allows for personal interpretation of an assignment."

PUBLIC CITIZEN, Suite 605, 2000 P St., Washington DC 20036. (202)293-9142. Editor: Catherine Baker. Emphasizes consumer issues for the membership of Public Citizen, a group founded by Ralph Nader in 1971. Bimonthly. Circ. 42,000. Accepts previously published material. Returns original artwork after publication. Sample copy available with 9x12 envelope SASE with first-class postage.
Illustrations: Buys up to 10/issue. Prefers contemporary, not cartoonish style. Prefers pen & ink; uses computer illustration also. "I use computer art when it is appropriate for a particular article." Send query letter with samples to be kept on file. Samples not filed are returned by SASE. Reports only if interested. Buys first rights or one-time rights. Pays $300, 3-color, cover; and $50-200, b&w or 2-color, inside; on publication.
Tips: "Frequently commissions more than one spot per artist. Also, send several keepable samples that show a range of styles and the ability to conceptualize. I do not want to see cartoons or buffoonery."

***PUBLIC RELATIONS JOURNAL**, 845 3rd Ave., New York NY 10022. (212)955-2230. Art Director: Susan Yip. Emphasizes issues and developments, both theory and practice, for public relations practitioners, educators and their managements. Monthly. Circ. 15,733. Accepts previously published material. Returns original artwork after publication. Art guidelines available.
Cartoons: Buys business cartoons. Send samples of style to be kept on file. Material not kept on file returned only if requested. Reports back only if interested. Negotiates rights purchased. Pays $50, b&w; $75-100, color; on publication.
Illustrations: Buys illustrations from freelancers. Themes and styles vary. Send brochure and samples to be kept on file. Prefers slides or photographs as samples. Samples not filed are returned only if requested. Reports back only if interested. Negotiates rights purchased. Pays $200 for color cover; $75 for b&w and $100 for color inside; on publication.

***PUBLISHER'S WEEKLY**, 249 W. 17th St., Fourth Floor, New York NY 10011. (212)645-9700. Art Director: Maureen Gleason. Magazine emphasizing book publishing for "people involved in the creative or the technical side of publishing." Weekly. 51 issues /year. Circ. 50,000. Original artwork is returned to the artist after publication. Sample copies available.
Illustrations: Buys 75 illustrations/year from freelancers. Works on assignment only. "Open to all styles, with book-oriented themes." Send query letter with brochure or resume, tear sheets, Photostats, photocopies, slides and photographs. Samples are filed. Samples not filed are returned by SASE. Reports back only if interested. To show a portfolio, mail appropriate materials. Generally buys reprint rights. Pays $100, b&w; $200, color, inside; on acceptance.
Tips: "Send promotional pieces and follow up with a phone call."

ELLERY QUEEN'S MYSTERY MAGAZINE, Davis Publications, 380 Lexington Ave., New York NY 10017. (212)557-9100. Editor: Eleanor Sullivan. Emphasizes mystery stories and reviews of mystery books. Reports within 1 month. Pays $25 minimum, line drawings. All other artwork is done inhouse. Pays on acceptance.

QUILT WORLD, 306 E. Parr Rd., Berne IN 46711. Editor: Sandra L. Hatch. Concerns patchwork and quilting. Bimonthly. SASE. Previously published work OK. Original artwork not returned after publication. Sample copy with 9x12 SASE with 66¢ postage.
Cartoons: Buys 2 cartoons/issue from freelancers. Receives 25 submissions/week from freelancers. Uses themes "poking gentle fun at quilters." Send finished cartoons. Reports in 3 weeks if not accepted. "I hold cartoons I can use until there is space." Buys all rights. Pays $15; on acceptance and/or publication.

R-A-D-A-R, 8121 Hamilton Ave., Cincinnati OH 45231. Editor: Margaret Williams. For children 3rd-6th grade in Christian Sunday schools. Original artwork not returned after publication.
Cartoons: Buys 1 cartoon/month on animals, school and sports. Prefers to see finished cartoons. Reports in 1-2 months. Pays $10-15; on acceptance.
Illustrations: Uses 5 or more illustrations/issue. "Art that accompanies nature or handicraft articles may be purchased, but almost everything is assigned." Send tear sheets to be kept on file. Samples returned by SASE. Reports in 1-2 months. Buys all rights on a work-for-hire basis. Pays $60, line drawing, cover; pays $35-40, inside.

RADIO-ELECTRONICS, 500-B Bi-County Blvd., Farmingdale NY 11735. (516)293-3000. Editorial Director: Arthur Kleiman. Monthly. For electronics professionals and hobbyists. Circ. 242,000. Previously published work OK. Free sample copy.
Cartoons: Buys 3 cartoons/issue on electronics, service, hi-fi, computers and TV games; single panel. Mail art. SASE. Reports in 1 week. Buys first or all rights. Pays $35 minimum, b&w washes; on acceptance.

RAG MAG, Box 12, Goodhue MN 55027. Contact: Beverly Voldseth. Emphasizes poetry, graphics, fiction and reviews for small press, writers, poets and editors. Semiannually: fall and spring. Circ. 300. Accepts previously published material. Send no original work. Sample copy $3; art guidelines free for SASE.
Cartoons: Buys 2 cartoons/issue from freelancers. Any theme or style. Prefers single panel or multiple panel with gagline; b&w line drawings. Send samples of styles or finished cartoons. Material returned in 2 months by SASE if unwanted. Reports within 2 months. Acquires first rights. Pays in copies only.
Illustrations: Buys 6 illustrations/issue from freelancers. Any style or theme. Send camera-ready copy. Samples returned by SASE. Reports within 1 month. Acquires first rights. Pays in copies for b&w cover and inside.
Tips: "Realize I publish only 2 issues per year. I can use only 10-12 art pieces per year. I don't hold a lot in my files because I think artists should be sending their art work around. And even if I like someone's art work very much, I like to use new people."

***THE READING TEACHER**, International Reading Association, 800 Barksdale Rd., Box 8139, Newark DE 19714-8139. (302)731-1600. Graphic Design Coordinator: Boni Nash. Journal (8½x11 perfect bound), emphasizing reading instruction at the elementary level for school reading specialists, classroom teachers, administrators, etc. Monthly (October-May). Circ. 50,000. Original artwork not returned after publication. Sample copy available.
Cartoons: Buys 1 cartoon/issue from freelancers. Considers themes related to reading or school. Prefers single panel with or without gagline; b&w line drawings or b&w washes. Send query letter with roughs or finished cartoons; call for appointment to show portfolio. Material not filed is returned by SASE. Reports within 1 month. Buys one-time rights. Pays $20, b&w; on acceptance.

REAL ESTATE CENTER JOURNAL, (formerly Tierra Grande), Real Estate Center, Texas A&M University, College Station TX 77843. (409)845-0369. Art Director: Bob Beals. Emphasizes real estate; "primarily for real estate practitioners, with a smattering of investors, attorneys, CPAs, architects and others interested in real estate." Quarterly. Circ. 75,000. Previously published material and simultaneous submissions OK. Free sample copy.
Illustrations: Uses 1-5 illustrations/issue; buys 1-5 from freelancers. Interested in "anything relating directly or indirectly to real estate." Works on assignment only. Send query letter. Provide samples and tear sheets to be kept on file for possible future assignments. Reports in 2 months. Negotiates rights purchased. Pays $20-200, inside b&w line drawings; $50-200, inside b&w washes; on acceptance.
Tips: "There are a great many talented artists, making it unnecessary to consider the marginally talented or those with less than professional presentation of their material. I especially like the artist to know printing production, and I want to know how well the artist works in 1 or 2 colors."

RELIX MAGAZINE, Box 94, Brooklyn NY 11229. (718)258-0009. Manager: Toni A. Brown. Emphasizes music—rock, 60's groups, particularly the Grateful Dead for audience 16-39 years of age, 68%

male, 32% female. Bimonthly. Circ. 15,000. Accepts previously published material. Original artwork not returned after publication. Sample copy $3; art guidelines for SASE.
Cartoons: Prefers music-related themes, especially "hippie humor." Prefers multi panel, with gagline; b&w line drawings. Send query letter with samples of style to be kept on file. Material not kept on file is returned by SASE. Reports only if interested. Buys all rights. Pay rate is open; pays on publication.
Illustrations: Uses 3-6 illustrations/issue. Prefers rock and roll themes. Send query letter with samples to be kept on file. Prefers Photostats or photographs as samples. Samples not kept on file are returned by SASE. Does not report back. Buys all rights. Pays $150, color, cover; negotiates payment for b&w, inside; pays on publication.
Tips: "We seriously consider anything. We have a lot of opportunities open including t-shirts. We are very accessible. We are especially looking for skeletal art—not morbid."

RENEGADE, 2705 E. 7th St., Long Beach CA 90814. Publisher: Deni Loubert. Publishes comic book series. Titles include *French Ice*, *Kilgore*, *Cases of Sherlock Holmes*, *The Silent Invasion* and *Neil the Horse*. Prints work "that hasn't been seen before." Circ. 12-15,000.
Illustrations: Send query letter with a one paragraph summary of the premise, and photocopies of a cover and an interior page. "The artist receives royalties based on sales. All titles are creator-owned, with the artist retaining the copyright."
Tips: "Artists who work for me need very little guidance. I work with people who write and draw the entire package and with people who have established themselves as a team."

RENTAL EQUIPMENT REGISTER, 2048 Cotner, Los Angeles CA 90025. (213)477-1033. Readers are independent owners of small and large rental centers including firms engaged in rental of tools and appliances, trucks, trailers, contractor equipment, home health care supplies and party goods. Monthly. Circ. 14,500.
Cartoons: Uses 2 cartoons/issue; buys all from freelancers. Interested in cartoons with slant to the rental center owner. Prefers single panel b&w line drawings or b&w washes. Send finished cartoons to Bob Keeley, editor. SASE. Reports in 2 weeks. Buys all rights. Pays $20-30 for b&w; on publication.

RESIDENT AND STAFF PHYSICIAN, 80 Shore Rd., Port Washington NY 11050. (516)883-6350. Executive Editor: Anne Mattarella. Emphasizes hospital medical practice from clinical, educational, economic and human standpoints. For hospital physicians, interns and residents. Monthly. Circ. 100,000.
Cartoons: Buys 3-4 cartoons/year. "We occasionally publish sophisticated cartoons in good taste dealing with medical themes." Interested in "inside" medical themes. Send query letter with brochure showing art style or resume, tear sheets, Photostats, photocopies, slides and photographs. Call or write to schedule an appointment to show a portfolio, which should include final reproduction/product, color, tear sheets and b&w. Reports in 2 weeks. Buys all rights. Pays $25; varies for color; also buys spots; pays $10-50; on acceptance.
Illustrations: "We commission qualified freelance medical illustrators to do covers and inside material. Artists should send sample work." Pays $600, color, cover; payment varies for inside work; on acceptance.
Tips: "We like to look at previous work to give us an idea of the artist's style. Since our publication is clinical, we require highly-qualified technical artists who are very familiar with medical illustration. Sometimes we have use for nontechnical work. We like to look at everything. We need material from the *doctor's* point of view, *not* the patient's."

RESTAURANT BUSINESS MAGAZINE, 633 Third Ave., New York NY 10017. Art Director: Charli Ornett. Emphasizes restaurants/food/business and management for restaurateurs. Monthly. Circ. 110,000. Original artwork returned after publication.
Illustrations: Uses 8-10 illustrations/issue. Works on assignment only. Drop off portfolio. Prefers to see b&w and color portfolio. Negotiates rights purchased and payment. Pays $1,000 color, cover; $75-250 b&w inside; $150-600 color inside; within 60 days.
Tips: "Show the kind of stuff you want to do."

RESTAURANT HOSPITALITY, 1100 Superior Ave., Cleveland OH 44114. (216)696-7000. Associate Editor: David Farkas. Emphasizes commercial food service industry for owners, managers, chefs, etc. Circ. 121,000. Accepts previously published material "if exclusive to foodservice trade press." Original artwork returned after publication. Sample copy $4.
Illustrations: "We have built a file of freelance illustrators but want to see the work of others to whom we can assign projects." Works on assignment only. Send query letter with brochure, resume, business card, samples and tear sheets to be kept on file. Prefers photographs as samples, 5x7 or larger, but will accept Photostats. Does not report back to the artist. Pays $350-400, cover; $100-300, inside; on acceptance.

THE RETIRED OFFICER, 201 N. Washington St., Alexandria VA 22314. (703)549-2311. Art Director: M.L. Woychik. For retired officers of the seven uniformed services; concerns current military/political affairs; recent military history, especially Vietnam and Korea; holiday anecdotes; travel; human interest; humor; hobbies; second-career job opportunities and military family lifestyle. Free sample copy for 9x12 SASE with $1.25 postage.
Illustrations: Buys illustrations on assigned themes. (Generally uses Washington DC area artists.) Send query letter with resume and samples.

RIP OFF PRESS, INC., Box 4686, Auburn CA 95604. (916)885-8183. Chief Copy Editor: Kathe Todd. Quarterly. Publishes comic books including *Fabulous Furry Freak Brothers*, *Rip Off Comics* and *Gyro Comics*. Genres: animal parodies and social parodies. Themes: social commentary and alternative lifestyles. "We publish 'underground' comix. Prefer submissions to be intelligent, funny and well-drawn, rather than heavily violent, graphically sexual or New Wave." Circ. 10-50,000. Original artwork returned after publication. Send $1 for catalog listing retail prices. Art guidelines for SASE with first-class postage.
Illustrations: Prefers three-tier page of 6 panels or format 2 wide by 3 tall. Send query letter with photocopies of representative pages or stories. Samples are filed "depending on merit." Samples not filed are returned by SASE if requested. Call or write to schedule an appointment to show a portfolio, which should include 4-5 photocopies of original inking. Buys U.S. comic rights and first refusal on subsequent collections. "Our advance ranges $75-100 per b&w finished page against 10% of cover price on net copies sold (divided by number of pages)." Pays on acceptance and publication when earned royalties exceed advance.
Tips: Looks for "knowledge of successful techniques for b&w reproduction; ability to use comic narrative techniques well; knowledge of and facility with anatomy and perspective."

RISK MANAGEMENT, 205 E. 42nd St., New York NY 10017. (212)286-9292. Graphics Design Manager: Linda Golden. Emphasizes the insurance trade for insurance buyers of Fortune 500 companies. Monthly. Circ. 10,500.
Illustrations: Uses 3-4 illustrations/issue; buys 2-4 every issue from freelancers. Prefers color illustration or stylized line; no humorous themes. Works on assignment only. Send card showing art style or tear sheets. Call for appointment to show portfolio, which should include original art and tear sheets. Prefers printed pieces as samples; original work will not be kept on file after 1 year. Samples not kept on file are returned only if requested. Buys one-time rights. Pays $100 color, cover (2nd use); $175-225 b&w and $250-300 color, inside; on acceptance.
Tips: When reviewing an artist's work, looks for "neatness, strong concepts, realism with subtle twists and sharply-defined illustrations."

ROAD KING MAGAZINE, Box 250, Park Forest IL 60466. (312)481-9240. Editor: George Friend. Emphasizes services for truckers, news of the field, CB radio and fiction; leisure-oriented. Readers are over-the-road truckers. Quarterly. Circ. 224,000.
Cartoons: Uses 4 cartoons/issue; buys all from freelancers. Receives 1-2 submissions/week from freelancers. Interested in over-the-road trucking experiences. Prefers single panel b&w line drawings with gagline. Send finished cartoons. SASE. Reports in 2-4 months. Buys first North American serial rights. Pays $25 and up for b&w; on acceptance.
Tips: "Stick to our subject matter. No matter how funny the cartoons are, we probably won't buy them unless they are about trucks and trucking."

RODALES PRACTICAL HOMEOWNER, 33 E. Minor St., Emmaus PA 18049. (215)967-5171. Art Director: John Pepper. Emphasizes "do-it-yourself home design, repair and management for 30-50-year-old, college-educated males; homeowners, handymen." Published 9 times/year. Circ. 700,000. Original artwork returned after publication "if requested." Sample copy for SASE "and samples of artist's work"; art guidelines available for SASE.
Illustrations: Buys 15-20 illustrations/issue from freelancers. Works on assignment only. Prefers technical illustrations in 4-color. Send business card, samples, and tear sheets to be kept on file for possible future assignments; call or write for appointment to show portfolio. Samples not kept on file are returned by SASE. Reports in 2-4 weeks. Pays $40-300, inside b&w line drawings; $50-1,500, inside color washes. Pays upon completion of assignment.
Tips: "Become familiar with the needs and style of publication. Have a unique, innovative, clear and accurate style that works with the nature of the magazine."

ROOM OF ONE'S OWN, Box 46160, Station G, Vancouver, British Columbia V6R 4G5 Canada. Contact: Editor. Literary journal. Emphasizes feminist literature for general and academic women, and libraries. Quarterly. Circ. 1,200. Original artwork returned after publication. Sample copy $2.75; art

guidelines for SAE (nonresidents include IRC).
Illustrations: Buys 3-5 illustrations/issue from freelancers. Prefers good b&w line drawings. Prefers pen & ink, then charcoal/pencil, colored pencil, watercolor and collage. Send samples to be kept on file. Accepts Photostats, photographs, slides or original work as samples. Samples not kept on file are returned by SAE (nonresidents include IRC). Reports within 1 month. Buys first rights. Pays $50, b&w, cover; $25, b&w, inside; on publication.
Tips: "Artwork is not a big deal except for the cover."

ROSICRUCIAN DIGEST, Rosicrucian Order, AMORC, San Jose CA 95191. (408)287-9171, ext. 320. Editor/Art Director: Mr. Robin M. Thompson. Fraternal magazine featuring articles on science, philosophy, psychology, metaphysics, mysticism, and the arts for men and women of all ages—"inquiring minds seeking answers to the important questions of life." Bimonthly. Circ. 70,000. Does not accept previously published material. Returns original artwork to the artist. Sample copy available.
Illustrations: Buys a maximum of 10/year. Send query letter with samples. Prefers Photostats, tear sheets and photocopies as samples. Samples returned with SASE. Reports back within 30-60 days. Pays $10 minimum. Pays on acceptance.
Tips: "We are looking for new, fresh unknown artists who want to break in. We offer the opportunity to show off their fine work in a scholarly publication. We are looking for thought-provoking artwork. Nothing sensational or trendy. Freelancers should be familiar with our magazine—the format, style, etc.—before sending their samples or especially their portfolios."

THE ROTARIAN, 1560 Sherman Ave., Evanston IL 60201. Editor: Willmon L. White. Associate Editor: Jo Nugent. Art Director: P. Limbos. Emphasizes general interest and business and management articles. Service organization for business and professional men, their families, and other subscribers. Monthly. Sample copy and editorial fact sheet available.
Cartoons: Buys 4-5 cartoons/issue. Interested in general themes with emphasis on business. Avoid topics of sex, national origin, politics. Send query letter to Cartoon Editor, Charles Pratt, with brochure showing art style. Reports in 1-2 weeks. Buys all rights. Pays $75 on acceptance.
Illustrations: Buys assigned themes. Most editorial illustrations are commissioned. Buys average 3 or more illustrations/issue; 6 humorous illustrations/year. Send query letter to Art Director with brochure showing art style. Reports within 10 working days. Buys all rights. Call to schedule an appointment to show a portfolio, which should include keyline paste-up, original/final art, final reproduction/product, color and photographs. Pays $250-1,000 on acceptance.
Tips: "Artists should set up appointments with art director to show their portfolios. Preference given to area talent." Conservative style and subject matter.

***ROUGH NOTES**, 1200 N. Meridian, Indianapolis IN 46204. Assistant Editor: Nancy Doucette.
Cartoons: Buys 2-3 cartoons/issue on property and casualty insurance, some life insurance and general humor. No risque material. Receives 30-40 cartoons/week from freelance artists. Submit art the third week of the month. SASE. Reports in 1 month. Buys all rights. Prefers 5x8 or 8x10 finished art. Pays $15, line drawings and halftones; on acceptance.
Tips: "Do not submit sexually discriminating materials. I have a tendency to disregard all of the material if I find any submissions of this type. Send several items for more variety in selection. We would prefer to deal only in finished art, not sketches."

RUNNER'S WORLD, 135 N. 6th St., Emmaus PA 18049. (215)967-5171. Art Director: Ken Kleppert. Emphasizes serious, recreational running. Monthly. Circ. 470,000. Returns original artwork after publication. Sample copy available.
Illustrations: Buys average of 6/issue from freelancers. "Styles include tightly rendered human athletes, caricatures, and cerebral interpretations of running themes. Also, *RW* uses medical illustration for features on biomechanics." Prefers pen & ink, airbrush, charcoal/pencil, colored pencil, watercolor, acrylics, oils, pastels, collage and mixed media. Works on assignment only. Send samples to be kept on file. Prefers tear sheets or slides as samples. Samples not filed are returned by SASE. Reports back only if interested. Buys one-time rights.
Tips: Portfolio should include "a maximum of 12 images. The portfolio should be as well thought out and designed as any illustration."

RUNNING TIMES, Suite 300, 9171 Wilshire Blvd., Beverly Hills CA. (213)858-7100. Publisher: Ed Ayres. Emphasizes distance running. Readers include road runners, cross country and adventure runners; people interested in fitness. Monthly. Sample copy $1.95.
Illustrations: Uses 3-5 illustrations/issue, all from freelancers. Prefers b&w line drawings for inside, and color illustrations for inside and cover. Especially needs color illustrations for feature articles and small b&w drawings. Prefers to see finished art, portfolio or tear sheet to be kept on file. SASE. Reports

in 4 weeks. Buys all rights on a work-for-hire basis. Pays $35-200 for inside and $250 minimum for cover; on publication. Buys first North American serial rights.
Tips: "We need more art and would like to see more samples or portfolios!"

RURAL KENTUCKIAN, Box 32170, Louisville KY 40232. Editor: Gary Luhr. Magazine emphasizing Kentucky-related and general feature material for Kentuckians living outside metropolitan areas. Monthly. Circ. 300,000. Accepts previously published material. Original artwork returned after publication if requested. Sample copy available. All artwork is solicited by the magazine to illustrate upcoming articles.
Illustrations: Buys 2-3 illustrations/issue from freelancers. Works on assignment only. Prefers b&w line art. Send query letter with resume and samples. Samples not filed are returned only if requested. Reports within 2 weeks. Buys one-time rights. Pays $50, b&w, cover; $30-50, b&w, inside; on acceptance.

SACRAMENTO MAGAZINE, Box 2424, Sacramento CA 95811. (916)446-7548. Art Director: Chuck Donald. Emphasizes Sacramento city living for audience 25-54 years old, executives/professionals, married, middle-upper income. Monthly. Circ. 30,000. Accepts previously published material and simultaneous submissions. Sample copy for SASE.
Cartoons: Buys 6 cartoons/issue. Pays $25 b&w.
Illustrations: Uses 5 illustrations/issue. Send query letter with brochure showing art style or tear sheets, Photostats, slides and photographs to be kept on file. Accepts any type of samples which fairly represent artist's work. Reports only if interested. Negotiates rights purchased. Call or write to schedule an appointment to show a portfolio, which should include original/final art and final reproduction/product. Pays $350 color, cover; $125 b&w and $200 color, inside; on acceptance.

***SAFE & VAULT TECHNOLOGY**, 5083 Danville Rd., Nicholasville Ky 40356. Editor: April Truitt. Estab. 1986. "Our subscribers maintain, service and sell safes and vaults for everyone from individual homeowners to banks, institutions and government installations." Monthly. Circ. 5,000. Accepts previously published material. Original artwork is not returned to the artist after publication unless requested. Sample copy $7. Art guidelines not available.
Cartoons: Prefers single panel with or without gagline; b&w line drawings and b&w washes. Send query letter with finished cartoons. Samples are not filed, but returned by SASE if requested. Reports back only if interested. Buys one-time rights. Pays $50, b&w.
Illustrations: Send query letter with brochure showing art style or tear sheets, Photostats or photocopies. Samples are not filed and returned only if requested. Reports back only if interested. To show a portfolio, mail appropriate materials. Buys reprint rights.

SAFETY & HEALTH, National Safety Council, 444 N. Michigan Ave., Chicago IL 60611-3991. (312)527-4800. Editor: Roy Fisher. For those responsible for developing and administering occupational and environmental safety and health programs. Monthly. Circ. 56,000. Original artwork returned after publication. Free sample copy and artist's guidelines. Also uses artists for 4-color cover design, publication redesign and layout mock-ups. Contact: Gordon Bieberle, Director of Publications Department.
Cartoons: Contact: Susan-Marie Kelly. Uses 4-6 cartoons/issue, all from freelancers. Interested in occupational safety and health; single, double or multi panel with gagline. Prefers to see roughs. SASE. Reports in 4 weeks. Buys first North American serial rights or all rights on a work-for-hire basis. Pays $10 minimum, b&w line drawings.

SAILING, 125 E. Main St., Port Washington WI 53074. (414)284-3494. Editor: Micca L. Hutchins. Emphasizes all aspects of sailing (sailboats only). Monthly. Circ. 35,000. Original artwork returned after publication upon special request. Previously published work OK. Sample copy $2.95.
Illustrations: Uses very few illustrations/year. Interested in action sailing only. Works primarily on assignment. Send resume, finished art, or samples of style. Samples returned by SASE, if requested. Provide letter of inquiry to be kept on file for future assignments. Reports in 2-3 weeks. Buys one-time North American rights.

SAILING WORLD, 111 E Ave., Norwalk CT 06851. (203)853-9921. Editor: John Burnham. Managing Editor: Douglas O. Logan. Emphasizes racing events and instructional articles for "performance-oriented sailors." Published 12 times/year. Circ. 62,000. Original artwork returned after publication. Sample copy $1.75.
Illustrations: Works on assignment only. Send query letter with roughs. Samples returned by SASE. Buys first rights. Pays on publication.

THE ST. LOUIS JOURNALISM REVIEW, 8380 Olive Blvd., St. Louis MO 63132. (314)991-1699. Contact: Charles L. Klotzer. Features critiques of primarily St. Louis but also national media—print, broadcasting, TV, cable, advertising, public relations and the communication industry. Monthly. Circ. 12,000.
Cartoons: Subject should pertain to the news media; preferably local. Query with samples. SASE. Reports in 4-7 weeks. Pays $15-25 on publication.
Illustrations: Query with samples. SASE. Reports in 4-6 weeks. Pays $15-25 each (negotiable) for b&w illustrations pertaining to the news media (preferably local); on publication.

SALT LICK PRESS, 1804 E. 38½ St., Austin TX 78722. Editor/Publisher: James Haining. Published irregularly. Circ. 1,500. Previously published material and simultaneous submissions OK. Original artwork returned after publication. Sample copy $3.
Illustrations: Uses 12 illustrations/issue; buys 2 from freelancers. Receives 2 illustrations/week from freelance artists. Interested in a variety of themes. Send brochure showing art style or tear sheets, Photostats, photocopies, slides and photographs. Samples returned by SASE. Reports in 6 weeks. To show a portfolio, mail roughs, Photostats, photographs and b&w. Negotiates payment; pays on publication. Buys first rights.

SALT WATER SPORTSMAN, 186 Lincoln St., Boston MA 02111. (617)426-4074. Editor-in-Chief/Art Director: Barry Gibson. Emphasizes resorts, areas, techniques, equipment and conservation. For saltwater fishermen, fishing equipment retailers and resort owners. Monthly. Circ. 135,000. Original artwork returned after publication. Free sample copy and artists' guidelines.
Illustrations: Buys 3 illustrations/issue from freelancers. Receives 3 submissions/week from freelancers. Works on assignment only. Interested in themes covering all phases of salt water sport fishing—mood, how-to, etc. Prefers pen & ink and charcoal/pencil. Send query letter with brochure to be kept on file. SASE. Reports in 4 weeks. Reports back on future assignment possibilities. Write to schedule an appointment to show a portfolio, which should include final reproduction/product. Buys first North American serial rights. Pays $600 b&w, cover, payment varies for inside; on acceptance.
Tips: "Let us see samples of work relevant to our topics/areas. New artists should strive for accuracy in portraying fish, equipment, etc."

***SALVAGE SELLER**, Suite 201, 6420 Zane Ave. N, Minneapolis MN 55429. (612)535-8383. Publisher: Ron Sauby. Emphasizes salvage. Monthly. Accepts previously published material. Returns original artwork after publication. Sample copy free for SASE; art guidelines available.
Cartoons: Themes, styles and format open. Send query letter with samples of style to be kept on file. Write or call for appointment to show portfolio. Material not filed is returned by SASE. Reports within 30 days. Negotiates rights purchased. Pays on acceptance.
Illustrations: Works on assignment only. Send query letter and samples to be kept on file. Write or call for appointment to show portfolio. Will review Photostats, tear sheets, photocopies, slides or photographs. Samples not filed are returned by SASE. Reports within 30 days. Negotiates rights purchased. Pays on acceptance.

SAN JOSE STUDIES, San Jose State University, San Jose CA 95192. (408)277-2841. Editor: Fauneil J. Rinn. Emphasizes the arts, humanities, business, science, social science; scholarly. Published 3 times/year. Circ. 500. Original artwork returned after publication. Sample copy $5.
Cartoons: Number of cartoons/issue varies. Interested in "anything that would appeal to the active intellect." Prefers single panel b&w line drawings. Send slides. SASE. Reports in 2 weeks. Buys first North American serial rights. Pays in 2 copies of publication, plus entry in $100 annual contest.
Illustrations: Number of illustrations/issue varies. Prefers b&w line drawings. Send slides. SASE. Reports in 2 weeks. To show a portfolio, mail Photostats, photographs and b&w. Buys first North American serial rights. Pays in 2 copies of publication, plus entry in $100 annual contest.
Tips: "We would be interested in cartoons, and humorous and cartoon-style illustrations especially if accompanied by some description of the artist's techniques, purpose, conception and development of the artwork."

SANTA BARBARA MAGAZINE, 216 E. Victoria St., Santa Barbara CA 93101. (805)965-5999. Art Director: Kimberly Kavish. Magazine emphasizing Santa Barbara culture and community. Bimonthly. Circ. 11,000. Original artwork returned after publication if requested. Sample copy $2.95.
Illustrations: Buys about 3 illustrations/issue from freelance artists. Works on assignment only. Send query letter with brochure, resume, tear sheets and photocopies. Reports back within 6 weeks. To show a portfolio, mail original/final art, final reproduction/product/color, tear sheet and b&w, will contact if interested. Buys first rights. Payment varies; on acceptance.

SATELLITE ORBIT, Box 53, Boise ID 83707. (208)322-2800. Contact: Art Director. Magazine emphasizing satellite television industry for home satellite dish owners and dealers. Monthly. Circ. 400,000. Accepts previously published material. Original artwork returned after publication.
Cartoons: Buys 1-3 cartoons/issue from freelancers. Prefers single panel, with gagline; b&w washes. Send query letter with samples of style to be kept on file. Material not kept on file is returned by SASE. Reports within 1 month. Negotiates rights purchased. Pays $75, b&w; $150, color.
Illustrations: Buys 5-15 illustrations/issue from freelancers. Works on assignment only. Send query letter with tear sheets, photocopies, slides and photographs. Samples not filed are returned only if requested. Reports within 1 month. To show a portfolio, mail color, tear sheet, photographs and b&w. Negotiates rights purchased. Negotiates payment. Pays on publication.

THE SATURDAY EVENING POST, The Saturday Evening Post Society, 1100 Waterway Blvd., Indianapolis IN 46202. (317)636-8881. General interest, family-oriented magazine. Published 9 times/year. Circ. 600,000. Sample copy $1.
Cartoons: Cartoon Editor: Stephen Pettinga. Buys 20 cartoons/issue. Prefers single panel with gaglines. Receives 100 batches of cartoons/week from freelance cartoonists. "We look for cartoons with neat line or tone art. The content should be in good taste, suitable for a general-interest, family magazine. It must not be offensive while remaining entertaining. We prefer that artists first send SASE for guidelines and then review recent issues. Political, violent or sexist cartoons are not used. Need all topics, but particularly medical, health, travel and financial." SASE. Reports in 1 month. Buys all rights. Pays $125, b&w line drawings and washes, no pre-screened art; on publication.
Illustrations: Art Director: Chris Wilhoite. Uses average of 3 illustrations/issue; buys 90% from freelancers. Send query letter with brochure showing art style or resume and samples. To show a portfolio, mail original/final art. Buys all rights, "generally. All ideas, sketchwork and illustrative art are handled through commissions only and thereby controlled by art direction. Do not send original material (drawings, paintings, etc.) or 'facsimiles of' that you wish returned." Cannot assume any responsibility for loss or damage. "If you wish to show your artistic capabilities, please send unreturnable, expendable/sampler material (slides, tear sheets, photocopies, etc.)."

SAVINGS INSTITUTIONS, 111 E. Wacker Dr., Chicago IL 60601. (312)644-3100. Art Director: George Glatter. Emphasizes the savings and loan business for people in savings and loan or related businesses. Monthly. Circ. 35,000. Accepts previously published material. Original artwork returned after publication. Sample copy available.
Cartoons: Buys 0-1 cartoons/issue from freelancers.
Illustrations: Buys 0-2 illustrations/issue from freelancers; some are humorous or cartoon-style illustrations. Works on assignment only. Send query letter with samples to be kept on file. Call for appointment to show portfolio. Samples not kept on file are returned only if requested. Reports only if interested. Buys first rights, one-time rights, reprint rights or negotiates rights purchased. Negotiates payment. Pays on acceptance.

SCHOOL SHOP, 416 Longshore Dr., Ann Arbor MI 48105. Publisher and Executive Editor: Alan H. Jones. Magazine emphasizes industrial technology and vocational-technical education. Audience is administrators and teachers in industrial arts, technology education and vo-tech education. Articles cover projects, tips, and new information in the field. Monthly. Circ. 45,000. Original artwork not returned to the artist after publication. Sample copies $2.
Cartoons: Buys 2 cartoons/issue; buys all from freelancers. Prefers industrial/technology and vocational-technical education themes. Prefers single panel with or without b&w line drawings. Send query letter with finished cartoons. Samples are not filed. Samples not filed are returned if requested by artist. Reports back within 4-6 weeks. Pays $20, b&w.
Tips: "All cartoons submitted must be educationally oriented in the fields mentioned."

SCIENCE AND CHILDREN, National Science Teachers Association, 1742 Connecticut Ave. NW, Washington DC 20009. (202)328-5800. Editor-in-Chief: Phyllis Marcuccio. For elementary and middle school science teachers, educators, administrators and personnel. Published 8 times/year. Circ. 17,000. Original artwork not returned after publication. Free sample copy.
Cartoons: Buys 1 cartoon/issue; buys all from freelancers. Interested in science-technology and environment; multi-panel with gaglines. Reports in 2 weeks. Prefers finished cartoons. SASE. Buys all rights. Payments negotiated. Pays on publication.
Illustrations: Buys 10-15 illustrations/issue from freelancers. Works on assignment only. Interested in education and environment; light, stylized, realistic science illustrations (no stock illustrations). Samples returned by SASE. Send resume, brochure, flyer or photocopy of work to be kept on file for future assignments. Reports in 2 weeks. Prefers to see portfolio with samples of style. Buys all rights on a work-for-hire basis. Payment negotiated; on publication.
Tips: "Looking for new talent. Realistic drawings of children important—scientific renderings secondary."

SCIENCE NEWS, 1719 N St. NW, Washington DC 20036. (202)785-2255. Art Director: Wendy McCarren. Emphasizes all sciences for teachers, students and scientists. Weekly. Circ. 235,000. Accepts previously published material. Original artwork returned after publication. Sample copy for SASE with 39¢ postage.
Illustrations: Buys 6 illustrations/year from freelancers. Prefers realistic style, scientific themes; uses some cartoon-style illustrations. Works on assignment only. Send query letter with Photostats or photocopies to be kept on file. Samples returned by SASE. Reports only if interested. Buys one-time rights. Write to schedule an appointment to show a portfolio, which should include original/final art. Pays $50-200; on acceptance.
Tips: Uses some cartoons and cartoon-style illustrations.

THE SCIENCE TEACHER, 1742 Connecticut Ave. NW, Washington DC 20009. (202)328-5800. Assistant Editor: Susan Burns. Emphasizes high school science. Features how-to and technical articles on new theories in science and science experiments for teenagers. Published 9 times/year. Circ. 24,000. Original artwork returned after publication upon request. Free sample copy.
Cartoons: Rarely buys cartoons.
Illustrations: Buys 2 illustrations/issue from freelancers. Works on assignment only. "Must be b&w—any medium accepted." Send query letter with photocopies. Samples are filed. Samples not filed are returned only if requested. Reports back only if interested. Call to schedule an appointment to show a portfolio or mail original/final art or tear sheets. Buys first rights. Pays $80-120, b&w; $150, color, cover (photography). Pays on acceptance.
Tips: Artists "should live in the DC area. We are in search of new artists and photographers constantly, especially photographers who can shoot in a high school."

SCOTT STAMP MONTHLY MAGAZINE, Box 828, Sidney OH 45365. Art Director: Edward Heys. Magazine emphasizing stamp collecting for beginning through advanced collectors. Monthly. Circ. 20,000. Accepts previously published material. Original artwork returned after publication. Sample copy available for SASE with $1.24 postage. Finds most artists through samples received through the mail.
Cartoons: Buys 1-2 cartoons/issue. Prefers single, double or multi panel with gagline; b&w line drawings; b&w washes. Send query letter with brochure showing art style, resume, tear sheets, Photostats, photocopies and slides. Material not kept on file is returned by SASE. Reports only if interested. Buys reprint rights. Pays $15, b&w.
Illustrations: Prefers fairly tight illustrations of historical persons, events; pen & ink, watercolor and calligraphy. Works on assignment only. Reports only if interested. To show a portfolio, mail roughs, Photostats and tear sheets. Samples not filed are returned by SASE. Buys one-time and reprint rights. Pays $400, color, cover; $25-100, b&w, and $50-200 color, inside; on acceptance. Also uses freelancers for paste-up.
Tips: Looks for "clean, accurate, meticuluous work. Portfolio should include very limited number of samples. Do not want to see anything with an excuse. Artists should target their samples to magazine's specific needs."

SCREEN PRINTING MAGAZINE, 407 Gilbert Ave., Cincinnati OH 45202. (513)421-2050. Art Director: Magno Relejo, Jr. Emphasizes screen printing for screen printers, distributors and manufacturers of screen printing equipment and screen printed products. Monthly. Also publishes *Visual Merchandising*, and *Signs of the Times*. Publishes books. All use freelance art work. Circ. 12,000. Accepts previously published material and simultaneous submissions in noncompeting magazines. Sometimes returns original artwork after publication. Sample copy available.
Illustrations: Uses 3 illustrations/issue. Send query letter with samples and tear sheets. Prefers Photostats as samples. Samples returned by SASE if requested. Reports only if interested. Call for appointment to show portfolio. Negotiates rights purchased. Pays for design and illustration by the project, $50-350. Pays on acceptance.
Tips: "Ask for sample copy of the magazine. Need competent technical illustrators with good sense of design. Large, student-type portfolio with loose dog-eared samples makes for a lousy impression."

SEA, Box 1579, Newport Beach CA 92663. (714)646-0173. Art Director: Jeffrey Fleming. Emphasizes recreational boating for owners or users of recreational boats, both power and sail, primarily for cruising and general recreation; some interest in boating competition; regionally oriented to 13 Western states. Monthly. Circ. 70,000. Whether original artwork returned after publication depends upon terms of purchase. Sample copy for SASE with first-class postage.
Illustrations: Uses 2 illustrations/issue; buys 90% from freelancers. "I often look for a humorous illustration to lighten a technical article." Works on assignment only. Send query letter with brochure. Samples filed. Samples not filed are returned by SASE. Reports in 6 weeks only if interested. Call to sched-

Close-up

Mary Grace Eubank

Illustrator

Dallas, Texas

Illustrating for the children's market has been a rewarding experience for Dallas artist Mary Grace Eubank. Although her work first appeared on giftwrap and greeting cards, she says her illustrations for the popular children's magazine, *Sesame Street*, have led to a seemingly endless variety of opportunities in book illustration, packaging and advertising projects.

Eubank has worked with *Sesame Street* for 10 years and is one of a handful of regular freelance artists who draws Jim Henson's Muppet characters for the magazine. Drawing the licensed characters is different from other editorial illustration, however, because the magazine maintains careful control over the size and proportion of the characters.

Magazines using licensed characters maintain consistency in a number of ways. While most give the artist a set of specifications from which to work before a drawing is made, *Sesame Street* looks over an artist's drawing first and then marks it for proper proportion. It is returned to the artist for adjustment. In this way the artist can draw the characters in his or her own style, she explains, yet the magazine retains control of the final drawing.

Eubank's colorful style has always been suited to young children. She specializes in cartoon-like animals, an ever-popular subject for children's magazines and books. For the magazine Eubank works in a combination of gouache and pencil, but in recent years she has switched to airbrush to get a more polished effect. Style and technique can determine the type of magazine interested in your work, she says. It's important to do research to find out which magazines are seeking your particular style.

"Having a good working relationship with a well-known magazine art director really helped open the door." The way to meet and work for these directors, she says, is to become an expert at self-promotion.

"All businesses advertise their products for sale—my art is my product so it makes sense to me to advertise it. The best advice I can give any freelance artist is to buy a page in one of the source books such as *Creative Black Book* or *American Showcase*. I know it can be expensive, but that one page will be seen by thousands of art directors. I spent about $4,000 for my first page, but it generated $40,000 in work for me in less than a year." In addition, she says, with the source book advertisement the artist receives a few thousand tear sheets that can be sent out as samples.

"All businesses advertise their products for sale—my art is my product so it makes sense for me to advertise it."

—Mary Eubank

If a page of advertisement in a source book is beyond your financial means, there are other ways to promote your work, Eubank says. Take time to create a good direct mail package. Include slides or c-prints, high-quality color photos of your art. "Also use a directory like *Artist's Market* to be sure you have the art director's name. A mailing sent to an address alone may not make it to the art director."

Although she continues to illustrate *Sesame Street* and draw the characters for other products, Eubank contacted the toy companies about two years ago to let them know she was interested in other projects. Since that time her work has appeared on toy packages, greeting cards and even on children's meal boxes for fast-food restaurants. Still, she says her magazine experience was a "springboard" for her success.

—Robin Gee

Mary Eubank does freelance illustration for* Sesame Street. *"The magazine paid $750 for this illustration, rendered in gouache and pencil." Her magazine work led to assignments for toy companies and book publishers.

ule an appointment to show a portfolio, which should include original/final art, tear sheets, color and b&w. Negotiates rights purchased. Pays $100, b&w; $250, color, inside; on publication (negotiable).
Tips: "We will accept students for portfolio review with an eye to obtaining quality art at a reasonable price. We will help start career for illustrators and hope that they will remain loyal to the publication which helped launch their career."

SECURITY MANAGEMENT, c/o ASIS, Suite 1200, 1655 N. Fort Myer Dr., Arlington VA 22209. (703)522-5800. Art Director: Roy Comiskey. For security managers who protect assets of businesses and government. Monthly. Circ. 25,000. Original artwork returned after publication.
Cartoons: Rarely use cartoons. SASE.
Illustrations: Uses 7-8 illustrations/issue; buys all from freelancers. Prefers airbrush, colored pencil, watercolor, acrylics, oils, pastels and collage. Works on assignment only. Send query letter with business card, tear sheets and/or promotional pieces to be kept on file. "Show twenty pieces or less. Show me a good sampling of what you can do and what I can expect from you. Art directors hate to see surprises at deadlines. I like to see talent and professionalism. Pays $600-800, cover; $100-200, b&w and $200-500, color, inside; on publication.
Tips: "We primarily use color in our magazine but still like to use strong black-and-white work on occassion. Local and national talent are represented on our pages. We are always looking for new people with strong conceptual ideas and technical expertise. Send samples; it's a great way to let us know you're out there and available to work."

SEEK, 8121 Hamilton Ave., Cincinnati OH 45231. (513)931-4050, ext. 365. Emphasizes religion/faith. Readers are young adult to middle-aged adults who attend church and Bible classes. Quarterly in weekly issues. Circ. 45,000. Free sample copy and guidelines; SASE appreciated.
Cartoons: Editor: Eileen H. Wilmoth. Uses 1-2 cartoons/quarter. Buys "church or Bible themes—contemporary situations of applied Christianity." Prefers single panel b&w line drawings with gagline. Send finished cartoons, photocopies and photographs. SASE. Reports in 3-6 weeks. Buys first North American serial rights. Pays $10-15 on acceptance.
Illustrations: Art Director: Frank Sutton. Buys 1-2 illustrations/issue. Uses cover & inside b&w line drawings and washes. Works on assignment only; needs vary with articles used. Arrange appointment to show portfolio. Reports in 1 week. Pays $60, cover or full page art; $40, inside pieces; on acceptance. Buys first North American serial rights.
Tips: "We use only 2-color work. The art needs to be attractive as well as realistic. I look for detail, shading and realism."

THE SENSIBLE SOUND, 403 Darwin Dr., Snyder NY 14226. Editor: John A. Horan. Emphasizes audio equipment for hobbyists. Quarterly. Circ. 5,800. Accepts previously published material and simultaneous submissions. Original artwork returned after publication. Sample copy $2.
Cartoons: Uses 4 cartoons/year. Prefers single panel, with or without gagline; b&w line drawings. Send samples of style and roughs to be kept on file. Material not kept on file is returned by SASE. Reports within 30 days. Negotiates rights purchased. Pay rate varies; pays on publication.

SERVICE BUSINESS, 1916 Pike Pl., #345, Seattle WA 98101. (206)622-4241. Publisher: Bill Griffin. Submissions Editor: Martha M. Ireland. Technical, management and human relations emphasis for self-employed cleaning and maintenance service contractors. Quarterly. Circ. 6,000. Prefers first publication material, simultaneous submissions OK "if to non-competing publications." Original artwork returned after publication if requested by SASE. Sample copy $3.
Cartoons: Uses 1-2 cartoons/issue; buys all from freelancers. Must be relevant to magazine's readership. Prefers b&w line drawings.
Illustrations: Uses approximately 12 illustrations/issue including some humorous and cartoon-style illustrations; buys all from freelancers. Send query letters with samples. Samples returned by SASE. Buys first publication rights. Reports only if interested. Pays for design by the hour, $10-15. Pays for illustration by the project, $3-15. Pays on publication.
Tips: "Our budget is extremely limited. Those who require high fees are really wasting their time. However, we are interested in people with talent and ability who seek exposure and publications. Our readership is people who work and own businesses in the cleaning industry. If you have materical relevant to this specific audience, we would definitely be interest in hearing from your. Better yet, send samples."

***SESAME STREET**, Children's Television Workshop, One Lincoln Plaza, New York NY 10023. Art Director: Paul Richer. Aimed at pre-schoolers. Articles use Muppet characters to teach pre-reading skills to 2-6 year olds. Published 10 times/year. Circ. 1.3 million.
Illustrations: Buys artwork for 10-15 articles/month. Works on assignment only. "All art is four-col-

or. Become familiar with the characters by reviewing the magazine and by watching the TV show, which offers insights into the different personalities of the characters and how they relate to children." Send query letter with samples and SASE. Reports back within 1 week. Buys reprint or all rights. Pays $600-900/spread; within 30 days of completion of work.

S/F MAGAZINE, 755 Mt. Auburn St., Watertown MA 02172. (617)924-2422. Editor-in-Chief: Alan R. Earls. Magazine for real estate and other professionals in New England. Monthly. Circ. 18,000. Sample copy for $2 postage or money order.
Cartoons: Buys 1-2 cartoons/issue from freelancers on assignment only. Prefers single panel. Send samples of style. Reports back within 1 month. Buys all rights. Pays $50 and up; on publication.
Illustrations: Works on assignment only. Send query letter with brochure showing art style to be kept on file. Prefers Photostats as samples. Samples not filed are returned by SASE only if requested by artist. Reports back only if interested. Material copyrighted. Payment varies. Pays on publication.

THE SHINGLE, One Reading Center, Philadelphia PA 19107. (215)238-6300. Managing Editor: Nancy L. Hebble. Law-related articles, opinion pieces, news features, book reviews, poetry and fiction for the Philadelphia Bar Association membership (10,500 members). Quarterly. Circ. 11,000. Sample copy free for SASE.
Illustrations: Buys 2 illustrations/issue. Works on assignment only. Prefers fine line drawings; themes vary with editorial content. Prefers pen & ink. Send query letter with brochure, resume, business card and Photostats to be kept on file. Samples not kept on file are not returned. Reports only if interested. Pay rate varies; pays on acceptance.
Tips: "No cartoons. Portfolios should contain any work that was done for a specific assignment detailed by an editor or a publisher, as well as assignments the artist was given a free hand."

***SHINING STAR**, Box 299, Carthage IL 62332-0299. (217)357-3981. Art Director: Tom Sjoerdsma. Magazine emphasizing Christian education. It is sent to teachers who reproduce the artwork for classroom use. it is used by children in kindergarten through eigth grade. Published 5 times/year. Combined circ. 100,000.
Illustrations: Art is 60% freelanced. "Art must be easily reproduced. It should use clean, black lines" Prefers pen & ink. "Two- and three-color overlays are also used." Send query letter with photocopies. Samples are filed. Reports back withn 2 weeks only if interested. Buys all rights. Work-for-hire. Pays $5/hour.

SHUTTLE SPINDLE & DYEPOT, 102 Mountain Ave., Bloomfield CT 06002. (203)233-5124. Art Director: Tracy McHugh. Editor: Judy Robbins. Emphasizes weaving and fiber arts for hobbyists and professionals. Quarterly. Circ. 18,500. Accepts simultaneous submissions. Original artwork returned after publication. Sample copy $6.50; art guidelines for SASE.
Illustrations: Uses 20-30 illustrations/issue; buys "very few" from freelancers. Works on assignment only. Prefers b&w line drawings. Send query letter with resume tear sheets, photocopies and slides to be kept on file. Reports within 6 weeks. To show a portfolio, mail color and b&w or write to schedule an appointment. Buys first American serial rights. Honorarium only on publication; no payment. Credit line given.

***SIERRA**, 730 Polk St., San Francisco CA 94109. (415)776-2211. Art Director: Martha Geering. Emphasizes conservation and environmental politics for young adults on up who are well educated, activists, outdoor-oriented and politically well informed with a dedication to conservation. Bimonthly. Circ. 310,000. SASE. Reports in 4 weeks.
Illustrations: Buys 1-2 illustrations/issue from freelancers. Interested in all styles—images of politically aware environmental concerns and also humorous illustrations. Works on assignment only. Send resume, business card, tear sheet and copies of illustrations to be kept on file for future assignments. SASE if material is to be returned. Buys one-time rights. Payment varies; pays on publication.

***SIGNS OF THE TIMES MAGAZINE**, 1350 North King's Rd., Nampa ID 83687. (208)465-2591 or 465-2500. Art Director/Designer: Ed Guthero. Magazine emphasizing Christian lifestyle. "Looks at contemporary issues, from a Christian viewpoint—news, health, self-help, etc., covers a wide variety of topics. We attempt to show that Biblical principles are relevant to all of life. Our audience is the general public." Monthly. Circ. 370,000. Accepts previously published material. Original artwork is returned to the artist after publication.
Cartoons: Buys when applicable. Prefers "any contemporary style, also,—airbrush, and "David-Levine" type of editorial style for black & white. We don't use a lot of cartooning, but we use some." Send query letter with samples. Samples are filed. Samples not filed are returned if requested by artist. Reports back only if interested. Buys one-time rights. Pays approximately $300-450, color, full page.

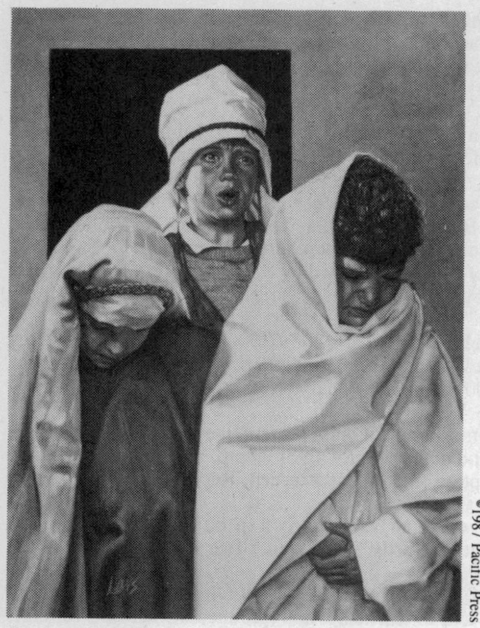
©1987 Pacific Press

This editorial illustration by Lars Justinen of Nampa, Idaho for* Signs of the Times Magazine *is based on a true story. During a Christmas pageant, a boy playing the innkeeper instantly regrets turning away Mary and Joseph and spontaneously offers, "Wait, you can have my room." Justinen completed the piece in oil on masonite board in two weeks. Designer Ed Guthero says, "I appreciated the way the artist used models and took sufficient reference photos, coaxing the children to have the right expressions." Justinen sold all rights for $450. He feels that there is not a big gulf between fine art and illustration. "My paintings attract art directors, who see them in galleries and like their realistic treatments."

Illustrations: Buys 6-10 illustration/issue from freelancers. Buys 72-120 illustrations/year from freelancers. Works on assignment only. Prefers contemporary editorial illustration, "conceptual in approach as well as contemporary realism." Prefers mixed media, then pen & ink, airbrush, colored pencil, watercolor, acrylics, oils, pastels, collage and calligraphy. Call or send query letter with tear sheets and slides. Samples are filed. Samples not filed are returned only if requested by artist. Reports back only if interested. Call or write to schedule an appointment to show a portfolio or mail final reproduction/product, slides, color and b&w. Buys one-time rights. Pays approximately $500 + , color, cover; $80-300, b&w; $(1 page)450 + average, color, inside. Pays on acceptance (30 days). *Fees are negotiable depending on needs and placement, size, etc. in the magazine.
Tips: "Artists are invited to send a mini-portfolio of 35mm slides, and some tear sheets of published work if possible. Portfolio should show styles applied to original subject matter. Many young illustrators show work using popular movie stars, photos, etc, as reference-I like to see the techniques done using their own original reference; it better show their ability to do original work."

THE SINGLE PARENT, 8807 Colesville Rd., Silver Spring MD 20910. (301)588-9354. Editor: Donna Duvall. Assistant Editor: Jackie Conciatore. Emphasizes family life in all aspects—raising children, psychology, divorce, remarriage, etc.—for all single parents and their children. Bimonthly. Circ. 200,000. Accepts simultaneous submissions and occasionally accepts previously published material. Original artwork returned after publication. Sample copy available for 10"x12" SASE with 48¢ postage.
Cartoons: Rarely uses cartoons.
Illustrations: Uses 5-6 illustrations/issue; buys all from freelancers. Works on assignment for all stories. Assignments based on artist's style. Send query letter with brochure, samples to be kept on file. Write or call for appointment to show portfolio. Prefers Photostats, photographs, tear sheets as samples. Reports within 6 weeks. Negotiates rights purchased. Pays $75, b&w, cover; $50-75, b&w, inside. Pays on publication.

SKI, 380 Madison Ave., New York NY 10017. Editor: Richard Needham. Emphasizes instruction, resorts, equipment and personality profiles. For new and expert skiers. Published 8 times/year. Previously published work OK "if we're notified."
Cartoons: Especially needs cartoons of skiers with gagline. "Artist/cartoonist must remember he is reaching experienced skiers who enjoy 'subtle' humor." Mail art. SASE. Reports immediately. Buys first serial rights. Pays $100, b&w skiing themes; on publication.
Illustrations: Mail art. SASE. Reports immediately. Buys one-time rights. Pays $300-750, full-color art; on acceptance.

SKIING, 1515 Broadway, New York NY 10036. (212)719-6600. Art Director: Jeffrey Tennyson. Emphasizes skiing, ski areas, ski equipment, instruction for young adults and professionals; good incomes. Published 7 times a year, September-March. Circ. 445,000. Original artwork returned after publication. Sample copy free for SASE.
Illustrations: Uses 2 illustrations/issue on average. Works on assignment basis. Send query letter with samples to be kept on file. Drop-off portfolio policy. Prefers Photostats, photocopies or printed samples. Samples returned by SASE if not kept on file. Reports only if interested. Buys first or one-time rights. Pays $75-250, b&w, inside; on acceptance. Color rates based on size.
Tips: "Know the magazine."

SKY AND TELESCOPE, 49 Bay State Rd., Cambridge MA 02238. Editor: L.J. Robinson. Art Director: Mr. Kelly Beatty. Concerns astronomy, building telescopes and space exploration for enthusiasts and professionals. Monthly. Circ. 75,000. Buys one-time rights. Pays on publication.
Cartoons: Buys 4/year on astronomy, telescopes and space exploration; single panel preferred. Pays $25-50, b&w line drawings, washes and gray opaques. Send query letter with samples.
Illustrations: Buys assigned themes. Send query letter with previously published work. Pays $50-150.

SMALL BOAT JOURNAL, Box 1066, Bennington VT 05201. (802)442-3101. Editor: Thomas Baker. Editorial Assistant: Janet Thompson. Magazine emphasizing boats and boating for recreation boaters of all types—sailors, powerboaters and rowers. Bimonthly.
Illustrations: Works with 4 artists/year. Uses artists for illustrating technical details, boat building and repair techniques, perspective and profile views of boats. Prefers illustrations of small boats, technical/representative illustrations. Prefers pen & ink, charcoal/pencil, watercolor, acrylics and oils. Cartoon ideas also welcomed. Send query letter with brochure or samples. Reports back only if interested. Call to schedule an appointment to show a portfolio, which should include roughs and original/final art. Pays by the piece, $25-350.
Tips: "Ability to render people is a plus. Familiarity with boats and nautical subjects is necessary."

THE SMALL POND MAGAZINE OF LITERATURE, Box 664, Stratford CT 06497. Emphasizes poetry and short prose. Readers are people who enjoy literature—primarily college-educated. Published 3 times/year. Circ. 300. Sample copy $2.50; art guidelines for SASE.
Illustrations: Editor: Napoleon St. Cyr. Uses 1-5 illustrations/issue. Receives 50-75 illustrations/year. Uses "line drawings (inside and on cover) which generally relate to natural settings, but have used abstract work completely unrelated." Especially needs line drawings; "fewer wildlife drawings and more unrelated-to-wildlife material." Send query letter with finished art or production quality photocopies, 2x3 minimum, 8x11 maximum. SASE. Reports in 1-2 months. Pays 2 copies of issue in which work appears on publication. Buys copyright in convention countries.
Tips: "Need cover art work, but inquire first or send for sample copy." Especially looks for "smooth clean lines, original movements, an overall impact. Don't send a heavy portfolio, but rather 4-6 black-and-white representative samples with SASE. Better still, send for copy of magazine ($2.50)."

SOAP OPERA DIGEST, 45 W. 25th St., New York NY 10010. Art Director: Andrea Wagner. Emphasizes soap opera and prime-time drama synopses and news. Biweekly. Circ. 825,000. Accepts previously published material. Returns original artwork after publication upon request. Sample copy available, with SASE.
Cartoons: Publishes 3/issue. Seeks humor on soaps, drama or TV. Accepts single or double panel with or without gagline; b&w line drawings, b&w washes. Send query letter to Lynn Davey, Managing Editor with samples of style to be kept on file. Material not filed is returned by SASE. Pays $50, b&w; on publication.
Illustrations: Buys 2 illustrations/issue from freelancers. Works on assignment only. Prefers humor and caricatures. Prefers pen & ink, airbrush and watercolor. Send query letter with brochure showing art style or resume, tear sheets and photocopies to be kept on file. Call to schedule an appointment to show a portfolio, which should include original/final art and tear sheets. Negotiates rights purchased. Pays $200-300 for b&w and $300-500 for color, inside; on publication. All original artwork is returned after publication.
Tips: "I do not want to see package design. I know you are applying for a publication design job, keep your book targeted to the job."

***SOARING**, Soaring Society of America, Box E, Hobbs NM 88240. Editor: Mark Kennedy. "We are a low-budget magazine and depend on society members for art." Monthly. Circ. 16,000. Receives several cartoons and illustrations/week from freelance artists. Original artwork returned after publication, if requested. Sample copy $2.50.
Cartoons: Uses less than 1 cartoon/issue. Prefers to see finished cartoons. Reports in 1 month. Buys

one-time rights. No payment.
Illustrations: Uses less than 1 illustration/issue. Interested in cutaway 3-dimension technical illustrations and illustrations for realism in flight stories. We will return promptly. Reports in 1 week. Cover: Pays $58. Inside: No payment for line drawings, pen and ink, and washes.
Tips: "Readership is nuts-and-bolts oriented. We are leery of nonrepresentational art, though not adamant. We receive many flight stories which call for illustration. Occasional articles offer opportunity for quick sketch or cartoon-type treatment. Technical cutaway drawing for display of aircraft very desirable."

SOCIAL POLICY, 33 W. 42nd St., New York NY 10036. (212)840-7619. Managing Editor: Audrey Gartner. Emphasizes the human services—education, health, mental health, self-help, consumer education, neighborhood movement, employment. For social action leaders, academics, social welfare practitioners. Quarterly. Circ. 5,000. Accepts simultaneous submissions. Original artwork returned after publication. Sample copy $2.50.
Cartoons: Accepts b&w only, "with social consciousness." Sometimes uses humorous illustrations; often uses cartoon-style illustrations. Call for appointment to show portfolio. Reports only if interested. Buys one-time rights. Pays on publication.
Illustrations: Buys 4-6 illustrations/issue from freelancers. Accepts b&w only, "with social consciousness." Prefers pen & ink and charcoal/pencil. Send query letter and tear sheets to be kept on file.

Jackie Conciatore, assistant editor of* The Single Parent *in Silver Spring, Maryland, commissioned illustrator Sonia Safier-Kerzner of Bethesda, Maryland to illustrate a humorous short story about a father who is confused by "expert" advice on parenting. The pen-and-ink illustration was completed within two weeks. The artist found the magazine listed in the* Artist's Market *when she had just moved to the Washington, D.C. area. "The magazine appealed to me because of its focus on human interest." Safier-Kerzner is also exhibiting work in galleries.

Call for appointment to show portfolio, which should include original/final art, final reproduction/product, tear sheets and b&w. Reports only if interested. Buys one-time rights. Pays $100, cover; $25, b&w, inside. Pays on publication.
Tips: When reviewing an artist's work, looks for "sensitivity to the subject matter being illustrated."

SOLDIERS MAGAZINE, Cameron Station, Alexandria VA 22304-5050. (202)274-6671. Editor-in-Chief: Lt. Col. Donald Maple. Lighter Side Compiler: Thomas Kiddoo. Provides "timely and factual information on topics of interest to members of the Active Army, Army National Guard, Army Reserve and Department of Army civilian employees." Monthly. Circ. 250,000. Previously published material and simultaneous submissions OK. Samples available upon request.
Cartoons: Purchases approximately 60 cartoons/year. Should be single panel with gagline. Prefers military and general audience humor. Submit work; reports within 3 weeks. Buys all rights. Pays $25/cartoon on acceptance.
Tips: "We are actively seeking new ideas, fresh humor and looking for new talent—people who haven't been published before. We recommend a review of back issues before making submission. Issues available upon request. Remember that we are an inhouse publication—anti-Army humor, sexist or racist material is totally unacceptable."

SOLIDARITY MAGAZINE, Published by United Auto Workers, 8000 E. Jefferson, Detroit MI 48214. (313)926-5291. Editor: David Elsila. "1.5 million member trade union representing U.S. and Canadian workers in auto, aerospace, agricultural-implement and other industries."
Illustrations: Works with 10-12 artists/year for illustrations. Uses artists for posters and magazine illustrations. Interested in graphic designs of publications, topical art for magazine covers with liberal-labor political slant. Especially needs illustrations for articles on unemployment, economy. Prefers Detroit-area artists, but not essential. Looks for "ability to grasp publication's editorial slant" when reviewing artist's work. Send query letter with resume, flyer and/or tear sheet. Samples to be kept on file. Pays $75/small b&w spot illustration; up to $400 for color covers; $400 + /designing small pamphlet.

SONOMA BUSINESS MAGAZINE, Box 11298, Santa Rosa CA 95403. Art Director: Candi Cohen. Monthly. Tabloid emphasizing business with very local editorial content. Relates to business owners in Sonoma County. Circ. 10,000. Accepts previously published material. Returns original artwork after publication. Sample copy $3.50 with 12x9 SASE. Art guidelines not available.
Illustrations: Buys 1-3 illustrations/issue from freelancers. Works on assignment only. Send query letter with brochure. Samples are filed. Reports back only if interested. Write to schedule an appointment to show a portfolio, which should include original/final art, tear sheets, final reproduction/product, b&w and color. Buys one-time rights. Pays $50-125 b&w; $200, color, cover; on acceptance.
Tips: "Keep trying. Must be well-drawn, clever, and we usually buy b&w."

SOUTH CAROLINA WILDLIFE, Box 167, Columbia SC 29202. (803)758-0001. Editor: John Davis. Art Director: Linda Laffitte. Deals with wildlife, outdoor recreation, natural history and environmental concerns. Bimonthly. Circ. 70,000. Previously published work OK. Sample copy and guidelines available.
Illustrations: Uses 10-20 illustrations/issue. Interested in wildlife art; all media; b&w line drawings, washes, full-color illustrations. "Particular need for natural history illustrations of good quality. They must be technically accurate." Subject matter must be appropriate for South Carolina. Prefers to see finished art, portfolio, samples of style, slides, or transparencies. Send resume, brochure, or flyer to be kept on file. SASE. Reports in 2-8 weeks. Acquires one-time rights. Does not buy art; accepts donations.
Tips: "We are interested in unique illustrations—something that would be impossible to photograph. Make sure proper research has been done and that the art is technically accurate."

SOUTH FLORIDA HOME BUYERS GUIDE, Suite 300, 251 W. Hillsboro Blvd., Deerfield Beach FL 33442. (305)428-5602. Managing Editor: Dee Krams. Emphasizes real estate (new developments) and is directed to newcomers to South Florida; homebuyers. Bimonthly. Circ. 80,000. Accepts previously published material. Does not return original artwork after publication. Sample copy available.
Cartoons: Send query letter with samples of style to be kept on file. Material not filed is returned by SASE. Reports within 1 month. Write for appointment to show portfolio. Buys first rights. Negotiates payment; pays on acceptance.
Illustrations: Buys "a few" illustrations/issue from freelancers. Works on assignment only. Send query letter with samples to be kept on file. Write for appointment to show portfolio. Prefers tear sheets or photographs as samples. Samples not filed are returned by SASE. Reports within 1 month. Buys first rights. Negotiates payment; pays on acceptance.

SOUTHERN MOTOR CARGO, Box 40169, Memphis TN 38104. (901)276-5424. Contact: Pearce Hammond. For trucking management and maintenance personnel of private, contract and for-hire carriers in 16 southern states (Alabama, Arkansas, Delaware, Florida, Georgia, Kentucky, Louisana, Maryland, Mississippi, North Carolina, Oklahoma, South Carolina, Tennessee, Texas, Virginia and West Virginia) and the Disrict of Columbia. Special issues include "ATA Conventions," October; "Transportation Graduate Directory," February. Monthly. Circ. 56,000.
Cartoons: Buys various cartoons/issue on truck management situations. "Stay away from stereotyped 'truckin' on' theme." Mail roughs. Pays $20, b&w; on publication. SASE. Reports in 6 weeks.

SOUTHWEST DIGEST, 510 E. 23rd St., Lubbock TX 79404. (806)762-3612. Co-Publisher-Managing Editor: Eddie P. Richardson. Newspaper emphasizing positive black images, and community building and rebuilding "primarily oriented to the black community and basically reflective of the black community, but serving all people." Weekly. Accepts previously published material. Original work returned after publication.
Cartoons: Number of cartoons purchased/issue from freelancers varies. Prefers economic development, community development, community pride and awareness, and black uplifting themes. Single, double or multi-panel with gagline; b&w line drawings. Send query letter with samples of style, roughs or finished cartoons to be kept on file. Write or call for appointment to show portfolio. Material not filed returned by SASE only if requested. Buys first, one-time, reprint, or all rights; or negotiates rights purchased. Pays on publication.
Illustrations: Send query letter with brochure or samples to be kept on file. Write or call for appointment to show portfolio which should include Photostats, tear sheets, photocopies, photographs, etc. as samples. Samples not filed returned by SASE only if requested. Reports only if interested. Negotiates rights purchased. Pays on publication.

SPACE AND TIME, 4B, 138 W. 70th St., New York NY 10023-4432. Editor: Gordon Linzner. Emphasizes fantasy and science fiction stories. "Readers are sf/fantasy fans looking for an alternative to the newsstand magazines." Biannually. Circ. 450. Original artwork returned after publication. Sample copy $4.
Cartoons: Buys 1-2 cartoons/issue from freelancers. Considers sf/fantasy themes—any style. Prefers single panel with or without gagline; b&w line drawings. Send finished cartoons to be kept on file if accepted for publication. Material not filed is returned by SASE. Reports within 3 months. Buys first rights. Pays $5, b&w; on acceptance.
Illustrations: Buys 20-25 illustrations from freelancers. Assigns themes or styles illustrating specific stories. "We use all styles, but could use more representational material." Prefers pen & ink. Works on assignment only. Send query letter with brochure showing art style. Samples not filed are returned by SASE. Reports within 3 months. To show a portfolio, mail original/final art, Photostats and b&w. Buys first rights. Pays $2, b&w, inside; on acceptance.
Tips: "Show a variety of samples with fantastic and realistic themes. I do not want to see exclusively weird work which might not give an idea of your range."

SPACE WORLD MAGAZINE, 922 Pennsylvania Ave., SE, Washington DC 20003. (202)543-3991. Editor: John Rhea. Feature magazine popularizing and advancing space exploration for the general public interested in all aspects of space program.
Illustrations: Works with 15-20 freelance artists/year. Uses for magazine illustration. "We are looking for original artwork on space themes, either conceptual or representing specific designs, events, etc." Prefers acrylics, then oils and collage. Send query letter with photographs to Kate McMains, Associate Editor. "Color slides are best." Samples not filed are returned by SASE. Reports back within 6 weeks. Pays for illustration by the project, $25-150. "We do not generally commission original art. These fees are for one-time reproduction of existing artwork. Considers rights purchased when establishing payment.
Tips: "Show a set of slides showing planetary art, space craft and people working in space. I do not want to see 'science-fiction' art."

SPITBALL, the Literary Baseball Magazine, 6224 Collegevue Pl., Cincinnati OH 45224. (513)541-4296. Editor: Mike Shannon. Magazine emphasizing baseball exclusively, for well-educated, literate baseball fans. Quarterly. Returns original artwork after publication if the work is donated; does not return if purchases work. Sample copy $1; art guidelines for SASE with first-class postage.
Cartoons: Prefers single panel without gagline, b&w line drawings. Query with samples of style, roughs and finished cartoons. Samples not filed are returned by SASE. Reports back within 1 week. Negotiates rights purchased.
Illustrations: We need three types of art: cover work, illustration (for a story, essay or poem), and filler. All work must be baseball-related; prefers pen & ink, airbrush, charcoal/pencil and collage. Some-

times we assign the cover piece on a particular subject; sometimes we just use a drawing we like. Interested artists should write to set out needs for future covers and specific illustration." Buys 3 or 4 illustration/issue. Send query letter with original b&w illustrations. Samples not filed are returned by SASE. Reports back within 1 week. To show a portfolio, mail appropriate materials. Artists should target their samples to magazine's needs. Negotiates rights purchased. Pays $10 minimum; on acceptance.

SPORTING CLASSICS, Box 1017, Camden SC 29020. (803)425-1003. Design Director: Duncan Grant. Magazine emphasizing outdoor sports such as hunting and fishing for "sophisticated, educated, high-income, well-traveled sportsmen" who love art, decoys, collect guns, knives, etc. Circ. 85,000. Accepts previously published material. Original artwork returned after publication. Sample copy for SASE with 80¢ postage.
Illustrations: Uses 10-15 illustrations/issue. Works on assignment only. Prefers sporting, wildlife, outdoor, hunting and fishing themes. Send query letter with brochure showing art style or samples, tear sheets, Photostats, photocopies, slides and photographs. Reports only if interested. Write to schedule an appointment to show a portfolio, which should include color, tear sheets and photographs. Buys one-time rights. Pays $500, b&w and $1,200, color, cover; $50-250, b&w and $250-1,000, color, inside on publication.

***S.P.O.R.T.S. (Sports Periodical on Research and Technology in Sports)**, 333 River Rd., Ottawa, Ontario K1L 8H9 Canada. (613)748-5624. Editor: Paul Patterson. Circ. 2,500. For high-level coaches and sports-related people (e.g., researches, teachers, athletes). Topic areas include nutrition, sports medicine, biomechanics, physiology, research and psychology. Receives 2-3 cartoons and 2-3 illustrations/week from freelance artists. Especially needs good practical applied information that is original; creative illustration; sport specific and life-like illustration. Original artwork returned after publication. Free sample copy.
Cartoons: Buys 4 cartoons/issue from freelancers. Interested in coaching-related situations. Prefers single panel b&w line drawings with or without gaglines. Send query letter with brochure showing art style or slides. Reports in 2 weeks. Pays $25-50, b&w; on publication. Buys one-time rights.
Illustrations: Buys 2-8 illustrations/issue from freelancers. Illustrations should be in "creative realism . . . depicting athletes in action." Prefers color washes for cover and inside; b&w line drawings for inside. Reports in 2 weeks. Call to schedule an appointment to show a portfolio, which should include color, tear sheets, Photostats and b&w. Pays $400, b&w and $600, color cover; $250-450, b&w; on acceptance.
Tips: "There is a trend toward 'realistic illustration showing coaching techniques. Read the magazine before sending in work."

SPORTS AFIELD MAGAZINE, 250 W. 55th St., New York NY 10019. (212)649-2000. Art Director: Gary Gretter. Magazine emphasizing outdoor activities—fishing, hunting and camping. Monthly. Circ. 600,000. Does not accept previously published material. Returns original artwork after publication.
Illustrations: Buys 2-3/issue. Works on assignment only. Send query letter with samples to be kept on file except for material not of interest. Prefers slides as samples. Samples not filed are returned by SASE. Call for appointment to show portfolio. Buys first rights or negotiates rights purchased. Payment negotiated.

STARWIND, Box 98, Ripley OH 45167. Contact: Editor. Emphasizes science fiction, fantasy and nonfiction of scientific and technological interest. Quarterly. Circ. 2,500. Sample copy $3.50; art guidelines for SASE.
Cartoons: Buys 5-8 cartoons/issue from freelancers. Interested in science fiction and fantasy subjects. Format: single and multi panel b&w line drawings. Prefers finished cartoons. SASE. Reports in 2-3 months. Buys first North American serial rights. Pays on publication.
Illustrations: Uses 10-15 illustrations/issue. Sometimes uses humorous and cartoon-style illustrations depending on the type of work being published. Works on assignment only. Samples returned by SASE. Reports back on future assignment possibilities. Send resume or brochure and samples of style to be kept on file for future assignments. Illustrates stories rather extensively (normally an 8x11 and an interior illustration). Format: b&w line drawings (pen & ink and similar media). SASE. Reports in 2-3 months. Buys first North American rights. Pays on publication.
Tips: "We first of all look for work that falls into science fiction genre; if an artist has a feel for and appreciation of science fiction he/she is more likely to be able to meet our needs. We look to see that the artist can do well what he/she tried to do—for example, draw the human figure well. We are especially attracted to work that is clean and spare, not cluttered, and that has a finished, not sketchy quality. If an artist also does technical illustrations, we are interested in seeing samples of this style too. Would specifically like to see samples of work that we'd be capable of reproducing and that are compatible with our magazine's subject matter. We prefer to see photocopies rather than slides. We also like to be able to keep samples on file, rather than have to return them."

STOCK CAR RACING MAGAZINE, Box 715, Ipswich MA 90138. Editor: Dick Berggren. For stock car racing, fans and competitors. Monthly. Circ. 120,000.
Cartoons: Uses 4 cartoons/issue; all from freelancers. Receives 4 cartoons from freelancers/week. Interested in cartoons pertaining to racing. Format: single or multipanel b&w line drawings with gag line. Prefers samples of style or finished cartoons. SASE. Reports in 2 weeks. Buys all rights. Pays $20-35 on publication.
Illustrations: Number of illustrations/issue varies. Format: b&w line drawings. Prefers finished art. SASE. Buys all rights. Pays on publication.

STONE COUNTRY, Box 132, Menemsha MA 02552. Editor-in-Chief: Judith Neeld. Art Editor: Pat McCormick. Submit to 69 Central Ave., Madison NJ 07940. For serious poets and poetry supporters. Published 2 times/year. Circ. 800. Previously published artwork OK. Sample copy $3.50; $2.50 for tear sheets and sample covers (postage included).
Illustrations: Uses 2 covers/year and 6-7 illustrations/issue. Receives 1 illustration/month from freelance artists. Must be camera-ready. Cover design should fit 5½x8½, "no lettering" inside drawings no larger than 3x4. Interested in b&w drawings only, no washes or pencil shading; to achieve shading, use fine b&w lines. Any style or theme; size is important. "We are interested in abstract as well as from-nature representational work. Rarely use the human form or face on a cover. Art students welcome." Send query letter with brochure showing art style or resume, tear sheets, Photostats and photocopies, "submit completed work directly to art editor." Reports in 6-8 weeks. "We don't view portfolios." Buys first North American serial rights. Cover: Pays $15, b&w; on publication. Inside: Pays 1 contributor's copy, b&w.
Tips: "Send original graphics directly to art editor with SASE. Or, to save both of us if the work isn't what we look for, order samples through general editor."

STONE SOUP, The Magazine by Children, Box 83, Santa Cruz CA 95063. (408)426-5557. Editor: Gerry Mandel. Literary magazine emphasizing writing and art by children up to age 13. Features adventure, ethnic, experimental, fantasy, humorous and science fiction articles. "We publish writing and art by children up to age 13. We look for artwork that reveals that the artist is closely observing his or her world." Bimonthly. Circ. 10,000. Original artwork is sometimes returned after publication. Sample copies available. Art guidelines for SASE with first-class postage.
Illustrations: Buys 5 illustrations/issue from freelancers. Complete and detailed scenes from real life. Send query letter with Photostats, photocopies, slides and photographs. Samples are filed. Samples not filed are returned by SASE. Reports back within 6 weeks. Buys all rights. Pays $10, b&w; $10, color, inside; on acceptance.
Tips: "We accept artwork by children only, up to age 13."

***STORK MAGAZINE**, 1100 Waterway Blvd., Box 567, Indianapolis IN 46206. (317)636-8881. Art Director: Rick Gonzalez. Emphasizes health, nutrition, exercise and safety for infants. Monthly except bimonthly February/March, April/May, June/July and August/September. Accepts previously published material and simultaneous submissions. Original artwork not returned after publication. Sample copy 75¢; art guidelines for SASE.
Illustrations: Buys 15-30 illustrations/issue from freelancers. Interested in "stylized, humorous, realistic and cartooned themes; also nature and health." Especially needs b&w and 2-color artwork for line or halftone reproduction; full-color text and cover art. Works on assignment only. Send query letter with resume, stats or good photocopies, slides and tear sheets to be kept on file. Samples not kept on file returned by SASE. Reports only if interested. Buys all rights. To show a portfolio, mail final reproduction/product, color, tear sheets, b&w and 2-color. Pays $225, 4-color, cover; $25-100, b&w and 2-color and $60-125, 4-color, inside; on publication.
Tips: "Be sure to send in appropriate material for the magazine (example: do not send *New Yorker* illustrations for a children's magazine for ages 2-5)."

***STUDENT LAWYER**, 750 N. Lake Shore Dr., Chicago IL 60611. (312)988-6049. Editor: Sarah Hoban. Art Director: Robert Woolley. Trade journal emphasizing legal education and social/legal issues. "*Student Lawyer* is a monthly legal affairs magazine published by the Law Student Division of the American Bar Association. It has a circulation of approximately 40,000, most of whom are law students. It is not a legal journal. It is a features magazine, competing for a share of law students' limited spare time—so the articles we publish must be informative, lively good reads. We have no interest whatsoever in anything that resembles a footnoted, academic article. We are interested in professional and legal education education issues, sociolegal phenomena, legal career features, profiles of lawyers who are making an impact on the profession, and the (very) occasional piece of fiction." Monthly (September-May). Circ. 32,000. Accepts previously published material. Original artwork is returned to the artist after publication. Samples copies $3. Art guidelines free for SASE with first-class postage.

Illustrations: Buys 8 illustrations/issue from freelancers. Buys 75 illustrations/year from freelancers. Works on assignment only. Send query letter with brochure, tear sheets and photographs. Samples are filed. Samples not filed are returned by SASE. Reports back within 3 weeks only if interested. Call to schedule an appointment to show a portfolio, which should include original/final art and tear sheets. Buys one-time rights. Pays $75-350; on acceptance.
Tips: "Be familiar with the magazine."

***SUDS 'N' STUFF**, Box 6402, Oceanside CA 92056. Publisher: Michael J. Bosak, III. Newsletter emphasizing beer. "Interested in new beers on the market, interesting stories regarding old breweries, mini-breweries, national and international events concerning beer, interesting people in the beer industry, historical events concerning beer. Example: Why did the Pilgrims land at Plymouth Rock? They ran out of beer. Readers are all ages, mostly college graduates." Circ. 8,000. Accepts previously published material. Original artwork is returned to artist after publication. Sample copies free for SASE with 50¢ postage.
Cartoons: Prefers multiple panel without gagline; b&w line drawings. Send query letter. Samples not filed are not returned. Reports back within 1 month. Negotiates rights purchased.
Illustrations: Send query letter with brochure.

***SUN DOG**, English Department, Florida State University, Tallahassee FL 32306. Editors: Craig Stroupe and Kevin Murphy. Biannual. Circ. 2,000. Emphasizes literature for college students, faculty and educated readers. Samples copy $3.
Illustrations: Interested in b&w line drawings and 4-color covers. Also occasionally features one artist in an issue. Send query letter and samples. Samples returned by SASE. Reports within 3 months.

THE SUN, 412 W. Rosemary, Chapel Hill NC 27514. (919)942-5282. Editor: Sy Safransky. Magazine of ideas. Monthly. Circ. 10,000. Accepts previously published material. Original artwork returned after publication. Sample copy $3. Art guidelines free for SASE with first-class postage.
Cartoons: Buys various cartoons/issue from freelancers. Send finished cartoons. Material not kept on file is returned by SASE. Reports within 1 month. Buys first rights. Pays $25 and up, b&w; plus copies and subscription.
Illustrations: Buys various illustrations/issue from freelancers. Send query letter with samples. Samples not filed are returned by SASE. Reports within 1 month. To show a portfolio, mail appropriate materials. Buys first rights. Pays $25 and up; plus copies and subscription. Pays on publication.

THE SUNDAY OREGONIAN'S NORTHWEST MAGAZINE, 1320 SW Broadway, Portland OR 97201. (503)221-8235. Graphic Coordinator: Kevin Murphy. Magazine emphasizing stories with Northwest orientation for aged 25-45 and upwardly mobile people. Weekly. Circ. 430,000. Original artwork returned after publication. Sample copy for SASE.
Illustrations: Buys 2 illustrations/issue from freelancers. Preference given to Northwest illustrators. Works on assignment only. Send query letter with brochure showing art style or resume and slides. Samples not filed are returned only if requested. Reports only if interested. Call or write to schedule an appointment to show a portfolio, which should include original/final art, color, photographs and slides. Buys first or one-time rights. Negotiates payment. Pays on publication.

SWIFTSURE, 33 Chester Rd., Northwood, Middlesex HA6 1BG England. Editor: Martin Lock. Estab. 1985. Publishes comic books. Genres: adventure, fantasy and science fiction. Themes: outer space and social commentary. "*Swiftsure* is SF-based series/anthology title, aimed at comics readers who go beyond superhero comics." Bimonthly. Circ. 2,000. Original artwork returned after publication. Sample copy $1.
Illustrations: Prefers narrative, representational style. Prefers pen & ink. Uses three-tier page of 6 panels, vertical panels, horizontal panels, inset panels, borderless panels and circular panels. Uses freelance artists for inking, lettering, pencilling and covers. Send query letter with photocopies only. Samples are filed. Samples not filed are returned by a SAE (nonresidents include IRC). Reports back within 2 months. To show a portfolio, mail photocopies of original pencil art or inking reduced to 8½x11

"Your portfolio should be as well thought out and designed as any illustration."

—Ken Kleppert, Runner's World
Emmaus, Pennsylvania

of display pieces, action continuity, and lettering. Buys first rights. Payment is on profit-sharing basis, based on actual print order. Pays on publication.

***TANNING TRENDS**, 8888 Thorne Rd., Horton MI 49246. (517)563-2600. Managing Editor: Carol Genee. "A business publication for indoor tanning salon management covering advertising, marketing, finance, legal and medical issues, industry news, new product announcements and salon profiles." Monthly. Circ. 24,000. Accepts previously published material "as long as not published in competing magazine." Original artwork is sometimes returned to the artist after publication. Samples copies available. Art guidelines not available.
Illustrations: Buys 1 illustration/issue from freelancers. Works on assignment only. Send query letter with brochure showing art style or resume, tear sheets, Photostats, photocopies, slides or photographs. Samples are filed. Samples not filed are returned only if requested. Reports back within 2 weeks only if interested. Write to schedule an appointment to show a portfolio, or mail thumbnails, roughs, original/final art, tear sheets, final reproduction/product, Photostats, photographs, slides, color and b&w. Negotiates rights purchased. Pays $30 minimum, b&w; $50 minimum, color, inside; on acceptance.
Tips: "Send query letter with photocopied samples. We prefer to work on an assignment basis."

TEACHING AND COMPUTERS, SCHOLASTIC, INC., 730 Broadway, New York NY 10003. Art Director: Shelley Laroche. Emphasizes teaching K-8th grade with computers for teachers and students. Monthly. Circ. 65,000. Accepts previously published material. Original artwork returned after publication. Sample copy and art guidelines available. Send SASE.
Cartoons: Buys 4 cartoons/issue from freelancers. Themes, style and format open. Send query letter with samples of styles to be kept on file; drop off portfolio. Material not filed is returned only if requested. Reports only if interested. Buys first rights or one-time rights depending on job. Payment open; pays on acceptance.
Illustrations: Buys 10-12 illustrations/issue from freelancers. Works on assignment only. Send query letter with brochure, resume, business card and samples to be kept on file; drop off portfolio. Prefers tearsheets or photographs as samples. Samples not filed are returned only if requested. Reports only if interested. Buys one-time rights. Payment open, b&w and color, inside: pays on acceptance.

***TEDDY BEAR**, 12th Floor, 170 Fifth Ave., New York NY 10010. (212)989-8700. Art Director: Diane Lemonides. Magazine emphasizing collecting. Quarterly. Original artwork is returned to the artist after publication. Sample copies free for SASE with first-class postage. Art guidelines available.
Cartoons: Prefers teddy bears as subjects. Samples are filed. Samples not filed returned if requested by artist. Buys first rights.
Illustrations: Buys 3 illustrations/issue from freelancers. Buys various amount of illustrations/year from freelancers. Works on assignment only. Send query letter with brochure, tear sheets, Photostats, photocopies, slides and photographs. Samples are filed. Samples not filed are returned only if requested by artist. Reports back only if interested. Call to schedule an appointment to show a portfolio, which should include final reproduction/product, Photostats, photographs, color and b&w. Buys first rights; negotiates rights purchased. Pays on publication.

'TEEN, Petersen Publishing Co., 8490 Sunset Blvd., Los Angeles CA 90069. (213)854-2222. Art Director: Laurel Finnerty. Deals with self-development for girls 12-19. Circ. 1,000,000.
Illustrations: Buys 2-3 illustrations/issue for fiction, fashion and beauty sections. Contact only through artist's agent or send query letter with brochure showing art style or tear sheets, slides and photographs. Works on assignment only. Will see artists and photographers with finished and professional portfolios. Call to schedule an appointment to show a portfolio, which should include original/final art, final reproduction/product, color, tear sheets, photographs and b&w. Buys all rights. Pays $25-150, b&w and $150-250, color, inside; on acceptance. Other assignments are negotiable.
Tips: "Youth today are more involved and the keyword is *active*. Prefer youthful upbeat look. We're appealing to an audience that is bright, young and active."

TENNIS, 5520 Park Ave., Trumbull CT 06611. (203)373-7000. Art Director: Kathleen Burke. For young, affluent tennis players. Monthly. Circ. 500,000.
Cartoons: Buys 3 cartoons/issue from freelancers. Receives 6 submissions/week from freelancers on tennis. Prefers finished cartoons, single panel. Reports in 2 weeks. Pays $75, b&w.
Illustrations: Buys 5 illustrations/issue from freelancers. Works on assignment only. Send query letter with tear sheets. To show a portfolio, mail appropriate materials or call to schedule an appointment; portfolio should include original/final art, final reproduction/product, color, tear sheets and photographs. Pays $400, color; on acceptance.
Tips: "Prospective contributors should first look through an issue of the magazine to make sure their style is appropriate for us."

TENNIS BUYER'S GUIDE, 5520 Park Ave., Trumbull CT. 06611. (203)373-7000. Art Director: Lori Wendino. Magazine emphasizing the tennis retailing industry. Bimonthly. Circ. 12,000.
Illustrations: Buys 4-6 illustrations/issue from freelancers. Works on assignment only. Soft goods oriented. Illustrations often used for conceptual pieces. Send query letter with brochure or tear sheets, slides and photographs. Reports back within 2 weeks. Call to schedule an appointment to show a portfolio, which should include thumbnails, roughs, original/final art, tear sheets, final reproduction/product, color and b&w. Buys one-time reproduction rights on a work-for-hire basis. Payment negotiated; pays on acceptance.

THE TEXAS OBSERVER, 307 W. 7th., Austin TX 78701. (512)477-0746. Contact: Art Director. Emphasizes Texas political, social and literary topics. Biweekly. Circ. 12,000. Accepts previously published material. Returns original artwork after publication. Sample copy for SASE with postage for two ounces; art guidelines for SASE with first class postage.
Illustrations: Buys 2 illustrations/issue from freelancers. "We only print black and white, so pen & ink is best, washes are fine." Send Photostats, tear sheets, photocopies, slides or photographs to be kept on file. Samples not filed are returned by SASE. Reports within 1 month. Write or call for appointment to show portfolio. Buys one-time rights. Pays $35 for b&w cover; $20, inside; on publication.

TFR—THE FREELANCERS' REPORT, Box 93, Poquonock CT 06064. (203)688-5496. Editor: Pat McDonald. Estab 1986. Monthly magazine emphasizing freelancing writers (all genres), illustrators and photographers. Circ. 200 at first issue Jan '87. Accepts previously published material. Returns original artwork to the artist after publication if requested. Sample copy $3.
Cartoons: Uses 3 cartoons/issue from freelancers. Buys 36 cartoons/year from freelancers. Prefers gag cartoons, caricatures and humorous illustrations. Prefers single panel, with gagline; b&w line drawings. Send finished cartoons. Samples not filed are returned by SASE only if requested by artist. Reports back within 60 days. Requires first rights or reprint rights. Pays 1 copy of publication and 2 tearsheets.
Illustrations: Uses 3 illustrations/issue from freelancers. Buys 36 illustrations/year from freelancers. Prefers anything b&w which appeals to us and can be reproduced clearly by a quality photocopier. Send samples. Samples not filed are returned by SASE if requested. Reports back within 60 days. To show a portfolio, mail final reproduction/product, tear sheets, b&w and clear photocopies of original. Buys first rights or reprint rights. Pays 1 copy of publication and two tear sheets.
Tips: "Contact us by letter with actual submission, clear photocopies suggested. Queries discouraged due to small overworked staff. The majority of our art needs are cover and cartoon stock."

THRUST—Science Fiction & Fantasy Review, 8217 Langport Terrace, Gaithersburg MD 20877. Publisher/Editor: D. Douglas Fratz. Emphasizes science fiction and fantasy literature for highly knowledgeable science fiction professionals and well-read fans. Quarterly. Circ. 1,800. Accepts previously published material. Returns original artwork after publication. Sample copy $2.50. Art guidelines for SASE with first-class postage.
Cartoons: Buys 1-2/issue from freelance artists. Themes must be related to science fiction or fantasy. Prefers single panel; b&w line drawings. Send query letter with samples of style to be kept on file unless SASE included. Reports within 4 weeks. Buys one-time rights. Pays $2-4, b&w; on publication.
Illustrations: Buys 9-10/issue from freelance artists. Prefers "sharp, bold b&w art." Science fiction or fantasy themes only. Prefers pen & ink, then airbrush and charcoal/pencil. Send query letter with tear sheets, Photostats or photocopies to be kept on file unless SASE included. Accepts any style. Samples not filed are returned by SASE. Reports within 4 weeks. To show a portfolio, mail appropriate materials, which should include original/final art, final reproduction/product, tear sheets and b&w. Buys one-time rights. Pays $25, b&w, cover; and $15/page, b&w, inside; on publication.
Tips: "Show us only science fiction work." Overall, "there is better realistic art, as well as more interesting experimentation in science-fiction/fantasy art."

***TIKKUN MAGAZINE**, 5100 Leona St., Oakland CA 94619. (415)482-0805. Publisher: Nan Fink. Estab. 1986. It is a "Jewish critique of politics, culture and society. Includes articles regarding Jewish and non-Jewish issues, left of center politically. Bimonthly. Circ. 40,000. Accepts previously published material. Original artwork is returned to the artist after publication. Sample copies free for SASE with first-class postage.
Illustrations: Buys 0-8 illustrations/issue from freelancers. Prefers line drawings: (filed, payment on use). Send query letter with brochure, resume, tear sheets, Photostats, photocopies, slides and photographs. Samples are filed. Reports back within weeks only if interested. To show a portfolio, mail appropriate materials. Buys one-time rights. Pays $25, b&w; cover: cover, $250 on publication.
Tips: "Send samples of line drawings for inside or slides for cover."

TODAY'S FIREMAN, Box 875108, Los Angeles CA 90087. Editor: Don Mack. Trade journal emphasizing the fire service. Features general interest, humor and technical articles. "Readers are firefigh-

ters—items should be of interest to the fire service." Quarterly. Circ. 10,000. Accepts previously published material. Original artwork is not returned after publication.
Cartoons: Prefers single panel with gagline; b&w line drawings. Send query letter with samples of style, roughs or finished cartoons. Reports back only if interested. Buys one-time rights. Pays $4.

TODAY'S POLICEMAN, Box 875108, Los Angeles CA 90087. Editor: Don Mack. For persons employed in and interested in police services. Semiannualy. Circ. 10,000.
Cartoons: Buys 6 cartoons/issue dealing with law enforcement and politics. Send finished art. SASE. Pays $2.50 for b&w.

TOURIST ATTRACTIONS AND PARKS, Suite 226, 401 N. Broad St., Philadelphia PA 19108. (215)925-9744. President: Scott Borowsky. Deals with arenas, attractions, fairgrounds, stadiums, concerts, theme and amusement parks. Published 6 times/year. Circ. 20,000. Also uses freelance artists for cover, layout and paste-up (each issue). Pays $7-8/hour for paste-up.
Illustrations: Buys 6/issue. Send query letter with resume and samples. SASE. Buys all rights. Cover: Pays $50 minimum, gray opaques; on publication. Inside: Buys gray opaques.

***TOY & MODEL TRAINS**, 1027 N. 7th St., Milwaukee WI 53233. Art Director: Lawrence Luser. Magazine emphasizing model railroading and toy trains. Bimonthly. Circ. 73,000. Accepts previously published material. Original artwork is sometimes returned to the artist after publication. Sample copies and art guidelines available.
Illustrations: Works on assignment only. Technical illustration "with flair." Send query letter with brochure. Samples are filed. Samples not filed are returned only if requested by artist. Reports back only if interested. Write to schedule an appointment to show a portfolio or mail original/final art, tear sheets, final reproduction/product, photographs, slides, color and b&w. Negotiates rights purchased.

TQ, (Teen Quest, formerly Young Ambassador), Box 82808, Lincoln NE 68501. (402)474-4567. Art Director: Victoria Valentine. "Our main purpose is to help Christian teens live consistently for Christ, and to help them grow in their knowledge of the Bible and its principles for living." Monthly. Circ. 80,000. Original artwork returned after publication. Free sample copy.
Cartoons: Managing Editor: Barbara Comito. Buys 2-3 cartoons/issue from freelancers. Receives 4 submissions/week from freelancers. Interested in wholesome humor for teens; prefer cartoons with teens as main characters; single panel. Prefers to see finished cartoons. Reports in 4-6 weeks. Buys first rights on a work-for-hire basis.
Illustrations: Some illustrations purchased on assignment only. Submit samples with query letter. Pays $250-500 per page for 4-color art.

TRADITION, 106 Navajo, Council Bluffs IA 51501. (712)366-1136. Editor-in-Chief/Art Director: Robert Everhart. "For players and listeners of traditional and country music. We are a small, nonprofit publication and will use whatever is sent to us. A first time gratis use is the best way to establish communication." Monthly. Circ. 2,000. Simultaneous submissions and previously published work OK. Buys one-time rights. Free sample copy.
Cartoons: Buys 1/issue on country music; single panel with gagline. Receives 10-15 cartoons/week from freelance artists. Mail roughs. Pays $5-15, b&w line drawings; on publication.
Illustrations: Buys 1/issue on country music. Query with resume and samples. SASE. Cover: Pays $5-15, b&w line drawings. Inside: Pays $5-15, b&w line drawings; on publication. Reports in 4 weeks.
Tips: "We'd like to see an emphasis on traditional country music."

TRAINING: THE MAGAZINE OF HUMAN RESOURCES DEVELOPMENT, 50 S. Ninth St., Minneapolis MN 55402. Editor: Jack Gordon. Art Director: Jodi Scharff. Covers "job-related training and education in business and industry, both theory and practice." Audience: "training directors, personnel managers, sales and data processing managers, general managers, etc." Monthly. Circ. 51,000. Especially needs cartoons on adult education on the job. Original artwork returned after publication "on request." Sample copy $3 plus 9x11 SASE.
Cartoons: Buys 2-4 cartoons/issue from freelancers. "We buy a wide variety of styles. The themes relate directly to our editorial content, which is training in the work place." Prefers airbrush, watercolor, and acrylics. Samples not filed are returned by SASE only if requested. Reports in 4 weeks. Buys reprint rights. Pays $25, b&w, on acceptance.
Illustrations: Buys 5-8 illustrations/issue from freelancers. Send query letter with photocopies or Photostats to be kept on file. Call (612)333-0471 or write art director for appointment to show portfolio. Samples not filed are returned only if requested and only by SASE. Reports within 4 weeks. Buys reprint rights. Pays $400 and up for color, cover; $75-200 for b&w, inside; $250 for color, inside; on acceptance.

Tips: "Show a wide variety of work in different media and with different subject matter. For my magazine, good renditions of people are very important."

***TRANSAMERICA**, Transamerica Corp., 600 Montgomery St., San Francisco CA 94111. (415)983-4295. Editor: Beth Quartarolo. For employees. Quarterly. Circ. 35,000. SASE. Previously published work OK. Pays on acceptance.
Illustrations: Buys 3-4/year on assigned themes. Cover: Uses color illustrations. Query with previously published work or arrange interview to show portfolio. Negotiates pay.
Tips: "When trying to sell your work, give some general rates. I need some idea of what the artist is going to charge."

***TRANSITIONS ABROAD: The Magazine of Overseas Opportunities**, 18 Hulst Rd., Box 344, Amherst MA 01004. Editor: Clayton A. Hubbs. Emphasizes educational low-budget and special interest overseas travel for those who travel to learn and to participate. Bimonthly. Circ. 10,000. Original artwork returned after publication. Sample copy $3.50; art guidelines for SASE.
Illustrations: Uses 6 illustrations/issue; buys 4 from freelancers. Receives 1 illustration/week from freelance artists. Especially needs illustrations of American travelers in overseas settings; work, travel and study around the world. Send roughs to be kept on file. Samples not kept on file are returned by SASE. Reports in 4 weeks. Buys one-time rights. Pays $25-100, cover b&w line drawings; $30-100, cover b&w washes; on publication.
Tips: The trend is toward "more and more interest in budget travel and travel which involves interaction with people in the host country, with a formal or informal educational component. We usually commission graphics to fit specific features. Inclusion of article with graphics vastly increases likelihood of acceptance. Artists should study the publication and determine its needs."

TRAVEL & LEISURE, 1120 6th Ave., New York NY 10036. (212)382-5600. Design/Art Director: Bob Ciano. Associate Art Directors: Joseph Paschke and Joan Ferrell. Emphasizes travel, resorts, dining and entertainment. Monthly. Circ. 1,000,000. Original artwork returned after publication. Art guidelines for SASE.
Illustrations: Uses 1-15 illustrations/issue, all from freelancers. Interested in travel and leisure-related themes. Prefers pen & ink, airbrush, colored pencil, watercolor, acrylics, oils, pastels, collage, mixed media and calligraphy. "Illustrators are selected by excellence and relevance to the subject." Works on assignment only. Provide business card to be kept on file for future assignment; samples returned by SASE. Reports in 1 week. Buys world serial rights. Pays a minimum of $150 inside b&w and $800-1,500 maximum, inside color; on publication.

TRUE WEST, Box 2107, Stillwater OK 74076. Editor: John Joerschke. Emphasizes American Western history from 1830 to 1910 for a primarily rural and suburban audience, middle-age and older, interested in Old West history, horses, cowboys, art, clothing, and all things western. Monthly. Circ. 90,000. Accepts previously published material and considers some simultaneous submissions. Original artwork returned after publication. Sample copy $1. Art guidelines for SASE.
Illustrations: Buys 5-10 illustrations/issue from freelancers. "Inside illustrations are usually, but not always, pen & ink line drawings; covers are Western paintings." Send query letter with samples to be kept on file; "we return anything on request." "For inside illustrations, we want samples of artist's line drawings. For covers, we need to see full-color transparencies." Reports within 30 days. Call or write for appointment to show portfolio. Buys one-time rights. Pays $75-150, for color transparency for cover; $15-40, b&w, inside. "We're paying about twelve months after acceptance but are slowly speeding that up."

***TURF AND SPORT DIGEST**, 511-513 Oakland Ave., Baltimore MD 21212. Publisher: Allen L. Mitzel Jr. Emphasizes thoroughbred racing coverage, personalities, events and handicapping methods for fans of thoroughbred horseracing.
Cartoons: Interested in horse racing themes. Pays $10; on publication.

TURTLE MAGAZINE FOR PRESCHOOL KIDS, 1100 Waterway Blvd., Box 567, Indianapolis IN 46206. (317)636-8881. Art Director: Rick Gonzalez. Emphasizes health, nutrition, exercise and safety for children 2-5 years. Monthly except bimonthly February/March, April/May, June/July and August/September. Accepts previously published material and simultaneous submissions. Original artwork not returned after publication. Sample copy 75¢; art guidelines for SASE. Finds most artists through portfolio reviews and samples received in mail.
Illustrations: Buys 15-30 illustrations/issue from freelancers. Interested in "stylized, humorous, realistic and cartooned themes; also nature and health." Especially needs b&w and 2-color artwork for line or halftone reproduction; full-color text and cover art. Works on assignment only. Send query letter with

resume, stats or good photocopies, slides and tear sheets to be kept on file. Samples not kept on file returned by SASE. Reports only if interested. Buys all rights. To show a portfolio, mail final reproduction/product, color, tear sheets, b&w and 2-color. Negotiates payment. Pays on publication.
Tips: "Be sure to send in appropriate material for the magazine (example: do not send *New Yorker* illustrations for a children's magazine for ages 2-5)."

TV GUIDE, Radnor PA 19088. Cartoon Editor: M.E. Bilisnansky. Emphasizes news, personalities and programs of television for a general audience. Weekly. Query. Reports in 2 weeks. Buys all rights. Pays on acceptance.
Cartoons: Buys about 35 cartoons/year on TV themes. Pays $200, single cartoon. Also uses cartoons for editorial features. Line drawings and halftones. Buys only single panel cartoons. No cartoon strips.

TWIN CITIES, 7831 East Bush Lake Rd., Minneapolis MN 55435. (612)835-6855. Art Director: Kathleen Timmerman. Magazine emphasizing lifestyle and general local interest for upscale, wealthy, well-educated men and women. Monthly. Circ. 48,000. Original artwork returned after publication. Sample copy $3.
Illustrations: Buys 2-6 illustrations/issue from freelancers. Works on assignment only. Prefers original styles that illuminate the editorial theme. Send query letter with resume, tear sheets and photocopies. Samples not filed are returned by SASE. Reports only if interested. Call to schedule an appointment to show a portfolio, which should include roughs, original/final art, final reproduction/product, color, tear sheets, Photostats, photographs and b&w. Buys one-time rights. Pays for design by the hour $25-40. Pays for illustration by the project, $150-600.
Tips: "I look for uniqueness of style and prefer to see published editorial work. I think our readership is quite sophisticated and the illustrators we choose must appeal to a target group."

THE UNITED METHODIST PUBLISHING HOUSE, Publishing Division, 201 Box 801, Eighth Ave. S, Nashville TN 37202. (615)749-6000. Art Procurement Supervisor: David Dawson. Publishes 60 + magazines, and church and home leaflets for ages 1½ years to senior citizens. Uses 30-40 illustrations/publication. Assigns 500-1,000 jobs/year.
Illustrations: Works with 25-50 freelance artists/year. Seeks "artists with editorial and publishing experience. Also seeks artists of ethnic background—Korean, Hispanic and black. We need illustrators who can do people well." Works on assignment only. Send brochure showing art style or slides, Photostats, photographs and tear sheets to be kept on file. Samples not filed are returned only if requested. Reports only if interested. Considers complexity of project, skill and experience of artist, project's budget and rights purchased when establishing payment. Buys all rights. Pays for covers by the project, $250 minimum for full-color. Pays for text illustration by the project, negotiates. Automatically pays on the 5th and 20th of each month.
Tips: "The ability to render the human figure is important, good graphic design is helpful, other kinds of illustrations considered; how-to, game boards, mazes, etc. If you feel professionally competent in any of these areas please respond."

USA TODAY, 99 W. Hawthorne Ave., Valley Stream NY 11580. (516)568-9191. Contact: Bob Rothenberg. For intellectual college graduates. Monthly. Circ. 235,000. Free sample copy.
Illustrations: Buys 70-80 illustrations/year on assigned themes. Uses only New York artists in the metropolitan area. Send query letter with samples. SASE. Reports in 1 week. Buys all rights. Cover: pays $200, color. Inside: Pays $25-75, b&w line drawings; on publication.

***VARBUSINESS**, 600 Community Dr., Manhasset NY 11030. (516)365-4600. Art Director: Joe McNeill. Emphasizes computer business. "Aimed to and about people; hardware and technology is downplayed. The art is in a lighter, less technical vein." Monthly. Circ. 75,000. Original artwork is returned to the artist after publication. Art guidelines not available.
Illustrations: Buys 20 illustrations/issue from freelancers. Works on assignment only. Prefers pop, illustrative style. Prefers airbrush, then pen & ink, colored pencil, acrylics, pastels and computer illustration. Send query letter with tear sheets. Samples are filed. Samples not filed are returned only if requested. Reports back only if interested. Call or write to schedule an appointment to show a portfolio, which should include tear sheets, final reproduction/product and slides. Buys one-time rights. Pays $2-3,000, color, cover; $750-1,500, color, inside; on publication.
Tips: "Show printed pieces or suitable color reproductions, I do not want to see photocopies or stats."

VEGETARIAN TIMES, Box 570, Oak Park IL 60303. (312)848-8120. Art Director: Gregory Chambers. Consumer food magazine with emphasis on fitness and health for readers 30-50, 75% women. Monthly. Circ. 100,000. Accepts previously published material. Original artwork returned after publi-

cation. Sample copy $2.
Illustrations: Buys 4 illustrations/issue from freelancers. Send query letter with samples showing art style. To show a portfolio, mail appropriate materials or call to schedule an appointment; portfolio should include roughs, original/final art, color, tear sheets, photographs and b&w. Pays $30-300, inside; on publication.
Tips: "I work primarily with food/health-related topics, and look for someone who is familiar with or sympathetic to vegetarianism and whole foods cuisine."

VENTURE, Box 150, Wheaton IL 60189. (312)665-0630. Art Director: Lawrence Libby. For boys 10-15. "We seek to promote consciousness, acceptance of and personal commitment to Jesus Christ." Published 6 times/year. Circ. 25,000. Simultaneous submissions and previously published work OK. Original artwork returned after publication. Sample copy $1.50 with large SASE; artists' guidelines with SASE.
Cartoons: Send to attention of cartoon editor. Uses 1-3 cartoons/issue; buys all from freelancers. Receives 2 submissions/week from freelancers, on nature, sports, school, camping, hiking; single panel with gagline. "Keep it clean." Prefers finished cartoons. SASE. Reports in 2-4 weeks. Buys first-time rights. Pays $20 minimum, b&w line drawings; on acceptance.
Illustrations: Contact art director. Uses 3 illustrations/issue; buys 2/issue from freelancers, on education, family life and camping; b&w only. Works on assignment only. Send business card, tear sheets and photocopies of samples to be kept on file for future assignments. Samples returned by SASE. Reports back on future assignment possibilities. SASE. Reports in 2 weeks. Buys first time rights. Pays $100-150 for inside use of b&w line drawings and washes; on publication.

VERDICT MAGAZINE, 124 Truxtun Ave., Bakersfield CA 93301. (805)325-7124. Managing Editor: Steve Walsh. Emphasizes law for insurance defense lawyers. Circ. 5,000. Accepts previously published material. Original artwork returned after publication. Sample copy for SASE with $3 postage; art guidelines for SASE with first-class postage.
Cartoons: Buys 4 cartoons/issue from freelancers. Legal theme. Prefers single panel with gagline; b&w line drawings or b&w washes. Send finished cartoons to be kept on file. Material not filed is returned by SASE. Reports only if interested. Buys one-time rights or reprint rights. Write for appointment to show portfolio. Pays $5, b&w; on publication.
Illustrations: Buys 4 illustrations/issue from freelancers. Theme: legal. Prefers pen & ink and charcoal/pencil. Send Photostats, tear sheets or photocopies to be kept on file. Samples not filed are returned by SASE. Reports only if interested. Write for appointment to show portfolio. Buys one-time rights or reprint rights. Pays $10, color, cover; $5, b&w, inside; on publication.
Tips: "Send copies of original art—not original art."

VICTIMOLOGY: AN INTERNATIONAL JOURNAL, 5535 Lee Hwy., Arlington VA 22207. (703)536-1750. Editor-in-Chief: Emilio Viano. For professionals, lawyers, criminologists, medical personnel and others helping child/spouse abuse programs, hotlines, rape crisis centers and other victim programs. "By 'victim,' we mean not only those victimized by crime but earthquakes, the environment, accidents, pollution and the state." Quarterly. Circ. 2,500. Send query letter with samples. SASE. Reports in 4 weeks. Buys all rights. Pays on publication. Sample copy $5. Write to be put on mailing list to receive periodical announcements.
Illustrations: Buys several illustrations/year on victimization. "We like to see illustrations on what is done in behalf of the victim." Pays $200, color, cover; $100, b&w. Pays $30, b&w, inside. Pays $50 for brochure work.

VIDEO REVIEW, 902 Broadway, New York NY 10010. (212)477-2200. Art Director: Rob Allen. Emphasizes home video for owners and prospective owners of home video equipment. Monthly. Circ. 475,000. Original artwork returned after publication.
Illustrations: Uses 1-2 illustrations/issue; buys all from freelancers. Prefers airbrush, line drawings, sculpture and color. Works on assignment only. Send samples of style. Samples not returned. Reports when an assignment is available. Call or write for appointment. Negotiates rights purchased.

VIRGINIA BAR NEWS, Suite 1000, Ross Building, 801 East Main St., Richmond VA 23219. (804)786-2061. Coordinator of Public Information and Publications: Caroline Bolte. Magazine emphasizing legal profession for members of the bar throughout the state. Bimonthly. Circ. 22,000. Sample copy for SASE.
Illustrations: Buys various illustrations/issue from freelancers. Works on assignment only. Send query letter with resume, tear sheets, Photostats, photocopies and photographs. Samples not filed are returned only if requested. Reports within 1 month. Portfolio should include original/final art, photographs and b&w. Pays $150-200, b&w, cover; $25-75, b&w, inside; on publication.

VIRTUE MAGAZINE, Box 850, Sisters OR 97759. (503)549-8261. Art Director: Dennis Mortenson. Magazine aimed at Christian homemakers. The majority are ages 25-45, married, and have children living at home. Publishes 10 issues/year. Circ. 125,000. Accepts previously published material. Original artwork returned after publication. Sample copy $2 plus postage or SASE. Art guidelines for SASE with first-class postage.
Cartoons: Buys 1-4 cartoons/issue from freelancers. Cartoons should involve family, children, homemaking, marriage or incidents in a woman's everyday life. They should be aimed at women. Prefers single panel with or without gagline; b&w line drawings or b&w washes. Send samples of style and finished cartoons. Samples not filed are returned by SASE. Reports within 5-10 days. Buys first rights. Pays $25-40, b&w.
Illustrations: Buys 4-6 illustrations/issue from freelancers. Works on assignment only. Send query letter with brochure showing art style or resume, tear sheets, Photostats, photocopies, slides or photographs. Prefers samples that can be filed. Samples not filed are returned by SASE. To show a portfolio, mail appropriate materials or call to schedule an appointment; portfolio should include original/final art and tear sheets. Buys first rights. Pays $50-125, b&w, and $100-250, color, inside; on publication.
Tips: "Artists should have knowledge of good leading lines, color and anatomy. We use mostly realistic art, though I'm leaning to 3-D and graphics/collage."

VISIONS, THE INTERNATIONAL MAGAZINE OF ILLUSTRATED POETRY, Black Buzzard Press, 4705 S. 8th Rd., Arlington VA 22204. Editors: Bradley R. Strahan, Ursula Gill and Shirley Sullivan. Emphasizes literature and the illustrative arts for "well educated, very literate audience, very much into art and poetry." Published 3 times/year. Circ. 675. Only accepts previously published material under very special circumstances. Original artwork returned after publication only if requested. Sample copy $3 (latest issue $3.50); art guidelines for SASE.
Illustrations: Buys approximately 21/issue, 58 illustrations/year from freelancers. Works on assignment only. Representational to surrealistic and some cubism. Send query letter with SASE and samples to be kept on file. Samples should clearly show artist's style and capability; no slides or originals. Samples not filed are returned by SASE. Reports within 2 months. Buys first rights. "For information on releases on artwork, please contact the editors at the above address." Pays by the project, in copies or up to $10.
Tips: "Don't send slides. We might lose them. We don't use color, anyway."

VOGUE, 350 Madison Ave., New York NY 10017. (212)880-8914. Art Director: Roger Schoening. Emphasizes fashion, health, beauty, culture and decorating for women. Write and send resume; will then review portfolio; works primarily with New York area artists. Leave photocopies for referral.

VOLKSWAGEN'S WORLD, Volkswagen of America, Troy MI 48099. (313)362-6770. Editor: Marlene Goldsmith. For Volkswagen owners. Quarterly. Circ. 300,000.
Cartoons: Seldom purchases cartoons unless the subject matter is particularly unique. Send query letter with samples. SASE. Reports in 6 weeks. Buys all rights. Pays $15 minimum, halftones and washes; on acceptance.
Illustrations: Send query letter with samples. SASE. Reports in 6 weeks. Buys all rights. Cover: pays $250 minimum, color. Inside: pays $15 minimum, b&w and color; on acceptance.
Tips: "We're happy to send sample issues to prospective contributors. It's the best way of seeing what our needs are."

***THE WAR CRY, Magazine of The Salvation Army**, 799 Bloomfield Ave., Verona NJ 07044. Art Director: Warren L. Maye. Emphasizes the work of The Salvation Army worldwide, inspirational fiction and nonfiction with a "Christian-oriented, social service focus: helping others in need, homeless, disaster victims, etc., food, shelter, and other resources." Biweekly. Circ. 350,000. Accepts previously published material. Original artwork is sometimes returned to the artist after publication. Sample copies for SASE with first-class postage. Art guidelines available.
Illustrations: Buys 0-1 illustration/issue from freelancers. Buys 8-10 illustrations/year from freelancers. Prefers realistic, color religious illustration. Send query letter with brochure showing art style or resume, tear sheets, slides and photographs. Samples are filed. Samples not filed are returned by SASE. Reports back within 2 weeks. To show a portfolio, mail tear sheets, photographs, slides, color and b&w. Buys reprint rights or all rights. Pays $60-75, 2/color; $75-300, 4/color, inside; on acceptance.
Tips: "Read an issue first. Gain an understanding of the organization through a local corps, hospital or rehabilitation center."

THE WASHINGTON MONTHLY, 1711 Connecticut Ave. NW, Washington DC 20009. (202)462-0128. Art Director: R.J. Matson. For journalists, government officials and general public interested in public affairs. "We examine government's failures and suggest solutions." Monthly. Circ. 30,000. Pre-

viously published and photocopied submissions OK.
Illustrations: Buys 20-40 illustrations/year on politics and government. Local artists preferred. Send query letter with samples or arrange interview to show Portfolio. SASE. Reports in 4 weeks. Buys one-time rights. Pays $50-125, b&w line drawings and washes, inside; pay is negotiable for color-separated work; $100 minimum, b&w, cover; on publication.
Tips: "We need fast turn-around; artist should read articles before attempting work."

THE WASHINGTONIAN MAGAZINE, Suite 200, 1828 L St. NW, Washington DC 20036. (202)296-3600. Emphasizes politics, cultural events, personalities, entertainment and dining. About Washington, for Washingtonians. Monthly. Circ. 150,000. Simultaneous submissions and previously published work OK. Original artwork returned after publication if requested. No artists' guidelines available.
Cartoons: Buys 5 cartoons/issue from freelancers, on "sophisticated topics, urban life"; single and double panel with gagline. Uses b&w line drawings, gray opaques, b&w washes, and opaque watercolors. Prefers finished cartoons. Reports in 4-6 weeks. Buys one-time rights. Pays $50, b&w; on publication.
Illustrations: Design Director: Lynne Mannino. Uses up to 5 illustrations/issue. Works on assignment only. Uses b&w line drawings, gray opaques, b&w washes, color washes and opaque watercolor. Any medium used. Send business card and tear sheets to be kept on file. Returns samples if requested. Does not report back on future assignment possibilities. Prefers to see Portfolio and samples of style. SASE. Reports in 1 week. Buys one-time rights. Pay is negotiable; on publication.
Tips: "I like to see in your samples how illustration is used for a client. Include tearsheets so I can see how the piece will print. I don't want to see school work, work that isn't for a client."

WATER SKI MAGAZINE, Box 2456, Winter Park FL 32790. (305)628-4802. Publisher: Terry Snow. Send query letters to: Terry Temple, editor. Emphasizes water skiing for an audience generally 18-34 years old, 80% male, active, educated, affluent. Published 8 times/year. Circ. 72,000. Accepts previously published material and simultaneous submissions. Original artwork returned after publication. Query for guidelines.
Cartoons: Uses 1-4 cartoons/issue, buys all from freelancers. 90% assigned. Prefers single panel with gagline, color or b&w washes or b&w line drawings. Prefers to receive query letter with samples or roughs first, but will review finished work. Samples returned. Reports within 3 weeks. Negotiates rights purchased. Negotiates payment, usually $15-30, b&w; up to $300, color, depending on topic. Pays 30 days after publication.
Illustrations: Uses 10 illustrations/issue; buys 5 illustrations/issue from freelancers. Prefers strong lines in a realistic style. Works on assignment "most of the time." Send query letter with resume, samples and tear sheets to be kept on file. Samples returned by SASE if not kept on file. Reports within 3 weeks. May also submit portfolio. Negotiates payment and rights purchased. Pays on publication.

WEBB CO., 1999 Shepard Rd., St. Paul MN 55116. Creative Director: Jerald Johnson.
Illustrations: Uses 1 illustration/issue from freelancer. Receives 1 submission/week from freelancers. Interested in themes for 10 agriculture magazines, 1 horticulture magazine, 1 home magazine, 1 snowmobile magazine, 13 consumer magazines. Buys business and general interest themes. Works on assignment only. Provide brochure, flyer, tear sheet and slides to be kept on file for future assignments. Prefers to see Portfolio and samples of style. Samples not kept on file are returned by SASE. Buys all rights on a work-for-hire basis and one-time publication rights. Pays $50-1,000, b&w or color; on acceptance.

WEIGHT WATCHERS MAGAZINE, 360 Lexington Ave., New York NY 10017. (212)370-0644. Art Director: Alan Richardson. Emphasizes food, health, fashion, beauty for the weight and beauty conscious, 25-45 years old. Monthly. Circ. 875,000. Original artwork returned after publication.
Illustrations: Uses 6 illustrations/issue. Works on assignment only. Send query letter with brochure to be kept on file. Reports only if interested. Portfolios seen by drop-off only. Buys one-time rights. Pays on acceptance.

WEST, 750 Ridder Park Dr., San Jose CA 95190. (408)920-5795. Editor: Jeffrey Klein. Art Director: Bambi Nicklen. General interest magazine for subscribers of the *San Jose Mercury News*. Circ. 307,000. Weekly. Free sample copy.
Illustrations: Buys 2-3/issue on all themes except erotica. Query with resume and samples or previously published work, or arrange interview to show Portfolio. Cover: pays up to $700, opaque watercolors, oils, acrylics or mixed media. Inside: pays $125-400, b&w line drawings, washes and gray opaques; $150-400, color washes, opaque watercolors, oils, acrylics or mixed media. Pays on acceptance.

WESTERN OUTDOORS,3197-E Airport Loop Dr., Costa Mesa CA 92626. (714)546-4370. Art Director: Gayle Radestock. Emphasizes hunting and fishing and related activities in the western states; directed to men and women interested in pursuing these activities in the 11 contiguous western states plus Alaska, Hawaii, British Columbia and western Mexico. Published 10 times/year. Circ. 150,000. Returns original artwork after publication.
Illustrations: Works on assignment only. Send query letter with samples to be kept on file. Accepts photocopies as samples. Samples not filed are returned by SASE. Reports within 30 days. Write for appointment to show portfolio. Buys first rights. Pays on acceptance.

***THE WESTERN PRODUCER**, Box 2500, Saskatoon, Saskatchewan S7K 2C4 Canada. (306)665-3500. For farm families in western Canada. Weekly. Circ. 140,000.
Cartoons: Receives 12/week from freelance artists. Uses only cartoons about rural life. SASE (nonresidents include IRC). Reports in 3 weeks. Buys first Canadian rights. Pays $15, b&w line drawings; on acceptance. No illustrations.

WESTERN RV TRAVELER, Suite 226, 2033 Clement Ave., Alameda CA 94501. (415)769-8338. Art Director: David Angelo. "RV magazine of the west" for RV-owners and travel-oriented readers. Monthly. Circ. 100,000. Accepts previously published material. Original artwork returned after publication. Sample copy available.
Cartoons: Buys 1-5 cartoons/issue from freelancers. Prefers single panel with or without gagline; b&w line drawings or b&w washes. Send query letter with finished cartoons. Write to schedule an appointment to show a portfolio. Material not kept on file is returned by SASE. Reports only if interested. Buys one-time rights. Pays $5, b&w.
Illustrations: Buys 5-10 illustrations/issue from freelancers. Prefers line drawings for newsprint publication. Send query letter with resume, tear sheets, Photostats, photocopies and photographs. Samples not filed are returned by SASE. Reports only if interested. Write to schedule an appointment to show a portfolio, which should include original/final art, final reproduction/product, tear sheets, Photostats, photographs and three-dimensional work. Buys one-time rights. Pays $100, color, cover; $5, b&w, inside; on publication.

WESTERN SPORTSMAN, Box 737, Regina, Saskatchewan S4P 3A8 Canada. (306)352-8384. Editor-in-Chief: Rick Bates. For fishermen, hunters, campers and outdoorsmen. Bimonthly. Circ. 30,000. Original artwork returned after publication. Sample copy $3.50; artist's guidelines for SASE (nonresidents include IRC).
Cartoons: Buys 90 cartoons/year on the outdoors; single panel with gaglines. Send art or query with samples. SASE (nonresidents include IRC). Reports in 3-8 weeks. Buys first North American serial rights. Pays $20, b&w line drawings; on acceptance.
Illustrations: Buys 8 illustrations/year on the outdoors. Mail art or query with samples. SASE (nonresidents include IRC). Reports in 3-8 weeks. Buys first North American serial rights. Pays $50-200, b&w line drawings, inside; on acceptance.

WHISPERING WIND MAGAZINE, 8009 Wales St., New Orleans LA 70126. Editor: Jack B. Heriard. Magazine emphasizing American Indian crafts and culture. Features historical and how-to articles and ethnic and historical native American (Indian) essays. "Readership is 52% Indian, 49% 15-35 years of age." Bimonthly. Circ. 4,000. Accepts previously published material. Original artwork returned after publication if requested. Sample copy $3.
Cartoons: Uses 3 cartoons/year from freelancers. "Must be Indian-oriented—no stereotypes." Prefers single panel with gagline, b&w line drawings. Send query letter with roughs. Samples are returned by SASE. Reports back within 5 days. Negotiates rights purchased. No payment.
Illustrations: Works on assignment only. Prefers traditional style. Looks for "attention to detail, accuracy of subjects and clothing from a historical perspective. Avoid, stereotyping Indian clothing (all Indians wear war bonnets, etc.)." Send query letter with photocopies. Samples are returned by SASE. Reports back within 5 days. Negotiates rights purchased. No payment.

***WILDFIRE**, Box 148, Tum Tum WA 99034. (509)326-6561. Managing Editor: Matthew Ryan. Magazine emphasizing nature, Native American values, spirituality and new art topics. "We promote Native American spirituality, earth awareness, ecology, natural child birth/raising, sexuality and relationships, alternative lifestyles, earth changes and prophecy." Quarterly. Circ. 11,000. Accepts previously published material. Original artwork is returned to the artist after publication. Sample copies $2.50.
Cartoons: Buys 3 cartoons/issue from freelancers. "Am looking for more.". Prefers themes featuring nature vs. technology or common sense vs. experts, "non-sarcastic." Prefers b&w line drawings or b&w washes. Send samples of style. Samples are filed. Samples not filed are returned by SASE if requested by artist. Reports back within 1 month. Buys first rights. Pays $20 (varies), b&w.

Illustrations: "Have not bought illustrations in the past, but am interested." Send query letter with brochure. Samples are filed. Samples not filed are returned only if requested by artist. Reports back within months. Write to schedule an appointment to show a portfolio, which should include b&w tear sheets. Buys first rights. Pays $25 (varies), b&w.
Tips: "Read sample copy! Send samples of work and orientation (what can you create specifically for our view). I would like to see color work and fine line graphics in a portfolio."

WILSON LIBRARY BULLETIN, 950 University Ave., Bronx NY 10452. (212)588-8400. Editor: Milo Nelson. Emphasizes the issues and the practice of library science. Published 10 times/year. Circ. 25,000. Free sample copy.
Cartoons: Buys 2-3 cartoons/issue on education and library science; single panel with gagline. Mail finished art. SASE. Reports back only if interested. Buys first rights. Pays $100, b&w line drawings and washes; on acceptance.
Illustrations: Uses 1-2 illustrations/issue; buys all from freelancers. Works on assignment only. Send query letter, business card and samples to be kept on file. Reports back only if interested. Call for appointment to show portfolio. Buys first rights. Cover: pays $300, color washes. Inside: pays $100-200, b&w line drawings and washes; $20, spot drawings. Pays on publication.

WINDSOR THIS MONTH MAGAZINE, Box 1029, Station A, Windsor, Ontario N9A 6P4 Canada. (519)966-7411. Publisher: J.S. Woloschuk. Features Windsor-oriented issues, people interviews, opinion, entertainment. Published 12 times/year. Circ. 24,000.
Illustrations: Buys 3/issue on assigned themes. Send query letter with samples. Include SASE (nonresidents include IRC). Reports in 1 month. Buys first North American serial rights. Negotiates payment, color and b&w; pays on publication.
Tips: "Send sample of published work."

WINES & VINES, 1800 Lincoln Ave., San Rafael CA 94901. (415)453-9700. Editor: Philip E. Hiaring. Emphasizes the grape and wine industry in North America for the trade—growers, winemakers, merchants. Monthly. Circ. 5,800. Accepts previously published material. Original artwork not returned after publication.
Cartoons: Buys approximately 3 cartoons/year. Prefers single panel with gagline; b&w line drawings. Send query letter with roughs to be kept on file. Material not kept on file is not returned. Reports within 1 month. Buys first rights. Pays $10.
Illustrations: Send query letter to be kept on file. Reports within 1 month. Buys first rights. Pays $50-100, color, cover; $15, b&w, inside. Pays on acceptance.

WINNING, 15115 S. 76 E. Ave., Bixby OK 74008. (918)366-4441. Editors: Janna Pirtle and Gordon Sprouse. Newspaper emphasizing contests, sweepstakes and lottery. Monthly. Circ. 250,000. Accepts previously published material after publication. Sample copy $2.
Cartoons: Buys 2-3 cartoons/issue from freelancers. Prefers contests, sweepstakes and lottery as themes. Prefers single, double or multiple panel, with or without gagline; b&w line drawings. Send samples of style to be kept on file. Material not kept on file is returned by SASE. Reports only if interested. Negotiates rights purchased.
Illustrations: Buys 2-3 illustrations/issue from freelancers. Send query letter with tear sheets. Samples not filed are returned by SASE. Does not report back.

WIRE JOURNAL INTERNATIONAL, 1570 Boston Post Rd., Guilford CT 06437. (203)453-2777. Contact: Art Director. Emphasizes the wire industry worldwide, members of Wire Association International, industry suppliers, manufacturers, research/developers, engineers, etc. Monthly. Circ. 12,500. Original artwork not returned after publication. Free sample copy and art guidelines.
Illustrations: Uses "no set number" of illustrations/issue; illustrations are "used infrequently." Works on assignment only. Provide samples, business card and tear sheets to be kept on file for possible future assignments. Call for appointment or submit portfolio. Reports "as soon as possible." Buys all rights. Pay is negotiable; on publication.
Tips: "Show practical artwork that relates to industrial needs and avoid bringing samples of surrealism art, for example. Also, show a better variety of techniques—and know something about who we are and the industry we serve."

WISCONSIN RESTAURATEUR, 122 W. Washington, Madison WI 53703. (608)251-3663. Editor: Jan Simonson. Emphasizes the restaurant industry. Readers are "restaurateurs, hospitals, schools, institutions, cafeterias, food service students, chefs, etc." Monthly. Circ. 3,850, except convention issue (March), 8,000. Original artwork returned after publication. Free sample copy; art guidelines for SASE. Especially needs cover material.

Cartoons: Buys 1 cartoon/issue from freelancer. Receives 5 cartoons/week from freelancers. "Uses much material pertaining to conventions, food shows, etc. Sanitation issue good. Cartoons about employees. No off-color material." Prefers b&w line drawings with gaglines. Send finished cartoons. SASE. Reports in 2 weeks. Buys first North American serial rights. Pays $8 on publication.
Illustrations: Uses 5 illustrations/issue; buys 1/issue from freelancer. Receives 1 illustration/week from freelance artists. Freelancers chosen "at random, depending on theme and articles featured for the month." Looks for "the unusual, pertaining to the food service industry. No offbeat or questionable material." Prefers b&w line drawings and washes for covers. Send brochure showing art style or resume to be kept on file for future assignments. Buys first North American serial rights. To show a portfolio, mail appropriate materials, which should include roughs, original/final art and b&w. Pays $25, b&w and $50, color, cover; $15, b&w, $20, color, inside; Pays on acceptance.
Tips: Trends within the field include "seafood, low-calorie beverages and more convenience foods." Changes within the magazine include "new cover design, and the use of more freelance material—pictures and illustrations. Study back issues."

***WISCONSIN REVIEW**, Box 158, Radford Hall, University of Wisconsin-Oshkosh, Oshkosh WI 54901. (414)424-2267. Editor: Brenda Cardenas Christians. Emphasizes literature (poetry, short fiction, reviews) and the arts. Tri-annual. Circ. 2,000. Original artwork returned after publication "if requested." Sample copy $2; art guidelines available for SASE.
Illustrations: Uses 5-10 illustrations/issue. "Cover submissions can be color, size 5 1/2x8 1/2 or smaller or slides. Submissions for inside must be black-and-white, size 5 1/2x8 1/2 or smaller unless artist allows reduction of a larger size submission. We are primarily interested in material that in one way or another attempts to elucidate, explain, discover or otherwise untangle the manifestly complex circumstances in which we find ourselves in the 1980s." Provide samples and tear sheets with "updated address and phone number" to be kept on file for possible future assignments. Send query letter with roughs, finished art or samples of style. Samples returned by SASE. Reports in 5 months. Pays in 2 contributor's copies.

WISCONSIN TRAILS, Box 5650, Madison WI 53705. (608)231-2444. Production Manager: Nancy Mead. Concerns travel, recreation, history, industry and personalities in Wisconsin. Published 6 times/year. Circ. 30,000. Previously published and photocopied submissions OK. Artists' guidelines for SASE.
Illustrations: Buys 6 illustrations/issue from freelancers. Receives less than 1 submission/week from freelancers. "Art work is done on assignment, to illustrate specific articles. All articles deal with Wisconsin. We allow artists considerable stylistic latitude." Send samples (photocopies OK) of style; indication of artist's favorite topics; name, address and phone number to be kept on file for future assignments. SASE. Reporting time varies. Buys one-time rights on a work-for-hire basis. Pays $25-300, inside; on publication.

***WOMAN BEAUTIFUL**, Allied Publications, 1776 Lake Worth Rd., Lake Worth FL 33460. Contact: Editor. For students at beauty schools and people who patronize beauty salons. Bimonthly. Circ. 12,000.
Cartoons: Buys 2 cartoons/issue on any subject. Send finished art. SASE. Reports in 2 months. Pays $10 for b&w; on publication.

***WOMEN'S VOICE OF COLUMBUS**, 2470 E. Main St., Columbus OH 43209. Publisher/Editor: Linda Katz. Estab. 1986. "Encouraging women to define their own happiness and go for it, keeping in mind a sense of responsibility to other people. We provide readers with info on choices—social, professional, financial, spiritual." Quarterly. Circ. 25,000. Accepts previously published material. Original artwork is returned to the artist after publication. Sample copies and art guidelines available.
Cartoons: Buys 1 cartoon/issue from freelancers. Prefers single panel or double panel with gagline; b&w line drawings or b&w washes. Prefers pen & ink caricatures. Send query letter with samples of style. Samples are filed. Samples not filed are returned by SASE. Reports only if interested. Call to schedule an appointment to show a portfolio, or mail roughs, original/final art, and tear sheets. Buys first rights or reprint rights. Pays $150, color, cover; $50, b&w, inside; on publication.
Tips: "Send copies of sketches then call."

WOODENBOAT, Box 78, Brooklin ME 04616. Editor: Jonathan A. Wilson. Executive Editor: Billy R. Sims. Contributing Editor: Peter H. Spectre. Managing Editor: Jennifer Buckley. Concerns designing, building, repairing, using and maintaining wooden boats. Bimonthly. Circ. 110,000. Previously published work OK. Sample copy $4.
Illustrations: Buys 48/year on wooden boats or related items. Send query letter with samples. SASE for return of material. Reports in 1-2 months. "We are always in need of high quality technical draw-

ings. Rates vary, but usually $25-350. Buys first North American serial rights. Pays on publication. **Tips:** "We work with several professionals on an assignment basis, but most of the illustrative material that we use in the magazine is submitted with a feature article. When we need additional material, however, we will try to contact a good freelancer in the appropriate geographic area."

WOODMEN OF THE WORLD, 1700 Farnam St., Omaha NE 68102. (402)342-1890. Editor-in-Chief: Leland A. Larson. For members of the Woodmen of the World Life Insurance Society and their families. Emphasizes Society activities, children's and women's interests and humor. Monthly. Circ. 470,000. Previously published work OK. Original artwork returned after publication, if arrangements are made. Free sample copy.
Cartoons: Buys 1-6 cartoons/issue from freelancers. Receives 10-50 submissions/week from freelancers. Especially needs cartoons. Interested in general interest subjects; single panel. Send finished cartoons. SASE. Reports in 2 weeks. Buys various rights. Pays $10, b&w line drawings, washes and halftones; on acceptance.
Illustrations: Uses 5-10 illustrations/year; buys 3-4/year from freelancers. Interested in lodge activities, seasonal, humorous and human interest themes. Prefers mixed media. Works on assignment only. Send brochure showing art style or flyers to be kept on file. Prefers to see finished art. SASE. Reports in 2 weeks. Buys one-time rights. Payment varies according to job.

WRITER'S DIGEST, 1507 Dana Avenue, Cincinnati OH 45207. Art Director: Carole Winters. Assistant Editor: Bill Strickland (for cartoons). Emphasizes freelance writing for freelance writers. Monthly. Circ. 200,000. Original artwork returned after publication. Sample copy $2.
Cartoons: Buys 3 cartoons/issue from freelancers. Theme: the writing life—cartoons that deal with writers and the trials of writing and selling their work. Also, writing from a historical standpoint (past works), language use and other literary themes. Prefers single panel with or without gagline. Send finished cartoons. Material returned by SASE. Reports within 1 month. Buys first rights or one-time rights. Pays $50-85, b&w; on acceptance.
Illustrations: Buys 4 illustrations/month from freelancers. Theme: the writing life (b&w line art primarily). Works on assignment only. Send brochure and nonreturnable samples to be kept on file. Accepts photocopies as samples. Write for appointment to show portfolio. Buys one-time rights. Pays $400, color, cover; $50-200, inside, b&w. Pays on acceptance.

WRITER'S YEARBOOK, 1507 Dana Ave., Cincinnati OH 45207. Submissions Editor: Bill Strickland. Emphasizes writing and marketing techniques, business topics for writers and writing opportunities for freelance writers and people trying to get started in writing. Annually. Original artwork returned with one copy of the issue in which it appears. Sample copy $3.95. Affiliated with *Writer's Digest*. Cartoons submitted to either publication are considered for both.
Cartoons: Uses 6-10 freelance cartoons/issue. "All cartoons must pertain to writing—its joys, agonies, quirks. All styles accepted, but high-quality art is a must." Prefers single panel, with or without gagline, b&w line drawings or washes. "Verticals are always considered, but horizontals—especially severe horizontals—are hard to come by." Send finished cartoons. Samples returned by SASE. Reports within 3 weeks. Buys first North American serial rights, one-time use. Pays $50 minimum, b&w. Pays on acceptance.
Tips: "A cluttery style does not appeal to us. Send finished, not rough art, with clearly typed gaglines. Cartoons without gaglines must be particularly well executed."

YACHTING, 5 River Rd., Box 1200, Cos Cob CT 06807. (203)629-8300. Editor: Roy Attaway. For top-level participants in yachting in all its forms, power and sail. Monthly. Circ. 135,000. Art guidelines for SASE.
Illustrations: Buys many spot illustrations/year. Query. Frank Rothmann, Design Director. SASE. Reports in 2-3 weeks. Buys all rights. Pays $50, b&w, inside.

YANKEE MAGAZINE, Main St., Dublin NH 03444. (603)563-8111. Design Editor: J. Porter. Regional magazine about New England. Monthly. Circ. 1 million. Accepts previously published material. Returns original artwork after publication. Sample copy $1.95.
Cartoons: Buys 4 cartoons/issue from freelancers. Cartoons must be "very funny and relative to New England lifestyle." Send query letter with samples of style to be kept on file. Material not filed is returned by SASE. Reports only if interested. Buys one-time rights. Pays $50 second rights, $100 first rights, b&w.
Illustrations: Buys various number/issue from freelancers. Send query letter with tear sheets, slides or photographs to be kept on file. Samples not filed are returned by SASE. Reports only if interested. Buys one-time rights. Pays $200-650, color, cover; $100-550 for b&w and $150-750 for color, inside; on acceptance.

Newspapers & Newsletters

Newspapers are changing the way they convey information by emphasizing their visual appearance. By increasing their use of color and informational graphics, they have replaced the "grey" look of yesterday's papers. This adds up to more assignments for freelance artists.

Artwork has a more direct purpose in newspapers than in magazines, because an illustration is used as a captionless photograph to summarize a feature story, or, as a chart, to make difficult information more inviting. Illustrations are used in every section of a daily paper and also in Sunday supplements.

Newspapers need versatile artists to illustrate a variety of assignments. When submitting samples or showing your portfolio to newspaper art directors, show strong black-and-white work to demonstrate your ability to interpret a story; cut out a few headlines and lead paragraphs and illustrate them. Once you have an assignment, keep in contact with the art director, because more assignments will arise. Because of timeliness and short deadlines, newspapers prefer to work with local artists, so check your local papers first.

Political cartoons spice up the editorial page. Newspapers rely on the editorial cartoonist to prod the public's interest in political events and to create some controversy. To get started as a political cartoonist, check with your local paper. Show the editor samples of caricatures, especially of local figures. Often cartoonists prefer to work on the local or regional level because they are not limited to national topics and political figures that everyone else is lampooning. Also try alternative newsweeklies, which are known for their irreverence and humor that deviate from the norm.

Newsletters give specialized information to limited audiences. They can convey club news or supply up-to-the-minute tips about the corporate scene. Though page layout and paste-up have become computerized, newsletters still require illustration and cartoons. They use mostly black-and-white work, because few can afford color. Carefully study the focus of several newsletters, and submit samples to those that fit your interests and style. Often your interest in a certain subject inspires "something extra" that clinches a sale.

For further information and for extra names and addresses, consult *Writer's Market 1989*, *The Newspaper and Allied Services Directory*, *Gale Directory of Publications*, *Editor & Publisher*, and *The Newsletter Directory*. The Society of Newspaper Design publishes an annual directory which summarizes news and trends of the past year.

***ADVOCATE NEWSPAPERS—Valley, Hartford, Hew Haven, Fairfield Country**, 87 School St., Hatfield MA 01038. (413)247-9301. Editor: Kitty Axelson. Weekly newspaper emphasizing progressive political, social, environmental issues for "mostly college- or graduate-school-educated readers who are active and progressive in outlook." Circ. 250,000. Accepts previously published material. Returns original artwork after publication. Sample copy for SASE with first-class postage.
Cartoons: Send query letter. "Although we generally do not run cartoons other than those we are already using, we're not opposed to seeing new ones."

AMERICAN MEDICAL NEWS, 535 N. Dearborn St., Chicago IL 60610. (312)645-4441. Editor: Dick Walt. Emphasizes news and opinions on developments, legislation and business in medicine. For physicians. Weekly newspaper. Circ. 315,000. Original artwork not returned after publication. Free sample copy.
Cartoons: Graphics Editor: Kevin O'Neil. Uses 1 cartoon/issue, all from freelancers. Receives "doz-

ens" of submissions/week from freelancers. Interested in medical themes; single panel. Prefers to see finished cartoons. SASE. Reports in 4 weeks. Usually buys first North American rights. Pays up to $100, b&w; on acceptance.
Illustrations: Contact: Kevin O'Neil, graphics editor. Number illustrations used/issue varies; number bought/issue from freelancers varies. Prefers realistic style on a medical theme. Works on assignment only. Send query letter with brochure showing art style. Samples returned by SASE. "We don't look at many portfolios, but portfolio should include original/final art, color and tear sheets." Usually buys first North American rights. Pays $250-350; "we have paid as much as $600 for single illustration." Pays on acceptance.
Tips: "I will look at any cartoons. I usually work with artists only from the Chicago area, because we need to see them in person. Portfolios should include tear sheets and brochures."

THE AMERICAN NEWSPAPER CARRIER, Box 15300, Winston-Salem NC 27113. Editor: Marilyn H. Rollins. A monthly newsletter for pre-teen and teenage newspaper carriers. Original artwork not returned after publication. Sample copy and art guidelines free for SASE.
Cartoons: Uses freelance and staff cartoons. Publishes 2-3 single panel and 1 multiple panel per issue. Prefers original b&w line drawings. Usually buys all rights. Pays $25 minimum on acceptance.
Illustrations: Buys 1-2 per issue, all freelance. Prefers small comical, b&w illustrations. Prefers pen & ink. Works on assignment only. Send query letter with tear sheets and photocopies to be kept on file. Samples not returned. Usually buys all rights. Pays $50 minimum on acceptance.

AMERICANS FOR LEGAL REFORM AND CITIZENS LEGAL MANUAL SERIES, Suite 300, Halt, 1319 F St. NW, Washington DC 20004. Communications Director: Richard Hébert. Magazine emphasizing self-help law, consumer education, and legal reform issues. Circ. 115,000. Accepts previously published material. Original artwork returned after publication.
Cartoons: Buys 1-2 cartoons/issue from freelancers. Prefers current legal reform issues as themes. Prefers single, double or multiple panel with or without gagline; b&w line drawings or b&w washes. Send query letter with samples of style to be kept on file. Samples not filed are not returned. Reports only if interested. Write to schedule an appointment to show a portfolio. Buys one-time rights, reprint rights or negotiates rights purchased. Negotiates payment.
Illustrations: Prefers legal reform issues as themes. Prefers pen & ink and computer illustration. Send query letter with resume, photocopies, halftones and photos. Samples not filed are not returned. Write to schedule an appointment to show a portfolio, which should include thumbnails, roughs, original/final art, final reproduction/product and b&w. Negotiates rights purchased. Pays $150 and up, b&w cover; on acceptance.
Tips: "We do not want to see serial cartoons. Material should be in good taste."

ANCHOR BAY BEACON, 51170 Washington, New Baltimore MI 48047. (313)725-4531. Executive Editor: Michael Eckert. Newspaper emphasizing local news for paid readership in one city, one village and three townships. Weekly. Circ. 8,000. Accepts previously published material. Original work returned after publication. Sample copy free for large manila SASE with 50¢ postage.
Cartoons: Number of cartoons purchased/issue from freelancers is open. No color. Send query letter with samples of style to be kept on file. Material filed returned only if requested. Reports only if interested. Buys reprint rights. Negotiates pay rate; pays on publication.
Illustrations: Works on assignment only. Send query letter to be kept on file. Write for appointment to show portfolio. Reports only if interested. Buys reprint rights. Negotiates pay rate; pays on publication.

APA MONITOR, American Psychological Association, 1200 17th St. NW, Washington DC 20036. (202)955-7690. Editor: Kathleen Fisher. Managing Editor: Laurie Denton. Monthly tabloid newspaper for psychologists and other behavioral scientists. 72-80 pages. Circ. 75,000.
Cartoons: Buys 1-2 b&w cartoons/month from freelancers. Pays $50 on acceptance.
Illustrations: Buys 2-5 illustrations/month from freelancers. Uses 30 illustrations/year on current events and feature articles in behavioral sciences/mental health area. Washington area artists preferred. Works on assignment only. Query with resume, tear sheets and photocopies. Sample copy $3. SASE. To show a portfolio, mail appropriate materials or call to schedule an appointment; portfolio should include original/final art, final reproduction/product. Original artwork returned after publication, if requested. Buys first North American serial rights. Pays $200, b&w cover and inside; on publication.
Tips: "Be creative, think about topics relevant to psychology. I look for ability to develop simple, clean graphics to complement abstract, complex ideas."

***ARIZONA REPUBLIC**, 120 E. Van Buren, Phoenix AZ 85001. (602)271-8291. Art Director: Patti Valdez. General audience. Daily. Original artwork returned after publication.
Illustrations: Works on assignment with local artists. Send query letter with brochure, business card

and samples to be kept on file. Prefers Photostats, photographs or slides as samples. Samples not kept on file are returned by SASE. Call for appointment to show portfolio. Buys first rights or one-time rights; pays on publication.

***ASSOCIATED MEDIA CORPORATION**, 86 Viaduct Rd., Stamford CT 06907. Director of Design: Rosemarie Sunden. Publishes bi-monthly business magazine. Circ. 40,000. Accepts previously published material. Returns original artwork to the artist after publication. Sample copy for SASE with first-class postage. Art guidelines available.
Cartoons: Buys 1 cartoon/issue from freelancers. Buys 26 cartoons/year from freelancers. Prefers editorial or political cartoons, caricatures and humorous illustrations. Prefers local issues; "editorial guidance given." Prefers single panel with gagline; b&w line drawings. Prefers 8x10". Send query letter with samples of style and finished cartoons. Samples are filed. Samples not filed are not returned. Reports back only if interested. Buys one-time rights. Pays $50, b&w; $100, color; on publication.
Illustrations: Prefers line art and spot color. Prefers pen & ink, then markers and calligraphy. Works on assignment only. Send query letter with resume and samples. Samples are filed. Samples not filed are not returned. Reports back only if interested. Write to schedule an appointment to show a portfolio, which should include final reproduction/product, Photostats, printed samples, photocopies of b&w work. Buys first rights. Pays $50, b&w; $100, color, cover; $50, b&w, inside; on publication.
Tips: "I want to see printed examples of work. I don't need to see comps, ideas or mechanical."

BALLS AND STRIKES NEWSPAPER, 2801 N.E. 50th St., Oklahoma City OK 73111. (405)424-5266. Communications Director: Bill Plummer III. Official publication of the amateur softball association. Emphasizes amateur softball for "the more than 30 million people who play amateur softball; they come from all walks of life and hold varied jobs." Published 8 times/year. Circ. 275,000. Previously published material OK. Original work returned after publication. Free sample copy available.
Illustrations: Uses 2-4 illustrations/issue. No drug or alcohol themes. Works on assignment only. Send query letter with resume and business card to be kept on file. Samples returned. Reports in 3 days. Buys all rights. Pays on publication.

BARTER COMMUNIQUE, Box 2527, Sarasota FL 33578. (813)349-3300. Art Director: Robert J. Murley. Concerns bartering; for radio, TV stations, newspapers, magazines, travel and ad agencies. Quarterly tabloid. Circ. 50,000.
Cartoons: Buys 5/issue on barter situations. Send roughs. Pays $5, b&w; on publication.
Illustrations: Query with samples. SASE. Reports in 2 weeks. Pays $5, b&w; on publication.
Tips: Looks for "uniqueness" in reviewing samples.

BLACK VOICE NEWS, Box 1581, Riverside CA 92502. (714)889-0506 or 682-6111. Contact: Hardy Brown, Jr. Newspaper emphasizing general topics for "the black community with various backgrounds, and Hispanics and whites who are in tune with that community." Weekly. Circ. 5,000. Sample copy free for SASE.
Cartoons: Prefers political, historic and topical themes. Accepts single, double or multiple panel with or without gagline; b&w line drawings. Send query letter with samples of style to be kept on file. Material not filed is returned by SASE. Reports back only if interested. Write for appointment to show portfolio. Buys one-time or reprint rights; pays on publication.
Illustrations: Send query letter with samples to be kept on file; write for appointment to show portfolio. Samples not filed are returned by SASE. Reports back only if interested. Buys one-time or reprint rights; pays on publication.

BOOKPLATES IN THE NEWS, Apt. F, 605 N. Stoneman Ave., Alhambra CA 91801. (213)283-1936. Director: Audrey Spencer Arellanes. Emphasizes bookplates for those who use bookplates whether individuals or institutions, those who collect them, artists who design them, art historians, genealogists, historians, antiquarian booktrade and others for tracing provenance of a volume; also publishes yearbook annually. Quarterly. Circ. 250. Original work returned after publication. Previously published material OK "on occasion, usually from foreign publications." Sample copy $5; art guidelines for SASE with postage for 3 ounces.
Illustrations: Illustrations are bookplates. "Appearance of work in our publications should produce requests for bookplate commissions." Send query letter and finished art. Reports in 3 weeks. No payment.
Tips: "We only publish bookplates, those marks of ownership used by individuals and institutions. Some artists and owners furnish 250 original prints of their bookplate to be tipped-in quarterly. Membership is international; this is reflected in artwork from around the world."

THE BOSTON PHOENIX, 126 Brookline Ave., Boston MA 02215. (617)536-5390. Design Director: Cleo Leontis. Weekly. Circ. 150,000. Original work returned after publication by SASE. Sample copy

$3.50; send requests for sample copy to circulation department.
Illustrations: Uses 2-8 b&w illustrations/issue, occasional color; buys all from freelancers. On assignment only. Send samples of style (no originals) and resume to be kept on file for possible future assignments. Call for appointment. Buys one-time rights. Pays on publication.

THE BREAD RAPPER, 2103 Noyes, Evanston IL 60201. Editor-in-Chief: Laurie Lawlor. Concerns banking services and involvement of bank with community; received with checking account statement. Photocopied submissions OK. Sample copy and artist's guidelines with SASE.
Cartoons: Buys 1 cartoon/issue on banking; single panel with gagline. No negative bank slants (bank robberies, etc.), please. Mail art. SASE. Reports within 8 weeks. Buys all rights. Pays $20 minimum, b&w line drawings and washes; on publication.

***BRUM BEAT**, Box 944, Birmingham B16 8UT England. (021)454-7020. Editor: Jim Simpson. Newspaper emphasizing music and entertainment for ages 16 to 35 interested in music and music-related activities. Monthly. Circ. 40,000. Accepts previously published material. Original artwork returned after publication. Sample copy for SASE with 31 pence postage.
Cartoons: Currently buys no cartoons but will consider music-related ones. Send samples of style to be kept on file. Material not kept on file is returned by SASE. Reports only if interested. Buys one-time rights. Payment varied.
Illustrations; Buys few illustrations. Prefers music-related themes. Send samples. Samples not filed are returned by SASE. Reports only if interested. Pays on publication.

BUILDING BRIEFS, Dan Burch Associates, 2338 Frankfort Ave., Louisville KY 40206. (502)895-4881. Program Manager: Sharon Hall. Newsletter. Emphasizes design/build and conventional methods of construction for commercial and industrial buildings, plus other topics such as landscaping, security, and energy-saving ideas. Directed to potential clients of a building contractor in the nonresidential market, company presidents, board members and managerial personnel who will construct or renovate their buildings. Bimonthly. Circ. 25,000+. Original artwork returned after publication. Sample copy available.
Cartoons: Buys 1 cartoon/issue from freelancers. Prefers themes related to construction; light humor, simple line art. Prefers single panel with gagline; b&w line drawings. Send query letter with finished cartoons to be kept on file. Material not kept on file is returned. Reports only if interested. Buys one-time rights. Pays $50, b&w; on publication.
Tips: "Spend a little time researching the commercial building industry. Talk to a building contractor. Two industry publications where more can be learned are *Metal Construction News* and *Metal Building Review*."

THE BURLINGTON LOOK, Burlington Industries, Box 21207, Greensboro NC 27420. (919)379-2339. Publications Editor: Melissa Staples. Tabloid. Emphasizes textiles and home furnishings for all domestic employees of Burlington Industries plus opinion leaders in the plant communities. Published 6 times/year. Circ. 45,000. Accepts previously published material and simultaneous submissions. Original artwork not returned after publication unless requested. Sample copy for SASE.
Illustrations: Currently uses 1-2 illustrations/issue—"works with local artists mostly"; buys all from freelancers. Themes/styles vary depending on subject matter. Works on assignment only. Send query letter with resume, business card, samples and tear sheets to be kept on file. Prefers Photostats or photographs as samples; "I'd rather not have original work for fear it may be damaged or get lost." Samples not kept on file are returned only if requested. Reports within 2 weeks. Negotiates rights purchased. Pays $25-150; on acceptance.
Tips: "Looking for illustrators with the creativity to be able to illustrate and visually communicate various story concepts."

CARTOON WORLD, Box 30367, Lincoln NE 68503. (112)435-3191. Editor/Publisher: George Hartman. Newsletter "slanted to amateur and professional freelance cartoonists." Monthly. Circ. 300. Accepts previously published material. Returns original artwork after publication. Sample copy $5; art guidelines available.
Cartoons: Does not want individual cartoons; seeks articles on cartooning, illustrated with cartoons, that will benefit other cartoonists. Topics as how to cartoon, how to create ideas, cartoon business plans, hints and markets. Send query letter with originals only. Reports within 10 days. Material will not be returned nor considered for publication without return postage. To show a portfolio, mail appropriate materials, which should include final reproduction/product. Buys reprint rights. Pays $5/8½x11" page, on acceptance.
Tips: "Anything sent to us must be by professionals who had lots of experience on cartooning or gagwriting."

THE CHRISTIAN SCIENCE MONITOR, 1 Norway St., Boston MA 02115. (617)450-2361. Art Director: Heidi B. Mack. Newspaper emphasizing analytical reporting of current events; diverse features and news features for well-educated, well-informed readers in all fields—specifically politicians, educators, business people. Daily. Circ. 200,000. Original artwork returned after 3 months. Sample copy and art guidelines available.
Illustrations: Buys 1-2 illustrations/week from freelancers. Prefers editorial ("op-ed") conceptual themes; line, wash or scratchboard. Works on assignment only. Send samples to be filed. Samples should be 8½x11" photocopies; no originals. Samples not returned. Reports only if interested. Buys first rights. Pays $100-200, b&w; on publication.

THE CHRONICLE OF HIGHER EDUCATION, Suite 700, 1255 23rd St. NW, Washington DC 20037. (202)466-1035. Art Director: Peter Stafford. Emphasizes all aspects of higher education for college and university administrators, professors, students and staff. Weekly. Circ. 75,000. Sample copy available.
Cartoons: Uses approximately 30 cartoons/year. Prefers higher education related themes, i.e., sports, high cost of tuition, student loans, energy conservation on campus. Prefers single panel, with gagline; b&w line drawings or b&w washes. Send query letter with samples of style to be kept on file. Material not kept on file is returned only if requested. Reports only if interested. Buys one-time rights. Pays on publication.
Illustrations: Buys 1 illustration/week from freelancers. Uses 1 illustration/issue; buys all from freelancers. Uses a variety of styles, depending on the tone of the story. Works on assignment only. Send query letter with Photostats or good quality photocopy for line work; photographs or slides for halftone work, business card and tear sheets to be kept on file. Samples are returned only if requested. Reports only if interested. Buys one-time rights. Pays $100 and up depending on size, b&w, inside. Pays on publication.

CITROEN CAR CLUB NEWSLETTER,350 Hulbe Rd., Boise ID 83705. Editor: Karl Petersen. Emphasizing Citroen, Panhard and related cars, parts and international activities. Monthly. Circ. 1,200. Accepts previously published material. Original artwork returned after publication if requested. Art guidelines not available.
Cartoons: Send query letter with samples of style and finished cartoons. Samples are filed. Samples not filed are returned if requested. Reports back within 2 weeks. No payment.
Illustrations: Send query letter. Samples are filed. Samples not filed are returned if requested. Reports back within 2 weeks. Write to schedule an appointment to show a portfolio. No payment.
Tips "We have a limited forum of enthusiasts. We will give submissions international exposure at no cost to artist. We have done one-artist, seven illustration duotone calendar, for example, for Kojiro Imamura, Japan."

COA REVIEW: THE NEWSLETTER ABOUT CHILDREN OF ALCOHOLICS, Box 190, Rutherford NJ 07070. (201)777-2277. Managing Directors: Thomas W. Perrin or Janice A. Treggett. Bimonthly newsletter. Emphasizes children of alcoholics. Also covers co-dependency. "Articles appeal to the professional therapist and the lay person." Circ. 2,000. Sample copy $1.
Cartoons: "I have not been able to find any cartoonists as of yet." Prefers cartoons that lampoon psychologists or psychiatrists and the foibles of the client and aspects of his personality." Prefers single panel with gagline; b&w line drawings. Send roughs. Samples are filed. Samples not filed are returned. Reports back within 6 months. "If you don't hear from me after 6 months, forget it." Buys first rights. Pays $25, b&w; on publication.
Illustrations: Prefers pen & ink line drawings about alcoholic disorders. Works on assignment only. Send query letter with resume and samples. Samples are filed. Samples not filed are returned. Reports back within 6 months. To show a portfolio, mail tear sheets and photocopies. Buys first rights. Pays $75, b&w, cover; $25 for interior illustration. Pays on publication.
Tips: "Also interested in cover art for our catalog. We also publish books. If an artist can put together a catalog of his work, we will consider publishing a book."

THE COMDEX SHOW DAILY, 300 1st Ave., Needham MA 02194. (617)449-6600. Managing Editor: Ann Zennic. Tabloid. Emphasizes computers and computer-related products for attendees and exhibitors at the U.S. Comdex Shows. Seasonal: Fall, Spring. Circ. 40,000. Accepts previously published material. Original artwork returned after publication if requested. Sample copy free for SASE; art guidelines available.
Cartoons: Buys 50-100 cartoons/issue from freelancers; buys 300-400/year from freelancers. "Computer graphics used in cartoon illustration. Application ties in well as our newspaper is read by people in the computer industry." Wants anything related to computers, trade shows, Las Vegas, or Atlanta. Prefers single panel with or without gagline; b&w line drawings. Send query letter with roughs or finished cartoons to be kept on file. Material not filed is returned by SASE only if requested. Reports within sev-

eral weeks. Buys one-time rights. Pays $18; on acceptance.
Illustrations: Themes: computers/trade shows/computer related products. Humorous and cartoon-style illustrations used once a year. Works on assignment only. Send query letter with tear sheets, Photostats, photocopies, slides and photographs to be kept on file. Samples returned by SASE only if requested. Reports within several weeks only if interested. Call or write to schedule an appointment to show a portfolio, which should include final reproduction/product, tear sheets and Photostats. Buys one-time rights. Pays $50-100, b&w; on acceptance.

COMPUTERWORLD FOCUS, 375 Cochituate Rd., Framingham MA 01701. (617)879-0700. Art Director: Tom Monahan. Tabloid. Emphasizes news and products relating to the computer field. Monthly. Returns original artwork after publication.
Illustrations: Buys 2 illustrations/week. Themes depend on the storyline. Works on assignment only. Send query letter with brochure and photocopies or Photostats to be kept on file. Reports back only if interested. Buys first rights. To show portfolio, mail appropriate materials or call to schedule an appointment; portfolio should include original/final art, final reproduction/product, color, Photostats and b&w. Pays $200, b&w and $250-600 color, inside; on acceptance.

CONNECTICUT TRAVELER, 2276 Whitney Ave., Hamden CT 06518. (203)281-7505. Managing Director of Publications: Elke P. Martin. Newspaper. Estab. 1983. Emphasizes automobile travel, safety and maintenance, national and international travel and regional events (New England) for AAA members. Monthly. Circ. 155,000. Accepts previously published material. Returns original artwork after publication. Sample copy free for SASE; art guidelines available.
Illustrations: Buys b&w illustrations and 4-color cover/issue.
Cartoons: Buys 1 cartoon/issue from freelancers. Prefers single panel with gagline; b&w line drawings; b&w washes. Send query letter with samples of style to be kept on file. Reports within 2 weeks. Buys reprint rights or negotiates rights purchased. Pays on acceptance.

THE CONSTANTIAN, 123 Orr Rd., Pittsburgh PA 15241. (412)831-8750. Editor: Randall J. Dicks. "We (Constantian Society) are monarchists and royalists, interested in monarchy as a political system and royalty as persons and personalities." Bimonthly newsletter. Circ. 500. Previously published work OK. Sample copy for SASE with postage for 3 ounces.
Cartoons: "We have not used many cartoons but we are certainly willing to consider them. We take our subject seriously, but there is room for humor. It is best to write us about the idea first and send samples." Send query letter with resume and samples. To show a portfolio, mail appropriate materials. SASE. Reports within 1 month. Buys various rights. Pays $5-10, b&w line drawings; on acceptance or publication.
Illustrations: "We use a lot of decorative drawings and work which relate to our subject matter (heraldic items of different nationalities, coats of arms, monograms, etc.)." We have a number of new projects and publications in mind, and may need cover art and other illustrations for booklets or brochures. SASE. Reports within 1 month. Rights purchased vary. Pays $10 and up, b&w line drawings; on acceptance or publication.
Tips: "Now we are using a MacIntosh computer for our journal—it has new look, and there are changes in format. Artists should have some understanding of our subject—monarchy and royalty."

CONSTRUCTION SUPERVISION & SAFETY LETTER, 24 Rope Ferry Rd., Waterford CT 06386. (203)442-4365. Editor: DeLoris Lidestri. Emphasizes construction supervision for supervisors who work with their crews. Covers bricklayers, carpenters, electricians, painters, plasterers, plumbers and building laborers. Semimonthly. Circ. 3,700. Original artwork not returned after publication. Free sample copy.
Cartoons: Uses 1-3 cartoons/issue which are done by freelancers. Receives 5-7 submissions/week from freelancers. Uses "situations that deal with supervision in construction. Cartoons that depict both men and women as workers and/or supervisors needed. No sexist material, please." Format: single panel, b&w line drawings with gagline. Prefers to see finished cartoons. SASE. Reports in 2 weeks. Buys all rights. Pays $15 on acceptance.
Tips: "Send cartoons that deal with supervision to me. But any to do with construction safety send to Winifred Bonney, editor. CL has expanded from four pages to eight pages. We have a four-page safety section now. We want to see cartoons that do no harm to anyone gentle humor is fine. We do not want to see sexism or racism."

***CRAFTERS' LINK**, 59999 Myrtle Rd., South Bend IN 46614. (219)232-0939. Editor: Joanne Hill. Newsletter published 10 times/year emphasizing marketing of crafts "for the crafter who is new to the business or not fully developed as a business person." Circ. 300. Accepts previously published material. Returns original artwork after publication. Sample copy for postage for two ounces. Art guidelines

for SASE with first-class postage.
Cartoons: Buys 10-15 cartoons/year from free freelancers. Prefers gag cartoons and humorous illustrations with crafts or craft sales themes (festivals, mall shows). Prefers single panel with gagline; b&w line drawings. "Columns are 2¼ wide, generally use 3-4" for cartoon. Artwork can be reduced if proportioned appropriately." Send query letter with samples of style and roughs. Samples are filed. Samples not filed are returned by SASE only if requested. Reports back within 1 month. Negotiates rights purchased. Pays $10, b&w; on acceptance.
Illustrations: Buys 6-30 illustrations/year from freelancers. Prefers b&w line art—drawings pertaining to crafts and craft marketing theme. Send query letter with samples. Samples are filed. Samples not filed are returned by SASE. Reports back within 1 month. Portfolio should include roughs and tear sheets. Negotiates rights purchased. Pays $10, b&w; on acceptance.
Tips: "Interested in the promotion of craft marketing—need market scenes in artwork (best to query our needs). Cartoons easier—anything that will help crafter laugh at him/herself and the problems of marketing crafts. We do not want crafts as finished products or 'how-to': we write about marketing."

THE CRANSTON MIRROR, 250 Auburn St., Cranston RI 02910. (401)467-7474. Contact: Malcolm L. Daniels. Weekly newspaper. Circ. 10,000. Original artwork returned after publication. Prefers local artists. Also uses artists for layout, illustration, technical art, paste-up, lettering and retouching. Pays $175, booklet; $15-75, illustrations.
Cartoons: Uses 2 cartoons/issue; buys 1 or none/issue from freelancers. Receives 3-4 submissions/week from freelancers. Interested in local editorial subjects. Call for interview to show portfolio (except July and August). Prefers to see finished cartoons. Reports in 1 week. Pays $20, b&w.
Illustrations: Uses 2-4 illustrations/issue; buys 1-2/issue from freelancers. Send resume and photocopies to be kept on file for future assignments. Reports in 1 week. Call or write to schedule an appointment to show a portfolio, which should include original/final art and Photostats. Pays $30-50, b&w, cover; $25, b&w, inside; on publication.
Tips: Especially looks for "unique idea, quality workmanship and regard to detail. Ideas, however, are paramount. Be neat. Have material ready and know what you want to say for a portfolio review."

CYCLE NEWS, Box 498, Long Beach CA 90801. (213)427-7433. Editor: Jack Mangus. For the motorcycle enthusiast. Weekly newspaper. Circ. 75,000. Previously published work OK. Returns originals to artist after publication. Sample copy available. Art guidelines not available.
Cartoons: Buys 0-2 cartoons/issue. Send query letter with finished cartoons and SASE. Reports back only if interested. Negotiates payment and rights purchased. Pays on publication.
Illustrations: Buys varying number of illustrations/issue. Works on assignment only. Send query letter with photocopies and SASE. Reports only if interested. Negotiates payment and rights purchased. Pays on publication.

***THE EAST HARTFORD GAZETTE**, 54 Connecticut Blvd., East Hartford CT 06108. Editor: Bill Doak. Weekly newspaper emphasizing local news, politics, development. "A community newspaper with a hometown feel." Circ. 21,000. Accepts previously published material. Returns original artwork after publication. Sample copy available.
Cartoons: Prefers editorial or political cartoons and humorous illustrations on local issues. Prefers single panel with gagline; b&w line drawings, 5x7, 8x10. Send query letter with finished cartoons. Samples not filed are returned only if requested.

***EASY READER**, Box 726, 1233 Hermosa Ave., Hermosa Beach CA 90254. (213)372-4611. Editor: George Wiley. Weekly newspaper emphasizing local, regional and national news typical of the alternative press. "We concentrate largely on local issues of interest to readers in the South Bay area of Los Angeles. But we also use national material, particularly with an aggressive political slant. We want high-impact art. No Happy Faces." Circ. 60,000. Accepts previously published material sometimes. Returns original artwork to the artist after publication. Sample copy for SASE with first-class postage.
Cartoons: Occasionally buys cartoons from freelancers. Prefers editorial or political cartoons and caricatures. Style should be biting, no-holds-barred, "but no blue material.". Prefers b&w line drawings and b&w washes, 8½x11. Send query letter with samples of style, roughs and finished cartoons. Samples are filed. Samples not filed are returned by SASE. Reports back within 3 weeks. Buys first rights or one-time rights. Pays $25, b&w; $50, color; on publication. Color seldom used.
Illustrations: Buys 20 or more cover illustrations/year from freelancers. Works on assignment only. Send query letter with brochure, resume and samples. Samples are filed. Samples not filed are returned by SASE. Reports back within 3 weeks with SASE. Call to schedule an appointment to show a portfolio. Buys first rights or one-time rights. Pays $100, b&w; $150, color, cover; on publication.
Tips: "Nothing cute, nothing sentimental, nothing folksy—we want well-conceived artwork that concisely and simply makes its point. Irreverence is okay, even encouraged, as is caricature. A sense of humor helps."

THE ECO-HUMANE LETTER, The International Ecology Society, 1471 Barclay St., St. Paul MN 55106-1405. (612)774-4971. Editor: R.J.F. Kramer. Periodic newsletter. Emphasizes animals/environment. Features "select article reprints, action alerts, general data for those interested in the protection of animals and nature." Circ. 6,000. Accepts previously published material. Sample copy for SASE with first-class postage.
Cartoons: Prefers gag cartoons, editorial or political cartoons, caricatures and humorous illustrations. Prefers single panel, double panel, multi-panel with or without gagline; b&w line drawings and b&w washes. Prefers any size if readable. Send query letter with samples of style, roughs and finished cartoons. Samples are not filed. Samples are not returned. Reports back only if interested. Buys all rights. Pays $10, b&w; on publication.
Illustrations: Prefers line art. Send query letter or resume. Samples are not filed. Samples are not returned. Reports back only if interested. To show a portfolio, mail appropriate materials. Buys all rights. Pays $10, b&w, cover; $10, b&w, inside; on publication.
Tips: "Cover all bases. Volunteer for good causes."

***FIGHTING WOMAN NEWS**, Box 1459, Grand Central Station, New York NY 10163. Art Director: Muskat Buckby. Emphasizes women's martial arts for adult women actively practicing some form of martial art; 90% college graduates. Quarterly. Circ. 5,000. Accepts previously published material, "but we must be told about the previous publication." Sample copy $3.50; art guidelines for SASE with postage for two ounces.
Cartoons: Buys 0-1 cartoon/issue from freelancers. Cartoon format open; no color. Send query letter with samples of style to be kept on file. Material not filed is returned by SASE. Reports as soon as possible. Buys one-time rights. Pays in copies.
Illustrations: Buys 3-4 illustrations/issue from freelancers. "No woman black-belt beating up men or 'sexy' themes—done to death!" Send query letter with tear sheets and Photostats to be kept on file. Samples not filed are returned by SASE. Reports as soon as possible. Buys one-time rights. Pays $10, b&w, cover; in copies, b&w, inside; on publication.
Tips: "What works best for us, is to have a few samples on file plus a rough idea of the artist's interest and availability. Then we can send out stuff that needs an illustrations and ask if she can do it. Since *FWN* is basically a copy-paying market, we realize that people can't always be available when we need them."

***FOR PARENTS**, 3011 Schoolview Rd., Eden NY 14057. Editor: Carolyn Shadle. Bimonthly newsletter emphasizing parent-child communication for parents of school-age children interested in positive parenting and moral development. Circ. 4,000. Accepts previously published material. Sample copy for SASE with first-class postage.
Cartoons: Buys 2 cartoons/year from freelancers. Prefers editorial or political cartoons and humorous illustrations with sex education, conflict, communication themes. Prefers single panel with gagline; b&w line drawings and b&w washes, 2x2. Send query letter with samples of style, roughs or finished cartoons. Samples are filed. Samples not filed are not returned. Reports back only if interested. Negotiates rights purchased. Pays $15, b&w; on publication.
Illustrations: Buys 2 illustrations/year from freelancers. Prefers sex education, conflict, communication themes. Send query letter with brochure showing art style. Samples are filed. Reports back only if interested. To show a portfolio, mail thumbnails, roughs, original/final art, tear sheets, b&w. Pays $15, b&w; on publication.
Tips: "Don't call. Send samples or queries."

THE FOREMAN'S LETTER, 24 Rope Ferry Rd., Waterford CT 06386. (203)442-4365. Editor: Carl Thunberg. For industrial supervisors.
Cartoons: Usually uses 1 cartoon/issue; may buy up to 2/issue from freelancers. Receives 20 submissions/week from freelancers. Interested in "supervisor-worker relations; avoid sexism and other discriminatory situations." Prefers single panel, finished cartoons. Send query letter with brochure showing art style. SASE. Reports in 1 week. To show a portfolio, mail Photostats. Buys all rights. Pays $15-20; on acceptance.

FREEWAY, Box 632, Glen Ellyn IL 60138. (312)668-6000. Designer: Mardelle Ayers. Sunday School paper emphasizing Christian living for high school and college age teens from a conservative, evangelical Christian upbringing. Published 4 quarters a year, 13 issues per quarter. Circ. 60,000. Accepts previously published material. Sample copy free for SASE with first-class postage.
Cartoons: Buys 4-5 cartoons/quarter. Prefers any style or theme that appeals to teens. Prefers commissioned artwork for specific articles; b&w line drawings or b&w washes. Send query letter with samples. Material not kept on file is returned by SASE. Reports within 4 weeks. Buys first rights. Pays $15-20, b&w.

Illustrations: Buys 1-3 illustrations/issue from freelancers. Works on assignment only. Prefers any theme or style appealing to teens. Send query letter with resume, Photostats and photocopies. Samples not filed are returned by SASE if requested. Reports only if interested. To show a portfolio, mail Photostats and b&w photos. Pays $15-150.
Tips: Looks for "good contrast and composition along with a contemporary look in technique."

***THE GRAPEVINE WEEKLY**, 108 S. Albany St., Ithaca NY 14850. (607)272-3470. Managing Editor: Molly Keene. "We are an alternative newsweekly that covers the news, issues, people, arts and entertainment of Tompkins County, N.Y." Weekly. Circ. 18,000. Original artwork is returned after publication. Sample copies $.50.
Cartoons: Cartoon editor: Linda McCandless. Buys 3 cartoons/issue from freelancers. Buys 150 cartoons/year from freelancers. Prefers single or multiple panel; b&w line drawings. Send query letter with samples of style. Samples are filed. Samples not filed are returned by SASE. Reports back within 4 weeks. Buys first rights. Pays $5-10, b&w.
Illustrations: Buys 20 illustrations/issue from freelancers. Works on assignment only. Send query letter with tear sheets. Samples are filed. Reports back within 4 weeks. Call or write to schedule an appointment to show a portfolio, which should include thumbnails, tear sheets and b&w. Buys first rights. Pays $10-50, b&w, cover; $10-15, b&w inside; on publication.
Tips: "The artist should be from Tompkins County. We look for simple, line illustrations that reproduce cleanly without losing their intended shading. No intricate shading."

GUARDIAN,33 W. 17th ST., New York NY 10011. (212)691-0404. Photo/Graphics Editor: Anthony Parker. Independent radical newspaper with national and international news and cultural reviews for nonsectarian leftists and activists. Weekly. Circ. 20,000. Accepts previously published material. Original artwork returned by SASE after publication. Sample copy available; art guidelines free for SASE.
Cartoons: Buys 7 cartoons/issue from freelancers. Prefers b&w, pen & ink, scratch board; progressive themes. Prefers single, double or multiple panel; b&w line drawings. Send query letter with sample of style not larger than 8½x11" to be kept on file. Material not filed is returned by SASE. Reports only if interested. Write for appointment to show portfolio. Negotiates rights purchased. Pays $15, b&w; on publication.
Illustrations: Buys 3 illustrations/issue from freelancers. "We need left-wing political themes." Themes: progressive politics, issues. Send query letter and photocopies not larger than 8½x11" to be kept on file. Samples not filed are returned by SASE. Reports only if interested. To show a portfolio, mail original/final art, tear sheets, Photostats, photographs and b&w. Negotiates rights purchased. Pays $15, b&w, cover, inside; on publication.

HIGH COUNTRY NEWS, Box 1090, Paonia CO 81428. (303)527-4898. Editor: Betsy Marston. Emphasizes economic and environmental issues, Rocky Mountain regional pieces for national audience, all ages, occupations. Biweekly. Circ. 6,500. Accepts previously published material and simultaneous submissions. Original artwork returned after publication if accompanied by postage.
Illustrations: Uses 5 illustrations/issue; buys 3 illustrations/issue from freelancers. Send query letter with samples and/or tear sheets to be kept on file. Prefers photocopies as samples. Samples not kept on file are returned by SASE. Reports within 1 month. Buys one-time rights. Pays after publication.

***THE HOMESTEADER**, Oxford NY 13830. Editor: Richard Fahey. Bimonthly newsletter emphasizing Christian homesteading, handtools, nature for fairly well-educated Christians changing their lives from urban to country ways. Circ. 10,000. Accepts previously published material. Returns original artwork after publication if requested. Sample copy for SASE with first-class postage.
Illustrations: Buys 5 illustrations/issue from freelancers. Prefers line art. Works on assignment "mostly." Send query letter brochure showing art style or samples. Samples are filed. Samples not filed are returned by SASE. Reports back within several days. To show a portfolio, mail appropriate materials. Buys one-time rights or all rights. Pays $20, b&w; on publication.
Tips: Artist "should have an interest in nature, handtools, farm animals, and family."

***HOOT, Columbus' Cartoon Newspaper**, Box 28235, Columbus OH 43228. Editor: Irv Oslin. Estab. 1987. "A biweekly all-cartoon newspaper featuring nationally-syndicated cartoons (and internationally for that matter). Our appeal is to mature folks with a keen sense of humor." Circ. 15,000. Accepts previously published material. Returns original artwork after publication with SASE. Sample copy for SASE with postage for two ounces. Finds most artists through references/word-of-mouth and samples received through the mail.
Cartoons: Buys 3-4 cartoons/issue from freelancers. Prefers gag cartoons and editorial or political cartoons. Interested in the "off-beat. We're talking Larson (Far Side) or Toles in the editorial genre." Prefers single panel or multiple panel with or without gagline; b&w line drawings and b&w washes. Send

roughs and finished cartoons. Samples are filed. Samples not filed are returned by SASE. Reports back within weeks. Buys one-time rights. Pays $5-10, b&w; on publication.
Tips: "*Hoot* would like nothing better than to be the springboard for the next Gary Larson. We're looking to expose cartoonists who are offbeat and drifting somewhere along the fringe of the mainstream."

***INTENSIVE CARING UNLIMITED**, 910 Bent Lane, Philadelphia PA 19118. (215)233-4723. Editor-in-chief: Lenette Moses. Bimonthly newsletter. "Our publication provides support and information for parents whose children are premature or high-risk, those with handicaps or medical problems, or parents going through high-risk pregnancy." Circ. 3,000. Accepts previously published material. Returns original artwork after publication. Sample copy and art guidelines available.
Cartoons: Uses 1 cartoon/issue from freelancers. Prefers humorous illustrations. Interested in family issues. Prefers single panel with or without gagline; b&w line drawings, 4x2. Call editor, or send query letter with samples of style. Samples are filed. Samples not filed are returned. Reports back within 3 weeks.
Illustrations: Uses 12 illustrations/issue from freelancers. Prefers line art. Call editor, or send query letter with samples. Samples are filed. Samples not filed are returned if requested. Reports back within 3 weeks.
Tips: "As a non-profit organization, we are not able to pay for artwork. However, artists may retain all rights. We will use almost any quality line drawing of family topics, offering an artist exposure to our circulation of 3,000. Chance of acceptance is increased when artist contacts editor for list of upcoming article topics."

***JAPAN ECONOMIC SURVEY**, published by Japan Economic Institute of America, Inc., Suite 211, 1000 Connecticut Ave. NW, Washington DC 20036. Editor: Barbara P. Wanner. Newsletter emphasizing US-Japan economic and political issues/developments for opinionmakers in government, business and academia. Monthly. Circ. 3,500. Accepts previously published material. Original artwork usually returned after publication. Sample copy available.
Cartoons: Buys 3-4 cartoons/year from freelancers. Prefers single panel without gagline; b&w line drawings. Send query letter with samples of style to be kept on file. Reports only if interested. Buys one-time rights. Payment varies.
Illustrations: Buys 3-4 illustrations/year from freelancers. Works on assignment only. Send query letter with samples. Samples not filed are not returned. Reports only if interested. Write to schedule an appointment to show a portfolio. Buys one-time rights. Pays on acceptance.

***JEWISH VEGETARIAN SOCIETY NEWSLETTER**, Box 5722, Baltimore MD 21208-0722. (301)486-4948. Chairman: Izak Luchinsky. Quarterly newsletter emphasizing flesh-free diet based on Old Testament precepts for Jewish vegetarians. Circ. 1,300.
Illustrations: Works on assignment only. Send resume and samples. Samples are not filed. Reports back within 30 days. To show a portfolio, mail thumbnails, roughs, original/final art, tear sheets, final reproduction/product. Photostats, photographs, b&w and color. Buys one-time rights. Payment is negotiable. Pays on publication.

JEWS FOR JESUS NEWSLETTER, 60 Haight St., San Francisco CA 94102. (415)864-2600. Editor: Mrs. Ceil Rosen. Emphasizes Christian witness to Jews, evangelical Christian thought and humor to teach Christian truth for ministers and lay leaders who are evangelical, yet interested in Jews and Jewish customs. Monthly newsletter. Receives 6 cartoons and 12 illustrations/month from freelance artists. Simultaneous submissions OK. Original work not returned after publication. Free sample copy for SASE.
Illustrations: Uses 5-6 illustrations/issue; buys some from freelancers. Interested in religious humor. Send copies of finished art only. Samples returned by SASE. Reports in 6 weeks. Buys first rights or negotiates. Pays $25-100, cover and inside, color washes; $10-100 inside, b&w; on acceptance.
Tips: There is a trend toward "large evangelical magazines using more humor that helps us laugh at ourselves. Artists should show that they have an understanding of our beliefs and respect them."

THE JOURNAL, Addiction Research Foundation, 33 Russell St., Toronto, Ontario M5S 2S1 Canada. (416)595-6053. Editor: Anne MacLennan. Concerns drug and alcohol research, treatment, prevention and education. Monthly. Circ. 26,000. Free sample copy and guidelines.
Cartoons: Uses cartoons occasionally; buys 1/month from freelancers. Receives 1 submission/month from freelancers. Interested in "themes relating to alcohol and other drug use." Prefers finished cartoons. Pays from $30, 3x5 minimum cartoons; on publication.
Illustrations: Buys 1 illustration/month from freelancers. Send photocopies. Write to schedule an appointment to show a portfolio, which should include roughs and b&w. Pays $200 b&w, cover and inside; on publication.

THE JOURNAL NEWSPAPERS, The Journal, Springfield VA 22159. (703)750-8779. Entertainment Editor: Buzz McClain. Emphasizes daily news and features. Daily. Circ. 160,000. Accepts previously published material. Original artwork returned after publication.
Illustrations: Buys a few illustrations from freelancers. Works on assignment only. Send query letter with resume and tear sheets. Samples not filed are returned only if requested. Reports only if interested. Call to schedule an appointment to show a portfolio, which should include original/final art and tear sheets. Buys first rights. Pays on publication.

LIGHTWAVE, the Journal of Fiber Optics, 235 Bear Hill Rd., Waltham MA 02154. (617)890-2700. Editor: Sharon Scully. Contact: Beth Draper. Newspaper. Emphasizes fiber optics for communication and sensing for engineers. Monthly. Circ. 13,000. Sometimes accepts previously published material. Returns original artwork after publication on request. Sample copy $3.50 for paid subscribers; $4 nonsubscribers.
Cartoons: Considers b&w line drawings with or without gaglines. Send query letter with samples of style or roughs to be kept on file. Write for appointment to show portfolio. Material not filed returned by SASE. Reports only if interested. Buys first rights. Pays $100 for b&w; on acceptance.
Illustrations: Buys 2 illustrations/issue from freelancers. Prefers sketches of real people or objects. Send query letter with tear sheets or photocopies to be kept on file. Write for appointment to show portfolio. Samples not filed returned by SASE. Reports only if interested. Buys first rights. Pays $50-100 for b&w; on acceptance.

THE MANITOBA TEACHER, 191 Harcourt St., Winnipeg, Manitoba R3J 3H2 Canada. (204)888-7961. Editor: Mrs. Miep van Raalte. Emphasizes education for teachers and others in Manitoba. 4 issues/year between July 1 and June 30. Circ. 16,900. Free sample copy and art guidelines.
Cartoons: Uses less than 2 cartoons/year relating to education in Manitoba. Prefers single panel, b&w line drawings with gagline. Send roughs and samples of style. SAE (nonresidents include IRC). Reports in 1 month.
Illustrations: Interested in b&w line drawings for inside. Send roughs and samples of style. SAE (nonresidents include IRC). Reports in 1 month.
Tips: Especially needs cartoons and illustrations related directly to the Manitoba scene. "Inquire before sending work."

***MEDICAL ABSTRACTS NEWSLETTER**, Box 2170, Teaneck NJ 07666. Publisher: Toni L. Goldfarb. Monthly newsletter emphasizing health and medicine. "*Medical Abstracts Newsletter* summarizes research breakthroughs reported in over 150 scientific journals that doctors read. Each monthly issue provides about 40 brief, easy-to-understand abstracts, written especially for general readers." Circ. 10,000. Accepts previously published material. Returns original artwork to the artist after publication. Sample copy for SASE with first-class postage.
Cartoons: Buys 1 cartoon/issue from freelancers. Buys 12 cartoons/year from freelancers. Prefers gag cartoons. Prefers health or medicine as themes. Prefers single panel with gagline; b&w line drawings. "Must be easily reduced to approximately 3½x3½. Send query letter with samples of style. Samples are filed. Samples not filed are returned by SASE. Reports back within 2 weeks. Buys one-time or reprint rights. Pays $10 minimum ("usually more!"), on publication.
Tips: "We take cartoons that 'poke fun' at doctors, but none that 'draw blood'!"

THE MIAMI HERALD, One Herald Plaza, Miami FL 33132. (305)376-3431. Director of Editorial Art and Design: Randy Stano. Daily newspaper. Circ. 475,000 daily, over 500,000 on Sunday. Accepts previously published material. Original artwork returned after publication. Sample copy available on assignment.
Cartoons: Occasionally buys cartoons from freelancers. Material not filed is returned. Reports only if interested. Write or call for appointment to show portfolio. Buys one-time rights. Pays on acceptance.
Illustrations: Buys 1-6 illustrations/month from freelancers. Works on assignment only. Send resume, tear sheets and slides. Samples not filed are returned if requested. Reports only if interested. Call or write to schedule an appointment to show a portfolio, which should include final reproduction/product and tear sheets. Buys one-time or reprint rights. Pays $150-300 for b&w and $300-450 for color, cover. Pays on acceptance.
Tips: "Keep an open mind."

MIAMI TODAY, Box 1368, Miami FL 33101. (305)358-2663. Publisher: Michael Lewis. Weekly tabloid. Circ. 30,000. Accepts previously published material. Returns original artwork after publication. Sample copy free for SASE with $1.34 postage.
Cartoons: Occasionally buys cartoons from freelancers. Prefers business, real estate as themes. Prefers b&w line drawings and b&w washes. Send finished cartoons. Samples are not filed. Samples are re-

©1988 Ray Vella

This pen-and-ink piece by freelance artist Ray Vella illustrated an op-ed story in the **National Law Journal** ***about deterrent to criminal behavior. Vella says, "The clientele which reads the publication is a highly-educated group and can identify with a more conceptual drawing." The piece was assigned by art director Douglas Hunt on a Friday afternoon and was due the following Wednesday. Vella sold one-time rights. Hunt had worked with him at a previous job, where Vella was a staff illustrator. "He is very strong on ideation," says Hunt. "His ideas have real visual punch. His technique reproduces well in newsprint."***

turned by SASE. Reports back within weeks. Buys one-time and reprint rights. Pays $5-10, b&w; on publication.

Illustrations: Rarely buys illustrations from freelancers. Send query letter with brochure showing art style. Samples are returned by SASE. Reports back within weeks. Buys one-time and reprint rights. Pays $10, b&w.

NATIONAL ENQUIRER, Lantana FL 33464. Cartoon Editor: Michele L. Cooke. Weekly tabloid. Circ. 6,000,000.

Cartoons: Buys 450 cartoons/year on "all subjects the family reader can relate to, especially animal and husband-wife situations. Captionless cartoons have a better chance of selling here." Receives 2,000 cartoons/week from freelance artists, buys 8/week from freelancers. Especially needs Christmas cartoon spread (submit by August). Send query letter with original cartoons. Mail 8½x11" art. SASE. Reports in 2 weeks. "No portfolios, please." Buys first rights. Pays $300 maximum, b&w single panel; $40 every panel thereafter; pays on acceptance. "No critiques of artwork given."

Tips: "Study 5-6 issues before submitting. Check captions for spelling. New submitters should send introductory letter. All cartoonists should include phone and social security number on cartoon back. Know your market. We have no use for political or off-color gags. Neatness counts and sloppy, stained artwork registers a negative reaction. Besides neatness, we also look for "correct spelling and punctuation on captions and in the body of the cartoon, accurate rendering of the subject (if the subject is a duck, make it look like a duck and not a goose, swan or chicken), and *most important* is visual impact! Prefers 8½x11" instead of 'halfs."

THE NATIONAL LAW JOURNAL, Suite 900, 111 8th Ave., New York NY 10011. (212)741-8300. Art Director: Douglas Hunt. Tabloid emphasizing law for attorneys. Weekly. Circ. 38,000. Original artwork returned after publication. Sample copy $2.

Close-up

Andrew Grossman
Gag Writer

Jim Toomey
Cartoonist
Washington, D.C.

They say it takes two to tango, but sometimes it takes two to 'toon. Andrew Grossman and Jim Toomey combine their talents at writing and cartooning, respectively, to sell cartoons. Their work as a collaborative team, called A.J. Toos, appears in newspapers and magazines such as *The National Enquirer, The Boston Globe*, the *Washington Post*, *TV Guide* and *Reader's Digest*.

The story behind the team began in 1983. A writer and a poet, Grossman found he was also a pretty funny guy, ready with a one-liner for any occasion. As a writer, he knew that newspapers and magazines were his stage and that cartoons were his *schtick*. However, he couldn't draw. So he placed an advertisement on a college bulletin board for a cartoonist, and Jim Toomey responded.

"Jim did political cartoons for his college newspaper," says Grossman, who acts as spokesman for the team. "Unfortunately, those big heads political cartoonists put on their characters don't go over too well in gag cartoons. Once he broke that habit, it was smooth sailing." Now Grossman writes the cartoons, detailing the situation and the captions (if there is one) and sends them to Toomey, who draws the cartoons. Grossman checks the final art and submits them to newspapers and magazines.

Unlike most of today's top cartoonists, A.J. Toos works mostly with publications instead of supplementing editorial work with advertising and greeting card assignments. "I'm not putting those types of work down," says Grossman, "but I'm saying there is a good income to be made here."

Grossman has found there is a difference in working with newspapers as opposed to magazines. "A daily newspaper works fast, as in within a few hours, and almost always within a day." He has also found that newspapers assign work, whereas magazines use unsolicited work. "Newspapers, of course, are on porous paper, while many magazines are on glossy paper. This will decide whether or not you use wash or pen and ink with a screen for a newspaper assignment."

While Toomey 'toons away, Grossman markets their work. By working with many editors and art directors, he has learned what makes cartoons sell. "The biggest problem I had was in learning to send material that is properly angled to each publication. When I started out, I might send a general cartoon to *Physician's Management* instead of sending them medically-oriented work. I would simply hope that by some stroke of luck they would buy the cartoon. Luck is always nice, but being prepared through knowing your markets and creating work that fits those markets make someone lucky.

"Realizing that cartooning is a business and not a lucky shot-in-the-dark proposition was important to me. Young cartoonists seem to expect editors will throw open their arms to them without learning about specific needs of the markets. You have to know the markets by reading the publications and studying the cartoons they use. Then you have to create work that is comparable in quality and angled properly."

Coming up with the gags took some practice, too. He learned that what tickled his funnybone may not do the same for other people. "I had to learn how to create humor that other people could associate with." Humor, he says, is based on two things: ordinary people doing extraordinary things and extraordinary people doing ordinary things.

Grossman first began selling cartoons through the mail by sending promotional postcards, followed by a batch of cartoons to interested respondents, a practice he recommends for newcomers. Now that the team has become a well-known commodity, Grossman makes cold calls to editors of publications he has not worked with before. "I mention one or two of the bigger name magazines we work with. If the editor is interested, I send samples of our work and a cover letter stating our interest and our rates." Once the samples arrive, he calls again to gauge his reaction. "After I have established a relationship with a magazine, I will correspond through the mail."

Negotiating a price for a cartoon is possible, Grossman finds. Rates are firm for major publications, but others are willing to negotiate. Grossman has two standards for determining a fair price. He either charges the same rate for a cartoon as for an illustration or asks the editor what he thinks is fair. "Quoting a price that a publication cannot afford is a waste of time."

Grossman encourages all aspiring cartoonists to study what works for the pros but to develop their own style. "Don't compare yourself to the people who are mediocre. You should always be going against the best, because you are working to be as good as them."

—Susan Conner

"Geez, Dad, I wanted a <u>toy</u> dumptruck!"

***The National Enquirer** purchased first rights from A.J.Toos for $300. Grossman says, "The cartoon was sent in on an unsolicited basis in time for a Christmas issue, which means about four months in advance of Christmas."*

Cartoons: Buys 1 cartoon/issue from freelancers. Prefers single panel; b&w line drawings. Send query letter with samples of style or finished cartoons. Material not filed is returned. Reports within 2 weeks. Buys one-time rights. Pays $125, b&w; on acceptance.
Illustrations: Buys 4 illustrations/month from freelancers. Prefers pen & ink, then airbrush, charcoal/pencil, collage and computer illustration. Works on assignment only. Send query letter with brochure to be kept on file. Samples returned only if requested. Reports within 2 weeks. Buys one-time rights. Pays $150-250, b&w, cover and inside; $250-450 color, cover and inside; on acceptance.
Tips: "We are looking for high concepts and skilled execution."

NATIONAL LIBRARIAN, Box 586, Alma MI 48801. (517)463-7227. Editor: Peter Dollard. Emphasizes professional issues related to librarianship. Quarterly. Circ. 500. Original work returned after publication. Sample copy and publication guidelines for SASE.
Cartoons: Uses single panel b&w line drawings with gagline. Send query letter with finished cartoons. Samples returned. Reports in 2-4 weeks. Material not copyrighted. Pays $25, b&w; on acceptance.
Illustrations: Uses 1-2 illustrations/issue. Send query letter with finished art. Reports in 2 weeks. Material not copyrighted. Pays $25; on acceptance.

NEW ALASKAN, Rt. 1, Box 677, Ketchikan AK 99901. (907)247-2490. Editor: Bob Pickrell. Emphasizes Southeastern Alaska lifestyle, history and politics for general public in this area. Monthly. Circ. 6,000. Previously published material and simultaneous submissions OK. Original work returned after publication by SASE. Sample copy $1.50; art guidelines for SASE.
Cartoons: Uses 1 cartoon/issue; buys 1 from freelancers. Interested only in art with a Southeastern Alaska tie-in; single panel with or without gagline, b&w line drawings. Send roughs or samples of style. Samples returned by SASE. Reports in 6 months. Negotiates rights purchased. Pays $25 up, b&w; on publication.
Illustrations: Uses 2 illustrations/issue; buys 1 from freelancers. Interested only in art with a Southeastern Alaska tie-in. "We prefer mss with illustrations except for cover art which can stand by itself." Works on assignment only. Provide business card and samples to be kept on file for possible future assignments. Samples returned by SASE. Reports in 6 months. Negotiates rights purchased and payment; on publication.

NEW ENGLAND SENIOR CITIZEN/SENIOR AMERICAN NEWS, Prime National Publishing Corp., 470 Boston Post Rd., Weston MA 02193. (617)899-2702. Editor-in-Chief/Art Director: Ira Alterman. For men and women ages 60 and over who are interested in travel, retirement lifestyles and nostalgia. Monthly tabloid. Circ. 60,000. Previously published work OK. Sample copy 50¢.
Illustrations: Buys 1-4/issue. Query or mail samples. SASE. Reports in 6 months. Cover: Pays $10-50, b&w. Pays on publication.

NEWSDAY, 235 Pinelawn Rd., Melville NY 11050. (516)454-2303. Art Director: Jack Sherman. Daily newspaper. Circ. 500,000. Original artwork returned after publication. Sample copy and art guidelines available.
Illustrations: Buys 4-5 illustrations/week from freelancers. Send query letter with brochure showing art style. Samples not filed are returned. Reports only if interested. Call to schedule an appointment to show a portfolio, which should include original/final art, final reproduction/product, color, tear sheets, Photostats and b&w photos. Buys one-time rights. Pays $350 for b&w and $400 for color, cover; $100-250 for b&w; $150-300 for color, inside. Pays on publication.
Tips: "Let your portfolio talk for you."

***NORTH MYRTLE BEACH TIMES**, Box 725, North Myrtle Beach SC 29597. (803)249-1122 or 249-3525. Publisher:Pauline L. Lowman. Semiweekly. Circ. 9,500. Simultaneous submissions OK. Original work returned after publication if requested. Free sample copy and art guidelines.
Cartoons: Uses 2 cartoons/issue. Interested in editorial themes; double panel b&w line drawings with gagline. Send query letter with resume and samples of style. Samples returned by SASE. Reports in 2 weeks. To show a portfolio, mail appropriate materials or call to schedule an appointment. Material not copyrighted. Pays on acceptance.
Illustrations: Uses editorial themes. Send query letter with samples of style. Samples returned by SASE. Reports in 2 weeks. Material not copyrighted. Pays on publication.
Tips: "Be original and able to express ideas well. Be neat with work and have interesting samples to show."

NURSINGWORLD JOURNAL, 470 Boston Post Rd., Weston MA 02193. (617)899-270. Editor: Shirley Copithorne. Readers are "student and experienced nurses interested in keeping their skills current and seeking employment, trends in nursing, relocation or area hiring trends in nursing, reviews of nursing articles, feature stories." Specialty is health care publications. Monthly. Circ. 40,000. Sample copy $2.

Cartoons: Uses 1-3 cartoons/issue. Receives 25 submissions/month from freelancers. Interested in hospital or nursing themes. Prefers b&w line drawing with gagline. Send finished cartoons. SASE. Reports within 6 months. Buys one-time rights. Pays $5-10 for b&w; on publication.

Illustrations: Uses 3 illustrations/issue. Receives 10 submissions/month from freelancers. Interested in general illustrations that go along with editorial; usually people or nature. Works on assignment. "Freelancers call, send us samples, and we make a decision at that time if their style fits our paper. If it does, we keep their names on file, then contact them for assignments." Send roughs. SASE. Reports within 6 months. Prefers b&w line drawings. Buys all rights on a work-for-hire basis. Pays $50-100 for b&w or color cover, $50 for inside b&w. Pays on publication.

Tips: Interested in seeing "any articles you're interested in. Submissions from editor's point of view."

NUTRITION HEALTH REVIEW, 171 Madison Ave., New York NY 10016. (212)679-3590. Features Editor: Frank Ray Rifkin. Tabloid. Emphasizes physical health, mental health, nutrition, food preparation and medicine. For a general audience. Quarterly. Circ. 165,000 paid. Accepts simultaneous submissions. Sample copy for SASE with first-class postage.

Cartoons: Uses 10 cartoons/issue. Interested in health, diet, illness, medications and psychology. Prefers single panel with gagline; b&w line drawings, 5x4. Send finished cartoons; samples returned by SASE if not purchased. Reports within 30 days. Buys first rights. Pays $15 + , b&w; on acceptance.

Illustrations: Buys 10 illustrations/issue from freelancers. Send brochure showing art style to be kept on file; call or write for appointment to show portfolio, which should include roughs and original/final art. Samples returned by SASE. Reports back. Buys first rights. Pays $50 and up; on acceptance.

ON THE MARK: THE NEWSLETTER FOR MARK HAMILL FANS, Box 5276, Orange CA 92613-5276. Publisher: Lisa E. Cowan. Quarterly newsletter emphasizing the acting career of Mark Hamill. This is a 6-page offset printed newsletter on the past and present career of actor Mark Hamill and Star Wars articles. Circ. 500. Accepts previously published material. Original artwork returned after publication. Sample copy for SASE with first-class postage. Art guidelines for SASE with first-class postage.

Cartoons: Buys 2-3 cartoons/year from freelancers. Prefers gag cartoons and humorous illustrations featuring Mark Hamill. Prefers single panel with gagline; b&w line drawings 3½x3½. Send query letter with samples of style. Samples are filed. Samples not filed are returned only if requested by artist. Reports back within 8 days. Buys one-time rights. Pays $5 minimum, b&w on acceptance.

Illustrations: Buys 2-8 illustrations/year from freelancers. Prefers line art. Works on assignment usually. Send query letter with samples. Samples are filed. Samples not filed are returned if requested. Reports back within 10 days. To show a portfolio mail thumbnails, tear sheets, final reproduction/product and b&w. Buys one-time rights. Pays $5-10 b&w; on acceptance.

Tips: "We are mostly interested in quality line art of Mark Hamill in current roles. We want to see samples of people art, no Star Wars art."

PARENTGUIDE NEWS AND CITY NEWS, Suite 2012, 2 Park Ave., New York NY 10016. (212)213-8840. "*Parentguide* reaches parents of children from birth through their elementary school years. We are an upbeat newspaper for sophisticated parents. City News is for teenagers." Features general interest, how-to and personal experience. Monthly. Accepts previously published material. Sample copy $1.50.

Cartoons: Uses 2-3 cartoons/issue from freelancers. Themes and styles vary. Prefers b&w line drawings without gagline. Send query letter. Samples are filed. Samples not filed are returned by SASE. Reports back only if interested.

Illustrations: Uses 2-3 illustrations/issue from freelancers. Send query letter with resume, tear sheets and photocopies. Samples are filed. Samples not filed are returned by SASE. Reports back only if interested. Write to schedule an appointment to show a portfolio, which should include roughs, color, tear sheets, Photostats or b&w. Buys first and one-time rights.

***THE PATRIOT**, Box 346, Kutztown PA 19530. (215)683-7343. Editor: Stephen Fellman. For general audience. Weekly newspaper. Circ. 4,300. Originals returned to artist after publication.

Illustrations: Buys newspaper ad layouts and sales promotion art. Works on assignment only. Samples returned by SASE; reports back on future assignment possibilities. Provide business card to be kept on file for future assignments. Pays $5-10/sketch.

***PENNYWHISTLE PRESS (Gannett News)**, Suite 1000, 1000 Wilson Blvd., Arlington VA 22209. Art Director: Eileen Kelly. Weekly newspaper. "We are an eight-page, full-color weekly newspaper for children. We are primarily a Sunday supplement for approximately 50 papers nationwide." Circ. 2,500,000.

Illustrations: Buys from 30-40 freelance artists/year. Uses illustrations, spot drawings and full-color covers. "We use all media from pen & ink to oil paintings." Prefers, but not limited to, local artists. "Our readership is about 6 through 12 years old. Obviously, we will target that group." Works on assignment only. Send query letter with brochure or samples. Samples are filed. Samples not filed are returned by SASE if requested. Reports back only if interested. Write to schedule an appointment to show a portfolio, which should include final reproduction/product, Photostats, photographs, b&w, color, slides and transparencies. "Some work-for-hire. Some all rights." Pays $50-250; on acceptance.

PERSONNEL ADVISORY BULLETIN, Bureau of Business Practice, 24 Rope Ferry Rd., Waterford CT 06386. Editor: Jill Whitney. For personnel managers and practitioners in smaller companies—white collar and industrial. Features interviewing and hiring, training, benefits, career development, promotion practices, counseling, record keeping, etc. Bimonthly newsletter. Original artwork not returned after publication. No previously published material or simultaneous submissions. Free sample copy.
Cartoons: Uses 1 cartoon/issue; buys 1/issue from freelancers. Receives 15-20 submissions/week from freelancers. Buys 30/year on "personnel-oriented situations. Please, no sexist situations and male boss/dumb female secretary jokes." Prefers single panel. Mail finished art. SASE. Reports in 2 weeks. Buys all rights. Pays $15 for b&w line drawings. Pays on acceptance.
Tips: "We're trying to be more selective in choosing strictly personnel-oriented subject matter. Avoid anything smacking of sexism or other discriminatory attitudes. Don't overdo hiring-firing situations. Make captions *literate* and *funny*."

***POSTCARD CLASSICS**, Box 8, Norwood PA 19074. Editor: Dr. James Lewis Lowe. "A bimonthly journal for collectors, dealers, and archivists of antique (pre-1920) picture postcards including views, greetings, and picture postcards issued for special events, i.e., expositions, fairs, parades, elections, etc." Circ. 1,000. Returns original artwork after publication. Sample copy for SASE with first-class postage.
Cartoons: Seeks "dignified humor relating to postcards." Prefers single panel with gagline; b&w line drawings 4x5. Send finished cartoons. Samples are filed. Does not report back.

PUBLICATIONS CO., Suite 304, 5225 Wilshire Blvd., Los Angeles CA 90036. (213)933-2646. Editor: Lucie Dubovik. Emphasizes general business for companies, service organizations, etc. and journalism in schools. Monthly. Accepts previously published material. Sample copy and art guidelines free for SASE.
Cartoons: Buys several cartoons/issue from freelancers. Prefers business, industry, factory, schools, and teen situations, plus seasonal material as themes. Prefers single panel with gagline; b&w line drawings. Send query letter with samples of style or finished cartoons. Material not filed is returned by SASE. Reports within 1 month. Buys reprint rights. Pays on acceptance.
Illustrations: Buys several illustrations/issue from freelancers. Prefers business, industry, factory, school and teen situations plus seasonal material as themes. Send query letter with original art. Samples not filed are returned by SASE. Reports within 1 month. Buys reprint rights. Pays on acceptance.

***PURRRRR! The Newsletter for Cat Lovers**, HCR 227, Islesboro ME 04848. (207)734-6745. Publisher/Editor: Agatha Cabaniss. Bimonthly newsletter. "Want humorous, upbeat slant. Mixture of solid news and humor. Interested in people working with animal welfare. Includes cartoons and poems." Circ. 400+. Accepts previously published material. Returns original artwork after publication. Sample copy $2.
Cartoons: Buys 2-3 cartoons/issue from freelancers. Prefers gag cartoons or humorous illustrations featuring cats. Prefers single panel, double panel or multiple panel with or without gagline; b&w line drawings. Send query letter with samples of style, roughs or finished cartoons. Samples are filed "if we might want them in the future." Samples not filed are returned by SASE. Reports back within 7 days. Buys one-time rights. Pays $10, b&w; on acceptance.

SAN FRANCISCO BAY GUARDIAN, 2700 19th St., San Francisco CA 94110. (415)824-7660. Art Director: John Schmitz. For "a young, liberal, well-educated audience." Circ. 165,000. Weekly newspaper. SASE. Pays 60 days after publication.
Cartoons: "Almost all illustrations are assigned; we are, however, always looking for cartoons and strips that have a Bay Area theme. We pay, on the average, $15-50 for editorial carton/illustration.
Illustrations: Buys assigned themes. Pays $40-150. Arrange interview to show portfolio.
Tips: "I am always looking for artwork for our cover done by *Bay Area* artists. We are now looking for artists with national quality to deal with local and general issues."

SKYDIVING, Box 1520, Deland FL 32721. (904)736-9779. Editor: Michael Truffer. Emphasizes skydiving for sport parachutists, worldwide dealers and equipment manufacturers. Monthly. Circ. 7,800.

Cartoons: Uses 1-2 cartoons/issue; buys 0-1 from freelancers. Receives 1-2 submissions/week from freelancers. Interested in themes relating to skydiving or aviation. Prefers single panel b&w line drawings with gagline. Send finished cartoons or samples of style. SASE. Reports in 1 week. Buys one-time rights. Pays $10 minimum for b&w; on publication.
Tips: Artists "must *know* parachuting; cartoons must be funny."

SOUTHERN JEWISH WEEKLY, Box 3297, Jacksonville FL 32206. (904)634-1812. Editor/Publisher: Isadore Moscovitz. Emphasizes human interest material and short stories. "The only Jewish newspaper covering all of Florida and the Southeast." Weekly. Circ. 28,500.
Illustrations: Buys 12 illustrations/year on Jewish themes that pertain to newspaper's articles. Send query letter with resume and samples. Seasonal themes must arrive 2 weeks in advance of holiday. SASE. Reports in 1 week. Pays $10 minimum, b&w; on publication.
Tips: "Send samples of work along with resume to us two weeks or more in advance of Jewish holiday being featured."

SOUTHWEST DIGEST, 510 E. 23rd St., Lubbock TX 79404. (806)762-3612. Co-Publisher-Managing Editor: Eddie P. Richardson. Newspaper emphasizing positive black images, and community building and rebuilding "primarily oriented to the black community and basically reflective of the black community, but serving all people." Weekly. Accepts previously published material. Original work returned after publication.
Cartoons: Number of cartoons purchased/issue from freelancers varies. Prefers economic development, community development, community pride and awareness, and black uplifting themes. Single, double or multi-panel with gagline; b&w line drawings. Send query letter with samples of style, roughs or finished cartoons to be kept on file. Write or call for appointment to show portfolio. Material not filed returned by SASE only if requested. Buys first, one-time, reprint, or all rights; or negotiates rights purchased. Pays on publication.
Illustrations: Send query letter with brochure or samples to be kept on file. Write or call for appointment to show portfolio. Prefers Photostats, tear sheets, photocopies, photographs, etc. as samples. Samples not filed returned by SASE only if requested. Reports only if interested. Negotiates rights purchased. Pays $5 minimum on publication.

SPARKS JOURNAL, Society of Wireless Pioneers, Box 530, Santa Rosa CA 95402. Editor: William A. Breniman. For radio-telegraph men who handle(d) communications with ships and at-shore stations; included are military, commercial, aeronautical and governmental communications personnel. "Since many have earned their living aboard ships as 'Sparks,' we like to bring a nautical flavor to our pages." Quarterly tabloid newspaper. Circ. 5,000 (members) plus some libraries and museums. Accepts previously published material "if it fits."
Cartoons: Buys 15-20 cartoons/issue. Send query letter with samples. To show a portfolio, mail appropriate materials, which should include b&w drawings. Pays $2-30 for b&w; on acceptance.
Illustrations: Uses illustrative headings for various articles. Buys 4-10 illustrations/issue. Send query letter with brochure showing art style or tear sheets and photocopies. Uses b&w only; no color. Include SASE. Buys reprint rights. Pays $25-100 for b&w, cover; $10-25 for b&w, inside; on acceptance.
Tips: "Those who have a love of the sea and things nautical, and are also versed in wireless telegraph or transmission via Hertzian waves (communications), would probably be able to furnish the type of material we use. We are a professional, nonprofit organization; we do not cater to the amateur radio (including CB) field. We also publish *The Skipper's Log* (quarterly tabloid, members only), *Port's O'Call* (biennial), *Sparks* (in series, annual), and a book-format almanac."

SPORT SCENE: FOCUS ON YOUTH PROGRAMS, North American Youth Sport Institute, 4985 Oak Garden Dr., Kernersville NC 27284. (919)784-4926. Editor/Publisher: Jack Hutslar PhD. Quarterly newsletter emphasizing children in sport and recreation, ages 18 and younger. For parents, youth and school coaches, teachers and program directors. Circ. 15,000. Accepts previously published material. Original artwork returned to the artist after publication. Sample copy for SASE with first-class postage.
Cartoons: Prefers gag cartoons, caricatures and humorous illustrations. Prefers children, coaches, parents and referees, etc. as themes. Prefers single panel with or without gagline. Send query letter with samples of style. Samples are filed. Samples not filed are not returned. Reports back within 2 weeks. Negotiates rights purchased.
Illustrations: Send query letter with samples and business card. Samples are filed. Samples not filed are not returned. Reports back within 2 weeks. Negotiates rights purchased.
Tips: "Include work featuring children in a sport setting."

MAXWELL SROGE PUBLISHING, 731 N. Cascade Ave., Colorado Springs CO 80903. (303)633-5556. Associate Editor: Karen Pochert. Biweekly newsletters emphasizing catalog marketing, and di-

rect marketing. There are three publications: 1) Non-Store Marketing Report (executives in mail order business); 2) Catalog Marketer (management in catalog marketing business); 3) Business-To-Business Direct Marketer (management in business-to-business direct marketing). We reach a healthy percentage of the 6,000 catalog marketers in the U.S. with each of our publications. Sample copy and art guidelines available.
Illustrations: Works on assignment only. Send query letter or resume. Samples are filed. Reports back only if interested. "We will call to schedule an appointment to show a portfolio, which should include roughs, original/final art, tear sheets and final reproduction/product; on publication.
Tips: "We are primarily interested in paste-up artist to paste-up our three newsletters and to design and layout variable advertising and promotional materials.

THE STATE JOURNAL-REGISTER, 1 Copley Plaza, Box 219, Springfield IL 62705. (217)788-1477. Graphics Editor: Elizabeth Novickas. Emphasizes news and features for the town and surrounding area. Daily. Circ. 70,000. Sample copy and art guidelines for SASE.
Illustrations: "Uses approximately 6-7 photographs/issue and occasionally graphs, charts, maps, artwork. We buy only some illustrations from freelancers, not all. Staff does some work." Works on assignment only. Send query letter with samples to be kept on file. Samples are returned if not kept on file. Negotiates rights purchased. Pays $100-200, b&w and color, cover. Pays $50-150, b&w and color, inside; on publication.
Tips: "We use cartoons and illustrations, either straightforward or abstract styles. I do not want to see any layout or advertising."

***STETHOSCOPE, DIGEST**, Physicians Planning Service, 292 Madison Ave., New York NY 10017. (212)949-5900. Editor: Bill Valladares. Bimonthly economic newsletter geared toward doctors and residents. Circ. 50,000. Returns original artwork after publication. Sample copy for SASE with first-class postage.
Cartoons: Buys 1 cartoon/issue from freelancers. Prefers gag cartoons. Prefers single panel with or without gagline; b&w line drawings and b&w washes. Call or send query letter with roughs. Samples are filed. Samples not filed are returned by SASE. Reports back within 4 weeks only if interested. Negotiates rights purchased. Pays $25-50, b&w; on publication.

THE SUPERVISOR, Kemper Group, Long Grove IL 60049. (312)540-2094. Editor: Mary Puccinelli. Newsletter. Emphasizes industrial and fleet safety for supervisors responsible for industrial safety and/or fleet safety. Bimonthly. Circ. 50,000. Accepts simultaneous submissions. Original artwork not returned after publication. Sample copy free for SASE.
Cartoons: Uses 2 cartoons/issue; buys all from freelancers. Seeks "very funny cartoons;" can be "offbeat" but not offensive. Topics for the year are sent to prospective artists in June. Prefers single panel, with gagline; b&w line drawings. Send query letter with samples of style to be kept on file. Material not kept on file is returned by SASE. Reports within 1 month. Buys all rights. Payment varies; on acceptance.

SWCP CATALYST, (Self-Winding Clock Publications Catalyst), Box 7704, Long Beach CA 90807. (213)427-4202. Publisher: Dr. Bengt E. Honning. Emphasizes horology/clocks, the self-winding clock and other antique battery clocks for time standards department—USN, NASA, etc., Western Union, collectors, antique battery clock service. Bimonthly. Circ. 450. Accepts previously published material and simultaneous submissions. Original artwork returned after publication. Sample copy and art guidelines free for SASE.
Illustrations: Uses 3-4 illustrations/issue. Prefers horology themes. Send query letter with business card and samples. Prefers photocopies as samples; "dimensions of original if otherwise." Samples returned by SASE. Reports within 2 weeks. Original material not copyrighted.

> ***"There is more excitement in newspaper illustration. Illustrations make newspapers more reader friendly."***
>
> ***—Rosemarie Sander, Associated Media Corporation Stamford, Connecticut***

TEENS TODAY, 6401 The Paseo, Kansas City MO 64131. (816)333-7000. Editor: Karen De Sollar. For junior and senior high school students who attend Church of the Nazarene. Weekly. Circ. 60,000. Original work not returned after publication. Sample copy with SASE.
Illustrations: Uses 1-2 illustrations/issue; buys 1-2/issue from freelancers; all illustrations go with stories. Works on assignment only. Prefers to see resume, flyer and tear sheets to be kept on file. SASE. Reports in 6-8 weeks.

TELEBRIEFS, Illinois Bell Telephone Co., 225 W. Randolph, Chicago IL 60606. Contact: Editor. Monthly newsletter for telephone customers. Circ. 3,500,000. Original artwork not returned after publication. Free sample copy.
Cartoons: Uses 2 cartoons/issue, all from freelancers. Receives 8 submissions/month from freelancers. Cartoons "must be telephone company or telecommunications related." Single panel. "No ethnic humor. We reduce cartoons to 1¾x1¾ so we need few elements, drawn very boldly. Prefer strong visual with captions of 10 or fewer words." Prefers finished cartoons. SASE. Reports in 2 weeks. Buys all rights on a work-for-hire basis. Pays $40, line drawings with shading; on acceptance.
Illustrations: Buys 1 illustration/week from freelancers. Send photocopies. To show a portfolio, mail appropriate materials, which should include roughs, original/final art and Photostats.
Tips: "Since break up of Bell System, Illinois Bell is no longer in the business of leasing, selling, or installing telephone equipment. Cartoons should mainly imply telephone usage, such as speaking on phone."

TOWERS CLUB, USA NEWSLETTER, Box 2038, Vancouver WA 98668. (206)574-3084. Chief Executive Officer: Jerry Buchanan. Emphasizes "anything that offers a new entrepreneurial opportunity, especially through mail order. The newsletter for 'Find a Need and Fill It' people." Readers are 80% male with average age of 48 and income of $35,000. Monthly except May and December. Circ. 4,000. Previously published material and simultaneous submissions OK. Original work returned after publication by SASE. Sample copy $3.
Cartoons: Uses 1 cartoon/issue; buys all from freelancers. Interested in themes of selling how-to-do-it information, showing it as a profitable and honorable profession; single panel with gagline, b&w line drawings. Send finished cartoons. Samples returned by SASE. Reports in 1 week. Buys one-time rights. Pays $15-25, b&w; on publication.
Illustrations: Uses 5-7 illustrations/issue. Interested in realistic, illustrative art of typists, computers, small print shop operations, mail order, etc.; no comical themes. Especially needs line drawings of typists/writers/office workers, money, mail delivery, affluent people, intelligent and successful faces, etc. Send brochure showing art style. Provide samples to be kept on file for possible future assignments. Samples not kept on file are returned by SASE. Reports in 1 week. Buys one-time rights. Makes some permanent purchases. Pays $15, b&w; on acceptance.
Tips: "Newsletters are going more to using typesetting and artwork to brighten pages. Subscribe to our *Towers Club, USA* newsletter and study content and artwork used. Normally $60 per year, we will give 40% discount to artists who show us a portfolio of their work. Our theme will lead them to much other business, as we are about creative self-publishing/marketing exclusively. Many cartoonists have little or no genuine sense of humor. I suggest they tie in with someone who does and split the fee. Illustrators should see several copies of the publication they hope to draw for before submitting their samples. It could save a lot of postage. I do not want to see general, arty, avant-garde work."

***TRANSPORT WORLD**, Box 6782, Pawtucket RI 02940. President: Robert J. Andrews. Quarterly tabloid emphasizing transportation post cards for collectors. Circ. 300. Accepts previously published material. Original artwork returned after publication.
Cartoons: Prefers 8½x11 cartoons. Samples are filed. Samples not filed are returned only if requested by artist. No payment.
Illustrations: Samples are filed. Samples not filed are returned if requested. Reports back within 2 months. To show a portfolio, mail original/final art and color. No payment.

TRISTATE MAGAZINE, 617 Vine St., Cincinnati OH 45202. (513)721-2700. Editor: Alice Hornbaker. Design Artist: Marty Eggerding. Weekly. Circ. 330,000.
Illustrations: Uses 1-2 illustrations/issue on assigned themes. "We use, on rare occasion, unsolicited freelance art. Samples returned by SASE. Reports back on future assignment possibilities. Provide business card to be kept on file for future assignments. Reporting time varies. Buys all rights on a work-for-hire basis. Pays $50-200 maximum, b&w line drawings and washes; $150-350 maximum, color illustrations and cover.

***UMBILICUS**, 3127 Telegraph Ave., Oakland CA 94609. (415)428-1446. Editor: Ericka Huggins. Quarterly newsletter emphasizing pregnancy, birth and childrearing in the first year of life. "Our audi-

ence is pregnant women, new mothers and fathers, families with infants and toddlers. We offer choices in childbearing and childrearing through information, referral and support." Circ. 5,000. Accepts previously published material. Returns original artwork to the artist after publication.
Cartoons: Prefers cartoons and humorous illustrations. Prefers parenting or birthing themes. Prefers single panel with gagline; b&w line drawings. Send query letter with samples of style. Samples are filed. Samples not filed are returned by SASE. Reports back to within 7 days. Buys reprint rights. Payment is negotiated.
Illustrations: Prefers line art. Works on assignment only. Send brochure or samples. Samples are filed. Samples not filed are returned by SASE. Reports back within 7 days. Call or write to schedule an appointment to show a portfolio, which should include final reproduction/product, b&w and color. Buys reprint rights. Pays on publication.

VELO-NEWS, Box 1257, Brattleboro VT 05301. Editor: Geoff Drake. Tabloid. Emphasizes bicycle racing for competitors, coaches, officials, enthusiasts. Published 18 times/year. Circ. 15,000. Accepts previously published material and simultaneous submissions. Original artwork returned after publication.
Cartoons: Uses cartoons irregularly; buys from freelancers. Prefers single panel, with gagline; b&w line drawings. Send query letter with samples of style to be kept on file. Material not kept on file is returned by SASE. Reports within 2 weeks. Buys one-time rights. Pays $16.50, b&w; on publication.

WDS FORUM, 1507 Dana Ave., Cincinnati OH 45207. Editor: Ms. Kirk Polking. Sixteen-page quarterly newsletter emphasizing writing techniques and marketing for Writer's Digest School students. Circ. 13,000.
Cartoons: Needs work on "the joys and griefs of freelancing, that first check/rejection slip, trying to find time to write, postal problems, editor/author relations, etc." Send either finished art or roughs. SASE. Reports in 3 weeks. Pays $10, b&w.
Illustrations: "We might buy a few spot drawings, as fillers, of writer-related subject matter." SASE. Reports in 3 weeks. Send query letter with samples. Pays $5, each drawing; on acceptance. "Sorry our rates are so low but we carry no advertising and our newsletter is primarily a service to our students."

WESTERN CANADA OUTDOORS, Box 430, North Battleford, Saskatchewan S9A 2Y5 Canada. (306)445-4401. Publisher: S. Nowakowski. For hunting, fishing and outdoor families. Bimonthly newspaper. Circ. 42,000. Previously published work OK. Free sample copy.
Cartoons: Uses 3 cartoons/issue, all by freelancers. Receives 0-1 submission/week from freelancers. Interested in "an outdoor, conserving environment theme"; single panel. Prefers to see finished cartoons. SASE (nonresidents include SAE and International Reply Coupons). Reports in 1 month. Buys "once-rental" rights. Pays $5-10, halftones; on acceptance.
Illustrations: Uses 0-1 illustrations/issue, all from freelancers. Receives no submissions/week from freelancers. Interested in wildlife. Especially needs hunting and fishing related artwork; must have some interest for Western Canada. Prefers to see finished art. SASE (nonresidents include SAE and International Reply Coupons). Reports in 1 month. Buys "once-rental" rights. Pays on acceptance.

***WINNING SWEEPSTAKES NEWSLETTER**, Sebell Publishing Company, Inc., Box 400, Ashland MA 01721. (617)881-7400. Editor: Jeffrey Sklar. Monthly newsletter emphasizing consumer promotions and sweepstakes. Circ. 100,000. Sample copy for SASE with first-class postage.
Cartoons: Buys 20 cartoons/year from freelancers. Prefers gag cartoons and editorial or political cartoons on consumer, sweepstakes habits. Prefers multiple panel with gagline; b&w washes. Send roughs. Samples are filed. Samples not filed are returned only if requested. Reports back within 3 weeks. Buys all rights. Pays $50, b&w; on acceptance.
Illustrations: Buys 20-25 illustrations/year from freelancers. Works on assignment only. Send resume, business card and samples. Samples are filed. Samples not filed are returned if requested. Reports back within 3 weeks. Buys all rights. Pays on acceptance.

WORCESTER MAGAZINE, CENTRUMGUIDE, Box 1000, Worcester MA 01614. (617)799-0511. Art Director: Mark Minter. Concerns central Massachusetts. Weekly and monthly newspapers. Circ. 50,000.
Illustrations: Buys on assigned themes. Prefers line art with color for illustrations, b&w line art for spots. Send query letter with photocopies. Buys one-time rights. "Complicated projects or illustrations are reviewed on a case by case payment system. The base payment prices are as follows." Cover: Pays $75-100, gray opaques, b&w line drawings and washes; $100, color. Inside: Pays $15-50, gray opaques, b&w line drawings and washes; $5 for cartoons; on publication.
Tips: "I prefer pen & ink, color washes and watercolor."

Syndicates & Clip Art Firms

Almost every major daily paper buys syndicated cartoons. Syndicates play a major role in determining what people will chuckle at every day, and they are constantly on the lookout for cartoonists.

However, there's more to landing a syndicate contract than just being funny. You must also be able to sustain a consistently high level of humor, create enduring characters and develop a loyal following. Successful panels and strips are original, timely and have a widespread appeal. They feature either a strong central character or a unique theme or attitude, such as the zany zen of Bill Griffith's "Zippy the Pinhead."

If you have developed a strip with fresh ideas and a unique cast of characters, you could be on your way toward syndication. While syndicates search for originality, saleability and timeliness, you should be looking for syndicates that have a strong sales force and widespread distribution. Consult the listings in this section and also those in the *Editor & Publisher Directory of Syndicated Services* for addresses and contact information. Then send a sample package to your top choice. Your package should contain a cover letter stating your background and the main theme of your strip plus photocopies (not originals) of four to six weeks of *published* work. If you're not published, build up your portfolio by cartooning for local papers.

Your samples should be one-and-a-half times larger than the standard size for a daily strip. Most dailies conform to the Standard Advertising Unit of 38.6 picas (panels are 19 picas wide). Because strips are reduced when printed, focus on a simple drawing style with heavier lines.

As in any profession, it takes persistence to become syndicated. Syndicates listed in this section estimate that a newcomer faces 10-to-1 odds of being syndicated. Large syndicates cautiously introduce two or three new features a year, with the smaller ones attempting 12 to 15. Syndicates are choosy because they invest between $7,000 to $15,000 to introduce a new strip.

When you land a syndicate contract, consult an attorney before signing it. It is a complicated agreement that requires careful scrutiny. Read the Close-up of Richard Newcombe, president of Creators Syndicate, to get an idea of favorable contract terms.

Your payment will be a percentage of gross or net receipts. The amount you can earn depends upon the number of newspapers in which your strip appears and the size of those newspapers. Newspapers pay in the area of $8 to $12 a week for a daily feature. Usually the receipts for a strip are split between the syndicate and the cartoonist.

Licensing is another source of possible revenue. In this arrangement, you are granting other businesses the nonexclusive right to use your characters on their products and also in advertising or as endorsements for a fee. Syndicates handle character licensing to businesses, book publishers, advertising firms, television and motion picture companies.

Artists interested in approaching clip art firms with their work should keep in mind that most firms are looking for work that appeals to a mass audience. A variety of styles might be accepted, but the overwhelming priority is that the artwork reproduce well in black and white.

ADVENTURE FEATURE SYNDICATE, Suite 400, 329 Harvey Dr., Glendale CA 91206. (818)247-1721. Executive Editor: Orpha Harryman Barry. Syndicates to 200 newspaper and book publishers.
Needs: Buys from 20 freelance artists/year. Considers single, double and multi-panel cartoons. Prefers mystery, SF, adventure and drama as themes. Also needs comic strips, comic book, graphic novels and panel cartoonists.
First Contact & Terms: Send query letter with resume, Photostats and tear sheets to be kept on file. Samples not kept on file are returned by SASE. Reports within 30 days. Write for appointment to show portfolio. Pays 50% of gross income; on publication. Considers salability of artwork when establishing payment. Buys reprint rights; negotiates rights purchased.
Tips: "Comic strips need a four-week presentation package reduced to newspaper size. Include an outline of artwork's storyline that could be used for a promotional kit. We also must have return envelope and postage to return submissions!"

***ALL CHURCH TECHNICAL SERVICE**, 1640 Rockwood Trail, Fayetteville AR 72701. Owner: Wayne Summers. Publishes monthly and quarterly clip art for churches and Christian organizations to use in their newsletters, bulletins and promotions. Sales of clip art subscriptions are world-wide.
Needs: Requires over 500 spot art items/year in a variety of subjects and styles. Work is reproduced by offset press on 11"x8½" sheets, one subject per page, normally with 3 drawings in three sizes per page. Symbols, logos, collages, unique letter/with graphics, and person-oriented art items are oganized around the following themes: Bible Illustrations, Bible Study, Borders, Children, Devotional, Christian Growth, Enlistment and Announcement, Family, Fellowship, Ministry, Missions, Music, Outreach, Planning, Prayer, Recreation, Seasonal, Special Events, Stewardship, Training, Worship, and Youth.
First Contact & Terms: Submit black & white samples (copies acceptable) with short resume. Originals submitted will be purchased immediately, scheduled for future publication with commitment to buy, or returned to artist when accompanied by envelope and postage. Payment ranges from $5-50, depending on complexity and quality. Precise lettering can be added by publisher in situations when appropriate.
Tips: "Drawings should normally be no larger than 20 square inches. Use only black ink on white, with clarity and precision being critical. Smallest linewidth accepted is pen size 0, since drawings are reduced down to as small as 25% of original."

***AMERICAN-INTERNATIONAL SYNDICATE**, Suite 103 D, 3801 Oakland St., St. Joseph MO 64506. (816)271-5250. Art Director: W.E. Clark. Serves 8 outlets, including overseas newspapers and daily newspapers, plus magazines in the U.S. and Canada.
Needs: Published artists only. Considers comic strips and gag cartoons. Prefers single or multiple panel. Pen & ink only.
First Contact & Terms: Send brochure showing art style or photocopies. Samples are filed. Samples not filed are returned only if requested by artist. Reports back within 14 days only if interested. Write to schedule an appointment to show a portfolio, or mail b&w and Photostats. Pays 50% of gross income on publication. Considers skill and experience of artist and saleability of art work when establishing payment. Buys first rights.

ALFONSO

"This big, loveable creature is very childlike," says cartoonist Charles Russo of his character Alfonso. The strip was purchased by American International Syndicate. President Gerald Bennett says Russo shows "exceptional artistic talent in drawing feature material." Russo originally sent the syndicate photocopies of his work. "It gave me good exposure as a comic strip artist," says Russo. "This is something I have been trying to accomplish for ten years."

Tips: "Send about 10-12 photocopies (good clean—clear). One feature only. Send SASE if you wish material returned. Do not send large package with small SASE envelope requesting we write explaining why we did not buy your feature or what we liked or disliked about it. We are not a school; we do not have the time to reply to such mail."

AMERICAN NEWSPAPER SYNDICATE, 9 Woodrush Drive, Irvine CA 92714. (714) 559-8047. Executive Editor: Susan Smith. Syndicates to U.S. and Canadian medium and large-sized general interest and special interest newspapers.
Needs: Wants to syndicate 5 new cartoonists this year. Looking for comic strips, comic panels, editorial cartoons, illustrations, spot drawings, b&w and color. "We are particularly looking for humorous features that are fresh, contemporary and genuinely funny. We also will consider dramatic serial strip concepts that are unique and that have strong characters. We need features that can run daily and Sunday. Material should appeal to all ages, and can be on any subject."
First Contact & Terms: Send query letter with copies of 20 dailies. Samples not kept on file are returned by SASE. Please do *not* send original art. Reports within 3 weeks. Buys U.S. newspaper rights. Wants to sign contracts with cartoonists to produce material on a regular basis. Also looking for merchandising and licensing possibilities.
Tips: "We are willing to take on material that may be considered too unconventional by the other syndicates. Because of our understanding of the newspaper syndication market, we feel we can find a place for the previously unpublished cartoonists. We urge you to be fresh and original. Be yourself. Don't try to imitate other, well-known cartoonists. Develop three-dimensional characters in open-ended situations that will provide ample opportunities for comic possibilities. Ask yourself: do I *really like* these characters? Is this feature *really* funny? Would I want to read it every day? When you can honestly answer yes to these questions, you may have a feature that is a potential hit."

BLACK CONSCIENCE SYNDICATION, INC., 21 Bedford St., Wyandanch NY 11798. (516)491-7774. Director: Clyde R. Davis. Estab. 1987. Syndicate serving regional magazines, schools, daily newspapers and television.
Needs: Considers comic strips, gag cartoons, caricatures, editorial or political cartoons, illustrations and spot drawings. Prefers single, double or multi-panel cartoons. "All material must be of an importance to the Black community in America and the world." Especially needs material on gospel music and its history.
First Contact & Terms: Send query letter with resume, tear sheets and photocopies. Samples are filed. Samples not filed are returned by SASE only if requested by artist. Reports back within 2 months. Call to show a portfolio, which should include tear sheets. Pays 50% of gross income. Pays on publication. Considers client's preferences when establishing payment. Buys first rights.
Tips: "All material must be inspiring as well as informative. Our main search is for the truth."

B M ENTERPRISES, Box 421, Farrell PA 16121. President: William (Bill) Murray. Syndicates to 400 weekly newspapers, schools and national and regional magazines.
Needs: Buys from 12 freelance artists/year. Considers single, double and multiple panel cartoons; line and spot drawings; b&w. Prefers humorous themes. Also uses artists for advertising.
First Contact & Terms: Prefers published artists only; however, others may submit. Works on assignment only. Send query letter with resume and tear sheets to be kept on file. Write for artists' guidelines. Samples not kept on file are returned by SASE. Reports within 30 days. Write for appointment to show portfolio. Pays flat fee, $8-50. Pays on acceptance. Considers skill and experience of artist when establishing payment. Buys all rights.
Tips: "Submit only best work. Send only humorous or family-oriented work."

***BRILLIANT ENTERPRISES**, 117 W. Valerio St., Santa Barbara CA 93101. Art Director: Ashleigh Brilliant. Serves 100's of daily newspapers.
Needs: Buys from various numbers of freelance artists/year. Considers illustrations with text. Prefers pen & ink.
First Contact & Terms: Samples are not filed, and are returned by SASE. Reports back within 3 weeks. Pays flat fee of $50 minimum. Pays on acceptance. Buys all rights.
Tips: "Our products and publications are so unusual that freelancers who do not first carefully study our line will only be wasting their time and ours. First contact should be made by sending for our catalog $2+ SASE)."

The asterisk before a listing indicates that the listing is new in this edition. New markets are often the most receptive to freelance submissions.

CAROL BRYAN IMAGINES, THE LIBRARY IMAGINATION PAPER, 1000 Byus Dr., Charleston WV 25311. Editor: Carol Bryan. Syndicates clip art for 3,000 public and school libraries. Sample issue $1.
Needs: Buys 6-15 illustrations/issue. Considers gag cartoons, illustrations and spot drawings. Prefers single panel b&w line drawings. Prefers library themes—"not negative towards library or stereotyped (example: showing a spinster librarian with glasses and bun)."
First Contact & Terms: Send query letter with tear sheets, photocopies and finished cartoons. Samples are filed. Samples not filed are returned by SASE. Reports back within 3 weeks. Pays flat fee, $10-25; on publication. Buys one-time or reprint rights.
Tips: "Seeing a sample issue is mandatory—we have a specific style and have been very successful with it. Your style may blend with our philosophy. Need great cartoons that libraries can publish in their newsletters."

CHURCH BULLETIN & NEWSLETTER RESOURCE, Box 1149, Orange Park FL 32067-1149. (904)269-5139. Publisher: Wayne Hepburn. Clip art firm serving about 12,000 outlets, including churches, schools, associations and ministries.
Needs: Buys 40-60 cartoons and 200-1,000 illustrations/year from freelance artists. Prefers illustrations and single panel cartoons with gagline and b&w line art. Maximum size is 7x10 and must be reducible to 20% of size without losing detail. "We need very graphic material." Prefers religious or educational themes. "Looking for reproducible children's activity and learning material."
First Contact & Terms: Send photocopies. Samples not filed are returned by SASE. Guidelines and catalog available for 9x12 SASE with 2 first-class stamps. Reports back within 2 months. To show a portfolio, mail roughs and Photostats. Pays $5-50; on acceptance. Buys all rights.
Tips: "All our images are published as clip art to be reproduced by readers in their bulletins and newletters for churches, schools, associations, etc. We need art for holidays, seasons and activities; new material every 3 months. We want single-panel cartoons, not continuity strips."

CITY NEWS SERVICE, Box 39, Willow Springs MO 65793. (417)469-2423. President: Richard Weatherington. Editorial service providing editorial and graphic packages for magazines. Considers cartoons, caricature, tax and business subjects as themes; considers b&w line drawings and shading film.
Needs: Buys from 12 or more freelance artists/year.
First Contact & Terms: Send query letter with resume, tear sheets or photocopies. Samples should contain business subjects. Samples not filed are returned by SASE. Reports within 4-6 weeks. To show a portfolio, mail tear sheets or Photostats. Pays for illustration by the project, $25 minimum. "We may buy art outright or split percentage of sales." Considers complexity of project, skill and experience of artist, how work will be used and rights purchased when establishing payment.
Tips: "We have the markets for multiple sales of editorial support art. We need talented artists to supply specific projects. We will work with beginning artists."

CLASSIFIED INTERNATIONAL ADVERTISING SERVICES INC., 3211 N. 74th Ave., Hollywood FL 33024. Contact: Art & Research Director Clip Art Service. Clients: auto dealers, real estate agencies and newspapers.
Needs: B&w line drawings, cartoons and limited photography.
First Contact & Terms: Mail samples only, please. Samples returned by SASE. Reports only if interested. Works on assignment only. Pays by the project. Considers complexity of project, and skill and experience of artist when establishing payment.
Tips: "We provide work for classified departments of newspaper firms. We have three sections to our service: automotive, real estate and self-promotion. Our company provides our service to all parts of the country, so our needs range so as to provide for the variety of tastes in the field of art. We provide cartoons, illustrations and realism, depending on the particular idea we're trying to convey."

***COLUMBIA FEATURES, INC.**, 3500 S. Atlantic Ave., New Smyrna Beach FL 32069. (904)423-2329. Editor: Robert Ferguson. Serves 200 daily newspapers.
Needs: Buys from 4-12 freelance artists/year. Published artists only. Considers comic strips, gag cartoons, caricatures, editorial or political cartoons, illustrations, spot drawings and Macintosh graphics. Prefers pen & ink. Also needs artists for publicity.
First Contact & Terms: Send resume and Photostats. Samples are not filed and are returned by SASE. Reports back within 2 weeks. Pays 50% of gross income. Pays on publication. Considers skill and experience of artist, saleability of art work and client's preferences when establishing payment. Buys first rights.
Tips: "Please study newspapers for syndicated comics, panels, and illustrations to understand the market before submitting anything."

COMMUNITY AND SUBURBAN PRESS SERVICE, Box 639, Frankfort KY 40602. (502)223-1736. Editor/Publisher: Kennison Keene. Syndicates to 300 weekly, small daily and shopper publications throughout the USA, and 1,500 or more yearly.
Needs: Buys from 10 or more freelance artists/year. Considers double panel cartoons; illustrations and line drawings; b&w. Prefers humorous themes. Also uses artists for graduation and Christmas ads.
First Contact & Terms: Send samples. Write for artists' guidelines. Considers single panel cartoons. "Usually cartoon artists will submit 8 or 9 cartoons at a time, together with SASE." Samples not kept on file returned by SASE. Reports within 1 week. To show a portfolio, mail original/final art. "We pay $15/cartoon, if work is acceptable to us. Price to be negotiated on holiday greeting ads and graduation greeting ads." Pays on acceptance. Considers salability of artwork. Buys first rights.

COMMUNITY FEATURES, Dept. C, Box 1062, Berkeley CA 94701. Art Editor: B. Miller. Syndicates to 270 daily and weekly newspapers, shoppers, consumer magazines. Mails brochure of new syndicated offerings to 700+ newspapers. Guidelines $1 and #10 SASE. Specify "artists' guidelines."
Needs: Interested in professional quality b&w illustrations, spot drawings, line art, square single, double and multiple panel cartoons; illustrated educational panels, how-to, etc. Does not seek color. Looking for illustrators and editorial cartoonists for regular assignments.
First Contact & Terms: Send tear sheets, veloxes, PMTs or excellent photocopies (published and unpublished) that can be kept on file. Do not send art-boards. Reports within 3-6 weeks. Buys various rights. Purchases some one-shot. Will consider line-art on all topics listed in guidelines. Pays $20-500 flat rate for one-shot and occasional work; 50% commission for regularly appearing features. Pays on publication.
Tips: "We look for a bold, modern look. Submit very clear copies. Include SASE if return is desired. Often, freelancers go to too much trouble and expense in sending elaborate packages with long cover letters. The work always speaks for itself! Best to leave samples of your work on file with us and we will contact you as the need arises. (No art work is distributed to our clients without artist's written approval.) Pet peeve: misspelled captions!"

***MARY ELLEN CORBETT SYNDICATE**, Wheeler Rd., Brandon VT 05733. (802)247-3648. Editor: Mary Ellen Corbett. Serves daily newspapers coast to coast.
Needs: Buys from some freelance artists annually. "Number varies." Works on assignment only. Considers comic strips, gag cartoons, caricatures, editorial or political cartoons and illustrations. Prefers multiple panel cartoons. Prefers pen & ink, roughs only for consideration. Prefers women's issues.
First Contact & Terms: Send query letter with resume and samples. Samples are filed. Samples not filed are returned only if requested with SASE. Reports back within 4 weeks. Pays "percentage based upon material syndication potential." Considers skill and experience of artist and saleability of art work when establishing payment.
Tips: "Concepts are as important as art work. Ability to sustain quality of material is crucial. Roughs satisfactory for evaluation purposes. No need for sophisticated presentations."

***CREATORS SYNDICATE, INC.**, 1554 S. Sepulveda Blvd., Los Angeles CA 90025. (213)477-2776. President: Richard S. Newcombe. Estab. 1987. Serves 1,700 daily newspapers, weekly and monthly magazines.
Needs: Buys from 100 freelance writers and artists/year. Considers comic strips, gag cartoons, caricatures, editorial or political cartoons and one-shot articles and columns.
First Contact & Terms: Send query letter with brochure showing art style or resume and "anything but originals." Samples are not filed, but returned by SASE. Reports back within 2 months. Write to show a portfolio, which should include tear sheets and Photostats. Pays 50% of net proceeds. Considers saleability of art work and client's preferences when establishing payment. Negotiates rights purchased.

DYNAMIC GRAPHICS INC., 6000 N. Forest Park Dr., Peoria IL 61614-3592. (309)688-8800. Art Director: Frank Antal. Distributes to thousands of magazines, newspapers, agencies, industries and educational institutions.
Needs: Works with 30-40 artists/year. Illustrations, graphic design and elements; primarily b&w, but will consider some 2- and full-color. "We are currently seeking to contact established illustrators capable of handling b&w highly realistic illustration of contemporary people and situations."
First Contact & Terms: Submit portfolio. SASE. Reports within 1 month. Buys all rights. Negotiates payment. Pays on acceptance.
Tips: "Concentrate on mastering the basics in anatomy and figure illustration before settling into a 'personal' or 'interpretive' style!"

EDITOR'S CHOICE CLIP ART QUARTERLY, Box 529, Kitty Hawk NC 27979. (919)441-3141. Editor: Frances K. Ries. Clip art firm. Distributes quarterly to major corporations who publish employee

Close-up

Richard Newcombe

President, Creators Syndicate
Los Angeles, California

For the past year the big news in syndication circles has been the formation of Creators Syndicate whose founder, Richard Newcombe, caused a ruckus by touting artists' rights. "I was prepared to hit a nerve in the industry," Newcombe says, "but I hit an artery instead."

Newcombe says he founded Creators Syndicate (CS) for the opportunity to create the ideal syndicate. "Over the years, I have seen plenty of greedy syndicate contracts that took advantage of artists. So I finally decided it was time to set a higher standard of professionalism."

For cartoonists, syndication offers the pot of gold at the end of the rainbow. Whether they are able to bank the gold depends upon how much creative control they are able to hold. Newcombe feels many artists have signed unfair contracts in order to be in print. "Milton Caniff was so frustrated that he stopped writing and drawing 'Terry and the Pirates' more than 40 years ago because he was denied ownership of his creation. In fact, we are talking about industry practices that have existed ever since William Randolph Hearst sued Rudolph Dirks for ownership of the first comic strip ever syndicated—'The Katzenjammer Kids.' Hearst was allowed to keep the name and Dirks was allowed to keep the characters, which he used in his next strip. But the significance of CS is that we are challenging the foundation of an entire industry, forcing the major syndicates to abandon practices which reasonable people would call abusive."

Newcombe says syndicates have two ways to control their cartoonists—by owning the characters and automatic renewal of a five- or ten-year contract. They often combine one with another to sweeten the pot. Some syndicates ask for a 10-20 year contract but grant ownership rights, while others offer five-year contracts but keep ownership rights, while others offer five-year contracts but keep ownership of the characters. By owning the characters, a syndicate can hire another artist (on salary rather than on a royalty basis, as the creator was) to continue the feature after the original contract expires. Thus the creator must start a new feature and find another syndicate.

If syndicate contracts are so bad, why does everyone accept them? "Largely because they have had no choice," says Newcombe. "In many cases the only way they could become syndicated was to sign over ownership of their feature or sign a contract of extreme length. I know of one contract that runs into the middle of the next century."

To treat this injustice, Creators offers a five-year contract to new artists, who maintain ownership of the strip. CS asks for the five-year term because introducing a new artist is an investment. Newcombe estimates that it costs between $40,000 to $50,000 for the introduction. "We might spend as much as $1,000 to make a $25-per-week sale, and the syndicate is lucky to keep $12 each week after paying the artist."

In order to beat the 100-1 odds against a newcomer becoming syndicated, Newcombe is willing to give a chance to any strip that has sales potential. "The key to a successful strip or panel is to offer work that is entertaining and clever, that has either mass appeal or a small but vocal following." Newcombe cites Johnny Hart's "B.C." as the ideal strip. "It was not created with demographics in mind. What are the demographics for cave men? This strip flows from Johnny's incredibly creative mind. The ideas felt natural to him, and, as a result, they felt natural to millions upon millions of newspaper readers."

Most syndicates receive thousands of submissions each year, but they introduce, on the average, only three to six new comics a year. In order to increase your odds for successful syndication, Newcombe suggests that you develop your cartooning skills in a local newspaper and regional magazines. With a following behind you, the national syndicates will pay attention.

When approaching syndicates, first write for printed guidelines, then submit four weeks of samples (photocopies only). Newcombe says that most submissions are in the rough/draft category. But, he adds, "Remember, Charles Schultz is willing to discard 99 ideas to find exactly the right one for the gag you see in today's paper."

Asked how much money you can make in syndication, Newcombe says the amount depends on several factors. Successful cartoonists run in hundreds of newspapers, whose size affects the payoff. Also, they are published in books, greeting cards, character advertising endorsements, television, motion pictures and merchandising.

Newcombe sounds the call of a freedom fighter with his final advice to cartoonists: "As for syndicates that say, 'We give away ownership rights,' my response is to say, 'They're not yours to give.' My advice is to fight for your freedom and for the freedom of all cartoonists. Don't let your syndicate limit it."

—Susan Conner

Johnny Hart, the creator of the "B.C." comic series, was one of the first artists to join Creators Syndicate. He encourages all artists to retain ownership of their strips and sign shorter-term contracts.

newsletters or magazines.
Needs: Serious and humorous editorial illustrations, graphics, standing heads, etc. Works with 6-8 freelance artists/year. Prefers line illustrations in pen & ink, scratchboard, etc., or pencil illustration on textured board. Also buys graphic symbols. Work is related to business and industry, employee relations, health and wellness, physical fitness, family life, recreation, etc.
First Contact & Terms: Experienced illustrators and graphic designers only. Works on assignment only. Send query letter, resume and samples to be kept on file. Reports within 60 days. Prefers photocopies as samples. Samples returned by SASE if not kept on file. Original art not returned at job's completion. Buys all rights or negotiates limited use fee. Pays $30-100 for illustrations; negotiates payment amount, varies according to project. Pays on acceptance.
Tips: "Only accomplished illustrators will be considered. Amateurs need not apply. Send 10-12 samples that show an individual's diversity of styles and techniques. We need illustrations that are easily reproducible. Pen or pencil illustrations must be clear and of good quality. We have no use for color illustrations."

RICHARD R. FALK ASSOCIATES, 1472 Broadway, New York NY 10036. President: R. Falk. Syndicates to regional magazines and daily newspapers.
Needs: Buys from 3-4 freelance artists/year. Works on assignment only. Considers caricatures, editorial or political cartoons and spot drawings. Prefers line drawings. Prefers theatrical, entertainment themes.
First Contact & Terms: "Only send simple flyers, throwaway illustrations." Reports back only if interested. Pays flat fee; $50-250. Pays on acceptance. Considers clients' preferences. Buys one-time rights.
Tips: "Do not send original work, only nonreturnable photocopies."

FILLERS FOR PUBLICATIONS, 5225 Wilshire Blvd., Los Angeles CA 90036. (213)933-2646. President: Lucie Dubovik. Distributes to magazines and newspapers.
Needs: Buys 72 pieces/year. Considers single panel, 4x6 or 5x7 cartoons on current events, education, family life, retirement, factory and office themes. Clip art: inquire for subject matter and format.
First Contact & Terms: Send query letter with samples of style and SASE. Samples are returned. Reports in 3 weeks. Previously published and simultaneous submissions OK. Buys first rights. Pays $7, cartoons, line drawings; $25/page of clip art; on acceptance.

FOTO EXPRESSION INTERNATIONAL, Box 1268, Station "Q"., Toronto Ontario M4T 2P4 Canada. (416)736-0119 or (416)665-8459. Director: M.J. Kubik. Serving 35 outlets.
Needs: Buys from 80 freelance artists/year. Considers single, double and multiple panel cartoons, illustrations, spot drawings, b&w and color.
First Contact & Terms: Send query letter with brochure showing art style or resume, tear sheets, slides and photographs. Samples not filed returned by SASE. Reports within one month. To show a portfolio, mail final reproduction/product, color, photographs and b&w. Artist receives percentage; on publication. Considers skill and experience of artist and rights purchased when establishing payment. Negotiates rights purchased.
Tips: "Quality and content are essential. Resume and samples must be accompanied by a SASE or, out of Canada, International Reply Coupon is required."

PAULA ROYCE GRAHAM, 2770 W. 5th St., Brooklyn NY 11224. (718)372-1920. Contact: Paula Royce Graham. Syndicates to newspapers and magazines.
Needs: Considers illustrations; b&w. Also uses artists for advertising and graphics.
First Contact & Terms: Send business card and tear sheets to be kept on file. Write for artists' guidelines. Samples returned by SASE only if requested. Reports within days. Write for appointment to show portfolio. Pay is negotiable; on publication. Considers skill of artist, client's preferences and rights purchased when establishing payment. Buys all rights.

GRAPHIC ARTS COMMUNICATIONS, Box 421, Farrell PA 16121. (412)342-5300. President: Bill Murray. Syndicates to 200 newspapers and magazines. Buys 400 pieces/year.
Needs: Humor through youth and family themes for single panel, strips and multi-panel cartoons. Needs ideas for anagrams, editorial cartoons and puzzles, and for new comic panel "Sugar & Spike."
First Contact & Terms: Query for guidelines. SASE. Reports within 4-6 weeks. No originals returned. Buys all rights. Pays flat fee, $8-50.

GRAPHIC NEWS BUREAU, gabriel graphics, Box 38, Madison Square Station, New York NY 10010. (212)254-8863. Cable: NOLNOEL. Director: J.G. Bumberg. Custom syndications and promotions to customized lists, small dailies, suburbans and selected weeklies.

Needs: Represents 4-6 freelance artists/year. Prefers artists within easy access. No dogmatic, regional or pornographic themes. Uses single panel cartoons, illustration, halftones in line conversions and line drawings.
First Contact & Terms: Send query letter only. Reports within 4-6 weeks. Returns original art after reproduction on request with SASE. Provide 3x5 card to be kept on file for possible future assignments. Negotiates rights purchased; on publication.
Tips: "A new, added service provides for counselling in graphics/management/communications...when and where printing is an integral part of the promotion, product, service."

HISPANIC LINK NEWS SERVICE, 1420 N St. NW, Washington DC 20005. (202)234-0737. General Manager: Hector Ericksen-Mendoza. Syndicated column service to 200 newspapers and a newsletter serving 1,000 private subscribers, "movers and shakers in the Hispanic community in U.S., plus others interested in Hispanics."
Needs: Buys from 20 freelance artists/year. Considers single panel cartoons; b&w, pen & ink line drawings. Work should have a Hispanic angle; "most are editorial cartoons, some straight humor."
First Contact & Terms: Send query letter with resume and photocopies to be kept on file. Samples not filed returned by SASE. Reports within 3 weeks. Call for appointment to show portfolio or contact through artist's agent. Pays flat fee of $25 average; on acceptance. Considers clients' preferences when establishing payment. Buys reprint rights and negotiates rights purchased; "while we ask for reprint rights, we also allow the artist to sell later."
Tips: "While we accept work from all artists, we are particularly interested in helping Hispanic artists showcase their work. Cartoons should offer a Hispanic perspective on current events or a Hispanic view of life."

HOSPITAL PR GRAPHICS, Box 529, Kitty Hawk NC 27949. (919)441-3141. Editor: Frances K. Ries. Clip art firm. Distributes monthly to hospitals and other health care organizations.
Needs: Works wih 4-5 freelance artists/year (at present). Uses illustrations, line drawings, spot drawings and graphic symbols related to health care for use in brochures, folders, newsletters, etc. Prefers sensitive line illustrations, spot drawings and graphics related to hospitals, nurses, doctors, patients, technicians, medical apparatus. Also buys 12 cartoons/year maximum.
First Contact & Terms: Experienced illustrators only, preferably having hospital exposure or access to resource material. Works on assignment only. Send query letter, resume, Photostats or photocopies to be kept on file. Samples returned by SASE if not kept on file. Reports within 1 month. Original art not returned at job's completion. Buys all rights. Pays flat rate of $20-80 for illustrations; negotiates payment, varies according to project. Pays on acceptance.
Tips: "We are looking to establish a continuing relationship with at least 5-6 freelance graphic designers and illustrators. Illustration style should be serious, sensitive and somewhat idealized. Send enough samples to show the variety (if any) of styles you're capable of handling. Indicate the length of time it took to complete each illustration or graphic."

***INTERNATIONAL PHOTO NEWS**, Box 2405, West Palm Beach FL 33402. (305)793-3424. Photo Editor: Jay Kravetz. Serves 1,800 newspapers and magazines.
Needs: Buys from 100 freelance artists/year. Works on assignment only. Considers comic strips, caricatures, editorial or political cartoons and illustrations. Prefers double panel cartoons. Prefers pen & ink line drawings. Prefers political, celebrity, government subjects.
First Contact & Terms: Send query letter with resume and photocopies. Samples are filed. Samples not filed are returned. Write to shedule an appointment to show a portfolio, which should include tear sheets, Photostats and photographs. Pays 50% of gross income; on publication. Considers saleability of artwork when establishing payment. Buys one-time rights.

INTERPRESS OF LONDON AND NEW YORK, 400 Madison Ave., New York NY 10017. (212)832-2839. Editor/Publisher: Jeffrey Blyth. Syndicates to several dozen European magazines and newspapers.
Needs: Buys from 4-5 freelance artists/year. Prefers material which is universal in appeal; no "American only" material.
First Contact & Terms: Send query letter and photographs; write for artists' guidelines. Samples not kept on file returned by SASE. Reports within 3 weeks. Purchases European rights. Pays 60% of net proceeds on publication.

***JOURNAL PRESS SYNDICATE**, Box 931, Grand Central Station, New York NY 10017. Editor: Eugene R. Smith. Syndicates to newspapers.
Needs: Buys 3 pieces/year. Needs comic strips, panels and editorial cartoons.
First Contact & Terms: Query or submit photocopies (no originals) of material for consideration.

SASE. Reports in 6 weeks. Originals returned to artist. Buys all rights. Negotiates pay.
Tips: "We find that gag-a-day comic strips have almost altogether replaced continuity strips in newspapers. We do not encourage submission of continuities. Artistic value is not paramount. . . . We are marketers of materials to the newspaper industry. Our first question is always 'Will it sell?' "

***JSA PUBLICATIONS**, Box 37175, Oak Park MI 48237. (313)546-9123. Director: Joe Ajlouny. Serves 12 outlets, mainly magazines.
Needs: Buys from 24 freelance artists/year. Considers comic strips, gag cartoons, caricatures or editorial or political cartoons. Prefers pen & ink and airbrush.
First Contact & Terms: Send query letter with resume and samples. Samples are filed. Samples not filed are returned by SASE only if requested. Reports back within 4 weeks only if interested. Call to schedule an appointment to show a portfolio. Pays flat fee of $60-500; on publication. Considers client's preferences and rights purchased when establishing payment. Negotiates rights purchased.
Tips: "All submissions should be readable, not too small."

LANDMARK DESIGNS, INC., Box 2832, Eugene OR 97402. (503)345-3429. Vice President: Richard McAlexander. Serves 80 outlets, such as daily newspapers, magazines, books.
Needs: Buys from 2 freelancers/year. Works on assignment only. Considers architectual renderings and illustrations. Prefers pen & ink. Prefers architecture, residential themes. Also needs artists for advertising.
First Contact & Terms: Send query letter with brochure or samples. Samples are filed. Samples not filed are returned by SASE. Reports back within 10 days only if interested. Write to show a portfolio or mail b&w and tear sheets. Pays for design by the project, 25% commission. Pays for illustration by the project, $40 minimum. Pays on acceptance. Considers skill and experience of artist when establishing payment. Buys all rights.

***LEOLEEN-DURCK CREATIONS/LEONARD BRUCE DESIGNS**, Suite 226, Box 2767, Jackson TN 38302. (901)668-1205. Director/Cartoonist: Leonard Bruce. Serves 5 outlets. Serves daily and weekly newspapers, charities, local papers, national magazines and other syndicates.
Needs: Buys from 10 freelance artists/year. Works on assignment only. Considers comic strips, gag cartoons, caricatures and editorial or political cartoons. Prefers single panel cartoons. Prefers pen & ink, very detailed with washes. Prefers off-the-wall, science fiction, animals and pets, children's themes.
First Contact & Terms: Send brochure showing art style, resume and photocopies. Sample package should include background sheet of strip and artist, resume and photo of artist, 18 samples of previous published works and SASE. Samples are not filed and are returned by SASE. Reports back within 3 weeks only if interested. Write to schedule an appointment to show a portfolio or mail b&w and Photostats. Pays 10% of net proceeds; on publication. Considers skill and experience of artist and saleability of art work when establishing payment. Buys first rights.
Tips: "Send your best work, blocked out panel cartoons and print neatly. Be able to accept rejections and work to refine your material. Send resume, cover sheet explaining your panel or strip. Always send in an SASE with samples. We have just gotten back into the business, and if the artist will work with us on his/her strip panel we will do our best to educate, refine and eventually syndicate the artwork and help the artist grow. We are a small company and we will try to work with the artist and for the artist so that everyone will benefit."

LOS ANGELES TIMES SYNDICATE, 218 S. Spring St., Los Angeles CA 90012. (213)237-7987. Comics Editor: David Seidman, (213)237-5198.
Needs: Comic strips, panel cartoons and editorial cartoons. "We prefer humor to dramatic continuity. We consider only cartoons that run 6 or 7 days/week." Cartoons may be of any size as long as they're to scale with cartoons running in newspapers. (Strips usually run approximately 6 7/16x2", panel cartoons 3 1/8x4"; editorial cartoons vary.)
First Contact & Terms: Submit photocopies or Photostats of 24 dailies. Submitting Sunday cartoons is optional; if you choose to submit them, send at least four. Reports within 2 months. SASE. Syndicate buys all rights.
Tips: "Don't imitate cartoons that are already in the paper. Avoid linework or details that might bleed together, fade out or reproduce too small to see clearly. Keep sex, alcohol, violence and other potentially offensive subjects to a minimum. We hardly ever match artists with writers or vice versa. We prefer people or teams who can do the entire job of creating a feature."

MCLEAN PROVIDENCE JOURNAL AND ARLINGTON COURIER, Box 580, McLean VA 22101. Editor: David Dear. Syndicates to weekly newspapers.
Needs: Buys from 2 freelance artists/year. Prefers local or Virginia artists. Considers comic strips, gag cartoons, caricatures, editorial or political cartoons, illustrations and spot drawings. Prefers pen & ink with washes.

First Contact & Terms: Send query letter with brochure or resume and tear sheets. Samples are filed. Samples not filed are returned by SASE. Reports back only if interested. To show a portfolio, mail tear sheets. Pays flat fee, $5-90; on publication. Considers clients' preferences when establishing payment. Negotiates rights purchased.
Tips: "Best luck if they are local artists or if work has local theme or elements."

METRO CREATIVE GRAPHICS, INC., 33 W. 34th St., New York NY 10011. (800)223-1600. Contact: Andrew Shapiro. Clip art firm. Distributes to 6,000 daily and weekly paid and free circulation newspapers, schools, graphics and ad agencies and retail chains.
Needs: Buys from 100 freelance artists/year. Considers single panel illustrations and line and spot drawings; b&w and color. Prefers all categories of themes associated with retail, classified, promotion and advertising. Also needs artists for special-interest tabloid section covers.
First Contact & Terms: Send query letter with brochure showing style or Photostats, photocopies, slides, photographs and tear sheets to be kept on file. Samples not kept on file returned by SASE. Reports only if interested. To show a portfolio, mail appropriate materials or call to schedule an appointment. Works on assignment only. Pays flat fee of $25-1,000; on acceptance. Considers skill and experience of artist, saleability of artwork and clients' preferences when establishing payment.
Tips: "Metro provides steady work, lead time and prompt payment. All applicants are seriously considered. Don't rely on 1-2 samples to create interest. Show a variety of styles and special ability to draw people in realistic situations. If specialty is graphic design, think how you would use samples in advertising."

MINORITY FEATURES SYNDICATE, Box 421, Farrell PA 16121. (412)342-5300. Chairman of the Board: Bill Murray. Clip art firm serving approximately 500 outlets.
Needs: Buys from 600 freelance artists/year. Considers single, double and multi-panel cartoons; illustrations and spot drawings. Prefers b&w pen & ink line drawings with family themes. Also uses artists for advertising art. Also publishes comic books. Query first.
First Contact & Terms: Published artists only. Works on assignment only. Send query letter to be kept on file; write for artists' guidelines. Prefers photocopies as samples. Samples returned by SASE. Reports only if interested. Pays flat fee, $8-50; on acceptance. Considers rights purchased when establishing payment. Buys all rights.
Tips: "Submit only your best efforts."

***NATIONAL CATHOLIC NEWS SERVICE**, 1312 Massachusetts Ave. NW, Washington DC 20005. Picture Editor: Bob Strawn. Serves 150 outlets. Serves weekly newspapers.
Needs: Considers gag cartoons, illustrations and spot drawings. Prefers single panel cartoons. Prefers pen & ink line drawings. Prefers religious, family and Catholic themes.
First Contact & Terms: Send query letter with brochure, tear sheets, Photostats, photocopies and slides. Samples are filed. Samples not filed are returned by SASE. Reports back within 3 weeks. Call or write to schedule an appointment to show a portfolio, which should include original/final art, final reproduction/product, b&w, tear sheets, Photostats, photographs and slides. Pays flat fee of $75-150 for assignments; cartoons, $15; stock line art, $25; on acceptance. Considers skill and experience of artist when establishing payment. Buys one-time rights or all rights; negotiates rights purchased.
Tips: "Some knowledge of the Catholic Church can be very helpful but not absolutely required. Artists should be able to work in simple line style suitable for newspaper reproduction. We are looking for artists with a modern style, not so traditional. The right artist could get an assignment a week from us."

NATIONAL NEWS BUREAU, 2019 Chancellor St., Philadelphia PA 19103. (215)569-0700. Editor: Harry Jay Katz. Syndicates to 1,000 outlets and publishes entertainment newspapers on a contract basis.
Needs: Buys from 500 freelance artists/year. Prefers entertainment themes. Uses single, double and multiple panel cartoons, illustrations, line and spot drawings.
First Contact & Terms: Send samples and resume. Samples returned by SASE. Reports within 2 weeks. Returns original art after reproduction. Send resume and samples to be kept on file for future assignments. Negotiates rights purchased. Pays flat rate, $5-100 for each piece; on publication.

NEWSPAPER ENTERPRISE ASSOCIATION/UNITED FEATURE SYNDICATE, 200 Park Ave., New York NY 10166. Director of Comic Art: Sarah Gillespie. Syndicates to more than 1,500 newspapers.
Needs: Comic strip ideas, editorial cartoons and comic panels. Prefers pen & ink. Contact via mail. Send 4-6 weeks of dailies, short cover letter with bio. "I don't want to see long character descriptions, originals, oversize material or licensing samples." Send copies, not originals, and SASE for return. All submissions answered. If used in NEA Daily Service, pays flat fee. If used in syndicate division, 50% commission.
Tips: "We are looking for innovative comic features with interesting characters. There should be an

idea behind your feature that allows it to be open-ended. Whatever the 'staging,' you need an on-going narrative structure. The market is very, very tight. We take 3 new strips a year and get over 3,000 submissions. Concentrate on character more than subject matter."

OCEANIC PRESS SERVICE, Box 6538, Buena Park CA 90622-6538. (714)527-5651. Manager: Nat Carlton. Syndicates to 300 magazines, newspapers and subscribers in 30 countries.
Needs: Buys several hundred pieces/year. Considers cartoon strips (single, double and multiple panel) and illustrations. Prefers camera ready material (tear sheets or clippings). Themes include published sex cartoons, family cartoons, inflation, juvenile activities and jacket covers for paperbacks (color transparencies). Especially needs juvenile activity drawings and unusual sports cartoons; also sex cartoons. "God, sex and action is still a good formula. Poke fun at established TV shows. Bad economy means people must do their own home, car and other repairs. How-to articles with b&w line drawings are needed. Magazines will buy less and have more features staff-written. Quality is needed. People like to read more about celebrities, but it has to have a special angle, not the usual biographic run-of-the-mill profile. Much will be TV related. I'd like to see a good cartoon book on Sherlock Holmes, on Hollywood, on leading TV shows."
First Contact & Terms: Send query letter with Photostats and samples of previously published work. Accepts tear sheets and clippings. SASE. Reports within 1 month. Pays on publication. Originals returned to artist, or put on auction. Guidelines $1 with SASE.
Tips: "The trend is definitely toward women's market: money saving topics, service features—how to do home repair—anything to fight inflation; also unusual cartoons about unusual happenings; unusual sports; and cartoons with sophisticated international settings, credit cards, air travel. We would like to receive more clippings for foreign reprints. Competition is keen—artists should strive for better quality submissions."

PRESS ASSOCIATES INC., 806 15th St. NW, Washington DC 20005. (202)638-0444. Contact: Art Editor. News service serving "hundreds" of trade union newspapers and magazines.
Needs: Buys from 10-15 freelance artists/year. Considers single panel cartoons; line drawings; b&w. Prefers humorous and workplace themes—manufacturing, office, retail, etc.
First Contact & Terms: Send query letter with original cartoons. Samples not kept on file returned by SASE only if requested. Pays flat rate of $7.50; on acceptance. Considers clients' preferences when establishing payment. Buys first or reprint rights.
Tips: "We do not consider strips, only single-panel cartoons."

PROFESSIONAL ADVISORY COUNSEL, INC., Suite 106, 5815 Melton Dr., Oklahoma City OK 73132. President: Larry W. Beavers. Syndicate serving approximately 1,000 international outlets.
Needs: Buys from over 30 freelance artists/year. Considers illustrations and spot drawings, b&w and color. Prefers camera-ready artwork. Also uses artists for advertising. Considers any media.
First Contact & Terms: Works on assignment only. Send query letter with brochure, resume, business card and samples to be kept on file if interested. Samples not returned. Especially looks for "simplicity and fast-relating/assimilating potential." Reports only if interested. Write for appointment to show portfolio and for artists' guidelines. Pays flat fee, $10-100 average; on acceptance. Buys all rights.
Tips: "Make your contact quick, concise and to-the-point."

REPORTER, YOUR EDITORIAL ASSISTANT, Suite 304, 5225 Wilshire Blvd., Los Angeles CA 90036. (213)747-6542. Editor: George Dubow. Syndicates to newspapers and magazines from secondary level schools and colleges.
Needs: Considers single panel cartoons on teenage themes.
First Contact & Terms: Mail art. SASE. Reports in 2 weeks. Buys all rights. Originals returned to artist only upon request. Pays $5-10.

***REVIEWS AND PREVIEWS**, Box 112940, Miami FL 33111. Art Director: Andre DuMont. Serves 42 outlets such as foreign magazines, galleries, commercial buildings and private collections.
Needs: Considers illustrations and spot drawings. Prefers single panel cartoons. Prefers erotic, oriental or modern themes.
First Contact & Terms: Send query letter with brochure, Photostats, photocopies and slides. Samples are filed. Samples not filed are returned by SASE. Reports back within 2 weeks. Write to schedule an appointment to show a portfolio which should include original/final art, photographs and slides. Pays 75% of net proceeds. Pays on publication. Considers saleability of art work and client's preferences when establishing payment. Buys all rights; negotiates rights purchased.

SINGER MEDIA CORP., 3164 Tyler Ave., Anaheim CA 92801. (714)527-5650. Executive Vice President: Natalie Carlton. Syndicates to 300 magazines, newspapers, book publishers and poster firms;

strips include *They Changed History*, and *How It Began*. Artists' guidelines $1.
Needs: Buys several thousand pieces/year. Considers cartoon strips; single, double and multiple panel; family, children, sex, juvenile activities and games themes; universal material on current topics. Especially needs business, outerspace and credit card cartoons of 3-4 panels. Prefers to buy reprints or clips of previously published material.
First Contact & Terms: Send query letter with tear sheets. Show 10-12 samples. "Prefer to see tear sheets or camera ready copy or clippings." SASE. Reports within 2-3 weeks. Returns originals to artist at job's completion if requested at time of submission with SASE. Licenses reprint or all rights; prefers foreign reprint rights. Pays 50% commission.
Tips: "Send us cartoons on subjects like inflation, taxes, sports or Christmas; we get thousands on sex. Everyone wants new ideas—not the same old characters, same old humor at the doctor or psychiatrist or at the bar. More sophistication is needed. Background is also needed—not just 2 people talking."

TEENAGE CORNER INC., 70-540 Gardenia Ct., Rancho Mirage CA 92270. President: David J. Lavin. Syndicates rights.
Needs: Spot drawings and illustrations.
First Contact & Terms: Send query letter. SASE. Reports within 1 week. Buys one-time and reprint rights. Negotiates commission. Pays on publication.

TRIBUNE MEDIA SERVICES, INC., 64 E. Concord St., Orlando FL 32801. (305)839-5650. Editor: Mike Argirion. Syndicate serving daily and Sunday newspapers.
Needs: Seeks comic strips and newspaper panels.
First Contact & Terms: Send query letter with resume and photocopies. Samples not filed are returned. Reports within 2-4 weeks.

UNITED CARTOONIST SYNDICATE, Box 7081, Corpus Christi TX 78415. (512)855-2480. President: Pedro R. Moreno. Syndicate serving international and U.S. outlets. Regular outlets vary from church newsletters to major newspapers or international comic syndicates.
Needs: Buys from 12-24 freelance artists/year. Consider single, double or multiple panel cartoons; b&w or color on Sundays. Prefers (medium) line drawings of pen & ink or zip-a-tone (no washes). Prefers family entertainment (clean) as themes. "The humor in comics whould be of a clean-cut nature, not the aggressive sexual type."
First Contact & Terms: Send query letter with $5 for "comic guidelines." Reports within 7 days. To show a portfolio, mail tear sheets, b&w and reduced newspaper page size. Pays 40% of gross income on publication. Considers saleability of artwork when establishing payment. Negotiates rights purchased.
Tips: "Before submitting your artwork, reduce your comic panel or comic strip in a newspaper page size. The amount of 6-12 comics are required for a good evaluation for possible syndication. Comic strips and panels submitted must include SASE and $5 for "comic guidelines" or they will not be returned."

UNIVERSAL PRESS SYNDICATE, 4900 Main St., Kansas City MO 64112. Editorial Director: Lee Salem. Syndicate serving 2750 daily and weekly newspapers.
Needs: Comic strips and panels; text features. Considers single, double or multiple panel cartoons; b&w and color. Prefers photocopies of b&w, pen & ink, line drawings; other techniques are reviewed, but remember that this material will be published in newspapers.
First Contact & Terms: Reports within 4 weeks. To show a portfolio, mail Photostats. Buys syndication rights. Send query letter with resume and photocopies.
Tips: "A well-conceived comic strip with strong characters, good humor and a contemporary feel will almost always get a good response. Be original. Don't be afraid to try some new idea or technique. Don't be discouraged by rejection letters. Universal Press receives 100-150 comic submissions a week, and only takes on two or three a year, so keep plugging away. Talent has a way of rising to the top."

***WADE'S CARTOON SERVICE**, Suite #3, 1924 N. Talbott Ave., Indianapolis IN 46202. (317)925-6517. Contact: Harlan Wade. Serves 200 weeklies.
Needs: Buys from 40 freelance artists/year. Considers comic strips, gag cartoons and editorial or political cartoons. Prefers single panel, double panel and multiple panel; pen & ink, pen & ink with washes. Also uses artists for advertising.
First Contact & Terms: Send query letter with brochure showing art style or resume and samples. Samples are filed. Samples not filed are returned by SASE. Reports back within 2 weeks. Write to schedule an appointment to show a portfolio, or mail original/final art, b&w (8½x11). Pays 50% of gross income or flat fee of $50 maximum; on publication. Considers saleability of art work and client's preferences when establishing payment. Buys all rights.
Tips: "Cartoons and comic strips must be in good taste and very funny."

Artist's Resource List

The section introductions in this directory recommend the following additional reading material for names and addresses of art buyers. Most are available either in a library or bookstore or from the publisher. To insure accurate names and addresses, use copies of these resources that are no older than a year.

Advertising Age
740 Rush St., Chicago IL 60611
Adweek
A/S/M Communications, Inc., 49 E. 21st St., New York NY 10010
American Art Directory
R.R. Bowker Company, 245 W. 17th St., New York NY 10011
American Showcase
American Showcase, Inc., 724 Fifth Ave., New York NY 10019
The Art and Craft of Greeting Cards
(by Susan Evarts), North Light Publishing, 1507 Dana Ave., Cincinnati OH 45207
Art Business News
Myers Publishing Co., 60 Ridgeway Plaza, Stamford CT 06905
Art Directors Annual
Art Directors Club, 250 Park Ave. S., New York NY 10003
Art in America's Annual Guide to Galleries, Museums and Artists
980 Madison Ave., New York NY 10021
The Artist's Friendly Legal Guide
North Light Publishing, 1507 Dana Ave., Cincinnati OH 45207
The Artist's Guide to Philadelphia Galleries
(by Amy Orr), Box 8755, Philadelphia PA 19101
Audio Video Market Place
R.R. Bowker Company, 245 W. 17th St., New York NY 10011
Barron's Profiles of American Colleges
Barron's Educational Series, Inc., 113 Crossways Park Dr., Woodbury NY 11797
Better Homes & Gardens
Meredith Corporation, 1716 Locust St., Des Moines IA 50336
Books In Print
(vol. 4), R.R. Bowker Company, 245 W. 17th St., New York NY 10011
Cartoon World
Box 30367, Lincoln, NE 68503
Chicago Creative Directory
333 N. Michigan Ave., Chicago IL 60601
Collector's Mart
WEB Publications, Inc., 15100 W. Kellogg, Wichita KS 67235
Comparative Guide to American Colleges
Harper & Row, 10 E. 53rd St., New York NY 10022
Contracts for Artists
(by William Gignilliat), Words of Art, Inc., Box 2, Atlanta GA 30301
Creative Black Book
Creative Black Book, Inc., 401 Park Ave. S., New York NY 10016
Creative Source
Wilcord Publications Ltd., Suite 200, 206 Laird Dr., Toronto Ontario M4G 3W5
Dancemagazine
Dance Magazine Inc., 33 W. 60th St., New York NY 10036
Decor
Source List, Commerce Publishing Co., 408 Olive St., St. Louis MO 63102
The Design Directory
Wefler & Associates, Inc., Box 1591, Evanston IL 60204
Designing Greeting Cards and Paper Products
(by Ron Lister), Prentice-Hall, Inc., Englewood Cliffs NJ 07632
Directory of Directories
Gale Research Co., Book Tower, Detroit MI 48226
Editor & Publisher
The Editor & Publisher Co. Inc., 11 W. 19th St., New York NY 10011
Editor & Publisher's Syndicate Directory
The Editor & Publisher Co. Inc., 11 W. 19th St., New York NY 10011
Encyclopedia of Associations
Gale Research Co., Book Tower, Detroit MI 48226
The Gag Recap
Al Gottlieb, Box 86, East Meadow NY 11554
Gale Directory of Publications
Gale Research Company, Book Tower, Detroit MI 48226
Gebbie Press All-In-One-Directory
Gebbie Press, Box 1000, New Paltz NY 12561
Gifts and Decorative Accessories
Geyer-McAllister Publications, 51 Madison Ave., New York NY 10010. (Buyer's guide and December issue)
Giftware News
Talcott Communications Inc., 1414 The Merchandise Mart, Chicago IL 60654

The Graphic Artist's Guide to Marketing and Self-Promotion
(by Sally Davis), North Light Publishing, 1507 Dana Ave., Cincinnati, OH 45207

Graphic Artists Guild Directory
Graphic Artists Guild, 30 E. 20th St., New York NY 10003

Graphic Artist Guild Handbook: Pricing & Ethical Guidelines
Robert Silver Associates, 95 Madison Ave., New York NY 10016

Greetings Magazine
MacKay Publishing Corp., 309 Fifth Ave., New York NY 10016

Homesewing Trade News
Homesewing Trade News, Inc., 330 Sunrise Hwy., Box 286, Rockville Centre NY 11571

House Beautiful
Hearst Corporation, 1700 Broadway, New York NY 10019

How to Make Money in Newspaper Syndication
(by Susan Lane), Newspaper Syndication Specialists, Suite 326, Box 19654, Irvine, CA 92720

Interior Design
475 Park Ave. S., New York NY 10016

Internal Publications Directory
National Research Bureau, Suite 1150, 310 S. Michigan Ave., Chicago IL 60604

International Directory of Little Magazines and Small Presses
Dustbooks, Box 100, Paradise CA 95969

Legal Guide for the Visual Artist
Madison Square Press, Inc., 10 E. 23rd St., New York NY 10010

Literary Market Place
R.R. Bowker Company, 245 W. 17th St., New York NY 10011

Madison Avenue Handbook
Peter Glenn Publications, 17 E. 48th St., New York NY 10017

Medical Marketing & Media
CPS Communications, Inc., Suite 215, 7200 W. Camino Real, Boca Raton FL 33431. December issue

The National Art Museum and Gallery Guide
Art Now, Inc., 320 Bonnie Burn Rd., Box 219, Scotch Plains NJ 07076

The Newsletter Directory
Gale Research Co., Suite 300, 8800 Hwy. 7, Minneapolis MN 55426

O'Dwyer's Directory of Public Relations Firms
J.R. O'Dwyer Company, Inc., 271 Madison Ave., New York NY 10016

Plate World
Plate World Inc., 9200 N. Maryland Ave., Niles IL 60648

Publishers Weekly
205 W. 42nd St., New York NY 10017

Selling Your Graphic Design & Illustration
St. Martin's Press, 175 Fifth Ave., New York NY 10010

Standard Directory of Advertising Agencies
National Register Publishing Co., Inc., 3004 Glenview Rd., Wilmette IL 60091

Standard Periodical Directory
Oxbridge Communications, Inc., Room 301, 150 Fifth Ave., New York NY 10011

Standard Rate and Data Service
3004 Glenview Rd., Wilmette IL 60091. (Consumer magazine volume)

Step-by-Step Graphics
Dynamic Graphics, Inc., 6000 N. Forest Park Dr., Peoria IL 61614-3597.

This Business of Art
(by Diane Cochrane), Watson-Guptill Publications, 1515 Broadway, New York NY 10036

Thomas Register of Manufacturers
Thomas Publishing Co., 1 Penn Plaza, New York NY 10001

Trade Journal Recap
Al Gottlieb, Box 86, East Meadow NY 11554

Ulrich's International Periodicals Directory
R.R. Bowker Company, 245 W. 17th St., New York NY 10011

Visual Merchandising & Store Design
Signs of the Times Publishing Company, 407 Gilbert Ave., Cincinnati OH 45202

W
Fairchild Publications, 7 E. 12th St., New York NY 10003

Washington Art
Art Calendar, Box 1040, Great Falls VA 22066

Women's Wear Daily
Fairchild Publications, 7 E. 12th St., New York NY 10003

The Work Book
Scott & Daughters Publishing, #204, 1545 Wilcox Ave., Los Angeles CA 90028

Working Press of the Natiion
National Research Bureau, Suite 1150, 310 S. Michigan Ave., Chicago IL 60604

Writer's Market
Writer's Digest Books, 1507 Dana Ave., Cincinnati OH 45207

Glossary

Acceptance (payment on). The artist is paid for his work as soon as the buyer decides to use it.
Airbrush. Small pencil-shaped pressure gun used to spray ink, paint or dyes to obtain graduated tonal effects.
Architectural delineator. An illustrator who sketches preliminary ideas for a presentation to a client.
ASAP. Abbreviation for as soon as possible.
Ben-day. An artificial process of shading line illustrations, named after its inventor.
Biennially. Once every two years.
Bimonthly. Once every two months.
Biweekly. Once every two weeks.
Bleed. Area of a plate or print that extends (bleeds off) beyond the edge of trimmed sheet.
Buy-out. The sale of all reproduction rights, and sometimes the original work, by the artist; also subcontracted portions of a job resold at a cost or profit to the end client by the artist.
Calligraphy. The art of fine handwriting.
Camera-ready. Art that is completely prepared for copy camera platemaking.
Cel art. Artwork applied to plastic film, especially used in animation; also an abbreviation for artwork on celluoid.
Cibachrome. Trade mark for a full color positive print made from a transparency.
Collaterals. Accompanying or auxiliary pieces, especially in advertising.
Collotype. A screenless, flat, printing process in which plates are coated with gelatin, exposed to continuous-tone negatives and printed on lithographic presses.
Color separation. Photographic process of separating any multi-color image into its primary component parts (cyan, magenta, yellow and black) for printing.
Commission. 1. Percentage of retail price taken by a sponsor/salesman on artwork sold. 2. Assignment given to an artist.
Compact disc. A small disc, about 4.7" in diameter, which contains digitized music that is incorporated as miscroscopic pits in the aluminum base. Also called digital audio discs.
Comprehensive. Complete sketch of layout showing how a finished illustration will look when printed; also called a comp.
Consignment. Arrangement by which items are sent by an artist to a sales agent (gallery, shop, sales representative, etc.) for sale with the understanding the artist will not receive payment until work is sold. A commission is almost always charged for this service.
Direct-mail package. Sales or promotional material that is distributed by mail. Usually consists of an outer envelope, a cover letter, brochure or flyer, SASE, and postpaid reply card, or order form with business reply envelope.
Edition. The total number of prints published of one piece of art.
Elhi. Abbreviation for elementary/high school.
Etching. A print made by the intaglio process, creating a design in the surface of a metal or other plate with a needle and using a mordant to bite out the design.
Exclusive area representation. Requirement that an artist's work appear in only one outlet within a defined geographical area.
Gouache. Opaque watercolor with definite, appreciable film thickness and an actual paint layer.
Gagline. The words printed, usually directly beneath, a cartoon; also called a caption.
Halftone. Reproduction of a continuous tone illustration with the image formed by dots produced by a camera lens screen.
IRC. International Reply Coupon; purchased at the post office to enclose with artwork sent to a foreign buyer to cover his postage cost when replying.
Keyline. Identification, through signs and symbols, of the positions of illustrations and copy for the printer.
Kill fee. Portion of the agreed-upon price the artist receives for a job that was assigned, started, but then canceled.
Layout. Arrangement of photographs, illustrations, text and headlines for printed material.
Light table. Table with a light source beneath a glass top; especially useful in transferring art by tracing.
Line drawing. Illustration done with pencil or ink using no wash or other shading.
Lithography. Printing process based on a design made with a greasy substance on a limestone slab or metal plate and chemically treated so image areas take ink and non-image areas repel ink; during printing, non-image areas are kept wet with water.
Logotype. Name or design of a company or product used as a trademark on letterheads, direct mail packages, in advertising, etc., to establish visual identity; also called logo.
Mechanicals. Paste-up or preparation of work for printing.
Ms, mss. Abbreviation for manuscript(s).
Offset. Printing process in which a flat printing plate is treated to be ink-receptive in image areas and ink-repellent in non-image areas. Ink is transferred from the printing plate to a rubber plate, and then to the paper.

Overlay. Transparent cover over copy, where instructions, corrections or color location directions are given.
Panel. In cartooning, refers to the number of boxed-in illustrations, i.e. single panel, double panel or multipanel.
Paste-up. Procedure involving coating the backside of art, type, photostats, etc., with rubber cement or wax and adhering them in their proper positions to the mechanical board. The boards are then used as finished art by the printer.
Perspective. The ability to see objects in relation to their relative positions and distance, and depict the volume and spatial relationships on paper.
Photostat. Black-and-white copies produced by an inexpensive photographic process using paper negatives; only line values are held with accuracy. Also called stat.
Pin registration. The use of highly accurate holes and special pins on copy, film, plates and presses to insure proper positioning and alignment of colors.
PMT. Photostat produced without a negative, somewhat like the Polaroid process.
P-O-P. Point-of-purchase; a display device or structure located with the product in or at the retail outlet to advertise or hold the product to increase sales.
Print. An impression pulled from an original plate, stone, block, screen or negative; also a positive made from a photographic negative.
Publication (payment on). The artist is paid for his work when it is published.
Query. Letter of inquiry to an editor or buyer eliciting his interest in a work you want to do or sell.
Rendering. A drawn representation of a building, interior, etc., in perspective.
Retail. To sell directly to the consumer.
Roughs. Preliminary sketches or drawings.
Royalty. An agreed percentage paid by the publisher to the artist for each copy of his work sold.
SASE. Abbreviation for self-addressed, stamped envelope.
Semiannual. Once every six months.
Semimonthly. Once every two weeks.
Semiweekly. Twice a week.
Serigraph. Silkscreen; stencil method of printing involving a stencil adhered to a fine mesh cloth and stretched tightly over a wooden frame. Paint is forced through the holes of the screen not blocked by the stencil.
Simultaneous submissions. Submission of the same artwork to more than one potential buyer at the same time.
Speculation. Creating artwork with no assurance that the buyer will purchase it or reimburse expenses in any way, as opposed to creating artwork on assignment.
Spot drawing. Small illustration used to decorate or enhance a page of type, or to serve as a column ending.
Storyboard. Series of panels which illustrates a progressive sequence of graphics and story copy for a TV commercial, film or filmstrip. Serves as a guide for the eventual finished product.
Tabloid. Publication where an ordinary newspaper page is turned sideways.
Tear sheet. Published page containing an artist's illustration, cartoon, design or photograph.
Template. Plastic stencil containing various sizes of commonly used shapes, symbols or letters which can be traced one at a time.
Thumbnail. A rough layout in miniature.
Transparency. A photographic positive film such as a color slide.
Type spec. Type specification; determination of the size and style of type to be used in a layout.
UPS. Universal Postal Union, a coupon for return of first-class surface letters.
Velox. Photoprint of a continuous tone subject that has been transformed into line art by means of a halftone screen.
Video. General category comprised of videocassettes and videotapes.
Wash. Thin application of transparent color, or watercolor black, for a pastel or gray tonal effect.
Wholesale. To sell (usually in large quantities) to an outlet for resale rather than directly to the consumer.

Index

B

C

M

O

P

Q

R

S

T

U

V

W

X Y Z

1989 Close-up Personalities

Artist: Lee Hammond

Mary Eubank
Illustrator
Page 522

Mike Quon
Designer/Illustrator
Page 134

Terry Brown
Society of Illustrators
Page 185